# C++ HOW TO PROGRAM

Bhanu Satani

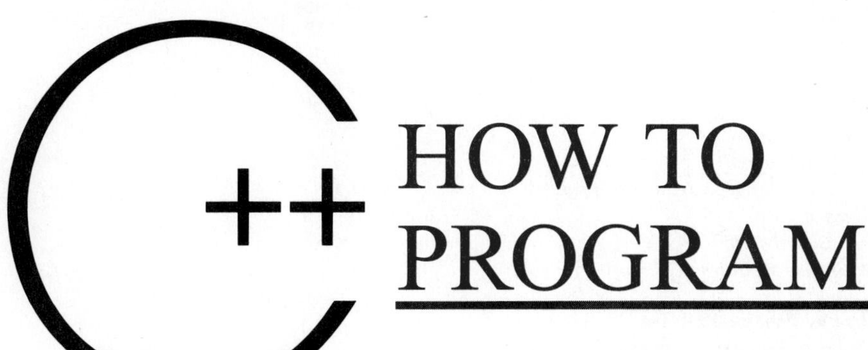


H. M. Deitel
Nova University
Deitel and Associates

P. J. Deitel
Deitel and Associates

PRENTICE HALL, Englewood Cliffs, New Jersey 07632

Library of Congress Cataloging-in-Publication Data

Deitel, Harvey M.
C ++ how to program / H.M. Deitel, P.J. Deitel.
p. cm.
Includes bibliographical references and index.
ISBN 0-13-117334-0
1. C++ (Computer program language) I. Deitel, Paul J.
II. Title.
QA76.73.C153D45 1994
005.13'3--dc20 94-11656
CIP

Acquisitions Editor: ***Alan Apt***
Production Editor: ***Joe Scordato***
Copy Editor: ***Michael Schiaparelli***
Chapter Opener and Cover Designer: ***Jeannette Jacobs***
Buyer: ***Linda Behrens***
Supplements Editor: ***Alice Dworkin***
Editorial Assistant: ***Shirley McGuire***

**A Simon & Schuster Company**
**Englewood Cliffs, New Jersey 07632**



Printed in the United States of America

20 19 18 17 16 15 14 13 12

ISBN 0-13-117334-0

Prentice-Hall International (UK) Limited, London
Prentice-Hall of Australia Pty. Limited, Sydney
Prentice-Hall Canada Inc., Toronto
Prentice-Hall Hispanoamericana, S.A., Mexico
Prentice-Hall of India Private Limited, New Delhi
Prentice-Hall of Japan, Inc., Tokyo
Simon & Schuster of Asia Pte. Ltd., Singapore
Editora Prentice-Hall do Brasil, Ltda., Rio de Janeiro

**TO**

*Dr. Stephen Feldman, President of Nova Southeastern University and to Dr. Edward Lieblein, Dean of the Nova Southeastern University Center for Computer and Information Sciences.*

*For their vision of an institution for advanced scientific and computer science education and research in South Florida, and for their indefatigable efforts in realizing that vision in this young university.*

*H. M. D.*

**TO**

*My teachers at Lawrenceville and M.I.T.*

*For instilling in me a love of learning and writing.*

*P. J. D.*

# Contents

# Illustrations

# Preface

Welcome to C++! This book is by an old guy and a young guy. The old guy (HMD; Massachusetts Institute of Technology 1967) has been programming and/or teaching programming for more than 30 years. The young guy (PJD; MIT 1991) has been programming for a dozen years and has caught the teaching and writing "bug." The old guy programs and teaches from experience; the young guy does so from an inexhaustible reserve of energy. The old guy wants clarity; the young guy wants performance. The old guy appreciates elegance and beauty; the young guy wants results. We got together to produce a book we hope you will find informative, interesting, and entertaining.

In most educational environments, C++ is normally taught only to experienced C programmers. Many educators believe that the complexity of C++, and a number of other difficulties, make C++ unworthy for a first programming course—precisely the target course for this book. So why did we write this text?

C++ is beginning to replace C as the systems implementation language of choice in industry, and there is good reason to believe that C++ will emerge as the dominant language of the mid-to-late 1990s. Harvey Deitel has been teaching introductory programming courses in university environments for two decades with an emphasis on developing clearly written, well-structured programs. Much of what is taught in these courses is the basic principles of programming with an emphasis on the effective use of control structures and functionalization. We have presented this material exactly the way HMD has done in his university courses. There are some pitfalls, but where these occur, we point them out and explain procedures for dealing with them effectively. Our experience has been that students handle the course in about the same manner as they handle introductory Pascal or C courses. There is one noticeable difference though: Students are highly motivated by the fact that they are learning a leading-edge language (C++) and a leading-edge programming paradigm (object-oriented programming) that will be immediately useful to them as they leave the university environment. This increases their enthusiasm for the material—a big help when you consider that C++ is more difficult to learn than Pascal or C.

Our goal was clear: Produce a C++ programming textbook for introductory university-level courses in computer programming for students with little or no programming experience, yet offer the depth and the rigorous treatment of theory and practice demanded by traditional, upper-level C++ courses. To meet these goals, we produced a book larger than other C++ texts—this because our text also patiently teaches the principles of both procedural programming and object-oriented programming. Hundreds of students have studied this material in our courses. Tens of thousands of students worldwide learned C from, and were introduced to C++ in, our related text, *C How to Program,* now in its second edition.

## Introducing Object Orientation from Chapter 1!

We faced a difficult challenge in designing this book. Should the book present a pure object-oriented approach? Or should it present a hybrid approach balancing procedural programming with object-oriented programming?

Most college professors who will teach from this text have been teaching procedural programming for many years (probably in C or Pascal) and have perhaps modest experience teaching object-oriented programming. C++ itself is not a purely object-oriented language. Rather it is a hybrid language that enables procedural programming and OOP.

So we chose the following approach. The first five chapters of the book introduce procedural programming in C++. They present computer concepts, control structures, functions, arrays, pointers and strings. These chapters cover the ANSI C components of C++ and the C++ enhancements to C.

We have done something to make these first five chapters really unique. At the end of each of these chapters, we have included a special section entitled, "Thinking About Objects." These sections introduce the concepts and terminology of object orientation to help students start familiarizing themselves with what objects are and how they behave.

The Chapter 1 "Thinking About Objects" section introduces the concepts and terminology of object orientation. The Chapters 2 through 5 sections present a requirements specification for a substantial object-oriented system project, namely building an elevator simulator, and carefully guide the student through the typical phases of the object-oriented design process. These sections discuss how to identify the objects in a problem, how to specify the objects' attributes and behaviors, and how to specify the interactions among objects. By the time the student has finished Chapter 5, he or she has completed a careful object-oriented design of the elevator simulator and is ready—if not anxious—to begin programming the elevator in C++.

Chapters 6, 7, and 8 cover data abstraction, classes and operator overloading in C++. These chapters also contain "Thinking About Objects" sections that ease students through the various stages of programming their elevators in C++. In a moment we will do a detailed tour of the remainder of the text.

## About this Book

*C++ How to Program* contains a rich collection of examples, exercises, and projects drawn from many fields to provide the student with a chance to solve interesting real-world problems. The book concentrates on the principles of good software engineering and stresses program clarity. We avoid arcane terminology and syntax specifications in favor of teaching by example.

This book is written by two educators who spend most of their time teaching edge-of-the-practice topics in university courses and professional seminars. The text places a strong emphasis on pedagogy. For example, virtually every new concept of either C++ or object-oriented programming is presented in the context of a complete, working C++ program immediately followed by a window showing the program's output. Reading these programs is much like entering and running them on a computer.

Among the other pedagogical devices in the text are a set of objectives and an outline at the beginning of every chapter; common programming errors, good programming practices, performance tips, portability tips, and software engineering observations enumerated in each chapter and summarized at the end of each chapter; comprehensive bullet-list-style and alphabetized terminology sections in each chapter; self-review exercises and answers in each chapter; and the richest collection of exercises in any C++ book.

The exercises range from simple recall questions to lengthy programming problems to major projects. Instructors requiring substantial term projects will find many appropriate problems listed in the exercises for Chapters 3 through 18. We have put a great deal of effort into the exercises to enhance the value of this course for the student. An instructor's manual is available on PC-format disks and Macintosh-format disks with the programs in the main text and answers to almost all of the exercises at the end of each chapter.

In writing this book, we have used a variety of C++ compilers running on Sun SPARCstations, Apple Macintosh (Symantech C++), IBM PC (Turbo C++, Borland C++, IBM's CSET++, and Microsoft C/C++ version 7 and Visual C++), and DEC VAX/VMS (DEC C++). For the most part, the programs in the text will work on all these compilers with little or no modification. We published the versions we developed on Borland C++.

This text follows the evolving ANSI C++ draft standard. See the reference manuals for your particular system for more details about the language, or obtain a copy of "Working Paper for Draft Proposed International Standard for Information Systems—Programming Language C++" from the American National Standards Institute (ANSI) standards Secretariat: CBEMA, 1250 Eye Street NW, Suite 200, Washington DC 20005. We have used various materials from this document with the express written permission of ANSI/CBEMA. The credit line for this permission follows.

> The material described herein is taken from the working paper for the draft proposed American National Standard, Programming Language C++. Approval and technical development work is being conducted by Accredited Standards Committee X3, Information Technology and its Technical Committee X3J16, Programming Language C++, respectively. For further details, contact X3 Secretariat, 1250 Eye Street, NW, Washington, DC 20005.

This book has many features that help the student learn.

*Objectives*

Each chapter begins with a statement of objectives. This tells the student what to expect and gives the student an opportunity, after reading the chapter, to determine if he or she has met these objectives. It is a confidence builder and a source of positive reinforcement.

*Quotations*

The learning objectives are followed by a series of quotations. Some are humorous, some are philosophical, and some offer interesting insights. Our students enjoy relating the quotes to the chapter material. [Trivia: The book has 2,132,722 characters.]

*Outline*

The chapter outline helps the student approach the material in top-down fashion. This, too, helps students anticipate what is to come and set a comfortable and effective learning pace. [Trivia: The book has 342,980 words.]

*Sections*

Each chapter is organized into small sections that address key areas. We prefer a large number of small sections, rather than the opposite.

*329 Example Programs (and Program Outputs and Illustrations)*

C++ features are presented in the context of complete, working C++ programs. Each program is immediately followed by a window containing the output produced when the program is run. This enables the student to confirm that the programs run as expected. Relating outputs back to the program statements that produce those outputs is an excellent way to learn and reinforce concepts. Our programs exercise the diverse features of C++. Reading the book carefully is much like entering and running these programs on a computer.

*Illustrations*

An abundance of charts and line drawings is included. The discussion of control structures features carefully drawn flowcharts. (Note: We do not teach the use of flowcharting as a program development tool, but we do use brief flowchart-oriented presentation to specify the precise operation of C++'s control structures.) Chapter 15, "Data Structures," uses line drawings to illustrate the creation and maintenance of linked lists, queues, stacks, and binary trees.

*Helpful Design Elements*

We have included five design elements to help students focus on important aspects of program development, testing and debugging, performance, and portability. We highlight hundreds of these tips in the form of Good Programming Practices, Common Programming Errors, Performance Tips, Portability Tips, and Software Engineering

Observations. These tips and practices represent the best we have been able to glean from a combined four decades of programming and teaching experience. One of our students—a mathematics major—told us recently that she feels this approach is somewhat like the highlighting of axioms, theorems, and corollaries in mathematics books; it provides a basis on which to build good software.

*111 Good Programming Practices*

Good Programming Practices are highlighted in the text. They call the student's attention to techniques that help produce better programs. When we teach introductory courses to nonprogrammers, we state that the "buzzword" of the course is "clarity," and we tell the students that we will highlight (in these Good Programming Practices) every possible technique for writing programs that are clearer, more understandable, more debuggable, and more maintainable.

*171 Common Programming Errors*

Students learning a language—especially in their first programming course—tend to make certain kinds of errors frequently. Focusing the students' attention on these Common Programming Errors helps the student avoid making the same errors. It also helps reduce the long lines outside instructors' offices during office hours!

*49 Performance Tips*

In our experience, teaching students to write clear and understandable programs is by far the most important goal for a first programming course. But students want to write the programs that run the fastest, use the least memory, require the smallest number of keystroke, or dazzle in other nifty ways. Students really care about performance. They want to know what they can do to "turbo charge" their programs. So we have include Performance Tips to highlight opportunities for improving program performance.

*28 Portability Tips*

Software development is a complex and expensive activity. Organizations that develop software must often produce versions customized to a variety of computers and operating systems. So there is a strong emphasis today on portability, i.e., on producing software that will run on a variety of computer systems with few, if any, changes. Many people tout C++ as an appropriate language for developing portable software, especially because of C++'s close relationship to ANSI C and the fact that an ANSI standard version of C++ will soon appear. Some people assume that if they implement an application in C++, the application will automatically be portable. This is simply not the case. Achieving portability requires careful and cautious design. There are many pitfalls. We include numerous Portability Tips to help students write portable code.

*106 Software Engineering Observations*

The object-oriented programming paradigm requires a complete rethinking about the way we build software systems. C++ is an effective language for performing good software engineering. The Software Engineering Observations highlight techniques, architectural issues, and design issues, etc. that affect the architecture and construction of software systems, especially large-scale systems. Much of what the student learns here will be useful in upper-level courses and in industry as the student begins to work with large, complex real-world systems.

*Summary*

Each chapter ends with additional pedagogical devices. We present a thorough, bullet-list-style summary of the chapter. This helps the students review and reinforce key concepts.

*Terminology*

We include a Terminology section with an alphabetized list of the important terms defined in the chapter—again, further confirmation.

*Summary of Tips, Practices, and Errors*

We summarize the Good Programming Practices, Common Programming Errors, Performance Tips, Portability Tips, and Software Engineering Observations.

*525 Self-Review Exercises and Answers (Count Includes Separate Parts)*

Extensive Self-Review Exercises and answers are included for self-study. This gives the student a chance to build confidence with the material and prepare to attempt the regular exercises.

*763 Exercises (Solutions in Instructor's Manual; Count Includes Separate Parts)*

Each chapter concludes with a substantial set of exercises including simple recall of important terminology and concepts; writing individual C++ statements; writing small portions of C++ functions and classes; writing complete C++ functions, classes, and programs; and writing major term projects. The large number of exercises enables instructors to tailor their courses to the unique needs of their audiences and to vary course assignments each semester. Instructors can use these exercises to form homework assignments, short quizzes, and major examinations. The solutions for the exercises are included in the *Instructor's Manual* and on the IBM-PC-format and Apple-Macintosh-format disks available to instructors through their Prentice-Hall representatives.

*3736 Index Entries (Many with Multiple Page References Each)*

We have included an extensive index at the back of the book. This helps the student find any term or concept by keyword. The Index is useful to people reading the book for the first time and is especially useful to practicing programmers who use the book as a reference. We have made sure that every term in the Terminology sections appears in the Index (along with many more index items from each chapter). Thus, the student can use the Index in conjunction with the Terminology sections to be sure he or she has covered the key material of each chapter.

## A Tour of the Book

The book is divided into several major parts. The first part, Chapters 1 through 5, presents a thorough treatment of procedural programming in C++ including data types, input/output, control structures, functions, arrays, pointers, and strings.

The second part, Chapters 6 through 8, presents a substantial treatment of data abstraction with classes, objects, and operator overloading. This section might effectively be called, "Programming with Objects."

The third part, Chapters 9 and 10, presents inheritance, virtual functions, and polymorphism—the root technologies of true object-oriented programming.

The next part, chapters 11 and 14, presents C++-style stream-oriented input/output including using stream I/O with the keyboard, the screen, files, and character arrays; both sequential file processing and direct-access (i.e., random access) file processing are discussed.

The next part, chapters 12 and 13, discusses two of the most recent major additions to the C++ language, namely templates and exception handling. Templates, also called parameterized types, encourage software reusability. Exceptions help programmers develop more robust, fault-tolerant, mission-critical systems.

The next part, Chapter 15, presents a thorough treatment of dynamic data structures such as linked lists, queues, stacks, and trees.

The last part of the main text, Chapters 16 through 18 discuss a variety of topics including bit, character, and string manipulation; the preprocessor, and miscellaneous "Other Topics."

The last part of the book includes substantial reference materials that support the main text including Appendices on C++ syntax, the standard function libraries, operator precedence, the ASCII character set, number systems (binary, decimal, octal, and hexadecimal) , and C++ resources (such as consortia, journals, and companies that make various key C++-related products). An extensive bibliography is included to encourage further reading. The text concludes with a detailed index that helps the reader locate any terms in the text by keyword. Now let us look at each of the chapters in detail.

Chapter 1, "Introduction to C++," discusses what computers are, how they work, and how they are programmed. It introduces the notion of structured programming and explains why this set of techniques has fostered a revolution in the way programs are written. The chapter gives a brief history of the development of programming languages from machine languages, to assembly languages, to high-level languages. The origin of the C++ programming language is discussed. The chapter includes an introduction to the a typical C++ programming environment and gives a concise introduction to writing C++ programs. A detailed treatment of decision making and arithmetic operations in C++ is presented. After studying this chapter, the student will understand how to write simple, but complete, C++ programs.

Chapter 2, "Control Structures," introduces the notion of algorithms (procedures) for solving problems. It explains the importance of using control structures effectively in producing programs that are understandable, debuggable, maintainable, and more likely to work properly on the first try. It introduces the sequence structure, selection structures (**if**, **if/else**, and **switch**), and repetition structures (**while**, **do/while**, and **for**). It examines repetition in detail, and compares the alternatives of counter-controlled loops and sentinel-controlled loops. It explains the technique of top-down, stepwise refinement that is critical to the production of properly structured programs, and presents the popular program design aid, pseudocode. The methods and approaches used in Chapter 2 are applicable to effective use of control structures in any programming language, not just C++. This chapter helps the student develop good programming habits in preparation for dealing with the more substantial programming tasks in the remainder of the text. The chapter concludes with a discussion of logical operators—**&&** (and), **||** (or), and **!** (not).

Chapter 3, "Functions," discusses the design and construction of program modules. C++'s function-related capabilities include standard library functions, programmer-defined functions, recursion, call-by-value, and call-by-reference capabilities. The techniques presented in Chapter 3 are essential to the production of properly structured programs, especially the kinds of larger programs and software that system programmers and application programmers are likely to develop in real-world applications. The "divide and conquer" strategy is presented as an effective means for solving complex problems by dividing them into simpler interacting components. Students enjoy the treatment of random numbers and simulation, and they appreciate the discussion of the dice game craps which makes elegant use of control structures. The chapter offers a solid introduction to recursion and includes a table summarizing the dozens of recursion examples and exercises distributed throughout the remainder of the book. Some texts leave recursion for a chapter late in the book; but we feel this topic is best covered gradually throughout the text. The extensive collection of 60 exercises at the end of the chapter includes several classical recursion problems such as the Towers of Hanoi. The chapter discusses the so-called "C++ enhancements to C," including inline functions, reference parameters, default arguments, the unary scope resolution operator, function overloading, and function templates.

Chapter 4, "Arrays," discusses the structuring of data into arrays, or groups, of related data items of the same type. The chapter presents numerous examples of both single-subscripted arrays and double-subscripted arrays. It is widely recognized that structuring data properly is just as important as using control structures effectively in the development of properly structured programs. Examples in the chapter investigate various common array manipulations, printing histograms, sorting data, passing arrays to functions, and an introduction to the field of survey data analysis (with simple statistics). A feature of this chapter is the discussion of elementary sorting and searching techniques and the presentation of binary searching as a dramatic improvement over linear searching. The 38 end-of-chapter exercises include a variety of interesting and challenging problems such as improved sorting techniques, the design of an airline reservations system, an introduction to the concept of turtle graphics (made famous in the LOGO language), and the Knight's Tour and Eight Queens problems that introduce the notions of heuristic programming so widely employed in the field of artificial intelligence. The exercises conclude with 8 recursion problems including the selection sort, palindromes, linear search, binary search, the eight queens, printing an array, printing a string backwards, and finding the minimum value in an array.

Chapter 5, "Pointers and Strings," presents one of the most powerful features of the C++ language. The chapter provides detailed explanations of pointer operators, call by reference, pointer expressions, pointer arithmetic, the relationship between pointers and arrays, arrays of pointers, and pointers to functions. There is an intimate relationships between pointers, arrays, and strings in C++, so we introduce basic string manipulation concepts and include a discussion of some of the most popular string handling functions, namely **getline** (input a line of text), **strcpy** and **strncpy** (copy a string), **strcat** and **strncat**, (concatenate two strings) **strcmp** and **strncmp** (compare two strings), **strtok** ("tokenize" a string into its pieces), and **strlen** (compute the length of a string). The 49 chapter exercises include a simulation of the classic race between the tortoise and the hare, card shuffling and dealing algorithms, recursive quicksort, and recursive maze traversals. A special section entitled "Building Your Own Computer" is also included. This section explains the notion of machine language programming and proceeds with a project involving the design and implementation of a computer simulator that allows the reader to write and run machine language programs. This unique feature of the text will be especially useful to the reader who wants to understand how computers really work. Our students enjoy this project and often implement substantial enhancements; many enhancements are suggested in the exercises. In Chapter 15, another special section guides the reader through building a compiler; the machine language produced by the compiler is then executed on the machine language simulator produced in Chapter 7. Information is communicated from the compiler to the simulator in sequential files (see Chapter 14). A second special section includes challenging string manipulation exercises related to text analysis, word processing, printing dates in various formats, check protection, writing the word equivalent of a check amount, Morse Code, and metric-to-English conversions.

Chapter 6, "Classes and Data Abstraction," begins our discussion of objects. The chapter represents a wonderful opportunity for teaching data abstraction the "right way"—through a language (C++) expressly devoted to implementing abstract data types (ADTs). In recent years, data abstraction has become a major topic in introductory computing courses. Chapters 6, 7, and 8 include a solid treatment of data abstraction. Chapter 6 discusses implementing ADTs as **struct**s, implementing ADTs as C++-style classes, accessing class members, separating interface from implementation, using access functions and utility functions, initializing objects with constructors, destroying objects with destructors, assignment by default memberwise copy, and software reusability. The chapter exercises challenge the student to develop classes for complex numbers, rational numbers, times, dates, rectangles, huge integers, and for playing tic-tac-toe. Students generally enjoy game-playing programs.

Chapter 7, "Classes Part II," continues the study of classes and data abstraction. The chapter discusses declaring and using constant objects, constant member functions, composition—the process of building classes that have objects of other classes as members, friend functions and friend classes that have special access rights to the private and protected members of classes, the **this** pointer that enables an object to know its own address, dynamic memory allocation, static class members for containing and manipulating class-wide data, examples of popular abstract data types (arrays, strings, and queues), container classes, and iterators. The chapter exercises ask the student to develop a savings account class and a class for holding sets of integers.

Chapter 8, "Operator Overloading," is one of the most popular topics in our C++ courses. Students really enjoy this material. They find it a perfect match with the discussion of abstract data types in Chapters 6 and 7. Operator overloading enables the programmer to tell the compiler how to use existing operators with objects of new types. C++ already knows how to use these operators with objects of built-in types such as integers, floats, and characters. But suppose we create a new string class. What does the plus sign mean? Many programmers use plus with strings to mean concatenation. In Chapter 8, the programmer will learn how to "overload" the plus sign so that when it is written between two string objects in an expression, the compiler will generate a function call to an "operator function" that will concatenate the two strings. The chapter discusses the fundamentals of operator overloading, restrictions in operator overloading, overloading with class member functions vs. with nonmember functions, overloading unary and binary operators, and converting between types. A feature of the chapter is the collection of substantial case studies including an array class, a string class, a date class, a huge integers class, and a complex numbers class (the last two appear with full source code in the exercises). The more mathematically inclined student will enjoy creating the polynomial class in the exercises.

Chapter 9, "Inheritance," deals with one of the most fundamental capabilities of object-oriented programming languages. Inheritance is a form of software reusability in which new classes are developed quickly and easily by absorbing the capabilities of existing classes and adding appropriate new capabilities. The chapter discusses the notions of base classes and derived classes, protected members, public inheritance, protected inheritance, private inheritance, direct base classes, indirect base classes, use of constructors and destructors in base classes and derived classes, and software engineering with inheritance. The chapter compares inheritance ("is a" relationships) with composition ("has a" relationships) and introduces "uses a" and "knows a" relationships. A feature of the chapter is its several substantial case studies. In particular, a lengthy case study implements a point, circle, cylinder class hierarchy. The chapter concludes with a case study on multiple inheritance—an advanced feature of C++ that enables a derived class to be formed by inheriting attributes and behaviors from several base classes. The exercises ask the student to compare the creation of new classes by inheritance vs. composition; to extend the various inheritance hierarchies discussed in the chapter; to write an inheritance hierarchy for quadrilaterals, trapezoids, parallelograms, rectangles, and squares; and to create a more general shape hierarchy with two-dimensional shapes and three-dimensional shapes.

Chapter 10, "Virtual Functions and Polymorphism," deals with another of the fundamental capabilities of object-oriented programming, namely polymorphic behavior. When many classes are related through inheritance to a common base class, each derived-class object may be treated as a base-class object. This enables programs to be written in a general manner independent of the specific types of the derived-class objects. New kinds of objects can be handled by the same program, thus making systems more extensible. Polymorphism enables programs to eliminate complex `switch` logic in favor of simpler "straight-line" logic. A screen manager of a video game, for example, can simply send a draw message to every object in a linked list of objects to be drawn. Each object knows how to draw itself. A new object can be added to the program without modifying that program as long as that new object also knows how to draw itself. This style of programming is typically used to implement today's popular graphical user interfaces. The chapter discusses the mechanics of achieving polymorphic behavior through the use of virtual functions. The chapter distinguishes between abstract classes (from which objects cannot be instantiated) and concrete classes (from which objects can be instantiated). Abstract classes are useful for providing an inheritable interface to classes throughout the hierarchy. A feature of the chapter is its two major polymorphism case studies—a payroll system and another version of the point, circle, cylinder shape hierarchy discussed in Chapter 9. The chapter exercises ask the student to discuss a number of conceptual issues and approaches, add abstract classes to the shape hierarchy, develop a basic graphics package, modify the chapter's employee class—and pursue all these projects with virtual functions and polymorphic programming.

Chapter 11, "Stream Input/Output," contains a comprehensive treatment of the new object-oriented style of input/output introduced in C++. The chapter discusses the various I/O capabilities of C++ including output with the stream insertion operator, input with the stream extraction operator, type-safe I/O (a nice improvement over C), formatted I/O, unformatted I/O (for performance), stream manipulators for controlling the stream base (decimal, octal, or hexadecimal), floating-point numbers, controlling field widths, user-defined manipulators, stream format states, stream error states, I/O of objects of user-defined types, and tying output streams to input streams (to ensure that prompts actually appear before the user is expected to enter responses). The extensive exercise set asks the student to write various programs that test virtually all the I/O capabilities discussed in the text.

Chapter 12, "Templates," discusses one of the more recent additions to the evolving C++ language. Function templates were introduced in Chapter 3. Chapter 12 presents an additional function template example. Class templates enable the programmer to capture the essence of an abstract data type (such as a stack, an array, or a queue) and then create—with minimal additional code—versions of that ADT for particular types (such as a queue of **`int`**, a queue of **`float`**, a queue of strings, etc.). For this reason, template classes are often called parameterized types. The chapter discusses using type parameters and nontype parameters and considers the interaction among templates and other C++ concepts, such as inheritance, friends, and static members. The exercises challenge the student to write a variety of function templates and class templates, and to employ these in complete programs.

Chapter 13, "Exception Handling," discusses the latest major addition to the C++ language. Exception handling enables the programmer to write programs that are more robust, more fault tolerant, and more appropriate for mission-critical environments. The chapter discusses when exception handling is appropriate; introduces the basics of exception handling with **`try`** blocks, **`throw`** statements, and **`catch`** blocks; indicates how and when to rethrow an exception; explains how to write an exception specification and process unexpected exceptions; and discusses the important ties between exceptions and constructors, destructors, and inheritance. A features of the chapter is its 43 exercises that walk the student through implementing programs that illustrate the diversity and power of C++'s exception handling capabilities.

Chapter 14, "File Processing and String Stream I/O," discusses the techniques used to process text files with sequential access and random access. The chapter begins with an introduction to the data hierarchy from bits, to bytes, to fields, to records, to files. Next, C++'s simple view of files and streams is presented. Sequential access files are discussed using a series of three programs that show how to open and close files, how to store data sequentially in a file, and how to read data sequentially from a file. Random access files are discussed using a series of four programs that show how to sequentially create a file for random access, how to read and write data to a file with random access, and how to read data sequentially from a randomly accessed file. The fourth random access program combines many of the techniques of accessing files both sequentially and randomly into a complete transaction processing program. Students in our industry seminars have told us that after studying the material on file processing, they were able to produce substantial file-processing programs that were immediately useful in their organizations. The chapter also discusses C++'s capabilities for inputting data from character arrays in memory and outputting data to character arrays in memory; these capabilities are often referred to as in-core formatting or string stream processing. The exercises ask the student to implement a variety of programs that build and process both sequential access files and random access files.

Chapter 15, "Data Structures," discusses the techniques used to create and manipulate dynamic data structures. The chapter begins with discussions of self-referential classes and dynamic memory allocation. The chapter proceeds with a discussion of how to create and maintain various dynamic data structures including linked lists, queues (or waiting lines), stacks, and trees. For each type of data structure, we present complete, working programs and show sample outputs. The chapter really helps the student master pointers. The chapter includes abundant examples using indirection and double indirection—a particularly difficult concept. One problem when working with pointers is that students have trouble visualizing the data structures and how their nodes are linked together. So we have included illustrations that show the links, and the sequence in which they are created. The binary tree example is a superb capstone for the study of pointers and dynamic data structures. This example creates a binary tree; enforces duplicate elimination; and introduces recursive preorder, inorder, and postorder tree traversals. Students have a genuine sense of accomplishment when they study and implement this example. They particularly appreciate seeing that the inorder traversal prints the node values in sorted order. The chapter includes a substantial collection of exercises. A highlight of the chapter is the special section "Building Your Own Compiler." The exercises walk the student through the development of an infix-to-postfix-conversion program and a postfix-expression-evaluation program. We then modify the postfix evaluation algorithm to generate machine-language code. The compiler places this code in a file (using the techniques of Chapter 1). Students then run the machine language produced by their compilers on the software simulators they built in the exercises of Chapter 7! The 35 exercises include a supermarket simulation using queueing, recursively searching a list, recursively printing a list backwards, binary tree node deletion, level-order traversal of a binary tree, printing trees, writing a portion of an optimizing compiler, writing an interpreter, inserting/deleting anywhere in a linked list, implementing lists and queues without tail pointers, analyzing the performance of binary tree searching and sorting, and implementing an indexed list class.

Chapter 16, "Bits, Characters, Strings, and Structures," presents a variety of important features. C++'s powerful bit manipulation capabilities enable programmers to write programs that exercise lower-level hardware capabilities. This helps programs process bit strings, set individual bits on or off, and store information more compactly. Such capabilities, often found only in low-level assembly languages, are valued by programmers writing system software such as operating systems and networking software. As you recall, we introduced string manipulation in Chapter 5 and presented the most popular string manipulation functions. In Chapter 16, we continue our presentation of characters and strings. We present the various character manipulation capabilities of the **ctype** library—these include the ability to test a character to see if it is a digit, an alphabetic character, an alphanumeric character, a hexadecimal digit, a lowercase letter, an uppercase letter, etc. We present the remaining string manipulation function of the various string-related libraries.; as always, every function is presented in the context of a complete, working C++ program. Structures are like records in Pascal and other languages—they group data items of various types. Structures are used in Chapter 14 to form files consisting of records of information. Structures are used in conjunction with pointers and dynamic memory allocation in Chapter 15 to form dynamic data structures such as linked lists, queues, stacks, and trees. A feature of the chapter is its revised, high-performance card shuffling and dealing simulation. This is an excellent opportunity for the instructor to emphasize the quality of algorithms. The 35 exercises encourage the student to try out most of the capabilities discussed in the chapter. The feature exercise leads the student through the development of a spell checker program.

Chapter 17, "The Preprocessor," provides detailed discussions of the preprocessor directives. The chapter includes more complete information on the **#include** directive that causes a copy of a specified file to be included in place of the directive before the file is compiled, and the **#define** directive that creates symbolic constants and macros. The chapter explains conditional compilation for enabling the programmer to control the execution of preprocessor directives, and the compilation of program code. The # operator that converts its operand to a string and the ## operator that concatenates two tokens are discussed. The five predefined symbolic constants (**__LINE__**, **__FILE__**, **__DATE__**, **__TIME__**, and **__STDC__**) are presented. Finally, macro **assert** of the **assert.h** header is discussed; **assert** is valuable in program testing, debugging, verification, and validation.

Chapter 18, "Other Topics," presents additional topics including several advanced topics not ordinarily covered in introductory courses. We show how to redirect input to a program to come from a file, redirect output from a program to be placed in a file, redirect the output of one program to be the input of another program (piping), and append the output of a program to an existing file., how to develop functions that use variable-length argument lists, how command-line arguments can be passed to function **main**, and used in a program, compiling programs whose components are spread across multiple files, registering functions with `atexit` to be executed at program termination, and terminating program execution with function `exit`, use the `const` and `volatile` type qualifiers, specify the type of a numeric constant using the integer and floating point suffixes, use the signal handling library to trap unexpected events, create and use dynamic arrays with `calloc` and `realloc`, use unions as a space saving technique, and use linkage specifications when C++ programs are to be linked with legacy C code.

Several Appendices provide valuable reference material. We present the C++ syntax summary in Appendix A; a summary of all standard library functions with explanations in Appendix B; an operator precedence and associativity chart in Appendix C; the set of ASCII character codes in Appendix D; a discussion of the binary, octal, decimal, and hexadecimal number systems in Appendix E; and various C++ and OOP resources such as journal names and addresses, company names and addresses, and consortia names and addresses in Appendix F. A Bibliography (184 entries) encourages the student to do further reading on C++ and OOP. The book contains a comprehensive index to enable the reader to locate by keyword any term or concept throughout the text.

In Appendix A, we have used extensive materials from the evolving C++ draft standard document. The permission credit for that material appears earlier in this Preface and in the front of Appendix A.

Appendix B and various figures were condensed from the ANSI/ISO standard document with the express written permission of the American National Standards Institute; this appendix is a detailed and valuable reference for the practicing C++ programmer. We sincerely appreciate the cooperation of Robert E. Hager—Acting Director of Publications for ANSI—for helping us obtain the necessary publication permissions. The permission credit for this material follows:

> Various figures and Appendix B: Standard Library have been condensed and adapted with permission from American National Standard for Information Systems—Programming Language C, ANSI/ISO 9899: 1990. Copies of this standard may be purchased from the American National Standards Institute at 11 West 42nd Street, New York, NY 10036.

*Acknowledgements*

One of the great pleasures of writing a textbook is acknowledging the efforts of the many people whose names may not appear on the cover, but without whose hard work, cooperation, friendship, and understanding producing this text would have been impossible.

HMD wants to thank his Nova University colleagues Ed Lieblein, Ed Simco, Clovis Tondo, Phil Adams, Raisa Szabo, Raul Salazar, Brian Ouellette, and Barbara Edge.

We would like to thank our friends at Digital Equipment Corporation (Stephanie Stosur Schwartz, Sue-Lane Garrett, Betsy Mills, Jennie Connolly, Barbara Couturier and Paul Sandore), Sun Microsystems (Gary Morin and Karine Shaw), Informative Stages (Don Hall and David Litwack), Semaphore Training (Clive Lee), Cambridge Technology Partners (Gart Davis, Paul Sherman, and Wilberto Martinez), and our many other corporate clients who have made teaching this material in an industrial setting such a joy.

We are fortunate to have been able to work on this project with a talented and dedicated team of publishing professionals at Prentice Hall. This book happened because of the encouragement, enthusiasm, and persistence of our publisher, Alan Apt, and his boss, Marcia Horton, Editor-in-Chief. Sondra Chavez coordinated the complex reviewer effort on the manuscript and was always incredibly helpful when we needed assistance—her ebullience and good cheer are sincerely appreciated. Joe Scordato did a marvelous job as project manager. Shirley McGuire was a superb editorial assistant.

We appreciate the efforts of our reviewers:

Tim Born (AT&T Bell Labs)

Tony L. Hansen (AT&T Bell Labs; Hansen is the author of *The C++ Answer Book*, Addison-Wesley 1990, that contains answers to the exercises in—and is widely used in conjunction with—*The C++ Programming Language*, the classic C++ text by Bjarne Stroustrup)

Clovis Tondo (T & T TechWork, Inc. and Nova Southeastern University; Tondo is the co-author of *The C Answer Book*, Prentice-Hall, 1989, that contains answers to the exercises in—and is widely used in conjunction with—*The C Programming Language*, the classic by Brian Kernighan and Dennis Ritchie)

R. Reid (Michigan State University)

Gene Spafford (Purdue University)

H. E. Dunsmore (Purdue University)

David Falconer (California State University at Fullerton)

David Finkel (Worcester Polytechnic)

Kenneth A. Reek (Rochester Institute of Technology)

Ken Arnold (Wildfire Communications)

Don Kostuch (You Can C Clearly Now)

Robert G. Plantz (Sonoma State University)

These people scrutinized every aspect of the text and made countless valuable suggestions for improving the accuracy and completeness of the presentation.

The authors would like to extend a special note of thanks to Ed Lieblein, one of the world's foremost authorities on software engineering, for his constructive comments and criticisms on enhancing the material on C++ and OOP. Dr. Lieblein is a friend and colleague of HMD at Nova Southeastern University in Ft. Lauderdale, Florida where he is Full Professor of Computer Science and Dean the Center for Computer and Information Sciences. Dr. Lieblein was previously Chief Technical Officer of Tartan Laboratories, a company specializing in compiler development. Before that, he served as Director of Computer Software and Systems in the Office of the Secretary of Defense. In that capacity, he managed the DoD Software Initiative, a special program to improve the nation's software capability for future mission-critical systems. He initiated the Pentagon's STARS program for software technology and reusability, guided the Ada program to international standardization, and played an important role in establishing the Software Engineering Institute at Carnegie Mellon University. It is a special privilege for HMD to be able to work with Dr. Lieblein at Nova Southeastern University.

Tem Nieto contributed long hours of painstaking effort helping us form the special section "Building Your Own Compiler" at the end of Chapter 15. Mr. Nieto is also working with us on the Instructor's Manual for the book.

Last, but certainly not least, we would like to thank Barbara and Abbey Deitel, for their love and understanding, and for their enormous efforts in helping prepare the manuscript. They contributed endless hours of effort; they tested every program in the text, assisted in every phase of the manuscript preparation, and proofread every draft of the text through to publication. Their sharp eyes prevented innumerable errors from finding a home in the manuscript. Barbara also researched the quotes, and Abbey suggested the title for the book.

We would greatly appreciate your comments, criticisms, corrections, and suggestions for improving the text. Please send us your suggestions for improving and adding to our list of Good Programming Practices, Common Programming Errors, Performance Tips, Portability Tips, and Software Engineering Observations. We will acknowledge all contributors in the next edition of our book. Please address all correspondence to our email address:

**deitel@world.std.com**

or write us as follows:

Harvey M. Deitel (author)
Paul J. Deitel (author)
c/o Computer Science Editor
College Book Editorial
Prentice Hall
Englewood Cliffs, New Jersey 07632

We will respond immediately.

Harvey M. Deitel
Paul J. Deitel

# C++ HOW TO PROGRAM

1

# Introduction to Computers and C++ Programming

## Objectives

- To understand basic computer science concepts.
- To become familiar with different types of programming languages.
- To understand the C++ program development environment.
- To be able to write simple computer programs in C++.
- To be able to use simple input and output statements.
- To become familiar with fundamental data types.
- To be able to use arithmetic operators.
- To understand the precedence of arithmetic operators.
- To be able to write simple decision-making statements.

*Our life is frittered away by detail ...Simplify, simplify.*
Henry Thoreau

*High thoughts must have high language.*
Aristophanes

*My object all sublime*
*I shall achieve in time.*
W.S. Gilbert

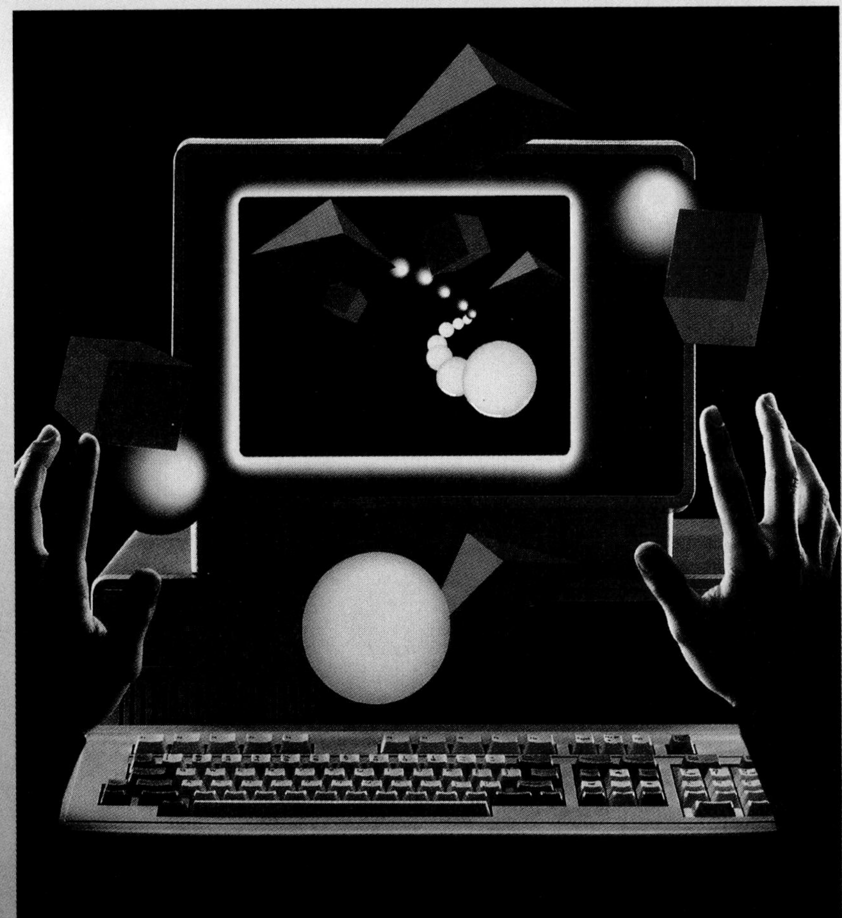

## Outline



## 1.1 Introduction

Welcome to C++! We have worked hard to create what we hope will be an informative, entertaining and challenging learning experience for you. C++ is a difficult language that is normally taught only to experienced programmers, so this book is unique among C++ textbooks:

- It is appropriate for technically oriented people with little or no programming experience.

- It is appropriate for experienced programmers who want a deeper treatment of the language.

How can one book appeal to both groups? The answer is that the common core of the book emphasizes achieving program *clarity* through the proven techniques of *structured programming* and *object-oriented programming.* Nonprogrammers will learn programming the right way from the beginning. We have attempted to write in a clear and straightforward manner. The book is abundantly illustrated. Perhaps most importantly, the book presents a huge number of working C++ programs and shows the outputs produced when those programs are run on a computer.

The first five chapters introduce the fundamentals of computers, computer programming, and the C++ computer programming language. Novices who have taken our courses tell us that the material in those chapters presents a solid foundation for the deeper treatment of C++ in Chapters 6 through 16. Experienced programmers typically read the first five chapters quickly and then find that the treatment of C++ in Chapters 6 through 16 is both rigorous and challenging.

Many experienced programmers have told us that they appreciate our treatment of structured programming. Often they have been programming in structured languages like C or Pascal, but because they were never formally introduced to structured programming, they are not writing the best possible code in these languages. As they review structured programming in the early chapters of this book, they are able to improve their C and Pascal programming styles as well. So whether you are a novice or an experienced programmer, there is much here to inform, entertain, and challenge you.

Most people are familiar with the exciting things computers do. Using this textbook, you will learn how to command computers to do those things. It is *software* (i.e., the instructions you write to command the computer to perform *actions* and make *decisions*) that controls computers (often referred to as *hardware*), and C++ is one of today's most popular software development languages. This text provides an introduction to programming in the version of C++ undergoing standardization in the United States through the *American National Standards Institute (ANSI).* Eventually, a worldwide standard version of C++ is likely to evolve through the efforts of the *International Standards Organization (ISO).*

The use of computers is increasing in almost every field of endeavor. In an era of steadily rising costs, computing costs have been decreasing dramatically because of the rapid developments in both hardware and software technology. Computers that might have filled large rooms and cost millions of dollars 25 years ago can now be inscribed on the surfaces of silicon chips smaller than a fingernail, and that cost perhaps a few dollars each. Ironically, silicon is one of the most abundant materials on the earth—it is an ingredient in common sand. Silicon chip technology has made computing so economical that approximately 200 million general-purpose computers are in use worldwide helping people in business, industry, government, and their personal lives. That number could easily double in a few years.

This book will challenge you for several reasons. Your peers over the last few years probably learned C or Pascal as their first programming language. You will actually learn both C and C++! Why? Simply because C++ includes *ANSI C* and adds much more.

Your peers probably learned the programming methodology called *structured programming.* You will learn both structured programming and the exciting newer methodology, *object-oriented programming.* Why do we teach both? We certainly anticipate that object-orientation will be the key programming methodology for the mid-to-late 1990s. So you will build and work with many *objects* in this course. But you will discover that the internal structure of those objects is often best built using structured programming techniques. Also, the logic of manipulating objects is occasionally best expressed with structured programming.

Another reason we present both methodologies is that over the next decade there will be a massive migration from C-based systems to C++-based systems. There is a huge amount of so-called "legacy C code" in place. C has been in use for about a quarter of a century and its use in recent years has been increasing dramatically. Once people learn C++, they find its features more powerful than those of C, and these people often choose to move to C++. They begin converting their legacy systems to C++, a process that is relatively straightforward. Then they begin using the various C++ features generally called "C++ enhancements to C" to improve their style of writing C-like programs. Finally, they begin employing the object-oriented programming capabilities of C++ to realize the full benefits of the language.

An interesting phenomenon occurring in the programming languages marketplace is that many of the key vendors now simply market a combined C/C++ product rather than offering separate products. This gives users the ability to continue programming in C if they wish, and then gradually migrate to C++ when appropriate.

C++ is certain to become the implementation language of choice in the 1990s. But can it be taught in a first programming course, the intended audience for this book? We think so. Two years ago we took on a similar challenge when Pascal was the entrenched language in first computer science courses. We wrote *C How to Program,* the sister book to this text. Hundreds of universities worldwide now use the second edition of *C How to Program.* Courses based on that book have proven to be equally effective to their Pascal-based predecessors. No significant differences have been observed, except that students are better motivated because they know they are more likely to use C rather than Pascal in their upper-level courses and in their careers. Students learning C also know that they will be better prepared to learn C++.

In the first five chapters of the book you will learn structured programming in C++, the "C portion" of C++, and the C++ enhancements to C. In the balance of the book you will learn object-oriented programming in C++. We do not want you to wait until Chapter 6, however, to begin appreciating object-orientation, so each of the first five chapters concludes with a section called "Thinking About Objects." These sections introduce basic concepts and terminology about object orientation. When we reach Chapter 6, you will be well prepared to start using C++ to build objects and write object-oriented programs.

This first chapter has three parts. The first part introduces the basics of computers and computer programming. The second part gets you started immediately writing some simple C++ programs. The third part gets you "thinking about objects."

So there you have it! You are about to start on a challenging and rewarding path. As you proceed, if you would like to communicate with us, send us email over the Internet at `deitel@world.std.com`. We will make every effort to respond quickly. Good luck!

## 1.2 What is a Computer?

A *computer* is a device capable of performing computations and making logical decisions at speeds millions, and even billions, of times faster than human beings can. For example, many of today's personal computers can perform tens of millions of additions per second. A person operating a desk calculator might require decades to complete the same number of calculations a powerful personal computer can perform in one second. (Points to ponder: How would you know whether the person added the numbers correctly? How would you know whether the computer added the numbers correctly?) Today's fastest *supercomputers* can perform hundreds of billions of additions per second—about as many calculations as hundreds of thousands of people could perform in one year! And trillion-instruction-per-second computers are already functioning in research laboratories.

Computers process *data* under the control of sets of instructions called *computer programs.* These computer programs guide the computer through orderly sets of actions specified by people called *computer programmers.*

The various devices (such as the keyboard, screen, disks, memory, and processing units) that comprise a computer system are referred to as *hardware.* The computer programs that run on a computer are referred to as *software.* Hardware costs have been declining dramatically in recent years, to the point that personal computers have become a commodity. Unfortunately, software development costs have been rising steadily as programmers develop ever more powerful and complex applications, without being able to improve the technology of software development. In this book you will learn proven software development methods that can reduce software development costs—structured programming, top-down stepwise refinement, functionalization and object-oriented programming.

## 1.3 Computer Organization

Regardless of differences in physical appearance, virtually every computer may be envisioned as being divided into six *logical units* or sections. These are:

1. *Input unit.* This is the "receiving" section of the computer. It obtains information (data and computer programs) from various *input devices* and places this information at the disposal of the other units so that the information may be processed. Most information is entered into computers today through typewriter-like keyboards and "mouse" devices. In the future, perhaps most information will be entered by speaking to your computer.

2. *Output unit.* This is the "shipping" section of the computer. It takes information that has been processed by the computer and places it on various *output devices* to make the information available for use outside the computer. Most information output from computers today is displayed on screens, printed on paper, or used to control other devices.

3. *Memory unit.* This is the rapid access, relatively low-capacity "warehouse" section of the computer. It retains information that has been entered through the input unit so that the information may be made immediately available for processing when it is needed. The memory unit also retains information that has already

been processed until that information can be placed on output devices by the output unit. The memory unit is often called either *memory* or *primary memory.*

4. *Arithmetic and logic unit (ALU).* This is the "manufacturing" section of the computer. It is responsible for performing calculations such as addition, subtraction, multiplication, and division. It contains the decision mechanisms that allow the computer, for example, to compare two items from the memory unit to determine whether or not they are equal.

5. *Central processing unit (CPU).* This is the "administrative" section of the computer. It is the computer's coordinator and is responsible for supervising the operation of the other sections. The CPU tells the input unit when information should be read into the memory unit, tells the ALU when information from the memory unit should be utilized in calculations, and tells the output unit when to send information from the memory unit to certain output devices.

6. *Secondary storage unit.* This is the long-term, high-capacity "warehousing" section of the computer. Programs or data not actively being used by the other units are normally placed on secondary storage devices (such as disks) until they are again needed, possibly hours, days, months, or even years later. Information in secondary storage takes much longer to access than information in primary memory. The cost per unit of secondary storage is much less than the cost per unit of primary memory.

## 1.4 Evolution of Operating Systems

Early computers were capable of performing only one *job* or *task* at a time. This form of computer operation is often called single-user *batch processing.* The computer runs a single program at a time while processing data in groups or *batches.* In these early systems, users generally submitted their jobs to the computer center on decks of punched cards. Users often had to wait hours or even days before printouts were returned to their desks.

Software systems called *operating systems* were developed to help make it more convenient to use computers. Early operating systems managed the smooth transition between jobs. This minimized the time it took for computer operators to switch between jobs, and hence increased the amount of work, or throughput, computers could process.

As computers became more powerful, it became evident that single-user batch processing rarely utilized the computer's resources efficiently. Instead, it was thought that many jobs or tasks could be made to *share* the resources of the computer to achieve better utilization. This is called *multiprogramming.* Multiprogramming involves the "simultaneous" operation of many jobs on the computer—the computer shares its resources among the jobs competing for its attention. With early multiprogramming operating systems, users still submitted jobs on decks of punched cards and waited hours or days for results.

In the 1960s, several groups in industry and the universities pioneered *timesharing* operating systems. Timesharing is a special case of multiprogramming in which users access the computer through *terminals*, typically devices with keyboards and screens. In a typical timesharing computer system, there may be dozens or even hundreds of users sharing the computer at once. The computer does not actually run all the users simultaneously. Rather, it runs a small portion of one user's job and then moves on to service the next user. The computer does this so quickly that it may provide service to each user several times per second. Thus the users' programs *appear* to be running simultaneously. An advantage of timesharing is that the user receives almost immediate responses to requests rather than having to wait long periods for results as with previous modes of computing.

## 1.5 Personal Computing, Distributed Computing, and Client/Server Computing

In 1977, Apple Computer popularized the phenomenon of *personal computing.* Initially, it was a hobbyist's dream. Computers became economical enough for people to buy them for their own personal or business use. In 1981, IBM, the world's largest computer vendor, introduced the IBM Personal Computer. Literally overnight, personal computing became legitimate in business, industry, and government organizations.

But these computers were "standalone" units—people did their work on their own machines and then transported disks back and forth to share information. Although early personal computers were not powerful enough to timeshare several users, these machines could be linked together in computer networks, sometimes over telephone lines and sometimes in *local area networks (LANs)* within an organization. This led to the phenomenon of *distributed computing* in which an organization's computing, instead of being performed strictly at some central computer installation, is distributed over networks to the sites at which the real work of the organization is performed. Personal computers were powerful enough to handle the computing requirements of individual users, and to handle the basic communications tasks of passing information back and forth electronically.

Today's most powerful personal computers are as powerful as the million dollar machines of just a decade ago. The most powerful desktop machines—called *workstations*—provide individual users with enormous capabilities. Information is easily shared across computer networks where some computers called *file servers* offer a common store of programs and data that may be used by *client* computers distributed throughout the network, hence the term *client/server computing.* C and C++ have become the programming languages of choice for writing software for operating systems, for computer networking, and for distributed client/server applications. Today's popular operating systems such as UNIX, OS/2, and Windows NT provide the kinds of capabilities discussed in this section.

## 1.6 Machine Languages, Assembly Languages, and High-level Languages

Programmers write instructions in various programming languages, some directly understandable by the computer and others that require intermediate *translation* steps. Hundreds of computer languages are in use today. These may be divided into three general types:

1. Machine languages
2. Assembly languages
3. High-level languages

Any computer can directly understand only its own *machine language.* Machine language is the "natural language" of a particular computer. It is defined by the hardware design of that computer. Machine languages generally consist of strings of numbers (ultimately reduced to 1s and 0s) that instruct computers to perform their most elementary operations one at a time. Machine languages are *machine-dependent,* i.e., a particular machine language can be used on only one type of computer. Machine languages are cumbersome for humans, as can be seen by the following section of a machine language program that adds overtime pay to base pay and stores the result in gross pay.

```
+1300042774
+1400593419
+1200274027
```

As computers became more popular, it became apparent that machine language programming was simply too slow and tedious for most programmers. Instead of using the strings of numbers that computers could directly understand, programmers began using English-like abbreviations to represent the elementary operations of the computer. These English-like abbreviations formed the basis of *assembly languages. Translator programs* called *assemblers* were developed to convert assembly language programs to machine language at computer speeds. The following section of an assembly language program also adds overtime pay to base pay and stores the result in gross pay, but more clearly than its machine language equivalent:

```
LOAD    BASEPAY
ADD     OVERPAY
STORE   GROSSPAY
```

Although such code is clearer to humans, it is incomprehensible to computers until translated to machine language.

Computer usage increased rapidly with the advent of assembly languages, but these still required many instructions to accomplish even the simplest tasks. To speed the programming process, *high-level languages* were developed in which single statements could be written to accomplish substantial tasks. The translator programs that convert high-level language programs into machine language are called *compilers.* High-level languages allow programmers to write instructions that look almost like everyday English and contain commonly used mathematical notations. A payroll program written in a high-level language might contain a statement such as:

```
grossPay = basePay + overTimePay
```

Obviously, high-level languages are much more desirable from the programmer's standpoint than either machine languages or assembly languages. C and C++ are among the most powerful and most widely-used high-level languages.

The process of compiling a high-level language program into machine language can take a considerable amount of computer time. *Interpreter* programs were developed that can directly execute high-level language programs without the need for compiling those programs into machine language. Although compiled programs execute faster than interpreted programs, interpreters are popular in program development environments in which programs are recompiled frequently as new features are added and errors are corrected. Once a program is developed, a compiled version can be produced to run most efficiently.

## 1.7 History of C++

C++ evolved from C which evolved from two previous languages, BCPL and B. BCPL was developed in 1967 by Martin Richards as a language for writing operating systems software and compilers. Ken Thompson modeled many features in his language B after their counterparts in BCPL and used B to create early versions of the UNIX operating system at Bell Laboratories in 1970 on a DEC PDP-7 computer. Both BCPL and B were "typeless" languages—every data item occupied one "word" in memory and the burden of treating a data item as a whole number or a real number, for example, fell on the shoulders of the programmer.

The C language was evolved from B by Dennis Ritchie at Bell Laboratories and was originally implemented on a DEC PDP-11 computer in 1972. C uses many important concepts of BCPL and B while adding data typing and other features. C initially became widely known as the development language of the UNIX operating system. Today, virtually all new major operating systems are written in C and/or C++. Over the past two decades, C has become available for most computers. C is hardware independent. With careful design, it is possible to write C programs that are *portable* to most computers.

By the late 1970s, C had evolved into what is now referred to as "traditional C," "classic C," or "Kernighan and Ritchie C." The publication by Prentice-Hall in 1978 of Kernighan and Ritchie's book, *The C Programming Language,* brought wide attention to the language (Ke78). This publication became one of the most successful computer science books of all time.

The widespread use of C with various types of computers (sometimes called *hardware platforms*) unfortunately led to many variations. These were similar, but often incompatible. This was a serious problem for program developers who needed to write portable programs that would run on several platforms. It became clear that a standard version of C was needed. In 1983, the X3J11 technical committee was created under the American National Standards Committee on Computers and Information Processing (X3) to "provide an unambiguous and machine-independent definition of the language." In 1989, the standard was approved. ANSI cooperated with the International Standards Organizations (ISO) to standardize C worldwide; the joint standard document was published in 1990 and is referred to as ANSI/ISO 9899: 1990. Copies of this document may be ordered from ANSI. The second edition of Kernighan and Ritchie, published in 1988, reflects this version called ANSI C, a version of the language now used worldwide (Ke88).

***Portability Tip 1.1***

*Because C is a standardized, hardware-independent, widely available language, applications written in C can often be run with little or no modifications on a wide range of different computer systems.*

C++, an extension of C, was developed by Bjarne Stroustrup in the early 1980s at Bell Laboratories. C++ provides a number of features that "spruce up" the C language, but more importantly, it provides capabilities for *object-oriented programming.*

There is a revolution brewing in the software community. Building software quickly, correctly, and economically remains an elusive goal, and this at a time when demands for new and more powerful software are soaring. *Objects* are essentially reusable software *components* that model items in the real world. Software developers are discovering that using a modular, object-oriented design and implementation approach can make software development groups much more productive than is possible with previous popular programming techniques such as structured programming. Object-oriented programs are easier to understand, correct and modify.

Many other object-oriented languages have been developed, including most notably, Smalltalk, developed at Xerox's Palo Alto Research Center (PARC). Smalltalk is a pure object-oriented language—literally everything is an object. C++ is a hybrid language—it is possible to program in either a C-like style, an object-oriented style, or both. It is widely believed that C++ will become the dominant systems-implementation language in the mid-to-late 1990s.

## 1.8 C++ Class Libraries and the C Standard Library

C++ programs consist of pieces called *classes* and *functions*. You can program each piece you may need to form a C++ program. But most C++ programmers take advantage of rich collections of existing classes and functions in C++ class libraries and the *ANSI C standard function library* (which C++ borrows from the ANSI C language). Thus, there are really two pieces to learning the C++ "world." The first is learning the C++ language itself, and the second is learning how to use the classes in various C++ class libraries and the functions in the ANSI C standard library. Throughout the book, we discuss many of these classes and functions. Appendix B (condensed and adapted from the ANSI C standard document itself) enumerates the functions available in the ANSI C standard library. The book by Plauger (Pl92) is must reading for programmers who need a deep understanding of the ANSI C library functions, how to implement them, and how to use them to write portable code. Class libraries are provided primarily by compiler vendors, but many class libraries are supplied by independent software vendors.

***Software Engineering Observation 1.1***

*Use a* building block approach *to creating programs. Avoid reinventing the wheel. Use existing pieces—this is called* software reuse *and it is central to object-oriented programming.*

***Software Engineering Observation 1.2***

*When programming in C++ you will typically use the following building blocks: classes from class libraries and functions from the ANSI C standard library, classes and functions you create yourself, and classes and functions other people create and make available to you.*

The advantage of creating your own functions and classes is that you will know exactly how they work. You will be able to examine the C++ code. The disadvantage is the time-consuming and complex effort that goes into designing and developing new functions and classes.

***Performance Tip 1.1***

*Using ANSI standard library functions instead of writing your own comparable versions can improve program performance because these functions are carefully written to perform efficiently.*

***Portability Tip 1.2***

*Using ANSI standard library functions instead of writing your own comparable versions can improve program portability because these functions are included in virtually all C++ implementations.*

## 1.9 Concurrent C++

Other versions of C and C++ have been developed through continuing research efforts at Bell Laboratories. Gehani (Ge89) has developed *Concurrent C* and *Concurrent C++*—both C extensions which include capabilities for specifying that multiple activities can be performed in parallel. Languages like these will become popular in the next decade as the use of *multiprocessors,* i.e., computers with more than one CPU, increases. As of this writing, Concurrent C and Concurrent C++ are still primarily research languages and have not gained commercial acceptance. Operating systems textbooks usually include substantial treatments of concurrent programming (De90).

## 1.10 Other High-level Languages

Hundreds of high-level languages have been developed, but only a few have achieved broad acceptance. *FORTRAN* (FORmula TRANslator) was developed by IBM Corporation between 1954 and 1957 to be used for scientific and engineering applications that require complex mathematical computations. FORTRAN is still widely used, especially in engineering applications.

*COBOL* (COmmon Business Oriented Language) was developed in 1959 by a group of computer manufacturers and government and industrial computer users. COBOL is used primarily for commercial applications that require precise and efficient manipulation of large amounts of data. Today, more than half of all business software is still programmed in COBOL. Approximately one million people are actively writing COBOL programs.

*Pascal* was designed at about the same time as C. It was created by Professor Nicklaus Wirth and was intended for academic use. We will say more about Pascal in the next section.

## 1.11 Structured Programming

During the 1960s, many large software development efforts encountered severe difficulties. Software schedules were typically late, costs greatly exceeded budgets, and the finished products were unreliable. People began to realize that software development was a far more complex activity than they had imagined. Research activity in the 1960s resulted in the evolution of *structured programming*—a disciplined approach to writing programs that are clearer than unstructured programs, easier to test and debug, and easier to modify.

Chapter 2 discusses the principles of structured programming. Chapters 3 through 5 develop many structured programs.

One of the more tangible results of this research was the development of the Pascal programming language by Nicklaus Wirth in 1971. Pascal, named after the seventeenth-century mathematician and philosopher Blaise Pascal, was designed for teaching structured programming in academic environments and rapidly became the preferred programming language in most universities. Unfortunately, the language lacks many features needed to make it useful in commercial, industrial, and government applications, so it has not been widely accepted in these environments.

The Ada programming language was developed under the sponsorship of the United States Department of Defense (DOD) during the 1970s and early 1980s. Hundreds of separate languages were being used to produce DOD's massive command-and-control software systems. DOD wanted a single language that would fulfill most of its needs. Pascal was chosen as a base, but the final Ada language is quite different from Pascal. The language was named after Lady Ada Lovelace, daughter of the poet Lord Byron. Lady Lovelace is generally credited with writing the world's first computer program in the early 1800s (for the Analytical Engine mechanical computing device designed by Charles Babbage). One important capability of Ada is called *multitasking;* this allows programmers to specify that many activities are to occur in parallel. The other widely used high-level languages we have discussed—including C and C++—generally allow the programmer to write programs that perform only one activity at a time.

## 1.12 Basics of a Typical C++ Environment

C++ systems generally consist of several parts: an environment, the language, the C Standard Library, and various class libraries. The following discussion explains a typical C++ program development environment shown in Fig. 1.1.

C++ programs typically go through six phases to be executed (Fig. 1.1). These are: *edit, preprocess, compile, link, load,* and *execute.* We concentrate on a typical UNIX-based C++ system here. If you are not using a UNIX system, refer to the manuals for your system, or ask your instructor how to accomplish these tasks in your environment.

The first phase consists of editing a file. This is accomplished with an *editor program.* The programmer types a C++ program with the editor and makes corrections if necessary. The program is then stored on a secondary storage device such as a disk. C++ program file names often end with the **.C** extension (note that **C** is in uppercase; some C++ environments require other extensions such as **.cpp** or **.cxx**; see the documentation for your C++ environment for more information). Two editors widely used on UNIX systems are **vi** and **emacs**. C++ software packages such as Borland C++ and Microsoft C/C++ for personal computers have built-in editors that are smoothly integrated into the programming environment. We assume the reader knows how to edit a program.

Next, the programmer gives the command to *compile* the program. The compiler translates the C++ program into machine language code (also referred to as *object code*). In a C++ system, a preprocessor program executes before the compiler's translation phase begins. The C++ preprocessor obeys special commands called *preprocessor directives* which indicate that certain manipulations are to be performed on the program before

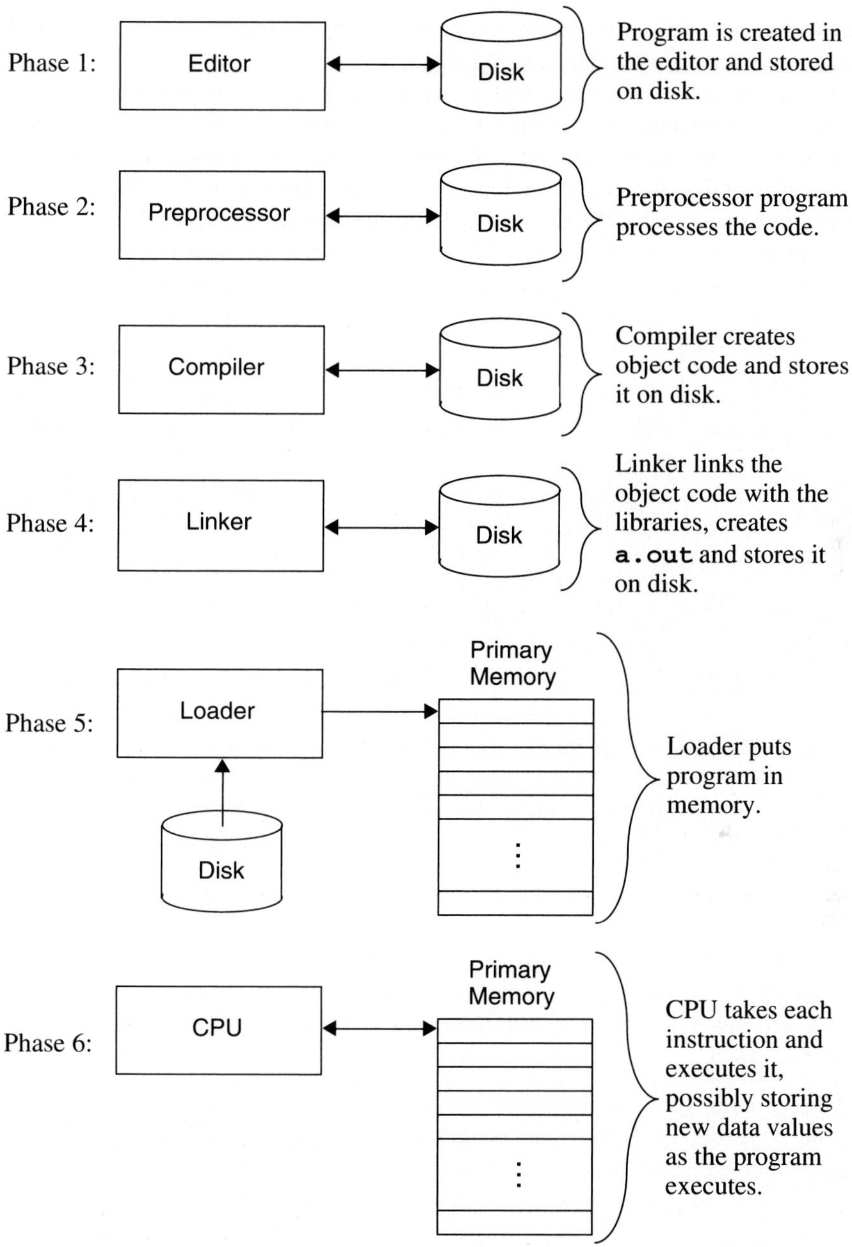


**Fig. 1.1** A typical C++ environment.

compilation. These manipulations usually consist of including other text files in the file to be compiled and performing various text replacements. The most common preprocessor directives are discussed in the early chapters; a detailed discussion of all the preprocessor features appears in the appendices. The preprocessor is invoked by the compiler before the program is converted to machine language.

The next phase is called *linking*. C++ programs typically contain references to functions defined elsewhere such as in the standard libraries or in the private libraries of groups of programmers working on a particular project. The object code produced by the C++ compiler typically contains "holes" due to these missing parts. A *linker* links the object code with the code for the missing functions to produce an *executable image* (with no missing pieces). On a typical UNIX-based system, the command to compile and link a C++ program is **`CC`**. To compile and link a program named **`welcome.C`** type

```
CC welcome.C
```

at the UNIX prompt and press the return key. If the program compiles and links correctly, a file called **`a.out`** will be produced. This is the executable image of our **`welcome.C`** program.

The next phase is called *loading*. Before a program can be executed, the program must first be placed in memory. This is done by the *loader* which takes the executable image from disk and transfers it to memory.

Finally, the computer, under the control of its CPU, executes the program one instruction at a time. To load and execute the program on a UNIX system, we type **`a.out`** at the UNIX prompt and press return.

Programs rarely work on the first try. Each of the preceding phases can fail because of various types of errors that we will discuss in this text. For example, an executing program might attempt to divide by zero (an illegal operation on computers just as it is in arithmetic). This would cause the computer to print an error message. The programmer would return to the edit phase, make the necessary corrections, and proceed through the remaining phases again to determine that the corrections work properly.

***Common Programming Error 1.1***

*Errors like division-by-zero errors occur as a program runs, so these errors are called* run-time errors *or* execution-time errors. *Divide-by-zero is generally a* fatal error, *i.e., an error that causes the program to terminate immediately without having successfully performed its job.* Nonfatal errors *allow programs to run to completion, often producing incorrect results.*

Most programs in C++ input and/or output data. Certain C++ functions take their input from **`cin`** (the *standard input stream*; pronounced "see-in") which is normally the keyboard, but **`cin`** can be connected to another device. Data is output to **`cout`** (the *standard output stream*; pronounced "see-out") which is normally the computer screen, but **`cout`** can be connected to another device. When we say that a program prints a result, we normally mean that the result is displayed on a screen. Data may be output to other devices such as disks and hardcopy printers. There is also a *standard error stream* referred to as **`cerr`**. The **`cerr`** stream (normally connected to the screen) is used for displaying error messages. It is common for users to route regular output data, i.e., **`cout`**, to a device other than the screen while keeping **`cerr`** assigned to the screen so the user can be immediately informed of errors.

## 1.13 General Notes About C++ and this Book

C++ is a difficult language. Experienced C++ programmers sometimes take pride in being able to create some weird, contorted, convoluted usage of the language. This is a poor programming practice. It makes programs more difficult to read, more likely to behave strangely, more difficult to test and debug, and more difficult to adapt to changing requirements. This book is geared for novice programmers, so we stress *clarity.* The following is our first "good programming practice."

***Good Programming Practice 1.1***

*Write your C++ programs in a simple and straightforward manner. This is sometimes referred to as KIS ("keep it simple"). Do not "stretch" the language by trying bizarre usages.*

We will include many of these tips throughout the text to highlight those practices that can help you write programs that are clearer, more understandable, more maintainable, and easier to test and debug. These practices are only guidelines; you will, no doubt, develop your own preferred programming style. We will also highlight common programming errors (problems to watch out for so you do not make these errors in your programs), performance tips (techniques that will help you write programs that run faster and use less memory), portability tips (techniques that will help you write programs that can run, with little or no modifications, on a variety of computers), and software engineering observations (thoughts and concepts that affect and improve the overall architecture of a software system, and particularly, of large software systems).

You have heard that C and C++ are portable languages, and that programs written in C and C++ can run on many different computers. *Portability is an elusive goal.* The ANSI C standard document (An90) contains a lengthy list of portability issues, and complete books have been written that discuss portability in C (Ja89) (Ra90).

***Portability Tip 1.3***

*Although it is possible to write portable programs, there are many problems among different C and C++ compilers and different computers that can make portability difficult to achieve. Simply writing programs in C and C++ does not guarantee portability. The programmer will often need to deal directly with compiler and computer variations.*

We have done a careful walkthrough of the evolving ANSI C++ standard document and audited our presentation against it for completeness and accuracy. However, C++ is a rich language, and there are some subtleties in the language and some advanced subjects we have not covered. If you need additional technical details on C++, we suggest that you read the most current draft of the ANSI C++ standard document. Another valuable source (although a bit out of date) is *The Annotated C++ Reference Manual* by Margaret Ellis and Bjarne Stroustrup (Addison Wesley Publishing Company, 1991). Our book contains an extensive bibliography of books and papers on the C++ language and object-oriented programming.

Many features of the current versions of C++ are not compatible with older C++ implementations, so you may find that some of the programs in this text do not work on older C++ compilers.

***Good Programming Practice 1.2***

*Read the manuals for the version of C++ you are using. Refer to these manuals frequently to be sure you are aware of the rich collection of C++ features and that you are using these features correctly.*

***Good Programming Practice 1.3***

*Your computer and compiler are good teachers. If after carefully reading your C++ language manual you are not sure how a feature of C++ works, experiment and see what happens. Set your compiler options for "maximum warnings." Study each message you get when you compile your programs and correct the programs to eliminate the messages.*

## 1.14 Introduction to C++ Programming

The C++ language facilitates a structured and disciplined approach to computer program design. We now introduce C++ programming and present several examples that illustrate many important features of C++. Each example is analyzed one statement at a time. In Chapter 2 we present a detailed treatment of *structured programming* in C++. We then use the structured approach through Chapter 5. Beginning with Chapter 6, we study object-oriented programming in C++. Again, because of the central importance of object-oriented programming in this book, each of the first five chapters concludes with a section entitled "Thinking About Objects." These special sections introduce the concepts of object orientation.

## 1.15 A Simple Program: Printing a Line of Text

C++ uses notations that may appear strange to nonprogrammers. We begin by considering a simple program that prints a line of text. The program and its screen output are shown in Fig. 1.2.

This program illustrates several important features of the C++ language. We consider each line of the program in detail. The line

```
// A first program in C++
#include <iostream.h>

main()
{
   cout << "Welcome to C++!\n";

   return 0;    // indicate that program ended successfully
}
```

```
Welcome to C++!
```

Fig. 1.2 Text printing program.

```
// A first program in C++
```

begins with **//** indicating that the remainder of the line is a *comment.* Programmers insert comments to *document* programs and improve program readability. Comments also help other people read and understand your program. Comments do not cause the computer to perform any action when the program is run. Comments are ignored by the C++ compiler and do not cause any machine language object code to be generated. The comment **A first program in C++** simply describes the purpose of the program. A comment that begins with **//** is called a *single-line comment* because the comment terminates at the end of the current line. Later, we will discuss an alternate comment notation that facilitates writing embedded comments and multiple-line comments.

***Good Programming Practice 1.4***

*Every program should begin with a comment describing the purpose of the program.*

The line

```
#include <iostream.h>
```

is a *preprocessor directive,* i.e., a message to the C++ preprocessor. Lines beginning with **#** are processed by the preprocessor before the program is compiled. This specific line tells the preprocessor to include the contents of the *input/output stream header file* **iostream.h** in the program. This file must be included for any program that outputs data to the screen or inputs data from the keyboard using C++-style stream input/output. The program in Fig. 1.2 outputs data to the screen, as we will soon see. The contents of **iostream.h** will be explained in more detail in Chapter 3.

***Common Programming Error 1.2***

*Forgetting to include the* **iostream.h** *file in a program that inputs data from the keyboard or outputs data to the screen.*

The line

```
main()
```

is a part of every C++ program. The parentheses after **main** indicate that **main** is a program building block called a *function.* C++ programs contain one or more functions, one of which must be **main**. The program in Fig. 1.2 contains only one function. C++ programs normally begin executing at function **main**, even if **main** is not the first function in the program.

The *left brace,* **{**, must begin the *body* of every function. A corresponding *right brace* must end each function. The line

```
cout << "Welcome to C++!\n";
```

instructs the computer to print on the screen the *string* of characters contained between the quotation marks. The entire line, including **cout**, the **<<** *operator,* the *string* **"Welcome to C++!\n"**, and the *semicolon* (**;**), is called a *statement.* Every statement must end with a semicolon (also known as the *statement terminator*). All output and input in

C++ is accomplished with *streams* of characters. Thus, when the preceding statement is executed, it sends the stream of characters **`Welcome to C++!`** to the *standard output stream object*—**`cout`**—which is normally "connected" to the screen. We will discuss **`cout`** in detail in Chapter 11, "Stream Input/Output."

The operator **`<<`** is referred to as the *stream insertion operator.* When this program executes, the value to the right of the operator, the right *operand,* is inserted in the output stream. The characters of the right operand normally print exactly as they appear between the double quotes. Notice, however, that the characters **`\n`** are not printed on the screen. The backslash (**`\`**) is called an *escape character.* It indicates that a "special" character is to be output. When a backslash is encountered in a string of characters, the next character is combined with the backslash to form an *escape sequence.* The escape sequence **`\n`** means *newline.* It causes the *cursor* (i.e., the current screen position indicator) to move to the beginning of the next line on the screen. Some other common escape sequences are listed in Fig. 1.3.

***Common Programming Error 1.3***

*Omitting the semicolon at the end of a statement is a* syntax error. *A syntax error is caused when the compiler can not recognize a statement. The compiler normally issues an error message to help the programmer locate and fix the incorrect statement. Syntax errors are violations of the language. Syntax errors are also called* compile errors, compile-time errors, *or* compilation errors *because they appear during the compilation phase.*

The line

```
return 0;    // indicate that program ended successfully
```

is included at the end of every **`main`** function. The C++ keyword **`return`** is one of several methods used to *exit a function.* When the **`return`** statement is used at the end of **`main`** as shown here, the value **`0`** indicates that the program has terminated successfully. In Chapter 3, we discuss functions in detail and the reasons for including this statement will become clear. For now, simply include this statement in each program, or the compiler may produce a warning on some systems.

| Escape Sequence | Description |
|---|---|
| `\n` | Newline. Position the cursor to the beginning of the next line. |
| `\t` | Horizontal tab. Move the cursor to the next tab stop. |
| `\r` | Carriage return. Position the cursor to the beginning of the current line; do not advance to the next line. |
| `\a` | Alert. Sound the system bell. |
| `\\` | Backslash. Used to print a backslash character. |
| `\"` | Double quote. Used to print a double quote character. |

**Fig. 1.3** Some common escape sequences.

The right brace, **}**, indicates the end of **main**.

*Good Programming Practice 1.5*

*The last character printed by a function that does any printing should be a newline (**\n**). This ensures that the function will leave the cursor positioned at the beginning of a new line. Conventions of this nature encourage software reusability—a key goal in software development environments.*

*Good Programming Practice 1.6*

*Indent the entire body of each function one level of indentation within the braces that define the body of the function. This makes the functional structure of a program stand out and helps make programs easier to read.*

*Good Programming Practice 1.7*

*Set a convention for the size of indent you prefer and then uniformly apply that convention. The tab key may be used to create indents, but tab stops may vary. We recommend using either 1/4-inch tab stops or (preferably) three spaces to form a level of indent.*

**Welcome to C++!** can be printed several ways. For example, the program of Fig. 1.4 uses multiple stream insertion statements, yet produces identical output to the program of Fig. 1.2. This works because each stream insertion statement resumes printing where the previous statement stopped printing. The first stream insertion prints **Welcome** followed by a space, and the second stream insertion begins printing on the same line immediately following the space. In general, C++ allows the programmer to express statements in a variety of ways.

A single statement can print multiple lines by using newline characters as in Fig. 1.5. Each time the **\n** (newline) escape sequence is encountered in the output stream, the cursor is positioned to the beginning of the next line. To get a blank line in your output, simply place two newline characters back-to-back.

```
// Printing a line with multiple statements
#include <iostream.h>

main()
{
   cout << "Welcome ";
   cout << "to C++!\n";

   return 0;   // indicate that program ended successfully
}
```

```
Welcome to C++!
```

Fig. 1.4 Printing on one line with separate statements using **cout**.

```
// Printing multiple lines with a single statement
#include <iostream.h>

main()
{
   cout << "Welcome\nto\nC++!\n";

   return 0;    // indicate that program ended successfully
}
```

```
Welcome
to
C++!
```

**Fig. 1.5** Printing on multiple lines with a single statement using **`cout`**.

## 1.16 Another Simple Program: Adding Two Integers

Our next program uses the input stream object **`cin`** and the *stream extraction operator,* **`>>`**, to obtain two integers typed by a user at the keyboard, computes the sum of these values, and outputs the result using **`cout`**. The program and sample output are shown in Fig. 1.6.

```
// Addition program
#include <iostream.h>

main()
{
   int integer1, integer2, sum;       // declaration

   cout << "Enter first integer\n";   // prompt
   cin >> integer1;                   // read an integer
   cout << "Enter second integer\n";  // prompt
   cin >> integer2;                   // read an integer
   sum = integer1 + integer2;         // assignment of sum
   cout << "Sum is " << sum << endl;  // print sum

   return 0;    // indicate that program ended successfully
}
```

```
Enter first integer
45
Enter second integer
72
Sum is 117
```

**Fig. 1.6** An addition program.

The comment

```
// Addition program
```

states the purpose of the program. The C++ preprocessor directive

```
#include <iostream.h>
```

includes the contents of the **iostream.h** header file in the program.

As stated earlier, every program begins execution with function **main**. The left brace marks the beginning of **main**'s body and the corresponding right brace marks the end of **main**. The line

```
int integer1, integer2, sum;        // declaration
```

is a *declaration.* The words **integer1**, **integer2**, and **sum** are the names of *variables.* A variable is a location in the computer's memory where a value can be stored for use by a program. This declaration specifies that the variables **integer1**, **integer2**, and **sum** are data of type ***int*** which means that these variables will hold *integer* values, i.e., whole numbers such as 7, –11, 0, 31914. All variables must be declared with a name and a data type before they can be used in a program. Several variables of the same type may be declared in one declaration or in multiple declarations. We could have written three declarations, one for each variable, but the preceding declaration is more concise.

We will soon discuss the data types **float** (for specifying real numbers, i.e., numbers with decimal points like 3.4, 0.0, –11.19) and **char** (for specifying character data; a **char** variable may hold only a single lowercase letter, a single uppercase letter, a single digit, or a single special character like a *, $, etc.).

***Good Programming Practice 1.8***

*Place a space after each comma (**,**) to make programs more readable.*

A variable name is any valid *identifier.* An identifier is a series of characters consisting of letters, digits, and underscores ( _ ) that does not begin with a digit. C++ allows identifiers of any length, but your system and/or C++ implementation may impose some restrictions on the length of identifiers. C++ is *case sensitive*—uppercase and lowercase letters are different, so **a1** and **A1** are different identifiers.

***Good Programming Practice 1.9***

*Choosing meaningful variable names helps a program to be "self-documenting," i.e., it becomes easier to understand the program simply by reading it rather than having to read manuals or use excessive comments.*

***Good Programming Practice 1.10***

*Avoid indentifiers that begin with underscores because a C++ compiler may use names like that for its own purposes internally. This will prevent names you choose from being confused with names the compiler chooses.*

Declarations can be placed almost anywhere in a function. However, the declaration of a variable must appear before the variable is used in the program. For example, in the program of Fig. 1.6, instead of using a single declaration for all three variables, three separate declarations could have been used. The declaration

```
int integer1;
```

could have been placed immediately before the line

```
cin >> integer1;
```

the declaration

```
int integer2;
```

could have been placed immediately before the line

```
cin >> integer2;
```

and the declaration

```
int sum;
```

could have been placed immediately before the line

```
sum = integer1 + integer2;
```

***Good Programming Practice 1.11***

*Always place a blank line before a declaration that appears between executable statements. This makes the declarations stand out in the program and contributes to program clarity.*

***Good Programming Practice 1.12***

*If you prefer to place declarations at the beginning of a function, separate those declarations from the executable statements in that function with one blank line to highlight where the declarations end and the executable statements begin.*

The statement

```
cout << "Enter first integer\n";   // prompt
```

prints the literal **`Enter first integer`** on the screen and positions to the beginning of the next line. This message is called a *prompt* because it tells the user to take a specific action. We like to pronounce the preceding statement as "**`cout`** *gets* the character string **`"Enter first integer\n"`**."

The statement

```
cin >> integer1;                   // read an integer
```

uses the *input stream object* **`cin`** and the *stream extraction operator*, **`>>`**, to obtain a value from the user. The **`cin`** object takes input from the standard input stream which is usually the keyboard. We like to pronounce the preceding statement as, "**`cin`** gives a value to **`integer1`**."

When the computer executes the preceding statement, it waits for the user to enter a value for variable **integer1**. The user responds by typing an integer and then pressing the *return key* (sometimes called the *enter key*) to send the number to the computer. The computer then assigns this number, or *value,* to the variable **integer1**. Any subsequent references to **integer1** in the program will use this same value.

The **cout** and **cin** stream objects facilitate interaction between the user and the computer. Because this interaction resembles a dialogue, it is often called *conversational computing* or *interactive computing.*

The statement

```
cout << "Enter second integer\n"; // prompt
```

prints the message **Enter second integer** on the screen, then positions to the beginning of the next line. This statement prompts the user to take action. The statement

```
cin >> integer2;                  // read an integer
```

obtains a value for variable **integer2** from the user.

The assignment statement

```
sum = integer1 + integer2;        // assignment of sum
```

calculates the sum of the variables **integer1** and **integer2**, and assigns the result to variable **sum** using the *assignment operator* **=**. The statement is read as, "**sum** *gets* the value of **integer1 + integer2**." Most calculations are performed in assignment statements. The **=** operator and the **+** operator are called *binary operators* because they each have two *operands.* In the case of the **+** operator, the two operands are **integer1** and **integer2**. In the case of the **=** operator, the two operands are **sum** and the value of the expression **integer1 + integer2**.

***Good Programming Practice 1.13***

*Place spaces on either side of a binary operator. This makes the operator stand out and makes the program more readable.*

The statement

```
cout << "Sum is " << sum << endl; // print sum
```

prints the character string **Sum is** followed by the numerical value of variable **sum** followed by **endl** (an abbreviation for "end line")—a so-called *stream manipulator.* The **endl** manipulator outputs a newline and then "flushes the output buffer." This simply means that on some systems where outputs accumulate in the machine until there are enough to "make it worthwhile to print on the screen," **endl** forces any accumulated outputs to be printed at that moment.

Note that the preceding statement outputs multiple values of different types. The stream insertion operator "knows" how to output each piece of data. Using multiple stream insertion operators (**<<**) in a single statement is referred to as *concatenating stream insertion operations.* Thus, it is unnecessary to have multiple output statements to output multiple pieces of data.

Calculations can also be performed in output statements. We could have combined the previous two statements into the statement

```
cout << "Sum is " << integer1 + integer2 << endl;
```

The right brace, **}**, informs the computer that the end of function **main** has been reached.

A powerful feature of C++ is that users can create their own data types (we will explore this in Chapter 6). Users can then "teach" C++ how to input and output values of these new data types using the **>>** and **<<** operators (this is called *operator overloading*—a topic we will explore in Chapter 8).

## 1.17 Memory Concepts

Variable names such as **integer1**, **integer2**, and **sum** actually correspond to *locations* in the computer's memory. Every variable has a *name*, a *type*, a *size* and a *value*.

In the addition program of Fig. 1.6, when the statement

```
cin >> integer1;
```

is executed, the value typed by the user is placed into a memory location to which the name **integer1** has been assigned by the compiler. Suppose the user enters the number **45** as the value for **integer1**. The computer will place **45** into location **integer1** as shown in Fig. 1.7.

Whenever a value is placed in a memory location, the value replaces the previous value in that location. The previous value is destroyed.

Returning to our addition program, when the statement

```
cin >> integer2;
```

is executed, suppose the user enters the value **72**. This value is placed into location **integer2**, and memory appears as in Fig. 1.8. Note that these locations need not be adjacent in memory.

| integer1 | 45 |
|---|---|

**Fig. 1.7** A memory location showing the name and value of a variable.

| integer1 | 45 |
|---|---|
| integer2 | 72 |

**Fig. 1.8** Memory locations after values for two variables have been input.

Once the program has obtained values for **integer1** and **integer2**, it adds these values and places the sum into variable **sum**. The statement

```
sum = integer1 + integer2;
```

that performs the addition also involves destroying a value. This occurs when the calculated sum of **integer1** and **integer2** is placed into location **sum** (without regard to what value may already be in **sum**). After **sum** is calculated, memory appears as in Fig. 1.9. Note that the values of **integer1** and **integer2** appear exactly as they did before they were used in the calculation of **sum**. These values were used, but not destroyed, as the computer performed the calculation. Thus, when a value is read out of a memory location, the process is nondestructive.

## 1.18 Arithmetic

Most programs perform arithmetic calculations. The *arithmetic operators* are summarized in Fig. 1.10. Note the use of various special symbols not used in algebra. The *asterisk* (*) indicates multiplication, and the *percent sign* (%) is the *modulus* operator which will be discussed shortly. The arithmetic operators in Fig. 1.10 are all binary operators. For example, the expression **integer1 + integer2** contains the binary operator **+** and the two operands **integer1** and **integer2**.

| | |
|---|---|
| integer1 | 45 |
| integer2 | 72 |
| sum | 117 |

Fig. 1.9 Memory locations after a calculation.

| C++ operation | Arithmetic operator | Algebraic expression | C++ expression |
|---|---|---|---|
| Addition | + | $f + 7$ | `f + 7` |
| Subtraction | - | $p - c$ | `p - c` |
| Multiplication | * | $bm$ | `b * m` |
| Division | / | $x / y$ *or* $\frac{x}{y}$ *or* $x \div y$ | `x / y` |
| Modulus | % | r mod s | `r % s` |

Fig. 1.10 Arithmetic operators.

*Integer division* yields an integer result; for example, the expression `7 / 4` evaluates to `1`, and the expression `17 / 5` evaluates to `3`. Note that any fractional part in integer division is simply discarded (i.e., truncated)—no rounding occurs. C++ provides the modulus operator, `%`, which yields the remainder after integer division. The modulus operator is an integer operator that can be used only with integer operands. The expression `x % y` yields the remainder after `x` is divided by `y`. Thus, `7 % 4` yields `3`, and `17 % 5` yields `2`. In later chapters, we will discuss many interesting applications of the modulus operator such as determining if one number is a multiple of another.

***Common Programming Error 1.4***

*Attempting to use the modulus operator,* `%`, *with noninteger operands is a syntax error.*

Arithmetic expressions in C++ must be written in *straight-line form* to facilitate entering programs into the computer. Thus, expressions such as "`a` divided by `b`" must be written as `a / b` so that all constants, variables, and operators appear in a straight line. The algebraic notation

$$\frac{a}{b}$$

is generally not acceptable to compilers, although some special-purpose software packages do exist that support more natural notation for complex mathematical expressions.

Parentheses are used in C++ expressions in much the same manner as in algebraic expressions. For example, to multiply `a` times the quantity `b + c` we write:

```
a * (b + c)
```

C++ applies the operators in arithmetic expressions in a precise sequence determined by the following *rules of operator precedence,* which are generally the same as those followed in algebra:

1. Operators in expressions contained within pairs of parentheses are evaluated first. Thus, *parentheses may be used to force the order of evaluation to occur in any sequence desired by the programmer.* Parentheses are said to be at the "highest level of precedence." In cases of *nested,* or *embedded,* parentheses, the operators in the innermost pair of parentheses are applied first.
2. Multiplication, division, and modulus operations are applied next. If an expression contains several multiplication, division, and modulus operations, operators are applied from left to right. Multiplication, division, and modulus are said to be on the same level of precedence.
3. Addition and subtraction operations are applied last. If an expression contains several addition and subtraction operations, operators are applied from left to right. Addition and subtraction also have the same level of precedence.

The rules of operator precedence enable C++ to apply operators in the correct order. When we say operators are applied from left to right, we are referring to the *associativity* of the operators. We will see that some operators associate from right to left. Fig. 1.11 summarizes these rules of operator precedence. This table will be expanded as additional C++ operators are introduced. A complete precedence chart is included in Appendix C.

| Operator(s) | Operation(s) | Order of evaluation (precedence) |
|---|---|---|
| `( )` | Parentheses | Evaluated first. If the parentheses are nested, the expression in the innermost pair is evaluated first. If there are several pairs of parentheses "on the same level" (i.e., not nested), they are evaluated left to right. |
| `*`, `/`, or `%` | Multiplication<br>Division<br>Modulus | Evaluated second. If there are several, they are evaluated left to right. |
| `+` or `-` | Addition<br>Subtraction | Evaluated last. If there are several, they are evaluated left to right. |

**Fig. 1.11** Precedence of arithmetic operators.

Now let us consider several expressions in light of the rules of operator precedence. Each example lists an algebraic expression and its C++ equivalent.

The following is an example of an arithmetic mean (average) of five terms:

Algebra: $m = \frac{a + b + c + d + e}{5}$

C++: `m = (a + b + c + d + e) / 5;`

The parentheses are required because division has higher precedence than addition. The entire quantity **`(a + b + c + d + e)`** is to be divided by **`5`**. If the parentheses are erroneously omitted, we obtain **`a + b + c + d + e / 5`** which evaluates as

$$a + b + c + d + \frac{e}{5}$$

The following is an example of the equation of a straight line:

Algebra: $y = mx + b$

C++: `y = m * x + b;`

No parentheses are required. The multiplication is applied first because multiplication has a higher precedence than addition.

The following example contains modulus (%), multiplication, division, addition, and subtraction operations:

Algebra: $z = pr \% q + w / x - y$

C++: `z = p * r % q + w / x - y;`

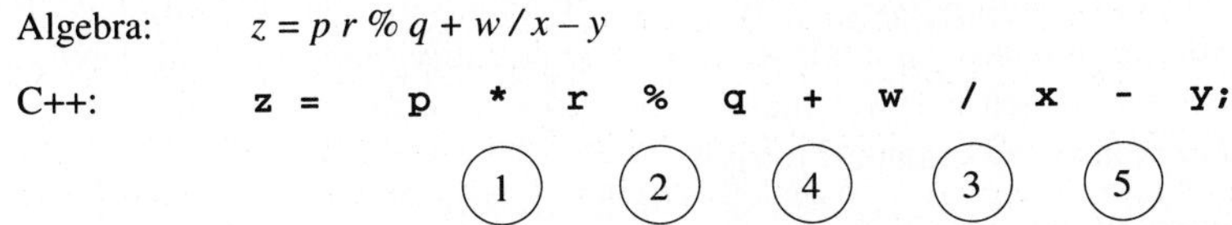

The circled numbers under the statement indicate the order in which C++ applies the operators. The multiplication, modulus, and division are evaluated first in left-to-right order (i.e., they associate from left to right) since they have higher precedence than addition and subtraction. The addition and subtraction are applied next. These are also applied left to right.

Not all expressions with several pairs of parentheses contain nested parentheses. For example, the expression

```
a * (b + c) + c * (d + e)
```

does not contain nested parentheses. Rather, the parentheses are said to be on the same level.

To develop a better understanding of the rules of operator precedence, consider how a second-degree polynomial is evaluated.

```
y =   a   *   x   *   x   +   b   *   x   +   c;
```

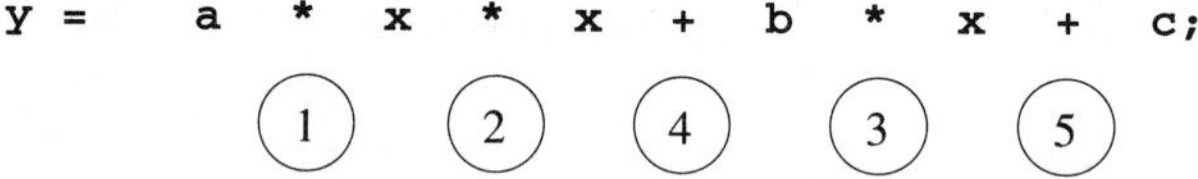


The circled numbers under the statement indicate the order in which C++ applies the operators. There is no arithmetic operator for exponentiation in C++, so we have represented $x^2$ as **x * x**. We will soon discuss the library function **pow** ("power") that performs exponentiation. Because of some subtle issues related to the data types required by **pow**, we defer a detailed explanation of **pow** until Chapter 3.

Suppose variables **a**, **b**, **c**, and **x** are initialized as follows: **a = 2**, **b = 3**, **c = 7**, and **x = 5**. Figure 1.12 illustrates the order in which the operators are applied in the preceding second degree polynomial.

As in algebra, it is acceptable to place unnecessary parentheses in an expression to make the expression clearer. These unnecessary parentheses are also called *redundant parentheses*. For example, the preceding assignment statement might be parenthesized as

```
y = (a * x * x) + (b * x) + c;
```

## 1.19 Decision Making: Equality and Relational Operators

This section introduces a simple version of C++'s *if structure* that allows a program to make a decision based on the truth or falsity of some *condition*. If the condition is met, i.e., the condition is *true*, the statement in the body of the **if** structure is executed. If the condition is not met, i.e., the condition is *false*, the body statement is not executed. We will see an example shortly.

Conditions in **if** structures can be formed by using the *equality operators* and *relational operators* summarized in Fig. 1.13. The relational operators all have the same level of precedence and associate left to right. The equality operators both have the same level of precedence, which is lower than the precedence of the relational operators. The equality operators also associate left to right.

***Common Programming Error 1.5***

*A syntax error will occur if the operators* **==**, **!=**, **>=**, *and* **<=** *contain spaces between their symbols.*

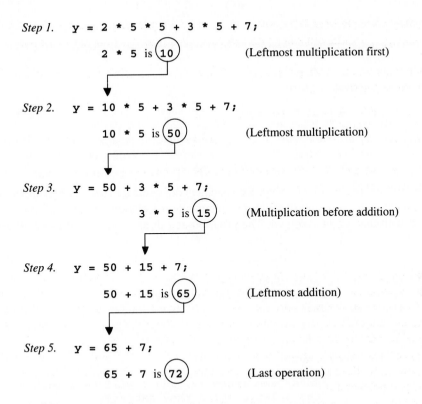

*Step 1.* `y = 2 * 5 * 5 + 3 * 5 + 7;`

`2 * 5` is `10` (Leftmost multiplication first)

*Step 2.* `y = 10 * 5 + 3 * 5 + 7;`

`10 * 5` is `50` (Leftmost multiplication)

*Step 3.* `y = 50 + 3 * 5 + 7;`

`3 * 5` is `15` (Multiplication before addition)

*Step 4.* `y = 50 + 15 + 7;`

`50 + 15` is `65` (Leftmost addition)

*Step 5.* `y = 65 + 7;`

`65 + 7` is `72` (Last operation)

**Fig. 1.12** Order in which a second degree polynomial is evaluated.

| Standard algebraic equality operator or relational operator | C++ equality or relational operator | Example of C++ condition | Meaning of C++ condition |
|---|---|---|---|
| Equality operators | | | |
| = | `==` | `x == y` | `x` is equal to `y` |
| ≠ | `!=` | `x != y` | `x` is not equal to `y` |
| Relational operators | | | |
| > | `>` | `x > y` | `x` is greater than `y` |
| < | `<` | `x < y` | `x` is less than `y` |
| ≥ | `>=` | `x >= y` | `x` is greater than or equal to `y` |
| ≤ | `<=` | `x <= y` | `x` is less than or equal to `y` |

**Fig. 1.13** Equality and relational operators.

***Common Programming Error 1.6***

*Reversing the operators* **!=**, **>=**, *and* **<=** *as in* **=!**, **=>**, *and* **=<**, *respectively. This causes a syntax error.*

***Common Programming Error 1.7***

*Confusing the equality operator* **==** *with the assignment operator* **=**. *The equality operator should be read "is equal to" and the assignment operator should be read "gets" or "gets the value of." Some people prefer to read the equality operator as "double equals." As we will soon see, confusing these operators may not necessarily cause an easy-to-recognize syntax error, but may cause extremely subtle logic errors.*

The following example uses six **if** statements to compare two numbers input by the user. If the condition in any of these **if** statements is satisfied, the output statement associated with that **if** is executed. The program and three sample outputs are shown in Fig. 1.14.

```
// Using if statements, relational
// operators, and equality operators
#include <iostream.h>

main()
{
   int num1, num2;

   cout << "Enter two integers, and I will tell you\n"
        << "the relationships they satisfy: ";
   cin >> num1 >> num2;    // read two integers

   if (num1 == num2)
      cout << num1 << " is equal to " << num2 << endl;

   if (num1 != num2)
      cout << num1 << " is not equal to " << num2 << endl;

   if (num1 < num2)
      cout << num1 << " is less than " << num2 << endl;

   if (num1 > num2)
      cout << num1 << " is greater than " << num2 << endl;

   if (num1 <= num2)
      cout << num1 << " is less than or equal to "
           << num2 << endl;

   if (num1 >= num2)
      cout << num1 << " is greater than or equal to "
           << num2 << endl;

   return 0;   // indicate program ended successfully
}
```

**Fig. 1.14** Using equality and relational operators (part 1 of 2).

```
Enter two integers, and I will tell you
the relationships they satisfy: 3 7
3 is not equal to 7
3 is less than 7
3 is less than or equal to 7
```

```
Enter two integers, and I will tell you
the relationships they satisfy: 22 12
22 is not equal to 12
22 is greater than 12
22 is greater than or equal to 12
```

```
Enter two integers, and I will tell you
the relationships they satisfy: 7 7
7 is equal to 7
7 is less than or equal to 7
7 is greater than or equal to 7
```

**Fig. 1.14** Using equality and relational operators (part 2 of 2).

Note that the program in Fig. 1.14 uses concatenated stream extraction operations to input two integers. First a value is read into variable **`num1`**, then a value is read into variable **`num2`**. Indentation in **`if`** statements enhances program readability. Also, notice that each of the **`if`** statements in Fig. 1.14 has a single statement in its body. In Chapter 2 we show how to specify **`if`** statements with multiple-statement bodies.

***Good Programming Practice 1.14***

*Indent the statement in the body of an* **`if`** *structure to make the body of the structure stand out and to enhance program readability.*

***Good Programming Practice 1.15***

*There should be no more than one statement per line in a program.*

***Common Programming Error 1.8***

*Placing a semicolon immediately after the right parenthesis after the condition in an* **`if`** *structure. The semicolon would cause the body of the* **`if`** *structure to be empty, so the* **`if`** *structure itself would perform no action regardless of whether or not its condition is true. Worse yet, the original body statement of the* **`if`** *structure would now become a statement in sequence with the* **`if`** *structure and would always be executed.*

Notice the use of spacing in Fig. 1.14. In C++ statements, *white space* characters such as tabs, newlines, and spaces are normally ignored by the compiler. So, statements may be split over several lines and may be spaced according to the programmer's preferences. It is incorrect to split identifiers.

***Good Programming Practice 1.16***

*A lengthy statement may be spread over several lines. If a single statement must be split across lines, choose breaking points that make sense such as after a comma in a comma-separated list, or after an operator in a lengthy expression. If a statement is split across two or more lines, indent all subsequent lines.*

The chart in Fig. 1.15 shows the precedence of the operators introduced in this chapter. The operators are shown top to bottom in decreasing order of precedence. Notice that all these operators, with the exception of the assignment operator =, associate from left to right. Addition is left associative, so an expression like **x + y + z** is evaluated as if it had been written **(x + y) + z**. The assignment operator = associates from right to left, so an expression like **x = y = 0** is evaluated as if it had been written **x = (y = 0)** which, as we will soon see, first assigns **0** to **y** and then assigns the result of that assignment—0—to **x**.

***Good Programming Practice 1.17***

*Refer to the operator precedence chart when writing expressions containing many operators. Confirm that the operators in the expression are performed in the order you expect. If you are uncertain about the order of evaluation in a complex expression, use parentheses to force the order, exactly as you would do in algebraic expressions. Be sure to observe that some operators such as assignment (=) associate right to left rather than left to right.*

We have introduced many important features of C++ including printing data on the screen, inputting data from the keyboard, performing calculations, and making decisions. In Chapter 2, we build on these techniques as we introduce *structured programming.* You will become more familiar with indentation techniques. We will study how to specify and vary the order in which statements are executed—this order is called *flow of control.*

## 1.20 Thinking About Objects

Now we begin our early introduction to object orientation. We will see that object orientation is a natural way of thinking about the world and of writing computer programs.

| Operators | Associativity | Type |
|---|---|---|
| `()` | left to right | parentheses |
| `*  /  %` | left to right | multiplicative |
| `+  -` | left to right | additive |
| `<  <=  >  >=` | left to right | relationals |
| `==  !=` | left to right | equalities |
| `<<  >>` | left to right | insertion/extraction |
| `=` | right to left | assignment |

**Fig. 1.15** Precedence and associativity of the operators discussed so far.

Why, then, did we not begin with object orientation on page one? Why are we deferring object-oriented programming in C++ until Chapter 6? The answer is that the objects we will build will be composed in part of structured program pieces, so we need to establish a basis in structured programming first.

In each of the first five chapters we concentrate on the "conventional" methodology of structured programming. Then we end each chapter with our continuing introduction to object-orientation. What will our strategy be in these sections on object orientation? In this first chapter, we introduce basic concepts (i.e., "object think") and terminology (i.e., "object speak"). In Chapters 2 through 5 we will consider more substantial issues and then attack a challenging problem with the techniques of *object-oriented design (OOD)*. We will analyze a typical problem statement that requires a system to be built, determine which objects are needed to implement the system, determine what attributes the objects will need to have, determine what behaviors these objects will need to exhibit, and specify how the objects will need to interact with one another to accomplish the overall system goals. We will do all this for a real-world problem rather than an artificial classroom example, and we will do it before we have learned how to write object-oriented C++ programs. When we get to Chapter 6, you will be ready to begin implementing object-oriented systems in C++.

We start by introducing some of the key terminology of object orientation. Look around you in the real world. Everywhere you look you see them—*objects*! People, animals, plants, cars, planes, buildings, lawnmowers, computers and the like. Humans think in terms of objects. We have the marvelous ability of *abstraction* that enables us to view screen images as objects such as people, planes, trees and mountains rather than as individual dots of color. We can, if we wish, think in terms of beaches rather than grains of sand, forests rather than trees, and houses rather than bricks.

We might be inclined to divide objects into two categories—animate objects and inanimate objects. Animate objects are "alive" in some sense. They move around and do things. Inanimate objects, like towels, seem not to do much at all. They just kind of "sit around." All these objects, however, do have some things in common. They all have *attributes* like size, shape, color, weight, and the like. And they all exhibit various *behaviors,* e.g., a ball rolls, bounces, inflates, and deflates; a baby cries, sleeps, crawls, walks, and blinks; a car accelerates, brakes, turns, etc.

Humans learn about objects by studying their attributes and observing their behaviors. Different objects can have many of the same attributes and exhibit similar behaviors. Comparisons can be made, for example, between babies and adults, and between humans and chimpanzees. Cars, trucks, little red wagons and roller skates have much in common.

*Object-oriented programming (OOP)* models real-world objects with software counterparts. It takes advantage of *class* relationships where objects of a certain class—such as a class of vehicles—have the same characteristics. It takes advantage of *inheritance* relationships, and even *multiple inheritance* relationships where newly created classes of objects are derived by inheriting characteristics of existing classes, yet contain unique characteristics of their own. Objects of class convertible certainly have the characteristics of class automobile, but the roof goes up and down.

Object-oriented programming gives us a more natural and intuitive way to view the programming process, namely by *modeling* real-world objects, their attributes, and their behaviors. OOP also models communication between objects. Just as people send *messages* to one another (e.g., a sergeant commanding troops to stand at attention), objects also communicate via messages.

OOP *encapsulates* data (attributes) and functions (behavior) into packages called *objects;* the data and functions of an object are intimately tied together. Objects have the property of *information hiding.* This means that although objects may know how to communicate with one another across well-defined *interfaces,* objects normally are not allowed to know how other objects are implemented—implementation details are hidden within the objects themselves. Surely it is possible to drive a car effectively without knowing the details of how engines, transmissions and exhaust systems work internally. We will see why information hiding is so crucial to good software engineering.

In C and other *procedural programming languages,* programming tends to be *action-oriented,* whereas in C++ programming tends to be *object-oriented.* In C, the unit of programming is the *function.* In C++, the unit of programming is the *class* from which objects are eventually *instantiated* (a fancy term for "created").

C programmers concentrate on writing functions. Groups of actions that perform some common task are formed into functions, and functions are grouped to form programs. Data is certainly important in C, but the view is that data exists primarily in support of the actions that functions perform. The *verbs* in a system specification help the C programmer determine the set of functions that work together to implement the system.

C++ programmers concentrate on creating their own *user-defined types* called *classes.* Each class contains data as well as the set of functions that manipulate the data. The data components of a class are called *data members.* The function components of a class are called *member functions.* Just as an instance of a built-in type such as **`int`** is called a *variable,* an instance of a user-defined type (i.e., a class) is called an *object.* The programmer uses built-in types as the building blocks for constructing user-defined types. The focus of attention in C++ is on objects rather than functions. The *nouns* in a system specification help the C++ programmer determine the set of classes from which objects will be created that will work together to implement the system.

In this chapter we introduced one of C++'s control structures, namely the **`if`** structure. In Chapter 2, we discuss the six remaining control structures, and we explain how to form structured programs by combining control structures with various action statements. We will discover that only three different types of control structures are needed, and that these need to be combined in only two different ways to form *any* possible C++ program. At the end of Chapter 2, we continue our early introduction to object orientation by identifying the objects that will be needed to implement a real-world system.

## Summary

- A computer is a device capable of performing computations and making logical decisions at speeds millions, and even billions, of times faster than human beings can.
- Computers process data under the control of computer programs.
- The various devices (such as the keyboard, screen, disks, memory, and processing units) that comprise a computer system are referred to as hardware.

- The computer programs that run on a computer are referred to as software.
- The input unit is the "receiving" section of the computer. Most information is entered into computers today through typewriter-like keyboards.
- The output unit is the "shipping" section of the computer. Most information is output from computers today by displaying it on screens or by printing it on paper.
- The memory unit is the "warehouse" section of the computer, and is often called either memory or primary memory.
- The arithmetic and logic unit (ALU) performs calculations and makes decisions.
- Programs or data not actively being used by the other units are normally placed on secondary storage devices (such as disks) until they are again needed.
- In single-user batch processing, the computer runs a single program at a time while processing data in groups or batches.
- Operating systems are software systems that make it more convenient to use computers and to get the best performance from computers.
- Multiprogramming operating systems enable the "simultaneous" operation of many jobs on the computer—the computer shares its resources among the jobs.
- Timesharing is a special case of multiprogramming in which users access the computer through terminals. The users' programs appear to be running simultaneously.
- With distributed computing, an organization's computing is distributed via networking to the sites where the real work of the organization is performed.
- File servers store programs and data that may be shared by client computers distributed throughout the network, hence the term client/server computing.
- Any computer can directly understand only its own machine language.
- Machine languages generally consist of strings of numbers (ultimately reduced to 1s and 0s) that instruct computers to perform their most elementary operations one at a time. Machine languages are machine-dependent.
- English-like abbreviations form the basis of assembly languages. Assemblers translate assembly language programs into machine language.
- Compilers translate high-level language programs into machine language. High-level languages contain English words and conventional mathematical notations.
- Interpreter programs directly execute high-level language programs without the need for compiling those programs into machine language.
- Although compiled programs execute faster than interpreted programs, interpreters are popular in program development environments in which programs are recompiled frequently as new features are added and errors are corrected. Once a program is developed, a compiled version can then be produced to run most efficiently.
- C is known as the development language of the UNIX operating system.

- It is possible to write programs in C and C++ that are portable to most computers.
- FORTRAN (FORmula TRANslator) is used for mathematical applications.
- COBOL (COmmon Business Oriented Language) is used primarily for commercial applications that require precise and efficient manipulation of large amounts of data.
- Structured programming is a disciplined approach to writing programs that are clearer than unstructured programs, easier to test and debug, and easier to modify.
- Pascal was designed for teaching structured programming in academic environments.
- Ada was developed under the sponsorship of the United States Department of Defense (DOD) using Pascal as a base.
- Multitasking allows programmers to specify parallel activities.
- All C++ systems consist of three parts: the environment, the language, and the standard libraries. Library functions are not part of the C++ language itself; these functions perform operations such as input/output and mathematical calculations.
- C++ programs typically go through six phases to be executed: edit, preprocess, compile, link, load, and execute.
- The programmer types a program with an editor and makes corrections if necessary. C++ file names on a typical UNIX-based system end with the **.C** extension.
- A compiler translates a C++ program into machine language code (or object code).
- The preprocessor obeys preprocessor directives which typically indicate that other files are to be included in the file to be compiled, and special symbols are to be replaced with program text.
- A linker links the object code with the code for missing functions to produce an executable image (with no missing pieces). On a typical UNIX-based system, the command to compile and link a C++ program is **CC**. If the program compiles and links correctly, a file called **a.out** is produced. This is the executable image of the program.
- A loader takes an executable image from disk and transfers it to memory.
- A computer, under the control of its CPU, executes a program one instruction at a time.
- Errors like division-by-zero errors occur as a program runs, so these errors are called run-time errors or execution-time errors.
- Divide-by-zero is generally a fatal error, i.e., an error that causes the program to terminate immediately without having successfully performed its job. Nonfatal errors allow programs to run to completion, often producing incorrect results.
- Certain C++ functions take their input from **cin** (the standard input stream) which is normally the keyboard, but **cin** can be connected to another device. Data is output to **cout** (the standard output stream) which is normally the computer screen, but **cout** can be connected to another device.

- There standard error stream is referred to as **`cerr`**. The **`cerr`** stream (normally connected to the screen) is used for displaying error messages.
- There are many problems between different C++ implementations and different computers that can make portability challenging.
- C++ provides capabilities to do object-oriented programming.
- Objects are essentially reusable software components that model items in the real world.
- Single-line comments begin with `//`. Programmers insert comments to document programs and improve their readability. Comments do not cause the computer to perform any action when the program is run.
- The line **`#include <iostream.h>`** tells the C++ preprocessor to include the contents of the input/output stream header file in the program. This file contains information necessary to compile programs that use **`cin`** and **`cout`**.
- C++ programs normally begin executing at the function **`main`**.
- The output stream object **`cout`**—normally connected to the screen—is used to output data. Multiple data items can be output by concatenating stream insertion (**`<<`**) operators.
- The input stream object **`cin`**—normally connected to the keyboard—is used to input data. Multiple data items can be input by concatenating stream extraction (**`>>`**) operators.
- All variables in a C++ program must be declared before they can be used.
- A variable name in C++ is any valid identifier. An identifier is a series of characters consisting of letters, digits, and underscores ( _ ). Identifiers cannot start with a digit. C++ identifiers can be any length; however, some systems and/or C++ implementations may impose some restrictions on the length of identifiers.
- C++ is case sensitive.
- Most calculations are performed in assignment statements.
- Every defined variable stored in the computer's memory has a name, a value, a type and a size.
- Whenever a new value is placed in a memory location, it replaces the previous value in that location. The previous value is destroyed.
- When a value is read from memory, the process is nondestructive, i.e., a copy of the value is read leaving the original value undisturbed in the memory location.
- C++ evaluates arithmetic expressions in a precise sequence determined by the rules of operator precedence and associativity.
- The **`if`** statement allows a program to make a decision when a certain condition is met. The format for an **`if`** statement is

```
if (condition)
   statement;
```

If the condition is true, the statement in the body of the `if` to be executed. If the condition is not met, i.e., the condition is false, the body statement is skipped.

- Conditions in `if` statements are commonly formed by using equality operators and relational operators. The result of using these operators is always simply the observation of "true" or "false."
- Object-orientation is a natural way of thinking about the world and of writing computer programs.
- All objects have attributes like size, shape, color, weight, and the like. And they all exhibit various behaviors.
- Humans learn about objects by studying their attributes and observing their behaviors.
- Different objects can have many of the same attributes and exhibit similar behaviors.
- Object-oriented programming (OOP) models real-world objects with software counterparts. It takes advantage of class relationships where objects of a certain class have the same characteristics. It takes advantage of inheritance relationships, and even multiple inheritance relationships where newly created classes are derived by inheriting characteristics of existing classes, yet contain unique characteristics of their own.
- Object-oriented programming provides an intuitive way to view the programming process, namely by modeling real-world objects, their attributes, and their behaviors.
- OOP also models communication between objects via messages.
- OOP encapsulates data (attributes) and functions (behavior) into objects.
- Objects have the property of information hiding. Although objects may know how to communicate with one another across well-defined interfaces, objects normally are not allowed to know implementation details of other objects.
- Information hiding is crucial to good software engineering.
- In C and other procedural programming languages, programming tends to be action-oriented. Data is certainly important in C, but the view is that data exists primarily in support of the actions that functions perform.
- C++ programmers concentrate on creating their own user-defined types called classes. Each class contains data as well as the set of functions that manipulate the data. The data components of a class are called data members. The function components of a class are called member functions.

## Terminology

abstraction
action
ANSI C
arithmetic and logic unit (ALU)
arithmetic operators
assembly language
assignment operator (`=`)
associativity of operators

attributes of an object
behaviors of an object
binary operators
body of a function
C
C standard library
C++
C++ class libraries
case sensitive
central processing unit (CPU)
class
client/server computing
comment (`//`)
compile error
compile-time error
compiler
computer
computer program
condition
CPU
data
data member
decision
declaration
distributed computing
editor
encapsulation
equality operators
  `==` "is equal to"
  `!=` "is not equal to"
escape character (`\`)
escape sequence
execution-time error
fatal error
file server
flow of control
function
hardware
high-level language
identifier
**`if`** structure
information hiding
inheritance
input device
input/output (I/O)
integer (**`int`**)
integer division
interface
interpreter
linking
loading
logic error
machine dependent
machine independent
machine language
**`main`**
member function
memory
memory location
message
modeling
modulus operator (`%`)
multiple inheritance
multiplication operator (`*`)
multiprocessor
multiprogramming
multitasking
newline character (`\n`)
nested parentheses
nonfatal error
object
object-oriented design (OOD)
object-oriented programming (OOP)
"object speak"
"object think"
operand
operator
output device
parentheses `()`
precedence
preprocessor
primary memory
procedural programming
programming language
prompt
relational operators
  `>` "is greater than"
  `<` "is less than"
  `>=` "is greater than or equal to"
  `<=` "is less than or equal to"
reserved words
right-to-left associativity
rules of operator precedence
run-time error
semicolon (`;`) statement terminator
software
software reusability
standard error (**`cerr`**)

standard input (**cin**)
standard output (**cout**)
statement
statement terminator (**;**)
string
structured programming
syntax error
terminal
translator program
user-defined type
variable
variable name
variable value
white space characters

## Common Programming Errors

**1.1** Errors like division-by-zero errors occur as a program runs, so these errors are called run-time errors or execution-time errors. Divide-by-zero is generally a fatal error, i.e., an error that causes the program to terminate immediately without having successfully performed its job. Nonfatal errors allow programs to run to completion, often producing incorrect results.

**1.2** Forgetting to include the **iostream.h** file in a program that inputs data from the keyboard or outputs data to the screen.

**1.3** Omitting the semicolon at the end of a statement is a syntax error. A syntax error is caused when the compiler cannot recognize a statement. The compiler normally issues an error message to help the programmer locate and fix the incorrect statement. Syntax errors are violations of the language. Syntax errors are also called compile errors, compile-time errors, or compilation errors because they appear during the compilation phase.

**1.4** Attempting to use the modulus operator, **%**, with noninteger operands is a syntax error.

**1.5** A syntax error will occur if the operators **==**, **!=**, **>=**, and **<=** contain spaces between their symbols.

**1.6** Reversing the operators **!=**, **>=**, and **<=** as in **=!**, **=>**, and **=<**, respectively. This causes a syntax error.

**1.7** Confusing the equality operator **==** with the assignment operator **=**. The equality operator should be read "is equal to" and the assignment operator should be read "gets" or "gets the value of." Some people prefer to read the equality operator as "double equals." Confusing these operators may not necessarily cause an easy-to-recognize syntax error, but may cause extremely subtle logic errors.

**1.8** Placing a semicolon immediately after the right parenthesis after the condition in an ***if*** structure. The semicolon would cause the body of the ***if*** structure to be empty, so the ***if*** structure itself would perform no action regardless of whether or not its condition is true. Worse yet, the original body statement of the ***if*** structure would now become a statement in sequence with the ***if*** structure and would always be executed.

## Good Programming Practices

**1.1** Write your C++ programs in a simple and straightforward manner. This is sometimes referred to as KIS ("keep it simple"). Do not "stretch" the language by trying bizarre usages.

**1.2** Read the manuals for the version of C++ you are using. Refer to these manuals frequently to be sure you are aware of the rich collection of C++ features and that you are using these features correctly.

**1.3** Your computer and compiler are good teachers. If after carefully reading your C++ language manual you are not sure how a feature of C++ works, experiment and see what happens. Set your compiler options for "maximum warnings." Study each message you get when you compile your programs and correct the programs to eliminate the messages.

**1.4** Every program should begin with a comment describing the purpose of the program.

**1.5** The last character printed by a function that does any printing should be a newline (`\n`). This ensures that the function will leave the cursor positioned at the beginning of a new line. Conventions of this nature encourage software reusability—a key goal in software development environments.

**1.6** Indent the entire body of each function one level of indentation (three spaces) within the braces that define the body of the function. This makes the functional structure of a program stand out and helps make programs easier to read.

**1.7** Set a convention for the size of indent you prefer and then uniformly apply that convention. The tab key may be used to create indents, but tab stops may vary. We recommend using either 1/4-inch tab stops or (preferably) three spaces to form a level of indent.

**1.8** Place a space after each comma (`,`) to make programs more readable.

**1.9** Choosing meaningful variable names helps a program to be "self-documenting," i.e., it becomes easier to understand the program simply by reading it rather than having to read manuals or use excessive comments.

**1.10** Avoid indentifiers that begin with underscores because a C++ compiler may use names like that for its own purposes internally. This will prevent names you choose from being confused with names the compiler chooses.

**1.11** Always place a blank line before a declaration that appears between executable statements. This makes the declarations stand out in the program and contributes to program clarity.

**1.12** If you prefer to place declarations at the beginning of a function, separate those declarations from the executable statements in that function with one blank line to highlight where the declarations end and the executable statements begin.

**1.13** Place spaces on either side of a binary operator. This makes the operator stand out and makes the program more readable.

**1.14** Indent the statement in the body of an `if` structure to make the body of the structure stand out and to enhance program readability.

**1.15** There should be no more than one statement per line in a program.

**1.16** A lengthy statement may be spread over several lines. If a single statement must be split across lines, choose breaking points that make sense such as after a comma in a comma-separated list, or after an operator in a lengthy expression. If a statement is split across two or more lines, indent all subsequent lines.

**1.17** Refer to the operator precedence chart when writing expressions containing many operators. Confirm that the operators in the expression are performed in the order you expect. If you are uncertain about the order of evaluation in a complex expression, use parentheses to force the order, exactly as you would do in algebraic expressions. Be sure to observe that some operators such as assignment (`=`) associate right to left rather than left to right.

## *Performance Tips*

**1.1** Using ANSI standard library functions instead of writing your own comparable versions can improve program performance because these functions are carefully written to perform efficiently.

## *Portability Tips*

**1.1** Because C is a standardized, hardware-independent, widely available language, applications written in C can often be run with little or no modifications on a wide range of different computer systems.

1.2 Using ANSI C standard library functions instead of writing your own comparable versions can improve program portability because these functions are included in virtually all C++ implementations.

1.3 Although it is possible to write portable programs, there are many problems among different C and C++ compilers and different computers that can make portability difficult to achieve. Simply writing programs in C and C++ does not guarantee portability. The programmer will often need to deal directly with compiler and computer variations.

## *Software Engineering Observations*

1.1 Use a building block approach to creating programs. Avoid reinventing the wheel. Use existing pieces—this is called software reuse and it is central to object-oriented programming.

1.2 When programming in C++ you will typically use the following building blocks: classes from class libraries and functions from the ANSI C standard library, classes and functions you create yourself, and classes and functions other people create and make available to you.

## *Self-Review Exercises*

1.1 Fill in the blanks in each of the following:

a) The company that popularized personal computing was __________.

b) The computer that made personal computing legitimate in business and industry was the __________.

c) Computers process data under the control of sets of instructions called computer __________.

d) The six key logical units of the computer are the __________, __________, __________, __________, __________, and the __________.

e) The three classes of languages discussed in the chapter are __________, __________, and __________.

f) The programs that translate high-level language programs into machine language are called __________.

g) C is widely known as the development language of the __________ operating system.

h) The __________ language was developed by Wirth for teaching structured programming in universities.

i) The Department of Defense developed the Ada language with a capability called __________ which allows programmers to specify that many activities can proceed in parallel.

1.2 Fill in the blanks in each of the following sentences about the C++ environment.

a) C++ programs are normally typed into a computer using an __________ program.

b) In a C++ system, a __________ program executes before the compiler's translation phase begins.

c) The __________ program combines the output of the compiler with various library functions to produce an executable image.

d) The __________ program transfers the executable image of a C++ program from disk to memory.

1.3 Fill in the blanks in each of the following.

a) Every C++ program begins execution at the function __________.

b) The __________ begins the body of every function and the __________ ends the body of every function.

c) Every statement ends with a _________.
d) The escape sequence `\n` represents the _________ character which causes the cursor to position to the beginning of the next line on the screen.
e) The _________ statement is used to make decisions.

**1.4** State whether each of the following is true or false. If false, explain why.
a) Comments cause the computer to print the text after the `//` on the screen when the program is executed.
b) The escape sequence `\n` when output with `cout` causes the cursor to position to the beginning of the next line on the screen.
c) All variables must be declared before they are used.
d) All variables must be given a type when they are declared.
e) C++ considers the variables `number` and `NuMbEr` to be identical.
f) Declarations can appear almost anywhere in the body of a C++ function.
g) The modulus operator (`%`) can be used only with integer operands.
h) The arithmetic operators `*`, `/`, `%`, `+`, and `-` all have the same level of precedence.
i) A C++ program that prints three lines of output must contain three output statements using `cout`.

**1.5** Write a single C++ statement to accomplish each of the following:
a) Declare the variables `c`, `thisIsAVariable`, `q76354`, and `number` to be of type `int`.
b) Prompt the user to enter an integer. End your prompting message with a colon (`:`) followed by a space and leave the cursor positioned after the space.
c) Read an integer from the keyboard and store the value entered in integer variable `age`.
d) If the variable `number` is not equal to 7, print `"The variable number is not equal to 7."`
e) Print the message `"This is a C++ program"` on one line.
f) Print the message `"This is a C++ program"` on two lines where the first line ends with `C++`.
g) Print the message `"This is a C++ program"` with each word on a separate line.
h) Print the message `"This is a C++ program"` with each word separated from the next by a tab.

**1.6** Write a statement (or comment) to accomplish each of the following:
a) State that a program will calculate the product of three integers.
b) Declare the variables `x`, `y`, `z`, and `result` to be of type `int`.
c) Prompt the user to enter three integers.
d) Read three integers from the keyboard and store them in the variables `x`, `y`, and `z`.
e) Compute the product of the three integers contained in variables `x`, `y`, and `z`, and assign the result to the variable `result`.
f) Print `"The product is "` followed by the value of the variable `result`.
g) Return a value from `main` indicating that the program terminated successfully.

**1.7** Using the statements you wrote in Exercise 1.6, write a complete program that calculates and prints the product of three integers.

**1.8** Identify and correct the errors in each of the following statements:
a)
```
if (c < 7);
   cout << "c is less than 7\n";
```
b)
```
if (c => 7)
   cout << "c is equal to or greater than 7\n";
```

**1.9** Fill the correct "object speak" term into the blanks in each of the following:

a) Humans can look at a TV screen and see dots of color, or they can step back and see three people sitting at a conference table; this is an example of a capability called ________.

b) If we view a car as an object, the fact that the car is a convertible is a(an) attribute/behavior (pick one) ________ of the car.

c) The fact that a car can accelerate or decelerate, turn left or turn right, or go forward or backward are all examples of ________ of a car object.

d) When a new type of class obtains characteristics from several different types of existing classes, this is called ________ inheritance .

e) Objects communicate by sending each other ________.

f) Objects communicate with one another across well-defined ________.

g) Each object is ordinarily not allowed to know how other objects are implemented; this property is called ________.

h) The ________ in a system specification help the C++ programmer determine the classes that will be needed to implement the system.

i) The data components of a class are called ________ and the function components of a class are called ________.

j) An instance of a user-defined type is called a(n) ________.

## Answers to Self-Review Exercises

**1.1** a) Apple. b) IBM Personal Computer. c) programs. d) input unit, output unit, memory unit, arithmetic and logic unit, central processing unit, secondary storage unit. e) machine languages, assembly languages, high-level languages. f) compilers. g) UNIX. h) Pascal. i) multitasking.

**1.2** a) editor. b) preprocessor. c) linker. d) loader.

**1.3** a) `main`. b) Left brace (`{`), right brace (`}`). c) Semicolon. d) newline. e) `if`.

**1.4** a) False. Comments do not cause any action to be performed when the program is executed. They are used to document programs and improve their readability.

b) True.

c) True.

d) True.

e) False. C++ is case sensitive, so these variables are unique.

f) True.

g) True.

h) False. The operators `*`, `/`, and `%` are on the same level of precedence, and the operators `+` and `-` are on a lower level of precedence.

i) False. A single output statement using `cout` containing multiple `\n` escape sequences can print several lines.

**1.5**

a)
```
int c, thisIsAVariable, q76354, number;
```
b)
```
cout << "Enter an integer: ";
```
c)
```
cin >> age;
```
d)
```
if (number != 7)
   cout << "The variable number is not equal to 7.\n";
```
e)
```
cout << "This is a C++ program.\n";
```
f)
```
cout << "This is a C++\nprogram.\n";
```
g)
```
cout << "This\nis\na\nC++\nprogram.\n";
```
h)
```
cout << "This\tis\ta\tC++\tprogram.\n";
```

**1.6** a) `// Calculate the product of three integers`
b) `int x, y, z, result;`
c) `cout << "Enter three integers: ";`
d) `cin >> x >> y >> z;`
e) `result = x * y * z;`
f) `cout << "The product is " << result << '\n';`
g) `return 0;`

**1.7**

```
// Calculate the product of three integers
#include <iostream.h>

main()
{
   int x, y, z, result;

   cout << "Enter three integers: ";
   cin >> x >> y >> z;
   result = x * y * z;
   cout << "The product is " << result << '\n';

   return 0;
}
```

**1.8** a) Error: Semicolon after the right parenthesis of the condition in the `if` statement. Correction: Remove the semicolon after the right parenthesis. Note: The result of this error is that the output statement will be executed whether or not the condition in the `if` statement is true. The semicolon after the right parenthesis is considered an empty statement—a statement that does nothing. We will learn more about the empty statement in the next chapter.

b) Error: The relational operator `=>`. Correction: Change `=>` to `>=`.

**1.9** a) abstraction. b) attribute. c) behaviors. d) multiple. e) messages. f) interfaces. g) information hiding. h) nouns. i) data members, member functions. j) object.

## Exercises

**1.10** Categorize each of the following items as either hardware or software:
a) CPU
b) C++ compiler
c) ALU
d) C++ preprocessor
e) input unit
f) an editor program

**1.11** Why might you want to write a program in a machine-independent language instead of a machine-dependent language? Why might a machine-dependent language be more appropriate for writing certain types of programs?

**1.12** Fill in the blanks in each of the following statements:
a) Which logical unit of the computer receives information from outside the computer for use by the computer? __________.
b) The process of instructing the computer to solve specific problems is called __________.
c) What type of computer language uses English-like abbreviations for machine language instructions? __________.

d) Which logical unit of the computer sends information that has already been processed by the computer to various devices so that the information may be used outside the computer? __________.
e) Which logical unit of the computer retains information? __________.
f) Which logical unit of the computer performs calculations? __________.
g) Which logical unit of the computer makes logical decisions? __________.
h) The level of computer language most convenient to the programmer for writing programs quickly and easily is __________.
i) The only language that a computer can directly understand is called that computer's __________.
j) Which logical unit of the computer coordinates the activities of all the other logical units? __________.

**1.13** Discuss the meaning of each of the following objects:
a) `cin`
b) `cout`
c) `cerr`

**1.14** Why is so much attention today focused on object-oriented programming in general and C++ in particular?

**1.15** Fill in the blanks in each of the following:
a) __________ are used to document a program and improve its readability.
b) The object used to print information on the screen is __________.
c) A C++ statement that makes a decision is __________.
d) Calculations are normally performed by __________ statements.
e) The __________ object inputs values from the keyboard.

**1.16** Write a single C++ statement or line that accomplishes each of the following:
a) Print the message `"Enter two numbers."`
b) Assign the product of variables `b` and `c` to variable `a`.
c) State that a program performs a sample payroll calculation (i.e., use text that helps to document a program).
d) Input three integer values from the keyboard and place these values in integer variables `a`, `b`, and `c`.

**1.17** State which of the following are true and which are false. Explain your answers.
a) C++ operators are evaluated from left to right.
b) The following are all valid variable names: `_under_bar_`, `m928134`, `t5`, `j7`, `her_sales`, `his_account_total`, `a`, `b`, `c`, `z`, `z2`.
c) The statement `cout << "a = 5;";` is a typical example of an assignment statement.
d) A valid C++ arithmetic expression with no parentheses is evaluated from left to right.
e) The following are all invalid variable names: `3g`, `87`, `67h2`, `h22`, `2h`.

**1.18** Fill in the blanks in each of the following:
a) What arithmetic operations are on the same level of precedence as multiplication? __________.
b) When parentheses are nested, which set of parentheses is evaluated first in an arithmetic expression? __________.
c) A location in the computer's memory that may contain different values at various times throughout the execution of a program is called a __________.

**1.19** What, if anything, prints when each of the following C++ statements is performed? If nothing prints, then answer "nothing." Assume `x = 2` and `y = 3`.

a) `cout << x;`
b) `cout << x + x;`
c) `cout << "x=";`
d) `cout << "x = " << x;`
e) `cout << x + y << " = " << y + x;`
f) `z = x + y;`
g) `cin >> x >> y;`
h) `// cout << "x + y = " << x + y;`
i) `cout << "\n";`

**1.20** Which of the following C++ statements contain variables whose values are destroyed?

a) `cin >> b >> c >> d >> e >> f;`
b) `p = i + j + k + 7;`
c) `cout << "variables whose values are destroyed";`
d) `cout << "a = 5";`

**1.21** Given the equation $y = ax^3 + 7$, which of the following, if any, are correct C++ statements for this equation?

a) `y = a * x * x * x + 7;`
b) `y = a * x * x * (x + 7);`
c) `y = (a * x) * x * (x + 7);`
d) `y = (a * x) * x * x + 7;`
e) `y = a * (x * x * x) + 7;`
f) `y = a * x * (x * x + 7);`

**1.22** State the order of evaluation of the operators in each of the following C++ statements, and show the value of **x** after each statement is performed.

a) `x = 7 + 3 * 6 / 2 - 1;`
b) `x = 2 % 2 + 2 * 2 - 2 / 2;`
c) `x = (3 * 9 * (3 + (9 * 3/ (3))));`

**1.23** Write a program that asks the user to enter two numbers, obtains the two numbers from the user, and prints the sum, product, difference, and quotient of the two numbers.

**1.24** Write a program that prints the numbers 1 to 4 on the same line with each pair of adjacent numbers separated by one space. Write the program using the following methods.

a) Using one output statement with one stream insertion operator.
b) Using one output statement with four stream insertion operators.
c) Using four output statements.

**1.25** Write a program that asks the user to enter two integers, obtains the numbers from the user, and then prints the larger number followed by the words "**is larger**." If the numbers are equal, print the message "**These numbers are equal**."

**1.26** Write a program that inputs three integers from the keyboard, and prints the sum, average, product, smallest, and largest of these numbers. The screen dialogue should appear as follows:

```
Input three different integers: 13 27 14
Sum is 54
Average is 18
Product is 4914
Smallest is 13
Largest is 27
```

**1.27** Write a program that reads in the radius of a circle and prints the circle's diameter, circumference, and area. Use the constant value 3.14159 for $\pi$. Do these calculations in output statements. (Note: In this chapter, we have discussed only integer constants and variables. In Chapter 3 we will discuss floating point numbers, i.e., values that can have decimal points.)

**1.28** Write a program that prints a box, an oval, an arrow, and a diamond as follows:

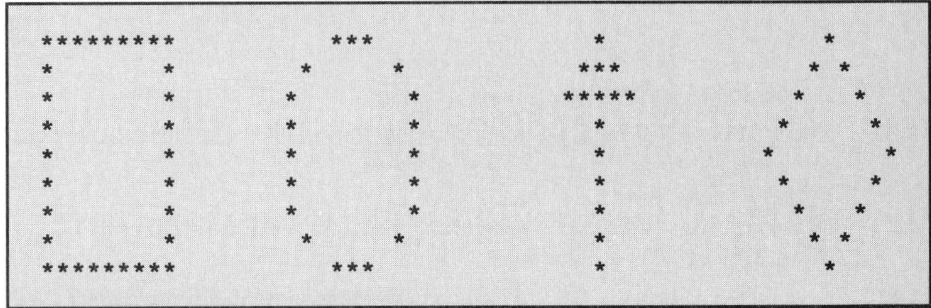

**1.29** What does the following code print?

```
cout << "*\n**\n***\n****\n*****\n";
```

**1.30** Write a program that reads in five integers and determines and prints the largest and the smallest integers in the group. Use only the programming techniques you learned in this chapter.

**1.31** Write a program that reads an integer and determines and prints whether it is odd or even. (Hint: Use the modulus operator. An even number is a multiple of two. Any multiple of two leaves a remainder of zero when divided by 2.)

**1.32** Write a program that reads in two integers and determines and prints if the first is a multiple of the second. (Hint: Use the modulus operator.)

**1.33** Display a checkerboard pattern with eight output statements, and then display the same pattern with as few output statements as possible.

**1.34** Distinguish between the terms fatal error and nonfatal error. Why might you prefer to experience a fatal error rather than a nonfatal error?

**1.35** Here's a peek ahead. In this chapter you learned about integers and the type `int`. C++ can also represent uppercase letters, lowercase letters, and a considerable variety of special symbols. C++ uses small integers internally to represent each different character. The set of characters a computer uses and the corresponding integer representations for those characters is called that computer's character set. You can print a character by simply enclosing that character in single quotes as with

```
cout << 'A';
```

You can print the integer equivalent of a character by preceding that character with **(int)**—this is called a cast (we will say more about casts in Chapter 2).

```
cout << (int) 'A';
```

When the preceding statement executes, it prints the value 65 (on systems that use the so-called ASCII character set). Write a program that prints the integer equivalents of some uppercase letters, lowercase letters, digits and special symbols. At a minimum, determine the integer equivalents of the following: **A B C a b c 0 1 2 $ * + /** and the blank character.

**1.36** Write a program that inputs a five-digit number, separates the number into its individual digits and prints the digits separated from one another by three spaces each. For example, if the user types in **42339** the program should print

```
4   2   3   3   9
```

**1.37** Using only the techniques you learned in this chapter, write a program that calculates the squares and cubes of the numbers from 0 to 10 and uses tabs to print the following table of values:

```
number  square  cube
0       0       0
1       1       1
2       4       8
3       9       27
4       16      64
5       25      125
6       36      216
7       49      343
8       64      512
9       81      729
10      100     1000
```

**1.38** Give a brief answer to each of the following "object think" questions:

a) Why does this text choose to discuss structured programming in detail before proceeding with an in-depth treatment of object-oriented programming?
b) What are the typical steps (mentioned in the text) of an object-oriented design process?
c) How is multiple inheritance exhibited by human beings?
d) What kinds of messages do people send to one another?
e) Objects send messages to one another across well-defined interfaces. What interfaces does a car radio (object) present to its user (a person object)?

**1.39** You are probably wearing on your wrist one of the world's most common types of objects—a watch. Discuss how each of the following terms and concepts applies to the notion of a watch: object, attributes, behaviors, class, inheritance (consider, for example, an alarm clock), abstraction, modeling, messages, encapsulation, interface, information hiding, data members, and member functions.

# 2

# Control Structures

**Objectives**

- To understand basic problem solving techniques.
- To be able to develop algorithms through the process of top-down, stepwise refinement.
- To be able to use the `if`, `if/else`, and `switch` selection structures to choose among alternative actions.
- To be able to use the `while`, `do/while` and `for` repetition structures to execute statements in a program repeatedly.
- To understand counter-controlled repetition and sentinel-controlled repetition.
- To be able to use the increment, decrement, assignment, and logical operators.
- To be able to use the `break` and `continue` program control statements.

*Let's all move one place on.*
Lewis Carroll

*The wheel is come full circle.*
William Shakespeare, King Lear

*Who can control his fate?*
William Shakespeare, Othello

*The used key is always bright.*
Benjamin Franklin

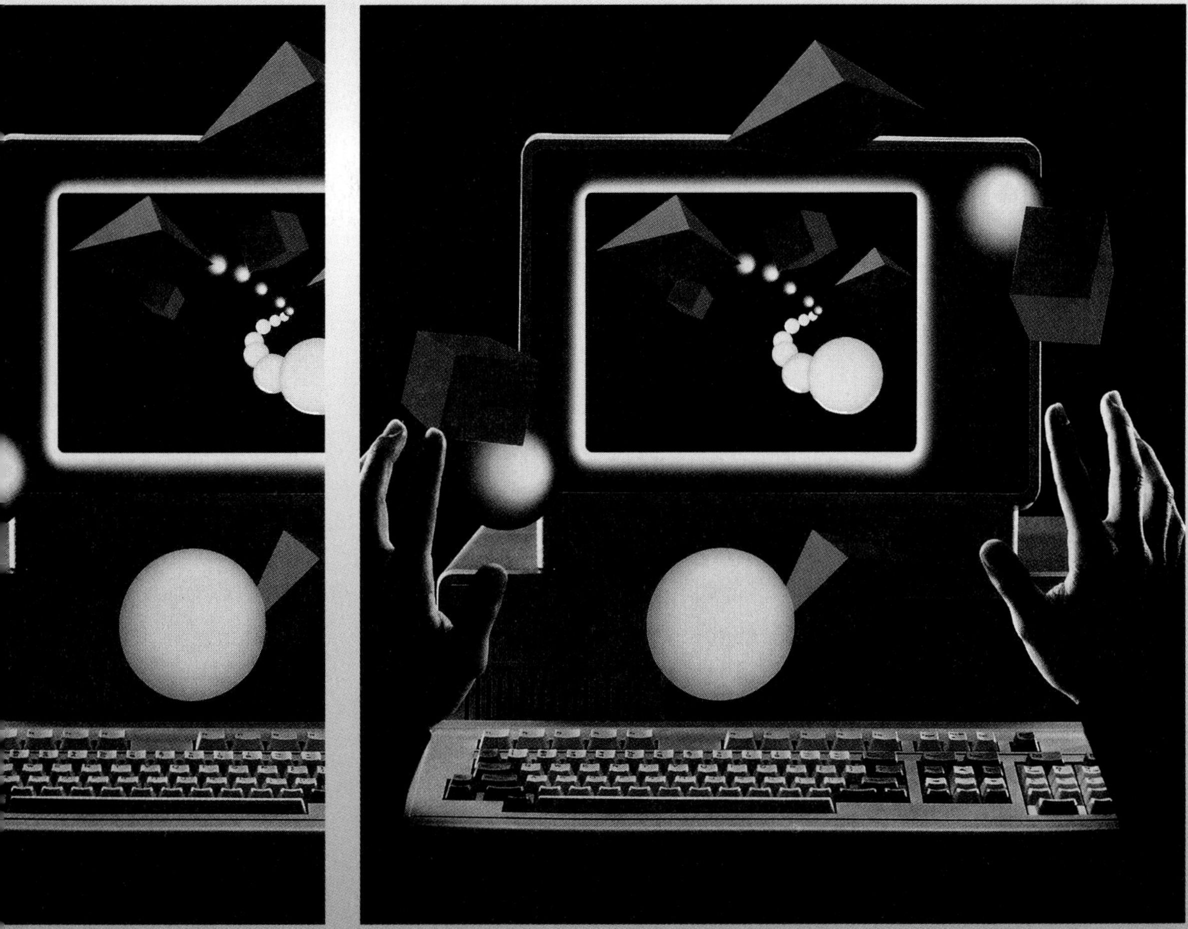

## Outline



## 2.1 Introduction

Before writing a program to solve a particular problem, it is essential to have a thorough understanding of the problem and a carefully planned approach to solving the problem. When writing a program, it is equally essential to understand the types of building blocks that are available and to employ proven program construction principles. In this chapter we discuss all of these issues in our presentation of the theory and principles of structured programming. The techniques that you will learn here are applicable to most high-level languages including C++. When we begin our treatment of object-oriented programming in C++ in Chapter 6, we will see that the control structures we study here in Chapter 2 are helpful in building and manipulating objects.

## 2.2 Algorithms

Any computing problem can be solved by executing a series of actions in a specific order. A *procedure* for solving a problem in terms of

1. the *actions* to be executed, and
2. the *order* in which these actions are to be executed

is called an *algorithm*. The following example demonstrates that correctly specifying the order in which the actions are to be executed is important.

Consider the "rise-and-shine algorithm" followed by one junior executive for getting out of bed and going to work: (1) Get out of bed, (2) take off pajamas, (3) take a shower, (4) get dressed, (5) eat breakfast, (6) carpool to work.

This routine gets the executive to work well prepared to make critical decisions. Suppose, however, that the same steps are performed in a slightly different order: (1) Get out of bed, (2) take off pajamas, (3) get dressed, (4) take a shower, (5) eat breakfast, (6) carpool to work.

In this case, our junior executive shows up for work soaking wet. Specifying the order in which statements are to be executed in a computer program is called *program control*. In this chapter, we investigate the program control capabilities of C++.

## 2.3 Pseudocode

*Pseudocode* is an artificial and informal language that helps programmers develop algorithms. The pseudocode we present here is particularly useful for developing algorithms that will be converted to structured C++ programs. Pseudocode is similar to everyday English; it is convenient and user-friendly although it is not an actual computer programming language.

Pseudocode programs are not actually executed on computers. Rather, they help the programmer "think out" a program before attempting to write it in a programming language such as C++. In this chapter, we give several examples of how pseudocode may be used effectively in developing structured C++ programs.

The style of pseudocode we present consists purely of characters, so programmers may conveniently type pseudocode programs using an editor program. The computer can display a fresh copy of a pseudocode program on demand. A carefully prepared pseudocode program may be converted easily to a corresponding C++ program. This is done in many cases simply by replacing pseudocode statements with their C++ equivalents.

Pseudocode consists only of executable statements—those that are executed when the program has been converted from pseudocode to C++ and is run. Declarations are not executable statements. For example, the declaration

```
int i;
```

simply tells the compiler the type of variable `i` and instructs the compiler to reserve space in memory for the variable. But this declaration does not cause any action—such as input, output, or a calculation—to occur when the program is executed. Some programmers choose to list variables and briefly mention the purpose of each at the beginning of a pseudocode program.

## 2.4 Control Structures

Normally, statements in a program are executed one after the other in the order in which they are written. This is called *sequential execution.* Various C++ statements we will soon discuss enable the programmer to specify that the next statement to be executed may be other than the next one in sequence. This is called *transfer of control.*

During the 1960s, it became clear that the indiscriminate use of transfers of control was the root of much difficulty experienced by software development groups. The finger of blame was pointed at the ***goto*** *statement* that allows the programmer to specify a transfer of control to one of a very wide range of possible destinations in a program. The notion of so-called *structured programming* became almost synonymous with *"**goto** elimination."*

The research of Bohm and Jacopini[1] had demonstrated that programs could be written without any **goto** statements. The challenge of the era became for programmers to shift their styles to "**goto**-less programming." It was not until the 1970s that programmers started taking structured programming seriously. The results have been impressive as software development groups have reported reduced development times, more frequent on-time delivery of systems, and more frequent within-budget completion of software projects. The key to these successes is that structured programs are clearer, easier to debug and modify, and more likely to be bug-free in the first place.

Bohm and Jacopini's work demonstrated that all programs could be written in terms of only three *control structures,* namely the *sequence structure,* the *selection structure,* and the *repetition structure.* The sequence structure is built into C++. Unless directed otherwise, the computer executes C++ statements one after the other in the order in which they are written. The *flowchart* segment of Fig. 2.1 illustrates a typical sequence structure in which two calculations are performed in order.

A flowchart is a graphical representation of an algorithm or of a portion of an algorithm. Flowcharts are drawn using certain special-purpose symbols such as rectangles, diamonds, ovals, and small circles; these symbols are connected by arrows called *flowlines.*

Like pseudocode, flowcharts are useful for developing and representing algorithms, although pseudocode is strongly preferred by most programmers. Flowcharts show clearly how control structures operate; that is all we use them for in this text.

Consider the flowchart segment for the sequence structure in Fig. 2.1. We use the *rectangle symbol,* also called the *action symbol,* to indicate any type of action including a calculation or an input/output operation. The flowlines in the figure indicate the order in

---

[1] Bohm, C. , and G. Jacopini, "Flow Diagrams, Turing Machines, and Languages with Only Two Formation Rules," *Communications of the ACM,* Vol. 9, No. 5, May 1966, pp. 336-371.

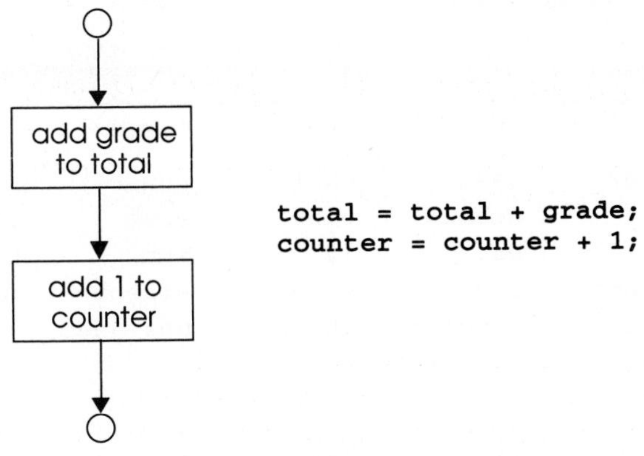


**Fig. 2.1** Flowcharting C++'s sequence structure.

which the actions are to be performed—first, **`grade`** is to be added to **`total`** then **`1`** is to be added to **`counter`**. C++ allows us to have as many actions as we want in a sequence structure. As we will soon see, anywhere a single action may be placed, we may place several actions in sequence.

When drawing a flowchart that represents a *complete* algorithm, an *oval symbol* containing the word "Begin" is the first symbol used in the flowchart; an oval symbol containing the word "End" is the last symbol used. When drawing only a portion of an algorithm as in Fig. 2.1, the oval symbols are omitted in favor of using *small circle symbols* also called *connector symbols*.

Perhaps the most important flowcharting symbol is the *diamond symbol*, also called the *decision symbol*, which indicates that a decision is to be made. We will discuss the diamond symbol in the next section.

C++ provides three types of selection structures; we discuss each of these in this chapter. The **`if`** selection structure either performs (selects) an action if a condition is true or skips the action if the condition is false. The **`if/else`** selection structure performs an action if a condition is true and performs a different action if the condition is false. The **`switch`** selection structure performs one of many different actions depending on the value of an expression.

The **`if`** structure is called a *single-selection structure* because it selects or ignores a single action. The **`if/else`** structure is called a *double-selection structure* because it selects between two different actions. The **`switch`** structure is called a *multiple-selection structure* because it selects among many different actions.

C++ provides three types of repetition structures, namely **`while`**, **`do/while`** and **`for`**. Each of the words **`if`**, **`else`**, **`switch`**, **`while`**, **`do`**, and **`for`** are C++ *keywords*. These words are reserved by the language to implement various features such as C++'s control structures. Keywords may not be used as identifiers such as for variable names. A complete list of C++ keywords is shown in Fig. 2.2.

***Common Programming Error 2.1***

*Using a keyword as an identifier.*

**C++ Keywords**

*C and C++*

| | | | | | |
|---|---|---|---|---|---|
| `auto` | `break` | `case` | `char` | `const` | `continue` |
| `default` | `do` | `double` | `else` | `enum` | `extern` |
| `float` | `for` | `goto` | `if` | `int` | `long` |
| `register` | `return` | `short` | `signed` | `sizeof` | `static` |
| `struct` | `switch` | `typedef` | `union` | `unsigned` | `void` |
| `volatile` | `while` | | | | |

*C++ only*

| | | | | | |
|---|---|---|---|---|---|
| `asm` | `catch` | `class` | `delete` | `friend` | `inline` |
| `new` | `operator` | `private` | `protected` | `public` | `template` |
| `this` | `throw` | `try` | `virtual` | | |

**Fig. 2.2** C++ keywords.

Well, that is all there is. C++ has only seven control structures: sequence, three types of selection and three types of repetition. Each C++ program is formed by combining as many of each type of control structure as is appropriate for the algorithm the program implements. As with the sequence structure of Fig. 2.1, we will see that each control structure is flowcharted with two small circle symbols, one at the entry point to the control structure and one at the exit point. These *single-entry/single-exit control structures* make it easy to build programs—the control structures are attached to one another by connecting the exit point of one control structure to the entry point of the next. This is similar to the way a child stacks building blocks, so we call this *control-structure stacking*. We will learn that there is only one other way control structures may be connected—a method called *control-structure nesting*. Thus, any C++ program we will ever build can be constructed from only seven different types of control structures combined in only two ways.

## 2.5 The If Selection Structure

A selection structure is used to choose among alternative courses of action. For example, suppose the passing grade on an exam is 60. The pseudocode statement

*If student's grade is greater than or equal to 60*
    *Print "Passed"*

determines if the condition "student's grade is greater than or equal to 60" is true or false. If the condition is true, then "Passed" is printed, and the next pseudocode statement in order is "performed" (remember that pseudocode is not a real programming language). If the condition is false, the print statement is ignored, and the next pseudocode statement in order is performed. Note that the second line of this selection structure is indented. Such indentation is optional, but it is highly recommended because it emphasizes the inherent structure of structured programs. The C++ compiler ignores *whitespace characters* like blanks, tabs and newlines used for indentation and vertical spacing.

***Good Programming Practice 2.1***

*Consistently applying reasonable indentation conventions throughout your programs greatly improves program readability. We suggest a fixed-size tab of about 1/4 inch or three blanks per indent.*

The preceding pseudocode *If* statement may be written in C++ as

```
if (grade >= 60)
   cout << "Passed" << endl;
```

Notice that the C++ code corresponds closely to the pseudocode. This is one of the properties of pseudocode that makes it such a useful program development tool.

***Good Programming Practice 2.2***

*Pseudocode is often used to "think out" a program during the program design process. Then the pseudocode program is converted to C++.*

The flowchart of Fig. 2.3 illustrates the single-selection **`if`** structure. This flowchart contains what is perhaps the most important flowcharting symbol—the *diamond symbol*, also called the *decision symbol,* which indicates that a decision is to be made. The decision symbol contains an expression, such as a condition, that can be either true or false. The decision symbol has two flowlines emerging from it. One indicates the direction to be taken when the expression in the symbol is true; the other indicates the direction to be taken when the expression is false. We learned in Chapter 1 that decisions can be made based on conditions containing relational or equality operators. Actually, a decision can be made on any expression—if the expression evaluates to zero, it is treated as false, and if the expression evaluates to nonzero, it is treated as true.

Note that the **`if`** structure, too, is a single-entry/single-exit structure. We will soon learn that the flowcharts for the remaining control structures also contain (besides small circle symbols and flowlines) only rectangle symbols to indicate the actions to be performed, and diamond symbols to indicate decisions to be made. This is the *action/decision model of programming* we have been emphasizing.

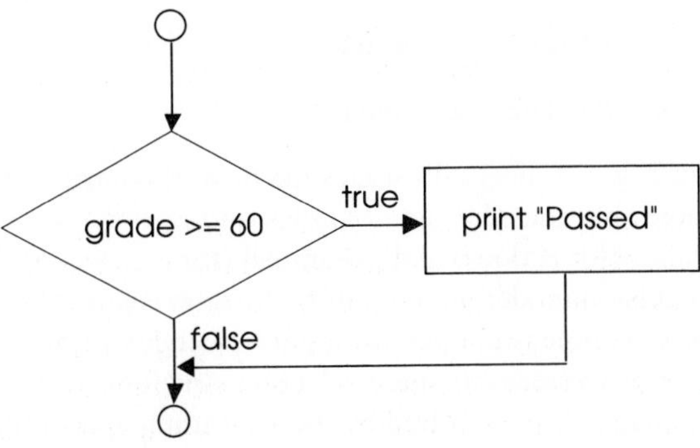


**Fig. 2.3** Flowcharting the single-selection **`if`** structure.

We can envision seven bins, each containing only control structures of one of the seven types. These control structures are empty. Nothing is written in the rectangles or in the diamonds. The programmer's task, then, is assembling a program from as many of each type of control structure as the algorithm demands, combining those control structures in only two possible ways (stacking or nesting), and then filling in the actions and decisions in a manner appropriate for the algorithm. We will discuss the variety of ways in which actions and decisions may be written.

## 2.6 The If/Else Selection Structure

The **if** selection structure performs an indicated action only when the condition is true; otherwise the action is skipped. The **if/else** selection structure allows the programmer to specify that a different action is to be performed when the condition is true than when the condition is false. For example, the pseudocode statement

*If student's grade is greater than or equal to 60*
    *Print "Passed"*
*else*
    *Print "Failed"*

prints *Passed* if the student's grade is greater than or equal to 60 and prints *Failed* if the student's grade is less than 60. In either case, after printing occurs, the next pseudocode statement in sequence is "performed." Note that the body of the *else* is also indented.

***Good Programming Practice 2.3***

*Indent both body statements of an* **if/else** *structure.*

Whatever indentation convention you choose should be carefully applied throughout your programs. It is difficult to read programs that do not obey uniform spacing conventions.

***Good Programming Practice 2.4***

*If there are several levels of indentation, each level should be indented the same additional amount of space.*

The preceding pseudocode *If/else* structure may be written in C++ as

```
if (grade >= 60)
   cout << "Passed" << endl;
else
   cout << "Failed" << endl;
```

The flowchart of Fig. 2.4 nicely illustrates the flow of control in the **if/else** structure. Once again, note that (besides small circles and arrows) the only symbols in the flowchart are rectangles (for actions) and a diamond (for a decision). We continue to emphasize this action/decision model of computing. Imagine again a deep bin containing as many empty double-selection structures as might be needed to build any C++ program. The programmer's job is to assemble these selection structures (by stacking and nesting) with any other control structures required by the algorithm, and to fill in the empty rectangles and empty diamonds with actions and decisions appropriate to the algorithm being implemented.

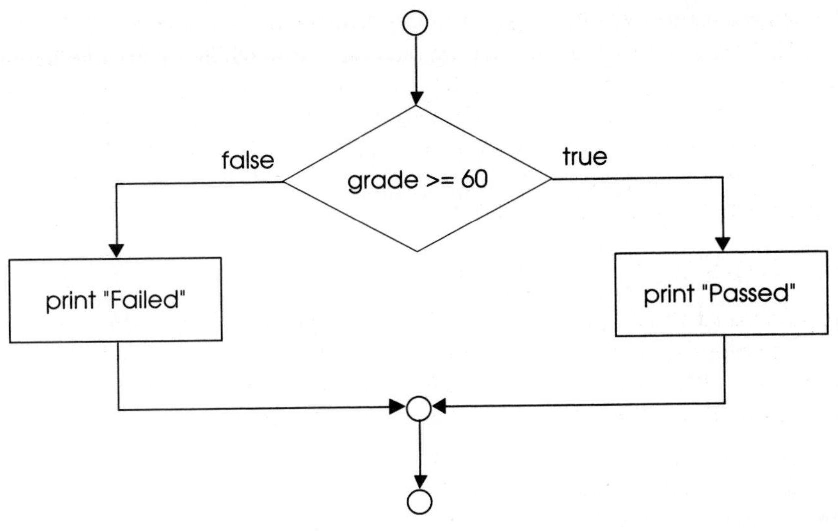


**Fig. 2.4** Flowcharting the double-selection `if/else` structure.

C++ provides the *conditional operator* (`?:`) which is closely related to the **`if/else`** structure. The conditional operator is C++'s only *ternary operator*—it takes three operands. The operands together with the conditional operator form a *conditional expression.* The first operand is a condition, the second operand is the value for the entire conditional expression if the condition is true, and the third operand is the value for the entire conditional expression if the condition is false. For example, the output statement

```
cout << (grade >= 60 ? "Passed" : "Failed") << endl;
```

contains a conditional expression that evaluates to the string **`"Passed"`** if the condition **`grade >= 60`** is true and evaluates to the string **`"Failed"`** if the condition is false. Thus, the statement with the conditional operator performs essentially the same as the preceding **`if/else`** statement. As we will see, the precedence of the conditional operator is low, so the parentheses in the preceding expression are required. Without these parentheses, the compiler would attempt to output grade with **`cout << grade`**, which is clearly not the intent of the programmer. A variety of syntax errors would then occur including the compiler's attempt to find a meaning for **`"Failed" << endl`**.

The values in a conditional expression can also be actions to be executed. For example, the conditional expression

```
grade >= 60 ? cout << "Passed\n" : cout << "Failed\n";
```

is read, "If **`grade`** is greater than or equal to **`60`** then **`cout << "Passed\n"`**, otherwise **`cout << "Failed\n"`**." This, too, is comparable to the preceding **`if/else`** structure. We will see that conditional operators can be used in some situations where **`if/else`** statements cannot.

*Nested* **`if/else`** *structures* test for multiple cases by placing **`if/else`** structures inside **`if/else`** structures. For example, the following pseudocode statement will print

**A** for exam grades greater than or equal to 90, **B** for grades in the range 80 to 89, **C** for grades in the range 70 to 79, **D** for grades in the range 60 to 69, and **F** for all other grades.

*If student's grade is greater than or equal to 90*
*Print "A"*
*else*
*If student's grade is greater than or equal to 80*
*Print "B"*
*else*
*If student's grade is greater than or equal to 70*
*Print "C"*
*else*
*If student's grade is greater than or equal to 60*
*Print "D"*
*else*
*Print "F"*

This pseudocode may be written in C++ as

```
if (grade >= 90)
   cout << "A" << endl;
else
   if (grade >= 80)
      cout << "B" << endl;
   else
      if (grade >= 70)
         cout << "C" << endl;
      else
         if (grade >= 60)
            cout << "D" << endl;
         else
            cout << "F" << endl;
```

If **grade** is greater than or equal to 90, the first four conditions will be true, but only the **cout** statement after the first test will be executed. After that **cout** is executed, the **else**-part of the "outer" **if/else** statement is skipped. Most C++ programmers prefer to write the preceding **if** structure as

```
if (grade >= 90)
   cout << "A" << endl;
else if (grade >= 80)
   cout << "B" << endl;
else if (grade >= 70)
   cout << "C" << endl;
else if (grade >= 60)
   cout << "D" << endl;
else
   cout << "F" << endl;
```

Both forms are equivalent. The latter form is popular because it avoids the deep indentation of the code to the right. Such indentation often leaves little room on a line, forcing lines to be split and decreasing program readability.

The **if** selection structure normally expects only one statement in its body. To include several statements in the body of an **if**, enclose the statements in braces ( **{** and **}**). A set of statements contained within a pair of braces is called a *compound statement*.

***Software Engineering Observation 2.1***

*A compound statement can be placed anywhere in a program that a single statement can be placed.*

The following example includes a compound statement in the **else** part of an **if/else** structure.

```
if (grade >= 60)
   cout << "Passed." << endl;
else {
   cout << "Failed." << endl;
   cout << "You must take this course again." << endl;
}
```

In this case, if **grade** is less than 60, the program executes both statements in the body of the **else** and prints

```
Failed.
You must take this course again.
```

Notice the braces surrounding the two statements in the **else** clause. These braces are important. Without the braces, the statement

```
cout << "You must take this course again." << endl;
```

would be outside the body of the **else**-part of the **if**, and would execute regardless of whether the grade is less than 60.

***Common Programming Error 2.2***

*Forgetting one or both of the braces that delimit a compound statement.*

A syntax error is caught by the compiler. A *logic error* has its effect at execution time. A *fatal logic error* causes a program to fail and terminate prematurely. A *nonfatal logic error* allows a program to continue executing but the program produces incorrect results.

***Software Engineering Observation 2.2***

*Just as a compound statement can be placed anywhere a single statement can be placed, it is also possible to have no statement at all, i.e., the empty statement. The empty statement is represented by placing a semicolon (* **;** *) where a statement would normally be.*

***Common Programming Error 2.3***

*Placing a semicolon after the condition in an* **if** *structure leads to a logic error in single-selection* **if** *structures and a syntax error in double-selection* **if** *structures (if the* **if***-part contains an actual body statement).*

***Good Programming Practice 2.5***

*Some programmers prefer to type the beginning and ending braces of compound statements before typing the individual statements within the braces. This helps avoid omitting one or both of the braces.*

In this section, we introduced the notion of a compound statement. A compound statement may contain declarations (as does the body of **`main`**, for example). If so, the compound statement is called a *block*. The declarations in a block are commonly placed first in the block before any action statements, but declarations may be intermixed with action statements. We will discuss the use of blocks in Chapter 3. The reader should avoid using blocks (other than as the body of **`main`**, of course) until that time.

## 2.7 The While Repetition Structure

A *repetition structure* allows the programmer to specify that an action is to be repeated while some condition remains true. The pseudocode statement

*While there are more items on my shopping list*
    *Purchase next item and cross it off my list*

describes the repetition that occurs during a shopping trip. The condition, "there are more items on my shopping list" may be true or false. If it is true, then the action, "Purchase next item and cross it off my list" is performed. This action will be performed repeatedly while the condition remains true. The statement(s) contained in the *while* repetition structure constitute the body of the *while*. The *while* structure body may be a single statement or a compound statement. Eventually, the condition will become false (when the last item on the shopping list has been purchased and crossed off the list). At this point, the repetition terminates, and the first pseudocode statement after the repetition structure is executed.

***Common Programming Error 2.4***

*Not providing in the body of a* **`while`** *structure an action that eventually causes the condition in the* **`while`** *to become false. Normally, such a repetition structure will never terminate—an error called an "infinite loop."*

***Common Programming Error 2.5***

*Spelling the keyword* **`while`** *with an uppercase* **`W`** *as in* **`While`** *(remember that C++ is a case-sensitive language). All of C++'s reserved keywords such as* **`while`**, **`if`**, *and* **`else`** *contain only lowercase letters.*

As an example of an actual **`while`**, consider a program segment designed to find the first power of 2 larger than 1000. Suppose the integer variable **`product`** has been initialized to 2. When the following **`while`** repetition structure finishes executing, **`product`** will contain the desired answer:

```
int product = 2;
while (product <= 1000)
   product = 2 * product;
```

The flowchart of Fig. 2.5 nicely illustrates the flow of control in the **while** repetition structure that corresponds to the preceding **while** structure. Once again, note that (besides small circles and arrows) the flowchart contains only a rectangle symbol and a diamond symbol. Imagine, again, a deep bin of empty **while** structures that may be stacked and nested with other control structures to form a structured implementation of an algorithm's flow of control. The empty rectangles and diamonds are then filled in with appropriate actions and decisions. The flowchart clearly shows the repetition. The flowline emerging from the rectangle wraps back to the decision which is tested each time through the loop until the decision eventually becomes false. At this point, the **while** structure is exited and control passes to the next statement in the program.

When the **while** structure is entered, the value of **product** is 2. The variable **product** is repeatedly multiplied by 2, taking on the values 4, 8, 16, 32, 64, 128, 256, 512, and 1024 successively. When **product** becomes 1024, the condition in the **while** structure, **product <= 1000**, becomes false. This terminates the repetition with the final value of **product** being 1024. Program execution continues with the next statement after the **while**.

## 2.8 Formulating Algorithms: Case Study 1 (Counter-Controlled Repetition)

To illustrate how algorithms are developed, we solve several variations of a class averaging problem. Consider the following problem statement:

> *A class of ten students took a quiz. The grades (integers in the range 0 to 100) for this quiz are available to you. Determine the class average on the quiz.*

The class average is equal to the sum of the grades divided by the number of students. The algorithm for solving this problem on a computer must input each of the grades, perform the averaging calculation, and print the result.

Let us use pseudocode to list the actions to be executed and specify the order in which these actions should be executed. We use *counter-controlled repetition* to input the grades one at a time. This technique uses a variable called a *counter* to specify the num-

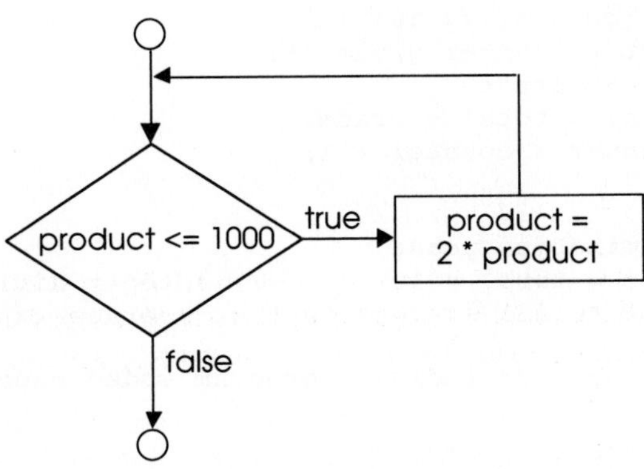


**Fig. 2.5** Flowcharting the **while** repetition structure.

ber of times a set of statements should execute. In this example, repetition terminates when the counter exceeds 10. In this section, we present a pseudocode algorithm (Fig. 2.6) and the corresponding program (Fig. 2.7). In the next section, we show how pseudocode algorithms are developed. Counter-controlled repetition is often called *definite repetition* because the number of repetitions is known before the loop begins executing.

*Set total to zero*
*Set grade counter to one*

*While grade counter is less than or equal to ten*
    *Input the next grade*
    *Add the grade into the total*
    *Add one to the grade counter*

*Set the class average to the total divided by ten*
*Print the class average*

**Fig. 2.6** Pseudocode algorithm that uses counter-controlled repetition to solve the class average problem.

```
// Class average program with
// counter-controlled repetition
#include <iostream.h>

main()
{
   int counter, grade, total, average;

   // initialization phase
   total = 0;
   counter = 1;

   // processing phase
   while (counter <= 10) {
      cout << "Enter grade: ";
      cin >> grade;
      total = total + grade;
      counter = counter + 1;
   }

   // termination phase
   average = total / 10;        // integer division
   cout << "Class average is " << average << endl;

   return 0;   // indicate program ended successfully
}
```

**Fig. 2.7** C++ program and sample execution for the class average problem with counter-controlled repetition (part 1 of 2).

```
Enter grade: 98
Enter grade: 76
Enter grade: 71
Enter grade: 87
Enter grade: 83
Enter grade: 90
Enter grade: 57
Enter grade: 79
Enter grade: 82
Enter grade: 94
Class average is 81
```

**Fig. 2.7** C++ program and sample execution for the class average problem with counter-controlled repetition (part 2 of 2).

Note the references in the algorithm to a total and a counter. A *total* is a variable used to accumulate the sum of a series of values. A counter is a variable used to count—in this case, to count the number of grades entered. Variables used to store totals should normally be initialized to zero before being used in a program; otherwise the sum would include the previous value stored in the total's memory location. Counter variables are normally initialized to zero or one, depending on their use (we will present examples showing each of these uses). An uninitialized variable contains a *"garbage" value*—the value last stored in the memory location reserved for that variable.

***Common Programming Error 2.6***

*If a counter or total is not initialized, the results of your program will probably be incorrect. This is an example of a logic error.*

***Good Programming Practice 2.6***

*Initialize counters and totals.*

Note that the averaging calculation in the program produced an integer result. Actually, the sum of the grades in this example is 817 which when divided by 10 should yield 81.7, i.e., a number with a decimal point. We will see how to deal with such numbers (called floating-point numbers) in the next section.

## 2.9 Formulating Algorithms with Top-down, Stepwise Refinement: Case Study 2 (Sentinel-Controlled Repetition)

Let us generalize the class average problem. Consider the following problem:

*Develop a class averaging program that will process an arbitrary number of grades each time the program is run.*

In the first class average example, the number of grades (10) was known in advance. In this example, no indication is given of how many grades are to be entered. The program must process an arbitrary number of grades. How can the program determine when to stop the input of grades? How will it know when to calculate and print the class average?

One way to solve this problem is to use a special value called a *sentinel value* (also called a *signal value*, a *dummy value*, or a *flag value*) to indicate "end of data entry." The user types grades in until all legitimate grades have been entered. The user then types the sentinel value to indicate that the last grade has been entered. Sentinel-controlled repetition is often called *indefinite repetition* because the number of repetitions is not known before the loop begins executing.

Clearly, the sentinel value must be chosen so that it cannot be confused with an acceptable input value. Because grades on a quiz are normally nonnegative integers, –1 is an acceptable sentinel value for this problem. Thus, a run of the class average program might process a stream of inputs such as 95, 96, 75, 74, 89, and –1. The program would then compute and print the class average for the grades 95, 96, 75, 74, and 89 (–1 is the sentinel value, so it should not enter into the averaging calculation).

***Common Programming Error 2.7***

---

*Choosing a sentinel value that is also a legitimate data value.*

We approach the class average program with a technique called *top-down, stepwise refinement*, a technique that is essential to the development of well-structured programs. We begin with a pseudocode representation of the *top:*

*Determine the class average for the quiz*

The top is a single statement that conveys the overall function of the program. As such, the top is, in effect, a complete representation of a program. Unfortunately, the top (as in this case) rarely conveys a sufficient amount of detail from which to write the C++ program. So we now begin the refinement process. We divide the top into a series of smaller tasks and list these in the order in which they need to be performed. This results in the following *first refinement*.

*Initialize variables*
*Input, sum, and count the quiz grades*
*Calculate and print the class average*

Here, only the sequence structure has been used—the steps listed are to be executed in order, one after the other.

***Software Engineering Observation 2.3***

---

*Each refinement, as well as the top itself, is a complete specification of the algorithm; only the level of detail varies.*

To proceed to the next level of refinement, i.e., the *second refinement*, we commit to specific variables. We need a running total of the numbers, a count of how many numbers have been processed, a variable to receive the value of each grade as it is input, and a variable to hold the calculated average. The pseudocode statement

*Initialize variables*

may be refined as follows:

*Initialize total to zero*
*Initialize counter to zero*

Notice that only the variables *total* and *counter* need to be initialized before they are used; the variables *average* and *grade* (for the calculated average and the user input, respectively) need not be initialized because their values will be written over as they are calculated or input.

The pseudocode statement

*Input, sum, and count the quiz grades*

requires a repetition structure (i.e., a loop) that successively inputs each grade. Because we do not know in advance how many grades are to be processed, we will use sentinel-controlled repetition. The user will type legitimate grades in one at a time. After the last legitimate grade is typed, the user will type the sentinel value. The program will test for the sentinel value after each grade is input and will terminate the loop when the sentinel value is entered by the user. The second refinement of the preceding pseudocode statement is then

*Input the first grade*
*While the user has not as yet entered the sentinel*
    *Add this grade into the running total*
    *Add one to the grade counter*
    *Input the next grade (possibly the sentinel)*

Notice that in pseudocode, we do not use braces around the set of statements that form the body of the *while* structure. We simply indent all these statements under the *while* to show that they all belong to the *while*. Again, pseudocode is only an informal program development aid.

The pseudocode statement

*Calculate and print the class average*

may be refined as follows:

*If the counter is not equal to zero*
    *Set the average to the total divided by the counter*
    *Print the average*
*else*
    *Print "No grades were entered"*

Notice that we are being careful here to test for the possibility of division by zero—a *fatal logic error* that if undetected would cause the program to fail (often called *"bombing"* or *"crashing"*). The complete second refinement of the pseudocode for the class average problem is shown in Fig. 2.8.

**Common Programming Error 2.8**

*An attempt to divide by zero causes a fatal error.*

**Good Programming Practice 2.7**

*When performing division by an expression whose value could be zero, explicitly test for this case and handle it appropriately in your program (such as printing an error message) rather than allowing the fatal error to occur.*

*Initialize total to zero*
*Initialize counter to zero*

*Input the first grade*
*While the user has not as yet entered the sentinel*
    *Add this grade into the running total*
    *Add one to the grade counter*
    *Input the next grade (possibly the sentinel)*

*If the counter is not equal to zero*
    *Set the average to the total divided by the counter*
    *Print the average*
*else*
    *Print "No grades were entered"*

**Fig. 2.8** Pseudocode algorithm that uses sentinel-controlled repetition to solve the class average problem.

In Fig. 2.6 and Fig. 2.8, we include some completely blank lines in the pseudocode to make the pseudocode more readable. The blank lines separate these programs into their various phases.

***Software Engineering Observation 2.4***

*Many programs can be divided logically into three phases: an initialization phase that initializes the program variables; a processing phase that inputs data values and adjusts program variables accordingly; and a termination phase that calculates and prints the final results.*

The pseudocode algorithm in Fig. 2.8 solves the more general class averaging problem. This algorithm was developed after only two levels of refinement. Sometimes more levels are necessary.

***Software Engineering Observation 2.5***

*The programmer terminates the top-down, stepwise refinement process when the pseudocode algorithm is specified in sufficient detail for the programmer to be able to convert the pseudocode to C++. Implementing the C++ program is then normally straightforward.*

The C++ program and a sample execution are shown in Fig. 2.9. Although only integer grades are entered, the averaging calculation is likely to produce a number with a decimal point (i.e., a real number). The type `int` cannot represent real numbers. The program introduces the data type `float` to handle numbers with decimal points (also called *floating-point numbers*) and introduces a special operator called a *cast operator* to handle the averaging calculation. These features are explained in detail after the program is presented.

```
// Class average program with
// sentinel-controlled repetition.
#include <iostream.h>
#include <iomanip.h>

main()
{
   float average;            // number with decimal point
   int counter, grade, total;

   // initialization phase
   total = 0;
   counter = 0;

   // processing phase
   cout << "Enter grade, -1 to end: ";
   cin >> grade;

   while (grade != -1) {
      total = total + grade;
      counter = counter + 1;
      cout << "Enter grade, -1 to end: ";
      cin >> grade;
   }

   // termination phase
   if (counter != 0) {
      average = (float) total / counter;
      cout << "Class average is " << setprecision(2)
           << setiosflags(ios::fixed | ios::showpoint)
           << average << endl;
   }
   else
      cout << "No grades were entered" << endl;

   return 0;   // indicate program ended successfully
}
```

```
Enter grade, -1 to end: 75
Enter grade, -1 to end: 94
Enter grade, -1 to end: 97
Enter grade, -1 to end: 88
Enter grade, -1 to end: 70
Enter grade, -1 to end: 64
Enter grade, -1 to end: 83
Enter grade, -1 to end: 89
Enter grade, -1 to end: -1
Class average is 82.50
```

**Fig. 2.9** C++ program and sample execution for the class average problem with sentinel-controlled repetition.

Notice the compound statement in the **while** loop in Fig 2.9. Without the braces, the last three statements in the body of the loop would fall outside the loop, causing the computer to interpret this code incorrectly as follows

```
while(grade != -1)
   total = total + grade;
counter = counter + 1;
cout << "Enter grade, -1 to end: ";
cin >> grade;
```

This would cause an infinite loop if the user does not input –1 for the first grade.

***Good Programming Practice 2.8***

---

*In a sentinel-controlled loop, the prompts requesting data entry should explicitly remind the user what the sentinel value is.*

Averages do not always evaluate to integer values. Often, an average is a value such as 7.2 or -93.5 that contains a fractional part. These values are referred to as floating-point numbers and are represented by the data type **float**. The variable **average** is declared to be of type **float** to capture the fractional result of our calculation. However, the result of the calculation **total / counter** is an integer because **total** and **counter** are both integer variables. Dividing two integers results in *integer division* in which any fractional part of the calculation is lost (i.e., *truncated*). Because the calculation is performed first, the fractional part is lost before the result is assigned to **average**. To produce a floating-point calculation with integer values, we must create temporary values that are floating-point numbers for the calculation. C++ provides the *unary cast operator* to accomplish this task. The statement

```
average = (float) total / counter;
```

includes the cast operator **(float)** which creates a temporary floating-point copy of its operand, **total**. Using a cast operator in this manner is called *explicit conversion.* The value stored in **total** is still an integer. The calculation now consists of a floating-point value (the temporary **float** version of **total**) divided by the integer **counter**.

The C++ compiler only knows how to evaluate expressions in which the data types of the operands are identical. To ensure that the operands are of the same type, the compiler performs an operation called *promotion* (also called *implicit conversion*) on selected operands. For example, in an expression containing the data types **int** and **float**, **int** operands are *promoted* to **float**. In our example, after **counter** is promoted to **float**, the calculation is performed and the result of the floating-point division is assigned to **average**. Later in this chapter we discuss all the standard data types and their order of promotion.

Cast operators are available for any data type. The cast operator is formed by placing parentheses around a data type name. The cast operator is a *unary operator*, i.e., an operator that takes only one operand. In Chapter 1, we studied the binary arithmetic operators. C++ also supports unary versions of the plus (**+**) and minus (**-**) operators, so the programmer can write expressions like **-7** or **+5**. Cast operators associate from right to left and have the same precedence as other unary operators such as unary **+** and unary **-**. This precedence is one level higher than that of the *multiplicative operators* `*`, `/`, and `%`, and one level lower than that of parentheses. We indicate the cast operator with the notation *(type)* in our precedence charts.

The formatting capabilities in Fig. 2.9 are explained in depth in Chapter 11 and discussed here briefly. The call **setprecision(2)** in the output statement

```
cout << "Class average is " << setprecision(2)
     << setiosflags(ios::fixed | ios::showpoint)
     << average << endl;
```

indicates that **float** variable **average** is to be printed with two digits of *precision* to the right of the decimal point (e.g., 92.37). This call is referred to as a *parameterized stream manipulator*. Programs that use these calls must contain the preprocessor directive

```
#include <iomanip.h>
```

Note that **endl** is a *nonparameterized stream manipulator* and does not require the **iomanip.h** header file. If the precision is not specified, floating-point values are normally output with six digits of precision (i.e., the *default precision*), although we will see an exception to this in a moment.

The stream manipulator **setiosflags(ios::fixed | ios::showpoint)** in the preceding statement sets two output formatting options, namely **ios::fixed** and **ios::showpoint**. The vertical bar character (**|**) separates multiple options in a **setiosflags** call (we will explain the **|** notation in depth in Chapter 16). The option **ios::fixed** causes a floating-point value to be output in so-called *fixed-point format* (as opposed to *scientific notation* which we will discuss in Chapter 11). The **ios::showpoint** option forces the decimal point and trailing zeros to print even if the value is a whole number amount such as 88.00. Without the **ios::showpoint** option, such a value prints in C++ as 88 without the trailing zeros and without the decimal point. When the preceding formatting is used in a program, the printed value is *rounded* to the indicated number of decimal positions, although the value in memory remains unaltered. For example, the values 87.945 and 67.543 are output as 87.95 and 67.54, respectively.

***Common Programming Error 2.9***

*Using floating-point numbers in a manner that assumes they are represented precisely can lead to incorrect results. Floating-point numbers are represented only approximately by most computers.*

***Good Programming Practice 2.9***

*Do not compare floating-point values for equality or inequality. Rather, test that the difference is less than a specified small value.*

Despite the fact that floating-point numbers are not always "100% precise," they have numerous applications. For example, when we speak of a "normal" body temperature of 98.6 we do not need to be precise to a large number of digits. When we view the temperature on a thermometer and read it as 98.6, it may actually be 98.5999473210643. The point here is that calling this number simply 98.6 is fine for most applications.

Another way floating-point numbers develop is through division. When we divide 10 by 3, the result is 3.3333333... with the sequence of 3s repeating infinitely. The computer allocates only a fixed amount of space to hold such a value, so clearly the stored floating-point value can only be an approximation.

## 2.10 Formulating Algorithms with Top-down, Stepwise Refinement: Case Study 3 (Nested Control Structures)

Let us work another complete problem. We will once again formulate the algorithm using pseudocode and top-down, stepwise refinement, and write a corresponding C++ program. We have seen that control structures may be stacked on top of one another (in sequence) just as a child stacks building blocks. In this case study we will see the only other structured way control structures may be connected in C++, namely through *nesting* of one control structure within another.

Consider the following problem statement:

*A college offers a course that prepares students for the state licensing exam for real estate brokers. Last year, several of the students who completed this course took the licensing examination. Naturally, the college wants to know how well its students did on the exam. You have been asked to write a program to summarize the results. You have been given a list of these 10 students. Next to each name is written a 1 if the student passed the exam and a 2 if the student failed.*

Your program should analyze the results of the exam as follows:

1. Input each test result (i.e., a 1 or a 2). Display the message "Enter result" on the screen each time the program requests another test result.
2. Count the number of test results of each type.
3. Display a summary of the test results indicating the number of students who passed and the number of students who failed.
4. If more than 8 students passed the exam, print the message "Raise tuition."

After reading the problem statement carefully, we make the following observations:

1. The program must process 10 test results. A counter-controlled loop will be used.
2. Each test result is a number—either a 1 or a 2. Each time the program reads a test result, the program must determine if the number is a 1 or a 2. We test for a 1 in our algorithm. If the number is not a 1, we assume that it is a 2. (An exercise at the end of the chapter considers the consequences of this assumption.)
3. Two counters are used—one to count the number of students who passed the exam and one to count the number of students who failed the exam.
4. After the program has processed all the results, it must decide if more than 8 students passed the exam.

Let us proceed with top-down, stepwise refinement. We begin with a pseudocode representation of the top:

*Analyze exam results and decide if tuition should be raised*

Once again, it is important to emphasize that the top is a complete representation of the program, but several refinements are likely to be needed before the pseudocode can be naturally evolved into a C++ program. Our first refinement is

*Initialize variables*
*Input the ten quiz grades and count passes and failures*
*Print a summary of the exam results and decide if tuition should be raised*

Here, too, even though we have a complete representation of the entire program, further refinement is necessary. We now commit to specific variables. Counters are needed to record the passes and failures, a counter will be used to control the looping process, and a variable is needed to store the user input. The pseudocode statement

*Initialize variables*

may be refined as follows:

*Initialize passes to zero*
*Initialize failures to zero*
*Initialize student to one*

Notice only the counters and totals are initialized. The pseudocode statement

*Input the ten quiz grades and count passes and failures*

requires a loop that successively inputs the result of each exam. Here it is known in advance that there are precisely ten exam results, so counter-controlled looping is appropriate. Inside the loop (i.e., *nested* within the loop) a double-selection structure will determine whether each exam result is a pass or a failure, and will increment the appropriate counter accordingly. The refinement of the preceding pseudocode statement is then

```
While student counter is less than or equal to ten
    Input the next exam result

    If the student passed
        Add one to passes
    else
        Add one to failures

    Add one to student counter
```

Notice the use of blank lines to set off the *If/else* control structure to improve program readability. The pseudocode statement

*Print a summary of the exam results and decide if tuition should be raised*

may be refined as follows:

```
Print the number of passes
Print the number of failures
If eight or more students passed
    Print "Raise tuition"
```

The complete second refinement appears in Fig. 2.10. Notice that blank lines are also used to set off the *while* structure for program readability.

*Initialize passes to zero*
*Initialize failures to zero*
*Initialize student to one*

*While student counter is less than or equal to ten*
    *Input the next exam result*

    *If the student passed*
        *Add one to passes*
    *else*
        *Add one to failures*

    *Add one to student counter*

*Print the number of passes*
*Print the number of failures*
*If eight or more students passed*
    *Print "Raise tuition"*

**Fig. 2.10** Pseudocode for examination results problem.

This pseudocode is now sufficiently refined for conversion to C++. The C++ program and two sample executions are shown in Fig. 2.11. Note that we have taken advantage of a feature of C++ that allows variable initialization to be incorporated into declarations. Looping programs may require initialization at the beginning of each repetition; such initialization would normally occur in assignment statements.

***Good Programming Practice 2.10***

*Initializing variables when they are declared helps the programmer avoid the problems of uninitialized data.*

***Software Engineering Observation 2.6***

*Experience has shown that the most difficult part of solving a problem on a computer is developing the algorithm for the solution. Once a correct algorithm has been specified, the process of producing a working C++ program from the algorithm is normally straightforward.*

***Software Engineering Observation 2.7***

*Many experienced programmers write programs without ever using program development tools like pseudocode. These programmers feel that their ultimate goal is to solve the problem on a computer, and that writing pseudocode merely delays the production of final outputs. Although this may work for simple and familiar problems, it can lead to serious errors on large, complex projects.*

```
// Analysis of examination results
#include <iostream.h>

main()
{
   // initializing variables in declarations
   int passes = 0, failures = 0, student = 1, result;

   // process 10 students; counter-controlled loop
   while (student <= 10) {
      cout << "Enter result (1=pass,2=fail): ";
      cin >> result;

      if (result == 1)         // if/else nested in while
         passes = passes + 1;
      else
         failures = failures + 1;

      student = student + 1;
   }

   cout << "Passed " << passes << endl;
   cout << "Failed " << failures << endl;

   if (passes > 8)
      cout << "Raise tuition " << endl;

   return 0;   // successful termination
}
```

```
Enter Result (1=pass,2=fail): 1
Enter Result (1=pass,2=fail): 2
Enter Result (1=pass,2=fail): 2
Enter Result (1=pass,2=fail): 1
Enter Result (1=pass,2=fail): 1
Enter Result (1=pass,2=fail): 1
Enter Result (1=pass,2=fail): 2
Enter Result (1=pass,2=fail): 1
Enter Result (1=pass,2=fail): 1
Enter Result (1=pass,2=fail): 2
Passed 6
Failed 4
```

**Fig. 2.11** C++ program and sample executions for examination results problem (part 1 of 2).

## 2.11 Assignment Operators

C++ provides several assignment operators for abbreviating assignment expressions. For example the statement

```
c = c + 3;
```

```
Enter Result (1=pass,2=fail): 1
Enter Result (1=pass,2=fail): 1
Enter Result (1=pass,2=fail): 1
Enter Result (1=pass,2=fail): 2
Enter Result (1=pass,2=fail): 1
Enter Result (1=pass,2=fail): 1
Enter Result (1=pass,2=fail): 1
Enter Result (1=pass,2=fail): 1
Enter Result (1=pass,2=fail): 1
Enter Result (1=pass,2=fail): 1
Passed 9
Failed 1
Raise tuition
```

**Fig. 2.11** C++ program and sample executions for examination results problem (part 2 of 2).

can be abbreviated with the *addition assignment operator* **+=** as

```
c += 3;
```

The **+=** operator adds the value of the expression on the right of the operator to the value of the variable on the left of the operator and stores the result in the variable on the left of the operator. Any statement of the form

*variable* **=** *variable operator expression***;**

where *operator* is one of the binary operators **+**, **-**, *****, **/**, or **%** (or others we will discuss later in the text), can be written in the form

*variable operator***=** *expression***;**

Thus the assignment **c += 3** adds **3** to **c**. Figure 2.12 shows the arithmetic assignment operators, sample expressions using these operators, and explanations.

| Assignment operator | Sample expression | Explanation | Assigns |
|---|---|---|---|
| Assume : `int c = 3, d = 5, e = 4, f = 6, g = 12;` | | | |
| `+=` | `c += 7` | `c = c + 7` | `10` to `c` |
| `-=` | `d -= 4` | `d = d - 4` | `1` to `d` |
| `*=` | `e *= 5` | `e = e * 5` | `20` to `e` |
| `/=` | `f /= 3` | `f = f / 3` | `2` to `f` |
| `%=` | `g %= 9` | `g = g % 9` | `3` to `g` |

**Fig. 2.12** Arithmetic assignment operators.

***Performance Tip 2.1***

*Programmers can write programs a bit faster and compilers can compile programs a bit faster when the "abbreviated" assignment operators are used. Some compilers generate code that runs faster when "abbreviated" assignment operators are used.*

***Performance Tip 2.2***

*Many of the performance tips we mention in this text result in nominal improvements, so the reader may be tempted to ignore them. Significant performance improvement is often realized when a supposedly nominal improvement is placed in a loop that may repeat a large number of times.*

## 2.12 Increment and Decrement Operators

C++ also provides the unary *increment operator*, `++`, and the unary *decrement operator*, `--`, which are summarized in Fig. 2.13. If a variable `c` is incremented by 1, the increment operator `++` can be used rather than the expressions `c = c + 1` or `c += 1`. If an increment or decrement operator is placed before a variable, it is referred to as the *preincrement* or *predecrement operator,* respectively. If an increment or decrement operator is placed after a variable, it is referred to as the *postincrement* or *postdecrement operator,* respectively. Preincrementing (predecrementing) a variable causes the variable to be incremented (decremented) by 1, then the new value of the variable is used in the expression in which it appears. Postincrementing (postdecrementing) the variable causes the current value of the variable to be used in the expression in which it appears, then the variable value is incremented (decremented) by 1.

The program of Fig. 2.14 demonstrates the difference between the preincrementing version and the postincrementing version of the `++` operator. Postincrementing the variable `c` causes it to be incremented after it is used in the output statement. Preincrementing the variable `c` causes it to be incremented before it is used in the output statement.

The program displays the value of `c` before and after the `++` operator is used. The decrement operator (`--`) works similarly.

| Operator | Called | Sample expression | Explanation |
|---|---|---|---|
| `++` | preincrement | `++a` | Increment `a` by 1 then use the new value of `a` in the expression in which `a` resides. |
| `++` | postincrement | `a++` | Use the current value of `a` in the expression in which `a` resides, then increment `a` by 1. |
| `--` | predecrement | `--b` | Decrement `b` by 1 then use the new value of `b` in the expression in which `b` resides. |
| `--` | postdecrement | `b--` | Use the current value of `b` in the expression in which `b` resides, then decrement `b` by 1. |

**Fig. 2.13** The increment and decrement operators.

```
// Preincrementing and postincrementing
#include <iostream.h>

main()
{
   int c;

   c = 5;
   cout << c << endl;
   cout << c++ << endl;     // postincrement
   cout << c << endl << endl;

   c = 5;
   cout << c << endl;
   cout << ++c << endl;     // preincrement
   cout << c << endl;

   return 0;   // successful termination
}
```

```
5
5
6

5
6
6
```

**Fig. 2.14** The difference between preincrementing and postincrementing.

***Good Programming Practice 2.11***

*Unary operators should be placed next to their operands with no intervening spaces.*

The three assignment statements in Fig 2.11

```
passes = passes + 1;
failures = failures + 1;
student = student + 1;
```

can be written more concisely with assignment operators as

```
passes += 1;
failures += 1;
student += 1;
```

with preincrement operators as

```
++passes;
++failures;
++student;
```

or with postincrement operators as

```
passes++;
failures++;
student++;
```

It is important to note here that when incrementing or decrementing a variable in a statement by itself, the preincrement and postincrement forms have the same effect, and the predecrement and postdecrement forms have the same effect. It is only when a variable appears in the context of a larger expression that preincrementing the variable and postincrementing the variable have different effects (and similarly for predecrementing and postdecrementing).

For now, only a simple variable name may be used as the operand of an increment or decrement operator (we will see later that increment or decrement operators may be used on so-called lvalues).

***Common Programming Error 2.10***

*Attempting to use the increment or decrement operator on an expression other than a simple variable name, e.g., writing* `++(x + 1)` *is a syntax error.*

The chart in Fig. 2.15 shows the precedence and associativity of the operators introduced to this point. The operators are shown top-to-bottom in decreasing order of precedence. The second column describes the associativity of the operators at each level of precedence. Notice that the conditional operator (`?:`), the unary operators increment (`++`), decrement (`--`), plus (`+`), minus (`-`) and casts, and the assignment operators `=`, `+=`, `-=`, `*=`, `/=` and `%=` associate from right to left. All other operators in the operator precedence chart of Fig. 2.15 associate from left to right. The third column names the various groups of operators.

| Operators | | | | | | Associativity | Type |
|---|---|---|---|---|---|---|---|
| `()` | | | | | | left to right | parentheses |
| `++` | `--` | `+` | `-` | `(type)` | | right to left | unary |
| `*` | `/` | `%` | | | | left to right | multiplicative |
| `+` | `-` | | | | | left to right | additive |
| `<<` | `>>` | | | | | left to right | insertion/extraction |
| `<` | `<=` | `>` | `>=` | | | left to right | relational |
| `==` | `!=` | | | | | left to right | equality |
| `?:` | | | | | | right to left | conditional |
| `=` | `+=` | `-=` | `*=` | `/=` | `%=` | right to left | assignment |

**Fig. 2.15** Precedence of the operators encountered so far in the text.

## 2.13 Essentials of Counter-Controlled Repetition

Counter-controlled repetition requires:

1. The *name* of a control variable (or loop counter).
2. The *initial value* of the control variable.
3. The *increment* (or *decrement*) by which the control variable is modified each time through the loop.
4. The condition that tests for the *final value* of the control variable (i.e., whether looping should continue).

Consider the simple program shown in Fig. 2.16, which prints the numbers from 1 to 10. The declaration

```
int counter = 1;
```

*names* the control variable (**counter**), declares it to be an integer, reserves space for it in memory, and sets it to an *initial value* of **1**. Declarations that require initialization are, in effect, executable statements.

```
// Counter-controlled repetition

#include <iostream.h>

main()
{
   int counter = 1;                  // initialization

   while (counter <= 10) {           // repetition condition
      cout << counter << endl;
      ++counter;                     // increment
   }

   return 0;
}
```

```
1
2
3
4
5
6
7
8
9
10
```

**Fig. 2.16** Counter-controlled repetition.

The declaration and initialization of **counter** could also have been accomplished with the statements

```
int counter;
counter = 1;
```

The declaration is not executable, but the assignment is. We use both methods of initializing variables.

The statement

```
++counter;
```

*increments* the loop counter by 1 each time the loop is performed. The loop-continuation condition in the **while** structure tests if the value of the control variable is less than or equal to **10** (the last value for which the condition is true). Note that the body of this **while** is performed even when the control variable is **10**. The loop terminates when the control variable exceeds **10** (i.e., **counter** becomes **11**).

The program in Fig. 2.16 can be made more concise by initializing **counter** to **0** and by replacing the **while** structure with

```
while (++counter <= 10)
   cout << counter << endl;
```

This code saves a statement because the incrementing is done directly in the **while** condition before the condition is tested. Also, this code eliminates the braces around the body of the **while** because the **while** now contains only one statement. Coding in such a condensed fashion takes some practice.

***Common Programming Error 2.11***

*Because floating-point values may be approximate, controlling counting loops with floating-point variables may result in imprecise counter values and inaccurate tests for termination.*

***Good Programming Practice 2.12***

*Control counting loops with integer values.*

***Good Programming Practice 2.13***

*Indent the statements in the body of each control structure.*

***Good Programming Practice 2.14***

*Put a blank line before and after each major control structure to make it stand out in the program.*

***Good Programming Practice 2.15***

*Too many levels of nesting can make a program difficult to understand. As a general rule, try to avoid using more than three levels of indentation.*

***Good Programming Practice 2.16***

*Vertical spacing above and below control structures, and indentation of the bodies of control structures within the control structure headers gives programs a two-dimensional appearance that greatly improves readability.*

## 2.14 The For Repetition Structure

The **for** repetition structure handles all the details of counter-controlled repetition. To illustrate the power of **for**, let us rewrite the program of Fig. 2.16. The result is shown in Fig. 2.17. The program operates as follows.

When the **for** structure begins executing, the control variable **counter** is initialized to 1. Then, the loop-continuation condition **counter <= 10** is checked. Because the initial value of **counter** is 1, the condition is satisfied, so the body statement prints the value of **counter**, namely 1. The control variable **counter** is then incremented in the expression **counter++**, and the loop begins again with the loop-continuation test. Because the control variable is now equal to 2, the final value is not exceeded, so the program performs the body statement again. This process continues until the control variable **counter** is incremented to 11—this causes the loop-continuation test to fail and repetition terminates. The program continues by performing the first statement after the **for** structure (in this case, the **return** statement at the end of the program).

Figure 2.18 takes a closer look at the **for** structure of Fig. 2.17. Notice that the **for** structure "does it all"—it specifies each of the items needed for counter-controlled repetition with a control variable. If there is more than one statement in the body of the **for**, braces are required to define the body of the loop.

Notice that Fig. 2.17 uses the loop-continuation condition **counter <= 10**. If the programmer incorrectly wrote **counter < 10**, then the loop would only be executed 9 times. This is a common logic error called an *off-by-one error*.

***Common Programming Error 2.12***

*Using an incorrect relational operator or using an incorrect final value of a loop counter in the condition of a* **while** *or* **for** *structure can cause off-by-one errors.*

```
// Counter-controlled repetition with the for structure
#include <iostream.h>

main()
{
   // Initialization, repetition condition, and incrementing
   // are all included in the for structure header.
   for (int counter = 1; counter <= 10; counter++)
      cout << counter << endl;

   return 0;
}
```

**Fig. 2.17** Counter-controlled repetition with the **for** structure.

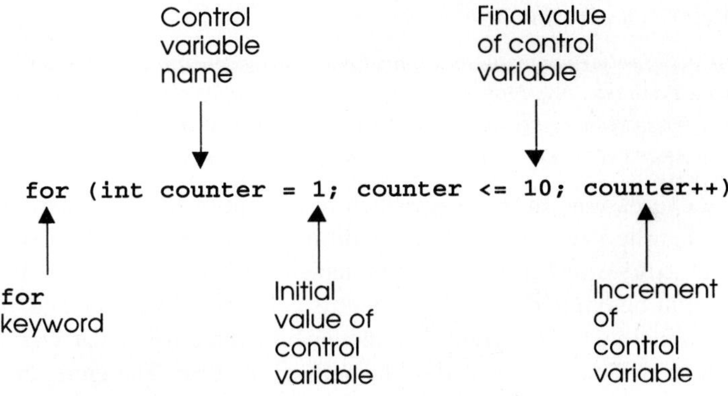


**Fig. 2.18** Components of a typical `for` header.

*Good Programming Practice 2.17*

*Using the final value in the condition of a* `while` *or* `for` *structure and using the* `<=` *relational operator will help avoid off-by-one errors. For a loop used to print the values 1 to 10, for example, the loop-continuation condition should be* `counter <= 10` *rather than* `counter < 10` *(which is an off-by-one error) or* `counter < 11` *(which is nevertheless correct).*

The general format of the `for` structure is

```
for (expression1; expression2; expression3)
    statement
```

where *expression1* initializes the loop's control variable, *expression2* is the loop-continuation condition, and *expression3* increments the control variable. In most cases the `for` structure can be represented with an equivalent `while` structure as follows:

```
expression1;

while (expression2) {
    statement
    expression3;
}
```

There is an exception to this rule which we will discuss in Section 2.18.

Sometimes, *expression1* and *expression3* are comma-separated lists of expressions. The commas as used here are *comma operators* that guarantee lists of expressions evaluate left to right. The comma operator has the lowest precedence of all operators in C++. The value and type of a comma-separated list of expressions is the value and type of the rightmost expression in the list. The comma operator is most often used in `for` structures. Its primary application is to enable the programmer to use multiple initialization expressions and/or multiple increment expressions. For example, there may be several control variables in a single `for` structure that must be initialized and incremented.

***Good Programming Practice 2.18***

*Place only expressions involving the control variables in the initialization and increment sections of a* **for** *structure. Manipulations of other variables should appear either before the loop (if they execute only once like initialization statements) or in the loop body (if they execute once per repetition like incrementing or decrementing statements).*

The three expressions in the **for** structure are optional. If *expression2* is omitted, C++ assumes that the loop-continuation condition is true, thus creating an infinite loop. One might omit *expression1* if the control variable is initialized elsewhere in the program. *expression3* might be omitted if the increment is calculated by statements in the body of the **for** or if no increment is needed. The increment expression in the **for** structure acts like a stand-alone statement at the end of the body of the **for**. Therefore, the expressions

```
counter = counter + 1
counter += 1
++counter
counter++
```

are all equivalent in the incrementing portion of the **for** structure. Many programmers prefer the form **counter++** because the incrementing occurs after the loop body is executed. The postincrementing form therefore seems more natural. Because the variable being incremented here does not appear in an expression, both forms of incrementing have the same effect. The two semicolons in the **for** structure are required.

***Common Programming Error 2.13***

*Using commas instead of semicolons in a* **for** *header.*

***Common Programming Error 2.14***

*Placing a semicolon immediately to the right of the right parenthesis of a* **for** *header makes the body of that* **for** *structure an empty statement. This is normally a logic error.*

The initialization, loop-continuation condition, and increment portions of a **for** structure can contain arithmetic expressions. For example, assume that **x = 2** and **y = 10**. If **x** and **y** are not modified in the loop body, the statement

```
for (int j = x; j <= 4 * x * y; j += y / x)
```

is equivalent to the statement

```
for (int j = 2; j <= 80; j += 5)
```

The "increment" of a **for** structure may be negative (in which case it is really a decrement and the loop actually counts downwards).

If the loop-continuation condition is initially false, the body of the **for** structure is not performed. Instead, execution proceeds with the statement following the **for**.

The control variable is frequently printed or used in calculations in the body of a **for** structure, but it does not have to be. It is common to use the control variable for controlling repetition while never mentioning it in the body of the **for** structure.

***Good Programming Practice 2.19***

*Although the value of the control variable can be changed in the body of a* **`for`** *loop, avoid doing so because this practice can lead to subtle errors.*

The **`for`** structure is flowcharted much like the **`while`** structure. For example, the flowchart of the **`for`** statement

```
for (int counter = 1; counter <= 10; counter++)
   cout << counter << endl;
```

is shown in Fig. 2.19. This flowchart makes it clear that the initialization occurs only once and that incrementing occurs each time *after* the body statement is performed. Note that (besides small circles and arrows) the flowchart contains only rectangle symbols and a diamond symbol. Imagine, again, that the programmer has access to a deep bin of empty **`for`** structures—as many as the programmer might need to stack and nest with other control structures to form a structured implementation of an algorithm's flow of control. And again, the rectangles and diamonds are then filled with actions and decisions appropriate to the algorithm.

## 2.15 Examples Using the For Structure

The following examples show methods of varying the control variable in a **`for`** structure. In each case, we write the appropriate **`for`** header. Note the change in the relational operator for loops that decrement the control variable.

a) Vary the control variable from **`1`** to **`100`** in increments of **`1`**.

```
for (int i = 1; i <= 100; i++)
```

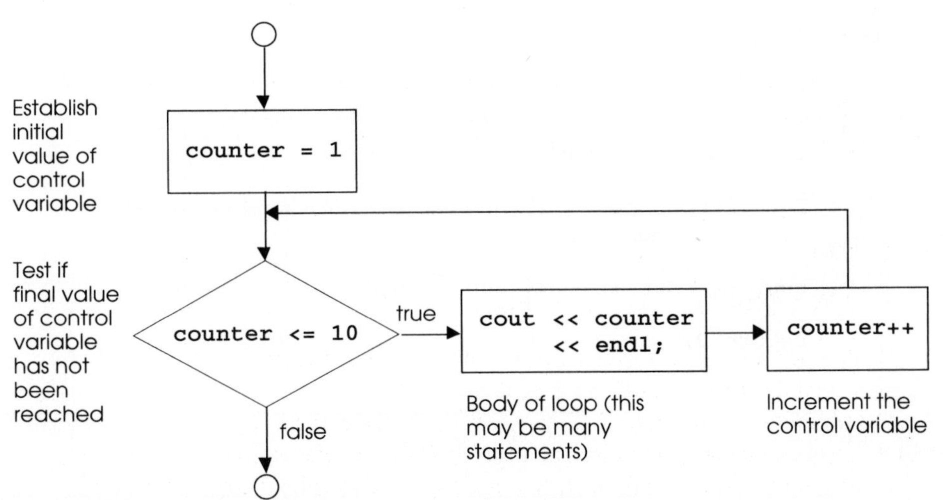


**Fig. 2.19** Flowcharting a typical **`for`** structure.

b) Vary the control variable from **100** to **1** in increments of **-1** (decrements of **1**).

```
for (int i = 100; i >= 1; i--)
```

*Common Programming Error 2.15*

---

*Not using the proper relational operator in the loop-continuation condition of a loop that counts downwards (such as using* `i <= 1` *in a loop counting down to 1).*

c) Vary the control variable from **7** to **77** in steps of **7**.

```
for (int i = 7; i <= 77; i += 7)
```

d) Vary the control variable from **20** to **2** in steps of **-2**.

```
for (int i = 20; i >= 2; i -= 2)
```

e) Vary the control variable over the following sequence of values: **2, 5, 8, 11, 14, 17, 20**.

```
for (int j = 2; j <= 20; j += 3)
```

f) Vary the control variable over the following sequence of values: **99, 88, 77, 66, 55, 44, 33, 22, 11, 0**.

```
for (int j = 99; j >= 0; j -= 11)
```

The next two examples provide simple applications of the **for** structure. The program of Fig. 2.20 uses the **for** structure to sum all the even integers from **2** to **100**.

```
// Summation with for
#include <iostream.h>

main()
{
   int sum = 0;

   for (int number = 2; number <= 100; number += 2)
      sum += number;

   cout << "Sum is " << sum << endl;

   return 0;
}
```

```
Sum is 2550
```

**Fig. 2.20** Summation with **for**.

Note that the body of the **for** structure in Fig. 2.20 could actually be merged into the rightmost portion of the **for** header by using the comma operator as follows:

```
for (int number = 2; number <= 100; sum += number, number += 2)
   ;
```

The initialization **sum = 0** could also be merged into the initialization section of the **for**.

***Good Programming Practice 2.20***

*Although statements preceding a **for** and statements in the body of a **for** can often be merged into the **for** header, avoid doing so because it makes the program more difficult to read.*

***Good Programming Practice 2.21***

*Limit the size of control structure headers to a single line if possible.*

The next example computes compound interest using the **for** structure. Consider the following problem statement:

*A person invests $1000.00 in a savings account yielding 5 percent interest. Assuming that all interest is left on deposit in the account, calculate and print the amount of money in the account at the end of each year for 10 years. Use the following formula for determining these amounts:*

$$a = p(1 + r)^n$$

where

$p$ is the original amount invested (i.e., the principal)
$r$ is the annual interest rate
$n$ is the number of years
$a$ is the amount on deposit at the end of the $n$th year.

This problem involves a loop that performs the indicated calculation for each of the 10 years the money remains on deposit. The solution is shown in Fig. 2.21.

The **for** structure executes the body of the loop 10 times, varying a control variable from 1 to 10 in increments of 1. Although C++ does not include an exponentiation operator, we can, however, use the standard library function **pow** for this purpose. The function **pow(x, y)** calculates the value of **x** raised to the **y**th power. Function **pow** takes two arguments of type **double** and returns a **double** value. The type **double** is a floating-point type much like **float**, but a variable of type **double** can store a value of much greater magnitude with greater precision than **float**. Constants (like **1000.0** and **.05** in Fig. 2.21) are treated as being type **double** by C++.

This program would not compile without the inclusion of **math.h**. Function **pow** requires two **double** arguments. Note that **year** is an integer. The **math.h** file includes information that tells the compiler to convert the value of **year** to a temporary **double** representation before calling the function. This information is contained in **pow**'s *function prototype*. Function prototypes are explained in Chapter 3. We provide a summary of the **pow** function and other math library functions in Chapter 3.

```
// Calculating compound interest

#include <iostream.h>
#include <iomanip.h>
#include <math.h>

main()
{
   double amount, principal = 1000.0, rate = .05;

   cout << "Year" << setw(21) << "Amount on deposit" << endl;

   for (int year = 1; year <= 10; year++) {
      amount = principal * pow(1.0 + rate, year);
      cout << setw(4) << year
           << setiosflags(ios::fixed | ios::showpoint)
           << setw(21) << setprecision(2) << amount << endl;
   }

   return 0;
}
```

```
Year    Amount on deposit
   1              1050.00
   2              1102.50
   3              1157.62
   4              1215.51
   5              1276.28
   6              1340.10
   7              1407.10
   8              1477.46
   9              1551.33
  10              1628.89
```

**Fig. 2.21** Calculating compound interest with `for`.

***Common Programming Error 2.16***

*Forgetting to include the* `math.h` *file in a program that uses math library functions.*

Notice that we have declared the variables **`amount`**, **`principal`**, and **`rate`** to be of type **`double`**. We have done this for simplicity because we are dealing with fractional parts of dollars and we need a type that allows decimal points in its values. Unfortunately, this can cause trouble. Here is a simple explanation of what can go wrong when using **`float`** or **`double`** to represent dollar amounts (assuming printing is done with **`setprecision(2)`**): Two **`float`** dollar amounts stored in the machine could be 14.234 (which prints as 14.23) and 18.673 (which prints as 18.67). When these amounts are added, they produce the internal sum 32.907 which prints as 32.91. Thus your printout could appear as

```
   14.23
+  18.67
 -------
   32.91
```

but a person adding the individual numbers as printed would expect the sum 32.90! You have been warned!

***Good Programming Practice 2.22***

*Do not use variables of type* **float** *or* **double** *to perform monetary calculations. The imprecision of floating-point numbers can cause errors that will result in incorrect monetary values. In the exercises, we explore the use of integers to perform monetary calculations. Note: C++ class libraries are becoming available for properly performing monetary calculations.*

The output statement

```
cout << setw(4) << year
     << setiosflags(ios::fixed | ios::showpoint)
     << setw(21) << setprecision(2) << amount << endl;
```

prints the values of the variables **year** and **amount** with the formatting specified by the parameterized stream manipulators **setw**, **setiosflags** and **setprecision**. The call **setw(4)** specifies that the next value output is printed in a *field width* of 4, i.e., the value is printed with at least 4 character positions. If the value to be output is less than 4 character positions wide, the value is *right justified* in the field by default. If the value to be output is more than 4 character positions wide, the field width is extended to accommodate the entire value. The call **setiosflags(ios::left)** can be used to specify that values should be output *left justified.*

The remainder of the formatting in the preceding output statement indicates that variable **amount** is printed as a fixed-point value with a decimal point (specified with **setiosflags(ios::fixed | ios::showpoint)**) right-justified in a field of 21 character positions (specified with **setw(21)**) and two digits of precision to the right of the decimal point (specified with **setprecision(2)**). We will discuss the powerful input/output formatting capabilities of C++ in detail in Chapter 11.

Note that the calculation **1.0 + rate** which appears as an argument to the **pow** function is contained in the body of the **for** statement. In fact, this calculation produces the same result each time through the loop, so repeating the calculation is wasteful.

***Performance Tip 2.3***

*Avoid placing expressions whose values do not change inside loops. But even if you do, many of today's sophisticated optimizing compilers will automatically place such expressions outside loops in the generated machine language code.*

## 2.16 The Switch Multiple-Selection Structure

We have discussed the **if** single-selection structure and the **if/else** double-selection structure. Occasionally, an algorithm will contain a series of decisions in which a variable or expression is tested separately for each of the constant integral values it may assume, and different actions are taken. C++ provides the **switch** multiple-selection structure to handle such decision making.

The **switch** structure consists of a series of **case** labels, and an optional **default** case. The program in Fig. 2.22 uses **switch** to count the number of each different letter grade that students earned on an exam.

In the program, the user enters letter grades for a class. Inside the **while** header,

```
while ( ( grade = cin.get() ) != EOF)
```

the parenthesized assignment **( grade = cin.get() )** is executed first. The **cin.get()** function reads one character from the keyboard and stores that character in integer variable **grade**. The dot notation used in **cin.get()** will be explained in Chapter 6, "Classes." Characters are normally stored in variables of type **char**. However, an important feature of C++ is that characters can be stored in any integer data type because they are represented as 1-byte integers in the computer. Thus, we can treat a character as either an integer or a character depending on its use. For example, the statement

```
cout << "The character (" << 'a' << ") has the value "
     << (int) 'a' << endl;
```

prints the character **a** and its integer value as follows

```
The character (a) has the value 97
```

The integer 97 is the character's numerical representation in the computer. Many computers today use the *ASCII (American Standard Code for Information Interchange) character set* in which 97 represents the lowercase letter **'a'**. A list of the ASCII characters and their decimal values is presented in Appendix D.

Assignment statements as a whole have the value that is assigned to the variable on the left side of the **=**. Thus, the value of the assignment **grade = cin.get()** is the same as the value returned by **cin.get()** and assigned to the variable **grade**.

The fact that assignment statements have values can be useful for initializing several variables to the same value. For example,

```
a = b = c = 0;
```

first evaluates the assignment **c = 0** (because the **=** operator associates from right to left). The variable **b** is then assigned the value of the assignment **c = 0** (which is 0). Then, the variable **a** is assigned the value of the assignment **b = (c = 0)** (which is also 0). In the program, the value of the assignment **grade = cin.get()** is compared with the value of **EOF** (a symbol whose acronym stands for "end-of-file"). We use **EOF** (which normally has the value –1) as the sentinel value. The user types a system-dependent keystroke combination to mean "end-of-file," i.e., "I have no more data to enter." **EOF** is a symbolic integer constant defined in the **<iostream.h>** header file. If the value assigned to **grade** is equal to **EOF**, the program terminates. We have chosen to represent characters in this program as **int**s because **EOF** has an integer value (again, normally –1).

```
// Counting letter grades
#include <iostream.h>

main()
{
   int grade;
   int aCount = 0, bCount = 0, cCount = 0,
       dCount = 0, fCount = 0;

   cout << "Enter the letter grades." << endl
        << "Enter the EOF character to end input." << endl;

   while ( ( grade = cin.get() ) != EOF ) {

      switch (grade) {          // switch nested in while

         case 'A': case 'a':    // Grade was uppercase A
            ++aCount;           // or lowercase a.
            break;

         case 'B': case 'b':    // Grade was uppercase B
            ++bCount;           // or lowercase b.
            break;

         case 'C': case 'c':    // Grade was uppercase C
            ++cCount;           // or lowercase c.
            break;

         case 'D': case 'd':    // Grade was uppercase D
            ++dCount;           // or lowercase d.
            break;

         case 'F': case 'f':    // Grade was uppercase F
            ++fCount;           // or lowercase f.
            break;

         case '\n': case ' ':   // ignore these in input
            break;

         default:               // catch all other characters
            cout << "Incorrect letter grade entered."
                 << " Enter a new grade." << endl;
            break;
      }
   }

   cout << endl << "Totals for each letter grade are:"
        << endl << "A: " << aCount << endl << "B: " << bCount
        << endl << "C: " << cCount << endl << "D: " << dCount
        << endl << "F: " << fCount << endl;

   return 0;
}
```

**Fig. 2.22** An example using **switch** (part 1 of 2).

```
Enter the letter grades.
Enter the EOF character to end input.
A
B
C
C
A
D
F
C
E
Incorrect letter grade entered. Enter a new grade.
D
A
B

Totals for each letter grade are:
A: 3
B: 2
C: 3
D: 2
F: 1
```

**Fig. 2.22** An example using **`switch`** (part 2 of 2).

***Portability Tip 2.1***

*The keystroke combinations for entering end-of-file are system dependent.*

***Portability Tip 2.2***

*Testing for the symbolic constant* **`EOF`** *rather than –1 makes programs more portable. The ANSI standard states that* **`EOF`** *is a negative integral value (but not necessarily –1). Thus,* **`EOF`** *could have different values on different systems.*

On UNIX systems and many others, end-of-file is entered by typing the sequence

*<ctrl-d>*

on a line by itself. This notation means to simultaneously press both the **`ctrl`** key and the **`d`** key. On other systems such as Digital Equipment Corporation's VAX VMS or Microsoft Corporation's MS-DOS, end-of-file can be entered by typing

*<ctrl-z>*

The user enters grades at the keyboard. When the return (or enter) key is pressed, the characters are read by the **`cin.get()`** function one character at a time. If the character entered is not end-of-file, the **`switch`** structure is entered. The keyword **`switch`** is followed by the variable name **`grade`** in parentheses. This is called the *controlling expression.* The value of this expression is compared with each of the ***`case`*** *labels.* Assume the user has entered the letter **C** as a grade. **C** is automatically compared to each **case** in the **switch**. If a match occurs (**case 'C':**), the statements for that **case** are executed. For the letter **C**, **cCount** is incremented by **1**, and the **switch** structure is exited immediately with the **break** statement.

The **break** statement causes program control to proceed with the first statement after the **switch** structure. The **break** statement is used because the **case**s in a **switch** statement would otherwise run together. If **break** is not used anywhere in a **switch** structure, then each time a match occurs in the structure, the statements for all the remaining **case**s will be executed. (This feature is rarely useful, although it is perfect for programming the iterative song "The Twelve Days of Christmas!") If no match occurs, the **default** case is executed and an error message is printed.

Each **case** can have one or more actions. The **switch** structure is different from all other structures in that braces are not required around multiple actions in a **case** of a **switch**. The general **switch** multiple-selection structure (using a **break** in each **case**) is flowcharted in Fig. 2.23.

The flowchart makes it clear that each **break** statement at the end of a **case** causes control to immediately exit the **switch** structure. Again, note that (besides small circles and arrows) the flowchart contains only rectangle symbols and diamond symbols. Imagine, again, that the programmer has access to a deep bin of empty **switch** structures—as many as the programmer might need to stack and nest with other control structures to form a structured implementation of an algorithm's flow of control. And again, the rectangles and diamonds are then filled with actions and decisions appropriate to the algorithm. Nested control structures are common, but it is rare to find nested **switch** structures in a program.

***Common Programming Error 2.17***

*Forgetting a* **break** *statement when one is needed in a* **switch** *structure.*

***Common Programming Error 2.18***

*Omitting the space between the word* **case** *and the integral value being tested in a* **switch** *structure can cause a logic error. For example, writing* **case3:** *instead of writing* **case 3:** *simply creates an unused label (we will say more about this in Chapter 18). The problem is that the* **switch** *structure will not perform the appropriate actions when the* **switch***'s controlling expression has a value of 3.*

***Good Programming Practice 2.23***

*Provide a* **default** *case in* **switch** *statements. Cases not explicitly tested in a* **switch** *statement without a* **default** *case are ignored. Including a* **default** *case focuses the programmer on the need to process exceptional conditions. There are situations in which no* **default** *processing is needed.*

***Good Programming Practice 2.24***

*Although the* **case** *clauses and the* **default** *case clause in a* **switch** *structure can occur in any order, it is considered a good programming practice to place the* **default** *clause last.*

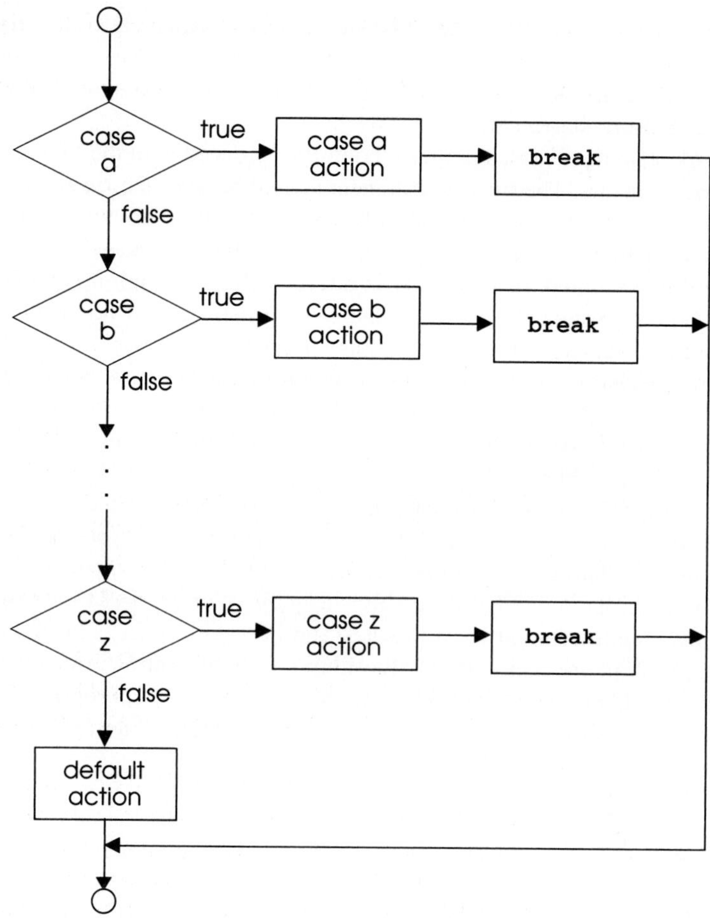


**Fig. 2.23** The **`switch`** multiple-selection structure.

*Good Programming Practice 2.25*

*In a* **`switch`** *structure when the* **`default`** *clause is listed last, the* **`break`** *statement is not required. Some programmers include this* **`break`** *for clarity and symmetry with other cases.*

In the **`switch`** structure of Fig. 2.22, the lines

```
case '\n': case ' ':
   break;
```

cause the program to skip newline and blank characters. Reading characters one at a time can cause some problems. To have the program read the characters, they must be sent to the computer by pressing the *return key* on the keyboard. This causes the newline character to be placed in the input after the character we wish to process. Often, this newline character must be specially processed to make the program work correctly. By including the preceding cases in our **switch** structure, we prevent the error message in the **default** case from being printed each time a newline or space is encountered in the input.

***Common Programming Error 2.19***

*Not processing newline characters in the input when reading characters one at a time can cause logic errors.*

***Good Programming Practice 2.26***

*Remember to provide processing capabilities for newline and other whitespace characters in the input when processing characters one at a time.*

Note that several case labels listed together (such as **case 'D': case 'd':** in Fig. 2.22) simply means that the same set of actions is to occur for each of the cases.

When using the **switch** structure, remember that it can only be used for testing a *constant integral expression,* i.e., any combination of character constants and integer constants that evaluates to a constant integer value. A character constant is represented as the specific character in single quotes such as **'A'**. An integer constant is simply an integer value.

When we get to the part of the book on object-oriented programming, we will present a more elegant way to implement **switch** logic. We will use a technique called polymorphism to create programs that are often clearer, easier to maintain, and easier to extend than programs using **switch** logic.

Portable languages like C++ must have flexible data type sizes. Different applications may need integers of different sizes. C++ provides several data types to represent integers. The range of integer values for each type depends on the particular computer's hardware. In addition to the types **int** and **char**, C++ provides the types **short** (an abbreviation of **short int**) and **long** (an abbreviation of **long int**). The minimum range of values for **short** integers is ±32767. For the vast majority of integer calculations, **long** integers are sufficient. The minimum range of values for **long** integers is ±2147483647. On most computers, **int**s are equivalent either to **short** or to **long**. The range of values for an **int** is at least the same as the range for **short** integers and no larger than the range for **long** integers. The data type **char** can be used to represent any of the characters in the computer's character set. The data type **char** can also be used to represent small integers.

***Portability Tip 2.3***

*Because **ints** vary in size between systems, use **long** integers if you expect to process integers outside the range ±32767 and you would like to be able to run the program on several different computer systems.*

***Performance Tip 2.4***

*In performance-oriented situations where memory is at a premium or execution speed is crucial, it may be desirable to use smaller integer sizes.*

## 2.17 The Do/While Repetition Structure

The `do/while` repetition structure is similar to the `while` structure. In the `while` structure, the loop-continuation condition is tested at the beginning of the loop before the body of the loop is performed. The `do/while` structure tests the loop-continuation condition *after* the loop body is performed, therefore the loop body will be executed at least once. When a `do/while` terminates, execution continues with the statement after the `while` clause. Note that it is not necessary to use braces in the `do/while` structure if there is only one statement in the body. However, the braces are usually included to avoid confusion between the `while` and `do/while` structures. For example,

```
while (condition)
```

is normally regarded as the header to a `while` structure. A `do/while` with no braces around the single statement body appears as

```
do
   statement
while (condition);
```

which can be confusing. The last line—`while (`*condition*`);`—may be misinterpreted by the reader as a `while` structure containing an empty statement. Thus, the `do/while` with one statement is often written as follows to avoid confusion:

```
do {
   statement
} while (condition);
```

***Good Programming Practice 2.27***

*Some programmers always include braces in a* `do/while` *structure even if the braces are not necessary. This helps eliminate ambiguity between the* `while` *structure and the* `do/while` *structure containing one statement.*

***Common Programming Error 2.20***

*Infinite loops are caused when the loop-continuation condition in a* `while`, `for`, *or* `do/while` *structure never becomes false. To prevent this, make sure there is not a semicolon immediately after the header of a* `while` *structure. In a counter-controlled loop, make sure the control variable is incremented (or decremented) in the body of the loop. In a sentinel-controlled loop, make sure the sentinel value is eventually input.*

The program in Fig. 2.24 uses a `do/while` structure to print the numbers from 1 to 10. Note that the control variable `counter` is preincremented in the loop-continuation test. Note also the use of the braces to enclose the single-statement body of the `do/while`.

The `do/while` structure is flowcharted in Fig. 2.25. This flowchart makes it clear that the loop-continuation condition is not executed until after the action is performed at least once. Again, note that (besides small circles and arrows) the flowchart contains only a rectangle symbol and a diamond symbol. Imagine, again, that the programmer has ac-

```
// Using the do/while repetition structure
#include <iostream.h>

main()
{
   int counter = 1;

   do {
      cout << counter << "  ";
   } while (++counter <= 10);

   return 0;
}
```

```
 1  2  3  4  5  6  7  8  9  10
```

Fig. 2.24 Using the **do/while** structure.

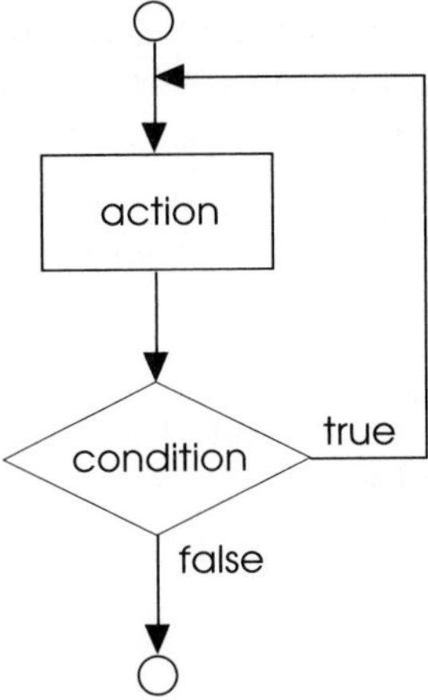


Fig. 2.25 The **do/while** repetition structure.

cess to a deep bin of empty **do/while** structures—as many as the programmer might need to stack and nest with other control structures to form a structured implementation of an algorithm's flow of control. And again, the rectangles and diamonds are then filled with actions and decisions appropriate to the algorithm.

## 2.18 The Break and Continue Statements

The **break** and **continue** statements alter the flow of control. The **break** statement, when executed in a **while**, **for**, **do/while**, or **switch** structure, causes immediate exit from that structure. Program execution continues with the first statement after the structure. Common uses of the **break** statement are to escape early from a loop, or to skip the remainder of a **switch** structure (as in Fig. 2.22). Figure 2.26 demonstrates the break statement in a **for** repetition structure. When the **if** structure detects that **x** has become 5, **break** is executed. This terminates the **for** statement and the program continues with the **cout** after the **for**. The loop fully executes only four times.

The **continue** statement, when executed in a **while**, **for**, or **do/while** structure, skips the remaining statements in the body of that structure, and proceeds with the next iteration of the loop. In **while** and **do/while** structures, the loop-continuation test is evaluated immediately after the **continue** statement is executed. In the **for** structure, the increment expression is executed, then the loop-continuation test is evaluated. Earlier, we stated that the **while** structure could be used in most cases to represent the **for** structure. The one exception occurs when the increment expression in the **while** structure follows the **continue** statement. In this case, the increment is not executed before the repetition-continuation condition is tested, and the **while** does not execute in the same manner as the **for**. Figure 2.27 uses the **continue** statement in a **for** structure to skip the output statement in the structure and begin the next iteration of the loop.

***Good Programming Practice 2.28***

*Some programmers feel that* **break** *and* **continue** *violate structured programming. Because the effects of these statements can be achieved by structured programming techniques we will soon learn, these programmers do not use* **break** *and* **continue**.

***Performance Tip 2.5***

*The* **break** *and* **continue** *statements, when used properly, perform faster than the corresponding structured techniques we will soon learn.*

```
// Using the break statement in a for structure
#include <iostream.h>

main()
{
   for (int x = 1; x <= 10; x++) {

      if (x == 5)
         break;      // break loop only if x == 5

      cout << x << " ";
   }

   cout << endl << "Broke out of loop at x == " << x << endl;
   return 0;
}
```

```
1 2 3 4
Broke out of loop at x == 5
```

Fig. 2.26 Using the **break** statement in a **for** structure.

```
// Using the continue statement in a for structure
#include <iostream.h>

main()
{
   for (int x = 1; x <= 10; x++) {

      if (x == 5)
         continue;   // skip remaining code in loop
                     // only if x == 5

      cout << x << " ";
   }

   cout << endl << "Used continue to skip printing the value 5"
        << endl;
   return 0;
}
```

```
1 2 3 4 6 7 8 9 10
Used continue to skip printing the value 5
```

**Fig. 2.27** Using the `continue` statement in a `for` structure.

***Software Engineering Observation 2.8***

*There is a tension between achieving quality software engineering and achieving the best performing software. Often, one of these goals is achieved at the expense of the other.*

## 2.19 Logical Operators

So far we have studied only *simple conditions* such as **counter <= 10**, **total > 1000**, and **number != sentinelValue**. We have expressed these conditions in terms of the relational operators **>**, **<**, **>=**, and **<=**, and the equality operators **==** and **!=**. Each decision tested precisely one condition. If we wanted to test multiple conditions in the process of making a decision, we had to perform these tests in separate statements or in nested **if** or **if/else** structures.

C++ provides *logical operators* that may be used to form more complex conditions by combining simple conditions. The logical operators are **&&** *(logical AND)*, **||** *(logical OR)*, and **!** *(logical NOT* also called *logical negation)*. We will consider examples of each of these.

Suppose we wish to ensure at some point in a program that two conditions are *both* true before we choose a certain path of execution. In this case we can use the logical **&&** operator as follows:

```
if (gender == 1 && age >= 65)
   ++seniorFemales;
```

This **if** statement contains two simple conditions. The condition **gender == 1** might be evaluated, for example, to determine if a person is a female. The condition **age >= 65** is evaluated to determine if a person is a senior citizen. The two simple conditions are evaluated first because the precedences of **==** and **>=** are both higher than the precedence of **&&**. The **if** statement then considers the combined condition

```
gender == 1 && age >= 65
```

This condition is true if and only if both of the simple conditions are true. Finally, if this combined condition is indeed true, then the count of **seniorFemales** is incremented by **1**. If either or both of the simple conditions are false, then the program skips the incrementing and proceeds to the statement following the **if**. The preceding combined condition can be made more readable by adding redundant parentheses

```
(gender == 1) && (age >= 65)
```

The table of Fig. 2.28 summarizes the **&&** operator. The table shows all four possible combinations of zero (false) and nonzero (true) values for expression1 and expression2. Such tables are often called *truth tables.* C++ evaluates to 0 or 1 all expressions that include relational operators, equality operators, and/or logical operators. Although C++ returns 1 for a true result, it accepts *any* nonzero value as true.

Now let us consider the **||** (logical OR) operator. Suppose we wish to ensure at some point in a program that either *or* both of two conditions are true before we choose a certain path of execution. In this case we use the **||** operator as in the following program segment:

```
if (semesterAverage >= 90 || finalExam >= 90)
   cout << "Student grade is A" << endl;
```

This statement also contains two simple conditions. The condition **semesterAverage >= 90** is evaluated to determine if the student deserves an "A" in the course because of a solid performance throughout the semester. The condition **finalExam >= 90** is evaluated to determine if the student deserves an "A" in the course because of an outstanding performance on the final exam. The **if** statement then considers the combined condition

```
semesterAverage >= 90 || finalExam >= 90
```

| expression1 | expression2 | expression1 && expression2 |
|---|---|---|
| 0 | 0 | 0 |
| 0 | nonzero | 0 |
| nonzero | 0 | 0 |
| nonzero | nonzero | 1 |

**Fig. 2.28** Truth table for the **&&** (logical AND) operator.

and awards the student an "A" if either or both of the simple conditions are true. Note that the message "**Student grade is A**" is not printed only when both of the simple conditions are false (zero). Figure 2.29 is a truth table for the logical OR operator (||).

The **&&** operator has a higher precedence than the **||** operator. Both operators associate from left to right. An expression containing **&&** or **||** operators is evaluated only until truth or falsehood is known. Thus, evaluation of the expression

```
gender == 1 && age >= 65
```

will stop immediately if **gender** is not equal to **1** (i.e., the entire expression is false), and continue if **gender** is equal to **1** (i.e., the entire expression could still be true if the condition **age >= 65** is true).

***Common Programming Error 2.21***

*In expressions using operator* **&&**, *it is possible that a condition—we will call this the dependent condition—may require another condition to be true for it to be meaningful to evaluate the dependent condition. In this case, the dependent condition should be placed after the other condition or an error might occur.*

***Performance Tip 2.6***

*In expressions using operator* **&&**, *if the separate conditions are independent of one another make the condition that is most likely to be false the leftmost condition. In expressions using operator* **||**, *make the condition that is most likely to be true the leftmost condition. This can reduce a program's execution time.*

C++ provides the **!** (logical negation) operator to enable a programmer to "reverse" the meaning of a condition. Unlike the **&&** and **||** operators, which combine two conditions (and are therefore binary operators), the logical negation operator has only a single condition as an operand (and is therefore a unary operator). The logical negation operator is placed before a condition when we are interested in choosing a path of execution if the original condition (without the logical negation operator) is false, such as in the following program segment:

```
if ( !(grade == sentinelValue) )
   cout << "The next grade is " << grade << endl;
```

| expression1 | expression2 | expression1 \|\| expression2 |
|---|---|---|
| 0 | 0 | 0 |
| 0 | nonzero | 1 |
| nonzero | 0 | 1 |
| nonzero | nonzero | 1 |

**Fig. 2.29** Truth table for the logical OR (||) operator.

The parentheses around the condition **grade == sentinelValue** are needed because the logical negation operator has a higher precedence than the equality operator. Figure 2.30 is a truth table for the logical negation operator.

In most cases, the programmer can avoid using logical negation by expressing the condition differently with an appropriate relational or equality operator. For example, the preceding statement may also be written as follows:

```
if (grade != sentinelValue)
   cout << "The next grade is " << grade << endl;
```

This flexibility can often help a programmer express a condition in a more "natural" or convenient manner.

The chart in Fig. 2.31 shows the precedence and associativity of the C++ operators introduced to this point. The operators are shown from top to bottom in decreasing order of precedence.

| expression | ! expression |
|---|---|
| 0 | 1 |
| nonzero | 0 |

**Fig. 2.30** Truth table for operator ! (logical negation).

| Operators | | | | | | Associativity | Type |
|---|---|---|---|---|---|---|---|
| () | | | | | | left to right | parentheses |
| ++ | -- | + | - | ! | (*type*) | right to left | unary |
| * | / | % | | | | left to right | multiplicative |
| + | - | | | | | left to right | additive |
| << | >> | | | | | left to right | insertion/extraction |
| < | <= | > | >= | | | left to right | relational |
| == | != | | | | | left to right | equality |
| && | | | | | | left to right | logical AND |
| \|\| | | | | | | left to right | logical OR |
| ?: | | | | | | right to left | conditional |
| = | += | -= | *= | /= | %= | right to left | assignment |
| , | | | | | | left to right | comma |

**Fig. 2.31** Operator precedence and associativity.

## 2.20 Confusing Equality (==) and Assignment (=) Operators

There is one type of error that C++ programmers, no matter how experienced, tend to make so frequently that we felt it was worth a separate section. That error is accidentally swapping the operators `==` (equality) and `=` (assignment). What makes these swaps so damaging is the fact that they do not ordinarily cause syntax errors. Rather, statements with these errors ordinarily compile correctly, and the programs run to completion probably generating incorrect results through run-time logic errors.

There are two aspects of C++ that cause these problems. One is that any expression that produces a value can be used in the decision portion of any control structure. If the value is 0, it is treated as false, and if the value is nonzero, it is treated as true. The second is that C++ assignments produce a value, namely the value that is assigned to the variable on the left side of the assignment operator. For example, suppose we intend to write

```
if (payCode == 4)
   cout << "You get a bonus!" << endl;
```

but we accidentally write

```
if (payCode = 4)
   cout << "You get a bonus!" << endl;
```

The first **`if`** statement properly awards a bonus to the person whose **`paycode`** is equal to 4. The second **`if`** statement—the one with the error—evaluates the assignment expression in the **`if`** condition to the constant 4. Because any nonzero value is interpreted as "true," the condition in this **`if`** statement is always true, and the person always receives a bonus regardless of what the actual paycode is! Even worse, the paycode has been modified when it was only supposed to be examined!

***Common Programming Error 2.22***

*Using operator == for assignment, or using operator = for equality.*

Programmers normally write conditions such as **`x == 7`** with the variable name on the left and the constant on the right. By reversing these so that the constant is on the left and the variable name is on the right as in **`7 == x`**, the programmer who accidentally replaces the `==` operator with `=` will be protected by the compiler. The compiler will treat this as a syntax error because only a variable name can be placed on the left-hand side of an assignment statement. At least this will prevent the potential devastation of a run-time logic error.

Variable names are said to be *lvalues* (for "left values") because they can be used on the left side of an assignment operator. Constants are said to be *rvalues* (for "right values") because they can be used on only the right side of an assignment operator. Note that lvalues can also be used as rvalues, but not vice versa.

***Good Programming Practice 2.29***

*When an equality expression has a variable and a constant as in* **`x == 1`**, *some programmers prefer to write the expression with the constant on the left and the variable name on the right as protection against the logic error that occurs when the programmer accidentally replaces the == operator with =.*

The other side of the coin can be equally unpleasant. Suppose the programmer wants to assign a value to a variable with a simple statement like

```
x = 1;
```

but instead writes

```
x == 1;
```

Here, too, this is not a syntax error. Rather the compiler simply evaluates the conditional expression. If **x** is equal to **1**, the condition is true and the expression returns the value 1. If **x** is not equal to **1**, the condition is false and the expression returns the value 0. Regardless of what value is returned, there is no assignment operator, so the value is simply lost, and the value of **x** remains unaltered, probably causing an execution-time logic error. Unfortunately, we do not have a handy trick available to help you with this problem!

## 2.21 Structured Programming Summary

Just as architects design buildings by employing the collective wisdom of their profession, so should programmers design programs. Our field is younger than architecture is, and our collective wisdom is considerably sparser. We have learned that structured programming produces programs that are easier than unstructured programs to understand and hence are easier to test, debug, modify, and even prove correct in a mathematical sense.

Figure 2.32 summarizes C++'s control structures. Small circles are used in the figure to indicate the single entry point and the single exit point of each structure. Connecting individual flowchart symbols arbitrarily can lead to unstructured programs. Therefore, the programming profession has chosen to combine flowchart symbols to form a limited set of control structures, and to build structured programs by properly combining control structures in two simple ways. For simplicity, only single-entry/single-exit control structures are used—there is only one way to enter and only one way to exit each control structure. Connecting control structures in sequence to form structured programs is simple—the exit point of one control structure is connected directly to the entry point of the next control structure, i.e., the control structures are simply placed one after another in a program; we have called this "control structure stacking." The rules for forming structured programs also allow for control structures to be nested.

Figure 2.33 shows the rules for forming properly structured programs. The rules assume that the rectangle flowchart symbol may be used to indicate any action including input/output.

Applying the rules of Fig. 2.33 always results in a structured flowchart with a neat, building-block appearance. For example, repeatedly applying rule 2 to the simplest flowchart results in a structured flowchart containing many rectangles in sequence (Fig. 2.35). Notice that rule 2 generates a stack of control structures; so let us call rule 2 the *stacking rule*.

Rule 3 is called the *nesting rule*. Repeatedly applying rule 3 to the simplest flowchart results in a flowchart with neatly nested control structures. For example, in Fig. 2.36, the rectangle in the simplest flowchart is first replaced with a double-selection (**if/else**)

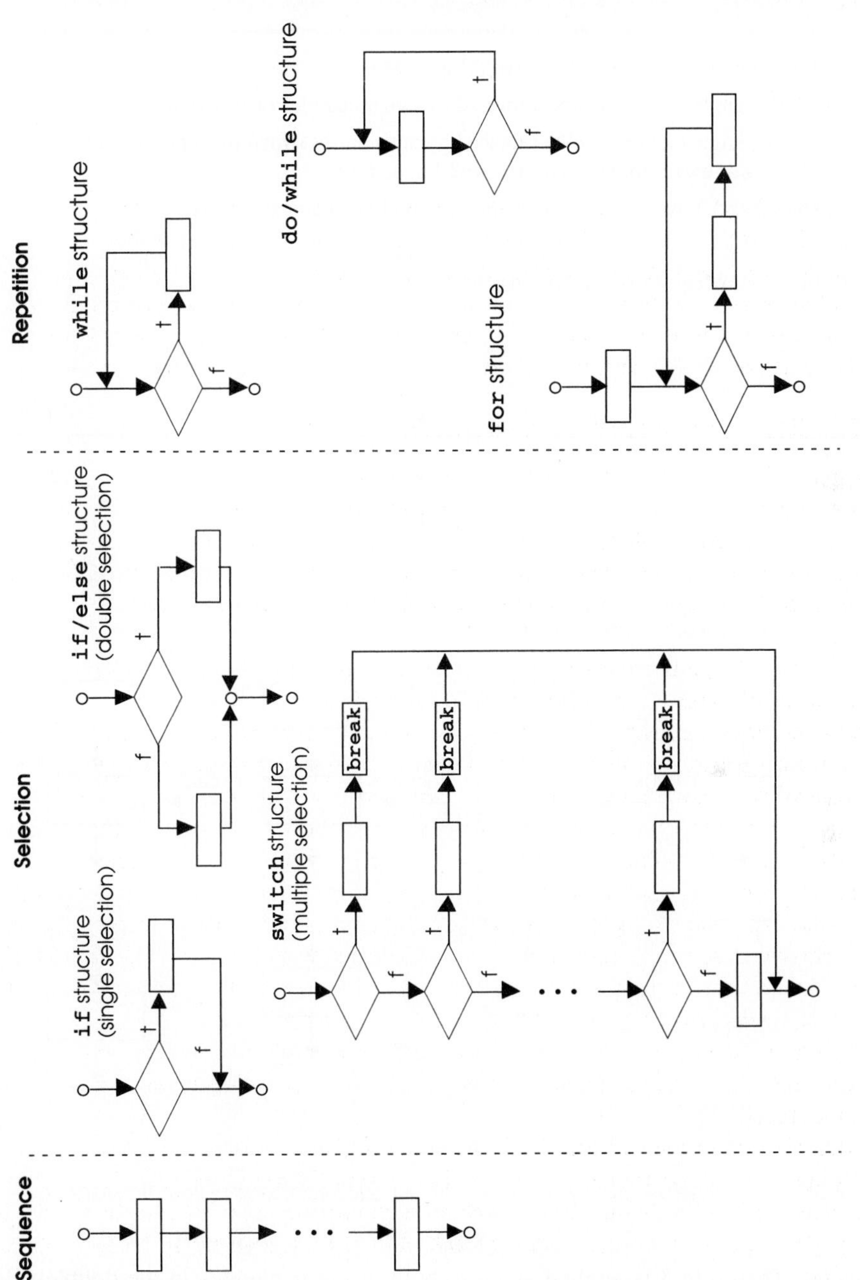


**Fig. 2.32** C++'s single-entry/single-exit sequence, selection, and repetition structures.

**Rules for Forming Structured Programs**

1) Begin with the "simplest flowchart" (Fig. 2.34).
2) Any rectangle (action) can be replaced by two rectangles (actions) in sequence.
3) Any rectangle (action) can be replaced by any control structure (sequence, **`if`**, **`if/else`**, **`switch`**, **`while`**, **`do/while`**, or **`for`**).
4) Rules 2 and 3 may be applied as often as you like and in any order.

**Fig. 2.33** Rules for forming structured programs.

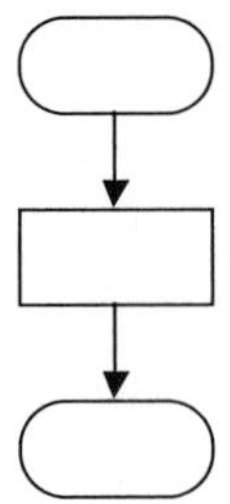

**Fig. 2.34** The simplest flowchart.

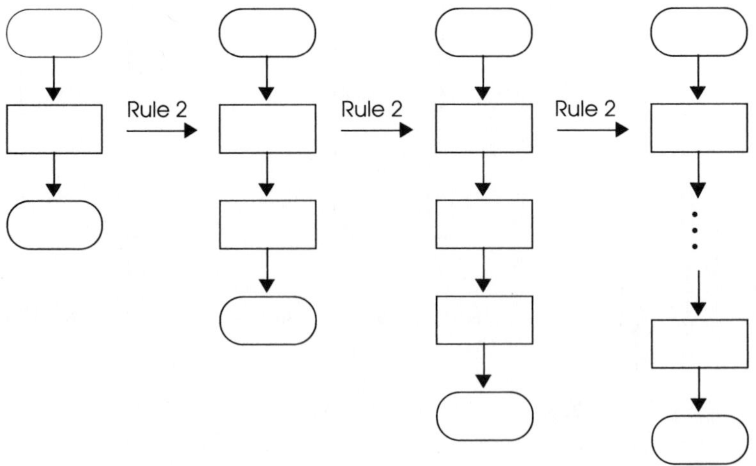


**Fig. 2.35** Repeatedly applying rule 2 of Fig. 2.33 to the simplest flowchart.

structure. Then rule 3 is applied again to both of the rectangles in the double-selection structure, replacing each of these rectangles with double-selection structures. The dashed boxes around each of the double-selection structures represent the rectangle that was replaced.

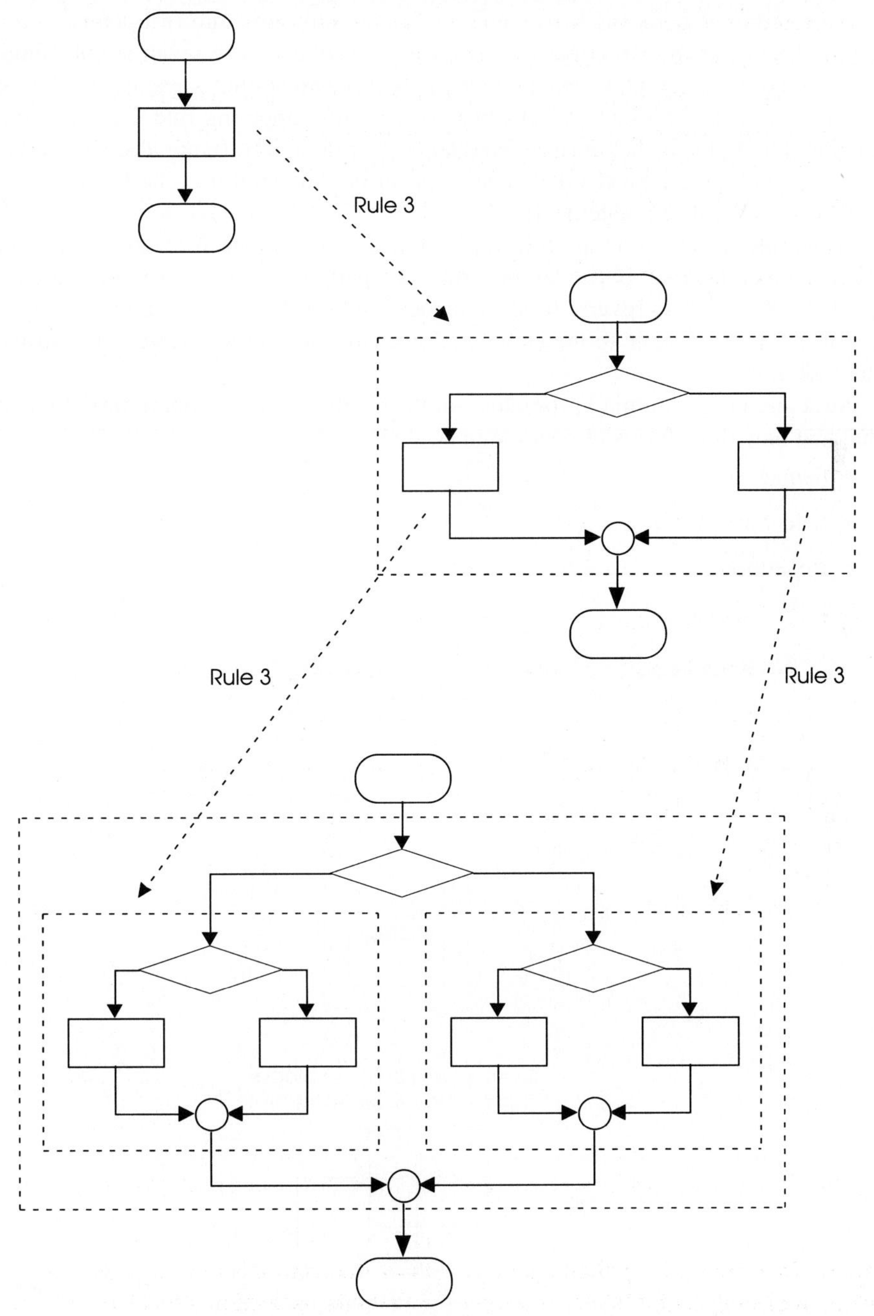


**Fig. 2.36** Applying rule 3 of Fig. 2.33 to the simplest flowchart.

Rule 4 generates larger, more involved, and more deeply nested structures. The flowcharts that emerge from applying the rules in Fig. 2.33 constitute the set of all possible structured flowcharts and hence the set of all possible structured programs.

The beauty of the structured approach is that we use only seven simple single-entry/single-exit pieces, and we assemble them in only two simple ways. Figure 2.37 shows the kinds of stacked building blocks that emerge from applying rule 2 and the kinds of nested building blocks that emerge from applying rule 3. The figure also shows the kind of overlapped building blocks that cannot appear in structured flowcharts (because of the elimination of the `goto` statement).

If the rules in Fig. 2.33 are followed, an unstructured flowchart (such as that in Fig. 2.38) cannot be created. If you are uncertain if a particular flowchart is structured, apply the rules of Fig. 2.33 in reverse to try to reduce the flowchart to the simplest flowchart. If the flowchart is reducible to the simplest flowchart, the original flowchart is structured; otherwise, it is not.

Structured programming promotes simplicity. Bohm and Jacopini have given us the result that only three forms of control are needed:

- Sequence
- Selection
- Repetition

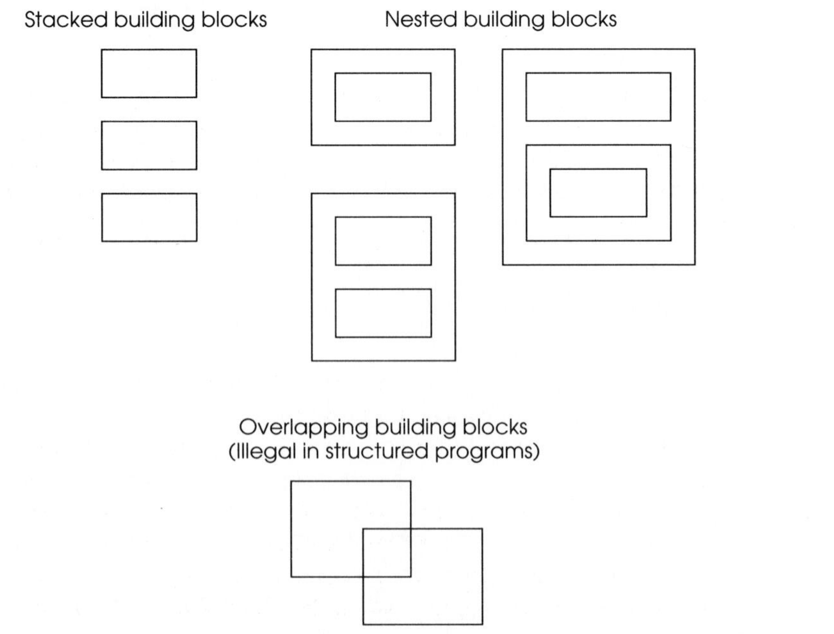


**Fig. 2.37** Stacked building blocks, nested building blocks, and overlapped building blocks.

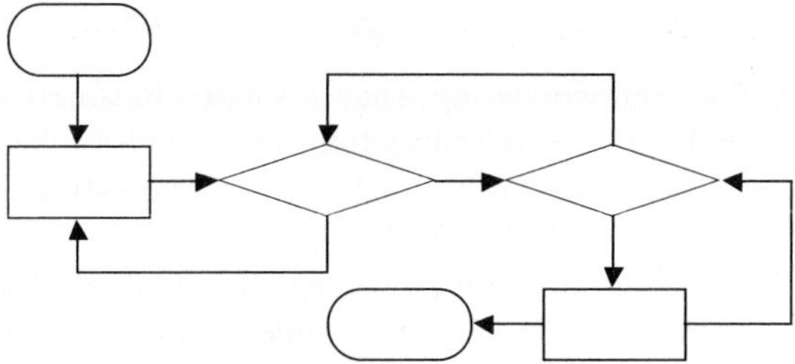

Fig. 2.38 An unstructured flowchart.

Sequence is trivial. Selection is implemented in one of three ways:

- **`if`** structure (single selection)
- **`if/else`** structure (double selection)
- **`switch`** structure (multiple selection)

In fact, it is straightforward to prove that the simple **`if`** structure is sufficient to provide any form of selection—everything that can be done with the **`if/else`** structure and the **`switch`** structure can be implemented by combining **`if`** structures (although perhaps not as smoothly).

Repetition is implemented in one of three ways:

- **`while`** structure
- **`do/while`** structure
- **`for`** structure

It is straightforward to prove that the **`while`** structure is sufficient to provide any form of repetition. Everything that can be done with the **`do/while`** structure and the **`for`** structure can be done with the **`while`** structure (although perhaps not as smoothly).

Combining these results illustrates that any form of control ever needed in a C++ program can be expressed in terms of:

- sequence
- **`if`** structure (selection)
- **`while`** structure (repetition)

And these control structures can be combined in only two ways—stacking and nesting. Indeed, structured programming promotes simplicity.

In this chapter, we discussed how to compose programs from control structures containing only actions and decisions. In Chapter 3, we introduce another program structuring unit called the *function*. We will learn to compose large programs by combining functions which, in turn, are composed of control structures. We will also discuss how using functions promotes software reusability. In Chapter 6, we introduce C++'s other program structuring unit called the *class*. We will then create objects from classes and proceed with our treatment of object-oriented programming. Now, we continue our introduction to objects by introducing a problem that the reader will attack with the techniques of object-oriented design.

## 2.22 Thinking About Objects: Identifying the Objects in a Problem

Here you are, new at C++ and wondering what this marvelous new technology called object-orientation is all about. These special sections at the ends of the next several chapters will ease you into object-orientation by means of an interesting and challenging real-world case study on building an elevator simulator.

In Chapters 2 through 5, you will perform the various steps of an object-oriented design (OOD). Beginning in Chapter 6, you will implement the elevator simulator using the techniques of object-oriented programming (OOP) in C++. For now, this assignment may seem a bit complex. Please do not be concerned. You will attempt only a small portion of the problem in this chapter.

***Problem Statement***

A company intends to build a two-story office building and equip it with the "latest" in elevator technology. The company wants you to develop an object-oriented software simulator that models the operation of the elevator to determine if this elevator will meet their needs.

The elevator, which has a capacity of one person, is designed to conserve energy, so it only moves when necessary. The elevator starts the day waiting with its doors shut on floor 1 of the building. The elevator, of course, alternates directions—first up, then down.

Your simulator includes a clock that begins the day set to time 0 and that "ticks" once per second. The "scheduler" component of the simulator randomly schedules the arrival of the first person on each floor (you will learn how to schedule random arrivals in Chapter 3). When the clock's time becomes equal to the time of the first arrival, the simulator "creates" a new person for the specified floor, and places the person on that floor. The person then presses the up-button or the down-button on that floor. The person's destination floor is never equal to the floor on which that person arrives.

If the first person of the day arrives at floor 1, the person can immediately get on the elevator (after pressing the up-button and waiting for the elevator's doors to open, of course!). If the first person arrives at floor 2, the elevator proceeds to floor 2 to pick up that person. The elevator requires five ticks of the clock to travel between floors.

The elevator signals its arrival at a floor by turning on a light above the elevator door on that floor and by sounding a bell. The buttons on the floor and the buttons in the elevator for that floor are reset, the elevator opens its door, the passenger—if there is one whose destination is that floor—gets out of the elevator, another passenger—if there is one waiting on that floor—gets into the elevator and presses a destination button, and the elevator closes its doors. If the elevator needs to begin moving, it determines in which direction it should go (a simple decision on a two-story elevator!), and begins moving to the next floor. For simplicity, assume that all of the events that happen once the elevator reaches a floor, and until the elevator closes its doors on that floor, take zero time. The elevator always knows what floor it is on and what floor it is going to.

At most, one person can be waiting on each floor at any time, so if a floor is occupied when a new person (i.e., not a person already on the elevator) is due to arrive at that floor, the new arrival is rescheduled for one second later. For simplicity, only one person can be "created" in the simulation at any given time, so there is never a duplicate arrival time for the next person in the building. Assume that people arrive at random on each floor every

5 to 20 seconds—in Chapter 3 you will learn how to use random number generation to simulate this arrival rate.

Your goal (over these special sections in Chapters 2 through 8) is to implement a working software simulator program that runs according to these specifications. Your program should simulate several minutes of the elevator's operation and determine if the elevator will successfully meet the anticipated traffic requirements in this office building.

***Elevator Laboratory Assignment 1***

In this and the next few assignments, you will perform the separate steps of an object-oriented design. The first step is to *identify the objects* in your problem. You will eventually describe these objects in a formal way and implement them in C++. For this assignment, all you should do is

1. Identify the objects in this elevator simulation problem. The problem statement specifies many objects working together to simulate the elevator and its interactions with the various people, floors of the building, buttons, etc. Locate the *nouns* from the problem statement; with high likelihood, these represent most of the objects necessary to implement the elevator simulation.
2. For each object you identify, write one precisely worded paragraph that captures all the facts about that object from the problem statement.

***Notes***

1. This is a good team exercise. Ideally you should work in a group of two to four people. This will help you and your teammates reinforce one another's efforts, and challenge and refine each other's design and implementation approaches.
2. Your group should compete with other groups in your class to develop the "best" design and implementation.
3. You will learn how to implement "randomness" in the next chapter where we study random number generation. Random number generation helps you do things like simulate coin tossing and dice rolling. It will also help you implement people arriving at random to use the elevator.
4. We have made a number of simplifying assumptions. You may decide to supply additional details.
5. Because the real world is so object oriented, it will be quite natural for you to pursue this project even though you have not yet formally studied object orientation.
6. Do not worry about perfection. System design is not a perfect and complete process, so you should pursue this project only on a best-efforts basis.

***Questions***

1. How might you decide if the elevator is able to handle the anticipated traffic volume?
2. Why is it so much more complicated to implement a three-story (or larger) building?
3. We will see later that once we have created one elevator object, it is easy to create as many as we want. What problems do you foresee in having several elevators, each of which may pick up and discharge passengers at every floor in the building?
4. For simplicity, we have given our elevator and each of the floors a capacity of one passenger. What problems do you foresee in being able to increase these capacities?

## *Summary*


- A procedure for solving a problem in terms of the actions to be executed and the order in which these actions should be executed is called an algorithm.
- Specifying the order in which statements are to be executed in a computer program is called program control.
- Pseudocode helps the programmer "think out" a program before attempting to write it in a programming language such as C++.
- Declarations are messages to the compiler telling it the names and attributes of variables and telling it to reserve space for variables.
- A selection structure is used to choose among alternative courses of action.
- The **`if`** selection structure executes an indicated action only when the condition is true.
- The **`if/else`** selection structure specifies separate actions to be executed when the condition is true and when the condition is false.
- Whenever more than one statement is to be executed where normally only a single statement is expected, these statements must be enclosed in braces forming a compound statement. A compound statement can be placed anywhere a single statement can be placed.
- An empty statement indicating that no action is to be taken is indicated by placing a semicolon (`;`) where a statement would normally be.
- A repetition structure specifies that an action is to be repeated while some condition remains true.
- The format for the **`while`** repetition structure is

```
while (condition)
    statement
```

- A value that contains a fractional part is referred to as a floating-point number and is represented by the data type **`float`**.
- The unary cast operator **`(float)`** creates a temporary floating-point copy of its operand.
- C++ provides the arithmetic assignment operators `+=`, `-=`, `*=`, `/=`, and `%=` that help abbreviate certain common types of expressions.
- C++ provides the increment operator, `++`, and the decrement operator, `--`, to increment or decrement a variable by 1. If the operator is prefixed to the variable, the variable is incremented or decremented by 1 first, then used in its expression. If the operator is postfixed to the variable, the variable is used in its expression, then incremented or decremented by 1.
- A loop is a group of instructions the computer executes repeatedly until some terminating condition is satisfied. Two forms of repetition are counter-controlled repetition and sentinel-controlled repetition.

- A loop counter is used to count the number of times a group of instructions should be repeated. It is incremented (or decremented) usually by 1 each time the group of instructions is performed.
- Sentinel values are generally used to control repetition when the precise number of repetitions is not known in advance and the loop includes statements that obtain data each time the loop is performed. A sentinel value is entered after all valid data items have been supplied to the program. Sentinels should be different from valid data items.
- The **for** repetition structure handles all the details of counter-controlled repetition. The general format of the **for** structure is

  ```
  for (expression1; expression2; expression3)
      statement
  ```

  where *expression1* initializes the loop's control variable, *expression2* is the loop-continuation condition, and *expression3* increments the control variable.
- The **do/while** repetition structure tests the loop-continuation condition at the end of the loop, so the body of the loop will be executed at least once. The format for the **do/while** structure is

  ```
  do
      statement
  while (condition);
  ```

- The **break** statement, when executed in one of the repetition structures (**for**, **while**, and **do/while**), causes immediate exit from the structure.
- The **continue** statement, when executed in one of the repetition structures (**for**, **while**, and **do/while**), skips any remaining statements in the body of the structure, and proceeds with the next iteration of the loop.
- The **switch** statement handles a series of decisions in which a particular variable or expression is tested for values it may assume, and different actions are taken. In most programs, it is necessary to include a **break** statement after the statements for each **case**. Several **case**s can execute the same statements by listing the **case** labels together before the statements. The **switch** structure can only test constant integral expressions.
- On UNIX systems and many others, end-of-file is entered by typing the sequence

  *<ctrl-d>*

  on a line by itself. On VMS and DOS, end-of-file is entered by typing

  *<ctrl-z>*

- Logical operators may be used to form complex conditions by combining conditions. The logical operators are **&&**, **||**, and **!**, meaning logical AND, logical OR, and logical NOT (negation), respectively.
- A true value is any nonzero value; a false value is 0 (zero).

## Terminology

**&&** operator
**||** operator
**!** operator
**--** operator
**++** operator
**?:** operator
action
action/decision model
algorithm
arithmetic assignment operators: **+=**, **-=**, ***=**, **/=**, and **%=**
ASCII character set
block
body of a loop
**break**
**case** label
cast operator
**char**
**cin.get()** function
compound statement
conditional operator (**?:**)
**continue**
control structure
counter-controlled repetition
decision
decrement operator (**--**)
**default** case in **switch**
definite repetition
**do/while** repetition structure
**double**
double-selection structure
empty statement (**;**)
**EOF**
fatal error
field width
fixed-point format
**float**
**for** repetition structure
**if** selection structure
**if/else** selection structure
increment operator (**++**)
indefinite repetition
infinite loop
initialization
integer division
**ios::fixed**
**ios::left**
**ios::showpoint**
keyword
logic error
logical AND (**&&**)
logical negation (**!**)
logical operators
logical OR (**||**)
**long**
loop counter
looping
loop-continuation condition
lvalue ("left value")
multiple selection
multiple-selection structure
nested control structures
nonfatal error
off-by-one error
parameterized stream manipulator
postdecrement operator
postincrement operator
**pow** function
predecrement operator
preincrement operator
pseudocode
repetition
repetition structures
rvalue("right value")
selection
sentinel value
sequential execution
**setiosflags** stream manipulator
**setprecision** stream manipulator
**setw** stream manipulator
**short**
single-entry/single-exit control structures
single-selection structure
stacked control structures
structured programming
**switch** selection structure
syntax error
ternary operator
top-down, stepwise refinement
transfer of control
unary operator
**while** repetition structure
whitespace characters

## Common Programming Errors

**2.1** Using a keyword as an identifier.

**2.2** Forgetting one or both of the braces that delimit a compound statement.

**2.3** Placing a semicolon after the condition in an `if` structure leads to a logic error in single selection `if` structures and a syntax error in double selection `if` structures (if the `if`-part contains an actual body statement).

**2.4** Not providing in the body of a `while` structure an action that eventually causes the condition in the `while` to become false. Normally, such a repetition structure will never terminate—an error called an "infinite loop."

**2.5** Spelling the keyword `while` with an uppercase `W` as in `While` (remember that C++ is a case-sensitive language). All of C++'s reserved keywords such as `while`, `if`, and `else` contain only lowercase letters.

**2.6** If a counter or total is not initialized, the results of your program will probably be incorrect. This is an example of a logic error.

**2.7** Choosing a sentinel value that is also a legitimate data value.

**2.8** An attempt to divide by zero causes a fatal error.

**2.9** Using floating-point numbers in a manner that assumes they are represented precisely can lead to incorrect results. Floating-point numbers are represented only approximately.

**2.10** Attempting to use the increment or decrement operator on an expression other than a simple variable name, e.g., writing `++(x + 1)` is a syntax error.

**2.11** Because floating-point values may be approximate, controlling counting loops with floating-point variables may result in imprecise counter values and inaccurate termination tests.

**2.12** Using an incorrect relational operator or using an incorrect final value of a loop counter in the condition of a `while` or `for` structure can cause off-by-one errors.

**2.13** Using commas instead of semicolons in a `for` header.

**2.14** Placing a semicolon immediately to the right of a `for` header makes the body of that `for` structure an empty statement. This is normally a logic error.

**2.15** Not using the proper relational operator in the loop-continuation condition of a loop that counts downwards (such as using `i <= 1` in a loop counting down to 1).

**2.16** Forgetting to include the `math.h` file in a program that uses math library functions.

**2.17** Forgetting a `break` statement when one is needed in a `switch` structure.

**2.18** Omitting the space between the word `case` and the integral value being tested in a `switch` structure can cause a logic error. For example, writing `case3:` instead of writing `case 3:` simply creates an unused label (we will say more about this in Chapter 18). The problem is that the `switch` structure will not perform the appropriate actions when the `switch`'s controlling expression has a value of 3.

**2.19** Not processing newline characters in the input when reading characters one at a time can cause logic errors.

**2.20** Infinite loops are caused when the loop-continuation condition in a `while`, `for`, or `do/while` structure never becomes false. To prevent this, make sure there is not a semicolon immediately after the header of a `while` structure. In a counter-controlled loop, make sure the control variable is incremented (or decremented) in the body of the loop. In a sentinel-controlled loop, make sure the sentinel value is eventually input.

**2.21** In expressions using operator `&&`, it is possible that a condition—we will call this the dependent condition—may require another condition to be true for it to be meaningful to evaluate the dependent condition. In this case, the dependent condition should be placed after the other condition or an error might occur.

**2.22** Using operator `==` for assignment, or using operator `=` for equality.

## *Good Programming Practices*

**2.1** Consistently applying reasonable indentation conventions throughout your programs greatly improves program readability. We suggest a fixed-size tab of about 1/4 inch or three blanks per indent.

**2.2** Pseudocode is often used to "think out" a program during the program design process. Then the pseudocode program is converted to C++.

**2.3** Indent both body statements of an `if/else` structure.

**2.4** If there are several levels of indentation, each level should be indented the same additional amount of space.

**2.5** Some programmers prefer to type the beginning and ending braces of compound statements before typing the individual statements within the braces. This helps avoid omitting one or both of the braces.

**2.6** Initialize counters and totals.

**2.7** When performing division by an expression whose value could be zero, explicitly test for this case and handle it appropriately in your program (such as printing an error message) rather than allowing the fatal error to occur.

**2.8** In a sentinel-controlled loop, the prompts requesting data entry should explicitly remind the user what the sentinel value is.

**2.9** Do not compare floating-point values for equality or inequality. Rather, test that the difference is less than a specified small value.

**2.10** Initializing variables when they are declared helps avoid the problems of uninitialized data.

**2.11** Unary operators should be placed next to their operands with no intervening spaces.

**2.12** Control counting loops with integer values.

**2.13** Indent the statements in the body of each control structure.

**2.14** Put a blank line before and after each major control structure to make it stand out in the program.

**2.15** Too many levels of nesting can make a program difficult to understand. As a general rule, try to avoid using more than three levels of indentation.

**2.16** Vertical spacing above and below control structures, and indentation of the bodies of control structures within the control structure headers gives programs a two-dimensional appearance that greatly improves readability.

**2.17** Using the final value in the condition of a `while` or `for` structure and using the `<=` relational operator will help avoid off-by-one errors. For a loop used to print the values 1 to 10, for example, the loop-continuation condition should be `counter <= 10` rather than `counter < 10` (which is an off-by-one error) or `counter < 11` (which is nevertheless correct).

**2.18** Place only expressions involving the control variables in the initialization and increment sections of a `for` structure. Manipulations of other variables should appear either before the loop (if they are to be executed only once like initialization statements) or in the loop body (if they are to executed once per repetition like incrementing or decrementing statements).

**2.19** Although the value of the control variable can be changed in the body of a `for` loop, avoid doing so because this practice can lead to subtle errors.

**2.20** Although statements preceding a `for` and statements in the body of a `for` can be merged into the `for` header, avoid doing so because it makes the program more difficult to read.

**2.21** Limit the size of control structure headers to a single line if possible.

**2.22** Do not use variables of type `float` or `double` to perform monetary calculations. The imprecision of floating-point numbers can cause errors that will result in incorrect monetary values. In the exercises, we explore the use of integers to perform monetary calculations. Note: C++ class libraries are becoming available for properly performing monetary calculations.

**2.23** Provide a **`default`** case in **`switch`** statements. As occurs with single selection **`if`** structures, cases not explicitly tested are ignored. The **`default`** case helps prevent this by focusing the programmer on the need to process exceptional conditions. There will be cases in which no default processing is needed.

**2.24** Although the **`case`** clauses and the **`default`** case clause in a **`switch`** structure can occur in any order, it is considered a good programming practice to place the **`default`** clause last.

**2.25** In a **`switch`** structure when the **`default`** clause is listed last, the **`break`** statement is not required. But some programmers include this **`break`** for clarity and symmetry with other **`case`**s.

**2.26** Remember to provide processing capabilities for newline and other whitespace characters in the input when processing characters one at a time.

**2.27** Some programmers always include braces in a **`do/while`** structure even if the braces are not necessary. This helps eliminate ambiguity between the **`do/while`** structure containing one statement and the **`while`** structure.

**2.28** Some programmers feel that **`break`** and **`continue`** violate structured programming. Because the effects of these statements can be achieved by structured programming techniques we will soon learn, these programmers do not use **`break`** and **`continue`**.

**2.29** When an equality expression has a variable and a constant as in **`x == 1`**, some programmers prefer to write the expression with the constant on the left and the variable name on the right as protection against the logic error that occurs when the programmer accidentally replaces the **`==`** operator with **`=`**.

## *Performance Tips*

**2.1** Programmers can write programs a bit faster and compilers can compile programs a bit faster when the "abbreviated" assignment operators are used. Some compilers generate code that runs faster when "abbreviated" assignment operators are used.

**2.2** Many of the performance tips we mention in this text result in nominal improvements, so the reader may be tempted to ignore them. Significant performance improvement is often realized when a supposedly nominal improvement is placed in a loop that may repeat a large number of times.

**2.3** Avoid placing expressions whose values do not change inside loops. But even if you do, many of today's sophisticated optimizing compilers will automatically place such expressions outside loops in the generated machine language code.

**2.4** In performance-oriented situations where memory is at a premium or execution speed is crucial, it may be desirable to use smaller integer sizes.

**2.5** The **`break`** and **`continue`** statements, when used properly, perform faster than the corresponding structured techniques we will soon learn.

**2.6** In expressions using operator **`&&`**, make the condition that is most likely to be false the leftmost condition. In expressions using operator **`||`**, make the condition that is most likely to be true the leftmost condition. This can reduce a program's execution time.

## *Portability Tips*

**2.1** The keystroke combinations for entering end-of-file are system dependent.

2.2 Testing for the symbolic constant **EOF** rather than –1 makes programs more portable. The ANSI standard states that **EOF** is a negative integral value (but not necessarily –1). Thus, **EOF** could have different values on different systems.

2.3 Because **int**s vary in size between systems, use **long** integers if you expect to process integers outside the range ±32767, and you would like to be able to run the program on several different computer systems.

## *Software Engineering Observations*

2.1 A compound statement can be placed anywhere in a program that a single statement can be placed.

2.2 Just as a compound statement can be placed anywhere a single statement can be placed, it is also possible to have no statement at all, i.e., the empty statement. The empty statement is represented by placing a semicolon (**;**) where a statement would normally be.

2.3 Each refinement, as well as the top itself, is a complete specification of the algorithm; only the level of detail varies.

2.4 Many programs can be divided logically into three phases: An initialization phase that initializes the program variables; a processing phase that inputs data values and adjusts program variables accordingly; and a termination phase that calculates and prints the final results.

2.5 The programmer terminates the top-down, stepwise refinement process when the pseudocode algorithm is specified in sufficient detail for the programmer to be able to convert the pseudocode to C++. Implementing the C++ program is then normally straightforward.

2.6 Experience has shown that the most difficult part of solving a problem on a computer is developing the algorithm. Once a correct algorithm has been specified, the process of producing a working C++ program from the algorithm is normally straightforward.

2.7 Many experienced programmers write programs without ever using program development tools like pseudocode. These programmers feel that their ultimate goal is to solve the problem on a computer, and that writing pseudocode merely delays the production of final outputs. Although this may work for simple and familiar problems, it can lead to serious errors on large, complex projects.

2.8 There is a tension between achieving quality software engineering and achieving the best performing software. Often one of these goals is achieved at the expense of the other.

## *Self-Review Exercises*

***Exercises 2.1 through 2.10 correspond to Sections 2.1 through 2.12.***
***Exercises 2.11 through 2.13 correspond to Sections 2.13 through 2.21.***

2.1 Answer each of the following questions.

a) All programs can be written in terms of three types of control structures:__________, __________, and __________.

b) The __________selection structure is used to execute one action when a condition is true and another action when that condition is false.

c) Repetition of a set of instructions a specific number of times is called ________ repetition.

d) When it is not known in advance how many times a set of statements will be repeated, a __________value can be used to terminate the repetition.

2.2 Write four different C++ statements that each add 1 to integer variable **x**.

**2.3** Write C++ statements to accomplish each of the following:

a) Assign the sum of **x** and **y** to **z** and increment the value of **x** by 1 after the calculation.
b) Test if the value of the variable **count** is greater than 10. If it is, print "**Count is greater than 10**"
c) Decrement the variable **x** by 1 then subtract it from the variable **total**.
d) Calculate the remainder after **q** is divided by **divisor** and assign the result to **q**. Write this statement two different ways.

**2.4** Write a C++ statement to accomplish each of the following tasks.

a) Declare variables **sum** and **x** to be of type **int**.
b) Initialize variable **x** to **1**.
c) Initialize variable **sum** to **0**.
d) Add variable **x** to variable **sum** and assign the result to variable **sum**.
e) Print **"The sum is: "** followed by the value of variable **sum**.

**2.5** Combine the statements that you wrote in Exercise 2.4 into a program that calculates and prints the sum of the integers from 1 to 10. Use the **while** structure to loop through the calculation and increment statements. The loop should terminate when the value of **x** becomes 11.

**2.6** Determine the values of each variable after the calculation is performed. Assume that when each statement begins executing all variables have the integer value 5.

a) `product *= x++;`
b) `quotient /= ++x;`

**2.7** Write single C++ statements that

a) Input integer variable **x** with **cin** and **>>**.
b) Input integer variable **y** with **cin** and **>>**.
c) Initialize integer variable **i** to **1**.
d) Initialize integer variable **power** to **1**.
e) Multiply variable **power** by **x** and assign the result to **power**.
f) Increment variable **y** by **1**.
g) Test **y** to see if it is less than or equal to **x**.
h) Output integer variable **power** with **cout** and **<<**.

**2.8** Write a C++ program that uses the statements in Exercise 2.7 to calculate **x** raised to the **y** power. The program should have a **while** repetition control structure.

**2.9** Identify and correct the errors in each of the following:

a)
```
while (c <= 5) {
   product *= c;
   ++c;
```
b)
```
cin << value;
```
c)
```
if (gender == 1)
   cout << "Woman" << endl;
else;
   cout << "Man" << endl;
```

**2.10** What is wrong with the following **while** repetition structure:

```
while (z >= 0)
   sum += z;
```

**2.11** State whether the following are true or false. If the answer is false, explain why.

a) The **default** case is required in the **switch** selection structure.
b) The **break** statement is required in the default case of a **switch** selection structure.

c) The expression **(x > y && a < b)** is true if either **x > y** is true or **a < b** is true.

d) An expression containing the **||** operator is true if either or both of its operands is true.

**2.12** Write a C++ statement or a set of C++ statements to accomplish each of the following:

a) Sum the odd integers between 1 and 99 using a **for** structure. Assume the integer variables **sum** and **count** have been declared.

b) Print the value **333.546372** in a field width of **15** characters with precisions of **1**, **2**, and **3**. Print each number on the same line. Left justify each number in its field. What three values print?

c) Calculate the value of **2.5** raised to the power of **3** using the **pow** function. Print the result with a precision of **2** in a field width of **10** positions. What prints?

d) Print the integers from 1 to 20 using a **while** loop and the counter variable **x**. Assume that the variable **x** has been declared, but not initialized. Print only 5 integers per line. Hint: Use the calculation **x % 5**. When the value of this is 0, print a newline character, otherwise print a tab character.

e) Repeat Exercise 2.3 (d) using a **for** structure.

**2.13** Find the error in each of the following code segments and explain how to correct it.

a)
```
x = 1;
while (x <= 10);
    x++;
}
```

b)
```
for (y = .1; y != 1.0; y += .1)
    cout << y << endl;
```

c)
```
switch (n) {
    case 1:
        cout << "The number is 1" << endl;
    case 2:
        cout << "The number is 2" << endl;
        break;
    default:
        cout << "The number is not 1 or 2" << endl;
        break;
}
```

d) The following code should print the values 1 to 10.
```
n = 1;
while (n < 10)
    cout << n++ << endl;
```

## Answers to Self-Review Exercises

**2.1** a) Sequence, selection, and repetition. b) **if/else**. c) Counter-controlled or definite. d) Sentinel, signal, flag, or dummy.

**2.2**
```
x = x + 1;
x += 1;
++x;
x++;
```

**2.3** a)
```
z = x++ + y;
```
b)
```
if (count > 10)
    cout << "Count is greater than 10" << endl;
```

c) `total -= --x;`
d) `q %= divisor;`
`q = q % divisor;`

2.4 a) `int sum, x;`
b) `x = 1;`
c) `sum = 0;`
d) `sum += x;` or `sum = sum + x;`
e) `cout << "The sum is: " << sum << endl;`

2.5
```
// Calculate the sum of the integers from 1 to 10
#include <iostream.h>

main()
{
   int sum, x;
   x = 1;
   sum = 0;
   while (x <= 10) {
      sum += x;
      ++x;
   }
   cout << "The sum is: " << sum << endl;
}
```

2.6 a) `product = 25, x = 6;`
b) `quotient = 0, x = 6;`

2.7 a) `cin >> x;`
b) `cin >> y;`
c) `i = 1;`
d) `power = 1;`
e) `power *= x;` or `power = power * x;`
f) `y++;`
g) `if (y <= x)`
h) `cout << power << endl;`

2.8
```
// raise x to the y power
#include <iostream.h>

main()
{
   int x, y, i, power;

   i = 1;
   power = 1;
   cin >> x;
   cin >> y;

   while (i <= y) {
      power *= x;
      ++i;
   }

   cout << power << endl;
   return 0;
}
```

**2.9** a) Error: Missing the closing right brace of the `while` body.
Correction: Add closing right brace after the statement `++c;`.
b) Error: Used stream insertion instead of stream extraction.
Correction: Change `<<` to `>>`.
c) Error: Semicolon after `else` results in a logic error. The second output statement will always be executed.
Correction: Remove the semicolon after `else`.

**2.10** The value of the variable `z` is never changed in the `while` structure. Therefore, if the loop-continuation condition `(z >= 0)` is true, an infinite loop is created. To prevent the infinite loop, `z` must be decremented so that it eventually becomes less than 0.

**2.11** a) False. The `default` case is optional. If no default action is needed, then there is no need for a `default` case.
b) False. The `break` statement is used to exit the `switch` structure. The `break` statement is not required when the `default` case is the last case.
c) False. Both of the relational expressions must be true in order for the entire expression to be true when using the `&&` operator.
d) True.

**2.12** a)
```
sum = 0;
for (count = 1; count <= 99; count += 2)
   sum += count;
```
b)
```
cout << setiosflags(ios::fixed | ios::showpoint |
ios::left)
     << setprecision(1) << setw(15) << 333.546372
     << setprecision(2) << setw(15) << 333.546372
     << setprecision(3) << setw(15) << 333.546372 << endl;
```
Output is:
```
333.5          333.55         333.546
```
c)
```
cout << setiosflags(ios::fixed | ios::showpoint)
     << setprecision(2) << setw(10) << pow(2.5, 3) << endl;
```
Output is:
```
     15.63
```
d)
```
x = 1;
while (x <= 20) {
   cout << x;
   if (x % 5 == 0)
      cout << endl;
   else
      cout << '\t';
   x++;
}
```
e)
```
for (x = 1; x <= 20; x++) {
   cout << x;
   if (x % 5 == 0)
      cout << endl;
   else
      cout << '\t';
}
```

or

```
for (x = 1; x <= 20; x++)
   if (x % 5 == 0)
      cout << x << endl;
   else
      cout << x << '\t';
```

**2.13** a) Error: The semicolon after the `while` header causes an infinite loop.
Correction: Replace the semicolon by a `{` or remove both the `;` and the `}`.

b) Error: Using a floating-point number to control a `for` repetition structure.
Correction: Use an integer, and perform the proper calculation in order to get the values you desire.

```
for (y = 1; y != 10; y++)
   cout << ( (float) y / 10 ) << endl;
```

c) Error: Missing `break` statement in the statements for the first `case`.
Correction: Add a `break` statement at the end of the statements for the first `case`. Note that this is not necessarily an error if the programmer wants the statement of `case 2:` to execute every time the `case 1:` statement executes.

d) Error: Improper relational operator used in the while repetition-continuation condition.
Correction: Use `<=` rather than `<` or change `10` to `11`.

## Exercises

***Exercises 2.14 through 2.38 correspond to Sections 2.1 through 2.12.***
***Exercises 2.39 through 2.66 correspond to Sections 2.13 through 2.21.***

**2.14** Identify and correct the errors in each of the following (Note: there may be more than one error in each piece of code):

a)
```
if (age >= 65);
   cout << "Age is greater than or equal to 65" << endl;
else
   cout << "Age is less than 65 << endl";
```

b)
```
int x = 1, total;
while (x <= 10) {
   total += x;
   ++x;
}
```

c)
```
While (x <= 100)
   total += x;
   ++x;
```

d)
```
while (y > 0) {
   cout << y << endl;
   ++y;
}
```

**2.15** What does the following program print?

```
#include <iostream.h>
main()
{
   int y, x = 1, total = 0;
   while (x <= 10) {
      y = x * x;
      cout << y << endl;
      total += y;
      ++x;
   }
   cout << "Total is " << total << endl;
   return 0;
}
```

**For Exercises 2.16 to 2.19 perform each of these steps:**

1. Read the problem statement.
2. Formulate the algorithm using pseudocode and top-down, stepwise refinement.
3. Write a C++ program.
4. Test, debug, and execute the C++ program.

**2.16** Because of the high price of gasoline, drivers are concerned with the mileage obtained by their automobiles. One driver has kept track of several tankfuls of gasoline by recording miles driven and gallons used for each tankful. Develop a C++ program that will input the miles driven and gallons used for each tankful. The program should calculate and display the miles per gallon obtained for each tankful. After processing all input information, the program should calculate and print the combined miles per gallon obtained for all tankfuls.

```
Enter the gallons used (-1 to end): 12.8
Enter the miles driven: 287
The miles / gallon for this tank was 22.421875

Enter the gallons used (-1 to end): 10.3
Enter the miles driven: 200
The miles / gallon for this tank was 19.417475

Enter the gallons used (-1 to end): 5
Enter the miles driven: 120
The miles / gallon for this tank was 24.000000

Enter the gallons used (-1 to end): -1

The overall average miles/gallon was 21.601423
```

**2.17** Develop a C++ program that will determine if a department store customer has exceeded the credit limit on a charge account. For each customer, the following facts are available:

1. Account number (an integer)
2. Balance at the beginning of the month
3. Total of all items charged by this customer this month
4. Total of all credits applied to this customer's account this month
5. Allowed credit limit

The program should input each of these facts, calculate the new balance (= beginning balance + charges - credits), and determine if the new balance exceeds the customer's credit limit. For those customers whose credit limit is exceeded, the program should display the customer's account number, credit limit, new balance, and the message "Credit limit exceeded."

```
Enter account number (-1 to end): 100
Enter beginning balance: 5394.78
Enter total charges: 1000.00
Enter total credits: 500.00
Enter credit limit: 5500.00
Account:       100
Credit limit: 5500.00
Balance:       5894.78
Credit Limit Exceeded.

Enter account number (-1 to end): 200
Enter beginning balance: 1000.00
Enter total charges: 123.45
Enter total credits: 321.00
Enter credit limit: 1500.00

Enter account number (-1 to end): 300
Enter beginning balance: 500.00
Enter total charges: 274.73
Enter total credits: 100.00
Enter credit limit: 800.00

Enter account number (-1 to end): -1
```

**2.18** One large chemical company pays its salespeople on a commission basis. The salespeople receive $200 per week plus 9 percent of their gross sales for that week. For example, a salesperson who sells $5000 worth of chemicals in a week receives $200 plus 9 percent of $5000, or a total of $650. Develop a C++ program that will input each salesperson's gross sales for last week and will calculate and display that salesperson's earnings. Process one salesperson's figures at a time.

```
Enter sales in dollars (-1 to end): 5000.00
Salary is: $650.00

Enter sales in dollars (-1 to end): 1234.56
Salary is: $311.11

Enter sales in dollars (-1 to end): 1088.89
Salary is: $298.00

Enter sales in dollars (-1 to end): -1
```

**2.19** Develop a C++ program that will determine the gross pay for each of several employees. The company pays "straight-time" for the first 40 hours worked by each employee and pays "time-and-a-half" for all hours worked in excess of 40 hours. You are given a list of the employees of the company, the number of hours each employee worked last week, and the hourly rate of each employee. Your program should input this information for each employee, and should determine and display the employee's gross pay.

```
Enter hours worked (-1 to end): 39
Enter hourly rate of the worker ($00.00): 10.00
Salary is $390.00

Enter hours worked (-1 to end): 40
Enter hourly rate of the worker ($00.00): 10.00
Salary is $400.00

Enter hours worked (-1 to end): 41
Enter hourly rate of the worker ($00.00): 10.00
Salary is $415.00

Enter hours worked (-1 to end): -1
```

**2.20** The process of finding the largest number (i.e., the maximum of a group of numbers) is used frequently in computer applications. For example, a program that determines the winner of a sales contest would input the number of units sold by each salesperson. The salesperson who sells the most units wins the contest. Write a pseudocode program and then a C++ program that inputs a series of 10 numbers, and determines and prints the largest of the numbers. Hint: Your program should use three variables as follows:

**`counter:`** A counter to count to 10 (i.e., to keep track of how many numbers have been input, and to determine when all 10 numbers have been processed).
**`number:`** The current number input to the program.
**`largest:`** The largest number found so far.

**2.21** Write a C++ program that utilizes looping and the tab escape sequence **`\t`** to print the following table of values:

```
N       10*N    100*N   1000*N

1       10      100     1000
2       20      200     2000
3       30      300     3000
4       40      400     4000
5       50      500     5000
```

**2.22** Using an approach similar to Exercise 2.20, find the *two* largest values of the 10 numbers. Note: You may input each number only once.

**2.23** Modify the program in Fig. 2.11 to validate its inputs. On any input, if the value entered is other than 1 or 2, keep looping until the user enters a correct value.

**2.24** What does the following program print?

```
#include <iostream.h>
main()
{
   int count = 1;
   while (count <= 10) {
      cout << (count % 2 ? "****" : "++++++++")
           << endl;
      ++count;
   }
   return 0;
}
```

**2.25** What does the following program print?

```
#include <iostream.h>

main()
{
   int row = 10, column;
   while (row >= 1) {
      column = 1;
      while (column <= 10) {
         cout << (row % 2 ? "<" : ">");
         ++column;
      }
      --row;
      cout << endl;
   }
   return 0;
}
```

**2.26** *(Dangling Else Problem)* Determine the output for each of the following when **x** is **9** and **y** is **11** and when **x** is **11** and **y** is **9**. Note that the compiler ignores the indentation in a C++ program. Also, the C++ compiler always associates an **else** with the previous **if** unless told to do otherwise by the placement of braces **{}**. Because, on first glance, the programmer may not be sure which **if** an **else** matches, this is referred to as the "dangling else" problem. We have eliminated the indentation from the following code to make the problem more challenging. (Hint: Apply indentation conventions you have learned.)

a)
```
if (x < 10)
if (y > 10)
cout << "*****" << endl;
else
cout << "#####" << endl;
cout << "$$$$$" << endl;
```

b)
```
if (x < 10) {
if (y > 10)
cout << "*****" << endl;
}
else {
cout << "#####" << endl;
cout << "$$$$$" << endl;
}
```

**2.27** *(Another Dangling Else Problem)* Modify the following code to produce the output shown. Use proper indentation techniques. You may not make any changes other than inserting braces. The compiler ignores indentation in a C++ program. We have eliminated the indentation from the following code to make the problem more challenging. Note: It is possible that no modification is necessary.

```
if (y == 8)
if (x == 5)
cout << "@@@@@" << endl;
else
cout << "#####" << endl;
cout << "$$$$$" << endl;
cout << "&&&&&" << endl;
```

a) Assuming **x = 5** and **y = 8**, the following output is produced.

```
@@@@@
$$$$$
&&&&&
```

b) Assuming **x = 5** and **y = 8**, the following output is produced.

```
@@@@@
```

c) Assuming **x = 5** and **y = 8**, the following output is produced.

```
@@@@@
&&&&&
```

d) Assuming **x = 5** and **y = 7**, the following output is produced. Note: The last three output statements after the **else** are all part of a compound statement.

```
#####
$$$$$
&&&&&
```

**2.28** Write a program that reads in the size of the side of a square and then prints a hollow square of that size out of asterisks and blanks. Your program should work for squares of all side sizes between 1 and 20. For example, if your program reads a size of 5, it should print

```
*****
*   *
*   *
*   *
*****
```

**2.29** A palindrome is a number or a text phrase that reads the same backwards as forwards. For example, each of the following five-digit integers are palindromes: 12321, 55555, 45554 and 11611. Write a program that reads in a five-digit integer and determines whether or not it is a palindrome. (Hint: Use the division and modulus operators to separate the number into its individual digits.)

**2.30** Input an integer containing only 0s and 1s (i.e., a "binary" integer) and print its decimal equivalent. (Hint: Use the modulus and division operators to pick off the "binary" number's digits one at a time from right to left. Just as in the decimal number system where the rightmost digit has a positional value of 1, and the next digit left has a positional value of 10, then 100, then 1000, etc., in the binary number system the rightmost digit has a positional value of 1, the next digit left has a positional value of 2, then 4, then 8, etc. Thus the decimal number 234 can be interpreted as 4 * 1 + 3 * 10 + 2 * 100. The decimal equivalent of binary 1101 is 1 * 1 + 0 * 2 + 1 * 4 + 1 * 8 or 1 + 0 + 4 + 8 or 13.)

**2.31** Write a program that displays the following checkerboard pattern

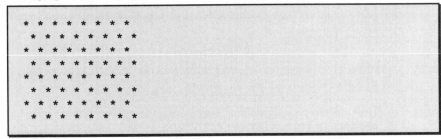

```
* * * * * * * *
 * * * * * * * *
* * * * * * * *
 * * * * * * * *
* * * * * * * *
 * * * * * * * *
* * * * * * * *
 * * * * * * * *
```

Your program may use only three output statements, one of the form

```
cout << "* ";
```

one of the form

```
cout << ' ';
```

and one of the form

```
cout << endl;
```

**2.32** Write a program that keeps printing the multiples of the integer 2, namely 2, 4, 8, 16, 32, 64, etc. Your loop should not terminate (i.e., you should create an infinite loop). What happens when you run this program?

**2.33** Write a program that reads the radius of a circle (as a `float` value) and computes and prints the diameter, the circumference, and the area. Use the value 3.14159 for π.

**2.34** What's wrong with the following statement? Provide the correct statement to accomplish what the programmer was probably trying to do.

```
cout << ++(x + y);
```

**2.35** Write a program that reads three nonzero `float` values and determines and prints if they could represent the sides of a triangle.

**2.36** Write a program that reads three nonzero integers and determines and prints if they could be the sides of a right triangle.

**2.37** A company wants to transmit data over the telephone, but they are concerned that their phones may be tapped. All of their data is transmitted as four-digit integers. They have asked you to write a program that will encrypt their data so that it may be transmitted more securely. Your program should read a four-digit integer and encrypt it as follows: Replace each digit by *(the sum of that digit plus 7) modulus 10*. Then, swap the first digit with the third, and swap the second digit with the fourth. Then print the encrypted integer. Write a separate program that inputs an encrypted four-digit integer, and decrypts it to form the original number.

**2.38** The factorial of a nonnegative integer $n$ is written $n!$ (pronounced "$n$ factorial") and is defined as follows:

$$n! = n \cdot (n - 1) \cdot (n - 2) \cdot \ldots \cdot 1 \quad \text{(for values of } n \text{ greater than or equal to 1)}$$

and

$$n! = 1 \quad (\text{for } n = 0).$$

For example, $5! = 5 \cdot 4 \cdot 3 \cdot 2 \cdot 1$ which is 120.

a) Write a program that reads a nonnegative integer and computes and prints its factorial.
b) Write a program that estimates the value of the mathematical constant $e$ by using the formula:

$$e = 1 + \frac{1}{1!} + \frac{1}{2!} + \frac{1}{3!} + \ldots$$

c) Write a program that computes the value of $e^x$ by using the formula

$$e^x = 1 + \frac{x}{1!} + \frac{x^2}{2!} + \frac{x^3}{3!} + \ldots$$

**2.39** Find the error in each of the following (Note: there may be more than one error):

a)
```
For (x = 100, x >= 1, x++)
    cout << x << endl;
```

b) The following code should print whether integer **value** is odd or even:
```
switch (value % 2) {
    case 0:
        cout << "Even integer" << endl;
    case 1:
        cout << "Odd integer" << endl;
}
```

c) The following code should output the odd integers from 19 to 1:
```
for (x = 19; x >= 1; x += 2)
    cout << x << endl;
```

d) The following code should output the even integers from 2 to 100:
```
counter = 2;
do {
    cout << counter << endl;
    counter += 2;
} While (counter < 100);
```

**2.40** Write a program that sums a sequence of integers. Assume that the first integer read specifies the number of values remaining to be entered. Your program should read only one value per input statement. A typical input sequence might be

```
5 100 200 300 400 500
```

where the **5** indicates that the subsequent **5** values are to be summed.

**2.41** Write a program that calculates and prints the average of several integers. Assume the last value read is the sentinel **9999**. A typical input sequence might be

```
10 8 11 7 9 9999
```

indicating that the average of all the values preceding **9999** is to be calculated.

**2.42** What does the following program do?

```
#include <iostream.h>
main()
{
    int x, y;
    cout << "Enter two integers in the range 1-20: ";
    cin >> x >> y;
    for (int i = 1; i <= y; i++) {
        for (int j = 1; j <= x; j++)
            cout << '@';
        cout << endl;
    }
    return 0;
}
```

**2.43** Write a program that finds the smallest of several integers. Assume that the first value read specifies the number of values remaining.

**2.44** Write a program that calculates and prints the product of the odd integers from 1 to 15.

**2.45** The *factorial* function is used frequently in probability problems. The factorial of a positive integer *n* (written *n!* and pronounced "n factorial") is equal to the product of the positive integers from 1 to *n*. Write a program that evaluates the factorials of the integers from 1 to 5. Print the results in tabular format. What difficulty might prevent you from calculating the factorial of 20?

**2.46** Modify the compound interest program of Section 2.15 to repeat its steps for interest rates of 5 percent, 6 percent, 7 percent, 8 percent, 9 percent, and 10 percent. Use a `for` loop to vary the interest rate.

**2.47** Write a program that prints the following patterns separately one below the other. Use `for` loops to generate the patterns. All asterisks (`*`) should be printed by a single statement of the form `cout << '*';` (this causes the asterisks to print side by side). Hint: The last two patterns require that each line begin with an appropriate number of blanks. Extra credit: Combine your code from the four separate problems into a single program that prints all four patterns side by side making clever use of nested `for` loops.

```
(A)            (B)            (C)                (D)
*              **********     **********                  *
**             *********       *********                 **
***            ********         ********                ***
****           *******           *******               ****
*****          ******             ******              *****
******         *****               *****             ******
*******        ****                 ****            *******
********       ***                   ***           ********
*********      **                     **          *********
**********     *                       *         **********
```

**2.48** One interesting application of computers is drawing graphs and bar charts (sometimes called "histograms"). Write a program that reads five numbers (each between 1 and 30). For each number read, your program should print a line containing that number of adjacent asterisks. For example, if your program reads the number seven, it should print `*******`.

**2.49** A mail order house sells five different products whose retail prices are product 1 — $2.98, product 2—$4.50, product 3—$9.98, product 4—$4.49, and product 5—$6.87. Write a program that reads a series of pairs of numbers as follows:

1. Product number
2. Quantity sold for one day

Your program should use a `switch` statement to help determine the retail price for each product. Your program should calculate and display the total retail value of all products sold last week.

**2.50** Modify the program of Fig. 2.22 so that it calculates the grade point average for the class. A grade of 'A' is worth 4 points, 'B' is worth 3 points, etc.

**2.51** Modify the program in Fig. 2.21 so that it uses only integers to calculate the compound interest. (Hint: Treat all monetary amounts as integral numbers of pennies. Then "break" the result into its dollar portion and cents portion by using the division and modulus operations respectively. Insert a period.)

**2.52** Assume `i = 1`, `j = 2`, `k = 3`, and `m = 2`. What does each of the following statements print? Are the parentheses necessary in each case?

a) `cout << (i == 1) << endl;`
b) `cout << (j == 3) << endl;`
c) `cout << (i >= 1 && j < 4) << endl;`

d) `cout << (m <= 99 && k < m) << endl;`
e) `cout << (j >= i || k == m) <, endl;`
f) `cout << (k + m < j || 3 - j >= k) << endl;`
g) `cout << (!m) << endl;`
h) `cout << ( !(j - m) ) << endl;`
i) `cout << ( !(k > m) ) << endl;`

**2.53** Write a program that prints a table of the binary, octal, and hexadecimal equivalents of the decimal numbers in the range 1 through 256. If you are not familiar with these number systems, read Appendix E first.

**2.54** Calculate the value of π from the infinite series

$$\pi = 4 - \frac{4}{3} + \frac{4}{5} - \frac{4}{7} + \frac{4}{9} - \frac{4}{11} + \ldots$$

Print a table that shows the value of π approximated by 1 term of this series, by two terms, by three terms, etc. How many terms of this series do you have to use before you first get 3.14? 3.141? 3.1415? 3.14159?

**2.55** *(Pythagorean Triples)* A right triangle can have sides that are all integers. The set of three integer values for the sides of a right triangle is called a Pythagorean triple. These three sides must satisfy the relationship that the sum of the squares of two of the sides is equal to the square of the hypotenuse. Find all Pythagorean triples for **side1**, **side2**, and the **hypotenuse** all no larger than 500. Use a triple-nested **for**-loop that tries all possibilities. This is an example of "brute force" computing. You will learn in more advanced computer science courses that there are large numbers of interesting problems for which there is no known algorithmic approach other than using sheer brute force.

**2.56** A company pays its employees as managers (who receive a fixed weekly salary), hourly workers (who receive a fixed hourly wage for up to the first 40 hours they work and "time-and-a-half," i.e., 1.5 times their hourly wage, for overtime hours worked), commission workers (who receive a $250 plus 5.7% of their gross weekly sales), or pieceworkers (who receive a fixed amount of money per item for each of the items they produce—each pieceworker in this company works on only one type of item). Write a program to compute the weekly pay for each employee. You do not know the number of employees in advance. Each type of employee has its own pay code: Managers have paycode 1, hourly workers have code 2, commission workers have code 3 and pieceworkers have code 4. Use a **switch** to compute each employee's pay based on that employee's paycode. Within the **switch**, prompt the user (i.e., the payroll clerk) to enter the appropriate facts your program needs to calculate each employee's pay based on that employee's paycode.

**2.57** *(De Morgan's Laws)* In this chapter, we discussed the logical operators `&&`, `||`, and `!`. De Morgan's Laws can sometimes make it more convenient for us to express a logical expression. These laws state that the expression `!(`*condition1* `&&` *condition2*`)` is logically equivalent to the expression `(!`*condition1* `||` `!`*condition2*`)`. Also, the expression `!(`*condition1* `||` *condition2*`)` is logically equivalent to the expression `(!`*condition1* `&&` `!`*condition2*`)`. Use De Morgan's Laws to write equivalent expressions for each of the following, and then write a program to show that both the original expression and the new expression in each case are equivalent:

a) `!(x < 5) && !(y >= 7)`
b) `!(a == b) || !(g != 5)`
c) `!((x <= 8) && (y > 4))`
d) `!((i > 4) || (j <= 6))`

**2.58** Write a program that prints the following diamond shape. You may use output statements that print either a single asterisk (`*`) or a single blank. Maximize your use of repetition (with nested **for** structures) and minimize the number of output statements.

**2.59** Modify the program you wrote in Exercise 2.58 to read an odd number in the range 1 to 19 to specify the number of rows in the diamond. Your program should then display a diamond of the appropriate size.

**2.60** A criticism of the **break** statement and the **continue** statement is that each is unstructured. Actually **break** statements and **continue** statements can always be replaced by structured statements, although doing so can be awkward. Describe in general how you would remove any **break** statement from a loop in a program and replace that statement with some structured equivalent. (Hint: The **break** statement leaves a loop from within the body of the loop. The other way to leave is by failing the loop-continuation test. Consider using in the loop-continuation test a second test that indicates "early exit because of a 'break' condition.") Use the technique you developed here to remove the break statement from the program of Fig. 2.26.

**2.61** What does the following program segment do?

```
for (i = 1; i <= 5; i++) {
   for (j = 1; j <= 3; j++) {
      for (k = 1, k <= 4; k++)
         cout << '*';
      cout << endl;
   }
   cout << endl;
}
```

**2.62** Describe in general how you would remove any **continue** statement from a loop in a program and replace that statement with some structured equivalent. Use the technique you developed here to remove the **continue** statement from the program of Fig. 2.27.

**2.63** *("The Twelve Days of Christmas" Song)* Write a program that uses repetition and **switch** structures to print the song "The Twelve Days of Christmas." One **switch** structure should be used to to print the day (i.e., "First," "Second," etc.). A separate **switch** structure should be used to print the remainder of each verse.

### *Exercise 2.64 corresponds to Section 2.22, "Thinking About Objects."*

**2.64** Describe in 200 words or less what an automobile is and does. List the nouns and verbs separately. In the text, we stated that each noun may correspond to an object that will need to be built to implement a system, in this case a car. Pick five of the objects you listed and for each list several attributes and several behaviors. Describe briefly how these objects interact with one another and other objects in your description. You have just performed several of the key steps in a typical object-oriented design.

# 3

# Functions

**Objectives**

- To understand how to construct programs modularly from small pieces called functions.
- To introduce the common math functions available in the C standard library.
- To be able to create new functions.
- To understand the mechanisms used to pass information between functions.
- To introduce simulation techniques using random number generation.
- To understand how the visibility of identifiers is limited to specific regions of programs.
- To understand how to write and use functions that call themselves.

*Form ever follows function.*
Louis Henri Sullivan

*E pluribus unum.*
*(One composed of many.)*
Virgil

*O! call back yesterday, bid time return.*
William Shakespeare, Richard II

*Call be Ishmael.*
Herman Melville, Moby Dick

*When you call me that, smile.*
Owen Wister

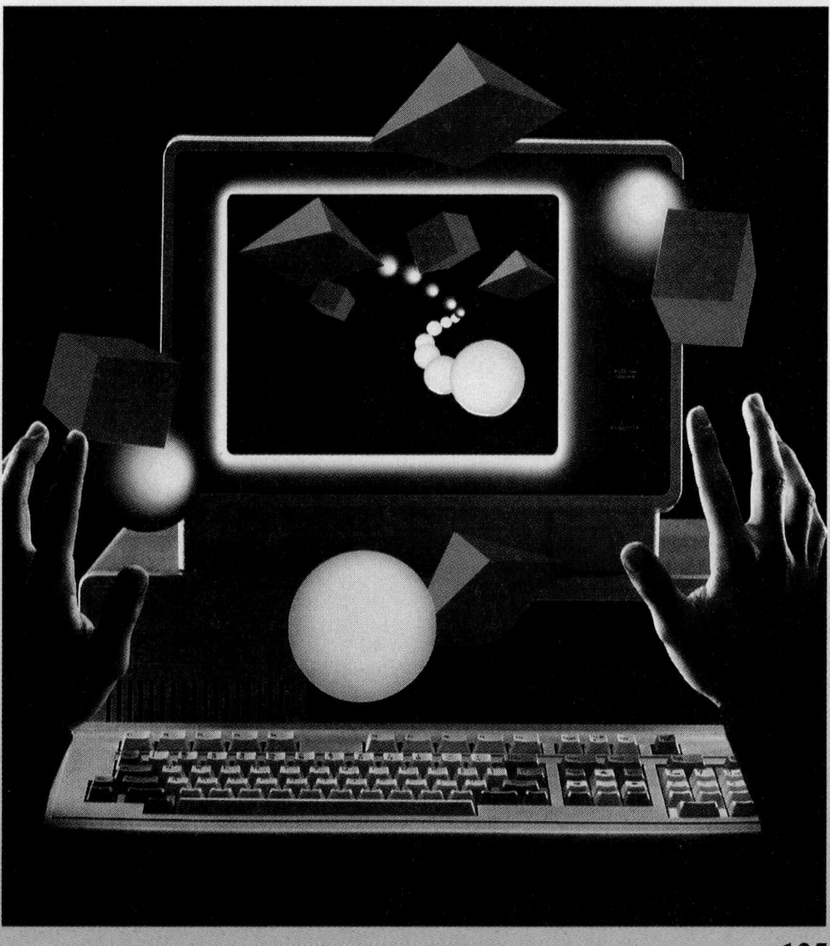

## Outline



## 3.1 Introduction

Most computer programs that solve real-world problems are much larger than the programs presented in the first few chapters. Experience has shown that the best way to develop and maintain a large program is to construct it from smaller pieces or *modules* each of which is more manageable than the original program. This technique is called *divide and conquer.* This chapter describes many key features of the C++ language that facilitate the design, implementation, operation, and maintenance of large programs.

## 3.2 Program Modules in C++

Modules in C++ are called *functions* and *classes.* C++ programs are typically written by combining new functions the programmer writes with "pre-packaged" functions available in the *C standard library,* and by combining new classes the programmer writes with "pre-packaged" classes available in various class libraries. In this chapter, we concentrate on functions; we will discuss classes in detail beginning with Chapter 6.

The C standard library provides a rich collection of functions for performing common mathematical calculations, string manipulations, character manipulations, input/output, error checking, and many other useful operations. This makes the programmer's job easier because these functions provide many of the capabilities programmers need. The C standard library functions are provided as part of the C++ programming environment.

***Good Programming Practice 3.1***

*Familiarize yourself with the rich collection of functions in the ANSI C standard library and with the rich collections of classes available in various class libraries .*

***Software Engineering Observation 3.1***

*Avoid reinventing the wheel. When possible, use ANSI C standard library functions instead of writing new functions. This reduces program development time.*

***Portability Tip 3.1***

*Using the functions in the ANSI C standard library helps make programs more portable.*

The programmer can write functions to define specific tasks that may be used at many points in a program. These are sometimes referred to as *programmer-defined functions.* The actual statements defining the function are written only once and these statements are hidden from other functions.

A function is *invoked* (i.e., made to perform its designated task) by a *function call.* The function call specifies the function name and provides information (as *arguments*) that the called function needs to do its job. A common analogy for this is the hierarchical form of management. A boss (the *calling function* or *caller*) asks a worker (the *called function*) to perform a task and *return* (i.e., report back) the results when the task is done. The boss function does not know *how* the worker function performs its designated tasks. The worker may call other worker functions, and the boss will be unaware of this. We will soon see how this "hiding" of implementation details promotes good software engineering. Figure 3.1 shows the **main** function communicating with several worker functions in a hierarchical manner. Note that **worker1** acts as a boss function to **worker4** and **worker5**. Relationships among functions may be other than the hierarchical structure shown in this figure.

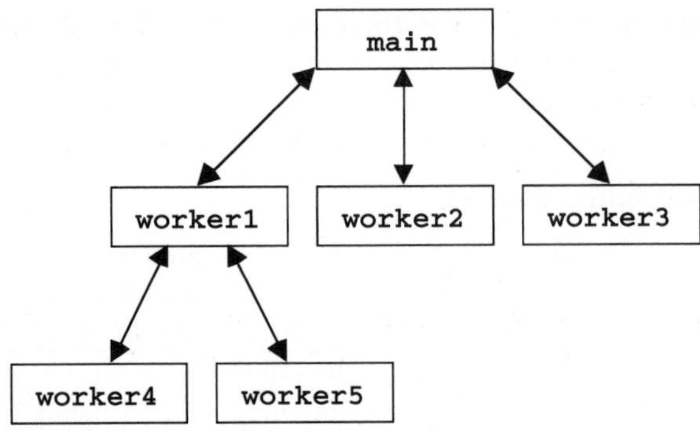


**Fig. 3.1** Hierarchical boss function/worker function relationship.

## 3.3 Math Library Functions

Math library functions allow the programmer to perform certain common mathematical calculations. We use various math library functions here to introduce the concept of functions. Later in the book, we will discuss many of the other functions in the C standard library. A complete list of the C standard library functions is provided in Appendix B.

Functions are normally called by writing the name of the function followed by a left parenthesis followed by the *argument* (or a comma separated list of arguments) of the function followed by a right parenthesis. For example, a programmer desiring to calculate and print the square root of **900.0** might write

```
cout << sqrt(900.0);
```

When this statement is executed, the math library function **sqrt** is called to calculate the square root of the number contained in the parentheses (**900.0**). The number **900.0** is the *argument* of the **sqrt** function. The preceding statement would print **30**. The **sqrt** function takes an argument of type **double** and returns a result of type **double**. All functions in the math library return the data type **double**.

***Good Programming Practice 3.2***

*Include the math header file by using the preprocessor directive* **#include <math.h>** *when using functions in the math library.*

***Common Programming Error 3.1***

*Forgetting to include the math header file when using math library functions results in a compile-time error. A standard header file must be included for every standard library function used in a program.*

Function arguments may be constants, variables, or expressions. If **c1 = 13.0**, **d = 3.0**, and **f = 4.0**, then the statement

```
cout << sqrt(c1 + d * f);
```

calculates and prints the square root of `13.0 + 3.0 * 4.0 = 25.0`, namely `5` (because C++ does not ordinarily print trailing zeros or the decimal point in a floating point number that has no fractional part).

Some math library functions are summarized in Fig. 3.2. In the figure, the variables **x** and **y** are of type **double**.

## 3.4 Functions

Functions allow the programmer to modularize a program. All variables declared in function definitions are *local variables*—they are known only in the function in which they are defined. Most functions have a list of *parameters* that provide the means for communicating information between functions. A function's parameters are also local variables.

| Function | Description | Example |
|---|---|---|
| **sqrt(x)** | square root of *x* | **sqrt(900.0)** is **30.0**<br>**sqrt(9.0)** is **3.0** |
| **exp(x)** | exponential function $e^x$ | **exp(1.0)** is **2.718282**<br>**exp(2.0)** is **7.389056** |
| **log(x)** | natural logarithm of *x* (base e) | **log(2.718282)** is **1.0**<br>**log(7.389056)** is **2.0** |
| **log10(x)** | logarithm of *x* (base 10) | **log10(1.0)** is **0.0**<br>**log10(10.0)** is **1.0**<br>**log10(100.0)** is **2.0** |
| **fabs(x)** | absolute value of *x* | if **x > 0** then **fabs(x)** is **x**<br>if **x = 0** then **fabs(x)** is **0.0**<br>if **x < 0** then **fabs(x)** is **-x** |
| **ceil(x)** | rounds *x* to the smallest integer not less than *x* | **ceil(9.2)** is **10.0**<br>**ceil(-9.8)** is **-9.0** |
| **floor(x)** | rounds *x* to the largest integer not greater than *x* | **floor(9.2)** is **9.0**<br>**floor(-9.8)** is **-10.0** |
| **pow(x, y)** | *x* raised to power *y* ($x^y$) | **pow(2, 7)** is **128.0**<br>**pow(9, .5)** is **3.0** |
| **fmod(x, y)** | remainder of *x/y* as a floating point number | **fmod(13.657, 2.333)** is **1.992** |
| **sin(x)** | trigonometric sine of *x* (*x* in radians) | **sin(0.0)** is **0.0** |
| **cos(x)** | trigonometric cosine of *x* (*x* in radians) | **cos(0.0)** is **1.0** |
| **tan(x)** | trigonometric tangent of *x* (*x* in radians) | **tan(0.0)** is **0.0** |

**Fig. 3.2** Commonly used math library functions.

***Software Engineering Observation 3.2***

*In programs containing many functions,* **`main`** *should be implemented as a group of calls to functions that perform the bulk of the program's work.*

There are several motivations for "functionalizing" a program. The divide-and-conquer approach makes program development more manageable. Another motivation is *software reusability*—using existing functions as building blocks to create new programs. Software reusability is a major factor in the object-oriented programming movement. With good function naming and definition, programs can be created from standardized functions that accomplish specific tasks, rather than being built by using customized code. A third motivation is to avoid repeating code in a program. Packaging code as a function allows the code to be executed from several locations in a program simply by calling the function.

***Software Engineering Observation 3.3***

*Each function should be limited to performing a single, well-defined task, and the function name should effectively express that task. This promotes software reusability.*

***Software Engineering Observation 3.4***

*If you cannot choose a concise name that expresses what the function does, it is possible that your function is attempting to perform too many diverse tasks. It is usually best to break such a function into several smaller functions.*

## 3.5 Function Definitions

Each program we have presented has consisted of a function called **`main`** that called standard library functions to accomplish its tasks. We now consider how programmers write their own customized functions.

Consider a program that uses a function **`square`** to calculate the squares of the integers from 1 to 10 (Fig. 3.3).

***Good Programming Practice 3.3***

*Place a blank line between function definitions to separate the functions and enhance program readability.*

Function **`square`** is *invoked* or *called* in **`main`** with the call

```
square(x)
```

Function **`square`** receives a copy of the value of **`x`** in the *parameter* **`y`**. Then **`square`** calculates **`y * y`**. The result is passed back to the point in **`main`** where **`square`** was invoked, and the result is displayed. This process is repeated ten times using the **`for`** repetition structure.

The definition of **`square`** shows that **`square`** expects an integer parameter **`y`**. The keyword **`int`** preceding the function name indicates that **`square`** returns an integer result. The **`return`** statement in **`square`** passes the result of the calculation back to the calling function.

```
// A programmer-defined square function

#include <iostream.h>

int square(int);    // function prototype

main()
{
   for (int x = 1; x <= 10; x++)
      cout << square(x) << "  ";

   cout << endl;

   return 0;
}

// Function definition
int square(int y)
{
   return y * y;
}
```

```
 1  4  9  16  25  36  49  64  81  100
```

**Fig. 3.3** Using a programmer-defined function.

The line

```
int square(int);
```

is a *function prototype*. The data type **int** in parentheses informs the compiler that function **square** expects an integer value from the caller. The data type **int** to the left of the function name **square** informs the compiler that **square** returns an integer result to the caller. The compiler refers to the function prototype to check that calls to **square** contain the correct return type, the correct number of arguments, the correct argument types, and that the arguments are in the correct order. Function prototypes are discussed in detail in Section 3.6.

The format of a function definition is

```
return-value-type  function-name(parameter-list)
{
   declarations  and  statements
}
```

The *function-name* is any valid identifier. The *return-value-type* is the data type of the result returned from the function to the caller. The return-value-type **void** indicates that a function does not return a value. An unspecified return-value-type is assumed by the compiler to be **int**.

***Common Programming Error 3.2***

*Omitting the return-value-type in a function definition causes a syntax error if the function prototype specifies a return type other than* `int`.

***Common Programming Error 3.3***

*Forgetting to return a value from a function that is supposed to return a value can lead to unexpected errors. The C++ language specification states that the result of this omission is undefined. C++ compilers will generally issue a warning message.*

***Common Programming Error 3.4***

*Returning a value from a function whose return type has been declared* `void` *causes a syntax error.*

***Good Programming Practice 3.4***

*Even though an omitted return type defaults to* `int`, *always state the return type explicitly. The return type for* `main`, *however, is normally omitted.*

The *parameter-list* is a comma-separated list containing the declarations of the parameters received by the function when it is called. If a function does not receive any values, *parameter-list* is `void`. A type must be listed explicitly for each parameter in the parameter list of a function.

***Common Programming Error 3.5***

*Declaring function parameters of the same type as* `float x, y` *instead of* `float x, float y`. *The parameter declaration* `float x, y` *would actually report a compilation error because types are required for each parameter in the parameter list.*

***Common Programming Error 3.6***

*Placing a semicolon after the right parenthesis enclosing the parameter list of a function definition is a syntax error.*

***Common Programming Error 3.7***

*Defining a function parameter again as a local variable in the function is a syntax error.*

***Good Programming Practice 3.5***

*Although it is not incorrect to do so, do not use the same names for the arguments passed to a function and the corresponding parameters in the function definition. This helps avoid ambiguity.*

The *declarations* and *statements* within braces form the *function body.* The function body is also referred to as a *block.* A block is simply a compound statement that includes declarations. Variables can be declared in any block, and blocks can be nested. *A function cannot be defined inside another function under any circumstances.*

***Common Programming Error 3.8***

*Defining a function inside another function is a syntax error.*

***Good Programming Practice 3.6***

*Choosing meaningful function names and meaningful parameter names makes programs more readable and helps avoid excessive use of comments.*

***Software Engineering Observation 3.5***

*A function should usually be no longer than one page. Better yet, a function should usually be no longer than half a page. Regardless of how long a function is, it should perform one task well. Small functions promote software reusability.*

***Software Engineering Observation 3.6***

*Programs should be written as collections of small functions. This makes programs easier to write, debug, maintain and modify.*

***Software Engineering Observation 3.7***

*A function requiring a large number of parameters may be performing too many tasks. Consider dividing the function into smaller functions that perform the separate tasks. The function header should fit on one line if possible.*

***Software Engineering Observation 3.8***

*The function prototype, function header, and function calls should all agree in the number, type, and order of arguments and parameters, and in the type of return value.*

There are three ways to return control to the point at which a function was invoked. If the function does not return a result, control is returned simply when the function-ending right brace is reached, or by executing the statement

```
return;
```

If the function does return a result, the statement

```
return expression;
```

returns the value of *expression* to the caller.

Our second example uses a programmer-defined function **maximum** to determine and return the largest of three integers (Fig. 3.4). The three integers are input. Next, the integers are passed to **maximum** which determines the largest integer. This value is returned to main by the **return** statement in **maximum**. The value returned is assigned to the variable **largest** which is then printed.

## 3.6 Function Prototypes

One of the most important features of C++ is the *function prototype.* A function prototype tells the compiler the type of data returned by the function, the number of parameters the function expects to receive, the types of the parameters, and the order in which these parameters are expected. The compiler uses function prototypes to validate function calls. Early versions of C did not perform this kind of checking, so it was possible to call func-

```
// Finding the maximum of three integers
#include <iostream.h>

int maximum(int, int, int);    // function prototype

main()
{
   int a, b, c;

   cout << "Enter three integers: ";
   cin >> a >> b >> c;
   cout << "Maximum is: " << maximum(a, b, c) << endl;

   return 0;
}

// Function maximum definition
int maximum(int x, int y, int z)
{
   int max = x;

   if (y > max)
      max = y;

   if (z > max)
      max = z;

   return max;
}
```

```
Enter three integers: 22 85 17
Maximum is: 85
```

```
Enter three integers: 92 35 14
Maximum is: 92
```

```
Enter three integers: 45 19 98
Maximum is: 98
```

**Fig. 3.4** Programmer-defined `maximum` function.

tions improperly without the compiler detecting the errors. Such calls could result in fatal execution-time errors or nonfatal errors that caused subtle, difficult to detect logic errors. Function prototypes correct this deficiency.

***Software Engineering Observation 3.9***

*Function prototypes are required in C++. Use* **#include** *preprocessor directives to obtain function prototypes for the standard library functions from the header files for the appropriate libraries. Also use* **#include** *to obtain header files containing function prototypes used by you and/or your group members.*

The function prototype for **maximum** in Fig. 3.4 is

```
int maximum(int, int, int);
```

This prototype states that **maximum** takes three arguments of type **int**, and returns a result of type **int**. Notice that the function prototype is the same as the header of the function definition of **maximum** except the names of the parameters (**x**, **y**, and **z**) are not included.

***Good Programming Practice 3.7***

*Parameter names can be included in function prototypes for documentation purposes. The compiler ignores these names.*

***Common Programming Error 3.9***

*Forgetting the semicolon at the end of a function prototype causes a syntax error.*

A function call that does not match the function prototype causes a syntax error. A syntax error is also generated if the function prototype and the function definition disagree. For example, in Fig. 3.4, if the function prototype had been written

```
void maximum(int, int, int);
```

the compiler would report an error because the **void** return type in the function prototype would differ from the **int** return type in the function header.

Another important feature of function prototypes is the *coercion of arguments,* i.e., the forcing of arguments to the appropriate type. For example, the math library function **sqrt** can be called with an integer argument even though the function prototype in **math.h** specifies a **double** argument, and the function will still work correctly. The statement

```
cout << sqrt(4);
```

correctly evaluates **sqrt(4)**, and prints the value **2**. The function prototype causes the compiler to convert the integer value **4** to the **double** value **4.0** before the value is passed to **sqrt**. In general, argument values that do not correspond precisely to the parameter types in the function prototype are converted to the proper type before the function is called. These conversions can lead to incorrect results if C++'s *promotion rules* are not followed. The promotion rules specify how types can be converted to other types without losing data. In our **sqrt** example above, an **int** is automatically converted to a **double** without changing its value. However, a **double** converted to an **int** truncates the fractional part of the **double** value. Converting large integer types to small integer types (e.g., **long** to **short**) may also result in changed values.

The promotion rules apply to expressions containing values of two or more data types; such expressions are also referred to as *mixed-type expressions*. The type of each value in a mixed-type expression is promoted to the "highest" type in the expression (actually a temporary version of each value is created and used for the expression—the original values remain unchanged). Figure 3.5 lists the built-in data types in order from highest type to lowest type.

Converting values to lower types can result in incorrect values. Therefore, a value can only be converted to a lower type by explicitly assigning the value to a variable of lower type, or by using a cast operator. Function argument values are converted to the parameter types in a function prototype as if they are being assigned directly to variables of those types. If our **`square`** function that uses an integer parameter (Fig. 3.3) is called with a floating-point argument, the argument is converted to **`int`** (a lower type), and **`square`** usually returns an incorrect value. For example, **`square(4.5)`** would return **`16`** not **`20.25`**.

***Common Programming Error 3.10***

*Converting from a higher data type in the promotion hierarchy to a lower type can change the data value.*

***Common Programming Error 3.11***

*Forgetting a function prototype when a function is not defined before it is first invoked causes a syntax error.*

***Software Engineering Observation 3.10***

*A function prototype placed outside any function definition applies to all calls to the function appearing after the function prototype in the file. A function prototype placed in a function applies only to calls made in that function.*

| Data types | |
|---|---|
| `long double` | |
| `double` | |
| `float` | |
| `unsigned long int` | (synonymous with `unsigned long`) |
| `long int` | (synonymous with `long`) |
| `unsigned int` | (synonymous with `unsigned`) |
| `int` | |
| `unsigned short int` | (synonymous with `unsigned short`) |
| `short int` | (synonymous with `short`) |
| `unsigned char` | |
| `char` | |

**Fig. 3.5** Promotion hierarchy for built-in data types.

## 3.7 Header Files

Each standard library has a corresponding *header file* containing the function prototypes for all the functions in that library and definitions of various data types and constants needed by those functions. Figure 3.6 lists alphabetically the ANSI/ISO C standard library header files that may be included in C++ programs. The term "macros" that is used several times in Fig. 3.6 is discussed in detail in Chapter 17, "Preprocessor." We will discuss various C++ specific header files later in the book.

| Standard library header file | Explanation |
|---|---|
| `<assert.h>` | Contains macros and information for adding diagnostics that aid program debugging. |
| `<ctype.h>` | Contains function prototypes for functions that test characters for certain properties, and function prototypes for functions that can be used to convert lowercase letters to uppercase letters and vice versa. |
| `<errno.h>` | Defines macros that are useful for reporting error conditions. |
| `<float.h>` | Contains the floating point size limits of the system. |
| `<limits.h>` | Contains the integral size limits of the system. |
| `<locale.h>` | Contains function prototypes and other information that enables a program to be modified for the current locale on which it is running. The notion of locale enables the computer system to handle different conventions for expressing data like dates, times, dollar amounts, and large numbers in different areas throughout the world. |
| `<math.h>` | Contains function prototypes for math library functions. |
| `<setjmp.h>` | Contains function prototypes for functions that allow bypassing of the usual function call and return sequence. |
| `<signal.h>` | Contains function prototypes and macros to handle various conditions that may arise during program execution. |
| `<stdarg.h>` | Defines macros for dealing with a list of arguments to a function whose number and types are unknown. |
| `<stddef.h>` | Contains definitions of types used for performing certain calculations. |
| `<stdio.h>` | Contains function prototypes for the standard input/output library functions, and information used by them. |
| `<stdlib.h>` | Contains function prototypes for conversions of numbers to text and text to numbers, memory allocation, random numbers, and other utility functions. |
| `<string.h>` | Contains function prototypes for string processing functions. |
| `<time.h>` | Contains function prototypes and types for manipulating the time and date. |

**Fig. 3.6** The standard library header files.

The programmer can create custom header files. Programmer-defined header files should also end in **.h**. A programmer-defined header file can be included by using the **#include** preprocessor directive. For example, the header file **square.h** can be included in our program by the directive

```
#include "square.h"
```

at the top of the program. Section 17.2 presents additional information on including header files.

## 3.8 Random Number Generation

We now take a brief and, it is hoped, entertaining diversion into a popular programming application, namely simulation and game playing. In this section and the next section, we will develop a nicely structured game-playing program that includes multiple functions. The program uses most of the control structures we have studied.

There is something in the air of a gambling casino that invigorates every type of person from the high-rollers at the plush mahogany-and-felt craps tables to the quarter-poppers at the one-armed bandits. It is the *element of chance,* the possibility that luck will convert a pocketful of money into a mountain of wealth. The element of chance can be introduced into computer applications by using the **rand** function in the C standard library.

Consider the following statement:

```
i = rand();
```

The **rand** function generates an integer between 0 and **RAND_MAX** (a symbolic constant defined in the **<stdlib.h>** header file). The value of **RAND_MAX** must be at least 32767—the maximum positive value for a two-byte (i.e., 16-bit) integer. The programs in this section were tested on a system with a maximum value of 32767 for **RAND_MAX**. If **rand** truly produces integers at random, every number between 0 and **RAND_MAX** has an equal *chance* (or *probability*) of being chosen each time **rand** is called.

The range of values produced directly by **rand** is often different than what is needed in a specific application. For example, a program that simulates coin tossing might require only 0 for "heads" and 1 for "tails." A program that simulates rolling a six-sided die would require random integers in range 1 to 6. A program that randomly predicts the next type of spaceship (out of four possibilities) that will fly across the horizon in a video game would require random integers in the range 1 through 4.

To demonstrate **rand**, let us develop a program to simulate 20 rolls of a six-sided die and print the value of each roll. The function prototype for the **rand** function can be found in **<stdlib.h>**. We use the modulus operator (**%**) in conjunction with **rand** as follows

```
rand() % 6
```

to produce integers in the range 0 to 5. This is called *scaling*. The number 6 is called the *scaling factor.* We then *shift* the range of numbers produced by adding 1 to our previous result. Figure 3.7 confirms that the results are in the range 1 to 6.

```
// Shifted, scaled integers produced by 1 + rand() % 6
#include <iostream.h>
#include <iomanip.h>
#include <stdlib.h>

main()
{
   for (int i = 1; i <= 20; i++) {
      cout << setw(10) << 1 + rand() % 6;

      if (i % 5 == 0)
         cout << endl;
   }

   return 0;
}
```

```
         5         5         3         5         5
         2         4         2         5         5
         5         3         2         2         1
         5         1         4         6         4
```

**Fig. 3.7** Shifted, scaled integers produced by `1 + rand() % 6`.

To show that these numbers occur approximately with equal likelihood, let us simulate 6000 rolls of a die with the program of Fig. 3.8. Each integer from 1 to 6 should appear approximately 1000 times.

As the program output shows, by scaling and shifting we have utilized the **rand** function to realistically simulate the rolling of a six-sided die. Note that *no* **default** case is provided in the **switch** structure. After we study arrays in Chapter 4, we will show how to replace the entire **switch** structure elegantly with a single-line statement.

Executing the program of Fig. 3.7 again produces

```
         5         5         3         5         5
         2         4         2         5         5
         5         3         2         2         1
         5         1         4         6         4
```

Notice that exactly the same sequence of values was printed. How can these be random numbers? Ironically, this repeatability is an important characteristic of the **rand** function. When debugging a program, this repeatability is essential for proving that corrections to a program work properly.

The **rand** function actually generates *pseudo-random numbers*. Calling **rand** repeatedly produces a sequence of numbers that appears to be random. However, the sequence repeats itself each time the program is executed. Once a program has been thoroughly debugged, it can be conditioned to produce a different sequence of random num-

```
// Roll a six-sided die 6000 times
#include <iostream.h>
#include <iomanip.h>
#include <stdlib.h>

main()
{
   int frequency1 = 0, frequency2 = 0,
       frequency3 = 0, frequency4 = 0,
       frequency5 = 0, frequency6 = 0;

   for (int roll = 1; roll <= 6000; roll++) {
      int face = 1 + rand() % 6;

      switch (face) {
         case 1:
            ++frequency1;
            break;
         case 2:
            ++frequency2;
            break;
         case 3:
            ++frequency3;
            break;
         case 4:
            ++frequency4;
            break;
         case 5:
            ++frequency5;
            break;
         case 6:
            ++frequency6;
            break;
      }
   }

   cout << "Face" << setw(13) << "Frequency"
        << endl << "   1" << setw(13) << frequency1
        << endl << "   2" << setw(13) << frequency2
        << endl << "   3" << setw(13) << frequency3
        << endl << "   4" << setw(13) << frequency4
        << endl << "   5" << setw(13) << frequency5
        << endl << "   6" << setw(13) << frequency6 << endl;

   return 0;
}
```

**Fig. 3.8** Rolling a six-sided die 6000 times (part 1 of 2).

bers for each execution. This is called *randomizing,* and is accomplished with the standard library function **srand**. The **srand** function takes an **unsigned** integer argument and *seeds* the **rand** function to produce a different sequence of random numbers for each execution of the program.

```
Face    Frequency
   1          987
   2          984
   3         1029
   4          974
   5         1004
   6         1022
```

**Fig. 3.8** Rolling a six-sided die 6000 times (part 2 of 2).

The use of **srand** is demonstrated in Fig. 3.9. In the program, we use the data type **unsigned** which is short for **unsigned int**. An **int** is stored in at least two bytes of memory and can have positive and negative values. A variable of type **unsigned int** is also stored in at least two bytes of memory. A two-byte **unsigned int** can have only positive values in the range 0 to 65535. A four-byte **unsigned int** can have only positive values in the range 0 to 4294967295. The **srand** function takes an **unsigned int** value as an argument. The function prototype for the **srand** function is found in the header file **<stdlib.h>**.

Let us run the program several times and observe the results. Notice that a *different* sequence of random numbers is obtained each time the program is run provided that a different seed is supplied.

```
// Randomizing die-rolling program

#include <iostream.h>
#include <iomanip.h>
#include <stdlib.h>

main()
{
   unsigned seed;

   cout << "Enter seed: ";
   cin >> seed;
   srand(seed);

   for (int i = 1; i <= 10; i++) {
      cout << setw(10) << 1 + rand() % 6;

      if (i % 5 == 0)
         cout << endl;
   }

   return 0;
}
```

**Fig. 3.9** Randomizing the die-rolling program (part 1 of 2).

```
Enter seed: 67
           1           6           5           1           4
           5           6           3           1           2
```

```
Enter seed: 432
           4           2           6           4           3
           2           5           1           4           4
```

```
Enter seed: 67
           1           6           5           1           4
           5           6           3           1           2
```

**Fig. 3.9** Randomizing the die-rolling program (part 2 of 2).

If we wish to randomize without the need for entering a seed each time, we may use a statement like

```
srand(time(NULL));
```

This causes the computer to read its clock to obtain the value for the seed automatically. The **time** function (with the argument **NULL** as written in the preceding statement) returns the current "calendar time" in seconds. This value is converted to an unsigned integer and used as the seed to the random number generator. The function prototype for **time** is in **<time.h>**.

The values produced directly by **rand** are always in the range:

```
0 ≤ rand() ≤ RAND_MAX
```

Previously we demonstrated how to write a single statement to simulate the rolling of a six-sided die with the statement:

```
face = 1 + rand() % 6;
```

which always assigns an integer (at random) to variable **face** in the range 1 ≤ **face** ≤ 6. Note that the width of this range (i.e., the number of consecutive integers in the range) is 6 and the starting number in the range is 1. Referring to the preceding statement, we see that the width of the range is determined by the number used to scale **rand** with the modulus operator (i.e., 6), and the starting number of the range is equal to the number (i.e., 1) that is added to **rand % 6**. We can generalize this result as follows

```
n = a + rand() % b;
```

where **a** is the *shifting value* (which is equal to the first number in the desired range of consecutive integers), and **b** is the scaling factor (which is equal to the width of the desired range of consecutive integers). In the exercises, we will see that it is possible to choose integers at random from sets of values other than ranges of consecutive integers.

***Common Programming Error 3.12***

*Using **`srand`** in place of **`rand`** to generate random numbers.*

## 3.9 Example: A Game of Chance

One of the most popular games of chance is a dice game known as "craps," which is played in casinos and back alleys throughout the world. The rules of the game are straightforward:

> *A player rolls two dice. Each die has six faces. These faces contain 1, 2, 3, 4, 5, and 6 spots. After the dice have come to rest, the sum of the spots on the two upward faces is calculated. If the sum is 7 or 11 on the first throw, the player wins. If the sum is 2, 3, or 12 on the first throw (called "craps"), the player loses (i.e., the "house" wins). If the sum is 4, 5, 6, 8, 9, or 10 on the first throw, then that sum becomes the player's "point." To win, you must continue rolling the dice until you "make your point." The player loses by rolling a 7 before making the point.*

The program in Fig. 3.10 simulates the game of craps. Figure 3.11 shows several sample executions.

Notice that the player must roll two dice on the first roll, and must do so later on all subsequent rolls. We define a function **`rollDice`** to roll the dice and compute and print their sum. Function **`rollDice`** is defined once, but it is called from two places in the program. Interestingly, **`rollDice`** takes no arguments, so we have indicated **`void`** in the parameter list. The function **`rollDice`** does return the sum of the two dice, so a return type of **`int`** is indicated in the function header.

The game is reasonably involved. The player may win or lose on the first roll, or may win or lose on any subsequent roll. The variable **`gameStatus`** is used to keep track of this. Variable **`gameStatus`** is declared to be of a type called **`Status`**. The line

```
enum Status { CONTINUE, WON, LOST };
```

creates a *user-defined type* called an *enumeration.* An enumeration, introduced by the keyword **`enum`** and followed by a *type name* (in this case, **`Status`**), is a set of integer constants represented by identifiers. The values of these *enumeration constants* start at **`0`**, unless specified otherwise, and are incremented by **`1`**. In the preceding enumeration, **`CONTINUE`** is assigned the value 0, **`WON`** is assigned the value 1 and **`LOST`** is assigned the value 2. The identifiers in an **`enum`** must be unique, but separate enumeration constants can have the same integer value.

***Good Programming Practice 3.8***

*Capitalize the first letter of an identifier used as a user-defined type name.*

Variables of user-defined type **`Status`** can only be assigned one of the three values declared in the enumeration. When the game is won, **`gameStatus`** is set to **`WON`**. When the game is lost, **`gameStatus`** is set to **`LOST`**. Otherwise, **`gameStatus`** is set to **`CONTINUE`** so the dice can be rolled again.

```
// Craps
#include <iostream.h>
#include <stdlib.h>
#include <time.h>

int rollDice(void);

main()
{
   enum Status { CONTINUE, WON, LOST };
   int sum, myPoint;
   Status gameStatus;

   srand(time(NULL));
   sum = rollDice();              // first roll of the dice

   switch(sum) {
      case 7: case 11:            // win on first roll
         gameStatus = WON;
         break;
      case 2: case 3: case 12:    // lose on first roll
         gameStatus = LOST;
         break;
      default:                    // remember point
         gameStatus = CONTINUE;
         myPoint = sum;
         cout << "Point is " << myPoint << endl;
         break;
   }

   while (gameStatus == CONTINUE) {    // keep rolling
      sum = rollDice();

      if (sum == myPoint)         // win by making point
         gameStatus = WON;
      else
         if (sum == 7)            // lose by rolling 7
            gameStatus = LOST;
   }

   if (gameStatus == WON)
      cout << "Player wins" << endl;
   else
      cout << "Player loses" << endl;

   return 0;
}
```

**Fig. 3.10** Program to simulate the game of craps (part 1 of 2).

***Common Programming Error 3.13***

*Assigning the integer equivalent of an enumeration constant to a variable of the enumeration type reports a warning from the compiler.*

```
int rollDice(void)
{
   int die1, die2, workSum;

   die1 = 1 + rand() % 6;
   die2 = 1 + rand() % 6;
   workSum = die1 + die2;
   cout << "Player rolled " << die1 << " + " << die2
        << " = " << workSum << endl;

   return workSum;
}
```

**Fig. 3.10** Program to simulate the game of craps (part 2 of 2).

```
Player rolled 6 + 5 = 11
Player wins
```

```
Player rolled 6 + 6 = 12
Player loses
```

```
Player rolled 4 + 6 = 10
Point is 10
Player rolled 2 + 4 = 6
Player rolled 6 + 5 = 11
Player rolled 3 + 3 = 6
Player rolled 6 + 4 = 10
Player wins
```

```
Player rolled 1 + 3 = 4
Point is 4
Player rolled 1 + 4 = 5
Player rolled 5 + 4 = 9
Player rolled 4 + 6 = 10
Player rolled 6 + 3 = 9
Player rolled 1 + 2 = 3
Player rolled 5 + 2 = 7
Player loses
```

**Fig. 3.11** Sample runs for the game of craps.

Another popular enumeration is

```
enum Months {JAN = 1, FEB, MAR, APR, MAY, JUN, JUL, AUG,
             SEP, OCT, NOV, DEC};
```

which creates user-defined type **Months** with enumeration constants representing the months of the year. Because the first value in the preceding enumeration is explicitly set to **1**, the remaining values are incremented from **1** resulting in the values **1** through **12**. Any enumeration constant can be assigned an integer value in the enumeration definition.

***Common Programming Error 3.14***

*After an enumeration constant has been defined, attempting to assign another value to the enumeration constant is a syntax error.*

***Good Programming Practice 3.9***

*Use only uppercase letters in the names of enumeration constants. This makes these constants stand out in a program and reminds the programmer that enumeration constants are not variables.*

***Good Programming Practice 3.10***

*Using enumerations rather than integer constants makes programs more readable.*

After the first roll, if the game is won, the **while** structure is skipped because **gameStatus** is not equal to **CONTINUE**. The program proceeds to the **if/else** structure which prints "**Player wins**" if **gameStatus** is equal to **WON** and "**Player loses**" if **gameStatus** is equal to **LOST**.

After the first roll, if the game is not over, **sum** is saved in **myPoint**. Execution proceeds with the **while** structure because **gameStatus** is equal to **CONTINUE**. Each time through the **while**, **rollDice** is called to produce a new **sum**. If **sum** matches **myPoint**, **gameStatus** is set to **WON**, the **while**-test fails, the **if/else** structure prints "**Player wins**" and execution terminates. If **sum** is equal to **7**, **gameStatus** is set to **LOST**, the **while**-test fails, the **if/else** statement prints "**Player loses**" and execution terminates.

Note the interesting use of the various program control mechanisms we have discussed. The craps program uses two functions—**main** and **rollDice**—and the **switch**, **while**, **if/else**, and nested **if** structures. In the exercises, we investigate various interesting characteristics of the game of craps.

## 3.10 Storage Classes

In Chapters 1 through 3, we have used identifiers for variable names. The attributes of variables include name, type, size, and value. In this chapter, we also use identifiers as names for user-defined functions. Actually, each identifier in a program has other attributes including *storage class*, *scope* and *linkage*.

C++ provides four *storage class specifiers:* ***auto***, ***register***, ***extern***, and ***static***. An identifier's storage class specifier helps determine its storage class, scope, and linkage.

An identifier's *storage class* determines the period during which that identifier exists in memory. Some identifiers exist briefly, some are repeatedly created and destroyed, and others exist for the entire execution of a program.

An identifier's *scope* is where the identifier can be referenced in a program. Some identifiers can be referenced throughout a program, while others can be referenced from only limited portions of a program.

An identifier's *linkage* determines for a multiple-source-file program (a topic we will begin investigating in Chapter 6) whether an identifier is known only in the current source file or in any source file with proper declarations.

This section discusses the four storage class specifiers and the two storage classes. Section 3.11 discusses the scope of identifiers.

The storage class specifiers can be split into two storage classes: *automatic storage class* and *static storage class*. The **auto** and **register** keywords are used to declare variables of the automatic storage class. Such variables are created when the block in which they are declared is entered, they exist while the block is active, and they are destroyed when the block is exited.

Only variables can be of automatic storage class. A function's local variables and parameters normally are of automatic storage class. The storage class specifier **auto** explicitly declares variables of automatic storage class. For example, the following declaration indicates that **float** variables **x** and **y** are local variables of automatic storage class, i.e., they exist only in the body of the function in which the declaration appears:

```
auto float x, y;
```

Local variables are of automatic storage class by default, so the **auto** keyword is rarely used. For the remainder of the text, we will refer to variables of automatic storage class simply as automatic variables.

***Performance Tip 3.1***

*Automatic storage is a means of conserving memory because automatic storage class variables are created when the block in which they are declared is entered and are destroyed when the block is exited.*

***Software Engineering Observation 3.11***

*Automatic storage is yet another example of the principle of least privilege. Why have variables stored in memory and accessible when they are not needed?*

Data in the machine language version of a program are normally loaded into registers for calculations and other processing.

***Performance Tip 3.2***

*The storage class specifier* **register** *can be placed before an automatic variable declaration to suggest that the compiler maintain the variable in one of the computer's high-speed hardware registers rather than in memory. If intensely used variables such as counters or totals can be maintained in hardware registers, the overhead of repeatedly loading the variables from memory into the registers and storing the results back into memory can be eliminated.*

***Common Programming Error 3.15***

*Using multiple storage class specifiers for an identifier. Only one storage class specifier can be applied to an identifier. For example, if you include* `register`*, do not also include* `auto`*.*

The compiler may ignore `register` declarations. For example, there may not be a sufficient number of registers available for the compiler to use. The following declaration *suggests* that the integer variable `counter` be placed in one of the computer's registers; regardless of whether the compiler does this, `counter` is initialized to 1:

```
register int counter = 1;
```

The `register` keyword can be used only with local variables and function parameters.

***Performance Tip 3.3***

*Often,* `register` *declarations are unnecessary. Today's optimizing compilers are capable of recognizing frequently used variables and can decide to place them in registers without the need for a* `register` *declaration from the programmer.*

The keywords `extern` and `static` are used to declare identifiers for variables and functions of the static storage class. Such variables exist from the point at which the program begins execution. For variables, storage is allocated and initialized once when the program begins execution. For functions, the name of the function exists when the program begins execution. However, even though the variables and the function names exist from the start of program execution, this does not mean that the these identifiers can be used throughout the program. Storage class and scope (where a name can be used) are separate issues as we will see in Section 3.11.

There are two types of identifiers with static storage class: external identifiers (such as global variables and function names) and local variables declared with the storage class specifier `static`. Global variables and function names default to storage class specifier `extern`. Global variables are created by placing variable declarations outside any function definition. Global variables retain their values throughout the execution of the program. Global variables and functions can be referenced by any function that follows their declarations or definitions in the file.

***Software Engineering Observation 3.12***

*Declaring a variable as global rather than local allows unintended side effects to occur when a function that does not need access to the variable accidentally or maliciously modifies it. In general, use of global variables should be avoided except in certain situations with unique performance requirements (as discussed in Chapter 18).*

***Good Programming Practice 3.11***

*Variables used only in a particular function should be declared as local variables in that function rather than as global variables.*

Local variables declared with the keyword `static` are still known only in the function in which they are defined, but unlike automatic variables, `static` local variables retain their value when the function is exited. The next time the function is called, the

**static** local variable contains the value it had when the function last exited. The following statement declares local variable **count** to be **static** and to be initialized to 1.

```
static int count = 1;
```

All numeric variables of the static storage class are initialized to zero if they are not explicitly initialized by the programmer. (Static pointer variables, discussed in Chapter 5, are also initialized to zero.)

The storage class specifiers **extern** and **static** have special meaning when they are explicitly applied to external identifiers. In Chapter 18, "Other Topics," we discuss the explicit use of **extern** and **static** with external identifiers and multiple-source-file programs.

## 3.11 Scope Rules

The *scope* of an identifier is the portion of the program in which the identifier can be referenced. For example, when we declare a local variable in a block, it can be referenced only in that block or in blocks nested within that block. The four scopes for an identifier are *function scope, file scope, block scope,* and *function-prototype scope.*

An identifier declared outside any function has *file scope*. Such an identifier is "known" in all functions from the point at which the identifier is declared until the end of the file. Global variables, function definitions, and function prototypes placed outside a function all have file scope.

Labels (an identifier followed by a colon such as **start:**) are the only identifiers with *function scope.* Labels can be used anywhere in the function in which they appear, but cannot be referenced outside the function body. Labels are used in **switch** structures (as **case** labels) and in **goto** statements (see Chapter 18, "Other Topics"). Labels are implementation details that functions hide from one another. This hiding—more formally called *information hiding*—is one of the most fundamental principles of good software engineering.

Identifiers declared inside a block have *block scope.* Block scope begins at the identifier's declaration and ends at the terminating right brace (**}**) of the block. Local variables declared at the beginning of a function have block scope as do function parameters, which are also local variables of the function. Any block may contain variable declarations. When blocks are nested, and an identifier in an outer block has the same name as an identifier in an inner block, the identifier in the outer block is "hidden" until the inner block terminates. This means that while executing in the inner block, the inner block sees the value of its own local identifier and not the value of the identically named identifier in the enclosing block. Local variables declared **static** still have block scope even though they exist from the time the program begins execution. Thus, storage duration does not affect the scope of an identifier.

The only identifiers with *function-prototype scope* are those used in the parameter list of a function prototype. As mentioned previously, function prototypes do not require names in the parameter list—only types are required. If a name is used in the parameter list of a function prototype, the compiler ignores the name. Identifiers used in a function prototype can be reused elsewhere in the program without ambiguity.

***Common Programming Error 3.16***

*Accidentally using the same name for an identifier in an inner block as is used for an identifier in an outer block, when in fact, the programmer wants the identifier in the outer block to be active for the duration of the inner block.*

***Good Programming Practice 3.12***

*Avoid variable names that hide names in outer scopes. This can be accomplished by avoiding the use of duplicate identifiers in a program.*

The program of Fig. 3.12 demonstrates scoping issues with global variables, automatic local variables, and **static** local variables.

```
// A scoping example

#include <iostream.h>

void a(void);    // function prototype
void b(void);    // function prototype
void c(void);    // function prototype

int x = 1;       // global variable

main()
{
   int x = 5;    // local variable to main

   cout << "local x in outer scope of main is " << x << endl;

   {             // start new scope
      int x = 7;

      cout << "local x in inner scope of main is " << x << endl;
   }             // end new scope

   cout << "local x in outer scope of main is " << x << endl;

   a();          // a has automatic local x
   b();          // b has static local x
   c();          // c uses global x
   a();          // a reinitializes automatic local x
   b();          // static local x retains its previous value
   c();          // global x also retains its value

   cout << "local x in main is " << x << endl;

   return 0;
}
```

**Fig. 3.12** A scoping example (part 1 of 2).

```
void a(void)
{
   int x = 25;  // initialized each time a is called

   cout << endl << "local x in a is " << x
        << " after entering a" << endl;
   ++x;
   cout << "local x in a is " << x
        << " before exiting a" << endl;
}

void b(void)
{
    static int x = 50;   // Static initialization only
                         // first time b is called.
    cout << endl << "local static x is " << x
         << " on entering b" << endl;
    ++x;
    cout << "local static x is " << x
         << " on exiting b" << endl;
}
void c(void)
{
   cout << endl << "global x is " << x
        << " on entering c" << endl;
   x *= 10;
   cout << "global x is " << x << " on exiting c" << endl;
}
```

```
local x in outer scope of main is 5
local x in inner scope of main is 7
local x in outer scope of main is 5

local x in a is 25 after entering a
local x in a is 26 before exiting a

local static x is 50 on entering b
local static x is 51 on exiting b

global x is 1 on entering c
global x is 10 on exiting c

local x in a is 25 after entering a
local x in a is 26 before exiting a

local static x is 51 on entering b
local static x is 52 on exiting b

global x is 10 on entering c
global x is 100 on exiting c
local x in main is 5
```

**Fig. 3.12** A scoping example (part 2 of 2).

A global variable **x** is declared and initialized to 1. This global variable is hidden in any block (or function) in which a variable named **x** is declared. In **main**, a local variable **x** is declared and initialized to 5. This variable is printed to show that the global **x** is hidden in **main**. Next, a new block is defined in **main** with another local variable **x** initialized to 7. This variable is printed to show that it hides **x** in the outer block of **main**. The variable **x** with value 7 is automatically destroyed when the block is exited, and the local variable **x** in the outer block of **main** is printed to show that it is no longer hidden. The program defines three functions—each takes no arguments and returns nothing. Function **a** defines automatic variable **x** and initializes it to 25. When **a** is called, the variable is printed, incremented, and printed again before exiting the function. Each time this function is called, automatic variable **x** is recreated and initialized to 25. Function **b** declares **static** variable **x** and initializes it to 50. Local variables declared as **static** retain their values even when they are out of scope. When **b** is called, **x** is printed, incremented, and printed again before exiting the function. In the next call to this function, **static** local variable **x** will contain the value 51. Function **c** does not declare any variables. Therefore, when it refers to variable **x**, the global **x** is used. When **c** is called, the global variable is printed, multiplied by 10, and printed again before exiting the function. The next time function **c** is called, the global variable has its modified value, 10. Finally, the program prints the local variable **x** in **main** again to show that none of the function calls modified the value of **x** because the functions all referred to variables in other scopes.

## 3.12 Recursion

The programs we have discussed are generally structured as functions that call one another in a disciplined, hierarchical manner. For some problems, it is useful to have functions call themselves. A *recursive function* is a function that calls itself either directly or indirectly through another function. Recursion is an important topic discussed at length in upper-level computer science courses. In this section and the next, simple examples of recursion are presented. This book contains an extensive treatment of recursion. Figure 3.17 (at the end of Section 3.14) summarizes the recursion examples and exercises in the book.

We consider recursion conceptually first, and then examine several programs containing recursive functions. Recursive problem solving approaches have a number of elements in common. A recursive function is called to solve a problem. The function actually knows how to solve only the simplest case(s), or so-called *base case(s)*. If the function is called with a base case, the function simply returns a result. If the function is called with a more complex problem, the function divides the problem into two conceptual pieces: a piece that the function knows how to do and a piece that the function does not know how to do. To make recursion feasible, the latter piece must resemble the original problem, but be a slightly simpler or slightly smaller version of the original problem. Because this new problem looks like the original problem, the function launches (calls) a fresh copy of itself to go to work on the smaller problem—this is referred to as a *recursive call* and is also called the *recursion step*. The recursion step also includes the keyword **return** because its result will be combined with the portion of the problem the function knew how to solve to form a result that will be passed back to the original caller, possibly **main**.

The recursion step executes while the original call to the function is still open, i.e., it has not yet finished executing. The recursion step can result in many more such recursive calls as the function keeps dividing each new subproblem the function is called with into two conceptual pieces. In order for the recursion to eventually terminate, each time the function calls itself with a slightly simpler version of the original problem, this sequence of smaller and smaller problems must eventually converge on the base case. At that point, the function recognizes the base case, returns a result to the previous copy of the function, and a sequence of returns ensues all the way up the line until the original call of the function eventually returns the final result to **main**. All of this sounds quite exotic compared to the kind of conventional problem solving we have been using to this point. As an example of these concepts at work, let us write a recursive program to perform a popular mathematical calculation.

The factorial of a nonnegative integer *n,* written *n!* (and pronounced "*n* factorial"), is the product

$$n \cdot (n - 1) \cdot (n - 2) \cdot \ldots \cdot 1$$

with 1! equal to 1, and 0! defined to be 1. For example, 5! is the product $5 \cdot 4 \cdot 3 \cdot 2 \cdot 1$, which is equal to 120.

The factorial of an integer, **number**, greater than or equal to 0, can be calculated *iteratively* (nonrecursively) using **for** as follows:

```
factorial = 1;
for (int counter = number; counter >= 1; counter--)
   factorial *= counter;
```

A recursive definition of the factorial function is arrived at by observing the following relationship:

$$n! = n \cdot (n - 1)!$$

For example, 5! is clearly equal to 5 * 4! as is shown by the following:

$$5! = 5 \cdot 4 \cdot 3 \cdot 2 \cdot 1$$
$$5! = 5 \cdot (4 \cdot 3 \cdot 2 \cdot 1)$$
$$5! = 5 \cdot (4!)$$

The evaluation of 5! would proceed as shown in Fig. 3.13. Figure 3.13a shows how the succession of recursive calls proceeds until 1! is evaluated to be 1, which terminates the recursion. Figure 3.13b shows the values returned from each recursive call to its caller until the final value is calculated and returned.

The program of Fig. 3.14 uses recursion to calculate and print the factorials of the integers 0 to 10 (the choice of the data type **unsigned long** will be explained momentarily). The recursive function **factorial** first tests to see if a terminating condition is true, i.e., is **number** less than or equal to 1. If **number** is indeed less than or equal to 1, **factorial** returns 1, no further recursion is necessary, and the program terminates. If **number** is greater than 1, the statement

```
return number * factorial(number - 1);
```

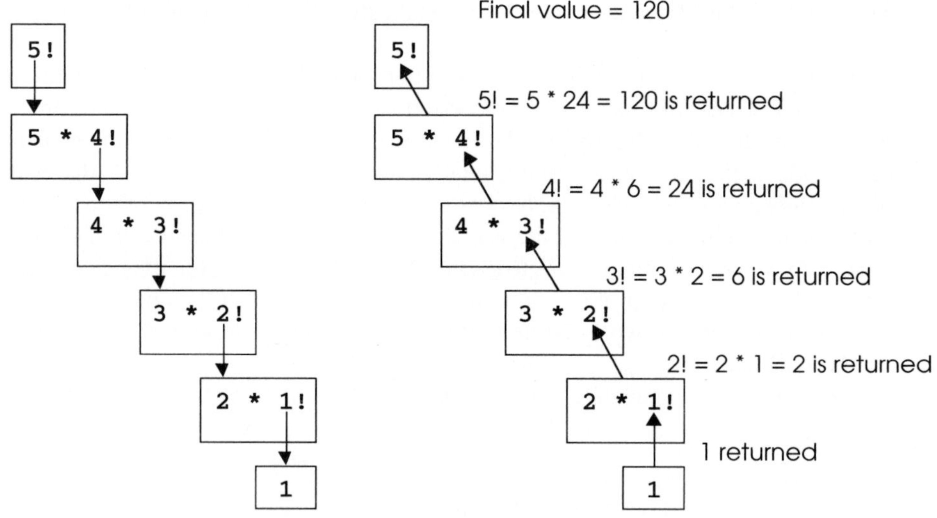


**Fig. 3.13** Recursive evaluation of 5!.

expresses the problem as the product of **`number`** and a recursive call to **`factorial`** evaluating the factorial of **`number - 1`**. Note that **`factorial(number - 1)`** is a slightly simpler problem than the original calculation **`factorial(number)`**.

Function **`factorial`** has been declared to receive a parameter of type **`unsigned long`** and return a result of type **`unsigned long`**. This is shorthand notation for **`unsigned long int`**. The C++ language specification requires that a variable of type **`unsigned long int`** is stored in at least 4 bytes (32 bits), and thus may hold a value at least in the range 0 to 4294967295. (The data type **`long int`** is also stored in at least 4 bytes and may hold a value at least in the range ±2147483647.) As can be seen in Fig. 3.14, factorial values become large quickly. We have chosen the data type **`unsigned long`** so the program can calculate factorials greater than 7! on computers with small (such as 2-byte) integers. Unfortunately, the **`factorial`** function produces large values so quickly that even **`unsigned long`** does not help us print many factorial values before the size of a **`unsigned long`** variable is exceeded.

As we explore in the exercises, **`float`** and **`double`** may ultimately be needed by the user desiring to calculate factorials of larger numbers. This points to a weakness in most programming languages, namely that the languages are not easily extended to handle the unique requirements of various applications. As we will see in the section of the book on object-oriented programming, C++ is an extensible language that allows us to create arbitrarily large integers if we wish.

***Common Programming Error 3.17***

*Forgetting to return a value from a recursive function when one is needed. Most compilers produce a warning message.*

```
// Recursive factorial function
#include <iostream.h>
#include <iomanip.h>

unsigned long factorial(unsigned long);

main()
{
   for (int i = 0; i <= 10; i++)
      cout << setw(2) << i << "! = " << factorial(i) << endl;

   return 0;
}

// Recursive definition of function factorial
unsigned long factorial(unsigned long number)
{
   if (number <= 1)
      return 1;
   else
      return number * factorial(number - 1);
}
```

```
 0! = 1
 1! = 1
 2! = 2
 3! = 6
 4! = 24
 5! = 120
 6! = 720
 7! = 5040
 8! = 40320
 9! = 362880
10! = 3628800
```

**Fig. 3.14** Calculating factorials with a recursive function.

***Common Programming Error 3.18***

*Either omitting the base case, or writing the recursion step incorrectly so that it does not converge on the base case, will cause infinite recursion, eventually exhausting memory. This is analogous to the problem of an infinite loop in an iterative (nonrecursive) solution. Infinite recursion can also be caused by providing an unexpected input.*

## 3.13 Example Using Recursion: The Fibonacci Series

The Fibonacci series

0, 1, 1, 2, 3, 5, 8, 13, 21, …

begins with 0 and 1 and has the property that each subsequent Fibonacci number is the sum of the previous two Fibonacci numbers.

The series occurs in nature and, in particular, describes a form of spiral. The ratio of successive Fibonacci numbers converges on a constant value of 1.618.... This number, too, repeatedly occurs in nature and has been called the *golden ratio* or the *golden mean.* Humans tend to find the golden mean aesthetically pleasing. Architects often design windows, rooms, and buildings whose length and width are in the ratio of the golden mean. Postcards are often designed with a golden mean length/width ratio.

The Fibonacci series may be defined recursively as follows:

$$fibonacci(0) = 0$$
$$fibonacci(1) = 1$$
$$fibonacci(n) = fibonacci(n-1) + fibonacci(n-2)$$

Figure 3.15 calculates the $i^{th}$ Fibonacci number recursively using function **fibonacci**. Notice that Fibonacci numbers tend to become large quickly. Therefore, we have chosen the data type **unsigned long** for the parameter type and the return type in function **fibonacci**. In Fig. 3.15, each pair of output lines shows a separate run of the program.

The call to **fibonacci** from **main** is not a recursive call, but all subsequent calls to **fibonacci** are recursive. Each time **fibonacci** is invoked, it immediately tests for the base case—**n** equal to 0 or 1. If this is true, **n** is returned. Interestingly, if **n** is greater than 1, the recursion step generates *two* recursive calls, each of which is for a slightly simpler problem than the original call to **fibonacci**. Figure 3.16 shows how function **fibonacci** would evaluate **fibonacci(3)**—we abbreviate **fibonacci** simply as **f** to make the figure more readable.

```
// Recursive fibonacci function
#include <iostream.h>

unsigned long fibonacci(unsigned long);

main()
{
   unsigned long result, number;

   cout << "Enter an integer: ";
   cin >> number;
   result = fibonacci(number);
   cout << "Fibonacci(" << number << ") = " << result << endl;
   return 0;
}

// Recursive definition of function fibonacci
unsigned long fibonacci(unsigned long n)
{
   if (n == 0 || n == 1)
      return n;
   else
      return fibonacci(n - 1) + fibonacci(n - 2);
}
```

**Fig. 3.15** Recursively generating Fibonacci numbers (part 1 of 2).

```
Enter an integer: 0
Fibonacci(0) = 0

Enter an integer: 1
Fibonacci(1) = 1

Enter an integer: 2
Fibonacci(2) = 1

Enter an integer: 3
Fibonacci(3) = 2

Enter an integer: 4
Fibonacci(4) = 3

Enter an integer: 5
Fibonacci(5) = 5

Enter an integer: 6
Fibonacci(6) = 8

Enter an integer: 10
Fibonacci(10) = 55

Enter an integer: 20
Fibonacci(20) = 6765

Enter an integer: 30
Fibonacci(30) = 832040

Enter an integer: 35
Fibonacci(35) = 9227465
```

**Fig. 3.15** Recursively generating Fibonacci numbers (part 2 of 2).

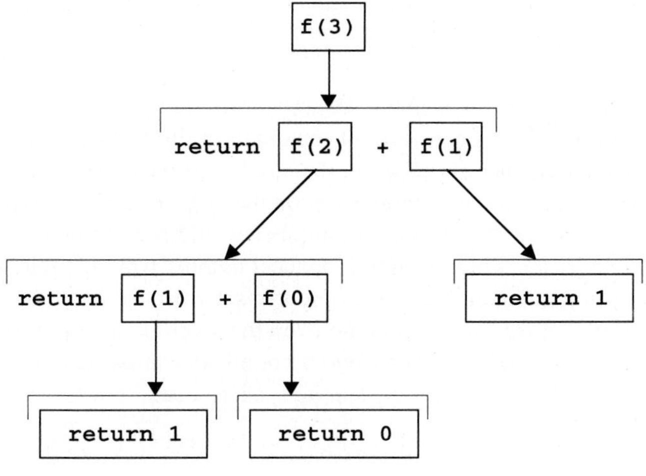


**Fig. 3.16** Set of recursive calls to function `fibonacci`.

This figure raises some interesting issues about the order in which C++ compilers will evaluate the operands of operators. This is a different issue from the order in which operators are applied to their operands, namely the order dictated by the rules of operator precedence. From Fig. 3.16 it appears that while evaluating `f(3)`, two recursive calls will be made, namely `f(2)` and `f(1)`. But in what order will these calls be made?

Most programmers simply assume the operands will be evaluated left to right. Strangely, the C++ language does not specify the order in which the operands of most operators (including `+`) are to be evaluated. Therefore, the programmer may make no assumption about the order in which these calls will execute. The calls could in fact execute `f(2)` first and then `f(1)`, or the calls could execute in the reverse order, `f(1)` then `f(2)`. In this program and in most other programs, it turns out the final result would be the same. But in some programs the evaluation of an operand may have *side effects* that could affect the final result of the expression. The C++ language specifies the order of evaluation of the operands of only four operators—namely `&&`, `||`, the comma (`,`) operator, and `?:`. The first three of these are binary operators whose two operands are guaranteed to be evaluated left to right. The last operator is C++'s only ternary operator. Its leftmost operand is always evaluated first; if the leftmost operand evaluates to nonzero, the middle operand is evaluated next and the last operand is ignored; if the leftmost operand evaluates to zero, the third operand is evaluated next and the middle operand is ignored.

***Common Programming Error 3.19***

*Writing programs that depend on the order of evaluation of the operands of operators other than `&&`, `||`, `?:`, and the comma (`,`) operator can lead to errors because compilers may not necessarily evaluate the operands in the order the programmer expects.*

***Portability Tip 3.2***

*Programs that depend on the order of evaluation of the operands of operators other than `&&`, `||`, `?:`, and the comma (`,`) operator can function differently on systems with different compilers.*

A word of caution is in order about recursive programs like the one we use here to generate Fibonacci numbers. Each level of recursion in the **`fibonacci`** function has a doubling effect on the number of calls, i.e., the number of recursive calls that will be executed to calculate the *n*th Fibonacci number is on the order of $2^n$. This rapidly gets out of hand. Calculating only the 20th Fibonacci number would require on the order of $2^{20}$ or about a million calls, calculating the 30th Fibonacci number would require on the order of $2^{30}$ or about a billion calls, and so on. Computer scientists refer to this as *exponential complexity*. Problems of this nature humble even the world's most powerful computers! Complexity issues in general, and exponential complexity in particular, are discussed in detail in the upper-level computer science curriculum course generally called "Algorithms."

***Performance Tip 3.4***

*Avoid fibonacci-style recursive programs which result in an exponential "explosion" of calls.*

## 3.14 Recursion vs. Iteration

In the previous sections, we studied two functions that can easily be implemented either recursively or iteratively. In this section we compare the two approaches and discuss why the programmer might choose one approach over the other in a particular situation.

Both iteration and recursion are based on a control structure: Iteration uses a repetition structure; recursion uses a selection structure. Both iteration and recursion involve repetition: Iteration explicitly uses a repetition structure; recursion achieves repetition through repeated function calls. Iteration and recursion each involve a termination test: Iteration terminates when the loop-continuation condition fails; recursion terminates when a base case is recognized. Iteration with counter-controlled repetition and recursion each gradually approach termination: Iteration keeps modifying a counter until the counter assumes a value that makes the loop-continuation condition fail; recursion keeps producing simpler versions of the original problem until the base case is reached. Both iteration and recursion can occur infinitely: An infinite loop occurs with iteration if the loop-continuation test never becomes false; infinite recursion occurs if the recursion step does not reduce the problem each time in a manner that converges on the base case.

Recursion has many negatives. It repeatedly invokes the mechanism, and consequently the overhead, of function calls. This can be expensive in both processor time and memory space. Each recursive call causes another copy of the function (actually only the function's variables) to be created; this can consume considerable memory. Iteration normally occurs within a function so the overhead of repeated function calls and extra memory assignment is omitted. So why choose recursion?

***Software Engineering Observation 3.13***

*Any problem that can be solved recursively can also be solved iteratively (nonrecursively). A recursive approach is normally chosen in preference to an iterative approach when the recursive approach more naturally mirrors the problem and results in a program that is easier to understand and debug. Another reason to choose a recursive solution is that an iterative solution may not be apparent.*

***Performance Tip 3.5***

*Avoid using recursion in performance situations. Recursive calls take time and consume additional memory.*

***Common Programming Error 3.20***

*Accidentally having a nonrecursive function call itself either directly, or indirectly through another function.*

Most programming textbooks introduce recursion much later than we have done here. We feel that recursion is a sufficiently rich and complex topic that it is better to introduce it earlier and spread the examples over the remainder of the text. Figure 3.17 summarizes the recursion examples and exercises in the text.

Let us reconsider some observations that we make repeatedly throughout the book. Good software engineering is important. High performance is often important. Unfortunately, these goals are often at odds with one another. Good software engineering is key

| Chapter | Recursion Examples and Exercises |
|---|---|
| *Chapter 3* | Factorial function<br>Fibonacci functions<br>Greatest common divisor<br>Sum of two integers<br>Multiply two integers<br>Raising an integer to an integer power<br>Towers of Hanoi<br>Recursive `main`<br>Printing keyboard inputs in reverse<br>Visualizing recursion |
| *Chapter 4* | Sum the elements of an array<br>Print an array<br>Print an array backwards<br>Print a string backwards<br>Check if a string is a palindrome<br>Minimum value in an array<br>Selection sort<br>Eight Queens<br>Linear search<br>Binary search |
| *Chapter 5* | Quicksort<br>Maze traversal<br>Printing a string input at the keyboard backwards |
| *Chapter 15* | Linked list insert<br>Linked list delete<br>Search a linked list<br>Print a linked list backwards<br>Binary tree insert<br>Preorder traversal of a binary tree<br>Inorder traversal of a binary tree<br>Postorder traversal of a binary tree |

**Fig. 3.17** Summary of recursion examples and exercises in the text.

to making more manageable the task of developing the larger and more complex software systems we need. High performance in these systems is key to realizing the systems of the future that will place ever greater computing demands on hardware. Where do functions fit in here?

***Software Engineering Observation 3.14***

*Functionalizing programs in a neat, hierarchical manner promotes good software engineering. But it has a price.*

***Performance Tip 3.6***

*A heavily functionalized program—as compared to a monolithic (i.e., one-piece) program without functions—makes potentially large numbers of function calls and these consume execution time and space on a computer's processor(s). But monolithic programs are difficult to program, test, debug, maintain, and evolve.*

So functionalize your programs judiciously, always keeping in mind the delicate balance between performance and good software engineering.

## 3.15 Functions with Empty Parameter Lists

In C++, an empty parameter list is specified by writing either **void** or nothing at all in parentheses. The declaration

```
void print();
```

specifies that function **print** does not take any arguments and does not return a value. Figure 3.18 demonstrates both C++ ways of declaring and using functions that do not take arguments.

```
// Functions that take no arguments
#include <iostream.h>

void f1();
void f2(void);

main()
{
   f1();
   f2();

   return 0;
}

void f1()
{
   cout << "Function f1 takes no arguments" << endl;
}

void f2(void)
{
   cout << "Function f2 also takes no arguments" << endl;
}
```

```
Function f1 takes no arguments
Function f2 also takes no arguments
```

**Fig. 3.18** Two ways to declare and use functions that take no arguments.

***Portability Tip 3.3***

*The meaning of an empty function parameter list in C++ is dramatically different than in C. In C, it means all argument checking is disabled (i.e., the function call can pass any arguments it wants). In C++, it means that the function takes no arguments. Thus, C programs using this feature may report syntax errors when compiled in C++.*

Now that we are discussing omitting things, it should be noted that a function defined in a file before any call to the function does not require a separate function prototype. In this case, the function header acts as the function prototype.

***Common Programming Error 3.21***

*C++ programs do not compile unless function prototypes are provided for every function or each function is defined before it is used.*

## 3.16 Inline Functions

Implementing a program as a set of functions is good from a software engineering standpoint, but function calls involve execution-time overhead. C++ provides *inline functions* to help reduce function-call overhead—especially for small functions. The qualifier **`inline`** before a function's return type in the function definition "advises" the compiler to generate a copy of the function's code in place (when appropriate) to avoid a function call. The tradeoff is that multiple copies of the function code are inserted in the program rather than having a single copy of the function to which control is passed each time the function is called. The compiler can ignore the **`inline`** qualifier and typically does so for all but the smallest functions.

***Software Engineering Observation 3.15***

*Any change to an* **`inline`** *function may require all clients of the function to be recompiled. This may be significant in some program development and maintenance situations.*

***Good Programming Practice 3.13***

*The* **`inline`** *qualifier should be used only with small, frequently used functions.*

***Performance Tip 3.7***

*Using* **`inline`** *functions can reduce execution time, but can increase program size.*

The program of Fig. 3.19 uses **`inline`** function **`cube`** to calculate the volume of a cube of side **`s`**. The keyword **`const`** in the parameter list of function **`cube`** tells the compiler that the function does not modify variable **`s`**. The **`const`** keyword is discussed in detail in Chapters 4, 5, and 7.

## 3.17 References and Reference Parameters

Two ways to invoke functions in many programming languages are *call-by-value* and *call-by-reference*. When an argument is passed call-by-value, a *copy* of the argument's value is made and passed to the called function. Changes to the copy do not affect the

```
// Using an inline function to calculate
// the volume of a cube.
#include <iostream.h>

inline float cube(const float s) { return s * s * s; }

main()
{
   cout << "Enter the side length of your cube:  ";

   float side;

   cin >> side;
   cout << "Volume of cube with side "
        << side << " is " << cube(side) << endl;

   return 0;
}
```

```
Enter the side length of your cube:  3.5
Volume of cube with side 3.5 is 42.875
```

**Fig. 3.19** Using an **inline** function to calculate the volume of a cube.

original variable's value in the caller. This prevents the accidental *side effects* that so greatly hinder the development of correct and reliable software systems. Each of the arguments that have been passed in the programs in this chapter so far have been passed call-by-value. One disadvantage of call-by-value is that if a large data item is being passed, making a copy of that data can take a considerable amount of execution time.

In this section we introduce *reference parameters*—the first of two means C++ provides for performing call-by-reference. With call-by-reference, the caller gives the called function the ability to directly access the caller's data, and to modify that data if the called function so chooses. Call-by-reference is good for performance reasons because it eliminates the overhead of copying large amounts of data, but call-by-reference can weaken security because the called function can corrupt the caller's data.

A reference parameter is an alias for its corresponding argument. To indicate that a function parameter is passed by reference, simply follow the parameter's type in the function prototype by an ampersand (**&**); use the same convention when listing the parameter's type in the function header. For example, the declaration

```
int &count
```

in a function header may be pronounced "**count** is a reference to an **int**." In the function call, simply mention the variable by name and it will be passed by reference. Then, mentioning the variable by its parameter name in the body of the called function actually refers to the original variable in the calling function, and the original variable can be modified directly by the called function.

Figure 3.20 compares call-by-value and call-by-reference with reference parameters. The "styles" of the arguments in the calls to **squareByValue** and **squareByReference** are identical, i.e., both variables are simply mentioned by name. Without checking the function prototypes or function definitions, it is not possible to tell from the calls alone whether either function can modify its arguments.

***Common Programming Error 3.22***

*Because reference parameters are mentioned only by name in the body of the called function, the programmer might inadvertently treat reference parameters as call-by-value parameters. This can cause unexpected side effects if the original copies of the variables are changed by the calling function.*

In Chapter 5 we discuss pointers; we will see that pointers enable an alternate form of call-by-reference in which the style of the call clearly indicates call-by-reference (and the potential for modifying the caller's arguments).

```
// Comparing call-by-value and call-by-reference
// with references.
#include <iostream.h>

int squareByValue(int);
void squareByReference(int &);

main()
{
   int x = 2, z = 4;

   cout << "x = " << x << " before squareByValue" << endl
        << "Value returned by squareByValue: "
        << squareByValue(x) << endl
        << "x = " << x << " after squareByValue" << endl << endl;

   cout << "z = " << z << " before squareByReference" << endl;
   squareByReference(z);
   cout << "z = " << z << " after squareByReference" << endl;

   return 0;
}

int squareByValue(int a)
{
   return a *= a;     // caller's argument not modified
}

void squareByReference(int &cRef)
{
   cRef *= cRef;      // caller's argument modified
}
```

Fig. 3.20 An example of call-by-reference (part 1 of 2).

```
x = 2 before squareByValue
Value returned by squareByValue: 4
x = 2 after squareByValue

z = 4 before squareByReference
z = 16 after squareByReference
```

**Fig. 3.20** An example of call-by-reference (part 2 of 2).

***Performance Tip 3.8***

*For passing large objects, use a constant reference parameter to simulate the appearance and security of call-by-value and avoid the overhead of passing a copy of the large object.*

To specify a reference to a constant, place the **`const`** qualifier before the type specifier in the parameter declaration.

Note the placement of **`&`** in the parameter list of the **`squareByReference`** function. Some C++ programmers prefer to write **`int& cRef`** rather than **`int &cRef`**.

***Common Programming Error 3.23***

*Declaring multiple references in one statement while assuming that the* **`&`** *distributes across a comma-separated list of variable names. To declare variables* **`x`**, **`y`**, *and* **`z`** *all as references to integer, use the notation* **`int &x, &y, &z;`** *rather than the incorrect notation* **`int& x, y, z;`** *or the other common incorrect notation* **`int &x, y, z;`**.

***Software Engineering Observation 3.16***

*For the combined reasons of clarity and performance, many C++ programmers prefer that modifiable arguments be passed to functions by using pointers, small non-modifiable arguments be passed call-by-value, and large non-modifiable arguments be passed to functions by using references to constants.*

References can also be used as aliases for other variables within a function (although there is little reason for doing so). For example, the code

```
int count = 1;          // declare integer variable count
int &cRef = count;      // create cRef as an alias for count
++cRef;                 // increment count (using its alias)
```

increments variable **`count`** using its alias **`cRef`**. Reference variables must be initialized in their declarations (see Fig. 3.21 and Fig. 3.22), and cannot be reassigned as aliases to other variables. Once a reference is declared as an alias for another variable, all operations supposedly performed on the alias (i.e., the reference) are actually performed on the original variable itself. The alias is simply another name for the original variable—no space is reserved for the alias. Taking the address of a reference and comparing references does not cause syntax errors; rather each operation actually occurs on the variable for which the reference is an alias. A reference argument must be an lvalue, not a constant or expression that returns an rvalue.

```
// References must be initialized
#include <iostream.h>

main()
{
   int x = 3, &y;     // Error: y must be initialized

   cout << "x = " << x << endl << "y = " << y << endl;
   y = 7;
   cout << "x = " << x << endl << "y = " << y << endl;

   return 0;
}
```

```
Compiling FIG3_21.CPP:
Error FIG3_21.CPP 6: Reference variable 'y' must be
   initialized
```

**Fig. 3.21** Attempting to use an uninitialized reference.

```
// References must be initialized
#include <iostream.h>

main()
{
   int x = 3, &y = x;  // y is now an alias for x

   cout << "x = " << x << endl << "y = " << y << endl;
   y = 7;
   cout << "x = " << x << endl << "y = " << y << endl;

   return 0;
}
```

```
x = 3
y = 3
x = 7
y = 7
```

**Fig. 3.22** Using an initialized reference.

Functions can return references, but this can be dangerous. When returning a reference to a variable declared in the called function, the variable should be declared **`static`** within that function. Otherwise the reference refers to an automatic variable that is discarded when the function terminates; such a variable is said to be "undefined" and the program's behavior would be unpredictable.

***Common Programming Error 3.24***

*Not initializing a reference variable when it is declared.*

***Common Programming Error 3.25***

*Attempting to reassign a previously declared reference to be an alias to another variable.*

***Common Programming Error 3.26***

*Returning a pointer or reference to an automatic variable in a called function.*

## 3.18 Default Arguments

Function calls may commonly pass a particular value of an argument. The programmer can specify that such an argument is a *default argument,* and the programmer can provide a default value for that argument. When a default argument is omitted in a function call, the default value of that argument is automatically passed in the call.

Default arguments must be the rightmost (trailing) arguments in a function's parameter list. When calling a function with two or more default arguments, if an omitted argument is not the rightmost argument in the argument list, all arguments to the right of that argument must also be omitted. Default arguments should be specified with the first occurrence of the function name—typically in the prototype. Default values can be constants, global variables, or function calls. Default arguments also can be used with **inline** functions.

Figure 3.23 demonstrates using default arguments in calculating the volume of a box.

```
// Using default arguments
#include <iostream.h>

// Calculate the volume of a box
inline int boxVolume(int length = 1, int width = 1,
                     int height = 1)
   { return length * width * height; }

main()
{
   cout << "The default box volume is: "
        << boxVolume() << endl << endl
        << "The volume of a box with length 10," << endl
        << "width 1 and height 1 is: "
        << boxVolume(10) << endl << endl
        << "The volume of a box with length 10," << endl
        << "width 5 and height 1 is: "
        << boxVolume(10, 5) << endl << endl
        << "The volume of a box with length 10," << endl
        << "width 5 and height 2 is: "
        << boxVolume(10, 5, 2)
        << endl;

   return 0;
}
```

**Fig. 3.23** Using default arguments (part 1 of 2).

```
The default box volume is: 1

The volume of a box with length 10,
width 1 and height 1 is: 10

The volume of a box with length 10,
width 5 and height 1 is: 50

The volume of a box with length 10,
width 5 and height 2 is: 100
```

**Fig. 3.23** Using default arguments (part 2 of 2).

All three arguments have been given default values of **1**. The first call to **inline** function **boxVolume** specifies no arguments, and thus uses all three default values. The second call passes a **length** argument, and thus uses default values for the **width** and **height** arguments. The third call passes arguments for **length** and **width**, and thus uses a default value for the **height** argument. The last call passes arguments for **length**, **width**, and **height** thus using no default values.

***Good Programming Practice 3.14***

*Using default arguments can simplify writing function calls. However, some programmers feel that specifying all arguments explicitly is clearer.*

***Common Programming Error 3.27***

*Specifying and attempting to use a default argument that is not a rightmost (trailing) argument (while not simultaneously defaulting all the rightmost arguments).*

## 3.19 Unary Scope Resolution Operator

It is possible to declare local and global variables of the same name. C++ provides the *unary scope resolution operator* (**::**) to access a global variable when a local variable of the same name is in scope. The unary scope resolution operator cannot be used to access a local variable of the same name in an outer block. A global variable may be accessed directly without the unary scope resolution operator if the name of the global variable is not the same as the name of a local variable in scope. In Chapter 6, we discuss the use of the *binary scope resolution operator* with classes.

Figure 3.24 demonstrates the unary scope resolution operator with local variables and global variables of the same name. To emphasize that the local and global versions of variable **value** are distinct, the program declares one of the variables **float** and the other **int**.

***Common Programming Error 3.28***

*Attempting to access a non-global variable in an outer block using the unary scope resolution operator.*

```
// Using the unary scope resolution operator
#include <iostream.h>

float value = 1.2345;

main()
{
   int value = 7;

   cout << "Local value = " << value << endl
        << "Global value = " << ::value << endl;

   return 0;
}
```

```
Local value = 7
Global value = 1.2345
```

**Fig. 3.24** Using the unary scope resolution operator.

***Good Programming Practice 3.15***

*Avoid using variables of the same name for different purposes in a program. Although this is allowed in various circumstances, it can be confusing.*

## 3.20 Function Overloading

C++ enables several functions of the same name to be defined as long as these functions have different sets of parameters (at least as far as their types are concerned). This capability is called *function overloading*. When an overloaded function is called, the C++ compiler selects the proper function by examining the number, types, and order of the arguments in the call. Function overloading is commonly used to create several functions of the same name that perform similar tasks, but on different data types.

***Good Programming Practice 3.16***

*Overloading functions that perform closely related tasks can make programs more readable and understandable.*

Figure 3.25 uses overloaded function **`square`** to calculate the square of an **`int`** and the square of a **`double`**. In Chapter 8, we discuss how to overload operators to define how they should operate on objects of user-defined data types. (In fact, we have been using many overloaded operators to this point, including the stream insertion operator `<<` and the stream extraction operator `>>`. We will say more about overloading `<<` and `>>` in Chapter 8.) Section 3.21 introduces template functions for performing identical tasks on many different data types. Chapter 12 discusses template functions and template classes in detail.

```
// Using overloaded functions
#include <iostream.h>

int square(int x) { return x * x; }

double square(double y) { return y * y; }

main()
{
   cout << "The square of integer 7 is "
        << square(7) << endl
        << "The square of double 7.5 is "
        << square(7.5) << endl;

   return 0;
}
```

```
The square of integer 7 is 49
The square of double 7.5 is 56.25
```

**Fig. 3.25** Using overloaded functions.

Overloaded functions are distinguished by their *signature*—a combination of the function's name and its parameter types. The compiler encodes each function identifier (sometimes referred to as *name mangling* or *name decoration*) with the number and types of its parameters to enable *type-safe linkage*. Type-safe linkage ensures that the proper overloaded function is called and that the arguments conform to the parameters. Linkage errors are detected and reported by the compiler. The program of Fig. 3.26 was compiled on the Borland C++ compiler. Rather than showing the execution output of the program (as we normally would), we have shown the encoded function names produced in assembly language by Borland C++. Each mangled name begins with **@** followed by the function name. The encoded parameter list begins with **$q**. In the parameter list for function **nothing2**, **zc** represents a **char**, **i** represents an **int**, **pf** represents a **float ***, and **pd** represents a **double ***. In the parameter list for function **nothing1**, **i** represents an **int**, **f** represents a **float**, **zc** represents a **char**, and **pi** represents an **int ***. The two **square** functions are distinguished by their parameter lists; one specifies **d** for double and the other specifies **i** for **int**. The return types of the functions are not specified in the encoded names. Encoding of function names is compiler specific. Overloaded functions can have different return types, but must have different parameter lists.

***Common Programming Error 3.29***

*Creating overloaded functions with identical parameter lists and different return types causes a syntax error.*

The compiler uses only the parameter lists to distinguish between functions of the same name. Overloaded functions need not have the same number of parameters. Programmers should use caution when overloading functions with default parameters as this may cause ambiguity.

```
// Name mangling
int square(int x) { return x * x; }

double square(double y) { return y * y; }

void nothing1(int a, float b, char c, int *d)
   { }  // empty function body

char *nothing2(char a, int b, float *c, double *d)
   { return 0; }

main()
{
   return 0;
}
```

```
public  _main
public  @nothing2$qzcipfpd
public  @nothing1$qifzcpi
public  @square$qd
public  @square$qi
```

**Fig. 3.26** Name mangling to enable type-safe linkage.

***Common Programming Error 3.30***

*A function with default arguments omitted might be called identically to another overloaded function; this is a syntax error.*

## 3.21 Function Templates

Overloaded functions are normally used to perform similar operations on different types of data. If the operations are identical for each type, this may be performed more compactly and conveniently using *function templates*, a capability introduced in recent versions of C++. The programmer writes a single function template definition. Based on the argument types provided in calls to this function, C++ automatically generates separate functions to handle each type of call appropriately. Thus, defining a single template defines a whole family of solutions.

All function template definitions begin with the **`template`** keyword followed by a list of formal type parameters to the function template enclosed in angle brackets (< and >). Every formal type parameter is preceded by the **`class`** keyword. The formal type parameters are built-in types or user-defined types used to specify the types of the arguments to the function, to specify the return type of the function, and to declare variables within the body of the function definition. The function definition follows and is defined like any other function.

The following template function definition is also used in the complete program of Fig. 3.27.

```
template <class T>
T maximum(T value1, T value2, T value3)
{
   T max = value1;

   if (value2 > max)
      max = value2;

   if (value3 > max)
      max = value3;

   return max;
}
```

This function template declares a single formal parameter **T** as the type of the data to be tested by function **maximum**. When the compiler detects a **maximum** invocation in the program source code, the type of the data passed to **maximum** is substituted for **T** throughout the template definition and C++ creates a complete function for determining the maximum of three values of the specified data type. Then, the newly created function is compiled. Thus, templates really are a means of code generation. In Fig. 3.27, three functions are instantiated—one expects three **int** values, one expects three **double** values, and one expects three **char** values. The instantiation for type **int** is:

```
int maximum(int value1, int value2, int value3)
{
   int max = value1;

   if (value2 > max)
      max = value2;

   if (value3 > max)
      max = value3;

   return max;
}
```

Every formal parameter in the template definition must appear in the function's parameter list at least once. The name of a formal parameter must be unique in the formal parameter list of a particular template definition.

Figure 3.27 illustrates the use of the **maximum** template function to determine the largest of three integer values, three **double** values, and three character values.

***Common Programming Error 3.31***

*Not placing keyword* **class** *before every formal parameter of a function template.*

***Common Programming Error 3.32***

*Not using every formal parameter of a function template in the function signature.*

## 3.22 Thinking About Objects: Identifying an Object's Attributes

In the "Thinking About Objects" section at the end of Chapter 2, we began the first phase of an object-oriented design for our elevator simulator, namely identifying the objects needed to implement the simulator. As a starting point, you were encouraged to list the

```
// Using template functions
#include <iostream.h>

template <class T>
T maximum(T value1, T value2, T value3)
{
   T max = value1;

   if (value2 > max)
      max = value2;

   if (value3 > max)
      max = value3;

   return max;
}

main()
{
   int int1, int2, int3;
   cout << "Input three integer values: ";
   cin >> int1 >> int2 >> int3;
   cout << "The maximum integer value is: "
        << maximum(int1, int2, int3);           // int version

   double double1, double2, double3;
   cout << endl << "Input three double values: ";
   cin >> double1 >> double2 >> double3;
   cout << "The maximum double value is: "
        << maximum(double1, double2, double3);   // double version

   char char1, char2, char3;
   cout << endl << "Input three characters: ";
   cin >> char1 >> char2 >> char3;
   cout << "The maximum character value is: "
        << maximum(char1, char2, char3) << endl; // char version
   return 0;
}
```

```
Input three integer values: 1 2 3
The maximum integer value is: 3
Input three double values: 3.3 2.2 1.1
The maximum double value is: 3.3
Input three characters: A C B
The maximum character value is: C
```

**Fig. 3.27** Using template functions.

nouns in the problem statement. In doing so, you discovered that some of the objects in your simulator were the elevator itself, people, floors, the building, various buttons, a clock, lights and bells on each floor, etc.

In our introduction to objects in Chapter 1, we indicated that objects have attributes and behaviors. Object attributes are represented in C++ programs by data; object behaviors are represented by functions. In this assignment we concentrate on determining the attributes of the objects needed to implement the elevator simulator. In Chapter 4, we will concentrate on behaviors. In Chapter 5, we will concentrate on the interactions between the objects in the elevator simulator.

Let us discuss attributes of real-world objects before we begin the assignment. A person's attributes include height and weight. A radio's attributes include whether it is set to AM or FM, station setting, and current volume setting. A car's attributes include current speedometer and odometer readings. A house's attributes include style ("colonial," "ranch," etc.), number of rooms, square footage, and lot size. A personal computer's attributes include manufacturer (Apple, IBM, Compaq, etc.), type of screen (monochrome or color), main memory size (in megabytes), hard disk size (in megabytes), etc.

***Elevator Laboratory Assignment 2***

1. To get the process started, type into a word processor or editor program the text of the problem statement for the elevator simulation (from Section 2.22).
2. Extract all the facts from the problem. Eliminate all irrelevant text and place each fact on a separate line of your text file (there are approximately 60 facts in the problem statement). Here is the first portion of what your fact file might look like:

   *Fact File*
   two-story office building
   elevator
   person on the elevator
   doors
   floor 1
   directions—up and down
   clock
   time 0
   "ticks" once per second
   scheduler component of the simulator
   randomly schedule the arrival of the first person on each floor
   time of the first arrival
   simulator
   "creates" a new person for the specified floor
   places the person on that floor
   person then presses the up-button or the down-button on that floor
   up-button or the down-button on a floor
   person's destination floor
   floor on which a person arrives
   first person of the day arrives at floor 1
   person arrives at floor 1
   person gets on the elevator
   person presses the up-button

3. Group all your facts by object. This will help confirm that you properly identified the objects in the laboratory exercises in Chapter 2. Use an outline form in which the ob-

ject is listed at the left margin of the page and the facts related to an object are listed below that object and indented one tab. Some facts mention only one object while other facts mention several objects. Each fact should initially be listed under every object the fact mentions. Note that some facts like "directions—up and down" do not explicitly mention an object, but should nevertheless be grouped with an object (in this case, the direction is clearly the direction in which the elevator is moving). This outline file will be used in this assignment and in the next several assignments.

4. Now separate the facts for each object into two groups. Label the first group *Attributes* and the second group *Other Facts*. For now, actions (behaviors) should be grouped under *Other Facts*. As you place an action under *Other Facts* consider creating an additional entry under *Attributes* if appropriate. For example, the fact "elevator closes its doors" is an action that for now is grouped under *Other Facts*, but it indicates that an attribute of doors is that that they are either open or shut. The fact, "floor is occupied" is an attribute of floor, more specifically, floor is either occupied (by one person) or unoccupied at any time. Some attributes of the elevator are: whether it is moving or stopped, whether it does or does not have a passenger, and if it is moving—whether it is moving up or down. An attribute of a button is whether it is "on" or "off." An attribute of a person is the person's destination floor. And so on.

***Notes***

1. Begin by listing the object attributes that are explicitly mentioned in the problem statement. Then list attributes that are directly implied in the problem statement.
2. Add appropriate attributes as it becomes apparent that they are needed.
3. System design is not a perfect and complete process. Do the best you can for now. Be prepared to modify the design as this exercise proceeds in subsequent chapters.
4. One object can be an attribute of another object. This is called composition. For example, there are a button objects inside the elevator for floor 1 and for floor 2—the person presses one of these buttons to select a destination floor. For the purposes of this laboratory exercise, treat all the objects separately—do not allow composition. We will incorporate composition into the elevator simulator in Chapter 5.
5. In this chapter, you learned how to implement "randomness." When you eventually implement the elevator simulator, the statement

```
arrivalTime = currentTime + (5 + rand() % 16);
```

can be used to randomly schedule the next arrival of a person on a floor.

## Summary

- The best way to develop and maintain a large program is to divide it into several smaller program modules each of which is more manageable than the original program. Modules are written in C++ as classes and functions.
- A function is invoked by a function call. The function call mentions the function by name and provides information (as arguments) that the called function needs to perform its task.

- The purpose of information hiding is for functions to have access only to the information they need to complete their tasks. This is a means of implementing the principle of least privilege, one of the most important principles of good software engineering.
- Functions are normally invoked in a program by writing the name of the function followed by the arguments of the function followed in parentheses.
- Data type **`double`** is a floating-point type like **`float`**. A variable of type **`double`** can store a value of much greater magnitude and precision than **`float`** can store.
- Each argument of a function may be a constant, a variable, or an expression.
- A local variable is known only in a function definition. Functions are not allowed to know the implementation details of any other function (including local variables).
- The general format for a function definition is

  *return-value-type function-name* ( *parameter-list* )
  {
      *declarations and statements*
  }

  The *return-value-type* states the type of the value returned to the calling function. If a function does not return a value, the *return-value-type* is declared as **`void`**. The *function-name* is any valid identifier. The *parameter-list* is a comma-separated list containing the declarations of the variables that will be passed to the function. If a function does not receive any values, *parameter-list* is declared as **`void`**. The *function-body* is the set of declarations and statements that constitute the function.
- The arguments passed to a function should match in number, type, and order with the parameters in the function definition.
- When a program encounters a function, control is transferred from the point of invocation to the called function, the function is executed, and control returns to the caller.
- A called function can return control to the caller in one of three ways. If the function does not return a value, control is returned when the function-ending right brace is reached, or by executing the statement

  ```
  return;
  ```

  If the function does return a value, the statement

  **`return`** *expression*;

  returns the value of *expression*.
- A function prototype declares the return-type of the function and declares the number, the types, and order of the parameters the function expects to receive.
- Function prototypes enable the compiler to verify that functions are called correctly.
- The compiler ignores variable names mentioned in the function prototype.
- Each standard library has a corresponding header file containing the function prototypes for all the functions in that library, as well as definitions of various symbolic constants needed by those functions.

- Programmers can and should create and include their own header files.
- When an argument is passed call-by-value, a *copy* of the variable's value is made and the copy is passed to the called function. Changes to the copy in the called function do not affect the original variable's value.
- The **rand** function generates an integer between 0 and **RAND_MAX** which is defined to be at least 32767.
- The function prototypes for **rand** and **srand** are contained in **<stdlib.h>**.
- Values produced by **rand** can be scaled and shifted to produce values in a specific range.
- To randomize a program, use the C standard library function **srand**.
- The **srand** statement is ordinarily inserted in a program only after the program has been thoroughly debugged. While debugging, it is better to omit **srand**. This ensures repeatability, which is essential to proving that corrections to a random number generation program work properly.
- To randomize without the need for entering a seed each time, we may use **srand(time(NULL))**. The **time** function normally returns "calendar time" in seconds. The **time** function prototype is located in the header **<time.h>**.
- The general equation for scaling and shifting a random number is

  ```
  n = a + rand() % b;
  ```

  where **a** is the shifting value (which is equal to the first number in the desired range of consecutive integers), and **b** is the scaling factor (which is equal to the width of the desired range of consecutive integers).
- An enumeration, introduced by the keyword ***enum*** and followed by a type name, is a set of integer constants represented by identifiers.
- The values of these enumeration constants start at **0**, unless specified otherwise, and are incremented by **1**.
- The identifiers in an **enum** must be unique, but separate enumeration constants can have the same integer value.
- Any enumeration constant can be explicitly assigned an integer value in the enumeration definition.
- Each variable identifier has the attributes storage class, scope and linkage.
- C++ provides four storage class specifiers: **auto**, **register**, **extern**, and **static**.
- An identifier's storage class determines when that identifier exists in memory.
- An identifier's scope is where the identifier can be referenced in a program.
- An identifier's linkage determines for a multiple-source-file program if an identifier is known only in the current source file or in any source file with proper declarations.

- Variables of automatic storage class are created when the block in which they are declared is entered, exist while the block is active, and are destroyed when the block is exited. A function's local variables normally are of automatic storage class.
- The storage class specifier `register` can be placed before an automatic variable declaration to suggest that the compiler maintain the variable in one of the computer's high-speed hardware registers. The compiler may ignore `register` declarations. The `register` keyword can be used only with variables of the automatic storage class.
- The keywords `extern` and `static` are used to declare identifiers for variables and functions of static storage class.
- Static storage class variables are allocated and initialized when the program begins execution.
- Two types of identifiers have static storage class: external identifiers and local variables declared with the storage class specifier `static`.
- Global variables are created by placing variable declarations outside any function definition, and they retain their values throughout the execution of the program.
- Local variables declared `static` retain their value when the function in which they are declared is exited.
- All numeric variables of static storage class are initialized to zero if they are not explicitly initialized by the programmer.
- The four scopes for an identifier are function scope, file scope, block scope, and function-prototype scope.
- Labels are the only identifiers with function scope. Labels can be used anywhere in the function in which they appear, but can not be referenced outside the function body.
- An identifier declared outside any function has file scope. Such an identifier is "known" from the point at which the identifier is declared until the end of the file.
- Identifiers declared inside a block have block scope. Block scope ends at the terminating right brace (`}`) of the block.
- Local variables declared at the beginning of a function have block scope as do function parameters, which are considered local variables by the function.
- Any block may contain variable declarations. When blocks are nested, and an identifier in an outer block has the same name as an identifier in an inner block, the identifier in the outer block is "hidden" until the inner block terminates.
- The only identifiers with function-prototype scope are those used in the parameter list of a function prototype. Identifiers used in a function prototype can be reused elsewhere in the program without ambiguity.
- A recursive function is a function that calls itself either directly or indirectly.
- If a recursive function is called with a base case, the function simply returns a result. If the function is called with a more complex problem, the function divides the problem

into two conceptual pieces: a piece that the function knows how to do and a slightly smaller version of the original problem. Because this new problem looks like the original problem, the function launches a recursive call to work on the smaller problem.

- For recursion to terminate, each time the recursive function calls itself with a slightly simpler version of the original problem, the sequence of smaller and smaller problems must converge on the base case. When the function recognizes the base case, the result is returned to the previous function call, and a sequence of returns ensues all the way up the line until the original call of the function eventually returns the final result.
- The ANSI standard does not specify the order in which the operands of most operators are to be evaluated. C++ specifies the order of evaluation of the operands of the operators **&&**, **||**, the comma (**,**) operator, and **?:**. The first three are binary operators whose operands are evaluated left to right. The last operator is C++'s only ternary operator. Its leftmost operand is evaluated first; if it evaluates to nonzero, the middle operand is evaluated next and the last operand is ignored; if it evaluates to zero, the third operand is evaluated next and the middle operand is ignored.
- Both iteration and recursion are based on a control structure: Iteration uses a repetition structure; recursion uses a selection structure.
- Both iteration and recursion involve repetition: Iteration explicitly uses a repetition structure; recursion achieves repetition through repeated function calls.
- Iteration and recursion each involve a termination test: Iteration terminates when the loop-continuation condition fails; recursion terminates when a base case is recognized.
- Iteration and recursion can occur infinitely: An infinite loop occurs with iteration if the loop-continuation test never becomes false; infinite recursion occurs if the recursion step does not reduce the problem in a manner that converges on the base case.
- Recursion repeatedly invokes the mechanism, and consequently the overhead, of function calls. This can be expensive in both processor time and memory space.
- C++ programs do not compile unless a function prototype is provided for every function or a function is defined before it is used.
- A function that does not return a value is declared with a **void** return type. If an attempt is made either to return a value from the function or to use the result of the function invocation in the calling function, the compiler reports an error.
- An empty parameter list is specified with empty parentheses or **void** in parentheses.
- Inline functions eliminate function-call overhead. The programmer uses the keyword **inline** to advise the compiler to generate function code in line (when possible) to minimize function calls. The compiler may choose to ignore the **inline** advice.
- C++ offers a direct form of call-by-reference using reference parameters. To indicate that a function parameter is passed by reference, follow the parameter's type in the function prototype by an **&**. In the function call, mention the variable by name and it will be passed call-by-reference. In the called function, mentioning the variable by its

local name actually refers to the original variable in the calling function. Thus, the original variable can be modified directly by the called function.

- Reference parameters can also be created for local use as aliases for other variables within a function. Reference variables must be initialized in their declarations, and they cannot be reassigned as aliases to other variables. Once a reference variable is declared as an alias for another variable, all operations supposedly performed on the alias are actually performed on the variable.
- The `const` qualifier also can create "constant variables." A constant variable must be initialized with a constant expression when the variable is declared, and cannot be modified thereafter. Constant variables are often called named constants or read-only variables. Constant variables can be placed anywhere a constant expression is expected. Another common use of the `const` qualifier is creating references to constants.
- C++ allows the programmer to specify default arguments and their default values. If a default argument is omitted in a call to a function, the default value of that argument is used. Default arguments must be the rightmost (trailing) arguments in a function's parameter list. Default arguments should be specified with the first occurrence of the function name. Default values can be constants, global variables, or function calls.
- The unary scope resolution operator (`::`) enables a program to access a global variable when a local variable of the same name is in scope.
- It is possible to define several functions with the same name but with different parameter types. This is called function overloading. When an overloaded function is called, the compiler selects the proper function by examining the number and types of arguments in the call.
- Overloaded functions can have different return values, and must have different parameter lists. Two functions differing only by return type will result in a compilation error.
- Function templates enable the creation of functions that perform the same operations on different types of data, but the function template is defined only once.

## Terminology

ampersand (`&`) suffix
argument in a function call
`auto` storage class specifier
automatic storage
automatic storage class
automatic variable
base case in recursion
block
block scope
C standard library
call a function
call-by-reference
call-by-value
called function
caller
calling function
coercion of arguments
`const`
constant variable
copy of a value
default function arguments
divide and conquer
element of chance
`enum`

enumeration
enumeration constant
**`extern`** storage class specifier
factorial function
file scope
function
function call
function declaration
function definition
function overloading
function prototype
function scope
global variable
header file
information hiding
**`inline`** function
invoke a function
iteration
linkage
linkage specifications
local variable
math library functions
mixed-type expression
modular program
named constant
optimizing compiler
overloading
parameter in a function definition
principle of least privilege
programmer-defined function
promotion hierarchy
**`rand`**
random number generation
randomize
**`RAND_MAX`**
read-only variable
recursion
recursive call
recursive function
reference parameter
reference types
**`register`** storage class specifier
**`return`**
return-value-type
scaling
scope
shifting
side effects
signature
simulation
software engineering
software reusability
**`srand`**
standard library header files
**`static`** storage class specifier
static storage duration
**`static`** variable
storage class specifier
storage class
**`template`**
template function
**`time`**
type-safe linkage
unary scope resolution operator (**`::`**)
**`unsigned`**
**`void`**

## *Common Programming Errors*

**3.1** Forgetting to include the math header file when using math library functions results in a compile-time error. A standard header file must be included for every standard library function used in a program.

**3.2** Omitting the return-value-type in a function definition causes a syntax error if the function prototype specifies a return type other than **`int`**.

**3.3** Forgetting to return a value from a function that is supposed to return a value can lead to unexpected errors. The ANSI standard states that the result of this omission is undefined. C++ compilers will generally issue a warning message.

**3.4** Returning a value from a function whose return type has been declared **`void`** causes a syntax error.

**3.5** Declaring function parameters of the same type as **`float x, y`** instead of **`float x, float y`**. The parameter declaration **`float x, y`** would actually report a compilation error because types are required for each parameter in the parameter list.

3.6 Placing a semicolon after the right parenthesis enclosing the parameter list of a function definition is a syntax error.

3.7 Defining a function parameter again as a local variable within the function is a syntax error.

3.8 Defining a function inside another function is a syntax error.

3.9 Forgetting the semicolon at the end of a function prototype causes a syntax error at compilation time.

3.10 Converting from a higher data type in the promotion hierarchy to a lower type can change the data value.

3.11 Forgetting a function prototype when a functions is not defined before it is first invoked causes a syntax error.

3.12 Using **`srand`** in place of **`rand`** to generate random numbers.

3.13 Assigning the integer equivalent of an enumeration constant to a variable of the enumeration type reports a warning from the compiler.

3.14 After an enumeration constant has been defined, attempting to assign another value to the enumeration constant is a syntax error.

3.15 Using multiple storage class specifiers for an identifier. Only one storage class specifier can be applied to an identifier. For example, if you include **`register`**, do not also include **`auto`**.

3.16 Accidentally using the same name for an identifier in an inner block as is used for an identifier in an outer block, when in fact, the programmer wants the identifier in the outer block to be active for the duration of the inner block.

3.17 Forgetting to return a value from a recursive function when one is needed. The compiler produces a warning message.

3.18 Either omitting the base case or writing the recursion step incorrectly so that it does not converge on the base case will cause infinite recursion, eventually exhausting memory. This is analogous to the problem of an infinite loop in an iterative (nonrecursive) solution. Infinite recursion can also be caused by providing an unexpected input.

3.19 Writing programs that depend on the order of evaluation of the operands of operators other than **`&&`**, **`||`**, **`?:`**, and the comma (**`,`**) operator can lead to errors because compilers may not necessarily evaluate the operands in the order the programmer expects.

3.20 Accidentally having a nonrecursive function call itself either directly or indirectly through another function.

3.21 C++ programs do not compile unless function prototypes are provided for every function, or each function is defined before it is used.

3.22 Because reference parameters are mentioned only by name in the body of the called function, the programmer might inadvertently treat reference parameters as call-by-value parameters. This can cause unexpected side effects if the original copies of the variables are changed by the calling function.

3.23 Declaring multiple references in one statement while assuming that the **`&`** distributes across a comma-separated list of variable names. To declare variables **`x`**, **`y`**, and **`z`** all as references to integer, use the notation **`int &x, &y, &z;`** rather than the incorrect notation **`int& x, y, z;`** or the other common incorrect notation **`int &x, y, z;`**.

3.24 Not initializing a reference variable when it is declared.

3.25 Attempting to reassign a previously declared reference to be an alias to another variable.

3.26 Returning a pointer or reference to an automatic variable in a called function.

3.27 Specifying and attempting to use a default argument that is not a rightmost (trailing) argument (while not simultaneously defaulting all the rightmost arguments).

3.28 Attempting to access a non-global variable in an outer block using the unary scope resolution operator.

**3.29** Creating overloaded functions with identical parameter lists and different return types causes a syntax error.

**3.30** A function with default arguments omitted might be called identically to another overloaded function; this is a syntax error.

**3.31** Not placing keyword **`class`** before every formal parameter of a function template.

**3.32** Not using every formal parameter of a function template in the function signature.

## Good Programming Practices

**3.1** Familiarize yourself with the rich collection of functions in the ANSI C standard library and with the rich collections of classes available in various class libraries .

**3.2** Include the math header file by using the preprocessor directive **`#include <math.h>`** when using functions in the math library.

**3.3** Place a blank line between function definitions to separate the functions and enhance program readability.

**3.4** Even though an omitted return type defaults to **`int`**, always state the return type explicitly. The return type for **`main`**, however, is normally omitted.

**3.5** Although it is not incorrect to do so, do not use the same names for the arguments passed to a function and the corresponding parameters in the function definition. This helps avoid ambiguity.

**3.6** Choosing meaningful function names and meaningful parameter names makes programs more readable and helps avoid excessive use of comments.

**3.7** Parameter names are sometimes included in function prototypes for documentation purposes. The compiler ignores these names.

**3.8** Capitalize the first letter of an identifier used as a user-defined type name.

**3.9** Use only uppercase letters in the names of enumeration constants. This makes these constants stand out in a program and reminds the programmer that enumeration constants are not variables.

**3.10** Using enumerations rather than integer constants makes programs more readable.

**3.11** Variables used only in a particular function should be declared as local variables in that function rather than as global variables.

**3.12** Avoid variable names that hide names in outer scopes. This can be accomplished by avoiding the use of duplicate identifiers in a program.

**3.13** The **`inline`** qualifier should be used only with small, frequently used functions.

**3.14** Using default arguments can simplify writing function calls. However, some programmers feel that specifying all arguments explicitly is clearer.

**3.15** Avoid using variables of the same name for different purposes in a program. Although this is allowed in various circumstances, it can be confusing.

**3.16** Overloading functions that perform closely related tasks can make programs more readable and understandable.

## Performance Tips

**3.1** Automatic storage is a means of conserving memory because automatic storage class variables are created when the block in which they are declared is entered and are destroyed when the block is exited.

**3.2** The storage class specifier **`register`** can be placed before an automatic variable declaration to suggest that the compiler maintain the variable in one of the computer's high-speed hardware registers rather than in memory. If you include **`register`**, do not also include

**auto**—only one storage class specifier can be used in a variable declaration. If intensely used variables such as counters or totals can be maintained in hardware registers, the overhead of repeatedly loading the variables from memory into the registers and storing the results back into memory can be eliminated.

**3.3** Often, **register** declarations are unnecessary. Today's optimizing compilers are capable of recognizing frequently used variables and can decide to place them in registers without the need for a **register** declaration from the programmer.

**3.4** Avoid fibonacci-style recursive programs which result in an exponential "explosion" of calls.

**3.5** Avoid using recursion in performance situations. Recursive calls take time and consume additional memory.

**3.6** A heavily functionalized program—as compared to a monolithic (i.e., one-piece) program without functions—makes potentially large numbers of function calls and these consume execution time on a computer's processor(s). But monolithic programs are difficult to program, test, debug, maintain, and evolve.

**3.7** Using **inline** functions can reduce execution time, but can increase program size.

**3.8** For passing large objects, use a constant reference parameter to simulate the appearance and security of call-by-value and avoid the overhead of passing a copy of the large object.

## *Portability Tips*

**3.1** Using the functions in the ANSI C standard library helps make programs more portable.

**3.2** Programs that depend on the order of evaluation of the operands of operators other than **&&**, **||**, **?:**, and the comma (**,**) operator can function differently on systems with different compilers.

**3.3** The meaning of an empty function parameter list in C++ is dramatically different than in C. In C, it means all argument checking is disabled (i.e., the function call can pass any arguments it wants). In C++, it means that the function takes no arguments. Thus, C programs using this feature may report syntax errors when compiled in C++.

## *Software Engineering Observations*

**3.1** Avoid reinventing the wheel. When possible, use ANSI C standard library functions instead of writing new functions. This reduces program development time.

**3.2** In programs containing many functions, **main** should be implemented as a group of calls to functions that perform the bulk of the program's work.

**3.3** Each function should be limited to performing a single, well-defined task, and the function name should effectively express that task. This promotes software reusability.

**3.4** If you cannot choose a concise name that expresses what the function does, it is possible that your function is attempting to perform too many diverse tasks. It is usually best to break such a function into several smaller functions.

**3.5** A function should be no longer than one page. Better yet, a function should be no longer than half a page. Regardless of how long a function is, it should perform one task well. Small functions promote software reusability.

**3.6** Programs should be written as collections of small functions. This makes programs easier to write, debug, maintain and modify.

**3.7** A function requiring a large number of parameters may be performing too many tasks. Consider dividing the function into smaller functions that perform the separate tasks. The function header should fit on one line if possible.

**3.8** The function prototype, function header, and function calls should all agree in the number, type, and order of arguments and parameters, and in the type of return value.

**3.9** Function prototypes are required in C++. Use `#include` preprocessor directives to obtain function prototypes for the standard library functions from the header files for the appropriate libraries. Also use `#include` to obtain header files containing function prototypes used by you and/or your group members.

**3.10** A function prototype placed outside any function definition applies to all calls to the function appearing after the function prototype in the file. A function prototype placed in a function applies only to calls made in that function.

**3.11** Automatic storage is yet another example of the principle of least privilege. Why have variables stored in memory and accessible when they are not needed?

**3.12** Declaring a variable as global rather than local allows unintended side effects to occur when a function that does not need access to the variable accidentally or maliciously modifies it. In general, use of global variables should be avoided except in certain situations with unique performance requirements (as discussed in Chapter 18).

**3.13** Any problem that can be solved recursively can also be solved iteratively (nonrecursively). A recursive approach is normally chosen in preference to an iterative approach when the recursive approach more naturally mirrors the problem and results in a program that is easier to understand and debug. Another reason to choose a recursive solution is that an iterative solution may not be apparent.

**3.14** Functionalizing programs in a neat, hierarchical manner promotes good software engineering. But it has a price.

**3.15** Any change to an `inline` function may require all clients of the function to be recompiled. This may be significant in some program development and maintenance situations.

**3.16** For the combined reasons of clarity and performance, many C++ programmers prefer that modifiable arguments be passed to functions by using pointers, small non-modifiable arguments be passed call-by-value, and large non-modifiable arguments be passed to functions by using references to constants.

## *Self-Review Exercises*

**3.1** Answer each of the following:

a) Program modules in C++ are called __________ and__________.
b) A function is invoked with a __________.
c) A variable that is known only within the function in which it is defined is called a __________.
d) The __________ statement in a called function is used to pass the value of an expression back to the calling function.
e) The keyword __________ is used in a function header to indicate that a function does not return a value or to indicate that a function contains no parameters.
f) The __________ of an identifier is the portion of the program in which the identifier can be used.
g) The three ways to return control from a called function to a caller are __________, __________, and __________.
h) A __________ allows the compiler to check the number, types, and order of the arguments passed to a function.
i) The __________ function is used to produce random numbers.
j) The __________ function is used to set the random number seed to randomize a program.

k) The storage class specifiers are __________, __________, __________, and__________.
l) Variables declared in a block or in the parameter list of a function are assumed to be of storage class __________ unless specified otherwise.
m) The storage class specifier __________ is a recommendation to the compiler to store a variable in one of the computer's registers.
n) A variable declared outside any block or function is an __________ variable.
o) For a local variable in a function to retain its value between calls to the function, it must be declared with the __________ storage class specifier.
p) The four possible scopes of an identifier are __________, __________, __________, and __________.
q) A function that calls itself either directly or indirectly is a __________ function.
r) A recursive function typically has two components: one that provides a means for the recursion to terminate by testing for a __________ case, and one that expresses the problem as a recursive call for a slightly simpler problem than the original call.
s) In C++, it is possible to have various functions with the same name that each operate on different types and/or numbers of arguments. This is called function __________.
t) The __________ enables access to a global variable with the same name as a variable in the current scope.
u) The __________ qualifier is used to declare read-only variables.
v) __________ functions enable a single function to be defined to perform a task on many different data types.

**3.2** For the following program, state the scope (either function scope, file scope, block scope, or function prototype scope) of each of the following elements.

a) The variable **x** in **main**.
b) The variable **y** in **cube**.
c) The function **cube**.
d) The function **main**.
e) The function prototype for **cube**.
f) The identifier **y** in the function prototype for **cube**.

```
#include <iostream.h>
int cube(int y);

main()
{
    int x;

    for (x = 1; x <= 10; x++)
        cout << cube(x) << endl;
}

int cube(int y)
{
    return y * y * y;
}
```

**3.3** Write a program that tests if the examples of the math library function calls shown in Fig. 3.2 actually produce the indicated results.

**3.4** Give the function header for each of the following functions.

a) Function **hypotenuse** that takes two double-precision, floating-point arguments, **side1** and **side2**, and returns a double-precision, floating-point result.

b) Function **smallest** that takes three integers, **x**, **y**, **z**, and returns an integer.

c) Function **instructions** that does not receive any arguments and does not return a value. (Note: Such functions are commonly used to display instructions to a user.)

d) Function **intToFloat** that takes an integer argument, **number**, and returns a floating-point result.

**3.5** Give the function prototype for each of the following:

a) The function described in Exercise 3.4a.

b) The function described in Exercise 3.4b.

c) The function described in Exercise 3.4c.

d) The function described in Exercise 3.4d.

**3.6** Write a declaration for each of the following:

a) Integer **count** that should be maintained in a register. Initialize **count** to **0**.

b) Floating point variable **lastVal** that is to retain its value between calls to the function in which it is defined.

c) External integer **number** whose scope should be restricted to the remainder of the file in which it is defined.

**3.7** Find the error in each of the following program segments and explain how the error can be corrected (see also Exercise 3.53):

a)
```
int g(void) {
   cout << "Inside function g" << endl;

   int h(void) {
      cout << "Inside function h" << endl;
   }
}
```

b)
```
int sum(int x, int y) {
   int result;

   result = x + y;
}
```

c)
```
int sum(int n) {
   if (n == 0)
      return 0;
   else
      n + sum(n - 1);
}
```

d)
```
void f(float a); {
   float a;

   cout << a << endl;
}
```

e)
```
void product(void) {
   int a, b, c, result;
   cout << "Enter three integers: "
   cin >> a >> b >> c;
   result = a * b * c;
   cout << "Result is " << result;
   return result;
}
```

**3.8** Why would a function prototype contain a parameter type declaration such as **`float&`**?

**3.9** (True/False) All calls in C++ are performed call-by-value.

**3.10** Write a complete C++ program that uses an **`inline`** function **`sphereVolume`** to prompt the user for the radius of a sphere, and to calculate and print the volume of that sphere using the assignment **`volume = (4/3) * 3.14159 * pow(radius, 3)`**.

## *Answers to Self-Review Exercises*

**3.1** a) Functions and classes. b) Function call. c) Local variable. d) **`return`**. e) **`void`**. f) Scope. g) **`return;`** or **`return expression;`** or encountering the closing right brace of a function. h) Function prototype. i) **`rand`**. j) **`srand`**. k) **`auto`**, **`register`**, **`extern`**, **`static`**. l) Automatic. m) **`register`**. n) External, global. o) **`static`**. p) Function scope, file scope, block scope, function prototype scope. q) Recursive. r) Base. s) Overloading. t) Unary scope resolution operator (**`::`**). u) **`const`**. v) Template.

**3.2** a) Block scope. b) Block Scope. c) File scope. d) File scope. e) File scope. f) Function prototype scope.

**3.3**

```
/* Testing the math library functions */
#include <iostream.h>
#include <iomanip.h>
#include <math.h>
main()
{
   cout << setiosflags(ios::fixed | ios::showpoint)
        << setprecision(1)
        << "sqrt(" << 900.0 << ") = " << sqrt(900.0) << endl
        << "sqrt(" << 9.0 << ") = " << sqrt(9.0) << endl
        << "exp(" << 1.0 << ") = " << setprecision(6)
        << exp(1.0) << endl << "exp(" << setprecision(1) << 2.0
        << ") = " << setprecision(6) << exp(2.0) << endl
        << "log(" << 2.718282 << ") = " << setprecision(1)
        << log(2.718282) << endl << "log(" << setprecision(6)
        << 7.389056 << ") = " << setprecision(1)
        << log(7.389056) << endl;
   cout << "log10(" << 1.0 << ") = " << log10(1.0) << endl
        << "log10(" << 10.0 << ") = " << log10(10.0) << endl
        << "log10(" << 100.0 << ") = " << log10(100.0) << endl
        << "fabs(" << 13.5 << ") = " << fabs(13.5) << endl
        << "fabs(" << 0.0 << ") = " << fabs(0.0) << endl;
        << "fabs(" << -13.5 << ") = " << fabs(-13.5) << endl
   cout << "ceil(" << 9.2 << ") = " << ceil(9.2) << endl
        << "ceil(" << -9.8 << ") = " << ceil(-9.8) << endl
        << "floor(" << 9.2 << ") = " << floor(9.2) << endl
        << "floor(" << -9.8 << ") = " << floor(-9.8) << endl;
   cout << "pow(" << 2.0 << ", " << 7.0 << ") = " << pow(2.0, 7.0)
        << endl << "pow(" << 9.0 << ", " << 0.5 << ") = "
        << pow(9.0, 0.5) << endl << setprecision(3) << "fmod("
        << 13.675 << ", " << 2.333 << ") = " << fmod(13.675, 2.333)
        << endl << setprecision(1) << "sin(" << 0.0 << ") = "
        << sin(0.0) << endl << "cos(" << 0.0 << ") = " << cos(0.0)
        << endl << "tan(" << 0.0 << ") = " << tan(0.0) << endl;
   return 0;
}
```

```
sqrt(900.0) = 30.0
sqrt(9.0) = 3.0
exp(1.0) = 2.718282
exp(2.0) = 7.389056
log(2.718282) = 1.0
log(7.389056) = 2.0
log10(1.0) = 0.0
log10(10.0) = 1.0
log10(100.0) = 2.0
fabs(13.5) = 13.5
fabs(0.0) = 0.0
fabs(-13.5) = 13.5
ceil(9.2) = 10.0
ceil(-9.8) = -9.0
floor(9.2) = 9.0
floor(-9.8) = -10.0
pow(2.0, 7.0) = 128.0
pow(9.0, 0.5) = 3.0
fmod(13.675, 2.333) = 2.010
sin(0.0) = 0.0
cos(0.0) = 1.0
tan(0.0) = 0.0
```

**3.4**
a) `double hypotenuse(double side1, double side2)`
b) `int smallest(int x, int y, int z)`
c) `void instructions(void) // in C++ (void) can be written ()`
d) `float intToFloat(int number)`

**3.5**
a) `double hypotenuse(double, double);`
b) `int smallest(int, int, int);`
c) `void instructions(void); // in C++ (void) can be written ()`
d) `float intToFloat(int);`

**3.6**
a) `register int count = 0;`
b) `static float lastVal;`
c) `static int number;`
Note: This would appear outside any function definition.

**3.7**
a) Error: Function `h` is defined in function `g`.
Correction: Move the definition of `h` out of the definition of `g`.

b) Error: The function is supposed to return an integer, but does not.
Correction: Delete variable `result` and place the following statement in the function:

```
return x + y;
```

c) Error: The result of `n + sum(n - 1)` is not returned; `sum` returns an improper result.
Correction: Rewrite the statement in the `else` clause as

```
return n + sum(n - 1);
```

d) Error: Semicolon after the right parenthesis that encloses the parameter list, and redefining the parameter `a` in the function definition.
Correction: Delete the semicolon after the right parenthesis of the parameter list, and delete the declaration `float a;`.

e) Error: The function returns a value when it is not supposed to.
Correction: Eliminate the **return** statement.

**3.8** Because the programmer is declaring a reference parameter of type "reference to" **float** to get access through call-by-reference to the original argument variable.

**3.9** False. C++ allows direct call-by-reference via the use of reference parameters in addition to the use of pointers.

**3.10**
```
// Inline function that calculates the volume of a sphere
#include <iostream.h>

const float PI = 3.14159;

inline float sphereVolume(const float r) {return
                         4.0 / 3.0 * PI * r * r * r;}

main()
{
   float radius;

   cout << "Enter the length of the radius of your sphere: ";
   cin >> radius;
   cout << "Volume of sphere with radius " << radius <<
           "is " << sphereVolume(radius) << '\n';
   return 0;
}
```

## Exercises

**3.11** Show the value of x after each of the following statements is performed:

a) `x = fabs(7.5)`
b) `x = floor(7.5)`
c) `x = fabs(0.0)`
d) `x = ceil(0.0)`
e) `x = fabs(-6.4)`
f) `x = ceil(-6.4)`
g) `x = ceil(-fabs(-8+floor(-5.5)))`

**3.12** A parking garage charges a $2.00 minimum fee to park for up to three hours. The garage charges an additional $0.50 per hour for each hour *or part thereof* in excess of three hours. The maximum charge for any given 24-hour period is $10.00. Assume that no car parks for longer than 24 hours at a time. Write a program that will calculate and print the parking charges for each of 3 customers who parked their cars in this garage yesterday. You should enter the hours parked for each customer. Your program should print the results in a neat tabular format, and should calculate and print the total of yesterday's receipts. The program should use the function **calculate-Charges** to determine the charge for each customer. Your outputs should appear in the following format:

```
Car          Hours          Charge
1              1.5            2.00
2              4.0            2.50
3             24.0           10.00
TOTAL         29.5           14.50
```

**3.13** An application of function **floor** is rounding a value to the nearest integer. The statement

```
y = floor(x + .5);
```

will round the number **x** to the nearest integer and assign the result to **y**. Write a program that reads several numbers and uses the preceding statement to round each of these numbers to the nearest integer. For each number processed, print both the original number and the rounded number.

**3.14** Function **floor** may be used to round a number to a specific decimal place. The statement

```
y = floor(x * 10 + .5) / 10;
```

rounds **x** to the tenths position (the first position to the right of the decimal point). The statement

```
y = floor(x * 100 + .5) / 100;
```

rounds **x** to the hundredths position (i.e., the second position to the right of the decimal point). Write a program that defines four functions to round a number **x** in various ways:

a) **roundToInteger(number)**
b) **roundToTenths(number)**
c) **roundToHundredths(number)**
d) **roundToThousandths(number)**

For each value read, your program should print the original value, the number rounded to the nearest integer, the number rounded to the nearest tenth, the number rounded to the nearest hundredth, and the number rounded to the nearest thousandth.

**3.15** Answer each of the following questions.

a) What does it mean to choose numbers "at random?"
b) Why is the **rand** function useful for simulating games of chance?
c) Why would you randomize a program by using **srand**? Under what circumstances is it desirable not to randomize?
d) Why is it often necessary to scale and/or shift the values produced by **rand**?
e) Why is computerized simulation of real-world situations a useful technique?

**3.16** Write statements that assign random integers to the variable $n$ in the following ranges:

a) $1 \le n \le 2$
b) $1 \le n \le 100$
c) $0 \le n \le 9$
d) $1000 \le n \le 1112$
e) $-1 \le n \le 1$
f) $-3 \le n \le 11$

**3.17** For each of the following sets of integers, write a single statement that will print a number at random from the set.

a) 2, 4, 6, 8, 10.
b) 3, 5, 7, 9, 11.
c) 6, 10, 14, 18, 22.

**3.18** Write a function **integerPower(base, exponent)** that returns the value of

$$base^{\,exponent}$$

For example, **integerPower(3,4) = 3 * 3 * 3 * 3**. Assume that **exponent** is a positive, nonzero integer, and **base** is an integer. The function **integerPower** should use **for** or **while** to control the calculation. Do not use any math library functions.

**3.19** Define a function **hypotenuse** that calculates the length of the hypotenuse of a right triangle when the other two sides are given. Use this function in a program to determine the length of the hypotenuse for each of the following triangles. The function should take two arguments of type **double** and return the hypotenuse as a **double**.

| Triangle | Side 1 | Side 2 |
|---|---|---|
| 1 | 3.0 | 4.0 |
| 2 | 5.0 | 12.0 |
| 3 | 8.0 | 15.0 |

**3.20** Write a function **multiple** that determines for a pair of integers whether the second integer is a multiple of the first. The function should take two integer arguments and return 1 (true) if the second is a multiple of the first, and 0 (false) otherwise. Use this function in a program that inputs a series of pairs of integers.

**3.21** Write a program that inputs a series of integers and passes them one at a time to function **even** which uses the modulus operator to determine if an integer is even. The function should take an integer argument and return 1 if the integer is even and 0 otherwise.

**3.22** Write a function that displays at the left margin of the screen a solid square of asterisks whose side is specified in integer parameter **side**. For example, if **side** is **4**, the function displays

```
****
****
****
****
```

**3.23** Modify the function created in Exercise 3.22 to form the square out of whatever character is contained in character parameter **fillCharacter**. Thus if **side** is 5 and **fillCharacter** is "**#**" then this function should print

```
#####
#####
#####
#####
#####
```

**3.24** Use techniques similar to those developed in Exercises 3.22 and 3.23 to produce a program that graphs a wide range of shapes.

**3.25** Write program segments that accomplish each of the following:

a) Calculate the integer part of the quotient when integer **a** is divided by integer **b**.
b) Calculate the integer remainder when integer **a** is divided by integer **b**.
c) Use the program pieces developed in a) and b) to write a function that inputs an integer between 1 and 32767 and prints it as a series of digits, each pair of which is separated by two spaces. For example, the integer 4562 should be printed as

```
4  5  6  2
```

**3.26** Write a function that takes the time as three integer arguments (for hours, minutes, and seconds), and returns the number of seconds since the last time the clock "struck 12." Use this function to calculate the amount of time in seconds between two times, both of which are within one 12-hour cycle of the clock.

**3.27** Implement the following integer functions:

a) Function **`celsius`** returns the Celsius equivalent of a Fahrenheit temperature.

b) Function **`fahrenheit`** returns the Fahrenheit equivalent of a Celsius temperature.

c) Use these functions to write a program that prints charts showing the Fahrenheit equivalents of all Celsius temperatures from 0 to 100 degrees, and the Celsius equivalents of all Fahrenheit temperatures from 32 to 212 degrees. Print the outputs in a neat tabular format that minimizes the number of lines of output while remaining readable.

**3.28** Write a function that returns the smallest of three floating-point numbers.

**3.29** An integer number is said to be a *perfect number* if its factors, including 1 (but not the number itself), sum to the number. For example, 6 is a perfect number because 6 = 1 + 2 + 3. Write a function **`perfect`** that determines if parameter **`number`** is a perfect number. Use this function in a program that determines and prints all the perfect numbers between 1 and 1000. Print the factors of each perfect number to confirm that the number is indeed perfect. Challenge the power of your computer by testing numbers much larger than 1000.

**3.30** An integer is said to be *prime* if it is divisible only by 1 and itself. For example, 2, 3, 5, and 7 are prime, but 4, 6, 8, and 9 are not.

a) Write a function that determines if a number is prime.

b) Use this function in a program that determines and prints all the prime numbers between 1 and 10,000. How many of these 10,000 numbers do you really have to test before being sure that you have found all the primes?

c) Initially you might think that $n/2$ is the upper limit for which you must test to see if a number is prime, but you need only go as high as the square root of $n$. Why? Rewrite the program, and run it both ways. Estimate the performance improvement.

**3.31** Write a function that takes an integer value and returns the number with its digits reversed. For example, given the number 7631, the function should return 1367.

**3.32** The *greatest common divisor (GCD)* of two integers is the largest integer that evenly divides each of the two numbers. Write a function **`gcd`** that returns the greatest common divisor of two integers.

**3.33** Write a function **`qualityPoints`** that inputs a student's average and returns 4 if a student's average is 90-100, 3 if the average is 80-89, 2 if the average is 70-79, 1 if the average is 60-69, and 0 if the average is lower than 60.

**3.34** Write a program that simulates coin tossing. For each toss of the coin the program should print **`Heads`** or **`Tails`**. Let the program toss the coin 100 times, and count the number of times each side of the coin appears. Print the results. The program should call a separate function **`flip`** that takes no arguments and returns `0` for tails and `1` for heads. *Note:* If the program realistically simulates the coin tossing, then each side of the coin should appear approximately half the time.

**3.35** Computers are playing an increasing role in education. Write a program that will help an elementary school student learn multiplication. Use **`rand`** to produce two positive one-digit integers. It should then type a question such as:

```
How much is 6 times 7?
```

The student then types the answer. Your program checks the student's answer. If it is correct, print **`"Very good!"`** and then ask another multiplication question. If the answer is wrong, print **`"No. Please try again."`** and then let the student try the same question again repeatedly until the student finally gets it right.

**3.36** The use of computers in education is referred to as *computer-assisted instruction* (CAI). One problem that develops in CAI environments is student fatigue. This can be eliminated by varying the computer's dialogue to hold the student's attention. Modify the program of Exercise 3.35 so the various comments are printed for each correct answer and each incorrect answer as follows:

Responses to a correct answer

```
Very good!
Excellent!
Nice work!
Keep up the good work!
```

Responses to an incorrect answer

```
No. Please try again.
Wrong. Try once more.
Don't give up!
No. Keep trying.
```

Use the random number generator to choose a number from 1 to 4 to select an appropriate response to each answer. Use a `switch` structure to issue the responses.

**3.37** More sophisticated computer-aided instructions systems monitor the student's performance over a period of time. The decision to begin a new topic is often based on the student's success with previous topics. Modify the program of Exercise 3.36 to count the number of correct and incorrect responses typed by the student. After the student types 10 answers, your program should calculate the percentage of correct responses. If the percentage is lower than 75 percent, your program should print `"Please ask your instructor for extra help"` and then terminate.

**3.38** Write a program that plays the game of "guess the number" as follows: Your program chooses the number to be guessed by selecting an integer at random in the range 1 to 1000. The program then types:

```
I have a number between 1 and 1000.
Can you guess my number?
Please type your first guess.
```

The player then types a first guess. The program responds with one of the following:

```
1. Excellent! You guessed the number!
   Would you like to play again (y or n)?
2. Too low. Try again.
3. Too high. Try again.
```

If the player's guess is incorrect, your program should loop until the player finally gets the number right. Your program should keep telling the player `Too high` or `Too low` to help the player "zero in" on the correct answer. Note: The searching technique employed in this problem is called *binary search.* We will say more about this in the next problem.

**3.39** Modify the program of Exercise 3.38 to count the number of guesses the player makes. If the number is 10 or fewer, print `Either you know the secret or you got lucky!` If the player guesses the number in 10 tries, then print `Ahah! You know the secret!` If the player makes more than 10 guesses, then print `You should be able to do better!` Why should it take no more than 10 guesses? Well with each "good guess" the player should be able to eliminate half of the numbers. Now show why any number 1 to 1000 can be guessed in 10 or fewer tries.

**3.40** Write a recursive function **`power (base, exponent)`** that when invoked returns

$$base^{exponent}$$

For example, **`power(3, 4)`** `= 3 * 3 * 3 * 3`. Assume that **`exponent`** is an integer greater than or equal to 1. *Hint:* The recursion step would use the relationship

$$base^{exponent} = base \cdot base^{exponent - 1}$$

and the terminating condition occurs when **`exponent`** is equal to **`1`** because

$$base^1 = base$$

**3.41** The Fibonacci series

0, 1, 1, 2, 3, 5, 8, 13, 21, ...

begins with the terms 0 and 1 and has the property that each succeeding term is the sum of the two preceding terms. a) Write a *nonrecursive* function **`fibonacci(n)`** that calculates the *n*th Fibonacci number. b) Determine the largest Fibonacci number that can be printed on your system. Modify the program of part a) to use **`double`** instead of **`int`** to calculate and return Fibonacci numbers, and use this modified program to repeat part b).

**3.42** *(Towers of Hanoi)* Every budding computer scientist must grapple with certain classic problems, and the Towers of Hanoi (see Fig. 3.28) is one of the most famous of these. Legend has it that in a temple in the Far East, priests are attempting to move a stack of disks from one peg to another. The initial stack had 64 disks threaded onto one peg and arranged from bottom to top by decreasing size. The priests are attempting to move the stack from this peg to a second peg under the constraints that exactly one disk is moved at a time, and at no time may a larger disk be placed above a smaller disk. A third peg is available for temporarily holding disks. Supposedly the world will end when the priests complete their task, so there is little incentive for us to facilitate their efforts.

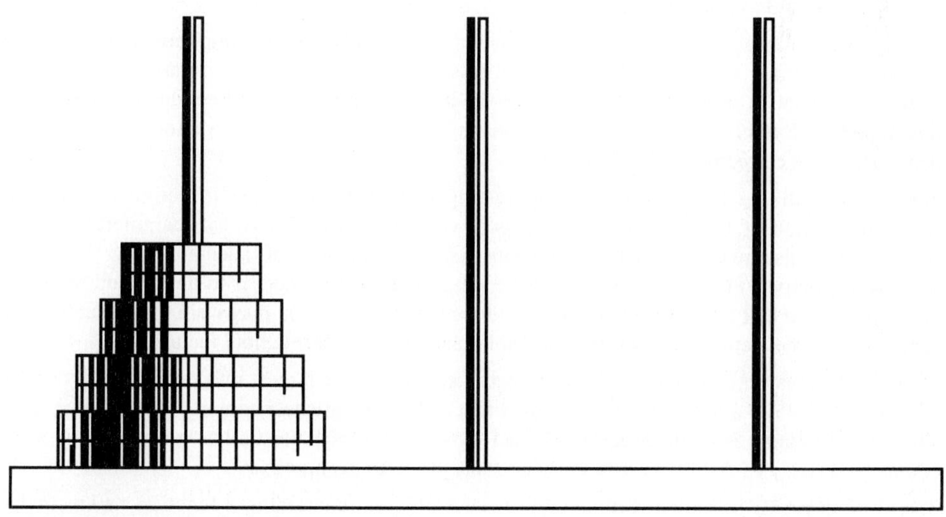

**Fig. 3.28** The Towers of Hanoi for the case with four disks.

Let us assume that the priests are attempting to move the disks from peg 1 to peg 3. We wish to develop an algorithm that will print the precise sequence of peg-to-peg disk transfers.

If we were to approach this problem with conventional methods, we would rapidly find ourselves hopelessly knotted up in managing the disks. Instead, if we attack the problem with recursion in mind, it immediately becomes tractable. Moving *n* disks can be viewed in terms of moving only *n* - 1 disks (and hence the recursion) as follows:

1. Move *n* - 1 disks from peg 1 to peg 2, using peg 3 as a temporary holding area.
2. Move the last disk (the largest) from peg 1 to peg 3.
3. Move the *n* - 1 disks from peg 2 to peg 3, using peg 1 as a temporary holding area.

The process ends when the last task involves moving *n* = 1 disk, i.e., the base case. This is accomplished by trivially moving the disk without the need for a temporary holding area.

Write a program to solve the Towers of Hanoi problem. Use a recursive function with four parameters:

1. The number of disks to be moved
2. The peg on which these disks are initially threaded
3. The peg to which this stack of disks is to be moved
4. The peg to be used as a temporary holding area

Your program should print the precise instructions it will take to move the disks from the starting peg to the destination peg. For example, to move a stack of three disks from peg 1 to peg 3, your program should print the following series of moves:

1 → 3 (This means move one disk from peg 1 to peg 3.)

1 → 2

3 → 2

1 → 3

2 → 1

2 → 3

1 → 3

**3.43** Any program that can be implemented recursively can be implemented iteratively, although sometimes with more difficulty and less clarity. Try writing an iterative version of the Towers of Hanoi. If you succeed, compare your iterative version with the recursive version you developed in Exercise 3.42. Investigate issues of performance, clarity, and your ability to demonstrate the correctness of the programs.

**3.44** (Visualizing Recursion) It is interesting to watch recursion "in action." Modify the factorial function of Fig. 3.14 to print its local variable and recursive call parameter. For each recursive call, display the outputs on a separate line and add a level of indentation. Do your utmost to make the outputs clear, interesting, and meaningful. Your goal here is to design and implement an output format that helps a person understand recursion better. You may want to add such display capabilities to the many other recursion examples and exercises throughout the text.

**3.45** The greatest common divisor of integers **`x`** and **`y`** is the largest integer that evenly divides both **`x`** and **`y`**. Write a recursive function **`gcd`** that returns the greatest common divisor of **`x`** and **`y`**. The **`gcd`** of **`x`** and **`y`** is defined recursively as follows: If **`y`** is equal to **`0`**, then **`gcd(x, y)`** is **`x`**; otherwise **`gcd(x, y)`** is **`gcd(y, x % y)`** where **`%`** is the modulus operator.

**3.46** Can **`main`** be called recursively? Write a program containing a function **`main`**. Include **`static`** local variable **`count`** initialized to 1. Postincrement and print the value of **`count`** each time **`main`** is called. Run your program. What happens?

**3.47** Exercises 3.35 through 3.37 developed a computer-assisted instruction program to teach an elementary school student multiplication. This exercise suggests enhancements to that program.

a) Modify the program to allow the user to enter a grade-level capability. A grade level of 1 means to use only single-digit numbers in the problems, a grade level of two means to use numbers as large as two-digits, etc.

b) Modify the program to allow the user to pick the type of arithmetic problems he or she wishes to study. An option of 1 means addition problems only, 2 means subtraction problems only, 3 means multiplication problems only, 4 means division problems only, and 5 means to randomly intermix problems of all these types.

**3.48** Write function **`distance`** that calculates the distance between two points (x1, y1) and (x2, y2). All numbers and return values should be of type **`float`**.

**3.49** What does the following program do?

```
#include <iostream.h>

main()
{
   int c;

   if ( ( c = cin.get() ) != EOF) {
      main();
      cout << c;
   }

   return 0;
}
```

**3.50** What does the following program do?

```
#include <iostream.h>

int mystery(int, int);

main()
{
   int x, y;

   cout << "Enter two integers: ";
   cin >> x >> y;
   cout << "The result is " << mystery(x, y) << endl;
   return 0;
}

// Parameter b must be a positive
// integer to prevent infinite recursion
int mystery(int a, int b)
{
   if (b == 1)
      return a;
   else
      return a + mystery(a, b - 1);
}
```

**3.51** After you determine what the program of Exercise 3.50 does, modify the program to function properly after removing the restriction of the second argument being nonnegative.

**3.52** Write a program that tests as many of the math library functions in Fig. 3.2 as you can. Exercise each of these functions by having your program print out tables of return values for a diversity of argument values.

**3.53** Find the error in each of the following program segments and explain how to correct it:

a)
```
float cube(float);      /* function prototype */
...
cube(float number)      /* function definition */
{
   return number * number * number;
}
```
b)
```
register auto int x = 7;
```
c)
```
int randomNumber = srand();
```
d)
```
float y = 123.45678;
int x;

x = y;
cout << (float) x << endl;
```
e)
```
double square(double number)
{
   double number;
   return number * number;
}
```
f)
```
int sum(int n)
{
   if (n == 0)
      return 0;
   else
      return n + sum(n);
}
```

**3.54** Modify the craps program of Fig. 3.10 to allow wagering. Package as a function the portion of the program that runs one game of craps. Initialize variable **bankBalance** to 1000 dollars. Prompt the player to enter a **wager**. Use a **while** loop to check that **wager** is less than or equal to **bankBalance** and if not prompt the user to reenter **wager** until a valid **wager** is entered. After a correct **wager** is entered, run one game of craps. If the player wins, increase **bankBalance** by **wager** and print the new **bankBalance**. If the player loses, decrease **bankBalance** by **wager**, print the new **bankBalance**, check if **bankBalance** has become zero, and if so print the message **"Sorry. You busted!"** As the game progresses, print various messages to create some "chatter" such as **"Oh, you're going for broke, huh?"**, or **"Aw cmon, take a chance!"**, or **"You're up big. Now's the time to cash in your chips!"**.

**3.55** Write a C++ program that uses an **inline** function **circleArea** to prompt the user for the radius of a circle, and to calculate and print the area of that circle.

**3.56** Write a complete C++ program with the two alternate functions specified below that each simply triple the variable **count** defined in **main**. Then compare and contrast the two approaches. These two functions are

a) Function **tripleCallByValue** that passes a copy of **count** call-by-value, triples the copy, and returns the new value.

b) Function **tripleByReference** that passes **count** with true call-by-reference via a reference parameter, and triples the original copy of **count** through its alias (i.e., the reference parameter).

**3.57** What is the purpose of the unary scope resolution operator?

**3.58** Write a program that uses a function template called **min** to determine the smaller of two arguments. Test the program using integer, character, and floating-point number pairs.

**3.59** Write a program that uses a function template called **max** to determine the larger of three arguments. Test the program using integer, character, and floating-point number pairs.

**3.60** Determine if the following program segments contain errors. For each error, explain how it can be corrected. Note: For a particular program segment, it is possible that no errors are present in the segment.

a)
```
template <class A>
int sum(int num1, int num2, int num3)
{
    return num1 + num2 + num3;
}
```
b)
```
void printResults(int x, int y)
{
    cout << "The sum is " << x + y << '\n';
    return x + y;
}
```
c)
```
template <A>
A product(A num1, A num2, A num3)
{
    return num1 * num2 * num3;
}
```
d)
```
double cube(int);
int cube(int);
```

# 4

# Arrays

## Objectives

- To introduce the array data structure.
- To understand the use of arrays to store, sort, and search lists and tables of values.
- To understand how to declare an array, initialize an array, and refer to individual elements of an array.
- To be able to pass arrays to functions.
- To understand basic sorting techniques.
- To be able to declare and manipulate multiple-subscript arrays.

*With sobs and tears he sorted out*
*Those of the largest size . . .*
Lewis Carroll

*Attempt the end, and never stand to doubt;*
*Nothing's so hard, but search will find it out.*
Robert Herrick

*Now go, and write it before them in a table,*
*and note it in a book.*
Isaiah 30:8

*'Tis in my memory lock'd,*
*And you yourself shall keep the key of it.*
William Shakespeare

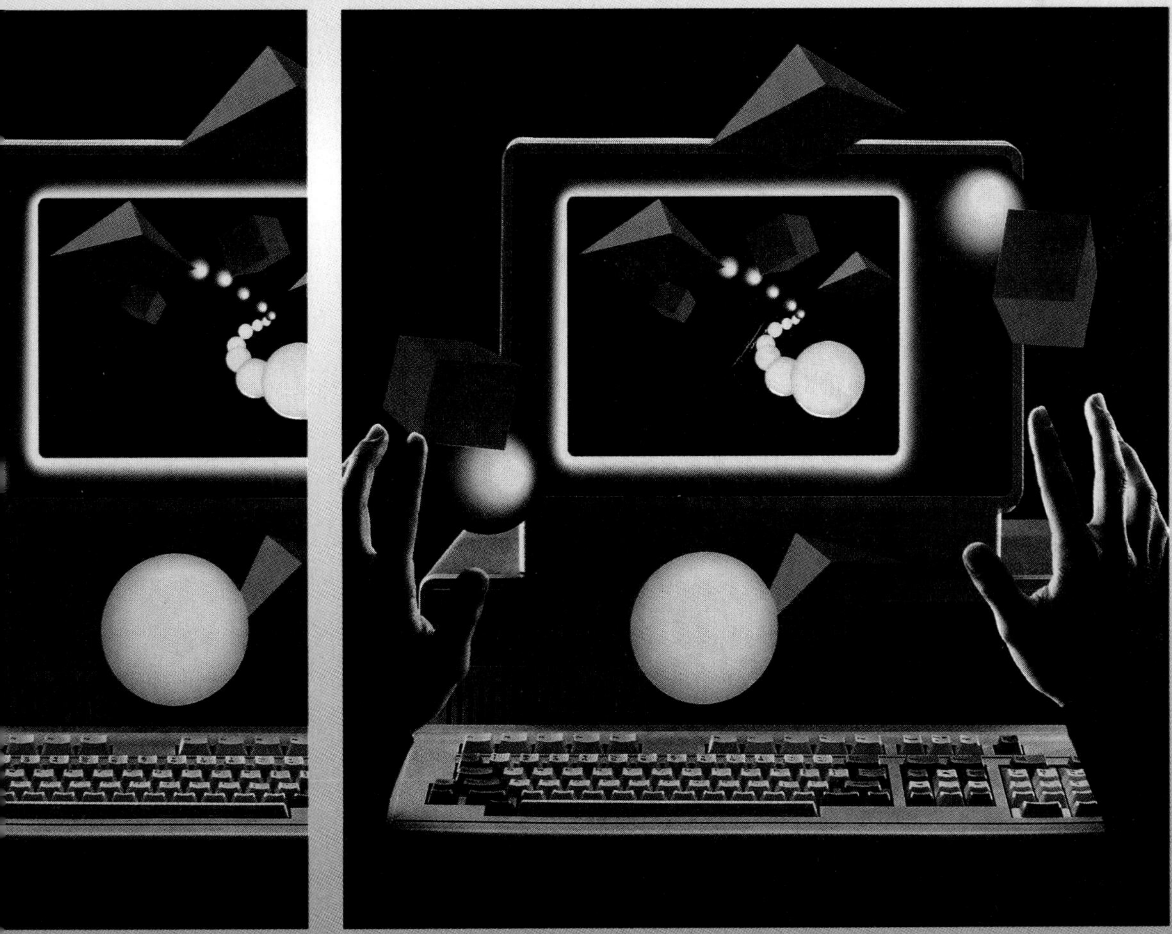

# Outline



## 4.1 Introduction

This chapter serves as an introduction to the important topic of data structures. *Arrays* are data structures consisting of related data items of the same type. In Chapter 6, we discuss the notions of *structures* and *classes*—each capable of holding related data items of possibly different types. Arrays and structures are "static" entities in that they remain the same size throughout program execution (they may, of course, be of automatic storage class and hence created and destroyed each time the blocks in which they are defined are entered and exited). In Chapter 15, we introduce dynamic data structures such as lists, queues, stacks, and trees that may grow and shrink as programs execute.

## 4.2 Arrays

An array is a consecutive group of memory locations that all have the same name and the same type. To refer to a particular location or element in the array, we specify the name of the array and the *position number* of the particular element in the array.

Figure 4.1 shows an integer array called `c`. This array contains twelve *elements.* Any one of these elements may be referred to by giving the name of the array followed by the position number of the particular element in square brackets (`[]`). The first element in every array is the *zeroth element.* Thus, the first element of array `c` is referred to as `c[0]`, the second element of array `c` is referred to as `c[1]`, the seventh element of array `c` is referred to as `c[6]`, and, in general, the *i*th element of array `c` is referred to as `c[i-1]`. Array names follow the same conventions as other variable names.

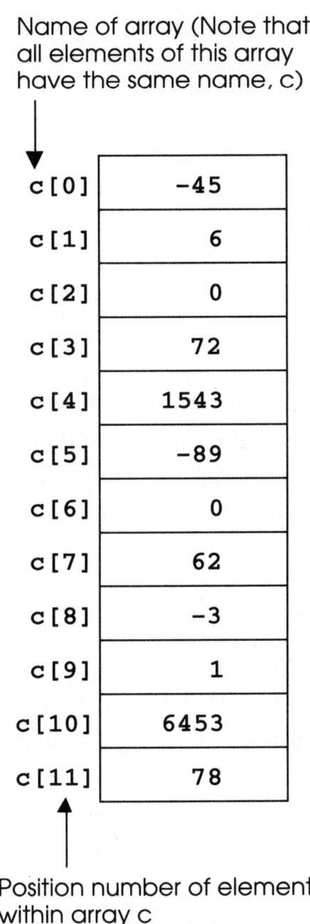


**Fig. 4.1** A 12-element array.

The position number contained within square brackets is more formally called a *subscript.* A subscript must be an integer or an integer expression. If a program uses an expression as a subscript, then the expression is evaluated to determine the subscript. For example, if we assume that variable **a** is equal to **5** and that variable **b** is equal to **6**, then the statement

```
c[a + b] += 2;
```

adds 2 to array element **c[11]**. Note that a subscripted array name is an lvalue—it can be used on the left side of an assignment.

Let us examine array **c** in Fig. 4.1 more closely. The *name* of the array is **c**. Its twelve elements are referred to as **c[0]**, **c[1]**, **c[2]**, ..., **c[11]**. The *value* of **c[0]** is **-45**, the value of **c[1]** is **6**, the value of **c[2]** is **0**, the value of **c[7]** is **62**, and the value of **c[11]** is **78**. To print the sum of the values contained in the first three elements of array **c**, we would write

```
cout << c[0] + c[1] + c[2] << endl;
```

To divide the value of the seventh element of array **c** by **2** and assign the result to the variable **x**, we would write

```
x = c[6] / 2;
```

***Common Programming Error 4.1***

*It is important to note the difference between the "seventh element of the array" and "array element seven." Because array subscripts begin at 0, the "seventh element of the array" has a subscript of 6, while "array element seven" has a subscript of 7 and is actually the eighth element of the array. This is a source of "off-by-one" errors.*

The brackets used to enclose the subscript of an array are actually considered to be an operator in C++. Brackets have the same level of precedence as parentheses. The chart in Fig. 4.2 shows the precedence and associativity of the operators introduced to this point in the text. They are shown top to bottom in decreasing order of precedence with their associativity and type.

## 4.3 Declaring Arrays

Arrays occupy space in memory. The programmer specifies the type of each element and the number of elements required by each array so that the compiler may reserve the appropriate amount of memory. To tell the compiler to reserve 12 elements for integer array **c**, the declaration

```
int c[12];
```

| Operators | Associativity | Type |
|---|---|---|
| `()` `[]` | left to right | highest |
| `++` `--` `!` `(`*type*`)` | right to left | unary |
| `*` `/` `%` | left to right | multiplicative |
| `+` `-` | left to right | additive |
| `<<` `>>` | left to right | insertion/extraction |
| `<` `<=` `>` `>=` | left to right | relational |
| `==` `!=` | left to right | equality |
| `&&` | left to right | logical and |
| `\|\|` | left to right | logical or |
| `?:` | right to left | conditional |
| `=` `+=` `-=` `*=` `/=` `%=` | right to left | assignment |
| `,` | left to right | comma |

**Fig. 4.2** Operator precedence.

is used. Memory may be reserved for several arrays with a single declaration. The following declaration reserves 100 elements for integer array **b** and 27 elements for integer array **x**.

```
int b[100], x[27];
```

Arrays may be declared to contain other data types. For example, an array of type **char** can be used to store a character string. Character strings and their similarity to arrays, and the relationship between pointers and arrays, are discussed in Chapter 5.

## 4.4 Examples Using Arrays

The program in Fig. 4.3 uses a **for** repetition structure to initialize the elements of a ten-element integer array **n** to zeros, and prints the array in tabular format. The first output statement displays the column heads for the columns printed in the **for** structure. Remember that **setw** specifies the field width in which the *next* value is to be output.

```
// initializing an array
#include <iostream.h>
#include <iomanip.h>

main()
{
   int n[10];

   for (int i = 0; i < 10; i++)     // initialize array
      n[i] = 0;

   cout << "Element" << setw(13) << "Value" << endl;

   for(i = 0; i < 10; i++)          // print array
      cout << setw(7) << i << setw(13) << n[i] << endl;

   return 0;
}
```

```
Element        Value
      0            0
      1            0
      2            0
      3            0
      4            0
      5            0
      6            0
      7            0
      8            0
      9            0
```

**Fig. 4.3** Initializing the elements of an array to zeros.

The elements of an array can also be initialized in the array declaration by following the declaration with an equal sign and a comma-separated list (enclosed in braces) of *initializers.* The program in Fig. 4.4 initializes an integer array with ten values and prints the array in tabular format.

If there are fewer initializers than elements in the array, the remaining elements are automatically initialized to zero. For example, the elements of the array **n** in Fig. 4.3 could have been initialized to zero with the declaration

```
int n[10] = {0};
```

which explicitly initializes the first element to zero and implicitly initializes the remaining nine elements to zero because there are fewer initializers than elements in the array. Remember that automatic arrays are not implicitly initialized to zero. The programmer must at least initialize the first element to zero for the remaining elements to be automatically zeroed. The method used in Fig. 4.3 can be done repeatedly as a program executes.

***Common Programming Error 4.2***

*Forgetting to initialize the elements of an array whose elements should be initialized.*

```
// Initializing an array with a declaration
#include <iostream.h>
#include <iomanip.h>

main()
{
   int n[10] = {32, 27, 64, 18, 95, 14, 90, 70, 60, 37};

   cout << "Element" << setw(13) << "Value" << endl;

   for (int i = 0; i < 10; i++)
      cout << setw(7) << i << setw(13) << n[i] << endl;

   return 0;
}
```

```
Element        Value
      0           32
      1           27
      2           64
      3           18
      4           95
      5           14
      6           90
      7           70
      8           60
      9           37
```

**Fig. 4.4** Initializing the elements of an array with a declaration.

The following array declaration

```
int n[5] = {32, 27, 64, 18, 95, 14};
```

would cause a syntax error because there are 6 initializers and only 5 array elements.

***Common Programming Error 4.3***

*Providing more initializers in an array initializer list than there are elements in the array is a syntax error.*

If the array size is omitted from a declaration with an initializer list, the number of elements in the array will be the number of elements in the initializer list. For example,

```
int n[] = {1, 2, 3, 4, 5};
```

would create a five-element array.

The program in Fig. 4.5 initializes the elements of a ten-element array **s** to the integers **2**, **4**, **6**, ..., **20**, and prints the array in tabular format. These numbers are generated by multiplying each successive value of the loop counter by **2** and adding **2**.

```
// Initialize array s to the even integers from 2 to 20.
#include <iostream.h>
#include <iomanip.h>

main()
{
   const int arraySize = 10;
   int s[arraySize];

   for (int j = 0; j < arraySize; j++)    // set the values
      s[j] = 2 + 2 * j;

   cout << "Element" << setw(13) << "Value" << endl;

   for (j = 0; j < arraySize; j++)    // print the values
      cout << setw(7) << j << setw(13) << s[j] << endl;

   return 0;
}
```

```
Element        Value
      0            2
      1            4
      2            6
      3            8
      4           10
      5           12
      6           14
      7           16
      8           18
      9           20
```

**Fig. 4.5** Generating the values to be placed into elements of an array.

The line

```
const int arraySize = 10;
```

uses the **`const`** qualifier to declare a so-called *constant variable* **`arraySize`** whose value is `10`. Constant variables must be initialized with a constant expression when they are declared and cannot be modified thereafter (Fig. 4.6 and Fig. 4.7). Constant variables are also called *named constants* or *read-only variables.* Note that the term "constant variable" is an oxymoron—a contradiction in terms like "jumbo shrimp" or "freezer burn." (Please send your favorite oxymorons to our email address listed in the Preface. Thanks!)

***Common Programming Error 4.4***

*Assigning a value to a constant variable in an executable statement is a syntax error.*

```
// A const object must be initialized
main()
{
   const int x;   // Error: x must be initialized

   x = 7;         // Error: cannot modify a const variable

   return 0;
}
```

```
Compiling FIG4_6.CPP:
Error FIG4_6.CPP 4: Constant variable 'x' must be
   initialized
Error FIG4_6.CPP 6: Cannot modify a const object
```

**Fig. 4.6** A **`const`** object must be initialized.

```
// Using a properly initialized constant variable
#include <iostream.h>

main()
{
   const int x = 7;  // initialized constant variable

   cout << "The value of constant variable x is: "
        << x << '\n';

   return 0;
}
```

```
The value of constant variable x is: 7
```

**Fig. 4.7** Correctly initializing and using a constant variable.

Constant variables can be placed anywhere a constant expression is expected. In Fig. 4.5, constant variable **arraySize** is used to specify the size of array **s** in the declaration

```
int s[arraySize];
```

Only constants can be used to declare automatic and static arrays.

Using constant variables to specify array sizes makes programs more *scalable*. In Fig. 4.5, the first **for** loop could fill a 1000-element array by simply changing the value of **arraySize** in its declaration from **10** to **1000**. If the constant variable **arraySize** had not been used, we would have to change the program in three separate places to scale the program to handle 1000 array elements. As programs get larger, this technique becomes more useful for writing clear programs.

***Software Engineering Observation 4.1***

*Defining the size of each array as a constant variable makes programs more scalable.*

***Common Programming Error 4.5***

*Ending a* **#include** *preprocessor directive with a semicolon. Remember that preprocessor directives are not C++ statements.*

The program in Fig. 4.8 sums the values contained in the twelve-element integer array **a**. The statement in the body of the **for** loop does the totaling. It is important to remember that the values being supplied as initializers for array **a** normally would be read into the program from the user at the keyboard. For example, the following **for** structure

```
for (int j = 0; j < arraySize; j++)
   cin >> a[j];
```

reads one value at a time from the keyboard and stores the value in element **a[j]**.

```
// Compute the sum of the elements of the array
#include <iostream.h>

main()
{
   const int arraySize = 12;
   int a[arraySize] = {1, 3, 5, 4, 7, 2, 99, 16, 45, 67, 89, 45};
   int total = 0;

   for (int i = 0; i < arraySize ; i++)
      total += a[i];

   cout << "Total of array element values is " << total << endl;
   return 0;
}
```

```
Total of array element values is 383
```

**Fig. 4.8** Computing the sum of the elements of an array.

Our next example uses arrays to summarize the results of data collected in a survey. Consider the problem statement:

*Forty students were asked to rate the quality of the food in the student cafeteria on a scale of 1 to 10 (1 means awful and 10 means excellent). Place the forty responses in an integer array and summarize the results of the poll.*

This is a typical array application (see Fig. 4.9). We wish to summarize the number of responses of each type (i.e., 1 through 10). The array **responses** is a 40-element array of the students' responses. We use an eleven-element array **frequency** to count the number of occurrences of each response. We ignore the first element, **frequency[0]**, because it is more logical to have the response 1 increment **frequency[1]** than **frequency[0]**. This allows us to use each response directly as the subscript in the **frequency** array.

```
// Student poll program
#include <iostream.h>
#include <iomanip.h>

main()
{
   const int responseSize = 40, frequencySize = 11;
   int responses[responseSize] = {1, 2, 6, 4, 8, 5, 9, 7, 8,
       10, 1, 6, 3, 8, 6, 10, 3, 8, 2, 7, 6, 5, 7, 6, 8, 6, 7,
       5, 6, 6, 5, 6, 7, 5, 6, 4, 8, 6, 8, 10};
   int frequency[frequencySize] = {0};

   for (int answer = 0; answer < responseSize; answer++)
      ++frequency[responses[answer]];

   cout << "Rating" << setw(17) << "Frequency" << endl;

   for (int rating = 1; rating < frequencySize; rating++)
      cout << setw(6) << rating
           << setw(17) << frequency[rating] << endl;

   return 0;
}
```

```
Rating         Frequency
     1                 2
     2                 2
     3                 2
     4                 2
     5                 5
     6                11
     7                 5
     8                 7
     9                 1
    10                 3
```

Fig. 4.9 A simple student poll analysis program.

***Good Programming Practice 4.1***

*Strive for program clarity. It is sometimes worthwhile to trade off the most efficient use of memory or processor time in favor of writing clearer programs.*

***Performance Tip 4.1***

*Sometimes performance considerations far outweigh clarity considerations.*

The first **`for`** loop takes the responses one at a time from the array **`response`** and increments one of the ten counters (**`frequency[1]`** to **`frequency[10]`**) in the **`frequency`** array. The key statement in the loop is

```
++frequency[responses[answer]];
```

This statement increments the appropriate **`frequency`** counter depending on the value of **`responses[answer]`**. For example, when the counter **`answer`** is **`0`**, **`responses[answer]`** is **`1`**, so **`++frequency[responses[answer]];`** is actually interpreted as

```
++frequency[1];
```

which increments array element one. When **`answer`** is **`1`**, **`responses[answer]`** is **`2`**, so **`++frequency[responses[answer]];`** is interpreted as

```
++frequency[2];
```

which increments array element two. When **`answer`** is **`2`**, **`responses[answer]`** is **`6`**, so **`++frequency[responses[answer]];`** is interpreted as

```
++frequency[6];
```

which increments array element six, and so on. Note that regardless of the number of responses processed in the survey, only an eleven-element array is required (ignoring element zero) to summarize the results. If the data contained invalid values such as 13, the program would attempt to add **`1`** to **`frequency[13]`**. This would be outside the bounds of the array. *C++ has no array bounds checking to prevent the computer from referring to an element that does not exist.* Thus, an executing program can walk off either end of an array without warning. The programmer should ensure that all array references remain within the bounds of the array. C++ is an extensible language. In Chapter 8, we will extend C++ by implementing an array as a user-defined type with classes. Our new array definition will enable us to perform many operations that are not standard for C++'s built-in arrays. For example, we will be able to compare arrays directly, assign one array to another, input and output entire arrays with **`cin`** and **`cout`**, initialize arrays automatically, prevent access to array elements not in the array bounds, and change the range of subscripts so that the first element of an array is not required to be element 0.

***Common Programming Error 4.6***

*Referring to an element outside the array bounds.*

*Good Programming Practice 4.2*

*When looping through an array, the array subscript should never go below 0 and should always be less than the total number of elements in the array (one less than the size of the array). Make sure the loop terminating condition prevents accessing elements outside this range.*

*Good Programming Practice 4.3*

*Programs should validate the correctness of all input values to prevent erroneous information from affecting a program's calculations.*

*Portability Tip 4.1*

*The (normally serious) effects of referencing elements outside the array bounds are system dependent.*

Our next example (Fig. 4.10) reads numbers from an array and graphs the information in the form of a bar chart or histogram—each number is printed, and then a bar consisting of that many asterisks is printed beside the number. The nested **for** loop actually draws the bars. Note the use of **endl** to end a histogram bar.

In Chapter 3 we stated that we would show a more elegant method of writing the dice-rolling program of Fig. 3.8. The problem was to roll a single six-sided die 6000 times to test whether the random number generator actually produces random numbers. An array version of this program is shown in Fig. 4.11.

```
// Histogram printing program
#include <iostream.h>
#include <iomanip.h>

main()
{
   const int arraySize = 10;
   int n[arraySize ] = {19, 3, 15, 7, 11, 9, 13, 5, 17, 1};

   cout << "Element" << setw(13) << "Value"
        << setw(17) << "Histogram" << endl;

   for (int i = 0; i < arraySize ; i++) {
      cout << setw(7) << i << setw(13) << n[i] << "        ";

      for(int j = 1; j <= n[i]; j++)    // print one bar
         cout << '*';

      cout << endl;
   }

   return 0;
}
```

Fig. 4.10 A program that prints histograms (part 1 of 2).

```
Element        Value       Histogram
   0              19       *******************
   1               3       ***
   2              15       ***************
   3               7       *******
   4              11       ***********
   5               9       *********
   6              13       *************
   7               5       *****
   8              17       *****************
   9               1       *
```

Fig. 4.10 A program that prints histograms (part 2 of 2).

```
// Roll a six-sided die 6000 times
#include <iostream.h>
#include <iomanip.h>
#include <stdlib.h>
#include <time.h>

main()
{
   const int arraySize = 7;
   int face, frequency[arraySize ] = {0};

   srand(time(NULL));

   for (int roll = 1; roll <= 6000; roll++) {
      face = rand() % 6 + 1;
      ++frequency[face];          // replaces 20-line switch
   }                              // of Fig. 3.10

   cout << "Face" << setw(17) << "Frequency" << endl;

   for (face = 1; face < arraySize ; face++)  // ignore element 0
      cout << setw(4) << face
           << setw(17) << frequency[face] << endl;

   return 0;
}
```

```
Face        Frequency
   1             1037
   2              987
   3             1013
   4             1028
   5              952
   6              983
```

Fig. 4.11 Dice-rolling program using arrays instead of `switch`.

To this point we have discussed only integer arrays. However, arrays may be of any type. We now discuss storing strings in character arrays. So far, the only string processing capability we have introduced is outputting a string with **cout** and **<<**. A string such as "**hello**" is really an array of characters. Character arrays have several unique features.

A character array can be initialized using a string literal. For example, the declaration

```
char string1[] = "first";
```

initializes the elements of array **string1** to the individual characters in the string literal **"first"**. The size of array **string1** in the preceding declaration is determined by the compiler based on the length of the string. It is important to note that the string **"first"** contains five characters *plus* a special string termination character called the *null character*. Thus, array **string1** actually contains six elements. The character constant representation of the null character is **'\0'**. All strings end with this character. A character array representing a string should always be declared large enough to hold the number of characters in the string and the terminating null character.

Character arrays also can be initialized with individual character constants in an initializer list. The preceding declaration is equivalent to

```
char string1[] = {'f', 'i', 'r', 's', 't', '\0'};
```

Because a string is an array of characters, we can access individual characters in a string directly using array subscript notation. For example, **string1[0]** is the character **'f'** and **string1[3]** is the character **'s'**.

We also can input a string directly into a character array from the keyboard using **cin** and **>>**. For example, the declaration

```
char string2[20];
```

creates a character array capable of storing a string of 19 characters and a terminating null character. The statement

```
cin >> string2;
```

reads a string from the keyboard into **string2**. Note in the preceding statement that only the name of the array is supplied to **cin**; no information about the size of the array is provided. It is the programmer's responsibility to ensure that the array into which the string is read is capable of holding any string the user types at the keyboard. **cin** reads characters from the keyboard until the first whitespace character is encountered—it does not care how large the array is. Thus, **cin** can insert data beyond the end of the array (see Section 5.12 for information on preventing insertion beyond the end of a character array).

***Common Programming Error 4.7***

*Not providing* **cin** *with a character array large enough to store a string typed at the keyboard can result in loss of data in a program and other run-time errors.*

A character array representing a string can be output with **cout** and **<<**. The array **string2** is printed with the statement

```
cout << string2 << endl;
```

Note that **cout**, like **cin**, does not care how large the character array is. The characters of the string are printed until a terminating null character is encountered.

Figure 4.12 demonstrates initializing a character array with a string literal, reading a string into a character array, printing a character array as a string, and accessing individual characters of a string.

Figure 4.12 uses a **for** structure to loop through the **string1** array and print the individual characters separated by spaces. The condition in the **for** structure, **string1[i] != '\0'**, is true while the terminating null character has not been encountered in the string.

Chapter 3 discussed the storage class specifier **static**. A **static** local variable in a function definition exists for the duration of the program but is only visible in the function body. We can apply **static** to a local array declaration so the array is not created and initialized each time the function is called, and the array is not destroyed each time the function is exited in the program.

Arrays that are declared **static** are initialized when the program is loaded. If a **static** array is not explicitly initialized by the programmer, that array is initialized to zero by the compiler.

```
// Treating character arrays as strings
#include <iostream.h>

main()
{
   char string1[20], string2[] = "string literal";

   cout << "Enter a string: ";
   cin >> string1;
   cout << "string1 is: " << string1 << endl
        << "string2 is: " << string2 << endl
        << "string1 with spaces between characters is:"
        << endl;

   for (int i = 0; string1[i] != '\0'; i++)
      cout << string1[i] << ' ';

   cout << endl;
   return 0;
}
```

```
Enter a string: Hello there
string1 is: Hello
string2 is: string literal
string1 with spaces between characters is:
H e l l o
```

**Fig. 4.12** Treating character arrays as strings.

Figure 4.13 demonstrates function **staticArrayInit** with a local array declared **static** and function **automaticArrayInit** with an automatic local array. Function **staticArrayInit** is called twice. The **static** local array is initialized to zero by the compiler. The function prints the array, adds 5 to each element, and prints the array again. The second time the function is called, the **static** array contains the values stored during the first function call. Function **automaticArrayInit** is also called twice. The elements of the automatic local array are initialized with the values 1, 2, and 3. The function prints the array, adds 5 to each element, and prints the array again. The second time the function is called, the array elements are initialized to 1, 2, and 3 again because the array has automatic storage class.

***Common Programming Error 4.8***

*Assuming that elements of a function's local* **static** *array are initialized to zero every time the function is called.*

```
// Static arrays are initialized to zero
#include <iostream.h>

void staticArrayInit(void);
void automaticArrayInit(void);

main()
{
  cout << "First call to each function:" << endl;
  staticArrayInit();
  automaticArrayInit();

  cout << endl << endl << "Second call to each function:" << endl;
  staticArrayInit();
  automaticArrayInit();

  return 0;
}

// function to demonstrate a static local array
void staticArrayInit(void)
{
  static int array1[3];

  cout << endl << "Values on entering staticArrayInit:" << endl;

  for (int i = 0; i < 3; i++)
     cout << "array1[" << i << "] = " << array1[i] << "  ";

  cout << endl << "Values on exiting staticArrayInit:" << endl;

  for (i = 0; i < 3; i++)
     cout << "array1[" << i << "] = " << (array1[i] += 5) << "  ";
}
```

Fig. 4.13 Comparing **static** array initialization and automatic array initialization (part 1 of 3).

```
// function to demonstrate an automatic local array
void automaticArrayInit(void)
{
   int array2[3] = {1, 2, 3};

   cout << endl << endl
        << "Values on entering automaticArrayInit:" << endl;

   for (int i = 0; i < 3; i++)
      cout << "array2[" << i << "] = " << array2[i] << "  ";

   cout << endl << "Values on exiting automaticArrayInit:"
        << endl;

   for (i = 0; i < 3; i++)
      cout << "array2[" << i << "] = "
           << (array2[i] += 5) << "  ";
}
```

**Fig. 4.13** Comparing `static` array initialization and automatic array initialization (part 2 of 3).

```
First call to each function:

Values on entering staticArrayInit:
array1[0] = 0  array1[1] = 0  array1[2] = 0
Values on exiting staticArrayInit:
array1[0] = 5  array1[1] = 5  array1[2] = 5

Values on entering automaticArrayInit:
array2[0] = 1  array2[1] = 2  array2[2] = 3
Values on exiting automaticArrayInit:
array2[0] = 6  array2[1] = 7  array2[2] = 8

Second call to each function:

Values on entering staticArrayInit:
array1[0] = 5  array1[1] = 5  array1[2] = 5
Values on exiting staticArrayInit:
array1[0] = 10  array1[1] = 10  array1[2] = 10

Values on entering automaticArrayInit:
array2[0] = 1  array2[1] = 2  array2[2] = 3
Values on exiting automaticArrayInit:
array2[0] = 6  array2[1] = 7  array2[2] = 8
```

**Fig. 4.13** Comparing `static` array initialization and automatic array initialization (part 3 of 3).

## 4.5 Passing Arrays to Functions

To pass an array argument to a function, specify the name of the array without any brackets. For example, if array **hourlyTemperatures** has been declared as

```
int hourlyTemperatures[24];
```

the function call statement

```
modifyArray(hourlyTemperatures, 24);
```

passes array **hourlyTemperatures** and its size to function **modifyArray**. When passing an array to a function, the array size is often passed so the function can process the specific number of elements in the array. In Chapter 8, when we introduce the **Array** class, we will build the size of the array into the user-defined type—every **Array** object that we create will "know" its own size. Thus, when we pass an **Array** object into a function we no longer will have to pass the size of the array as an argument.

C++ automatically passes arrays to functions using simulated call-by-reference—the called functions can modify the element values in the callers' original arrays. The value of the name of the array is the address of the first element of the array. Because the starting address of the array is passed, the called function knows precisely where the array is stored. Therefore, when the called function modifies array elements in its function body, it is modifying the actual elements of the array in their original memory locations.

***Performance Tip 4.2***

*Passing arrays simulated call-by-reference makes sense for performance reasons. If arrays were passed call-by-value, a copy of each element would be passed. For large, frequently passed arrays, this would be time consuming and would consume considerable storage for the copies of the arrays.*

***Software Engineering Observation 4.2***

*It is possible to pass an array by value by using a simple trick we explain in Chapter 6.*

Although entire arrays are passed simulated call-by-reference, individual array elements are passed call-by-value exactly as simple variables are. Such simple single pieces of data are called *scalars* or *scalar quantities.* To pass an element of an array to a function, use the subscripted name of the array element as an argument in the function call. In Chapter 5, we show how to simulate call-by-reference for scalars (i.e., individual variables and array elements).

For a function to receive an array through a function call, the function's parameter list must specify that an array will be received. For example, the function header for function **modifyArray** might be written as

```
void modifyArray(int b[], int arraySize)
```

indicating that **modifyArray** expects to receive an array of integers in parameter **b** and the number of array elements in parameter **arraySize**. The size of the array is not required between the array brackets. If it is included, the compiler will ignore it. Because arrays are passed simulated call-by-reference, when the called function uses the array name **b**, it will in fact be referring to the actual array in the caller (array **hourlyTemperatures** in the preceding call). In Chapter 5, we introduce other notations for indicating that an array is being received by a function. As we will see, these notations are based on the intimate relationship between arrays and pointers.

Note the strange appearance of the function prototype for **modifyArray**

```
void modifyArray(int [], int);
```

This prototype could have been written

```
void modifyArray(int anyArrayName[], int anyVariableName)
```

but as we learned in Chapter 3, C++ compilers ignore variable names in prototypes.

***Good Programming Practice 4.4***

*Some programmers include variable names in function prototypes to make programs clearer. The compiler ignores these names.*

Remember, the prototype tells the compiler the number of arguments and the types of each argument (in the order in which the arguments are expected to appear).

The program in Fig. 4.14 demonstrates the difference between passing an entire array and passing an array element. The program first prints the five elements of integer array **a**. Next, **a** and its size are passed to function **modifyArray** where each of **a**'s elements is multiplied by 2. Then **a** is reprinted in **main**. As the output shows, the elements of **a** are indeed modified by **modifyArray**. Now the program prints the value of **a[3]** and passes it to function **modifyElement**. Function **modifyElement** multiplies its argument by 2 and prints the new value. Note that when **a[3]** is reprinted in **main**, it has not been modified because individual array elements are passed call-by-value.

There may be situations in your programs in which a function should not be allowed to modify array elements. Because arrays are always passed simulated call-by-reference, modification of values in an array is difficult to control. C++ provides the type qualifier **const** to prevent modification of array values in a function. When an array parameter is preceded by the **const** qualifier, the elements of the array become constant in the function body, and any attempt to modify an element of the array in the function body results in a compile time error. This enables the programmer to correct a program so it does not attempt to modify array elements.

Figure 4.15 demonstrates the **const** qualifier. Function **tryToModifyArray** is defined with parameter **const int b[]** which specifies that array **b** is constant and cannot be modified. The output shows the error messages produced by the Borland C++ compiler. Each of the three attempts by the function to modify array elements results in the compiler error "**Cannot modify a const object**." The **const** qualifier will be discussed again in Chapter 7.

***Software Engineering Observation 4.3***

*The* **const** *type qualifier can be applied to an array parameter in a function definition to prevent the original array from being modified in the function body. This is another example of the principle of least privilege. Functions should not be given the capability to modify an array unless it is absolutely necessary.*

```
// Passing arrays and individual array elements to functions
#include <iostream.h>
#include <iomanip.h>

void modifyArray(int [], int);  // appears strange
void modifyElement(int);

main()
{
   const int arraySize = 5;
   int a[arraySize] = {0, 1, 2, 3, 4};

   cout << "Effects of passing entire array call-by-reference:"
        << endl << endl
        << "The values of the original array are:" << endl;

   for (int i = 0; i < arraySize; i++)
      cout << setw(3) << a[i];

   cout << endl;

   modifyArray(a, arraySize);  // array a passed call-by-reference

   cout << "The values of the modified array are:" << endl;

   for (i = 0; i < arraySize; i++)
      cout << setw(3) << a[i];

   cout << endl << endl << endl
        << "Effects of passing array element call-by-value:"
        << endl << endl << "The value of a[3] is "
        << a[3] << endl;

   modifyElement(a[3]);

   cout << "The value of a[3] is " << a[3] << endl;

   return 0;
}

void modifyArray(int b[], int sizeOfArray)
{
   for (int j = 0; j < sizeOfArray; j++)
      b[j] *= 2;
}

void modifyElement(int e)
{
   cout << "Value in modifyElement is "
        << (e *= 2) << endl;
}
```

**Fig. 4.14** Passing arrays and individual array elements to functions (part 1 of 2).

```
Effects of passing entire array call-by-reference:

The values of the original array are:
  0  1  2  3  4
The values of the modified array are:
  0  2  4  6  8


Effects of passing array element call-by-value:

The value of a[3] is 6
Value in modifyElement is 12
The value of a[3] is 6
```

**Fig. 4.14** Passing arrays and individual array elements to functions (part 2 of 2).

```
// Demonstrating the const type qualifier
#include <iostream.h>

void tryToModifyArray(const int []);

main()
{
   int a[] = {10, 20, 30};

   cout << a[0] << ' ' << a[1] << ' ' << a[2] << endl;
   return 0;
}

void tryToModifyArray(const int b[])
{
   b[0] /= 2;    // error
   b[1] /= 2;    // error
   b[2] /= 2;    // error
}
```

```
Compiling FIG4_15.CPP:
Error FIG4_15.CPP 16: Cannot modify a const object
Error FIG4_15.CPP 17: Cannot modify a const object
Error FIG4_15.CPP 18: Cannot modify a const object
Warning FIG4_15.CPP 19: Parameter 'b' is never used
```

**Fig. 4.15** Demonstrating the `const` type qualifier.

## 4.6 Sorting Arrays

*Sorting* data (i.e., placing the data into some particular order such as ascending or descending) is one of the most important computing applications. A bank sorts all checks by account number so that it can prepare individual bank statements at the end of each month. Telephone companies sort their lists of accounts by last name and, within that, by first name to make it easy to find phone numbers. Virtually every organization must sort some data and in many cases massive amounts of data. Sorting data is an intriguing problem which has attracted some of the most intense research efforts in the field of computer science. In this chapter we discuss the simplest known sorting scheme. In the exercises and in Chapter 15, we investigate more complex schemes that yield superior performance.

***Performance Tip 4.3***

*Often, the simplest algorithms perform poorly. Their virtue is that they are easy to write, test and debug. However, more complex algorithms are often needed to realize maximum performance.*

The program in Fig. 4.16 sorts the values of the ten-element array **a** into ascending order. The technique we use is called the *bubble sort* or the *sinking sort* because the smaller values gradually "bubble" their way upward to the top of the array like air bubbles rising in water, while the larger values sink to the bottom of the array. The technique is to make several passes through the array. On each pass, successive pairs of elements are compared. If a pair is in increasing order (or the values are identical), we leave the values as they are. If a pair is in decreasing order, their values are swapped in the array.

First the program compares **a[0]** to **a[1]**, then **a[1]** to **a[2]**, then **a[2]** to **a[3]**, and so on until it completes the pass by comparing **a[8]** to **a[9]**. Although there are 10 elements, only nine comparisons are performed. Because of the way the successive comparisons are made, a large value may move down the array many positions on a single pass, but a small value may move up only one position. On the first pass, the largest value is guaranteed to sink to the bottom element of the array, **a[9]**. On the second pass, the second largest value is guaranteed to sink to **a[8]**. On the ninth pass, the ninth largest value sinks to **a[1]**. This leaves the smallest value in **a[0]**, so only nine passes are needed to sort a 10-element array.

The sorting is performed by the nested **for** loop. If a swap is necessary, it is performed by the three assignments

```
hold = a[i];
a[i] = a[i + 1];
a[i + 1] = hold;
```

where the extra variable **hold** temporarily stores one of the two values being swapped. The swap cannot be performed with only the two assignments

```
a[i] = a[i + 1];
a[i + 1] = a[i];
```

If, for example, **a[i]** is **7** and **a[i + 1]** is **5**, after the first assignment both values will be **5** and the value **7** will be lost. Hence the need for the extra variable **hold**.

The chief virtue of the bubble sort is that it is easy to program. However, the bubble sort runs slowly. This becomes apparent when sorting large arrays. In the exercises, we will develop more efficient versions of the bubble sort and investigate some far more efficient sorts than the bubble sort. More advanced courses investigate sorting and searching in greater depth.

```
// This program sorts an array's values into
// ascending order
#include <iostream.h>
#include <iomanip.h>

main()
{
   const int arraySize = 10;
   int a[arraySize ] = {2, 6, 4, 8, 10, 12, 89, 68, 45, 37};
   int hold;

   cout << "Data items in original order" << endl;

   for (int i = 0; i < arraySize; i++)
      cout << setw(4) << a[i];

   for (int pass = 1; pass < arraySize; pass++) // passes

      for (i = 0; i < arraySize - 1; i++)       // one pass

         if (a[i] > a[i + 1]) {          // one comparison
            hold = a[i];                       // one swap
            a[i] = a[i + 1];
            a[i + 1] = hold;
         }

   cout << endl << "Data items in ascending order" << endl;

   for (i = 0; i < arraySize; i++)
      cout << setw(4) << a[i];

   cout << endl;
   return 0;
}
```

```
Data items in original order
   2   6   4   8  10  12  89  68  45  37
Data items in ascending order
   2   4   6   8  10  12  37  45  68  89
```

**Fig. 4.16** Sorting an array with bubble sort.

## 4.7 Case Study: Computing Mean, Median, and Mode Using Arrays

We now consider a larger example. Computers are commonly used to compile and analyze the results of surveys and opinion polls. The program in Fig. 4.17 uses array **response** initialized with 99 (represented by constant variable **responseSize**) responses to a survey. Each of the responses is a number from 1 to 9. The program computes the mean, median, and mode of the 99 values.

```
// This program introduces the topic of survey data analysis.
// It computes the mean, median, and  mode of the data.
#include <iostream.h>
#include <iomanip.h>

void mean(const int [], int);
void median(const int [], int);
void mode(const int [], int [], int);
void bubbleSort(int[], int);
void printArray(const int[], int);

main()
{
   const int responseSize = 99;
   int frequency[10] = {0},
       response[responseSize] = {6, 7, 8, 9, 8, 7, 8, 9, 8, 9,
                                 7, 8, 9, 5, 9, 8, 7, 8, 7, 8,
                                 6, 7, 8, 9, 3, 9, 8, 7, 8, 7,
                                 7, 8, 9, 8, 9, 8, 9, 7, 8, 9,
                                 6, 7, 8, 7, 8, 7, 9, 8, 9, 2,
                                 7, 8, 9, 8, 9, 8, 9, 7, 5, 3,
                                 5, 6, 7, 2, 5, 3, 9, 4, 6, 4,
                                 7, 8, 9, 6, 8, 7, 8, 9, 7, 8,
                                 7, 4, 4, 2, 5, 3, 8, 7, 5, 6,
                                 4, 5, 6, 1, 6, 5, 7, 8, 7};

   mean(response, responseSize);
   median(response, responseSize);
   mode(frequency, response, responseSize);

   return 0;
}

void mean(const int answer[], int arraySize)
{
   int total = 0;

   cout << "********" << endl << "  Mean" << endl
        << "********" << endl;

   for (int j = 0; j < arraySize; j++)
      total += answer[j];

   cout << "The mean is the average value of the data" << endl
        << "items. The mean is equal to the total of" << endl
        << "all the data items divided by the number" << endl
        << "of data items (" << arraySize
        << "). The mean value for" << endl << "this run is: "
        << total << " / " << arraySize << " = "
        << setiosflags(ios::fixed | ios::showpoint)
        << setprecision(4) << (float) total / arraySize
        << endl << endl;
}
```

Fig. 4.17 Survey data analysis program (part 1 of 3).

```
void median(const int answer[], int size)
{
   cout << endl << "********" << endl << " Median" << endl
        << "********" << endl
        << "The unsorted array of responses is";

   printArray(answer, size);
   bubbleSort(answer, size);
   cout << endl << endl << "The sorted array is";
   printArray(answer, size);
   cout << endl << endl << "The median is element " << size / 2
        << " of" << endl << "the sorted " << size
        << " element array." << endl
        << "For this run the median is "
        << answer[size / 2] << endl << endl;
}

void mode(const int freq[], int answer[], int size)
{
   int largest = 0, modeValue = 0;

   cout << endl << "********" << endl << "  Mode" << endl
        << "********" << endl;

   for (int rating = 1; rating <= 9; rating++)
      freq[rating] = 0;

   for (int j = 0; j < size; j++)
      ++freq[answer[j]];

   cout << "Response"<< setw(11) << "Frequency"
        << setw(19) << "Histogram" << endl << endl << setw(54)
        << "1    1    2    2" << endl << setw(54)
        << "5    0    5    0    5" << endl << endl;

   for (rating = 1; rating <= 9; rating++) {
      cout << setw(8) << rating << setw(11)
           << freq[rating] << "          ";

      if (freq[rating] > largest) {
         largest = freq[rating];
         modeValue = rating;
      }

      for (int h = 1; h <= freq[rating]; h++)
         cout << '*';

      cout << endl;
   }

   cout << "The mode is the most frequent value." << endl
        << "For this run the mode is " << modeValue
        << " which occurred " << largest << " times." << endl;
}
```

**Fig. 4.17** Survey data analysis program (part 2 of 3).

```
void bubbleSort(int a[], int size)
{
   int hold;

   for (int pass = 1; pass < size; pass++)

      for (int j = 0; j < size - 1; j++)

         if (a[j] > a[j+1]) {
            hold = a[j];
            a[j] = a[j+1];
            a[j+1] = hold;
         }
}

void printArray(const int a[], int size)
{
   for (int j = 0; j < size; j++) {

      if (j % 20 == 0)
         cout << endl;

      cout << setw(2) << a[j];
   }
}
```

**Fig. 4.17** Survey data analysis program (part 3 of 3).

The mean is the arithmetic average of the 99 values. Function **mean** computes the mean by totaling the 99 elements and dividing the result by 99.

The median is the "middle value." Function **median** determines the median by calling function **bubbleSort** to sort the array of responses into ascending order, and picking the middle element, **answer[responseSize / 2]**, of the sorted array. Note that when there is an even number of elements, the median should be calculated as the mean of the two middle elements. Function **median** does not currently provide this capability. Function **printArray** is called to output the **response** array.

The mode is the value that occurs most frequently among the 99 responses. Function **mode** determines the mode by counting the number of responses of each type, then selecting the value with the greatest count. This version of function **mode** does not handle a tie (see Exercise 4.14). Function **mode** also produces a histogram to aid in determining the mode graphically. Fig. 4.18 contains a sample run of this program. This example includes most of the common manipulations usually required in array problems, including passing arrays to functions.

## 4.8 Searching Arrays: Linear Search and Binary Search

Often, a programmer will be working with large amounts of data stored in arrays. It may be necessary to determine whether an array contains a value that matches a certain *key value*. The process of finding a particular element of an array is called *searching*. In this section we discuss two searching techniques—the simple *linear search* technique and the

```
********
  Mean
********
The mean is the average value of the data
items. The mean is equal to the total of
all the data items divided by the number
of data items (99). The mean value for
this run is: 681 / 99 = 6.8788


********
 Median
********
The unsorted array of responses is
 6 7 8 9 8 7 8 9 8 9 7 8 9 5 9 8 7 8 7 8
 6 7 8 9 3 9 8 7 8 7 7 8 9 8 9 8 9 7 8 9
 6 7 8 7 8 7 9 8 9 2 7 8 9 8 9 8 9 7 5 3
 5 6 7 2 5 3 9 4 6 4 7 8 9 6 8 7 8 9 7 8
 7 4 4 2 5 3 8 7 5 6 4 5 6 1 6 5 7 8 7

The sorted array is
 1 2 2 2 3 3 3 3 4 4 4 4 4 5 5 5 5 5 5 5
 5 6 6 6 6 6 6 6 6 6 7 7 7 7 7 7 7 7 7 7
 7 7 7 7 7 7 7 7 7 7 7 7 7 8 8 8 8 8 8 8
 8 8 8 8 8 8 8 8 8 8 8 8 8 8 8 8 8 8 8 8
 9 9 9 9 9 9 9 9 9 9 9 9 9 9 9 9 9 9 9

The median is element 49 of
the sorted 99 element array.
For this run the median is 7


********
  Mode
********
Response  Frequency          Histogram

                                     1    1    2    2
                                5    0    5    0    5

      1          1           *
      2          3           ***
      3          4           ****
      4          5           *****
      5          8           ********
      6          9           *********
      7         23           ***********************
      8         27           ***************************
      9         19           *******************
The mode is the most frequent value.
For this run the mode is 8 which occurred 27 times.
```

**Fig. 4.18** Sample run for the survey data analysis program.

more efficient *binary search* technique. Exercises 4.33 and 4.34 at the end of this chapter ask you to implement recursive versions of the linear search and the binary search.

The linear search (Fig. 4.19) compares each element of the array with the *search key*. Since the array is not in any particular order, it is just as likely that the value will be found in the first element as the last. On average, therefore, the program will have to compare the search key with half the elements of the array.

```
// Linear search of an array
#include <iostream.h>

int linearSearch(int [], int, int);

main()
{
   const int arraySize = 100;
   int a[arraySize], searchKey, element;

   for (int x = 0; x < arraySize; x++)   // create some data
      a[x] = 2 * x;

   cout << "Enter integer search key:" << endl;
   cin >> searchKey;
   element = linearSearch(a, searchKey, arraySize);

   if (element != -1)
      cout << "Found value in element " << element << endl;
   else
      cout << "Value not found" << endl;

   return 0;
}

int linearSearch(int array[], int key, int sizeOfArray)
{
   for (int n = 0; n < sizeOfArray; n++)
      if (array[n] == key)
         return n;

   return -1;
}
```

```
Enter integer search key:
36
Found value in element 18
```

```
Enter integer search key:
37
Value not found
```

Fig. 4.19 Linear search of an array.

The linear searching method works well for small arrays or for unsorted arrays. However, for large arrays linear searching is inefficient. If the array is sorted, the high-speed binary search technique can be used.

The binary search algorithm eliminates one half of the elements in the array being searched after each comparison. The algorithm locates the middle element of the array and compares it to the search key. If they are equal, the search key is found and the array subscript of that element is returned. Otherwise, the problem is reduced to searching one half of the array. If the search key is less than the middle element of the array, the first half of the array is searched, otherwise the second half of the array is searched. If the search key is not the middle element in the specified subarray (piece of the original array), the algorithm is repeated on one quarter of the original array. The search continues until the search key is equal to the middle element of a subarray or until the subarray consists of one element that is not equal to the search key (i.e., the search key is not found).

In a worst case scenario, searching an array of 1024 elements will take only 10 comparisons using a binary search. Repeatedly dividing 1024 by 2 (because after each comparison we are able to eliminate half of the array) yields the values 512, 256, 128, 64, 32, 16, 8, 4, 2, and 1. The number 1024 ($2^{10}$) is divided by 2 only ten times to get the value 1. Dividing by 2 is equivalent to one comparison in the binary search algorithm. An array of 1048576 ($2^{20}$) elements takes a maximum of 20 comparisons to find the search key. An array of one billion elements takes a maximum of 30 comparisons to find the search key. This is a tremendous increase in performance over the linear search that required comparing the search key to an average of half the elements in the array. For a one billion element array, this is a difference between an average of 500 million comparisons and a maximum of 30 comparisons! The maximum number of comparisons needed for the binary search of any sorted array can be determined by finding the first power of 2 greater than the number of elements in the array.

Figure 4.20 presents the iterative version of function **binarySearch**. The function receives four arguments—an integer array **b**, an integer **searchKey**, the **low** array subscript, and the **high** array subscript. If the search key does not match the middle element of a subarray, the **low** subscript or **high** subscript is adjusted so a smaller subarray can be searched. If the search key is less than the middle element, the **high** subscript is set to **middle - 1**, and the search is continued on the elements from **low** to **middle - 1**. If the search key is greater than the middle element, the **low** subscript is set to **middle + 1**, and the search is continued on the elements from **middle + 1** to **high**. The program uses an array of 15 elements. The first power of 2 greater than the number of elements in this array is 16 ($2^4$), so a maximum of 4 comparisons are required to find the search key. Function **printHeader** outputs the array subscripts and function **printRow** to output each subarray during the binary search process. The middle element in each subarray is marked with an asterisk (*) to indicate the element to which the search key is compared.

## 4.9 Multiple-Subscripted Arrays

Arrays in C++ can have multiple subscripts. A common use of multiple-subscripted arrays is to represent *tables* of values consisting of information arranged in *rows* and *columns*. To identify a particular table element, we must specify two subscripts: The first

```
// Binary search of an array
#include <iostream.h>
#include <iomanip.h>

int binarySearch(int [], int, int, int, int);
void printHeader(int);
void printRow(int [], int, int, int, int);

main()
{
   const int arraySize = 15;
   int a[arraySize], key, result;

   for (int i = 0; i < arraySize; i++)
      a[i] = 2 * i;    // place some data in array

   cout << "Enter a number between 0 and 28: ";
   cin >> key;

   printHeader(arraySize);
   result = binarySearch(a, key, 0, arraySize - 1, arraySize);

   if (result != -1)
      cout << endl << key << " found in array element "
           << result << endl;
   else
      cout << endl << key << " not found" << endl;

   return 0;
}

// Binary search
int binarySearch(int b[], int searchKey, int low, int high,
                 int size)
{
   int middle;

   while (low <= high) {
      middle = (low + high) / 2;

      printRow(b, low, middle, high, size);

      if (searchKey == b[middle])  // match
         return middle;
      else if (searchKey < b[middle])
         high = middle - 1;        // search low end of array
      else
         low = middle + 1;         // search high end of array
   }

   return -1;   // searchKey not found
}
```

**Fig. 4.20** Binary search of a sorted array (part 1 of 3).

```
// Print a header for the output
void printHeader(int size)
{
   cout << endl << "Subscripts:" << endl;

   for (int i = 0; i < size; i++)
      cout << setw(3) << i << ' ';

   cout << endl;

   for (i = 0; i < size; i++)
      cout << "----";

   cout << endl;
}

// Print one row of output showing the current
// part of the array being processed.
void printRow(int b[], int low, int mid, int high, int size)
{
   for (int i = 0; i < size; i++)
      if (i < low || i > high)
         cout << "    ";
      else if (i == mid)
         cout << setw(3) << b[i] << '*';  // mark middle value
      else
         cout << setw(3) << b[i] << ' ';

   cout << endl;
}
```

**Fig. 4.20** Binary search of a sorted array (part 2 of 3).

(by convention) identifies the element's row, and the second (by convention) identifies the element's column. Tables or arrays that require two subscripts to identify a particular element are called *double-subscripted arrays.* Note that multiple-subscripted arrays can have more than two subscripts. C++ compilers support at least 12 array subscripts.

Fig. 4.21 illustrates a double-subscripted array, **a**. The array contains three rows and four columns, so it is said to be a 3-by-4 array. In general, an array with $m$ rows and $n$ columns is called an *m-by-n array.*

Every element in array **a** is identified in Fig. 4.21 by an element name of the form **a[i][j]**; **a** is the name of the array, and **i** and **j** are the subscripts that uniquely identify each element in **a**. Notice that the names of the elements in the first row all have a first subscript of **0**; the names of the elements in the fourth column all have a second subscript of **3**.

***Common Programming Error 4.9***

*Referencing a double-subscripted array element* **a[x][y]** *incorrectly as* **a[x, y]**. *Actually,* **a[x, y]** *is treated as* **a[y]** *because C++ evaluates the expression (containing a comma operator)* **x, y** *simply as* **y** *(the last of the comma-separated expressions).*

```
Enter a number between 0 and 28: 25

Subscripts:
  0   1   2   3   4   5   6   7   8   9  10  11  12  13  14
------------------------------------------------------------
  0   2   4   6   8  10  12  14* 16  18  20  22  24  26  28
                                 16  18  20  22* 24  26  28
                                                 24  26* 28
                                                 24*

25 not found
```

```
Enter a number between 0 and 28: 8

Subscripts:
  0   1   2   3   4   5   6   7   8   9  10  11  12  13  14
------------------------------------------------------------
  0   2   4   6   8  10  12  14* 16  18  20  22  24  26  28
  0   2   4   6*  8  10  12
                  8  10* 12
                  8*

8 found in array element 4
```

```
Enter a number between 0 and 28: 6

Subscripts:
  0   1   2   3   4   5   6   7   8   9  10  11  12  13  14
------------------------------------------------------------
  0   2   4   6   8  10  12  14* 16  18  20  22  24  26  28
  0   2   4   6*  8  10  12

6 found in array element 3
```

**Fig. 4.20** Binary search of a sorted array (part 3 of 3).

A multiple-subscripted array can be initialized in its declaration much like a single subscripted array. For example, a double-subscripted array `b[2][2]` could be declared and initialized with

```
int b[2][2] = {{1, 2}, {3, 4}};
```

The values are grouped by row in braces. So, `1` and `2` initialize `b[0][0]` and `b[0][1]`, and `3` and `4` initialize `b[1][0]` and `b[1][1]`. If there are not enough initializers for a given row, the remaining elements of that row are initialized to `0`. Thus, the declaration

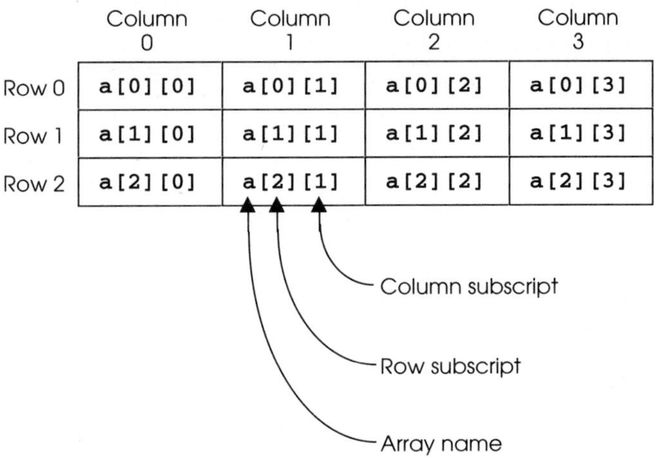


**Fig. 4.21** A double-subscripted array with three rows and four columns.

```
int b[2][2] = {{1}, {3, 4}};
```

would initialize **b[0][0]** to **1**, **b[0][1]** to **0**, **b[1][0]** to **3** and **b[1][1]** to **4**.

Figure 4.22 demonstrates initializing double-subscripted arrays in declarations. The program declares three arrays, each with two rows and three columns. The declaration of **array1** provides six initializers in two sublists. The first sublist initializes the first row of the array to the values 1, 2, and 3; and the second sublist initializes the second row of the array to the values 4, 5, and 6. If the braces around each sublist are removed from the **array1** initializer list, the compiler automatically initializes the elements of the first row followed by the elements of the second row.

The declaration of **array2** provides five initializers. The initializers are assigned to the first row then the second row. Any elements that do not have an explicit initializer are initialized to zero automatically, so **array2[1][2]** is initialized to 0.

The declaration of **array3** provides three initializers in two sublists. The sublist for the first row explicitly initializes the first two elements of the first row to 1 and 2. The third element is automatically initialized to zero. The sublist for the second row explicitly initializes the first element to 4. The last two elements are automatically initialized to zero.

The program calls function **printArray** to output each array's elements. Notice that the function definition specifies the array parameter as **int a[][3]**. When we receive a single-subscripted array as an argument to a function, the array brackets are empty in the function's parameter list. The size of first subscript of a multiple-subscripted array is not required either, but all subsequent subscript sizes are required. The compiler uses these sizes to determine the locations in memory of elements in multiple-subscripted arrays. All array elements are stored consecutively in memory regardless of the number of subscripts. In a double-subscripted array, the first row is stored in memory followed by the second row.

```
// Initializing multidimensional arrays
#include <iostream.h>

void printArray(int [][3]);

main()
{
   int array1[2][3] = { {1, 2, 3}, {4, 5, 6} },
       array2[2][3] = { 1, 2, 3, 4, 5 },
       array3[2][3] = { {1, 2}, {4} };

   cout << "Values in array1 by row are:" << endl;
   printArray(array1);

   cout << "Values in array2 by row are:" << endl;
   printArray(array2);

   cout << "Values in array3 by row are:" << endl;
   printArray(array3);

   return 0;
}

void printArray(int a[][3])
{
   for (int i = 0; i <= 1; i++) {

      for (int j = 0; j <= 2; j++)
         cout << a[i][j] << ' ';

      cout << endl;
   }
}
```

```
Values in array1 by row are:
1 2 3
4 5 6
Values in array2 by row are:
1 2 3
4 5 0
Values in array3 by row are:
1 2 0
4 0 0
```

**Fig. 4.22** Initializing multidimensional arrays.

Providing the subscript values in a parameter declaration enables the compiler to tell the function how to locate an element in the array. In a double-subscripted array, each row is basically a single-subscripted array. To locate an element in a particular row, the function must know exactly how many elements are in each row so it can skip the proper number of memory locations when accessing the array. Thus, when accessing **a[1][2]**, the function knows to skip the first row's three elements in memory to get to the second row (row 1). Then, the function accesses the third element of that row (element 2).

Many common array manipulations use **for** repetition structures. For example, the following **for** structure sets all the elements in the third row of array **a** in Fig. 4.21 to zero:

```
for (column = 0; column < 4; column++)
   a[2][column] = 0;
```

We specified the *third* row, therefore we know that the first subscript is always **2** (**0** is the first row, and **1** is the second row). The **for** loop varies only the second subscript (i.e., the column subscript). The preceding **for** structure is equivalent to the assignment statements:

```
a[2][0] = 0;
a[2][1] = 0;
a[2][2] = 0;
a[2][3] = 0;
```

The following nested **for** structure determines the total of all the elements in array **a**.

```
total = 0;

for (row = 0; row < 3; row++)
   for (column = 0; column < 4; column++)
      total += a[row][column];
```

The **for** structure totals the elements of the array one row at a time. The outer **for** structure begins by setting **row** (i.e., the row subscript) to **0** so the elements of the first row may be totaled by the inner **for** structure. The outer **for** structure then increments **row** to **1**, so the elements of the second row can be totaled. Then, the outer **for** structure increments **row** to **2**, so the elements of the third row can be totaled. The result is printed when the nested **for** structure terminates.

The program of Fig. 4.23 performs several other common array manipulations on 3-by-4 array **studentGrades**. Each row of the array represents a student and each column represents a grade on one of the four exams the students took during the semester. The array manipulations are performed by four functions. Function **minimum** determines the lowest grade of any student for the semester. Function **maximum** determines the highest grade of any student for the semester. Function **average** determines a particular student's semester average. Function **printArray** outputs the double-subscripted array in a neat, tabular format.

Functions **minimum**, **maximum**, and **printArray** each receive three arguments—the **studentGrades** array (called **grades** in each function), the number of students (rows of the array), and the number of exams (columns of the array). Each function loops through array **grades** using nested **for** structures. The following nested **for** structure is from the function **minimum** definition:

```
for (i = 0; i < pupils; i++)
   for (j = 0; j < tests; j++)
      if (grades[i][j] < lowGrade)
         lowGrade = grades[i][j];
```

```
// Double-subscripted array example
#include <iostream.h>
#include <iomanip.h>

const int students = 3;    // number of students
const int exams = 4;       // number of exams

int minimum(int [][exams], int, int);
int maximum(int [][exams], int, int);
float average(int [], int);
void printArray(int [][exams], int, int);

main()
{
   int studentGrades[students][exams] = {{77, 68, 86, 73},
                                          {96, 87, 89, 78},
                                          {70, 90, 86, 81}};

   cout << "The array is:" << endl;
   printArray(studentGrades, students, exams);
   cout << endl << endl << "Lowest grade: "
        << minimum(studentGrades, students, exams) << endl
        << "Highest grade: "
        << maximum(studentGrades, students, exams) << endl;

   for (int person = 0; person < students; person++)
      cout << "The average grade for student " << person << " is "
           << setiosflags(ios::fixed | ios::showpoint)
           << setprecision(2)
           << average(studentGrades[person], exams) << endl;

   return 0;
}

// Find the minimum grade
int minimum(int grades[][exams], int pupils, int tests)
{
   int lowGrade = 100;

   for (int i = 0; i < pupils; i++)
      for (int j = 0; j < tests; j++)
         if (grades[i][j] < lowGrade)
            lowGrade = grades[i][j];

   return lowGrade;
}
```

**Fig. 4.23** Example of using double-subscripted arrays (part 1 of 2).

The outer **for** structure begins by setting **i** (i.e., the row subscript) to **0** so the elements of the first row can be compared to variable **lowGrade** in the body of the inner **for** structure. The inner **for** structure loops through the four grades of a particular row and compares each grade to **lowGrade**. If a grade is less than **lowGrade**, **lowGrade** is set

```
// Find the maximum grade
int maximum(int grades[][exams], int pupils, int tests)
{
   int highGrade = 0;

   for (int i = 0; i < pupils; i++)
      for (int j = 0; j < tests; j++)
         if (grades[i][j] > highGrade)
            highGrade = grades[i][j];

   return highGrade;
}

// Determine the average grade for a particular exam
float average(int setOfGrades[], int tests)
{
   int total = 0;

   for (int i = 0; i < tests; i++)
      total += setOfGrades[i];

   return (float) total / tests;
}

// Print the array
void printArray(int grades[][exams], int pupils, int tests)
{
   cout << "                    [0]  [1]  [2]  [3]";

   for (int i = 0; i < pupils; i++) {
      cout << endl << "studentGrades[" << i << "] ";

      for (int j = 0; j < tests; j++)
         cout << setiosflags(ios::left) << setw(5)
              << grades[i][j];
   }
}
```

```
The array is:
                 [0]  [1]  [2]  [3]
studentGrades[0] 77   68   86   73
studentGrades[1] 96   87   89   78
studentGrades[2] 70   90   86   81

Lowest grade: 68
Highest grade: 96
The average grade for student 0 is 76.00
The average grade for student 1 is 87.50
The average grade for student 2 is 81.75
```

**Fig. 4.23** Example of using double-subscripted arrays (part 2 of 2).

to that grade. The outer **for** structure then increments the row subscript to **1**. The elements of the second row are compared to variable **lowGrade**. The outer **for** structure then increments the row subscript to **2**. The elements of the third row are compared to variable **lowGrade**. When execution of the nested structure is complete, **lowGrade** contains the smallest grade in the double-subscripted array. Function **maximum** works similarly to function **minimum**.

Function **average** takes two arguments—a single-subscripted array of test results for a particular student and the number of test results in the array. When **average** is called, the first argument is **studentGrades[student]** which specifies that a particular row of the double-subscripted array **studentGrades** is to be passed to **average**. For example, the argument **studentGrades[1]** represents the four values (a single-subscripted array of grades) stored in the second row of the double-subscripted array **studentGrades**. A double-subscripted array could be considered an array with elements that are single-subscripted arrays. Function **average** calculates the sum of the array elements, divides the total by the number of test results, and returns the floating-point result.

## 4.10 Thinking About Objects: Identifying an Object's Behaviors

In the "Thinking About Objects" sections at the ends of Chapters 2 and 3, we performed the first two phases of an object-oriented design for our elevator simulator, namely identifying the objects needed to implement the simulator and identifying the attributes of those objects.

In this assignment we concentrate on determining the behaviors of the objects needed to implement the elevator simulator. In Chapter 5, we will concentrate on the interactions between the objects.

Let us consider the behaviors of some real-world objects. A radio's behaviors include having its station set and having its volume set. A car's behaviors include accelerating (by pressing the accelerator pedal) and decelerating (by pressing the brake pedal).

As we will see, objects do not ordinarily perform their behaviors spontaneously. Rather, a specific behavior is normally invoked when a *message* is sent to the object, requesting that the object perform that specific behavior. This sounds like a function call—precisely how messages are sent to objects in C++.

***Elevator Laboratory Assignment 3***

1. Continue working with the facts file you created in Chapter 3. You had separated the facts related to each object into two groups. You labeled the first group *Attributes* and the second group *Other Facts*.

2. For each object, add a third group called *Behaviors*. Place in this group every behavior of an object that can be invoked by telling the object to do something, i.e., by sending the object a message. For example, a button can be pushed (by a person), so list *pushButton* as a behavior of a button object. Function *pushButton* and the other behaviors of the button object are called *member functions* of the button object. The object's attributes (such as whether a button is "on" or "off") are called *data members* of the button object. An object's member functions typically manipulate the

object's data members (such as *pushButton* changing one of the button's attributes to "on"). Member functions also typically send messages to other objects (such as the button object sending a *comeGetMe* message to summon the elevator). Assume that the elevator will have thermal buttons that are illuminated when someone presses them. When the elevator arrives at a floor, the elevator will want to send a *resetButton* message to turn the button's light off. The elevator may want to determine if a particular button has been pressed, so we can provide another behavior called *getButton* which simply examines a button and returns 1 or 0 to indicate that the button is currently "on" or "off." You will probably want the elevator's doors to respond to messages *openDoors* and *closeDoors*. And so on.

3. For each behavior you assign to an object, provide a brief description of what the behavior does. List any attribute changes the behavior causes, and list any messages the behavior sends to other objects.

***Notes***

1. Begin by listing the object behaviors that are explicitly mentioned in the problem statement. Then list behaviors that are directly implied in the problem statement.
2. Add appropriate behaviors as it becomes apparent they are needed.
3. Again, system design is not a perfect and complete process, so do the best you can for now and be prepared to modify your design as you proceed with this exercise in subsequent chapters.
4. As we will see, it is difficult to glean all possible behaviors at this phase of the design. You will probably add behaviors to your objects as you continue this exercise in Chapter 5.

## Summary

- C++ stores lists of values in arrays. An array is a consecutive group of related memory locations. These locations are related by the fact that they all have the same name and the same type. To refer to a particular location or element within the array, we specify the name of the array and the subscript.
- A subscript may be an integer or an integer expression. If a program uses an expression as a subscript, then the expression is evaluated to determine the particular element of the array.
- It is important to note the difference when referring to the seventh element of the array as opposed to array element seven. The seventh element has a subscript of `6`, while array element seven has a subscript of `7` (actually the eighth element of the array). This is a source of "off-by-one" errors.
- Arrays occupy space in memory. To reserve 100 elements for integer array **`b`** and 27 elements for integer array **`x`**, the programmer writes

```
int b[100], x[27];
```

- An array of type **`char`** can be used to store a character string.

- The elements of an array can be initialized three ways: by declaration, by assignment, and by input.
- If there are fewer initializers than elements in the array, the remaining elements are initialized to zero.
- C++ does not prevent referencing elements beyond the bounds of an array.
- A character array can be initialized using a string literal.
- All strings end with the null character (`'\0'`).
- Character arrays can be initialized with character constants in an initializer list.
- Individual characters in a string stored in an array can be accessed directly using array subscript notation.
- To pass an array to a function, the name of the array is passed. To pass a single element of an array to a function, simply pass the name of the array followed by the subscript (contained in square brackets) of the particular element.
- Arrays are passed to functions using simulated call-by-reference—the called functions can modify the element values in the callers' original arrays. The value of the name of the array is the address of the first element of the array. Because the starting address of the array is passed, the called function knows precisely where the array is stored.
- To receive an array argument, the function's parameter list must specify that an array will be received. The size of the array is not required in the array brackets.
- C++ provides the type qualifier **`const`** that enables programs to prevent modification of array values in a function. When an array parameter is preceded by the **`const`** qualifier, the elements of the array become constant in the function body, and any attempt to modify an element of the array in the function body results in a compile-time error.
- An array can be sorted using the bubble-sort technique. Several passes of the array are made. On each pass, successive pairs of elements are compared. If a pair is in order (or the values are identical), it is left as is. If a pair is out of order, the values are swapped. For small arrays, the bubble sort is acceptable, but for larger arrays it is inefficient compared to other more sophisticated sorting algorithms.
- The linear search compares each element of the array with the search key. Since the array is not in any particular order, it is just as likely that the value will be found in the first element as the last. On average, therefore, the program will have to compare the search key with half the elements of the array. The linear searching method works well for small arrays and is acceptable for unsorted arrays.
- The binary search eliminates one half of the elements in the array after each comparison. The algorithm locates the middle element of the array and compares it to the search key. If they are equal, the search key is found and the array subscript of that element is returned. Otherwise, the problem is reduced to searching one half of the array.
- In a worst case scenario, searching an array of 1024 elements will take only 10 comparisons using a binary search.

- Arrays may be used to represent tables of values consisting of information arranged in rows and columns. To identify a particular element of a table, two subscripts are specified: The first (by convention) identifies the row in which the element is contained, and the second (by convention) identifies the column in which the element is contained. Tables or arrays that require two subscripts to identify a particular element are called double-subscripted arrays.
- When we receive a single-subscripted array as an argument to a function, the array brackets are empty in the function's parameter list. The size of the first subscript of a multiple-subscripted array is not required either, but all subsequent subscript sizes are required. The compiler uses these sizes to determine the locations in memory of elements in multiple-subscripted arrays.
- To pass one row of a double-subscripted array to a function that receives a single-subscripted array, simply pass the name of the array followed by the first subscript.

## Terminology

`a[i]`
`a[i][j]`
array
array initializer list
binary search of an array
bounds checking
bubble sort
column subscript
`const` type qualifier
constant variable
declare an array
double-subscripted array
element of an array
initialize an array
initializer
linear search of an array
m-by-n array
multiple-subscripted array
name of an array
named constant
null character (`'\0'`)
off-by-one error
pass-by-reference
pass of a bubble sort
passing arrays to functions
position number
row subscript
scalability
scalar
search key
searching an array
simulated call-by-reference
single-subscripted array
sinking sort
sorting
sorting an array
square brackets `[]`
string
subscript
table of values
tabular format
temporary area for exchange of values
triple-subscripted array
value of an element
"walk off" an array
zeroth element

## Common Programming Errors

**4.1** It is important to note the difference between the "seventh element of the array" and "array element seven." Because array subscripts begin at 0, the "seventh element of the array" has a subscript of `6`, while "array element seven" has a subscript of `7` and is actually the eighth element of the array. This is a source of "off-by-one" errors.

**4.2** Forgetting to initialize the elements of an array whose elements should be initialized.

4.3 Providing more initializers in an array initializer list than there are elements in the array is a syntax error.

4.4 Assigning a value to a constant variable in an executable statement is a syntax error.

4.5 Ending a **#include** preprocessor directive with a semicolon. Remember that preprocessor directives are not C++ statements.

4.6 Referring to an element outside the array bounds.

4.7 Not providing **cin** with a character array large enough to store a string typed at the keyboard can result in loss of data in a program and other run-time errors.

4.8 Assuming that elements of a function's local **static** array are initialized to zero every time the function is called.

4.9 Referencing a double-subscripted array element ***a[x][y]*** incorrectly as ***a[x, y]***. Actually, ***a[x, y]*** is treated as ***a[y]*** because C++ evaluates the expression (containing a comma operator) ***x, y*** simply as ***y*** (the last of the comma-separated expressions).

## Good Programming Practices

4.1 Strive for program clarity. It is sometimes worthwhile to trade off the most efficient use of memory or processor time in favor of writing clearer programs.

4.2 When looping through an array, the array subscript should never go below 0 and should always be less than the total number of elements in the array (one less than the size of the array). Make sure the loop terminating condition prevents accessing elements outside this range.

4.3 Programs should validate the correctness of all input values to prevent erroneous information from affecting a program's calculations.

4.4 Some programmers include variable names in function prototypes to make programs clearer. The compiler ignores these names.

## Performance Tips

4.1 Sometimes performance considerations far outweigh clarity considerations.

4.2 Passing arrays simulated call-by-reference makes sense for performance reasons. If arrays were passed call-by-value, a copy of each element would be passed. For large, frequently passed arrays, this would be time consuming and would consume considerable storage for the copies of the arrays.

4.3 Often, the simplest algorithms perform poorly. Their virtue is that they are easy to write, test and debug. However, more complex algorithms are often needed to realize maximum performance.

## Portability Tip

4.1 The (normally serious) effects of referencing elements outside the array bounds are system dependent.

## Software Engineering Observations

4.1 Defining the size of each array as a constant variable makes programs more scalable.

4.2 It is possible to pass an array by value by using a simple trick we explain in Chapter 6.

4.3 The **const** type qualifier can be applied to an array parameter in a function definition to prevent the original array from being modified in the function body. This is another example of the principle of least privilege. Functions should not be given the capability to modify an array unless it is absolutely necessary.

## Self-Review Exercises

**4.1** Answer each of the following:

a) Lists and tables of values are stored in __________.

b) The elements of an array are related by the fact that they have the same __________ and __________.

c) The number used to refer to a particular element of an array is called its __________.

d) A __________ should be used to declare the size of an array because it makes the program more scalable.

e) The process of placing the elements of an array in order is called __________ the array.

f) The process of determining if an array contains a certain key value is called __________ the array.

g) An array that uses two subscripts is referred to as a __________ array.

**4.2** State whether the following are true or false. If the answer is false, explain why.

a) An array can store many different types of values.

b) An array subscript should normally be of data type `float`.

c) If there are fewer initializers in an initializer list than the number of elements in the array, the remaining elements are automatically initialized to the last value in the list of initializers.

d) It is an error if an initializer list contains more initializers than there are elements in the array.

e) An individual array element that is passed to a function and modified in that function will contain the modified value when the called function completes execution.

**4.3** Answer the following questions regarding an array called `fractions`.

a) Define a constant variable `arraySize` initialized to 10.

b) Declare an array with `arraySize` elements of type `float` and initialize the elements to `0`.

c) Name the fourth element from the beginning of the array.

d) Refer to array element 4.

e) Assign the value `1.667` to array element 9.

f) Assign the value `3.333` to the seventh element of the array.

g) Print array elements 6 and 9 with two digits of precision to the right of the decimal point and show the output that is actually displayed on the screen.

h) Print all the elements of the array using a `for` repetition structure. Define the integer variable `x` as a control variable for the loop. Show the output.

**4.4** Answer the following questions regarding an array called `table`.

a) Declare the array to be an integer array and to have 3 rows and 3 columns. Assume the constant variable `arraySize` has been defined to be 3.

b) How many elements does the array contain?

c) Use a `for` repetition structure to initialize each element of the array to the sum of its subscripts. Assume the integer variables `x` and `y` are declared as control variables.

d) Write a program segment to print the values of each element of array `table` in tabular format with 3 rows and 3 columns. Assume the array was initialized with the declaration,

```
int table[arraySize][arraySize] = {{1, 8}, {2, 4, 6}, {5}};
```

and the integer variables **x** and **y** are declared as control variables. Show the output.

**4.5** Find the error in each of the following program segments and correct the error.

a) `#include <iostream.h>;`

b) `arraySize = 10;   // arraySize was declared const`

c) Assume `int b[10] = {0};`
```
for (int i = 0; i <= 10; i++)
   b[i] = 1;
```

d) Assume `int a[2][2] = {{1, 2}, {3, 4}};`
```
a[1, 1] = 5;
```

## *Answers to Self-Review Exercises*

**4.1** a) Arrays. b) Name, type. c) Subscript. d) Constant variable. e) Sorting. f) Searching. g) Double-subscripted.

**4.2**
a) False. An array can store only values of the same type.
b) False. An array subscript should normally be an integer or an integer expression.
c) False. The remaining elements are automatically initialized to zero.
d) True.
e) False. Individual elements of an array are passed call-by-value. If the entire array is passed to a function, then any modifications will be reflected in the original.

**4.3**
a) `const int arraySize = 10;`
b) `float fractions[arraySize] = {0};`
c) `fractions[3]`
d) `fractions[4]`
e) `fractions[9] = 1.667;`
f) `fractions[6] = 3.333;`
g)
```
cout << setiosflags(ios::fixed | ios::showpoint)
     << setprecision(2) << fractions[6] << ' '
     << fractions[9] << endl;
```
*Output:* `3.33 1.67.`

h)
```
for (int x = 0; x < arraySize; x++)
   cout << "fractions[" << x << "] = " << fractions[x]
        << endl;
```

*Output:*
```
fractions[0] = 0
fractions[1] = 0
fractions[2] = 0
fractions[3] = 0
fractions[4] = 0
fractions[5] = 0
fractions[6] = 3.333
fractions[7] = 0
fractions[8] = 0
fractions[9] = 1.667
```

**4.4**
a) `int table[arraySize][arraySize];`
b) Nine.

c)
```
for (x = 0; x < arraySize; x++)
   for (y = 0; y < arraySize; y++)
      table[x][y] = x + y;
```
d)
```
cout << "     [0]  [1]  [2]" << endl;
for (int x = 0; x < arraySize; x++) {
   cout << '[' << x << "] ";

   for (int y = 0; y < arraySize; y++)
      cout << setw(3) << table[x][y] << "  ";

   cout << endl;
}
```
*Output:*
```
     [0]  [1]  [2]
[0]   1    8    0
[1]   2    4    6
[2]   5    0    0
```

**4.5** a) Error: Semicolon at end of **#include** preprocessor directive.
Correction: Eliminate semicolon.

b) Error: Assigning a value to a constant variable using an assignment statement.
Correction: Assign a value to the constant variable in a **const int arraySize** declaration.

c) Error: Referencing an array element outside the bounds of the array (**b[10]**).
Correction: Change the final value of the control variable to **9**.

d) Error: Array subscripting done incorrectly.
Correction: Change the statement to **a[1][1] = 5;**

## Exercises

**4.6** Fill in the blanks in each of the following:

a) C++ stores lists of values in __________.

b) The elements of an array are related by the fact that they __________.

c) When referring to an array element, the position number contained within parentheses is called a __________.

d) The names of the four elements of array **p** are __________, __________, __________, and __________.

e) Naming an array, stating its type, and specifying the number of elements in the array is called __________ the array.

f) The process of placing the elements of an array into either ascending or descending order is called __________.

g) In a double-subscripted array, the first subscript (by convention) identifies the __________ of an element, and the second subscript (by convention) identifies the __________ of an element.

h) An m-by-n array contains __________ rows, __________ columns, and __________ elements.

i) The name of the element in row 3 and column 5 of array **d** is __________.

**4.7** State which of the following are true and which are false; for those that are false, explain why they are false.

a) To refer to a particular location or element within an array, we specify the name of the array and the value of the particular element.

b) An array declaration reserves space for the array.

c) To indicate that 100 locations should be reserved for integer array **p**, the programmer writes the declaration

```
p[100];
```

d) A C++ program that initializes the elements of a 15-element array to zero must contain at least one **for** statement.

e) A C++ program that totals the elements of a double-subscripted array must contain nested **for** statements.

**4.8** Write C++ statements to accomplish each of the following:

a) Display the value of the seventh element of character array **f**.

b) Input a value into element 4 of single-subscripted floating-point array **b**.

c) Initialize each of the 5 elements of single-subscripted integer array **g** to **8**.

d) Total and print the elements of floating-point array **c** of 100 elements.

e) Copy array **a** into the first portion of array **b**. Assume **float a[11], b[34];**

f) Determine and print the smallest and largest values contained in 99-element floating-point array **w**.

**4.9** Consider a 2-by-3 integer array **t**.

a) Write a declaration for **t**.

b) How many rows does **t** have?

c) How many columns does **t** have?

d) How many elements does **t** have?

e) Write the names of all the elements in the second row of **t**.

f) Write the names of all the elements in the third column of **t**.

g) Write a single statement that sets the element of **t** in row 1 and column 2 to zero.

h) Write a series of statements that initializes each element of **t** to zero. Do not use a repetition structure.

i) Write a nested **for** structure that initializes each element of **t** to zero.

j) Write a statement that inputs the values for the elements of **t** from the terminal.

k) Write a series of statements that determines and prints the smallest value in array **t**.

l) Write a statement that displays the elements of the first row of **t**.

m) Write a statement that totals the elements of the fourth column of **t**.

n) Write a series of statements that prints the array **t** in neat, tabular format. List the column subscripts as headings across the top and list the row subscripts at the left of each row.

**4.10** Use a single-subscripted array to solve the following problem. A company pays its salespeople on a commission basis. The salespeople receive $200 per week plus 9 percent of their gross sales for that week. For example, a salesperson who grosses $5000 in sales in a week receives $200 plus 9 percent of $5000, or a total of $650. Write a program (using an array of counters) that determines how many of the salespeople earned salaries in each of the following ranges (assume that each salesperson's salary is truncated to an integer amount):

1. $200-$299
2. $300-$399
3. $400-$499
4. $500-$599
5. $600-$699
6. $700-$799
7. $800-$899

**8.** \$900-\$999

**9.** \$1000 and over

**4.11** The bubble sort presented in Fig. 4.16 is inefficient for large arrays. Make the following simple modifications to improve the performance of the bubble sort.

a) After the first pass, the largest number is guaranteed to be in the highest-numbered element of the array; after the second pass, the two highest numbers are "in place," and so on. Instead of making nine comparisons on every pass, modify the bubble sort to make eight comparisons on the second pass, seven on the third pass, and so on.

b) The data in the array may already be in the proper order or near-proper order, so why make nine passes if fewer will suffice? Modify the sort to check at the end of each pass if any swaps have been made. If none has been made, then the data must already be in the proper order, so the program should terminate. If swaps have been made, then at least one more pass is needed.

**4.12** Write single statements that perform the following single-subscripted array operations:

a) Initialize the 10 elements of integer array **`counts`** to zeros.

b) Add 1 to each of the 15 elements of integer array **`bonus`**.

c) Read 12 values for **`float`** array **`monthlyTemperatures`** from the keyboard.

d) Print the 5 values of integer array **`bestScores`** in column format.

**4.13** Find the error(s) in each of the following statements:

a) Assume: **`char str[5];`**
```
cin >> str;     // User types hello
```
b) Assume: **`int a[3];`**
```
cout << a[1] << " " << a[2] << " " << a[3] << endl;
```
c)
```
float f[3] = {1.1, 10.01, 100.001, 1000.0001};
```
d) Assume: **`double d[2][10];`**
```
d[1, 9] = 2.345;
```

**4.14** Modify the program of Fig. 4.17 so function **`mode`** is capable of handling a tie for the mode value. Also modify function **`median`** so the two middle elements are averaged in an array with an even number of elements.

**4.15** Use a single-subscripted array to solve the following problem. Read in 20 numbers, each of which is between 10 and 100, inclusive. As each number is read, print it only if it is not a duplicate of a number already read. Provide for the "worst case" in which all 20 numbers are different. Use the smallest possible array to solve this problem.

**4.16** Label the elements of 3-by-5 double-subscripted array **`sales`** to indicate the order in which they are set to zero by the following program segment:

```
for (row = 0; row < 3; row++)
   for (column = 0; column < 5; column++)
      sales[row][column] = 0;
```

**4.17** Write a program that simulates the rolling of two dice. The program should use **`rand`** to roll the first die, and should use **`rand`** again to roll the second die. The sum of the two values should then be calculated. *Note:* Since each die can show an integer value from 1 to 6, then the sum of the two values will vary from 2 to 12 with 7 being the most frequent sum and 2 and 12 being the least frequent sums. Figure 4.24 shows the 36 possible combinations of the two dice. Your program should roll the two dice 36,000 times. Use a single-subscripted array to tally the numbers of times each possible sum appears. Print the results in a tabular format. Also, determine if the totals are reasonable, i.e., there are six ways to roll a 7, so approximately one sixth of all the rolls should be 7.

| | 1 | 2 | 3 | 4 | 5 | 6 |
|---|---|---|---|---|---|---|
| 1 | 2 | 3 | 4 | 5 | 6 | 7 |
| 2 | 3 | 4 | 5 | 6 | 7 | 8 |
| 3 | 4 | 5 | 6 | 7 | 8 | 9 |
| 4 | 5 | 6 | 7 | 8 | 9 | 10 |
| 5 | 6 | 7 | 8 | 9 | 10 | 11 |
| 6 | 7 | 8 | 9 | 10 | 11 | 12 |

**Fig. 4.24** The 36 possible outcomes of rolling two dice.

**4.18** What does the following program do?

```
#include <iostream.h>

int whatIsThis(int [], int);

main()
{
   const int arraySize = 10;
   int a[arraySize] = {1, 2, 3, 4, 5, 6, 7, 8, 9, 10};

   int result = whatIsThis(a, arraySize);

   cout << "Result is " << result << endl;
   return 0;
}

int whatIsThis(int b[], int size)
{
   if (size == 1)
      return b[0];
   else
      return b[size - 1] + whatIsThis(b, size - 1);
}
```

**4.19** Write a program that runs 1000 games of craps and answers the following questions:

a) How many games are won on the first roll, second roll, ..., twentieth roll, and after the twentieth roll?

b) How many games are lost on the first roll, second roll, ..., twentieth roll, and after the twentieth roll?

c) What are the chances of winning at craps? (*Note:* You should discover that craps is one of the fairest casino games. What do you suppose this means?)

d) What is the average length of a game of craps?

e) Do the chances of winning improve with the length of the game?

**4.20** (*Airline Reservations System*) A small airline has just purchased a computer for its new automated reservations system. You have been asked to program the new system. You are to write a program to assign seats on each flight of the airline's only plane (capacity: 10 seats).

Your program should display the following menu of alternatives:

```
Please type 1 for "smoking"
Please type 2 for "nonsmoking"
```

If the person types 1, then your program should assign a seat in the smoking section (seats 1-5). If the person types 2, then your program should assign a seat in the nonsmoking section (seats 6-10). Your program should then print a boarding pass indicating the person's seat number and whether it is in the smoking or nonsmoking section of the plane.

Use a single-subscripted array to represent the seating chart of the plane. Initialize all the elements of the array to 0 to indicate that all seats are empty. As each seat is assigned, set the corresponding elements of the array to 1 to indicate that the seat is no longer available.

Your program should, of course, never assign a seat that has already been assigned. When the smoking section is full, your program should ask the person if it is acceptable to be placed in the nonsmoking section (and vice versa). If yes, then make the appropriate seat assignment. If no, then print the message **"Next flight leaves in 3 hours."**

**4.21** What does the following program do?

```
#include <iostream.h>

void someFunction(int [], int);

main()
{
   const int arraySize = 10;
   int a[arraySize] = {32, 27, 64, 18, 95, 14, 90, 70, 60, 37};

   cout << "The values in the array are:" << endl;
   someFunction(a, arraySize);
   cout << endl;
   return 0;
}

void someFunction(int b[], int size)
{
   if (size > 0) {
      someFunction(&b[1], size - 1);
      cout << b[0] << "  ";
   }
}
```

**4.22** Use a double-subscripted array to solve the following problem. A company has four salespeople (1 to 4) who sell five different products (1 to 5). Once a day, each salesperson passes in a slip for each different type of product sold. Each slip contains:

1. The salesperson number
2. The product number
3. The total dollar value of that product sold that day

Thus, each salesperson passes in between 0 and 5 sales slips per day. Assume that the information from all of the slips for last month is available. Write a program that will read all this information for last month's sales, and summarize the total sales by salesperson by product. All totals should be stored in the double-subscripted array **sales**. After processing all the information for last month, print the results in tabular format with each of the columns representing a particular salesperson and each of the rows representing a particular product. Cross total each row to get the total sales of each product for last month; cross total each column to get the total sales by salesperson for last month.

Your tabular printout should include these cross totals to the right of the totaled rows and to the bottom of the totaled columns.

**4.23** (*Turtle Graphics*) The Logo language, which is particularly popular among personal computer users, made the concept of *turtle graphics* famous. Imagine a mechanical turtle that walks around the room under the control of a C++ program. The turtle holds a pen in one of two positions, up or down. While the pen is down, the turtle traces out shapes as it moves; while the pen is up, the turtle moves about freely without writing anything. In this problem you will simulate the operation of the turtle and create a computerized sketchpad as well.

Use a 20-by-20 array `floor` which is initialized to zeros. Read commands from an array that contains them. Keep track of the current position of the turtle at all times and whether the pen is currently up or down. Assume that the turtle always starts at position 0,0 of the floor with its pen up. The set of turtle commands your program must process are as follows:

| Command | Meaning |
|---|---|
| `1` | Pen up |
| `2` | Pen down |
| `3` | Turn right |
| `4` | Turn left |
| `5,10` | Move forward 10 spaces (or a number other than 10) |
| `6` | Print the 20-by-20 array |
| `9` | End of data (sentinel) |

Suppose that the turtle is somewhere near the center of the floor. The following "program" would draw and print a 12-by 12-square leaving the pen in the up position:

```
2
5,12
3
5,12
3
5,12
3
5,12
1
6
9
```

As the turtle moves with the pen down, set the appropriate elements of array `floor` to `1`s. When the `6` command (print) is given, wherever there is a `1` in the array, display an asterisk, or some other character you choose. Wherever there is a zero display a blank. Write a program to implement the turtle graphics capabilities discussed here. Write several turtle graphics programs to draw interesting shapes. Add other commands to increase the power of your turtle graphics language.

**4.24** (*Knight's Tour*) One of the more interesting puzzlers for chess buffs is the Knight's Tour problem, originally proposed by the mathematician Euler. The question is this: Can the chess piece called the knight move around an empty chessboard and touch each of the 64 squares once and only once? We study this intriguing problem in depth here.

The knight makes L-shaped moves (over two in one direction and then over one in a perpendicular direction). Thus, from a square in the middle of an empty chessboard, the knight can make eight different moves (numbered 0 through 7) as shown in Fig. 4.25.

a) Draw an 8-by-8 chessboard on a sheet of paper and attempt a Knight's Tour by hand. Put a `1` in the first square you move to, a `2` in the second square, a `3` in the third, etc. Before starting the tour, estimate how far you think you will get, remembering that a full tour consists of 64 moves. How far did you get? Was this close to your estimate?

b) Now let us develop a program that will move the knight around a chessboard. The board is represented by an 8-by-8 double-subscripted array **`board`**. Each of the squares is initialized to zero. We describe each of the eight possible moves in terms of both their horizontal and vertical components. For example, a move of type 0 as shown in Fig. 4.25 consists of moving two squares horizontally to the right and one square vertically upward. Move 2 consists of moving one square horizontally to the left and two squares vertically upward. Horizontal moves to the left and vertical moves upward are indicated with negative numbers. The eight moves may be described by two single-subscripted arrays, **`horizontal`** and **`vertical`**, as follows:

| | 0 | 1 | 2 | 3 | 4 | 5 | 6 | 7 |
|---|---|---|---|---|---|---|---|---|
| 0 | | | | | | | | |
| 1 | | | | 2 | | 1 | | |
| 2 | | | 3 | | | | 0 | |
| 3 | | | | | K | | | |
| 4 | | | 4 | | | | 7 | |
| 5 | | | | 5 | | 6 | | |
| 6 | | | | | | | | |
| 7 | | | | | | | | |

**Fig. 4.25** The eight possible moves of the knight.

```
horizontal[0] = 2
horizontal[1] = 1
horizontal[2] = -1
horizontal[3] = -2
horizontal[4] = -2
horizontal[5] = -1
horizontal[6] = 1
horizontal[7] = 2

vertical[0] = -1
vertical[1] = -2
vertical[2] = -2
vertical[3] = -1
vertical[4] = 1
vertical[5] = 2
vertical[6] = 2
vertical[7] = 1
```

Let the variables **currentRow** and **currentColumn** indicate the row and column of the knight's current position. To make a move of type **moveNumber**, where **moveNumber** is between 0 and 7, your program uses the statements

```
currentRow += vertical[moveNumber];
currentColumn += horizontal[moveNumber];
```

Keep a counter that varies from **1** to **64**. Record the latest count in each square the knight moves to. Remember to test each potential move to see if the knight has already visited that square. And, of course, test every potential move to make sure that the knight does not land off the chessboard. Now write a program to move the knight around the chessboard. Run the program. How many moves did the knight make?

c) After attempting to write and run a Knight's Tour program, you have probably developed some valuable insights. We will use these to develop a *heuristic* (or strategy) for moving the knight. Heuristics do not guarantee success, but a carefully developed heuristic greatly improves the chance of success. You may have observed that the outer squares are more troublesome than the squares nearer the center of the board. In fact, the most troublesome, or inaccessible, squares are the four corners.

Intuition may suggest that you should attempt to move the knight to the most troublesome squares first and leave open those that are easiest to get to so when the board gets congested near the end of the tour there will be a greater chance of success.

We may develop an "accessibility heuristic" by classifying each of the squares according to how accessible they are, and then always moving the knight to the square (within the knight's L-shaped moves, of course) that is most inaccessible. We label a double-subscripted array **accessibility** with numbers indicating from how many squares each particular square is accessible. On a blank chessboard, each center square is rated as **8**, each corner square is rated as **2**, and the other squares have accessibility numbers of **3**, **4**, or **6** as follows:

```
2  3  4  4  4  4  3  2
3  4  6  6  6  6  4  3
4  6  8  8  8  8  6  4
4  6  8  8  8  8  6  4
4  6  8  8  8  8  6  4
4  6  8  8  8  8  6  4
3  4  6  6  6  6  4  3
2  3  4  4  4  4  3  2
```

Now write a version of the Knight's Tour program using the accessibility heuristic. At any time, the knight should move to the square with the lowest accessibility number. In case of a tie, the knight may move to any of the tied squares. Therefore, the tour may begin in any of the four corners. (*Note:* As the knight moves around the chessboard, your program should reduce the accessibility numbers as more and more squares become occupied. In this way, at any given time during the tour, each available square's accessibility number will remain equal to precisely the number of squares from which that square may be reached.) Run this version of your program. Did you get a full tour? Now modify the program to run 64 tours, one starting from each square of the chessboard. How many full tours did you get?

d) Write a version of the Knight's Tour program which, when encountering a tie between two or more squares, decides what square to choose by looking ahead to those squares reachable from the "tied" squares. Your program should move to the square for which the next move would arrive at a square with the lowest accessibility number.

**4.25** (*Knight's Tour: Brute Force Approaches*) In Exercise 4.24 we developed a solution to the Knight's Tour problem. The approach used, called the "accessibility heuristic," generates many solutions and executes efficiently.

As computers continue increasing in power, we will be able to solve more problems with sheer computer power and relatively unsophisticated algorithms. Let us call this approach "brute force" problem solving.

a) Use random number generation to enable the knight to walk around the chess board (in its legitimate L-shaped moves, of course) at random. Your program should run one tour and print the final chessboard. How far did the knight get?
b) Most likely, the preceding program produced a relatively short tour. Now modify your program to attempt 1000 tours. Use a single-subscripted array to keep track of the number of tours of each length. When your program finishes attempting the 1000 tours, it should print this information in neat tabular format. What was the best result?
c) Most likely, the preceding program gave you some "respectable" tours but no full tours. Now "pull all the stops out" and simply let your program run until it produces a full tour. (*Caution:* This version of the program could run for hours on a powerful computer.) Once again, keep a table of the number of tours of each length, and print this table when the first full tour is found. How many tours did your program attempt before producing a full tour? How much time did it take?
d) Compare the brute force version of the Knight's Tour with the accessibility heuristic version. Which required a more careful study of the problem? Which algorithm was more difficult to develop? Which required more computer power? Could we be certain (in advance) of obtaining a full tour with the accessibility heuristic approach? Could we be certain (in advance) of obtaining a full tour with the brute force approach? Argue the pros and cons of brute force problem solving in general.

**4.26** (*Eight Queens*) Another puzzler for chess buffs is the Eight Queens problem. Simply stated: Is it possible to place eight queens on an empty chessboard so that no queen is "attacking" any other, i.e., no two queens are in the same row, the same column, or along the same diagonal? Use the thinking developed in Exercise 4.24 to formulate a heuristic for solving the Eight Queens problem. Run your program. (*Hint:* It is possible to assign a value to each square of the chessboard indicating how many squares of an empty chessboard are "eliminated" if a queen is placed in that square. Each of the corners would be assigned the value 22, as in Fig. 4.26.) Once these "elimination numbers" are placed in all 64 squares, an appropriate heuristic might be: Place the next queen in the square with the smallest elimination number. Why is this strategy intuitively appealing?

Fig. 4.26 The 22 squares eliminated by placing a queen in the upper left corner.

**4.27** (*Eight Queens: Brute Force Approaches*) In this exercise you will develop several brute force approaches to solving the Eight Queens problem introduced in Exercise 4.26.

a) Solve the Eight Queens exercise, using the random brute force technique developed in Exercise 4.25.
b) Use an exhaustive technique, i.e., try all possible combinations of eight queens on the chessboard.
c) Why do you suppose the exhaustive brute force approach may not be appropriate for solving the Knight's Tour problem?
d) Compare and contrast the random brute force and exhaustive brute force approaches in general.

**4.28** (*Knight's Tour: Closed Tour Test*) In the Knight's Tour, a full tour occurs when the knight makes 64 moves touching each square of the chess board once and only once. A closed tour occurs when the 64th move is one move away from the location in which the knight started the tour. Modify the Knight's Tour program you wrote in Exercise 4.24 to test for a closed tour if a full tour has occurred.

**4.29** (*The Sieve of Eratosthenes*) A prime integer is any integer that is evenly divisible only by itself and 1. The Sieve of Eratosthenes is a method of finding prime numbers. It operates as follows:

1) Create an array with all elements initialized to 1 (true). Array elements with prime subscripts will remain 1. All other array elements will eventually be set to zero.
2) Starting with array subscript 2 (subscript 1 must be prime), every time an array element is found whose value is 1, loop through the remainder of the array and set to zero every element whose subscript is a multiple of the subscript for the element with value 1. For array subscript 2, all elements beyond 2 in the array that are multiples of 2 will be set to zero (subscripts 4, 6, 8, 10, etc.); for array subscript 3, all elements beyond 3 in the array that are multiples of 3 will be set to zero (subscripts 6, 9, 12, 15, etc.); and so on.

When this process is complete, the array elements that are still set to one indicate that the subscript is a prime number. These subscripts can then be printed. Write a program that uses an array of 1000 elements to determine and print the prime numbers between 1 and 999. Ignore element 0 of the array.

**4.30** (*Bucket Sort*) A bucket sort begins with a single-subscripted array of positive integers to be sorted, and a double-subscripted array of integers with rows subscripted from 0 to 9 and columns subscripted from 0 to $n$ - 1 where $n$ is the number of values in the array to be sorted. Each row of the double-subscripted array is referred to as a bucket. Write a function `bucketSort` that takes an integer array and the array size as arguments and performs as follows:

1) Place each value of the single-subscripted array into a row of the bucket array based on the value's ones digit. For example, 97 is placed in row 7, 3 is placed in row 3, and 100 is placed in row 0. This is called a "distribution pass."

2) Loop through the bucket array row-by-row and copy the values back to the original array. This is called a "gathering pass." The new order of the preceding values in the single-subscripted array is 100, 3, and 97.
3) Repeat this process for each subsequent digit position (tens, hundreds, thousands, etc.).

On the second pass, 100 is placed in row 0, 3 is placed in row 0 (because 3 has no tens digit), and 97 is placed in row 9. After the gathering pass, the order of the values in the single-subscripted array is 100, 3, and 97. On the third pass, 100 is placed in row 1, 3 is placed in row zero and 97 is placed in row zero (after the 3). After the last gathering pass, the original array is now in sorted order.

Note that the double-subscripted array of buckets is ten times the size of the integer array being sorted. This sorting technique provides better performance than a bubble sort, but requires much more memory. The bubble sort requires space for only one additional element of data. This is an example of the space-time tradeoff: The bucket sort uses more memory than the bubble sort, but performs better. This version of the bucket sort requires copying all the data back to the original array on each pass. Another possibility is to create a second double-subscripted bucket array and repeatedly swap the data between the two bucket arrays.

## Recursion Exercises

**4.31** (*Selection Sort*) A selection sort searches an array looking for the smallest element in the array. Then, the smallest element is swapped with the first element of the array. The process is repeated for the subarray beginning with the second element of the array. Each pass of the array results in one element being placed in its proper location. This sort performs comparably to the bubble sort—for an array of $n$ elements, $n - 1$ passes must be made, and for each subarray, $n - 1$ comparisons must be made to find the smallest value. When the subarray being processed contains one element, the array is sorted. Write recursive function `selectionSort` to perform this algorithm.

**4.32** (*Palindromes*) A palindrome is a string that is spelled the same way forwards and backwards. Some examples of palindromes are: "radar," "able was i ere i saw elba," and (if blanks are ignored) "a man a plan a canal panama." Write a recursive function `testPalindrome` that returns 1 if the string stored in the array is a palindrome, and 0 otherwise. The function should ignore spaces and punctuation in the string.

**4.33** (*Linear Search*) Modify Fig. 4.19 to use recursive function `linearSearch` to perform a linear search of the array. The function should receive an integer array and the size of the array as arguments. If the search key is found, return the array subscript; otherwise, return –1.

**4.34** (*Binary Search*) Modify the program of Fig. 4.20 to use a recursive function `binarySearch` to perform the binary search of the array. The function should receive an integer array and the starting subscript and ending subscript as arguments. If the search key is found, return the array subscript; otherwise, return –1.

**4.35** (*Eight Queens*) Modify the Eight Queens program you created in Exercise 4.26 to solve the problem recursively.

**4.36** (*Print an array*) Write a recursive function `printArray` that takes an array and the size of the array as arguments and returns nothing. The function should stop processing and return when it receives an array of size zero.

**4.37** (*Print a string backwards*) Write a recursive function `stringReverse` that takes a character array containing a string as an argument, prints the string backwards, and returns nothing. The function should stop processing and return when the terminating null character is encountered.

**4.38** (*Find the minimum value in an array*) Write a recursive function `recursiveMinimum` that takes an integer array and the array size as arguments and returns the smallest element of the array. The function should stop processing and return when it receives an array of 1 element.

# 5

# Pointers and Strings

**Objectives**

- To be able to use pointers.
- To be able to use pointers to pass arguments to functions call-by-reference.
- To understand the close relationships among pointers, arrays, and strings.
- To understand the use of pointers to functions.
- To be able to declare and use arrays of strings.

*Addresses are given to us to conceal our whereabouts.*
Saki (H.H. Munro)

*By indirections find directions out.*
William Shakespeare, Hamlet

*Many things, having full reference*
*To one consent, may work contrariously.*
William Shakespeare, King Henry V

*You will find it a very good practice always to verify your references, sir!*
Dr. Routh

*You can't trust code that you did not totally create yourself. (Especially code from companies that employ people like me.)*
Ken Thompson, 1983 Turing Award Lecture
Association for Computing Machinery, Inc.

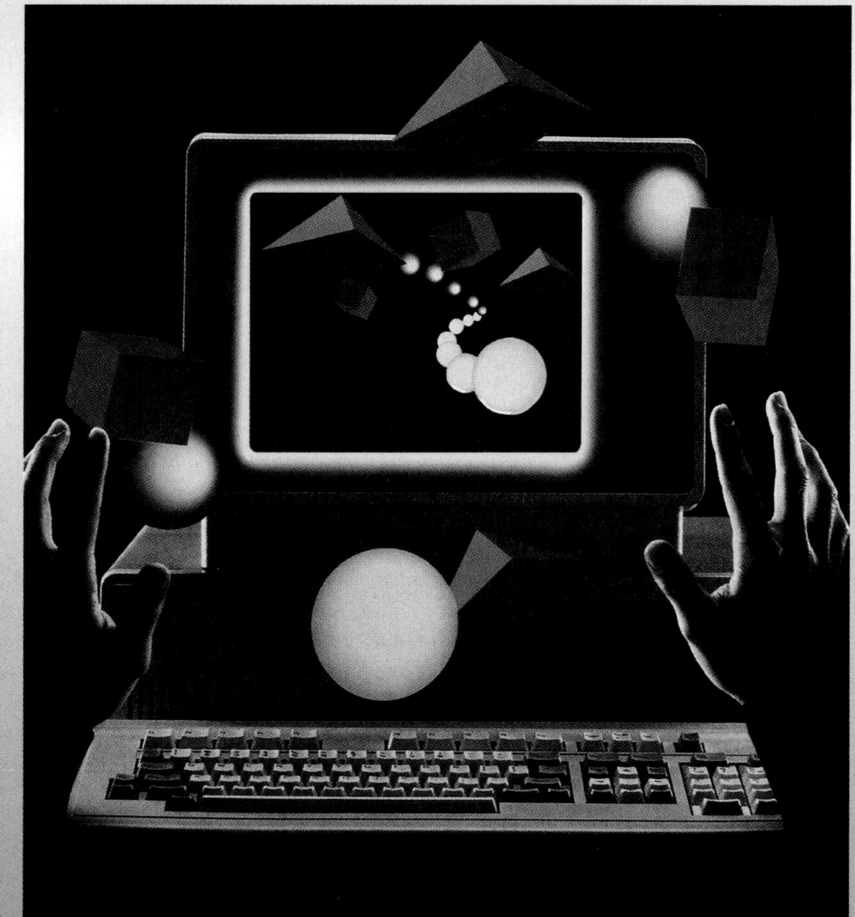

## Outline



## 5.1 Introduction

In this chapter, we discuss one of the most powerful features of the C++ programming language, the *pointer.* Pointers are among C++'s most difficult capabilities to master. In Chapter 3, we saw that references can be used to perform call-by-reference. Pointers enable programs to simulate call-by-reference, and to create and manipulate dynamic data structures, i.e., data structures that can grow and shrink, such as linked lists, queues, stacks, and trees. This chapter explains basic pointer concepts. This chapter also reinforces the intimate relationship between arrays, pointers, and strings, and includes a nice collection of string processing exercises.

Chapter 6 examines the use of pointers with structures. Chapter 15 introduces dynamic memory management techniques and presents examples of creating and using dynamic data structures.

## 5.2 Pointer Variable Declarations and Initialization

Pointers are variables that contain memory addresses as their values. Normally a variable directly contains a specific value. A pointer, on the other hand, contains an address of a variable that contains a specific value. In this sense, a variable name *directly* references a value and a pointer *indirectly* references a value (Fig. 5.1). Referencing a value through a pointer is called *indirection.*

Pointers, like any other variables, must be declared before they can be used. The declaration

```
int *countPtr, count;
```

declares the variable **countPtr** to be of type **int *** (i.e., a pointer to an integer value) and is read, "**countPtr** is a pointer to **int**" or "**countPtr** points to an object of type integer." Also, variable **count** is declared to be an integer, not a pointer to an integer. The * only applies to **countPtr** in the declaration. Each variable being declared as a pointer must be preceded by an asterisk (*). For example, the declaration

```
float *xPtr, *yPtr;
```

indicates that both **xPtr** and **yPtr** are pointers to **float** values. When * is used in this manner in a declaration, it indicates that the variable being declared is a pointer. Pointers can be declared to point to objects of any data type.

***Common Programming Error 5.1***

*The indirection operator * does not distribute to all variable names in a declaration. Each pointer must be declared with the * prefixed to the name.*

***Good Programming Practice 5.1***

*Although it is not required to do so, include the letters* `Ptr` *in pointer variable names to make it clear that these variables are pointers and need to be handled appropriately.*

Pointers should be initialized either when they are declared or in an assignment statement. A pointer may be initialized to **0**, **NULL**, or an address. A pointer with the value **0** or **NULL** points to nothing. **NULL** is a symbolic constant defined in the header file

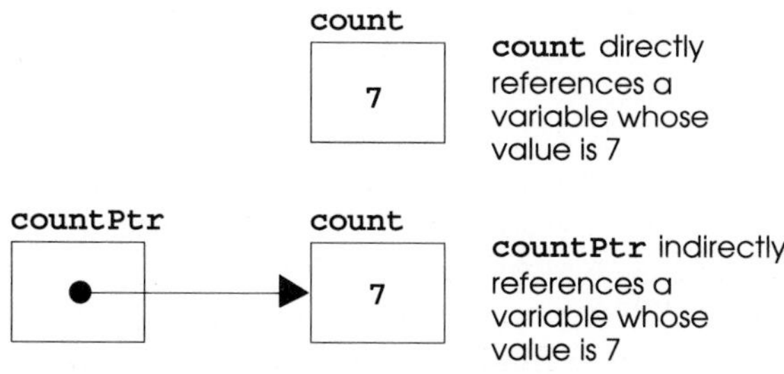


**Fig. 5.1** Directly and indirectly referencing a variable.

(**<iostream.h>** and in several C standard library header files). Initializing a pointer to **NULL** is equivalent to initializing a pointer to **0**, but in C++ **0** is preferred. When **0** is assigned, it is converted to a pointer of the appropriate type. The value **0** is the only integer value that can be assigned directly to a pointer variable without casting the integer to a pointer type first. Assigning a variable's address to a pointer is discussed in Section 5.3.

***Good Programming Practice 5.2***

*Initialize pointers to prevent unexpected results.*

## 5.3 Pointer Operators

The **&**, or *address operator*, is a unary operator that returns the address of its operand. For example, assuming the declarations

```
int y = 5;
int *yPtr;
```

the statement

```
yPtr = &y;
```

assigns the address of the variable **y** to pointer variable **yPtr**. Variable **yPtr** is then said to "point to" **y**. Figure 5.2 shows a schematic representation of memory after the preceding assignment is executed. In the figure, we show the "pointing relationship" by drawing an arrow from the pointer to the object it points to.

Figure 5.3 shows the representation of the pointer in memory assuming that integer variable **y** is stored at location **600000**, and pointer variable **yPtr** is stored at location **500000**. The operand of the address operator must be an lvalue (i.e., something to which a value can be assigned such as a variable); the address operator cannot be applied to constants, to expressions that do not result in references, or to variables declared with the storage class **register**.

The ***** *operator*, commonly referred to as the *indirection operator* or *dereferencing operator,* returns the value of the object to which its operand (i.e., a pointer) points. For example (referring again to Fig. 5.2), the statement

```
cout << *yPtr << endl;
```

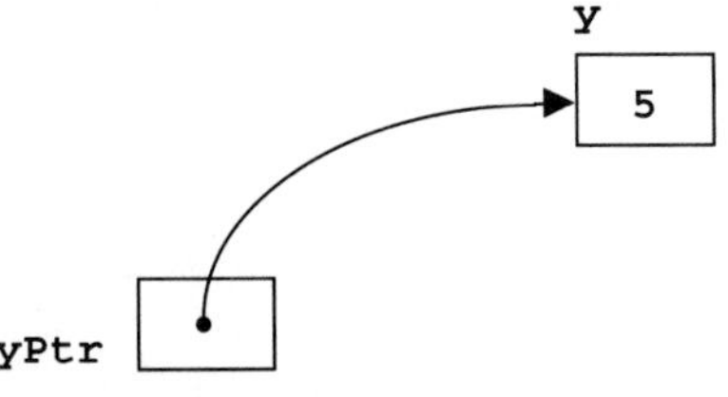


**Fig. 5.2** Graphical representation of a pointer pointing to an integer variable in memory.

**Fig. 5.3** Representation of **y** and **yPtr** in memory.

prints the value of variable **y**, namely 5. Using ***** in this manner is called *dereferencing a pointer.*

***Common Programming Error 5.2***

*Dereferencing a pointer that has not been properly initialized, or that has not been assigned to point to a specific location in memory. This could cause a fatal execution time error, or it could accidentally modify important data and allow the program to run to completion providing incorrect results.*

The program in Fig. 5.4 demonstrates the pointer operators. Memory locations are output as hexadecimal integers by **cout** (see Appendix E, "Number Systems," for more information on hexadecimal integers). Notice that the address of **a** and the value of **aPtr** are identical in the output, confirming that the address of **a** is indeed assigned to the pointer variable **aPtr**. The **&** and ***** operators are complements of one another—when they are both applied consecutively to **aPtr** in either order, the same result is printed. The chart in Fig. 5.5 shows the precedence and associativity of the operators introduced to this point.

```
// Using the & and * operators
#include <iostream.h>

main()
{
   int a;           // a is an integer
   int *aPtr;       // aPtr is a pointer to an integer

   a = 7;
   aPtr = &a;      // aPtr set to address of a

   cout << "The address of a is " << &a << endl
        << "The value of aPtr is " << aPtr << endl << endl;

   cout << "The value of a is " << a << endl
        << "The value of *aPtr is " << *aPtr << endl << endl;

   cout << "Proving that * and & are complements of "
        << "each other." << endl << "&*aPtr = " << &*aPtr
        << endl << "*&aPtr = " << *&aPtr << endl;
   return 0;
}
```

**Fig. 5.4** The **&** and ***** pointer operators (part 1 of 2).

```
The address of a is 0xfff4
The value of aPtr is 0xfff4

The value of a is 7
The value of *aPtr is 7

Proving that * and & are complements of each other.
&*aPtr = 0xfff4
*&aPtr = 0xfff4
```

**Fig. 5.4** The **&** and ***** pointer operators (part 2 of 2).

| Operators | Associativity | Type |
|---|---|---|
| `()` `[]` | left to right | highest |
| `+` `-` `++` `--` `!` `*` `&` `(type)` | right to left | unary |
| `*` `/` `%` | left to right | multiplicative |
| `+` `-` | left to right | additive |
| `<<` `>>` | left to right | insertion/extraction |
| `<` `<=` `>` `>=` | left to right | relational |
| `==` `!=` | left to right | equality |
| `&&` | left to right | logical and |
| `\|\|` | left to right | logical or |
| `?:` | right to left | conditional |
| `=` `+=` `-=` `*=` `/=` `%=` | right to left | assignment |
| `,` | left to right | comma |

**Fig. 5.5** Operator precedence.

## 5.4 Calling Functions by Reference

There are three ways to pass arguments to a function—*call-by-value*, *call-by-reference with reference arguments*, and *call-by-reference with pointer arguments*. In Chapter 3, we compared and contrasted call-by-value and call-by-reference with reference arguments. In this chapter, we concentrate on call-by-reference with pointer arguments.

As we saw in Chapter 3, **return** can be used to return one value from a called function to a caller (or to return control from a called function without passing back a value). We also saw that arguments can be passed to a function using reference arguments to enable the function to modify the original values of the arguments (thus, more than one value can be "returned" from a function), or to pass large data objects to a function and avoid the overhead of passing the objects call-by-value (which, of course, requires making a copy of the object). Pointers, like references, also can be used to modify one or more variables in the caller, or to pass pointers to large data objects to avoid the overhead of passing the objects call-by-value.

In C++, programmers can use pointers and the indirection operator to simulate call-by-reference. When calling a function with arguments that should be modified, the addresses of the arguments are passed. This is normally accomplished by applying the address operator (**&**) to the variable whose value will be modified. As we saw in Chapter 4, arrays are not passed using operator **&** because the name of the array is the starting location in memory of the array (the name of an array is equivalent to **&arrayName[0]**). When the address of a variable is passed to a function, the indirection operator (*****) may be used in the function to modify the value (if the variable is not declared **const**) at that location in the caller's memory.

The programs in Fig. 5.6 and Fig. 5.7 present two versions of a function that cubes an integer—**cubeByValue** and **cubeByReference**. The program in Fig. 5.6 passes the variable **number** to function **cubeByValue** using call-by-value. Function **cubeByValue** cubes its argument and passes the new value back to **main** using a **return** statement. The new value is assigned to **number** in **main**. The key point of call-by-value is that you have the opportunity to examine the result of the function call before modifying a variable's value. For example, in this program, we could have stored the result of **cubeByValue** in another variable, examined its value, and assigned the result to **number** after checking the value.

```
// Cube a variable using call-by-value
#include <iostream.h>

int cubeByValue(int);    // prototype

main()
{
   int number = 5;

   cout << "The original value of number is " << number << endl;
   number = cubeByValue(number);
   cout << "The new value of number is " << number << endl;
   return 0;
}

int cubeByValue(int n)
{
   return n * n * n;    // cube local variable n
}
```

```
The original value of number is 5
The new value of number is 125
```

**Fig. 5.6** Cube a variable using call-by-value.

The program of Fig. 5.7 passes the variable **number** using call-by-reference—the address of **number** is passed—to function **cubeByReference**. Function **cubeByReference** takes **nPtr** (a pointer to **int**) as an argument. The function dereferences the pointer and cubes the value to which **nPtr** points. This changes the value of **number** in **main**. Figures 5.8 and 5.9 analyze graphically the programs in Fig. 5.6 and Fig. 5.7, respectively.

***Common Programming Error 5.3***

*Not dereferencing a pointer when it is necessary to do so to obtain the value to which the pointer points.*

A function receiving an address as an argument must define a pointer parameter to receive the address. For example, the header for function **cubeByReference** is

```
void cubeByReference(int *nPtr)
```

The function header specifies that function **cubeByReference** receives the address of an integer variable as an argument, stores the address locally in **nPtr**, and does not return a value.

The function prototype for **cubeByReference** contains **int *** in parentheses. As with other variable types, it is not necessary to include names of pointers in function prototypes. Names included for documentation purposes are ignored by the compiler.

```
// Cube a variable using call-by-reference with a pointer argument
#include <iostream.h>

void cubeByReference(int *);    // prototype

main()
{
   int number = 5;

   cout << "The original value of number is " << number << endl;
   cubeByReference(&number);
   cout << "The new value of number is " << number << endl;
   return 0;
}

void cubeByReference(int *nPtr)
{
   *nPtr = *nPtr * *nPtr * *nPtr;  // cube number in main
}
```

```
The original value of number is 5
The new value of number is 125
```

**Fig. 5.7** Cube a variable using call-by-reference with a pointer argument.

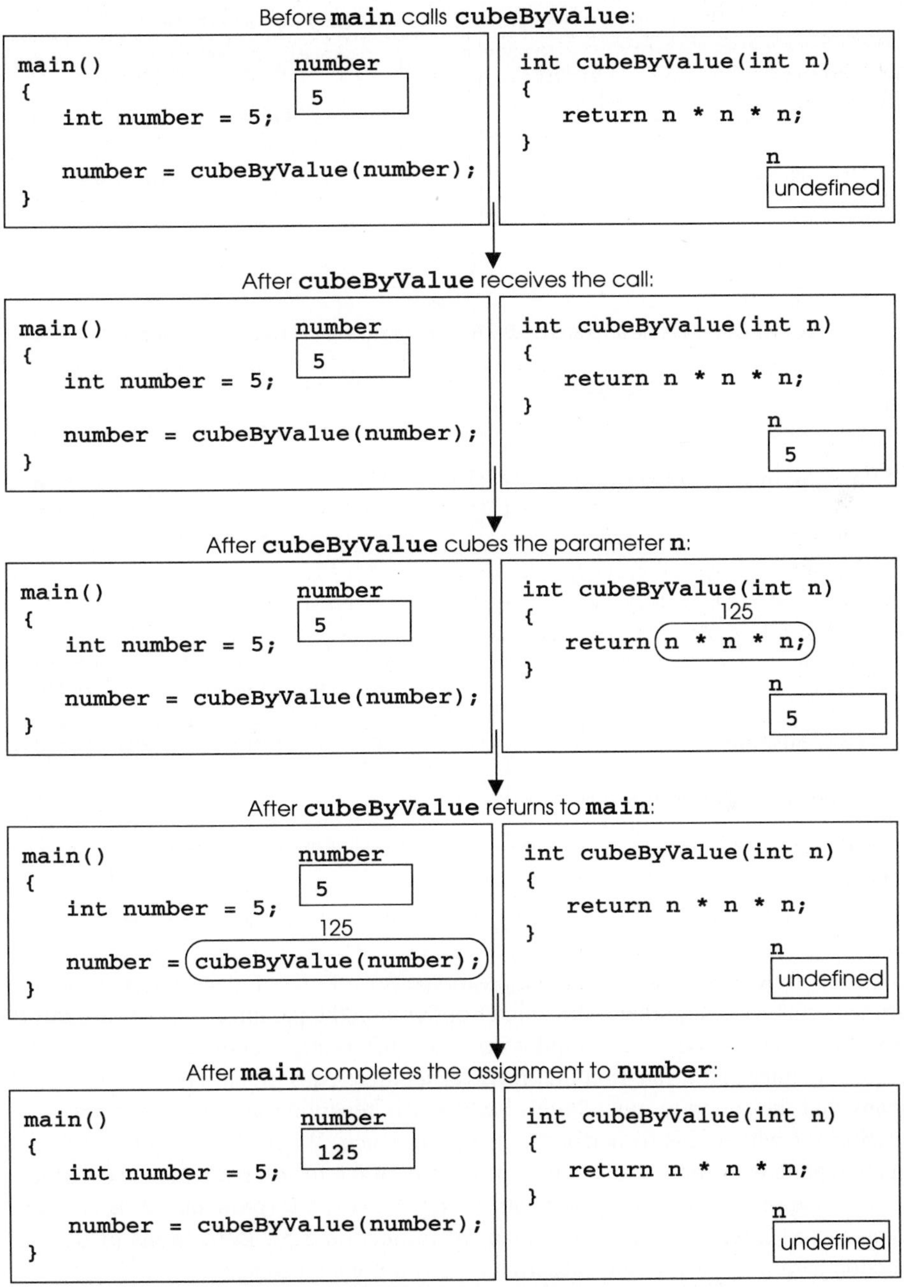

Before **main** calls **cubeByValue**:

```
main()                              number
{                                   5
   int number = 5;

   number = cubeByValue(number);
}
```

```
int cubeByValue(int n)
{
   return n * n * n;
}
                                    n
                                    undefined
```

After **cubeByValue** receives the call:

```
main()                              number
{                                   5
   int number = 5;

   number = cubeByValue(number);
}
```

```
int cubeByValue(int n)
{
   return n * n * n;
}
                                    n
                                    5
```

After **cubeByValue** cubes the parameter **n**:

```
main()                              number
{                                   5
   int number = 5;

   number = cubeByValue(number);
}
```

```
int cubeByValue(int n)
{               125
   return (n * n * n;)
}
                                    n
                                    5
```

After **cubeByValue** returns to **main**:

```
main()                              number
{                                   5
   int number = 5;
                        125
   number = (cubeByValue(number);)
}
```

```
int cubeByValue(int n)
{
   return n * n * n;
}
                                    n
                                    undefined
```

After **main** completes the assignment to **number**:

```
main()                              number
{                                   125
   int number = 5;

   number = cubeByValue(number);
}
```

```
int cubeByValue(int n)
{
   return n * n * n;
}
                                    n
                                    undefined
```

**Fig. 5.8** Analysis of a typical call-by-value.

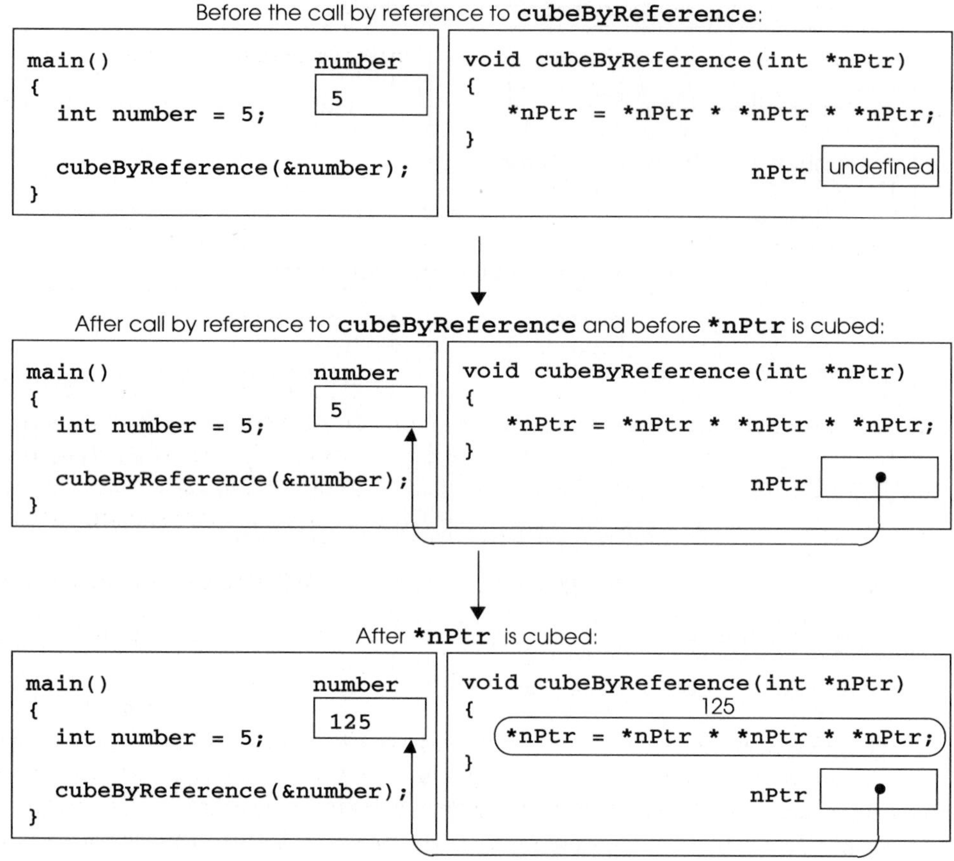


**Fig. 5.9** Analysis of a typical call-by-reference with a pointer argument.

In the function header and in the prototype for a function that expects a single-subscripted array as an argument, the pointer notation in the parameter list of **cubeByReference** may be used. The compiler does not differentiate between a function that receives a pointer and a function that receives a single-subscripted array. This, of course, means that the function must "know" when it is receiving an array or simply a single variable for which it is to perform call-by-reference. When the compiler encounters a function parameter for a single-subscripted array of the form **int b[]**, the compiler converts the parameter to the pointer notation **int * const b** (pronounced "**b** is a constant pointer to an integer—**const** is explained in Section 5.5). Both forms of declaring a function parameter as a single-subscripted array are interchangeable.

***Good Programming Practice 5.3***

*Use call-by-value to pass arguments to a function unless the caller explicitly requires that the called function modify the value of the argument variable in the caller's environment. This is another example of the principle of least privilege.*

## 5.5 Using the Const Qualifier with Pointers

The `const` *qualifier* enables the programmer to inform the compiler that the value of a particular variable should not be modified.

***Software Engineering Observation 5.1***

*The `const` qualifier can be used to enforce the principle of least privilege. Using the principle of least privilege to properly design software tremendously reduces debugging time and improper side effects, and makes a program easier to modify and maintain.*

***Portability Tip 5.1***

*Although `const` is well defined in ANSI C, some compilers do not enforce it.*

Over the years, a large base of legacy code was written in early versions of C that did not use `const` because it was not available. For this reason, there are tremendous opportunities for improvement in the software engineering of old C code. Also, many programmers currently using ANSI C do not use `const` in their programs because they began programming in early versions of C. These programmers are omitting many opportunities for good software engineering.

Six possibilities exist for using (or not using) `const` with function parameters—two with call-by-value parameter passing and four with call-by-reference parameter passing. How do you choose one of the six possibilities? Let the principle of least privilege be your guide. Always award a function enough access to the data in its parameters to accomplish its specified task, but no more.

In Chapter 3, we explained that when a function is called using call-by-value, a copy of the argument (or arguments) in the function call is made and passed to the function. If the copy is modified in the function, the original value is maintained without change in the caller. In many cases, a value passed to a function is modified so the function can accomplish its task. However, in some instances, the value should not be altered in the called function even though the called function manipulates a copy of the original value.

Consider a function that takes a single-subscripted array and its size as arguments and prints the array. Such a function should loop through the array and output each array element individually. The size of the array is used in the function body to determine the high subscript of the array so the loop can terminate when the printing is completed. The size of the array does not change in the function body.

***Software Engineering Observation 5.2***

*If a value does not (or should not) change in the body of a function to which it is passed, the parameter should be declared `const` to ensure that it is not accidentally modified.*

If an attempt is made to modify a `const` value, the compiler catches it and issues either a warning or an error depending on the particular compiler.

***Software Engineering Observation 5.3***

*Only one value can be altered in a calling function when call-by-value is used. That value must be assigned from the return value of the function. To modify multiple values in a calling function, call-by-reference must be used.*

***Good Programming Practice 5.4***

*Before using a function, check the function prototype for the function to determine if the function is able to modify the values passed to it.*

There are four ways to pass a pointer to a function: a non-constant pointer to non-constant data, a non-constant pointer to constant data, a constant pointer to non-constant data, and a constant pointer to constant data. Each combination provides a different level of access privileges.

The highest access is granted by a non-constant pointer to non-constant data—the data can be modified through the dereferenced pointer and the pointer can be modified to point to other data. Declaration for non-constant pointers to non-constant data do not include **const**. Such a pointer can be used to receive a string in a function that uses pointer arithmetic to process (and possibly modify) each character in the string. Function **convertToUppercase** of Fig. 5.10 declares parameter **sPtr** (**char *sPtr**) to be a non-constant pointer to non-constant data. The function processes the string **s** one character at a time using pointer arithmetic. Characters in the range **'a'** to **'z'** are converted to their corresponding uppercase letters by function **toupper**; others remain unchanged. Function **toupper** takes a character as an argument. If the character is a lowercase letter, the corresponding uppercase letter is returned; otherwise, the original character is returned. Function **toupper** is part of the character handling library **ctype.h** (see Chapter 16, "Characters, Strings, Structures, and Bit Manipulation").

```
// Converting lowercase letters to uppercase letters
// using a non-constant pointer to non-constant data
#include <iostream.h>
#include <ctype.h>

void convertToUppercase(char *);

main()
{
   char string[] = "characters and $32.98";

   cout << "The string before conversion is: " << string << endl;
   convertToUppercase(string);
   cout << "The string after conversion is:  " << string << endl;
   return 0;
}

void convertToUppercase(char *sPtr)
{
   while (*sPtr != '\0') {
      *sPtr = toupper(*sPtr);  // convert to uppercase letter
      ++sPtr;  // increment sPtr to point to the next character
   }
}
```

**Fig. 5.10** Converting a string to uppercase (part 1 of 2).

```
The string before conversion is: characters and $32.98
The string after conversion is:  CHARACTERS AND $32.98
```

**Fig. 5.10** Converting a string to uppercase (part 2 of 2).

A non-constant pointer to constant data is a pointer that can be modified to point to any data item of the appropriate type, but the data to which it points cannot be modified. Such a pointer might be used to receive an array argument to a function that will process each element of the array without modifying the data. For example, function **`printCharacters`** of Fig. 5.11 declares parameters **`sPtr`** to be of type **`const char *`**. The declaration is read from right to left as "**`sPtr`** is a pointer to a character constant." The body of the function uses a **`for`** structure to output each character in the string until the null character is encountered. After each character is printed, pointer **`sPtr`** is incremented to point to the next character in the string.

```
// Printing a string one character at a time using
// a non-constant pointer to constant data
#include <iostream.h>

void printCharacters(const char *);

main()
{
   char string[] = "print characters of a string";

   cout << "The string is:" << endl;
   printCharacters(string);
   cout << endl;
   return 0;
}

// In printCharacters, sPtr is a pointer to a character constant.
// Characters cannot be modified through sPtr
// (i.e., sPtr is a "read-only" pointer).
void printCharacters(const char *sPtr)
{
   for ( ; *sPtr != '\0'; sPtr++)    // no initialization
      cout << *sPtr;
}
```

```
The string is:
print characters of a string
```

**Fig. 5.11** Printing a string one character at a time using a non-constant pointer to constant data.

Figure 5.12 demonstrates the error messages produced by the Borland C++ compiler when attempting to compile a function that receives a non-constant pointer to constant data, and then tries to use that pointer to modify the data.

As we know, arrays are aggregate data types that store related data items of the same type under one name. In Chapter 6, we will discuss another form of aggregate data type called a *structure* (sometimes called a *record* in other languages). A structure is capable of storing related data items of different data types under one name (for example, storing information about each employee of a company). When a function is called with an array as an argument, the array is automatically passed to the function simulated call-by-reference. However, structures are always passed call-by-value—a copy of the entire structure is passed. This requires the execution-time overhead of making a copy of each data item in the structure and storing it on the computer's function call stack (the place where the local variables used in the function call are stored while the function is executing). When structure data must be passed to a function, we can use pointers to constant data to get the performance of call-by-reference and the protection of call-by-value. When a pointer to a structure is passed, only a copy of the address at which the structure is stored must be made. On a machine with 4-byte addresses, a copy of 4 bytes of memory is made rather than a copy of possibly hundreds or thousands of bytes of the structure.

```
// Attempting to modify data through a
// non-constant pointer to constant data.
#include <iostream.h>

void f(const int *);

main()
{
   int y;

   f(&y);       // f attempts illegal modification

   return 0;
}

// In f, xPtr is a pointer to an integer constant
void f(const int *xPtr)
{
   *xPtr = 100;  // cannot modify a const object
}
```

```
Compiling FIG5_12.CPP:
Error FIG5_12.CPP 19: Cannot modify a const object
Warning FIG5_12.CPP 20: Parameter 'xPtr' is never used
```

**Fig. 5.12** Attempting to modify data through a non-constant pointer to constant data.

***Performance Tip 5.1***

*Pass large objects such as structures using pointers to constant data, or references to constant data, to obtain the performance benefits of call-by-reference and the security of call-by-value.*

A constant pointer to non-constant data is a pointer that always points to the same memory location, and the data at that location can be modified through the pointer. This is the default for an array name. An array name is a constant pointer to the beginning of the array. All data in the array can be accessed and changed by using the array name and array subscripting. A constant pointer to non-constant data can be used to receive an array as an argument to a function that accesses array elements using only array subscript notation. Pointers that are declared **const** must be initialized when they are declared (if the pointer is a function parameter, it is initialized with a pointer that is passed to the function). The program of Fig. 5.13 attempts to modify a constant pointer. Pointer **ptr** is declared to be of type **int * const**. The declaration is read from right to left as "**ptr** is a constant pointer to an integer." The pointer is initialized with the address of integer variable **x**. The program attempts to assign the address of **y** to **ptr**, but an error message is generated. Note that no error is produced when the value **7** is assigned to ***ptr**—the value to which **ptr** points is still modifiable.

***Common Programming Error 5.4***

*Not initializing a pointer that is declared* **const** *results in a compile error.*

```
// Attempting to modify a constant pointer to
// non-constant data
#include <iostream.h>

main()
{
   int x, y;

   int * const ptr = &x;    // ptr is a constant pointer to an
                            // integer. An integer can be modified
                            // through ptr, but ptr always points
                            // to the same memory location.
   *ptr = 7;
   ptr = &y;    // ERROR: Cannot modify a const object

   return 0;
}
```

```
Compiling FIG5_13.CPP:
Error FIG5_13.CPP 14: Cannot modify a const object
Warning FIG5_13.CPP 17: 'y' is declared but never used
```

**Fig. 5.13** Attempting to modify a constant pointer to non-constant data.

The least amount of access privilege is granted by a constant pointer to constant data. Such a pointer always points to the same memory location, and the data at that memory location cannot be modified. This is how an array should be passed to a function that only looks at the array using array subscript notation and does not modify the array. The program of Fig. 5.14 declares pointer variable **ptr** to be of type **const int * const**. This declaration is read from right to left as "**ptr** is a constant pointer to an integer constant." The figure shows the error messages generated when an attempt is made to modify the data to which **ptr** points and when an attempt is made to modify the address stored in the pointer variable. Note that no error is generated when we attempt to output the value to which **ptr** points because nothing is being modified in the output statement.

## 5.6 Bubble Sort Using Call-by-reference

Let us modify the bubble sort program of Fig. 4.16 to use two functions—**bubbleSort** and **swap** (Fig. 5.15). Function **bubbleSort** performs the sort of the array. It calls function **swap** to exchange the array elements **array[j]** and **array[j + 1]**. Remember that C++ enforces information hiding between functions, so **swap** does not have access to individual array elements in **bubbleSort**. Because **bubbleSort** *wants* **swap** to have access to the array elements to be swapped, **bubbleSort** passes each of these elements call-by-reference to **swap**—the address of each array element is passed

```
// Attempting to modify a constant pointer to
// constant data.
#include <iostream.h>

main()
{
   int x = 5, y;

   const int *const ptr = &x;   // ptr is a constant pointer to a
                                // constant integer. ptr always
                                // points to the same location and
                                // the integer at that location
                                // cannot be modified.
   cout << *ptr << endl;
   *ptr = 7;    // ERROR: Cannot modify a const object
   ptr = &y;    // ERROR: Cannot modify a const object

   return 0;
}
```

```
Compiling FIG5_14.CPP:
Error FIG5_14.CPP 15: Cannot modify a const object
Error FIG5_14.CPP 16: Cannot modify a const object
Warning FIG5_14.CPP 19: 'y' is declared but never used
```

**Fig. 5.14** Attempting to modify a constant pointer to constant data.

explicitly. Although entire arrays are automatically passed call-by-reference, individual array elements are scalars and are ordinarily passed call-by-value. Therefore, **bubbleSort** uses the address operator (**&**) on each array element in the **swap** call as follows

```
swap(&array[j], &array[j + 1]);
```

to effect call-by-reference. Function **swap** receives **&array[j]** in pointer variable **element1Ptr**. Because of information hiding, **swap** is not allowed to know the name **array[j]**, but **swap** can use ***element1Ptr** as a synonym for **array[j]**. Thus, when **swap** references ***element1Ptr**, it is actually referencing **array[j]** in **bubbleSort**. Similarly, when **swap** references ***element2Ptr**, it is actually referencing **array[j + 1]** in **bubbleSort**. Even though **swap** is not allowed to say

```
temp = array[j];
array[j] = array[j + 1];
array[j + 1] = temp;
```

precisely the same effect is achieved by

```
temp = *element1Ptr;
*element1Ptr = *element2Ptr;
*element2Ptr = temp;
```

in the **swap** function of Fig. 5.15.

```
// This program puts values into an array, sorts the values into
// ascending order, and prints the resulting array.
#include <iostream.h>
#include <iomanip.h>

void bubbleSort(int *, const int);

main()
{
   const int arraySize = 10;
   int a[arraySize] = {2, 6, 4, 8, 10, 12, 89, 68, 45, 37};

   cout << "Data items in original order" << endl;

   for (int i = 0; i < arraySize; i++)
      cout << setw(4) << a[i];

   bubbleSort(a, arraySize);             // sort the array
   cout << endl << "Data items in ascending order" << endl;

   for (i = 0; i < arraySize; i++)
      cout << setw(4) << a[i];

   cout << endl;
   return 0;
}
```

**Fig. 5.15** Bubble sort with call-by-reference (part 1 of 2).

```
void bubbleSort(int *array, const int size)
{
   void swap(int *, int *);

   for (int pass = 1; pass < size; pass++)

      for (int j = 0; j < size - 1; j++)

         if (array[j] > array[j + 1])
            swap(&array[j], &array[j + 1]);
}

void swap(int *element1Ptr, int *element2Ptr)
{
   int temp = *element1Ptr;
   *element1Ptr = *element2Ptr;
   *element2Ptr = temp;
}
```

```
Data items in original order
   2   6   4   8  10  12  89  68  45  37
Data items in ascending order
   2   4   6   8  10  12  37  45  68  89
```

**Fig. 5.15** Bubble sort with call-by-reference (part 2 of 2).

Several features of function **bubbleSort** should be noted. The function header declares **array** as **int *array** rather than **int array[]** to indicate that **bubbleSort** receives a single-subscripted array as an argument (again, these notations are interchangeable). Parameter **size** is declared **const** to enforce the principle of least privilege. Although parameter **size** receives a copy of a value in **main** and modifying the copy cannot change the value in **main**, **bubbleSort** does not need to alter **size** to accomplish its task. The size of the array remains fixed during the execution of **bubbleSort**. Therefore, **size** is declared **const** to ensure that it is not modified. If the size of the array is modified during the sorting process, the sorting algorithm would not run correctly.

The prototype for function **swap** is included in the body of function **bubbleSort** because it is the only function that calls **swap**. Placing the prototype in **bubbleSort** restricts proper calls of **swap** to those made from **bubbleSort**. Other functions that attempt to call **swap** do not have access to a proper function prototype. This normally results in a compiler error because C++ requires function prototypes.

***Software Engineering Observation 5.4***

*Placing function prototypes in the definitions of other functions enforces the principle of least privilege by restricting proper function calls to the functions in which the prototypes appear.*

Note that function **bubbleSort** receives the size of the array as a parameter. The function must know the size of the array to sort the array. When an array is passed to a function, the memory address of the first element of the array is received by the function. The array size must be passed separately to the function.

By defining function **bubbleSort** so it receives the array size as a parameter, we enable the function to be used by any program that sorts single-subscripted integer arrays, and the arrays can be any size.

***Software Engineering Observation 5.5***

*When passing an array to a function, also pass the size of the array (rather than building into the function knowledge of the array size). This helps make the function more general. General functions are often reusable in many programs.*

The size of the array could have been programmed directly into the function. This restricts the use of the function to an array of a specific size and reduces its reusability. Only programs processing single-subscripted integer arrays of the specific size coded into the function can use the function.

C++ provides the *unary operator* ***sizeof*** to determine the size of an array (or any other data type) in bytes during program compilation. When applied to the name of an array as in Fig. 5.16, the **sizeof** operator returns the total number of bytes in the array as a value of type **size_t** which is usually **unsigned int**. Note that variables of type **float** are normally stored in 4 bytes of memory, and **array** is declared to have 20 elements. Therefore, **array** uses 80 bytes in memory.

The number of elements in an array also can be determined using the results of two **sizeof** operations. For example, consider the following array declaration:

```
double realArray[22];
```

```
// The sizeof operator used with an array name
// returns the number of bytes in the array.
#include <iostream.h>

main()
{
   float array[20];

   cout << "The number of bytes in the array is "
        << sizeof(array) << endl;

   return 0;
}
```

```
The number of bytes in the array is 80
```

**Fig. 5.16** The **sizeof** operator when applied to an array name returns the number of bytes in the array.

Variables of data type **double** normally are stored in 8 bytes of memory. Thus, array **realArray** contains a total of 176 bytes. To determine the number of elements in the array, the following expression can be used:

```
sizeof(realArray) / sizeof(double)
```

The expression determines the number of bytes in array **realArray** and divides that value by the number of bytes used in memory to store a **double** value.

The program of Fig. 5.17 uses the **sizeof** operator to calculate the number of bytes used to store each of the standard data types on popular personal computers.

***Portability Tip 5.2***

*The number of bytes used to store a particular data type may vary between systems. When writing programs that depend on data type sizes, and that will run on several computer systems, use* **sizeof** *to determine the number of bytes used to store the data types.*

```
// Demonstrating the sizeof operator
#include <iostream.h>

main()
{
   int array[20], *ptr = array;

   cout << "         sizeof(char) = " << sizeof(char) << endl
        << "        sizeof(short) = " << sizeof(short) << endl
        << "          sizeof(int) = " << sizeof(int) << endl
        << "         sizeof(long) = " << sizeof(long) << endl
        << "        sizeof(float) = " << sizeof(float) << endl
        << "       sizeof(double) = " << sizeof(double) << endl
        << "sizeof(long double) = " << sizeof(long double) << endl
        << "         sizeof array = " << sizeof array << endl
        << "           sizeof ptr = " << sizeof ptr << endl
        << endl;
   return 0;
}
```

```
       sizeof(char) = 1
      sizeof(short) = 2
        sizeof(int) = 2
       sizeof(long) = 4
      sizeof(float) = 4
     sizeof(double) = 8
sizeof(long double) = 10
       sizeof array = 40
         sizeof ptr = 2
```

Fig. 5.17 Using the **sizeof** operator to determine standard data type sizes.

Operator **sizeof** can be applied to any variable name, type name, or constant value. When applied to a variable name (which is not an array name) or a constant value, the number of bytes used to store the specific type of variable or constant is returned. Note that the parentheses used with **sizeof** are required if a type name is supplied as its operand. The parentheses used with **sizeof** are not required if a variable name is supplied as its operand.

***Common Programming Error 5.5***

*Omitting the parentheses in a* **sizeof** *operation when the operand is a type name results in a syntax error.*

## 5.7 Pointer Expressions and Pointer Arithmetic

Pointers are valid operands in arithmetic expressions, assignment expressions, and comparison expressions. However, not all the operators normally used in these expressions are valid with pointer variables. This section describes the operators that can have pointers as operands, and how these operators are used.

A limited set of arithmetic operations may be performed on pointers. A pointer may be incremented (++) or decremented (--), an integer may be added to a pointer (+ or +=), an integer may be subtracted from a pointer (- or -=), or one pointer may be subtracted from another.

Assume that array **int v[10]** has been declared and its first element is at location **3000** in memory. Assume pointer **vPtr** has been initialized to point to **v[0]**, i.e., the value of **vPtr** is **3000**. Figure 5.18 diagrams this situation for a machine with 4-byte integers. Note that **vPtr** can be initialized to point to array **v** with either of the following statements

```
vPtr = v;
vPtr = &v[0];
```

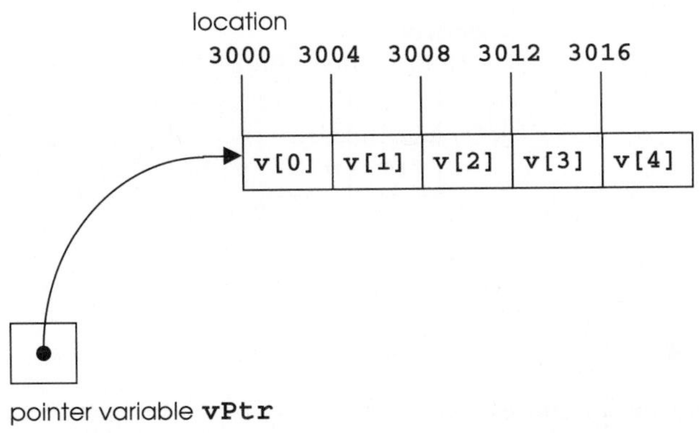


**Fig. 5.18** The array **v** and a pointer variable **vPtr** that points to **v**.

*Portability Tip 5.3*

*Most computers today have 2-byte or 4-byte integers. Some of the newer machines use 8-byte integers. Because the results of pointer arithmetic depend on the size of the objects a pointer points to, pointer arithmetic is machine dependent.*

In conventional arithmetic, the addition **3000 + 2** yields the value **3002**. This is normally not the case with pointer arithmetic. When an integer is added to or subtracted from a pointer, the pointer is not simply incremented or decremented by that integer, but by that integer times the size of the object to which the pointer refers. The number of bytes depends on the object's data type. For example, the statement

```
vPtr += 2;
```

would produce **3008** (**3000 + 2 * 4**) assuming an integer is stored in 4 bytes of memory. In the array **v**, **vPtr** would now point to **v[2]** (Fig. 5.19). If an integer is stored in 2 bytes of memory, then the preceding calculation would result in memory location **3004** (**3000 + 2 * 2**). If the array were of a different data type, the preceding statement would increment the pointer by twice the number of bytes it takes to store an object of that data type. When performing pointer arithmetic on a character array, the results will be consistent with regular arithmetic because each character is one byte long.

If **vPtr** had been incremented to **3016**, which points to **v[4]**, the statement

```
vPtr -= 4;
```

would set **vPtr** back to **3000**—the beginning of the array. If a pointer is being incremented or decremented by one, the increment (**++**) and decrement (**--**) operators can be used. Each of the statements

```
++vPtr;
vPtr++;
```

increments the pointer to point to the next location in the array. Each of the statements

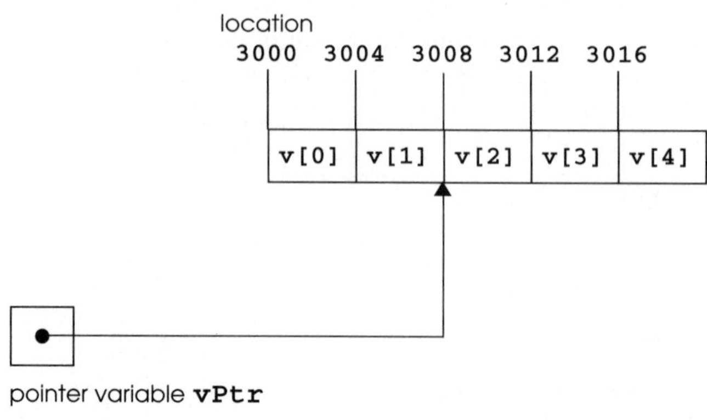


**Fig. 5.19** The pointer **vPtr** after pointer arithmetic.

```
--vPtr;
vPtr--;
```

decrements the pointer to point to the previous element of the array.

Pointer variables may be subtracted from one another. For example, if **vPtr** contains the location **3000**, and **v2Ptr** contains the address **3008**, the statement

```
x = v2Ptr - vPtr;
```

would assign to **x** the number of array elements from **vPtr** to **v2Ptr**, in this case, **2**. Pointer arithmetic is meaningless unless performed on an array. We cannot assume that two variables of the same type are stored contiguously in memory unless they are adjacent elements of an array.

***Common Programming Error 5.6***

*Using pointer arithmetic on a pointer that does not refer to an array of values.*

***Common Programming Error 5.7***

*Subtracting or comparing two pointers that do not refer to elements of the same array.*

***Common Programming Error 5.8***

*Running off either end of an array when using pointer arithmetic.*

A pointer can be assigned to another pointer if both pointers are of the same type. Otherwise, a cast operator must be used to convert the value of the pointer on the right of the assignment to the pointer type on the left of the assignment. The exception to this rule is the pointer to **void** (i.e., **void ***) which is a generic pointer capable of representing any pointer type. All pointer types can be assigned a pointer to **void** without casting. However, a pointer to **void** cannot be assigned directly to a pointer of another type—the **void** pointer must first be cast to the proper pointer type.

A **void *** pointer cannot be dereferenced. For example, the compiler knows that a pointer to **int** refers to four bytes of memory on a machine with 4-byte integers, but a pointer to **void** simply contains a memory location for an unknown data type—the precise number of bytes to which the pointer refers is not known by the compiler. The compiler must know the data type to determine the number of bytes to be dereferenced for a particular pointer. In the case of a pointer to **void**, this number of bytes cannot be determined from the type.

***Common Programming Error 5.9***

*Assigning a pointer of one type to a pointer of another (other than* **void *** *) causes a syntax error.*

***Common Programming Error 5.10***

*Dereferencing a* **void *** *pointer.*

Pointers can be compared using equality and relational operators, but such comparisons are meaningless unless the pointers point to members of the same array. Pointer comparisons compare the addresses stored in the pointers. A comparison of two pointers pointing to the same array could show, for example, that one pointer points to a higher-numbered element of the array than the other pointer does. A common use of pointer comparison is determining whether a pointer is 0.

## 5.8 The Relationship between Pointers and Arrays

Arrays and pointers are intimately related in C++ and may be used *almost* interchangeably. An array name can be thought of as a constant pointer. Pointers can be used to do any operation involving array subscripting.

***Good Programming Practice 5.5***

*Use array notation instead of pointer notation when manipulating arrays. Although the program may take slightly longer to compile, it will probably be clearer.*

Assume that integer array `b[5]` and integer pointer variable `bPtr` have been declared. Because the array name (without a subscript) is a pointer to the first element of the array, we can set `bPtr` to the address of the first element in array `b` with the statement

```
bPtr = b;
```

This is equivalent to taking the address of the first element of the array as follows

```
bPtr = &b[0];
```

Array element `b[3]` can alternatively be referenced with the pointer expression

```
*(bPtr + 3)
```

The `3` in the above expression is the *offset* to the pointer. When the pointer points to the beginning of an array, the offset indicates which element of the array should be referenced, and the offset value is identical to the array subscript. The preceding notation is referred to as *pointer/offset notation.* The parentheses are necessary because the precedence of `*` is higher than the precedence of `+`. Without the parentheses, the above expression would add `3` to the value of the expression `*bPtr` (i.e., `3` would be added to `b[0]` assuming `bPtr` points to the beginning of the array). Just as the array element can be referenced with a pointer expression, the address

```
&b[3]
```

can be written with the pointer expression

```
bPtr + 3
```

The array itself can be treated as a pointer and used in pointer arithmetic. For example, the expression

```
*(b + 3)
```

also refers to the array element `b[3]`. In general, all subscripted array expressions can be written with a pointer and an offset. In this case, pointer/offset notation was used with the name of the array as a pointer. Note that the preceding statement does not modify the array name in any way; **b** still points to the first element in the array.

Pointers can be subscripted exactly as arrays can. For example, the expression

```
bPtr[1]
```

refers to the array element **b[1]**; this expression is referred to as *pointer/subscript notation.*

Remember that an array name is essentially a constant pointer; it always points to the beginning of the array. Thus, the expression

```
b += 3
```

is invalid because it attempts to modify the value of the array name with pointer arithmetic.

***Common Programming Error 5.11***

*Although array names are pointers to the beginning of the array, and pointers can be modified in arithmetic expressions, array names cannot be modified in arithmetic expressions.*

The program in Fig. 5.20 uses the four methods we have discussed for referring to array elements—array subscripting, pointer/offset with the array name as a pointer, pointer subscripting, and pointer/offset with a pointer—to print the four elements of the integer array **b**.

To further illustrate the interchangeability of arrays and pointers, let us look at the two string copying functions—**copy1** and **copy2**—in the program of Fig. 5.21. Both functions copy a string into a character array. After a comparison of the function prototypes for **copy1** and **copy2**, the functions appear identical. They accomplish the same task, but they are implemented differently.

Function **copy1** uses array subscript notation to copy the string in **s2** to the character array **s1**. The function declares an integer counter variable **i** to use as the array subscript. The **for** structure header performs the entire copy operation—its body is the empty statement. The header specifies that **i** is initialized to zero and incremented by one on each iteration of the loop. The condition in the **for**, **(s1[i] = s2[i]) != '\0'**, performs the copy operation character by character from **s2** to **s1**. When the null character is encountered in **s2**, it is assigned to **s1**, and the loop terminates because the the null character is equal to **'\0'**. Remember that the value of an assignment statement is the value assigned to the left argument.

Function **copy2** uses pointers and pointer arithmetic to copy the string in **s2** to the character array **s1**. Again, the **for** structure header performs the entire copy operation. The header does not include any variable initialization. As in function **copy1**, the condition **(*s1 = *s2) != '\0'** performs the copy operation. Pointer **s2** is dereferenced and the resulting character is assigned to the dereferenced pointer **s1**. After the assignment in the condition, the pointers are incremented to point to the next element of array **s1** and the next character of string **s2**, respectively. When the null character is encountered in **s2**, it is assigned to the dereferenced pointer **s1** and the loop terminates.

```
// Using subscripting and pointer notations with arrays
#include <iostream.h>

main()
{
   int b[] = {10, 20, 30, 40};
   int *bPtr = b;    // set bPtr to point to array b

   cout << "Array b printed with:" << endl
        << "Array subscript notation" << endl;

   for (int i = 0; i <= 3; i++)
      cout << "b[" << i << "] = " << b[i] << endl;


   cout << endl << "Pointer/offset notation where" << endl
        << "the pointer is the array name" << endl;

   for (int offset = 0; offset <= 3; offset++)
      cout << "*(b + " << offset << ") = "
           << *(b + offset) << endl;


   cout << endl << "Pointer subscript notation" << endl;

   for (i = 0; i <= 3; i++)
      cout << "bPtr[" << i << "] = " << bPtr[i] << endl;


   cout << endl << "Pointer/offset notation" << endl;

   for (offset = 0; offset <= 3; offset++)
      cout << "*(bPtr + " << offset << ") = "
           << *(bPtr + offset) << endl;

   return 0;
}
```

**Fig. 5.20** Using four methods of referencing array elements (part 1 of 2).

Note that the first argument to both **copy1** and **copy2** must be an array large enough to hold the string in the second argument. Otherwise, an error may occur when an attempt is made to write into a memory location beyond the boundary of the array. Also, note that the second parameter of each function is declared as **const char *** (a constant string). In both functions, the second argument is copied into the first argument—characters are copied from the second argument one at a time, but the characters are never modified. Therefore, the second parameter is declared to point to a constant value so the principle of least privilege is enforced. Neither function requires the capability of modifying the second argument, so neither function is provided with the capability of modifying the second argument.

```
Array b printed with:
Array subscript notation
b[0] = 10
b[1] = 20
b[2] = 30
b[3] = 40

Pointer/offset notation where
the pointer is the array name
*(b + 0) = 10
*(b + 1) = 20
*(b + 2) = 30
*(b + 3) = 40

Pointer subscript notation
bPtr[0] = 10
bPtr[1] = 20
bPtr[2] = 30
bPtr[3] = 40

Pointer/offset notation
*(bPtr + 0) = 10
*(bPtr + 1) = 20
*(bPtr + 2) = 30
*(bPtr + 3) = 40
```

**Fig. 5.20** Using four methods of referencing array elements (part 2 of 2).

```
// Copying a string using array notation
// and pointer notation.
#include <iostream.h>

void copy1(char *, const char *);
void copy2(char *, const char *);

main()
{
   char string1[10], *string2 = "Hello",
        string3[10], string4[] = "Good Bye";

   copy1(string1, string2);
   cout << "string1 = " << string1 << endl;

   copy2(string3, string4);
   cout << "string3 = " << string3 << endl;

   return 0;
}
```

**Fig. 5.21** Copying a string using array notation and pointer notation (part 1 of 2).

```
// copy s2 to s1 using array notation
void copy1(char *s1, const char *s2)
{
   for (int i = 0; (s1[i] = s2[i]) != '\0'; i++)
      ;   // do nothing in body
}

// copy s2 to s1 using pointer notation
void copy2(char *s1, const char *s2)
{
   for ( ; (*s1 = *s2) != '\0'; s1++, s2++)
      ;   // do nothing in body
}
```

```
string1 = Hello
string3 = Good Bye
```

Fig. 5.21 Copying a string using array notation and pointer notation (part 2 of 2).

## 5.9 Arrays of Pointers

Arrays may contain pointers. A common use of such a data structure is to form an array of strings, referred to simply as a *string array.* Each entry in the array is a string, but in C++ a string is essentially a pointer to its first character. So each entry in an array of strings is actually a pointer to the first character of a string. Consider the declaration of string array **suit** that might be useful in representing a deck of cards.

```
char *suit[4] = {"Hearts", "Diamonds", "Clubs", "Spades"};
```

The **suit[4]** portion of the declaration indicates an array of 4 elements. The **char *** portion of the declaration indicates that each element of array **suit** is of type "pointer to **char**." The four values to be placed in the array are **"Hearts"**, **"Diamonds"**, **"Clubs"**, and **"Spades"**. Each of these is stored in memory as a null-terminated character string that is one character longer than the number of characters between quotes. The four strings are 7, 9, 6, and 7 characters long, respectively. Although it appears as though these strings are being placed in the **suit** array, only pointers are actually stored in the array (Fig. 5.22). Each pointer points to the first character of its corresponding

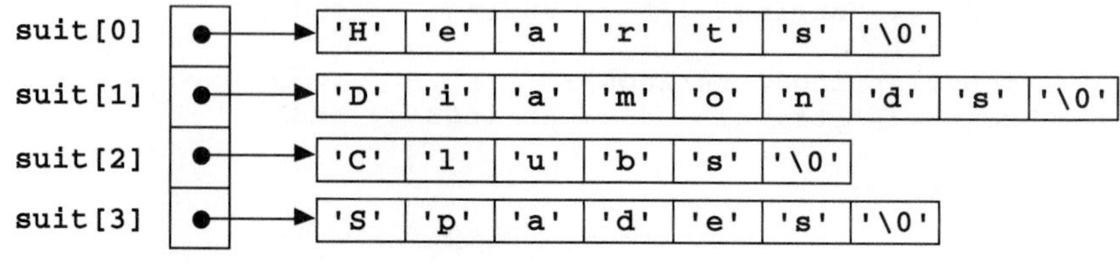


Fig. 5.22 A graphical representation of the **suit** array.

string. Thus, even though the **suit** array is fixed in size, it provides access to character strings of any length. This flexibility is one example of C++'s powerful data structuring capabilities.

The suit strings could be placed into a double-subscripted array in which each row represents one suit, and each column represents one of the letters of a suit name. Such a data structure must have a fixed number of columns per row and that number must be as large as the largest string. Therefore, considerable memory is wasted when a large number of strings is stored with most strings shorter than the longest string. We use arrays of strings to represent a deck of cards in the next section.

## 5.10 Case Study: A Card Shuffling and Dealing Simulation

In this section, we use random number generation to develop a card shuffling and dealing simulation program. This program can then be used to implement programs that play specific card games. To reveal some subtle performance problems, we have intentionally used sub-optimal shuffling and dealing algorithms. In the exercises and later in the text, we develop more efficient algorithms.

Using the top-down, stepwise refinement approach, we develop a program that will shuffle a deck of 52 playing cards, and then deal each of the 52 cards. The top-down approach is particularly useful in attacking larger, more complex problems than we have seen in the early chapters.

We use a 4-by-13 double-subscripted array **deck** to represent the deck of playing cards (Fig. 5.23). The rows correspond to the suits—row 0 corresponds to hearts, row 1 to diamonds, row 2 to clubs, and row 3 to spades. The columns correspond to the face values of the cards—columns 0 through 9 correspond to faces ace through ten respectively,

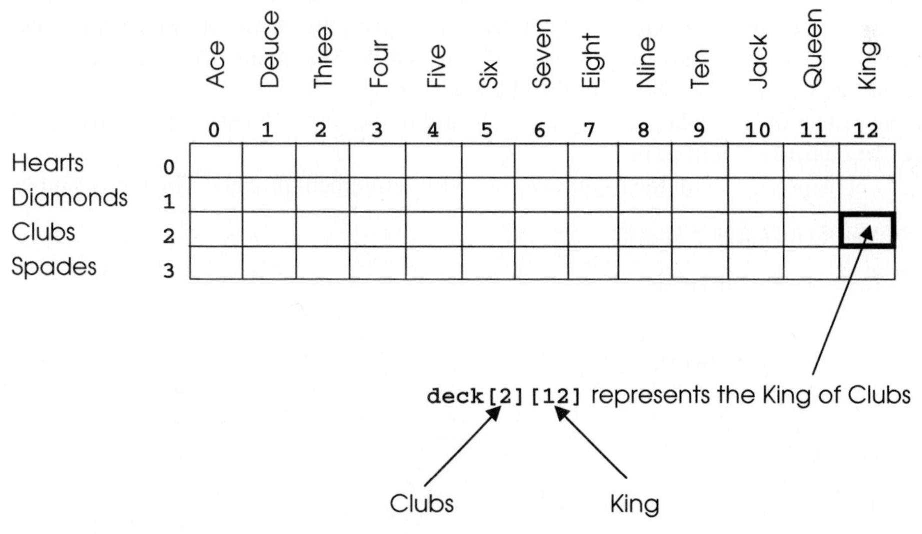


**Fig. 5.23** Double-subscripted array representation of a deck of cards.

and columns 10 through 12 correspond to jack, queen, and king. We shall load string array `suit` with character strings representing the four suits, and string array `face` with character strings representing the thirteen face values.

This simulated deck of cards may be shuffled as follows. First the array `deck` is cleared to zeros. Then, a `row` (0–3) and a `column` (0–12) are chosen at random. The number 1 is inserted in array element `deck[row][column]` to indicate that this card is going to be the first one dealt from the shuffled deck. This process continues with the numbers 2, 3, …, 52 being randomly inserted in the `deck` array to indicate which cards are to be placed second, third, …, and fifty-second in the shuffled deck. As the `deck` array begins to fill with card numbers, it is possible that a card will be selected twice, i.e., `deck[row][column]` will be nonzero when it is selected. This selection is simply ignored and other `row`s and `column`s are repeatedly chosen at random until an unselected card is found. Eventually, the numbers 1 through 52 will occupy the 52 slots of the `deck` array. At this point, the deck of cards is fully shuffled.

This shuffling algorithm could execute indefinitely if cards that have already been shuffled are repeatedly selected at random. This phenomenon is known as *indefinite postponement.* In the exercises we discuss a better shuffling algorithm that eliminates the possibility of indefinite postponement.

***Performance Tip 5.2***

*Sometimes an algorithm that emerges in a "natural" way can contain subtle performance problems such as indefinite postponement. Seek algorithms that avoid indefinite postponement.*

To deal the first card we search the array for `deck[row][column] == 1`. This is accomplished with a nested `for` structure that varies `row` from 0 to 3 and `column` from 0 to 12. What card does that slot of the array correspond to? The `suit` array has been preloaded with the four suits, so to get the suit we print the character string `suit[row]`. Similarly, to get the face value of the card, we print the character string `face[column]`. We also print the character string `" of "`. Printing this information in the proper order enables us to print each card in the form `"King of Clubs"`, `"Ace of Diamonds"`, and so on.

Let us proceed with the top-down, stepwise refinement process. The top is simply

*Shuffle and deal 52 cards*

Our first refinement yields:

*Initialize the suit array*
*Initialize the face array*
*Initialize the deck array*
*Shuffle the deck*
*Deal 52 cards*

"Shuffle the deck" may be expanded as follows:

*For each of the 52 cards*
*Place card number in randomly selected unoccupied slot of deck*

"Deal 52 cards" may be expanded as follows:

*For each of the 52 cards*
*Find card number in deck array and print face and suit of card*

Incorporating these expansions yields our complete second refinement:

*Initialize the suit array*
*Initialize the face array*
*Initialize the deck array*

*For each of the 52 cards*
*Place card number in randomly selected unoccupied slot of deck*
*For each of the 52 cards*
*Find card number in deck array and print face and suit of card*

"Place card number in randomly selected unoccupied slot of deck" may be expanded as follows:

*Choose slot of deck randomly*
*While chosen slot of deck has been previously chosen*
*Choose slot of deck randomly*
*Place card number in chosen slot of deck*

"Find card number in deck array and print face and suit of card" may be expanded as follows:

*For each slot of the deck array*
*If slot contains card number*
*Print the face and suit of the card*

Incorporating these expansions yields our third refinement:

*Initialize the suit array*
*Initialize the face array*
*Initialize the deck array*

*For each of the 52 cards*
*Choose slot of deck randomly*
*While slot of deck has been previously chosen*
*Choose slot of deck randomly*
*Place card number in chosen slot of deck*

*For each of the 52 cards*
*For each slot of deck array*
*If slot contains desired card number*
*Print the face and suit of the card*

This completes the refinement process. Note that this program is more efficient if the shuffle and deal portions of the algorithm are combined so each card is dealt as it is placed in the deck. We have chosen to program these operations separately because normally cards are dealt after they are shuffled (not while they are shuffled).

The card shuffling and dealing program is shown in Fig. 5.24 and a sample execution is shown in Fig. 5.25. Note the output formatting used in function deal:

```
cout << setw(5) << setiosflags(ios::right)
     << wFace[column] << " of "
     << setw(8) << setiosflags(ios::left)
     << wSuit[row] << (card % 2 == 0 ? '\n' : '\t');
```

```
// Card dealing program
#include <iostream.h>
#include <iomanip.h>
#include <stdlib.h>
#include <time.h>

void shuffle(int [][13]);
void deal(const int [][13], const char *[], const char *[]);

main()
{
   char *suit[4] = {"Hearts", "Diamonds", "Clubs", "Spades"};
   char *face[13] = {"Ace", "Deuce", "Three", "Four",
                     "Five", "Six", "Seven", "Eight",
                     "Nine", "Ten", "Jack", "Queen", "King"};
   int deck[4][13] = {0};

   srand(time(NULL));

   shuffle(deck);
   deal(deck, face, suit);

   return 0;
}

void shuffle(int wDeck[][13])
{
   int row, column;

   for (int card = 1; card <= 52; card++) {
      row = rand() % 4;
      column = rand() % 13;

      while(wDeck[row][column] != 0) {
         row = rand() % 4;
         column = rand() % 13;
      }

      wDeck[row][column] = card;
   }
}
```

**Fig. 5.24** Card dealing program (part 1 of 2).

The preceding output statement causes the face to be output right justified in a field of 5 characters and the suit to be output left justified in a field of 8 characters. The output is printed in two column format. If the card being output is in the first column, a tab is output after the card to move to the second column; otherwise, a newline is output.

```
void deal(const int wDeck[][13], const char *wFace[],
          const char *wSuit[])
{
   for (int card = 1; card <= 52; card++)

      for (int row = 0; row <= 3; row++)

         for (int column = 0; column <= 12; column++)
            if (wDeck[row][column] == card)
               cout << setw(5) << setiosflags(ios::right)
                    << wFace[column] << " of "
                    << setw(8) << setiosflags(ios::left)
                    << wSuit[row] << (card % 2 == 0 ? '\n' : '\t');
}
```

**Fig. 5.24** Card dealing program (part 2 of 2).

```
  Six of Clubs          Seven of Diamonds
  Ace of Spades           Ace of Diamonds
  Ace of Hearts         Queen of Diamonds
Queen of Clubs          Seven of Hearts
  Ten of Hearts         Deuce of Clubs
  Ten of Spades         Three of Spades
  Ten of Diamonds        Four of Spades
 Four of Diamonds         Ten of Clubs
  Six of Diamonds         Six of Spades
Eight of Hearts         Three of Diamonds
 Nine of Hearts         Three of Hearts
Deuce of Spades           Six of Hearts
 Five of Clubs          Eight of Clubs
Deuce of Diamonds       Eight of Spades
 Five of Spades          King of Clubs
 King of Diamonds        Jack of Spades
Deuce of Hearts         Queen of Hearts
  Ace of Clubs           King of Spades
Three of Clubs           King of Hearts
 Nine of Clubs           Nine of Spades
 Four of Hearts         Queen of Spades
Eight of Diamonds        Nine of Diamonds
 Jack of Diamonds       Seven of Clubs
 Five of Hearts          Five of Diamonds
 Four of Clubs           Jack of Hearts
 Jack of Clubs          Seven of Spades
```

**Fig. 5.25** Sample run of card dealing program.

There is a weakness in the dealing algorithm. Once a match is found, even if it is found on the first try, the two inner **for** structures continue searching the remaining elements of **deck** for a match. In the exercises and in a case study in Chapter 16, we correct this deficiency.

## 5.11 Function Pointers

A pointer to a function contains the address of the function in memory. In Chapter 4, we saw that an array name is really the address in memory of the first element of the array. Similarly, a function name is really the starting address in memory of the code that performs the function's task. Pointers to functions can be passed to functions, returned from functions, stored in arrays, and assigned to other function pointers.

To illustrate the use of pointers to functions, we have modified the bubble sort program of Fig. 5.15 to form the program of Fig. 5.26. Our new program consists of **main**,

```
// Multipurpose sorting program using function pointers
#include <iostream.h>
#include <iomanip.h>

void bubble(int *, const int, int (*)(int, int));
int ascending(const int, const int);
int descending(const int, const int);

main()
{
   const int arraySize = 10;
   int order, a[arraySize] = {2, 6, 4, 8, 10, 12, 89, 68, 45,
37};

   cout << "Enter 1 to sort in ascending order," << endl
        << "Enter 2 to sort in descending order: ";
   cin >> order;
   cout << endl << "Data items in original order" << endl;

   for (int counter = 0; counter < arraySize; counter++)
      cout << setw(4) << a[counter];

   if (order == 1) {
      bubble(a, arraySize, ascending);
      cout << endl << "Data items in ascending order" << endl;
   }
   else {
      bubble(a, arraySize, descending);
      cout << endl << "Data items in descending order" << endl;
   }

   for (counter = 0; counter < arraySize; counter++)
      cout << setw(4) << a[counter];

   cout << endl;
   return 0;
}
```

**Fig. 5.26** Multipurpose sorting program using function pointers (part 1 of 2).

```
void bubble(int *work, const int size, int (*compare)(int, int))
{
   void swap(int *, int *);

   for (int pass = 1; pass < size; pass++)

      for (int count = 0; count < size - 1; count++)

         if ((*compare)(work[count], work[count + 1]))
            swap(&work[count], &work[count + 1]);
}

void swap(int *element1Ptr, int *element2Ptr)
{
   int temp;

   temp = *element1Ptr;
   *element1Ptr = *element2Ptr;
   *element2Ptr = temp;
}

int ascending(const int a, const int b)
{
   return b < a;
}

int descending(const int a, const int b)
{
   return b > a;
}
```

**Fig. 5.26** Multipurpose sorting program using function pointers (part 2 of 2).

and the functions **bubble**, **swap**, **ascending**, and **descending**. Function **bubbleSort** receives a pointer to a function—either function **ascending** or function **descending**—as an argument in addition to an integer array and the size of the array. The program prompts the user to choose if the array should be sorted in ascending order or in descending order. If the user enters 1, a pointer to function **ascending** is passed to function **bubble** causing the array to be sorted into increasing order. If the user enters 2, a pointer to function **descending** is passed to function **bubble** causing the array to be sorted into decreasing order. The output of the program is shown in Fig. 5.27.

The following parameter appears in the function header for **bubble**:

```
int (*compare)(int, int)
```

This tells **bubble** to expect a parameter that is a pointer to a function that receives two integer parameters and returns an integer result. Parentheses are needed around ***compare** because ***** has a lower precedence than the parentheses enclosing the function parameters. If we had not included the parentheses, the declaration would have been

```
int *compare(int, int)
```

```
Enter 1 to sort in ascending order,
Enter 2 to sort in descending order: 1

Data items in original order
   2   6   4   8  10  12  89  68  45  37
Data items in ascending order
   2   4   6   8  10  12  37  45  68  89
```

```
Enter 1 to sort in ascending order,
Enter 2 to sort in descending order: 2

Data items in original order
   2   6   4   8  10  12  89  68  45  37
Data items in descending order
  89  68  45  37  12  10   8   6   4   2
```

**Fig. 5.27** The outputs of the bubble sort program in Fig. 5.26.

which declares a function that receives two integers as parameters and returns a pointer to an integer.

The corresponding parameter in the function prototype of **bubble** is

```
int (*)(int, int)
```

Note that only types have been included, but for documentation purposes the programmer can include names that the compiler will ignore.

The function passed to **bubble** is called in an **if** statement as follows

```
if ((*compare)(work[count], work[count + 1]))
```

Just as a pointer to a variable is dereferenced to access the value of the variable, a pointer to a function is dereferenced to use the function.

The call to the function could have been made without dereferencing the pointer as in

```
if (compare(work[count], work[count + 1]))
```

which uses the pointer directly as the function name. We prefer the first method of calling a function through a pointer because it explicitly illustrates that **compare** is a pointer to a function that is dereferenced to call the function. The second method of calling a function through a pointer makes it appear as though **compare** is an actual function. This may be confusing to a user of the program who would like to see the definition of function **compare** and finds that it is never defined in the file.

A common use of function pointers is in so-called menu driven systems. A user is prompted to select an option from a menu (possibly from 1 to 5). Each option is serviced by a different function. Pointers to each function are stored in an array of pointers to functions. The user's choice is used as a subscript into the array, and the pointer in the array is used to call the function.

The program of Fig. 5.28 provides a generic example of the mechanics of declaring and using an array of pointers to functions. Three functions are defined—**function1**, **function2**, and **function3**— that each take an integer argument and return nothing. Pointers to these three functions are stored in array **f** which is declared as follows:

```
void (*f[3])(int) = {function1, function2, function3};
```

```
// Demonstrating an array of pointers to functions
#include <iostream.h>

void function1(int);
void function2(int);
void function3(int);

main()
{
   void (*f[3])(int) = {function1, function2, function3};
   int choice;

   cout << "Enter a number between 0 and 2, 3 to end: ";
   cin >> choice;

   while (choice >= 0 && choice < 3) {
      (*f[choice])(choice);
      cout << "Enter a number between 0 and 2, 3 to end: ";
      cin >> choice;
   }

   cout << "You entered 3 to end" << endl;
   return 0;
}

void function1(int a)
{
   cout << "You entered " << a << " so function1 was called"
        << endl << endl;
}

void function2(int b)
{
   cout << "You entered " << b << " so function2 was called"
        << endl << endl;
}

void function3(int c)
{
   cout << "You entered " << c << " so function3 was called"
        << endl << endl;
}
```

**Fig. 5.28** Demonstrating an array of pointers to functions (part 1 of 2).

```
Enter a number between 0 and 2, 3 to end: 0
You entered 0 so function1 was called

Enter a number between 0 and 2, 3 to end: 1
You entered 1 so function2 was called

Enter a number between 0 and 2, 3 to end: 2
You entered 2 so function3 was called

Enter a number between 0 and 2, 3 to end: 3
You entered 3 to end
```

**Fig. 5.28** Demonstrating an array of pointers to functions (part 2 of 2).

The declaration is read beginning in the leftmost set of parentheses, "**f** is an array of 3 pointers to functions that take an **int** as an argument and that return **void**." The array is initialized with the names of the three functions. When the user enters a value between 0 and 2, the value is used as the subscript into the array of pointers to functions. The function call is made as follows:

```
(*f[choice])(choice);
```

In the call, **f[choice]** selects the pointer at location **choice** in the array. The pointer is dereferenced to call the function and **choice** is passed as the argument to the function. Each function prints its argument's value and its function name to indicate that the function is called correctly. In the exercises, you will develop a menu-driven system.

## 5.12 Introduction to Character and String Processing

In this section, we introduce some common C standard library functions that facilitate string processing. The techniques discussed here are appropriate for developing text editors, word processors, page layout software, computerized typesetting systems, and other kinds of text-processing software.

### 5.12.1 Fundamentals of Characters and Strings

Characters are the fundamental building blocks of C++ source programs. Every program is composed of a sequence of characters that—when grouped together meaningfully—is interpreted by the computer as a series of instructions used to accomplish a task. A program may contain *character constants.* A character constant is an integer value represented as a character in single quotes. The value of a character constant is the integer value of the character in the machine's character set. For example, **'z'** represents the integer value of **z**, and **'\n'** represents the integer value of newline.

A string is a series of characters treated as a single unit. A string may include letters, digits, and various *special characters* such as **+**, **-**, *****, **/**, **$**, and others. *String literals* or *string constants* in C++ are written in double quotation marks as follows:

| | |
|---|---|
| "John Q. Doe" | (a name) |
| "9999 Main Street" | (a street address) |
| "Waltham, Massachusetts" | (a city and state) |
| "(201) 555-1212" | (a telephone number) |

A string in C++ is an array of characters ending in the *null character* (`'\0'`). A string is accessed via a pointer to the first character in the string. The value of a string is the address of its first character. Thus in C++ it is appropriate to say that *a string is a pointer*—in fact a pointer to the string's first character. In this sense, strings are like arrays, because an array is also a pointer to its first element.

A string may be assigned in a declaration to either a character array or a variable of type **`char *`**. The declarations

```
char color[] = "blue";
char *colorPtr = "blue";
```

each initialize a variable to the string **`"blue"`**. The first declaration creates a 5-element array **`color`** containing the characters **`'b'`**, **`'l'`**, **`'u'`**, **`'e'`**, and **`'\0'`**. The second declaration creates pointer variable **`colorPtr`** that points to the string **`"blue"`** somewhere in memory.

***Portability Tip 5.4***

*When a variable of type* **`char *`** *is initialized with a string literal, some compilers may place the string in a location in memory where the string cannot be modified. If you may need to modify a string literal, it should be stored in a character array to ensure modifiability on all systems.*

The declaration **`char color[] = {"blue"};`** could also be written

```
char color[] = {'b', 'l', 'u', 'e', '\0'};
```

When declaring a character array to contain a string, the array must be large enough to store the string and its terminating null character. The preceding declaration determines the size of the array automatically based on the number of initializers provided in the initializer list.

***Common Programming Error 5.12***

*Not allocating sufficient space in a character array to store the null character that terminates a string.*

***Common Programming Error 5.13***

*Creating or using a "string" that does not contain a terminating null character.*

***Good Programming Practice 5.6***

*When storing a string of characters in a character array, be sure the array is large enough to hold the largest string that will be stored. C++ allows strings of any length to be stored. If a string is longer than the character array in which it is to be stored, characters beyond the end of the array will overwrite data in memory following the array.*

A string can be assigned to an array using stream extraction with **cin**. For example, the following statement can be used to assign a string to character array **word[20]**.

```
cin >> word;
```

The string entered by the user is stored in **word**. The preceding statement reads characters until a space, tab, newline, or end-of-file indicator is encountered. Note that the string should be no longer than 19 characters to leave room for the terminating null character. The **setw** stream manipulator introduced in Chapter 2 can be used to ensure that the string read into **word** does not exceed the size of the array. For example, the statement

```
cin >> setw(20) >> word;
```

specifies that **cin** should read a maximum of 19 characters into array **word** and save the 20th character in the array to store the terminating null character for the string. The **setw** stream manipulator only applies to the next value being input.

In some cases, it is desirable to input an entire line of text into an array. For this purpose, C++ provides the function **cin.getline**. The **cin.getline** function takes three arguments—a character array in which the line of text will be stored, a length, and a delimiter character. For example, the program segment

```
char sentence[80];
cin.getline(sentence, 80, '\n');
```

declares array **sentence** of 80 characters, then reads a line of text from the keyboard into the array. The function stops reading characters when the delimiter character **'\n'** is encountered, when the end-of-file indicator is entered, or when the number of characters read so far is one less than the length specified in the second argument (the last character in the array is reserved for the terminating null character). If the delimiter character is encountered, it is read and discarded. The third argument to **cin.getline** has **'\n'** as a default value, so the preceding function call could have been written as follows:

```
cin.getline(sentence, 80);
```

Chapter 11, "Stream Input/Output," provides a detailed discussion of **cin.getline** and other input/output functions.

***Common Programming Error 5.14***

*Processing a single character as a string. A string is a pointer—probably a respectably large integer. However, a character is a small integer (ASCII values range 0-255). On many systems this causes an error because low memory addresses are reserved for special purposes such as operating system interrupt handlers—so, "access violations" occur.*

***Common Programming Error 5.15***

*Passing a character as an argument to a function when a string is expected.*

***Common Programming Error 5.16***

*Passing a string as an argument to a function when a character is expected.*

## 5.12.2 String Manipulation Functions of the String Handling Library

The string handling library provides many useful functions for manipulating string data, comparing strings, searching strings for characters and other strings, tokenizing strings (separating strings into logical pieces), and determining the length of strings. This section presents some common string manipulation functions of the string handling library (from the C standard library). The functions are summarized in Fig. 5.29.

Note that several functions in Fig. 5.29 contain parameters with data type **size_t**. This type is defined in the header file **stddef.h** (from the C standard library) to be an unsigned integral type such as **unsigned int** or **unsigned long**.

***Common Programming Error 5.17***

*Forgetting to include the* **<string.h>** *header file when using functions from the string handling library.*

| Function prototype | Function description |
|---|---|
| `char *strcpy(char *s1, const char *s2)` | Copies the string **s2** into the character array **s1**. The value of **s1** is returned. |
| `char *strncpy(char *s1, const char *s2, size_t n)` | Copies at most **n** characters of the string **s2** into the character array **s1**. The value of **s1** is returned. |
| `char *strcat(char *s1, const char *s2)` | Appends the string **s2** to the string **s1**. The first character of **s2** overwrites the terminating null character of **s1**. The value of **s1** is returned. |
| `char *strncat(char *s1, const char *s2, size_t n)` | Appends at most **n** characters of string **s2** to string **s1**. The first character of **s2** overwrites the terminating null character of **s1**. The value of **s1** is returned. |
| `int strcmp(const char *s1, const char *s2)` | Compares the string **s1** to the string **s2**. The function returns a value of 0, less than 0, or greater than 0 if **s1** is equal to, less than, or greater than **s2**, respectively. |
| `int strncmp(const char *s1, const char *s2, size_t n)` | Compares up to **n** characters of the string **s1** to the string **s2**. The function returns 0, less than 0, or greater than 0 if **s1** is equal to, less than, or greater than **s2**, respectively. |

**Fig. 5.29** The string manipulation functions of the string handling library (part 1 of 2).

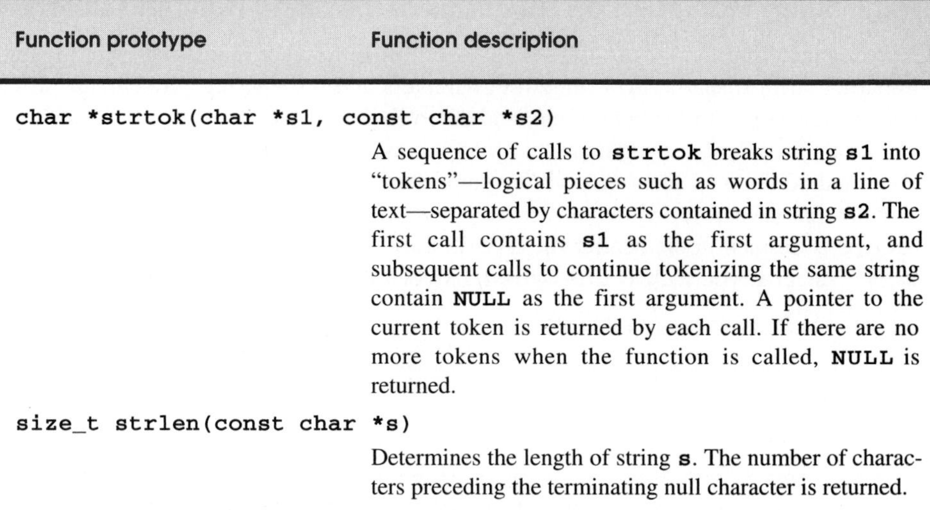

| Function prototype | Function description |
|---|---|
| `char *strtok(char *s1, const char *s2)` | A sequence of calls to **strtok** breaks string **s1** into "tokens"—logical pieces such as words in a line of text—separated by characters contained in string **s2**. The first call contains **s1** as the first argument, and subsequent calls to continue tokenizing the same string contain **NULL** as the first argument. A pointer to the current token is returned by each call. If there are no more tokens when the function is called, **NULL** is returned. |
| `size_t strlen(const char *s)` | Determines the length of string **s**. The number of characters preceding the terminating null character is returned. |

**Fig. 5.29** The string manipulation functions of the string handling library (part 2 of 2).

Function ***strcpy*** copies its second argument—a string—into its first argument—a character array that must be large enough to store the string and its terminating null character which is also copied. Function ***strncpy*** is equivalent to **strcpy** except that **strncpy** specifies the number of characters to be copied from the string into the array. Note that function **strncpy** does not necessarily copy the terminating null character of its second argument—a terminating null character is written only if the number of characters to be copied is at least one more than the length of the string. For example, if **"test"** is the second argument, a terminating null character is written only if the third argument to **strncpy** is at least **5** (4 characters in **"test"** plus 1 terminating null character). If the third argument is larger than **5**, null characters are appended to the array until the total number of characters specified by the third argument are written.

***Common Programming Error 5.18***

*Not appending a terminating null character to the first argument of a* **strncpy** *when the third argument is less than or equal to the length of the string in the second argument.*

The program in Fig. 5.30 uses **strcpy** to copy the entire string in array **x** into array **y**, and uses **strncpy** to copy the first **14** characters of array **x** into array **z**. A null character (**'\0'**) is appended to array **z** because the call to **strncpy** in the program does not write a terminating null character (the third argument is less than the string length of the second argument).

Function ***strcat*** appends its second argument—a string—to its first argument—a character array containing a string. The first character of the second argument replaces the null (**'\0'**) that terminates the string in the first argument. The programmer must ensure that the array used to store the first string is large enough to store the combination of the first string, the second string, and the terminating null character (copied from the second

```
// Using strcpy and strncpy
#include <iostream.h>
#include <string.h>

main()
{
   char x[] = "Happy Birthday to You";
   char y[25], z[15];

   cout << "The string in array x is: " << x << endl
        << "The string in array y is: " << strcpy(y, x)
        << endl;
   strncpy(z, x, 14);
   z[14] = '\0';
   cout << "The string in array z is: " << z << endl;

   return 0;
}
```

```
The string in array x is: Happy Birthday to You
The string in array y is: Happy Birthday to You
The string in array z is: Happy Birthday
```

**Fig. 5.30** Using `strcpy` and `strncpy`.

string). Function ***strncat*** appends a specified number of characters from the second string to the first string. A terminating null character is appended to the result. The program of Fig. 5.31 demonstrates function `strcat` and function `strncat`.

```
// Using strcat and strncat
#include <iostream.h>
#include <string.h>

main()
{
   char s1[20] = "Happy ";
   char s2[] = "New Year ";
   char s3[40] = "";

   cout << "s1 = " << s1 << endl << "s2 = " << s2 << endl;
   cout << "strcat(s1, s2) = " << strcat(s1, s2) << endl;
   cout << "strncat(s3, s1, 6) = " << strncat(s3, s1, 6) << endl;
   cout << "strcat(s3, s1) = " << strcat(s3, s1) << endl;

   return 0;
}
```

**Fig. 5.31** Using `strcat` and `strncat` (part 1 of 2).

```
s1 = Happy
s2 = New Year
strcat(s1, s2) = Happy New Year
strncat(s3, s1, 6) = Happy
strcat(s3, s1) = Happy Happy New Year
```

**Fig. 5.31** Using **strcat** and **strncat** (part 2 of 2).

The program of Fig. 5.32 compares three strings using functions ***strcmp*** and ***strncmp***. Function **strcmp** compares its first string argument to its second string argument character by character. The function returns 0 if the strings are equal, a negative value if the first string is less than the second string, and a positive value if the first string is greater than the second string. Function **strncmp** is equivalent to **strcmp** except that **strncmp** compares up to a specified number of characters. Function **strncmp** does not compare characters following a null character in a string. The program prints the integer value returned by each function call.

***Common Programming Error 5.19***

*Assuming that **strcmp** and **strncmp** return 1 when their arguments are equal. Both functions return 0 (C++'s false value) for equality. Therefore, when testing two strings for equality, the result of the **strcmp** or **strncmp** function should be compared with 0 to determine if the strings are equal.*

```
// Using strcmp and strncmp
#include <iostream.h>
#include <iomanip.h>
#include <string.h>

main()
{
   char *s1 = "Happy New Year";
   char *s2 = "Happy New Year";
   char *s3 = "Happy Holidays";

   cout << "s1 = " << s1 << endl << "s2 = " << s2 << endl
        << "s3 = " << s3 << endl << endl << "strcmp(s1, s2) = "
        << setw(2) << strcmp(s1, s2) << endl << "strcmp(s1, s3) =
"
        << setw(2) << strcmp(s1, s3) << endl << "strcmp(s3, s1) =
"
        << setw(2) << strcmp(s3, s1) << endl << endl;
   cout << "strncmp(s1, s3, 6) = " << setw(2) << strncmp(s1, s3,
6)
        << endl << "strncmp(s1, s3, 7) = " << setw(2)
        << strncmp(s1, s3, 7) << endl << "strncmp(s3, s1, 7) = "
        << setw(2) << strncmp(s3, s1, 7) << endl;
   return 0;
}
```

**Fig. 5.32** Using **strcmp** and **strncmp** (part 1 of 2).

```
s1 = Happy New Year
s2 = Happy New Year
s3 = Happy Holidays

strcmp(s1, s2) =  0
strcmp(s1, s3) =  6
strcmp(s3, s1) = -6

strncmp(s1, s3, 6) =  0
strncmp(s1, s3, 7) =  6
strncmp(s3, s1, 7) = -6
```

**Fig. 5.32** Using **`strcmp`** and **`strncmp`** (part 2 of 2).

To understand just what it means for one string to be "greater than" or "less than" another string, consider the process of alphabetizing a series of last names. The reader would, no doubt, place "Jones" before "Smith" because the first letter of "Jones" comes before the first letter of "Smith" in the alphabet. But the alphabet is more than just a list of 26 letters—it is an ordered list of characters. Each letter occurs in a specific position within the list. "Z" is more than just a letter of the alphabet; "Z" is specifically the twenty-sixth letter of the alphabet.

How does the computer know that one letter comes before another? All characters are represented inside the computer as numeric codes; when the computer compares two strings, it actually compares the numeric codes of the characters in the strings.

***Portability Tip 5.5***

*The internal numeric codes used to represent characters may be different on different computers.*

In an effort at standardizing character representations, most computer manufacturers have designed their machines to utilize one of two popular coding schemes—*ASCII* or *EBCDIC.* ASCII stands for "American Standard Code for Information Interchange," and EBCDIC stands for "Extended Binary Coded Decimal Interchange Code." There are other coding schemes, but these two are the most popular.

ASCII and EBCDIC are called *character codes* or *character sets.* String and character manipulations actually involve the manipulation of the appropriate numeric codes and not the characters themselves. This explains the interchangeability of characters and small integers in C++. Since it is meaningful to say that one numeric code is greater than, less than, or equal to another numeric code, it becomes possible to relate various characters or strings to one another by referring to the character codes. Appendix D contains a list of ASCII character codes.

Function **`strtok`** is used to break a string into a series of *tokens.* A token is a sequence of characters separated by *delimiting characters* (usually spaces or punctuation marks). For example, in a line of text, each word can be considered a token and the spaces separating the words can be considered delimiters.

Multiple calls to **strtok** are required to break a string into tokens (assuming the string contains more than one token). The first call to **strtok** contains two arguments, a string to be tokenized, and a string containing characters that separate the tokens (i.e., delimeters). In the program of Fig. 5.33, the statement

```
tokenPtr = strtok(string, " ");
```

assigns **tokenPtr** a pointer to the first token in **string**. The second argument of **strtok**, **" "**, indicates that tokens in **string** are separated by spaces. Function **strtok** searches for the first character in **string** that is not a delimiting character (space). This begins the first token. The function then finds the next delimiting character in the string and replaces it with a null (**'\0'**) character. This terminates the current token. Function **strtok** saves a pointer to the next character following the token in **string**, and returns a pointer to the current token.

```
// Using strtok
#include <iostream.h>
#include <string.h>

main()
{
   char string[] = "This is a sentence with 7 tokens";
   char *tokenPtr;

   cout << "The string to be tokenized is:" << endl << string
        << endl << endl << "The tokens are:" << endl;

   tokenPtr = strtok(string, " ");

   while (tokenPtr != NULL) {
      cout << tokenPtr << endl;
      tokenPtr = strtok(NULL, " ");
   }

   return 0;
}
```

```
The string to be tokenized is:
This is a sentence with 7 tokens

The tokens are:
This
is
a
sentence
with
7
tokens
```

**Fig. 5.33** Using **strtok**.

Subsequent calls to **strtok** to continue tokenizing **string** contain **NULL** as the first argument. The **NULL** argument indicates that the call to **strtok** should continue tokenizing from the location in **string** saved by the last call to **strtok**. If no tokens remain when **strtok** is called, **strtok** returns **NULL**. The program of Fig. 5.33 uses **strtok** to tokenize the string **"This is a sentence with 7 tokens"**. Each token is printed separately. Note that **strtok** modifies the input string; therefore, a copy of the string should be made if the string will be used again in the program after the calls to **strtok**.

***Common Programming Error 5.20***

*Not realizing that **strtok** modifies the string being tokenized, and then attempting to use that string as if it were the original unmodified string.*

Function ***strlen*** takes a string as an argument, and returns the number of characters in the string—the terminating null character is not included in the length. The program of Fig. 5.34 demonstrates function **strlen**.

## 5.13 Thinking About Objects: Interactions Among Objects

This is the last of our object-oriented design assignments before we begin our study of object-oriented programming in C++ in Chapter 6. After you complete this assignment

```
// Using strlen
#include <iostream.h>
#include <string.h>

main()
{
   char *string1 = "abcdefghijklmnopqrstuvwxyz";
   char *string2 = "four";
   char *string3 = "Boston";

   cout << "The length of \"" << string1
        << "\" is " << strlen(string1) << endl
        << "The length of \"" << string2
        << "\" is " << strlen(string2) << endl
        << "The length of \"" << string3
        << "\" is " << strlen(string3) << endl;

   return 0;
}
```

```
The length of "abcdefghijklmnopqrstuvwxyz" is 26
The length of "four" is 4
The length of "Boston" is 6
```

**Fig. 5.34** Using **strlen**.

and finish reading Chapter 6, you will be prepared (and probably eager) to begin coding your elevator simulator. To complete the elevator simulator as defined in Chapter 2, you will need the C++ techniques discussed in Chapters 6, 7, and 8. We will then suggest modifications to the simulator that will require the techniques of Chapters 9 and 10 on inheritance and polymorphism.

In this section we concentrate on the interactions between objects. We hope this section will help you "tie it all together." You will probably add to the lists of objects, their attributes and their behaviors that you developed in the lab assignments in Chapters 2, 3, and 4.

We have learned that most C++ objects do not do things spontaneously. Rather, the objects respond to stimuli in the form of messages that are actually function calls to the objects' member functions.

Let us consider several of the interactions among objects in the elevator simulation. The problem statement says, "Person presses the up-button or the down-button on that floor." The "subject" of that clause is person and the object is button. This is an example of an interaction between objects. The person object sends a message to the button object. We call that message *pushButton*. In the last chapter we made the message a member function of the button object.

At this point, under *Other Facts* for each of the objects in your simulation, about all you should have left are interactions between objects. Some of these explicitly show the interactions among objects. But consider the statement

*"person waits for elevator doors to open"*

In the last chapter, we listed two behaviors of the elevator's doors, namely *openDoors* and *closeDoors*. But now we want to determine which objects send these messages. It is not explicitly stated in the preceding quoted statement. So we think about this a bit and we realize that the elevator itself sends these messages to the doors. These interactions between objects are implicit in the problem statement.

Now continue refining the *Other Facts* sections for each of the objects in your elevator simulator. These sections should now contain mostly interactions among objects. View each of these as

1. a sending object
2. sending a particular message
3. to a particular receiving object

Under each object, add the section *Messages Sent to Other Objects* and list the remaining interactions between objects, i.e., under the person object, include the entry

*person sends pushButton message to the button on that floor*

Under the button object under *Messages Sent to Other Objects* place the message

*button sends comeGetMe message to elevator*

As you make these entries, you may add attributes and behaviors to your objects. This is perfectly natural.

As you complete this laboratory exercise, you will have a reasonably complete listing of the objects you will need to implement your elevator simulator. And for each object you will have a reasonably complete listing of that object's attributes and behaviors, and the messages that object sends to other objects.

In the next chapter, we begin our study of object-oriented programming in C++. You will learn how to create new classes. Once you have read Chapter 6, you will be ready to write a substantial portion of the elevator simulation in C++. After completing Chapters 7 and 8, you will have learned enough to implement a working elevator simulator.

Let us summarize the object-oriented design process we have presented in Chapters 2 through 5.

1. Type the problem statement into a text file.
2. Discard unimportant text.
3. Extract all the facts. Arrange the facts one per line in a facts file.
4. Scan the facts looking for nouns; these are with high likelihood many of the objects you will need. Make one top-level outline item per object.
5. For each fact, place that fact as a second-level outline item below the appropriate object. If a fact mentions several objects (as many facts will), place it below each of the objects it mentions.
6. Now refine the set of facts below each of the objects. List three subheads below each object, namely *Attributes, Behaviors,* and *Messages Sent to Other Objects.*
7. Under *Attributes,* list the data associated with each object.
8. Under *Behaviors,* list those actions the object can perform in response to receiving a message. Each behavior is a member function of the object.
9. Under *Messages Sent to Other Objects*, list the messages this object sends to other objects and the objects that receive these messages.
10. At this point your design probably still has a few missing pieces. These will probably become apparent as you proceed with implementing your system in C++ after reading Chapter 6.

## Summary

- Pointers are variables that contain as their values addresses of other variables.
- Pointers must be declared before they can be used.
- The declaration

```
int *ptr;
```

  declares **ptr** to be a pointer to an object of type **int**, and is read, "**ptr** is a pointer to **int**." The * as used here in a declaration indicates that the variable is a pointer.
- There are three values that can be used to initialize a pointer: **0**, **NULL**, or an address of an object of the same type. Initializing a pointer to **0** and initializing that same pointer to **NULL** are identical.
- The only integer that can be assigned to a pointer is 0.

- The `&` (address) operator returns the address of its operand.
- The operand of the address operator must be a variable; the address operator cannot be applied to constants, to expressions that do not return a reference, or to variables declared with the storage class **`register`**.
- The `*` operator, referred to as the indirection or dereferencing operator, returns the value of the object that its operand points to in memory. This is called dereferencing the pointer.
- When calling a function with an argument that the caller wants the called function to modify, the address of the argument may be passed. The called function then uses the indirection operator (`*`) to modify the value of the argument in the calling function.
- A function receiving an address as an argument must include a pointer as its corresponding formal parameter.
- It is not necessary to include the names of pointers in function prototypes; it is only necessary to include the pointer types. Pointer names may be included for documentation reasons, but the compiler ignores them.
- The **`const`** qualifier enables the programmer to inform the compiler that the value of a particular variable should not be modified.
- If an attempt is made to modify a value that is declared **`const`**, the compiler catches it and issues either a warning or an error depending on the particular compiler.
- There are four ways to pass a pointer to a function: a non-constant pointer to non-constant data, a constant pointer to non-constant data, a constant pointer to non-constant data, and a constant pointer to constant data.
- Arrays are automatically passed by reference using pointers because the value of the array name is the address of the array.
- To pass a single element of an array call-by-reference using pointers, the address of the specific array element must be passed.
- C++ provides the special unary operator **`sizeof`** to determine the size of an array (or any other data type) in bytes during program compilation.
- When applied to the name of an array, the **`sizeof`** operator returns the total number of bytes in the array as an integer.
- Operator **`sizeof`** can be applied to any variable name, type, or constant.
- The arithmetic operations that may be performed on pointers are incrementing (`++`) a pointer, decrementing (`--`) a pointer, adding (`+` or `+=`) a pointer and an integer, subtracting (`-` or `-=`) a pointer and an integer, and subtracting one pointer from another.
- When an integer is added or subtracted from a pointer, the pointer is incremented or decremented by that integer times the size of the object pointed to.
- Pointer arithmetic operations should only be performed on contiguous portions of memory such as an array. All elements of an array are stored contiguously in memory.

- When performing pointer arithmetic on a character array, the results are like regular arithmetic because each character is stored in one byte of memory.
- Pointers can be assigned to one another if both pointers are of the same type. Otherwise, a cast must be used. The exception to this is a pointer to **`void`** which is a generic pointer type that can hold pointers of any type. Pointers to **`void`** can be assigned pointers of other types. A void pointer can be assigned to a pointer of another type only with an explicit type cast.
- A pointer to **`void`** may not be dereferenced.
- Pointers can be compared using the equality and relational operators. Pointer comparisons are normally meaningful only if the pointers point to members of the same array.
- Pointers can be subscripted exactly as array names can.
- An array name is equivalent to a pointer to the first element of the array.
- In pointer/offset notation, the offset is the same as an array subscript.
- All subscripted array expressions can be written with a pointer and an offset using either the name of the array as a pointer, or a separate pointer that points to the array.
- An array name is a constant pointer that always points to the same location in memory. Array names cannot be modified as conventional pointers can.
- It is possible to have arrays of pointers.
- It is possible to have pointers to functions.
- A pointer to a function is the address where the code for the function resides.
- Pointers to functions can be passed to functions, returned from functions, stored in arrays, and assigned to other pointers.
- A common use of function pointers is in so called menu-driven systems. The function pointers are used to select which function to call for a particular menu item.
- Function **`strcpy`** copies its second argument—a string—into its first argument—a character array. The programmer must ensure that the array is large enough to store the string and its terminating null character.
- Function **`strncpy`** is equivalent to **`strcpy`** except that a call to **`strncpy`** specifies the number of characters to be copied from the string into the array. The terminating null character will only be copied if the number of characters to be copied is one more than the length of the string.
- Function **`strcat`** appends its second string argument—including the terminating null character—to its first string argument. The first character of the second string replaces the null (`'\0'`) character of the first string. The programmer must ensure that the array used to store the first string is large enough to store both the first string and the second string.
- Function **`strncat`** appends a specified number of characters from the second string to the first string. A terminating null character is appended to the result.

- Function **strcmp** compares its first string argument to its second string argument character-by-character. The function returns 0 if the strings are equal, a negative value if the first string is less than the second string, and a positive value if the first string is greater than the second string.
- Function **strncmp** is equivalent to **strcmp** except that **strncmp** compares a specified number of characters. If the number of characters in one of the strings is less than the number of characters specified, **strncmp** compares characters until the null character in the shorter string is encountered.
- A sequence of calls to **strtok** breaks a string into tokens that are separated by characters contained in a second string argument. The first call contains the string to be tokenized as the first argument, and subsequent calls to continue tokenizing the same string contain **NULL** as the first argument. A pointer to the current token is returned by each call. If there are no more tokens when **strtok** is called, **NULL** is returned.
- Function **strlen** takes a string as an argument, and returns the number of characters in the string—the terminating null character is not included in the length of the string.

## Terminology

adding a pointer and an integer
address operator (**&** )
appending strings to other strings
array of pointers
array of strings
ASCII
call-by-reference
call-by-value
character code
character constant
character pointer
character set
comparing strings
**const**
constant pointer
constant pointer to constant data
constant pointer to non-constant data
copying strings
decrement a pointer
delimiter
dereference a pointer
dereferencing operator (*****)
directly reference a variable
EBCDIC
function pointer
increment a pointer
indefinite postponement
indirection
indirection operator (*****)
indirectly reference a variable
initializing pointers
length of a string
linked list
literal
non-constant pointer to constant data
non-constant pointer to non-constant data
**NULL** pointer
numeric code representation of a character
offset
pointer
pointer arithmetic
pointer assignment
pointer comparison
pointer expression
pointer indexing
pointer subscripting
pointer to a function
pointer to **void** (**void ***)
pointer types
pointer/offset notation
principle of least privilege
simulated call-by-reference
**sizeof**
**strcat**
**strcmp**

**strcpy**
string
string concatenation
string constant
string literal
string processing
**string.h**
**strlen**
**strncat**
**strncmp**
**strncpy**
**strtok**
subtracting an integer from a pointer
subtracting two pointers
token
tokenizing strings
**void *** (pointer to **void**)
white space characters
word processing

## *Common Programming Errors*

**5.1** The indirection operator * does not distribute to all variable names in a declaration. Each pointer must be declared with the * prefixed to the name.

**5.2** Dereferencing a pointer that has not been initialized, or that has not been assigned to point to a specific location in memory. This could cause a fatal execution time error, or it could accidentally modify important data and allow the program to run to completion providing incorrect results.

**5.3** Not dereferencing a pointer when it is necessary to do so to obtain the value to which the pointer points.

**5.4** Not initializing a pointer that is declared ***const*** results in a compile error.

**5.5** Omitting the parentheses in a ***sizeof*** operation when the operand is a type name results in a syntax error.

**5.6** Using pointer arithmetic on a pointer that does not refer to an array of values.

**5.7** Subtracting or comparing two pointers that do not refer to elements of the same array.

**5.8** Running off either end of an array when using pointer arithmetic.

**5.9** Assigning a pointer of one type to a pointer of another (other than **void ***) causes a syntax error.

**5.10** Dereferencing a **void *** pointer.

**5.11** Although array names are pointers to the beginning of the array, and pointers can be modified in arithmetic expressions, array names cannot be modified in arithmetic expressions.

**5.12** Not allocating sufficient space in a character array to store the null character that terminates a string.

**5.13** Creating or using a "string" that does not contain a terminating null character.

**5.14** Processing a single character as a string. A string is a pointer—probably a respectably large integer. However, a character is a small integer (ASCII values range 0-255). On many systems this causes an error because low memory addresses are reserved for special purposes such as operating system interrupt handlers—so, "access violations" occur.

**5.15** Passing a character as an argument to a function when a string is expected.

**5.16** Passing a string as an argument to a function when a character is expected.

**5.17** Forgetting to include the **<string.h>** header file when using functions from the string handling library.

**5.18** Not appending a terminating null character to the first argument of a **strncpy** when the third argument is less than or equal to the length of the string in the second argument.

**5.19** Assuming that **strcmp** and **strncmp** return 1 when their arguments are equal. Both functions return 0 (C++'s false value) for equality. Therefore, when testing two strings for equality, the result of the **strcmp** or **strncmp** function should be compared with 0 to determine if the strings are equal.

5.20 Not realizing that **strtok** modifies the string being tokenized, and then attempting to use that string as if it were the original unmodified string.

## Good Programming Practices

5.1 Although it is not required to do so, include the letters **Ptr** in pointer variable names to make it clear that these variables are pointers and need to be handled appropriately.

5.2 Initialize pointers to prevent unexpected results.

5.3 Use call-by-value to pass arguments to a function unless the value of the variable must be modified. This is an example of the principle of least privilege. Some people prefer call-by-reference for performance reasons because the overhead of copying values is avoided.

5.4 Before using a function, check the function prototype for the function to determine if the function is able to modify the values passed to it.

5.5 Use array notation instead of pointer notation when manipulating arrays. Although the program may take slightly longer to compile, it will probably be clearer.

5.6 When storing a string of characters in a character array, be sure the array is large enough to hold the largest string that will be stored. C++ allows strings of any length to be stored. If a string is longer than the character array in which it is to be stored, characters beyond the end of the array will overwrite data in memory following the array.

## Performance Tips

5.1 Pass large objects such as structures using pointers to constant data, or references to constant data, to obtain the performance benefits of call-by-reference and the security of call-by-value.

5.2 Sometimes an algorithm that emerges in a "natural" way can contain subtle performance problems such as indefinite postponement. Seek algorithms that avoid indefinite postponement.

## Portability Tips

5.1 Although **const** is well defined in ANSI C, some compilers do not enforce it.

5.2 The number of bytes used to store a particular data type may vary between systems. When writing programs that depend on data type sizes, and that will run on several computer systems, be sure to use **sizeof** to determine the number of bytes used to store the data types.

5.3 Most computers today have 2-byte or 4-byte integers. Some of the newer machines use 8-byte integers. Because the results of pointer arithmetic depend on the size of the objects a pointer points to, pointer arithmetic is machine dependent.

5.4 When a variable of type **char *** is initialized with a string literal, some compilers may place the string in a location in memory where the string cannot be modified. If you may need to modify a string literal, it should be stored in a character array to ensure modifiability on all systems.

5.5 The internal numeric codes used to represent characters may be different on different computers.

## Software Engineering Observations

5.1 The **const** qualifier can be used to enforce the principle of least privilege. Using the principle of least privilege to properly design software tremendously reduces debugging time and improper side effects, and makes a program easier to modify and maintain.

5.2 If a value does not (or should not) change in the body of a function to which it is passed, the parameter should be declared `const` to ensure that it is not accidentally modified.

5.3 Only one value can be altered in a calling function when call-by-value is used. That value must be assigned from the return value of the function. To modify multiple values in a calling function, call-by-reference must be used.

5.4 Placing function prototypes in function definitions enforces the principle of least privilege by restricting proper function calls to the functions in which the prototypes appear.

5.5 When passing an array to a function, also pass the size of the array (rather than building into the function knowledge of the array size). This helps make the function more general. General functions are often reusable in many programs.

## Self-Review Exercises

5.1 Answer each of the following:

a) A pointer is a variable that contains as its value the ________ of another variable.

b) The three values that can be used to initialize a pointer are ________, ________, or ________.

c) The only integer that can be assigned to a pointer is ________.

5.2 State whether the following are true or false. If the answer is false, explain why.

a) The address operator `&` can only be applied to constants, to expressions, and to variables declared with the storage class `register`.

b) A pointer that is declared to be `void` can be dereferenced.

c) Pointers of different types may not be assigned to one another without a cast operation.

5.3 Answer each of the following. Assume that single-precision, floating-point numbers are stored in 4 bytes, and that the starting address of the array is at location 1002500 in memory. Each part of the exercise should use the results of previous parts where appropriate.

a) Declare an array of type `float` called `numbers` with 10 elements, and initialize the elements to the values `0.0`, `1.1`, `2.2`, ..., `9.9`. Assume the symbolic constant `SIZE` has been defined as `10`.

b) Declare a pointer `nPtr` that points to an object of type `float`.

c) Print the elements of array `numbers` using array subscript notation. Use a `for` structure, and assume the integer control variable `i` has been declared. Print each number with 1 position of precision to the right of the decimal point.

d) Give two separate statements that assign the starting address of array `numbers` to the pointer variable `nPtr`.

e) Print the elements of array `numbers` using pointer/offset notation with pointer `nPtr`.

f) Print the elements of array `numbers` using pointer/offset notation with the array name as the pointer.

g) Print the elements of array `numbers` by subscripting pointer `nPtr`.

h) Refer to element 4 of array `numbers` using array subscript notation, pointer/offset notation with the array name as the pointer, pointer subscript notation with `nPtr`, and pointer/offset notation with `nPtr`.

i) Assuming that `nPtr` points to the beginning of array `numbers`, what address is referenced by `nPtr + 8`? What value is stored at that location?

j) Assuming that `nPtr` points to `numbers[5]`, what address is referenced by `nPtr` after `nPtr -= 4` is executed. What is the value stored at that location?

5.4 For each of the following, write a single statement that performs the indicated task. Assume that floating-point variables `number1` and `number2` have been declared, and that `number1` has been initialized to `7.3`. Also, assume that variable `ptr` is of type `char *` and arrays `s1[100]` and `s2[100]` are of type `char`.

a) Declare the variable `fPtr` to be a pointer to an object of type `float`.
b) Assign the address of variable `number1` to pointer variable `fPtr`.
c) Print the value of the object pointed to by `fPtr`.
d) Assign the value of the object pointed to by `fPtr` to variable `number2`.
e) Print the value of `number2`.
f) Print the address of `number1`.
g) Print the address stored in `fPtr`. Is the value printed the same as the address of `number1`?
h) Copy the string stored in array `s2` into array `s1`.
i) Compare the string in `s1` to the string in `s2`. Print the result.
j) Append 10 characters from the string in `s2` to the string in `s1`.
k) Determine the length of the string in `s1`. Print the result.
l) Assign to `ptr` the location of the first token in `s2`. Tokens in `s2` are separated by commas (`,`).

**5.5** Do each of the following:

a) Write the function header for a function called `exchange` that takes two pointers to floating-point numbers `x` and `y` as parameters, and does not return a value.
b) Write the function prototype for the function in part (a).
c) Write the function header for a function called `evaluate` that returns an integer and that takes as parameters integer `x` and a pointer to function `poly`. Function `poly` takes an integer parameter and returns an integer.
d) Write the function prototype for the function in part (c).
e) Show two different methods of initializing character array `vowel` with the string of vowels, `"AEIOU"`.

**5.6** Find the error in each of the following program segments. Assume

```
int *zPtr;   // zPtr will reference array z
int *aPtr = NULL;
void *sPtr = NULL;
int number, i;
int z[5] = {1, 2, 3, 4, 5};

sPtr = z;
```

a)
```
++zptr;
```
b)
```
// use pointer to get first value of array
number = zPtr;
```
c)
```
// assign array element 2 (the value 3) to number
number = *zPtr[2];
```
d)
```
// print entire array z
for (i = 0; i <= 5; i++)
   cout << zPtr[i] << endl;
```
e)
```
// assign the value pointed to by sPtr to number
number = *sPtr;
```
f)
```
++z;
```
g)
```
char s[10];
cout << strncpy(s, "hello", 5) << endl;
```
h)
```
char s[12];
strcpy(s, "Welcome Home");
```

i)
```
if ( strcmp(string1, string2) )
    cout << "The strings are equal" << endl;
```

**5.7** What (if anything) prints when each of the following statements is performed? If the statement contains an error, describe the error and indicate how to correct it. Assume the following variable declarations:

```
char s1[50] = "jack", s2[50] = " jill", s3[50], *sptr;
```

a) `cout << strcpy(s3, s2) << endl;`
b) `cout << strcat(strcat(strcpy(s3, s1), " and "), s2) << endl;`
c) `cout << strlen(s1) + strlen(s2) << endl;`
d) `cout << strlen(s3) << endl;`

## *Answers to Self-Review Exercises*

**5.1** a) address. b) `0`, `NULL`, an address. c) `0`.

**5.2** a) False. The address operator can only be applied to variables, and it cannot be applied to constants, expressions, or variables declared with storage class **`register`**.
b) False. A pointer to **`void`** cannot be dereferenced because there is no way to know exactly how many bytes of memory should be dereferenced.
c) False. Pointers of type **`void`** can be assigned pointers of other types. Pointers of type **`void`** can be assigned to pointers of other types only with an explicit type cast.

**5.3** a)
```
float numbers[SIZE] = {0.0, 1.1, 2.2, 3.3, 4.4, 5.5,
                       6.6, 7.7, 8.8, 9.9};
```
b)
```
float *nPtr;
```
c)
```
cout << setiosflags(ios::fixed | ios::showpoint)
     << setprecision(1);
for (i = 0; i < SIZE; i++)
   cout << numbers[i] << ' ';
```
d)
```
nPtr = numbers;
nPtr = &numbers[0];
```
e)
```
cout << setiosflags(ios::fixed | ios::showpoint)
     << setprecision(1);
for (i = 0; i < SIZE; i++)
   cout << *(nPtr + i) << ' ';
```
f)
```
cout << setiosflags(ios::fixed | ios::showpoint)
     << setprecision(1);
for (i = 0; i < SIZE; i++)
   cout << *(numbers + i) << ' ';
```
g)
```
cout << setiosflags(ios::fixed | ios::showpoint)
     << setprecision(1);
for (i = 0; i < SIZE; i++)
   cout << nPtr[i] << ' ';
```
h)
```
numbers[4]
*(numbers + 4)
nPtr[4]
*(nPtr + 4)
```
i) The address is `1002500 + 8 * 4 = 1002532`. The value is `8.8`.
j) The address of `numbers[5]` is `1002500 + 5 * 4 = 1002520`.
The address of `nPtr -= 4` is `1002520 - 4 * 4 = 1002504`.
The value at that location is `1.1`.

5.4 a) `float *fPtr;`
b) `fPtr = &number1;`
c) `cout << "The value of *fPtr is " << *fPtr << endl;`
d) `number2 = *fPtr;`
e) `cout << "The value of number2 is " << number2 << endl;`
f) `cout << "The address of number1 is " << &number1 << endl;`
g) `cout << "The address stored in fPtr is " << fPtr << endl;`
Yes, the value is the same.
h) `strcpy(s1, s2);`
i) `cout << "strcmp(s1, s2) = " << strcmp(s1, s2) << endl;`
j) `strncat(s1, s2, 10);`
k) `cout << "strlen(s1) = " << strlen(s1) << endl;`
l) `ptr = strtok(s2, ",");`

5.5 a) `void exchange(float *x, float *y)`
b) `void exchange(float *, float *);`
c) `int evaluate(int x, int (*poly)(int))`
d) `int evaluate(int, int (*)(int));`
e) `char vowel[] = "AEIOU";`
`char vowel[] = {'A', 'E', 'I', 'O', 'U', '\0'};`

5.6 a) Error: `zPtr` has not been initialized.
Correction: Initialize `zPtr` with `zPtr = z;`
b) Error: The pointer is not dereferenced.
Correction: Change the statement to `number = *zPtr;`
c) Error: `zPtr[2]` is not a pointer and should not be dereferenced.
Correction: Change `*zPtr[2]` to `zPtr[2]`.
d) Error: Referring to an array element outside the array bounds with pointer subscripting.
Correction: Change the relational operator in the `for` structure to `<` to avoid walking off the end of the array.
e) Error: Dereferencing a void pointer.
Correction: In order to dereference the pointer, it must first be cast to an integer pointer. Change the above statement to `number = *(int *)sPtr;`
f) Error: Trying to modify an array name with pointer arithmetic.
Correction: Use a pointer variable instead of the array name to accomplish pointer arithmetic, or subscript the array name to refer to a specific element.
g) Error: Function `strncpy` does not write a terminating null character to array `s` because its third argument is equal to the length of the string `"hello"`.
Correction: Make the third argument of `strncpy` `6` or assign `'\0'` to `s[5]` to ensure that the terminating null character is added to the string.
h) Error: Character array `s` is not large enough to store the terminating null character.
Correction: Declare the array with more elements.
i) Error: Function `strcmp` will return 0 if the strings are equal, therefore the condition in the `if` structure will be false, and the output statement will not be executed.
Correction: Explicitly compare the result of `strcmp` with `0` in the condition of the `if` structure.

5.7 a) `jill`
b) `jack and jill`
c) `8`
d) `13`

## Exercises

**5.8** State whether the following are true or false. If false, explain why.

a) Two pointers that point to different arrays cannot be compared meaningfully.

b) Because the name of an array is a pointer to the first element of the array, array names may be manipulated in precisely the same manner as pointers.

**5.9** Answer each of the following. Assume that unsigned integers are stored in 2 bytes, and that the starting address of the array is at location 1002500 in memory.

a) Declare an array of type **`unsigned int`** called **`values`** with 5 elements, and initialize the elements to the even integers from 2 to 10. Assume the symbolic constant **`SIZE`** has been defined as **`5`**.

b) Declare a pointer **`vPtr`** that points to an object of type **`unsigned int`**.

c) Print the elements of array **`values`** using array subscript notation. Use a **`for`** structure and assume integer control variable **`i`** has been declared.

d) Give two separate statements that assign the starting address of array **`values`** to pointer variable **`vPtr`**.

e) Print the elements of array **`values`** using pointer/offset notation.

f) Print the elements of array **`values`** using pointer/offset notation with the array name as the pointer.

g) Print the elements of array **`values`** by subscripting the pointer to the array.

h) Refer to element 5 of array **`values`** using array subscript notation, pointer/offset notation with the array name as the pointer, pointer subscript notation, and pointer/offset notation.

i) What address is referenced by **`vPtr + 3`**? What value is stored at that location?

j) Assuming **`vPtr`** points to **`values[4]`**, what address is referenced by **`vPtr -= 4`**. What value is stored at that location?

**5.10** For each of the following, write a single statement that performs the indicated task. Assume that long integer variables **`value1`** and **`value2`** have been declared, and that **`value1`** has been initialized to **`200000`**.

a) Declare the variable **`lPtr`** to be a pointer to an object of type **`long`**.

b) Assign the address of variable **`value1`** to pointer variable **`lPtr`**.

c) Print the value of the object pointed to by **`lPtr`**.

d) Assign the value of the object pointed to by **`lPtr`** to variable **`value2`**.

e) Print the value of **`value2`**.

f) Print the address of **`value1`**.

g) Print the address stored in **`lPtr`**. Is the value printed the same as the address of **`value1`**?

**5.11** Do each of the following.

a) Write the function header for function **`zero`** which takes a long integer array parameter **`bigIntegers`** and does not return a value.

b) Write the function prototype for the function in part **(a)**.

c) Write the function header for function **`add1AndSum`** which takes an integer array parameter **`oneTooSmall`** and returns an integer.

d) Write the function prototype for the function described in part **(c)**.

***Note: Exercises 5.12 through 5.15 are reasonably challenging. Once you have done these problems, you ought to be able to implement most popular card games easily.***

**5.12** Modify the program in Fig. 5.24 so that the card dealing function deals a five-card poker hand. Then write the following additional functions:

a) Determine if the hand contains a pair.
b) Determine if the hand contains two pairs.
c) Determine if the hand contains three of a kind (e.g., three jacks).
d) Determine if the hand contains four of a kind (e.g., four aces).
e) Determine if the hand contains a flush (i.e., all five cards of the same suit).
f) Determine if the hand contains a straight (i.e., five cards of consecutive face values).

**5.13** Use the functions developed in Exercise 5.12 to write a program that deals two five-card poker hands, evaluates each hand, and determines which is the better hand.

**5.14** Modify the program developed in Exercise 5.13 so that it can simulate the dealer. The dealer's five-card hand is dealt "face down" so the player cannot see it. The program should then evaluate the dealer's hand and, based on the quality of the hand, the dealer should draw one, two, or three more cards to replace the corresponding number of unneeded cards in the original hand. The program should then reevaluate the dealer's hand. (*Caution:* This is a difficult problem!)

**5.15** Modify the program developed in Exercise 5.14 so that it can handle the dealer's hand automatically, but the player is allowed to decide which cards of the player's hand to replace. The program should then evaluate both hands and determine who wins. Now use this new program to play 20 games against the computer. Who wins more games, you or the computer? Have one of your friends play 20 games against the computer. Who wins more games? Based on the results of these games, make appropriate modifications to refine your poker playing program (this, too, is a difficult problem). Play 20 more games. Does your modified program play a better game?

**5.16** In the card shuffling and dealing program of Fig. 5.24, we intentionally used an inefficient shuffling algorithm that introduced the possibility of indefinite postponement. In this problem, you will create a high-performance shuffling algorithm that avoids indefinite postponement.

Modify the program of Fig. 5.24 as follows. Begin by initializing the **`deck`** array as shown in Fig. 5.35. Modify the **`shuffle`** function to loop row-by-row and column-by-column through the array touching every element once. Each element should be swapped with a randomly selected element of the array.

Print the resulting array to determine if the deck is satisfactorily shuffled (as in Fig. 5.36, for example). You may want your program to call the **`shuffle`** function several times to ensure a satisfactory shuffle.

| | 0 | 1 | 2 | 3 | 4 | 5 | 6 | 7 | 8 | 9 | 10 | 11 | 12 |
|---|---|---|---|---|---|---|---|---|---|---|---|---|---|
| 0 | 1 | 2 | 3 | 4 | 5 | 6 | 7 | 8 | 9 | 10 | 11 | 12 | 13 |
| 1 | 14 | 15 | 16 | 17 | 18 | 19 | 20 | 21 | 22 | 23 | 24 | 25 | 26 |
| 2 | 27 | 28 | 29 | 30 | 31 | 32 | 33 | 34 | 35 | 36 | 37 | 38 | 39 |
| 3 | 40 | 41 | 42 | 43 | 44 | 45 | 46 | 47 | 48 | 49 | 50 | 51 | 52 |

**Fig. 5.35** Unshuffled **`deck`** array.

| | 0 | 1 | 2 | 3 | 4 | 5 | 6 | 7 | 8 | 9 | 10 | 11 | 12 |
|---|---|---|---|---|---|---|---|---|---|---|---|---|---|
| 0 | 19 | 40 | 27 | 25 | 36 | 46 | 10 | 34 | 35 | 41 | 18 | 2 | 44 |
| 1 | 13 | 28 | 14 | 16 | 21 | 30 | 8 | 11 | 31 | 17 | 24 | 7 | 1 |
| 2 | 12 | 33 | 15 | 42 | 43 | 23 | 45 | 3 | 29 | 32 | 4 | 47 | 26 |
| 3 | 50 | 38 | 52 | 39 | 48 | 51 | 9 | 5 | 37 | 49 | 22 | 6 | 20 |

**Fig. 5.36** Sample shuffled **`deck`** array.

Note that although the approach in this problem improves the shuffling algorithm, the dealing algorithm still requires searching the **deck** array for card 1, then card 2, then card 3, and so on. Worse yet, even after the dealing algorithm locates and deals the card, the algorithm continues searching through the remainder of the deck. Modify the program of Fig. 5.24 so that once a card is dealt, no further attempts are made to match that card number, and the program immediately proceeds with dealing the next card. In Chapter 16, we develop a dealing algorithm that requires only one operation per card.

**5.17** (*Simulation: The Tortoise and the Hare*) In this problem you will recreate one of the truly great moments in history, namely the classic race of the tortoise and the hare. You will use random number generation to develop a simulation of this memorable event.

Our contenders begin the race at "square 1" of 70 squares. Each square represents a possible position along the race course. The finish line is at square 70. The first contender to reach or pass square 70 is rewarded with a pail of fresh carrots and lettuce. The course weaves its way up the side of a slippery mountain, so occasionally the contenders lose ground.

There is a clock that ticks once per second. With each tick of the clock, your program should adjust the position of the animals according to the following rules:

| Animal | Move type | Percentage of the time | Actual move |
|---|---|---|---|
| Tortoise | Fast plod | 50% | 3 squares to the right |
| | Slip | 20% | 6 squares to the left |
| | Slow plod | 30% | 1 square to the right |
| Hare | Sleep | 20% | No move at all |
| | Big hop | 20% | 9 squares to the right |
| | Big slip | 10% | 12 squares to the left |
| | Small hop | 30% | 1 square to the right |
| | Small slip | 20% | 2 squares to the left |

Use variables to keep track of the positions of the animals (i.e., position numbers are 1-70). Start each animal at position 1 (i.e., the "starting gate"). If an animal slips left before square 1, move the animal back to square 1.

Generate the percentages in the preceding table by producing a random integer, i, in the range $1 \leq i \leq 10$. For the tortoise, perform a "fast plod" when $1 \leq i \leq 5$, a "slip" when $6 \leq i \leq 7$, or a "slow plod" when $8 \leq i \leq 10$. Use a similar technique to move the hare.

Begin the race by printing

```
BANG !!!!!
AND THEY'RE OFF !!!!!
```

Then, for each tick of the clock (i.e., each repetition of a loop), print a 70-position line showing the letter **T** in the position of the tortoise and the letter **H** in the position of the hare. Occasionally, the contenders will land on the same square. In this case, the tortoise bites the hare and your program should print **OUCH!!!** beginning at that position. All print positions other than the **T**, the **H**, or the **OUCH!!!** (in case of a tie) should be blank.

After each line is printed, test if either animal has reached or passed square 70. If so, then print the winner and terminate the simulation. If the tortoise wins, print **TORTOISE WINS!!!**

`YAY!!!` If the hare wins, print `Hare wins. Yuch.` If both animals win on the same tick of the clock, you may want to favor the turtle (the "underdog"), or you may want to print `It's a tie`. If neither animal wins, perform the loop again to simulate the next tick of the clock. When you are ready to run your program, assemble a group of fans to watch the race. You'll be amazed at how involved your audience gets!

## Special Section: Building Your Own Computer

In the next several problems, we take a temporary diversion away from the world of high-level language programming. We "peel open" a computer and look at its internal structure. We introduce machine language programming and write several machine language programs. To make this an especially valuable experience, we then build a computer (through the technique of software-based *simulation)* on which you can execute your machine language programs!

**5.18** (*Machine Language Programming*) Let us create a computer we will call the Simpletron. As its name implies, it is a simple machine, but, as we will soon see, a powerful one as well. The Simpletron runs programs written in the only language it directly understands, that is, Simpletron Machine Language, or SML for short.

The Simpletron contains an *accumulator*—a "special register" in which information is put before the Simpletron uses that information in calculations or examines it in various ways. All information in the Simpletron is handled in terms of *words.* A word is a signed four-digit decimal number such as `+3364`, `-1293`, `+0007`, `-0001`, etc. The Simpletron is equipped with a 100-word memory, and these words are referenced by their location numbers `00`, `01`, ..., `99`.

Before running an SML program, we must *load* or place the program into memory. The first instruction (or statement) of every SML program is always placed in location `00`. The simulator will start executing at this location.

Each instruction written in SML occupies one word of the Simpletron's memory (and hence instructions are signed four-digit decimal numbers). We shall assume that the sign of an SML instruction is always plus, but the sign of a data word may be either plus or minus. Each location in the Simpletron's memory may contain either an instruction, a data value used by a program, or an unused (and hence undefined) area of memory. The first two digits of each SML instruction are the *operation code,* which specifies the operation to be performed. SML operation codes are summarized in Fig. 5.37.

| Operation code | Meaning |
|---|---|
| *Input/output operations:* | |
| `#define READ 10` | Read a word from the terminal into a specific location in memory. |
| `#define WRITE 11` | Write a word from a specific location in memory to the terminal. |

**Fig. 5.37** Simpletron Machine Language (SML) operation codes (part 1 of 2).

| Operation code | Meaning |
|---|---|
| *Load/store operations:* | |
| `#define LOAD 20` | Load a word from a specific location in memory into the accumulator. |
| `#define STORE 21` | Store a word from the accumulator into a specific location in memory. |
| *Arithmetic operations:* | |
| `#define ADD 30` | Add a word from a specific location in memory to the word in the accumulator (leave result in accumulator). |
| `#define SUBTRACT 31` | Subtract a word from a specific location in memory from the word in the accumulator (leave result in accumulator). |
| `#define DIVIDE 32` | Divide a word from a specific location in memory into the word in the accumulator (leave result in accumulator). |
| `#define MULTIPLY 33` | Multiply a word from a specific location in memory by the word in the accumulator (leave result in accumulator). |
| *Transfer of control operations:* | |
| `#define BRANCH 40` | Branch to a specific location in memory. |
| `#define BRANCHNEG 41` | Branch to a specific location in memory if the accumulator is negative. |
| `#define BRANCHZERO 42` | Branch to a specific location in memory if the accumulator is zero. |
| `#define HALT 43` | Halt, i.e., the program has completed its task. |

**Fig. 5.37** Simpletron Machine Language (SML) operation codes (part 2 of 2).

The last two digits of an SML instruction are the *operand,* which is the address of the memory location containing the word to which the operation applies. Now let us consider several simple SML programs.

The first SML program (Example 1) reads two numbers from the keyboard and computes and prints their sum. The instruction `+1007` reads the first number from the keyboard and places it into location `07` (which has been initialized to zero). Then instruction `+1008` reads the next number into location `08`. The *load* instruction, `+2007`, puts the first number into the accumulator, and the *add* instruction, `+3008`, adds the second number to the number in the accumulator. *All SML arithmetic instructions leave their results in the accumulator.* The *store* instruction, `+2109`, places the result back into memory location `09` from which the *write* instruction, `+1109`, takes the number and prints it (as a signed four-digit decimal number). The *halt* instruction, `+4300`, terminates execution.

| Example 1<br>Location | Number | Instruction |
|---|---|---|
| 00 | +1007 | (Read A) |
| 01 | +1008 | (Read B) |
| 02 | +2007 | (Load A) |
| 03 | +3008 | (Add B) |
| 04 | +2109 | (Store C) |
| 05 | +1109 | (Write C) |
| 06 | +4300 | (Halt) |
| 07 | +0000 | (Variable A) |
| 08 | +0000 | (Variable B) |
| 09 | +0000 | (Result C) |

| Example 2<br>Location | Number | Instruction |
|---|---|---|
| 00 | +1009 | (Read A) |
| 01 | +1010 | (Read B) |
| 02 | +2009 | (Load A) |
| 03 | +3110 | (Subtract B) |
| 04 | +4107 | (Branch negative to 07) |
| 05 | +1109 | (Write A) |
| 06 | +4300 | (Halt) |
| 07 | +1110 | (Write B) |
| 08 | +4300 | (Halt) |
| 09 | +0000 | (Variable A) |
| 10 | +0000 | (Variable B) |

This SML program reads two numbers from the keyboard and determines and prints the larger value. Note the use of the instruction `+4107` as a conditional transfer of control, much the same as C++'s `if` statement. Now write SML programs to accomplish each of the following tasks.

a) Use a sentinel-controlled loop to read 10 positive numbers and compute and print their sum.

b) Use a counter-controlled loop to read seven numbers, some positive and some negative, and compute and print their average.

c) Read a series of numbers and determine and print the largest number. The first number read indicates how many numbers should be processed.

**5.19** (*A Computer Simulator*) It may at first seem outrageous, but in this problem you are going to build your own computer. No, you will not be soldering components together. Rather, you will use the powerful technique of *software-based simulation* to create a *software model* of the Simpletron. You will not be disappointed. Your Simpletron simulator will turn the computer you are using into a Simpletron, and you will actually be able to run, test, and debug the SML programs you wrote in Exercise 5.18.

When you run your Simpletron simulator, it should begin by printing:

```
*** Welcome to Simpletron! ***

*** Please enter your program one instruction ***
*** (or data word) at a time. I will type the ***
*** location number and a question mark (?).  ***
*** You then type the word for that location. ***
*** Type the sentinel -99999 to stop entering ***
*** your program. ***
```

Simulate the memory of the Simpletron with a single-subscripted array **`memory`** that has 100 elements. Now assume that the simulator is running, and let us examine the dialog as we enter the program of Example 2 of Exercise 5.18:

```
00 ? +1009
01 ? +1010
02 ? +2009
03 ? +3110
04 ? +4107
05 ? +1109
06 ? +4300
07 ? +1110
08 ? +4300
09 ? +0000
10 ? +0000
11 ? -99999

*** Program loading completed ***
*** Program execution begins  ***
```

The SML program has now been placed (or loaded) in array **`memory`**. Now the Simpletron executes your SML program. Execution begins with the instruction in location `00` and, like C++, continues sequentially, unless directed to some other part of the program by a transfer of control.

Use the variable **`accumulator`** to represent the accumulator register. Use the variable **`instructionCounter`** to keep track of the location in memory that contains the instruction being performed. Use the variable **`operationCode`** to indicate the operation currently being performed, i.e., the left two digits of the instruction word. Use the variable **`operand`** to indicate the memory location on which the current instruction operates. Thus, **`operand`** is the rightmost two digits of the instruction currently being performed. Do not execute instructions directly from memory. Rather, transfer the next instruction to be performed from memory to a variable called **`instructionRegister`**. Then "pick off" the left two digits and place them in **`operationCode`**, and "pick off" the right two digits and place them in **`operand`**.

When Simpletron begins execution, the special registers are initialized as follows:

```
accumulator          +0000
instructionCounter      00
instructionRegister  +0000
operationCode           00
operand                 00
```

Now let us "walk through" the execution of the first SML instruction, **`+1009`** in memory location `00`. This is called an *instruction execution cycle.*

The **instructionCounter** tells us the location of the next instruction to be performed. We *fetch* the contents of that location from **memory** by using the C++ statement

```
instructionRegister = memory[instructionCounter];
```

The operation code and the operand are extracted from the instruction register by the statements

```
operationCode = instructionRegister / 100;
operand = instructionRegister % 100;
```

Now the Simpletron must determine that the operation code is actually a *read* (versus a *write*, a *load*, etc.). A **switch** differentiates among the twelve operations of SML.

In the **switch** structure, the behavior of various SML instructions is simulated as follows (we leave the others to the reader):

*read:* `cin >> memory[operand];`
*load:* `accumulator = memory[operand];`
*add:* `accumulator += memory[operand];`
Various branch instructions: We'll discuss these shortly.
*halt:* This instruction prints the message
**`*** Simpletron execution terminated ***`**

and then prints the name and contents of each register as well as the complete contents of memory. Such a printout is often called a *computer dump* (and, no, a computer dump is not a place where old computers go). To help you program your dump function, a sample dump format is shown in Fig. 5.38. Note that a dump after executing a Simpletron program would show the actual values of instructions and data values at the moment execution terminated.

Let us proceed with the execution of our program's first instruction, namely the **+1009** in location **00**. As we have indicated, the **switch** statement simulates this by performing the C++ statement

```
cin >> memory[operand];
```

A question mark (**?**) should be displayed on the screen before the **cin** is executed to prompt the user for input. The Simpletron waits for the user to type a value and then press the *Return key*. The value is then read into location **09**.

At this point, simulation of the first instruction is completed. All that remains is to prepare the Simpletron to execute the next instruction. Since the instruction just performed was not a transfer of control, we need merely increment the instruction counter register as follows:

```
++instructionCounter;
```

This completes the simulated execution of the first instruction. The entire process (i.e., the instruction execution cycle) begins anew with the fetch of the next instruction to be executed.

Now let us consider how the branching instructions—the transfers of control—are simulated. All we need to do is adjust the value in the instruction counter appropriately. Therefore, the unconditional branch instruction (**40**) is simulated within the **switch** as

```
instructionCounter = operand;
```

The conditional "branch if accumulator is zero" instruction is simulated as

```
if (accumulator == 0)
   instructionCounter = operand;
```

At this point you should implement your Simpletron simulator and run each of the SML programs you wrote in Exercise 5.18. You may embellish SML with additional features and provide for these in your simulator.

```
REGISTERS:
accumulator            +0000
instructionCounter        00
instructionRegister    +0000
operationCode             00
operand                   00

MEMORY:
       0     1     2     3     4     5     6     7     8     9
 0 +0000 +0000 +0000 +0000 +0000 +0000 +0000 +0000 +0000 +0000
10 +0000 +0000 +0000 +0000 +0000 +0000 +0000 +0000 +0000 +0000
20 +0000 +0000 +0000 +0000 +0000 +0000 +0000 +0000 +0000 +0000
30 +0000 +0000 +0000 +0000 +0000 +0000 +0000 +0000 +0000 +0000
40 +0000 +0000 +0000 +0000 +0000 +0000 +0000 +0000 +0000 +0000
50 +0000 +0000 +0000 +0000 +0000 +0000 +0000 +0000 +0000 +0000
60 +0000 +0000 +0000 +0000 +0000 +0000 +0000 +0000 +0000 +0000
70 +0000 +0000 +0000 +0000 +0000 +0000 +0000 +0000 +0000 +0000
80 +0000 +0000 +0000 +0000 +0000 +0000 +0000 +0000 +0000 +0000
90 +0000 +0000 +0000 +0000 +0000 +0000 +0000 +0000 +0000 +0000
```

**Fig. 5.38** A sample dump.

Your simulator should check for various types of errors. During the program loading phase, for example, each number the user types into the Simpletron's **`memory`** must be in the range **`-9999`** to **`+9999`**. Your simulator should use a **`while`** loop to test that each number entered is in this range, and, if not, keep prompting the user to reenter the number until the user enters a correct number.

During the execution phase, your simulator should check for various serious errors, such as attempts to divide by zero, attempts to execute invalid operation codes, accumulator overflows (i.e., arithmetic operations resulting in values larger than **`+9999`** or smaller than **`-9999`**), and the like. Such serious errors are called *fatal errors*. When a fatal error is detected, your simulator should print an error message such as:

```
*** Attempt to divide by zero ***
*** Simpletron execution abnormally terminated ***
```

and should print a full computer dump in the format we have discussed previously. This will help the user locate the error in the program.

## More Pointer Exercises

**5.20** Modify the card shuffling and dealing program of Fig. 5.24 so the shuffling and dealing operations are performed by the same function (**`shuffleAndDeal`**). The function should contain one nested looping structure that is similar to function **`shuffle`** in Fig. 5.24.

**5.21** What does this program do?

```
#include <iostream.h>

void mystery1(char *, const char *);

main()
{
   char string1[80], string2[80];

   cout << "Enter two strings: ";
   cin >> string1 >> string2;
   mystery1(string1, string2);
   cout << string1 << endl;
   return 0;
}

void mystery1(char *s1, const char *s2)
{
   while (*s1 != '\0')
      ++s1;

   for ( ; *s1 = *s2; s1++, s2++)
      ;   // empty statement
}
```

**5.22** What does this program do?

```
#include <iostream.h>

int mystery2(const char *);

main()
{
   char string[80];

   cout << "Enter a string: ";
   cin >> string;
   cout << mystery2(string) << endl;
   return 0;
}

int mystery2(const char *s)
{
   for (int x = 0; *s != '\0'; s++)
      ++x;

   return x;
}
```

**5.23** Find the error in each of the following program segments. If the error can be corrected, explain how.

a)
```
int *number;
cout << number << endl;
```

b)
```
float *realPtr;
long *integerPtr;
integerPtr = realPtr;
```

c)
```
int * x, y;
x = y;
```
d)
```
char s[] = "this is a character array";
for ( ; *s != '\0'; s++)
   cout << *s << ' ';
```
e)
```
short *numPtr, result;
void *genericPtr = numPtr;
result = *genericPtr + 7;
```
f)
```
float x = 19.34;
float xPtr = &x;
cout << xPtr << endl;
```
g)
```
char *s;
cout << s << endl;
```

**5.24** (*Quicksort*) In the examples and exercises of Chapter 4, we discussed the sorting techniques of bubble sort, bucket sort, and selection sort. We now present the recursive sorting technique called Quicksort. The basic algorithm for a single-subscripted array of values is as follows:

1) *Partitioning Step:* Take the first element of the unsorted array and determine its final location in the sorted array. This occurs when all values to the left of the element in the array are less than the element, and all values to the right of the element in the array are greater than the element. We now have one element in its proper location and two unsorted subarrays.
2) *Recursive Step:* Perform step 1 on each unsorted subarray.

Each time step 1 is performed on a subarray, another element is placed in its final location of the sorted array, and two unsorted subarrays are created. When a subarray consists of one element, it must be sorted, therefore that element is in its final location.

The basic algorithm seems simple enough, but how do we determine the final position of the first element of each subarray. As an example, consider the following set of values (the element in bold is the partitioning element—it will be placed in its final location in the sorted array):

**37** 2 6 4 89 8 10 12 68 45

1) Starting from the rightmost element of the array, compare each element to **37** until an element less than **37** is found, then swap **37** and that element. The first element less than **37** is 12, so **37** and 12 are swapped. The new array is:

   *12* 2 6 4 89 8 10 **37** 68 45

   Element 12 is in italic to indicate that it was just swapped with **37**.
2) Starting from the left of the array, but beginning with the element after 12, compare each element to **37** until an element greater than **37** is found, then swap **37** and that element. The first element greater than **37** is 89, so **37** and 89 are swapped. The new array is:

   12 2 6 4 **37** 8 10 *89* 68 45

3) Starting from the right, but beginning with the element before 89, compare each element to **37** until an element less than **37** is found, then swap **37** and that element. The first element less than **37** is 10, so **37** and 10 are swapped. The new array is:

   12 2 6 4 *10* 8 **37** 89 68 45

4) Starting from the left, but beginning with the element after 10, compare each element to **37** until an element greater than **37** is found, then swap **37** and that element. There are no more elements greater than **37**, so when we compare **37** to itself we know that **37** has been placed in its final location of the sorted array.

Once the partition has been applied on the above array, there are two unsorted subarrays. The subarray with values less than 37 contains 12, 2, 6, 4, 10, and 8. The subarray with values greater than 37 contains 89, 68, and 45. The sort continues with both subarrays being partitioned in the same manner as the original array.

Based on the preceding discussion, write recursive function **quickSort** to sort a single-subscripted integer array. The function should receive as arguments an integer array, a starting subscript, and an ending subscript. Function **partition** should be called by **quickSort** to perform the partitioning step.

**5.25** (*Maze Traversal*) The following grid of **#**s and dots (**.**) is a double-subscripted array representation of a maze.

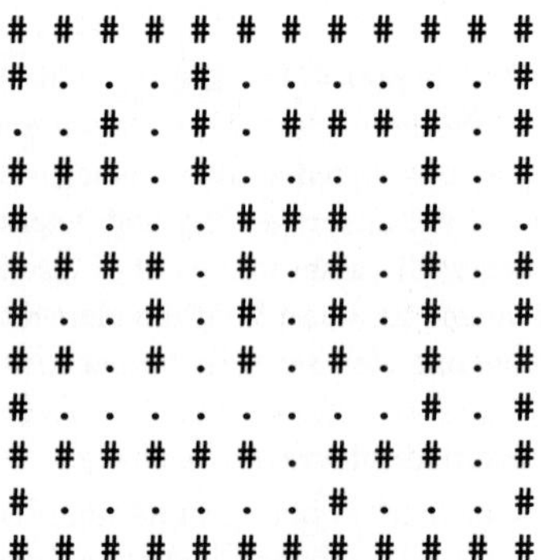

```
# # # # # # # # # # # #
# . . . # . . . . . . #
. . # . # . # # # # . #
# # # . # . . . . # . #
# . . . . # # # . # . .
# # # # . # . # . # . #
# . . # . # . # . # . #
# # . # . # . # . # . #
# . . . . . . . . # . #
# # # # # # . # # # . #
# . . . . . . # . . . #
# # # # # # # # # # # #
```

In the preceding double-subscripted array, the **#**s represent the walls of the maze and the dots represent squares in the possible paths through the maze. Moves can only be made to a location in the array that contains a dot.

There is a simple algorithm for walking through a maze that guarantees finding the exit (assuming there is an exit). If there is not an exit, you will arrive at the starting location again. Place your right hand on the wall to your right and begin walking forward. Never remove your hand from the wall. If the maze turns to the right, you follow the wall to the right. As long as you do not remove your hand from the wall, eventually you will arrive at the exit of the maze. There may be a shorter path than the one you have taken, but you are guaranteed to get out of the maze if you follow the algorithm.

Write recursive function **mazeTraverse** to walk through the maze. The function should receive as arguments a 12-by-12 character array representing the maze, and the starting location of the maze. As **mazeTraverse** attempts to locate the exit from the maze, it should place the character **X** in each square in the path. The function should display the maze after each move so the user can watch as the maze is solved.

**5.26** (*Generating Mazes Randomly*) Write a function **mazeGenerator** that takes as an argument a double-subscripted 12-by-12 character array and randomly produces a maze. The function should also provide the starting and ending locations of the maze. Try your function **mazeTraverse** from Exercise 5.25 using several randomly generated mazes.

**5.27** (*Mazes of Any Size*) Generalize functions **mazeTraverse** and **mazeGenerator** of Exercises 5.25 and 5.26 to process mazes of any width and height.

**5.28** (*Arrays of Pointers to Functions*) Rewrite the program of Fig. 4.23 to use a menu-driven interface. The program should offer the user 4 options as follows (these should be displayed on the screen):

```
Enter a choice:
  0  Print the array of grades
  1  Find the minimum grade
  2  Find the maximum grade
  3  Print the average on all tests for each student
  4  End program
```

One restriction on using arrays of pointers to functions is that all the pointers must have the same type. The pointers must be to functions of the same return type that receive arguments of the same type. For this reason, the functions in Fig. 4.23 must be modified so they each return the same type and take the same parameters. Modify functions **minimum** and **maximum** to print the minimum or maximum value and return nothing. For option 3, modify function **average** of Fig. 4.23 to output the average for each student (not a specific student). Function **average** should return nothing and take the same parameters as **printArray**, **minimum**, and **maximum**. Store the pointers to the four functions in array **processGrades** and use the choice made by the user as the subscript into the array for calling each function.

**5.29** (*Modifications to the Simpletron Simulator*) In Exercise 5.19, you wrote a software simulation of a computer that executes programs written in Simpletron Machine Language (SML). In this exercise, we propose several modifications and enhancements to the Simpletron Simulator. In Exercises 15.26 and 15.27, we propose building a compiler that converts programs written in a high-level programming language (a variation of BASIC) to Simpletron Machine Language. Some of the following modifications and enhancements may be required to execute the programs produced by the compiler.

a) Extend the Simpletron Simulator's memory to contain 1000 memory locations to enable the Simpletron to handle larger programs.
b) Allow the simulator to perform modulus calculations. This requires an additional Simpletron Machine Language instruction.
c) Allow the simulator to perform exponentiation calculations. This requires an additional Simpletron Machine Language instruction.
d) Modify the simulator to use hexadecimal values rather than integer values to represent Simpletron Machine Language instructions.
e) Modify the simulator to allow output of a newline. This requires an additional Simpletron Machine Language instruction.
f) Modify the simulator to process floating-point values in addition to integer values.
g) Modify the simulator to handle string input. Hint: Each Simpletron word can be divided into two groups, each holding a two-digit integer. Each two-digit integer represents the ASCII decimal equivalent of a character. Add a machine language instruction that will input a string and store the string beginning at a specific Simpletron memory location. The first half of the word at that location will be a count of the number of characters in the string (i.e., the length of the string). Each succeeding half-word contains one ASCII character expressed as two decimal digits. The machine language instruction converts each character into its ASCII equivalent and assigns it to a half-word.
h) Modify the simulator to handle output of strings stored in the format of part (g). Hint: Add a machine language instruction that will print a string beginning at a certain Simpletron memory location. The first half of the word at that location is a count of the number of characters in the string (i.e., the length of the string). Each succeeding half-word contains one ASCII character expressed as two decimal digits. The machine language instruction checks the length and prints the string by translating each two-digit number into its equivalent character.

**5.30** What does this program do?

```
#include <iostream.h>

int mystery3(const char *, const char *);

main()
{
   char string1[80], string2[80];

   cout << "Enter two strings: ";
   cin >> string1 >> string2;
   cout << "The result is "
        << mystery3(string1, string2) << endl;

   return 0;
}

int mystery3(const char *s1, const char *s2)
{
   for ( ; *s1 != '\0' && *s2 != '\0'; s1++, s2++)

      if (*s1 != *s2)
         return 0;

   return 1;
}
```

## *String Manipulation Exercises*

**5.31** Write a program that uses function **strcmp** to compare two strings input by the user. The program should state whether the first string is less than, equal to, or greater than the second string.

**5.32** Write a program that uses function **strncmp** to compare two strings input by the user. The program should input the number of characters to be compared. The program should state whether the first string is less than, equal to, or greater than the second string.

**5.33** Write a program that uses random number generation to create sentences. The program should use four arrays of pointers to **char** called **article**, **noun**, **verb**, and **preposition**. The program should create a sentence by selecting a word at random from each array in the following order: **article**, **noun**, **verb**, **preposition**, **article**, and **noun**. As each word is picked, it should be concatenated to the previous words in an array which is large enough to hold the entire sentence. The words should be separated by spaces. When the final sentence is output, it should start with a capital letter and end with a period. The program should generate 20 such sentences.

The arrays should be filled as follows: the **article** array should contain the articles **"the"**, **"a"**, **"one"**, **"some"**, and **"any"**; the **noun** array should contain the nouns **"boy"**, **"girl"**, **"dog"**, **"town"**, and **"car"**; the **verb** array should contain the verbs **"drove"**, **"jumped"**, **"ran"**, **"walked"**, and **"skipped"**; the **preposition** array should contain the prepositions **"to"**, **"from"**, **"over"**, **"under"**, and **"on"**.

After the preceding program is written and working, modify the program to produce a short story consisting of several of these sentences. (How about the possibility of a random term paper writer!)

**5.34** *(Limericks)* A limerick is a humorous five-line verse in which the first and second lines rhyme with the fifth, and the third line rhymes with the fourth. Using techniques similar to those developed in Exercise 5.33, write a C++ program that produces random limericks. Polishing this program to produce good limericks is a challenging problem, but the result will be worth the effort!

**5.35** Write a program that encodes English language phrases into pig Latin. Pig Latin is a form of coded language often used for amusement. Many variations exist in the methods used to form pig Latin phrases. For simplicity, use the following algorithm:

To form a pig Latin phrase from an English language phrase, tokenize the phrase into words with function `strtok`. To translate each English word into a pig Latin word, place the first letter of the English word at the end of the English word, and add the letters "`ay`." Thus the word "`jump`" becomes "`umpjay`," the word "`the`" becomes "`hetay`," and the word "`computer`" becomes "`omputercay`." Blanks between words remain as blanks. Assume the following: The English phrase consists of words separated by blanks, there are no punctuation marks, and all words have two or more letters. Function `printLatinWord` should display each word. Hint: Each time a token is found in a call to `strtok`, pass the token pointer to function `printLatinWord`, and print the pig Latin word.

**5.36** Write a program that inputs a telephone number as a string in the form `(555) 555-5555`. The program should use function `strtok` to extract the area code as a token, the first three digits of the phone number as a token, and the last four digits of the phone number as a token. The seven digits of the phone number should be concatenated into one string. The program should convert the area code string to `int` and convert the phone number string to `long`. Both the area code and the phone number should be printed.

**5.37** Write a program that inputs a line of text, tokenizes the line with function `strtok`, and outputs the tokens in reverse order.

**5.38** Use the string comparison functions discussed in Section 5.12.2 and the techniques for sorting arrays developed in Chapter 4 to write a program that alphabetizes a list of strings. Use the names of 10 or 15 towns in your area as data for your program.

**5.39** Write two versions of each of the string copy and string concatenation functions in Fig. 5.29. The first version should use array subscripting, and the second version should use pointers and pointer arithmetic.

**5.40** Write two versions of each string comparison function in Fig. 5.29. The first version should use array subscripting, and the second version should use pointers and pointer arithmetic.

**5.41** Write two versions of function `strlen` in Fig. 5.29. The first version should use array subscripting, and the second version should use pointers and pointer arithmetic.

## Special Section: Advanced String Manipulation Exercises

The preceding exercises are keyed to the text and designed to test the reader's understanding of fundamental string manipulation concepts. This section includes a collection of intermediate and advanced string manipulation exercises. The reader should find these problems challenging yet enjoyable. The problems vary considerably in difficulty. Some require an hour or two of program writing and implementation. Others are useful for lab assignments that might require two or three weeks of study and implementation. Some are challenging term projects.

**5.42** *(Text Analysis)* The availability of computers with string manipulation capabilities has resulted in some rather interesting approaches to analyzing the writings of great authors. Much attention has been focused on whether William Shakespeare ever lived. Some scholars believe there is substantial evidence indicating that Christopher Marlowe or other authors actually penned the masterpieces attributed to Shakespeare. Researchers have used computers to find similarities in the writings of these two authors. This exercise examines three methods for analyzing texts with a computer.

a) Write a program that reads several lines of text from the keyboard and prints a table indicating the number of occurrences of each letter of the alphabet in the text. For example, the phrase

```
To be, or not to be: that is the question:
```

contains one "a," two "b's," no "c's," etc.

b) Write a program that reads several lines of text and prints a table indicating the number of one-letter words, two-letter words, three-letter words, etc. appearing in the text. For example, the phrase

```
Whether 'tis nobler in the mind to suffer
```

contains

| Word length | Occurrences |
|---|---|
| 1 | 0 |
| 2 | 2 |
| 3 | 2 |
| 4 | 2 (including 'tis) |
| 5 | 0 |
| 6 | 2 |
| 7 | 1 |

c) Write a program that reads several lines of text and prints a table indicating the number of occurrences of each different word in the text. The first version of your program should include the words in the table in the same order in which they appear in the text. For example, the lines

```
To be, or not to be: that is the question:
Whether 'tis nobler in the mind to suffer
```

contain the words "to" three times, the word "be" two times, the word "or" once, etc. A more interesting (and useful) printout should then be attempted in which the words are sorted alphabetically.

**5.43** *(Word Processing)* One important function in word processing systems is *type-justification*—the alignment of words to both the left and right margins of a page. This generates a professional-looking document that gives the appearance of being set in type rather than prepared on a typewriter. Type-justification can be accomplished on computer systems by inserting blank characters between each of the words in a line so that the rightmost word aligns with the right margin.

Write a program that reads several lines of text and prints this text in type-justified format. Assume that the text is to be printed on 8 1/2-inch-wide paper, and that one-inch margins are to be allowed on both the left and right sides of the printed page. Assume that the computer prints 10 characters to the horizontal inch. Therefore, your program should print 6 1/2 inches of text or 65 characters per line.

**5.44** *(Printing Dates in Various Formats)* Dates are commonly printed in several different formats in business correspondence. Two of the more common formats are:

```
07/21/55 and July 21, 1955
```

Write a program that reads a date in the first format and prints that date in the second format.

**5.45** *(Check Protection)* Computers are frequently employed in check-writing systems such as payroll and accounts payable applications. Many strange stories circulate regarding weekly paychecks being printed (by mistake) for amounts in excess of $1 million. Weird amounts are printed by computerized check-writing systems because of human error and/or machine failure. Systems designers build controls into their systems to prevent such erroneous checks from being issued.

Another serious problem is the intentional alteration of a check amount by someone who intends to cash a check fraudulently. To prevent a dollar amount from being altered, most computerized check-writing systems employ a technique called *check protection.*

Checks designed for imprinting by computer contain a fixed number of spaces in which the computer may print an amount. Suppose a paycheck contains eight blank spaces in which the computer is supposed to print the amount of a weekly paycheck. If the amount is large, then all eight of those spaces will be filled, for example:

```
1,230.60 (check amount)
--------
12345678  (position numbers)
```

On the other hand, if the amount is less than $1000, then several of the spaces would ordinarily be left blank. For example,

```
   99.87
--------
12345678
```

contains three blank spaces. If a check is printed with blank spaces, it is easier for someone to alter the amount of the check. To prevent a check from being altered, many check-writing systems insert *leading asterisks* to protect the amount as follows:

```
***99.87
--------
12345678
```

Write a program that inputs a dollar amount to be printed on a check, and then prints the amount in check-protected format with leading asterisks if necessary. Assume that nine spaces are available for printing an amount.

**5.46** *(Writing the Word Equivalent of a Check Amount)* Continuing the discussion of the previous example, we reiterate the importance of designing check-writing systems to prevent alteration of check amounts. One common security method requires that the check amount be written both in numbers, and "spelled out" in words as well. Even if someone is able to alter the numerical amount of the check, it is extremely difficult to change the amount in words.

Many computerized check-writing systems do not print the amount of the check in words. Perhaps the main reason for this omission is the fact that most high-level languages used in commercial applications do not contain adequate string manipulation features. Another reason is that the logic for writing word equivalents of check amounts is somewhat involved.

Write a C++ program that inputs a numeric check amount and writes the word equivalent of the amount. For example, the amount 112.43 should be written as

```
ONE HUNDRED TWELVE and 43/100
```

**5.47** *(Morse Code)* Perhaps the most famous of all coding schemes is the Morse code, developed by Samuel Morse in 1832 for use with the telegraph system. The Morse code assigns a series of dots and dashes to each letter of the alphabet, each digit, and a few special characters (such as period, comma, colon, and semicolon). In sound-oriented systems, the dot represents a short sound and the dash represents a long sound. Other representations of dots and dashes are used with light-oriented systems and signal-flag systems.

Separation between words is indicated by a space, or, quite simply, the absence of a dot or dash. In a sound-oriented system, a space is indicated by a short period of time during which no sound is transmitted. The international version of the Morse code appears in Fig. 5.39.

Write a program that reads an English language phrase and encodes the phrase into Morse code. Also write a program that reads a phrase in Morse code and converts the phrase into the English language equivalent. Use one blank between each Morse-coded letter and three blanks between each Morse-coded word.

**5.48** *(A Metric Conversion Program)* Write a program that will assist the user with metric conversions. Your program should allow the user to specify the names of the units as strings (i.e., centimeters, liters, grams, etc. for the metric system and inches, quarts, pounds, etc. for the English system) and should respond to simple questions such as

| Character | Code | Character | Code |
|---|---|---|---|
| A | .- | T | - |
| B | -... | U | ..- |
| C | -.-. | V | ...- |
| D | -.. | W | .-- |
| E | . | X | -..- |
| F | ..-. | Y | -.-- |
| G | --. | Z | --.. |
| H | .... | | |
| I | .. | **Digits** | |
| J | .--- | 1 | .---- |
| K | -.- | 2 | ..--- |
| L | .-.. | 3 | ...-- |
| M | -- | 4 | ....- |
| N | -. | 5 | ..... |
| O | --- | 6 | -.... |
| P | .--. | 7 | --... |
| Q | --.- | 8 | ---.. |
| R | .-. | 9 | ----. |
| S | ... | 0 | ----- |

**Fig. 5.39** The letters of the alphabet as expressed in international Morse code.

```
"How many inches are in 2 meters?"
"How many liters are in 10 quarts?"
```

Your program should recognize invalid conversions. For example, the question

```
"How many feet in 5 kilograms?"
```

is not meaningful because `"feet"` are units of length while `"kilograms"` are units of weight.

## A challenging string manipulation project

**5.49** *(A Crossword Puzzle Generator)* Most people have worked a crossword puzzle, but few have ever attempted to generate one. Generating a crossword puzzle is a difficult problem. It is suggested here as a string manipulation project requiring substantial sophistication and effort. There are many issues the programmer must resolve to get even the simplest crossword puzzle generator program working. For example, how does one represent the grid of a crossword puzzle inside the computer? Should one use a series of strings, or should double-subscripted arrays be used? The programmer needs a source of words (i.e., a computerized dictionary) that can be directly referenced by the program. In what form should these words be stored to facilitate the complex manipulations required by the program? The really ambitious reader will want to generate the "clues" portion of the puzzle in which the brief hints for each "across" word and each "down" word are printed for the puzzle worker. Merely printing a version of the blank puzzle itself is not a simple problem.

# 6

# Classes and Data Abstraction

## Objectives

- To understand the software engineering concepts of encapsulation and data hiding.
- To understand the notions of data abstraction and abstract data types (ADTs).
- To be able to create C++ ADTs, namely classes.
- To understand how to create, use, and destroy class objects.
- To be able to control access to object data members and member functions.
- To begin to appreciate the value of object orientation.

*My object all sublime*
*I shall achieve in time.*
W. S. Gilbert

*Is it a world to hide virtues in?*
William Shakespeare, Twelfth Night

*Your public servants serve you right.*
Adlai Stevenson

*Private faces in public places*
*Are wiser and nicer*
*Than public faces in private places.*
W. H. Auden

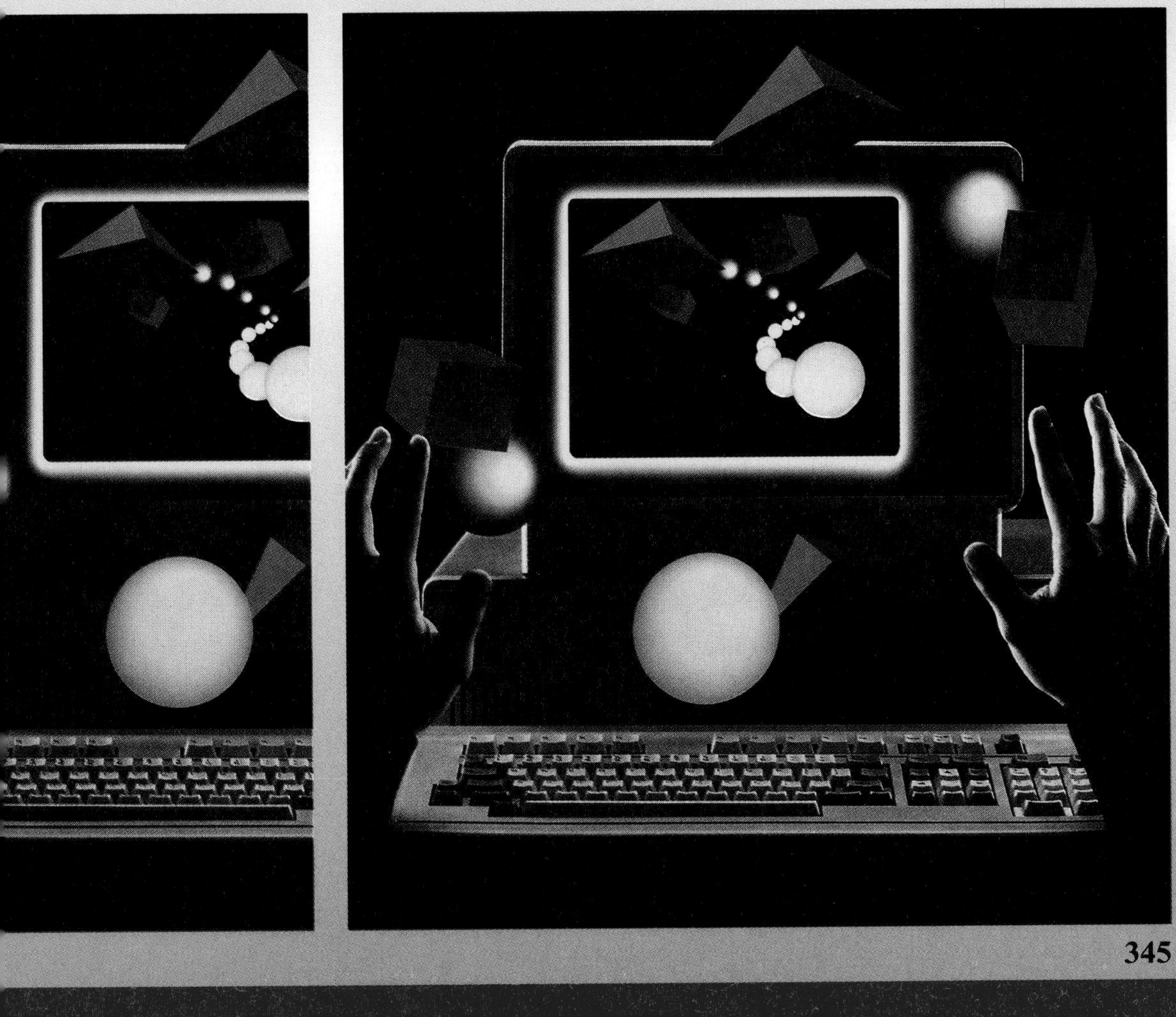

# Outline



## 6.1 Introduction

Now we begin our introduction to object orientation in C++. Why have we deferred object-oriented programming in C++ until Chapter 6? The answer is that the objects we will build will be composed in part of structured program pieces, so we needed to establish a basis in structured programming first.

Through our "Thinking About Objects" sections at the ends of Chapters 1 through 5, we have introduced the basic concepts (i.e., "object think") and terminology (i.e., "object speak") of object-oriented programming in C++. In these special sections, we also discussed the techniques of *object-oriented design (OOD):* We analyzed a typical problem statement that required a system (i.e., the elevator simulator) to be built, determined what objects were needed to implement the systems, determined what attributes the objects needed to have, determined what behaviors these objects needed to exhibit, and specified how the objects needed to interact with one another to accomplish the overall goals of the system.

Let us briefly review some key concepts and terminology of object orientation. OOP *encapsulates* data (attributes) and functions (behavior) into packages called *objects;* the data and functions of an object are intimately tied together. Objects have the property of *information hiding.* This means that although objects may know how to communicate with one another across well-defined *interfaces,* objects normally are not allowed to know how other objects are implemented—implementation details are hidden within the objects themselves. Surely it is possible to drive a car effectively without knowing the details of how engines, transmissions and exhaust systems work internally. We will see why information hiding is so crucial to good software engineering.

In C and other *procedural programming languages,* programming tends to be *action-oriented,* whereas ideally in C++ programming is *object-oriented.* In C, the unit of programming is the *function.* In C++, the unit of programming is the *class* from which objects are eventually *instantiated* (i.e., created).

C programmers concentrate on writing functions. Groups of actions that perform some task are formed into functions, and functions are grouped to form programs. Data is certainly important in C, but the view is that data exists primarily in support of the actions that functions perform. The *verbs* in a system specification help the C programmer determine the set of functions that will work together to implement the system.

C++ programmers concentrate on creating their own *user-defined types* called *classes.* Classes are also referred to as *programmer-defined types.* Each class contains data as well as the set of functions that manipulate the data. The data components of a class are called *data members.* The function components of a class are called *member functions.* Just as an instance of a built-in type such as **int** is called a *variable,* an instance of a user-defined type (i.e., a class) is called an *object.* The focus of attention in C++ is on objects rather than functions. The *nouns* in a system specification help the C++ programmer determine a set of classes. These classes are used to create objects that will work together to implement the system.

Classes in C++ are a natural evolution of the C notion of **struct**. Before proceeding with the specifics of developing classes in C++, we discuss structures, and we build a user-defined type based on a structure. The weaknesses we expose in this approach will help motivate the notion of a class.

## 6.2 Structure Definitions

Structures are aggregate data types built using things of other types. Consider the following structure definition:

```
struct Time {
   int hour;      // 0-23
   int minute;    // 0-59
   int second;    // 0-59
};
```

The keyword **struct** introduces the structure definition. The identifier **Time** is the *structure tag*. The structure tag names the structure definition and is used to declare variables of the *structure type*. In this example, the new type name is **Time**. The names declared in the braces of the structure definition are the structure's *members*. Members of the same structure must have unique names, but two different structures may contain members of the same name without conflict. Each structure definition must end with a semicolon. The preceding explanation is valid for classes also as we will soon see.

The definition of **Time** contains three members of type **int**—**hour**, **minute**, and **second**. Structure members can be any type, and one structure can contain members of many different types. A structure cannot, however, contain an instance of itself. For example, a member of type **Time** cannot be declared in the structure definition for **Time**. A pointer to another **Time** structure, however, can be included. A structure containing a member that is a pointer to the same structure type is referred to as a *self-referential structure*. Self-referential structures are useful for forming linked data structures (see Chapter 15).

The preceding structure definition does not reserve any space in memory; rather, the definition creates a new data type that is used to declare variables. Structure variables are declared like variables of other types. The declaration

```
Time timeObject, timeArray[10], *timePtr;
```

declares **timeObject** to be a variable of type **Time**, **timeArray** to be an array with 10 elements of type **Time**, and **timePtr** to be a pointer to a **Time** object.

## 6.3 Accessing Members of Structures

Members of a structure (or of a class) are accessed using the *member access operators*—the *dot operator* (**.**) and the *arrow operator* (**->**). The dot operator accesses a structure (or class) member via the variable name for the object or via a reference to the object. For example, to print member **hour** of structure **timeObject** use the statement

```
cout << timeObject.hour;
```

The arrow operator—consisting of a minus (**-**) sign and a greater than (**>**) sign with no intervening spaces—accesses a structure (or class) member via a pointer to the object. Assume that the pointer **timePtr** has been declared to point to a **Time** object, and that the address of structure **timeObject** has been assigned to **timePtr**. To print member **hour** of structure **timeObject** with pointer **timePtr**, use the statement

```
cout << timePtr->hour;
```

The expression **timePtr->hour** is equivalent to **(*timePtr).hour** which dereferences the pointer and accesses the member **hour** using the dot operator. The parentheses are needed here because the dot operator (**.**) has a higher precedence than the pointer dereferencing operator (*****). The arrow operator and structure member operator, along with parentheses and brackets (**[]**), have the second highest operator precedence (after the scope resolution operator introduced in Chapter 3) and associate from left to right.

## 6.4 Implementing a User-Defined Type Time With a Struct

Figure 6.1 creates the user-defined structure type **`Time`** with three integer members: **`hour`**, **`minute`**, and **`second`**. The program defines a single **`Time`** structure called **`dinnerTime`** and uses the dot operator to initialize the structure members with the values **`18`** for **`hour`**, **`30`** for **`minute`**, and **`0`** for **`second`**. The program then prints the time in military format and standard format. Note that the print functions receive references to constant **`Time`** structures. This causes **`Time`** structures to be passed to the print functions by reference—thus eliminating the copying overhead associated with passing structures to functions by value—and the use of **`const`** prevents the **`Time`** structure from being modified by the print functions. In Chapter 7, we discuss **`const`** objects and **`const`** member functions.

***Performance Tip 6.1***

*Structures ordinarily pass call-by-value. To avoid the overhead of copying a structure, pass the structure call-by-reference.*

***Performance Tip 6.2***

*To avoid the overhead of call-by-value yet still gain the benefit that the caller's original data is protected from modification, pass large-size arguments as* **`const`** *references.*

There are drawbacks to creating new data types with structures in this manner. Since initialization is not specifically required, it is possible to have uninitialized data and the consequent problems. Even if the data is initialized, it may not be initialized correctly. Invalid values can be assigned to the members of a structure (as we did in Fig. 6.1) because the program has direct access to the data. The program assigned bad values to all three members of the **`Time`** object **`dinnerTime`**. If the implementation of the **`struct`** is changed (e.g., the time is now represented as the number of seconds since midnight), all programs that use the **`struct`** must be changed. This is because the programmer directly manipulates the data type. There is no "interface" to it to ensure that the programmer uses the data type correctly and to ensure that the data remains in a consistent state.

***Software Engineering Observation 6.1***

*It is important to write programs that are understandable and easy to maintain. Change is the rule rather than the exception. Programmers should anticipate that their code will be modified. As we will see, classes facilitate program modifiability.*

There are other problems associated with C-style structures. In C, structures cannot be printed as a unit, rather their members must be printed and formatted one at a time. A function could be written to print the members of a structure in some appropriate format. Chapter 8, "Operator Overloading," illustrates how to overload the **`<<`** operator to enable objects of a structure—C++ enhances the notion of structure—or class type to be printed easily. In C, structures may not be compared in their entirety; they must be compared member by member. Chapter 8, also illustrates how to overload equality operators and relational operators to compare objects of (C++) structure and class types.

The following section reimplements our **`Time`** structure as a class and demonstrates some of the advantages to creating so-called *abstract data types* as classes. We will see

```
// FIG6_1.CPP
// Create a structure, set its members, and print it.
#include <iostream.h>

struct Time {       // structure definition
   int hour;        // 0-23
   int minute;      // 0-59
   int second;      // 0-59
};

void printMilitary(const Time &);   // prototype
void printStandard(const Time &);   // prototype

main()
{
   Time dinnerTime;      // variable of new type Time

   // set members to valid values
   dinnerTime.hour = 18;
   dinnerTime.minute = 30;
   dinnerTime.second = 0;

   cout << "Dinner will be held at ";
   printMilitary(dinnerTime);
   cout << " military time," << endl << "which is ";
   printStandard(dinnerTime);
   cout << " standard time." << endl;

   // set members to invalid values
   dinnerTime.hour = 29;
   dinnerTime.minute = 73;
   dinnerTime.second = 103;

   cout << endl << "Time with invalid values: ";
   printMilitary(dinnerTime);
   cout << endl;
   return 0;
}

// Print the time in military format
void printMilitary(const Time &t)
{
   cout << (t.hour < 10 ? "0" : "") << t.hour << ":"
        << (t.minute < 10 ? "0" : "") << t.minute << ":"
        << (t.second < 10 ? "0" : "") << t.second;
}

// Print the time in standard format
void printStandard(const Time &t)
{
   cout << ((t.hour == 0 || t.hour == 12) ? 12 : t.hour % 12)
        << ":" << (t.minute < 10 ? "0" : "") << t.minute
        << ":" << (t.second < 10 ? "0" : "") << t.second
        << (t.hour < 12 ? " AM" : " PM");
}
```

**Fig. 6.1** Create a structure, set its members, and print it (part 1 of 2).

```
Dinner will be held at 18:30:00 military time,
which is 6:30:00 PM standard time.

Time with invalid values: 29:73:103
```

Fig. 6.1 Create a structure, set its members, and print it (part 2 of 2).

that classes and structures can be used almost identically in C++. The difference between the two is in the default accessibility associated with the members of each. This will be explained shortly.

## 6.5 Implementing a Time Abstract Data Type with a Class

Classes enable the programmer to model objects that have *attributes* (represented as *data members*) and *behaviors* or *operations* (represented as *member functions*). Types containing data members and member functions are normally defined in C++ using the keyword **class**.

Member functions are sometimes called *methods* in other object-oriented programming languages, and are invoked in response to *messages* sent to an object. A message corresponds to a member-function call.

Once a class has been defined, the class name can be used to declare objects of that class. Figure 6.2 contains a simple definition for class **Time**.

Our **Time** class definition begins with the keyword **class**. The *body* of the class definition is delineated with left and right braces (**{** and **}**). The class definition terminates with a semicolon. Our **Time** class definition and our **Time** structure definition each contain the three integer members **hour**, **minute**, and **second**.

***Common Programming Error 6.1***

*Forgetting the semicolon at the end of a class (or structure) definition.*

The remaining parts of the class definition are new. The **public:** and **private:** labels are called *member access specifiers*. Any data member or member function de-

```
class Time {
public:
   Time();
   void setTime(int, int, int);
   void printMilitary();
   void printStandard();
private:
   int hour;     // 0 - 23
   int minute;   // 0 - 59
   int second;   // 0 - 59
};
```

Fig. 6.2 Simple definition of **class Time**.

clared after member access specifier **public:** (and before the next member access specifier) is accessible wherever the program has access to an object of class **Time**. Any data member or member function declared after member access specifier **private:** (and up to the next member access specifier) is accessible only to member functions of the class. Member access specifiers always end with a colon (**:**) and can appear multiple times and in any order in a class definition. For the remainder of the text, we will refer to the member access specifiers as **public** and **private** (without the colon).

***Good Programming Practice 6.1***

*Use each member access specifier only once in a class definition for clarity and readability. Place public members first where they are easy to locate.*

The class definition contains prototypes for the following four member functions after the **public** member access specifier—**Time**, **setTime**, **printMilitary**, and **printStandard**. These are the *public member functions,* or *public services* or *interface* of the class. These functions will be used by *clients* (i.e., portions of a program that are users) of the class to manipulate the data of the class.

Notice the member function with the same name as the class; it is called a *constructor* function of that class. A constructor is a special member function that initializes the data members of a class object. A class's constructor function is called automatically when an object of that class is created. We will see that it is common to have several constructors for a class; this is accomplished through function overloading.

The three integer members appear after the **private** member access specifier. This indicates that these data members of the class are only accessible to member functions—and as we will see in the next chapter, "friends"—of the class. Thus, the data members can only be accessed by the four functions whose prototypes appear in the class definition (or by friends of the class). Data members are normally listed in the **private** portion of a class and member functions are normally listed in the **public** portion. It is possible to have **private** member functions and **public** data as we will see later; the latter is uncommon and is considered a poor programming practice.

Once the class has been defined, it can be used as a type in declarations as follows:

```
Time sunset,                  // object of type Time
     arrayOfTimes[5],         // array of Time objects
     *pointerToTime,          // pointer to a Time object
     &dinnerTime = sunset;    // reference to a Time object
```

The class name becomes a new type specifier. There may be many objects of a class, just as there may be many variables of a type such as **int**. The programmer can create new class types as needed. This is one of many reasons why C++ is an *extensible language.*

Figure 6.3 uses the **Time** class. The program instantiates a single object of class **Time** called **t**. When the object is instantiated, the **Time** constructor is called automatically and explicitly initializes each private data member to **0**. The time is then printed in military and standard formats to confirm that the members have been initialized properly. The time is then set using the **setTime** member function and the time is printed again in both formats. Then member function **setTime** attempts to set the data members to invalid values, and the time is again printed in both formats.

```
// FIG6_3.CPP
// Time class.
#include <iostream.h>

// Time abstract data type (ADT) definition
class Time {
public:
   Time();                        // constructor
   void setTime(int, int, int);   // set hour, minute and second
   void printMilitary();          // print military time format
   void printStandard();          // print standard time format
private:
   int hour;      // 0 - 23
   int minute;    // 0 - 59
   int second;    // 0 - 59
};

// Time constructor initializes each data member to zero.
// Ensures all Time objects start in a consistent state.
Time::Time() { hour = minute = second = 0; }

// Set a new Time value using military time. Perform validity
// checks on the data values. Set invalid values to zero.
void Time::setTime(int h, int m, int s)
{
   hour = (h >= 0 && h < 24) ? h : 0;
   minute = (m >= 0 && m < 60) ? m : 0;
   second = (s >= 0 && s < 60) ? s : 0;
}

// Print Time in military format
void Time::printMilitary()
{
   cout << (hour < 10 ? "0" : "") << hour << ":"
        << (minute < 10 ? "0" : "") << minute << ":"
        << (second < 10 ? "0" : "") << second;
}

// Print time in standard format
void Time::printStandard()
{
   cout << ((hour == 0 || hour == 12) ? 12 : hour % 12)
        << ":" << (minute < 10 ? "0" : "") << minute
        << ":" << (second < 10 ? "0" : "") << second
        << (hour < 12 ? " AM" : " PM");
}
```

Fig. 6.3 Abstract data type **Time** implementation as a class (part 1 of 2).

Again, note that the data members **hour**, **minute**, and **second** are preceded by the **private** member access specifier. Private data members of a class are normally not accessible outside the class. (Again, we will see in Chapter 7 that friends of a class may access the class's private members.) The philosophy here is that the actual data represen-

```
// Driver to test simple class Time
main()
{
   Time t;  // instantiate object t of class Time

   cout << "The initial military time is ";
   t.printMilitary();
   cout << endl << "The initial standard time is ";
   t.printStandard();

   t.setTime(13, 27, 6);
   cout << endl << endl << "Military time after setTime is ";
   t.printMilitary();
   cout << endl << "Standard time after setTime is ";
   t.printStandard();

   t.setTime(99, 99, 99);  // attempt invalid settings
   cout << endl << endl << "After attempting invalid settings:"
        << endl << "Military time: ";
   t.printMilitary();
   cout << endl << "Standard time: ";
   t.printStandard();
   cout << endl;
   return 0;
}
```

```
The initial military time is 00:00:00
The initial standard time is 12:00:00 AM

Military time after setTime is 13:27:06
Standard time after setTime is 1:27:06 PM

After attempting invalid settings:
Military time: 00:00:00
Standard time: 12:00:00 AM
```

**Fig. 6.3** Abstract data type **Time** implementation as a class (part 2 of 2).

tation used within the class is of no concern to the class's clients. For example, it would be perfectly reasonable for the class to represent the time internally as the number of seconds since midnight. Clients could use the same public member functions and get the same results without being aware of this. In this sense, the implementation of a class is said to be *hidden* from its clients. Such *information hiding* promotes program modifiability and simplifies the client's perception of a class.

***Software Engineering Observation 6.2***

*Clients of a class use the class without knowing the internal details of how the class is implemented. If the class implementation is changed (to improve performance, for example), provided the class's interface remains constant, the class's client source code need not change. This makes it much easier to modify systems.*

In this program, the **Time** constructor simply initializes the data members to 0 (i.e., the military time equivalent of 12 AM). This ensures that the object is in a consistent state when it is created. Invalid values cannot be stored in the data members of a **Time** object because the constructor is automatically called when the **Time** object is created and all subsequent attempts by a client to modify the data members are scrutinized by the function **setTime**.

***Software Engineering Observation 6.3***

*Member functions are usually shorter than equivalent functions in non-object-oriented programs because the data stored in data members has ideally been validated by a constructor and/or by member functions that store new data.*

Note that the data members of a class cannot be initialized where they are declared in the class body. These data members should be initialized by the class's constructor, or they can be assigned values by "set" functions.

***Common Programming Error 6.2***

*Attempting to explicitly initialize a data member of a class in the class definition.*

The function with the same name as the class but preceded with a *tilde character (~)* is called the *destructor* of that class (this example does not include a destructor). The destructor does "termination housekeeping" on each class object before the memory for the object is reclaimed by the system. We will discuss constructors and destructors in more detail later in this chapter and in Chapter 7.

Note that the functions the class provides to the outside world are preceded by the **public** label. Public functions implement the capabilities the class provides to its clients. The public functions of a class are referred to as the class's *interface* or *public interface.*

***Software Engineering Observation 6.4***

*Clients have access to a class's interface but should not have access to a class's implementation.*

The class definition contains declarations of the class's data members and the class's member functions. The member function declarations are the function prototypes we discussed in earlier chapters. Member functions can be defined inside a class, but it is a good programming practice to define the functions outside the class definition.

***Software Engineering Observation 6.5***

*Declaring member functions inside a class definition and defining those member functions outside that class definition separates the interface of a class from its implementation. This promotes good software engineering.*

Note the use of the *binary scope resolution operator (::)* in each member function definition following the class definition in Fig. 6.3. Once a class is defined and its member functions are declared, the member functions must be defined. Each member function of the class can be defined directly in the class body (rather than including the function prototype of the class), or the member function can be defined after the class body. When a member function is defined after its corresponding class definition, the function name is preceded by the class name and the binary scope resolution operator (**::**). Because different classes can have the same member names, the scope resolution operator "ties" the member name to the class name to uniquely identify the member functions of a particular class.

Even though a member function declared in a class definition may be defined outside that class definition, that member function is still within that *class's scope,* i.e., its name is known only to other members of the class unless referred to via an object of the class, a reference to an object of the class, or a pointer to an object of the class. We will say more about class scope shortly.

If a member function is defined in a class definition, the member function is automatically inlined. Member functions defined outside a class definition may be made inline by explicitly using the keyword **inline**. Remember that the compiler reserves the right not to inline any function.

***Performance Tip 6.3***

*Defining a small member function inside the class definition automatically inlines the member function (if the compiler chooses to do so). This can improve performance, but it does not promote the best software engineering.*

It is interesting that the **printMilitary** and **printStandard** member functions take no arguments. This is because member functions implicitly know that they are to print the data members of the particular **Time** object for which they are invoked. This makes member function calls more concise than conventional function calls in procedural programming. It also reduces the likelihood of passing the wrong arguments, the wrong types of arguments, and/or the wrong number of arguments.

***Software Engineering Observation 6.6***

*Using an object-oriented programming approach can often simplify function calls by reducing the number of parameters to be passed. This benefit of object-oriented programming derives from the fact that encapsulation of data members and member functions within an object gives the member functions the right to access the data members.*

Classes simplify programming because the client (or user of the class object) need only be concerned with the operations encapsulated or embedded in the object. Such operations are usually designed to be client-oriented rather than implementation-oriented. Clients need not be concerned with a class's implementation. Interfaces do change, but less frequently than implementations. When an implementation changes, implementation-dependent code must change accordingly. By hiding the implementation we eliminate the possibility of other program parts becoming dependent on the details of the class implementation.

Often, classes do not have to be created "from scratch." Rather, they may be *derived* from other classes that provide operations the new classes can use. Or classes can include objects of other classes as members. Such *software reuse* can greatly enhance programmer productivity. Deriving new classes from existing classes is called *inheritance* and is discussed in detail in Chapter 9. Including classes as members of other classes is called *composition* and is discussed in Chapter 7.

## 6.6 Class Scope and Accessing Class Members

A class's data members (variables declared in the class definition) and member functions (functions declared in the class definition) belong to that *class's scope*. Nonmember functions are defined at *file scope*.

Within a class's scope, class members are immediately accessible by all of that class's member functions and can be referenced simply by name. Outside a class's scope, class members are referenced through either an object name, a reference to an object, or a pointer to an object.

Member functions of a class can be overloaded, but only by other member functions of the class. To overload a member function, simply provide in the class definition a prototype for each version of the overloaded function, and provide a separate function definition for each version of the function.

***Common Programming Error 6.3***

*Attempting to overload a member function of a class with a function not in that class's scope.*

Member functions have *function scope* within a class—variables defined in a member function are known only to that function. If a member function defines a variable with the same name as a variable with class scope, the class-scope variable is hidden by the function-scope variable within the function scope. Such a hidden variable can be accessed via the scope resolution operator by preceding the operator with the class name. Hidden global variables can be accessed with the unary scope resolution operator (see Chapter 3).

The operators used to access class members are identical to the operators used to access structure members. The *dot member selection operator* (`.`) is combined with an object's name or with a reference to an object to access the object's members. The *arrow member selection operator* (`->`) is combined with a pointer to an object to access that object's members.

The program of Fig. 6.4 uses a simple class called `Count` with public data member `x` of type `int`, and public member function `print` to illustrate accessing the members of a class with the member selection operators. The program instantiates three variables related to type `Count`—`counter`, `counterRef` (a reference to a `Count` object), and `counterPtr` (a pointer to a `Count` object). Variable `counterRef` is declared to reference `counter`, and variable `counterPtr` is declared to point to `counter`. *It is important to note that data member* `x` *has been made public here simply to demonstrate how public members are accessed. As we have stated, data is typically made private as we will do in all subsequent examples.*

## 6.7 Separating Interface from Implementation

One of the most fundamental principles of good software engineering is to separate interface from implementation. This makes it easier to modify programs. As far as clients of a class are concerned, changes in the class's implementation do not affect the client as long as the class's interface originally provided to the client is unchanged (the class's functionality could be expanded beyond the original interface).

*Software Engineering Observation 6.7*

*Place the class declaration in a header file to be included by any client that wants to use the class. This forms the class's public interface. Place the definitions of the class member functions in a source file. This forms the implementation of the class.*

*Software Engineering Observation 6.8*

*Clients of a class do not need access to the class's source code in order to use the class. The clients do, however, need to be able to link to the class's object code.*

```
// FIG6_4.CPP
// Demonstrating the class member access operators . and ->
//
// CAUTION: IN FUTURE EXAMPLES WE AVOID PUBLIC DATA!
#include <iostream.h>

// Simple class Count
class Count {
public:
   int x;
   void print() { cout << x << endl; }
};

main()
{
   Count counter,                   // create counter object
         *counterPtr = &counter, // pointer to counter
         &counterRef = counter;  // reference to counter

   cout << "Assign 7 to x and print using the object's name: ";
   counter.x = 7;        // assign 7 to data member x
   counter.print();      // call member function print

   cout << "Assign 8 to x and print using a reference: ";
   counterRef.x = 8;     // assign 8 to data member x
   counterRef.print();   // call member function print

   cout << "Assign 10 to x and print using a pointer: ";
   counterPtr->x = 10;  // assign 10 to data member x
   counterPtr->print(); // call member function print
   return 0;
}
```

```
Assign 7 to x and print using the object's name: 7
Assign 8 to x and print using a reference: 8
Assign 10 to x and print using a pointer: 10
```

**Fig. 6.4** Accessing an object's data members and member functions through the object's name, through a reference, and through a pointer to the object.

This encourages independent software vendors (ISVs) to provide class libraries for sale or license. The ISVs provide in their products only the header files and the object modules. No proprietary information is revealed—as would be the case if source code were provided. The C++ user community benefits by having more ISV-produced class libraries available.

Actually, things are not quite this rosy. Header files do contain some portion of the implementation and hints about other portions of the implementation. Inline member functions, for example, need to be in a header file, so that when the compiler compiles a client, the client can include the inline function definition in place. Private members are listed in the class definition in the header file, so these members are visible to clients even though the clients may not access the private members.

***Software Engineering Observation 6.9***

*Information important to the interface to a class should be included in the header file. Information that will be used only internally in the class and will not be needed by clients of the class should be included in the unpublished source file. This is yet another example of the principle of least privilege.*

Figure 6.5 splits the program of Fig. 6.3 into multiple files. When building a C++ program, each class definition is normally placed in a *header file,* and that class's member function definitions are placed in *source-code files* of the same base name. The header files are included (via **#include**) in each file in which the class is used, and the source-code file is compiled and linked with the file containing the main program. See your compiler's documentation to determine how to compile and link programs consisting of multiple source files.

```
// TIME1.H
// Declaration of the Time class.
// Member functions are defined in TIME.CPP

// prevent multiple inclusions of header file
#ifndef TIME1_H
#define TIME1_H

// Time abstract data type definition
class Time {
public:
   Time();                          // constructor
   void setTime(int, int, int);     // set hour, minute and second
   void printMilitary();            // print military time format
   void printStandard();            // print standard time format
private:
   int hour;      // 0 - 23
   int minute;    // 0 - 59
   int second;    // 0 - 59
};

#endif
```

**Fig. 6.5** **Time** class header file (part 1 of 3).

```
// TIME1.CPP
// Member function definitions for Time class.

#include <iostream.h>
#include "time1.h"

// Time constructor initializes each data member to zero.
// Ensures all Time objects start in a consistent state.
Time::Time() { hour = minute = second = 0; }

// Set a new Time value using military time.
// Perform validity checks on the data values.
// Set invalid values to zero (consistent state).
void Time::setTime(int h, int m, int s)
{
   hour = (h >= 0 && h < 24) ? h : 0;
   minute = (m >= 0 && m < 60) ? m : 0;
   second = (s >= 0 && s < 60) ? s : 0;
}

// Print Time in military format
void Time::printMilitary()
{
   cout << (hour < 10 ? "0" : "") << hour << ":"
        << (minute < 10 ? "0" : "") << minute << ":"
        << (second < 10 ? "0" : "") << second;
}

// Print time in standard format
void Time::printStandard()
{
   cout << ((hour == 0 || hour == 12) ? 12 : hour % 12)
        << ":" << (minute < 10 ? "0" : "") << minute
        << ":" << (second < 10 ? "0" : "") << second
        << (hour < 12 ? " AM" : " PM");
}
```

**Fig. 6.5** **Time** class member function definitions source file (part 2 of 3).

Figure 6.5 consists of the header file **time1.h** in which class **Time** is declared, the file **time1.cpp** in which the member functions of class **Time** are defined, and the file **fig6_5.cpp** in which function **main** is defined. The output for this program is identical to the output of Fig. 6.3.

Note that the class declaration is enclosed in the following preprocessor code (see Chapter 17):

```
// prevent multiple inclusions of header file

#ifndef TIME1_H
#define TIME1_H
   ...
#endif
```

```
// FIG6_5.CPP
// Driver for Time1 class
// NOTE: Compile with TIME1.CPP
#include <iostream.h>
#include "time1.h"

// Driver to test simple class Time
main()
{
   Time t;  // instantiate object t of class time

   cout << "The initial military time is ";
   t.printMilitary();
   cout << endl << "The initial standard time is ";
   t.printStandard();

   t.setTime(13, 27, 6);
   cout << endl << endl << "Military time after setTime is ";
   t.printMilitary();
   cout << endl << "Standard time after setTime is ";
   t.printStandard();

   t.setTime(99, 99, 99);  // attempt invalid settings
   cout << endl << endl << "After attempting invalid settings:"
        << endl << "Military time: ";
   t.printMilitary();
   cout << endl << "Standard time: ";
   t.printStandard();
   cout << endl;
   return 0;
}
```

```
The initial military time is 00:00:00
The initial standard time is 12:00:00 AM

Military time after setTime is 13:27:06
Standard time after setTime is 1:27:06 PM

After attempting invalid settings:
Military time: 00:00:00
Standard time: 12:00:00 AM
```

**Fig. 6.5** Driver program for **Time** class (part 3 of 3).

When we build larger programs, other definitions and declarations will also be placed in header files. The preceding preprocessor directives prevent the code between **#ifndef** and **#endif** from being included if the name **TIME1_H** has been defined. If the header has not been included previously in a file, the name **TIME1_H** is defined by the **#define** directive and the header file statements are included. If the header has been included previously, **TIME1_H** is defined already and the header file is not included again.

Attempts to include a header file multiple times typically occur in large programs with many header files that may themselves include other header files. Note: The convention we use for the symbolic constant name in the preprocessor directives is simply the header file name with the underscore character replacing the period.

***Good Programming Practice 6.2***

*Use* **#ifndef***,* **#define** *and* **#endif** *preprocessor directives to prevent header files from being included more than once in a program.*

***Good Programming Practice 6.3***

*Use the name of the header file with the period replaced by an underscore in the* **#ifndef** *and* **#define** *preprocessor directives of a header file.*

## 6.8 Controlling Access to Members

The member access specifiers **public** and **private** (and **protected** as we will see in Chapter 9, "Inheritance") are used to control access to a class's data members and member functions. The default access mode for classes is **private** so all members after the class header and before the first label are private. After each label, the mode that was invoked by that label applies until the next label or until the terminating right brace (**}**) of the class definition. The labels **public**, **private**, and **protected** may be repeated, but such usage is rare and can be confusing.

Private class members can be accessed only by member functions (and friend functions) of that class. The public members of a class may be accessed by any function in the program.

The primary purpose of public members is to present to the class's clients a view of the *services* the class provides. This set of services forms the *public interface* of the class. Clients of the class need not be concerned with how the class accomplishes its tasks. The private members of a class as well as the definitions of its public member functions are not accessible to the clients of a class. These components form the *implementation* of the class.

***Software Engineering Observation 6.10***

*C++ encourages programs to be implementation independent. When the implementation of a class used by implementation-independent code changes, that code need not be modified, but it may need to be recompiled.*

***Common Programming Error 6.4***

*An attempt by a function which is not a member of a particular class (or a friend of that class) to access a private member of that class.*

Figure 6.6 demonstrates that private class members are only accessible through the public class interface using public member functions. When this program is compiled, the compiler generates two errors stating that the private member specified in each statement is not accessible. Figure 6.6 includes **time1.h** and is compiled with **time1.cpp** from Fig. 6.5.

```
// FIG6_6.CPP
// Demonstrate errors resulting from attempts
// to access private class members.
#include <iostream.h>
#include "time1.h"

main()
{
   Time t;

   // Error: 'Time::hour' is not accessible
   t.hour = 7;

   // Error: 'Time::minute' is not accessible
   cout << "minute = " << t.minute;

   return 0;
}
```

```
Compiling FIG6_6.CPP:
Error FIG6_6.CPP 12: 'Time::hour' is not accessible
Error FIG6_6.CPP 15: 'Time::minute' is not accessible
```

**Fig. 6.6** Erroneous attempt to access private members of a class.

***Good Programming Practice 6.4***

*If you choose to list the private members first in a class definition, explicitly use the* **`private`** *label despite the fact that* **`private`** *is assumed by default. This improves program clarity. Our preference is to list the* **`public`** *members of a class first.*

***Good Programming Practice 6.5***

*Despite the fact that the* **`public`** *and* **`private`** *labels may be repeated and intermixed, list all the public members of a class first in one group and then list all the private members in another group. This focuses the client's attention on the class's public interface, rather than on the class's implementation.*

***Software Engineering Observation 6.11***

*Keep all the data members of a class private. Provide public member functions to set the values of private data members and to get the values of private data members. This architecture helps hide the implementation of a class from its clients, which reduces bugs and improves program modifiability.*

A client of a class may be a member function of another class or it may be a global function.

The default access for members of a class is **`private`**. Access to members of a class may be explicitly set to **`public`**, **`protected`** (as we will see in Chapter 9), or **`pri-`**

**vate**. The default access for **struct** members is **public**. Access to members of a **struct** also may be explicitly set to **public**, **protected**, or **private**.

***Software Engineering Observation 6.12***

*Class designers use private, protected, and public members to enforce the notion of information hiding and the principle of least privilege.*

Note that the members of a class are private by default, so it is never necessary to use the **private** member access specifier explicitly. Many programmers prefer, however, to list the interface to a class (i.e., the class's public members) first; then the private members are listed, thus requiring the explicit use of the **private** member access specifier in the class definition.

***Good Programming Practice 6.6***

*Using the member access specifiers* **public**, **protected**, *and* **private** *only once each in any class definition avoids confusion.*

Just because class data is **private** does not necessarily mean that clients cannot effect changes to that data. The data can be changed by member functions or friends of that class. As we will see, these functions should be designed to ensure the integrity of the data.

Access to a class's private data should be carefully controlled by the use of member functions, called *access functions*. For example, to allow clients to read the value of private data, the class can provide a *"get" function.* To enable clients to modify private data, the class can provide a *"set" function.* Such modification would seem to violate the notion of private data. But a *set* member function can provide data validation capabilities (such as range checking) to ensure that the value is set properly. A *set* function can also translate between the form of the data used in the interface and the form used in the implementation. A *get* function need not expose the data in "raw" format; rather the *get* function can edit the data and limit the view of the data the client will see.

***Software Engineering Observation 6.13***

*The class designer need not provide* set *and/or* get *functions for each private data item; these capabilities should be provided only when it makes sense and after careful thought by the class designer.*

***Software Engineering Observation 6.14***

*Making the data members of a class private and the member functions of the class public facilitates debugging because problems with data manipulations are localized to either the class's member functions or the friends of the class.*

## 6.9 Access Functions and Utility Functions

Not all member functions need be made public to serve as part of the interface of a class. Some member functions remain private and serve as *utility functions* to the other functions of the class.

*Software Engineering Observation 6.15*

*Member functions tend to fall into a number of different categories: functions that read and return the value of private data members; functions that set the value of private data members; functions that implement the features of the class; and functions that perform various mechanical chores for the class such as initializing class objects, assigning class objects, converting between classes and built-in types or between classes and other classes, and handling memory for class objects.*

Access functions can read or display data. Another common use for access functions is to test the truth or falsity of conditions—such functions are often called *predicate functions.* An example of a predicate function would be an **isEmpty** function for any container class—a class capable of holding many objects—such as a linked list, a stack or a queue. A program would test **isEmpty** before attempting to read another item from the container object. An **isFull** predicate function might test a container class object to determine if it has no additional room.

Figure 6.7 demonstrates the notion of a *utility function.* A utility function is not part of a class's interface. Rather, it is a private member function that supports the operation of the class's public member functions. Utility functions are not intended to be used by clients of a class.

Class **SalesPerson** has an array of 12 monthly sales figures initialized by the constructor to zero and set to user-supplied values by function **setSales**. Public member function **printAnnualSales** prints the total sales for the last 12 months. Utility function **totalAnnualSales** totals the 12 monthly sales figures for the benefit of **printAnnualSales**. Member function **printAnnualSales** edits the sales figures into dollar amount format.

```
// SALESP.H
// SalesPerson class definition
// Member functions defined in SALESP.CPP

#ifndef SALESP_H
#define SALESP_H

class SalesPerson {
public:
   SalesPerson();                  // constructor
   void setSales(int, double);     // User supplies one month's
                                   // sales figures.
   void printAnnualSales();

private:
   double sales[12];               // 12 monthly sales figures
   double totalAnnualSales();      // utility function
};

#endif
```

**Fig. 6.7** Using a utility function (part 1 of 3).

```
// SALESP.CPP
// Member functions for class SalesPerson
#include <iostream.h>
#include <iomanip.h>
#include "salesp.h"

// Constructor function initializes array
SalesPerson::SalesPerson()
{
   for (int i = 0; i < 12; i++)
      sales[i] = 0.0;
}

// Function to set one of the 12 monthly sales figures
void SalesPerson::setSales(int month, double amount)
{
   if (month >= 1 && month <= 12 && amount > 0)
      sales[month - 1] = amount;
   else
      cout << "Invalid month or sales figure" << endl;
}

// Private utility function to total annual sales
double SalesPerson::totalAnnualSales()
{
   double total = 0.0;

   for (int i = 0; i < 12; i++)
      total += sales[i];

   return total;
}

// Print the total annual sales
void SalesPerson::printAnnualSales()
{
   cout << setprecision(2)
        << setiosflags(ios::fixed | ios::showpoint)
        << endl << "The total annual sales are: $"
        << totalAnnualSales() << endl;
}
```

Fig. 6.7 Using a utility function (part 2 of 3).

## 6.10 Initializing Class Objects: Constructors

When an object is created, its members can be initialized by a *constructor* function. A constructor is a class member function with the same name as the class. The programmer provides the constructor which is then invoked automatically each time an object of that class is created (instantiated). *Data members of a class cannot be initialized in the class definition.* Rather, data members must either be initialized in a constructor of the class, or

```
// FIG6_7.CPP
// Demonstrating a utility function
// Compile with SALESP.CPP
#include <iostream.h>
#include "salesp.h"

main()
{
   SalesPerson s;          // create SalesPerson object s
   double salesFigure;

   for (int i = 1; i <= 12; i++) {
      cout << "Enter sales amount for month "
           << i << ": ";
      cin >> salesFigure;
      s.setSales(i, salesFigure);
   }

   s.printAnnualSales();

   return 0;
}
```

```
Enter sales amount for month 1: 5314.76
Enter sales amount for month 2: 4292.38
Enter sales amount for month 3: 4589.83
Enter sales amount for month 4: 5534.03
Enter sales amount for month 5: 4376.34
Enter sales amount for month 6: 5698.45
Enter sales amount for month 7: 4439.22
Enter sales amount for month 8: 5893.57
Enter sales amount for month 9: 4909.67
Enter sales amount for month 10: 5123.45
Enter sales amount for month 11: 4024.97
Enter sales amount for month 12: 5923.92

Total annual sales: $60120.58
```

**Fig. 6.7** Using a utility function (part 3 of 3).

their values may be set later after the object is created. Constructors cannot specify return types or return values. Constructors may be overloaded to provide a variety of means for initializing objects of a class.

***Common Programming Error 6.5***

*Attempting to declare a return type for a constructor, and/or attempting to return a value from a constructor.*

***Good Programming Practice 6.7***

*When appropriate (almost always), provide a constructor to ensure that every object is properly initialized with meaningful values.*

*Good Programming Practice 6.8*

*Every member function (and friend) that modifies the private data members of an object should ensure that the data remains in a consistent state.*

When an object of a class is declared, *initializers* can be provided in parentheses to the right of the object name and before the semicolon. These initializers are passed as arguments to the class's constructor. We will soon see several examples of these *constructor calls.*

## 6.11 Using Default Arguments with Constructors

The constructor from **time1.cpp** (Fig. 6.5) initialized **hour**, **minute**, and **second** to **0** (i.e., 12 midnight in military time). Constructors can contain default arguments. Figure 6.8 redefines the **Time** constructor function to include default arguments of zero for each variable. By providing default arguments to the constructor, even if no values are provided in a constructor call, the object is still guaranteed to be in a consistent state due to the default arguments. A programmer-supplied constructor that defaults all its arguments (or requires no arguments) is also a *default constructor*, i.e., a constructor that can be invoked with no arguments. The can be only one default constructor per class. In this program, the constructor calls member function **setTime** with the values passed to the constructor (or the default values) to ensure that the value supplied for **hour** is in the range 0 to 23, and that the values for **minute** and **second** are each in the range 0 to 59. If a value is out of range, it is set to zero by **setTime** (this is an example of ensuring that a data member remains in a consistent state).

```
// TIME2.H
// Declaration of the Time class.
// Member functions defined in TIME2.CPP

// prevent multiple inclusions of header file
#ifndef TIME2_H
#define TIME2_H

class Time {
public:
   Time(int = 0, int = 0, int = 0);  // default constructor
   void setTime(int, int, int);
   void printMilitary();
   void printStandard();
private:
   int hour;
   int minute;
   int second;
};

#endif
```

Fig. 6.8 Using a constructor with default arguments (part 1 of 4).

```
// TIME2.CPP
// Member function definitions for Time class.

#include <iostream.h>
#include "time2.h"

// Constructor function to initialize private data.
// Default values are 0 (see class definition).
Time::Time(int hr, int min, int sec)
   { setTime(hr, min, sec); }

// Set values of hour, minute, and second.
// Invalid values are set to 0.
void Time::setTime(int h, int m, int s)
{
   hour = (h >= 0 && h < 24) ? h : 0;
   minute = (m >= 0 && m < 60) ? m : 0;
   second = (s >= 0 && s < 60) ? s : 0;
}

// Display time in military format: HH:MM:SS
void Time::printMilitary()
{
   cout << (hour < 10 ? "0" : "") << hour << ":"
        << (minute < 10 ? "0" : "") << minute << ":"
        << (second < 10 ? "0" : "") << second;
}

// Display time in standard format: HH:MM:SS AM (or PM)
void Time::printStandard()
{
   cout << ((hour == 0 || hour == 12) ? 12 : hour % 12)
        << ":" << (minute < 10 ? "0" : "") << minute
        << ":" << (second < 10 ? "0" : "") << second
        << (hour < 12 ? " AM" : " PM");
}
```

**Fig. 6.8** Using a constructor with default arguments (part 2 of 4).

Note that the **Time** constructor could be written to include the same statements as member function **setTime**. This may be slightly more efficient because the extra call to **setTime** is eliminated. However, coding the **Time** constructor and member function **setTime** identically makes maintenance of this program more difficult. If the implementation of member function **setTime** changes, the implementation of the **Time** constructor should change accordingly. Having the **Time** constructor call **setTime** directly, requires any changes to the implementation of **setTime** to be made only once. This reduces the likelihood of a programming error when altering the implementation. Also, the performance of the **Time** constructor can be enhanced by explicitly declaring the constructor **inline** or by defining the constructor in the class definition (which implicitly inlines the function definition).

```
// FIG6_8.CPP
// Demonstrating a default constructor
// function for class Time.
#include <iostream.h>
#include "time2.h"

main()
{
   Time t1, t2(2), t3(21, 34), t4(12, 25, 42),
        t5(27, 74, 99);

   cout << "Constructed with:" << endl
        << "all arguments defaulted:" << endl << "   ";
   t1.printMilitary();
   cout << endl << "   ";
   t1.printStandard();

   cout << endl << "hour specified; minute and second defaulted:"
        << endl << "   ";
   t2.printMilitary();
   cout << endl << "   ";
   t2.printStandard();

   cout << endl << "hour and minute specified; second defaulted:"
        << endl << "   ";
   t3.printMilitary();
   cout << endl << "   ";
   t3.printStandard();

   cout << endl << "hour, minute, and second specified:"
        << endl << "   ";
   t4.printMilitary();
   cout << endl << "   ";
   t4.printStandard();

   cout << endl << "all invalid values specified:"
        << endl << "   ";
   t5.printMilitary();
   cout << endl << "   ";
   t5.printStandard();
   cout << endl;

   return 0;
}
```

**Fig. 6.8** Using a constructor with default arguments (part 3 of 4).

***Software Engineering Observation 6.16***

*If a member function of a class already provides all or part of the functionality required by a constructor (or other member function) of the class, call that member function from the constructor (or other member function). This simplifies the maintenance of the code and reduces the likelihood of an error if the implementation of the code is modified.*

```
Constructed with:
all arguments defaulted:
   00:00:00
   12:00:00 AM
hour specified; minute and second defaulted:
   02:00:00
   2:00:00 AM
hour and minute specified; second defaulted:
   21:34:00
   9:34:00 PM
hour, minute, and second specified:
   12:25:42
   12:25:42 PM
all invalid values specified:
   00:00:00
   12:00:00 AM
```

**Fig. 6.8** Using a constructor with default arguments (part 4 of 4).

***Good Programming Practice 6.9***

*Declare default function arguments only in the function prototype within the class definition in the header file.*

***Common Programming Error 6.6***

*Specifying default initializers for the same member function in both a header file and in the member function definition.*

The program of Fig. 6.8 initializes five **Time** objects—one with all three arguments defaulted in the constructor call, one with one argument specified, one with two arguments specified, one with three arguments specified, and one with three invalid arguments specified. The contents of each object's data members after instantiation and initialization are displayed.

If no constructor is defined for a class, the compiler creates a default constructor. Such a constructor does not perform any initialization, so when the object is created, it is not guaranteed to be in a consistent state.

## 6.12 Using Destructors

A *destructor* is a special member function of a class. The name of the destructor for a class is the *tilde (~)* character followed by the class name. This naming convention has intuitive appeal, because as we will see in a later chapter the tilde operator is the bitwise complement operator, and, in a sense, the destructor is the complement of the constructor.

A class's destructor is called when an object is destroyed—e.g., when program execution leaves the scope in which an object of that class was instantiated. The destructor itself does not actually destroy the object—it performs *termination housekeeping* before the system reclaims the object's memory space so that it may be used to hold new objects.

A destructor receives no parameters and returns no value. A class may have only one destructor—destructor overloading is not allowed.

***Common Programming Error 6.7***

*Attempting to pass arguments to a destructor, to return values from a destructor, or to overload a destructor.*

Notice that destructors have not been provided for the classes presented so far. Actually, destructors are rarely used with simple classes. In Chapter 8, we will see that destructors are appropriate for classes whose objects contain dynamically allocated storage (for arrays and strings, for example). In Chapter 7, we discuss how to dynamically allocate and deallocate storage.

## 6.13 When Destructors and Constructors are Called

Constructors and destructors are called automatically. The order in which these function calls are made depends on the order in which execution enters and leaves the scope in which objects are instantiated. Generally, destructor calls are made in the reverse order of the constructor calls. However, the storage class of objects can alter the order in which the destructors are called.

Constructors are called for objects declared in global scope before any other function (including **main**) in that file begins execution. The corresponding destructors are called when **main** terminates or the **exit** function is called (see Chapter 18, "Other Topics").

Constructors are called for automatic local objects when execution reaches the point where the objects are declared. The corresponding destructors are called when the objects leave scope (i.e., the block in which they are declared is exited). Constructors and destructors for automatic objects are called each time the objects enter and leave scope.

Constructors are called for static local objects once when execution reaches the point where the objects are first declared. Corresponding destructors are called when **main** terminates or the **exit** function is called.

The program of Fig. 6.9 demonstrates the order in which constructors and destructors are called for objects of type **CreateAndDestroy** in several scopes. The program declares **first** in global scope. Its constructor is called as the program begins execution and its destructor is called at program termination after all other objects are destroyed.

Function **main** declares three objects. Objects **second** and **fourth** are local automatic objects, and object **third** is a static local object. The constructors for each of these objects are called when execution reaches the point where each object is declared. The destructors for objects **fourth** and **second** are called in that order when the end of **main** is reached. Because object **third** is static, it exists until program termination. The destructor for object **third** is called before the destructor for **first**, but after all other objects are destroyed.

Function **create** declares three objects—**fifth** and **seventh** are local automatic objects, and **sixth** is a static local object. The destructors for objects **seventh** and **fifth** are called in that order when the end of **create** is reached. Because **sixth** is static, it exists until program termination. The destructor for **sixth** is called before the destructors for **third** and **first**, but after all other objects are destroyed.

```
// CREATE.H
// Definition of class CreateAndDestroy.
// Member functions defined in CREATE.CPP.

#ifndef CREATE_H
#define CREATE_H

class CreateAndDestroy {
public:
   CreateAndDestroy(int);  // constructor
   ~CreateAndDestroy();    // destructor
private:
   int data;
};

#endif
```

**Fig. 6.9** Demonstrating the order in which constructors and destructors are called (part 1 of 3).

```
// CREATE.CPP
// Member function definitions for class CreateAndDestroy
#include <iostream.h>
#include "create.h"

CreateAndDestroy::CreateAndDestroy(int value)
{
   data = value;
   cout << "Object " << data << "   constructor";
}

CreateAndDestroy::~CreateAndDestroy()
   { cout << "Object " << data << "   destructor " << endl; }
```

**Fig. 6.9** Demonstrating the order in which constructors and destructors are called (part 2 of 3).

## 6.14 Using Data Members and Member Functions

Private data members can be manipulated only by member functions (and friends) of the class. A typical manipulation might be the adjustment of a customer's bank balance (e.g., a private data member of a class **BankAccount**) by a member function **computeInterest**.

Classes often provide public member functions to allow clients of the class to set (i.e., write) or get (i.e., read) the values of private data members. These functions need not be called "set" and "get" specifically, but they often are. More specifically, a member function that sets data member **interestRate** would typically be named **setInterestRate**, and a member function that gets the **interestRate** would typically be called **getInterestRate**. Get functions are also commonly called "query" functions.

```
// FIG6_9.CPP
// Demonstrating the order in which constructors and
// destructors are called.
#include <iostream.h>
#include "create.h"

void create(void);   // prototype

CreateAndDestroy first(1);  // global object

main()
{
   cout << "   (global created before main)" << endl;

   CreateAndDestroy second(2);        // local object
   cout << "   (local automatic in main)" << endl;

   static CreateAndDestroy third(3);  // local object
   cout << "   (local static in main)" << endl;

   create();  // call function to create objects

   CreateAndDestroy fourth(4);        // local object
   cout << "   (local automatic in main)" << endl;
   return 0;
}

// Function to create objects
void create(void)
{
   CreateAndDestroy fifth(5);
   cout << "   (local automatic in create)" << endl;

   static CreateAndDestroy sixth(6);
   cout << "   (local static in create)" << endl;

   CreateAndDestroy seventh(7);
   cout << "   (local automatic in create)" << endl;
}
```

```
Object 1   constructor   (global created before main)
Object 2   constructor   (local automatic in main)
Object 3   constructor   (local static in main)
Object 5   constructor   (local automatic in create)
Object 6   constructor   (local static in create)
Object 7   constructor   (local automatic in create)
Object 7   destructor
Object 5   destructor
Object 4   constructor   (local automatic in main)
Object 4   destructor
Object 2   destructor
Object 6   destructor
Object 3   destructor
Object 1   destructor
```

**Fig. 6.9** Demonstrating the order in which constructors and destructors are called (part 3 of 3).

It would seem that providing both set and get capabilities would be essentially the same as making the data members public. This is yet another subtlety of C++ that makes the language so desirable for software engineering. If a data member is public, then the data member may be read or written at will by any function in the program. If a data member is private, a public "get" function would certainly seem to allow other functions to read the data at will but the get function could control the formatting and display of the data. A public "set" function could—and most likely would—carefully scrutinize any attempt to modify the value of the data member. This would ensure that the new value is appropriate for that data item. For example, an attempt to set the day of the month to 37 would be rejected, an attempt to set a person's weight to a negative value would be rejected, an attempt to set a numeric quantity to an alphabetic value would be rejected, an attempt to set a grade on an exam to 185 (when the proper range is zero to 100) would be rejected, and so on.

***Software Engineering Observation 6.17***

*Making data members private and controlling access, especially write access, to those data members through public member functions helps ensure data integrity.*

The benefits of data integrity are not automatic simply because data members are made private—the programmer must provide the validity checking. C++ does, however, provide a framework in which programmers can design better programs in a convenient manner.

***Good Programming Practice 6.10***

*Member functions that set the values of private data should verify that the intended new values are proper; if they are not, the set functions should place the private data members into an appropriate consistent state.*

The client of a class should be notified when an attempt is made to assign an invalid value to a data member. For this reason, a class's set functions are often written to return values indicating that an attempt was made to assign invalid data to an object of the class. This enables clients of the class to test the return values of set functions to determine if the object they are manipulating is a valid object and to take appropriate action if the object they are manipulating is not valid. In the exercises, you are asked to modify the program of Fig 6.10 to return appropriate error values from set functions.

Figure 6.10 extends our **`Time`** class to include get and set functions for the **`hour`**, **`minute`**, and **`second`** private data members. The set functions strictly control the setting of the data members. Attempts to set any data member to an incorrect value cause the data member to be set to zero (thus leaving the data member in a consistent state). Each get function simply returns the appropriate data member's value. The program first uses the set functions to set the private data members of **`Time`** object **`t`** to valid values, then uses the get functions to retrieve the values for output. Next the set functions attempt to set the **`hour`** and **`second`** members to invalid values and the **`minute`** member to a valid value, and then the get functions retrieve the values for output. The output confirms that the invalid values cause the data members to be set to zero. Finally, the program sets the time to **`11:58:00`** and increments the minute value by 3 with a call to function **`incrementMinutes`**. Function **`incrementMinutes`** is a nonmember function that uses the get and set member functions to increment the **minute** member properly. Although this works, it incurs the performance burden of issuing multiple function calls. In the next chapter, we discuss the notion of friend functions as a means of eliminating this performance burden.

***Common Programming Error 6.8***

*A constructor can call other member functions of the class such as set or get functions, but because the constructor is initializing the object, the data members may not yet be in a consistent state. Using data members before they have been properly initialized can cause errors.*

Set functions are certainly important from a software engineering standpoint because they can perform validity checking. Set and get functions have another important software engineering advantage.

```
// TIME3.H
// Declaration of the Time class.
// Member functions defined in TIME3.CPP

// prevent multiple inclusions of header file
#ifndef TIME3_H
#define TIME3_H

class Time {
public:
   Time(int = 0, int = 0, int = 0);  // constructor

   // set functions
   void setTime(int, int, int);  // set hour, minute, second
   void setHour(int);        // set hour
   void setMinute(int);      // set minute
   void setSecond(int);      // set second

   // get functions
   int getHour();            // return hour
   int getMinute();          // return minute
   int getSecond();          // return second

   void printMilitary();     // output military time
   void printStandard();     // output standard time

private:
   int hour;                 // 0 - 23
   int minute;               // 0 - 59
   int second;               // 0 - 59
};

#endif
```

Fig. 6.10 Declaration of the **Time** class (part 1 of 4).

```
// TIME3.CPP
// Member function definitions for Time class.
#include "time3.h"
#include <iostream.h>

// Constructor function to initialize private data.
// Calls member function setTime to set variables.
// Default values are 0 (see class definition).
Time::Time(int hr, int min, int sec) { setTime(hr, min, sec); }

// Set the values of hour, minute, and second.
void Time::setTime(int h, int m, int s)
{
   hour = (h >= 0 && h < 24) ? h : 0;
   minute = (m >= 0 && m < 60) ? m : 0;
   second = (s >= 0 && s < 60) ? s : 0;
}

// Set the hour value
void Time::setHour(int h) { hour = (h >= 0 && h < 24) ? h : 0; }

// Set the minute value
void Time::setMinute(int m)
   { minute = (m >= 0 && m < 60) ? m : 0; }

// Set the second value
void Time::setSecond(int s)
   { second = (s >= 0 && s < 60) ? s : 0; }

// Get the hour value
int Time::getHour() { return hour; }

// Get the minute value
int Time::getMinute() { return minute; }

// Get the second value
int Time::getSecond() { return second; }

// Display military format time: HH:MM:SS
void Time::printMilitary()
{
   cout << (hour < 10 ? "0" : "") << hour << ":"
        << (minute < 10 ? "0" : "") << minute << ":"
        << (second < 10 ? "0" : "") << second;
}

// Display standard format time: HH:MM:SS AM (or PM)
void Time::printStandard()
{
   cout << ((hour == 0 || hour == 12) ? 12 : hour % 12) << ":"
        << (minute < 10 ? "0" : "") << minute << ":"
        << (second < 10 ? "0" : "") << second
        << (hour < 12 ? " AM" : " PM");
}
```

**Fig. 6.10** Member function definitions for `Time` class (part 2 of 4).

```
// FIG6_10.CPP
// Demonstrating the Time class set and get functions
#include <iostream.h>
#include "time3.h"

void incrementMinutes(Time &, int);

main()
{
   Time t;

   t.setHour(17);
   t.setMinute(34);
   t.setSecond(25);

   cout << "Result of setting all valid values:" << endl
        << "  Hour: " << t.getHour()
        << "  Minute: " << t.getMinute()
        << "  Second: " << t.getSecond() << endl << endl;

   t.setHour(234);        // invalid hour set to 0
   t.setMinute(43);
   t.setSecond(6373);     // invalid second set to 0

   cout << "Result of attempting to set invalid hour and"
        << " second:" << endl << "  Hour: " << t.getHour()
        << "  Minute: " << t.getMinute()
        << "  Second: " << t.getSecond() << endl << endl;

   t.setTime(11, 58, 0);
   incrementMinutes(t, 3);
   return 0;
}

void incrementMinutes(Time &tt, int count)
{
   cout << "Incrementing minute " << count
        << " times:" << endl << "Start time: ";
   tt.printStandard();

   for (int i = 1; i <= count; i++) {
      tt.setMinute((tt.getMinute() + 1) % 60);

      if (tt.getMinute() == 0)
         tt.setHour((tt.getHour() + 1) % 24);

      cout << endl << "minute + 1: ";
      tt.printStandard();
   }

   cout << endl;
}
```

**Fig. 6.10** Using set and get functions (part 3 of 4).

```
Result of setting all valid values:
  Hour: 17  Minute: 34  Second: 25

Result of attempting to set invalid hour and second:
  Hour: 0  Minute: 43  Second: 0

Incrementing minute 3 times:
Start time: 11:58:00 AM
minute + 1: 11:59:00 AM
minute + 1: 12:00:00 PM
minute + 1: 12:01:00 PM
```

**Fig. 6.10** Using set and get functions (part 4 of 4).

***Software Engineering Observation 6.18***

*Accessing private data through set and get member functions not only protects the data members from receiving invalid values, but it also insulates clients of the class from the representation of the data members. Thus, if the representation of the data changes for some reason (typically to reduce the amount of storage required or to improve performance), only the member functions need to change—the clients need not change as long as the interface provided by the member functions remains the same. The clients may, however, need to be recompiled.*

## 6.15 A Subtle Trap: Returning a Reference to Private Data Member

A reference to an object is an alias for the object itself and hence may be used on the left side of an assignment statement. In this context, the reference makes a perfectly acceptable lvalue that can receive a value. One way to use this capability (unfortunately!) is to have a public member function of a class return a non-**const** reference to a private data member of that class.

Figure 6.11 uses a simplified version of the **Time** class to demonstrate returning a reference to a private data member. Such a return actually makes a call to function **badSetHour** an alias for the private data member **hour**. The function call can be used in any way the private data member can be used, including as an lvalue in an assignment statement!

***Good Programming Practice 6.11***

*Never have a public member function return a non-**const** reference (or a pointer) to a private data member. Returning such a reference violates the encapsulation of the class.*

The program begins by declaring **Time** object **t** and reference **hourRef** that is assigned the reference returned by the call **t.badSetHour(20)**. The program displays the value of the alias **hourRef**. Next, the alias is used to set the value of **hour** to 30 (an invalid value) and the value is displayed again. Finally, the function call itself is used as an lvalue and assigned the value 74 (another invalid value), and the value is displayed.

```
// TIME4.H
// Declaration of the Time class.
// Member functions defined in TIME4.CPP

// prevent multiple inclusions of header file
#ifndef TIME4_H
#define TIME4_H

class Time {
public:
   Time(int = 0, int = 0, int = 0);
   void setTime(int, int, int);
   int getHour();
   int &badSetHour(int);   // DANGEROUS reference return
private:
   int hour;
   int minute;
   int second;
};

#endif
```

**Fig. 6.11** Returning a reference to a private data member (part 1 of 3) .

```
// TIME4.CPP
// Member function definitions for Time class.
#include "time4.h"
#include <iostream.h>

// Constructor function to initialize private data.
// Calls member function setTime to set variables.
// Default values are 0 (see class definition).
Time::Time(int hr, int min, int sec) { setTime(hr, min, sec); }

// Set the values of hour, minute, and second.
void Time::setTime(int h, int m, int s)
{
   hour = (h >= 0 && h < 24) ? h : 0;
   minute = (m >= 0 && m < 60) ? m : 0;
   second = (s >= 0 && s < 60) ? s : 0;
}

// Get the hour value
int Time::getHour() { return hour; }

// BAD PROGRAMMING PRACTICE:
// Returning a reference to a private data member.
int &Time::badSetHour(int hh)
{
   hour = (hh >= 0 && hh < 24) ? hh : 0;

   return hour;   // DANGEROUS reference return
}
```

**Fig. 6.11** Returning a reference to a private data member (part 2 of 3).

```
// FIG6_11.CPP
// Demonstrating a public member function that
// returns a reference to a private data member.
// Time class has been trimmed for this example.

#include <iostream.h>
#include "time4.h"

main()
{
   Time t;
   int &hourRef = t.badSetHour(20);

   cout << "Hour before modification: " << hourRef << endl;
   hourRef = 30;  // modification with invalid value
   cout << "Hour after modification: " << t.getHour() << endl;

   // Dangerous: Function call that returns
   // a reference can be used as an lvalue.
   t.badSetHour(12) = 74;
   cout << endl << "**********************************" << endl
        << "BAD PROGRAMMING PRACTICE!!!!!!!!!" << endl
        << "badSetHour as an lvalue, Hour: "
        << t.getHour()
        << endl << "**********************************" << endl;

   return 0;
}
```

```
Hour before modification: 20
Hour after modification: 30

**********************************
BAD PROGRAMMING PRACTICE!!!!!!!!!
badSetHour as an lvalue, Hour: 74
**********************************
```

**Fig. 6.11** Returning a reference to a private data member (part 3 of 3).

## 6.16 Assignment by Default Memberwise Copy

The assignment operator (=) is used to assign an object to another object of the same type. Such assignment is normally performed by *memberwise copy*—each member of one object is copied individually to the same member in another object (see Fig. 6.12). (Note: Memberwise copy can cause serious problems when used with a class whose data members contain dynamically allocated storage; in Chapter 8, "Operator Overloading," we will discuss these problems and show how to deal with them.)

Objects may be passed as function arguments and may be returned from functions. Such passing and returning is performed call-by-value by default—a copy of the object is passed or returned (we present several examples in Chapter 8, "Operator Overloading").

```
// FIG6_12.CPP
// Demonstrating that class objects can be assigned
// to each other using default memberwise copy
#include <iostream.h>

// Simple Date class
class Date {
public:
   Date(int = 1, int = 1, int = 1990);  // default constructor
   void print();
private:
   int month;
   int day;
   int year;
};

// Simple Date constructor with no range checking
Date::Date(int m, int d, int y)
{
   month = m;
   day = d;
   year = y;
}

// Print the Date in the form mm-dd-yyyy
void Date::print()
   { cout << month << '-' << day << '-' << year; }

main()
{
   Date date1(7, 4, 1993), date2;  // d2 defaults to 1/1/90

   cout << "date1 = ";
   date1.print();
   cout << endl << "date2 = ";
   date2.print();

   date2 = date1;   // assignment by default memberwise copy
   cout << endl << endl
        << "After default memberwise copy, date2 = ";
   date2.print();
   cout << endl;

   return 0;
}
```

```
date1 = 7-4-1993
date2 = 1-1-1990

After default memberwise copy, date2 = 7-4-1993
```

**Fig. 6.12** Assigning one object to another with default memberwise copy.

***Performance Tip 6.4***

*Passing an object call-by-value is good from a security standpoint because the called function has no access to the original object, but call-by-value can degrade performance when making a copy of a large object. An object can be passed call-by-reference by passing either a pointer or a reference to the object. Call-by-reference offers good performance but is weaker from a security standpoint because the called function is given access to the original object. Call-by-`const`-reference is a safe alternative.*

## 6.17 Software Reusability

People who write object-oriented programs concentrate on implementing useful classes. There is a tremendous opportunity to capture and catalog classes so that they can be accessed by large segments of the programming community. Many *class libraries* exist and others are being developed worldwide. There are efforts to make these libraries broadly accessible. Software could then be constructed from existing, well-defined, carefully tested, well-documented, portable, widely available components. This kind of software reusability can speed the development of powerful, high-quality software. *Rapid applications development (RAD)* becomes possible.

Significant problems must be solved, however, before the full potential of software reusability can be realized. We need cataloging schemes, licensing schemes, protection mechanisms to ensure that master copies of classes are not corrupted, description schemes so that designers of new systems can determine if existing objects meet their needs, browsing mechanisms to determine what classes are available and how closely they meet software developer requirements, and the like. Many interesting research and development problems need to be solved. These problems *will* be solved because the potential value of their solutions is enormous.

## 6.18 Case Study: Programming the Classes for the Elevator Simulator

In the "Thinking About Objects" sections of Chapters 1 through 5 we introduced the fundamentals of object orientation and walked you through an object-oriented design for an elevator simulator. In the body of Chapter 6, we introduced the details of programming and using C++ classes. At this point, you are ready (and probably eager!) to begin programming your elevator simulator.

***Elevator Laboratory Assignment 5***

1. For each of the classes you identified in the "Thinking About Objects" sections of Chapters 2 through 5, write an appropriate C++ class definition. For each class, include both a header file and a member function definition source file.
2. Write a driver program that tests each of these classes, and that attempts to run the complete elevator simulation. CAUTION: You will probably need to wait until you have studied Chapter 7, "Classes: Part II," before you will be able to complete a reasonable working version of your simulator—so be patient and implement only those portions of the elevator simulator that you can with the knowledge you have gained

in Chapter 6. In Chapter 7 you will learn about composition, i.e., creating classes that contain other classes as members; this technique might help you represent the button objects inside the elevator as members of the elevator, for example. Also in Chapter 7, you will learn how to create and destroy objects dynamically with **`new`** and **`delete`**; this will help you create new person objects as new people arrive in the simulation and destroy these person objects as people leave the simulation (after getting off the elevator).

3. For the first version of your simulator, design only a simple, text-oriented output that displays a message for each significant event that occurs. Your messages might include strings such as: "Person 1 arrives on Floor 1," "Person 1 presses Up Button on Floor 1," "Elevator arrives on Floor 1," "Person 1 enters Elevator," etc. Note that we suggest you capitalize the words of each message that represent objects in your simulation. Note also that you may choose to defer this portion of the lab assignment until you have read Chapter 7.
4. The more ambitious students will want to use an animated graphical output that shows the elevator moving up and down on the screen.

## Summary

- Structures are aggregate data types built using data of other types.
- The keyword **`struct`** introduces a structure definition. The body of a structure is delineated by braces (**`{`** and **`}`**). Every structure definition must end with a semicolon.
- A structure tag name can be used to declare variables of a structure type.
- Structure definitions do not reserve space in memory; they create new data types that are used to declare variables.
- Members of a structure or a class are accessed using the member access operators—the dot operator (**`.`**) and the arrow operator (**`->`**). The dot operator accesses a structure member via the object's variable name or a reference to the object. The arrow operator accesses a structure member via a pointer to the object.
- Drawbacks to creating new data types with **`struct`**s are the possibility of having uninitialized data; improper initialization; all programs using a **`struct`** must be changed if the **`struct`** implementation changes; and no protection is provided to ensure that data is kept in a consistent state with proper data values.
- Classes enable the programmer to model objects with attributes and behaviors. Class types can be defined in C++ using the keywords **`class`** and **`struct`**, but keyword **`class`** is normally used for this purpose.
- The class name can be used to declare objects of that class.
- Class definitions begin with the keyword **`class`**. The body of the class definition is delineated with braces (**`{`** and **`}`**). Class definitions terminate with a semicolon.
- Any data member or member function declared after **`public:`** in a class is visible to any function with access to an object of the class.

- Any data member or member function declared after **`private:`** is only visible to friends and other members of the class.
- Member access specifiers always end with a colon (**`:`**) and can appear multiple times and in any order in a class definition.
- Private data are not accessible from outside the class.
- The implementation of a class is said to be hidden from its clients.
- A constructor is a special member function with the same name as the class that is used to initialize the members of a class object. Constructors are called when an object of their class is instantiated.
- The function with the same name as the class but preceded with a tilde character (~) is called a destructor.
- The set of public member functions of a class is called the class's interface or public interface.
- When a member function is defined outside the class definition, the function name is preceded by the class name and the binary scope resolution operator (**`::`**).
- Member functions defined using the scope resolution operator outside a class definition are within that class's scope.
- Member functions defined in a class definition are automatically inlined. The compiler reserves the right not to inline any function.
- Calling member functions is more concise than calling functions in procedural programming because most data used by the member function is directly accessible in the object.
- Within a class's scope, class members may be referenced simply by their names. Outside a class's scope, class members are referenced through either an object name, a reference to an object, or a pointer to an object.
- Member selection operators **`.`** and **`->`** are used to access class members.
- A fundamental principle of good software engineering is to separate interface from implementation for ease of program modifiability.
- Class definitions are normally placed in header files and member function definitions are normally placed in source-code files of the same base name.
- The default access mode for classes is **`private`** so all members after the class header and before the first label are considered to be private.
- Public class members present a view of the services the class provides to the clients of the class.
- Access to a class's private data can be carefully controlled by the use of member functions called access functions. If a class wants to allow clients to read private data, the class can provide a "get" function. To enable clients to modify private data, the class can provide a "set" function.

- Data members of a class are normally made private and member functions of a class are normally made public. Some member functions may be private and serve as utility functions to the other functions of the class.
- Data members of a class cannot be initialized in a class definition. They must be initialized in a constructor, or their values may be set after their object is created.
- Constructors can be overloaded.
- Once a class object is properly initialized, all member functions that manipulate the object should ensure that the object remains in a consistent state.
- When an object of a class is declared, initializers can be provided. These initializers are passed to the class's constructor.
- Constructors can specify default arguments.
- Constructors may not specify return types, nor may they attempt to return values.
- If no constructor is defined for a class, the compiler creates a default constructor. A default constructor supplied by the compiler does not perform any initialization, so when the object is created, it is not guaranteed to be in a consistent state.
- The destructor of an automatic object is called when the object goes out of scope. The destructor itself does not actually destroy the object, but it does perform termination housekeeping before the system reclaims the object's storage.
- Destructors do not receive parameters and do not return values. A class may have only one destructor.
- The assignment operator (`=`) is used to assign an object to another object of the same type. Such assignment is normally performed by memberwise copy. Memberwise copy is not ideal for all classes.

## *Terminology*

`&` reference operator
abstract data type (ADT)
access function
attribute
behavior
binary scope resolution operator (`::`)
**`class`**
class member selector operator (`.`)
class definition
class scope
client of a class
consistent state for a data member
constructor
data member
data type
default constructor
destructor
encapsulation
enter a scope
extensibility
file scope
get function
global object
header file
implementation of a class
information hiding
initialize a class object
inline member function
instance of a class
instantiate an object of a class
interface to a class
leave scope

member access control
member access specifiers
member function
member initializer
memberwise copy
message
nonmember function
nonstatic local object
object
object-oriented programming (OOP)
predicate function
principle of least privilege
`private:`
procedural programming
programmer-defined type
`protected:`
public interface of a class
`public:`
query function
rapid applications development (RAD)
reusable code
scope resolution operator (`::`)
services of a class
set function
software reusability
source-code file
static local object
tilde (~) in destructor name
user-defined type
utility function

## Common Programming Errors

**6.1** Forgetting the semicolon at the end of a class (or structure) definition.

**6.2** Attempting to explicitly initialize a data member of a class in the class definition.

**6.3** Attempting to overload a member function with a function not in that class's scope.

**6.4** An attempt by a function which is not a member of a particular class (or a friend of that class) to access a private member of that class.

**6.5** Attempting to declare a return type for a constructor, and/or attempting to return a value from a constructor.

**6.6** Specifying default initializers for the same member function in both a header file and in the member function definition.

**6.7** Attempting to pass arguments to a destructor, to return values from a destructor, or to overload a destructor.

**6.8** A constructor can call other member functions of the class such as set or get functions, but because the constructor is initializing the object, the data members may not yet be in a consistent state. Using data members before they have been properly initialized can cause errors.

## Good Programming Practices

**6.1** Use each member access specifier only once in a class definition for clarity and readability. Place public members first where they are easy to locate.

**6.2** Use **`#ifndef`**, **`#define`** and **`#endif`** preprocessor directives to prevent header files from being included more than once in a program.

**6.3** Use the name of the header file with the period replaced by an underscore in the **`#ifndef`** and **`#define`** preprocessor directives of a header file.

**6.4** If you choose to list the private members first in a class definition, explicitly use the **`private`** member access specifier even though **`private`** is assumed by default. This improves program clarity. Our preference is to list the **`public`** members of a class first.

**6.5** Despite the fact that the **`public`** and **`private`** member access specifiers may be repeated and intermixed, list all the public members of a class first in one group and then list all the private members in another group. This focuses the client's attention on the class's public interface, rather than on the class's implementation.

6.6 Using the member access specifiers `public`, `protected`, and `private` only once each in any class definition avoids confusion.

6.7 When appropriate (almost always), provide a constructor to ensure that every object is properly initialized with meaningful values.

6.8 Every member function (and friend) that modifies the private data members of an object should ensure that the data remains in a consistent state.

6.9 Declare default function arguments only in the function prototype within the class definition in the header file.

6.10 Member functions that set the values of private data should verify that the intended new values are proper; if they are not, the set functions should place the private data members into an appropriate consistent state.

6.11 Never have a public member function return a non-`const` reference (or a pointer) to a private data member. Returning such a reference violates the encapsulation of the class.

## *Performance Tips*

6.1 Structures ordinarily pass call-by-value. To avoid the overhead of copying a structure, pass the structure call-by-reference.

6.2 To avoid the overhead of call-by-value yet still gain the benefit that the caller's original data is protected from modification, pass large-size arguments as `const` references.

6.3 Defining a small member function inside the class definition automatically inlines the member function (if the compiler chooses to do so). This can improve performance, but it does not promote the best software engineering.

6.4 Passing an object call-by-value is good from a security standpoint because the called function has no access to the original object, but call-by-value can degrade performance when making a copy of a large object. An object can be passed call-by-reference by passing either a pointer or a reference to the object. Call-by-reference offers good performance but is weaker from a security standpoint because the called function is given access to the original object. Call-by-`const`-reference is a safe alternative.

## *Software Engineering Observations*

6.1 It is important to write programs that are understandable and easy to maintain. Change is the rule rather than the exception. Programmers should anticipate that their code will be modified. As we will see, classes facilitate program modifiability.

6.2 Clients of a class use the class without knowing the internal details of how the class is implemented. If the class implementation is changed (to improve performance, for example), provided the class's interface remains constant, the class's client source code need not change. This makes it much easier to modify systems.

6.3 Member functions are usually shorter than equivalent functions in non-object-oriented programs because the data stored in data members has ideally been validated by a constructor and/or by member functions that store new data.

6.4 Clients have access to a class's interface but should not have access to a class's implementation.

6.5 Declaring member functions inside a class definition and defining those member functions outside that class definition separates the interface of a class from its implementation. This promotes good software engineering.

**6.6** Using an object-oriented programming approach can often simplify function calls by reducing the number of parameters to be passed. This benefit of object-oriented programming derives from the fact that encapsulation of data members and member functions within an object gives the member functions the right to access the data members.

**6.7** Place the class declaration in a header file to be included by any client that wants to use the class. This forms the class's public interface. Place the definitions of the class member functions in a source file. This forms the implementation of the class.

**6.8** Clients of a class do not need access to the class's source code in order to use the class. The clients do, however, need to be able to link to the class's object code.

**6.9** Information important to the interface to a class should be included in the header file. Information that will be used only internally in the class and will not be needed by clients of the class should be included in the unpublished source file. This is yet another example of the principle of least privilege.

**6.10** C++ encourages programs to be implementation independent. When the implementation of a class used by implementation-independent code changes, that code need not be modified, but it may need to be recompiled.

**6.11** Keep all the data members of a class private. Provide public member functions to set the values of private data members and to get the values of private data members. This architecture helps hide the implementation of a class from its clients, which reduces bugs and improves program modifiability.

**6.12** Class designers use private, protected, and public members to enforce the notion of information hiding and the principle of least privilege.

**6.13** The class designer need not provide set and/or get functions for each private data item; these capabilities should be provided only when it makes sense and after careful thought by the class designer.

**6.14** Making the data members of a class private and the member functions of the class public facilitates debugging because problems with data manipulations are localized to either the class's member functions or the friends of the class.

**6.15** Member functions tend to fall into a number of different categories: functions that read and return the value of private data members; functions that set the value of private data members; functions that implement the features of the class; and functions that perform various mechanical chores for the class such as initializing class objects, assigning class objects, converting between classes and built-in types or between classes and other classes, and handling memory for class objects.

**6.16** If a member function of a class already provides all or part of the functionality required by a constructor (or other member function) of the class, call that member function from the constructor (or other member function). This simplifies the maintenance of the code and reduces the likelihood of an error if the implementation of the code is modified.

**6.17** Making data members private and controlling access, especially write access, to those data members through public member functions helps ensure data integrity.

**6.18** Accessing private data through set and get member functions not only protects the data members from receiving invalid values, but it also insulates clients of the class from the representation of the data members. Thus, if the representation of the data changes for some reason (typically to reduce the amount of storage required or to improve performance), only the member functions need to change—the clients need not change as long as the interface provided by the member functions remains the same. The clients may, however, need to be recompiled.

## Self-Review Exercises

**6.1** Fill in the blanks in each of the following:

a) The keyword ________ introduces a structure definition.

b) Class members are accessed via the ________ operator in conjunction with an object of the class or via the ________ operator in conjunction with a pointer to an object of the class.

c) Members of a class specified as ________ are accessible only to member functions of the class and friends of the class.

d) A ________ is a special member function used to initialize the data members of a class.

e) The default access for members of a class is ________ .

f) A ________ function is used to assign values to private data members of a class.

g) ________ can be used to assign an object of a class to another object of the same class.

h) Member functions of a class are normally made ________ and data members of a class are normally made ________.

i) A ________ function is used to retrieve values of private data of a class.

j) The set of public member functions of a class is referred to as the class's ________ .

k) A class implementation is said to be hidden from its clients or ________.

l) The keywords ________ and ________ can be used to introduce a class definition.

m) Members of a class specified as ________ are accessible anywhere an object of the class is in scope.

**6.2** Find the error(s) in each of the following and explain how to correct it.

a) Assume the following prototype is declared in class `Time`.

```
void ~Time(int);
```

b) The following is a partial definition of class `Time`.

```
class Time {
public:
   // function prototypes
private:
   int hour = 0;
   int minute = 0;
   int second = 0;
};
```

c) Assume the following prototype is declared in class `Employee`.

```
int Employee(const char *, const char *);
```

## Answers to Self-Review Exercises

**6.1** a) `struct`. b) dot (`.`), arrow (`->`). c) `private`. d) constructor. e) `private`. f) set. g) Default memberwise copy (performed by the assignment operator). h) `public`, `private`. i) get. j) interface. k) encapsulated. l) `class`, `struct`. m) `public`.

**6.2** a) Error: Destructors are not allowed to return values or take arguments.
Correction: Remove the return type `void` and the parameter `int` from the declaration.

b) Error: Members cannot be explicitly initialized in the class definition.
Correction: Remove the explicit initialization from the class definition and initialize the data members in a constructor.

c) Error: Constructors are not allowed to return values.
Correction: Remove the return type `int` from the declaration.

## Exercises

**6.3** What is the purpose of the scope resolution operator?

**6.4** Compare and contrast the notions of `struct` and `class` in C++.

**6.5** Provide a constructor that is capable of using the current time from the `time()` function—declared in the C Standard Library header `time.h`—to initialize an object of the `Time` class.

**6.6** Create a class called `Complex` for performing arithmetic with complex numbers. Write a driver program to test your class.

Complex numbers have the form

`realPart + imaginaryPart *` *i*

where *i* is

$$\sqrt{-1}$$

Use floating-point variables to represent the private data of the class. Provide a constructor function that enables an object of this class to be initialized when it is declared. The constructor should contain default values in case no initializers are provided. Provide public member functions for each of the following:

a) Addition of two `Complex` numbers: The real parts are added together and the imaginary parts are added together.
b) Subtraction of two `Complex` numbers: The real part of the right operand is subtracted from the real part of the left operand and the imaginary part of the right operand is subtracted from the imaginary part of the left operand.
c) Printing `Complex` numbers in the form `(a, b)` where `a` is the real part and `b` is the imaginary part.

**6.7** Create a class called `Rational` for performing arithmetic with fractions. Write a driver program to test your class.

Use integer variables to represent the private data of the class—the numerator and the denominator. Provide a constructor function that enables an object of this class to be initialized when it is declared. The constructor should contain default values in case no initializers are provided and should store the fraction in reduced form (i.e., the fraction

$$\frac{2}{4}$$

would be stored in the object as 1 in the numerator and 2 in the denominator). Provide public member functions for each of the following:

a) Addition of two `Rational` numbers. The result should be stored in reduced form.
b) Subtraction of two `Rational` numbers. The result should be stored in reduced form.
c) Multiplication of two `Rational` numbers. The result should be stored in reduced form.
d) Division of two `Rational` numbers. The result should be stored in reduced form.
e) Printing `Rational` numbers in the form `a/b` where `a` is the numerator and `b` is the denominator.
f) Printing `Rational` numbers in floating point format.

**6.8** Modify the `Time` class of Fig. 6.10 to include a `tick` member function that increments the time stored in a `Time` object by one second. The `Time` object should always remain in a consistent state. Write a driver program that tests the **tick** member function in a loop that prints the time in standard format during each iteration of the loop to illustrate that the **tick** member function works correctly. Be sure to test the following cases:

a) Incrementing into the next minute.
b) Incrementing into the next hour.
c) Incrementing into the next day (i.e., 11:59:59 PM to 12:00:00 AM).

**6.9** Modify the **Date** class of Fig. 6.12 to perform error checking on the initializer values for data members **month**, **day**, and **year**. Also, provide a member function **nextDay** to increment the day by one. The **Date** object should always remain in a consistent state. Write a driver program that tests the **nextDay** function in a loop that prints the date during each iteration of the loop to illustrate that the **nextDay** function works correctly. Be sure to test the following cases:

a) Incrementing into the next month.
b) Incrementing into the next year.

**6.10** Combine the modified **Time** class of Exercise 6.8 and the modified **Date** class of Exercise 6.9 into one class called **DateAndTime** (in Chapter 9 we will discuss inheritance which will enable us to accomplish this task quickly without modifying the existing class definitions). Modify the **tick** function to call the **nextDay** function if the time is incremented into the next day. Modify function **printStandard** and **PrintMilitary** to output the date in addition to the time. Write a driver program to test the new class **DateAndTime**. Specifically test incrementing the time into the next day.

**6.11** Modify the set functions in the program of Fig. 6.10 to return appropiate error values if an attempt is made to set a data member of an object of class **Time** to an invalid value.

**6.12** Create a class **Rectangle**. The class has attributes **length** and **width**, each of which defaults to 1. It has member functions that calculate the **perimeter** and the **area** of the rectangle. It has set and get functions for both **length** and **width**. The set functions should verify that **length** and **width** are each floating point numbers larger than 0.0 and less than 20.0.

**6.13** Create a more sophisticated **Rectangle** class than the one you created in Exercise 6.12. This class stores only the Cartesian coordinates of the four corners of the rectangle. The constructor calls a set function that accepts four sets of coordinates and verifies that each of these is in the first quadrant with no single x or y coordinate larger than 20.0. The set function also verifies that the supplied coordinates do, in fact, specify a rectangle. Member functions calculate the **length**, **width**, **perimeter**, and **area**. The length is the larger of the two dimensions. Include a predicate function **square** which determines if the rectangle is a square.

**6.14** Modify the **Rectangle** class of Exercise 6.13 to include a **draw** function that displays the rectangle inside a 25-by-25 box enclosing the portion of the first quadrant in which the rectangle resides. Include a **setFillCharacter** function to specify the character out of which the body of the rectangle will be drawn. Include a **setPerimeterCharacter** function to specify the character that will be used to draw the border of the rectangle. If you feel ambitious you might include functions to scale the size of the rectangle, rotate it, and move it around within the designated portion of the first quadrant.

**6.15** Create a class **HugeInteger** which uses a 40-element array of digits to store integers as large as 40-digits each. Provide member functions **inputHugeInteger**, **outputHugeInteger**, **addHugeIntegers**, and **substractHugeIntegers**. For comparing **HugeInteger** objects provide functions **isEqualTo**, **isNotEqualTo**, **isGreaterThan**, **isLessThan**, **IsGreaterThanOrEqualTo**, and **isLessThanOrEqualTo**—each of these is a "predicate" function that simply returns **1** (true) if the relationship holds between the two huge integers and returns 0 (false) if the relationship does not hold. Provide a predicate function **isZero**. If you feel ambitious, also provide member functions **`multiplyHugeIntegers`**, **`divideHugeIntegers`**, and **`modulusHugeIntegers`**.

**`6.16`** Create a class **`TicTacToe`** that will enable you to write a complete program to play the game of tic-tac-toe. The class contains as private data a 3-by-3 double array of integers. The constructor should initialize the empty board to all zeros. Allow two human players. Wherever the first player moves, place a 1 in the specified square; place a 2 wherever the second player moves. Each move must be to an empty square. After each move determine if the game has been won, or if the game is a draw. If you feel ambitious, modify your program so that the computer makes the moves for one of the players automatically. Also, allow the player to specify whether he or she wants to go first or second. If you feel exceptionally ambitious, develop a program that will play three-dimensional tic-tac-toe on a 4-by-4-by-4 board (Caution: This is an extremely challenging project that could take many weeks of effort!).

# 7

# Classes Part II

**Objectives**

- To be able to create and destroy objects dynamically.
- To be able to specify constant objects and constant member functions.
- To understand the purpose of friend functions and friend classes.
- To understand how to use static data members and member functions.
- To understand the concept of a container class.
- To understand the notion of iterator classes that walk through the elements of container classes.
- To understand the use of the `this` pointer.

*But what, to serve our private ends,*
*Forbids the cheating of our friends?*
Charles Churchill

*Instead of this absurd division into sexes they ought to class people as static and dynamic.*
Evelyn Waugh

*This above all: to thine own self be true.*
William Shakespeare, Hamlet

*Have no friends not equal to yourself.*
Confucius

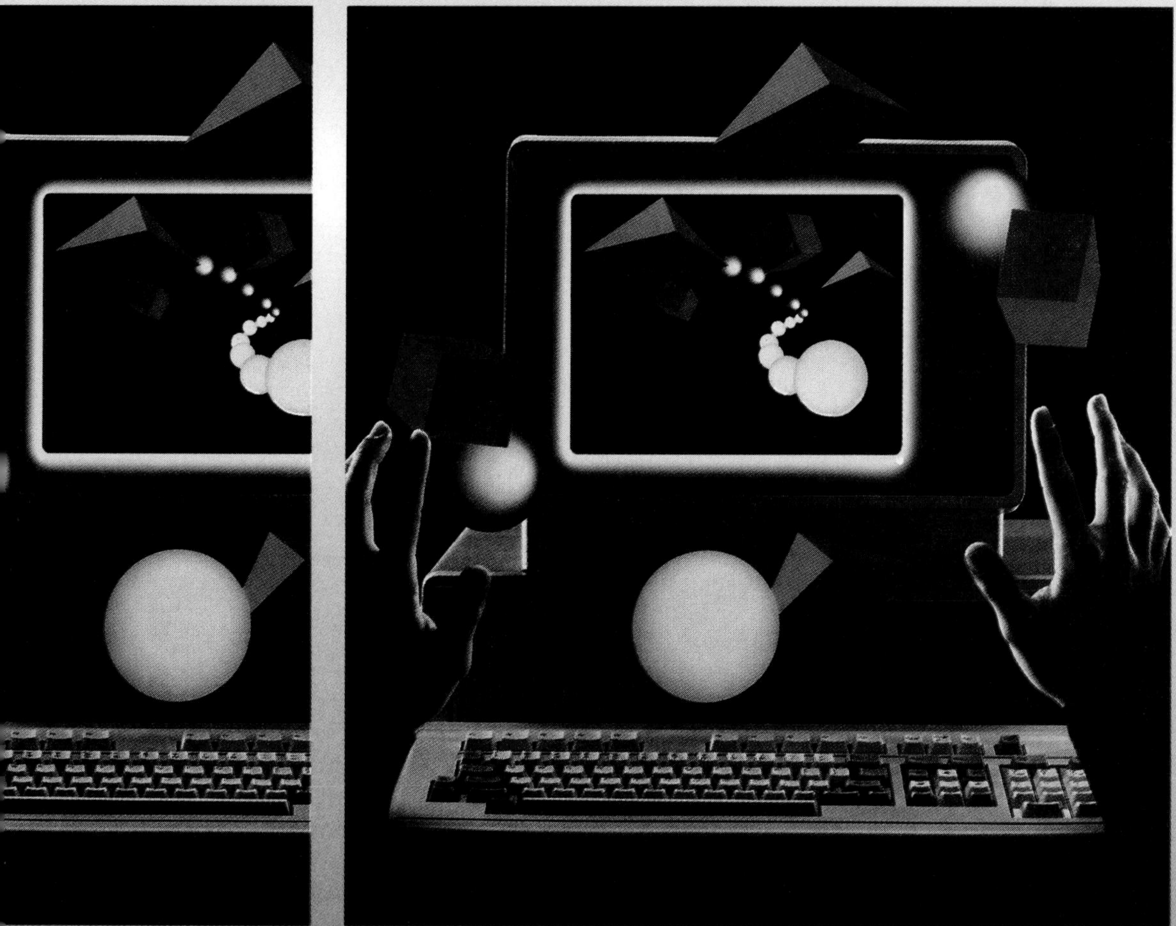

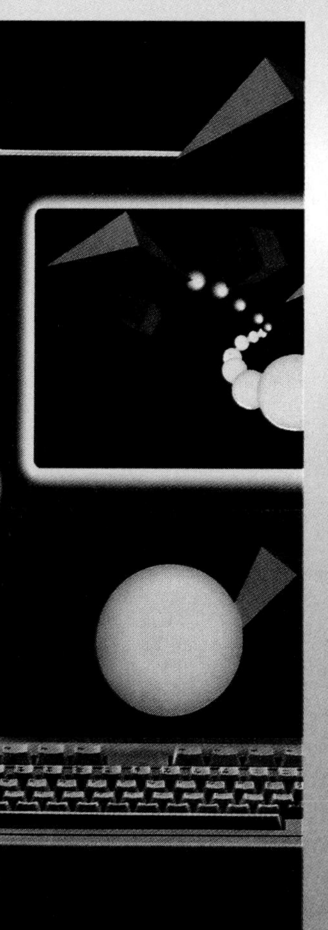

## Outline



## 7.1 Introduction

In this chapter we continue our study of classes and data abstraction. We discuss many more advanced topics and lay the groundwork for the discussion of classes and operator overloading in Chapter 8. The discussion in Chapters 6 through 8 encourages programmers to use objects. Then, Chapters 9 and 10 introduce inheritance and polymorphism—the techniques of truly object-oriented programming.

## 7.2 Constant Objects and Const Member Functions

We have repeatedly emphasized the *principle of least privilege* as one of the most fundamental principles of good software engineering. Let us see one way in which this principle applies to objects.

Some objects need to be modifiable and some do not. The programmer may use the keyword **`const`** to specify that an object is not modifiable, and that any attempt to modify the object is an error. For example,

```
const Time noon(12, 0, 0);
```

declares a **const** object **noon** of class **Time** and initializes it to 12 noon.

*Software Engineering Observation 7.1*

*Declaring an object as* `const` *helps enforce the principle of least privilege. Accidental attempts to modify the object are caught at compile time rather than causing execution-time errors.*

C++ compilers respect **const** declarations so rigidly that the compilers totally disallow any member function calls for **const** objects (some compilers provide only a warning). This is harsh because clients of the object will probably want to use various "get" member functions with the object, and these of course do not modify the object. To provide for this, the programmer may declare **const** member functions; only these can operate on **const** objects. Of course, **const** member functions cannot modify the object—the compiler disallows this.

A function is specified as **const** *both* in its declaration and in its definition by inserting the keyword **const** after the function's parameter list, and, in the case of the function definition, before the left brace that begins the function body. For example, the member function of some class **A**

```
int A::getValue() const {return privateDataMember};
```

which simply returns the value of one of the object's data members, is declared to be **const**. If a **const** member function is defined outside the class's definition, the member function's declaration and definition must each include **const**.

*Common Programming Error 7.1*

*Defining as* `const` *a member function that modifies a data member of an object.*

*Common Programming Error 7.2*

*Defining as* `const` *a member function that calls a non-*`const` *member function.*

*Common Programming Error 7.3*

*Calling a non-*`const` *member function for a* `const` *object.*

*Common Programming Error 7.4*

*Attempting to modify a* `const` *object.*

*Software Engineering Observation 7.2*

*A* `const` *member function can be overloaded with a non-*`const` *version. The choice of which overloaded member function to use is automatically made by the compiler based on whether the object has been declared* `const` *or not.*

An interesting problem arises here for constructors and destructors, each of which often needs to modify objects. The **const** declaration is not required for constructors and destructors of **const** objects. A constructor must be allowed to modify an object so that the object can be initialized properly. A destructor must be able to perform its termination housekeeping chores before an object is destroyed.

The program of Fig. 7.1 instantiates a constant object of class **Time** and attempts to modify the object with non-constant member functions **setHour**, **setMinute**, and **setSecond**. The warnings generated by the Borland C++ compiler are shown in the output window. A compiler option was set so that the compiler would not produce an executable file if any warning messages were produced.

*Good Programming Practice 7.1*

*Declare as* **const** *all member functions that are intended to be used with* **const** *objects.*

A **const** object cannot be modified by assignment so it *must* be initialized. When a a data member of a class is declared **const**, a *member initializer* must be used to provide the constructor with the initial value of the data member for an object of the class. Figure 7.2 demonstrates the uses of the member initializer syntax to initialize **const** data member **increment** of class **Increment**. The constructor for **Increment** is modified as follows (see page 400; below Fig. 7.1, part 3):

```
// TIME5.H
// Declaration of the class Time.
// Member functions defined in TIME5.CPP

#ifndef TIME5_H
#define TIME5_H

class Time {
public:
   Time(int = 0, int = 0, int = 0);  // default constructor

   // set functions
   void setTime(int, int, int);  // set time
   void setHour(int);        // set hour
   void setMinute(int);      // set minute
   void setSecond(int);      // set second

   // get functions (normally declared const)
   int getHour() const;     // return hour
   int getMinute() const; // return minute
   int getSecond() const; // return second

   // print functions (normally declared const)
   void printMilitary() const;   // print military time
   void printStandard() const;   // print standard time
private:
   int hour;                 // 0 - 23
   int minute;               // 0 - 59
   int second;               // 0 - 59
};

#endif
```

**Fig. 7.1** Using a **Time** class with **const** objects and **const** member functions (part 1 of 3).

```
// TIME5.CPP
// Member function definitions for Time class.
#include <iostream.h>
#include "time5.h"

// Constructor function to initialize private data.
// Default values are 0 (see class definition).
Time::Time(int hr, int min, int sec) { setTime(hr, min, sec); }

// Set the values of hour, minute, and second.
void Time::setTime(int h, int m, int s)
{
   hour = (h >= 0 && h < 24) ? h : 0;
   minute = (m >= 0 && m < 60) ? m : 0;
   second = (s >= 0 && s < 60) ? s : 0;
}

// Set the hour value
void Time::setHour(int h) { hour = (h >= 0 && h < 24) ? h : 0; }

// Set the minute value
void Time::setMinute(int m)
   { minute = (m >= 0 && m < 60) ? m : 0; }

// Set the second value
void Time::setSecond(int s)
   { second = (s >= 0 && s < 60) ? s : 0; }

// Get the hour value
int Time::getHour() const { return hour; }

// Get the minute value
int Time::getMinute() const { return minute; }

// Get the second value
int Time::getSecond() const { return second; }

// Display military format time: HH:MM:SS
void Time::printMilitary() const
{
   cout << (hour < 10 ? "0" : "") << hour << ":"
        << (minute < 10 ? "0" : "") << minute << ":"
        << (second < 10 ? "0" : "") << second;
}

// Display standard format time: HH:MM:SS AM (or PM)
void Time::printStandard() const
{
   cout << ((hour == 12) ? 12 : hour % 12) << ":"
        << (minute < 10 ? "0" : "") << minute << ":"
        << (second < 10 ? "0" : "") << second
        << (hour < 12 ? " AM" : " PM");
}
```

**Fig. 7.1** Using a **Time** class with **const** objects and **const** member functions (part 2 of 3).

```
// FIG7_1.CPP
// Attempting to access a const object with
// non-const member functions.

#include <iostream.h>
#include "time5.h"

main()
{
   const Time t(19, 33, 52);   // constant object

   t.setHour(12);     // ERROR: non-const member function
   t.setMinute(20);   // ERROR: non-const member function
   t.setSecond(39);   // ERROR: non-const member function

   return 0;
}
```

```
Compiling FIG7_1.CPP:
Warning FIG7_1.CPP: Non-const function
   Time::setHour(int) called for const object
Warning FIG7_1.CPP: Non-const function
   Time::setMinute(int) called for const object
Warning FIG7_1.CPP: Non-const function
   Time::setSecond(int) called for const object
```

**Fig. 7.1** Using a `Time` class with `const` objects and `const` member functions (part 3 of 3).

```
Increment::Increment(int c, int i)
   : increment(i)
{ count = c; }
```

The notation `: increment(i)` causes increment to be initialized to the value `i`. If multiple member initializers are needed, simply include them in a comma-separated list after the colon. All data members can be initialized using member initializer syntax.

Figure 7.3 illustrates the compiler errors issued by the Borland C++ compiler for a program that attempts to initialize `increment` with an assignment statement rather than with a member initializer.

***Common Programming Error 7.5***

*Not providing a member initializer for a* `const` *data member.*

***Software Engineering Observation 7.3***

*Constant class members (*`const` *objects and* `const` *"variables") must be initialized with member initializer syntax. Assignments are not allowed.*

```
// FIG7_2.CPP
// Using a member initializer to initialize a
// constant of a built-in data type.

#include <iostream.h>

class Increment {
public:
   Increment(int c = 0, int i = 1);
   void addIncrement() { count += increment; }
   void print() const;

private:
   int count;
   const int increment;        // const data member
};

// Constructor for class Increment
Increment::Increment(int c, int i)
   : increment(i)    // initializer for const member
{ count = c; }

// Print the data
void Increment::print() const
{
   cout << "count = " << count
        << ", increment = " << increment << endl;
}

main()
{
   Increment value(10, 5);

   cout << "Before incrementing: ";
   value.print();

   for (int j = 1; j <= 3; j++) {
      value.addIncrement();
      cout << "After increment " << j << ": ";
      value.print();
   }

   return 0;
}
```

```
Before incrementing: count = 10, increment = 5
After increment 1: count = 15, increment = 5
After increment 2: count = 20, increment = 5
After increment 3: count = 25, increment = 5
```

**Fig. 7.2** Using a member initializer to initialize a constant of a built-in data type.

```
// FIG7_3.CPP
// Attempting to initialize a constant of
// a built-in data type with an assignment.
#include <iostream.h>

class Increment {
public:
   Increment(int c = 0, int i = 1);
   void addIncrement() { count += increment; }
   void print() const;
private:
   int count;
   const int increment;
};

// Constructor for class Increment
Increment::Increment(int c, int i)
{              // Constant member 'increment' is not initialized
   count = c;
   increment = i;  // ERROR: Cannot modify a const object
}

// Print the data
void Increment::print() const
{
   cout << "count = " << count
        << ", increment = " << increment << endl;
}

main()
{
   Increment value(10, 5);

   cout << "Before incrementing: ";
   value.print();

   for (int j = 1; j <= 3; j++) {
      value.addIncrement();
      cout << "After increment " << j << ": ";
      value.print();
   }

   return 0;
}
```

```
Compiling FIG7_3.CPP:
Warning FIG7_3.CPP 18: Constant member 'increment' is
   not initialized
Error FIG7_3.CPP 20: Cannot modify a const object
Warning FIG7_3.CPP 21: Parameter 'i' is never used
```

**Fig. 7.3** Erroneous attempt to initialize a constant of a built-in data type by assignment.

## 7.3 Composition: Classes as Members of Other Classes

An **AlarmClock** class object needs to know when it is supposed to sound its alarm, so why not include a **Time** object as a member of the **AlarmClock** object? Such a capability is called *composition.* A class can have objects of other classes as members.

***Software Engineering Observation 7.4***

*One form of software reusability is composition in which a class has objects of other classes as members.*

When an object enters scope, its constructor is called automatically, so we need to specify how arguments are passed to member-object constructors. Member objects are constructed in the order in which they are declared (not in the order they are listed in the constructor's member initializer list) and before their enclosing class objects are constructed.

Figure 7.4 uses class **Employee** and class **Date** to demonstrate objects as members of other objects. Class **Employee** contains private data members **lastName**, **firstName**, **birthDate**, and **hireDate**. Members **birthDate** and **hireDate** are objects of class **Date** which contains private data members **month**, **day** and **year**. The program instantiates an **Employee** object, and initializes and displays its data members. Note the syntax of the function header in the **Employee** constructor definition:

```
Employee::Employee(char *fname, char *lname,
                   int bmonth, int bday, int byear,
                   int hmonth, int hday, int hyear)
   : birthDate(bmonth, bday, byear), hireDate(hmonth, hday, hyear)
```

```
// DATE1.H
// Declaration of the Date class.
// Member functions defined in DATE1.CPP
#ifndef DATE1_H
#define DATE1_H

class Date {
public:
   Date(int = 1, int = 1, int = 1900);  // default constructor
   void print() const;  // print date in month/day/year format
private:
   int month;  // 1-12
   int day;    // 1-31 based on month
   int year;   // any year

   // utility function to test proper day for month and year
   int checkDay(int);
};

#endif
```

**Fig. 7.4** Using member-object initializers (part 1 of 5).

```
// DATE1.CPP
// Member function definitions for Date class.

#include <iostream.h>
#include "date1.h"

// Constructor: Confirm proper value for month;
// call utility function checkDay to confirm proper
// value for day.
Date::Date(int mn, int dy, int yr)
{
   if (mn > 0 && mn <= 12)         // validate the month
      month = mn;
   else {
      month = 1;
      cout << "Month " << mn << " invalid. Set to month 1."
           << endl;
   }

   year = yr;                      // could also check
   day = checkDay(dy);             // validate the day

   cout << "Date object constructor for date ";
   print();
   cout << endl;
}

// Utility function to confirm proper day value
// based on month and year.
int Date::checkDay(int testDay)
{
   static int daysPerMonth[13] = {0, 31, 28, 31, 30,
               31, 30, 31, 31, 30,
               31, 30, 31};

   if (testDay > 0 && testDay <= daysPerMonth[month])
      return testDay;

   if (month == 2 &&      // February: Check for possible leap year
       testDay == 29 &&
       (year % 400 == 0 || (year % 4 == 0 && year % 100 != 0)))
      return testDay;

   cout << "Day " << testDay << " invalid. Set to day 1." << endl;

   return 1;  // leave object in consistent state if bad value
}

// Print Date object in form  month/day/year
void Date::print() const
   { cout << month << '/' << day << '/' << year; }
```

**Fig. 7.4** Using member-object initializers (part 2 of 5).

```
// EMPLY1.H
// Declaration of the Employee class.
// Member functions defined in EMPLY1.CPP
#ifndef EMPLY1_H
#define EMPLY1_H

#include "date1.h"

class Employee {
public:
   Employee(char *, char *, int, int, int, int, int, int);
   void print() const;
private:
   char lastName[25];
   char firstName[25];
   Date birthDate;
   Date hireDate;
};

#endif
```

Fig. 7.4 Using member-object initializers (part 3 of 5).

The constructor takes eight arguments (**fname**, **lname**, **bmonth**, **bday**, **byear**, **hmonth**, **hday**, and **hyear**). The colon in the header separates the member initializers from the parameter list. The member initializers specify the **Employee** arguments passed to the constructors of the member objects. Thus, **bmonth**, **bday**, and **byear** are passed to the **birthDate** constructor, and **hmonth**, **hday**, and **hyear** are passed to the **hireDate** constructor. Multiple member initializers are separated by commas.

A member object does not need to be initialized through a member initializer. If a member initializer is not provided, the member object's default constructor will be called automatically. Values, if any, established by the default constructor can then be overridden by set functions.

***Common Programming Error 7.6***

*Not providing a default constructor for a member object when no member initializer is provided for that member object. This can result in an uninitialized member object.*

***Performance Tip 7.1***

*Initialize member objects explicitly through member initializers. This eliminates the overhead of doubly initializing member objects—once when the member object's default constructor is called and again when set functions are used to initialize the member object.*

## 7.4 Friend Functions and Friend Classes

A *friend function* of a class is defined outside that class's scope, yet has the right to access **private** (and as we will see in Chapter 9, "Inheritance," **protected**) members of the class. A function or an entire class may be declared to be a **friend** of another class.

```
// EMPLY1.CPP
// Member function definitions for Employee class.
#include <iostream.h>
#include <string.h>
#include "emply1.h"
#include "date1.h"

Employee::Employee(char *fname, char *lname,
                   int bmonth, int bday, int byear,
                   int hmonth, int hday, int hyear)
   : birthDate(bmonth, bday, byear), hireDate(hmonth, hday, hyear)
{
   // copy fname into firstName and be sure that it fits
   int length = strlen(fname);
   length = length < 25 ? length : 24;
   strncpy(firstName, fname, length);
   firstName[length] = '\0';

   // copy lname into lastName and be sure that it fits
   length = strlen(lname);
   length = length < 25 ? length : 24;
   strncpy(lastName, lname, 24);
   lastName[length] = '\0';

   cout << "Employee object constructor: "
        << firstName << ' ' << lastName << endl;
}

void Employee::print() const
{
   cout << lastName << ", " << firstName << endl << "Hired: ";
   hireDate.print();
   cout << "  Birthday: ";
   birthDate.print();
   cout << endl;
}
```

Fig. 7.4 Using member-object initializers (part 4 of 5).

Friend functions are used to enhance performance. A mechanical example is shown here of how a friend function works. Later in the book, friend functions are used to overload operators for use with classes and to create iterator classes. Objects of an iterator class are used to successively select an item or perform an operation on an item in a container class (see Section 7.9) object. Objects of container classes are capable of storing many items in a similar fashion to an array.

To declare a function as a **friend** of a class, precede the function prototype in the class definition with the keyword **friend**. To declare class **ClassTwo** as a friend of class **ClassOne** place a declaration of the form

```
friend ClassTwo;
```

in the definition of class **ClassOne**.

```
// FIG7_4.CPP
// Demonstrating an object with a member object.
#include <iostream.h>
#include "emply1.h"

main()
{
   Employee e("Bob", "Jones", 7, 24, 49, 3, 12, 88);

   cout << endl;
   e.print();

   cout << endl << "Test Date constructor with invalid values:"
        << endl;
   Date d(14, 35, 94);  // invalid Date values

   return 0;
}
```

```
Date object constructor for date 7/24/49
Date object constructor for date 3/12/88
Employee object constructor: Bob Jones

Jones, Bob
Hired: 3/12/88  Birthday: 7/24/49

Test Date constructor with invalid values:
Month 14 invalid. Set month to 1.
Day 35 invalid. Set to day 1.
Date object constructor for date 1/1/94
```

**Fig. 7.4** Using member-object initializers (part 5 of 5).

***Software Engineering Observation 7.5***

*Member access notions of* `private`, `protected`, *and* `public` *are not relevant to friendship declarations, so friendship declarations can be placed anywhere in the class definition.*

***Good Programming Practice 7.2***

*Place all friendship declarations first in the class immediately after the class header and do not precede them with any member-access specifier.*

Friendship is granted, not taken, i.e., for class B to be a friend of class A, class A must declare that class B is its friend. Also, friendship is neither symmetric nor transitive, i.e., if class A is a friend of class B, and class B is a friend of class C, you cannot infer that class B is a friend of class A, that class C is a friend of class B, or that class A is a friend of class C.

***Software Engineering Observation 7.6***

*Some people in the OOP community feel that "friendship" corrupts information hiding and weakens the value of the object-oriented design approach.*

The program of Fig. 7.5 demonstrates the declaration and use of friend function **setX** for setting the private data member **x** of class **count**. Note that the **friend** declaration appears first (by convention) in the class declaration, even before public member functions are declared. The program of Fig. 7.6 demonstrates the messages produced by the compiler when non-friend function **cannotSetX** is called to modify private data member **x**. Figures 7.5 and 7.6 are intended to introduce the "mechanics" of using friend functions—practical examples of using friend functions appear in forthcoming chapters.

```
// FIG7_5.CPP
// Friends can access private members of a class.
#include <iostream.h>

// Modified Count class
class Count {
   friend void setX(Count &, int);  // friend declaration
public:
   Count() { x = 0; }                // constructor
   void print() const { cout << x << endl; }  // output
private:
   int x;   // data member
};

// Can modify private data of Count because
// setX is declared as a friend function of Count
void setX(Count &c, int val)
{
   c.x = val;  // legal: setX is a friend of Count
}

main()
{
   Count object;

   cout << "object.x after instantiation: ";
   object.print();
   cout << "object.x after call to setX friend function: ";
   setX(object, 8);  // set x with a friend
   object.print();

   return 0;
}
```

```
object.x after instantiation: 0
object.x after call to setX friend function: 8
```

**Fig. 7.5** Friends can access private members of a class.

```
// FIG7_6.CPP
// Non-friend/non-member functions cannot access
// private data of a class.
#include <iostream.h>

// Modified Count class
class Count {
public:
   Count() { x = 0; }                          // constructor
   void print() const { cout << x << endl; }  // output
private:
   int x;   // data member
};

// Function tries to modify private data of Count,
// but cannot because it is not a friend of Count.
void cannotSetX(Count &c, int val)
{
   c.x = val;  // ERROR: 'Count::x' is not accessible
}

main()
{
   Count object;

   cannotSetX(object, 3); // cannotSetX is not a friend

   return 0;
}
```

```
Compiling FIG7_6.CPP:
Error FIG7_6.CPP 17: 'Count::x' is not accessible
Warning FIG7_6.CPP 18: Parameter 'c' is never used
Warning FIG7_6.CPP 18: Parameter 'val' is never used
```

**Fig. 7.6** Non-friend/non-member functions cannot access private class members.

It is possible to specify overloaded functions as friends of a class. Each overloaded function intended to be a friend must be explicitly declared in the class definition as a friend of the class.

## 7.5 Using the `this` Pointer

When a member function references another member of a class for a specific object of that class, how does C++ ensure that the proper object is referenced? The answer is that each object maintains a pointer to itself—called the ***this** pointer*—that is an implicit argument in all references to members within that object. The **this** pointer may also be used explicitly. Each object can determine its own address by using the **this** keyword.

The **this** pointer is implicitly used to reference both the data members and member functions of an object. The type of the **this** pointer depends on the type of the object and whether the member function in which **this** is used is declared **const**. In a non-constant member function of class **Employee** the **this** pointer has type **Employee * const** (a constant pointer to an **Employee** object). In a constant member function of class **Employee** the **this** pointer has type **const Employee * const** (a constant pointer to an **Employee** object that is constant).

For now, we show a simple example of using the **this** pointer explicitly; later, we show some substantial and subtle examples of using **this**. Every member function has access to the **this** pointer to the object for which the member is being invoked.

***Performance Tip 7.2***

*For reasons of economy of storage, only one copy of each member function exists per class, and this member function is invoked by every object of that class. Each object, on the other hand, has its own copy of the class's data members.*

Figure 7.7 demonstrates the explicit use of the **this** pointer to enable a member function of class **Test** to print the private data **x** of a **Test** object.

```
// FIG7_7.CPP
// Using the this pointer to refer to object members.
#include <iostream.h>

class Test {
public:
   Test(int = 0);                    // default constructor
   void print() const;
private:
   int x;
};

Test::Test(int a) { x = a; }         // constructor

void Test::print() const
{
   cout << "        x = " << x << endl
        << "  this->x = " << this->x << endl
        << "(*this).x = " << (*this).x << endl;
}

main()
{
   Test a(12);

   a.print();

   return 0;
}
```

```
        x = 12
  this->x = 12
(*this).x = 12
```

Fig. 7.7 Using the **this** pointer.

For illustration purposes, the **print** member function in Fig. 7.7 first prints **x** directly. Then, the program uses two different notations for accessing **x** through the **this** pointer—the arrow operator (**->**) off the **this** pointer and the dot operator (**.**) off the dereferenced **this** pointer.

Note the parentheses around ***this** when used with the dot member selection operator (**.**). The parentheses are needed because the dot operator has higher precedence than the ***** operator. Without the parentheses, the expression

```
*this.x
```

would be evaluated as if it were parenthesized as follows:

```
*(this.x)
```

The C++ compiler would treat this expression as a syntax error because the member selection operator cannot be used with a pointer.

***Common Programming Error 7.7***

*Attempting to use the member selection operator (**.**) with a pointer to an object (the member selection operator may only be used with an object or with a reference to an object).*

One interesting use of the **this** pointer is to prevent an object from being assigned to itself. As we will see in Chapter 8, "Operator Overloading," self-assignment can cause serious errors when the objects contain pointers to dynamically allocated storage.

Another use of the **this** pointer is in enabling concatenated member function calls. Figure 7.8 illustrates returning a reference to a **Time** object to enable member function calls of class **Time** to be concatenated. Member functions **setTime**, **setHour**, **setMinute**, and **setSecond** each return ***this** with a return type of **Time &**.

Why does the technique of returning ***this** as a reference work? The dot operator (**.**) associates from left to right, so the expression

```
t.setHour(18).setMinute(30).setSecond(22);
```

first evaluates t.**setHour(18)** then returns a reference to object **t** as the value of this function call. The remaining expression is then interpreted as

```
t.setMinute(30).setSecond(22);
```

The **t.setMinute(30)** call executes and returns the equivalent of **t**. The remaining expression is interpreted as

```
t.setSecond(22);
```

Note the calls

```
t.setTime(20, 20, 20).printStandard();
```

also use the concatenation feature. These calls must appear in this order in this expression because **printStandard** as defined in the class does not return a reference to **t**. Placing the call to **printStandard** in the preceding statement before the call to **setTime** results in a syntax error.

```
// TIME6.H
// Declaration of class Time.
// Member functions defined in TIME6.CPP

#ifndef TIME6_H
#define TIME6_H

class Time {
public:
   Time(int = 0, int = 0, int = 0);  // default constructor

   // set functions
   Time &setTime(int, int, int);  // set hour, minute, second
   Time &setHour(int);     // set hour
   Time &setMinute(int);   // set minute
   Time &setSecond(int);   // set second

   // get functions (normally declared const)
   int getHour() const;    // return hour
   int getMinute() const; // return minute
   int getSecond() const; // return second

   // print functions (normally declared const)
   void printMilitary() const;  // print military time
   void printStandard() const;  // print standard time
private:
   int hour;               // 0 - 23
   int minute;             // 0 - 59
   int second;             // 0 - 59
};

#endif
```

**Fig. 7.8** Chaining member function calls (part 1 of 4).

```
// TIME6.CPP
// Member function definitions for Time class.
#include "time6.h"
#include <iostream.h>

// Constructor function to initialize private data.
// Calls member function setTime to set variables.
// Default values are 0 (see class definition).
Time::Time(int hr, int min, int sec) { setTime(hr, min, sec); }

// Set the values of hour, minute, and second.
Time &Time::setTime(int h, int m, int s)
{
   hour = (h >= 0 && h < 24) ? h : 0;
   minute = (m >= 0 && m < 60) ? m : 0;
   second = (s >= 0 && s < 60) ? s : 0;
   return *this;   // enables chaining
}
```

**Fig. 7.8** Chaining member function calls (part 2 of 4).

```
// TIME6.CPP: Continued

// Set the hour value
Time &Time::setHour(int h)
{
   hour = (h >= 0 && h < 24) ? h : 0;

   return *this;   // enables chaining
}

// Set the minute value
Time &Time::setMinute(int m)
{
   minute = (m >= 0 && m < 60) ? m : 0;

   return *this;   // enables chaining
}

// Set the second value
Time &Time::setSecond(int s)
{
   second = (s >= 0 && s < 60) ? s : 0;

   return *this;   // enables chaining
}

// Get the hour value
int Time::getHour() const { return hour; }

// Get the minute value
int Time::getMinute() const { return minute; }

// Get the second value
int Time::getSecond() const { return second; }

// Display military format time: HH:MM:SS
void Time::printMilitary() const
{
   cout << (hour < 10 ? "0" : "") << hour << ":"
        << (minute < 10 ? "0" : "") << minute << ":"
        << (second < 10 ? "0" : "") << second;
}

// Display standard format time: HH:MM:SS AM (or PM)
void Time::printStandard() const
{
   cout << ((hour == 0 || hour == 12) ? 12 : hour % 12) << ":"
        << (minute < 10 ? "0" : "") << minute << ":"
        << (second < 10 ? "0" : "") << second
        << (hour < 12 ? " AM" : " PM");
}
```

**Fig. 7.8** Chaining member function calls (part 3 of 4).

```
// FIG7_8.CPP
// Chaining member function calls together
// with the this pointer
#include <iostream.h>
#include "time6.h"

main()
{
   Time t;

   t.setHour(18).setMinute(30).setSecond(22);
   cout << "Military time: ";
   t.printMilitary();
   cout << endl << "Standard time: ";
   t.printStandard();

   cout << endl << endl << "New standard time: ";
   t.setTime(20, 20, 20).printStandard();
   cout << endl;

   return 0;
}
```

```
Military time: 18:30:22
Standard time: 6:30:22 PM

New standard time: 8:20:20 PM
```

**Fig. 7.8** Chaining member function calls (part 4 of 4).

## 7.6 Dynamic Memory Allocation with Operators New and Delete

The ***new*** and ***delete*** operators provide a nicer means of performing dynamic memory allocation (for any built-in or user-defined type) than with **malloc** and **free** function calls in C. Consider the following code

```
TypeName *typeNamePtr;
```

In ANSI C, to dynamically create an object of type **TypeName**, you would say

```
typeNamePtr = malloc(sizeof(TypeName));
```

This requires a function call to **malloc** and an explicit reference to the **sizeof** operator. In versions of C prior to ANSI C, you would also have to cast the pointer returned by **malloc** with the cast **(TypeName *)**. Function **malloc** does not provide any method of initializing the block of memory allocated. In C++, you simply write

```
typeNamePtr = new TypeName;
```

The **new** operator automatically creates an object of the proper size, calls the constructor for the object and returns a pointer of the correct type. If **new** is unable to find space, it returns a **0** pointer. To free the space for this object in C++ you must use the **delete** operator as follows:

```
delete typeNamePtr;
```

C++ allows you to provide an *initializer* for a newly created object as in:

```
float *thingPtr = new float (3.14159);
```

which initializes a newly created **float** object to **3.14159**.

An array can be created and assigned to **chessBoardPtr** as follows:

```
int *chessBoardPtr = new int[8][8];
```

This array can be deleted with the statement

```
delete [] chessBoardPtr;
```

As we will see, using **new** and **delete** instead of **malloc** and **free** offers other benefits as well. In particular, **new** automatically invokes the constructor, and **delete** automatically invokes the class's destructor.

***Common Programming Error 7.8***

*Mixing* **new***-and-***delete***-style dynamic memory allocation with* **malloc***-and-***free***-style dynamic memory allocation: Space created by* **malloc** *cannot be freed by* **delete***; objects created by* **new***, cannot be deleted by* **free***.*

***Good Programming Practice 7.3***

*Although C++ programs can contain storage created by* **malloc** *and deleted by* **free***, and objects created by* **new** *and deleted by* **delete***, it is best to use only* **new** *and* **delete***.*

## 7.7 Static Class Members

Normally, each object of a class has its own copy of all the data members of the class. In certain cases only one copy of a particular data member should be shared by all objects of a class. A static data member is used for these and other reasons. A static data member represents "class-wide" information. The declaration of a static member begins with the keyword **static**.

***Performance Tip 7.3***

*Use static data members to save storage when a single copy of the data will suffice.*

Although static data members may seem like global variables, static data members have class scope. Static members can be public, private or protected. Static data members *must* be initialized *once* (and only once) at file scope. Public static class members can be accessed through any object of that class, or they can be accessed through the class name using the binary scope resolution operator. Private and protected static class members must be accessed through public member functions of the class or through friends of the class. Static class members exist even when no objects of that class exist. To access a public static class member when no objects of the class exist, simply prefix the class name and the binary scope resolution operator to the data member. To access a private or protected static class member when no objects of the class exist, a public static member function must be provided and the function must be called by prefixing its name with the class name and binary scope resolution operator.

The program of Fig. 7.9 demonstrates the use of a private **static** data member and a public **static** member function. The data member **count** is initialized to zero at file scope with the statement

```
int Employee::count = 0;
```

Data member **count** maintains a count of the number of objects of class **Employee** that have been instantiated. When objects of class **Employee** exist, member **count** can be referenced through any member function of an **Employee** object—in this example, **count** is referenced by both the constructor and the destructor. When no objects of class **Employee** exist, member **count** can still be referenced, but only through a call to static member function **getCount** as follows:

```
Employee::getCount()
```

```
// EMPLOY1.H
// An employee class
#ifndef EMPLOY1_H
#define EMPLOY1_H

class Employee {
public:
   Employee(const char*, const char*); // constructor
   ~Employee();                        // destructor
   const char *getFirstName() const;   // return first name
   const char *getLastName() const;    // return last name

   // static member function
   static int getCount();  // return # objects instantiated

private:
   char *firstName;
   char *lastName;

   // static data member
   static int count;  // number of objects instantiated
};

#endif
```

Fig 7.9 Using a static data member to maintain a count of the number of objects of a class (part 1 of 5).

```
// EMPLOY1.CPP
// Member functions definitions for class Employee
#include <iostream.h>
#include <string.h>
#include <assert.h>
#include "employ1.h"

// Initialize the static data member
int Employee::count = 0;

// Define the static member function that
// returns the number of employee objects instantiated.
int Employee::getCount() { return count; }

// Constructor dynamically allocates space for the
// first and last name and uses strcpy to copy
// the first and last names into the object
Employee::Employee(const char *first, const char *last)
{
   firstName = new char[ strlen(first) + 1 ];
   assert(firstName != 0);   // ensure memory allocated
   strcpy(firstName, first);

   lastName = new char[ strlen(last) + 1 ];
   assert(lastName != 0);    // ensure memory allocated
   strcpy(lastName, last);

   ++count;  // increment static count of employees
   cout << "Employee constructor for " << firstName
        << ' ' << lastName << " called." << endl;
}

// Destructor deallocates dynamically allocated memory
Employee::~Employee()
{
   cout << "~Employee() called for " << firstName
        << ' ' << lastName << endl;
   delete [] firstName;  // recapture memory
   delete [] lastName;   // recapture memory
   --count;  // decrement static count of employees
}

// Return first name of employee
const char *Employee::getFirstName() const
{
   // Const before return type prevents client modifying private
   // data. Client should copy returned string before destructor
   // deletes dynamic storage to prevent undefined pointer.
   return firstName;
}
```

**Fig. 7.9** Using a static data member to maintain a count of the number of objects of a class (part 2 of 5).

```
// EMPLOY1.CPP: Continued

// Return last name of employee
const char *Employee::getLastName() const
{
   // Const before return type prevents client modifying private
   // data. Client should copy returned string before destructor
   // deletes dynamic storage to prevent undefined pointer.
   return lastName;
}
```

Fig. 7.9 Using a static data member to maintain a count of the number of objects of a class (part 3 of 5).

```
// FIG7_9.CPP
// Driver to test the employee class
#include <iostream.h>
#include "employ1.h"

main()
{
   cout << "Number of employees before instantiation is "
        << Employee::getCount() << endl;    // use class name

   Employee *e1Ptr = new Employee("Susan", "Baker");
   Employee *e2Ptr = new Employee("Robert", "Jones");

   cout << "Number of employees after instantiation is "
        << e1Ptr->getCount() << endl;

   cout << endl << "Employee 1: "
        << e1Ptr->getFirstName()
        << " " << e1Ptr->getLastName()
        << endl << "Employee 2: "
        << e2Ptr->getFirstName()
        << " " << e2Ptr->getLastName() << endl << endl;

   delete e1Ptr;    // recapture memory
   delete e2Ptr;    // recapture memory

   cout << "Number of employees after deletion is "
        << Employee::getCount() << endl;
   return 0;
}
```

Fig. 7.9 Using a static data member to maintain a count of the number of objects of a class (part 4 of 5).

In this example, function **getCount** is used to determine the number of **Employee** objects currently instantiated. Note that when there are no objects instantiated in the program, the **Employee::getCount()** function call is issued. However, when there are objects instantiated function **getCount** can be called through one of the objects as in

```
e1Ptr->getCount()
```

```
Number of employees before instantiation is 0
Employee constructor for Susan Baker called.
Employee constructor for Robert Jones called.
Number of employees after instantiation is 2

Employee 1: Susan Baker
Employee 2: Robert Jones

~Employee() called for Susan Baker
~Employee() called for Robert Jones
Number of employees after deletion is 0
```

**Fig. 7.9** Using a static data member to maintain a count of the number of objects of a class (part 5 of 5).

A member function may be declared **static** if it does not access nonstatic class members. Unlike nonstatic member functions, a static member function has no **this** pointer because static data members and static member functions exist independent of any objects of a class.

Note the use of ***assert*** in the **Employee** constructor function, **getFirstName** function, and **getLastName** function. The **assert** utility—defined in the **assert.h** header file—tests the value of an expression. If the value of the expression is **0** (false), then **assert** prints an error message and calls function ***abort*** (of the general utilities library—**stdlib.h**) to terminate program execution. This is a useful debugging tool for testing if a variable has a correct value. In this program, **assert** determines if the **new** operator was able to fulfill the request for memory to be allocated dynamically. For example, in the **Employee** constructor function, the following line (which is also called an *assertion*)

```
assert(firstName != 0);
```

tests pointer **firstName** to determine if it is not equal to **0** (null). If the condition in the preceding assertion is true, the program continues without interruption. If the condition in the preceding assertion is false, an error message containing the line number, the condition being tested, and the file name in which the assertion appears is printed, and the program terminates. The programmer may then concentrate on this area of the code to find the error. In Chapter 13, "Exception Handling", we will provide a better method of dealing with execution time errors.

Assertions do not have to be removed from the program when debugging is completed. When assertions are no longer needed for debugging purposes in a program, the line

```
#define NDEBUG
```

is inserted at the beginning of the program file. This causes the preprocessor to ignore all assertions instead of the programmer deleting each assertion manually.

*Common Programming Error 7.9*

*Referring to the* `this` *pointer within a static member function.*

*Common Programming Error 7.10*

*Declaring a static member function* `const`.

*Software Engineering Observation 7.7*

*Static data members and static member functions exist and can be used even if no objects of that class have been instantiated.*

Note that the implementations of functions **`getFirstName`** and **`getLastName`** return to the client of the class constant character pointers. In this implementation, if the client wishes to retain a copy of the first name or last name, the client is responsible for copying the dynamically allocated memory in the **`Employee`** object after obtaining the constant character pointer from the object. Note that it is also possible to implement **`getFirstName`** and **`getLastName`** so the client is required to pass a character array and the size of the array to each function. Then, the functions could copy the first or last name into the character array provided by the client.

## 7.8 Data Abstraction and Information Hiding

Classes normally hide their implementation details from the clients of the classes. This is called information hiding. As an example of information hiding, let us consider a data structure called a *stack.*

Think of a stack in terms of a pile of dishes. When a dish is placed on the pile, it is always placed at the top (referred to as *pushing onto the stack*), and when a dish is removed from the pile, it is always removed from the top (referred to as *popping off the stack*). Stacks are known as *last-in, first-out (LIFO) data structures*—the last item pushed (inserted) on the stack is the first item popped (removed) from the stack.

The programmer may create a stack class and hide from its clients the implementation of the stack. Stacks can easily be implemented with arrays and other methods (such as linked lists; see Chapter 15, "Data Structures"). A client of a stack class need not know how the stack is implemented. What the client simply requires is that when data items are placed in the stack, the data items will be recalled in last-in, first-out order. This concept is referred to as *data abstraction,* and C++ classes define *abstract data types (ADTs).* Although users may happen to know the details of how a class is implemented, users may not write code that depends on these details. This means that a particular class (such as one that implements a stack and its operations of ***`push`*** and ***`pop`***) can be replaced with another version without affecting the rest of the system, as long as the public interface to that class does not change.

The job of a high-level language is to create a view convenient for programmers to use. There is no single accepted standard view—that is one reason why there are so many programming languages. Object-oriented programming in C++ presents yet another view.

Most programming languages emphasize actions. In these languages, data exists in support of the actions programs need to take. Data is "less interesting" than actions, anyway. Data is "crude." There are only a few built-in data types, and it is difficult for programmers to create their own new data types.

This view changes with C++ and the object-oriented style of programming. C++ elevates the importance of data. The primary activity in C++ is creating new data types (i.e., classes) and expressing the interactions among objects of those data types.

To move in this direction, the programming-languages community needed to formalize some notions about data. The formalization we consider is the notion of abstract data types (ADTs). ADTs receive as much attention today as structured programming did over the last two decades. ADTs do not replace structured programming. Rather, they provide an additional formalization that can further improve the program development process.

What is an abstract data type? Consider the built-in type **`int`**. What comes to mind is the notion of an integer in mathematics, but **`int`** on a computer is not precisely what an integer is in mathematics. In particular, computer **`int`**s are normally quite limited in size. For example, **`int`** on a 32-bit machine may be limited approximately to the range -2 billion to +2 billion. If the result of a calculation falls outside this range, an error occurs and the machine responds in some machine-dependent manner, including the possibility of "quietly" producing an incorrect result. Mathematical integers do not have this problem. So the notion of a computer **`int`** is really only an approximation to the notion of a real-world integer. The same is true with **`float`**.

Even **`char`** is an approximation; **`char`** values are normally 8-bit patterns that look nothing like the characters they are supposed to represent such as a capital **`Z`**, a lowercase **`z`**, a dollar sign (**`$`**), a digit (**`5`**), and so on. Values of type **`char`** on most computers are quite limited compared to the range of real-world characters. The 7-bit ASCII character set provides for 127 different character values. This is completely inadequate for representing languages such as Japanese and Chinese that require thousands of characters.

The point is that even the built-in data types provided with programming languages like C++ are really only approximations or models of real-world concepts and behaviors. We have taken **`int`** for granted until this point, but now you have a new perspective to consider. Types like **`int`**, **`float`**, **`char`** and others are all examples of abstract data types. They are essentially ways of representing real-world notions to some satisfactory level of precision within a computer system.

An abstract data type actually captures two notions, namely a data representation and the operations that are allowed on that data. For example, the notion of **`int`** defines addition, subtraction, multiplication, division, and modulus operations in C++, but division by zero is undefined; and these allowed operations perform in a manner sensitive to machine parameters such as the fixed-word size of the underlying computer system. Another example is the notion of negative integers whose operations and data representation are clear, but the operation of taking the square root of a negative integer is undefined. In C++, the programmer uses classes to implement abstract data types.

### 7.8.1 Example: Array Abstract Data Type

We discussed arrays in Chapter 4. An array is not much more than a pointer and some space. This primitive capability is acceptable for performing array operations if the programmer is cautious and undemanding. There are many operations that would be nice to perform with arrays, but that are not built into C++. With C++ classes, the programmer can develop an array ADT that is preferable to "raw" arrays. The array class can provide many helpful new capabilities such as

- Subscript range checking.
- An arbitrary range of subscripts.
- Array assignment.
- Array comparison.
- Array input/output.
- Arrays that know their sizes.

The weakness here is that we are creating a customized, nonstandard data type which is not likely to be available in precisely this form across most C++ implementations. The use of C++ and object-oriented programming is increasing rapidly. It is crucial that the programming profession work towards the large-scale standardization and distribution of class libraries to realize the full potential of object orientation.

C++ has a small set of built-in types. ADTs extend the base programming language.

*Software Engineering Observation 7.8*

*The programmer is able to create new types through the use of the class mechanism. These new types may be designed to be used as conveniently as the built-in types. Thus, C++ is an extensible language. Although the language is easy to extend with these new types, the base language itself is not changeable.*

New ADTs created in C++ environments can be proprietary to an individual, to small groups, or to companies. ADTs can also be placed in standard class libraries intended for wide distribution. This does not necessarily promote standards although de facto standards are likely to emerge. The full value of C++ will be realized only when substantial and standardized class libraries become widely available. A formal process needs to be put in place to encourage the development of standardized libraries. In the United States, such standardization often happens through ANSI, the American National Standards Institute. ANSI is currently evolving a standard version of C++. Regardless of how these libraries ultimately appear, the reader who learns C++ and object-oriented programming will be ready to take advantage of the new kinds of rapid, component-oriented software development made possible with libraries of ADTs.

### 7.8.2 Example: String Abstract Data Type

C++ is an intentionally sparse language that provides programmers with only the raw capabilities needed to build a broad range of systems. The language is designed to minimize performance burdens. C++ is appropriate for both applications programming and systems programming—the latter places extraordinary performance demands on programs. Certainly, it would have been possible to include a string data type among C++'s built-in data types. Instead, the language was designed to include mechanisms for creating and implementing string abstract data types through classes. We will develop our own string ADT in Chapter 8.

### 7.8.3 Example: Queue Abstract Data Type

Each of us stands in line from time to time. A waiting line is also called a *queue.* We wait in line at the supermarket checkout counter, we wait in line to get gasoline, we wait in line to board a bus, we wait in line to pay a toll on the highway, and students know all too well about waiting in line during registration to get the courses they want. Computer systems use many waiting lines internally, so we need to write programs that simulate what queues are and do.

A queue is a good example of an abstract data type. A queue offers well-understood behavior to its clients. Clients put things in a queue one at a time—using an *enqueue* operation, and the clients get those things back one at a time on demand—using a *dequeue* operation. Conceptually, a queue can become infinitely long. A real queue, of course, is finite. Items are returned from a queue in *first-in, first-out (FIFO)* order—the first item inserted in the queue is the first item removed from the queue.

The queue hides an internal data representation that somehow keeps track of the items currently waiting in line, and it offers a set of operations to its clients, namely *enqueue* and *dequeue.* The clients are not concerned about the implementation of the queue. Clients merely want the queue to operate "as advertised." When a client enqueues a new item, the queue should accept that item and place it internally in some kind of first-in, first-out data structure. When the client wants the next item from the front of the queue, the queue should remove the item from its internal representation and should deliver the item to the outside world in FIFO order, i.e., the item that has been in the queue the longest should be the next one returned by the next *dequeue* operation.

The queue ADT guarantees the integrity of its internal data structure. Clients may not manipulate this data structure directly. Only the queue ADT has access to its internal data. Clients may cause only allowable operations to be performed on the data representation; operations not provided in the ADT's public interface are rejected by the ADT in some appropriate manner. This could mean issuing an error message, terminating execution, or simply ignoring the operation request.

## 7.9 Container Classes and Iterators

Among the most popular types of classes are *container classes* (also called *collection classes*), i.e., classes designed to hold collections of objects. Container classes commonly provide services such as insertion, deletion, searching, sorting, testing an item for membership in the class, and the like. Arrays, stacks, queues, and linked lists are examples of container classes.

It is common to associate *iterator objects*—or more simply *iterators*—with collection classes. An iterator is an object that returns the next item of a collection (or performs some action on the next item of a collection). Once an iterator for a class has been written, obtaining the next element from the class can be expressed simply. Iterators are normally written as friends of the classes through which they iterate; this enables iterators to have direct access to the private data of the classes through which they iterate. Just as a book being shared by several people could have several bookmarks in it at once, a container class can have several iterators operating on it at once. Each iterator maintains its own "position" information.

## 7.10 Thinking About Objects: Using Composition and Dynamic Object Management in the Elevator Simulator

In Chapters 2 through 5 you designed your elevator simulator and in Chapter 6 you began programming the simulator. In the body of Chapter 7, we discussed the remaining techniques that you will need to implement a complete, working elevator simulator. In particular, we discussed dynamic object management techniques that enable you to use **`new`** and **`delete`** to create and destroy objects as necessary as your simulator executes. We also discussed composition, a capability that allows you to create classes that have other classes as members. Composition enables you to create a building class that contains the elevator and the floors, and, in turn, create an elevator class that contains buttons.

***Elevator Laboratory Assignment 6***

1. Each time another person enters the simulator, you should use **`new`** to create a Person object to represent that person. Note that **`new`** causes the constructor to be invoked for the object being created, and, of course, the constructor should properly initialize the object. Each time a person leaves the simulator (after getting off the elevator) you should use **`delete`** to destroy the person object and reclaim the storage occupied by that object.
2. Enumerate the composition relationships among the classes you have implemented for your elevator simulator. Modify the class definitions you created in the "Thinking About Objects" section in Chapter 6 to reflect these composition relationships.
3. Complete the implementation of a working simulator program. We will suggest enhancements to the elevator simulator in subsequent chapters.

### Summary

- The keyword **`const`** specifies that an object is not modifiable.
- The C++ compiler disallows non-**`const`** member function calls for a **`const`** object.
- **`const`** member functions cannot modify an object.
- A function is specified as **`const`** both in its declaration and its definition.
- A **`const`** member function may be overloaded with a non-**`const`** version. The choice of which overloaded member function to use is automatically made by the compiler based on whether the object has been declared **`const`** or not.
- A **`const`** object must be initialized in its declaration.
- Member initializers must be provided in the constructor of a class when that class contains **`const`** data members.
- Classes can be composed of objects of other classes.
- Member objects are constructed in the order in which they are declared and before their enclosing class objects are constructed.
- If a member initializer is not provided for a member object, the member object's default constructor is called.

- A friend function of a class is a function defined outside that class and has the right to access **private** and **protected** members of the class.
- Friendship declarations can be placed anywhere in the class definition.
- Each overloaded function intended to be a friend must be explicitly declared as a friend of the class.
- Each object maintains a pointer to itself—called the **this** pointer—that becomes an implicit argument in all references to members within that object. The **this** pointer is implicitly used to reference both the member functions and data members of an object.
- Each object can determine its own address by using the **this** keyword.
- The **this** pointer may be used explicitly, but it is most often used implicitly.
- The **new** operator automatically creates an object of the proper size, and returns a pointer of the correct type. To free the space for this object, use the **delete** operator.
- An array of objects can be allocated dynamically with **new** as in

  ```
  int *ptr = new int[100];
  ```

  which allocates an array of 100 integers and assigns the starting location of the array to **ptr**. The preceding array of integers can be deleted with the statement

  ```
  delete [] ptr;
  ```

- A static data member represents "class-wide" information. The declaration of a static member begins with the keyword **static**.
- Static data members have class scope.
- Static members of a class can be accessed through an object of that class or through the class name using the scope resolution operator (if the member is public).
- A member function may be declared static if it does not access nonstatic class members. Unlike nonstatic member functions, a static member function has no **this** pointer. This is because static data members and static member functions exist independent of any objects of a class.

## *Terminology*

binary scope resolution operator (**::**)
chaining member function calls
class scope
composition
**const** member function
**const** object
constructor
container classes
default constructor
default destructor
**delete** operator
**delete[]** operator
destructor
dynamic objects
extensibility
**friend** class
**friend** function
iterator
member selection operator (**.**)
member access specifiers

member initializer
member object
member object constructor
nested class
**new** operator
pointer member selection operator (**->**)
principle of least privilege
static data member
static member function
**this** pointer

## Common Programming Errors

7.1 Defining as **const** a member function that modifies a data member of an object.

7.2 Defining as **const** a member function that calls a non-**const** member function.

7.3 Calling a non-**const** member function for a **const** object.

7.4 Attempting to modify a **const** object.

7.5 Not providing a member initializer for a **const** data member.

7.6 Not providing a default constructor for a member object when no member initializer is provided for that member object. This can result in an uninitialized member object.

7.7 Attempting to use the member selection operator (**.**) with a pointer to an object (the member selection operator may only be used with a member object or with a reference to an object).

7.8 Mixing **new**-and-**delete**-style dynamic memory allocation with **malloc**-and-**free**-style dynamic memory allocation: Space created by **malloc** cannot be freed by **delete**; objects created by **new**, cannot be deleted by **free**.

7.9 Referring to the **this** pointer within a static member function.

7.10 Declaring a static member function **const**.

## Good Programming Practices

7.1 Declare as **const** all member functions that are intended to be used with **const** objects.

7.2 Place all friendship declarations first in the class immediately after the class header and do not precede them with any member-access specifier.

7.3 Although C++ programs can contain storage created by **malloc** and deleted by **free**, and objects created by **new** and deleted by **delete**, it is best to use only **new** and **delete**.

## Performance Tips

7.1 Initialize member objects explicitly through member initializers. This eliminates the overhead of doubly initializing member objects—once when the member object's default constructor is called and again when set functions are used to initialize the member object.

7.2 For reasons of economy of storage, only one copy of each member function exists per class, and this member function is invoked by every object of that class. Each object, on the other hand, has its own copy of the class's data members.

7.3 Use static data members to save storage when a single copy of the data will suffice.

## Software Engineering Observations

7.1 Declaring objects **const** helps enforce the principle of least privilege. Accidental attempts to modify the object are caught at compile time rather than causing execution-time errors.

7.2 A **const** member function can be overloaded with a non-**const** version. The choice of which overloaded member function to use is made by the compiler based on whether the object has been declared **const** or not.

7.3 Constant class members (**const** objects and **const** "variables") must be initialized with member initializer syntax. Assignments are not allowed.

7.4 One form of software reusability is composition in which a class has objects of other classes as members.

7.5 Member access specifiers **private**, **protected**, and **public** are not relevant to friendship declarations, so such declarations can be placed anywhere in the class definition.

7.6 Some people in the OOP community feel that "friendship" corrupts information hiding and weakens the value of the object-oriented design approach.

7.7 Static data members and static member functions exist and can be used even if no objects of that class have been instantiated.

7.8 The programmer is able to create new types through the use of the class mechanism. These new types may be designed to be used as conveniently as the built-in types. Thus, C++ is an extensible language. Although the language is easy to extend with these new types, the base language itself is not changeable.

## *Self-Review Exercises*

7.1 Fill in the blanks in each of the following:

a) __________ syntax is used to initialize constant members of a class.

b) A nonmember function must be declared as a __________ of a class to have access to that class's **private** data members.

c) The __________ operator dynamically allocates memory for an object of a specified type and returns a __________ to that type.

d) A constant object must be __________; it cannot be modified after it is created.

e) A __________ data member represents class-wide information.

f) An object's member functions maintain a pointer to the object called the _____ pointer.

g) The keyword __________ specifies that an object or variable is not modifiable after it is initialized.

h) If a member initializer is not provided for a member object of a class, the object's __________ is called.

i) A member function can be declared **static** if it does not access ____ classmembers.

j) Friend functions can access the __________ and __________ members of a class.

k) Member objects are constructed __________ their enclosing class object.

l) The __________ operator reclaims memory previously allocated by **new**.

7.2 Find the error(s) in each of the following and explain how to correct it.

a)
```
class Example {
public:
   Example( int y = 10 ) { data = y; }
   int getIncrementedData() const { return ++data; }
   static int getCount()
   {
      cout << "Data is " << data << endl;
      return count;
   }
private:
   int data;
   static int count;
};
```

b)
```
char *string;
string = new char[20];
free(string);
```

## *Answers to Self-Review Exercises*

**7.1** a) Member initializer. b) **friend**. c) **new**, pointer. d) initialized. e) **static**. f) **this**. g) **const**. h) default constructor. i) nonstatic. j) **private**, **protected**. k) before. l) **delete**.

**7.2** a) Error: The class definition for **Example** has two errors. The first occurs in function **getIncrementedData**. The function is declared **const**, but it modifies the object.
Correction: To correct the first error, remove the **const** keyword from the definition of **getIncrementedData**.

Error: The second error occurs in function **getCount**. This function is declared **static**, so it is not allowed to access any nonstatic member of the class.
Correction: To correct the second error, remove the output line from the definition of **getCount**.

b) Error: Memory dynamically allocated by **new** is deleted by the C standard library function **free**.
Correction: Use C++'s **delete** operator to reclaim the memory. C-style dynamic memory allocation should not be mixed with C++'s **new** and **delete** operators.

## *Exercises*

**7.3** Compare and contrast dynamic memory allocation with the C++ operators **new** and **delete**, with dynamic memory allocation with the C Standard Library functions **malloc** and **free**.

**7.4** Explain the notion of friendship in C++. Explain the negative aspects of friendship as described in the text.

**7.5** Can a correct **Time** class definition include both of the following constructors?

```
Time (int h = 0, int m = 0, int s = 0);
Time();
```

**7.6** What happens when a return type, even **void**, is specified for a constructor or destructor?

**7.7** Create a **Date** class with the following capabilities:

a) Output the date in multiple formats such as

```
DDD YYYY
MM/DD/YY
June 14, 1992
```

b) Use overloaded constructors to create **Date** objects initialized with dates of the formats in part (a).

c) Create a **Date** constructor that reads the system date using the standard library functions of the **time.h** header and sets the **Date** members.

In Chapter 8, we will be able to create operators for testing the equality of two dates and for comparing dates to determine if one date is prior to or after another.

**7.8** Create a **SavingsAccount** class. Use a static data member to contain the **annualInterestRate** for each of the savers. Each member of the class contains a private data member **savingsBalance** indicating the amount the saver currently has on deposit. Provide a **calculateMonthlyInterest** member function that calculates the monthly interest by multiplying the **balance** by **annualInterestRate** divided by 12; this interest should be added to **savingsBalance**. Provide a static member function **modifyInterestRate** that sets the static **annualInterestRate** to a new value. Write a driver program to test class **SavingsAccount**. Instantiate two different **savingsAccount** objects, **saver1** and **saver2**, with balances of $2000.00 and $3000.00, respectively. Set **annualInterestRate** to 3%, then calculate the monthly interest and print the new balances for each of the savers. Then set the **annualInterestRate** to 4% and calculate the next month's interest and print the new balances for each of the savers.

**7.9** Create a class **IntegerSet**. Each object of the class can hold integers in the range 0 through 100. A set is represented internally as an array of ones and zeros. Array element **a[i]** is 1 if integer *i* is in the set. Array element **a[j]** is 0 if integer *j* is not in the set. The default constructor initializes a set to the so-called "empty set," i.e., a set whose array representation contains all zeros.

Provide member functions for the common set operations. For example, provide a **unionOfIntegerSets** member function that creates a third set which is the set-theoretic union of two existing sets (.i.e., an element of the third set's array is set to 1 if that element is 1 in either or both of the existing sets, and an element of the third set's array is set to 0 if that element is 0 in each of the existing sets).

Provide an **intersectionOfIntegerSets** member function that creates a third set which is the set-theoretic intersection of two existing sets i.e., an element of the third set's array is set to 0 if that element is 0 in either or both of the existing sets, and an element of the third set's array is set to 1 if that element is 1 in each of the existing sets).

Provide an **insertElement** member function that inserts a new integer *k* into a set (by setting **a[k]** to 1). Provide a **deleteElement** member function that deletes integer *m* (by setting **a[m]** to 0).

Provide a **settPrint** member function that prints a set as a list of numbers separated by spaces. Print only those elements that are present in the set. Print **---** for an empty set.

Provide an **isEqualTo** member function that determines if two sets are equal.

Provide an additional constructor to take five integer arguments which can be used to initialize a set object. If you want to provide fewer than five elements in the set, use default arguments of -1 for the others.

Now write a driver program to test your **IntegerSet** class. Instantiate several **IntegerSet** objects. Test that all your member functions work properly.

# 8

# Operator Overloading

## Objectives

- To understand how to redefine operators to work with new types.
- To understand how to convert objects from one class to another class.
- To learn when to, and when not to, overload operators.
- To study several interesting classes that use overloaded operators.
- To create Array, String, and Date abstract data types.

*The whole difference between construction and creation is exactly this: that a thing constructed can only be loved after it is constructed; but a thing created is loved before it exists.*
Gilbert Keith Chesterton, Preface to Dickens, Pickwick Papers

*The die is cast.*
Julius Caesar

*Our doctor would never really operate unless it was necessary. He was just that way. If he didn't need the money, he wouldn't lay a hand on you.*
Herb Shriner

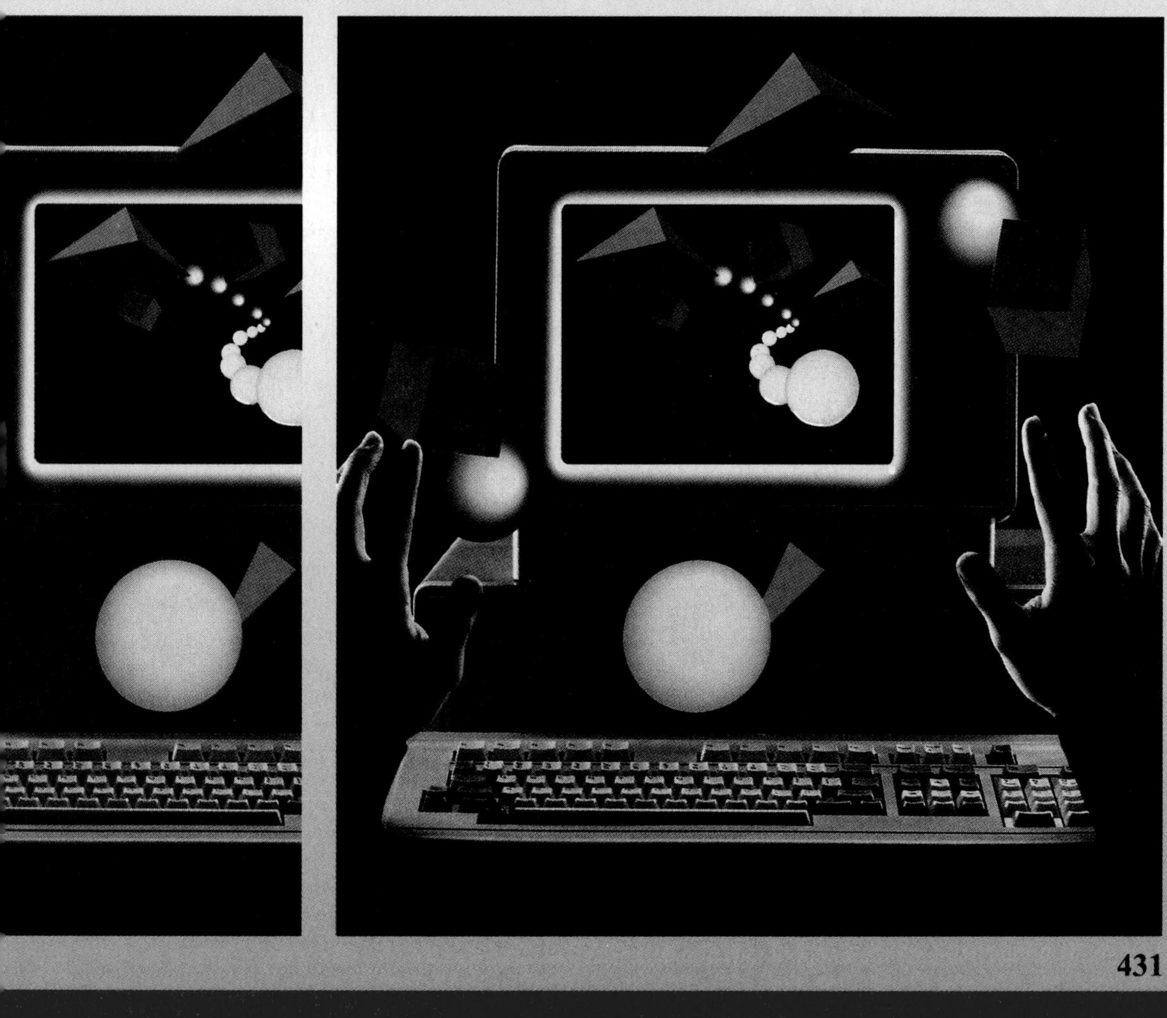

## Outline



## 8.1 Introduction

In Chapters 6 and 7 we introduced the basics of C++ classes and the notion of abstract data types (ADTs). Manipulations on class objects (i.e., instances of ADTs) were accomplished by sending messages (in the form of member function calls) to the objects. This function-call notation is cumbersome for certain kinds of classes, especially mathematical classes. For these kinds of classes it would be nice to use C++'s rich set of built-in operators to specify object manipulations. In this chapter, we show how to enable C++'s operators to work with class objects. This process is called *operator overloading*. It is straightforward and natural to extend C++ with these new capabilities.

The operator `<<` is used for multiple purposes in C++—as the stream-insertion operator and as the left-shift operator. This is an example of operator overloading. Similarly, `>>` is also overloaded; it is used both as the stream-extraction operator and as the right-shift operator. Both of these operators are overloaded in the C++ class library. The C++ language itself overloads `+` and `-`. These operators perform differently depending on their context in integer arithmetic, floating-point arithmetic, and pointer arithmetic.

C++ enables the programmer to overload most operators to be sensitive to the context in which they are used. The compiler generates the appropriate code based on the manner in which the operator is used. Some operators are overloaded frequently, especially the assignment operator and various arithmetic operators such as `+` and `-`. The job performed by overloaded operators can also be performed by explicit function calls, but operator notation is usually easier to read.

We will discuss when to use operator overloading and when not to. We show how to overload operators, and we present many complete programs using overloaded operators.

## 8.2 Fundamentals of Operator Overloading

C++ programming is a type-sensitive and type-focused process. Programmers can use built-in types and can define new types. The built-in types can be used with C++'s rich collection of operators. Operators provide programmers with a concise notation for expressing manipulations of objects of built-in types.

Programmers can use operators with user-defined types as well. Although C++ does not allow new operators to be created, it does allow existing operators to be overloaded so that when these operators are used with class objects, the operators have meaning appropriate to the new types. This is one of C++'s most powerful features.

***Software Engineering Observation 8.1***

*Operator overloading contributes to C++'s extensibility, surely one of the language's most appealing attributes.*

***Good Programming Practice 8.1***

*Use operator overloading when it makes a program clearer than accomplishing the same operations with explicit function calls.*

***Good Programming Practice 8.2***

*Avoid excessive or inconsistent use of operator overloading as this can make a program cryptic and difficult to read.*

Although operator overloading may sound like an exotic capability, most programmers implicitly use overloaded operators regularly. For example, the addition operator (`+`) operates quite differently on integers, floats, and doubles. But addition nevertheless works fine with variables of type **`int`**, **`float`**, **`double`**, and a number of other built-in types because the addition operator (`+`) has been overloaded in the C++ language itself.

Operators are overloaded by writing a function definition (with a header and body) as you normally would, except that the function name now becomes the keyword **`operator`** followed by the symbol for the operator being overloaded. For example, the function name **`operator+`** would be used to overload the addition operator.

To use an operator on class objects, that operator *must* be overloaded—with two exceptions. The assignment operator (`=`) may be used with every class without explicit overloading. The default behavior of the assignment operator is a *memberwise copy* of the data members of the class. We will soon see that such default memberwise copy is dangerous for classes with members that point to dynamically allocated storage; we will explicitly overload the assignment operator for such classes. The address operator (`&`) may also be used with objects of any class without overloading; it simply returns the address of the object in memory. The address operator can also be overloaded.

Overloading is most appropriate for mathematical classes. These often require that a substantial set of operators be overloaded to ensure consistency with the way these mathematical classes are handled in the real world. For example, it would be unusual to overload only addition for a complex number class because other arithmetic operators are also commonly used with complex numbers.

C++ is an operator-rich language. C++ programmers who understand the meaning and context of each operator are likely to make reasonable choices when it comes to overloading operators for new classes.

The point of operator overloading is to provide the same concise expressions for user-defined types that C++ provides with its rich collection of operators for built-in types. Operator overloading is not automatic, however; the programmer must write operator overloading functions to perform the desired operations. Sometimes these functions are best made member functions; sometimes they are best as friend functions; and occasionally they can be made nonmember, nonfriend functions.

Extreme misuses of overloading would be to overload the + operator to perform subtraction-like operations or to overload the / operator to perform multiplication-like operations. Such use of overloading can make a program confusing.

***Good Programming Practice 8.3***

*Overload operators to perform the same function or closely similar functions on class objects as the operators perform on objects of built-in types. Avoid nonintuitive uses of operators.*

***Good Programming Practice 8.4***

*Before writing C++ programs with overloaded operators, consult the manuals for your C++ compiler to become aware of various restrictions and requirements unique to particular operators.*

## 8.3 Restrictions on Operator Overloading

Most of C++'s operators can be overloaded. These are shown in Fig. 8.1. Figure 8.2 shows the operators that cannot be overloaded.

| Operators that can be overloaded | | | | | | | |
|---|---|---|---|---|---|---|---|
| + | - | * | / | % | ^ | & | \| |
| ~ | ! | = | < | > | += | -= | *= |
| /= | %= | ^= | &= | \|= | << | >> | >>= |
| <<= | == | != | <= | >= | && | \|\| | ++ |
| -- | ->* | , | -> | [] | () | new | delete |

**Fig. 8.1** Operators that can be overloaded.

| Operators that cannot be overloaded | | | | |
|---|---|---|---|---|
| `.` | `.*` | `::` | `?:` | `sizeof` |

**Fig. 8.2** Operators that cannot be overloaded.

***Common Programming Error 8.1***

*Attempting to overload a nonoverloadable operator.*

The precedence of an operator cannot be changed by overloading. This can lead to awkward situations in which an operator is overloaded in a manner for which its fixed precedence is inappropriate. However, parentheses can be used to force the order of evaluation of overloaded operators in an expression.

The associativity of an operator cannot be changed by overloading. Default arguments cannot be used with an overloaded operator.

It is not possible to change the number of operands an operator takes: Overloaded unary operators remain as unary operators; overloaded binary operators remain as binary operators. C++'s only ternary operator (`?:`) cannot be overloaded. Operators `&`, `*`, `+` and `-` each have unary and binary versions; these unary and binary versions can be overloaded separately.

It is not possible to create new operators; only existing operators may be overloaded. This prevents the programmer from using popular notations like the `**` operator used in BASIC for exponentiation

***Common Programming Error 8.2***

*Attempting to create new operators.*

The meaning of how an operator works on objects of built-in types cannot be changed by operator overloading. The programmer cannot, for example, change the meaning of how `+` adds two integers. Operator overloading works only with objects of user-defined types or with a mixture of an object of a user-defined type and an object of a built-in type.

***Common Programming Error 8.3***

*Attempting to modify how an operator works with objects of built-in types.*

***Software Engineering Observation 8.2***

*At least one argument of an operator function must be a class object or a reference to a class object. This prevents programmers from changing how operators work on objects of built-in types.*

Overloading an assignment operator and an addition operator to allow statements such as

```
object2 = object2 + object1;
```

does not imply that the += operator is also overloaded to allow statements such as

```
object2 += object1;
```

Such behavior can be achieved by explicitly overloading the += operator for that class.

***Common Programming Error 8.4***

*Assuming that overloading an operator (such as +) automatically overloads related operators (such as += ). Operators can be overloaded only explicitly; there is no implicit overloading.*

***Good Programming Practice 8.5***

*To ensure consistency among related operators, use one to implement the others (i.e., use an overloaded + operator to implement an overloaded += operator).*

## 8.4 Operator Functions as Class Members vs. as Friend Functions

Operator functions can be member functions or nonmember functions; nonmember functions are normally friends. The member functions use the **`this`** pointer implicitly to obtain one of their class object arguments. That class argument must be explicitly listed in a nonmember function call.

When overloading **`()`**, **`[]`**, **`->`**, or =, the operator overloading function must be declared as a class member. For the other operators, the operator overloading functions can be nonmember functions (normally friends).

Whether an operator function is implemented as a member function or as a nonmember function, the operator is still used the same way in expressions. So which implementation is best?

When an operator function is implemented as a member function, the leftmost (or only) operand must be a class object (or a reference to a class object) of the operator's class. If the left operand must be an object of a different class or a built-in type, this operator function must be implemented as a nonmember function exactly as we will do in Section 8.5 when overloading << and >> as the stream-insertion and stream-extraction operators, respectively. An operator function implemented as a nonmember function needs to be a friend if that function must access private or protected members of that class directly.

The overloaded << operator must have a left operand of type **`ostream &`** (such as **`cout`** in the expression **`cout << classObject`**), so it must be a nonmember function. Similarly, the overloaded >> operator must have a left operand of type **`istream &`** (such as **`cin`** in the expression **`cin >> classObject`**), so it, too, must be a nonmember function. Also, each of these overloaded operator functions may require access to the private data members of the class object being output or input, so these overloaded operator functions are sometimes made friend functions of the class for performance reasons.

***Performance Tip 8.1***

*It is possible to overload an operator as a nonmember, nonfriend function, but such a function needing access to a class's private or protected data would need to use set or get functions provided in that class's public interface. The overhead of calling these functions could cause poor performance.*

Operator member functions are called only when the left operand of a binary operator is specifically an object of that class, or when the single operand of a unary operator is an object of that class.

Another reason why one might choose a nonmember function to overload an operator is to enable the operator to be commutative. For example, suppose we have an object, **number**, of type **long int**, and an object **bigInteger1**, of class **HugeInteger** (a class in which integers may be arbitrarily large rather than being limited by the machine word size of the underlying hardware; class **HugeInteger** is developed in the chapter exercises). The addition operator (**+**) produces a temporary **HugeInteger** object as the sum of a **HugeInteger** and a **long int** (as in the expression **bigInteger1 + number**), or as the sum of a **long int** and a **HugeInteger** (as in the expression **number + bigInteger1**). Thus, we require the addition operator to be commutative (exactly as it is normally). The problem is that the class object must appear on the left of the addition if the operator is to be overloaded as a member function. So, we overload the operator as a friend to allow the **HugeInteger** to appear on the right of the addition. The **operator+** function that deals with the **HugeInteger** on the left can still be a member function.

## 8.5 Overloading Stream-Insertion and Stream-Extraction Operators

C++ is able to input and output the standard data types using the stream-extraction operator **>>** and stream-insertion operator **<<**. These operators are overloaded (in the class libraries provided with C++ compilers) to process each standard data type including strings and memory addresses. The stream-insertion and stream-extraction operators also can be overloaded to perform input and output for user-defined types. Figure 8.3 demonstrates overloading the stream-extraction and stream-insertion operators to handle data of a user-defined telephone number class called **PhoneNumber**. This program assumes telephone numbers are input correctly. We leave it to the exercises to provide error-checking.

In Fig. 8.3, the stream-extraction operator function (**operator>>**) takes an **istream** reference called **input** and a reference called **num** to the user-defined type **PhoneNumber** as arguments, and returns an **istream** reference. Operator function **operator>>** is used to input phone numbers of the form

```
(800) 555-1212
```

into objects of class **PhoneNumber**. When the compiler sees the expression

```
cin >> phone
```

in **main**, the compiler generates the function call

```
operator>>(cin, phone);
```

When this call is executed, parameter **input** becomes an alias for **cin** and parameter **num** becomes an alias for **phone**. The operator function uses **istream** member function **getline** to read as strings the three parts of the telephone number into the **areaCode**, **exchange**, and **line** members of the referenced **PhoneNumber** object (**num** in the operator function and **phone** in **main**). Function **getline** is explained in detail

```
// FIG8_3.CPP
// Overloading the stream-insertion and
// stream-extraction operators.
#include <iostream.h>

class PhoneNumber {
   friend ostream &operator<<(ostream &, const PhoneNumber &);
   friend istream &operator>>(istream &, PhoneNumber &);
private:
   char areaCode[4];  // 3-digit area code and null
   char exchange[4];  // 3-digit exchange and null
   char line[5];      // 4-digit line and null
};

// Overloaded stream-insertion operator (cannot be
// a member function).
ostream &operator<<(ostream &output, const PhoneNumber &num)
{
   output << "(" << num.areaCode << ") "
          << num.exchange << "-" << num.line;

   return output;     // enables cout << a << b << c;
}

// overloaded stream-extraction operator
istream &operator>>(istream &input, PhoneNumber &num)
{
   input.ignore();                    // skip (
   input.getline(num.areaCode, 4); // input area code
   input.ignore(2);                   // skip ) and space
   input.getline(num.exchange, 4); // input exchange
   input.ignore();                    // skip dash (-)
   input.getline(num.line, 5);     // input line

   return input;      // enables cin >> a >> b >> c;
}

main()
{
   PhoneNumber phone; // create object phone

   cout << "Enter a phone number in the "
        << "form (123) 456-7890:" << endl;

   // cin >> phone invokes operator>> function by
   // issuing the call operator>>(cin, phone).
   cin >> phone;

   // cout << phone invokes operator<< function by
   // issuing the call operator<<(cout, phone).
   cout << "The phone number entered was:" << endl
        << phone << endl;
   return 0;
}
```

**Fig. 8.3** User-defined stream-insertion and stream-extraction operators (part 1 of 2).

```
Enter a phone number in the form (123) 456-7890:
(800) 555-1212
The phone number entered was:
(800) 555-1212
```

**Fig. 8.3** User-defined stream-insertion and stream-extraction operators (part 2 of 2).

in Chapter 11. The parentheses, space, and dash characters are skipped by calling **`istream`** member function **`ignore`** which discards the specified number of characters in the input stream (one character by default). Function **`operator>>`** returns **`istream`** reference **`input`** (i.e., **`cin`**). This enables input operations on **`PhoneNumber`** objects to be concatenated with input operations on other **`PhoneNumber`** objects or on objects of other data types. We have also called such concatenation "chaining." For example, two **`PhoneNumber`** objects could be input as follows:

```
cin >> phone1 >> phone2;
```

First, the expression **`cin >> phone1`** would execute by making the call

```
operator>>(cin, phone1);
```

This call would then return a reference to **`cin`** as the value of **`cin >> phone1`** so the remaining portion of the expression would be interpreted simply as **`cin >> phone2`**. This would execute by making the call

```
operator>>(cin, phone2);
```

The stream-insertion operator takes an **`ostream`** reference (**`output`**) and a reference (**`num`**) to a user-defined type (**`PhoneNumber`**) as arguments, and returns an **`ostream`** reference. Function **`operator<<`** displays objects of type **`PhoneNumber`**. When the compiler sees the expression

```
cout << phone
```

in **`main`**, the compiler generates the function call

```
operator<<(cout, phone);
```

Function **`operator<<`** displays the parts of the telephone number as strings because they are stored in string format (**`istream`** member function **`getline`** stores a null character after it completes its input).

Note that the functions **`operator>>`** and **`operator<<`** are declared in **`class PhoneNumber`** as nonmember, friend functions. These operators must be nonmembers because the object of class **`PhoneNumber`** appears in each case as the right operand of the operator; the class operand must appear on the left in order to overload the operator as a member function. Overloaded input and output operators must be declared as friends if they must access non-public class members directly for performance reasons.

***Software Engineering Observation 8.3***

*New input/output capabilities for user-defined types can be added to C++ without modifying the declarations or private data members for either the* **`ostream`** *class or the* **`istream`** *class. This is another example of the extensibility of the C++ programming language.*

## 8.6 Overloading Unary Operators

A unary operator for a class can be overloaded as a non-static member function with no arguments or as a nonmember function with one argument; that argument must be either an object of the class or a reference to an object of the class. Member functions that implement overloaded operators must be non-static so they can access the data of the class. Remember that static member functions can only access the static data members of the class.

Later in this chapter, we will overload unary operator **`!`** to test if an object of the **`String`** class is empty. When overloading a unary operator such as **`!`** as a nonstatic member function with no arguments, if **`s`** is a **`String`** class object or a reference to a **`String`** class object, when the compiler sees the expression **`!s`** the compiler generates the call **`s.operator!()`**. The operand **`s`** is the class object for which the **`String`** class member function **`operator!`** is being invoked. The function is declared in the class definition as follows:

```
class String {
public:
   int operator!() const;
   ...
};
```

A unary operator such as **`!`** may be overloaded as a nonmember function with one argument two different ways—either with an argument that is an object (this requires a copy of the object, so the side effects of the function are not applied to the original object), or with an argument that is a reference to an object (no copy of the original object is made, so all side effects of this function are applied to the original object). If **`s`** is a **`String`** class object (or a reference to a **`String`** class object), then **`!s`** is treated as if the call **`operator!(s)`** had been written, invoking the nonmember friend function of class **`String`** declared below:

```
class String {
   friend int operator!(const String &);
   ...
};
```

***Good Programming Practice 8.6***

*When overloading unary operators, it is preferable to make the operator functions class members instead of nonmember friend functions. Friend functions and friend classes should be avoided unless they are absolutely necessary. The use of friends violates the encapsulation of a class.*

## 8.7 Overloading Binary Operators

A binary operator can be overloaded as a nonstatic member function with one argument, or as a nonmember function with two arguments (one of those arguments must be either a class object or a reference to a class object).

Later in this chapter, we will overload **+=** to indicate concatenation of two string objects. When overloading binary operator **+=** as a nonstatic member function of a **String** class with one argument, if **y** and **z** are **String** class objects, then **y += z** is treated as if **y.operator+=(z)** had been written, invoking the **operator+=** member function declared below

```
class String {
public:
   String &operator+=(const String &);
   ...
};
```

Binary operator **+=** may be overloaded as a nonmember function with two arguments—one of which must be a class object or a reference to a class object. If **y** and **z** are **String** class objects or references to **String** class objects, then **y += z** is treated as if the call **operator+=(y, z)** had been written in the program, invoking nonmember, friend function **operator+=** declared below

```
class String {
   friend String &operator+=(String &, const String &);
   ...
};
```

## 8.8 Case Study: An Array Class

Arrray notation in C++ is just an alternative to pointers, so arrays have much potential for errors. For example, a program can easily "walk off" an array because C++ does not check whether subscripts fall outside the range of an array. Arrays of size $n$ must number their elements 0, ..., $n - 1$; alternate subscript ranges are not allowed. An entire array cannot be input or output at once; each array element must be read or written individually. Two arrays cannot be compared with equality operators or relational operators. When an array is passed to a general-purpose function designed to handle arrays of any size, the size of the array must be passed as an additional argument. One array cannot be assigned to another with the assignment operator(s). These and other capabilities certainly seem like "naturals" for dealing with arrays, but C++ does not provide such capabilities. However, C++ does provide the means to implement such array capabilities through the mechanisms of operator overloading.

In this example, we develop an array class that performs range checking to ensure that subscripts remain within the bounds of the array. The class allows one array object to be assigned to another with the assignment operator. Objects of this array class automatically know their size so the size does not need to be passed separately as an argument when passing an array to a function. Entire arrays can be input or output with the stream-extraction and stream-insertion operators, respectively. Array comparisons can be made with the equality operators **==** and **!=**. Our array class uses a static member to keep track of the number of array objects that have been instantiated in the program. This example will sharpen your appreciation of data abstraction. You will probably want to suggest many enhancements to this array class. Class development is an interesting, creative, and intellectually challenging activity.

The program of Fig. 8.4 demonstrates class **Array** and its overloaded operators. First we walk through the driver program in **main**. Then we consider the class definition and each of the class's member function and friend function definitions.

Static data member **arrayCount** of class **Array** contains the number of **Array** objects instantiated during program execution. The program begins by using static member function **getArrayCount** to retrieve the number of arrays instantiated so far. Next, the program instantiates two objects of class **Array**—**integers1** with seven elements and **integers2** with default size ten elements (the default value specified by the **Array** constructor). Static member function **getArrayCount** is used again to retrieve this value. Member function **getSize** returns the size of the **integers1** array. The program outputs the size of array **integers1**, then outputs the array itself using the

```
// ARRAY1.H
// Simple class Array (for integers)
#ifndef ARRAY1_H
#define ARRAY1_H

#include <iostream.h>

class Array {
   friend ostream &operator<<(ostream &, const Array &);
   friend istream &operator>>(istream &, Array &);
public:
   Array(int = 10);                        // default constructor
   Array(const Array &);                   // copy constructor
   ~Array();                               // destructor
   int getSize() const;                    // return size
   const Array &operator=(const Array &);  // assign arrays
   int operator==(const Array &) const;    // compare equal
   int operator!=(const Array &) const;    // compare !equal
   int &operator[](int);                   // subscript operator
   static int getArrayCount();             // Return count of
                                           // arrays instantiated.

private:
   int *ptr; // pointer to first element of array
   int size; // size of the array
   static int arrayCount;  // # of Arrays instantiated
};

#endif
```

Fig. 8.4 Definition of class **Array** (part 1 of 7).

```
// ARRAY1.CPP
// Member function definitions for class Array
#include <iostream.h>
#include <stdlib.h>
#include <assert.h>
#include "array1.h"

// Initialize static data member at file scope
int Array::arrayCount = 0;    // no objects yet

// Default constructor for class Array
Array::Array(int arraySize)
{
   ++arrayCount;               // count one more object
   size = arraySize;           // default size is 10
   ptr = new int[size];        // create space for array
   assert(ptr != 0);           // terminate if memory not allocated

   for (int i = 0; i < size; i++)
      ptr[i] = 0;              // initialize array
}

// Copy constructor for class Array
Array::Array(const Array &init)
{
   ++arrayCount;               // count one more object
   size = init.size;           // size this object
   ptr = new int[size];        // create space for array
   assert(ptr != 0);           // terminate if memory not allocated

   for (int i = 0; i < size; i++)
      ptr[i] = init.ptr[i];    // copy init into object
}

// Destructor for class Array
Array::~Array()
{
   --arrayCount;               // one fewer objects
   delete [] ptr;              // reclaim space for array
}

// Get the size of the array
int Array::getSize() const { return size; }
```

**Fig. 8.4** Member function definitions for class **Array** (part 2 of 7).

overloaded stream-insertion operator to confirm that the array elements were initialized correctly by the constructor. Next, the size of array **integers2** is output, then the array is output using the overloaded stream-insertion operator.

The user is prompted to input 17 integers. The overloaded stream-extraction operator is used to read these values into both arrays with the statement

```
cin >> integers1 >> integers2;
```

```
// Overloaded assignment operator
const Array &Array::operator=(const Array &right)
{
   if (&right != this) {     // check for self-assignment
      delete [] ptr;         // reclaim space
      size = right.size;     // resize this object
      ptr = new int[size];   // create space for array copy
      assert(ptr != 0);      // terminate if memory not allocated

      for (int i = 0; i < size; i++)
         ptr[i] = right.ptr[i];  // copy array into object
   }

   return *this;    // enables x = y = z;
}

// Determine if two arrays are equal and
// return 1 if true, 0 if false.
int Array::operator==(const Array &right) const
{
   if (size != right.size)
      return 0;     // arrays of different sizes

   for (int i = 0; i < size; i++)
      if (ptr[i] != right.ptr[i])
         return 0; // arrays are not equal

   return 1;        // arrays are equal
}

// Determine if two arrays are not equal and
// return 1 if true, 0 if false.
int Array::operator!=(const Array &right) const
{
   if (size != right.size)
      return 1;          // arrays of different sizes

   for (int i = 0; i < size; i++)
      if (ptr[i] != right.ptr[i])
         return 1;       // arrays are not equal

   return 0;             // arrays are equal
}

// Overloaded subscript operator
int &Array::operator[](int subscript)
{
   // check for subscript out of range error
   assert(0 <= subscript && subscript < size);

   return ptr[subscript];   // reference return creates lvalue
}
```

**Fig. 8.4** Member function definitions for class **Array** (part 3 of 7).

```
// Return the number of Array objects instantiated
int Array::getArrayCount() { return arrayCount; }

// Overloaded input operator for class Array;
// inputs values for entire array.
istream &operator>>(istream &input, Array &a)
{
   for (int i = 0; i < a.size; i++)
      input >> a.ptr[i];

   return input;    // enables cin >> x >> y;
}

// Overloaded output operator for class Array
ostream &operator<<(ostream &output, const Array &a)
{
   for (int i = 0; i < a.size; i++) {
      output << a.ptr[i] << ' ';

      if ((i + 1) % 10 == 0)
         output << endl;
   }

   if (i % 10 != 0)
      output << endl;

   return output;    // enables cout << x << y;
}
```

**Fig. 8.4** Member function definitions for class `Array` (part 4 of 7).

```
// FIG8_4.CPP
// Driver for simple class Array
#include <iostream.h>
#include "array1.h"

main()
{
   // no objects yet
   cout << "# of arrays instantiated = "
        << Array::getArrayCount() << endl;

   // create two arrays and print Array count
   Array integers1(7), integers2;
   cout << "# of arrays instantiated = "
        << Array::getArrayCount() << endl << endl;

   // print integers1 size and contents
   cout << "Size of array integers1 is "
        << integers1.getSize() << endl
        << "Array after initialization:" << endl
        << integers1 << endl;
```

**Fig. 8.4** Driver for class `Array` (part 5 of 7).

```
   // print integers2 size and contents
   cout << "Size of array integers2 is "
        << integers2.getSize() << endl
        << "Array after initialization:" << endl
        << integers2 << endl;

   // input and print integers1 and integers2
   cout << "Input 17 integers:" << endl;
   cin >> integers1 >> integers2;
   cout << "After input, the arrays contain:" << endl
        << "integers1: " << integers1
        << "integers2: " << integers2 << endl;

   // use overloaded inequality (!=) operator
   cout << "Evaluating: integers1 != integers2" << endl;
   if (integers1 != integers2)
      cout << "They are not equal" << endl;

   // create array integers3 using integers1 as an
   // initializer; print size and contents
   Array integers3(integers1);

   cout << endl << "Size of array integers3 is "
        << integers3.getSize() << endl
        << "Array after initialization:" << endl
        << integers3 << endl;

   // use overloaded assignment (=) operator
   cout << "Assigning integers2 to integers1:" << endl;
   integers1 = integers2;
   cout << "integers1: " << integers1
        << "integers2: " << integers2 << endl;

   // use overloaded equality (==) operator
   cout << "Evaluating: integers1 == integers2" << endl;
   if (integers1 == integers2)
      cout << "They are equal" << endl << endl;

   // use overloaded subscript operator to create rvalue
   cout << "integers1[5] is " << integers1[5] << endl;

   // use overloaded subscript operator to create lvalue
   cout << "Assigning 1000 to integers1[5]" << endl;
   integers1[5] = 1000;
   cout << "integers1: " << integers1 << endl;

   // attempt to use out of range subscript
   cout << "Attempt to assign 1000 to integers1[15]" << endl;
   integers1[15] = 1000;  // ERROR: out of range

   return 0;
}
```

**Fig. 8.4** Driver for class **Array** (part 6 of 7).

```
# of arrays instantiated = 0
# of arrays instantiated = 2

Size of array integers1 is 7
Array after initialization:
0 0 0 0 0 0 0

Size of array integers2 is 10
Array after initialization:
0 0 0 0 0 0 0 0 0 0

Input 17 integers:
1 2 3 4 5 6 7 8 9 10 11 12 13 14 15 16 17
After input, the arrays contain:
integers1: 1 2 3 4 5 6 7
integers2: 8 9 10 11 12 13 14 15 16 17

Evaluating: integers1 != integers2
They are not equal

Size of array integers3 is 7
Array after initialization:
1 2 3 4 5 6 7

Assigning integers2 to integers1:
integers1: 8 9 10 11 12 13 14 15 16 17
integers2: 8 9 10 11 12 13 14 15 16 17

Evaluating: integers1 == integers2
They are equal

integers1[5] is 13
Assigning 1000 to integers1[5]
integers1: 8 9 10 11 12 1000 14 15 16 17

Attempt to assign 1000 to integers1[15]
Assertion failed: 0 <= subscript && subscript < size,
   file ARRAY1.CPP, line 93
Abnormal program termination
```

**Fig. 8.4** Output from driver for class **Array** (part 7 of 7).

The user is prompted to input 17 integers. The overloaded stream-extraction operator is used to read these values into both arrays with the statement

```
cin >> integers1 >> integers2;
```

The first seven values are stored in **integers1** and the remaining values are stored in **integers2**. The two arrays are output with the stream-insertion operator to confirm that the input was performed correctly.

Next the program tests the overloaded inequality operator by evaluating the condition

```
integers1 != integers2
```

and the program reports that the arrays are indeed not equal.

The program instantiates a third array called **integers3** and initializes it with array **integers1**. The program outputs the size of array **integers3**, then outputs the array itself using the overloaded stream-insertion operator to confirm that the array elements were initialized correctly by the constructor.

Next the program tests the overloaded assignment operator (=) with the expression **integers1 = integers2**. Both arrays are then printed to confirm that the assignment was correct. It is interesting to note that **integers1** originally held 7 integers and needed to be resized to hold a copy of the 10 elements in **integers2**. As we will see, the overloaded assignment operator performs this resizing in a manner transparent to the invoker of the operator.

Next the program uses the overloaded equality operator (==) to see that objects **integers1** and **integers2** are indeed identical after the assignment.

The program then uses the overloaded subscript operator to reference element **integers1[5]**—an in-range element of **integers1**. This subscripted name is then used as an rvalue to print the value in **integers1[5]**, and the name is then used as an lvalue on the left side of an assignment statement to receive a new value, 1000, for **integers1[5]**. Note that **operator[]** provides the reference and assigns the value.

The program then attempts to assign the value 1000 to **integers1[15]**—an out-of-range element. The program catches this error and terminates abnormally.

Interestingly, the array subscript operator **[]** is not restricted for use only with arrays; it can be used to select elements from other kinds of container classes such as linked lists, strings, dictionaries, and so on. Also, subscripts no longer have to be integers; characters or strings could be used, for example.

Now that we have seen how this program operates, let us walk through the class header and the member function definitions. The lines

```
int *ptr;                 // pointer to first element of array
int size;                 // size of the array
static int arrayCount;    // # of Arrays instantiated
```

represent the private data members of the class. The array consists of a pointer, **ptr** (to the appropriate type, in this case **int**), a **size** member indicating the number of elements in the array, and static member **arrayCount** indicating the number of array objects that have been instantiated.

The lines

```
friend ostream &operator<<(ostream &, const Array &);
friend istream &operator>>(istream &, Array &);
```

declare the overloaded stream-insertion operator and the overloaded stream-extraction operator to be friends of class **Array**. When the compiler sees an expression like

```
cout << arrayObject
```

it invokes the **operator<<** function by generating the call

```
operator<<(cout, arrayObject)
```

When the compiler sees an expression like

```
cin >> arrayObject
```

it invokes the **operator>>** function by generating the call

```
operator>>(cin, arrayObject)
```

We note again that these operator functions cannot be members of class **Array** because the **Array** object is always mentioned on the right side of the stream-insertion operator and the stream-extraction operator. Function **operator<<** prints the number of elements indicated by the **size** from the array stored at **ptr**. Function **operator>>** inputs directly into the array pointed to by **ptr**. Each of these operator functions returns an appropriate reference to enable concatenated calls.

The line

```
Array(int arraySize = 10);          // default constructor
```

declares the default constructor for the class and specifies that the array size defaults to 10 elements. When the compiler sees a declaration like

```
Array integers1(7);
```

or the equivalent form

```
Array integers1 = 7;
```

it invokes the default constructor. The default constructor member function **Array** increments **arrayCount**, copies the argument into the **size** data member, uses **new** to obtain the space to hold the internal representation of this array and assigns the pointer returned by **new** to data member **ptr**, uses **assert** to test that **new** was successful, then uses a **for** loop to initialize all the elements of the array to zero. It is possible to have an **Array** class that does not initialize its members if, for example, these members are to be read at some later time. But this is considered to be a poor programming practice. Arrays should be maintained in a properly initialized and consistent state.

The line

```
Array(const Array &);               // copy constructor
```

is a *copy constructor*. It initializes an **Array** object by making a copy of an existing **Array** object. Such copying must be done carefully to avoid the pitfall of leaving both **Array** objects pointing to the same dynamically allocated storage, exactly the problem that would occur with default memberwise copy. Copy constructors are invoked whenever a copy of an object is needed such as in call-by-value, when returning an object from a called function, or when initializing an object to be a copy of another object of the same class. The copy constructor is called in a declaration when an object of class **Array** is instantiated and initialized with another object of class **Array** as in the following declaration:

```
Array integers3(integers1);
```

or the equivalent declaration

```
Array integers3 = integers1;
```

Note that the copy constructor *must* use call-by-reference not call-by-value. Otherwise, the copy constructor call results in infinite recursion because, for call-by-value, a copy of the object passed to the copy constructor must be made which results in the copy constructor being called again!

The copy constructor member function **Array** increments **arrayCount**, copies the **size** of the array used for initialization into the **size** data member, uses **new** to obtain the space to hold the internal representation of this array and assigns the pointer returned by **new** to data member **ptr**, uses **assert** to test that **new** was successful, then uses a **for** loop to copy all the elements of the initializer array into this array. It is important to note that if the copy constructor simply copied the **ptr** in the source object to the target object's **ptr**, then both objects would point to the same dynamically allocated storage. The first destructor to execute would then delete the dynamically allocated storage and the other object's **ptr** would then be undefined, a situation likely to cause a serious runtime error.

*Good Programming Practice 8.7*

*A constructor, a destructor, an overloaded assignment operator, and a copy constructor are usually provided as a group for a class that uses dynamically allocated memory.*

The line

```
~Array();                              // destructor
```

declares the destructor for the class. The destructor is invoked automatically when the life of an object of class **Array** is terminated. The destructor decrements **arrayCount** then uses **delete** to reclaim the dynamic storage created by **new** in the constructor.

The line

```
int getSize() const;                   // return size
```

declares a function that reads the size of the array.

The line

```
const Array &operator=(const Array &);      // assign arrays
```

declares the overloaded assignment operator function for the class. When the compiler sees an expression like

```
integers1 = integers2;
```

it invokes the **operator=** function by generating the call

```
integers1.operator=(integers2)
```

The **operator=** member function tests for self assignment. If a self assignment is being attempted, the assignment is skipped (i.e., the object already is itself; in a moment we will see why self-assignment is dangerous). If it this not a self assignment, then the member function uses **delete** to reclaim the space originally allocated in the target array, copies the **size** of the source array to the **size** of the target array, uses **new** to allocate that amount of space for the target array and places the pointer returned by **new** into the array's **ptr** member, uses **assert** to verify that **new** succeeded, then uses a **for** loop to copy the array elements from the source array to the target array. Regardless of whether this is a self assignment or not, the member function then returns the current object (i.e., ***this**) as a constant reference; this enables concatenated **Array** assignments such as **x = y = z**. If the test for self assignment were omitted, the member function would begin by deleting the target array's space. Because this is also the source array in a self assignment, the array would have been destroyed.

***Common Programming Error 8.5***

*Not testing for and avoiding self assignment when overloading the assignment operator for a class that includes a pointer to dynamic storage.*

***Common Programming Error 8.6***

*Not providing an overloaded assignment operator and a copy constructor for a class when objects of that class contain pointers to dynamically allocated storage.*

***Software Engineering Observation 8.4***

*It is possible to prevent one class object from being assigned to another. This is done by defining the assignment operator as a private member of the class.*

***Software Engineering Observation 8.5***

*It is possible to prevent class objects from being copied; to do this, simply make both the overloaded assignment operator and the copy constructor private.*

The line

```
int operator==(const Array &) const; // compare equal
```

declares the overloaded equality operator (==) for the class. When the compiler sees the expression

```
integers1 == integers2
```

in **main**, the compiler invokes the **operator==** member function by generating the call

```
integers1.operator==(integers2)
```

The **operator==** member function immediately returns 0 (false) if the **size** members of the arrays are different. Otherwise, the member function compares each pair of elements. If they are all the same, 1 (true) is returned. The first pair of elements to differ causes 0 (false) to be returned immediately.

The line

```
int operator!=(const Array &) const; // compare !equal
```

declares the overloaded inequality operator (**!=**) for the class. The **operator!=** member function is invoked and operates similarly to the overloaded equality operator function. Note that the overloaded **operator!=** function could be written in terms of the overloaded **operator==** function as follows:

```
int Array::operator!=(const Array &right) const
   { return !(*this == right); }
```

The preceding function definition uses the overloded **operator==** function to determine if one **Array** is equal to another, then returns the opposite of that result. Writing the **operator!=** function in this manner enables the programmer to reuse the **operator==** function and reduces the amount of code that must be written from scratch in the class.

The line

```
int &operator[](int);                  // subscript operator
```

declares the overloaded subscript operator for the class. When the compiler sees the expression

```
integers1[5]
```

in **main**, the compiler invokes the overloaded **operator[]** member function by generating the call

```
integers1.operator[](5)
```

The **operator[]** member function tests if the subscript is in range, and if it is not, the program terminates abnormally. If the subscript is in range, the appropriate element of the array is returned as a reference so that it may be used as an lvalue (for example, on the left side of an assignment statement).

The line

```
static int getArrayCount();          // return count of Arrays
```

declares static member function **getArrayCount** that returns the value of static data member **arrayCount**, even if no objects of class **Array** exist.

## 8.9 Converting Between Types

Most programs process information of a variety of types. Sometimes all the operations "stay within a type." For example, adding an integer to an integer produces an integer (as long as the result is not too large to be represented as an integer). But, it is often necessary to convert data of one type to data of another type. This can happen in assignments, in calculations, in passing values to functions, and in returning values from functions. The compiler knows how to perform certain conversions among built-in types. Programmers can force conversions among built-in types by casting.

But what about user-defined types? The compiler cannot automatically know how to convert among user-defined types and built-in types. The programmer must specify how such conversions are to occur. Such conversions can be performed with *conversion constructors*—single-argument constructors that turn objects of other types (including built-in types) into objects of a particular class. We will use a conversion constructor later in this chapter to convert ordinary **char *** strings into **String** class objects.

A *conversion operator* (also called a *cast operator*) can be used to convert an object of one class into an object of another class or into an object of a built-in type. Such a conversion operator must be a nonstatic member function; this kind of conversion operator cannot be a friend function.

The function prototype

```
A::operator char *() const;
```

declares an overloaded cast operator function for creating a temporary **char *** object out of an object of user-defined type **A**. An overloaded cast operator function does not specify a return type—the return type is the type to which the object is being converted. If **s** is a class object, when the compiler sees the expression **(char *) s** the compiler generates the call **s.operator char *()**. The operand **s** is the class object **s** for which the member function **operator char *** is being invoked.

Overloaded cast operator functions can be defined for converting objects of user-defined types into built-in types or into objects of other user-defined types. The prototypes

```
A::operator int() const;
A::operator otherClass() const;
```

declare overloaded cast operator functions for converting an object of user-defined type **A** into an integer and for converting an object of user-defined type **A** into an object of user-defined type **otherClass**.

One of the nice features of cast operators and conversion constructors is that, when necessary, the compiler can call these functions automatically to create temporary objects. For example, if an object **s** of a user-defined **String** class appears in a program at a location where an ordinary **char *** is expected, such as

```
cout << s;
```

the compiler calls the overloaded cast operator function **operator char *** to convert the object into a **char *** and uses the resulting **char *** in the expression. With this cast operator provided for our **String** class, the stream-insertion operator does not have to be overloaded to output a **String** using **cout**.

## 8.10 Case Study: A String Class

As a capstone exercise to our study of overloading, we will build a class that handles the creation and manipulation of strings. C++ does not have a built-in string data type. But

C++ enables us to add our own string type as a class, and—through the mechanisms of overloading—provides a collection of operators for conveniently manipulating strings. The various parts of Fig. 8.5 include a class header, member function definitions, and a driver program to test our new class **String**.

First, we will present the header for class **String**. We discuss the private data used for representing **String** objects. Then we walk through the class's public interface, discussing each of the services the class provides.

Next, we will walk through the driver program in **main**. We will discuss the coding style we "aspire to," i.e., the kinds of operator-intensive expressions we would like to be able to write with objects of our new **String** class and with the class's collection of overloaded operators.

Then we discuss the member function definitions for class **String**. For each of the overloaded operators, we show the code in the driver program that invokes the overloaded operator function, and we explain how the overloaded operator function works.

```
// STRING2.H
// Definition of a String class
#ifndef STRING1_H
#define STRING1_H

#include <iostream.h>

class String {
   friend ostream &operator<<(ostream &, const String &);
   friend istream &operator>>(istream &, String &);
public:
   String(const char * = ""); // conversion constructor
   String(const String &);    // copy constructor
   ~String();                 // destructor
   const String &operator=(const String &);  // assignment
   String &operator+=(const String &);      // concatenation
   int operator!() const;                   // is String empty?
   int operator==(const String &) const;    // test s1 == s2
   int operator!=(const String &) const;    // test s1 != s2
   int operator<(const String &)  const;    // test s1 < s2
   int operator>(const String &)  const;    // test s1 > s2
   int operator>=(const String &) const;    // test s1 >= s2
   int operator<=(const String &) const;    // test s1 <= s2
   char &operator[](int);          // return char reference
   String operator()(int, int);    // return a substring
   int getLength() const;          // return string length

private:
   char *sPtr;                     // pointer to start of string
   int length;                     // string length
};

#endif
```

Fig. 8.5 Definition of a basic **String** class (part 1 of 7).

```
// STRING2.CPP
// Member function definitions for class String
#include <iostream.h>
#include <iomanip.h>
#include <string.h>
#include <assert.h>
#include "string2.h"

// Conversion constructor: Convert char * to String
String::String(const char *s)
{
   cout << "Conversion constructor: " << s << endl;
   length = strlen(s);            // compute length
   sPtr = new char[length + 1]; // allocate storage
   assert(sPtr != 0);  // terminate if memory not allocated
   strcpy(sPtr, s);               // copy literal to object
}

// Copy constructor
String::String(const String &copy)
{
   cout << "Copy constructor: " << copy.sPtr << endl;
   length = copy.length;          // copy length
   sPtr = new char[length + 1]; // allocate storage
   assert(sPtr != 0);             // ensure memory allocated
   strcpy(sPtr, copy.sPtr);       // copy string
}

// Destructor
String::~String()
{
   cout << "Destructor: " << sPtr << endl;
   delete [] sPtr;                // reclaim string
}

// Overloaded = operator; avoids self assignment
const String &String::operator=(const String &right)
{
   cout << "operator= called" << endl;

   if (&right != this) {            // avoid self assignment
      delete [] sPtr;               // prevents memory leak
      length = right.length;        // new String length
      sPtr = new char[length + 1]; // allocate memory
      assert(sPtr != 0);            // ensure memory allocated
      strcpy(sPtr, right.sPtr);     // copy string
   }
   else
      cout << "Attempted assignment of a String to itself" << endl;

   return *this;   // enables concatenated assignments
}
```

Fig. 8.5 Member function definitions for class `String` (part 2 of 7).

```
// Concatenate right operand to this object and
// store in this object.
String &String::operator+=(const String &right)
{
   char *tempPtr = sPtr;         // hold to be able to delete
   length += right.length;       // new String length
   sPtr = new char[length + 1]; // create space
   assert(sPtr != 0);    // terminate if memory not allocated

   strcpy(sPtr, tempPtr);        // left part of new String
   strcat(sPtr, right.sPtr);     // right part of new String
   delete [] tempPtr;            // reclaim old space

   return *this;                 // enables concatenated calls
}

// Is this String empty?
int String::operator!() const { return length == 0; }

// Is this String equal to right String?
int String::operator==(const String &right) const
   { return strcmp(sPtr, right.sPtr) == 0; }

// Is this String not equal to right String?
int String::operator!=(const String &right) const
   { return strcmp(sPtr, right.sPtr) != 0; }

// Is this String less than right String?
int String::operator<(const String &right) const
   { return strcmp(sPtr, right.sPtr) < 0; }

// Is this String greater than right String?
int String::operator>(const String &right) const
   { return strcmp(sPtr, right.sPtr) > 0; }

// Is this String greater than or equal to right String?
int String::operator>=(const String &right) const
   { return strcmp(sPtr, right.sPtr) >= 0; }

// Is this String less than or equal to right String?
int String::operator<=(const String &right) const
   { return strcmp(sPtr, right.sPtr) <= 0; }

// Return a reference to a character in a String.
char &String::operator[](int subscript)
{
   // First test for subscript out of range
   assert(subscript >= 0 && subscript < length);

   return sPtr[subscript];  // creates lvalue
}
```

**Fig. 8.5** Member function definitions for class **String** (part 3 of 7).

```
// Return a substring beginning at index and
// of length subLength as a reference to a String object.
String String::operator()(int index, int subLength)
{
   // ensure index is in range and substring length >= 0
   assert(index >= 0 && index < length && subLength >= 0);

   String sub;                 // empty String

   // determine length of substring
   if ((subLength == 0) || (index + subLength > length))
      sub.length = length - index + 1;
   else
      sub.length = subLength + 1;

   // allocate memory for substring
   delete sub.sPtr;          // delete character from object
   sub.sPtr = new char[sub.length];
   assert(sub.sPtr != 0); // ensure space allocated

   // copy substring into new String
   strncpy(sub.sPtr, &sPtr[index], sub.length);
   sub.sPtr[sub.length] = '\0'; // terminate new String

   return sub;               // return copy of String sub
}

// Return string length
int String::getLength() const { return length; }

// Overloaded output operator
ostream &operator<<(ostream &output, const String &s)
{
   output << s.sPtr;
   return output;    // enables concatenation
}

// Overloaded input operator
istream &operator>>(istream &input, String &s)
{
   char temp[100];    // buffer to store input

   input >> setw(100) >> temp;
   s = temp;          // use String class assignment operator
   return input;      // enables concatenation
}
```

**Fig. 8.5** Member function definitions for class **String** (part 4 of 7).

We begin with the internal representation of a **String**. The lines

```
private:
   char *sPtr;                  // pointer to start of string
   int length;                  // string length
```

```
// FIG8_5.CPP
// Driver for class String
#include <iostream.h>
#include "string2.h"

main()
{
   String s1("happy"), s2(" birthday"), s3;

   // test overloaded equality and relational operators
   cout << "s1 is \"" << s1 << "\"; s2 is \"" << s2
        << "\"; s3 is \"" << s3 << '\"' << endl
        << "The results of comparing s2 and s1:" << endl
        << "s2 == s1 yields " << (s2 == s1) << endl
        << "s2 != s1 yields " << (s2 != s1) << endl
        << "s2 >  s1 yields " << (s2 > s1) << endl
        << "s2 <  s1 yields " << (s2 < s1) << endl
        << "s2 >= s1 yields " << (s2 >= s1) << endl
        << "s2 <= s1 yields " << (s2 <= s1) << endl << endl;

   // test overloaded String empty (!) operator
   cout << "Testing !s3:" << endl;
   if (!s3) {
      cout << "s3 is empty; assigning s1 to s3;" << endl;
      s3 = s1;               // test overloaded assignment
      cout << "s3 is \"" << s3 << "\"" << endl << endl;
   }

   // test overloaded String concatenation operator
   cout << "s1 += s2 yields s1 = ";
   s1 += s2;                 // test overloaded concatenation
   cout << s1 << endl << endl;

   // test conversion constructor
   cout << "s1 += \" to you\" yields" << endl;
   s1 += " to you";          // test conversion constructor
   cout << "s1 = " << s1 << endl << endl;

   // test overloaded function call operator () for substring
   cout << "The substring of s1 starting at" << endl
        << "location 0 for 14 characters, s1(0, 14), is: "
        << s1(0, 14) << endl << endl;

   // test substring "to-end-of-String" option
   cout << "The substring of s1 starting at" << endl
        << "location 15, s1(15, 0), is: "
        << s1(15, 0) << endl << endl;  // 0 is "to end of string"
```

**Fig. 8.5** Driver for testing class **String** (part 5 of 7).

declare the private data members of the class. A **String** object has a pointer to its dynamically allocated storage representing the character string and has a length field which represents the number of characters in the string not including the null character at the end of the character string.

```
    // test copy constructor
    String *s4Ptr = new String(s1);
    cout << "*s4Ptr = " << *s4Ptr << endl << endl;

    // test assignment (=) operator with self-assignment
    cout << "assigning *s4Ptr to *s4Ptr" << endl;
    *s4Ptr = *s4Ptr;          // test overloaded assignment
    cout << "*s4Ptr = " << *s4Ptr << endl;

    // test destructor
    delete s4Ptr;

    // test using subscript operator to create lvalue
    s1[0] = 'H';
    s1[6] = 'B';
    cout << endl << "s1 after s1[0] = 'H' and s1[6] = 'B' is: "
         << s1 << endl << endl;

    // test subscript out of range
    cout << "Attempt to assign 'd' to s1[30] yields:" << endl;
    s1[30] = 'd';      // ERROR: subscript out of range

    return 0;
}
```

**Fig. 8.5** Driver for testing class **String** (part 6 of 7).

Now we walk through the **String** class header file in Fig. 8.5. The lines

```
friend ostream &operator<<(ostream &, const String &);
friend istream &operator>>(istream &, String &);
```

declare the overloaded stream-insertion operator function **operator<<** and the overloaded stream-extraction operator function **operator>>** as friends of the class. The implementation of these is straightforward.

The line

```
String(const char * = ""); // conversion constructor
```

declares a conversion constructor. This constructor takes a **char *** argument (that defaults to the empty string) and instantiates a **String** object which includes that same character string. Any single argument constructor can be thought of as a conversion constructor. As we will see, such constructors are helpful when we are doing any **String** operation using **char *** arguments. The conversion constructor converts the conventional string into a **String** object that is then assigned to the target **String** object. The availability of this conversion constructor means that it is not necessary to supply an overloaded assignment operator for specifically assigning character strings to **String** objects. The compiler automatically invokes the conversion constructor to create a temporary **String** object containing the character string. Then, the overloaded assignment operator is invoked to assign the temporary **String** object to another **String** object.

```
Conversion constructor: happy
Conversion constructor:  birthday
Conversion constructor:
s1 is "happy"; s2 is " birthday"; s3 is ""
The results of comparing s2 and s1:
s2 == s1 yields 0
s2 != s1 yields 1
s2 >  s1 yields 0
s2 <  s1 yields 1
s2 >= s1 yields 0
s2 <= s1 yields 1

Testing !s3:
s3 is empty; assigning s1 to s3;
operator= called
s3 is "happy"

s1 += s2 yields s1 = happy birthday

s1 += " to you" yields
Conversion constructor:  to you
Destructor:  to you
s1 = happy birthday to you

Conversion constructor:
The substring of s1 starting at
location 0 for 14 characters, s1(0, 14), is: happy birthday

Conversion constructor:
The substring of s1 starting at
location 15, s1(15, 0), is: to you

Copy constructor: happy birthday to you
*s4Ptr = happy birthday to you

assigning *s4Ptr to *s4Ptr
operator= called
Attempted assignment of a String to itself
*s4Ptr = happy birthday to you
Destructor: happy birthday to you

s1 after s1[0] = 'H' and s1[6] = 'B' is: Happy Birthday to you

Attempt to assign 'd' to s1[30] yields:
Assertion failed: subscript >= 0 && subscript < length,
   file STRING2.CPP, line 99
Abnormal program termination
```

**Fig. 8.5** Output from driver for testing class **String** (part 7 of 7).

***Software Engineering Observation 8.6***

*When a conversion constructor is used to perform an implicit conversion, C++ can only apply a single implicit constructor call to try to match the needs of another overloaded operator. It is not possible to match an overloaded operator's needs by performing a series of implicit, user-defined conversions.*

The **String** conversion constructor could be invoked in a declaration such as **String s1("happy")**. The conversion constructor member function calculates the length of the character string and assigns this to private data member **length**, uses **new** to assign a sufficient amount of space to private data member **sPtr**, uses **assert** to test that **new** succeeded and, if it did, uses **strcpy** to copy the character string into the object.

The line

```
String(const String &);     // copy constructor
```

is a copy constructor. It initializes a **String** object by making a copy of an existing **String** object. Such copying must be done carefully to avoid the pitfall of leaving both **String** objects pointing to the same dynamically allocated storage, exactly the problem that would occur with default memberwise copy. The copy constructor operates similarly to the conversion constructor except that it simply copies the **length** member from the source **String** object to the target **String** object. Note that the copy constructor creates new space for the target object's internal character string. If it simply copied the **sPtr** in the source object to the target object's **sPtr**, then both objects would point to the same dynamically allocated storage. The first destructor to execute would then delete the dynamically allocated storage and the other object's **sPtr** would then be undefined, a situation likely to cause a serious run-time error.

The line

```
~String();                              // destructor
```

declares the destructor for class **String**. The destructor uses **delete** to reclaim the dynamic storage obtained by **new** to provide the space for the character string.

The line

```
const String &operator=(const String &);      // assignment
```

declares the overloaded assignment operator. When the compiler sees an expression like **string1 = string2**, the compiler generates the function call

```
string1.operator=(string2);
```

The overloaded assignment operator function **operator=** tests for self-assignment, exactly as the copy constructor did. If this is a self-assignment, the function simply returns because the object is already itself. If this test were omitted, the function would immediately delete the space in the target object and thus lose the character string. Assuming that it is not a self-assignment, the function does delete the space, copies the length field of the source object to the target object, creates new space for the target object, uses **assert** to determine if **new** succeeded, and then uses **strcpy** to copy the character string from the source object to the target object. Whether or not this is a self-assignment, ***this** is returned to enable concatenated assignments.

The line

```
String &operator+=(const String &);     // concatenation
```

declares the overloaded string concatenation operator. When the compiler sees the expression **s1 += s2** in **main**, the function call **s1.operator+=(s2)** is generated. Function **operator+=** creates a temporary pointer to hold the current object's character string until the character string's memory can be deleted, calculates the combined length of the concatenated string, uses **new** to reserve space for the string, uses **assert** to test that **new** succeeded, uses **strcpy** to copy the original string into the newly allocated space, uses **strcat** to concatenate the source object's character string to the newly allocated space, uses **delete** to reclaim the space occupied by this object's original character string, and returns ***this** as a **String &** to enable concatenation of **+=** operators.

Do we need a second overloaded concatenation operator to allow concatenation of a **String** and a **char ***? No. The **const char *** conversion constructor converts a conventional string into a temporary **String** object which then matches the existing overloaded concatenation operator. C++ can perform such conversions only one level deep to facilitate a match. C++ can also perform an implicit compiler-defined conversion between built-in types before it performs the conversion between a built-in type and a class. Note that when a temporary **String** object is created, the conversion constructor and the destructor are called (see the output resulting from **s1 += " to you"** in Fig. 8.5). This is an example of function call overhead that is hidden from the client of the class when temporary class objects are created and destroyed during implicit conversions. Similar overhead is generated by copy constructors in call-by-value parameter passing and returning class objects by value.

***Performance Tip 8.2***

*Having the overloaded* **+=** *concatenation operator that takes a single argument of type* **const char *** *executes more efficiently than having to do the implicit conversion first, then the concatenation. Implicit conversions require less code and cause fewer errors.*

The line

```
int operator!() const;                   // is String empty?
```

declares the overloaded negation operator. This operator is commonly used with string classes to test if a string is empty. For example, when the compiler sees the expression **!string1**, it generates the function call

```
string1.operator!()
```

This function simply returns the result of testing if **length** is equal to zero.

The lines

```
int operator==(const String &) const;   // test s1 == s2
int operator!=(const String &) const;   // test s1 != s2
int operator<(const String &)  const;   // test s1 < s2
int operator>(const String &)  const;   // test s1 > s2
int operator>=(const String &) const;   // test s1 >= s2
int operator<=(const String &) const;   // test s1 <= s2
```

declare the overloaded equality operators and the overloaded relational operators for the **String** class. These are all similar, so let us discuss one example, namely overloading the `>=` operator. When the compiler sees the expression `string1 >= string2`, the compiler generates the function call

```
string1.operator>=(string2)
```

which returns 1 (true) if `string1` is greater than or equal to `string2`. Each of these operators uses `strcmp` to compare the character strings in the `String` objects. Note that each of the relational and equality operators are implemented using the function `strcmp` from the C standard library. Many C++ programmers advocate using some of the overloaded operator functions to implement others. For example, overloaded function `operator>=` could be implemented as follows:

```
int String::operator>=(const String &right) const
   { return (*this > right || *this == right) ? 1 : 0; }
```

The preceding `operator>=` definition uses the overloaded `>` and `==` operators to determine if one `String` object is greater than or equal to another. Implementing member functions using previously defined member functions enables the programmer to reduce the amount of code that must be written from scratch and increases the amount of code that is reused within the class.

The line

```
char &operator[](int);          // return char reference
```

declares the overloaded subscript operator. When the compiler sees an expression like `string1[0]`, the compiler generates the function call `string1.operator[](0)`. Function `operator[]` first uses `assert` to perform a range check on the subscript; if the subscript is out of range, the program will print an error message and terminate abnormally. If the subscript is within range, `operator[]` returns as a `char &` the appropriate character of the `String` object; this `char &` may be used as an lvalue to modify the designated character of the `String` object.

The line

```
String operator()(int, int); // return a substring
```

declares the *overloaded function call operator*. In string classes, it is common to overload this operator to select a substring from a `String` object. The two integer parameters specify the start location and the length of the substring being selected from the `String`. If the start location is out of range or the substring length is negative, an error message is generated. By convention, if the substring length is 0, then the substring is selected all the way to the end of the `String` object. For example, suppose `string1` is a `String` object containing the character string `"AEIOU"`. When the compiler sees the expression `string1(2, 2)`, it generates the function call `string1.operator()(2,2)`. When this call executes, it produces a temporary `String` object containing the string `"IO"` and returns a copy of this object.

Overloading the function call operator `()` is powerful because functions can take arbitrarily long and complex parameter lists. So we can use this capability for many interesting purposes. One such use of the function call operator is an alternate array subscripting notation: Instead of using C's awkward double square bracket notation for double arrays such as in **a[b][c]**, for example, some programmers prefer to overload the function call operator to enable the notation **a(b, c)**. The overloaded function call operator can only be a nonstatic member function. This operator is used only when the "function name" is an object of class **String**.

The line

```
int getLength() const;          // return string length
```

declares a function that returns the length of the **String** object. Note that this function obtains the length by returning the value of the private data of class **String**.

At this point, the reader should now step through the code in **main**, examine the output window, and check each use of an overloaded operator.

## 8.11 Overloading ++ and --

The increment and decrement operators—preincrement, postincrement, predecrement, and postdecrement—all can be overloaded. We will see how the compiler distinguishes between the prefix version or the postfix version of an increment or decrement operator.

To overload the increment operator to allow both preincrement and postincrement usage, each overloaded operator function must have a distinct signature so the compiler will be able to determine which version of **++** is intended. The prefix versions are overloaded exactly as any other prefix unary operator would be.

Suppose, for example, that we want to add 1 to the day in **Date** object **d1**. When the compiler sees the preincrementing expression

```
++d1
```

the compiler generates the member function call

```
d1.operator++()
```

whose prototype would be

```
Date operator++();
```

If the preincrementing is implemented as a nonmember function, when the compiler sees the expression

```
++d1
```

the compiler generates the function call

```
operator++(d1)
```

whose prototype would be declared in the **Date** class as

```
friend Date operator++(Date &);
```

Overloading the postincrementing operator presents a bit of a challenge because the compiler must be able to distinguish between the signatures of the overloaded preincrement and postincrement operator functions. The convention that has been adopted in C++ is that when the compiler sees the postincrementing expression

```
d1++
```

it will generate the member function call

```
d1.operator++(0)
```

whose prototype is

```
Date operator++(int)
```

The 0 is strictly a dummy value to make the argument list of **operator++** used for postincrementing distinguishable from the argument list of **operator++** used for preincrementing.

If the postincrementing is implemented as a nonmember function, when the compiler sees the expression

```
d1++
```

the compiler generates the function call

```
operator++(d1, 0)
```

whose prototype would be

```
friend Date operator++(Date &, int);
```

Once again, the **0** argument is used by the compiler so the argument list of **operator++** used for postincrementing is distinguishable from the argument list for preincrementing.

Everything stated in this section for overloading preincrement and postincrement operators applies to overloading predecrement and postdecrement operators. Next, we examine a **Date** class with overloaded preincrement and postincrement operators.

## 8.12 Case Study: A Date Class

Figure 8.6 illustrates a **Date** class. The class uses overloaded preincrement and postincrement operators to add 1 to the day in a **Date** object, while causing appropriate increments to the month and year if necessary.

The class provides the following member functions: an overloaded stream-insertion operator, a default constructor, a **setDate** function, an overloaded preincrement operator function, an overloaded postincrement operator function, an overloaded addition assignment operator (+=), a function to test for leap years, and a function to determine if a day is the last day of the month.

The driver program in **main** creates the date objects **d1** which is initialized by default to January 1, 1900; **d2** which is initialized to December 27, 1992; and **d3** which the program attempts to initialize to an invalid date. The **Date** constructor calls **setDate** to validate the month, day, and year specified. If the month is invalid, it is set to 1. An invalid year is set to 1900. An invalid day is set to 1.

```
// DATE1.H
// Definition of class Date
#ifndef DATE1_H
#define DATE1_H
#include <iostream.h>

class Date {
   friend ostream &operator<<(ostream &, const Date &);
public:
   Date(int m = 1, int d = 1, int y = 1900); // def. constructor
   void setDate(int, int, int);  // set the date
   Date operator++();            // preincrement
   Date operator++(int);         // postincrement
   const Date &operator+=(int);  // add days, modify object
   int leapYear(int);            // is this a leap year?
   int endOfMonth(int);          // is this end of month?
private:
   int month;
   int day;
   int year;
   static int days[];     // array of days per month
   void helpIncrement();  // utility function
};

#endif
```

**Fig. 8.6** Definition of class `Date` (part 1 of 6).

```
// DATE1.CPP
// Member function definitions for Date class
#include <iostream.h>
#include "date1.h"

// Initialize static member at file scope;
// one class-wide copy.
int Date::days[] = {0, 31, 28, 31, 30, 31, 30,
                    31, 31, 30, 31, 30, 31};

// Date constructor
Date::Date(int m, int d, int y) { setDate(m, d, y); }

// Set the date
void Date::setDate(int mm, int dd, int yy)
{
   month = (mm >= 1 && mm <= 12) ? mm : 1;
   year = (yy >= 1900 && yy <= 2100) ? yy : 1900;

   if (month == 2 && leapYear(year))   // test for a leap year
      day = (dd >= 1 && dd <= 29) ? dd : 1;
   else
      day = (dd >= 1 && dd <= days[month]) ? dd : 1;
}
```

**Fig. 8.6** Member function definitions for class `Date` (part 2 of 6).

```
// Preincrement operator overloaded as a member function.
Date Date::operator++()
{
   helpIncrement();
   return *this;   // value return; not a reference return
}

// Postincrement operator overloaded as a member function.
// Note that the dummy integer parameter does not have a
// parameter name.
Date Date::operator++(int)
{
   Date temp = *this;
   helpIncrement();

   // return non-incremented, saved, temporary object
   return temp;    // value return; not a reference return
}

// Add a specific number of days to a date
const Date &Date::operator+=(int additionalDays)
{
   for (int i = 1; i <= additionalDays; i++)
      helpIncrement();

   return *this;     // enables concatenation
}

// Determine if the year is a leap year
int Date::leapYear(int y)
{
   if (y % 400 == 0 || (y % 100 != 0 && y % 4 == 0) )
      return 1;   // a leap year
   else
      return 0;   // not a leap year
}

// Determine if the day is the end of the month
int Date::endOfMonth(int d)
{
   if (month == 2 && leapYear(year))
      return d == 29; // last day of Feb. in leap year
   else
      return d == days[month];
}
```

**Fig. 8.6** Member function definitions for class **Date** (part 3 of 6).

The driver program outputs each of the constructed **Date** objects using the overloaded stream-insertion operator. The overloaded operator **+=** is used to add 7 days to **d2**. Then the **setDate** function is used to set **d3** to February 28, 1992. Next, a new **Date** object, **d4**, is set to March 18, 1969. Then **d4** is incremented by 1 with the overloaded preincrement operator. The date is printed before and after the preincrementing to con-

```
// Function to help increment the date
void Date::helpIncrement()
{
   if (endOfMonth(day) && month == 12) {  // end year
      day = 1;
      month = 1;
      ++year;
   }
   else if (endOfMonth(day)) {             // end month
      day = 1;
      ++month;
   }
   else       // not end of month or year; increment day
      ++day;
}

// Overloaded output operator
ostream &operator<<(ostream &output, const Date &d)
{
   static char *monthName[13] = {"", "January",
      "February", "March", "April", "May", "June",
      "July", "August", "September", "October",
      "November", "December"};

   output << monthName[d.month] << ' '
          << d.day << ", " << d.year;

   return output;    // enables concatenation
}
```

**Fig. 8.6** Member function definitions for class `Date` (part 4 of 6).

firm that it worked correctly. Finally, **d4** is incremented with the overloaded postincrement operator. The date is printed before and after the postincrementing to confirm that it worked correctly.

Overloading the preincrementing operator is straightforward. The program calls utility function **helpIncrement** to do the actual incrementing. This function must deal with wraparounds or carries that occur when we increment the last day of the month. These carries require that the month be incremented. If the month is already 12, then the year must also be incremented. Function **helpIncrement** uses functions **leapYear** and **endOfMonth** to increment the day correctly.

The overloaded preincrement operator returns an incremented *copy* of the current object. This occurs because the current object, ***this**, is returned as a **Date**, thus invoking the copy constructor.

Overloading the postincrement operator is a bit trickier. To emulate the effect of the postincrement, we must return an unincremented copy of the **Date** object. On entry to **operator++**, we save the current object (***this**) in **temp**. Then we call **helpIncrement** to increment the object. Then we return the unincremented copy of the object in **temp**. Note that this function cannot return a reference to a **Date** object because the value being returned is stored in a local variable in the function definition. Local variables

```
// FIG8_6.CPP
// Driver for class Date
#include <iostream.h>
#include "date1.h"

main()
{
   Date d1, d2(12, 27, 1992), d3(0, 99, 8045);
   cout << "d1 is " << d1 << endl
        << "d2 is " << d2 << endl
        << "d3 is " << d3 << endl << endl;

   cout << "d2 += 7 is " << (d2 += 7) << endl << endl;

   d3.setDate(2, 28, 1992);
   cout << "  d3 is " << d3 << endl;
   cout << "++d3 is " << ++d3 << endl << endl;

   Date d4(3, 18, 1969);

   cout << "Testing the preincrement operator:" << endl
        << "  d4 is " << d4 << endl;
   cout << "++d4 is " << ++d4 << endl;
   cout << "  d4 is " << d4 << endl << endl;

   cout << "Testing the postincrement operator:" << endl
        << "  d4 is " << d4 << endl;
   cout << "d4++ is " << d4++ << endl;
   cout << "  d4 is " << d4 << endl;

   return 0;
}
```

**Fig.8.6** Driver for class **Date** (part 5 of 6).

are destroyed when the function in which they are declared is exited. Thus, declaring the return type to this function as **Date &** would result in a reference to an object that no longer exists being returned. Returning a reference to a local variable is a common error that is difficult to detect.

## Summary

- The operator **<<** is used for multiple purposes in C++—as the stream-insertion operator and as the left-shift operator. This is an example of operator overloading. Similarly, **>>** is also overloaded; it is used both as the stream-extraction operator and as the right-shift operator.
- More generally, C++ enables the programmer to overload most operators to be sensitive to the context in which they are used. The compiler generates the appropriate code based on the manner in which the operator is used.
- Operator overloading contributes to C++'s extensibility.

```
d1 is January 1, 1900
d2 is December 27, 1992
d3 is January 1, 1900

d2 += 7 is January 3, 1993

  d3 is February 28, 1992
++d3 is February 29, 1992

Testing the preincrement operator:
  d4 is March 18, 1969
++d4 is March 19, 1969
  d4 is March 19, 1969

Testing the postincrement operator:
  d4 is March 19, 1969
d4++ is March 19, 1969
  d4 is March 20, 1969
```

**Fig.8.6** Output from driver for class **Date** (part 6 of 6).

- Operators are overloaded by writing a function definition (with a header and body). The function name becomes the keyword **operator** followed by the symbol for the operator being overloaded.
- To use an operator on class objects, that operator *must* be overloaded—with two exceptions. The assignment operator (**=**) may be used with every class to perform a default memberwise copy without overloading. The address operator (**&**) may also be used with objects of any class without overloading; it simply returns the address of the object in memory.
- Operator overloading provides the same concise expressions for user-defined types that C++ provides with its rich collection of operators that work on built-in types.
- Most of C++'s operators can be overloaded.
- The precedence and associativity of an operator cannot be changed by overloading.
- Default arguments cannot be used to overload an operator.
- It is not possible to change the number of operands an operator takes: Overloaded unary operators remain as unary operators; overloaded binary operators remain as binary operators.
- It is not possible to create symbols for new operators; only existing operators may be overloaded.
- The meaning of how an operator works on objects of built-in types cannot be changed by overloading.
- When overloading **()**, **[]**, **->**, or =, the operator overloading function must be declared as a class member.

- Operator functions can be member functions or nonmember functions.
- When an operator function is implemented as a member function, the leftmost operand must be a class object (or a reference to a class object) of the operator's class.
- If the left operand must be an object of a different class, this operator function must be implemented as a nonmember function.
- Operator member functions are called only when the left operand of a binary operator is specifically an object of that class, or when the single operand of a unary operator is an object of that class.
- One might choose a nonmember function to overload an operator in order to enable the operator to be commutative (i.e., given the proper overloaded operator definitions, the left argument of an operator can be an object of another data type).
- A unary operator can be overloaded as a nonstatic member function with no arguments or as a nonmember function with one argument; that argument must be either an object of a user-defined type or a reference to an object of a user-defined type.
- A binary operator can be overloaded as a nonstatic member function with one argument, or as a nonmember function with two arguments (one of those arguments must be either a class object or a reference to a class object).
- The array subscript operator `[]` is not restricted for use only with arrays; it can be used to select elements from other kinds of container classes such as linked lists, strings, dictionaries, and so on. Also, subscripts no longer have to be integers; characters or strings could be used, for example.
- A copy constructor is used to initialize an object with another object of the same class. Copy constructors are also invoked whenever a copy of an object is needed, such as in call-by-value, and when returning a value from a called function. Copy constructors must receive reference parameters.
- The compiler does not automatically know how to convert between user-defined types and built-in types. The programmer must explicitly specify how such conversions are to occur. Such conversions can be performed with conversion constructors (i.e., single-argument constructors) that simply turn objects of other types into objects of a particular class.
- A conversion operator (or cast) can be used to convert an object of one class into an object of another class or into an object of a built-in type. Such a conversion operator must be a nonstatic member function; this kind of conversion operator cannot be a friend function.
- A conversion constructor is a single argument constructor used to convert the argument into an object of the constructor's class. The compiler can call such a constructor implicitly.
- The assignment operator is the most frequently overloaded operator. It is normally used to assign an object to another object of the same class, but through the use of conversion constructors it can also be used to assign between classes.

- If an overloaded assignment operator is not defined, assignment is still allowed, but it defaults to a memberwise copy of each data member. In some cases this is acceptable. For objects that contain pointers to dynamically allocated storage, memberwise copy results in two different objects pointing to the same dynamically allocated storage. When the destructor for either of these objects is called, the dynamically allocated storage is released. If the other object then refers to that storage, the result is undefined.
- To overload the increment operator to allow both preincrement and postincrement usage, each overloaded operator function must have a distinct signature so the compiler will be able to determine which version of `++` is intended. The prefix versions are overloaded exactly as any other prefix unary operator. Providing a unique signature to the postincrement operator function is achieved by providing a second argument—which must be of type `int`. Actually, the user does not supply a value for this special integer argument. It is there simply to help the compiler distinguish between prefix and postfix versions of increment and decrement operators.

## Terminology

built-in type
class `Array`
class `Date`
class `String`
concatenated function calls
conversion ambiguity resolution
conversion constructor
conversion function
conversion operator
conversions between class types
conversions between built-in types and classes
copy constructor
explicit type conversions (with casts)
friend function overloaded operator
implicit type conversions
member function overloaded operator
nonoverloadable operators
`operator` keyword
operator overloading
operators as functions
overloadable operators
overloaded `==` operator
overloaded `!=` operator
overloaded `<` operator
overloaded `<=` operator
overloaded `>` operator
overloaded `>=` operator
overloaded assignment (`=`) operator
overloaded `[]` operator
overloading
overloading a binary operator
overloading a unary operator
postfix operator overloading
prefix operator overloading
user-defined conversion
user-defined type

## Common Programming Errors

**8.1** Attempting to overload a nonoverloadable operator.

**8.2** Attempting to create new operators.

**8.3** Attempting to modify how an operator works with objects of built-in types.

**8.4** Assuming that overloading an operator (such as `+`) automatically overloads related operators (such as `+=` ). Operators can be overloaded only explicitly; there is no implicit overloading.

**8.5** Not testing for and avoiding self assignment when overloading the assignment operator for a class that includes a pointer to dynamic storage.

**8.6** Not providing an overloaded assignment operator and a copy constructor for a class when objects of that class contain pointers to dynamically allocated storage.

## Good Programming Practices

**8.1** Use operator overloading when it makes a program clearer than accomplishing the same operations with explicit function calls.

**8.2** Avoid excessive or inconsistent use of operator overloading as this can make a program cryptic and difficult to read.

**8.3** Overload operators to perform the same function or closely similar functions on class objects as the operators perform on objects of built-in types. Avoid nonintuitive uses of operators.

**8.4** Before writing C++ programs with overloaded operators, consult the manuals for your C++ compiler to become aware of various restrictions and requirements unique to particular operators.

**8.5** To ensure consistency among related operators, use one to implement the others (i.e., use an overloaded + operator to implement an overloaded += operator).

**8.6** When overloading unary operators, it is preferable to make the operator functions class members instead of nonmember friend functions. Friend functions and classes should be avoided unless they are absolutely necessary. The use of friends violates the encapsulation of a class.

**8.7** A constructor, a destructor, an overloaded assignment operator, and a copy constructor are usually provided as a group for a class that uses dynamically allocated memory.

## Performance Tips

**8.1** It is possible to overload an operator as a nonmember, nonfriend function, but such a function needing access to a class's private or protected data would need to use set or get functions provided in that class's public interface. The overhead of calling these functions could cause poor performance.

**8.2** Having the overloaded += concatenation operator that takes a single argument of type `const char *` executes more efficiently than having to do the implicit conversion first, then the concatenation. Implicit conversions require less code and cause fewer errors.

## Software Engineering Observations

**8.1** Operator overloading contributes to C++'s extensibility, surely one of the language's most appealing attributes.

**8.2** At least one argument of an operator function must be a class object or a reference to a class object. This prevents programmers from changing the meaning of how operators work on objects of built-in types.

**8.3** New input/output capabilities for user-defined types can be added to C++ without modifying the declarations or private data members for either the `ostream` class or the `istream` class. This is another example of the extensibility of the C++ programming language.

**8.4** It is possible to prevent one class object from being assigned to another. This is done by defining the assignment operator as a private member of the class.

**8.5** It is possible to prevent class objects from being copied; to do this, simply make both the overloaded assignment operator and the copy constructor private.

**8.6** When a conversion constructor is used to perform an implicit conversion, C++ can only apply a single implicit constructor call to try to match the needs of another overloaded operator. It is not possible to match an overloaded operator's needs by performing a series of implicit, user-defined conversions.

## Self-Review Exercises

**8.1** Fill in the blanks in each of the following:

a) Suppose `a` and `b` are integer variables and we form the sum `a + b`. Now suppose `c` and `d` are floating-point variables and we form the sum `c + d`. The two `+` operators here are clearly being used for different purposes. This is an example of __________.

b) The keyword __________ introduces an overloaded operator function definition.

c) To use operators on class objects, they must be overloaded with the exception of the operators __________ and __________.

d) The __________ and __________ of an operator cannot be changed by overloading the operator.

**8.2** Explain the multiple meanings of the operators `<<` and `>>` in C++.

**8.3** In what context might the name `operator/` be used in C++?

**8.4** (True/False) In C++, only existing operators can be overloaded.

**8.5** How does the precedence of an overloaded operator in C++ compare with the precedence of the original operator?

## Answers to Self-Review Exercises

**8.1** a) operator overloading. b) `operator`. c) assignment (`=`), address(`&`). d) precedence, associativity.

**8.2** The operator `>>` is both the right-shift operator and the stream-extraction operator depending on its context. The operator `<<` is both the left-shift operator and the stream-insertion operator depending on its context.

**8.3** For operator overloading: It would be the name of a function that would provide a new version of the `/` operator.

**8.4** True.

**8.5** Identical.

## Exercises

**8.6** Give as many examples as you can of operator overloading implicit in C. Give as many examples as you can of operator overloading implicit in C++. Give a reasonable example of a situation in which you might want to overload an operator explicitly in C++.

**8.7** The C++ operators that cannot be overloaded are _____, _____, _____, _____, and _____.

**8.8** String concatenation requires two operands—the two strings that are to be concatenated. In the text we showed how to implement an overloaded concatenation operator that concatenates the second `String` object to the right of the first `String` object, thus modifying the first `String` object. In some applications, it is desirable to produce a concatenated `String` object without modifying the two `String` arguments. Implement `operator+` to allow operations such as

```
string1 = string2 + string3;
```

**8.9** *(Ultimate operator overloading exercise)* To appreciate the care that should go into selecting operators for overloading, list each of C++'s overloadable operators and for each list a possible meaning (or several, if appropriate) for each of several classes you have studied in this course. We suggest you try:

a) Array
b) Stack
c) String

After doing this, comment on which operators seem to have meaning for a wide variety of classes. Which operators seem to be of little value for overloading? What operators seem ambiguous?

**8.10** Now work the process described in the previous problem in reverse. List each of C++'s overloadable operators. For each, list what you feel is perhaps the "ultimate operation" the operator should be used to represent. If there are several excellent operations, list them all.

**8.11** *(Project)* C++ is an evolving language, and new languages are always being developed. What additional operators would you recommend adding to C++ or to a future language like C++ that would support both procedural programming and object-oriented programming? Write a careful justification. You might consider sending your suggestions to the ANSI C++ Committee.

**8.12** One nice example of overloading the function call operator `()` is to allow the more common form of double array subscripting. Instead of saying

```
chessBoard[row][column]
```

for an array of objects, overload the function call operator to allow the alternate form

```
chessBoard(row, column)
```

**8.13** Overload the subscript operator to return a given member of a linked list.

**8.14** Overload the subscript operator to return the largest element of a collection, the second largest, the third largest, etc.

**8.15** Consider class **`Complex`** shown in Fig. 8.7. The class enables operations on so-called *complex numbers*. These are numbers of the form **`realPart + imaginaryPart *`** *i* where *i* has the value:

$$\sqrt{-1}$$

a) Modify the class to enable input and output of complex numbers through the overloaded `>>` and `<<` operators, respectively (you should remove the print function from the class).
b) Overload the multiplication operator to enable multiplication of two complex numbers as in algebra.
c) Overload the `==` and `!=` operators to allow comparisons of complex numbers.

**8.16** A machine with 32-bit integers can represent integers in the range of approximately –2 billion to +2 billion. This fixed-size restriction is rarely troublesome. But there are many applications in which we would like to be able to use a much wider range of integers. This is what C++ was built to do, namely create powerful new data types. Consider class **`HugeInt`** of Fig. 8.8. Study the class carefully, then

a) Describe precisely how it operates.
b) What restrictions does the class have?
c) Modify the class to be able to process arbitrarily large integers. (Hint: Use a linked list to represent a **`HugeInt`**.)
d) Overload the `*` multiplication operator.
e) Overload the `/` division operator.
f) Overload all the relational and equality operators.

```
// COMPLEX1.H
// Definition of class Complex
#ifndef COMPLEX1_H
#define COMPLEX1_H

class Complex {
public:
   Complex(double = 0.0, double = 0.0);       // constructor
   Complex operator+(const Complex &) const; // addition
   Complex operator-(const Complex &) const; // subtraction
   Complex &operator=(const Complex &);       // assignment
   void print() const;                        // output
private:
   double real;       // real part
   double imaginary;  // imaginary part
};

#endif
```

Fig. 8.7 Definition of class **Complex** (part 1 of 5).

```
// COMPLEX1.CPP
// Member function definitions for class Complex
#include <iostream.h>
#include "complex1.h"

// Constructor
Complex::Complex(double r, double i)
{
   real = r;
   imaginary = i;
}

// Overloaded addition operator
Complex Complex::operator+(const Complex &operand2) const
{
   Complex sum;
   sum.real = real + operand2.real;
   sum.imaginary = imaginary + operand2.imaginary;
   return sum;
}

// Overloaded subtraction operator
Complex Complex::operator-(const Complex &operand2) const
{
   Complex diff;
   diff.real = real - operand2.real;
   diff.imaginary = imaginary - operand2.imaginary;
   return diff;
}
```

Fig. 8.7 Member function definitions for class **Complex** (part 2 of 5).

```
// Overloaded = operator
Complex& Complex::operator=(const Complex &right)
{
   real = right.real;
   imaginary = right.imaginary;
   return *this;    // enables concatenation
}

// Display a Complex object in the form: (a, b)
void Complex::print() const
   { cout << '(' << real << ", " << imaginary << ')'; }
```

**Fig. 8.7** Member function definitions for class `Complex` (part 3 of 5).

```
// FIG8_7.CPP
// Driver for class Complex
#include <iostream.h>
#include "complex1.h"

main()
{
   Complex x, y(4.3, 8.2), z(3.3, 1.1);

   cout << "x: ";
   x.print();
   cout << endl << "y: ";
   y.print();
   cout << endl << "z: ";
   z.print();

   x = y + z;
   cout << endl << endl << "x = y + z:" << endl;
   x.print();
   cout << " = ";
   y.print();
   cout << " + ";
   z.print();

   x = y - z;
   cout << endl << endl << "x = y - z:" << endl;
   x.print();
   cout << " = ";
   y.print();
   cout << " - ";
   z.print();
   cout << endl;

   return 0;
}
```

**Fig. 8.7** Driver for class `Complex` (part 4 of 5).

```
x: (0, 0)
y: (4.3, 8.2)
z: (3.3, 1.1)

x = y + z:
(7.6, 9.3) = (4.3, 8.2) + (3.3, 1.1)

x = y - z:
(1, 7.1) = (4.3, 8.2) - (3.3, 1.1)
```

**Fig. 8.7** Output from driver for class **Complex** (part 5 of 5).

```
// HUGEINT1.H
// Definition of the HugeInt class
#ifndef HUGEINT1_H
#define HUGEINT1_H

#include <iostream.h>

class HugeInt {
   friend ostream &operator<<(ostream &, HugeInt &);
public:
   HugeInt(long = 0);             // conversion constructor
   HugeInt(const char *);         // conversion constructor
   HugeInt operator+(HugeInt &); // addition
private:
   short integer[30];
};

#endif
```

**Fig. 8.8** A user-defined huge integer class (part 1 of 4).

```
// HUGEINT1.CPP
// Member and friend function definitions for class HugeInt
#include <string.h>
#include "hugeint1.h"

// Conversion constructor
HugeInt::HugeInt(long val)
{
   for (int i = 0; i <= 29; i++)
      integer[i] = 0;   // initialize array to zero

   for (i = 29; val != 0 && i >= 0; i--) {
      integer[i] = val % 10;
      val /= 10;
   }
}
```

**Fig. 8.8** A user-defined huge integer class (part 2 of 4).

```
HugeInt::HugeInt(const char *string)
{
   int i, j;

   for (i = 0; i <= 29; i++)
      integer[i] = 0;

   for (i = 30 - strlen(string), j = 0; i <= 29; i++, j++)
      integer[i] = string[j] - '0';
}

// Addition
HugeInt HugeInt::operator+(HugeInt &op2)
{
   HugeInt temp;
   int carry = 0;

   for (int i = 29; i >= 0; i--) {
      temp.integer[i] = integer[i] + op2.integer[i] + carry;

      if (temp.integer[i] > 9) {
         temp.integer[i] %= 10;
         carry = 1;
      }
      else
         carry = 0;
   }

   return temp;
}

ostream& operator<<(ostream &output, HugeInt &num)
{
   for (int i = 0; (num.integer[i] == 0) && (i <= 29); i++)
      ; // skip leading zeros

   if (i == 30)
      output << 0;
   else
      for ( ; i <= 29; i++)
         output << num.integer[i];

   return output;
}
```

**Fig. 8.8** A user-defined huge integer class (part 3 of 4).

**8.17** Create a class `rationalNumber` (fractions) with the following capabilities:

a) Create a constructor that prevents a 0 denominator in a fraction, reduces or simplifies fractions that are not in reduced form, and avoids negative denominators.

b) Overload the addition, subtraction, multiplication and division operators for this class.

c) Overload the relational and equality operators for this class.

**8.18** Study the C string handling library functions and implement each of the functions as part of the `String` class. Then, use these functions to perform text manipulations.

```
// FIG8_8.CPP
// Test driver for HugeInt class
#include <iostream.h>
#include "hugeint1.h"

main()
{
   HugeInt n1(7654321), n2(7891234),
           n3("99999999999999999999999999999"),
           n4("1"), n5;

   cout << "n1 is " << n1 << endl << "n2 is " << n2
        << endl << "n3 is " << n3 << endl << "n4 is " << n4
        << endl << "n5 is " << n5 << endl << endl;

   n5 = n1 + n2;
   cout << n1 << " + " << n2 << " = " << n5 << endl << endl;

   cout << n3 << " + " << n4 << endl << "= " << (n3 + n4)
        << endl << endl;

   n5 = n1 + 9;
   cout << n1 << " + " << 9 << " = " << n5 << endl << endl;

   n5 = n2 + "10000";
   cout << n2 << " + " << "10000" << " = " << n5 << endl << endl;

   return 0;
}
```

```
n1 is 7654321
n2 is 7891234
n3 is 99999999999999999999999999999
n4 is 1
n5 is 0

7654321 + 7891234 = 15545555

99999999999999999999999999999 + 1
= 100000000000000000000000000000

7654321 + 9 = 7654330

7891234 + 10000 = 7901234
```

Fig. 8.8 A user-defined huge integer class (part 4 of 4).

**8.19** Develop class **Polynomial**. The internal representation of a **Polynomial** is an array of terms. Each term contains a coefficient and an exponent. The term

$2x^4$

has a coefficient of 2 and an exponent of 4. Develop a full class containing proper constructor and destructor functions as well as *set* and *get* functions. The class should also provide the following overloaded operator capabilities:

a) Overload the addition operator (`+`) to add two **`Polynomials`**.
b) Overload the subtraction operator (`-`) to subtract two **`Polynomials`**.
c) Overload the assignment operator to assign one **`Polynomial`** to another.
d) Overload the multiplication operator (`*`) to multiply two **`Polynomials`**.
e) Overload the addition assignment operator (`+=`), the subtraction assignment operator (`-=`), the multiplication assignment operator (`*=`).

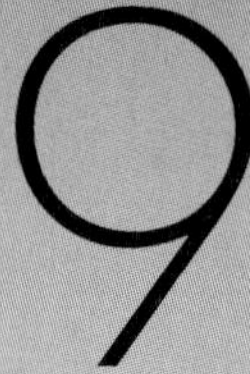

# Inheritance

## Objectives

- To be able to create new classes by inheriting from existing classes.
- To understand how inheritance promotes software reusability.
- To understand the notions of base classes and derived classes.
- To be able to use multiple inheritance to derive a class from several base classes.

*Say not you know another entirely, till you have divided an inheritance with him.*
Johann Kasper Lavater

*This method is to define as the number of a class the class of all classes similar to the given class.*
Bertrand Russell

*A deck of cards was built like the purest of hierarchies, with every card a master to those below it, a lackey to those above it.*
Ely Culbertson

*Good as it is to inherit a library, it is better to collect one.*
Augustine Birrell

*Save base authority from other's books.*
William Shakespeare, Lover's Labour's Lost

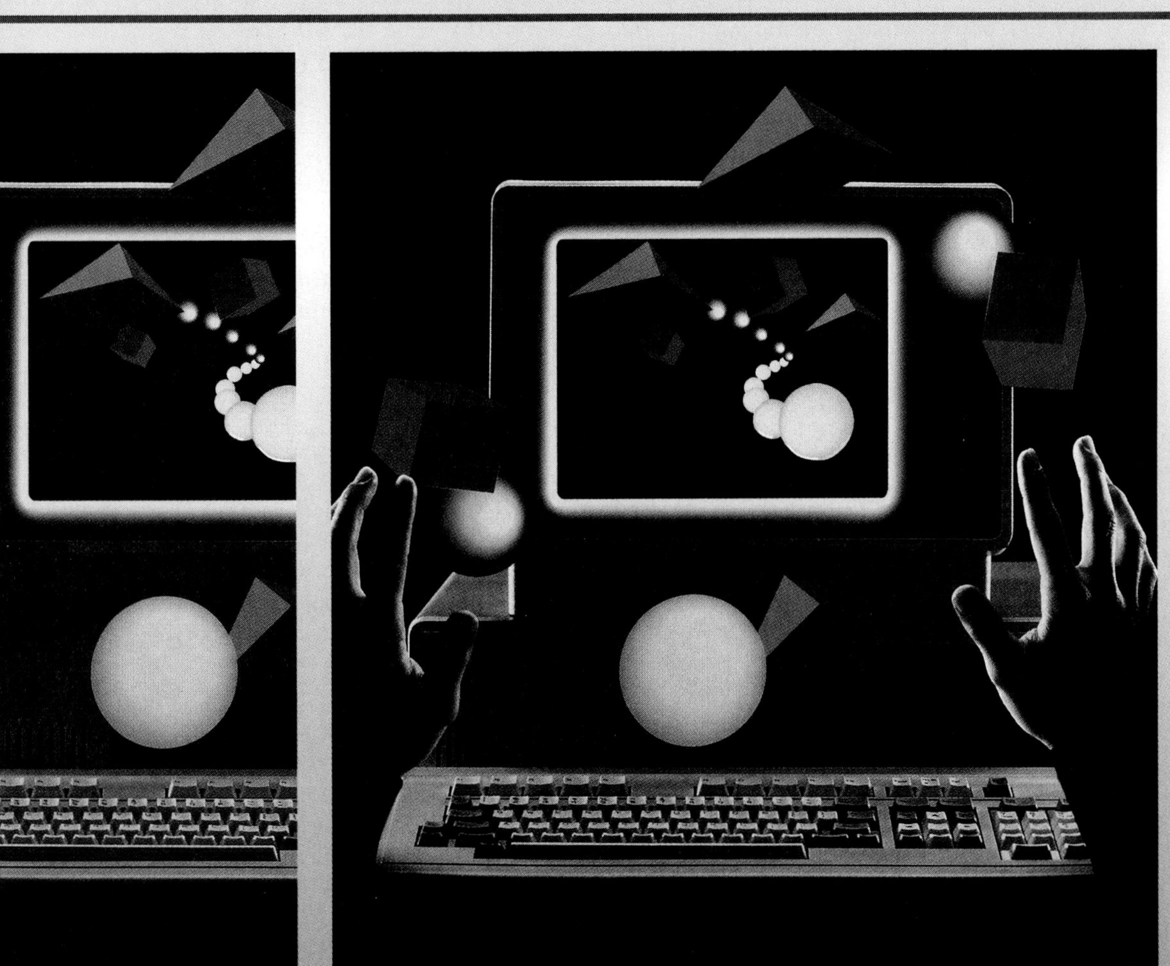

# Outline



## 9.1 Introduction

In this and the next chapter we discuss two of the most important capabilities object-oriented programming provides—*inheritance* and *polymorphism.* Inheritance is a form of software reusability in which new classes are created from existing classes by absorbing their attributes and behaviors and embellishing these with capabilities the new classes require. Software reusability saves time in program development. It encourages the reuse of proven and debugged high-quality software, thus reducing problems after a system becomes functional. These are exciting possibilities. Polymorphism enables us to write programs in a general fashion to handle a wide variety of existing and yet-to-be-specified related classes. Inheritance and polymorphism are effective techniques for dealing with software complexity.

When creating a new class, instead of writing completely new data members and member functions, the programmer can designate that the new class is to *inherit* the data members and member functions of a previously defined *base class.* The new class is referred to as a *derived class.* Each derived class itself becomes a candidate to be a base class for some future derived class. With *single inheritance,* a class is derived from one base class. With *multiple inheritance,* a derived class inherits from multiple (possibly unrelated) base classes.

A derived class normally adds data members and member functions of its own, so a derived class is generally larger than its base class. A derived class is more specific than its base class and represents a smaller group of objects. With single inheritance, the derived class starts out essentially the same as the base class. The real strength of inheritance comes from the ability to define in the derived class additions, replacements, or refinements to the features inherited from the base class.

Every object of a derived class is also an object of that derived class's base class. However, the converse is not true—base-class objects are not objects of that base class's derived classes. We will take advantage of this "derived-class-object-is-a-base-class-object" relationship to perform some interesting manipulations. For example, we can thread a wide variety of different objects related through inheritance into a linked list of base-class objects. This allows a variety of objects to be processed in a general way. As we will see in this and the next chapter, this is a key thrust of object-oriented programming.

We add a new form of member access control in this chapter, namely protected access. Derived classes and their friends receive favored treatment over other functions in accessing protected base-class members.

Experience in building software systems indicates that large portions of the code deal with closely related special cases. It becomes difficult in such systems to see the "big picture" because the designer and the programmer become preoccupied with the special cases. Object-oriented programming provides several ways of "seeing the forest through the trees"—a process sometimes called *abstraction.*

If a program is loaded with closely related special cases, then it is common to see **switch** statements that distinguish among the special cases and provide the processing logic to deal with each case individually. In Chapter 10, we show how to use inheritance and polymorphism to replace such **switch** logic with simpler logic.

We distinguish between *"is a" relationships* and *"has a" relationships.* "Is a" is inheritance. In an "is a" relationship, an object of a derived-class type may also be treated as an object of the base-class type. "Has a" is composition (see Fig. 7.4). In a "has a" relationship, a class object has one or more objects of other classes as members.

A derived class cannot access the private members of its base class; allowing this would violate the encapsulation of the base class. A derived class can, however, access the public and protected members of its base class. Base-class members that should not be accessible to a derived class via inheritance are declared private in the base class. A derived class can access private members of the base class only through access functions provided in the base class's public interface.

One problem with inheritance is that a derived class can inherit public member functions that it does not need to have or should expressly not have. When a base-class member is inappropriate for a derived class, that member can be redefined in the derived class with an appropriate implementation.

Perhaps most exciting is the notion that new classes can inherit from existing *class libraries.* Organizations develop their own class libraries and can take advantage of other libraries available worldwide. Someday software will be constructed from *standardized reusable components* just as hardware is often constructed today. This will help to meet the challenges of developing the ever more powerful software we will need in the future.

## 9.2 Base Classes and Derived Classes

Often an object of one class really "is an" object of another class as well. A rectangle certainly *is a* quadrilateral (as is a square, a parallelogram, and a trapezoid). Thus, class **Rectangle** can be said to *inherit* from class **Quadrilateral**. In this context, class **Quadrilateral** is called a *base class* and class **Rectangle** is called a *derived class.* A rectangle *is a* specific type of quadrilateral, but it is incorrect to claim that a quadrilateral *is a* rectangle. Figure 9.1 shows several simple inheritance examples.

Other object-oriented programming languages such as Smalltalk use different terminology: In inheritance, the base class is called the *superclass* (represents a superset of objects) and the derived class is called the *subclass* (represents a subset of objects). Because inheritance normally produces derived classes with *more* features than their base classes, the terms superclass and subclass can be confusing; we will avoid these terms.

Inheritance forms tree-like hierarchical structures. A base class exists in a hierarchical relationship with its derived classes. A class can certainly exist by itself, but it is when a class is used with the mechanism of inheritance that the class becomes either a base class that supplies attributes and behaviors to other classes, or the class becomes a derived class that inherits those attributes and behaviors.

Let us develop a simple inheritance hierarchy. A typical university community has thousands of people who are community members. These people consist of employees and students. Employees are either faculty members or staff members. Faculty members are either administrators (such as deans and department chairpersons) or teaching faculty. This yields the inheritance hierarchy shown in Fig. 9.2.

| Base class | Derived classes |
|---|---|
| `Student` | `GraduateStudent`<br>`UndergraduateStudent` |
| `Shape` | `Circle`<br>`Triangle`<br>`Rectangle` |
| `Loan` | `CarLoan`<br>`HomeImprovementLoan`<br>`MortgageLoan` |
| `Employee` | `FacultyMember`<br>`StaffMember` |
| `Account` | `CheckingAccount`<br>`SavingsAccount` |

**Fig. 9.1** Some simple inheritance examples.

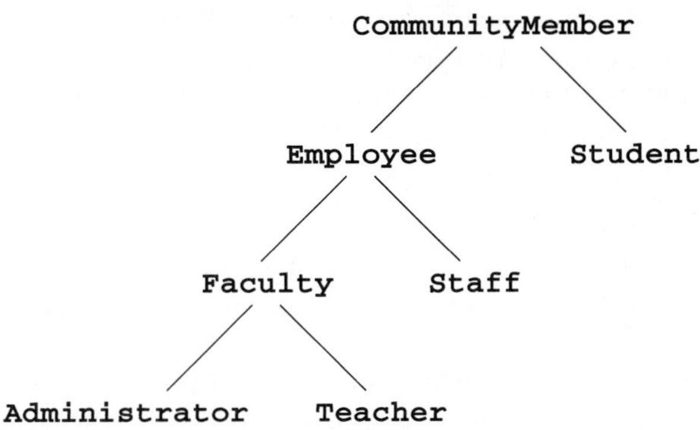


**Fig. 9.2** An inheritance hierarchy for university community members.

Another substantial inheritance hierarchy is the **`Shape`** hierarchy of Fig. 9.3. A common observation among students studying object-oriented programming for the first time is that there are abundant examples of hierarchies in the real world. It is just that these students are not accustomed to categorizing the real world in this manner, so it takes some adjustment in their thinking.

To specify that class **`CommissionWorker`** is derived from class **`Employee`**, class **`CommissionWorker`** would typically be defined as follows

```
class CommissionWorker : public Employee {
   ...
};
```

This is called *public inheritance* and is the type the reader is most likely to use. We will also discuss *private inheritance* and *protected inheritance.* With public inheritance, the public and protected members of the base class are inherited as public and protected members of the derived class, respectively. Remember that private members of a base class are not accessible from that class's derived classes.

It is possible to treat base-class objects and derived-class objects similarly; that commonality is expressed in the attributes and behaviors of the base class. Objects of any

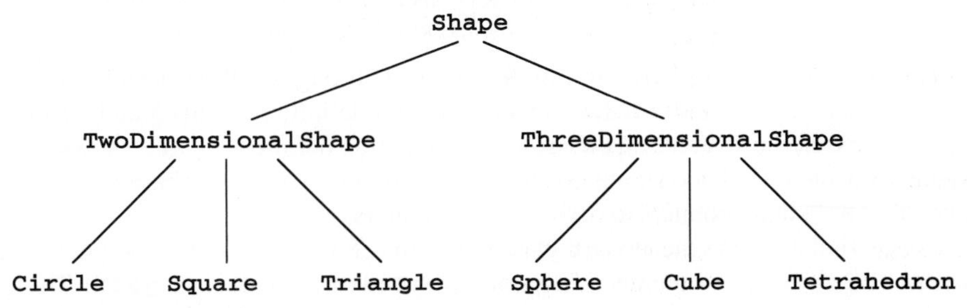


**Fig. 9.3** A portion of a **`Shape`** class hierarchy.

class publicly derived from a common base class can all be treated as objects of that base class.

We will consider many examples in which we can take advantage of this relationship with an ease of programming not available in non-object-oriented languages such as C.

## 9.3 Protected Members

Public members of a base class are accessible by all functions in the program. Private members of a base class are accessible only by member functions and friends of the base class.

Protected access serves as an intermediate level of protection between public access and private access. Protected members of a base class may be accessed only by members and friends of the base class and by members and friends of derived classes.

Derived-class members can refer to public and protected members of the base class simply by using the member names. Protcted data "breaks" encapsulation—a change to protected members of a base class may require modification of all derived classes.

## 9.4 Casting Base-Class Pointers to Derived-Class Pointers

An object of a publicly derived class can also be treated as an object of its corresponding base class. This makes possible some interesting manipulations. For example, despite the fact that objects of a variety of classes derived from a particular base class may be quite different from one another, we can still create a linked list of them—again, as long as we treat them as base-class objects. But the reverse is not true: A base-class object is not also automatically a derived-class object.

*Common Programming Error 9.1*

*Treating a base-class object as a derived-class object can cause errors.*

The programmer may, however, use an explicit cast to convert a base-class pointer to a derived-class pointer. But be careful—if such a pointer is to be dereferenced, then the programmer should be sure that the type of the pointer matches the type of the object to which it points.

*Common Programming Error 9.2*

*Explicitly casting a base-class pointer that points to a base-class object into a derived-class pointer and then referring to derived-class members that do not exist in that object.*

Our first example is shown in Fig. 9.4, parts 1 through 5. Parts 1 and 2 show the **Point** class definition and **Point** member function definitions. Parts 3 and 4 show the **Circle** class definition and **Circle** member function definition. Part 5 shows a driver program in which we demonstrate assigning derived-class pointers to base-class pointers and casting base-class pointers to derived-class pointers.

Let us first examine the **Point** class definition (Fig. 9.4, part 1). The public interface to **Point** contains member functions **setPoint**, **getX**, and **getY**. The data members **x** and **y** of **Point** are specified as **protected**. This prevents clients of **Point** objects from directly accessing the data, but enables classes derived from **Point**

```
// POINT.H
// Definition of class Point
#ifndef POINT_H
#define POINT_H

class Point {
   friend ostream &operator<<(ostream &, const Point &);
public:
   Point(float = 0, float = 0);       // default constructor
   void setPoint(float, float);       // set coordinates
   float getX() const { return x; }   // get x coordinate
   float getY() const { return y; }   // get y coordinate
protected:            // accessible by derived classes
   float x, y;        // x and y coordinates of the Point
};

#endif
```

**Fig. 9.4** Definition of class `Point` (part 1 of 5).

```
// POINT.CPP
// Member functions for class Point
#include <iostream.h>
#include "point.h"

// Constructor for class Point
Point::Point(float a, float b) { setPoint(a, b); }

// Set x and y coordinates of Point
void Point::setPoint(float a, float b)
{
   x = a;
   y = b;
}

// Output Point (with overloaded stream insertion operator)
ostream &operator<<(ostream &output, const Point &p)
{
   output << '[' << p.x << ", " << p.y << ']';

   return output;    // enables concatenated calls
}
```

**Fig. 9.4** Member function definitions for class `Point` (part 2 of 5).

to access the inherited data members directly. If the data were specified as **`private`**, the public member functions of **`Point`** must be used to access the data, even by derived classes. Note that the **`Point`** overloaded stream insertion operator function (Fig. 9.4, part 2) is able to reference variables **`x`** and **`y`** directly because the overloaded stream insertion operator function is a friend of class **`Point`**. Note also that it is necessary to reference **`x`** and **`y`** through objects as in **`p.x`** and **`p.y`**. This is because the overloaded stream insertion operator function is not a member function of the class **`Point`**.

```
// CIRCLE.H
// Definition of class Circle
#ifndef CIRCLE_H
#define CIRCLE_H

#include <iostream.h>
#include <iomanip.h>
#include "point.h"

class Circle : public Point {  // Circle inherits from Point
   friend ostream &operator<<(ostream &, const Circle &);
public:
   // default constructor
   Circle(float r = 0.0, float x = 0, float y = 0);

   void setRadius(float);        // set radius
   float getRadius() const;      // return radius
   float area() const;           // calculate area
protected:
   float radius;
};

#endif
```

**Fig. 9.4** Definition of class `Circle` (part 3 of 5).

```
// CIRCLE.CPP
// Member function definitions for class Circle
#include "circle.h"

// Constructor for Circle calls constructor for Point
// with a member initializer then initializes radius.
Circle::Circle(float r, float a, float b)
   : Point(a, b)         // call base-class constructor
{ radius = r; }

// Set radius of Circle
void Circle::setRadius(float r) { radius = r; }

// Get radius of Circle
float Circle::getRadius() const { return radius; }

// Calculate area of Circle
float Circle::area() const
   { return 3.14159 * radius * radius; }

// Output a Circle in the form:
// Center = [x, y]; Radius = #.##
ostream &operator<<(ostream &output, const Circle &c)
{
   output << "Center = [" << c.x << ", " << c.y
          << "]; Radius = " << setiosflags(ios::showpoint)
          << setprecision(2) << c.radius;

   return output;   // enables concatenated calls
}
```

**Fig. 9.4** Member function definition for class `Circle` (part 4 of 5).

```
// FIG9_4.CPP
// Casting base-class pointers to derived-class pointers
#include <iostream.h>
#include <iomanip.h>
#include "point.h"
#include "circle.h"

main()
{
   Point *pointPtr, p(3.5, 5.3);
   Circle *circlePtr, c(2.7, 1.2, 8.9);

   cout << "Point p: " << p << endl << "Circle c: " << c << endl;

   // Treat a Circle as a Point (see only the base class part)
   pointPtr = &c;   // assign address of Circle to pointPtr
   cout << endl << "Circle c (via *pointPtr): "
        << *pointPtr << endl;

   // Treat a Circle as a Circle (with some casting)
   pointPtr = &c;   // assign address of Circle to pointPtr
   circlePtr = (Circle *) pointPtr;  // cast base to derived
   cout << endl << "Circle c (via *circlePtr): " << endl
        << *circlePtr << endl << "Area of c (via circlePtr): "
        << circlePtr->area() << endl;

   // DANGEROUS: Treat a Point as a Circle
   pointPtr = &p;   // assign address of Point to pointPtr
   circlePtr = (Circle *) pointPtr;  // cast base to derived
   cout << endl << "Point p (via *circlePtr): "
        << endl << *circlePtr << endl
        << "Area of object circlePtr points to: "
        << circlePtr->area() << endl;

   return 0;
}
```

```
Point p: [3.5, 5.3]
Circle c: Center = [1.2, 8.9]; Radius = 2.70

Circle c (via *pointPtr): [1.20, 8.90]

Circle c (via *circlePtr):
Center = [1.20, 8.90]; Radius = 2.70
Area of c (via circlePtr): 22.90

Point p (via *circlePtr):
Center = [3.50, 5.30]; Radius = 4.02e-38
Area of object circlePtr points to: 0.00
```

**Fig. 9.4** Casting base-class pointers to derived-class pointers (part 5 of 5).

Class **Circle** (Fig. 9.4, part 3) inherits from class **Point** with public inheritance. This is specified in the first line of the class definition

```
class Circle : public Point {  // Circle inherits from Point
```

The colon (**:**) in the header of the class definition indicates inheritance. The keyword **public** indicates the type of inheritance (see Section 9.7). All the members of class **Point** are inherited into class **Circle**. This means that the public interface to **Circle** includes the **Point** public member functions as well as the **Circle** member functions **area**, **setRadius**, and **getRadius**.

The **Circle** constructor (Fig. 9.4, part 4) must invoke the **Point** constructor to initialize the base-class portion of a **Circle** object. This is accomplished with the member initializer syntax introduced in Chapter 7 as follows

```
Circle::Circle(float r, float a, float b)
   : Point(a, b)        // call base-class constructor
```

The second line of the constructor function header invokes the **Point** constructor by name. Values **a** and **b** are passed from the **Circle** constructor to the **Point** constructor to initialize the base-class members **x** and **y**. If the **Circle** constructor does not invoke the **Point** constructor explicitly, the **Point** constructor is invoked with the default values for **x** and **y** (i.e., 0 and 0). If the **Point** class does not provide a default constructor, the compiler generates an error.

Note that the **Circle** overloaded stream insertion operator function is able to reference variables **x** and **y** directly because these are protected members of base class **Point**. Note also that it is necessary to reference **x** and **y** through objects as in **c.x** and **c.y**. This is because the overloaded stream insertion operator function is not a member of the class **Circle**, but is a friend of the class.

The driver program (Fig. 9.4, part 5) creates **pointPtr** as a pointer to a **Point** object and instantiates **Point** object **p**, then creates **circlePtr** as a pointer to a **Circle** object and instantiates **Circle** object **c**. The objects **p** and **c** are output using their overloaded stream insertion operators to show that they were initialized correctly.

Next, the driver demonstrates assigning a derived-class pointer (the address of object **c**) to base-class pointer **pointPtr** and outputs the **Circle** object **c** using the overloaded stream insertion operator for **Point** and the dereferenced pointer ***pointPtr**. Note that only the **Point** portion of the **Circle** object **c** is displayed. It is always valid to assign a derived-class pointer to a base-class pointer because a derived-class object *is a* base-class object. The base-class pointer "sees" only the base-class part of the derived-class object. The compiler performs an implicit conversion of the derived-class pointer to a base-class pointer.

Then, the driver demonstrates assigning a derived-class pointer (the address of object **c**) to base-class pointer **pointPtr** and casting **pointPtr** back to a **Circle ***. The result of the cast operation is assigned to **circlePtr**. The **Circle** object **c** is output using the overloaded stream insertion operator for **Circle** and the dereferenced pointer ***circlePtr**. The area of **Circle** object **c** is output via **circlePtr**. This results in a valid area value because the pointers are always pointing to a **Circle** object.

A base-class pointer cannot be assigned directly to a derived-class pointer because this is an inherently dangerous assignment—derived-class pointers expect to be pointing to derived class-objects. The compiler does not perform an implicit conversion in this case. Using an explicit cast informs the compiler that the programmer knows this type of pointer conversion is dangerous—the programmer assumes responsibility for using the pointer appropriately.

Next, the driver demonstrates assigning a base-class pointer (the address of object `p`) to base-class pointer `pointPtr` and casting `pointPtr` back to a `Circle *`. The result of the cast operation is assigned to `circlePtr`. The `Point` object `p` is output using the overloaded stream insertion operator for `Circle` and the dereferenced pointer `*circlePtr`. Note the strange value output for the radius member. Outputting a `Point` as a `Circle` results in an invalid value for the `radius` because the pointers are always pointing to a `Point` object. A `Point` object does not have a `radius` member. Therefore, the program outputs whatever value happens to be in memory at the location that `circlePtr` expects the `radius` data member to be. The area of the object pointed to by `circlePtr` (`Point` object `p`) is also output via `circlePtr`. Note that the value for the area is 0.00 because this calculation is based on the nonexistent value of the `radius`. Obviously, accessing data members that are not there is dangerous. Calling member functions that do not exist can crash the program.

## 9.5 Using Member Functions

A derived class's member functions may need to access certain of its base class's data members and member functions.

***Software Engineering Observation 9.1***

*A derived class cannot directly access private members of its base class.*

This is a crucial aspect of software engineering in C++. If a derived class could access the base class's private members, this would violate the encapsulation of the base class. Hiding private members is a huge help in testing, debugging and correctly modifying systems. If a derived class could access its base class's private members, it would then be possible for classes derived from that derived class to access that data as well, and so on. This would propagate access to what is supposed to be private data, and the benefits of encapsulation would be lost throughout the class hierarchy.

## 9.6 Redefining Base-Class Members in a Derived Class

A derived class can redefine a base-class member function. When that function is mentioned by name in the derived class, the derived-class version is automatically selected. The scope-resolution operator may be used to access the base-class version from the derived class.

***Common Programming Error 9.3***

*When a base-class member function is redefined in a derived class, it is common to have the derived-class version call the base-class version and do some additional work. Not using the scope-resolution operator to reference the base class's member function causes infinite recursion because the derived-class member function actually calls itself.*

***Software Engineering Observation 9.2***

*A redefinition of a base-class member function in a derived class need not have the same signature as the base-class member function.*

Consider a simplified class **Employee**. It stores the employee's **firstName** and **lastName**. This information is common to all employees including those in classes derived from class **Employee**. From class **Employee** now derive classes **HourlyWorker**, **PieceWorker**, **Boss**, and **CommissionWorker**. The **HourlyWorker** gets paid by the hour with "time-and-a-half" for overtime hours in excess of 40 hours per week. The **PieceWorker** gets paid a fixed rate per item produced—for simplicity, assume this person makes only one type of item, so the private data members are number of items produced and rate per item. The **Boss** gets a fixed wage per week. The **CommissionWorker** gets a small fixed weekly base salary plus a fixed percentage of that person's gross sales for the week. For simplicity, we study only class **Employee** and derived class **HourlyWorker**.

Our next example is shown in Fig. 9.5, parts 1 through 5. Parts 1 and 2 show the **Employee** class definition and **Employee** member function definitions. Parts 3 and 4 show the **HourlyWorker** class definition and **HourlyWorker** member function definition. Part 5 shows a driver program for the **Employee/HourlyWorker** inheritance hierarchy that simply instantiates an **HourlyWorker** object, initializes it, and calls **HourlyWorker** member function **print** to output the object's data.

The **Employee** class definition (Fig. 9.5, part 1) consists of two private **char *** data members—**firstName** and **lastName**—and three member functions—a constructor, a destructor, and **print**. The constructor function (Fig. 9.5, part 2) receives two strings and dynamically allocates character arrays to store the strings. Note that the **assert** macro (discussed in Chapter 18, "Other Topics") is used to determine if memory was allocated to **firstName** and **lastName**. If not, the program terminates with an error message indicating the condition tested, the line number on which the condition

```
// EMPLOY.H
// Definition of class Employee
#ifndef EMPLOY_H
#define EMPLOY_H

class Employee {
public:
   Employee(const char*, const char*);  // constructor
   void print() const;  // output first and last name
   ~Employee();         // destructor
private:
   char *firstName;     // dynamically allocated string
   char *lastName;      // dynamically allocated string
};

#endif
```

Fig. 9.5 Definition of class **Employee** (part 1 of 5).

```
// EMPLOY.CPP
// Member function definitions for class Employee
#include <string.h>
#include <iostream.h>
#include <assert.h>
#include "employ.h"

// Constructor dynamically allocates space for the
// first and last name and uses strcpy to copy
// the first and last names into the object.
Employee::Employee(const char *first, const char *last)
{
   firstName = new char[ strlen(first) + 1 ];
   assert(firstName != 0); // terminate if memory not allocated
   strcpy(firstName, first);

   lastName = new char[ strlen(last) + 1 ];
   assert(lastName != 0);  // terminate if memory not allocated
   strcpy(lastName, last);
}

// Output employee name
void Employee::print() const
   { cout << firstName << ' ' << lastName; }

// Destructor deallocates dynamically allocated memory
Employee::~Employee()
{
   delete [] firstName;    // reclaim dynamic memory
   delete [] lastName;     // reclaim dynamic memory
}
```

**Fig. 9.5** Member function definitions for class **Employee** (part 2 of 5).

```
// HOURLY.H
// Definition of class HourlyWorker
#ifndef HOURLY_H
#define HOURLY_H

#include "employ.h"

class HourlyWorker : public Employee {
public:
   HourlyWorker(const char*, const char*, float, float);
   float getPay() const;  // calculate and return salary
   void print() const;    // redefined base-class print
private:
   float wage;            // wage per hour
   float hours;           // hours worked for week
};

#endif
```

**Fig. 9.5** Definition of class **HourlyWorker** (part 3 of 5).

```
// HOURLY_B.CPP
// Member function definitions for class HourlyWorker
#include <iostream.h>
#include <iomanip.h>
#include "hourly.h"

// Constructor for class HourlyWorker
HourlyWorker::HourlyWorker(const char *first, const char *last,
                           float initHours, float initWage)
   : Employee(first, last)   // call base-class constructor
{
   hours = initHours;
   wage = initWage;
}

// Get the HourlyWorker's pay
float HourlyWorker::getPay() const { return wage * hours; }

// Print the HourlyWorker's name and pay
void HourlyWorker::print() const
{
   cout << "HourlyWorker::print()" << endl;

   Employee::print();   // call base-class print function

   cout << " is an hourly worker with pay of"
        << " $" << setiosflags(ios::fixed | ios::showpoint)
        << setprecision(2) << getPay() << endl;
}
```

**Fig. 9.5** Member function definitions for class `HourlyWorker` (part 4 of 5).

```
// FIG9_5.CPP
// Redefining a base-class member function in a
// derived class.
#include <iostream.h>
#include "hourly.h"

main()
{
   HourlyWorker h("Bob", "Smith", 40.0, 7.50);
   h.print();
   return 0;
}
```

```
HourlyWorker::print()

Bob Smith is an hourly worker with pay of $300.00
```

**Fig. 9.5** Redefining a base-class member function in a derived class (part 5 of 5).

appears, and the file in which the condition is located. Because the data of **Employee** are **private**, the only access to the data is through member function **print** which simply outputs the first name and last name of the employee. The destructor function returns the dynamically allocated memory to the system.

Class **HourlyWorker** (Fig. 9.5, part 3) inherits from class **Employee** with public inheritance. Again, this is specified in the first line of the class definition as follows

```
class HourlyWorker : public Employee
```

The public interface to **HourlyWorker** includes the **Employee print** function and **HourlyWorker** member functions **getPay** and **print**. Note that class **HourlyWorker** defines its own **print** function. Therefore, class **HourlyWorker** has access to two **print** functions. Class **HourlyWorker** also contains private data members **wage** and **hours** for calculating the employee's weekly salary.

The **HourlyWorker** constructor (Fig. 9.5, part 4) uses member initializer syntax to pass the strings **first** and **last** to the **Employee** constructor so the base-class members can be initialized, then initializes members **wage** and **hours**. Member function **getPay** calculates the salary of the **HourlyWorker**.

**HourlyWorker** member function **print** is an example of a base-class member function being redefined in a derived class. Often base-class member functions are redefined in a derived-class to provide more functionality. The redefined functions sometimes call the base-class version of the function to perform part of the new task. In this example, the derived-class **print** function calls the base-class **print** function to output the employee's name (the base-class **print** is the only function with access to the private data of the base class). The derived-class **print** function also outputs the employee's pay. Note how the base class version of the print function is called

```
Employee::print();
```

Because the base-class function and derived-class function have the same name and signature, the base-class function must be preceded by its class name and the scope resolution operator. Otherwise, the derived-class version of the function is called which results in infinite recursion (the **HourlyWorker print** function calls itself).

## 9.7 Public, Protected, and Private Base Classes

When deriving a class from a base class, the base class may be inherited as **public**, **protected**, or **private**. Protected inheritance and private inheritance are rare and each should be used only with great care; we use only public inheritance in this book.

When deriving a class from a public base class, public members of the base class become public members of the derived class, and protected members of the base class become protected members of the derived class. Private members of a base class are never directly accessible from a derived class.

When deriving from a protected base class, public and protected members of the base class become protected members of the derived class. When deriving from a private base class, public and protected members of the base class become private members of the derived class. Private and protected inheritance are not "is a" relationships.

Figure 9.6 summarizes the accessibility of base-class members in a derived class based on the member access specifiers of the members in the base class and the type of inheritance. The first column contains the base-class member access specifier. The first row contains the type of inheritance. The remainder of the chart provides the access specifier that applies to a base class's members in a derived class and a brief description of how base-class members can be accessed.

## 9.8 Direct Base Classes and Indirect Base Classes

A base class may be a *direct base class* of a derived class, or a base class may be an *indirect base class* of a derived class. A direct base class of a derived class is explicitly listed in that derived class's header when that derived class is declared. An indirect base class is not explicitly listed in the derived class's header; rather the indirect base class is inherited from two or more levels up the class hierarchy.

| **Base class member access specifier** | **Type of Inheritance** | | |
|---|---|---|---|
| | `public` inheritance | `protected` inheritance | `private` inheritance |
| `public` | `public` in derived class.<br>Can be accessed directly by any non-static member functions, friend functions and non-member functions. | `protected` in derived class.<br>Can be accessed directly by all non-static member functions and friend functions. | `private` in derived class.<br>Can be accessed directly by all non-static member functions and friend functions. |
| `protected` | `protected` in derived class.<br>Can be accessed directly by all non-static member functions and friend functions. | `protected` in derived class.<br>Can be accessed directly by all non-static member functions and friend functions. | `private` in derived class.<br>Can be accessed directly by all non-static member functions and friend functions. |
| `private` | hidden in derived class.<br>Can be accessed by non-static member functions and friend functions through public or protected member functions of the base class. | hidden in derived class.<br>Can be accessed by non-static member functions and friend functions through public or protected member functions of the base class. | hidden in derived class.<br>Can be accessed by non-static member functions and friend functions through public or protected member functions of the base class. |

**Fig. 9.6** Summary of base-class member accessibility in a derived class.

## 9.9 Using Constructors and Destructors in Derived Classes

Because a derived class inherits its base class's members, when an object of a derived class is instantiated, the base class's constructor must be called to initialize the base-class members of the derived-class object. A *base-class initializer* (which uses the member-initializer syntax we have seen) can be provided in the derived-class constructor to call the base-class constructor explicitly, otherwise the derived class's constructor will call the base class's default constructor implicitly.

Base-class constructors and base-class assignment operators are not inherited by derived classes. Derived-class constructors and assignment operators, however, can call base-class constructors and assignment operators.

A derived-class constructor always calls the constructor for its base class first to initialize the derived class's base-class members. If the derived-class constructor is omitted, the derived class's default constructor calls the base-class constructor. Destructors are called in the reverse order of constructor calls, so a derived-class destructor is called before its base-class destructor.

***Software Engineering Observation 9.3***

*When an object of a derived class is created, first the base-class constructor executes, then the constructors for the derived class's member objects execute, then the derived class's constructor executes. Destructors are called in the reverse of the order in which their corresponding constructors are called.*

***Software Engineering Observation 9.4***

*The order in which member objects are constructed is the order in which those objects are declared within the class definition. The order in which the member initializers are listed does not affect construction.*

***Software Engineering Observation 9.5***

*In inheritance, base-class constructors are called in the order in which inheritance is specified in the derived-class definition. The order in which the base-class constructors are specified in the derived-class constructor does not affect construction.*

The program of Fig. 9.7 demonstrates the order in which base-class and derived-class constructors and destructors are called. The program consists of five parts. Parts 1 and 2 show a simple **`Point`** class containing a constructor, a destructor, and protected data members **`x`** and **`y`**. The constructor and destructor both print the **`Point`** object for which they are invoked. Parts 3 and 4 show a simple **`Circle`** class derived from **`Point`** with public inheritance containing a constructor, and destructor, and private data member **`radius`**. The constructor and destructor both print the **`Circle`** object for which they are invoked. The **`Circle`** constructor also invokes the **`Point`** constructor using member initializer syntax and passes the values **`a`** and **`b`** so the base-class data members can be initialized.

Part 5 shows a driver program for this **`Point/Circle`** hierarchy. The program begins by instantiating a **`Point`** object in its own scope inside **`main`**. The object goes in and out of scope immediately, so the **`Point`** constructor and destructor are both called.

```
// POINT2.H
// Definition of class Point
#ifndef POINT2_H
#define POINT2_H

class Point {
public:
   Point(float = 0.0, float = 0.0);   // default constructor
   ~Point();      // destructor
protected:        // accessible by derived classes
   float x, y;    // x and y coordinates of Point
};

#endif
```

**Fig. 9.7** Definition of class **Point** (part 1 of 5).

```
// POINT2.CPP
// Member function definitions for class Point
#include <iostream.h>
#include "point2.h"

// Constructor for class Point
Point::Point(float a, float b)
{
   x = a;
   y = b;

   cout << "Point  constructor: "
        << '[' << x << ", " << y << ']' << endl;
}

// Destructor for class Point
Point::~Point()
{
   cout << "Point  destructor:  "
        << '[' << x << ", " << y << ']' << endl;
}
```

**Fig. 9.7** Member function definitions for class **Point** (part 2 of 5).

The program then instantiates **Circle** object **circle1**. This invokes the **Point** constructor to perform output with values passed from the **Circle** constructor, then performs the output specified in the **Circle** constructor. **Circle** object **circle2** is instantiated next. Again, the **Point** and **Circle** constructors are both called. Note that the body of the **Point** constructor is performed before the body of the **Circle** constructor. The end of **main** is reached, so the destructors must be called for the **circle1** and **circle2** objects. Destructors are called in the reverse order of their corresponding constructors. Therefore, the **Circle** destructor and **Point** destructor are called in that order for object **circle2**, then the **Circle** destructor and **Point** destructor are called in that order for object **circle1**.

```
// CIRCLE2.H
// Definition of class Circle
#ifndef CIRCLE2_H
#define CIRCLE2_H

#include "point2.h"
#include <iomanip.h>

class Circle : public Point {
public:
   // default constructor
   Circle(float r = 0.0, float x = 0, float y = 0);

   ~Circle();        // destructor
private:
   float radius;     // radius of Circle
};

#endif
```

**Fig. 9.7** Definition of class `Circle` (part 3 of 5).

```
// CIRCLE2.CPP
// Member function definitions for class Circle
#include "circle2.h"

// Constructor for Circle calls constructor for Point
Circle::Circle(float r, float a, float b)
   : Point(a, b)     // call base-class constructor
{
   radius = r;

   cout << "Circle constructor: radius is "
        << radius << " [" << a << ", " << b << ']' << endl;
}

// Destructor for class Circle
Circle::~Circle()
{
   cout << "Circle destructor:  radius is "
        << radius << " [" << x << ", " << y << ']' << endl;
}
```

**Fig. 9.7** Member function definitions for class `Circle` (part 4 of 5).

## 9.10 Implicit Derived-Class Object to Base-Class Object Conversion

Despite the fact that a derived-class object also "is a" base-class object, the derived-class type and the base-class type are different. Derived-class objects can be treated as base-class objects. This makes sense because the derived class has members corresponding to each of the base-class members—remember that the derived class normally has more

```
// FIG9_7.CPP
// Demonstrate when base-class and derived-class
// constructors and destructors are called.

#include <iostream.h>
#include "point2.h"
#include "circle2.h"

main()
{
   // Show constructor and destructor calls for Point
   {
      Point p(1.1, 2.2);
   }

   cout << endl;
   Circle circle1(4.5, 7.2, 2.9);
   cout << endl;
   Circle circle2(10, 5, 5);
   cout << endl;
   return 0;
}
```

```
Point  constructor: [1.1, 2.2]
Point  destructor:  [1.1, 2.2]

Point  constructor: [7.2, 2.9]
Circle constructor: radius is 4.5 [7.2, 2.9]

Point  constructor: [5, 5]
Circle constructor: radius is 10 [5, 5]

Circle destructor:  radius is 10 [5, 5]
Point  destructor:  [5, 5]
Circle destructor:  radius is 4.5 [7.2, 2.9]
Point  destructor:  [7.2, 2.9]
```

**Fig. 9.7** Order in which base-class and derived-class constructors and destructors are called (part 5 of 5).

members than the base class has. Assignment in the other direction is not allowed because assigning a base-class object to a derived-class object would leave the additional derived-class members undefined. Although such assignment is not "naturally" allowed, it could be made legitimate by providing a properly overloaded assignment operator and/or conversion constructor.

***Common Programming Error 9.4***

*Assigning a derived-class object to an object of a corresponding base class, and then attempting to reference derived-class-only members in the new base-class object.*

A pointer to a derived-class object may be implicitly converted into a pointer to a base-class object because a derived-class object is a base-class object.

There are four possible ways to mix and match base-class pointers and derived-class pointers with base-class objects and derived-class objects:

1. Referring to a base-class object with a base-class pointer is straightforward.
2. Referring to a derived-class object with a derived-class pointer is straightforward.
3. Referring to a derived-class object with a base-class pointer is safe because the derived-class object is an object of its base class as well. Such code can only refer to base-class members. If this code refers to derived-class-only members through the base-class pointer, the compiler will report a syntax error.
4. Referring to a base-class object with a derived-class pointer is a syntax error. The derived-class pointer must first be cast to a base-class pointer.

***Common Programming Error 9.5***

*Casting a base-class pointer to a derived-class pointer can cause errors if that pointer is then used to reference a base-class object that does not have the desired derived-class members.*

As convenient as it may be to treat derived-class objects as base-class objects, and to do this by manipulating all these objects with base-class pointers, there is a problem. In a payroll system, for example, we would like to be able to walk through a linked list of employees and calculate the weekly pay for each person. But using base-class pointers enables the program to call only the base-class payroll calculation routine (if indeed there is such a routine in the base class). We need a way to invoke the proper payroll calculation routine for each object, whether it is a base-class object or a derived-class object, and to do this simply by using the base-class pointer. The solution is to use virtual functions and polymorphism as discussed in Chapter 10.

## 9.11 Software Engineering with Inheritance

We can use inheritance to customize existing software. We inherit the attributes and behaviors of an existing class, then add attributes and behaviors to customize the class to meet our needs. This is done in C++ without the derived class having access to the base class's source code, but the derived class does need to be able to link to the base class's object code. This powerful capability is attractive to independent software vendors (ISVs). The ISVs can develop proprietary classes for sale or license and make these classes available to users in object-code format. Users can then derive new classes from these library classes rapidly and without accessing the ISVs' proprietary source code. All the ISVs need to supply with the object code are the header files.

It can be difficult for students to appreciate the problems faced by designers and implementors on large-scale software projects. People experienced on such projects will invariably state that a key to improving the software development process is encouraging software reuse. Object-oriented programming in general, and C++ in particular, certainly do this.

It is the availability of substantial and useful class libraries that delivers the maximum benefits of software reuse through inheritance. As interest in C++ grows, interest in class libraries will increase. Just as shrink-wrapped software produced by independent software vendors became an explosive growth industry with the arrival of the personal computer, so, too, will the creation and sale of class libraries. Application designers will build their applications with these libraries, and library designers will be rewarded by having their libraries wrapped with the applications. Libraries currently being shipped with C++ compilers tend to be rather general-purpose and limited in scope. What we see coming is a massive worldwide commitment to the development of class libraries for a huge variety of applications arenas.

***Software Engineering Observation 9.6***

*Creating a derived class does not affect its base class's source code or object code; the integrity of a base class is preserved by inheritance.*

A base class specifies commonality. All classes derived from a base class inherit the capabilities of that base class. In the object-oriented design process, the designer looks for commonality and factors it out to form desirable base classes. Derived classes are then customized beyond the capabilities inherited from the base class.

Just as the designer of non-object-oriented systems seeks to avoid unnecessary proliferation of functions, the designer of object-oriented systems should avoid unnecessary proliferation of classes. Such a proliferation of classes creates management problems and can hinder software reusability simply because it is more difficult for a potential reuser of a class to locate that class in a huge collection. The tradeoff is to create fewer classes, each providing substantial additional functionality. Such classes might be a bit too rich for certain reusers; they can mask the excessive functionality, thus "toning down" the classes to meet their needs.

***Performance Tip 9.1***

*If classes produced through inheritance are larger than they need to be, memory and processing resources may be wasted. Inherit from the class "closest" to what you need.*

Note that reading a set of derived-class declarations can be confusing because inherited members are not shown, but inherited members are nevertheless present in the derived classes. A similar problem can exist in the documentation of derived classes.

***Software Engineering Observation 9.7***

*In an object-oriented system, classes are often closely related. "Factor out" common attributes and behavior and place these in a base class. Then use inheritance to form derived classes.*

***Software Engineering Observation 9.8***

*A derived class contains the attributes and behaviors of its base class. A derived class can also contain additional attributes and behaviors. With inheritance, the base class can be compiled independent of the derived class. Only the derived class's incremental attributes and behaviors need to be compiled to be able to combine these with the base class to form the derived class.*

*Software Engineering Observation 9.9*

*Modifications to a base class do not require derived classes to change as long as the public interface to the base class remains unchanged. Derived classes may, however, need to be recompiled.*

## 9.12 Composition Vs. Inheritance

We have discussed *is a* relationships which are supported by inheritance. We have also discussed *has a* relationships (and seen examples in preceding chapters) in which a class may have other classes as members—such relationships create new classes by *composition* of existing classes. For example, given the classes **`Employee`**, **`BirthDate`**, and **`TelephoneNumber`**, it is improper to say that an **`Employee`** *is a* **`BirthDate`** or that an **`Employee`** *is a* **`TelephoneNumber`**. But it is certainly appropriate to say that an **`Employee`** *has a* **`BirthDate`** and that an **`Employee`** *has a* **`TelephoneNumber`**.

*Software Engineering Observation 9.10*

*Program modifications to a class that is a member of another class do not require the enclosing class to change as long as the public interface to the member class remains unchanged. Note that the composite class may, however, need to be recompiled.*

## 9.13 "Uses A" and "Knows A" Relationships

Inheritance and composition each encourage software reuse by creating new classes that have much in common with existing classes. There are other ways to utilize the services of classes. Although a person object is not a car, and a person object does not contain a car, a person object certainly *uses a* car. A function uses an object simply by issuing a function call to a member function of that object.

An object can be *aware of* another object. Knowledge networks frequently have such relationships. One object can contain a pointer or a reference to another object to be aware of that object. In this case, one object is said to have a *knows a* relationship with the other object.

## 9.14 Case Study: Point, Circle, Cylinder

Now let us consider the capstone exercise for this chapter. We consider a point, circle, cylinder hierarchy. First we develop and use class **`Point`** (Fig. 9.8). Then we present an example in which we derive class **`Circle`** from class **`Point`** (Fig. 9.9). Finally, we present an example in which we derive class **`Cylinder`** from class **`Circle`** (Fig. 9.10).

Figure 9.8 shows class **`Point`**. Part 1 is the class **`Point`** definition. Note that **`Point`**'s data members are protected. Thus, when class **`Circle`** is derived from class **`Point`**, the member functions of class **`Circle`** will be able to directly reference coordinates **`x`** and **`y`** rather than using access functions. This may result in better performance.

Figure 9.8, part 2, shows the member function definitions for class **`Point`**. Figure 9.8, part 3, shows a driver program for class **`Point`**. Note that **`main`** must use the access functions **`getX`** and **`getY`** to read the values of protected data members **`x`** and **`y`**; remember that protected data members are accessible only to members and friends of their class and members and friends of their derived classes.

```
// POINT2.H
// Definition of class Point
#ifndef POINT2_H
#define POINT2_H

class Point {
   friend ostream &operator<<(ostream &, const Point &);
public:
   Point(float = 0, float = 0);       // default constructor
   void setPoint(float, float);       // set coordinates
   float getX() const { return x; }   // get x coordinate
   float getY() const { return y; }   // get y coordinate
protected:            // accessible to derived classes
   float x, y;        // coordinates of the Point
};

#endif
```

**Fig. 9.8** Definition of class `Point` (part 1 of 3).

```
// POINT2.CPP
// Member functions for class Point
#include <iostream.h>
#include "point2.h"

// Constructor for class Point
Point::Point(float a, float b) { setPoint(a, b); }

// Set the x and y coordinates
void Point::setPoint(float a, float b)
{
   x = a;
   y = b;
}

// Output the Point
ostream &operator<<(ostream &output, const Point &p)
{
   output << '[' << p.x << ", " << p.y << ']';

   return output;             // enables concatenation
}
```

**Fig. 9.8** Member functions for class `Point` (part 2 of 3).

Our next example is shown in Fig. 9.9, parts 1 through 3. The **`Point`** class definition and the member function definitions from Fig. 9.8 are reused here. Parts 1 through 3 show the **`Circle`** class definition, **`Circle`** member function definitions, and a driver program, respectively. Note that class **`Circle`** inherits from class **`Point`** with public inheritance. This means that the public interface to **`Circle`** includes the **`Point`** member functions as well as the **`Circle`** member functions **`setRadius`**, **`getRadius`**, and

```
// FIG9_8.CPP
// Driver for class Point
#include <iostream.h>
#include "point2.h"

main()
{
   Point p(7.2, 11.5);    // instantiate Point object p

   // protected data of Point inaccessible to main
   cout << "X coordinate is " << p.getX()
        << endl << "Y coordinate is " << p.getY();

   p.setPoint(10, 10);
   cout << endl << endl << "The new location of p is "
        << p << endl;

   return 0;
}
```

```
X coordinate is 7.2
Y coordinate is 11.5

The new location of p is [10, 10]
```

**Fig. 9.8** Driver for class `Point` (part 3 of 3).

```
// CIRCLE2.H
// Definition of class Circle
#ifndef CIRCLE2_H
#define CIRCLE2_H

#include "point2.h"

class Circle : public Point {
   friend ostream &operator<<(ostream &, const Circle &);
public:
   // default constructor
   Circle(float r = 0.0, float x = 0, float y = 0);
   void setRadius(float);        // set radius
   float getRadius() const;      // return radius
   float area() const;           // calculate area
protected:          // accessible to derived classes
   float radius;    // radius of the Circle
};

#endif
```

**Fig. 9.9** Definition of class `Circle` (part 1 of 3).

**area**. Note that the **Circle** overloaded stream insertion operator function is able to reference variables **x** and **y** directly because these are protected members of base class **Point**. Note also that it is necessary to reference **x** and **y** through objects, as in **c.x** and **c.y**. This is because the overloaded stream insertion operator function is not a member function of the class **Circle**. The driver program instantiates an object of class **Circle** then uses get functions to obtain the information about the **Circle** object. Again, **main** is neither a member function nor a friend of class **Circle** so it cannot directly reference the protected data of class **Circle**. The driver program then uses set functions **setRadius** and **setPoint** to reset the radius and coordinates of the center of the circle. Finally, the driver initializes reference variable **pRef** of type "reference to **Point** object" (**Point &**) to **Circle** object **c**. The driver then prints **pRef** which, despite the fact that it is initialized with a **Circle** object, "thinks" it is a **Point** object, so the **Circle** object actually prints as a **Point** object.

```
// CIRCLE2.CPP
// Member function definitions for class Circle

#include <iostream.h>
#include <iomanip.h>
#include "circle2.h"

// Constructor for Circle calls constructor for Point
// with a member initializer and initializes radius
Circle::Circle(float r, float a, float b)
   : Point(a, b)        // call base-class constructor
{ radius = r; }

// Set radius
void Circle::setRadius(float r) { radius = r; }

// Get radius
float Circle::getRadius() const { return radius; }

// Calculate area of Circle
float Circle::area() const
   { return 3.14159 * radius * radius; }

// Output a circle in the form:
// Center = [x, y]; Radius = #.##
ostream &operator<<(ostream &output, const Circle &c)
{
   output << "Center = [" << c.x << ", " << c.y
          << "]; Radius = " << setiosflags(ios::showpoint)
          << setprecision(2) << c.radius;

   return output;   //  enables concatenated calls
}
```

Fig. 9.9 Member function definitions for class **Circle** (part 2 of 3).

```
// FIG9_9.CPP
// Driver for class Circle
#include <iostream.h>
#include <iomanip.h>
#include "point2.h"
#include "circle2.h"

main()
{
   Circle c(2.5, 3.7, 4.3);

   cout << "X coordinate is " << c.getX()
        << endl << "Y coordinate is " << c.getY()
        << endl << "Radius is " << c.getRadius();

   c.setRadius(4.25);
   c.setPoint(2, 2);
   cout << setiosflags(ios::fixed | ios::showpoint);
   cout << endl << endl << "The new location and radius of c are"
        << endl << c << endl << "Area " << c.area() << endl;

   Point &pRef = c;
   cout << endl << "Circle printed as a Point is: "
        << pRef << endl;

   return 0;
}
```

```
X coordinate is 3.7
Y coordinate is 4.3
Radius is 2.5

The new location and radius of c are
Center = [2, 2]; Radius = 4.25
Area: 56.74

Circle printed as a Point is: [2.00, 2.00]
```

**Fig. 9.9** Driver for class **Circle** (part 3 of 3).

Our last example is shown in Fig. 9.10, parts 1 through 3. The **Point** class and **Circle** class definitions, and their member function definitions from Fig. 9.8 and Fig. 9.9 are reused here. Parts 1 through 3 show the **Cylinder** class definition, **Cylinder** member function definitions, and a driver program, respectively. Note that class **Cylinder** inherits from class **Circle** with public inheritance. This means that the public interface to **Cylinder** includes the **Circle** member functions as well as the **Cylinder** member functions **setHeight**, **getHeight**, **area** (redefined from **Circle**) and **volume**. Note that the **Cylinder** overloaded stream insertion operator function is able to reference variables **x**, **y**, and **radius** directly because these are protected members of base class **Circle** (**x** and **y** were inherited by **Circle** from **Point**). Note also that it is necessary to reference **x**, **y**, and **radius** through objects, as in **c.x**, **c.y**, and

**c.radius**. This is because the overloaded stream insertion operator function is not a member function of the class **Cylinder**, but is a friend of the class. The driver program instantiates an object of class **Cylinder** then uses get functions to obtain the information about the **Cylinder** object. Again, **main** is neither a member function nor a friend of class **Cylinder** so it cannot directly reference the protected data of class **Cylinder**. The driver program then uses set functions **setHeight**, **setRadius**, and **setPoint** to reset the height, radius, and coordinates of the cylinder. Finally, the driver initializes reference variable **pRef** of type "reference to **Point** object" (**Point &**) to **Cylinder** object **cyl**. It then prints **pRef** which, despite the fact that it is initialized with a **Cylinder** object, "thinks" it is a **Point** object, so the **Cylinder** object actually prints as a **Point** object. The driver then initializes reference variable **cRef** of type "reference to **Circle** object" (**Circle &**) to **Cylinder** object **cyl**. It then prints **cRef** which, despite the fact that it is initialized with a **Cylinder** object, "thinks" it is a **Circle** object, so the **Cylinder** object actually prints as a **Circle** object. The area of the **Circle** is also output.

This example nicely demonstrates public inheritance and defining and referencing protected data members. The reader should now be confident with the basics of inheritance. In the next chapter, we show how to program with inheritance hierarchies in a general manner using polymorphism. Data abstraction, inheritance, and polymorphism are the crux of object-oriented programming.

```
// CYLINDR2.H
// Definition of class Cylinder
#ifndef CYLINDR2_H
#define CYLINDR2_H

#include "circle2.h"

class Cylinder : public Circle {
   friend ostream& operator<<(ostream&, const Cylinder&);

public:
   // default constructor
   Cylinder(float h = 0.0, float r = 0.0,
            float x = 0.0, float y = 0.0);

   void setHeight(float);      // set height
   float getHeight() const;    // return height
   float area() const;         // calculate and return area
   float volume() const;       // calculate and return volume

protected:
   float height;               // height of the Cylinder
};

#endif
```

**Fig. 9.10** Definition of class **Cylinder** (part 1 of 3).

```
// CYLINDR2.CPP
// Member and friend function definitions
// for class Cylinder.

#include <iostream.h>
#include <iomanip.h>
#include "cylindr2.h"

// Cylinder constructor calls Circle constructor
Cylinder::Cylinder(float h, float r, float x, float y)
   : Circle(r, x, y)   // call base-class constructor
{ height = h; }

// Set height of Cylinder
void Cylinder::setHeight(float h) { height = h; }

// Get height of Cylinder
float Cylinder::getHeight() const { return height; }

// Calculate area of Cylinder (i.e., surface area)
float Cylinder::area() const
{
   return 2 * Circle::area() +
          2 * 3.14159 * radius * height;
}

// Calculate volume of Cylinder
float Cylinder::volume() const
   { return Circle::area() * height; }

// Output Cylinder dimensions
ostream& operator<<(ostream &output, const Cylinder& c)
{
   output << "Center = [" << c.x << ", " << c.y
          << "]; Radius = " << setiosflags(ios::showpoint)
          << setprecision(2) << c.radius
          << "; Height = " << c.height;

   return output;   // enables concatenated calls
}
```

**Fig. 9.10** Member function and friend function definitions for class `Cylinder` (part 2 of 3).

## 9.15 Multiple Inheritance

So far in this chapter, we have discussed single inheritance in which each class is derived from exactly one base class. A class may be derived from more than one base class; such derivation is called *multiple inheritance*. Multiple inheritance means that a derived class inherits the members of several base classes. This powerful capability encourages interesting forms of software reuse, but can cause a variety of ambiguity problems.

```
// FIG9_10.CPP
// Driver for class Cylinder
#include <iostream.h>
#include <iomanip.h>
#include "point2.h"
#include "circle2.h"
#include "cylindr2.h"

main()
{
   // create Cylinder object
   Cylinder cyl(5.7, 2.5, 1.2, 2.3);

   // use get functions to display the Cylinder
   cout << setiosflags(ios::fixed | ios::showpoint);
   cout << "X coordinate is " << cyl.getX() << endl
        << "Ycoordinate is " << cyl.getY() << endl
        << "Radius is " << cyl.getRadius() << endl
        << "Height is " << cyl.getHeight() << endl << endl ;

   // use set functions to change the Cylinder's attributes
   cyl.setHeight(10);
   cyl.setRadius(4.25);
   cyl.setPoint(2, 2);
   cout << "The new location, radius, "
        << "and height of cyl are:" << endl << cyl << endl;

   // display the Cylinder as a Point
   Point &pRef = cyl;   // pRef "thinks" it is a Point
   cout << endl << "Cylinder printed as a Point is: "
        << pRef << endl << endl;

   // display the Cylinder as a Circle
   Circle &cRef = cyl;  // cRef "thinks" it is a Circle
   cout << "Cylinder printed as a Circle is:" << endl << cRef
        << endl << "Area: " << cRef.area() << endl;

   return 0;
}
```

```
X coordinate is 1.2
Y coordinate is 2.3
Radius is 2.5
Height is 5.7

The new location, radius, and height of cyl are:
Center = [2, 2]; Radius = 4.25; Height = 10.00

Cylinder printed as a Point is: [2.00, 2.00]

Cylinder printed as a Circle is:
Center = [2.00, 2.00]; Radius = 4.25
Area: 56.74
```

**Fig. 9.10** Driver for class `Cylinder` (part 3 of 3).

*Good Programming Practice 9.1*

*Multiple inheritance is a powerful capability when used properly. Multiple inheritance should be used when an "is a" relationship exists between a new type and two or more existing types (i.e., type A "is a" type B and "is a" type C).*

Consider the multiple inheritance example in Fig. 9.11. Class **Base1** contains one protected data member—**int value**. **Base1** contains a constructor that sets **value** and public member function **getData** that returns **value**.

Class **Base2** is similar to class **Base1** except that its protected data is **char letter**. **Base2** also has a public member function **getData**, but this function returns the value of **char letter**.

Class **Derived** is inherited from both class **Base1** and class **Base2** through multiple inheritance. **Derived** has private data member **float real** and has public member function **getReal** that reads the value of **float real**.

```
// BASE1.H
// Definition of class Base1
#ifndef BASE1_H
#define BASE1_H

class Base1 {
public:
   Base1(int x) { value = x; }
   int getData() const { return value; }
protected:         // accessible to derived classes
   int value;      // inherited by derived class
};

#endif
```

**Fig. 9.11** Definition of class **Base1** (part 1 of 6).

```
// BASE2.H
// Definition of class Base2
#ifndef BASE2_H
#define BASE2_H

class Base2 {
public:
   Base2(char c) { letter = c; }
   char getData() const { return letter; }
protected:           // accessible to derived classes
   char letter;      // inherited by derived class
};

#endif
```

**Fig. 9.11** Definition of class **Base2** (part 2 of 6).

```
// DERIVED.H
// Definition of class Derived which inherits
// multiple base classes (Base1 and Base2).

#ifndef DERIVED_H
#define DERIVED_H

#include "base1.h"
#include "base2.h"

// multiple inheritance
class Derived : public Base1, public Base2 {
   friend ostream &operator<<(ostream &, const Derived &);

public:
   Derived(int, char, float);
   float getReal() const;

private:
   float real;    // derived class's private data
};

#endif
```

Fig. 9.11 Definition of class **Derived** (part 3 of 6).

```
// DERIVED.CPP
// Member function definitions for class Derived

#include <iostream.h>
#include "derived.h"

// Constructor for Derived calls constructors for
// class Base1 and class Base2.
Derived::Derived(int i, char c, float f)
   : Base1(i), Base2(c)   // call both base-class constructors
{ real = f; }

// Return the value of real
float Derived::getReal() const { return real; }

// Display all the data members of Derived
ostream &operator<<(ostream &output, const Derived &d)
{
   output << "     Integer: " << d.value << endl
          << "   Character: " << d.letter << endl
          << "Real number: " << d.real;

   return output;    // enables concatenated calls
}
```

Fig. 9.11 Member function definitions for class **Derived** (part 4 of 6).

```
// FIG9_11.CPP
// Driver for multiple inheritance example
#include <iostream.h>
#include "base1.h"
#include "base2.h"
#include "derived.h"

main()
{
   Base1 b1(10), *base1Ptr;     // create base-class object
   Base2 b2('Z'), *base2Ptr;    // create other base-class object
   Derived d(7, 'A', 3.5);      // create derived-class object

   // print data members of base class objects
   cout << "Object b1 contains integer "
        << b1.getData() << endl
        << "Object b2 contains character "
        << b2.getData() << endl
        << "Object d contains:" << endl << d << endl << endl;

   // print data members of derived class object
   // scope resolution operator resolves getData ambiguity
   cout << "Data members of Derived can be"
        << " accessed individually:" << endl
        << "    Integer: " << d.Base1::getData() << endl
        << "  Character: " << d.Base2::getData() << endl
        << "Real number: " << d.getReal() << endl << endl;

   cout << "Derived can be treated as an "
        << "object of either base class:" << endl;

   // treat Derived as a Base1 object
   base1Ptr = &d;
   cout << "base1Ptr->getData() yields "
        << base1Ptr->getData() << endl ;

   // treat Derived as a Base2 object
   base2Ptr = &d;
   cout << "base2Ptr->getData() yields "
        << base2Ptr->getData() << endl;

   return 0;
}
```

**Fig. 9.11** Driver for the multiple inheritance example (part 5 of 6).

Note how straightforward it is to indicate multiple inheritance by following the colon (**:**) after **class Derived** with a comma-separated list of base classes. Note also that constructor **Derived** calls base-class constructors for each of its base classes, **Base1** and **Base2**, through the member-initializer syntax. Again, base-class constructors are called in the order that the inheritance is specified, not in the order in which their constructors are mentioned

```
Object b1 contains integer 10
Object b2 contains character Z
Object d contains:
    Integer: 7
  Character: A
Real number: 3.5

Data members of Derived can be accessed individually:
    Integer: 7
  Character: A
Real number: 3.5

Derived can be treated as an object of either base class:
base1Ptr->getData() yields 7
base2Ptr->getData() yields A
```

Fig. 9.11 Driver for the multiple inheritance example (part 6 of 6).

The overloaded stream insertion operator for **Derived** uses dot notation off the derived object **d** to print **value**, **letter**, and **real**. This operator function is a friend of **Derived**, so **operator<<** can directly access private data member **real** of **Derived**. Also, because this operator is a friend of a derived class, it can access the protected members **value** and **letter** of **Base1** and **Base2**, respectively.

Now let us examine the driver program in **main**. We create object **b1** of class **Base1** and initialize it to **int** value **10**. We create object **b2** of class **Base2** and initialize it to **char** value **'Z'**. Then, we create object **d** of class **Derived** and initialize it to contain **int** value **7**, **char** value **'A'**, and **float** value **3.5**.

The contents of each of the base-class objects is printed by calling the **getData** member function for each object. Even though there are two **getData** functions, the calls are not ambiguous because they refer directly to the object **b1** version of **getData** and the object **b2** version of **getData**.

Next we print the contents of **Derived** object **d** with static binding. But we do have an ambiguity problem because this object contains two **getData** functions, one inherited from **Base1** and one inherited from **Base2**. This problem is easy to solve by using the binary scope resolution operator as in **d.Base1::getData()** to print the **int** in **value** and **d.Base2::getData()** to print the **char** in **letter**. The **float** value in **real** is printed without ambiguity with the call **d.getReal()**.

Next we demonstrate that the *is a* relationships of single inheritance also apply to multiple inheritance. We assign the address of derived object **d** to base-class pointer **base1Ptr**, and we print **int value** by invoking **Base1** member function **getData** off **base1Ptr**. We then assign the address of derived object **d** to base-class pointer **base2Ptr** and we print **char letter** by invoking **Base2** member function **getData** off **base2Ptr**.

This example showed the mechanics of multiple inheritance and introduced a simple ambiguity problem. Multiple inheritance is a complex topic dealt with in more detail in advanced C++ texts.

*Good Programming Practice 9.2*

*Multiple inheritance is a powerful feature, but it can introduce complexity into a system. Great care is required in the design of a system to use multiple inheritance profitably; it should not be used when single inheritance will do the job.*

## Summary

- One of the keys to the power of object-oriented programming is achieving software reusability through inheritance.
- The programmer can designate that the new class is to inherit the data members and member functions of a previously defined base class. In this case, the new class is referred to as a derived class.
- With single inheritance, a class is derived from only one base class. With multiple inheritance, a derived class inherits from multiple (possibly unrelated) base classes.
- A derived class normally adds data members and member functions of its own, so a derived class generally has a larger definition than its base class. A derived class is more specific than its base class and normally represents fewer objects.
- A derived class can not access the private members of its base class; allowing this would violate the encapsulation of the base class. A derived class can, however, access the public and protected members of its base class.
- A derived-class constructor always calls the constructor for its base class first to create and initialize the derived class's base-class members.
- Destructors are called in the reverse order of constructor calls, so a derived-class destructor is called before its base-class destructor.
- Inheritance enables software reusability which saves time in development and encourages the use of previously proven and debugged high-quality software.
- Inheritance can be accomplished from existing class libraries.
- Someday software for the most part will be constructed from standardized reusable components exactly as much hardware is constructed today.
- The implementor of a derived class does not need access to the source code of a base class, but does need the interface to the base class and the base class's object code.
- An object of a derived class can be treated as an object of its corresponding public base class. However, the reverse is not true.
- A base class exists in a hierarchical relationship with its singly derived classes.
- A class can exist by itself. When that class is used with the mechanism of inheritance, it becomes either a base class that supplies attributes and behaviors to other classes, or the class becomes a derived class that inherits those attributes and behaviors.
- An inheritance hierarchy can be arbitrarily deep within the physical limitations of a particular system.

- Hierarchies are useful tools for understanding and managing complexity. With software becoming increasingly complex, C++ provides mechanisms for supporting hierarchical structures through inheritance and polymorphism.
- An explicit cast can be used to convert a base-class pointer to a derived-class pointer. Such a pointer should not be dereferenced unless it actually points to an object of the derived class type.
- Protected access serves as an intermediate level of protection between public access and private access. Protected members of a base class may be accessed by members and friends of the base class and by members and friends of derived classes; no other functions can access the protected members of a base class.
- Protected members are used to extend privileges to derived classes while denying those privileges to non-class, non-friend functions.
- Multiple inheritance is indicated by placing a colon (`:`) after the derived-class name and following the colon with a comma-separated list of base classes. Member initializer syntax is used in the derived-class constructor to call base-class constructors.
- When deriving a class from a base class, the base class may be declared as either **`public`**, **`protected`**, or **`private`**.
- When deriving a class from a **`public`** base class, **`public`** members of the base class become **`public`** members of the derived class, and **`protected`** members of the base class become **`protected`** members of the derived class.
- When deriving a class from a **`protected`** base class, **`public`** and **`protected`** members of the base class become **`protected`** members of the derived class.
- When deriving a class from a **`private`** base class, **`public`** and **`protected`** members of the base class become **`private`** members of the derived class.
- A base class may be either a direct base class of a derived class or an indirect base class of a derived class. A direct base class is explicitly listed where the derived class is declared. An indirect base class is not explicitly listed; rather it is inherited from several levels up the class hierarchy tree.
- When a base-class member is inappropriate for a derived class, we may simply redefine that member in the derived class.
- It is important to distinguish between "is a" relationships and "has a" relationships. In a "has a" relationship, a class object has an object of another class as a member. In an "is a" relationship, an object of a derived-class type may also be treated as an object of the base-class type. "Is a" is inheritance. "Has a" is composition.
- A derived class object can be assigned to a base class object. This kind of assignment makes sense because the derived class has members corresponding to each of the base class members.
- A pointer to a derived-class object may be implicitly converted into a pointer for a base-class object.

- It is possible to convert a base-class pointer to a derived-class pointer by using an explicit cast. The target should be a derived class object.
- A base class specifies commonality. All classes derived from a base class inherit the capabilities of that base class. In the object-oriented design process, the designer looks for commonality and factors it out to form desirable base classes. Derived classes are then customized beyond the capabilities inherited from the base class.
- Reading a set of derived-class declarations can be confusing because not all the members of the derived class are present in these declarations. In particular, inherited members are not listed in the derived-class declarations, but these members are indeed present in the derived classes.
- "Has a" relationships are examples of creating new classes by composition of existing classes.
- "Knows a" relationships are examples of objects containing pointers or references to other objects so they can be aware of those objects.
- Member object constructors are called in the order in which the objects are declared. In inheritance, base-class constructors are called in the order in which inheritance is specified and before the derived-class constructor.
- For a derived-class object, first the base-class constructor is called, then the derived-class constructor is called (which may call member object constructors).
- When the derived-class object is destroyed, the destructors are called in the reverse order of the constructors—first the derived-class destructor is called, then the base-class destructor is called.
- A class may be derived from more than one base class; such derivation is called multiple inheritance.
- Indicate multiple inheritance by following the colon (`:`) inheritance indicator with a comma-separated list of base classes.
- The derived-class constructor calls base-class constructors for each of its base classes through the member-initializer syntax. Base-class constructors are called in the order in which the base classes are declared during inheritance.

## *Terminology*

abstraction
ambiguity in multiple inheritance
base class
base class default constructor
base-class constructor
base-class destructor
base-class initializer
base-class pointer
class hierarchy
class libraries
client of a class
composition
customize software
derived class
derived-class constructor
derived-class destructor
derived-class pointer
direct base class
directed acyclic graph (DAG)
friends of a base class

friends of a derived class
*has a* relationship
hierarchical relationship
indirect base class
infinite recursion error
inheritance
*is a* relationship
*knows a* relationship
member access control
member class
member object
multiple inheritance
object-oriented programming (OOP)
pointer to a base-class object
pointer to a derived-class object
private base class
private inheritance
protected base class
protected derivation
`protected` keyword
protected member of a class
public base class
public inheritance
redefine a base-class member
single inheritance
software reusability
standardized software components
subclass
superclass
*uses a* relationship

## Common Programming Errors

**9.1** Treating a base-class object as a derived-class object can cause errors.

**9.2** Explicitly casting a base-class pointer that points to a base-class object into a derived-class pointer and then referring to derived-class members that do not exist in that object.

**9.3** When a base-class member function is redefined in a derived class, it is common to have the derived-class version call the base-class version and do some additional work. Not using the scope-resolution operator to reference the base class's member function causes infinite recursion because the derived-class member function actually calls itself.

**9.4** Assigning a derived-class object to an object of a corresponding base class, and then attempting to reference derived-class-only members in the new base-class object.

**9.5** Casting a base-class pointer to a derived-class pointer can cause errors if that pointer is then used to reference a base-class object that does not have the desired derived-class members.

## Good Programming Practices

**9.1** Multiple inheritance is a powerful capability when used properly. Multiple inheritance should be used when an "is a" relationship exists between a new type and two or more existing types (i.e., type A "is a" type B and "is a" type C) .

**9.2** Multiple inheritance is a powerful feature, but it can introduce complexity into a system. Great care is required in the design of a system to use multiple inheritance profitably; it should not be used when single inheritance will do the job.

## Performance Tip

**9.1** If classes produced through inheritance are larger than they need to be, memory and processing resources may be wasted. Inherit from the class "closest" to what you need.

## Software Engineering Observations

**9.1** A derived class cannot directly access private members of its base class.

**9.2** A redefinition of a base-class member function in a derived class need not have the same signature as the base-class member function.

9.3 When an object of a derived class is created, first the base-class constructor executes, then the constructors for the derived class's member objects execute, then the derived class's constructor executes. Destructors are called in the reverse of the order in which their corresponding constructors are called.

9.4 The order in which member objects are constructed is the order in which those objects are declared within the class definition. The order in which the member initializers are listed does not affect construction.

9.5 In inheritance, base-class constructors are called in the order in which inheritance is specified in the derived-class definition. The order in which the base-class constructors are specified in the derived-class constructor does not affect construction.

9.6 Creating a derived class does not affect its base class's source code or object code; the integrity of a base class is preserved by inheritance.

9.7 In an object-oriented system, classes are often closely related. "Factor out" common attributes and behavior and place these in a base class. Then use inheritance to form derived classes.

9.8 A derived class contains the attributes and behaviors of its base class. A derived class can also contain additional attributes and behaviors. With inheritance, the base class can be compiled independent of the derived class. Only the derived class's incremental attributes and behaviors need to be compiled to be able to combine these with the base class to form the derived class.

9.9 Modifications to a base class do not require derived classes to change as long as the public interface to the base class remains unchanged. Derived classes may, however, need to be recompiled.

9.10 Modifications to a member class do not require its enclosing composed class to change as long as the public interface to the member class remains unchanged. Note that the composite class may, however, need to be recompiled.

## Self-Review Exercises

9.1 Fill in the blanks in each of the following:

a) If the class **`Alpha`** inherits from the class **`Beta`**, class **`Alpha`** is called the __________ class and class **`Beta`** is called the __________ class.

b) C++ provides for __________ which allows a derived class to inherit from many base classes, even if these base classes are unrelated.

c) Inheritance enables __________ which saves time in development, and encourages using previously proven and high-quality software.

d) An object of a __________ class can be treated as an object of its corresponding __________ class.

e) To convert a base-class pointer to a derived class pointer, a __________ must be used because the compiler considers this a dangerous operation.

f) The three member access specifiers are __________, __________, and __________.

g) When deriving a class from a base class with **`public`** inheritance, **`public`** members of the base class become __________ members of the derived class, and **`protected`** members of the base class become __________ members of the derived class.

h) When deriving a class from a base class with **`protected`** inheritance, **`public`** members of the base class become __________ members of the derived class, and **`protected`** members of the base class become __________ members of the derived class.

i) A "has a" relationship between classes represents __________ and an "is a" relationship between classes represents __________ .

## *Answers to Self-Review Exercises*

**9.1** a) derived, base. b) multiple inheritance. c) software reusability. d) derived, base. e) cast. f) **public**, **protected**, **private**. g) **public**, **protected**. h) **protected**, **protected**. i) composition, inheritance.

## *Exercises*

**9.2** Consider the class **bicycle**. Given your knowledge of some common components of bicycles, show a class hierarchy in which the class **bicycle** inherits from other classes, which, in turn, inherit from yet other classes. Discuss the instantiation of various objects of class **bicycle**. Discuss inheritance from class **bicycle** for other closely related derived classes.

**9.3** Briefly define each of the following terms: inheritance, multiple inheritance, base class, and derived class.

**9.4** Discuss why converting a base-class pointer to a derived-class pointer is considered dangerous by the compiler.

**9.5** Distinguish between single inheritance and multiple inheritance.

**9.6** (True/False) A derived class is often called a subclass because it represents a subset of its base class, i.e., a derived class is generally smaller than its base class.

**9.7** (True/False) A derived-class object is also an object of that derived class's base class.

**9.8** Some programmers prefer not to use **protected** access because it breaks the encapsulation of the base class. Discuss the relative merits of using **protected** access vs. insisting on using **private** access in base classes.

**9.9** Many programs written with inheritance could be solved with composition instead, and vice versa. Discuss the relative merits of these approaches in the context of the **Point**, **Circle**, **Cylinder** class hierarchy in this chapter. Rewrite the program of Fig. 9.10 (and the supporting classes) to use composition rather than inheritance. After you do this, reassess the relative merits of the two approaches both for the **Point**, **Circle**, **Cylinder** problem and for object-oriented programs in general.

**9.10** Rewrite the **Point**, **Circle**, **Cylinder** program of Fig. 9.10 as a Point, Square, Cube program. Do this two ways—once with inheritance and once with composition.

**9.11** In the chapter, we stated "When a base-class member is inappropriate for a derived class, that member can be redefined in the derived class with an appropriate implementation." If this is done, does the derived-class-is-a-base-class-object relationship still hold? Explain your answer.

**9.12** Study the inheritance hierarchy of Fig. 9.2. For each class, indicate some common attributes and behaviors consistent with the hierarchy. Add some other classes (i.e., **UndergraduateStudent**, **GraduateStudent**, **Freshman**, **Sophomore**, **Junior**, **Senior**, etc. to enrich the hierarchy.

**9.13** Write an inheritance hierarchy for class **Quadrilateral**, **Trapezoid**, **Parallelogram**, **Rectangle**, and **Square**. Use **Quadrilateral** as the base class of the hierarchy. Make the hierarchy as deep (i.e., as many levels) as possible. The private data of **Quadrilateral** should be the *(x, y)* coordinate pairs for the four endpoints of the **Quadrilateral**. Write a driver program that instantiates and displays objects of each of these classes.

**9.14** Write down all the shapes you can think of—both two-dimensional and three-dimensional—and form those shapes into a shape hierarchy. Your hierarchy should have base class

**Shape** from which class **TwoDimensionalShape** and class **ThreeDimensionalShape** are derived. Once you have developed the hierarchy, define each of the classes in the hierarchy. We will use this hierarchy in the exercises of Chapter 10 to process all shapes as objects of base-class **Shape**. This is a technique called polymorphism.

# 10

# Virtual Functions and Polymorphism

## Objectives

- To understand the notion of polymorphism.
- To understand how to declare and use virtual functions to effect polymorphism.
- To understand the distinction between abstract classes and concrete classes.
- To learn how to declare pure virtual functions to create abstract classes.
- To appreciate how polymorphism makes systems extensible and maintainable.

*O! Thou hast damnable iteration, and art indeed able to corrupt a saint.*
William Shakespeare, Henry IV, Part I

*General propositions do not decide concrete cases.*
Oliver Wendell Holmes

*A philosopher of imposing stature doesn't think in a vacuum. Even his most abstract ideas are, to some extent, conditioned by what is or is not known in the time when he lives.*
Alfred North Whitehead

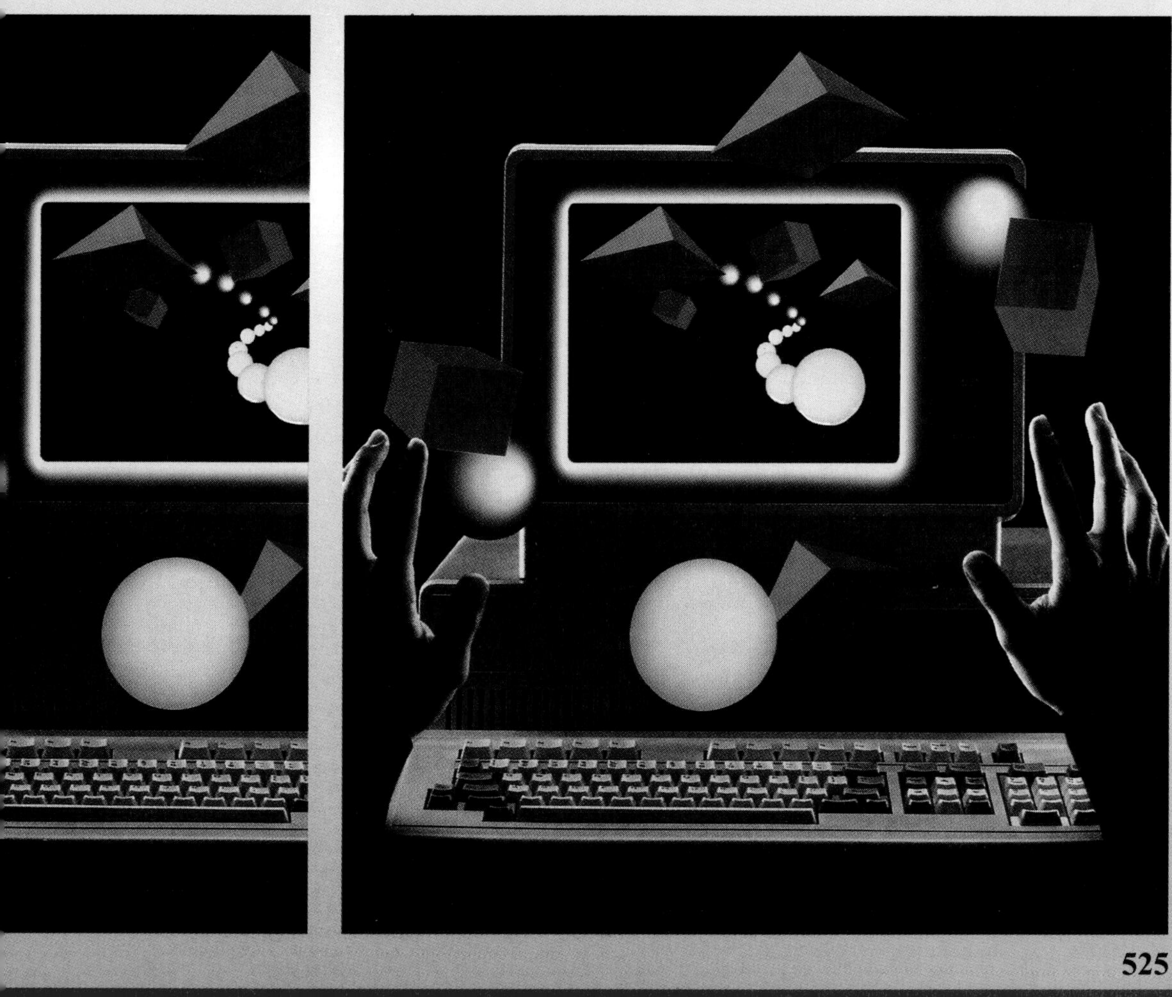

# Outline



## 10.1 Introduction

With *virtual functions* and *polymorphism,* it is possible to design and implement systems that are more easily *extensible.* Programs can be written to generically process—as base-class objects—objects of all existing classes in a hierarchy. Classes that do not exist during program development can be added with little or no modifications to the generic part of the program—as long as those classes are part of the hierarchy that is being processed generically. The only parts of a program that will need modification are those parts that require direct knowledge of the particular class that is added to the hierarchy.

## 10.2 Type Fields and Switch Statements

One means of dealing with objects of many different types is to use a **`switch`** statement to take an appropriate action on each object based on that object's type. For example, in a hierarchy of shapes in which each shape specifies its type as a data member, a **`switch`** structure could determine which **`print`** function to call based on the type of the particular object. There are many problems with using **`switch`** logic. The programmer might forget to make such a type test when one is warranted. The programmer may forget to test all possible cases in a **`switch`**. If a **`switch`**-based system is modified by adding new types, the programmer might forget to insert the new cases in existing **`switch`** statements. Every addition or deletion of a class to handle new types demands that every **`switch`** statement in the system be modified; tracking these down can be time consuming and error prone.

As we will see, virtual functions and polymorphic programming can eliminate the need for **switch** logic. The programmer can use the virtual function mechanism to perform the equivalent logic automatically, thus avoiding the kinds of errors typically associated with **switch** logic.

***Software Engineering Observation 10.1***

*An interesting consequence of using virtual functions and polymorphism is that programs take on a simplified appearance. They contain less branching logic in favor of simpler sequential code. This simplification facilitates testing, debugging, and program maintenance.*

## 10.3 Virtual Functions

Suppose a set of shape classes such as **Circle**, **Triangle**, **Rectangle**, **Square**, etc. are all derived from base class **Shape**. In object-oriented programming, each of these classes might be endowed with the ability to draw itself. Although each class has its own **draw** function, the **draw** function for each shape is quite different. When drawing a shape, whatever that shape may be, it would be nice to be able to treat all these shapes generically as objects of the base class **Shape**. Then to draw any shape, we could simply call function **draw** of base class **Shape** and let the program determine dynamically (i.e., at execution time) which derived class **draw** function to use.

To enable this kind of behavior, we declare **draw** in the base class as a *virtual function,* and then we *redefine* **draw** in each of the derived classes to draw the appropriate shape. A virtual function is declared by preceding the function's prototype with the keyword **virtual** in the base class. For example,

```
virtual void draw() const;
```

may appear in base-class **Shape**. The preceding prototype declares that function draw is a constant function that takes no arguments, returns nothing, and is a virtual function.

***Software Engineering Observation 10.2***

*Once a function has been declared virtual, it remains virtual all the way down the inheritance hierarchy from that point.*

***Good Programming Practice 10.1***

*Even though certain functions are implicitly virtual because of a declaration made higher in the class hierarchy, some programmers prefer to explicitly declare these virtual functions at every level of the hierarchy to promote program clarity.*

***Software Engineering Observation 10.3***

*When a derived class chooses not to define a virtual function, the derived class simply inherits its immediate base class's virtual function definition.*

If function **draw** in the base class has been declared **virtual**, and if we then use a base-class pointer to point to the derived-class object and invoke the **draw** function using this pointer (e.g., **shapePtr->draw()**), the program will choose the correct derived class's **draw** function dynamically (i.e., at execution time). This is called *dynamic binding* which will be illustrated in the case studies in Sections 10.6 and 10.9.

***Software Engineering Observation 10.4***

*Redefined virtual functions must have the same return type and signature as the base virtual function.*

***Common Programming Error 10.1***

*Redefining in a derived class a base-class virtual function and not ensuring that the derived function has the same return type and signature as the base class's version is a syntax error.*

When a virtual function is called by referencing a specific object by name and using the dot member selection operator (e.g., **squareObject.draw()**), the reference is resolved at compile time (this is called *static binding*), and the virtual function that is called is the one defined for (or inherited by) the class of that particular object.

## 10.4 Abstract Base Classes and Concrete Classes

When we think of a class as a type, we assume that objects of that type will be instantiated. However, there are cases in which it is useful to define classes for which the programmer never intends to instantiate any objects. Such classes are called *abstract classes.* Because these are used as base classes in inheritance situations, we will normally refer to them as *abstract base classes.* No objects of an abstract base class can be instantiated.

The sole purpose of an abstract class is to provide an appropriate base class from which classes may inherit interface and/or implementation. Classes from which objects can be instantiated are called *concrete classes.*

We could have an abstract base class **TwoDimensionalObject** and derive concrete classes such as **Square**, **Circle**, **Triangle**, etc. We could also have an abstract base class **ThreeDimensionalObject** and derive concrete classes such as **Cube**, **Sphere**, **Cylinder**, etc. Abstract base classes are too generic to define real objects; we need to be more specific before we can think of instantiating objects. That is what concrete classes do; they provide the specifics that make it reasonable to instantiate objects.

A class is made abstract by declaring one or more of its virtual functions to be pure. A *pure virtual function* is one with an *initializer of* **= 0** in its declaration as in

```
virtual float earnings() const = 0;    // pure virtual
```

***Software Engineering Observation 10.5***

*If a class is derived from a class with a pure virtual function, and if no definition is supplied for that pure virtual function in the derived class, then that virtual function remains pure in the derived class. Consequently, the derived class is also an abstract class.*

***Common Programming Error 10.2***

*Attempting to instantiate an object of an abstract class (i.e., a class that contains one or more pure virtual functions) is a syntax error.*

A hierarchy does not need to contain any abstract classes, but as we will see, many good object-oriented systems have class hierarchies headed by an abstract base class. In some cases, abstract classes constitute the top few levels of the hierarchy. A good example of this is a shape hierarchy. The hierarchy could be headed by abstract base class **Shape**. On the next level down, we can have two more abstract base classes, namely **TwoDimensionalShape** and **ThreeDimensionalShape**. The next level down would start defining concrete classes for two-dimensional shapes such as circles and squares, and concrete classes for three-dimensional shapes such as spheres and cubes.

## 10.5 Polymorphism

C++ enables *polymorphism*—the ability for objects of different classes related by inheritance to respond differently to the same member function call. If, for example, class **Rectangle** is derived from class **Quadrilateral**, then a **Rectangle** object *is a* more specific version of a **Quadrilateral** object. An operation (such as calculating the perimeter or the area) that can be performed on an object of class **Quadrilateral** can also be performed on an object of class **Rectangle**.

Polymorphism is implemented via virtual functions. When a request is made through a base-class pointer (or reference) to use a virtual function, C++ chooses the correct redefined function in the appropriate derived class associated with the object.

Sometimes a nonvirtual member function is defined in a base class and redefined in a derived class. If such a member function is called through a base-class pointer, the base-class version is used. If the member function is called through a derived-class pointer, the derived-class version is used. This is nonpolymorphic behavior.

Consider the following example using the **Employee** base class and **HourlyWorker** derived class of Fig. 9.5:

```
Employee e, *ePtr = &e;
HourlyWorker h, *hPtr = &h;
ePtr->print();     // call base-class print function
hPtr->print();     // call derived-class print function
```

Our **Employee** base class and **HourlyWorker** derived class both have their own **print** functions defined. Because the functions were not declared **virtual** and they have the same signature, calling the **print** function through an **Employee** pointer results in **Employee::print()** being called and calling the **print** function through an **HourlyWorker** pointer results in **HourlyWorker::print()** being called. The base-class **print** function is also a member of the derived class, but to call the base-class **print** for a derived-class object, the function must be called explicitly as follows:

```
hPtr->Employee::print();
```

This specifies that the base-class **print** should be called explicitly.

Through the use of virtual functions and polymorphism, one member function call can cause different actions to occur depending on the type of the object receiving the call (we will see that a small amount of additional overhead is required). This gives the programmer tremendous expressive capability. We will see examples of the power of polymorphism and virtual functions in the next several sections.

***Software Engineering Observation 10.6***

*With virtual functions and polymorphism, the programmer can deal in generalities and let the execution-time environment concern itself with the specifics. The programmer can command a wide variety of objects to behave in manners appropriate to those objects without even knowing the types of those objects.*

***Software Engineering Observation 10.7***

*Polymorphism promotes extensibility: Software written to invoke polymorphic behavior is written independently of the types of the objects to which messages are sent. Thus, new types of objects that can respond to existing messages can be added into such a system without modifying the base system. Except for client code that instantiates new objects, programs need not be recompiled.*

***Software Engineering Observation 10.8***

*An abstract class defines an interface for the various members of a class hierarchy. The abstract class contains pure virtual functions that will be defined in the derived classes. All functions in the hierarchy can use this same interface through polymorphism.*

Although we cannot instantiate objects of abstract base classes, we *can* declare pointers to abstract base classes. Such pointers can then be used to enable polymorphic manipulations of derived-class objects when such objects are instantiated from concrete classes.

Let us consider applications of polymorphism and virtual functions. A screen manager needs to display a variety of objects, including new types of objects that will be added to the system even after the screen manager is written. The system may need to display various shapes (i.e., the base class is **`Shape`**) such as squares, circles, triangles, rectangles, and the like (each of these shape classes is derived from the base class **`Shape`**). The screen manager uses base-class pointers (to **`Shape`**) to manage all the objects to be displayed. To draw any object (regardless of the level at which that object appears in the inheritance hierarchy), the screen manager uses a base-class pointer to the object and simply sends a **`draw`** message to the object. Function **`draw`** has been declared pure virtual in base class **`Shape`** and has been redefined in each of the derived classes. Each **`Shape`** object knows how to draw itself. The screen manager does not have to worry about what type each object is or whether the object is of a type the screen manager has seen before—the screen manager simply tells each object to draw itself.

Polymorphism is particularly effective for implementing layered software systems. In operating systems, for example, each type of physical device may operate quite differently from the others. Regardless of this, commands to *read* or *write* data from and to devices can have a certain uniformity. The *write* message sent to a device-driver object needs to be interpreted specifically in the context of that device driver and how that device driver manipulates devices of a specific type. However, the *write* call itself is really no different from the *write* to any other device in the system—simply place some number of bytes from memory onto that device. An object-oriented operating system might use an abstract base class to provide an interface appropriate for all device drivers. Then, through inheritance from that abstract base class, derived classes are formed that all operate similarly. The capabilities (i.e., the public interface) offered by the device drivers are provided as pure virtual functions in the abstract base class. The implementations of these virtual functions are provided in the derived classes that correspond to the specific types of device drivers.

In Chapter 7, we introduced the concept of iterators. It is common to define an *iterator class* that will walk through all the objects in a collection. If you want to print a list of objects in a linked list, for example, an iterator object can be instantiated that will return the next element of the linked list each time the iterator is called. Iterators are commonly used in polymorphic programming to walk through a linked list of objects from various levels of a hierarchy. The pointers in such a list would all be base-class pointers (see Chapter 15, "Data Structures," for more on linked lists and iterators). A list of objects of class **TwoDimensionalShape** could contain objects from the classes **Square**, **Circle**, **Triangle**, etc. Sending a message to draw each object in the list would, using polymorphism, draw the correct picture on the screen.

## 10.6 Case Study: A Payroll System Using Polymorphism

Let us use virtual functions and polymorphism to perform payroll calculations based on the type of an employee (Fig. 10.1). We use a base class **Employee**. The derived classes of **Employee** are **Boss** who gets paid a fixed weekly salary regardless of the number of hours worked, **CommissionWorker** who gets a flat base salary plus a percentage of sales, **PieceWorker** who gets paid by the number of items produced, and **HourlyWorker** who gets paid by the hour and receives overtime pay.

```
// EMPLOY2.H
// Abstract base class Employee
#ifndef EMPLOY2_H
#define EMPLOY2_H

class Employee {
public:
   Employee(const char *, const char *);
   ~Employee();
   const char *getFirstName() const;
   const char *getLastName() const;

   // Pure virtual functions make Employee abstract base class.
   virtual float earnings() const = 0; // pure virtual
   virtual void print() const = 0;     // pure virtual

private:
   char *firstName;
   char *lastName;
};

#endif
```

Fig. 10.1 Abstract base class **Employee** (part 1 of 12).

```
// EMPLOY2.CPP
// Member function definitions for
// abstract base class Employee.
//
// Note: No definitions given for pure virtual functions.
#include <iostream.h>
#include <string.h>
#include <assert.h>
#include "employ2.h"

// Constructor dynamically allocates space for the
// first and last name and uses strcpy to copy
// the first and last names into the object.
Employee::Employee(const char *first, const char *last)
{
   firstName = new char[ strlen(first) + 1 ];
   assert(firstName != 0);    // test that new worked
   strcpy(firstName, first);

   lastName = new char[ strlen(last) + 1 ];
   assert(lastName != 0);     // test that new worked
   strcpy(lastName, last);
}

// Destructor deallocates dynamically allocated memory
Employee::~Employee()
{
   delete [] firstName;
   delete [] lastName;
}

// Return a pointer to the first name
const char *Employee::getFirstName() const
{
   // Const prevents caller from modifying private data.
   // Caller should copy returned string before destructor
   // deletes dynamic storage to prevent undefined pointer.

   return firstName;   // caller must delete memory
}

// Return a pointer to the last name
const char *Employee::getLastName() const
{
   // Const prevents caller from modifying private data.
   // Caller should copy returned string before destructor
   // deletes dynamic storage to prevent undefined pointer.

   return lastName;   // caller must delete memory
}
```

**Fig. 10.1** Member function definitions for abstract base class `Employee` (part 2 of 12).

```
// BOSS1.H
// Boss class derived from Employee
#ifndef BOSS1_H
#define BOSS1_H
#include "employ2.h"

class Boss : public Employee {
public:
   Boss(const char *, const char *, float = 0.0);
   void setWeeklySalary(float);
   virtual float earnings() const;
   virtual void print() const;
private:
   float weeklySalary;
};

#endif
```

**Fig. 10.1** Class **Boss** derived from abstract base class **Employee** (part 3 of 12).

```
// BOSS1.CPP
// Member function definitions for class Boss
#include <iostream.h>
#include "boss1.h"

// Constructor function for class Boss
Boss::Boss(const char *first, const char *last, float s)
   : Employee(first, last)  // call base-class constructor
{ setWeeklySalary(s); }

// Set the Boss's salary
void Boss::setWeeklySalary(float s)
   { weeklySalary = s > 0 ? s : 0; }

// Get the Boss's pay
float Boss::earnings() const { return weeklySalary; }

// Print the Boss's name
void Boss::print() const
{
   cout << endl << "                   Boss: " << getFirstName()
        << ' ' << getLastName();
}
```

**Fig. 10.1** Member function definitions for class **Boss** (part 4 of 12).

An **earnings** function call certainly applies generically to all employees. But the way each person's earnings are calculated depends on the class of the employee, and these classes are all derived from the base class **Employee**. So **earnings** is declared **virtual** in base class **Employee** and appropriate implementations of **earnings** are provided for each of the derived classes. Then, to calculate any employee's earnings, the program simply uses a base-class pointer to that employee's object and invokes the

```
// COMMIS1.H
// CommissionWorker class derived from Employee
#ifndef COMMIS1_H
#define COMMIS1_H
#include "employ2.h"

class CommissionWorker : public Employee {
public:
   CommissionWorker(const char *, const char *,
                    float = 0.0, float = 0.0, unsigned = 0);
   void setSalary(float);
   void setCommission(float);
   void setQuantity(unsigned);
   virtual float earnings() const;
   virtual void print() const;

private:
   float salary;         // base salary per week
   float commission;     // amount per item sold
   unsigned quantity;    // total items sold for week
};

#endif
```

**Fig. 10.1** Class **CommissionWorker** derived from abstract base class **Employee** (part 5 of 12).

**earnings** function. In a real payroll system, the various employee objects might be pointed to by individual elements in an array of pointers of type **Employee ***. The program would simply walk through the array one element at a time using the **Employee *** pointers to invoke the **earnings** function of each object.

Let us consider the **Employee** class (Fig. 10.1, parts 1 and 2). The public member functions include a constructor that takes the first name and last name as arguments; a destructor that reclaims dynamically allocated memory; a *get* function that returns the first name; a *get* function that returns the last name; and finally, two pure virtual functions—**earnings** and **print**. Why are these functions pure virtual? The answer is that it does not make sense to provide implementations of these functions in the **Employee** class. We cannot calculate the earnings for a generic employee—we must first know what kind of employee it is—nor can we print the type of employee for a generic employee. By making these functions pure virtual we are indicating that we will provide implementations in derived classes, but not in the base class itself.

Class **Boss** (Fig. 10.1, parts 3 and 4) is derived from **Employee** with public inheritance. The public member functions include a constructor that takes a first name, a last name, and a weekly salary as arguments and passes the first name and last name to the **Employee** constructor to initialize the **firstName** and **lastName** members of the base-class part of the derived-class object; a *set* function to assign a new value to private data member **weeklySalary**; a virtual **earnings** function defining how to calculate a **Boss**'s earnings; and a virtual **print** function that outputs the type of the employee followed by the employee's name.

```
// COMMIS1.CPP
// Member function definitions for class CommissionWorker
#include <iostream.h>
#include "commis1.h"

// Constructor for class CommissionWorker
CommissionWorker::CommissionWorker(const char *first,
        const char *last, float s, float c, unsigned q)
   : Employee(first, last)  // call base-class constructor
{
   salary = s > 0 ? s : 0;
   commission = c > 0 ? c : 0;
   quantity = q > 0 ? q : 0;
}

// Set CommissionWorker's weekly base salary
void CommissionWorker::setSalary(float s)
   { salary = s > 0 ? s : 0; }

// Set CommissionWorker's commission
void CommissionWorker::setCommission(float c)
   { commission = c > 0 ? c : 0; }

// Set CommissionWorker's quantity sold
void CommissionWorker::setQuantity(unsigned q)
   { quantity = q > 0 ? q : 0; }

// Determine CommissionWorker's earnings
float CommissionWorker::earnings() const
   { return salary + commission * quantity; }

// Print the CommissionWorker's name
void CommissionWorker::print() const
{
   cout << endl << "Commission worker: " << getFirstName()
        << ' ' << getLastName();
}
```

**Fig. 10.1** Member function definitions for class **CommissionWorker** (part 6 of 12).

Class **CommissionWorker** (Fig. 10.1, parts 5 and 6) is derived from **Employee** with public inheritance. The public member functions include a constructor that takes a first name, a last name, a salary, a commission, and a quantity of items sold as arguments and passes the first name and last name to the **Employee** constructor; *set* functions to assign new values to private data members **salary**, **commission**, and **quantity**; a virtual **earnings** function defining how to calculate a **CommissionWorker**'s earnings; and a virtual **print** function that outputs the type of the employee followed by the employee's name.

Class **PieceWorker** (Fig. 10.1, parts 7 and 8) is derived from **Employee** with public inheritance. The public member functions include a constructor that takes a first

```
// PIECE1.H
// PieceWorker class derived from Employee
#ifndef PIECE1_H
#define PIECE1_H
#include "employ2.h"

class PieceWorker : public Employee {
public:
   PieceWorker(const char*, const char*, float = 0.0, unsigned = 0);
   void setWage(float);
   void setQuantity(unsigned);
   virtual float earnings() const;
   virtual void print() const;
private:
   float wagePerPiece; // wage for each piece output
   unsigned quantity;  // output for week
};

#endif
```

**Fig. 10.1** Class `PieceWorker` derived from abstract base class `Employee` (part 7 of 12).

```
// PIECE1.CPP
// Member function definitions for class PieceWorker
#include <iostream.h>
#include "piece1.h"

// Constructor for class PieceWorker
PieceWorker::PieceWorker(const char *first, const char *last,
                         float w, unsigned q)
   : Employee(first, last)  // call base-class constructor
{
   wagePerPiece = w > 0 ? w : 0;
   quantity = q > 0 ? q : 0;
}

// Set the wage
void PieceWorker::setWage(float w) { wagePerPiece = w > 0 ? w : 0; }

// Set the number of items output
void PieceWorker::setQuantity(unsigned q)
   { quantity = q > 0 ? q : 0; }

// Determine the PieceWorker's earnings
float PieceWorker::earnings() const
   { return quantity * wagePerPiece; }

// Print the PieceWorker's name
void PieceWorker::print() const
{
   cout << endl << "     Piece worker: " << getFirstName()
        << ' ' << getLastName();
}
```

**Fig. 10.1** Member function definitions for class `PieceWorker` (part 8 of 12).

```
// HOURLY1.H
// Definition of class HourlyWorker
#ifndef HOURLY1_H
#define HOURLY1_H
#include "employ2.h"

class HourlyWorker : public Employee {
public:
   HourlyWorker(const char *, const char *,
                float = 0.0, float = 0.0);
   void setWage(float);
   void setHours(float);
   virtual float earnings() const;
   virtual void print() const;
private:
   float wage;   // wage per hour
   float hours;  // hours worked for week
};

#endif
```

**Fig. 10.1** Class `HourlyWorker` derived from abstract base class `Employee` (part 9 of 12).

```
// HOURLY1.CPP
// Member function definitions for class HourlyWorker
#include <iostream.h>
#include "hourly1.h"

// Constructor for class HourlyWorker
HourlyWorker::HourlyWorker(const char *first, const char *last,
                           float w, float h)
   : Employee(first, last)   // call base-class constructor
{
   wage = w > 0 ? w : 0;
   hours = h >= 0 && h < 168 ? h : 0;
}

// Set the wage
void HourlyWorker::setWage(float w) { wage = w > 0 ? w : 0; }

// Set the hours worked
void HourlyWorker::setHours(float h)
   { hours = h >= 0 && h < 168 ? h : 0; }

// Get the HourlyWorker's pay
float HourlyWorker::earnings() const { return wage * hours; }

// Print the HourlyWorker's name
void HourlyWorker::print() const
{
   cout << endl << "    Hourly worker: " << getFirstName()
        << ' ' << getLastName();
}
```

**Fig. 10.1** Member function definitions for class `HourlyWorker` (part 10 of 12).

```
// FIG10_1.CPP
// Driver for Employee hierarchy

#include <iostream.h>
#include <iomanip.h>
#include "employ2.h"
#include "boss1.h"
#include "commis1.h"
#include "piece1.h"
#include "hourly1.h"

main()
{
   // set output formatting
   cout << setiosflags(ios::showpoint) << setprecision(2);

   Employee *ptr;  // base-class pointer

   Boss b("John", "Smith", 800.00);
   ptr = &b;  // base-class pointer to derived-class object
   ptr->print();                                // dynamic binding
   cout << " earned $" << ptr->earnings(); // dynamic binding
   b.print();                                   // static binding
   cout << " earned $" << b.earnings();    // static binding

   CommissionWorker c("Sue", "Jones", 200.0, 3.0, 150);
   ptr = &c;  // base-class pointer to derived-class object
   ptr->print();                                // dynamic binding
   cout << " earned $" << ptr->earnings(); // dynamic binding
   c.print();                                   // static binding
   cout << " earned $" << c.earnings();    // static binding

   PieceWorker p("Bob", "Lewis", 2.5, 200);
   ptr = &p;  // base-class pointer to derived-class object
   ptr->print();                                // dynamic binding
   cout << " earned $" << ptr->earnings(); // dynamic binding
   p.print();                                   // static binding
   cout << " earned $" << p.earnings();    // static binding

   HourlyWorker h("Karen", "Price", 13.75, 40);
   ptr = &h;  // base-class pointer to derived-class object
   ptr->print();                                // dynamic binding
   cout << " earned $" << ptr->earnings(); // dynamic binding
   h.print();                                   // static binding
   cout << " earned $" << h.earnings();    // static binding

   cout << endl;

   return 0;
}
```

**Fig. 10.1** `Employee` class derivation hierarchy that uses an abstract base class (part 11 of 12).

```
              Boss: John Smith earned $800.00
              Boss: John Smith earned $800.00
Commission worker: Sue Jones earned $650.00
Commission worker: Sue Jones earned $650.00
     Piece worker: Bob Lewis earned $500.00
     Piece worker: Bob Lewis earned $500.00
    Hourly worker: Karen Price earned $550.00
    Hourly worker: Karen Price earned $550.00
```

**Fig. 10.1** **Employee** class derivation hierarchy that uses an abstract base class (part 12 of 12).

name, a last name, a wage per piece, and a quantity of items produced as arguments and passes the first name and last name to the **Employee** constructor; *set* functions to assign new values to private data members **wagePerPiece** and **quantity**; a virtual **earnings** function defining how to calculate a **PieceWorker**'s earnings; and a virtual **print** function that outputs the type of the employee followed by the employee's name.

Class **HourlyWorker** (Fig. 10.1, parts 9 and 10) is derived from **Employee** with public inheritance. The public member functions include a constructor that takes a first name, a last name, a wage, and the number of hours worked as arguments and passes the first name and last name to the **Employee** constructor to initialize the **firstName** and **lastName** members of the base-class part of the derived-class object; *set* functions to assign new values to private data members **wage** and **hours**; a virtual **earnings** function defining how to calculate an **HourlyWorker**'s earnings; and a virtual **print** function that outputs the type of the employee followed by the employee's name.

The driver program (Fig. 10.1, parts 11 and 12) begins by declaring base-class pointer, **ptr**, of type **Employee ***. Each of the subsequent three code segments in **main** is similar, so we discuss only the first segment which deals with a **Boss** object.

The line

```
Boss b("John", "Smith", 800.00);
```

instantiates derived-class object **b** of class **Boss** and provides various constructor arguments including a first name, a last name, and a fixed weekly salary.

The line

```
ptr = &b;  // base-class pointer to derived-class object
```

places in base-class pointer **ptr** the address of derived class object **b**. This is precisely what we must do to effect polymorphic behavior.

The line

```
ptr->print();                          // dynamic binding
```

invokes the **print** member function of the object pointed to by **ptr**. Because **print** has been declared to be a virtual function in the base class, the system invokes the derived class object's **print** function—again, precisely what we call polymorphic behavior.

This function call is an example of dynamic binding—the function is invoked through a base-class pointer, so the decision as to what function to invoke is deferred until execution time.

The line

```
cout << " earned $" << ptr->earnings(); // dynamic binding
```

invokes the **earnings** member function of the object pointed to by **ptr**. Because **earnings** was declared to be a virtual function in the base class, the system invokes the derived-class object's **earnings** function. This is also an example of dynamic binding.

The line

```
b.print();                              // static binding
```

explicitly invokes the **Boss** version of member function **print** by using the dot member selection operator off the specific **Boss** object **b**. This is an example of static binding because the type of the object for which the function is called is known at compile time. This call is included for comparison purposes to illustrate that the correct **print** function is invoked using dynamic binding.

The line

```
cout << " earned $" << b.earnings();    // static binding
```

explicitly invokes the **Boss** version of member function **earnings** by using the dot member selection operator off the specific **Boss** object **b**. This is also an example of static binding. This call is included for comparison purposes to illustrate that the correct **earnings** function is invoked using dynamic binding.

## 10.7 New Classes and Dynamic Binding

Polymorphism and virtual functions could work nicely if all possible classes were known in advance. But they also work when new kinds of classes are added to systems.

New classes are accommodated by dynamic binding (also called *late binding*). An objects type need not be known at compile time for a virtual function call to be compiled. At execution time, the virtual function call is matched with the member function of the called object.

A screen manager program can now handle new display objects as they are added to the system without being recompiled. The **draw** function call remains the same. The new objects themselves contain the actual drawing capabilities. This makes it easy to add new capabilities to systems with minimal impact. It also promotes software reuse.

Dynamic binding enables independent software vendors (ISVs) to distribute software without revealing proprietary secrets. Software distributions can consist of only header files and object files. No source code needs to be revealed. Software developers can use inheritance to derive new classes from those provided by the ISVs. Software that works with the classes the ISVs provide will continue to work with the derived classes and will use (via dynamic binding) the redefined virtual functions provided in these classes.

The following paragraphs show how the compiler and the program (at run-time) handle polymorphism with little additional overhead.

Dynamic binding requires that at execution time, the call to a virtual member function be routed to the virtual function version appropriate for the class. A *virtual function table* called the *vtable* is implemented as an array containing function pointers. Each class that contains virtual functions has a *vtable*. For each virtual function in the class, the *vtable* has an entry containing a function pointer to the version of the virtual function to use for an object of that class. The virtual function to use for a particular class could be the function defined in that class or it could be a function inherited either directly or indirectly from a base class higher in the hierarchy.

When a base class provides a **`virtual`** member function, derived classes can redefine the function, but they do not have to redefine it. Thus, a derived class can use a base class's version of a virtual member function, and this would be indicated in the *vtable*.

Each object of a class with virtual functions contains a pointer to the *vtable* for that class. This pointer is not accessible to the programmer. At execution time, polymorphic calls to the virtual functions of the object dereference the *vtable* pointer in the object to obtain the *vtable* for the class. Then, the appropriate function pointer in the *vtable* is obtained and dereferenced to complete the call at execution time. This *vtable* lookup and pointer dereferencing requires nominal execution time overhead.

***Performance Tip 10.1***

*Polymorphism as implemented with virtual functions and dynamic binding is efficient. Programmers may use these capabilities with nominal impact on system performance.*

***Performance Tip 10.2***

*Virtual functions and dynamic binding enable polymorphic programming as opposed to* **`switch`** *logic programming. C++ optimizing compilers normally generate code that runs at least as efficiently as hand-coded* **`switch`***-based logic.*

## 10.8 Virtual Destructors

A problem can occur when using polymorphism to process dynamically allocated objects of a class hierarchy. If an object is destroyed explicitly by applying the **`delete`** operator to a base-class pointer to the object, the base-class destructor function is called on the object. This occurs regardless of the type of the object to which the base-class pointer is pointing and regardless of the fact that each class's destructor has a different name.

There is a simple solution to this problem—declare the base-class destructor virtual. This will automatically make all derived-class destructors virtual even though they do not have the same name as the base-class destructor. Now, if an object in the hierarchy is destroyed explicitly by applying the **`delete`** operator to a base-class pointer to a derived-class object, the destructor for the appropriate class is called. Remember that when a derived class is destroyed, the base-class part of the derived class is also destroyed. The base-class destuctor automatically executes after the derived-class destructor.

***Good Programming Practice 10.2***

*If a class has virtual functions, provide a virtual destructor even if one is not required for the class. Classes derived from this class may contain destructors that must be called properly.*

***Common Programming Error 10.3***

*Declaring a constructor as a virtual function. Constructors cannot be virtual.*

## 10.9 Case Study: Inheriting Interface and Implementation

Our next example (Fig. 10.2) re-examines the point, circle, cylinder hierarchy from the previous chapter except that we now head the hierarchy with abstract base class **Shape**. **Shape** has a pure virtual function—**printShapeName**—so **Shape** is an abstract base class. **Shape** contains two other virtual functions, namely **area** and **volume**, each of which has an implementation that returns a value of zero. **Point** inherits these imple-

```
// SHAPE.H
// Definition of abstract base class Shape
#ifndef SHAPE_H
#define SHAPE_H

class Shape {
public:
   virtual float area() const { return 0.0; }
   virtual float volume() const { return 0.0; }
   virtual void printShapeName() const = 0;   // pure virtual
   virtual void print() const = 0;            // pure virtual
};

#endif
```

**Fig. 10.2** Definition of abstract base class **Shape** (part 1 of 9).

```
// POINT1.H
// Definition of class Point
#ifndef POINT1_H
#define POINT1_H
#include <iostream.h>
#include "shape.h"

class Point : public Shape {
   friend ostream &operator<<(ostream &, const Point &);
public:
   Point(float = 0, float = 0);  // default constructor
   void setPoint(float, float);
   float getX() const { return x; }
   float getY() const { return y; }
   virtual void printShapeName() const { cout << "Point: "; }
   virtual void print() const;
private:
   float x, y;    // x and y coordinates of Point
};

#endif
```

**Fig. 10.2** Definition of class **Point** (part 2 of 9).

```
// POINT1.CPP
// Member function definitions for class Point
#include <iostream.h>
#include "point1.h"

Point::Point(float a, float b) { setPoint(a, b); }

void Point::setPoint(float a, float b)
{
   x = a;
   y = b;
}

void Point::print() const { cout << '[' << x << ", " << y << ']';
}

ostream &operator<<(ostream &output, const Point &p)
{
   p.print();        // call print to output the object

   return output;    // enables concatenated calls
}
```

**Fig. 10.2** Member function definitions for class **Point** (part 3 of 9).

```
// CIRCLE1.H
// Definition of class Circle
#ifndef CIRCLE1_H
#define CIRCLE1_H
#include "point1.h"

class Circle : public Point {
   friend ostream &operator<<(ostream &, const Circle &);
public:
   // default constructor
   Circle(float r = 0.0, float x = 0.0, float y = 0.0);

   void setRadius(float);
   float getRadius() const;
   virtual float area() const;
   virtual void printShapeName() const { cout << "Circle: "; }
   virtual void print() const;
private:
   float radius;    // radius of Circle
};

#endif
```

**Fig. 10.2** Definition of class **Circle** (part 4 of 9).

mentations from **Shape**. This makes sense because both the area and volume of a point are zero. **Circle** inherits the **volume** function from **Point**, but **Circle** provides its own implementation for the **area** function. **Cylinder** provides its own implementations for both the **area** function and the **volume** function.

```
// CIRCLE1.CPP
// Member function definitions for class Circle
#include <iostream.h>
#include <iomanip.h>
#include "circle1.h"

Circle::Circle(float r, float a, float b)
   : Point(a, b)  // call base-class constructor
{ radius = r > 0 ? r : 0; }

void Circle::setRadius(float r) { radius = r > 0 ? r : 0; }

float Circle::getRadius() const { return radius; }

float Circle::area() const { return 3.14159 * radius * radius; }

void Circle::print() const
{
   cout << '[' << getX() << ", " << getY()
        << "]; Radius = " << setiosflags(ios::showpoint)
        << setprecision(2) << radius;
}

ostream &operator<<(ostream &output, const Circle &c)
{
   c.print();        // call print to output the object
   return output;    // enables concatenated calls
}
```

Fig. 10.2 Member function definitions for class `Circle` (part 5 of 9).

```
// CYLINDR1.H
// Definition of class Cylinder
#ifndef CYLINDR1_H
#define CYLINDR1_H
#include "circle1.h"

class Cylinder : public Circle {
   friend ostream &operator<<(ostream &, const Cylinder &);
public:
   // default constructor
   Cylinder(float h = 0.0, float r = 0.0,
       float x = 0.0, float y = 0.0);

   void setHeight(float);
   virtual float area() const;
   virtual float volume() const;
   virtual void printShapeName() const { cout << "Cylinder: "; }
   virtual void print() const;
private:
   float height;   // height of Cylinder
};

#endif
```

Fig. 10.2 Definition of class `Cylinder` (part 6 of 9).

```
// CYLINDR1.CPP
// Member and friend function definitions for class Cylinder
#include <iostream.h>
#include <iomanip.h>
#include "cylindr1.h"

Cylinder::Cylinder(float h, float r, float x, float y)
   : Circle(r, x, y)  // call base-class constructor
{ height = h > 0 ? h : 0; }

void Cylinder::setHeight(float h) { height = h > 0 ? h : 0; }

float Cylinder::area() const
{
   // surface area of Cylinder
   return 2 * Circle::area() +
          2 * 3.14159 * Circle::getRadius() * height;
}

float Cylinder::volume() const { return Circle::area() * height; }

void Cylinder::print() const
{
   Circle::print();
   cout << "; Height = " << height;
}

ostream &operator<<(ostream &output, const Cylinder& c)
{
   c.print();         // call print to output the object
   return output;     // enables concatenated calls
}
```

**Fig. 10.2** Member function definitions for class **Cylinder** (part 7 of 9).

Note that although **Shape** is an abstract base class, it still contains implementations of certain member functions, and these implementations are inheritable. The **Shape** class provides an inheritable interface in the form of three virtual functions that all members of the hierarchy will contain. The **Shape** class also provides some implementations that derived classes in the first few levels of the hierarchy will use.

This case study emphasizes that a class can inherit interface and/or implementation from a base class. Hierarchies designed for implementation inheritance tend to have their functionality high in the hierarchy—each new class that is derived inherits one or more member functions that were defined in a base class and uses the base-class definitions. Hierarchies designed for interface inheritance tend to have their functionality lower in the hierarchy—a base class specifies one or more functions that should be called identically for each object in the hierarchy (i.e., they have the same signature), but the individual derived classes provide their own implementations of the function(s).

Base class **Shape** (Fig. 10.2, part 1) consists of four public virtual functions and does not contain any data. Functions **printShapeName** and **print** are pure virtual, so

```
// FIG10_2.CPP
// Driver for point, circle, cylinder hierarchy
#include <iostream.h>
#include <iomanip.h>
#include "shape.h"
#include "point1.h"
#include "circle1.h"
#include "cylindr1.h"

main()
{
   Point point(7, 11);                     // create a Point
   Circle circle(3.5, 22, 8);              // create a Circle
   Cylinder cylinder(10, 3.3, 10, 10);     // create a Cylinder

   point.printShapeName();     // static binding
   cout << point << endl;

   circle.printShapeName();    // static binding
   cout << circle << endl;

   cylinder.printShapeName();  // static binding
   cout << cylinder << "\n\n";

   cout << setiosflags(ios::showpoint) << setprecision(2);
   Shape *arrayOfShapes[3];    // array of base-class pointers

   // aim arrayOfShapes[0] at derived-class Point object
   // aim arrayOfShapes[1] at derived-class Circle object
   // aim arrayOfShapes[2] at derived-class Cylinder object
   arrayOfShapes[0] = &point;
   arrayOfShapes[1] = &circle;
   arrayOfShapes[2] = &cylinder;

   // Loop through arrayOfShapes and print the shape name,
   // area, and volume of each object to which the array points
   // using dynamic binding.
   for (int i = 0; i < 3; i++) {
      arrayOfShapes[i]->printShapeName();
      cout << endl;
      arrayOfShapes[i]->print();
      cout << "\nArea = " << arrayOfShapes[i]->area()
           << "\nVolume = " << arrayOfShapes[i]->volume()
           << endl << endl;
   }

   return 0;
}
```

**Fig. 10.2** Driver for point, circle, cylinder hierarchy (part 8 of 9).

they are redefined in each of the derived classes. Functions **area** and **volume** are defined to return **0.0**. These functions are redefined in derived classes when it is appropriate for those classes to have a different **area** calculation and/or a different **volume** calculation.

```
Point: [7, 11]
Circle: [22, 8]; Radius = 3.50
Cylinder: [10.00, 10.00]; Radius = 3.30; Height = 10.00

Point:
[7.00, 11.00]
Area = 0.00
Volume = 0.00

Circle:
[22.00, 8.00]; Radius=3.50
Area = 38.48
Volume = 0.00

Cylinder:
[10.00, 10.00]; Radius=3.30; Height=10.00
Area = 275.77
Volume = 342.12
```

**Fig. 10.2** Driver for point, circle, cylinder hierarchy (part 9 of 9).

Class **Point** (Fig. 10.2, parts 2 and 3) is derived from **Shape** with public inheritance. A **Point** does not have area or volume, so the base-class member functions **area** and **volume** are not redefined here—they are inherited as defined in **Shape**. Functions **printShapeName** and **print** are implementations of virtual function that were defined as pure virtual in the base class. Other member functions include a *set* function to assign new **x** and **y** coordinates to a **Point** and *get* functions to return the **x** and **y** coordinates of a **Point**.

Class **Circle** (Fig. 10.2, parts 4 and 5) is derived from **Point** with public inheritance. A **Circle** does not have volume, so base-class member function **volume** is not redefined here—it is inherited from **Shape** (and subsequently into **Point**). A **Circle** has area, so the **area** function is redefined in this class. Functions **printShapeName** and **print** are implementations of virtual function that were defined as pure virtual in the base class. If these functions are not redefined here, the **Point** versions of these functions would be inherited. Other member functions include a *set* function to assign a new **radius** to a **Circle** and a *get* function to return **radius** of a **Circle**.

Class **Cylinder** (Fig. 10.2, parts 6 and 7) is derived from **Circle** with public inheritance. A **Cylinder** has area and volume, so the **area** and **volume** functions are both redefined in this class. Functions **printShapeName** and **print** are implementations of virtual function that were defined as pure virtual in the base class. If these functions are not redefined here, the **Circle** versions of these functions would be inherited. Other member functions include a *set* function to assign a new **radius** to a **Circle** and a *get* function to return **radius** of a **Circle**.

The driver program (Fig. 10.2, parts 8 and 9) begins by instantiating **Point** object **point**, **Circle** object **circle**, and **Cylinder** object **cylinder**. Function **printShapeName** is invoked for each object and each object is output with its overloaded stream insertion operator to illustrate the objects are initialized correctly. Next, array **arrayOfShapes** of type **Shape *** is declared. This array of base-class pointers is used to point to each of the derived-class objects instantiated. First the address of the object **point** is assigned to array element **arrayOfShapes[0]**, the address of the object **circle** is assigned to array element **arrayOfShapes[1]**, and the address of the object **cylinder** is assigned to array element **arrayOfShapes[2]**. Next, a **for** structure is executed to walk through the array **arrayOfShapes** and the following calls are made during each iteration of the loop

```
arrayOfShapes[i]->printShapeName()
arrayOfShapes[i]->print()
arrayOfShapes[i]->area()
arrayOfShapes[i]->volume()
```

Each of the preceding calls invokes these functions on the object to which **arrayOfShapes[i]** is pointing. The output illustrates that the functions are invoked properly. First, the string **"Point: "** and the coordinates of the object **point** are output; the area and volume are both **0.00**. Next, the string **"Circle: "**, the coordinates of object **circle**, and the radius of object **circle** are output; the area of **circle** is calculated and the volume is **0.00**. Finally, the string **"Cylinder: "**, the coordinates of object **cylinder**, the radius of object **cylinder** and the height of object **cylinder** are output; the area of **cylinder** is calculated and the volume of **cylinder** is calculated. All the **printShapeName**, **print**, **area**, and **volume** function calls are resolved at run-time with dynamic binding.

## *Summary*

- With virtual functions and polymorphism, it becomes possible to design and implement systems that are more easily extensible. Programs can be written to process objects of types that may not exist when the program is under development.
- Virtual functions and polymorphic programming can eliminate the need for **switch** logic. The programmer can use the virtual function mechanism to perform the equivalent logic automatically, thus avoiding the kinds of errors typically associated with **switch** logic. Client code making decisions about object types and representations indicates poor class design.
- A virtual function is declared by preceding the function's prototype with the keyword **virtual** in the base class.
- Derived classes can provide their own implementations of a base class virtual function if necessary, but if they do not, the base class's implementation is used.
- If a virtual function is called by referencing a specific object by name and using the dot member selection operator, the reference is resolved at compile time (this is called *static binding*), and the virtual function that is called is the one defined for (or inherited by) the class of that particular object.
- There are many situations in which it is useful to define classes for which the programmer never intends to instantiate any objects. Such classes are called abstract

classes. Because these are used only as base classes, we will normally refer to them as abstract base classes. No objects of an abstract class may be instantiated in a program.

- Classes from which objects can be instantiated are called concrete classes.
- A class is made abstract by declaring one or more of its virtual functions to be pure. A pure virtual function is one with an initializer of `= 0` in its declaration.
- If a class is derived from a class with a pure virtual function without supplying a definition for that pure virtual function in the derived class, then that virtual function remains pure in the derived class. Consequently, the derived class is also an abstract class (and cannot have any objects).
- C++ enables polymorphism—the ability for objects of different classes related by inheritance to respond differently to the same member function call.
- Polymorphism is implemented via virtual functions.
- When a request is made through a base-class pointer to use a virtual function, C++ chooses the correct redefined function in the appropriate derived class associated with the object.
- Through the use of virtual functions and polymorphism, one member function call can cause different actions to occur depending on the type of the object receiving the call.
- Although we cannot instantiate objects of abstract base classes, we can declare pointers to abstract base classes. Such pointers can then be used to enable polymorphic manipulations of derived-class objects when such objects are instantiated from concrete classes.
- New kinds of classes are regularly added to systems. New classes are accommodated by dynamic binding (also called late binding). The type of an object need not be known at compile time for a virtual function call to be compiled. At execution time, the virtual function call is matched with the member function of the receiving object.
- Dynamic binding enables independent software vendors (ISVs) to distribute software without revealing proprietary secrets. Software distributions can consist of only header files and object files. No source code needs to be revealed. Software developers can then use inheritance to derive new classes from those provided by the ISVs. The software that works with the classes the ISVs provide will continue to work with the derived classes and will use (via dynamic binding) the redefined virtual functions provided in these classes.
- Dynamic binding requires that at execution time, the call to a virtual member function be routed to the virtual function version appropriate for the class. A virtual function table called the vtable is implemented as an array containing function pointers. Each class that contains virtual functions has a vtable. For each virtual function in the class, the vtable has an entry containing a function pointer to the version of the virtual function to use for an object of that class. The virtual function to use for a particular class could be the function defined in that class, or it could be a function inherited either directly or indirectly from a base class higher in the hierarchy.

- When a base class provides a virtual member function, derived classes can redefine the virtual function, but they do not have to redefine it. Thus a derived class can use a base class's version of a virtual member function, and this would be indicated in the vtable.
- Each object of a class with virtual functions contains a pointer to the vtable for that class. This pointer is not accessible to the programmer. The appropriate function pointer in the vtable is obtained and dereferenced to complete the call at execution time. This vtable lookup and pointer dereferencing require nominal execution time overhead, usually less than the best possible client code.
- Declare the base-class destructor virtual if the class contains virtual functions. This makes all derived-class destructors virtual even though they do not have the same name as the base-class destructor. If an object in the hierarchy is destroyed explicitly by applying the **`delete`** operator to a base-class pointer to a derived-class object, the destructor for the appropriate class is called.

## Terminology

abstract base class
abstract class
base-class **`virtual`** function
class hierarchy
convert derived-class pointer to base-class pointer
derived class
derived-class constructor
direct base class
dynamic binding
early binding
eliminating **`switch`** statements
explicit pointer conversion
extensibility
implicit pointer conversion
indirect base class
inheritance
late binding
pointer to a base class
pointer to a derived class
pointer to an abstract class
polymorphism
pure virtual function (`=0`)
redefined virtual function
reference to a base class
reference to a derived class
reference to an abstract class
software reusability
static binding
**`switch`** logic
virtual destructor
virtual function
**`virtual`** keyword
vtable

## Common Programming Errors

**10.1** Redefining in a derived class a base-class virtual function and not ensuring that the derived function has the same return type and signature as the base class's version is a syntax error.
**10.2** Attempting to instantiate an object of an abstract class (i.e., a class that contains one or more pure virtual functions) is a syntax error.
**10.3** Declaring a constructor as a virtual function. Constructors cannot be virtual.

## Good Programming Practices

**10.1** Even though certain functions are implicitly virtual because of a declaration made higher in the class hierarchy, some programmers prefer to explicitly declare these virtual functions at every level of the hierarchy to promote program clarity.

10.2 If a class has virtual functions, provide a virtual destructor even if one is not required for the class. Classes derived from this class may contain destructors that must be called properly.

## *Performance Tips*

10.1 Polymorphism as implemented with virtual functions and dynamic binding is efficient. Programmers may use these capabilities with nominal impact on system performance.

10.2 Virtual functions and dynamic binding enable polymorphic programming as opposed to **`switch`** logic programming. C++ optimizing compilers normally generate code that runs at least as efficiently as hand-coded **`switch`**-based logic.

## *Software Engineering Observations*

10.1 An interesting consequence of using virtual functions and polymorphism is that programs take on a simplified appearance. They contain less branching logic in favor of simpler sequential code. This simplification facilitates testing, debugging, and program maintenance.

10.2 Once a function has been declared virtual, it remains virtual all the way down the inheritance hierarchy from that point.

10.3 When a derived class chooses not to define a virtual function, the derived class simply inherits its immediate base class's virtual function definition.

10.4 Redefined virtual functions must have the same return type and signature as the base virtual function.

10.5 If a class is derived from a class with a pure virtual function, and if no definition is supplied for that pure virtual function in the derived class, then that virtual function remains pure in the derived class. Consequently, the derived class is also an abstract class.

10.6 With virtual functions and polymorphism, the programmer can deal in generalities and let the execution-time environment concern itself with the specifics. The programmer can command a wide variety of objects to behave in manners appropriate to those objects without even knowing the types of those objects. Except for client code that instantiates new objects, programs need not be recompiled.

10.7 Polymorphism promotes extensibility: Software written to invoke polymorphic behavior is written independently of the types of the objects to which messages are sent. Thus, new types of objects that can respond to existing messages can be added into such a system without modifying the base system.

10.8 An abstract class defines an interface for the various members of a class hierarchy. The abstract class contains pure virtual functions that will be defined in the derived classes. All functions in the hierarchy can use this same interface through polymorphism.

## *Self-Review Exercise*

10.1 Fill in the blanks in each of the following:

a) Using inheritance and polymorphism helps eliminate _________ logic.

b) A pure virtual function is specified by placing _________ at the end of its prototype in the class definition.

c) If a class contains one or more pure virtual functions, it is an _________.

d) A function call resolved at compile time is referred to as _________ binding.

e) A function call resolved at run time is referred to as _________ binding.

## Answers to Self-Review Exercise

**10.1** a) **`switch`**. b) **`= 0`**. c) abstract base class. d) static. e) dynamic.

## Exercises

**10.2** What are virtual functions? Describe a circumstance in which virtual functions would be appropriate.

**10.3** Given that constructors cannot be virtual, describe a scheme for how you might achieve a similar effect.

**10.4** How is it that polymorphism enables you to program "in the general" rather than "in the specific." Discuss the key advantages of programming "in the general."

**10.5** Discuss the problems of programming with **`switch`** logic. Explain why polymorphism is an effective alternative to using **`switch`** logic.

**10.6** Distinguish between static binding and dynamic binding. Explain the use of virtual functions and the vtable in dynamic binding.

**10.7** Distinguish between inheriting interface and inheriting implementation. How do inheritance hierarchies designed for inheriting interface differ from those designed for inheriting implementation?

**10.8** Distinguish between virtual functions and pure virtual functions.

**10.9** (True/False) All virtual functions in an abstract base class must be declared as pure virtual functions.

**10.10** Suggest one or more levels of abstract base classes for the **`Shape`** hierarchy discussed in this chapter (the first level is **`Shape`** and the second level consists of the classes **`TwoDimensionalShape`** and **`ThreeDimensionalShape`**).

**10.11** How does polymorphism promote extensibility?

**10.12** You have been asked to develop a flight simulator that will have elaborate graphical outputs. Explain why polymorphic programming would be especially effective for a problem of this nature.

**10.13** Develop a basic graphics package. Use the **`Shape`** class inheritance hierarchy from Chapter 9. Limit yourself to two-dimensional shapes such as squares, rectangles, triangles, and circles. Interact with the user. Let the user specify the position, size, shape, and fill characters to be used in drawing each shape. The user can specify many items of the same shape. As you create each shape, place a **`Shape *`** pointer to each new **`Shape`** object into an array. Each class has its own **`draw`** member function. Write a polymorphic screen manager that walks through the array (preferably using an iterator) sending **`draw`** messages to each object in the array to form a screen image. Redraw the screen image each time the user specifies an additional shape.

**10.14** Modify the payroll system of Fig. 10.1 to add private data members **`birthDate`** (a **`Date`** object) and **`departmentCode`** (an **`int`**) to class **`Employee`**. Assume this payroll is processed once per month. Then, as your program calculates the payroll for each **`Employee`** (polymorphically), add a $100.00 bonus to the person's payroll amount if this is the month in which the **`Employee`**'s birthday occurs.

**10.15** In Exercise 9.14, you developed a **`Shape`** class hierarchy and defined the classes in the hierarchy. Modify the hierarchy so that class **`Shape`** is an abstract base class containing the interface to the hierarchy. Derive **TwoDimensionalShape** and **ThreeDimensionalShape** from class **Shape**—these classes should also be abstract. Use a virtual **print** function to output the type and dimensions of each class. Also include virtual **area** and **volume** functions so these calculations can be performed for objects of each concrete class in the hierarchy. Write a driver program that tests the **Shape** class hierarchy.

# 11

# C++ Stream Input/Output

**Objectives**

- To understand how to use C++ object-oriented stream input/output.
- To be able to format inputs and outputs.
- To understand the stream I/O class hierarchy.
- To understand how to input/output objects of user-defined types.
- To be able to create user-defined stream manipulators.
- To be able to determine the success or failure of input/output operations.
- To be able to tie output streams to input streams.

*Consciousness . . . does not appear to itself chopped up in bits . . . A "river" or a "stream" are the metaphors by which it is most naturally described.*
William James

*All the news that's fit to print.*
Adolph S. Ochs

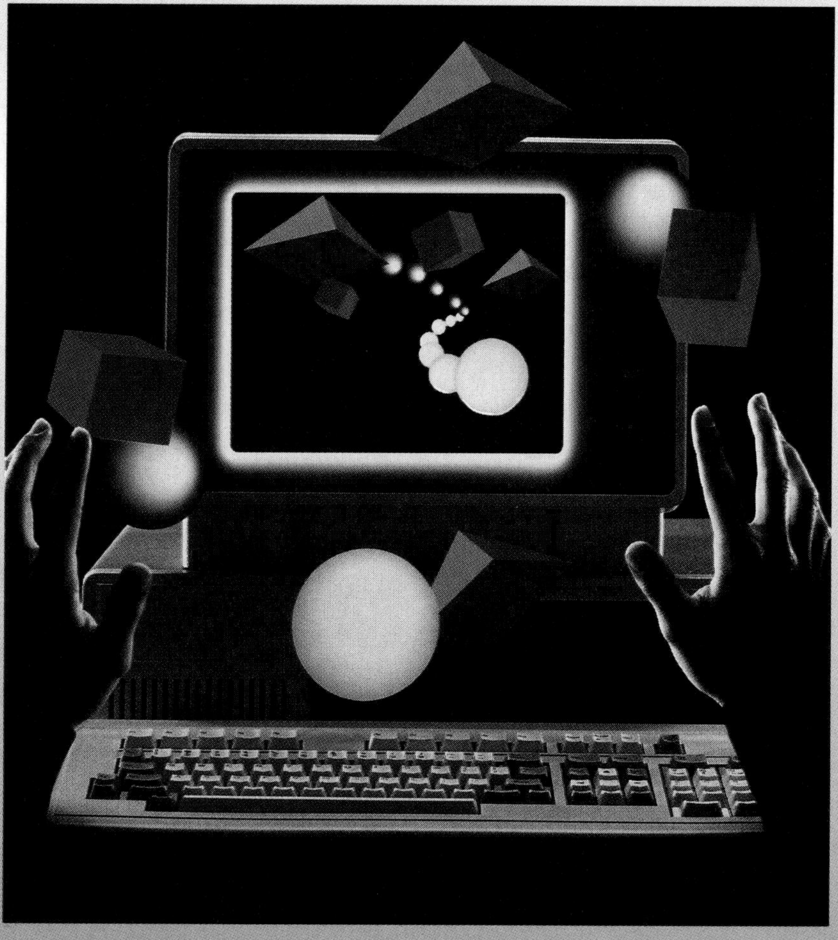

# Outline

## 11.1 Introduction

The C++ standard libraries provide an extensive set of input/output capabilities. This chapter discusses a range of capabilities sufficient for performing most common I/O operations and overviews the remaining capabilities. Some of the features presented here were discussed earlier in the text, but this chapter provides a more complete discussion of the input/output capabilities of C++.

Many of the I/O features described here are object-oriented. The reader should find it interesting to see how such capabilities are implemented. This style of I/O makes use of other C++ features such as references, function overloading, and operator overloading.

As we will see, C++ uses *type safe I/O*. Each I/O operation is automatically performed in a manner sensitive to the data type. If an I/O function has been properly defined to handle a particular data type, then that function is automatically called to handle that data type. If there is no match between the type of the actual data and a function for handling that data type, a compiler error indication is set. Thus, improper data cannot sneak through the system (as can occur in C—a hole in C that allows for some rather subtle and often bizarre errors).

Users may specify I/O of user-defined types as well as standard types. This *extensibility* is one of the most valuable features of C++.

***Good Programming Practice 11.1***

*Use the C++ form of I/O exclusively in C++ programs, despite the fact that C-style I/O is available to C++ programmers.*

***Software Engineering Observation 11.1***

*C++ style I/O is type safe.*

***Software Engineering Observation 11.2***

*C++ enables a common treatment of I/O of predefined types and user-defined types. This kind of commonality facilitates software development in general and software reuse in particular.*

## 11.2 Streams

C++ I/O occurs in *streams* of bytes. A stream is simply a sequence of bytes. In input operations, the bytes flow from a device (e.g., a keyboard, a disk drive, a network connection) to main memory. In output operations, bytes flow from main memory to a device (e.g., a display screen, a printer, a disk drive, a network connection).

The application associates meaning with bytes. The bytes may represent ASCII characters, internal format raw data, graphics images, digital speech, digital video or any other kind of information an application may require.

The job of the system I/O mechanisms is to move bytes from devices to memory and vice versa in a consistent and reliable manner. Such transfers often involve mechanical motion such as the rotation of a disk or a tape, or typing keystrokes at a keyboard. The time these transfers take is normally huge compared to the time the processor takes to manipulate data internally. Thus, I/O operations require careful planning and tuning to ensure maximum performance. Issues like this are discussed in depth in operating systems textbooks (De90).

C++ provides both "low-level" and "high-level" I/O capabilities. Low-level I/O capabilities (i.e., unformatted I/O) typically specify that some number of bytes should simply be transferred device-to-memory or memory-to-device. In such transfers, the individual byte is the item of interest. Such low-level capabilities do provide high-speed, high-volume transfers, but these capabilities are not particularly convenient for people.

People prefer a higher-level view of I/O, i.e., *formatted I/O,* in which bytes are grouped into meaningful units such as integers, floating-point numbers, characters, strings and user-defined types. These type-oriented capabilities are satisfactory for most I/O other than high-volume file processing.

***Performance Tip 11.1***

*Use unformatted I/O for the best performance in high-volume file processing.*

### 11.2.1 Iostream Library Header Files

The C++ **`iostream`** library provides hundreds of I/O capabilities. Several header files contain portions of the library interface.

Most C++ programs include the **`<iostream.h>`** header file which contains basic information required for all stream-I/O operations. The **`<iostream.h>`** header file contains the **`cin`**, **`cout`**, **`cerr`**, and **`clog`** objects which correspond to the standard input stream, standard output stream, the unbuffered standard error stream, and the buffered standard error stream. Both unformatted- and formatted-I/O capabilities are provided.

The **`<iomanip.h>`** header contains information useful for performing formatted I/O with so-called *parameterized stream manipulators.*

The **`<fstream.h>`** header contains information important for user-controlled file processing operations.

The **`<strstream.h>`** header contains information important for performing *in-memory formatting* (also called *in-core formatting*). This resembles file processing, but the "I/O" operations are performed to and from character arrays rather than files.

The **`<stdiostream.h>`** header contains information important for programs that mix the C and C++ styles of I/O. New programs should avoid C-style I/O, but people who need to modify existing C programs, or evolve C programs to C++, may find these capabilities useful.

Each C++ implementation generally contains other I/O-related libraries that provide system-specific capabilities such as controlling special-purpose devices for audio and video I/O.

### 11.2.2 Stream Input/Output Classes and Objects

The **`iostream`** library contains many classes for handling a wide variety of I/O operations. The **`istream`** class supports stream-input operations. The **`ostream`** class supports stream-output operations. The **`iostream`** class supports both stream-input and stream-output operations.

The **istream** class and the **ostream** class are each derived through single inheritance from the **ios** base class. The **iostream** class is derived through multiple inheritance from both the **istream** class and the **ostream** class. These inheritance relationships are summarized in Fig. 11.1.

Operator overloading provides a convenient notation for performing input/output. The left shift operator (<<) is overloaded to designate stream output and is referred to as the *stream-insertion operator*. The right shift operator (>>) is overloaded to designate stream input and is referred to as the *stream-extraction operator*. These operators are used with the standard stream objects **cin**, **cout**, **cerr**, and **clog**, and commonly with user-defined stream objects.

**cin** is an object of the **istream** class and is said to be "tied to" (or connected to) the standard input device, normally the keyboard. The stream-extraction operator as used in the following statement causes a value for integer variable **grade** (assuming **grade** has been declared as **int**) to be input from **cin** to memory:

```
cin >> grade;
```

Note that the stream-extraction operation is "smart enough" to "know" what the type of the data is. Assuming that **grade** has been properly declared, no additional type information needs to be specified for use with the stream-extraction operator (as is the case, incidentally, in C-style I/O).

**cout** is an object of the **ostream** class and is said to be "tied to" the standard output device, normally the display screen. The stream-insertion operator as used in the following statement causes the value of integer variable **grade** to be output from memory to the standard output device:

```
cout << grade;
```

Note that the stream-insertion operator is "smart enough" to "know" the type of **grade** (assuming it has been properly declared), so no additional type information needs to be specified for use with the stream-insertion operator.

**cerr** is an object of the **ostream** class and is said to be "tied to" the standard error device. Outputs to object **cerr** are unbuffered. This means that each insertion to **cerr** causes its output to appear immediately; this is appropriate for promptly notifying a user of trouble.

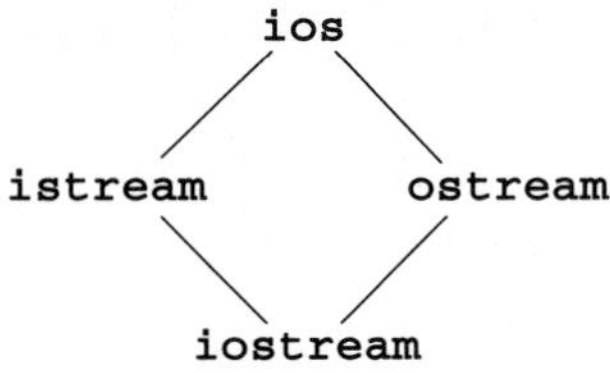


**Fig. 11.1** Portion of the stream I/O class hierarchy.

**`clog`** is an object of the **`ostream`** class and is also said to be "tied to" the standard error device. Outputs to **`clog`** are buffered. This means that each insertion to **`clog`** could cause its output to be held in a buffer until the buffer is filled or until the buffer is flushed.

C++ file processing uses the classes **`ifstream`** to perform file input operations, **`ofstream`** for file output operations, and **`fstream`** for file input/output operations. The **`ifstream`** class inherits from **`istream`**, the **`ofstream`** class inherits from **`ostream`**, and the **`fstream`** class inherits from **`iostream`**. The inheritance relationships of the I/O-related classes are summarized in Fig. 11.2. There are many more classes in the full stream-I/O class hierarchy supported at most installations, but the classes shown here provide the vast majority of the capabilities most programmers will need. See the class library reference for your C++ system for more file processing information.

## 11.3 Stream Output

The C++ **`ostream`** class provides the ability to perform formatted and unformatted output. Capabilities for output include: output of standard data types with the stream-insertion operator; output of characters with the **`put`** member function; unformatted output with the **`write`** member function (Section 11.5); output of integers in decimal, octal and hexadecimal formats (Section 11.6.1); output of floating-point values with various precisions (Section 11.6.2), with forced decimal points (Section 11.7.2), in scientific notation and in fixed notation (Section 11.7.6); output of data justified in fields of designated field widths (Section 11.7.3); output of data in fields padded with specified characters (Section 11.7.4); and output of uppercase letters in scientific notation and hexadecimal notation (Section 11.7.7).

### 11.3.1 Stream-insertion Operator

Stream output may be performed with the stream-insertion operator, i.e., the overloaded `<<` operator. The `<<` operator is overloaded to output data items of built-in types, to output strings and to output pointer values. Section 11.9 shows how to overload `<<` to output data items of user-defined types. Figure 11.3 demonstrates output of a string using a single stream-insertion statement. Multiple insertion statements may be used as in Fig. 11.4. When this program is run, it produces the same output as the previous program.

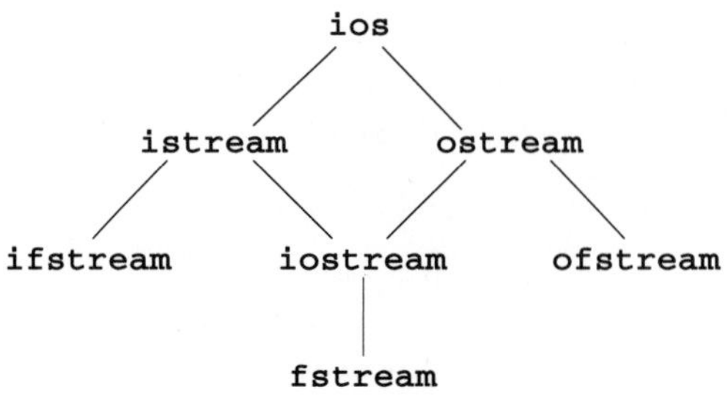


**Fig. 11.2** Portion of stream-I/O class hierarchy with key file-processing classes.

```
// fig11_03.cpp
// Outputting a string using stream insertion.

#include <iostream.h>

main()
{
   cout << "Welcome to C++!\n";

   return 0;
}
```

```
Welcome to C++!
```

Fig. 11.3 Outputting a string using stream insertion.

```
// fig11_04.cpp
// Outputting a string using two stream insertions.

#include <iostream.h>

main()
{
   cout << "Welcome to ";
   cout << "C++!\n";

   return 0;
}
```

```
Welcome to C++!
```

Fig. 11.4 Outputting a string using two stream insertions.

The effect of the **\n** (newline) escape sequence is also achieved by the **endl** (end line) *stream manipulator* as in Fig. 11.5. The **endl** stream manipulator issues a newline character and, in addition, flushes the output buffer (i.e., causes the output buffer to be output immediately even if it is not full). The output buffer may also be flushed simply by

```
cout << flush;
```

Stream manipulators are discussed in detail in Section 11.6.

Expressions can be output as shown in Fig. 11.6.

***Good Programming Practice 11.2***

*When outputting expressions, place them in parentheses to prevent operator precedence problems between the operators in the expression and the* **<<** *operator.*

```
// fig11_05.cpp
// Using the endl stream manipulator.
#include <iostream.h>

main()
{
   cout << "Welcome to ";
   cout << "C++!";
   cout << endl;   // end line stream manipulator

   return 0;
}
```

```
Welcome to C++!
```

Fig. 11.5 Using the **endl** stream manipulator.

```
// fig11_06.cpp
// Outputting expression values.
#include <iostream.h>

main()
{
   cout << "47 plus 53 is ";
   cout << (47 + 53);      // expression
   cout << endl;

   return 0;
}
```

```
47 plus 53 is 100
```

Fig. 11.6 Outputting expression values.

### 11.3.2 Concatenating Stream-Insertion/Extraction Operators

The overloaded **<<** and **>>** operators may each be used in a *concatenated form* as shown in Fig. 11.7.

The multiple stream insertions in Fig. 11.7 are executed as if they had been written:

```
(((cout << "47 plus 53 is ") << (47 + 53)) << endl);
```

i.e., **<<** associates from left to right. This kind of concatenation of stream-insertion operators is allowed because the overloaded **<<** operator returns a reference to its left-operand object, i.e., **cout**. Thus the leftmost parenthesized expression

```
(cout << "47 plus 53 is ")
```

```
// fig11_07.cpp
// Concatenating the overloaded << operator.
#include <iostream.h>

main()
{
   cout << "47 plus 53 is " << (47 + 53) << endl;

   return 0;
}
```

```
47 plus 53 is 100
```

Fig. 11.7 Concatenating the overloaded << operator.

outputs the specified character string and returns a reference to **cout**. This allows the middle parenthesized expression to be evaluated as

```
(cout << (47 + 53))
```

which outputs the integer value **100** and returns a reference to **cout**. The rightmost parenthesized expression is then evaluated as

```
cout << endl
```

which outputs a newline, flushes **cout**, and returns a reference to **cout**. This last return is not used.

### 11.3.3 Output of Char * Variables

In C-style I/O, it is necessary for the programmer to supply type information. C++ determines data types automatically—a nice improvement over C. But sometimes this "gets in the way." For example, we know that a character string is of type **char***. Suppose we want to print the value of that pointer, i.e., the memory address of the first character of that string. But the **<<** operator has been overloaded to print data of type **char*** as a null-terminated string. The solution is to cast the pointer to **void*** (this should be done to any pointer variable the programmer wishes to output as an address). Figure 11.8 demonstrates printing a **char*** variable in both string and address formats. Note that the address prints as a hexadecimal (base 16) number. Hexadecimal numbers in C++ begin with **0x** or **0X**. We say more about controlling the bases of numbers in Sections 11.6.1, 11.7.4, 11.7.5 and 11.7.7.

### 11.3.4 Character Output with the Put Member Function; Concatenating Puts

The **put** member function outputs one character as in

```
cout.put('A');
```

```
// fig11_08.cpp
// Printing the address stored in a char* variable
#include <iostream.h>

main()
{
   char *string = "test";

   cout << "Value of string is: " << string
        << "\nValue of (void *)string is: "
        << (void *)string << endl;
   return 0;
}
```

```
Value of string is: test
Value of (void *)string is: 0x00aa
```

**Fig. 11.8** Printing the address stored in a **char *** variable.

which displays **A** on the screen. Calls to **put** may be concatenated as in

```
cout.put('A').put('\n');
```

which outputs the letter **A** followed by a newline character. As with **<<**, the preceding statement executes in this manner because the dot operator (**.**) associates from left to right and the **put** member function returns a reference to the object through which the **put** call is invoked. The **put** function may also be called with an ASCII-valued expression as in **cout.put(65)** which also outputs **A**.

## 11.4 Stream Input

Now let us consider stream input. This may be performed with the stream-extraction operator, i.e., the overloaded **>>** operator. This operator normally skips *whitespace characters* (such as blanks, tabs, and newlines) in the input stream. Later we will see how to change this behavior. The stream-extraction operator returns zero (false) when end-of-file is encountered on a stream; otherwise, the stream extraction operator returns a reference to the object through which it is invoked. Each stream contains a set of *state bits* used to control the state of the stream (i.e., formatting, setting error states, etc.). Stream extraction causes the stream's **failbit** to be set if data of the wrong type is input, and causes the stream's **badbit** to be set if the operation fails. We will soon see how to test these bits after an I/O operation. Sections 11.7 and 11.8 discuss the stream state bits in detail.

### 11.4.1 Stream-Extraction Operator

To read two integers, use the **cin** object and the overloaded **>>** stream-extraction operator as in Fig. 11.9. Note that stream-extraction operations can also be concatenated.

The relatively high precedence of the **>>** and **<<** operators can cause problems. For example, the program of Fig. 11.10 will not compile properly without the parentheses around the conditional expression. The reader should verify this.

```
// fig11_09.cpp
// Calculating the sum of two integers
// input from the keyboard with cin
// and the stream-extraction operator.
#include <iostream.h>

main()
{
   int x, y;

   cout << "Enter two integers: ";
   cin >> x >> y;
   cout << "Sum of " << x << " and " << y << " is: "
        << (x + y) << endl;

   return 0;
}
```

```
Enter two integers: 30 92
Sum of 30 and 92 is: 122
```

**Fig. 11.9** Calculating the sum of two integers input from the keyboard with `cin` and the stream-extraction operator.

```
// fig11_10.cpp
// Revealing a precedence problem.
// Need parentheses around the conditional expression.
#include <iostream.h>

main()
{
   int x, y;

   cout << "Enter two integers: ";
   cin >> x >> y;
   cout << x << (x == y ? " is" : " is not")
        << " equal to " << y << endl;

   return 0;
}
```

```
Enter two integers: 7 5
7 is not equal to 5
```

```
Enter two integers: 8 8
8 is equal to 8
```

**Fig. 11.10** Avoiding a precedence problem between the stream-insertion operator and the conditional operator.

***Common Programming Error 11.1***

*Attempting to read from an ostream (or from any other output-only stream).*

***Common Programming Error 11.2***

*Attempting to write to an istream (or to any other input-only stream).*

***Common Programming Error 11.3***

*Not providing parentheses to force proper precedence when using the relatively high precedence stream-insertion operator << or stream-extraction operator >>.*

One popular way to input a series of values is to use the stream-extraction operation in the loop-continuation condition of a **`while`** loop. The extraction returns false (0) when end-of-file is encountered. Consider the program of Fig. 11.11 which finds the highest grade on an exam. Assume the number of grades is not known in advance and that the user will type end-of-file to indicate that all the grades have been entered. The **`while`** condition, **`(cin >> grade)`**, becomes 0 (i.e., false) when the user enters end-of-file.

```
// fig11_11.cpp
// Stream-extraction operator returning
// false on end-of-file.
#include <iostream.h>

main()
{
   int grade, highestGrade = -1;

   cout << "Enter grade (enter end-of-file to end): ";
   while (cin >> grade) {
      if (grade > highestGrade)
         highestGrade = grade;

      cout << "Enter grade (enter end-of-file to end): ";
   }

   cout << endl << "Highest grade is: " << highestGrade
        << endl;
   return 0;
}
```

```
Enter grade (enter end-of-file to end): 67
Enter grade (enter end-of-file to end): 87
Enter grade (enter end-of-file to end): 73
Enter grade (enter end-of-file to end): 95
Enter grade (enter end-of-file to end): 34
Enter grade (enter end-of-file to end): 99
Enter grade (enter end-of-file to end): ^Z

Highest grade is: 99
```

**Fig. 11.11** Stream-extraction operator returning false on end-of-file.

In Fig. 11.11, **cin >> grade** can be used as a condition because the base class **ios** (from which **istream** is inherited) provides an overloaded cast operator that converts a stream into a pointer of type **void ***. The value of the pointer is 0 if an error occurred while attempting to read a value or the end-of-file indicator was encountered. The compiler is able to use the **void *** cast operator implicitly.

### 11.4.2 Get and Getline Member Functions

The **get** member function with no arguments inputs one character from the designated stream (even if this is whitespace) and returns this character as the value of the function call. This version of **get** returns **EOF** when end-of-file on the stream is encountered.

Figure 11.12 demonstrates the use of member functions **eof** and **get** on input stream **cin** and member function **put** on output stream **cout**. The program first prints the value of **cin.eof()**, i.e., **0** (false) to show that end-of-file has not occurred on **cin**. The user enters a line of text followed by end-of-file (**<ctrl>-z** followed by **<return>** on IBM PC compatible systems, **<ctrl>-d** on UNIX and Macintosh systems). The program reads each character and outputs it to **cout** using member function **put**. When the end-of-file is encountered, the **while** ends, and **cin.eof()**—now **1** (true)—is printed again to show that end-of-file has been set on **cin**. Note that this program uses the version of **istream** member function **get** that takes no arguments and returns the character being input.

```
// fig11_12.cpp
// Using member functions get, put, and eof.
#include <iostream.h>

main()
{
   int c;

   cout << "Before input, cin.eof() is " << cin.eof() << endl
        << "Enter a sentence followed by end-of-file:" << endl;

   while ( ( c = cin.get() ) != EOF)
      cout.put(c);

   cout << endl << "EOF in this system is: " << c << endl;
   cout << "After input, cin.eof() is " << cin.eof() << endl;
   return 0;
}
```

```
Before input, cin.eof() is 0
Enter a sentence followed by end-of-file:
Testing the get and put member functions^Z
Testing the get and put member functions
EOF in this system is: -1
After input cin.eof() is 1
```

**Fig. 11.12** Using member functions **get**, **put**, and **eof**.

The **get** member function with a character argument inputs the next character from the input stream (even if this is a whitespace character) and stores it in the character argument. This version of **get** returns false when end-of-file is encountered; otherwise this version of **get** returns a reference to the **istream** object for which the **get** member function is being invoked.

A third version of the **get** member function takes three arguments—a character array, a size limit, and a delimiter (with default value **'\n'**). This version reads characters from the input stream. It reads up to one less than the specified maximum number of characters and terminates, or terminates as soon as the delimiter is read. A null character is inserted to terminate the input string in the character array used as a buffer by the program. The delimiter is not placed in the character array, but does remain in the input stream (the delimiter will be the next character read). Thus, the result of a second consecutive **get** is an empty line unless the delimeter character is flushed from the input stream. Figure 11.13 compares input using **cin** with stream extraction (which reads characters until a whitespace character is encountered) and input with **cin.get**. Note that the call to **cin.get** does not specify a delimiter character, so the default **'\n'** is used.

```
// fig11_13.cpp
// Contrasting input of a string with cin and cin.get.
#include <iostream.h>

const int SIZE = 80;

main()
{
   char buffer1[SIZE], buffer2[SIZE];

   cout << "Enter a sentence:" << endl;
   cin >> buffer1;
   cout << endl << "The string read with cin was:" << endl
        << buffer1 << endl << endl;

   cin.get(buffer2, SIZE);
   cout << "The string read with cin.get was:" << endl
        << buffer2 << endl;

   return 0;
}
```

```
Enter a sentence:
Contrasting string input with cin and cin.get

The string read with cin was:
Contrasting

The string read with cin.get was:
 string input with cin and cin.get
```

**Fig. 11.13** Contrasting input of a string using **cin** with stream extraction and input with **cin.get**.

The **getline** member function operates like the third version of the **get** member function and inserts a null character after the line in the character array. The **getline** function removes the delimiter from the stream (i.e., reads the character and discards it), but does not store it in the character array. The program of Fig. 11.14 demonstrates the use of the **getline** member function to input a line of text.

### 11.4.3 Other Istream Member Functions (Peek, Putback, Ignore)

The **ignore** member function skips over a designated number of characters (default is one character) or terminates upon encountering a designated delimiter (the default delimiter is **EOF** which causes **ignore** to skip to the end of file when reading from a file).

The **putback** member function places the previous character obtained by a **get** on an input stream back onto that stream. This function is useful for applications that scan an input stream looking for a field beginning with a specific character. When that character is input, the application puts that character back on the stream so the character can be included in the data about to be input.

The **peek** member function returns the next character from an input stream, but does not remove the character from the stream.

```
// fig11_14.cpp
// Character input with member function getline.

#include <iostream.h>

const int SIZE = 80;

main()
{
   char buffer[SIZE];

   cout << "Enter a sentence:" << endl;
   cin.getline(buffer, SIZE);

   cout << endl << "The sentence entered is:" << endl
        << buffer << endl;

   return 0;
}
```

```
Enter a sentence:
Using the getline member function

The sentence entered is:
Using the getline member function
```

Fig. 11.14 Character input with member function **getline**.

### 11.4.4 Type-Safe I/O

C++ offers *type-safe I/O*. The `<<` and `>>` operators are overloaded to accept data items of specific types. If unexpected data is processed, various error flags are set which the user may test to determine if an I/O operation succeeded or failed. In this manner the program "stays in control." We discuss these error flags in Section 11.8.

## 11.5 Unformatted I/O with `read`, `gcount` and `write`

*Unformatted input/output* is performed with the **`read`** and **`write`** member functions. Each of these inputs or outputs some number of bytes to or from a character array in memory. These bytes are not formatted in any way. They are simply input or output as raw bytes. For example, the call

```
char buffer[] = "HAPPY BIRTHDAY";
cout.write(buffer, 10);
```

outputs the first 10 bytes of **`buffer`** (including null characters that would cause output with **`cout`** and **`<<`** to terminate). Since a character string evaluates to the address of its first character, the call

```
cout.write("ABCDEFGHIJKLMNOPQRSTUVWXYZ", 10);
```

displays the first 10 characters of the alphabet.

The **`read`** member function inputs into a character array a designated number of characters. If fewer than the designated number of characters are read, **`failbit`** is set. We will soon see how to determine if **`failbit`** has been set (see Section 11.8).

The **`gcount`** member function reports the number of characters read by the last input operation.

Figure 11.15 demonstrates **`istream`** member functions **`read`** and **`gcount`** and **`ostream`** member function **`write`**. The program inputs 20 characters (from a longer input sequence) into character array **`buffer`** with **`read`**, determines the number of characters input with **`gcount`**, and outputs the characters in **`buffer`** with **`write`**.

## 11.6 Stream Manipulators

C++ provides various *stream manipulators* that perform formatting tasks. The stream manipulators provide capabilities such as setting field widths, setting precisions, setting and unsetting format flags, setting the fill character in fields, flushing streams, inserting a newline in the output stream and flushing the stream, inserting a null character in the output stream, and skipping whitespace in the input stream. These features are described in the following sections.

### 11.6.1 Integral Stream Base: `dec`, `oct`, `hex` and `setbase` Stream Manipulators

Integers are normally interpreted as decimal (base 10) values. To change the base in which integers are interpreted on a stream, insert the manipulator **`hex`** to set the base to hexadecimal (base 16) or insert the manipulator **`oct`** to set the base to octal (base 8). Insert the **`dec`** stream manipulator to reset the stream base to decimal.

```
// fig11_15.cpp
// Unformatted I/O with the read,
// gcount and write member functions.

#include <iostream.h>

const int SIZE = 80;

main()
{
   char buffer[SIZE];

   cout << "Enter a sentence:" << endl;
   cin.read(buffer, 20);
   cout << endl << "The sentence entered was:" << endl;
   cout.write(buffer, cin.gcount());
   cout << endl;

   return 0;
}
```

```
Enter a sentence:
Using the read, write, and gcount member functions

The sentence entered was:
Using the read, writ
```

**Fig. 11.15** Unformatted I/O with the **read**, **gcount** and **write** member functions.

The base of a stream may also be changed by the stream manipulator **setbase** which takes one integer argument of **10**, **8**, or **16** to set the base. Because **setbase** takes an argument, it is called a *parameterized stream manipulator*. Using **setbase** or any other parameterized manipulator requires the inclusion of the **<iomanip.h>** header file. The stream base remains the same until it is explicitly changed. Figure 11.16 shows the use of the **hex**, **oct**, **dec**, and **setbase** stream manipulators.

## 11.6.2 Floating-Point Precision (precision, setprecision)

We can control the *precision* of floating-point numbers, i.e., the number of digits to the right of the decimal point, by using either the **setprecision** stream manipulator or the **precision** member function. A call to either of these sets the precision for all subsequent output operations until the next precision-setting call. The **precision** member function with no argument returns the current precision setting. The program of Fig. 11.17 uses both the **precision** member function and the **setprecision** manipulator to print a table showing the square root of **2** with precisions varying from **0** through **9**. Note that precision **0** has special meaning. This restores the *default precision* value **6**.

```
// fig11_16.cpp
// Using hex, oct, dec and setbase stream manipulators.
#include <iostream.h>
#include <iomanip.h>

main()
{
   int n;

   cout << "Enter a decimal number: ";
   cin >> n;

   cout << n << " in hexadecimal is: "
        << hex << n << endl
        << dec << n << " in octal is: "
        << oct << n << endl
        << setbase(10) << n << " in decimal is: "
        << n << endl;

   return 0;
}
```

```
Enter a decimal number: 20
20 in hexadecimal is: 14
20 in octal is: 24
20 in decimal is: 20
```

**Fig. 11.16** Using the `hex`, `oct`, `dec` and `setbase` stream manipulators.

### 11.6.3 Field Width (`setw`, `width`)

The `ios` `width` member function sets the field width (i.e., the number of character positions in which a value should be output or the number of characters that should be input) and returns the previous width. If values processed are smaller than the field width, *fill characters* are inserted as *padding*. A value wider than the designated width will not be truncated—the full number will be printed. The width setting applies only for the next insertion or extraction; afterward, the width is implicitly set to `0`, i.e., output values will simply be as wide as they need to be. The `width` function with no argument returns the current setting.

*Common Programming Error 11.4*

*When not providing a sufficiently wide field to handle outputs, the outputs print as wide as they need to be, possibly causing difficult-to-read outputs.*

Figure 11.18 demonstrates the use of the `width` member function on both input and output. Note that on input, a maximum of one fewer characters than the width will be read because provision is made for the null character to be placed in the input string. Remember that stream extraction terminates when nonleading whitespace is encountered. The `setw` stream manipulator may also be used to set the field width.

```
// fig11_17.cpp
// Controlling precision of floating-point values
#include <iostream.h>
#include <iomanip.h>
#include <math.h>

main()
{
   double root2 = sqrt(2.0);

   cout << "Square root of 2 with precisions 0-9." << endl
        << "Precision set by the "
        << "precision member function:" << endl;

   for (int places = 0; places <= 9; places++) {
      cout.precision(places);
      cout << root2 << endl;
   }

   cout << endl << "Precision set by the "
        << "setprecision manipulator:" << endl;

   for (places = 0; places <= 9; places++)
      cout << setprecision(places) << root2 << endl;

   return 0;
}
```

```
Square root of 2 with precisions 0-9.
Precision set by the precision member function:
1.414214
1.4
1.41
1.414
1.4142
1.41421
1.414214
1.4142136
1.41421356
1.414213562

Precision set by the setprecision manipulator:
1.414214
1.4
1.41
1.414
1.4142
1.41421
1.414214
1.4142136
1.41421356
1.414213562
```

**Fig. 11.17** Controlling precision of floating-point values.

```
// fig11_18.cpp
// Demonstrating the width member function

#include <iostream.h>

main()
{
   int w = 4;
   char string[10];

   cout << "Enter a sentence:" << endl;
   cin.width(5);

   while (cin >> string) {
      cout.width(w++);
      cout << string << endl;
      cin.width(5);
   }

   return 0;
}
```

```
Enter a sentence:
This is a test of the width member function^Z
This
   is
     a
   test
      of
      the
      widt
          h
        memb
           er
          func
           tion
```

Fig. 11.18 Demonstrating the **width** member function.

### 11.6.4 User-Defined Manipulators

Users may create their own stream manipulators. Figure 11.19 shows the creation and use of new stream manipulators **bell**, **ret** (carriage return), **tab**, and **endLine**. Users may also create their own parameterized stream manipulators—consult your installation's manuals for instructions on how to do this.

## 11.7 Stream Format States

Various *format flags* specify the kinds of formatting to be performed during stream I/O operations. The **setf**, **unsetf**, and **flags** member functions control the flag settings.

```
// fig11_19.cpp
// Creating and testing user-defined, nonparameterized
// stream manipulators.
#include <iostream.h>

// bell manipulator (using escape sequence \a)
ostream& bell(ostream& output)
{
   return output << '\a';
}

// ret manipulator (using escape sequence \r)
ostream& ret(ostream& output)
{
   return output << '\r';
}

// tab manipulator (using escape sequence \t)
ostream& tab(ostream& output)
{
   return output << '\t';
}

// endLine manipulator (using escape sequence \n
// and the flush member function)
ostream& endLine(ostream& output)
{
   return output << '\n' << flush;
}

main()
{
   cout << "Testing the tab manipulator:" << endLine
        << 'a' << tab << 'b' << tab << 'c' << endLine
        << "Testing the ret and bell manipulators:"
        << endLine << "..........";

   for (int i = 1; i <= 100; i++)
      cout << bell;

   cout << ret << "-----" << endLine;

   return 0;
}
```

```
Testing the tab manipulator:
a       b       c
Testing the ret and bell manipulators:
-----.....
```

**Fig. 11.19** Creating and testing user-defined, nonparameterized stream manipulators.

### 11.7.1 Format State Flags

Each of the format state flags shown in Fig. 11.20 (and some that are not shown) is defined as an enumeration in class **ios** and is explained in the next several sections.

These flags can be controlled by the **flags**, **setf**, and **unsetf** member functions, but many C++ programmers prefer to use stream manipulators (see Section 11.7.8). The programmer may use the bitwise-or operation, **|**, to combine various options into a single **long** value (see Fig. 11.23). Calling the **flags** member function for a stream and specifying these "or-ed" options sets the options on that stream and returns a **long** value containing the prior options. This value is often saved so that **flags** may be called with this saved value to restore the previous stream options.

The **flags** function must specify a value representing the settings of all the flags. The one-argument **setf** function, on the other hand, specifies one or more "or-ed" flags and "ors" them with the existing flag settings to form a new format state.

The **setiosflags** parameterized stream manipulator performs the same functions as the **setf** member function. The **resetiosflags** stream manipulator performs the same functions as the **unsetf** member function. To use either of these stream manipulators, be sure to **#include <iomanip.h>**.

The **skipws** flag indicates that **>>** should skip whitespace on an input stream. The default behavior of **>>** is to skip whitespace. To change this, use the call **unsetf(ios::skipws)**. The **ws** stream manipulator may also be used to specify that whitespace should be skipped.

### 11.7.2 Trailing Zeros and Decimal Points (ios::showpoint)

The **showpoint** flag is set to force a floating-point number to be output with its decimal point and trailing zeros. A floating-point value of **79.0** will print as **79** without **showpoint** set and as **79.000000** (or as many trailing zeros as are specified by the current

```
ios::skipws

ios::left
ios::right
ios::internal

ios::dec
ios::oct
ios::hex

ios::showbase
ios::showpoint
ios::uppercase
ios::showpos

ios::scientific
ios::fixed
```

**Fig. 11.20** Format state flags.

precision) with **showpoint** set. The program in Fig. 11.21 shows the use of the **setf** member function to set the **showpoint** flag to control trailing zeros and the printing of the decimal point for floating-point values.

### 11.7.3 Justification (ios::left, ios::right, ios::internal)

The **left** and **right** flags enable fields to be left-justified with padding characters to the right, or right-justified with padding characters to the left, respectively. The character to be used for padding is specified by the **fill** member function or the **setfill** parameterized stream manipulator (see Section 11.7.4). Figure 11.22 shows the use of the **setw**, **setiosflags**, and **resetiosflags** manipulators and the **setf** and **unsetf** member functions to control the left- and right-justification of integer data in a field.

```
// fig11_21.cpp
// Controlling the printing of trailing
// zeros and decimal points when using
// floating-point values with float values.

#include <iostream.h>
#include <iomanip.h>
#include <math.h>

main()
{
   cout << "cout prints 9.9900 as: " << 9.9900 << endl
        << "cout prints 9.9000 as: " << 9.9000 << endl
        << "cout prints 9.0000 as: " << 9.0000 << endl << endl
        << "After setting the ios::showpoint flag" << endl;
   cout.setf(ios::showpoint);

   cout << "cout prints 9.9900 as: " << 9.9900 << endl
        << "cout prints 9.9000 as: " << 9.9000 << endl
        << "cout prints 9.0000 as: " << 9.0000 << endl;
   return 0;
}
```

```
cout prints 9.9900 as: 9.99
cout prints 9.9000 as: 9.9
cout prints 9.0000 as: 9

After setting the ios::showpoint flag
cout prints 9.9900 as: 9.990000
cout prints 9.9000 as: 9.900000
cout prints 9.0000 as: 9.000000
```

**Fig. 11.21** Controlling the printing of trailing zeros and decimal points with float values.

```
// fig11_22.cpp
// Left-justification and right-justification.

#include <iostream.h>
#include <iomanip.h>

main()
{
   int x = 12345;

   cout << "Default is right justified:" << endl
        << setw(10) << x << endl << endl
        << "USING MEMBER FUNCTIONS" << endl
        << "Use setf to set ios::left:" << endl << setw(10);

   cout.setf(ios::left, ios::adjustfield);
   cout << x << endl << "Use unsetf to restore default:" << endl;
   cout.unsetf(ios::left);
   cout << setw(10) << x << endl << endl
        << "USING PARAMETERIZED STREAM MANIPULATORS" << endl
        << "Use setiosflags to set ios::left:" << endl
        << setw(10) << setiosflags(ios::left) << x << endl
        << "Use resetiosflags to restore default:" << endl
        << setw(10) << resetiosflags(ios::left)
        << x << endl;
   return 0;
}
```

```
Default is right justified:
     12345

USING MEMBER FUNCTIONS
Use setf to set ios::left:
12345
Use unsetf to restore default:
     12345

USING PARAMETERIZED STREAM MANIPULATORS
Use setiosflags to set ios::left:
12345
Use resetiosflags to restore default:
     12345
```

**Fig. 11.22** Left-justification and right-justification.

The **internal** flag indicates that a number's sign (or base when the **ios::showbase** flag is set; see Section 11.7.5) should be left-justified within a field, the number's magnitude should be right-justified, and intervening spaces should be padded with the fill character. The **left**, **right**, and **internal** flags are contained in static data member **ios::adjustfield**. The **ios::adjustfield** argument must be provided as the second argument to **setf** when setting the **left**, **right**, or **internal** justification flags. This enables **setf** to ensure that only one of the three justification flags is set (they are mutually exclusive). Figure 11.23 shows the use of the **setiosflags** and **setw** stream manipulators to specify internal spacing. Note the use of the **ios::showpos** flag to force the printing of the plus sign.

### 11.7.4 Padding (Fill, Setfill)

The ***fill*** *member function* specifies the fill character to be used with adjusted fields; if no value is specified, spaces are used for padding. The **fill** function returns the prior padding character. The ***setfill*** *manipulator* also sets the padding character. Figure 11.24 demonstrates the use of the **fill** member function and the **setfill** manipulator to control the setting and resetting of the fill character.

### 11.7.5 Integral Stream Base (ios::dec, ios::oct, ios::hex, ios::showbase)

The ***ios::basefield*** *static member* (used similarly to **ios::adjustfield** with **setf**) includes the **ios::oct**, **ios::hex**, and **ios::dec** flag bits to specify that integers are to be treated as octal, hexadecimal, and decimal values, respectively. Stream insertions default to decimal if none of these bits is set. The default for stream extractions is to process the data in the form in which it is supplied—integers starting with **0** are treated as octal values, integers starting with **0x** or **0X** are treated as hexadecimal values, and all other integers are treated as decimal values. Once a particular base is specified for a stream, all integers on that stream are processed with that base until a new base is specified or until the end of the program.

```
// fig11_23.cpp
// Printing an integer with internal spacing and
// forcing the plus sign.

#include <iostream.h>
#include <iomanip.h>

main()
{
   cout << setiosflags(ios::internal | ios::showpos)
        << setw(10) << 123 << endl;

   return 0;
}
```

```
+       123
```

**Fig. 11.23** Printing an integer with internal spacing and forcing the plus sign.

```
// fig11_24.cpp
// Using the fill member function and the setfill
// manipulator to change the padding character for
// fields larger than the values being printed.

#include <iostream.h>
#include <iomanip.h>

main()
{
   int x = 10000;

   cout << x
        << " printed as int right and left justified" << endl
        << "and as hex with internal justification." << endl
        << "Using the default pad character (space):" << endl;
   cout.setf(ios::showbase);
   cout << setw(10) << x << endl;
   cout.setf(ios::left, ios::adjustfield);
   cout << setw(10) << x << endl;
   cout.setf(ios::internal, ios::adjustfield);
   cout << setw(10) << hex << x << endl << endl;

   cout << "Using various padding characters:" << endl;
   cout.setf(ios::right, ios::adjustfield);
   cout.fill('*');
   cout << setw(10) << dec << x << endl;
   cout.setf(ios::left, ios::adjustfield);
   cout << setw(10) << setfill('%') << x << endl;
   cout.setf(ios::internal, ios::adjustfield);
   cout << setw(10) << setfill('^') << hex
        << x << endl;

   return 0;
}
```

```
10000 printed as int right and left justified
and as hex with internal justification.
Using the default pad character (space):
     10000
10000
0x    2710

Using various padding characters:
*****10000
10000%%%%%
0x^^^^2710
```

**Fig. 11.24** Using the `fill` member function and the `setfill` manipulator to change the padding character for fields larger than the values being printed.

Set the **showbase** flag to force the base of an integral value to be output. Decimal numbers are output normally, octal numbers are output with a leading **0**, and hexadecimal numbers are output with either a leading **0x** or a leading **0X** (the **uppercase** flag determines which option is chosen; see Section 11.7.7). Figure 11.25 demonstrates the use of the **showbase** flag to force an integer to print in decimal, octal, and hexadecimal formats.

### 11.7.6 Floating-Point Numbers; Scientific Notation (ios::scientific, ios::fixed)

The ***ios::scientific** flag* and the ***ios::fixed** flag* are contained in the *static data member* ***ios::floatfield*** (used similarly to **ios::adjustfield** and **ios::basefield** in **setf**). These flags are used to control the output format of floating-point numbers. The **scientific** flag is set to force the output of a floating-point number in scientific format. The **fixed** flag forces a floating-point number to display a specific number of digits (as specified by the **precision** member function) to the right of the decimal point. Without these flags set, the value of the floating-point number determines the output format.

The call **cout.setf(0, ios::floatfield)** restores the system default format for outputting floating-point numbers. Figure 11.26 demonstrates the display of floating-point numbers in fixed and scientific formats using the two argument **setf** with **ios::floatfield**.

```
// fig11_25.cpp
// Using the ios::showbase flag
#include <iostream.h>
#include <iomanip.h>

main()
{
   int x = 100;

   cout << setiosflags(ios::showbase)
        << "Printing integers preceded by their base:" << endl
        << x << endl
        << oct << x << endl
        << hex << x << endl;
   return 0;
}
```

```
Printing integers preceded by their base:
100
0144
0x64
```

**Fig. 11.25** Using the **ios::showbase** flag.

```
// fig11_26.cpp
// Displaying floating-point values in system default,
// scientific, and fixed formats.

#include <iostream.h>

main()
{
   double x = .001234567, y = 1.946e9;

   cout << "Displayed in default format:" << endl
        << x << '\t' << y << endl;
   cout.setf(ios::scientific, ios::floatfield);
   cout << "Displayed in scientific format:" << endl
        << x << '\t' << y << endl;
   cout.unsetf(ios::scientific);
   cout << "Displayed in default format after unsetf:" << endl
        << x << '\t' << y << endl;
   cout.setf(ios::fixed, ios::floatfield);
   cout << "Displayed in fixed format:" << endl
        << x << '\t' << y << endl;

   return 0;
}
```

```
Displayed in default format:
0.001235    1.946e+09
Displayed in scientific format:
1.234567e-03   1.946e+09
Displayed in default format after unsetf:
0.001235    1.946e+09
Displayed in fixed format:
0.001235    1946000000
```

Fig. 11.26 Displaying floating-point values in system default, scientific, and fixed formats.

## 11.7.7 Uppercase/Lowercase Control (ios::uppercase)

The **ios::uppercase** flag is set to force an uppercase **X** or **E** to be output with hexadecimal integers or with scientific notation floating-point values, respectively (Fig. 11.27). When set, the **ios::uppercase** flag causes all letters in a hexadecimal value to be uppercase.

## 11.7.8 Setting and Resetting the Format Flags (Flags, Setiosflags, Resetiosflags)

The **flags** member function without an argument simply returns (as a **long** value) the current settings of the format flags. The **flags** member function with a **long** argument

```
// fig11_27.cpp
// Using the ios::uppercase flag
#include <iostream.h>
#include <iomanip.h>

main()
{
   cout << setiosflags(ios::uppercase)
        << "Printing uppercase letters in scientific" << endl
        << "notation exponents and hexadecimal values:" << endl
        << 4.345e10 << endl
        << hex << 123456789 << endl;
   return 0;
}
```

```
Printing uppercase letters in scientific
notation exponents and hexadecimal values:
4.345E+10
75BCD15
```

**Fig. 11.27** Using the **ios::uppercase** flag.

sets the format flags as specified by the argument and returns the prior flag settings. Any format flags not specified in the argument to **flags** are reset. Note that the initial settings of the flags on each system may differ. The program of Fig. 11.28 demonstrates the use of the **flags** member function to set a new format state and save the previous format state, then restore the original format settings.

The **setf** member function sets the format flags provided in its argument and returns the previous flag settings as a **long** value as in

```
long previousFlagSettings =
   cout.setf(ios::showpoint | ios::showpos);
```

The **setf** member function with two **long** arguments as in

```
cout.setf(ios::left, ios::adjustfield);
```

first clears the bits of **ios::adjustfield** and then sets the **ios::left** flag. This version of **setf** is used with the bit fields associated with **ios::basefield** (represented by **ios::dec**, **ios::oct**, and **ios::hex**), **ios::floatfield** (represented by **ios::scientific** and **ios::fixed**), and **ios::adjustfield** (represented by **ios::left**, **ios::right**, and **ios::internal**).

The **unsetf** member function resets the designated flags and returns the value of the flags prior to being reset.

## 11.8 Stream Error States

The state of a stream may be tested through bits in class **ios**—the base class for the classes **istream**, **ostream**, and **iostream** we are using for I/O.

```
// fig11_28.cpp
// Demonstrating the flags member function.
#include <iostream.h>

main()
{
   int i = 1000;
   double d = 0.0947628;

   cout << "The value of the flags variable is: "
        << cout.flags() << endl
        << "Print int and double in original format:" << endl
        << i << '\t' << d << endl << endl;
   long originalFormat = cout.flags(ios::oct | ios::scientific);
   cout << "The value of the flags variable is: "
        << cout.flags() << endl
        << "Print int and double in a new format" << endl
        << "specified using the flags member function:" << endl
        << i << '\t' << d << endl << endl;
   cout.flags(originalFormat);
   cout << "The value of the flags variable is: "
        << cout.flags() << endl
        << "Print values in original format again:" << endl
        << i << '\t' << d << endl;

   return 0;
}
```

```
The value of the flags variable is: 1
Print int and double in original format:
1000    0.094763

The value of the flags variable is: 4040
Print int and double in a new format
specified using the flags member function:
1750    9.47628e-02

The value of the flags variable is: 1
Print values in original format again:
1000    0.094763
```

**Fig. 11.28** Demonstrating the **flags** member function.

The **eofbit** is set automatically for an input stream when end-of-file is encountered. A program can use the **eof** member function to determine if end-of-file has been encountered on a stream. The call

```
cin.eof()
```

returns true if end-of-file has been encountered on **cin**, and false otherwise.

The **failbit** is set for a stream when a format error occurs on the stream, but characters have not been lost. The **fail** member function determines if a stream operation has failed; it is normally possible to recover from such errors.

The **badbit** is set for a stream when an error occurs that results in the loss of data. The **bad** member function determines if a stream operation has failed. Such serious failures are normally nonrecoverable.

The **goodbit** is set for a stream if none of the bits **eofbit**, **failbit**, or **badbit** are set for the stream.

The **good** member function returns true if the **bad**, **fail**, and **eof** functions would all return false. I/O operations should only be performed on "good" streams.

The **rdstate** member function returns the error state of the stream. A call to **cout.rdstate**, for example, would return the state of the stream which could then be tested by a **switch** statement that examines **ios::eofbit**, **ios::badbit**, **ios::failbit**, and **ios::goodbit**. The preferred means of testing the state of a stream is to use the member functions **eof**, **bad**, **fail**, and **good**—using these functions does not require the programmer to be familiar with particular status bits.

The **clear** member function is normally used to restore a stream's state to "good" so that I/O may proceed on that stream. The default argument for **clear** is **ios::goodbit**, so the statement

```
cin.clear();
```

clears **cin** and sets **goodbit** for the stream. The statement

```
cin.clear(ios::failbit)
```

actually sets the **failbit**. The user might want to do this when performing input on **cin** with a user-defined type and encountering a problem. The name **clear** seems inappropriate in this context, but it is correct.

The program of Fig. 11.29 illustrates the use of the **rdstate**, **eof**, **fail**, **bad**, **good**, and **clear** member functions.

The **operator!** member function returns true if either the **badbit** is set, the **failbit** is set, or both are set. The **operator void*** member function returns false if either the **badbit** is set, the **failbit** is set, or both are set. These functions are useful in file processing when a true/false condition is being tested in the condition of a selection structure or repetition structure.

## 11.9 I/O of User-Defined Types

C++ is able to input and output the standard data types using the stream-extraction operator **>>** and stream-insertion operator **<<**. These operators are overloaded to process each standard data type including strings and memory addresses. The programmer can overload the stream-insertion and -extraction operators to perform I/O for user-defined types. Figure 11.30 demonstrates overloading the stream-extraction and -insertion operators to handle data of a user-defined telephone number class called **PhoneNumber**. Note that this program assumes telephone numbers are input correctly. We leave it to the exercises to provide error-checking.

```
// fig11_29.cpp
// Testing error states.
#include <iostream.h>

main()
{
   int x;
   cout << "Before a bad input operation:" << endl
        << "cin.rdstate(): " << cin.rdstate() << endl
        << "    cin.eof(): " << cin.eof() << endl
        << "   cin.fail(): " << cin.fail() << endl
        << "    cin.bad(): " << cin.bad() << endl
        << "   cin.good(): " << cin.good() << endl << endl
        << "Expects an integer, but enter a character: ";
   cin >> x;

   cout << endl << "After a bad input operation:" << endl
        << "cin.rdstate(): " << cin.rdstate() << endl
        << "    cin.eof(): " << cin.eof() << endl
        << "   cin.fail(): " << cin.fail() << endl
        << "    cin.bad(): " << cin.bad() << endl
        << "   cin.good(): " << cin.good() << endl << endl;

   cin.clear();

   cout << "After cin.clear()" << endl
        << "cin.fail(): " << cin.fail()
        << "cin.good(): " << cin.good() << endl;
   return 0;
}
```

```
Before a bad input operation:
cin.rdstate(): 0
    cin.eof(): 0
   cin.fail(): 0
    cin.bad(): 0
   cin.good(): 1

Expects an integer, but enter a character: A

After a bad input operation:
cin.rdstate(): 2
    cin.eof(): 0
   cin.fail(): 2
    cin.bad(): 0
   cin.good(): 0

After cin.clear()
cin.fail(): 0
cin.good(): 1
```

**Fig. 11.29** Testing error states.

The stream-extraction operator takes an **istream** reference and a reference to a user-defined type (**PhoneNumber** in this instance) as arguments, and returns an **istream** reference. In Fig. 11.30, the overloaded stream-extraction operator is used to input phone numbers of the form

```
(800) 555-1212
```

into objects of type **PhoneNumber**. The operator function reads the three parts of a telephone number into the **areaCode**, **exchange**, and **line** members of the referenced **PhoneNumber** object (**num** in the operator function and **phone** in **main**). The parentheses, space, and dash characters are discarded by calling the **ignore istream** member function. The operator function returns the **input istream** reference. By returning the stream reference, input operations on **PhoneNumber** objects can be concatenated with input operations on other **PhoneNumber** objects or other data types. For example, two **PhoneNumber** objects could be input as follows:

```
cin >> phone1 >> phone2;
```

The stream-insertion operator takes an **ostream** reference and a reference to a user-defined type (**PhoneNumber** in this instance) as arguments, and returns an **ostream** reference. In Fig. 11.30, the overloaded stream-insertion operator displays objects of type **PhoneNumber** in the same form as they are input. The **operator** function displays the parts of the telephone number as strings because they are stored in string format (recall that **istream** member function **getline** stores a null character after it completes its input).

The overloaded **operator** functions are declared in **class PhoneNumber** as **friend** functions. Overloaded input and output operators must be declared as **friend**s if it is necessary to access non-public class members. Friends of a class can access the private class members.

***Software Engineering Observation 11.3***

*New input/output capabilities for user-defined types are added to C++ without modifying the declarations or private data members for either the* **ostream** *class or the* **istream** *class. This promotes the extensibility of the C++ programming language—one C++'s most attractive aspects.*

## 11.10 Tying an Output Stream to an Input Stream

Interactive applications generally involve an **istream** for input and an **ostream** for output. When a prompting message appears on the screen, the user responds by entering the appropriate data. Obviously, the prompt needs to appear before the input operation proceeds. With output buffering, outputs appear only when the buffer fills, when outputs are flushed explicitly by the program, or automatically at the end of the program. C++ provides the **tie** member function to synchronize (i.e., "tie together") the operation of an **istream** and an **ostream** to ensure that outputs appear before their subsequent inputs. A call such as

```
// fig11_30.cpp
// User-defined insertion and extraction operators

#include <iostream.h>

class PhoneNumber {
   friend ostream& operator<<(ostream&, PhoneNumber&);
   friend istream& operator>>(istream&, PhoneNumber&);
private:
   char areaCode[4];
   char exchange[4];
   char line[5];
};

ostream& operator<<(ostream& output, PhoneNumber& num)
{
   output << "(" << num.areaCode << ") "
          << num.exchange << "-" << num.line;

   return output;
}

istream& operator>>(istream& input, PhoneNumber& num)
{
   input.ignore();                        // skip (
   input.getline(num.areaCode, 4);
   input.ignore(2);                       // skip ) and space
   input.getline(num.exchange, 4);
   input.ignore();                        // skip -
   input.getline(num.line, 5);

   return input;
}

main()
{
   PhoneNumber phone;

   cout << "Enter a phone number in the "
        << "form (123) 456-7890:" << endl;
   cin >> phone;
   cout << "The phone number entered was:" << endl
        << phone << endl;

   return 0;
}
```

```
Enter a phone number in the form (123) 456-7890:
(800) 555-1212
The phone number entered was:
(800) 555-1212
```

**Fig. 11.30** User-defined stream-insertion and stream-extraction operators.

```
cin.tie(&cout);
```

ties **cout** (an **ostream**) to **cin** (an **istream**). Actually, this particular call is redundant because C++ performs this operation automatically to create a user's standard input/output environment. The user would, however, explicitly tie together other **istream/ostream** pairs. To untie an input stream, **inputStream**, from an output stream, use the call

```
inputStream.tie(0);
```

## Summary

- I/O operations are performed in a manner sensitive to the type of the data.
- C++ I/O occurs in streams of bytes. A stream is simply a sequence of bytes.
- I/O mechanisms of the system move bytes from devices to memory and vice versa in an efficient and reliable manner.
- C++ provides "low-level" and "high-level" I/O capabilities. Low-level I/O-capabilities specify that some number of bytes should be transferred device-to-memory or memory-to-device. High-level I/O is performed with bytes grouped into meaningful units such as integers, floats, characters, strings and user-defined types.
- C++ provides both unformatted I/O and formatted I/O operations. Unformatted I/O transfers are fast, but process raw data that is difficult for people to use. Formatted I/O processes data in meaningful units, but requires extra processing time that can negatively impact high-volume data transfers.
- Most C++ programs include the **<iostream.h>** header file that contains basic information required for all stream I/O operations.
- The **<iomanip.h>** header contains information for formatted input/output with parameterized stream manipulators.
- The **<fstream.h>** header contains information for file processing operations.
- The **<strstream.h>** header contains information for in-memory formatting.
- The **<stdiostream.h>** header contains information for programs that mix the C and C++ styles of I/O.
- The **istream** class supports stream input operations.
- The **ostream** class supports stream output operations.
- The **iostream** class supports both stream-input and stream-output operations.
- The **istream** class and the **ostream** class are each derived through single inheritance from the **ios** base class.
- The **iostream** class is derived through multiple inheritance from both the **istream** class and the **ostream** class.

- The left shift operator (<<) is overloaded to designate stream output and is referred to as the stream-insertion operator.
- The right shift operator (>>) is overloaded to designate stream input and is referred to as the stream-extraction operator.
- The **istream** object **cin** is tied to the standard input device, normally the keyboard.
- The **ostream** class object **cout** is tied to the standard output device, normally the display screen.
- The **ostream** class object **cerr** is tied to the standard error device. Outputs to **cerr** are unbuffered; each insertion to **cerr** appears immediately.
- Stream manipulator **endl** issues a newline character and flushes the output buffer.
- The C++ compiler determines data types automatically for input and output.
- Addresses are displayed in hexadecimal format by default.
- To print the address in a pointer variable cast the pointer to **void***.
- Member function **put** outputs one character. Calls to **put** may be concatenated.
- Stream input is performed with the stream-extraction operator **>>**. This operator automatically skips whitespace characters in the input stream.
- The **>>** operator returns false when end-of-file is encountered on a stream.
- Stream extraction causes **failbit** to be set for improper input, and **badbit** to be set if the operation fails.
- A series of values can be input using the stream extraction operation in a **while** loop header. The extraction returns false (0) when end-of-file is encountered.
- The **get** member function with no arguments inputs one character and returns the character; **EOF** is returned if end-of-file is encountered on the stream.
- The **get** member function with an argument of type **char** inputs one character. **EOF** is returned when end-of-file is encountered; otherwise, the **istream** object for which the **get** member function is being invoked is returned.
- The **get** member function with three arguments—a character array, a size limit, and a delimiter (with default value newline)—reads characters from the input stream up to a maximum of limit - 1 characters and terminates, or terminates when the delimiter is read. The input string is terminated with a null character. The delimiter is not placed in the character array, but remains in the input stream.
- The **getline** member function operates like the three argument **get** member function. The **getline** function removes the delimiter from the input stream, but does not store it in the string.
- Member function **ignore** skips the specified number of characters (default is one character) in the input stream; it terminates if the specified delimiter is encountered (the default delimiter is **EOF**).

- The **putback** member function places the previous character obtained by a **get** on a stream back onto that stream.
- The **peek** member function returns the next character from an input stream, but does not remove the character from the stream.
- C++ offers type-safe input/output. If unexpected data is processed by the **<<** and **>>** operators, various error flags are set which the user may test to determine if an I/O operation succeeded or failed.
- Unformatted I/O is performed with member functions **read** and **write**. These input or output some number of bytes to or from memory beginning at a designated memory address. They are input or output as raw bytes with no formatting.
- The **gcount** member function returns the number of characters input by the previous **read** operation on that stream.
- Member function **read** inputs a specified number of characters into a character array. **failbit** is set if fewer than the specified number of characters are read.
- To change the base in which integers output, use the manipulator **hex** to set the base to hexadecimal (base 16) or **oct** to set the base to octal (base 8). Use manipulator **dec** to reset the base to decimal. The base remains the same until explicitly changed.
- The parameterized stream manipulator **setbase** also sets the base for integer output. **setbase** takes one integer argument of **10**, **8**, or **16** to set the base.
- Floating-point precision can be controlled using either the **setprecision** stream manipulator or the **precision** member function. Both set the precision for all subsequent output operations until the next precision-setting call. The **precision** member function with no argument returns the current precision value. A precision of **0** specifies the default precision value (**6**).
- Parameterized manipulators require the inclusion of the **<iomanip.h>** header file.
- Member function **width** sets the field width and returns the previous width. Values smaller than the field are padded with fill characters. The field width setting applies only for the next insertion or extraction; the field width is implicitly set to **0** afterward (subsequent values will be output as large as they need to be). Values larger than a field are printed in their entirety. Function **width** with no argument returns the current width setting. Manipulator **setw** also sets the width.
- For input, the **setw** stream manipulator establishes a maximum string size; if a larger string is entered, the larger line is broken into pieces no larger than the designated size.
- Users may create their own stream manipulators.
- Member functions **setf**, **unsetf**, and **flags** control the flag settings.
- The **skipws** flag indicates that **>>** should skip whitespace on an input stream. The **ws** stream manipulator also skips over leading whitespace in an input stream.
- Format flags are defined as an enumeration in class **ios**.

- Format flags are controlled by the **flags** and **setf** member functions, but many C++ programmers prefer to use stream manipulators. The bitwise-or operation, **|**, can be used to combine various options into a single **long** value. Calling the **flags** member function for a stream and specifying these "or-ed" options sets the options on that stream and returns a **long** value containing the prior options. This value is often saved so **flags** may be called with this saved value to restore the previous stream options.
- The **flags** function must specify a value representing the total settings of all the flags. The **setf** function with one argument, on the other hand, automatically "ors" the specified flags with the existing flag settings to form a new format state.
- The **showpoint** flag is set to force a floating-point number to be output with a decimal point and number of significant digits specified by the precision.
- The **left** and **right** flags cause fields to be left-justified with padding characters to the right, or right-justified with padding characters to the left.
- The **internal** flag indicates that a number's sign (or base when the flag **ios::showbase** is set) should be left-justified within a field, magnitude should be right-justified, and intervening spaces should be padded with the fill character.
- **ios::adjustfield** contains the flags **left**, **right**, and **internal**.
- Member function **fill** specifies the fill character to be used with **left**, **right**, and **internal** adjusted fields (space is the default); the prior padding character is returned. Stream manipulator **setfill** also sets the fill character.
- Static member **ios::basefield** includes the **oct**, **hex**, and **dec** bits to specify that integers are to be treated as octal, hexadecimal, and decimal values, respectively. Integer output defaults to decimal if none of these bits is set; stream extractions process the data in the form in which it is supplied.
- Set the **showbase** flag to force the base of an integral value to be output.
- Static data member **ios::floatfield** contains the flags **scientific** and the **fixed**. Set the **scientific** flag to output a floating-point number in scientific format. Set the **fixed** flag to output a floating-point number with the precision specified by the **precision** member function.
- The call **cout.setf(0, ios::floatfield)** restores the default format for displaying floating-point numbers.
- Set the **uppercase** flag to force an uppercase **X** or **E** to be output with hexadecimal integers or with scientific notation floating-point values, respectively. When set, the **ios::uppercase** flag causes all letters in a hexadecimal value to be uppercase.
- Member function **flags** with no argument returns the **long** value of the current settings of the format flags. Member function **flags** with a **long** argument sets the format flags specified by the argument and returns the prior flag settings.
- Member function **setf** sets the format flags in its argument and returns the previous flag settings as a **long** value.

- Member function **`setf(long setBits, long resetBits)`** clears the bits of the **`resetBits`**, then sets the bit in **`setBits`**.
- Member function **`unsetf`** resets the designated flags and returns the value of the flags prior to being reset.
- Parameterized stream manipulator **`setiosflags`** performs the same functions as member function **`flags`**.
- Parameterized stream manipulator **`resetiosflags`** performs the same functions as member function **`unsetf`**.
- The state of a stream may be tested through bits in class **`ios`**.
- The **`eofbit`** is set for an input stream when end-of-file is encountered during an input operation. The **`eof`** member function is used to determine if the **`eofbit`** has been set.
- The **`failbit`** is set for a stream when a format error occurred on the stream, but characters have not been lost. The **`fail`** member function determines if a stream operation has failed; it is normally possible to recover from such errors.
- The **`badbit`** is set for a stream when an error occurred that resulted in the loss of data. The **`bad`** member function determines if a stream operation has failed. Such serious failures are normally nonrecoverable.
- The **`good`** member function returns true if the **`bad`**, **`fail`**, and **`eof`** functions would all return false. I/O operations should only be performed on "good" streams.
- The **`rdstate`** member function returns the error state of the stream.
- Member function **`clear`** is normally used to restore a stream's state to "good" so that I/O may proceed on that stream.
- The user can overload the stream insertion and extraction operators to perform I/O for user-defined types.
- The overloaded stream-extraction operator takes an **`istream`** reference and a reference to a user-defined type as arguments, and returns an **`istream`** reference.
- The overloaded stream-insertion operator takes an **`ostream`** reference and a reference to a user-defined type as arguments, and returns an **`ostream`** reference.
- Often, overloaded **`operator`** functions are declared as **`friend`** functions to a class; this enables access to non-public class members.
- C++ provides the **`tie`** member function to synchronize **`istream`** and **`ostream`** operations to ensure that outputs appear before subsequent inputs.

### *Terminology*

**`bad`** member function
**`badbit`**
**`cerr`**
**`cin`**
**`clear`** member function
**`clog`**
**`cout`**
**`dec`** stream manipulator

default fill character (space)
default precision
end-of-file
**endl**
**eof** member function
**eofbit**
extensibility
**fail** member function
**failbit**
field width
fill character
**fill** member function
**flags** member function
**flush** member function
**flush** stream manipulator
format flags
format states
formatted I/O
**fstream** class
**gcount** member function
**get** member function
**getline** member function
**good** member function
**hex** stream manipulator
**ifstream** class
**ignore** member function
in-core formatting
in-memory formatting
**<iomanip.h>** standard header file
**ios** class
**ios::adjustfield**
**ios::basefield**
**ios::fixed**
**ios::floatfield**
**ios::internal**
**ios::scientific**
**ios::showbase**
**ios::showpoint**
**ios::showpos**
**iostream** class
**istream** class
leading **0** (octal)
leading **0x** or **0X** (hexadecimal)
**left**
left-justified
**oct** stream manipulator
**ofstream** class
**operator!** member function
**operator void*** member function
**ostream** class
padding
parameterized stream manipulator
**peek** member function
**precision** member function
predefined streams
**put** member function
**putback** member function
**rdstate** member function
**read** member function
**resetiosflags** stream manipulator
right-justified
**setbase** stream manipulator
**setf** member function
**setfill** stream manipulator
**setiosflags** stream manipulator
**setprecision** stream manipulator
**setw** stream manipulator
**skipws**
stream class libraries
stream-extraction operator (**>>**)
stream input
stream-insertion operator (**<<**)
**stream** manipulator
stream output
**tie** member function
type-safe I/O
unformatted I/O
**unsetf** member function
**uppercase**
user-defined streams
whitespace characters
**width**
**write** member function
**ws** member function

## Common Programming Errors

**11.1** Attempting to read from an **ostream** (or from any other output-only stream).

**11.2** Attempting to write to an **istream** (or to any other input-only stream).

**11.3** Not providing parentheses to force proper precedence when using the relatively high precedence stream-insertion operator **<<** or stream-extraction operator **>>**.

**11.4** When not providing a sufficiently wide field to handle outputs, the outputs print as wide as they need to be, possibly causing difficult-to-read outputs.

## Good Programming Practices

**11.1** Use the C++ form of I/O exclusively in C++ programs, despite the fact that C-style I/O is available to C++ programmers.

**11.2** When outputting expressions, place them in parentheses to prevent operator precedence problems between the operators in the expression and the `<<` operator.

## Performance Tips

**11.1** Use unformatted I/O for the best performance in high-volume file processing.

## Software Engineering Observations

**11.1** C++ style I/O is type safe.

**11.2** C++ enables a common treatment of I/O of predefined types and user-defined types. This commonality facilitates software development in general and software reuse in particular.

**11.3** New input/output capabilities for user-defined types are added to C++ without modifying the declarations or private data members for either the `ostream` class or the `istream` class. This promotes the extensibility of the C++ programming language—one C++'s most attractive aspects.

## Self-Review Exercises

**11.1** Answer each of the following:

a) Overloaded stream operators are often defined as __________ functions of a class.
b) The format justification bits that can be set include __________, __________, and __________.
c) Input/output in C++ occurs as __________ of bytes.
d) Parameterized stream manipulators __________ and __________ can be used to set and reset format state flags.
e) Most C++ programs should include the __________ header file that contains basic information required for all stream I/O operations.
f) Member functions __________ and __________ are used to set and reset format state flags.
g) Header file __________ contains information for performing "in-memory" formatting.
h) When using parameterized manipulators, the header file __________ must be included.
i) Header file __________ contains information for user controlled file processing.
j) The __________ stream manipulator inserts a newline character in the output stream and flushes the output stream.
k) Header file __________ is used in programs that mix C-style and C++-style I/O.
l) The `ostream` member function __________ is used to perform unformatted output.
m) Input operations are supported by the __________ class.
n) Outputs to the standard error stream are directed to either the __________ or the __________ stream object.
o) Output operations are supported by the __________ class.
p) The symbol for the stream-insertion operator is __________.
q) The four objects that correspond to the standard devices on the system include __________, __________, __________, and __________.

r) The symbol for the stream-extraction operator is __________.
s) The stream manipulators __________, __________, and __________ are used to specify that integers should be displayed in octal, hexadecimal, and decimal formats.
t) The default precision for displaying floating-point values is __________.
u) When set, the __________ flag causes positive numbers to display with a plus sign.

**11.2** State whether the following are true or false. If the answer is false, explain why.

a) The stream member function `flags()` with a long argument sets the `flags` state variable to its argument and returns its previous value.
b) The stream-insertion operator `<<` and the stream-extraction operator `>>` are overloaded to handle all standard data types—including strings and memory addresses (stream-insertion only)—and all user-defined data types.
c) The stream member function `flags()` with no arguments resets all the flag bits in the `flags` state variable.
d) The stream-extraction operator `>>` can be overloaded with an operator function that takes an `istream` reference and a reference to a user-defined type as arguments and returns an `istream` reference.
e) The `ws` stream manipulator skips leading whitespace in an input stream.
f) The stream-insertion operator << can be overloaded with an operator function that takes an `istream` reference and a reference to a user-defined type as arguments and returns an `istream` reference.
g) Input with the stream-extraction operator `>>` always skips leading whitespace characters in the input stream.
h) The input and output features are provided as part of C++.
i) The stream member function `rdstate()` returns the state of the current stream.
j) The `cout` stream is normally connected to the display screen.
k) The stream member function `good()` returns true if the `bad()`, `fail()`, and `eof()` member functions all return false.
l) The `cin` stream is normally connected to the display screen.
m) If a nonrecoverable error occurs during a stream operation, the `bad` member function will return true.
n) Output to `cerr` is unbuffered and output to `clog` is buffered.
o) When the `ios::showpoint` flag is set, floating-point values are forced to print with the default six digits of precision—provided that the precision value has not been changed, in which case floating-point values print with the specified precision.
p) The `ostream` member function `put` outputs the specified number of characters.
q) The stream manipulators `dec`, `oct`, and `hex` only affect the next integer output operation.
r) When output, memory addresses are displayed as `long` integers by default.

**11.3** For each of the following, write a single statement that performs the indicated task.

a) Output the string `"Enter your name: "`.
b) Set a flag to cause the exponent in scientific notation and the letters in hexadecimal values to print in capital letters.
c) Output the address of the variable `string` of type `char *`.
d) Set a flag so that floating-point values print in scientific notation.
e) Output the address of the variable `integerPtr` of type `int *`.
f) Set a flag so that when integer values are output the integer base for octal and hexadecimal values is displayed.
g) Output the value pointed to by `floatPtr` of type `float *`.

h) Use a stream member function to set the fill character to `'*'` for printing in field widths larger than the values being output. Write a separate statement to do this with a stream manipulator.
i) Output the characters `'O'` and `'K'` in one statement with `ostream` function `put`.
j) Get the next character in the input stream without extracting it from the stream.
k) Input a single character into variable `c` of type `char` using the `istream` member function `get` in two different ways.
l) Input and discard the next six characters in the input stream.
m) Use the `istream` member function `read` to input 50 characters into array `line` of type `char`.
n) Read 10 characters into character array `name`. Stop reading characters if the `'.'` delimiter is encountered. Do not remove the delimiter from the input stream. Write another statement that performs this task and removes the delimiter from the input.
o) Use the `istream` member function `gcount` to determine the number of characters input into character array `line` by the last call to `istream` member function `read` and output that number of characters using `ostream` member function `write`.
p) Write separate statements to flush the output stream using a member function and a stream manipulator.
q) Output the following values: `124`, `18.376`, `'Z'`, `1000000`, and `"String"`.
r) Print the current precision setting using a member function.
s) Input an integer value into `int` variable `months` and a floating-point value into `float` variable `percentageRate`.
t) Print `1.92`, `1.925`, and `1.9258` with `3` digits of precision using a manipulator.
u) Print integer `100` in octal, hexadecimal, and decimal using stream manipulators.
v) Print integer `100` in decimal, octal, and hexadecimal using a single stream manipulator to change the base.
w) Print `1234` right-justified in a `10` digit field.
x) Read characters into character array `line` until the character `'z'` is encountered up to a limit of `20` characters (including a terminating null character). Do not extract the delimiter character from the stream.
y) Use integer variables `x` and `y` to specify the field width and precision used to display the `double` value `87.4573` and display the value.

**11.4** Identify the error in each of the following statements and explain how to correct it.

a)
```
cout << "Value of x <= y is: " << x <= y;
```
b) The following statement should print the integer value of `'c'`.
```
cout << 'c';
```
c)
```
cout << ""A string in quotes"";
```

**11.5** For each of the following, show the output.

a)
```
cout << "12345" << endl;
cout.width(5);
cout.fill('*');
cout << 123 << endl << 123;
```
b)
```
cout << setw(10) << setfill('$') << 10000;
```
c)
```
cout << setw(8) << setprecision(3) << 1024.987654;
```
d)
```
cout << setiosflags(ios::showbase) << oct << 99
     << endl << hex << 99;
```
e)
```
cout << 100000 << endl
     << setiosflags(ios::showpos) << 100000;
```

f)
```
cout << setw(10) << setprecision(2) <<
     << setiosflags(ios::scientific) << 444.93738;
```

## Answers to Self-Review Exercises

**11.1** a) `friend`. b) `ios::left`, `ios::right`, and `ios::internal`. c) streams. d) `setiosflags`, `resetiosflags`. e) `iostream.h`. f) `setf`, `unsetf`. g) `strstream.h`. h) `iomanip.h`. i) `fstream.h`. j) `endl`. k) `stdiostream.h`. l) `write`. m) `istream`. n) `cerr` or `clog`. o) `ostream`. p) `<<`. q) `cin`, `cout`, `cerr`, and `clog`. r) `>>`. s) `oct`, `hex`, `dec`. t) six digits of precision. u) `ios::showpos`.

**11.2**
- a) True.
- b) False. The stream insertion and stream extraction operators are not overloaded for all user-defined types. The programmer of a class must specifically provide the overloaded operator functions to overload the stream operators for use with each user-defined type.
- c) False. The stream member function `flags()` with no arguments simply returns the current value of the `flags` state variable.
- d) True.
- e) True.
- f) False. To overload the stream-insertion operator `<<`, the overloaded operator function must take an `ostream` reference and a reference to a user-defined type as arguments, and return an `ostream` reference.
- g) True. Unless `ios::skipws` is off.
- h) False. The I/O features of C++ are provided as part of the C++ standard library. The C++ language does not contain capabilities for input, output, or file processing.
- i) True.
- j) True.
- k) True.
- l) False. The `cin` stream is connected to the standard input of the computer which is normally the keyboard.
- m) True.
- n) True.
- o) True.
- p) False. The `ostream` member function `put` outputs its single character argument.
- q) False. The stream manipulators `dec`, `oct`, and `hex` set the output format state for integers to the specified base until the base is changed again or the program terminates.
- r) False. Memory addresses are displayed in hexadecimal format by default. To display addresses as `long` integers, the address must be cast to a `long` value.

**11.3**
- a) `cout << "Enter your name: ";`
- b) `cout.setf(ios::uppercase);`
- c) `cout << (void *) string;`
- d) `cout.setf(ios::scientific, ios::floatfield);`
- e) `cout << integerPtr;`
- f) `cout << setiosflags(ios::showbase);`
- g) `cout << *floatPtr;`
- h) `cout.fill('*');`
  `cout << setfill('*');`
- i) `cout.put('O').put('K');`
- j) `cin.peek();`

k) `c = cin.get();`
   `cin.get(c);`

l) `cin.ignore(6);`

m) `cin.read(line, 50);`

n) `cin.get(name, 10, '.');`
   `cin.getline(name, 10, '.');`

o) `cout.write(line, cin.gcount());`

p) `cout.flush();`
   `cout << flush;`

q) `cout << 124 << 18.376 << 'Z' << 1000000 << "String";`

r) `cout << cout.precision();`

s) `cin >> months >> percentageRate;`

t)
```
cout << setprecision(3) << 1.92 << '\t'
     << 1.925 << '\t' << 1.9258;
```

u) `cout << oct << 100 << hex << 100 << dec << 100;`

v) `cout << 100 << setbase(8) << 100 << setbase(16) << 100;`

w) `cout << setw(10) << 1234;`

x) `cin.get(line, 20, 'z');`

y) `cout << setw(x) << setprecision(y) << 87.4573;`

**11.4** a) Error: The precedence of the `<<` operator is higher than the precedence of `<=` which causes the statement to be evaluated improperly and causes a compiler error.
Correction: To correct the statement, add parentheses around the expression `x <= y`. This problem will occur with any expression that uses operators of lower precedence than the `<<` operator if the expression is not placed in parentheses.

b) Error: In C++, characters are not treated as small integers as they are in C.
Correction: To print the numerical value for a character in the computer's character set, the character must be cast to an integer value as in the following:

```
cout << int('c');
```

c) Error: Quote characters cannot be printed in a string unless an escape sequence is used.
Correction: Print the string in one of the following ways:

```
cout << '"' << "A string in quotes" << '"';
cout << "\"A string in quotes\"";
```

**11.5** a)
```
12345
**123
123
```

b) `$$$$$10000`

c) `1024.988`

d)
```
0143
0x63
```

e)
```
100000
+100000
```

f) `   4.45e+02`

## Exercises

**11.6** Write a statement for each of the following:

a) Print integer `40000` left-justified in a `15`-digit field.

b) Read a string into character array variable `state`.

c) Print `200` with and without a sign.
d) Print the decimal value `100` in hexadecimal form preceded by `0x`.
e) Read characters into array `s` until the character `'p'` is encountered up to a limit of 10 characters (including the terminating null character). Extract the delimiter from the input stream and discard it.
f) Print `1.234` in a `9`-digit field with preceding zeros.
g) Read a string of the form `"characters"` from the standard input. Store the string in character array `s`. Eliminate the quotation marks from the input stream. Read a maximum of 50 characters (including the terminating null character).

**11.7** Write a program to test inputting integer values in decimal, octal, and hexadecimal format. Output each integer read by the program in all three formats. Test the program with the following input data: 10, 010, 0x10.

**11.8** Write a program that prints pointer values using casts to all the integer data types. Which ones print strange values? Which ones cause errors?

**11.9** Write a program to test the results of printing the integer value `12345` and the floating-point value `1.2345` in various size fields. What happens when the values are printed in fields containing fewer digits than the values?

**11.10** Write a program that prints the value `100.453627` rounded to the nearest digit, tenth, hundredth, thousandth, and ten thousandth.

**11.11** Write a program that inputs a string from the keyboard and determines the length of the string. Print the string using twice the length as the field width.

**11.12** Write a program that converts integer Fahrenheit temperatures from `0` to `212` degrees to floating-point Celsius temperatures with `3` digits of precision. Use the formula

```
celsius = 5.0/9.0 * (fahrenheit - 32);
```

to perform the calculation. The output should be printed in two right-justified columns, and the Celsius temperatures should be preceded by a sign for both positive and negative values.

**11.13** In some programming languages, strings are entered surrounded by either single or double quotation marks. Write a program that reads the three strings `suzy`, `"suzy"`, and `'suzy'`. Are the single and double quotes ignored or read as part of the string?

**11.14** In Fig. 11.30, the stream-extraction and -insertion operators were overloaded for input and output of objects of the `PhoneNumber` class. Rewrite the stream-extraction operator to perform the following error checking on input. The `operator>>` function will need to be entirely recoded.

a) Input the entire phone number into an array. Test that the proper number of characters have been entered. There should be a total of 14 characters read for a phone number of the form `(800) 555-1212`. Use the stream member function `clear` to set `ios::failbit` for improper input.
b) The area code and exchange do not begin with `0` or `1`. Test the first digit of the area code and exchange portions of the phone number to be sure that neither begins with `0` or `1`. Use stream member function `clear` to set `ios::failbit` for improper input.
c) The middle digit of an area code is always `0` or `1`. Test the middle digit for a value of `0` or `1`. Use the stream member function `clear` to set `ios::failbit` for improper input. If none of the above operations results in `ios::failbit` being set for improper input, copy the three parts of the telephone number into the `areaCode`, `exchange`, and `line` members of the `PhoneNumber` object In the main program, if `ios::failbit` has been set on the input, have the program print an error message and end rather than print the phone number.

**11.15** Write a program that accomplishes each of the following:

a) Create the user-defined class `Point` that contains the private integer data members `xCoordinate` and `yCoordinate`, and declares stream-insertion and stream-extraction overloaded operator functions as `friend`s of the class.

b) Define the stream-insertion and stream-extraction operator functions. The stream-extraction operator function should determine if the data entered is valid data, and if not, it should set the `ios::failbit` to indicate improper input. The stream-insertion operator should not be able to display the point after an input error occurred.

c) Write a `main` function that tests input and output of user-defined class `Point` using the overloaded stream-extraction and stream-insertion operators.

**11.16** Write a program that accomplishes each of the following:

a) Create the user-defined class `Complex` that contains the private integer data members `real` and `imaginary`, and declares stream-insertion and stream-extraction overloaded operator functions as `friend`s of the class.

b) Define the stream-insertion and -extraction operator functions. The stream-extraction operator function should determine if the data entered is valid, and if not, it should set `ios::failbit` to indicate improper input. The input should be of the form:

```
3 + 8i
```

The values can be negative or positive, and it is possible that one of the two values is not provided. If a value is not provided, the appropriate data member should be set to `0`. The stream-insertion operator should not be able to display the point if an input error occurred. The output format should be identical to the input format shown above. For negative imaginary values, a minus sign should be printed rather than a plus sign.

c) Write a `main` function that tests input and output of user-defined class `Complex` using the overloaded stream-extraction and stream-insertion operators.

**11.17** Write a program that uses a `for` structure to print a table of ASCII values for the characters in the ASCII character set from `33` to `126`. The program should print the decimal value, octal value, hexadecimal value, and character value for each character. Use the stream manipulators `dec`, `oct`, and `hex` to print the integer values.

**11.18** Write a program to show that the `getline` and three-argument `get` istream member functions each end the input string with a string terminating null character. Also show that `get` leaves the delimiter character on the input stream while `getline` extracts the delimiter character and discards it. What happens to the unread characters in the stream?

**11.19** Write a program that creates the user-defined manipulator `skipwhite` to skip leading whitespace characters in the input stream. The manipulator should use the `isspace` function from the `ctype.h` library to test if the character is a whitespace character. Each character should be input using the `istream` member function `get`. When a non-whitespace character is encountered, the `skipwhite` manipulator finishes its job by placing the character back on the input stream and returning an `istream` reference.

Test the manipulator by creating a `main` function in which the `ios::skipws` flag is unset so that the stream-extraction operator does not automatically skip whitespace. Then test the manipulator on the input stream by entering a character preceded by whitespace as input. Print the character that was input to confirm that a whitespace character was not input.

# 12
# Templates

## Objectives

- To be able to use function templates to create a group of related (overloaded) functions.
- To be able to distinguish between function templates and template functions.
- To be able to use class templates to create a group of related types.
- To be able to distinguish between class templates and template classes.
- To understand how to overload template functions.
- To understand the relationships among templates, friends, inheritance, and static members.

*Behind that outside pattern*
*the dim shapes get clearer every day.*
*It is always the same shape, only very numerous.*
Charlotte Perkins Gilman

*If you are able to slip through the parameters*
*of the skies and the earth, then do so.*
The Koran

*A Mighty Maze! but not without a plan.*
Alexander Pope

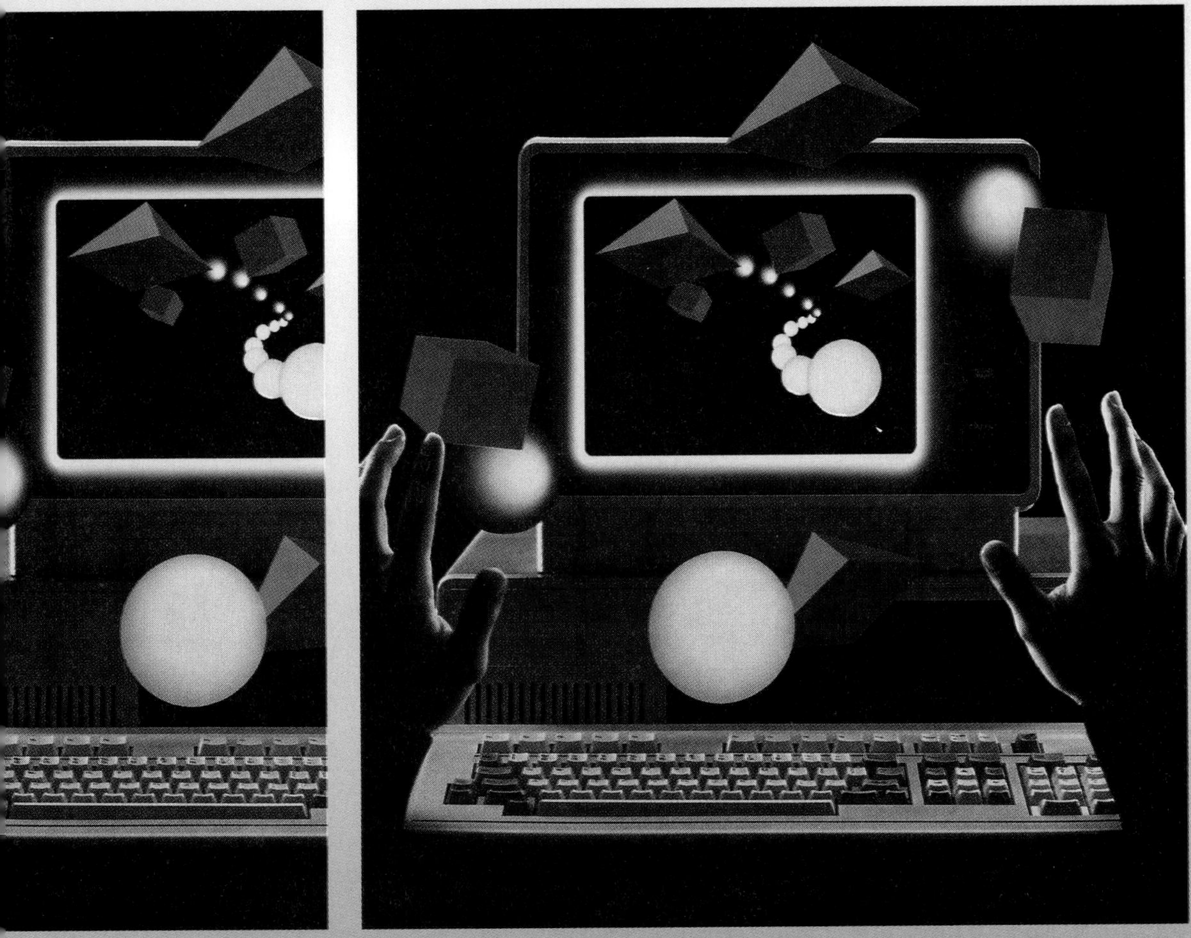

# Outline



## 12.1 Introduction

In this chapter we discuss one of the more recent features of the evolving C++ language standard, namely *templates.* Templates enable us to specify, with a single code segment, an entire range of related (overloaded) functions—called *template functions*—or an entire range of related classes—called *template classes.*

We might write a single *function template* for an array sort function and then have C++ automatically generate separate template functions that will sort an **`int`** array, sort a **`float`** array, sort an array of **`char *`** pointers, and so on.

We discussed function templates in Chapter 3. For the benefit of those readers who skipped that treatment, we present an additional discussion and example in this chapter.

We might write a single *class template* for a stack class and then have C++ automatically generate separate template classes such as a stack-of-**`int`** class, a stack-of-**`float`** class, a stack-of-**`char *`** pointers class, and so on.

Note the distinction between function templates and template functions: Function templates and class templates are like stencils out of which we trace shapes; template functions and template classes are like the separate tracings that all have the same shape but could be drawn in different colors, for example.

***Software Engineering Observation 12.1***

*Templates are one of C++'s many capabilities for software reuse.*

In this chapter, we will present examples of both function templates and class templates. We will also consider the relationships between templates and other C++ features such as overloading, inheritance, friends, and static members.

The design and details of the template mechanisms discussed here are based on the work of Bjarne Stroustrup as presented in his paper, *Parameterized Types for C++*, and published in the *Proceedings of the USENIX C++ Conference* held in Denver, Colorado in October, 1988.

## 12.2 Function Templates

Overloaded functions are normally used to perform *similar* operations on different types of data. If the operations are *identical* for each type, this may be performed more compactly and conveniently using *function templates*, a capability introduced in recent versions of C++. The programmer writes a single function template definition. Based on the argument types provided in calls to this function, the compiler automatically generates separate object-code functions to handle each type of call appropriately. In C, this task can be performed using macros created with the preprocessor directive **`#define`**. However, macros present the possibility for serious side effects and do not enable the compiler to perform type checking. Function templates provide a compact solution like macros, but enable full type-checking.

***Software Engineering Observation 12.2***

*Function templates, like macros, enable software reuse. But unlike macros, function templates benefit from the scrutiny of full C++ type checking.*

All function template definitions begin with keyword **`template`** followed by a list of formal parameters to the function template enclosed in *angle brackets (< and >)*; each formal parameter must be preceded by the keyword **`class`** as in

```
template<class T>
```

or

```
template<class ElementType>
```

or

```
template<class BorderType, class FillType>
```

The formal parameters of a template definition are used (as they would be with arguments of built-in types or user-defined types) to specify the *types* of the arguments to the function, to specify the return type of the function, and to declare variables within the function. The function definition follows and is defined like any other function. Note that keyword **`class`** used to specify function template type parameters actually means "any built-in type or user-defined type."

***Common Programming Error 12.1***

*Not placing* **`class`** *before every formal type parameter of a function template.*

Let us examine the **`printArray`** function template in Fig. 12.1. The function template is used in the complete program of Fig. 12.2.

The **`printArray`** function template declares a single formal parameter **`T`** (**`T`** could be any valid identifier) for the type of the array to be printed by function **`printArray`**;

```
template<class T>
void printArray(T *array, const int count)
{
   for (int i = 0; i < count; i++)
      cout << array[i] << " ";

   cout << endl;
}
```

**Fig. 12.1** A template function.

**T** is referred to as a *type parameter*. When the compiler detects a **printArray** function invocation in the program source code, the type of **printArray**'s first argument is substituted for **T** throughout the template definition, and C++ creates a complete template function for printing an array of the specified data type. Then, the newly created function is compiled. In Fig. 12.2, three **printArray** functions are instantiated—one expects an **int** array, one expects a **float** array, and one expects a **char** array. For example, the instantiation for type **int** is:

```
void printArray(int *array, const int count)
{
   for (int i = 0; i < count; i++)
      cout << array[i] << " ";

   cout << endl;
}
```

Every formal parameter in a function template definition must appear in the function's parameter list at least once. The name of a formal parameter can be used only once in the parameter list of a template header. Formal parameter names among template functions need not be unique.

***Common Programming Error 12.2***

*Not using every formal parameter of a function template in the function's parameter list.*

Figure 12.2 illustrates the use of the **printArray** function template. The program begins by instantiating **int** array **a**, **float** array **b**, and **char** array **c**, of sizes 5, 7, and 6, respectively. Then each of the arrays is printed by calling **printArray**—once with a first argument **a** of type **int ***, once with a first argument **b** of type **float ***, and once with a first argument **c** of type **char ***. The call

```
printArray(a, aCount);
```

for example, causes the compiler to instantiate a **printArray** template function for which type parameter **T** is **int**. The call

```
printArray(b, bCount);
```

causes the compiler to instantiate a second **printArray** template function for which type parameter **T** is **float**. The call

```
printArray(c, cCount);
```

```
// Using template functions
#include <iostream.h>

template<class T>
void printArray(T *array, const int count)
{
   for (int i = 0; i < count; i++)
      cout << array[i] << " ";

   cout << endl;
}

main()
{
   const int aCount = 5, bCount = 7, cCount = 6;
   int a[aCount] = {1, 2, 3, 4, 5};
   float b[bCount] = {1.1, 2.2, 3.3, 4.4, 5.5, 6.6, 7.7};
   char c[cCount] = "HELLO";   // 6th position for null

   cout << "Array a contains:" << endl;
   printArray(a, aCount);   // integer template function

   cout << "Array b contains:" << endl;
   printArray(b, bCount);   // float template function

   cout << "Array c contains:" << endl;
   printArray(c, cCount);   // character template function

   return 0;
}
```

```
Array a contains:
1 2 3 4 5
Array b contains:
1.1 2.2 3.3 4.4 5.5 6.6 7.7
Array c contains:
H E L L O
```

**Fig. 12.2** Using template functions.

causes the compiler to instantiate a third **`printArray`** template function for which type parameter **`T`** is **`char`**.

***Performance Tip 12.1***

*Templates certainly offer the benefits of software reusability. But keep in mind that multiple copies of template functions and template classes can be instantiated in a program. These copies can consume considerable memory.*

## 12.3 Overloading Template Functions

Template functions and overloading are intimately related. The related functions generated from a function template all have the same name, so the compiler uses overloading resolution to invoke the proper function.

A function template itself may be overloaded in several ways. We can provide other function templates that specify the same function name but different function parameters. For example, the **`printArray`** function template of Fig. 12.2 could be overloaded with another **`printArray`** function template with additional parameters **`lowSubscript`** and **`highSubscript`** to specify the portion of the array to be printed (see Exercise 12.4).

A function template can also be overloaded by providing other non-template functions with the same function name but different function arguments. For example, the **`printArray`** function template of Fig. 12.2 could be overloaded with a non-template version that specifically prints an array of character strings in neat, tabular, column format (see Exercise 12.5).

***Common Programming Error 12.3***

*If a template is invoked with a user-defined class type, and if that template uses operators (like ==, +, <=, etc.) with objects of that class type, then those operators must be overloaded! Forgetting to overload such operators causes linkage errors because the compiler, of course, still generates calls to the appropriate overloaded operator functions despite the fact that these functions are not present.*

The compiler performs a matching process to determine what function to call when a function is invoked. First the compiler tries to find and use a precise match in which the function names and argument types match perfectly with those of the function call. If this fails, the compiler checks if a function template is available that can generate a template function with a precise match of function name and argument types. If such a function template is found, the compiler generates and uses the appropriate template function. Note that this matching process with templates requires precise matches on all argument types—no automatic conversions are applied. Finally, the compiler proceeds with conventional overloading resolution as discussed in Chapter 3.

***Common Programming Error 12.4***

*The compiler performs a matching process to determine what function to call when a function is invoked. If no match can be found, or if the matching process produces multiple matches, a compiler error is generated.*

## 12.4 Class Templates

It is possible to understand what a stack is (a data structure into which we insert items in one order and retrieve them in last-in-first-out order) independent of the type of the items being placed in the stack. But when it comes to actually instantiating a stack, a data type must be specified. This creates a wonderful opportunity for software reusability. What we need are the means for describing the notion of a stack generically and instantiating classes that are type-specific versions of this generic class. This capability is provided by *class templates* in C++.

***Software Engineering Observation 12.3***

*Template classes encourage software reusability by enabling type-specific versions of generic classes to be instantiated.*

Class templates are called *parameterized types* because they require one or more type parameters to specify how to customize a generic class template to form a specific template class.

The programmer who wishes to use template classes simply writes one class template definition. Each time the programmer needs a new type-specific instantiation, the programmer uses a concise, simple notation and the compiler writes the source code for the template class the programmer requires. One **Stack** class template, for example, could thus become the basis for creating many **Stack** classes (such as "**Stack** of **float**," "**Stack** of **int**," "**Stack** of **char**," "**Stack** of **Employee**," etc.) used in a program.

Note the definition of the **Stack** class template in Fig. 12.3. It looks like a conventional class definition except that it is preceded by the header

```
template<class T>
```

to indicate that this is a class template definition with type parameter **T** indicating the type of the **Stack** class to be created. The programmer need not specifically use identifier **T**—any identifier can be used. The type of element to be stored on this **Stack** is mentioned only generically as **T** throughout the **Stack** class header and member function definitions.

Now let us consider the driver (function **main**) that exercises the **Stack** class template. The driver begins by instantiating object **floatStack** of size 5. This object is declared to be of class **Stack<float>** (pronounced "**Stack** of **float**"). The compiler associates type **float** with type parameter **T** in the template to produce the source code for a **Stack** class of type **float**.

```
// TSTACK1.H
// Simple template class Stack
#ifndef TSTACK1_H
#define TSTACK1_H

#include <iostream.h>

template<class T>
class Stack {
public:
   Stack(int = 10);      // default constructor (stack size 10)
   ~Stack() { delete [] stackPtr; } // destructor
   int push(const T&);   // push an element onto the stack
   int pop(T&);          // pop an element off the stack
   int isEmpty() const { return top == -1; } // 1 if empty
   int isFull() const { return top == size - 1; } // 1 if full
private:
   int size;             // # of elements in the stack
   int top;              // location of the top element
   T *stackPtr;          // pointer to the stack
};
```

**Fig. 12.3** Definition of class template **Stack** (part 1 of 4).

```
// Constructor with default size 10
template<class T>
Stack<T>::Stack(int s)
{
   size = s > 0 && s < 1000 ? s : 10;  // reasonable size
   top = -1;                           // Stack is initially empty
   stackPtr = new T[size];    // space allocated for Stack
elements
}

// Push an element onto the stack
// return 1 if successful, 0 otherwise
template<class T>
int Stack<T>::push(const T &item)
{
   if (!isFull()) {
      stackPtr[++top] = item;      // place item in Stack
      return 1;  // push successful
   }
   return 0;     // push unsuccessful
}

// Pop an element off the stack
template<class T>
int Stack<T>::pop(T &popValue)
{
   if (!isEmpty()) {
      popValue = stackPtr[top--];  // remove item from Stack
      return 1;  // pop successful
   }
   return 0;     // pop unsuccessful
}

#endif
```

**Fig. 12.3** Definition of class template **Stack** (part 2 of 4).

The driver then successively pushes the **float** values 1.1, 2.2, 3.3, 4.4 and 5.5 onto **floatStack**. The **push** loop terminates when the driver attempts to push a sixth value onto **floatStack** (which is already full because it was created to hold a maximum of 5 elements).

The driver now pops the five values off the stack (in last-in-first-out order). The driver attempts to pop a sixth value, but **floatStack** is now empty, so the **pop** loop terminates.

Next, the driver instantiates integer stack **intStack** with the declaration

```
Stack<int> intStack;
```

(pronounced "**intStack** is a **Stack** of **int**"). Because no size is specified, the size defaults to 10 as specified in the default constructor. Once again, the driver loops pushing values onto **intStack** until it is full, and then loops popping values off **intStack** until it is empty.

```
// FIG12_3.CPP
// Test driver for Stack template

#include <iostream.h>
#include "tstack1.h"

main()
{
   Stack<float> floatStack(5);
   float f = 1.1;
   cout << "Pushing elements onto floatStack" << endl;

   while (floatStack.push(f)) { // success (1 returned)
      cout << f << ' ';
      f += 1.1;
   }

   cout << endl << "Stack is full. Cannot push " << f << endl
        << endl << "Popping elements from floatStack" << endl;

   while (floatStack.pop(f))  // success (1 returned)
      cout << f << ' ';

   cout << endl << "Stack is empty. Cannot pop" << endl;

   Stack<int> intStack;
   int i = 1;
   cout << endl << "Pushing elements onto intStack" << endl;

   while (intStack.push(i)) { // success (1 returned)
      cout << i << ' ';
      i += 1;
   }

   cout << endl << "Stack is full. Cannot push " << i << endl
        << endl << "Popping elements from intStack" << endl;

   while (intStack.pop(i))  // success (1 returned)
      cout << i << ' ';

   cout << endl << "Stack is empty. Cannot pop" << endl;
   return 0;
}
```

**Fig. 12.3** Driver for class template **`Stack`** (part 3 of 4).

The member function definitions outside the class template header each begin with the header

```
template<class T>
```

Then each definition resembles a conventional function definition except that the **`Stack`** element type is always listed generically as type parameter **`T`**. The binary scope resolution operator is used with the class template name **`Stack<T>`** to tie each member function

```
Pushing elements onto floatStack
1.1 2.2 3.3 4.4 5.5
Stack is full. Cannot push 6.6

Popping elements from floatStack
5.5 4.4 3.3 2.2 1.1
Stack is empty. Cannot pop

Pushing elements onto intStack
1 2 3 4 5 6 7 8 9 10
Stack is full. Cannot push 11

Popping elements from intStack
10 9 8 7 6 5 4 3 2 1
Stack is empty. Cannot pop
```

**Fig. 12.3** Driver for class template **Stack** (part 4 of 4).

definition to the class template's scope. In this case, the class name is **Stack<T>**. When **floatStack** is instantiated to be of type **Stack<float>**, the **Stack** constructor creates an array of elements of type **float** to represent the stack. The statement

```
stackPtr = new T[size];
```

in the **Stack** class template definition is generated by the compiler in the **Stack<float>** template class as

```
stackPtr = new float[size];
```

***Common Programming Error 12.5***

*Although non-template classes can be nested, class templates cannot be nested. Attempting to nest one class template inside another is a syntax error.*

## 12.5 Class Templates and Non-Type Parameters

The **Stack** class template of the previous section used only type parameters in the template header. It is also possible to use non-type parameters. For example, the template header could be modified to take an **int elements** parameter as follows:

```
template<class T, int elements>   // note non-type parameter
```

Then, a declaration such as

```
Stack<float, 100> mostRecentSalesFigures;
```

would instantiate (at compile time) a 100-element **Stack** template class named **mostRecentSalesFigures** of **float** values; this template class would be of type **Stack<float, 100>**. The class header might then contain a private data member with an array declaration such as

```
T stackHolder[elements];    // array to hold stack contents
```

***Performance Tip 12.2***

*Specifying the size of a container class (such as an array class or a stack class) at compile time (possibly through a non-type template size parameter) eliminates the execution time overhead of creating the space dynamically with* **`new`**.

***Software Engineering Observation 12.4***

*Specifying the size of a container at compile time (possibly through a non-type template size parameter) avoids the possibility of a potentially fatal execution-time error if* **`new`** *is unable to obtain the needed memory.*

In the exercises, you will be asked to use a non-type parameter to help create a template for the **`Array`** class we developed in Chapter 8, "Overloading." This template will enable **`Array`** objects to be instantiated with a specified number of elements of a specified type at compile time, rather than dynamically creating space for the array objects at execution time.

A class for a specific type that does not match a common class template can be provided to override the class template for that type. For example, an **`Array`** template class can be used to instantiate an array of any type. The programmer may specifically choose to take control of instantiating the **`Array`** class of a specific type, such as **`Martian`**. This is done simply by forming the new class with a class name of **`Array<Martian>`**.

## 12.6 Templates and Inheritance

Templates and inheritance relate in several ways:

- A class template can be derived from a template class.
- A class template can be derived from a non-template class.
- A template class can be derived from a class template.
- A non-template class can be derived from a class template.

## 12.7 Templates and Friends

We have seen that functions and entire classes can be declared as friends of non-template classes. With class templates, the obvious kinds of friendship arrangements can be declared. Friendship can be established between a class template and a global function, a member function of another class (possibly a template class), or even an entire class (possible a template class). The notations required to establish these friendship relationships can be cumbersome.

Inside a class template for class **`X`** that has been declared with

```
template<class T> class X
```

a friendship declaration of the form

```
friend void f1();
```

makes function **`f1`** a friend of every template class instantiated from the preceding class template.

Inside a class template for class **X** that has been declared with

```
template<class T> class X
```

a friendship declaration of the form

```
friend void f2(X<T> &);
```

for a particular type **T** such as **float** makes function **f2(X<float> &)** a friend of **X<float>** only.

Inside a class template, you can declare that a member function of another class is a friend of any template class generated from the class template. Simply name the member function of the other class using the class name and the binary scope-resolution operator. For example, inside a class template for class **X** that has been declared with

```
template<class T> class X
```

a friendship declaration of the form

```
friend void A::f4();
```

makes member function **f4** of class **A** a friend of every template class instantiated from the preceding class template.

Inside a class template for class **X** that has been declared with

```
template<class T> class X
```

a friendship declaration of the form

```
friend void C<T>::f5(X<T> &);
```

for a particular type **T** such as **float** makes member function

```
C<float>::f5(X<float> &)
```

a friend function of *only* template class **X<float>**.

Inside a class template for class **X** that has been declared with

```
template<class T> class X
```

a second class **Y** can be declared with

```
friend class Y;
```

making every member function of class **Y** a friend of every template class produced from the class template for **X**.

Inside a class template for class **X** that has been declared with

```
template<class T> class X
```

a second class **Z** can be declared with

```
friend class Z<T>;
```

then when a template class is instantiated with a particular type for **T** such as **float**, all members of **class Z<float>** become friends of template class **X<float>**.

## 12.8 Templates and Static Members

What about `static` data members? Remember that with a non-template class, one copy of a `static` data member is shared among all objects of the class, and the `static` data member must be initialized at file scope.

Each template class instantiated from a class template has its own copy of each `static` data member of the class template; all objects of that template class share that one `static` data member. And as with `static` data members of non-template classes, `static` data members of template classes must also be initialized at file scope. Each template class gets its own copy of the class template's `static` member functions.

### *Summary*

- Templates enable us to specify a range of related (overloaded) functions—called template functions—or a range of related classes—called template classes.
- To use function templates, the programmer writes a single function template definition. Based on the argument types provided in calls to this function, C++ automatically generates separate object-code functions to handle each type of call appropriately.
- All function template definitions begin with keyword `template` followed by formal parameters to the function template enclosed in angle brackets (< and >); each formal parameter must be preceded by the keyword `class`. Keyword `class` used to specify function template type parameters means "any built-in type or user-defined type."
- Template definition formal parameters are used to specify the types of the arguments to the function, the return type of the function, and to declare variables in the function.
- Every formal parameter in a function template definition must appear in the function's parameter list at least once. The name of a formal parameter can be used only once in the parameter list of a template header. Formal parameter names among template functions need not be unique.
- A function template itself may be overloaded in several ways. We can provide other function templates that specify the same function name but different function parameters. A function template can also be overloaded by providing other non-template functions with the same function name but different function parameters.
- Class templates provide the means for describing a class generically and instantiating classes that are type-specific versions of this generic class.
- Class templates are called parameterized types; they require type parameters to specify how to customize a generic class template to form a specific template class.
- The programmer who wishes to use template classes writes one class template. When the programmer needs a new type-specific object, the programmer uses a concise notation and the compiler writes the source code for the template class.
- Note the definition of a class template looks like a conventional class definition except that it is preceded by the header `template<class T>` to indicate this is a class template definition with type parameter `T` indicating the type of the class to be created.

The type **`T`** is mentioned throughout the class header and member function definitions as a generic type name.

- The member function definitions outside the class template header each begin with the header **`template<class T>`**. Then each definition resembles a conventional function definition except that the generic data in the class is always listed generically as type parameter **`T`**. The binary scope resolution operator is used with the class template name to tie each member function definition to the class template's scope as in **`ClassName<T>`**.
- It is possible to use non-type parameters in the header of a class template.
- A class for a specific type can be provided to override the class template for that type.
- A class template can be derived from a template class. A class template can be derived from a non-template class. A template class can be derived from a class template. A non-template class can be derived from a class template.
- Functions and entire classes can be declared as friends of non-template classes. With class templates, the obvious kinds of friendship arrangements can be declared. Friendship can be established between a class template and a global function, a member function of another class (possibly a template class), or even an entire class (possible a template class).
- Each template class instantiated from a class template has its own copy of each **`static`** data member of the class template; all objects of that template class share that one **`static`** data member. And as with **`static`** data members of non-template classes, **`static`** data members of template classes must be initialized at file scope.
- Each template class gets a copy of the class template's **`static`** member functions.

## Terminology

angle brackets (**`<`** and **`>`**)
class template
class template name
formal parameter in a template header
friend of a template
function template
function template declaration
function template definition
keyword **`class`** in a template type parameter
keyword **`template`**
non-type parameter in a template header
overloading a template function
parameterized type
**`static`** data member of a class template
**`static`** data member of a template class
**`static`** member function of a class template
**`static`** member function of a template class
template class
template class member function
**`template<class T>`**
template function
template argument
template name
template parameter
type parameter in a template header

## Common Programming Errors

**12.1** Not placing ***`class`*** before every formal type parameter of a function template.

12.2 Not using every formal parameter of a function template in the function's parameter list.

12.3 If a template is invoked with a user-defined class type, and if that template uses operators (like `==`, `+`, `<=`, etc.) with objects of that class type, then those operators must be overloaded! Forgetting to overload such operators causes linkage errors because the compiler, of course, still generates calls to the appropriate overloaded operator functions despite the fact that these functions are not present.

12.4 The compiler performs a matching process to determine what function to call when a function is invoked. If no match can be found, or if the matching process produces multiple matches, a compiler error is generated.

12.5 Although non-template classes can be nested class templates can not be nested. Attempting to nest one class template inside another is a syntax error.

## Performance Tips

12.1 Templates certainly offer the benefits of software reusability. But keep in mind that multiple copies of template functions and template classes can be instantiated in a program. These copies can consume considerable memory.

12.2 Specifying the size of a container class (such as an array class or a stack class) at compile time (possibly through a non-type template size parameter) eliminates the execution time overhead of creating the space dynamically with **`new`**.

## Software Engineering Observations

12.1 Templates are one of C++'s many capabilities for software reuse.

12.2 Function templates, like macros, enable software reuse. But unlike macros, function templates benefit from the scrutiny of full C++ type checking.

12.3 Template classes encourage software reusability by enabling type-specific versions of generic classes to be instantiated.

12.4 Specifying the size of a container at compile time (possibly through a non-type template size parameter) avoids the possibility of a potentially fatal execution-time error if **`new`** is unable to obtain the needed memory.

## Self-Review Exercises

12.1 Answer each of the following true or false. For those that are false, state why.

a) A friend function of a function template must be a template function.

b) If several template classes are generated from a single class template with a single **`static`** data member, each of the template classes shares a single copy of the class template's **`static`** data member.

c) A template function can be overloaded by another template function with the same function name.

d) The name of a formal parameter can be used only once in the formal parameter list of the template definition. Formal parameter names among template definitions must be unique.

e) Keyword **`class`** as used with a template type parameter specifically means "any user-defined class type."

f) Template classes cannot be nested.

12.2 Fill in the blanks in each of the following:

a) Templates enable us to specify, with a single code segment, an entire range of related functions called __________, or an entire range of related classes called __________.

b) All function template definitions begin with keyword __________ followed by a list of formal parameters to the function template enclosed in __________.
c) The related functions generated from a function template all have the same name, so the compiler uses __________ resolution to invoke the proper function.
d) Class templates are also called __________ types.
e) The __________ operator is used with a template class name to tie each member function definition to the class template's scope.
f) As with **static** data members of non-template classes, **static** data members of template classes must also be initialized at __________ scope.

## Answers to Self-Review Exercises

**12.1** (a) False. It could be a non-template function. (b) False. Each template class will have a copy of the **static** data member. (c) True. (d) False. Formal parameter names among template functions need not be unique. e) False. Keyword **class** in this context also allows for a type parameter of a built-in type. (f) True.

**12.2** (a) template functions, template classes. (b) **template**, angle brackets (**<** and **>**). (c) overloading. (d) parameterized. e) binary scope resolution. (f) file.

## Exercises

**12.3** Write a function template **bubbleSort** based on the sort program of Fig. 5.15. Write a driver program that inputs, sorts, and outputs an **int** array and a **float** array.

**12.4** Overload function template **printArray** of Fig. 12.2 so that it takes two-additional integer arguments, namely **int lowSubscript** and **int highSubscript**. A call to this function will print only the designated portion of the array. Validate **lowSubscript** and **highSubscript**; if either is out-of-range or if **highSubscript** is less than or equal to **lowSubscript** the overloaded **printArray** function should return 0; otherwise, **printArray** should return the number of elements printed. Then modify **main** to exercise both versions of **printArray** on arrays **a**, **b**, and **c**. Be sure to test all capabilities of both versions of **printArray**.

**12.5** Overload function template **printArray** of Fig. 12.2 with a non-template version that specifically prints an array of character strings in neat, tabular, column format.

**12.6** Write a simple function template for predicate function **isEqualTo** that compares its two arguments with the equality operator (**==**) and returns 1 if they are equal and 0 if they are not equal. Use this function template in a program that calls **isEqualTo** only with a variety of built-in types. Now write a separate version of the program that calls **isEqualTo** with a user-defined class type, but does not overload the equality operator. What happens when you attempt to run this program? Now overload the equality operator (with operator function **operator==**). Now what happens when you attempt to run this program?

**12.7** Use a non-type parameter **numberOfElements** and a type parameter **elementType** to help create a template for the **Array** class we developed in Chapter 8, "Overloading." This template will enable **Array** objects to be instantiated with a specified number of elements of a specified element type at compile time.

**12.8** Write a program with class template **Array**. The template can instantiate an **Array** of any element type. Override the template with a specific definition for an **Array** of **float** elements (**class Array<float>**). The driver should demonstrate the instantiation of an **Array** of **int** through the template, and should show that an attempt to instantiate an **Array** of **float** uses the definition provided in **class Array<float>**.

**12.9** Distinguish between the terms function template and template function.

**12.10** Which is more like a stencil—a class template or a template class? Explain your answer.

**12.11** What is the relationship between function templates and overloading?

**12.12** Why might you choose to use a function template instead of a macro?

**12.13** What performance problem can result from using function templates and class templates?

**12.14** The compiler performs a matching process to determine the template function to call when a function is invoked. Under what circumstances does an attempt to make a match result in a compile error?

**12.15** Why is it appropriate to call a class template a parameterized type?

**12.16** Explain why you might use the statement

```
Array<Employee> workerList(100);
```

in a C++ program with template classes.

**12.17** Review your answer to Exercise 12.16. Now, why you might use the statement

```
Array<Employee> workerList;
```

in a C++ program with template classes?

**12.18** Explain the use of the following notation in a C++ program with template classes:

```
template<class T> Array<T>::Array(int s)
```

**12.19** Why might you typically use a non-type parameter with a class template for a container such as an array or stack?

**12.20** Describe how to provide a class for a specific type to override the class template for that type.

**12.21** Describe the relationship between class templates and inheritance.

**12.22** Suppose a class template has the header

```
template<class T1> class C1
```

Describe the friendship relationships established by placing each of the following friendship declarations inside this class template header. Identifiers beginning with "**f**" are functions, identifiers beginning with "**C**" are classes, and identifiers beginning with "**T**" can represent any type (i.e., built-in types or class types).

a) `friend void f1();`
b) `friend void f2(C1<T1> &);`
c) `friend void C2::f4();`
d) `friend void C3<T1>::f5(C1<T1> &);`
e) `friend class C5;`
f) `friend class C6<T1>;`

**12.23** Suppose class template **Employee** has a **static** data member **count**. Suppose three template classes are instantiated from the class template. How many copies of the **static** data member will exist? How will the use of each be constrained (if at all)?

# 13

# Exception Handling

## Objectives

- To understand exceptions and how to handle them.
- To be able to use try blocks to delineate code in which an exception may occur.
- To be able to throw exceptions of their point of origin.
- To be able to use catch blocks to specify exception handlers.
- To understand how uncaught exceptions and unexpected exceptions are processed.

*It is common sense to take a method and try it. If it fails, admit it frankly and try another. But above all, try something.*
Franklin Delano Roosevelt

*O! Throw away the worser part of it,*
*And live the purer with the other half.*
William Shakespeare

*If they're running and they don't look where they're going*
*I have to come out from somewhere and catch them.*
Jerome David Salinger

*And oftentimes excusing of a fault*
*Doth make the fault the worse by the excuse.*
William Shakespeare

*I never forget a face, but in your case I'll make an exception.*
Groucho (Julius Henry) Marx

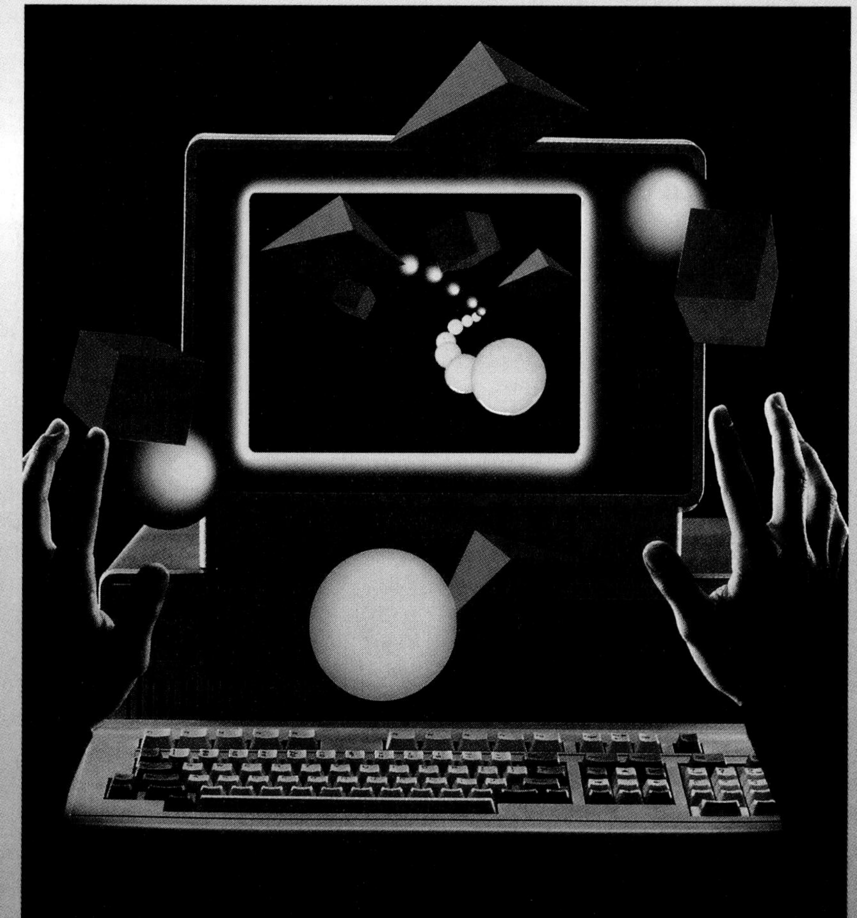

## Outline



## 13.1 Introduction

In this chapter, we introduce one of the latest additions to the evolving C++ language, namely *exception handling*. The extensibility of C++ can increase substantially the number and kinds of errors that can occur. Every new class adds its own error possibilities. The features presented here enable programmers to write clearer, more robust, more fault-tolerant programs. Recent systems (such as Microsoft's Windows NT operating system) developed with these and/or similar techniques have reported positive results. We also mention when exception handling should not be used.

The style and details of exception handling presented in this chapter are based on the work of Andrew Koenig and Bjarne Stroustrup as presented in their paper, "Exception Handling for C++ (revised)," published in the *Proceedings of the USENIX C++ Conference* held in San Francisco in April, 1990. Their work forms the basis of what is likely to become the ANSI standard version of exception handling.

Error-handling code varies in nature and amount among software systems depending on the application and whether or not the software is a product for release. Products tend to contain far more error handling code than "casual" software.

There are many popular means of dealing with errors. Most commonly, error handling code is interspersed throughout a system's code. Errors are dealt with at the places in the code where the errors can occur. The advantage to this approach is that a programmer reading code can see the error processing in the immediate vicinity of the code and determine if the proper error checking has been implemented.

The problem with this scheme is that the code in a sense becomes "polluted" with the error processing. It becomes more difficult for a programmer concerned with the application itself to read the code and determine if the code is functioning correctly. This makes it more difficult to understand and to maintain the code.

Some common examples of exceptions are memory exhaustion, an out-of-bounds array subscript, arithmetic overflow, division by zero, and invalid function parameters.

C++'s new exception handling features enable the programmer to remove the error-handling code from the "main line" of the program's execution. This improves program readability and modifiability. The separation of error-handling code from the main line of program code is consistent with the virtues of separability we have discussed in the contexts of both structured programming and object-oriented programming.

Another benefit of the new style of exception handling is that it becomes possible to catch all kinds of exceptions, or to catch all exceptions of a certain type, or to catch all exceptions of related types. This makes programs more robust by reducing the likelihood that errors will not be caught by a program.

Exception handling is provided to enable programs to catch and handle errors rather than letting them occur and suffering the consequences. With exception handling, if the programmer does not provide a means of handling a fatal error, the program terminates.

Exception handling is designed for dealing with *synchronous errors* such as an attempt to divide by zero (that occurs as the program executes the divide instruction). With exception handling, before the program executes the division, it checks the denominator and "throws" (issues) an exception if it is zero.

Exception handling is not designed to deal with asynchronous situations such as disk I/O completions, network message arrivals, mouse clicks, and the like; these are best handled through other means, such as interrupt processing.

Exception handling is used in situations in which the system can recover from the error causing the exception. The recovery procedure is called an *exception handler*.

Exception handling is typically used in situations in which the error will be dealt with by a different part of the program (i.e., a different scope) from that which detected the error. For example, a program that carries on an interactive dialog with a user should not use exceptions to process input errors.

***Good Programming Practice 13.1***

---

*Use exceptions for errors that must be processed in a different scope from where they occur. Use other means of error handling for errors that will be processed in the scope in which they occur.*

***Good Programming Practice 13.2***

---

*Avoid using exception handling for purposes other than error handling because this can reduce program clarity.*

There is another reason to avoid using exception handling techniques for conventional program control. Exception handling is designed for error processing which is an infrequent activity that is often used because a program is about to terminate. Given this, it is not required that C++ compiler writers implement exception handling for the kind of optimal performance that might be expected of regular application code.

***Performance Tip 13.1***

*Although it is possible to use exception handling for purposes other than error handling, this can reduce program performance.*

***Performance Tip 13.2***

*Exception handling is generally implemented in compilers in such a manner that when an exception does not occur, little or no overhead is imposed by the presence of exception handling code. When exceptions happen, they do incur execution-time overhead.*

***Software Engineering Observation 13.1***

*Flow of control with conventional control structures is generally clearer and more efficient than with exceptions.*

***Common Programming Error 13.1***

*Another reason exceptions can be dangerous as an alternative to normal flow of control is that the stack is unwound and resources allocated prior to the occurrence of the exception may not be freed. This problem can be avoided by careful programming.*

Exception handling helps improve a program's fault tolerance. It becomes "more pleasant" to write error-processing code, so programmers are more likely to provide it. It also becomes possible to catch exceptions in a variety of ways such as by type, or even to specify that exceptions of any type are to be caught. Exception handling provides the programmer with a rich, disciplined set of error-handling capabilities.

It is important to note that the vast majority of programs written today support only a single thread of execution. Multithreading is receiving great attention in recent operating systems like Windows NT, OS/2, and various versions of UNIX. The techniques discussed in this chapter apply even for multithreaded programs, although we do not discuss multithreaded programs specifically.

***Portability Tip 13.1***

*As of this writing, an ANSI standard for C++ has not yet been finalized, so it is possible that features described in this chapter may evolve somewhat over the next few years. As we completed this text, the major C++ compiler vendors were starting to introduce versions with exception handling. The experience gained over the next few years with these products should help lead toward a standard implementation.*

We will show how to deal with "uncaught" exceptions. We will consider how unexpected exceptions are handled. We will show how related exceptions can be represented by exception classes derived from a common base exception class.

The new exception handling features of C++ are likely to become widely used as a result of the ANSI C++ standardization effort. Such standardization is especially important on large software projects where dozens or even hundreds of people work on separate components of a system and these components need to be combined effectively for the overall system to function properly.

***Software Engineering Observation 13.2***

*Exception-handling is particularly well suited to systems of separately developed components. Such systems are typical of real-world software systems and products. Exception handling makes it easier to combine the components. Each component can perform its own exception detection separate from its handling.*

Exception handling can be viewed as another means of returning control from a function or exiting a block of code. Normally, when an exception occurs, it will be handled by a caller of the function generating the exception, by a caller of that caller, or however far back in the call chain it becomes necessary to go to find a handler for that exception.

## 13.2 When Exception Handling Should Be Used

Exception handling should be used

- to process only exceptional situations, despite the fact that there is nothing to prevent the programmer from using exceptions as an alternate for program control.
- to process exceptions for program components that are not geared to handling those exceptions directly.
- to process exceptions from software components such as functions, libraries, and classes that are likely to be widely used, and where it does not make sense for those components to handle their own exceptions.
- on large projects to handle error processing in a uniform manner project wide.

***Good Programming Practice 13.3***

*Use conventional error-handling techniques (rather than exception handling) for straightforward, local error-processing in which a program is easily able to deal with its own errors.*

***Software Engineering Observation 13.3***

*When dealing with libraries, the caller of the library function will likely have unique error processing in mind for an exception generated in the library function. It is unlikely that a library function will perform error processing that would meet the unique needs of all users. Therefore, exceptions are an appropriate means for dealing with errors produced by library functions.*

## 13.3 Other Error-Handling Techniques

We have presented a variety of ways of dealing with exceptional situations prior to this chapter.

- Use **`assert`** to test for coding an design errors. If the assertion is false, the program terminates and the code must be corrected. This is useful at debugging time.

- Simply ignore the exceptions. This would be devastating for software products released to the general public, or for special-purpose software needed for mission-critical situations. But for your own software developed for your own purposes, it is quite common to ignore many kinds of errors.
- Abort the program. This, of course, prevents a program from running to completion and producing incorrect results. Actually, for many types of errors this is a good strategy, especially for nonfatal errors that enable a program to run to completion, perhaps misleading the programmer to think that the program functioned correctly. Here, too, such a strategy is inappropriate for mission-critical applications. Resource issues are also important here. If a program obtains a resource, the program should normally return that resource before program termination.

***Common Programming Error 13.2***

*Aborting a program could leave a resource in a state in which other programs would not be able to acquire the resource, and hence we would have a so-called "resource leak."*

- Set some error indicator such as **`errno`**. The problem with this is that programs may not check these error indicators at all points at which the errors could be troublesome.
- Test for the error condition, issue an error message, and call **`exit`** to pass an appropriate error code to the program's environment.
- **`setjump`** and **`longjump`**. These capabilities, available through **`<setjmp.h>`** enable the programmer to specify an immediate jump out of deeply nested function calls back to an error handler. Without **`setjump/longjump`**, a program must execute several returns to get out of the deeply nested function calls. These could certainly be used to jump to some error handler. But they are dangerous in C++ because they unwind the stack without calling destructors for automatic objects. This can lead to a variety of serious problems.
- Certain specific kinds of errors have dedicated capabilities for handling them. For example, when **`new`** fails to allocate memory, it can cause a **`new_handler`** function to execute to deal with the error. This function can be varied by supplying a function name as the argument to **`set_new_handler`**.

## 13.4 The Basics of C++ Exception Handling

In this section we overview programming with exception handling. In subsequent sections, we examine exception handling in detail.

C++ exception handling is geared to situations in which the function that detects an error is unable to deal with it. Such a function will *throw an exception* (also called *raising an exception*). There is no guarantee that there will be "anything out there" (i.e., an *exception handler*) specifically geared to processing that kind of exception. If there is, the exception will be *caught* and *handled*. If there is no exception handler for that particular kind of exception, the program terminates.

The programmer encloses in a ***`try`*** *block* the code that may generate an error that will produce an exception. The **`try`** block is immediately followed by one or more

**catch** *blocks*. Each **catch** block specifies the type of exception it can catch and handle. Each **catch** block contains an exception handler.

If the exception matches the type of the parameter in one of the **catch** blocks, the code for that **catch** block is executed. Otherwise, function **terminate** is called, which by default calls function **abort**.

Program control on a thrown exception leaves the **try** block and searches the **catch** blocks in order for an appropriate handler (we will soon discuss what makes a handler "appropriate"). If no exceptions are thrown in the **try** block, the exception handlers for that block are skipped and the program resumes execution after the last **catch** block.

We can specify the exceptions a function throws. As an option, we can specify that a function shall not throw any exceptions at all.

The exception is thrown in a **try** block in the function, or the exception is thrown from a function called directly or indirectly from the **try** block.

The point at which the **throw** is executed is called the *throw point.* This term is also used to describe the **throw** expression itself.

Once an exception is thrown, control cannot return to the throw point.

When an exception occurs, it is possible to communicate information to the exception handler from the point of the exception. That information is the type of the thrown object itself or information placed into the thrown object.

The thrown object is typically a character string (for an error message) or a class object. The thrown object conveys information to the exception handler that will process that exception.

***Software Engineering Observation 13.4***

*A key to C++-style exception handling is that the portion of a program or system that will handle the exception can be quite different or distant from the portion of the program that detected and generated the exceptional situation.*

## 13.5 A Simple Exception Handling Example: Divide by Zero

Now let us consider a simple example of exception handling. The program of Fig. 13.1 uses **try**, **throw**, and **catch** to detect, indicate, and handle a divide-by-zero exception.

Consider the two output windows. The first shows a successful execution. In the second, a zero denominator is entered and the program detects the error and issues an error message.

Now consider the driver program in **main**. The program prompts for, and inputs, two integers. Note the "localized" declaration of **number1** and **number2**.

Next, the program proceeds with a **try** block which wraps the code that may throw an exception. Note that the actual division that may cause the error is not explicitly listed inside the **try** block. Rather, the call to function **quotient** invokes the code that attempts the actual division. Function **quotient** actually throws the divide-by-zero exception object as we will see momentarily. In general, errors may surface through explicitly mentioned code in the **try** block, through calls to a function, or even through deeply nested function calls initiated by code in the **try** block.

The **try** block is immediately followed by a **catch** block containing the exception handler for the divide-by-zero error. In general, when an exception is thrown within a **try** block, the exception is caught by a **catch** block that specifies the appropriate type that matches the thrown exception. In Fig. 13.1, the **catch** block specifies that it will catch exception objects of type **DivideByZeroError**; this type indeed matches the type of the object thrown in function **quotient**. The body of this exception handler simply issues an error message and returns, in this case with 1 indicating termination because of an error. Exception handlers can be much more elaborate than this.

If, when executed, the code in a **try** block does not throw an exception, then all the **catch** handlers immediately following the **try** block are skipped and execution resumes with the first line of code after the **catch** handlers; in Fig. 13.1 a **return** statement is executed that returns 0, indicating normal termination.

Now let us examine the definitions of class **DivideByZeroError** and function **quotient**. In function **quotient**, when the **if** statement determines that the denominator is zero, the body of the **if** statement issues a **throw** statement which specifies the name of the constructor for the exception object. This causes an object of class **DivideByZeroError** to be created. This object will be caught by the **catch** statement (specifying type **DivideByZeroError**) after the **try** block. The constructor for class **DivideByZeroError** simply copies the string **"Divide by zero"** into private data member **message**. The thrown object is received in the parameter specified in the **catch** handler (in this case, parameter **error**), and the message is printed there through a call to public access function **printMessage**.

```
// A simple exception handling example.
// Checking for a divide-by-zero error.
#include <iostream.h>

// Definition of class DivideByZeroError to be used in exception
// handling for throwing an exception on a division by zero.
class DivideByZeroError {
public:
   DivideByZeroError() : message("Divide by zero") { }
   void printMessage() const { cout << message; }
private:
   const char *message;
};

// Definition of function quotient. Used to demonstrate throwing
// an exception when a divide-by-zero error is encountered.
float quotient(int num1, int num2)
{
   if (num2 == 0)
      throw DivideByZeroError();

   return (float) num1 / num2;
}
```

**Fig. 13.1** A simple exception handling example with divide by zero (part 1 of 2).

```
// Driver program
main()
{
   cout << "Enter two integers to get their quotient: ";

   int number1, number2;
   cin >> number1 >> number2;

   try {   // wraps the code that may throw an exception
      float result = quotient(number1, number2);

      cout << "The quotient is: " << result << endl;
   }

   catch (DivideByZeroError error) {    // error handler
      cout << "ERROR: ";
      error.printMessage()
      cout << endl;

      return 1;   // terminate because of an error
   }

   return 0;      // terminate normally
}
```

```
Enter two integers to get their quotient: 7 3
The quotient is 2.333333
```

```
Enter two integers to get their quotient: 23 0
ERROR: Divide by zero
```

**Fig. 13.1** A simple exception handling example with divide by zero (part 2 of 2).

***Good Programming Practice 13.4***

*Avoid the name Exception for any exception class. This name is too likely to be used by libraries, possibly even the evolving ANSI C++ standard itself.*

***Good Programming Practice 13.5***

*Associating each type of execution-time error with an appropriately named exception object improves program clarity.*

## 13.6 Try Blocks

An exception that occurs in a `try` block is normally caught by a handler specified by a `catch` block immediately following that `try` block.

```
try {
    ...
}

catch(  ) {
    ...
}
```

A **try** block can be followed by zero or more **catch** blocks. If a **try** block executes and no exceptions are thrown, all the exception handlers are skipped and control resumes with the first statement after the last exception handler.

## 13.7 Throwing an Exception

The **throw** keyword is used to indicate that an exception has occurred. This is called *throwing an exception* or *raising an exception*. A throw normally specifies one operand (a special case we will discuss specifies no operands). The operand of a **throw** can be of any type. If the operand is an object, we call it an *exception object*. A conditional expression can be thrown instead of an object (see section 13.10). It is possible to throw objects not intended for error handling.

Where is an exception caught? Upon being thrown, the exception will be caught by the closest exception handler (for the **try** block from which the exception was thrown) specifying an appropriate type. The exception handlers for a **try** block are listed immediately following the **try** block.

As part of throwing an exception, a temporary copy of the **throw** operand is created and initialized. This temporary object then initializes the parameter in the exception handler. The temporary object is destroyed when the exception handler completes execution and exits.

***Software Engineering Observation 13.5***

*If it is necessary to pass information about the error that caused an exception, such information can be placed in the thrown object. The* **catch** *handler would then contain a parameter name through which that information could be referenced.*

***Software Engineering Observation 13.6***

*An object can be thrown without containing information to be passed; in this case, mere knowledge that an exception of this type has been raised may provide sufficient information for the handler to do its job correctly.*

When an exception is thrown, control exits the current **try** block and proceeds to an appropriate **catch** handler (if one exists) after that **try** block. It is possible that the **throw** point could be in a deeply nested scope within a **try** block; control will still proceed to the **catch** handler. It is also possible that the **throw** point could be in a deeply nested function call; still, control will proceed to the **catch** handler.

A **try** block may appear to contain no error checking and include no **throw** statements, but code referenced in the **try** block could certainly cause error checking code in constructors to execute. Code in a **try** block could perform array subscripting on an array class object whose **operator[]** member function could be overloaded to throw an exception on a subscript-out-of-range error. Any function call can invoke code that might throw an exception or call another function that throws an exception.

Although an exception can terminate program execution, it is not required to terminate program execution. However, an exception does terminate the block in which the exception occurred.

***Common Programming Error 13.3***

*Exceptions should be thrown only within a* **`try`** *block. An exception thrown outside a* **`try`** *block causes a call to* **`terminate`**.

## 13.8 Catching an Exception

Exception handlers are contained in **`catch`** blocks. Each **`catch`** block starts with the keyword **`catch`** followed by parentheses containing a type and an optional parameter name. This is followed by braces delineating the exception handling code. When an exception is caught, the code in the **`catch`** block is executed.

***Common Programming Error 13.4***

*Assuming that after an exception is processed, control will return to the first statement after the throw.*

The **`catch`** handler defines its own scope. A **`catch`** specifies in parentheses the type of the object to be caught. The parameter in a **`catch`** handler can be named or unnamed. If the parameter is named, the parameter can be referenced in the handler. If the parameter is unnamed, i.e., only a type is listed for purposes of matching with the thrown object type, then information is not conveyed from the **`throw`** point to the handler; only control passes from the **`throw`** point to the handler. For many exceptions, this is acceptable.

***Common Programming Error 13.5***

*Specifying a comma-separated list of catch arguments.*

An exception whose thrown object's type matches the type of the argument in the **`catch`** header causes the **`catch`** block, i.e., the exception handler for exceptions of that type, to execute.

The **`catch`** handler that catches an exception is the first one listed after the currently active **`try`** block that matches the type of the thrown object. The matching rules are discussed shortly.

An exception that is not be caught causes a call to **`terminate`** which by default terminates a program by calling **`abort`**. It is possible to specify customized behavior by designating another function to be executed by providing that function's name as the argument in a **`set_terminate`** function call.

A **`catch`** followed by parentheses enclosing an ellipsis

```
catch(...)
```

means to catch all exceptions.

***Common Programming Error 13.6***

*Placing* **catch(...)** *before other* **catch** *blocks would prevent those blocks from ever being executed;* **catch(...)** *should always be placed last in the list of handlers following a* **try** *block, or a syntax error occurs.*

***Software Engineering Observation 13.7***

*A weakness with catching exceptions with* **catch(...)** *is that you normally cannot be sure what the exception type is. Another weakness is that without a named parameter, there is no way to refer to the exception object inside the exception handler.*

It is possible that no handler will match a particular thrown object. This causes the search for a match to continue in the next enclosing **try** block. As this process continues, it may eventually be determined that there is no handler in the program that matches the type of the thrown object; in this case function **terminate** is called, which by default calls function **abort**.

***Software Engineering Observation 13.8***

*The programmer determines the order in which the exception handlers are listed. This order can affect how exceptions originating in that* **try** *block are handled.*

The exception handlers are searched in order for an appropriate match. The first handler that yields a match is executed. When that handler finishes executing, control resumes with the first statement after the last **catch** block, i.e., the first statement after the last exception handler for that **try** block.

It is possible that several exception handlers will provide an acceptable match to the type of the exception. In this case, the first exception handler that matches the exception type is executed. If several handlers match, and if each of these handles the exception differently, then the order of the handlers will affect the manner in which the exception is handled.

It is possible that several **catch** handlers could contain a class type that would match the type of a particular thrown object. This can happen for several reasons. First, there can be a "catch-all" handler **catch(...)** that will catch any exception. Second, because of inheritance hierarchies, it is possible that a derived-class object can be caught either by a handler specifying the derived-class type, or by handlers specifying the types of any base classes of that derived class.

***Common Programming Error 13.7***

*Placing a* **catch** *that catches a base class object before a* **catch** *that catches an object of a class derived from that base class is a syntax error. The base-class* **catch** *will catch all objects of classes derived from that base class, so the derived class* **catch** *would never be executed.*

Sometimes a program may process many closely related types of exceptions. Instead of providing separate exception classes and **catch** handlers for each, a programmer can provide a single exception class and **catch** handler for a group of exceptions. As each exception occurs, the exception object can be created with different private data. The **catch** handler can examine this private data to distinguish the type of the exception.

When does a match occur? The type of the **catch** handler parameter matches the type of the thrown object if

- they are indeed of the same type.
- the **catch** handler parameter type is a public base class of the class of the thrown object.
- the handler parameter is of a pointer type and the thrown object is of a pointer type convertible to the handler parameter type through an allowable pointer conversion. For example, a derived-class pointer is convertible to a base-class pointer through standard conversions.
- the **catch** handler is of the form **catch(...)**.

***Common Programming Error 13.8***

*Placing an exception handler with a* **void *** *argument type before exception handlers with other pointer types causes a syntax error. The* **void *** *handler would catch all exceptions of pointer types, so the other handlers would never execute.*

It is possible that even though a precise match is available, a match requiring standard conversions will be made because that handler appears before the one that would result in a precise match.

It is possible to throw **const** objects and **volatile** objects. In this case, the **catch** handler argument type must also be declared **const** or **volatile**, respectively.

By default, if no handler is found for an exception, the program terminates. Although this may seem like the right thing to do, it is not what programmers are necessarily used to doing. Rather, errors often simply happen and then program execution continues, possibly only "hobbling" along.

A **try** block followed by several exception handlers resembles a **switch** statement. It is interesting that it is not necessary to use **break** to exit an exception handler in a manner that skips over the remaining exception handlers. Each **catch** block defines a distinct scope whereas all the cases in a **switch** statement are contained within the scope of the **switch**.

An exception cannot access objects defined within it's **try** block because they have already been "unwound" (destroyed) when the handler begins executing (see Section 13.13).

What happens when an exception occurs in an exception handler? The original exception that was caught is officially handled when the exception handler begins executing. So exceptions occurring in an exception handler need to be processed outside the **try** block in which the original exception was thrown.

Exception handlers can be written in a variety of ways. They could take a closer look at an error and decide to call **terminate**. They could simply rethrow an exception (see Section 13.9). They could convert one type of exception into another by throwing a different exception. They could perform any necessary recovery and resume execution after the last exception handler. They could look at the situation causing the error, remove the cause of the error, and retry by calling the original function that caused an exception (this would not create infinite recursion). They could simply return some status value to their environment, etc.

***Software Engineering Observation 13.9***

*It is best to incorporate your exception handling strategy into a system from the inception of the design process. It is difficult to add effective exception handling after a system has been implemented.*

When a `try` block does not throw any exceptions, then when the `try` block completes normal execution, control passes to the first statement after the last `catch` handler following the `try` block.

It is not possible to return to the throw point by issuing a `return` statement in a `catch` handler. Such a `return` simply returns to the function that called the function containing the `catch` block.

***Software Engineering Observation 13.10***

*Another reason not to use exceptions for conventional flow of control is that these "additional" exceptions can get in the way of genuine error-type exceptions. It becomes more difficult for the programmer to keep track of the larger number of exception cases. For example, when a program processes an excessive variety of exceptions, can we really be sure of just what is being caught by a* `catch(...)`*? Exceptional situations should be rare, not commonplace.*

The order of `catch` handlers is important. Handlers that catch derived class objects should be placed before handlers that catch base class objects; otherwise, the base class handler catches both the base class objects and the objects of classes derived from that base class.

When an exception is caught, it is possible that resources may have been allocated but not yet released in the `try` block. The `catch` handler, if possible, should release these resources. For example, the `catch` handler should delete space allocated by `new` and should close any files opened in the `try` block that threw the exception. Automatic objects are destroyed (stack unwinding) before the handler begins executing.

A `catch` block can process the error in a manner that enables the program to continue executing correctly. Or the `catch` block can terminate the program.

A `catch` handler itself can discover an error and throw an exception. Such an exception will not be processed by `catch` handlers associated with the same `try` block as the `catch` handler throwing the exception. Rather the thrown exception will be caught, if possible, by a `catch` handler associated with the next outer `try` block.

***Common Programming Error 13.9***

*Assuming that an exception thrown from a* `catch` *handler will be processed by that handler or any other handler associated with the* `try` *block that threw the exception which caused the original* `catch` *handler to execute.*

## 13.9 Rethrowing an Exception

It is possible that the handler that catches an exception may decide that it cannot process the exception or it may simply want to release resources before letting someone else handle it. In this case, the handler can simply rethrow the exception with the statement

```
throw;
```

Such a **throw** with no arguments rethrows the exception. If no exception was thrown to begin with, then the rethrow causes a call to **terminate**. This **throw** statement should only appear in a **catch** handler; otherwise, it will cause a call to **terminate**.

***Common Programming Error 13.10***

*Placing an empty* **throw** *statement outside a* **catch** *handler; executing such a* **throw** *causes a call to* **terminate**.

Even if a handler can process an exception, and regardless of whether it does any processing on that exception, the handler can still rethrow the exception for further processing outside the handler.

A rethrown exception is detected by the next enclosing **try** block and is handled by an exception handler listed after that enclosing **try** block.

***Software Engineering Observation 13.11***

*Use* **catch(...)** *to perform recovery that does not depend on the type of the exception, such as releasing common resources. The exception can be rethrown to alert more specific enclosing* **catch** *blocks.*

## 13.10 Throwing a Conditional Expression

It is possible to throw a conditional expression. But be careful because promotion rules may cause the value returned by the conditional expression to be of a different type than you may expect. For example, when throwing an **int** or a **double** from the same conditional expression, the conditional expression will convert the **int** to a **double**. Therefore the result will always be caught by a **catch** with a **double** argument rather than sometimes catching **double** (for the actual **double**) and sometimes catching **int**.

## 13.11 Exception Specifications

An *exception specification* enables a list of exceptions that can be thrown by a function to be specified.

```
int g(float h) throw (a, b, c)
{
   // function body
}
```

It is possible to restrict the exception types that can be thrown from a particular function. The exception types are specified in the function declaration as an *exception specification;* this is also called a *throw list.* This exception specification lists the exceptions that may be thrown. A function may throw the indicated exceptions, or it may throw derived types. Despite this supposed guarantee that other exception types will not be thrown, it is possible to do so. If an exception not listed in the exception specification is thrown, function **unexpected** is called.

Placing **throw()** (i.e., an *empty exception specification*) after a function's parameter list states that the function will not throw any exceptions. Such a function could, in fact, throw an exception; this, too, would generate a call to **unexpected**.

***Common Programming Error 13.11***

*Throwing an exception not in a function's exception specification causes a call to* **`unexpected`**.

A function without an exception specification can throw any exception.

```
void g();     // this function can throw any exception
```

Functions that specify an empty exception specification do not throw exceptions.

```
void g()  throw (); // this function throws no exceptions
```

The meaning of **`unexpected`** can be redefined using **`set_unexpected`**.

One interesting aspect of exception handling is that the compiler will not consider it a compile error if a function contains a **`throw`** expression for an exception not listed in the function's exception specification. The function must attempt to throw that exception at execution time before the error will be caught.

If a function throws an exception of a particular class type, that function can also throw exceptions of all classes that can be publicly derived from that class.

No exception specification means any exception can be thrown in the function.

## 13.12 Processing Unexpected Exceptions

Function **`unexpected`** calls the function specified with the **`set_unexpected`** function. If no function has been specified in this manner, **`terminate`** is called by default.

Function **`terminate`** can be called various ways:

- explicitly,
- if a thrown exception can not be caught,
- if the stack is corrupted during exception handling,
- as the default action on a call to **`unexpected`**, and
- during stack unwinding initiated by an exception, an attempt by a destructor to throw an exception causes **`terminate`** to be called.

Function **`set_terminate`** can specify the function that will be called when **`terminate`** is called. Otherwise, **`terminate`** calls **`abort`**.

Prototypes for functions **`set_terminate`** and **`set_unexpected`** are found in header files **`<terminate.h>`** and **`<unexpected.h>`**, respectively.

Functions **`set_terminate`** and **`set_unexpected`** return pointers to the last function called by **`terminate`** and **`unexpected`**. This enables the programmer to save the function pointer so it can be restored later.

Functions **`set_terminate`** and **`set_unexpected`** take pointers to functions as arguments. Each argument must point to a function with **`void`** return type and no arguments.

If the last action of a user-defined termination function is not to exit a program, function **`abort`** will automatically be called to end program execution after the other statements of the user-defined termination function are executed.

## 13.13 Constructors, Destructors, and Exception Handling

First, let us deal with an issue we have mentioned, but that has yet to be satisfactorily resolved. What happens when an error is detected in a constructor? For example, how should a **String** constructor respond when **new** returns zero indicating that it was unable to obtain the space needed to hold the **String**'s internal representation? The problem is that a constructor cannot return a value, so how do we let the outside world know that the object has not been properly constructed? One scheme was simply to return the improperly constructed object and hope that anyone using the object would make appropriate tests to determine that the object was in fact bad. Another scheme is to set some variable outside the constructor. A thrown exception passes to the outside world the information about the failed constructor and the responsibility to deal with the failure.

To catch an exception, the exception handler must have access to a copy constructor for the thrown object (default memberwise copy is also valid).

Exceptions thrown in constructors cause destructors to be called for any objects built as part of the object being constructed before the exception is thrown.

Destructors are called for every automatic object constructed in a **try** block before an exception is thrown (this is called stack unwinding). An exception is handled at the moment the handler begins executing; stack unwinding is guaranteed to have been completed at that point. If a destructor invoked as a result of stack unwinding throws an exception, **terminate** is called.

If an object has member objects and if an exception is thrown before the outer object is fully constructed, then destructors will be executed for the member objects that have been constructed prior to the occurrence of the exception.

If an array of objects has been partially constructed when an exception occurs, only the destructors for the constructed array elements will be called.

Managing resources is tricky when an exception occurs. The exception could preclude the operation of code that would normally release the resource. One technique to resolve this problem is to initialize a local object when the resource is acquired. When an exception occurs, the destructor will be invoked and can free the resource.

It is possible to catch exceptions that are thrown from destructors. Simply enclose the function that calls the destructor in a **try** block and provide a **catch** handler with the proper type.

The thrown object's destructor executes after an exception handler completes execution.

## 13.14 Exceptions and Inheritance

Various exception classes can be derived from a common base class. If a **catch** is written to catch exception objects of a base class type, it can also catch all objects of classes derived from that base class. This can allow for polymorphic processing of related errors.

Using inheritance with exceptions enables an exception handler to catch related errors with a rather concise notation. One could certainly catch each type of derived class exception object individually, but it is more concise to catch the base class exception object instead. Also, catching derived class exception objects individually is subject to error if the programmer forgets to explicitly test for one or more of the derived class types.

## Summary


- Some common examples of exceptions are memory exhaustion, an out-of-bounds array subscript, arithmetic overflow, division by zero, and invalid function parameters.
- The spirit behind exception handling is to enable programs to catch and handle errors rather than letting them occur and simply suffering the consequences. With exception handling, if the programmer does not provide a means of handling a fatal error, the program will terminate; nonfatal errors normally allow a program to continue executing, but produce incorrect results.
- Exception handling is designed for dealing with synchronous errors, i.e., errors that occur as the result of a program's execution.
- Exception handling is not designed to deal with asynchronous situations such as disk I/O completions, network message arrivals, mouse clicks, and the like; these are best handled through other means, such as interrupt processing.
- Exception handling is typically used in situations in which the error will be dealt with by a different part of the program (i.e., a different scope) from that which detected the error.
- Exceptions should not be used as an alternate mechanism for specifying flow of control. Flow of control with conventional control structures is generally clearer and more efficient than with exceptions.
- Exception handling should be used to process exceptions for program components that are not geared to handling those exceptions directly.
- Exception handling should be used to process exceptions from software components such as functions, libraries, and classes that are likely to be widely used, and where it does not make sense for those components to handle their own exceptions.
- Exception handling should be used on large projects to handle error processing in a uniform manner for the entire project.
- C++ exception handling is geared to situations in which the function that detects an error is unable to deal with it. Such a function will throw an exception (also called raising an exception). If the exception matches the type of the parameter in one of the `catch` blocks, the code for that `catch` block is executed. Otherwise, function `terminate` is called, which by default calls function `abort`.
- The programmer encloses in a `try` block the code that may generate an error that will produce an exception. The `try` block is immediately followed by one or more `catch` blocks. Each `catch` block specifies the type of exception it can catch and handle. Each `catch` block contains an exception handler.
- Program control on a thrown exception leaves the `try` block and searches the `catch` blocks in order for an appropriate handler. If no exceptions are thrown in the `try` block, the exception handlers for that block are skipped and the program resumes execution after the last `catch` block.

- Exceptions are thrown in a **try** block in a function or from a function called directly or indirectly from the **try** block.
- Once an exception is thrown, control cannot return directly to the throw point.
- It is possible to communicate information to the exception handler from the point of the exception. That information is the type of thrown object or information placed into the thrown object.
- One of the most popular exception types thrown is **char ***. It is common to simply include an error message as the operand of the **throw**.
- The operand of a **throw** can be of any type. If the operand is an object, we call it an exception object.
- The exceptions thrown by a particular function can be specified with an exception specification. An empty exception specification states that the function will not throw any exceptions.
- Exceptions are caught by the closest exception handler (for the **try** block from which the exception was thrown) specifying an appropriate type.
- As part of throwing an exception, a temporary copy of the **throw** operand is created and initialized. This temporary object then initializes the proper variable in the exception handler. The temporary object is destroyed when the exception handler is exited.
- Errors are not always checked explicitly. A **try** block, for example, may appear to contain no error checking and include no **throw** statements. But code referenced in the **try** block could certainly cause error checking code in constructors to execute.
- An exception terminates the block in which the exception occurred.
- Exception handlers are contained in **catch** blocks. Each **catch** block starts with the keyword **catch** followed by parentheses containing a type and an optional parameter name. This is followed by braces delineating the exception handling code. When an exception is caught, the code in the **catch** block is executed.
- The **catch** handler defines its own scope.
- The parameter in a **catch** handler can be named or unnamed. If the parameter is named, the parameter can be referenced in the handler. If the parameter is unnamed, i.e., only a type is listed for the purpose of matching with the thrown object type or an elipsis for all types, then the handler will ignore the thrown object. The handler may rethrow the object to an outer try block.
- It is possible to specify customized behavior to replace function **terminate** by designating another function to be executed and providing that function's name as the argument in a **set_terminate** function call.
- **catch(...)** means to catch all exceptions.
- It is possible that no handler will match a particular thrown object. This causes the search for a match to continue in an enclosing **try** block.

- The exception handlers are searched in order for an appropriate match. The first handler that yields a match is executed. When that handler finishes executing, control resumes with the first statement after the last **`catch`** block.
- The order of the exception handlers affects how an exception is handled.
- A derived-class object can be caught either by a handler specifying the derived-class type or by handlers specifying the types of any base classes of that derived class.
- Sometimes a program may process many closely related types of exceptions. Instead of providing separate exception classes and **`catch`** handlers for each, a programmer can provide a single exception class and **`catch`** handler for a group of exceptions. As each exception occurs, the exception object can be created with different private data. The **`catch`** handler can examine this private data to distinguish the type of the exception.
- It is possible that even though a precise match is available, a match requiring standard conversions will be made because that handler appears before the one that would result in a precise match.
- By default, if no handler is found for an exception, the program terminates.
- An exception handler cannot directly access variables in the scope of its **`try`** block. Information the handler needs is normally passed in the thrown object.
- Exception handlers can take a closer look at an error and decide to call **`terminate`**. They can rethrow an exception. They can convert one type of exception into another by throwing a different exception. They can perform any necessary recovery and resume execution after the last exception handler. They can look at the situation causing the error, remove the cause of the error, and retry by calling the original function that caused an exception (this would not create infinite recursion). They can simply return some status value to their environment, etc.
- A handler that catches a derived class object should be placed before a handler that catches a base class object. If the base class handler were first, it would catch both the base class objects and the object of classes derived from that base class.
- When an exception is caught, it is possible that resources may have been allocated but not yet released in the **`try`** block. The **`catch`** handler should release these resources.
- It is possible that the handler that catches an exception may decide that it cannot process the exception. In this case, the handler can simply rethrow the exception. A **`throw`** with no arguments rethrows the exception. If no exception was thrown to begin with, then the rethrow causes a call to **`terminate`**.
- Even if a handler can process an exception, and regardless of whether it does any processing on that exception, the handler can rethrow the exception for further processing outside the handler. A rethrown exception is detected by the next enclosing **`try`** block and is handled by an exception handler listed after that enclosing **`try`** block.
- Absence of an exception specification means any exception can be thrown from the function.

- Function **unexpected** calls a function specified with function **set_unexpected**. If no function has been specified in this manner, **terminate** is called by default.
- Function **terminate** can be called in various ways: explicitly; if a thrown exception cannot be caught; if the stack is corrupted during exception handling; as the default action on a call to **unexpected**; or if during stack unwinding initiated by an exception, an attempt by a destructor to throw an exception causes **terminate** to be called.
- Prototypes for functions **set_terminate** and **set_unexpected** are found in header files **<terminate.h>** and **<unexpected.h>**, respectively.
- Functions **set_terminate** and **set_unexpected** return pointers to the last function called, by **terminate** and **unexpected**. This enables the programmer to save the function pointer so it can be restored later.
- Functions **set_terminate** and **set_unexpected** take pointers to functions as arguments. Each argument must point to a function with **void** return type and no arguments.
- If the last action of a user-defined termination function is not to exit a program, function **abort** will automatically be called to end program execution after the other statements of the user-defined termination function are executed.
- An exception thrown outside a **try** block will cause the program to terminate.
- If a handler cannot be found after a **try** block, stack unwinding continues until an appropriate handler is found. If a handler is ultimately not found, then **terminate** is called which by default aborts the program with **abort**.
- Exception specifications list the exceptions that may be thrown from a function. A function may throw the indicated exceptions, or it may throw derived types. If an exception not listed in the exception specification is thrown, **unexpected** is called.
- If a function throws an exception of a particular class type, that function can also throw exceptions of all classes that can be publicly derived from that class.
- To catch an exception, the exception handler must have access to a copy constructor for the thrown object.
- Exceptions thrown from constructors cause destructors to be called for all completed base and member objects of the object being constructed before the exception is thrown.
- If an array of objects has been partially constructed when an exception occurs, only the destructors for the constructed array elements will be called.
- Exceptions thrown from destructors can be caught by enclosing the function that calls the destructor in a **try** block and provide a **catch** handler with the proper type.
- A powerful reason for using inheritance with exceptions is for creating the ability to catch a variety of related errors easily with concise notation. One could certainly catch each type of derived class exception object individually, but it is much more concise to simply catch the base class exception object.

## Terminology

`abort()`
`assert` macro
asynchronous error
callback
catch a group of exceptions
catch all exceptions
catch an exception
`catch` argument
`catch` block
`catch` clause
`catch(...)`
default exception handler
ellipsis (`...`) as a catch type
empty exception specification
empty `throw` specification
enclosing try blocks
exception
exception declaration
exception handler
exception handling
exception list
exception object
exception specification
exceptional condition
`exit()`
fault tolerance
free store exhaustion
function with no exception specification
handle an exception
handler for a base class
handler for a derived class
handler list
mission critical applications
nested exception handlers
`new_handler`
non-error exceptions
raise an exception
resumption model of exception handling
rethrow an exception
robustness
`set_new_handler()`
`set_terminate()`
`set_unexpected()`
stack unwinding
synchronous error
`terminate()`
termination model of exception handling
throw an exception
throw an object
throw an unexpected exception
`throw` expression
`throw` list
`throw` point
`throw` without arguments
thrown argument
thrown exception
`try` block
`try` statement
type of a thrown object
`unexpected()`
uncaught exception
unwinding the stack

## Common Programming Errors

**13.1** Another reason exceptions can be dangerous as an alternative to normal flow of control is that the stack is unwound and resources allocated prior to the occurrence of the exception may not be freed. This problem can be avoided by careful programming.

**13.2** Aborting a program could leave a resource in a state in which other programs would not be able to acquire the resource, and hence we would have a so-called "resource leak."

**13.3** Exceptions should be thrown only within a `try` block. An exception thrown outside a `try` block causes a call to `terminate`.

**13.4** Assuming that after an exception is processed, control will return to the first statement after the throw.

**13.5** Specifying a comma-separated list of catch arguments.

**13.6** Placing `catch(...)` before other `catch` blocks would prevent those blocks from ever being executed; `catch(...)` should always be placed last in the list of handlers following a `try` block, or a syntax error occurs.

**13.7** Placing a `catch` that catches a base class object before a `catch` that catches an object of a class derived from that base class is a syntax error. The base-class `catch` will catch all objects of classes derived from that base class, so the derived class `catch` would never be executed.

**13.8** Placing an exception handler with a `void *` argument type before exception handlers with other pointer types. The `void *` handler will catch all exceptions of pointer types, so the other handlers would never execute.

**13.9** Assuming that an exception thrown from a `catch` handler will be processed by that handler or any other handler associated with the `try` block that threw the exception which caused the original `catch` handler to execute.

**13.10** Placing an empty `throw` statement outside a `catch` handler; executing such a `throw` causes a call to `terminate`.

**13.11** Throwing an exception not in a function's exception specification causes a call to `unexpected`.

## Good Programming Practices

**13.1** Use exceptions for errors that must be processed in a different scope from where they occur. Use other means of error handling for errors that will be processed in the scope in which they occur.

**13.2** Avoid using exception handling for purposes other than error handling because this can reduce program clarity.

**13.3** Use conventional error-handling techniques (rather than exception handling) for straightforward, local error-processing in which a program is easily able to deal with its own errors.

**13.4** Avoid the name Exception for any exception class. This name is too likely to be used by libraries, possibly even the evolving ANSI C++ standard itself.

**13.5** Associating each type of execution-time error with an appropriately named exception object improves program clarity.

## Performance Tips

**13.1** Although it is possible to use exception handling for purposes other than error handling, this can reduce program performance.

**13.2** Exception handling is generally implemented in compilers in such a manner that when an exception does not occur, little or no overhead is imposed by the presence of exception handling code. When exceptions happen, they do incur execution-time overhead.

## Portability Tips

**13.1** As of this writing, an ANSI standard for C++ has not yet been finalized, so it is possible that features described in this chapter may evolve somewhat over the next few years. As we completed this text, the major C++ compiler vendors were starting to introduce versions with exception handling. The experience gained over the next few years with these products should help lead toward a standard implementation.

## Software Engineering Observations

**13.1** Flow of control with conventional control structures is generally clearer and more efficient than with exceptions.

**13.2** Exception-handling is particularly well suited to systems of separately developed components. Such systems are typical of real-world software systems and products. Exception handling makes it easier to combine the components. Each component can perform its own exception detection separate from its handling.

**13.3** When dealing with libraries, the caller of the library function will likely have unique error processing in mind for an exception generated in the library function. It is unlikely that a library function will perform error processing that would meet the unique needs of all users. Therefore, exceptions are an appropriate means for dealing with errors produced by library functions.

**13.4** A key to C++-style exception handling is that the portion of a program or system that will handle the exception can be quite different or distant from the portion of the program that detected and generated the exceptional situation.

**13.5** If it is necessary to pass information about the error that caused an exception, such information can be placed in the thrown object. The `catch` handler would then contain a parameter name through which that information could be referenced.

**13.6** An object can be thrown without containing information to be passed; in this case, mere knowledge that an exception of this type has been raised may provide sufficient information for the handler to do its job correctly.

**13.7** A weakness with catching exceptions with `catch(...)` is that you normally cannot be sure what the exception type is. Another weakness is that without a named parameter, there is no way to refer to the exception object inside the exception handler.

**13.8** The programmer determines the order in which the exception handlers are listed. This order can affect how exceptions originating in that `try` block are handled.

**13.9** It is best to incorporate your exception handling strategy into a system from the inception of the design process. It is difficult to add effective exception handling after a system has been implemented.

**13.10** Another reason not to use exceptions for conventional flow of control is that these "additional" exceptions can get in the way of genuine error-type exceptions. It becomes more difficult for the programmer to keep track of the larger number of exception cases. For example, when a program processes an excessive variety of exceptions, can we really be sure of just what is being caught by a `catch(...)`? Exceptional situations should be rare, not commonplace.

**13.11** Use `catch(...)` to perform recovery that does not depend on the type of the exception, such as releasing common resources. The exception can be rethrown to alert more specific enclosing `catch` blocks.

## Self-Review Exercises

**13.1** List five common examples of exceptions.

**13.2** Give several reasons why exception handling techniques should not be used for conventional program control.

**13.3** Why are exceptions appropriate for dealing with errors produced by library functions?

**13.4** What is a "resource leak?"

**13.5** If no exceptions are thrown in a `try` block, where does control proceed to after the `try` block completes execution?

**13.6** What happens if an exception is thrown outside a `try` block?

**13.7** Give a key advantage and a key disadvantage of using `catch(...)`.

**13.8** What happens if no catch handler matches the type of a thrown object?

**13.9** What happens if several handlers match the type of the thrown object?

**13.10** Why would a programmer specify a base class type as the type of a **catch** handler and then throw objects of derived class types?

**13.11** How might a **catch** handler be written to process related types of errors without using inheritance among exception classes?

**13.12** What pointer type is used in a **catch** handler to catch any exception any pointer type?

**13.13** Suppose a **catch** handler with a precise match to an exception object type is available. Under what circumstances might a different handler be executed for exception objects of that type?

**13.14** Must throwing an exception cause program termination?

**13.15** What happens when a **catch** handler throws an exception?

**13.16** What does the statement **throw;** do?

**13.17** How does the programmer restrict the exception types that can be thrown from a function?

**13.18** What happens if a function does throw an exception of a type not allowed by the exception specification for the function?

**13.19** What happens to the automatic objects that have been constructed in a **try** block when that block throws an exception?

## Answers to Self-Review Exercises

**13.1** Memory exhaustion, array subscript out of bounds, arithmetic overflow, division by zero, invalid function parameters.

**13.2** (a) Exception handling is designed to handle infrequently occurring situations that often result in program termination, so compiler writers are not required to implement exception handling to perform optimally. (b) Flow of control with conventional control structures is generally clearer and more efficient than with exceptions. (c) Problems can occur because the stack is unwound when an exception occurs and resources allocated prior to the exception may not be freed. (d) The "additional" exceptions can get in the way of genuine error-type exceptions. It becomes more difficult for the programmer to keep track of the larger number of exception cases. What does a **catch(...)** really catch?

**13.3** It is unlikely that a library function will perform error processing that will meet the unique needs of all users.

**13.4** An aborting program could leave a resource in a state in which other programs would not be able to acquire the resource.

**13.5** The execption handlers (in the **catch** blocks) for that **try** block are skipped and the program resumes execution after the last **catch** block.

**13.6** An exception thrown outside a **try** block causes a call to **terminate**.

**13.7** The form **catch(...)** catches any type of error thrown in a **try** block. An advantage is that no thrown error can slip by. A disadvantage is that the **catch** handler has no parameter so it cannot reference information in the thrown object; hence, it cannot know the cause of the error.

**13.8** This causes the search for a match to continue in the next enclosing **try** block. As this process continues, it may eventually be determined that there is no handler in the program that matches the type of the thrown object; in this case **terminate** is called, which by default calls **abort**. An alternate **terminate** function can be provided as an argument to **set_terminate**.

**13.9** The first matching exception handler after the `try` block is executed.

**13.10** This is a nice way to catch related types of exceptions.

**13.11** Provide a single exception class and `catch` handler for a group of exceptions. As each exception occurs, the exception object can be created with different private data. The `catch` handler can examine this private data to distinguish the type of the exception.

**13.12** `void *`.

**13.13** A handler requiring standard conversions may appear before one with a precise match.

**13.14** No, but it does terminate the block in which the exception is thrown.

**13.15** The exception will be processed by a `catch` handler (if one exists) associated with the `try` block (if one exists) enclosing the `catch` handler that caused the exception.

**13.16** It rethrows the exception.

**13.17** Provide an exception specification listing the exception types that can be thrown from the function.

**13.18** Function `unexpected` is called.

**13.19** Through the process of stack unwinding, destructors are called for each of these objects.

## *Exercises*

**13.20** List the various exceptional conditions which have occurred in programs throughout this text. List as many additional exceptional conditions as you can. For each of these, describe briefly how a program would typically handle the exception using the exception handling techniques discussed in this chapter. Some typical exceptions are: Division by zero, arithmetic overflow, array subscript out of bounds, exhaustion of the free store, etc.

**13.21** Under what circumstances would the programmer not provide a parameter name when defining the type of the object that will be caught by a handler?

**13.22** A program contains the statement

```
throw;
```

Where would you normally expect to find such a statement? What if that statement appeared in a different part of a program?

**13.23** Under what circumstances would you use the following statement?

```
catch(...) { throw; }
```

**13.24** Compare and contrast exception handling with the various other error-processing schemes discussed in the text.

**13.25** List the benefits of exception handling over conventional means of error-processing.

**13.26** Give several reasons why exceptions should not be used as an alternate form of program control.

**13.27** Describe a technique for handling related exceptions.

**13.28** Until this chapter, we have found that dealing with errors detected by constructors is a bit awkward. Exceptions gives us a much better means of dealing with such errors. Consider a constructor for a `String` class. The constructor uses `new` to obtain space from the free store. Suppose `new` fails. Show how you would deal with this without exception handling. Discuss the key issues. Show how you would deal with such memory exhaustion with exception handling. Explain why the exception handling method is superior.

**13.29** Suppose a program throws an exception and the appropriate exception handler begins executing. Now suppose that the exception handler itself throws the same exception. Does this create an infinite recursion? Write a C++ program to check your observation.

**13.30** Use inheritance to create a base exception class and various derived exception classes. Then show that the `catch` handler specifying the base class catches derived class exceptions.

**13.31** Throwing exceptions with a conditional expression can be tricky. Show a conditional expression that returns either a `double` or an `int`. Provide an `int catch` handler and a `double catch` handler. Show that only the `double catch` handler executes regardless of whether the `int` or the `double` is returned.

**13.32** Write a C++ program designed to generate and handle a memory exhaustion error. Your program should loop on a request to create dynamic storage through operator `new`.

**13.33** Write a C++ program which shows that all destructors for objects constructed in a block are called before an exception is thrown from that block.

**13.34** Write a C++ program which shows that member object destructors are called for only those member objects that were constructed before an exception occurred.

**13.35** Write a C++ program that demonstrates how any exception is caught with `catch(...)`.

**13.36** Write a C++ program which shows that the order of exception handlers is important. The first matching handler is the one that executes. Compile and run your program two different ways to show that two different handlers execute with two different effects.

**13.37** Write a C++ program that shows a constructor passing information about constructor failure to an exception handler after a `try` block.

**13.38** Write a C++ program that uses a multiple inheritance hierarchy of exception classes to create a situation in which the order of exception handlers matters.

**13.39** Using `setjmp/longjmp`, a program can transfer control immediately to an error routine from a deeply nested function invocation. Unfortunately, as the stack is unwound, destructors are not called for the automatic objects that were created during the sequence of nested function calls. Write a C++ program which demonstrates that these destructors are, in fact, not called.

**13.40** Write a C++ program that illustrates rethrowing an exception.

**13.41** Write a C++ program that uses `set_unexpected` to set a user-defined function for `unexpected`, uses `set_unexpected` again, and then resets `unexpected` back to its previous function. Write a similar program to test `set_terminate` and `terminate`.

**13.42** Write a C++ program which shows that a function with its own `try` block does not have to catch every possible error generated within the `try`. Some exceptions can slip through to, and be handled in, other scopes.

**13.43** Write a C++ program that throws an error from a deeply nested function call and still has the `catch` handler following the `try` block enclosing the call chain catch the exception.

# 14

# File Processing and Stream I/O

## Objectives

- To be able to create, read, write, and update files.
- To become familiar with sequential access file processing.
- To become familiar with random access file processing.
- To be able to specify high-performance unformatted I/0 operations.
- To understand the differences between formatted and "raw data" file processing.
- To build a transaction processing program with random access file processing.
- To be able to perform input from, and output to, character strings.

*I read part of it all the way through.*
Samuel Goldwyn

*I can only assume that a "Do Not File" document is filed in a "Do Not File" file.*
Senator Frank Church
Senate Intelligence Subcommittee Hearing, 1975

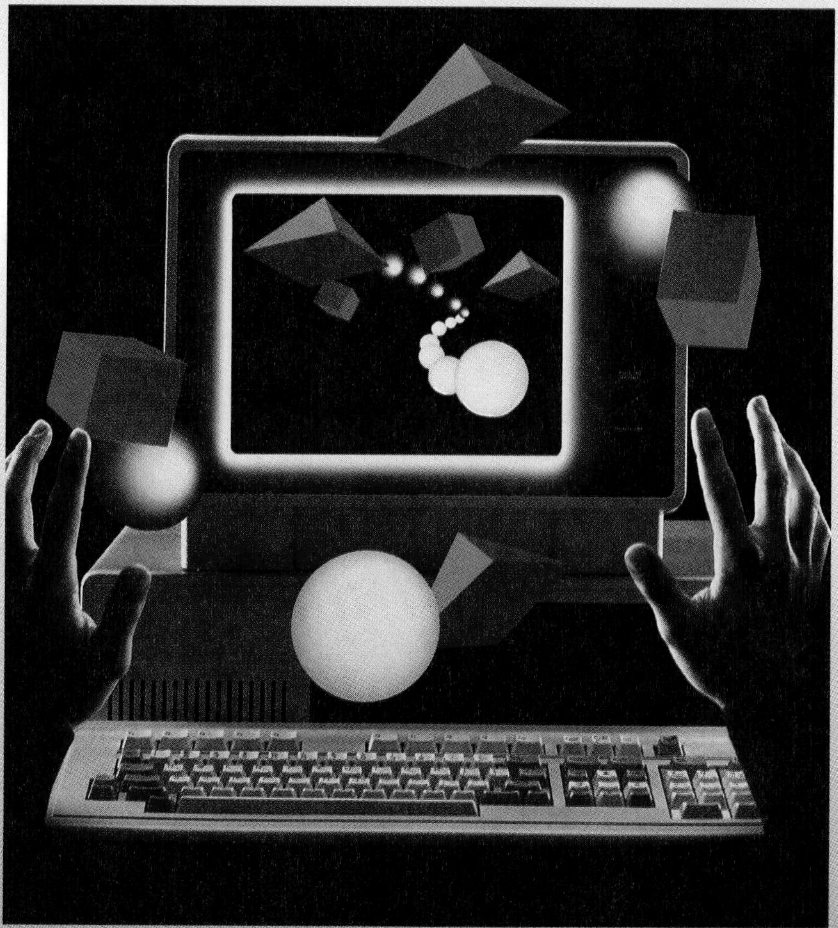

# Outline



## 14.1 Introduction

Storage of data in variables and arrays is temporary. *Files* are used for permanent retention of large amounts of data. Computers store files on *secondary storage devices* such as magnetic disks, optical disks and tapes. In this chapter, we explain how data files are created, updated, and processed by C++ programs. We consider both sequential access files and random access files. We compare formatted data file processing and raw data file processing. We examine the techniques for input of data from, and output of data to, character arrays rather than files.

## 14.2 The Data Hierarchy

Ultimately, all data items processed by a computer are reduced to combinations of zeros and ones. This occurs because it is simple and economical to build electronic devices that can assume two stable states—one state represents `0` and the other state represents `1`. It is remarkable that the impressive functions performed by computers involve only the most fundamental manipulations of `0`s and `1`s.

The smallest data item in a computer can assume the value `0` or the value `1`. Such a data item is called a *bit* (short for "*b*inary dig*it*"—a digit that can assume one of two values). Computer circuitry performs various simple bit manipulations such as examining the value of a bit, setting the value of a bit, and reversing a bit (from `1` to `0` or from `0` to `1`).

It is cumbersome for programmers to work with data in the low-level form of bits. Instead, programmers prefer to work with data in forms such as *decimal digits* (i.e., 0, 1, 2, 3, 4, 5, 6, 7, 8, and 9), *letters* (i.e., A through Z, and a through z), and *special symbols* (i.e., $, @, %, &, *, (, ), -, +, ", :, ?, /, and many others). Digits, letters, and special symbols are referred to as *characters.* The set of all characters used to write programs and represent data items on a particular computer is called that computer's *character set.* Since computers can process only `1`s and `0`s, every character in a computer's character set is represented as a pattern of `1`s and `0`s (called a *byte*). Bytes are most commonly composed of eight bits. Programmers create programs and data items with characters; computers manipulate and process these characters as patterns of bits.

Just as characters are composed of bits, *fields* are composed of characters (or bytes). A field is a group of characters that conveys meaning. For example, a field consisting solely of uppercase and lowercase letters can be used to represent a person's name.

Data items processed by computers form a *data hierarchy* in which data items become larger and more complex in structure as we progress from bits, to characters (bytes), to fields, and so on.

A *record* (i.e., a **`struct`** or a **`class`** in C++) is composed of several fields (called members in C++). In a payroll system, for example, a record for a particular employee might consist of the following fields:

1. Employee identification number
2. Name
3. Address
4. Hourly salary rate
5. Number of exemptions claimed
6. Year-to-date earnings
7. Amount of federal taxes withheld, etc.

Thus, a record is a group of related fields. In the preceding example, each of the fields belongs to the same employee. Of course, a particular company may have many employees, and will have a payroll record for each employee. A *file* is a group of related records. A company's payroll file normally contains one record for each employee. Thus, a payroll file for a small company might contain only 22 records, whereas a payroll file for a large company might contain 100,000 records. It is not unusual for a company to have many files, each containing millions of characters of information. Figure 14.1 illustrates the *data hierarchy.*

To facilitate the retrieval of specific records from a file, at least one field in each record is chosen as a *record key.* A record key identifies a record as belonging to a particular person or entity that is unique from all other records in the file. In the payroll record described previously, the employee identification number would normally be chosen as the record key.

There are many ways of organizing records in a file. The most common type of organization is called a *sequential file* in which records are typically stored in order by the

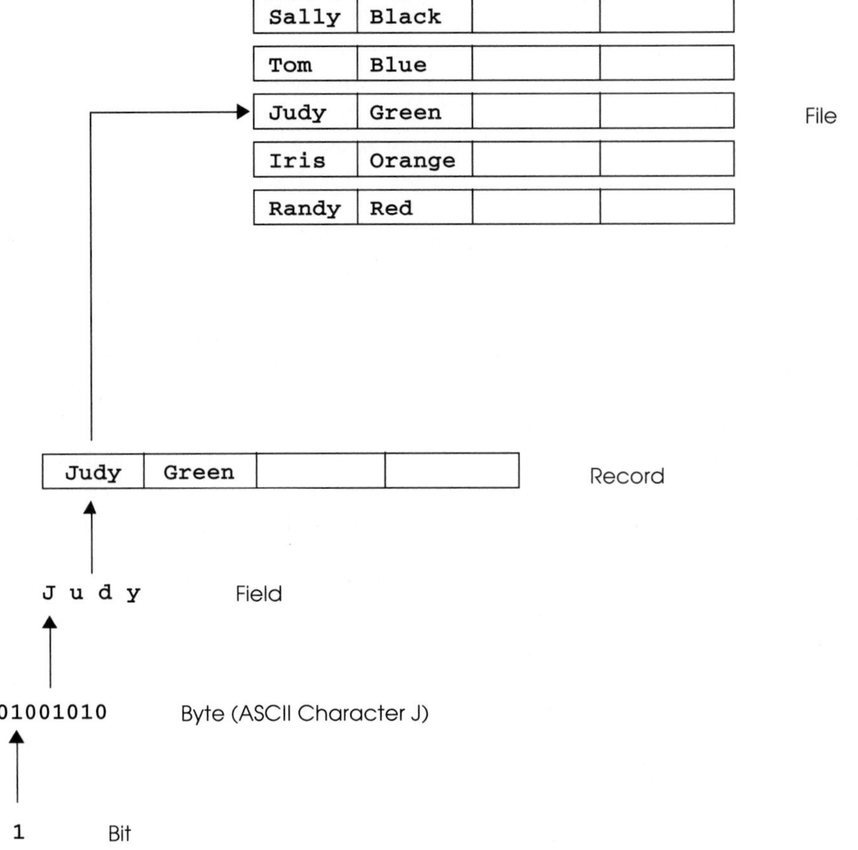


**Fig. 14.1** The data hierarchy.

record key field. In a payroll file, records are usually placed in order by employee identification number. The first employee record in the file contains the lowest employee identification number, and subsequent records contain increasingly higher employee identification numbers.

Most businesses utilize many different files to store data. For example, companies may have payroll files, accounts receivable files (listing money due from clients), accounts payable files (listing money due to suppliers), inventory files (listing facts about all the items handled by the business), and many other types of files. A group of related files is sometimes called a *database*. A collection of programs designed to create and manage databases is called a *database management system* (DBMS).

## 14.3 Files and Streams

C++ views each file simply as a sequential stream of bytes (Fig. 14.2). Each file ends either with an *end-of-file marker* or at a specific byte number recorded in a system-maintained, administrative data structure. When a file is *opened*, an object is created and a

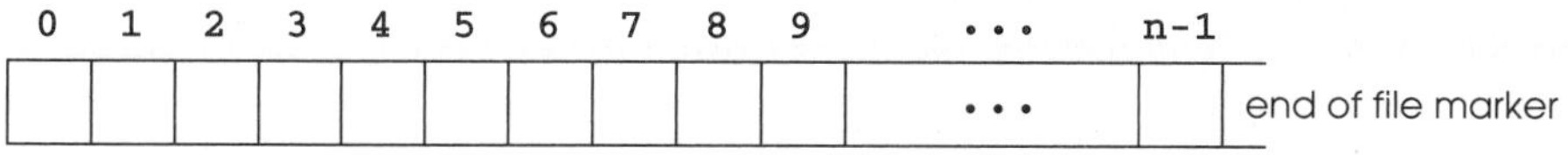

0 1 2 3 4 5 6 7 8 9 ... n-1

... end of file marker

**Fig. 14.2** C++'s view of a file of $n$ bytes.

stream is associated with the object. In Chapter 10, we saw that four objects are created for us automatically—**`cin`**, **`cout`**, **`cerr`**, and **`clog`**. The streams associated with these objects provide communication channels between a program and a particular file or device. For example, the **`cin`** object (standard input stream object) enables a program to input data from the keyboard, the **`cout`** object (standard output stream object) enables a program to output data to the screen, the **`cerr`** and **`clog`** objects (standard error stream objects) enable a program to output error messages to the screen.

To perform file processing in C++, the header files **`<iostream.h>`** and **`<fstream.h>`** must be included. The header **`<fstream.h>`** includes the definitions for the stream classes **`ifstream`** (for input from a file), **`ofstream`** (for output to a file), and **`fstream`** (for input to and output from a file). Files are opened by creating objects of these stream classes. These stream classes are derived from (i.e., inherit the functionality of) classes **`istream`**, **`ostream`**, and **`iostream`**, respectively. Thus, the member functions, operators, and manipulators described in Chapter 10, "C++ Stream Input/Output," can all be applied to file streams as well. The inheritance relationships of the I/O classes discussed to this point are summarized in Fig. 14.3.

## 14.4 Creating a Sequential Access File

C++ imposes no structure on a file. Thus, notions like "record" do not exist in C++ files. Therefore, the programmer must structure files to meet the requirements of applications. In the following example, we see how the programmer can impose a simple record structure on a file. First we present the program, then we analyze it in detail.

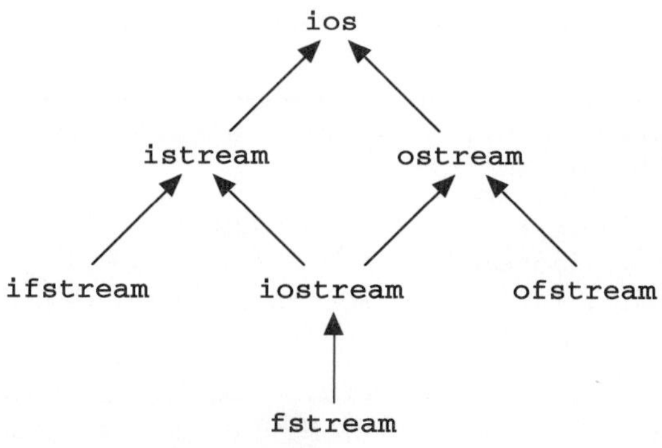


**Fig. 14.3** Portion of stream I/O class hierarchy.

Figure 14.4 creates a simple sequential access file that might be used in an accounts receivable system to help manage the money owed by a company's credit clients. For each client, the program obtains an account number, the client's name, and the client's balance (i.e., the amount the client still owes the company for goods and services received in the past). The data obtained for each client constitutes a record for that client. The account number is used as the record key in this application; that is, the file will be created and maintained in account number order. This program assumes the user enters the records in account number order. In a comprehensive accounts receivable system, a sorting capability would be provided so the user could enter the records in any order—the records would then be sorted and written to the file.

```
// fig14_4.cpp
// Creating a sequential file
#include <iostream.h>
#include <fstream.h>
#include <stdlib.h>

main()
{
   ofstream outClientFile("clients.dat", ios::out);

   if (!outClientFile) {
      cerr << "File could not be opened" << endl;
      exit(1);    // prototype in stdlib.h
   }

   cout << "Enter the account, name, and balance." << endl
        << "Enter EOF to end input." << endl << "? ";

   int account;
   char name[10];
   float balance;

   while (cin >> account >> name >> balance) {
      outClientFile << account << ' ' << name
                    << ' ' << balance << endl;
      cout << "? ";
   }

   return 0;
}
```

```
Enter the account, name, and balance.
Enter EOF to end input.
? 100 Jones 24.98
? 200 Doe 345.67
? 300 White 0.00
? 400 Stone -42.16
? 500 Rich 224.62
? ^Z
```

**Fig. 14.4** Creating a sequential file.

Now let us examine this program. As stated previously, files are opened by creating objects of stream classes **ifstream**, **ofstream**, or **fstream**. In Fig. 14.4, the file is to be opened for output, so an **ofstream** object is created. Two arguments are passed to the object's constructor—the *filename* and the *file open mode*. For an **ofstream** object, the file open mode can be either **ios::out** to output data to a file or **ios::app** to append data to the end of a file (without modifying any data already in the file). Existing files opened with mode **ios::out** are *truncated*—all data in the file is discarded. If the specified file does not yet exist, then a file is created with that filename. The declaration

```
ofstream outClientFile("clients.dat", ios::out);
```

creates an **ofstream** object named **outClientFile** associated with the file **clients.dat** that is opened for output. The arguments **"clients.dat"** and **ios::out** are passed to the **ofstream** constructor which opens the file. This establishes a "line of communication" with the file. The arguments are passed to the **ofstream** constructor function which opens the file. By default, **ofstream** objects are opened for output, so the statement

```
ofstream outClientFile("clients.dat");
```

could have been used to open **clients.dat** for output. Figure 14.5 lists the file open modes.

***Common Programming Error 14.1***

*Opening an existing file for output (**ios::out**) when, in fact, the user wants to preserve the file; the contents of the file are discarded without warning.*

***Common Programming Error 14.2***

*Using an incorrect **ofstream** object to refer to a file.*

| Mode | Description |
|---|---|
| **ios::app** | Write all output to the end of the file. |
| **ios::ate** | Move to the end of the original file when file is opened. Enable data to be written anywhere in the file. |
| **ios::in** | Open a file for input. |
| **ios::out** | Open a file for output. |
| **ios::trunc** | Discard the file's contents if it exists (this is also the default action for **ios::out**) |
| **ios::nocreate** | If the file does not exist, the open operation fails. |
| **ios::noreplace** | If the file exists, the open operation fails. |

**Fig. 14.5** File open modes.

An **ofstream** object can be created without opening a specific file—a file can be attached to the object later. For example, the declaration

```
ofstream outClientFile;
```

creates **ofstream** object named **outClientFile**. The **ofstream** member function **open** opens a file and attaches it to an existing **ofstream** object as follows:

```
outClientFile.open("clients.dat", ios::out);
```

*Common Programming Error 14.3*

*Not opening a file before attempting to reference it in a program.*

After creating an **ofstream** object and attempting to open it, the program tests whether the open operation was successful. The program segment

```
if (!outClientFile) {
   cerr << "File could not be opened" << endl;
   exit(1);
}
```

uses the overloaded **ios** operator member function **operator!** to determine if the open operation succeeded. The condition returns a nonzero (true) value if either the **failbit** or **badbit** are set for the stream on the **open** operation. Some possible errors are attempting to open a nonexistent file for reading, attempting to open a file for reading without permission, and opening a file for writing when no disk space is available.

When the condition indicates that the open attempt was unsuccessful, the error message "**File could not be opened**" is output, and function **exit** is called to end the program. The argument to **exit** is returned to the environment from which the program was invoked. Argument **0** indicates that the program terminated normally; any other value indicates that the program terminated due to an error. The value returned by **exit** is used by the calling environment (most likely the operating system) to respond appropriately to the error.

Another overloaded **ios** operator member function—**operator void***—converts the stream to a pointer so it can be tested as 0 (the null pointer) or nonzero (any other pointer value). If the **failbit** or **badbit** (see Chapter 10) have been set for the stream, **0** (false) is returned. The condition in the following **while** header automatically invokes the **operator void*** member function.

```
while (cin >> account >> name >> balance)
```

The condition will remain true as long as neither the **failbit** nor the **badbit** has been set for **cin**. Entering the end-of-file indicator sets the **failbit** for **cin**. The **operator void *** function can be used to test an input object for end-of-file instead of explicitly calling the **eof** member function on the input object.

If the file is opened successfully, the program begins processing data. The following statement prompts the user to enter the various fields for each record, or to enter end-of-file when data entry is complete:

```
cout << "Enter the account, name, and balance." << endl
     << "Enter EOF to end input." << endl << "? ";
```

Figure 14.6 lists the keyboard combinations for entering end-of-file for various computer systems.

The line

```
while (cin >> account >> name >> balance)
```

inputs each set of data and determines if end-of-file has been entered. When end-of-file or bad data is entered, the stream-extraction operation >> on **cin** returns **0** (normally this stream extraction returns **cin**) and the **while** structure terminates. The user enters end-of-file to inform the program that there is no more data to be processed. The end-of-file indicator is set when the end-of-file key combination is entered by the user. The **while** structure continues looping as long as the end-of-file indicator has not been entered.

The statement

```
outClientFile << account << " " << name
              << " " << balance << endl;
```

writes a set of data to the file **"clients.dat"** using the stream-insertion operator **<<** and the **outClientFile** object associated with the file at the beginning of the program. The data may be retrieved by a program designed to read the file (see Section 14.5). Note that the file created in Fig. 14.4 is a text file. It can be read by any text editor.

Once the end-of-file indicator is entered, **main** terminates. This causes the **outClientFile** object to be destroyed thus invoking its destructor function which closes the file **clients.dat**. An **ofstream** object can explicitly be closed by the programmer using member function **close** as follows:

```
outClientFile.close();
```

***Performance Tip 14.1***

*Explicitly close each file as soon as it is known that the program will not reference the file again. This can reduce resource usage in a program that will continue executing long after it no longer needs to be referencing a particular file. This practice also improves program clarity.*

| Computer system | Keyboard combination | |
|---|---|---|
| UNIX systems | <ctrl> **d** | (on a line by itself) |
| IBM PC and compatibles | <ctrl> **z** | |
| Macintosh | <ctrl> **d** | |
| VAX (VMS) | <ctrl> **z** | |

**Fig. 14.6** End-of-file key combinations for various popular computer systems.

In the sample execution for the program of Fig. 14.4, the user enters information for five accounts, and then signals that data entry is complete by entering end-of-file (**^Z** appears on screens of IBM PC compatibles). This dialog window does not show how the data records actually appear in the file. To verify that the file has been created successfully, in the next section we create a program to read the file and print its contents.

## 14.5 Reading Data from a Sequential Access File

Data are stored in files so that they may be retrieved for processing when needed. The previous section demonstrated how to create a file for sequential access. In this section, we discuss how to read data sequentially from a file.

The program of Fig. 14.7 reads records from the file **"clients.dat"** created by the program of Fig. 14.4 and prints the contents of the records. Files are opened for input by creating an **ifstream** class object. Two arguments are passed to the object—the filename and the file open mode. The declaration

```
ifstream inClientFile("clients.dat", ios::in);
```

creates an **ifstream** object called **inClientFile** and associates with it the file **clients.dat** that is to be opened for input. The arguments in parentheses are passed to the **ifstream** constructor function which opens the file and establishes a "line of communication" with the file. Objects of class **ifstream** are opened for input by default, so the statement

```
ifstream inClientFile("clients.dat");
```

could have been used to open **clients.dat** for input. Just as with an **ofstream** object, an **ifstream** object can be created without opening a specific file and a file can be attached to it later.

*Good Programming Practice 14.1*

*Open a file for input only (using* **ios::in***) if the contents of the file should not be modified. This prevents unintentional modification of the file's contents. This is an example of the principle of least privilege.*

The program uses the condition **!inClientFile** to determine whether the file was opened successfully before attempting to retrieve data from the file. The line

```
while (inClientFile >> account >> name >> balance)
```

reads a set of data (i.e., a record) from the file. After the preceding line is executed the first time, **account** has the value **100**, **name** has the value **"Jones"**, and **balance** has the value **24.98**. Each time the line is executed, another record is read from the file into the variables **account**, **name**, and **balance**. The records are displayed using function **outputLine** which uses parameterized stream manipulators to format the data for display. When the end of the file has been reached, the input sequence in the **while** structure returns **0** (normally the stream **inClientFile** is returned), the file is closed by the **ifstream** destructor function, and the program terminates.

```
// fig14_7.cpp
// Reading and printing a sequential file
#include <iostream.h>
#include <fstream.h>
#include <iomanip.h>
#include <stdlib.h>

void outputLine(int, char*, float);

main()
{
   ifstream inClientFile("clients.dat", ios::in);

   if (!inClientFile) {
      cerr << "File could not be opened" << endl;
      exit(1);
   }

   int account;
   char name[10];
   float balance;

   cout << setiosflags(ios::left) << setw(10) << "Account"
        << setw(13) << "Name" << "Balance" << endl;

   while (inClientFile >> account >> name >> balance)
      outputLine(account, name, balance);

   return 0;
}

void outputLine(int acct, char *name, float bal)
{
   cout << setiosflags(ios::left) << setw(10) << acct
        << setw(13) << name << setw(7) << setprecision(2)
        << setiosflags(ios::showpoint | ios::right)
        << bal << endl;
}
```

```
Account   Name         Balance
100       Jones          24.98
200       Doe           345.67
300       White           0.00
400       Stone         -42.16
500       Rich          224.62
```

**Fig. 14.7** Reading and printing a sequential file.

To retrieve data sequentially from a file, programs normally start reading from the beginning of the file, and read all the data consecutively until the desired data are found.

It may be necessary to process the file sequentially several times (from the beginning of the file) during the execution of a program. Both the **istream** class and the **ostream** class provide member functions for repositioning the *file position pointer* (the byte number of the next byte in the file to be read or written). These member functions are **seekg** ("seek get") for the **istream** class and **seekp** ("seek put") for the **ostream** class. Each **istream** object has a "get pointer" that indicates the byte number in the file from which the next input is to occur, and each **ostream** object has a "put pointer" that indicates the byte number in the file at which the next output is to be placed. The statement

```
inClientFile.seekg(0);
```

repositions the file position pointer to the beginning of the file (location **0**) attached to **inClientFile**. The argument to **seekg** is normally a **long** integer. A second argument can be specified to indicate the *seek direction*. The seek direction can be **ios::beg** (the default) for positioning relative to the beginning of a stream, **ios::cur** for positioning relative to the current position in a stream, and **ios::end** for positioning relative to the end of a stream. The file position pointer is an integer value that specifies the location in the file as a number of bytes from the starting location of the file (this is sometimes referred to as the *offset* from the beginning of the file). Some examples of positioning the "get" file position pointer are:

```
// position to the nth byte of fileObject
// assumes ios::beg
fileObject.seekg(n);

// position n bytes forward in fileObject
fileObject.seekg(n, ios::cur);

// position y bytes back from end of fileObject
fileObject.seekg(y, ios::end);

// position at end of fileObject
fileObject.seekg(0, ios::end);
```

The same operations can be performed with **ostream** member function **seekp**. Member functions **tellg** and **tellp** are provided to return the current locations of the "get" and "put" pointers, respectively. The following statement assigns the "get" file position pointer value to variable **location** of type **long**.

```
location = filObject.tellg();
```

The program of Fig. 14.8 enables a credit manager to display the account information for those customers with zero balances (i.e., customers who do not owe the company any money), credit balances (i.e., customers to whom the company owes money), and debit balances (i.e., customers who owe the company money for goods and services received in the past). The program displays a menu and allows the credit manager to enter one of three options to obtain credit information. Option 1 produces a list of accounts with zero balances. Option 2 produces a list of accounts with credit balances. Option 3 produces a list of accounts with debit balances. Option 4 terminates program execution. A sample output is shown in Fig. 14.9.

```
// fig14_8.cpp
// Credit inquiry program
#include <iostream.h>
#include <fstream.h>
#include <iomanip.h>
#include <stdlib.h>

void outputLine(int, char*, float);

main()
{
   ifstream inClientFile("clients.dat", ios::in);

   if (!inClientFile) {
      cerr << "File could not be opened" << endl;
      exit(1);
   }

   cout << "Enter request" << endl
        << " 1 - List accounts with zero balances" << endl
        << " 2 - List accounts with credit balances" << endl
        << " 3 - List accounts with debit balances" << endl
        << " 4 - End of run" << endl << "? ";

   int request;
   cin >> request;

   while (request != 4) {
      int account;
      char name[10];
      float balance;

      inClientFile >> account >> name >> balance;

      switch (request) {
         case 1:
            cout << endl << "Accounts with zero balances:" <<
endl;

            while (!inClientFile.eof()) {
               if (balance == 0)
                  outputLine(account, name, balance);

               inClientFile >> account >> name >> balance;
            }

            break;
         case 2:
            cout << endl << "Accounts with credit balances:"
                 << endl;

            while (!inClientFile.eof()) {
               if (balance < 0)
                  outputLine(account, name, balance);

               inClientFile >> account >> name >> balance;
            }

            break;
```

Fig. 14.8 Credit inquiry program (part 1 of 2).

```
            case 3:
               cout << endl << "Accounts with debit balances:"
                    << endl;

               while (!inClientFile.eof()) {
                  if (balance > 0)
                     outputLine(account, name, balance);

                  inClientFile >> account >> name >> balance;
               }

               break;
         }

         inClientFile.clear();   // reset eof for next input
         inClientFile.seekg(0); // position to beginning of file
         cout << endl << "? ";
         cin >> request;
      }

      cout << "End of run." << endl;

      return 0;
   }

   void outputLine(int acct, char *name, float bal)
   {
      cout << setiosflags(ios::left) << setw(10) << acct
           << setw(13) << name << setw(7) << setprecision(2)
           << setiosflags(ios::showpoint | ios::right)
           << bal << endl;
   }
```

**Fig. 14.8** Credit inquiry program (part 2 of 2).

## 14.6 Updating Sequential Access Files

Data that is formatted and written to a sequential access file as shown in Section 14.4 cannot be modified without the risk of destroying other data in the file. For example, if the name "`White`" needed to be changed to "`Worthington`", the old name cannot simply be overwritten. The record for `White` was written to the file as

```
300 White 0.00
```

If this record is rewritten beginning at the same location in the file using the longer name, the record would be

```
300 Worthington 0.00
```

The new record contains six more characters than the original record. Therefore, the characters beyond the second "`o`" in "`Worthington`" would overwrite the beginning of the next sequential record in the file. The problem here is that in the formatted input/output model using the insertion operator `<<` and the extraction operator `>>`, fields—

```
Enter request
 1 - List accounts with zero balances
 2 - List accounts with credit balances
 3 - List accounts with debit balances
 4 - End of run
? 1

Accounts with zero balances:
300         White              0.00

? 2

Accounts with credit balances:
400         Stone            -42.16

? 3

Accounts with debit balances:
100         Jones             24.98
200         Doe              345.67
500         Rich             224.62

? 4
End of run.
```

**Fig. 14.9** Sample output of the credit inquiry program of Fig. 14.8.

and hence records—can vary in size. For example, 7, 14, –117, 2074, and 27383 are all **int**s and each is stored in the same number of "raw data" bytes internally, but when these integers are output as formatted text to the screen or to a file on disk, they become different-sized fields. Therefore, the formatted input/output model is not usually used to update records in place.

Such updating can be done, but it is awkward. For example, to make the preceding name change, the records before **300 White 0.00** in a sequential access file could be copied to a new file, the updated record would then be written to the new file, and the records after **300 White 0.00** would be copied to the new file. This requires processing every record in the file to update one record. If many records are being updated in one pass of the file, then this technique can be acceptable.

## 14.7 Random Access Files

So far, we have seen how to create sequential access files and to search through them to locate particular information. Sequential access files are inappropriate for so-called *"instant-access" applications* in which a particular record of information must be located immediately, Some popular instant access applications are airline reservation systems, banking systems, point-of-sale systems, automated teller machines and other kinds of *transaction processing systems* that require rapid access to specific data. The bank at which you have your account may have hundreds of thousands or even millions of other customers, yet when you use an automated teller machine, your account is checked for sufficient funds in seconds. This kind of instant access is possible with *random access files*. Individual records of a random access file can be accessed directly (and quickly) without searching through other records.

As we have said, C++ does not impose structure on a file. So the application that wants to use random access files must literally create them. A variety of techniques can be used to create random access files. Perhaps the simplest is to require that all records in a file are of the same fixed length.

Using fixed length records makes it easy for a program to calculate (as a function of the record size and the record key) the exact location of any record relative to the beginning of the file. We will soon see how this facilitates immediate access to specific records, even in large files.

Figure 14.10 illustrates C++'s view of a random access file composed of fixed-length records (each record is 100 bytes long). A random access file is like a railroad train with many cars—some empty and some with contents.

Data can be inserted in a random access file without destroying other data in the file. Data stored previously also can be updated or deleted without rewriting the entire file. In the following sections we explain how to create a random access file, enter data, read the data both sequentially and randomly, update the data, and delete data no longer needed.

## 14.8 Creating a Random Access File

The **ostream** member function **write** outputs a fixed number of bytes beginning at a specific location in memory to the specified stream. When the stream is associated with a file, the data is written beginning at the location in the file specified by the "put" file position pointer. The **istream** member function **read** inputs a fixed number of bytes from the specified stream to an area in memory beginning at a specified address. If the stream is associated with a file, the bytes are input beginning at the location in the file specified by the "get" file position pointer.

Now, when writing an integer **number** to a file, instead of using

```
outFile << number;
```

which could print as few as 1 digit or as many as 11 digits (10 digits plus a sign, each of which requires 1 byte of storage) for a 4-byte integer, we can use

```
outFile.write((char *)&number, sizeof(number));
```

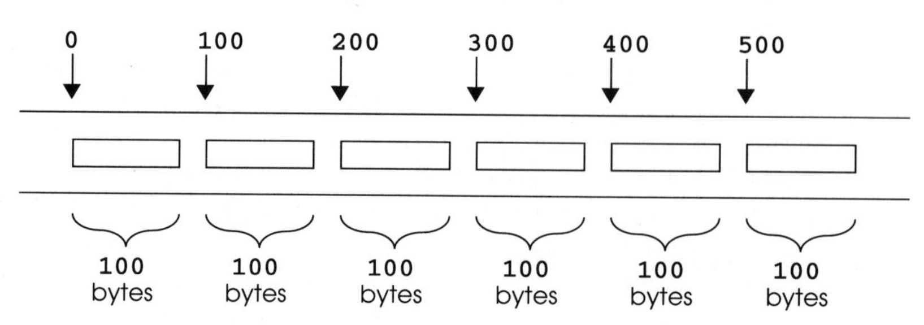


**Fig. 14.10** C++'s view of a random access file.

which always writes 4 bytes (on a machine with 4-byte integers). The **write** function expects a first argument of type **char ***, hence we used the **(char *)** cast. The second argument of **write** is an integer of type **size_t** specifying the number of bytes to be written. As we will see, **istream** function **read** can then be used to read the 4 bytes back into integer variable **number**.

Random access file processing programs rarely write a single field to a file. Normally, they write one **struct** or **class** object at a time, as we show in the following examples.

Consider the following problem statement:

*Create a credit processing program capable of storing up to 100 fixed-length records for a company that can have up to 100 customers. Each record should consist of an account number that will be used as the record key, a last name, a first name, and a balance. The program should be able to update an account, insert a new account, delete an account, and list all the account records in a formatted text file for printing.*

The next several sections introduce the techniques necessary to create this credit processing program. Figure 14.11 illustrates opening a random access file, defining the record format using a **struct**, and writing data to the disk. This program initializes all

```
// fig14_11.cpp
// Creating a random access file sequentially
#include <iostream.h>
#include <fstream.h>
#include <stdlib.h>

struct clientData {
   int acctNum;
   char lastName[15];
   char firstName[10];
   float balance;
};

main()
{
   ofstream outCredit("credit.dat", ios::out);

   if (!outCredit) {
      cerr << "File could not be opened." << endl;
      exit(1);
   }

   clientData blankClient = {0, "", "", 0.0};

   for (int i = 1; i <= 100; i++)
      outCredit.write((char *)&blankClient, sizeof(blankClient));

   return 0;
}
```

**Fig. 14.11** Creating a random access file sequentially.

100 records of the file **"credit.dat"** with empty **struct**s using function **write**. Each empty **struct** contains **0** for the account number, the null string (represented by empty quotation marks) for the last name, the null string for the first name, and **0.0** for the balance. The file is initialized the proper amount of empty space in which the account data will be stored, and to determine in subsequent programs if each record is empty or contains data.

In Fig. 14.11, the statement

```
outCredit.write((char *)&blankClient, sizeof(blankClient));
```

causes the structure **blankClient** of size **sizeof(blankClient)** to be written to the **credit.dat** file associated with **ofstream** object **outCredit**. Remember that operator **sizeof** returns the size in bytes of the object contained in parentheses (see Chapter 5).

## 14.9 Writing Data Randomly to a Random Access File

The program of Fig. 14.12 writes data to the file **"credit.dat"**. It uses the combination of **ostream** functions **seekp** and **write** to store data at exact locations in the file. Function **seekp** sets the "put" file position pointer to a specific position in the file, then **write** outputs the data. A sample execution is shown in Fig. 14.13.

The statement

```
outCredit.seekp((client.acctNum - 1) * sizeof(client));
```

positions the "put" file position pointer for object **outCredit** to the byte location calculated by **(client.acctNum - 1) * sizeof(client)**. Since the account number is between 1 and 100, 1 is subtracted from the account number when calculating the byte location of the record. Thus, for record 1, the file position pointer is set to byte 0 of the file. Note that the **ofstream** object **outCredit** is opened with file open mode **ios::ate**. The "put" file position pointer is set to the end of the file initially, but data can be written anywhere in the file.

## 14.10 Reading Data Sequentially from a Random Access File

In the previous sections, we created a random access file and wrote data to that file. In this section, we develop a program that reads through the file sequentially and prints only those records containing data. These programs produce an additional benefit. See if you can determine what it is; we will reveal it at the end of this section.

The **istream** function **read** inputs a specified number of bytes from the current position in the specified stream into an object. For example, the statement

```
inCredit.read((char *)&client, sizeof(client));
```

from Fig 14.14 reads the number of bytes specified by **sizeof(client)** from the file associated with **ifstream** object **inCredit** and stores the data in the structure **client**. Note that function **read** requires a first argument of type **char ***. Since **&client** is of type **clientData ***, **&client** must be cast to **char ***.

```
// fig14_12.cpp
// Writing to a random access file
#include <iostream.h>
#include <fstream.h>
#include <stdlib.h>

struct clientData {
   int acctNum;
   char lastName[15];
   char firstName[10];
   float balance;
};

main()
{
   ofstream outCredit("credit.dat", ios::ate);

   if (!outCredit) {
      cerr << "File could not be opened." << endl;
      exit(1);
   }

   cout << "Enter account number "
        << "(1 to 100, 0 to end input)" << endl << "? ";

   clientData client;
   cin >> client.acctNum;

   while (client.acctNum > 0 && client.acctNum <= 100) {
      cout << "Enter lastname, firstname, balance" << endl << "?
";
      cin >> client.lastName >> client.firstName >>
client.balance;
      outCredit.seekp((client.acctNum - 1) * sizeof(client));
      outCredit.write((char *)&client, sizeof(client));
      cout << "Enter account number" << endl << "? ";
      cin >> client.acctNum;
   }

   return 0;
}
```

**Fig. 14.12** Writing data randomly to a random access file.

The program of Fig. 14.14 reads sequentially through every record in the **"credit.dat"** file, checks each record to see if it contains data, and displays formatted outputs for records containing data. The condition

```
!inCredit.eof()
```

uses the **ios** member function **eof** to determine when the end of the file is reached and causes execution of the **while** structure to terminate. The data input from the file are output by function **outputLine** which takes two arguments—an **ostream** object and a **clientData** structure to be output.

```
Enter account number (1 to 100, 0 to end input)
? 37
Enter lastname, firstname, balance
? Barker Doug 0.00
Enter account number
? 29
Enter lastname, firstname, balance
? Brown Nancy -24.54
Enter account number
? 96
Enter lastname, firstname, balance
? Stone Sam 34.98
Enter account number
? 88
Enter lastname, firstname, balance
? Smith Dave 258.34
Enter account number
? 33
Enter lastname, firstname, balance
? Dunn Stacey 314.33
Enter account number
? 0
```

**Fig. 14.13** Sample execution of the program in Fig. 14.12.

What about that additional benefit we promised? If you examine the output window, you will notice that the records are listed in sorted order (by account number)! This is a simple consequence of the way we stored these records in the file using direct access techniques. Compared to the bubble sort we have seen (Chapter 4), sorting with direct access techniques is blazingly fast. The speed is achieved by making the file large enough to hold every possible record that might be created. This of course, means that the file could be sparsely occupied most of the time, a waste of storage. So here is yet another example of the space-time tradeoff: By using large amounts of space, we are able to develop a much faster sorting algorithm.

## 14.11 Example: A Transaction Processing Program

We now present a substantial transaction processing program (Fig. 14.15) using a random access file to achieve "instant" access processing. The program maintains a bank's account information. The program updates existing accounts, adds new accounts, deletes accounts, and stores a formatted listing of all the current accounts in a text file for printing. We assume that the program of Fig. 14.11 has been executed to create the file **`credit.dat`** and that the program of Fig. 14.12 has been executed to insert the initial data.

The program has five options. Option 1 calls function **`textFile`** to store a formatted list of all the account information in a text file called **`print.txt`** that may be printed later. Function **`textFile`** takes an **`fstream`** object as an argument to be used

```
// fig14_14.cpp
// Reading a random access file sequentially
#include <iostream.h>
#include <iomanip.h>
#include <fstream.h>
#include <stdlib.h>

struct clientData {
   int acctNum;
   char lastName[15];
   char firstName[10];
   float balance;
};

void outputLine(ostream&, clientData);

main()
{
   ifstream inCredit("credit.dat", ios::in);

   if (!inCredit) {
      cerr << "File could not be opened." << endl;
      exit(1);
   }

   cout << setiosflags(ios::left) << setw(6) << "Acct"
        << setw(16) << "Last Name" << setw(11)
        << "First Name" << setiosflags(ios::right)
        << setw(10) << "Balance" << endl;

   clientData client;

   inCredit.read((char *)&client, sizeof(clientData));

   while (!inCredit.eof()) {

      if (client.acctNum != 0)
         outputLine(cout, client);

      inCredit.read((char *)&client, sizeof(clientData));
   }

   return 0;
}

void outputLine(ostream &output, clientData c)
{
   output << setiosflags(ios::left) << setw(6) << c.acctNum
          << setw(16) << c.lastName << setw(11) << c.firstName
          << setw(10) << setprecision(2)
          << setiosflags(ios::showpoint | ios::right)
          << c.balance << endl;
}
```

**Fig. 14.14** Reading a random access file sequentially (part 1 of 2).

```
Acct  Last Name        First Name    Balance
29    Brown            Nancy          -24.54
33    Dunn             Stacey         314.33
37    Barker           Doug             0.00
88    Smith            Dave           258.34
96    Stone            Sam             34.98
```

**Fig. 14.14** Reading a random access file sequentially (part 2 of 2).

to input data from the **credit.dat** file. Function **textFile** uses **istream** member function **read** and the sequential file access techniques of Fig. 14.14 to input data from **credit.dat**. Function **outputLine** discussed in Section 14.10 is used to output the data to file **print.txt**. Note that **textFile** uses **istream** member function **seekg** to ensure that the file position pointer is at the beginning of the file. After choosing Option 1 the file **print.txt** contains:

```
Acct  Last Name        First Name    Balance
29    Brown            Nancy          -24.54
33    Dunn             Stacey         314.33
37    Barker           Doug             0.00
88    Smith            Dave           258.34
96    Stone            Sam             34.98
```

Option 2 calls the function **updateRecord** to update an account. The function will only update an existing record, so the function first determines if the specified record is empty. The record is read into structure **client** with **istream** member function **read**, then **client.acctNum** is compared to zero to determine if the record contains information. If **client.acctNum** is zero, a message is printed stating that the record is empty and the menu choices are displayed. If the record contains information, function **updateRecord** displays the record on the screen using function **outputLine**, inputs the transaction amount, calculates the new balance, and rewrites the record to the file. A typical output for Option 2 is:

```
Enter account to update (1 - 100): 37
37    Barker           Doug                0.00

Enter charge (+) or payment (-): +87.99
37    Barker           Doug               87.99
```

Option 3 calls the function **newRecord** to add a new account to the file. If the user enters an account number for an existing account, **newRecord** displays a message that the account exists, and displays the menu choices. This function adds a new account in the same manner as the program of Fig. 14.12. A typical output for Option 3 is:

```
Enter new account number (1 - 100): 22
Enter lastname, firstname, balance
? Johnston Sarah 247.45
```

Option 4 calls function **deleteRecord** to delete a record from the file. The user is prompted to enter the account number. Only an existing record may be deleted, so if the specified account is empty, an error message is issued. If the account exists, it is reinitialized by copying an empty record (**blankClient**) to the file. A message is displayed to inform the user that the record has been deleted. A typical output for Option 4 is

```
Enter account number to delete (1 - 100): 29
Account #29 deleted.
```

Option 5 terminates program execution. The program is shown in Fig. 14.15. The file **"credit.dat"** is opened by creating an **fstream** object for reading and writing using modes **ios::in** and **ios::out** "or-ed" together.

```
// fig14_15.cpp
// This program reads a random access file sequentially,
// updates data already written to the file, creates new
// data to be placed in the file, and deletes data
// already in the file.
#include <iostream.h>
#include <fstream.h>
#include <iomanip.h>
#include <stdlib.h>

struct clientData {
   int acctNum;
   char lastName[15];
   char firstName[10];
   float balance;
};

int enterChoice(void);
void textFile(fstream&);
void updateRecord(fstream&);
void newRecord(fstream&);
void deleteRecord(fstream&);
void outputLine(ostream&, clientData);
```

**Fig. 14.15** Bank account program (part 1 of 4).

```
main()
{
   fstream inOutCredit("credit.dat", ios::in | ios::out);

   if (!inOutCredit) {
      cerr << "File could not be opened." << endl;
      exit (1);
   }

   int choice;

   while ( ( choice = enterChoice() ) != 5 ) {

      switch (choice) {
         case 1:
            textFile(inOutCredit);
            break;
         case 2:
            updateRecord(inOutCredit);
            break;
         case 3:
            newRecord(inOutCredit);
            break;
         case 4:
            deleteRecord(inOutCredit);
            break;
         default:
            cerr << "Incorrect choice" << endl;
            break;
      }

      inOutCredit.clear();  // resets end-of-file indicator
   }

   return 0;
}

// Prompt for and input menu choice
int enterChoice(void)
{
   cout << endl << "Enter your choice" << endl
        << "1 - store a formatted text file of accounts" << endl
        << "    called \"print.txt\" for printing" << endl
        << "2 - update an account" << endl
        << "3 - add a new account" << endl
        << "4 - delete an account" << endl
        << "5 - end program" << endl << "? ";

   int menuChoice;
   cin >> menuChoice;
   return menuChoice;
}
```

**Fig. 14.15** Bank account program (part 2 of 4).

```
// Create formatted text file for printing
void textFile(fstream &readFromFile)
{
   ofstream outPrintFile("print.txt", ios::out);

   if (!outPrintFile) {
      cerr << "File could not be opened." << endl;
      exit(1);
   }

   outPrintFile << setiosflags(ios::left) << setw(6) << "Acct"
        << setw(16) << "Last Name" << setw(11) << "First Name"
        << setiosflags(ios::right) << setw(10) << "Balance" <<
endl;
   readFromFile.seekg(0);

   clientData client;
   readFromFile.read((char *)&client, sizeof(client));

   while (!readFromFile.eof()) {
      if (client.acctNum != 0)
         outputLine(outPrintFile, client);

      readFromFile.read((char *)&client, sizeof(client));
   }
}

// Update an account's balance
void updateRecord(fstream &updateFile)
{
   int account;

   do {
      cout << "Enter account to update (1 - 100): ";
      cin >> account;
   } while (account < 1 || account > 100);

   updateFile.seekg((account - 1) * sizeof(client));

   clientData client;
   updateFile.read((char *)&client, sizeof(client));

   if (client.acctNum != 0) {
      outputLine(cout, client);
      cout << endl << "Enter charge (+) or payment (-): ";

      float transaction;
      cin >> transaction;
      client.balance += transaction;
      outputLine(cout, client);
      updateFile.seekp((account - 1) * sizeof(client));
      updateFile.write((char *)&client, sizeof(client));
   }
   else
      cerr << "Acount #" << account
           << " has no information." << endl;
}
```

Fig. 14.15 Bank account program (part 3 of 4).

```
// Create and insert new record
void newRecord(fstream &insertInFile)
{
   cout << "Enter new account number (1 - 100): ";

   int account;
   cin >> account;
   insertInFile.seekg((account - 1) * sizeof(client));

   clientData client;
   insertInFile.read((char *)&client, sizeof(client));

   if (client.acctNum == 0) {
     cout << "Enter lastname, firstname, balance" << endl << "? ";
     cin >> client.lastName >> client.firstName >> client.balance;
     client.acctNum = account;
     insertInFile.seekp((account - 1) * sizeof(clientData));
     insertInFile.write((char *)&client, sizeof(clientData));
   }
   else
     cerr << "Account #" << account
          << " already contains information." << endl;
}

// Delete an existing record
void deleteRecord(fstream &deleteFromFile)
{
   cout << "Enter account number to delete (1 - 100): ";

   int account;
   cin >> account;
   deleteFromFile.seekg((account - 1) * sizeof(client));

   clientData client;
   deleteFromFile.read((char *)&client, sizeof(client));

   if (client.acctNum != 0) {
     clientData blankClient = {0, "", "", 0};

     deleteFromFile.seekp((account - 1) * sizeof(client));
     deleteFromFile.write((char *)&blankClient, sizeof(client));
     cout << "Account #" << account << " deleted." << endl;
   }
   else
     cout << "Account #" << account << " is empty." << endl;
}

// Output a line of client information
void outputLine(ostream &output, clientData c)
{
   output << setiosflags(ios::left)  << setw(6) << c.acctNum
          << setw(16) << c.lastName << setw(11) << c.firstName
          << setiosflags(ios::showpoint | ios::right)
          << setw(10) << setprecision(2) << c.balance << endl;
}
```

**Fig. 14.15** Bank account program (part 4 of 4).

## 14.12 String Stream Processing

In addition to standard stream I/O and file stream I/O, C++ stream I/O includes capabilities for inputting from character arrays in memory and outputting to character arrays in memory. These capabilities are often referred to as *in-core I/O, in-memory I/O,* or *string stream processing*.

Input from a character array is supported by class **istrstream**. Output to a character array is supported by class **ostrstream**. Class **istrstream** inherits the functionality of class **istream**. Class **ostrstream** inherits the functionality of class **ostream**. Programs that use in-core formatting must include the **<strstream.h>** and **<iostream.h>** header files.

One application of these techniques is data validation. A program can read an entire line at a time from the input stream into a character array. Then a validation routine can scrutinize the contents of the array and correct (or repair) the data, if necessary. Then the program can proceed to input from the character array, knowing that all the input data is in the proper format.

Outputting to a character array is a nice way to take advantage of the powerful output formatting capabilities of C++ streams. Data can be prepared in a character array to mimic the edited screen format. That array could then be written to a disk file to preserve the screen image.

An **ostrstream** object can be used two ways. The first use dynamically allocates a character array for output that is sent to the **ostrstream** object. Once output is complete, the object can be "frozen" with the **str** member function to prevent further output from being sent to the object. The **str** member function returns a **char*** pointer to the beginning of the array object in memory. This pointer can be assigned to a **char*** variable and referenced like any character array in C++.

Figure 14.16 demonstrates a dynamically allocated **ostrstream** object. The program creates **ostrstream** object **outputString** and uses the stream-insertion operator to output a series of strings and numerical values to the object. The stream manipulator **ends** inserts a null character (**'\0'**) at the end of the data output to **outputString**. The program then freezes the contents of **outputString** with the **str** member function and assigns pointer variable **result** a pointer to the beginning of the array in memory. The array is then output as a string. The program tests the state of the **outputString** stream before insertion and after function **str** is called on the stream and another insertion is attempted.

The second use of an **ostrstream** object passes three arguments to the **ostrstream** constructor—a character array, the length of the array, and a stream open mode (**ios::out** or **ios::app**). When **ios::app** is specified, the character array is assumed to be a null-terminated string, and insertion begins at the null character.

Figure 14.17 demonstrates the use of an **ostrstream** object with a previously defined array. The declaration

```
ostrstream outputString(buffer, size, ios::out);
```

creates the object **outputString** that will use character array **buffer** of **size** elements to store the output directed to **outputString**. Since the size of the array is

```
// fig14_16.cpp
// Using a dynamically allocated ostrstream object.
#include <iostream.h>
#include <strstream.h>

main()
{
   ostrstream outputString;
   char *s1 = "Output of several data types ",
        *s2 = "to an ostrstream object:",
        *s3 = "\n       double: ",
        *s4 = "\n          int: ",
        *s5 = "\naddress of int: ",
        *result;
   double d = 123.4567;
   int i = 22;

   cout << "outputString state before insertion: "
        << outputString.rdstate() << endl;

   outputString << s1 << s2 << s3 << d
                << s4 << i << s5 << &i << ends;

   result = outputString.str();

   outputString << "TEST INSERTION AFTER str IS CALLED";

   cout << endl << "outputString state after str is called" <<
endl
        << "and another insertion is attempted: "
        << outputString.rdstate() << endl << endl
        << "The dynamically created string contains:" << endl
        << endl << result << endl;

   return 0;
}
```

```
outputString state before insertion: 0

outputString state after str is called
and another insertion is attempted: 4

The dynamically created string contains:

Output of several data types to an ostrstream object:
       double: 123.4567
          int: 22
address of int: 0xffe0
```

**Fig. 14.16** Using a dynamically allocated **ostrstream** object.

known in advance, **outputString** can perform its own error checking. If an attempt is made to output data to **outputString** where the data would be stored past the end of array **buffer**, the **failbit** (which we have discussed in Chapter 10) will be set, and the output operation will not occur. The program outputs a string, an integer, and a terminating null character to **buffer**, then outputs the contents of **buffer**. The program tests the state of stream **outputString** before insertion and after attempting to insert past the end of array **buffer**.

An **istrstream** object inputs data from a character array in memory to program variables. The data are stored in an **istrstream** object as characters; however, input from the **istrstream** object works identically to input from any file in general or from standard input in particular. The terminating null character is interpreted by the object as end-of-file.

Figure 14.18 demonstrates input from an **istrstream** object. The declaration

```
istrstream inputBuffer(input, size);
```

```
// fig14_17.cpp
// Demonstrating an ostrstream object
// using a previously defined array.
#include <iostream.h>
#include <strstream.h>

main()
{
   const int size = 15;
   char buffer[size];

   ostrstream outputString(buffer, size, ios::out);
   cout << "outputString state before insertion: "
        << outputString.rdstate() << endl << endl;

   outputString << "Testing " << 123 << ends;

   cout << "The contents of buffer are:" << endl << buffer;

   outputString << "ATTEMPT TO INSERT PAST END OF ARRAY";
   cout << endl << endl << "outputString state after attempting"
        << endl << "to insert past the end of the string: "
        << outputString.rdstate() << endl;

   return 0;
}
```

```
outputString state before insertion: 0

The contents of buffer are:
Testing 123

outputString state after attempting
to insert past the end of the string: 4
```

**Fig. 14.17** Demonstrating an `ostrstream` object using a previously defined array.

creates **istrstream** object **inputBuffer**. The two arguments specify the array from which data will be read (**input**) and the number of elements in the array (**size**). The array input contains the following data

```
Input test 123 4.7 A
```

which when read as input to a program consists of two strings (**"Input"** and **"test"**), an integer value (**123**), a floating-point value (**4.7**), and a character (**'A'**). These data are input to variables **string1**, **string2**, **i**, **d**, and **c** respectively using the stream-extraction operator, then output to **cout**. The program tests stream state on **inputBuffer** before extraction is attempted and after extraction is attempted with no data remaining in the **input** array.

```
// fig14_18.cpp
// Demonstrating input from an istrstream object.
#include <iostream.h>
#include <strstream.h>

main()
{
   const int size = 80;
   char input[size] = "Input test 123 4.7 A";

   istrstream inputBuffer(input, size);

   cout << "inputBuffer state before extraction: "
        << inputBuffer.rdstate() << endl << endl;

   char string1[size], string2[size];
   int i;
   double d;
   char c;
   inputBuffer >> string1 >> string2 >> i >> d >> c;

   cout << "The following inputs were extracted" << endl
        << "from the istrstream object:" << endl
        << " String: " << string1 << endl
        << " String: " << string2 << endl
        << "Integer: " << i << endl
        << " Double: " << d << endl
        << "   Char: " << c << endl << endl;

   // attempt to read from empty stream
   long l;
   inputBuffer >> l;
   cout << "inputBuffer state after extraction on empty stream: "
        << inputBuffer.rdstate() << endl;

   return 0;
}
```

**Fig. 14.18** Demonstrating input from an **istrstream** object (part 1 of 2).

```
inputBuffer state before extraction: 0

The following inputs were extracted
from the istrstream object:
 String: Input
 String: test
Integer: 123
 Double: 4.7
   Char: A

inputBuffer state after extraction on empty stream: 2
```

**Fig. 14.18** Demonstrating input from an **istrstream** object (part 2 of 2).

## 14.13 Input/Output of Objects

In this chapter and Chapter 11 we discussed C++'s object-oriented style of input/output. But our examples concentrated on I/O of traditional data types rather than objects of user-defined classes. In Chapter 8, we showed how to input and output class objects using operator overloading. We accomplished object input by overloading the stream-extraction operator >> for the appropriate **istream** classes. We accomplished object output by overloading the stream-insertion operator << for the appropriate **ostream** classes. In both cases only an object's data members were input or output, and, in each case, in a form meaningful for objects of that particular abstract data type. An object's member functions are available internally in the computer and are combined with the data values as these data are input via the overloaded stream-insertion operator.

When object data members are output to a disk file, in a sense we lose the object's type information. We only have data, not type information, on a disk. If the program that is going to read this data knows what object type it corresponds to, then the data is simply read into objects of that type.

An interesting problem occurs when we store objects of different types in the same file. How can we distinguish them (or their collections of data members) as we read them into a program? The problem, of course, is that objects typically do not have type fields (we studied this issue carefully in Chapter 10, " Virtual Functions and Polymorphism").

One approach would be to have each overloaded output operator output a type code preceding each collection of data members that represents one object. Then object input would always begin by reading the type-code field and using a **switch** statement to invoke the proper overloaded function. Although this solution lacks the elegance of polymorphic programming, it provides a workable mechanism for retaining objects in files and retrieving them as needed.

### *Summary*

- All data items processed by a computer are reduced to combinations of zeros and ones.
- The smallest data item in a computer can assume the value 0 or the value 1. Such a data item is called a bit.

- Digits, letters, and special symbols are referred to as characters. The set of all characters that may be used to write programs and represent data items on a particular computer is called that computer's character set. Every character in the computer's character set is represented as a pattern of eight **1**s and **0**s (called a byte).
- A field is a group of characters (or bytes) that conveys meaning.
- A record is a group of related fields.
- At least one field in a record is chosen as a record key to identify a record as belonging to a particular person or entity that is unique from all other records in the file.
- Sequential access is the most popular method of accessing data in a file.
- A collection of programs designed to create and manage databases is called a database management system (DBMS).
- C++ views each file as a sequential stream of bytes.
- Each file ends in some machine-dependent form of end-of-file marker.
- Streams provide communication channels between files and programs.
- The header files **<iostream.h>** and **<fstream.h>** must be included in a program to perform C++ file I/O. Header **<fstream.h>** includes the definitions for the stream classes **ifstream**, **ofstream**, and **fstream**.
- Files are opened simply by instantiating objects of stream classes **ifstream**, **ofstream**, and **fstream**.
- C++ imposes no structure on a file. Thus, notions like "record" do not exist in C++. The programmer must structure a file appropriately to meet the requirements of a particular application.
- Files are opened for output by creating an **ofstream** class object. Two arguments are passed to the object—the filename and the file open mode. For an **ofstream** object, the file open mode can be either **ios::out** to output data to a file or **ios::app** to append data to the end of a file. Existing files opened with mode **ios::out** are truncated. Nonexistent files are created.
- The **ios** operator member function **operator!** returns a nonzero (true) value if either the **failbit** or **badbit** have been set for a stream on the **open** operation.
- The **ios** operator member function **operator void*** converts the stream to a pointer for comparison with **0** (the null pointer). If either the **failbit** or **badbit** have been set for the stream, 0 (false) is returned.
- Programs may process no files, one file, or several files. Each file has a unique name and is associated with an appropriate file stream object. All file processing functions must refer to a file with the appropriate object.
- A "get pointer" indicates the position in the file from which the next input is to occur, and a "put pointer" indicates the position in the file at which the next output is to be placed. Both the **istream** class and the **ostream** class provide member functions

for repositioning the file position pointer. The functions are **seekg** ("seek get") for the **istream** class and **seekp** ("seek put") for the **ostream** class.

- Member functions **tellp** and **tellg** return the current locations of the "put" and "get" pointers, respectively.
- A convenient way to implement random access files is by using only fixed-length records. Using this technique, a program can quickly calculate the exact location of a record relative to the beginning of the file.
- Data can be inserted in a random access file without destroying other data in the file. Data can be updated or deleted without rewriting the entire file.
- The **ostream** member function **write** outputs to a specified stream some number of bytes beginning at a designated location in memory. When the stream is associated with a file, the data is written beginning at the location specified by the '"put" file position pointer.
- The **istream** member function **read** inputs some number of bytes from the specified stream to an area in memory beginning of a designated address. The bytes are input beginning at the location specified by the "get" file position pointer.
- The **write** function expects a first argument of type **char***, so this argument must be cast to **char*** if it is of some other pointer type. The second argument is an integer that specifies the number of bytes to be written.
- The compile-time, unary operator **sizeof** returns the size in bytes of the object contained in parentheses; **sizeof** returns an unsigned integer.
- The **istream** member function **read** inputs a specified number of bytes from the designated stream into an object; **read** requires a first argument of type **char***.
- The **ios** member function **eof** determines if the end of the file indicator has been set for the designated stream. End-of-file is set after an attempted read fails.
- C++ stream I/O includes capabilities for input to character arrays in memory and output from character arrays in memory. These capabilities are often referred to as in-core I/O, in-memory I/O, or string stream processing.
- Input from a character array is supported by class **istrstream**. Output to a character array is supported by class **ostrstream**.
- Class **istrstream** is derived from class **istream**. Class **ostrstream** is derived from class **ostream**.
- Programs that use in-core formatting must include the **<strstream.h>** header file in addition to **<iostream.h>**.
- An **ostrstream** object can be used two ways. The first dynamically allocates a character array as the outputs are sent to the **ostrstream** object. Once output to the **ostrstream** object is complete, the object can be "frozen" with the **str** member function. The **str** member function returns a **char*** pointer to the beginning of the array in memory.

- The second way to use an **ostrstream** object is to pass three arguments to the constructor—a character array, the length of the array, and a file open mode (**ios::out** or **ios::app**). Data is output to the specified array. If **ios::app** is specified, the character array is assumed to be a null-terminated string, and insertions begin at the null character but cannot exceed the array's size.
- An **istrstream** object inputs data from a character array in memory to program variables. The terminating null character is interpreted as end-of-file.

## Terminology

alphabetic field
binary digit
bit
byte
**cerr** (standard error unbuffered)
character field
character set
**cin** (standard input)
**clog** (standard error buffered)
close a file
**close** member function
**cout** (standard output)
data hierarchy
database
database management system (DBMS)
decimal digit
end-of-file
end-of-file marker
**ends** stream manipulator
field
file
file name
file position pointer
**fstream** class
**fstream.h** header file
**ifstream** class
in-core I/O
in-memory I/O
input stream
**ios::app** file open mode
**ios::ate** file open mode
**ios::beg** seek starting point
**ios::cur** seek starting point
**ios::end** seek starting point
**ios::in** file open mode
**ios::out** file open mode
**ios::trunc** file open mode
**ios::nocreate** file open mode
**ios::noreplace** file open mode
**istream** class
**istrstream** class
numeric field
**ofstream** class
open a file
**open** member function
**operator!** member function
**operator void*** member function
**ostream** class
**ostrstream** class
output stream
random access file
record
record key
**seekg istream** member function
**seekp ostream** member function
sequential access file
special symbol
**str** string-stream member function
stream
string-stream processing
**strstream.h** header file
**tellg istream** member function
**tellp ostream** member function
truncate an existing file

## Common Programming Errors

**14.1** Opening an existing file for output (**ios::out**) when, in fact, the user wants to preserve the file; the contents of the file are discarded without warning.

**14.2** Using an incorrect `ofstream` object to refer to a file.
**14.3** Not opening a file before attempting to reference it in a program.

## Good Programming Practices

**14.1** Open a file for input only (using `ios::in`) if the contents of the file should not be modified. This prevents unintentional modification of the file's contents. This is an example of the principle of least privilege.

## Performance Tip

**14.1** Explicitly close each file as soon as it is known that the program will not reference the file again. This can reduce resource usage in a program that will continue executing long after it no longer needs to be referencing a particular file. This practice also improves program clarity.

## Self-Review Exercises

**14.1** Fill in the blanks in each of the following:

a) Ultimately, all data items processed by a computer are reduced to combinations of __________ and __________.
b) The smallest data item a computer can process is called a __________.
c) A __________ is a group of related records.
d) Digits, letters, and special symbols are referred to as __________.
e) A group of related files is called a __________.
f) Member function __________ of the file stream classes `fstream`, `ifstream`, and `ofstream` closes a file.
g) The `istream` member function __________ reads a character from the specified stream.
h) The `istream` member functions __________ and __________ read a line from the specified stream.
i) Member function __________ of the file stream classes `fstream`, `ifstream`, and `ofstream` opens a file.
j) The `istream` member function __________ is normally used when reading data from a file in random access applications.
k) Member functions __________ and __________ of the `istream` and `ostream` classes set the appropriate position pointer to a specific location in an input or output stream respectively.

**14.2** State which of the following are true and which are false (for those that are false, explain why):

a) Member function `read` cannot be used to read data from the input object `cin`.
b) The programmer must explicitly create the `cin`, `cout`, `cerr`, and `clog` objects.
c) A program must explicitly call function `close` to close a file associated with an `ifstream`, `ofstream`, or `fstream` object.
d) If the file position pointer points to a location in a sequential file other than the beginning of the file, the file must be closed and reopened to read from the beginning of the file.
e) The `ostream` member function `write` can write to standard output stream `cout`.
f) Data in sequential access files is always updated without overwriting nearby data.

g) It is not necessary to search through all the records in a random access file to find a specific record.
h) Records in random access files must be of uniform length.
i) Member functions **seekp** and **seekg** must seek relative to the beginning of a file.

**14.3** Assume that each of the following statements applies to the same program.
a) Write a statement that opens file **"oldmast.dat"** for input; use **ifstream** object **inOldMaster**.
b) Write a statement that opens file **"trans.dat"** for input; use **ifstream** object **inTransaction**.
c) Write a statement that opens file **"newmast.dat"** for output (and creation); use **ofstream** object **outNewMaster**.
d) Write a statement that reads a record from the file **"oldmast.dat"**. The record consists of integer **accountNum**, string **name**, and floating point **currentBalance**; use **ifstream** object **inOldMaster**.
e) Write a statement that reads a record from the file **"trans.dat"**. The record consists of integer **accountNum** and floating point **dollarAmount**; use **ifstream** object **inTransaction**.
f) Write a statement that writes a record to the file **"newmast.dat"**. The record consists of integer **accountNum**, string **name**, and floating point **currentBalance**; use **ofstream** object **outNewMaster**.

**14.4** Find the error and show how to correct it in each of the following.
a) File **"payables.dat"** referred to by **ofstream** object **outPayable** has not been opened.

```
outPayable << account << company << amount << endl;
```

b) The following statement should read a record from the file **"payables.dat"**. The **ifstream** object **inPayable** refers to this file, and **istream** object **inReceivable** refers to the file **"receivables.dat"**.

```
inReceivable >> account >> company >> amount;
```

c) The file **"tools.dat"** should be opened to add data to the file without discarding the current data.

```
ofstream outTools("tools.dat", ios::out);
```

## *Answers to Self-Review Exercises*

**14.1** a) 1s, 0s. b) Bit. c) File. d) Characters. e) Database. f) **close**. g) **get**. h) **get**, **getline**. i) **open**. j) **read**. k) **seekg**, **seekp**.

**14.2** a) False. Function **read** can be used to read from any input stream object derived from **istream**.
b) False. These four streams are created automatically for the programmer. The **<iostream.h>** header file must be included in a file to use them. This header includes declarations of each of these stream objects.
c) False. The files will be closed when destructors for **ifstream**, **ofstream**, or **fstream** objects are executed when the stream objects go out of scope or before program execution terminates, but it is a good programming practice to close all files explicitly with **close** once they are no longer needed.
d) False. Member function **seekp** or **seekg** can be used to reposition the put or get file position pointer to the beginning of the file.

e) True.
f) False. In most cases, sequential file records are not of uniform length. Therefore, it is possible that updating a record will cause other data to be overwritten.
g) True.
h) False. Records in a random access file are normally of uniform length.
i) False. It is possible to seek from the beginning of the file, from the end of the file, and from the current position in the file.

**14.3** a) `ifstream inOldMaster("oldmast.dat", ios::in);`
b) `ifstream inTransaction("trans.dat", ios::in);`
c) `ofstream outNewMaster("newmast.dat", ios::out);`
d) `inOldMaster >> accountNum >> name >> currentBalance;`
e) `inTransaction >> accountNum >> dollarAmount;`
f) `outNewMaster << accountNum << name << currentBalance;`

**14.4** a) Error: The file **"payables.dat"** has not been opened before the an attempt is made to output data to the stream.
Correction: Use **ostream** member function **open** to open **"payables.dat"** for output.
b) Error: The incorrect **istream** object is being used to read a record from file **"payables.dat"**.
Correction: Use **istream** object **inPayable** to refer to **"payables.dat"**.
c) Error: The contents of the file are discarded because the file is opened for output (**ios::out**).
Correction: To add data to the file, either open the file for updating (**ios::ate**) or open the file for appending (**ios::app**).

## *Exercises*

**14.5** Fill in the blanks in each of the following:
a) Computers store large amounts of data on secondary storage devices as _________.
b) A _________ is composed of several fields.
c) A field that may contain only digits, letters, and blanks is called an_________ field.
d) To facilitate the retrieval of specific records from a file, one field in each record is chosen as a _________.
e) The vast majority of information stored in computer systems is stored in files.
f) A group of related characters that conveys meaning is called a _________.
g) The standard stream objects declared by header file **<iostream.h>** are _________ , _________ , _________ , and_________ .
h) The **ostream** member function _________ outputs a character to the specified stream.
i) The **ostream** member function _________ is generally used to write data to a randomly accessed file.
j) The **istream** member function _________ repositions the file position pointer in a file.

**14.6** State which of the following are true and which are false (and for those that are false, explain why):
a) The impressive functions performed by computers essentially involve the manipulation of zeros and ones.

b) People prefer to manipulate bits instead of characters and fields because bits are more compact.
c) People specify programs and data items as characters; computers then manipulate and process these characters as groups of zeros and ones.
d) A person's 5-digit zip code is an example of a numeric field.
e) A person's street address is generally considered to be an alphabetic field in computer applications.
f) Data items represented in computers form a data hierarchy in which data items become larger and more complex as we progress from fields to characters to bits, etc.
g) A record key identifies a record as belonging to a particular field.
h) Most organizations store all their information in a single file to facilitate computer processing.
i) Each statement that processes a file in a C++ program explicitly refers to that file by name.
j) When a program creates a file, the file is automatically retained by the computer for future reference.

**14.7** Exercise 14.3 asked the reader to write a series of single statements. Actually, these statements form the core of an important type of file processing program, namely, a file-matching program. In commercial data processing, it is common to have several files in each application system. In an accounts receivable system, for example, there is generally a master file containing detailed information about each customer such as the customer's name, address, telephone number, outstanding balance, credit limit, discount terms, contract arrangements, and possibly a condensed history of recent purchases and cash payments.

As transactions occur (i.e., sales are made and cash payments arrive in the mail), they are entered into a file. At the end of each business period (i.e., a month for some companies, a week for others, and a day in some cases) the file of transactions (called `"trans.dat"` in Exercise 14.3) is applied to the master file (called `"oldmast.dat"` in Exercise 14.3), thus updating each account's record of purchases and payments. During an updating run, the master file is rewritten as a new file (`"newmast.dat"`), which is then used at the end of the next business period to begin the updating process again.

File-matching programs must deal with certain problems that do not exist in single-file programs. For example, a match does not always occur. A customer on the master file may not have made any purchases or cash payments in the current business period, and therefore no record for this customer will appear on the transaction file. Similarly, a customer who did make some purchases or cash payments may have just moved to this community, and the company may not have had a chance to create a master record for this customer.

Use the statements written in Exercise 14.3 as a basis for writing a complete file-matching accounts receivable program. Use the account number on each file as the record key for matching purposes. Assume that each file is a sequential file with records stored in increasing account number order.

When a match occurs (i.e., records with the same account number appear on both the master file and the transaction file), add the dollar amount on the transaction file to the current balance on the master file, and write the `"newmast.dat"` record. (Assume that purchases are indicated by positive amounts on the transaction file, and that payments are indicated by negative amounts.) When there is a master record for a particular account but no corresponding transaction record, merely write the master record to `"newmast.dat"`. When there is a transaction record but no corresponding master record, print the message `"Unmatched transaction record for account number ..."` (fill in the account number from the transaction record).

**14.8** After writing the program of Exercise 14.7, write a simple program to create some test data for checking out the program. Use the following sample account data:

Master file:

| Account number | Name | Balance |
|---|---|---|
| 100 | Alan Jones | 348.17 |
| 300 | Mary Smith | 27.19 |
| 500 | Sam Sharp | 0.00 |
| 700 | Suzy Green | -14.22 |

Transaction file:

| Account number | Dollar amount |
|---|---|
| 100 | 27.14 |
| 300 | 62.11 |
| 400 | 100.56 |
| 900 | 82.17 |

**14.9** Run the program of Exercise 14.7 using the files of test data created in Exercise 14.8. Print the new master file. Check that the accounts have been updated correctly.

**14.10** It is possible (actually common) to have several transaction records with the same record key. This occurs because a particular customer might make several purchases and cash payments during a business period. Rewrite your accounts receivable file-matching program of Exercise 14.7 to provide for the possibility of handling several transaction records with the same record key. Modify the test data of Exercise 14.8 to include the following additional transaction records:

| Account number | Dollar amount |
|---|---|
| 300 | 83.89 |
| 700 | 80.78 |
| 700 | 1.53 |

**14.11** Write a series of statements that accomplish each of the following. Assume the structure

```
struct person {
   char lastName[15];
   char firstName[15];
   char age[2];
};
```

has been defined, and that the random access file has been opened properly.

a) Initialize the file **"nameage.dat"** with 100 records containing **lastName = "unassigned"**, **firstName = ""**, and **age = "0"**.
b) Input 10 last names, first names, and ages, and write them to the file.
c) Update a record that has information in it, and if there is none tell the user **"No info"**.
d) Delete a record that has information by reinitializing that particular record.

**14.12** You are the owner of a hardware store and need to keep an inventory that can tell you what different tools you have, how many of each you have on hand, and the cost of each one. Write a program that initializes the random access file **"hardware.dat"** to one hundred empty records, lets you input the data concerning each tool, enables you to list all your tools, lets you delete a record for a tool that you no longer have, and lets you update *any* information in the file. The tool identification number should be the record number. Use the following information to start your file:

| Record # | Tool name | Quantity | Cost |
|---|---|---|---|
| 3 | Electric sander | 7 | 57.98 |
| 17 | Hammer | 76 | 11.99 |
| 24 | Jig saw | 21 | 11.00 |
| 39 | Lawn mower | 3 | 79.50 |
| 56 | Power saw | 18 | 99.99 |
| 68 | Screwdriver | 106 | 6.99 |
| 77 | Sledge hammer | 11 | 21.50 |
| 83 | Wrench | 34 | 7.50 |

**14.13** Modify the telephone number word generating program you wrote in Chapter 4 so that it writes its output to a file. This allows you to read the file at your convenience. If you have a computerized dictionary available, modify your program to look up the thousands of seven-letter words in the dictionary. Some of the interesting seven-letter combinations created by this program may consist of two or more words. For example, the phone number 8432677 produces "THEBOSS." Modify your program to use the computerized dictionary to check each possible seven-letter word to see if it is a valid one-letter word followed by a valid six-letter word, a valid two-letter word followed by a valid five-letter word, etc.

**14.14** Write a program that uses the **sizeof** operator to determine the sizes in bytes of the various data types on your computer system. Write the results to the file **"datasize.dat"** so you may print the results later. The format for the results in the file should be:

```
Data type                Size
char                        1
unsigned char               1
short int                   2
unsigned short int          2
int                         4
unsigned int                4
long int                    4
```

```
unsigned long int          4
float                      4
double                     8
long double               16
```

Note: The sizes of the built-in data types on your computer may differ from those listed above.

# 15

# Data Structures

## Objectives

- To be able to form linked data structures using pointers, self-referential classes, and recursion.
- To be able to allocate and free memory dynamically for creating and destroying data structure objects.
- To be able to create and manipulate dynamic data structures such as linked lists, queues, stacks, and binary trees.
- To understand various important applications of linked data structures.
- To understand how to create reusable data structures with class templates, inheritance, and composition.

*Much that I bound, I could not free;*
*Much that I freed returned to me.*
Lee Wilson Dodd

*'Will you walk a litter faster?' said a whiting to a snail,*
*'There's a porpoise close behind us, and he's treading on my tail.'*
Lewis Carroll

*Push on—keep moving.*
Thomas Morton

*I think that I shall never see*
*A poem lovely as a tree.*
Joyce Kilmer

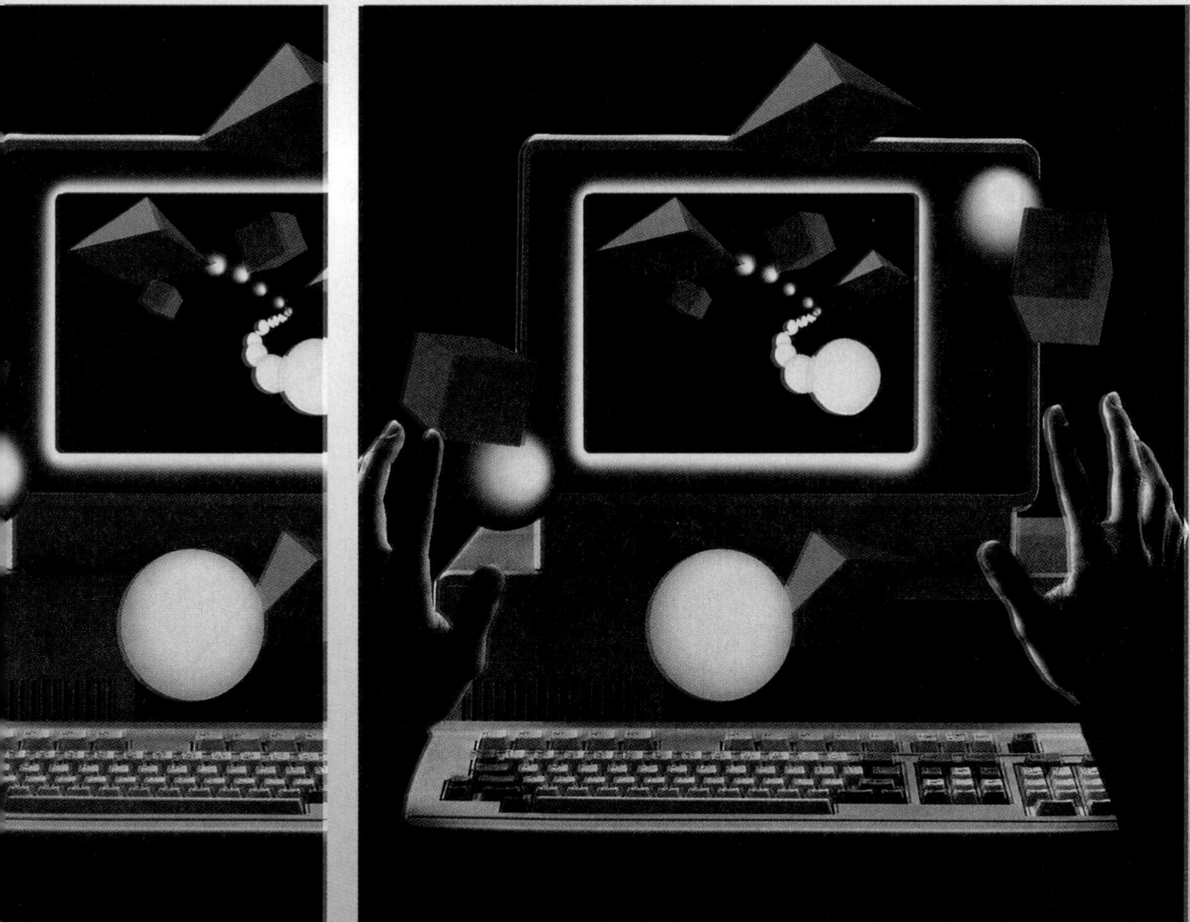

# Outline



## 15.1 Introduction

We have studied fixed-size *data structures* such as single-subscripted arrays, double-subscripted arrays, and `struct`s. This chapter introduces *dynamic data structures* that grow and shrink at execution time. *Linked lists* are collections of data items "lined up in a row"—insertions and deletions are made anywhere in a linked list. *Stacks* are important in compilers and operating systems—insertions and deletions are made only at one end of a stack—its *top*. *Queues* represent waiting lines; insertions are made at the back (also referred to as the *tail*) of a queue, and deletions are made from the front (also referred to as the *head*) of a queue. *Binary trees* facilitate high-speed searching and sorting of data, efficient elimination of duplicate data items, representing file system directories, and compiling expressions into machine language. These data structures have many other interesting applications.

We will discuss each of the major types of data structures and implement programs that create and manipulate these data structures. We use classes, class templates, inheritance, and composition to create and package these data structures for reusability and maintainability.

The chapter examples are practical programs that you will be able to use in more advanced courses and in industry applications. The programs are especially heavy on pointer manipulation. The exercises include a rich collection of useful applications.

We encourage you to attempt the major project described in the special section entitled "Building Your Own Compiler." You have been using a compiler to translate your C++ programs to machine language so that you could execute these programs on your computer. In this project, you will actually build your own compiler. It will read a file of statements written in a simple, yet powerful, high-level language similar to early versions of the popular language BASIC. Your compiler will translate these statements into a file of Simpletron Machine Language (SML) instructions—SML is the language you learned in the Chapter 5 special section, "Building Your Own Computer." Your Simpletron Simulator program will then execute the SML program produced by your compiler! Implementing this project using a heavily object-oriented approach will give you a wonderful opportunity to exercise most of what you have learned in this course. The special section carefully walks you through the specifications of the high-level language, and describes the algorithms you will need to convert each type of high-level language statement into machine language instructions. If you enjoy being challenged, you might attempt the many enhancements to both the compiler and the Simpletron Simulator suggested in the Exercises.

## 15.2 Self-Referential Classes

A *self-referential class* contains a pointer member that points to a class object of the same class type. For example, the definition

```
class Node {
public:
   Node(int);
   void setData(int);
   int getData() const;
   void setNextPtr(const Node *);
   const Node *getNextPtr() const;
private:
   int data;
   Node *nextPtr;
};
```

defines a type, **Node**. Type **Node** has two private data members—integer member **data** and pointer member **nextPtr**. Member **nextPtr** points to an object of type **Node**—an object of the same type as the one being declared here, hence the term "self-referential class." Member **nextPtr** is referred to as a *link*—i.e., **nextPtr** can be used to "tie" an object of type **Node** to another object of the same type. Type **Node** also has five member functions: a constructor that receives an integer to initialize member **data**, a **setData** function to set the value of member **data**, a **getData** function to return the value of member **data**, a **setNextPtr** function to set the value of member **nextPtr**, and a **getNextPtr** function to return the value of member **nextPtr**.

Self-referential class objects can be linked together to form useful data structures such as lists, queues, stacks, and trees. Figure 15.1 illustrates two self-referential class objects linked together to form a list. Note that a slash—representing a null (**0**) pointer—is placed in the link member of the second self-referential class object to indicate that the link does not point to another object. The slash is only for illustration purposes; it does not correspond to the backslash character in C++. A null pointer normally indicates the end of a data structure just as the null character (**'\0'**) indicates the end of a string.

***Common Programming Error 15.1***

*Not setting the link in the last node of a list to null (**0**).*

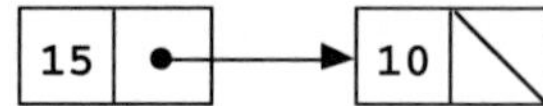


Fig. 15.1 Two self-referential class objects linked together.

## 15.3 Dynamic Memory Allocation

Creating and maintaining dynamic data structures requires *dynamic memory allocation*—the ability for a program to obtain more memory space at execution time to hold new nodes and to release space no longer needed. The limit for dynamic memory allocation can be as large as the amount of available physical memory in the computer or the amount of available virtual memory in a virtual memory system. Often, the limits are much smaller because available memory must be shared among many users.

Operators **new** and **delete** are essential to dynamic memory allocation. Operator **new** takes as an argument the type of the object being dynamically allocated and returns a pointer to an object of that type. For example, the statement

```
Node *newPtr = new Node(10);
```

allocates **sizeof(Node)** bytes and stores a pointer to this memory in **newPtr**. If no memory is available, **new** returns a zero pointer. The 10 is the node object's data.

The **delete** operator deallocates memory allocated with **new**—i.e., the memory is returned to the system so that the memory can be reallocated in the future. To free memory dynamically allocated by the preceding **new**, use the statement

```
delete newPtr;
```

Note that **newPtr** itself is not deleted; rather the space **newPtr** points to is deleted.

The following sections discuss lists, stacks, queues, and trees. These data structures are created and maintained with dynamic memory allocation and self-referential classes.

***Portability Tip 15.1***

*A class object's size is not necessarily the sum of the sizes of its data members. This is because of various machine-dependent boundary alignment requirements (see Chapter 16) and other reasons.*

***Common Programming Error 15.2***

*Assuming that the size of a class object is simply the sum of the sizes of its data members.*

***Good Programming Practice 15.1***

*When using* **new***, test for a null pointer return value. Perform appropriate error processing if the requested memory is not allocated.*

***Common Programming Error 15.3***

*Not returning dynamically allocated memory when it is no longer needed can cause the system to run out of memory prematurely. This is sometimes called a "memory leak."*

*Good Programming Practice 15.2*

*When memory that was dynamically allocated with* `new` *is no longer needed, use* `delete` *to return the memory to the system immediately.*

*Common Programming Error 15.4*

*Deleting memory with* `delete` *that was not allocated dynamically with* `new`*.*

*Common Programming Error 15.5*

*Referring to memory that has been deleted.*

## 15.4 Linked Lists

A *linked list* is a linear collection of self-referential class objects, called *nodes,* connected by pointer *links*—hence, the term "linked" list. A linked list is accessed via a pointer to the first node of the list. Subsequent nodes are accessed via the link-pointer member stored in each node. By convention, the link pointer in the last node of a list is set to null (zero) to mark the end of the list. Data are stored in a linked list dynamically—each node is created as necessary. A node can contain data of any type including objects of other classes. Stacks and queues are also linear data structures, and, as we will see, are constrained versions of linked lists. Trees are nonlinear data structures.

Lists of data can be stored in arrays, but linked lists provide several advantages. A linked list is appropriate when the number of data elements to be represented in the data structure at once is unpredictable. Linked lists are dynamic, so the length of a list can increase or decrease as necessary. The size of a "conventional" C++ array, however, cannot be altered, because the array size is fixed at compile time. "Conventional" arrays can become full. Linked lists become full only when the system has insufficient memory to satisfy dynamic storage allocation requests.

*Performance Tip 15.1*

*An array can be declared to contain more elements than the number of items expected, but this can waste memory. Linked lists can provide better memory utilization in these situations. Linked lists allow the program to adapt at run time.*

Linked lists can be maintained in sorted order simply by inserting each new element at the proper point in the list. Existing list elements do not need to be moved.

*Performance Tip 15.2*

*Insertion and deletion in a sorted array can be time consuming—all the elements following the inserted or deleted element must be shifted appropriately.*

*Performance Tip 15.3*

*The elements of an array are stored contiguously in memory. This allows immediate access to any array element because the address of any element can be calculated directly based on its position relative to the beginning of the array. Linked lists do not afford such immediate access to their elements.*

Linked list nodes are normally not stored contiguously in memory. Logically, however, the nodes of a linked list appear to be contiguous. Figure 15.2 illustrates a linked list with several nodes.

***Performance Tip 15.4***

*Using dynamic memory allocation (instead of arrays) for data structures that grow and shrink at execution time can save memory. Keep in mind, however, that pointers occupy space, and that dynamic memory allocation incurs the overhead of function calls.*

The program of Fig. 15.3 (whose output is shown in Fig. 15.4) uses a **`List`** class template (see Chapter 12, "Templates") to manipulate a list of integer values and a list of floating-point values. The driver program (**`driver.cpp`**) provides 5 options: 1) insert a value at the beginning of the list (function **`insertAtFront`**), 2) insert a value at the end of the list (function **`insertAtBack`**), 3) delete a value from the front of the list (function **`removeFromFront`**), 4) delete a value from the end of the list (function **`removeFromBack`**), and 5) terminate the list processing. A detailed discussion of the program follows. Exercise 15.20 asks you to implement a recursive function that prints a linked list backwards, and Exercise 15.21 asks you to implement a recursive function that searches a linked list for a particular data item.

The program of Fig. 15.3 consists of two class templates—**`ListNode`** and **`List`**. Encapsulated in each **`List`** object is a linked-list of **`ListNode`** objects. The **`ListNode`** class template consists of private members **`data`** and **`nextPtr`**. **`ListNode`** member **`data`** stores a value of type **`NODETYPE`**, the type parameter passed to the class template. **`ListNode`** member **`nextPtr`** stores a pointer to the next **`ListNode`** object in the linked list.

The **`List`** class template consists of private members **`firstPtr`** (a pointer to the first **`ListNode`** in a list object) and **`lastPtr`** (a pointer to the last **`ListNode`** in a **`List`** object). The default constructor initializes both pointers to **`0`** (null). The destructor ensures that all **`ListNode`** objects in a **`List`** object are destroyed when that **`List`** object is destroyed. The primary member functions of the **`List`** class template are **`insertAtFront`**, **`insertAtBack`**, **`removeFromFront`**, and **`removeFromBack`**. Function **`isEmpty`** is called a *predicate function*—it does not alter the list in any way; rather, it determines if the list is empty (i.e., the pointer to the first node of the list is null). If the list is empty, **`1`** is returned; otherwise, **`0`** is returned. Function **`print`** displays the list's contents.

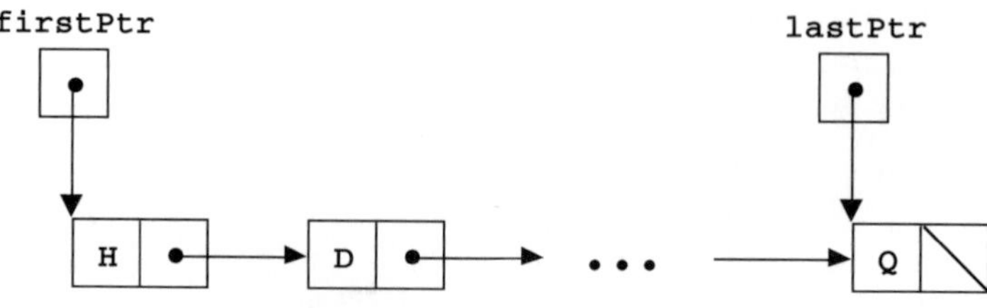


Fig. 15.2 A graphical representation of a list.

```
// LISTND.H: ListNode template definition
#ifndef LISTND_H
#define LISTND_H

template<class NODETYPE>
class ListNode {
   friend class List<NODETYPE>; // make List a friend
public:
   ListNode(const NODETYPE &);  // constructor
   NODETYPE getData() const;    // return the data in the node
private:
   NODETYPE data;               // data
   ListNode *nextPtr;           // next node in the list
};

// Constructor
template<class NODETYPE>
ListNode<NODETYPE>::ListNode(const NODETYPE &info)
{
   data = info;
   nextPtr = 0;
}

// Return a copy of the data in the node
template<class NODETYPE>
NODETYPE ListNode<NODETYPE>::getData() const { return data;}
#endif

// LIST.H: Template List class definition
#ifndef LIST_H
#define LIST_H
#include <iostream.h>
#include <assert.h>
#include "listnd.h"

template<class NODETYPE>
class List {
public:
   List();      // constructor
   ~List();     // destructor
   void insertAtFront(const NODETYPE &);
   void insertAtBack(const NODETYPE &);
   int removeFromFront(NODETYPE &);
   int removeFromBack(NODETYPE &);
   int isEmpty() const;
   void print() const;
private:
   ListNode<NODETYPE> *firstPtr;  // pointer to first node
   ListNode<NODETYPE> *lastPtr;   // pointer to last node
   ListNode<NODETYPE> *getNewNode(const NODETYPE &); // utility
};
```

**Fig. 15.3** Manipulating a linked list (part 1 of 6).

```
// Default constructor
template<class NODETYPE>
List<NODETYPE>::List() { firstPtr = lastPtr = 0; }

// Destructor
template<class NODETYPE>
List<NODETYPE>::~List()
{
   if (!isEmpty()) {    // List is not empty
      cout << "Destroying nodes ... " << endl;

      ListNode<NODETYPE> *currentPtr = firstPtr, *tempPtr;

      while (currentPtr != 0) {  // delete remaining nodes
         tempPtr = currentPtr;
         cout << tempPtr->data << endl;
         currentPtr = currentPtr->nextPtr;
         delete tempPtr;
      }
   }

   cout << "All nodes destroyed" << endl << endl;
}

// Insert a node at the front of the list
template<class NODETYPE>
void List<NODETYPE>::insertAtFront(const NODETYPE &value)
{
   ListNode<NODETYPE> *newPtr = getNewNode(value);

   if (isEmpty())  // List is empty
      firstPtr = lastPtr = newPtr;
   else {          // List is not empty
      newPtr->nextPtr = firstPtr;
      firstPtr = newPtr;
   }
}

// Insert a node at the back of the list
template<class NODETYPE>
void List<NODETYPE>::insertAtBack(const NODETYPE &value)
{
   ListNode<NODETYPE> *newPtr = getNewNode(value);

   if (isEmpty())  // List is empty
      firstPtr = lastPtr = newPtr;
   else {          // List is not empty
      lastPtr->nextPtr = newPtr;
      lastPtr = newPtr;
   }
}
```

**Fig. 15.3** Manipulating a linked list (part 2 of 6).

```
// Delete a node from the front of the list
template<class NODETYPE>
int List<NODETYPE>::removeFromFront(NODETYPE &value)
{
   if (isEmpty())                // List is empty
      return 0;                  // delete unsuccessful
   else {

      ListNode<NODETYPE> *tempPtr = firstPtr;

      if (firstPtr == lastPtr)
         firstPtr = lastPtr = 0;
      else
         firstPtr = firstPtr->nextPtr;

      value = tempPtr->data;  // data being removed
      delete tempPtr;
      return 1;                  // delete successful
   }
}

// Delete a node from the back of the list
template<class NODETYPE>
int List<NODETYPE>::removeFromBack(NODETYPE &value)
{
   if (isEmpty())
      return 0;   // delete unsuccessful
   else {
      ListNode<NODETYPE> *tempPtr = lastPtr;

      if (firstPtr == lastPtr)
         firstPtr = lastPtr = 0;
      else {
         ListNode<NODETYPE> *currentPtr = firstPtr;

         while (currentPtr->nextPtr != lastPtr)
            currentPtr = currentPtr->nextPtr;

         lastPtr = currentPtr;
         currentPtr->nextPtr = 0;
      }

      value = tempPtr->data;
      delete tempPtr;
      return 1;   // delete successful
   }
}

// Is the List empty?
template<class NODETYPE>
int List<NODETYPE>::isEmpty() const { return firstPtr == 0; }
```

**Fig. 15.3** Manipulating a linked list (part 3 of 6).

```
// Return a pointer to
// a newly allocated node.
template<class NODETYPE>
ListNode<NODETYPE> *List<NODETYPE>::getNewNode(const NODETYPE &value)
{
   ListNode<NODETYPE> *ptr = new ListNode<NODETYPE>(value);

   assert(ptr != 0);
   return ptr;
}

// Display the contents of the List
template<class NODETYPE>
void List<NODETYPE>::print() const
{
   if (isEmpty()) {
      cout << "The list is empty" << endl << endl;
      return;
   }

   ListNode<NODETYPE> *currentPtr = firstPtr;

   cout << "The list is: ";

   while (currentPtr != 0) {
      cout << currentPtr->data << ' ';
      currentPtr = currentPtr->nextPtr;
   }

   cout << endl << endl;
}

#endif

// DRIVER.CPP
// List class test

#include <iostream.h>
#include "list.h"

void testIntegerList();   // driver for integer List
void testFloatList();     // driver for float List
void instructions();      // instructions to user

main()
{
   testIntegerList();     // test the integer List
   testFloatList();       // test the float List

   return 0;
}
```

**Fig. 15.3** Manipulating a linked list (part 4 of 6).

```
// Function to test an integer List
void testIntegerList()
{
   cout << "Testing a List of integer values" << endl;

   List<int> integerList;

   instructions();

   int choice, value;

   do {
      cout << "? ";

      cin >> choice;

      switch (choice) {

         case 1:
            cout << "Enter an integer: ";
            cin >> value;
            integerList.insertAtFront(value);
            integerList.print();
            break;

         case 2:
            cout << "Enter an integer: ";
            cin >> value;
            integerList.insertAtBack(value);
            integerList.print();
            break;

         case 3:
            if (integerList.removeFromFront(value))
               cout << value << " removed from list" << endl;

            integerList.print();
            break;

         case 4:
            if (integerList.removeFromBack(value))
               cout << value << " removed from list" << endl;

            integerList.print();
            break;
      }

   } while (choice != 5);

   cout << "End test of integer List" << endl;
}
```

**Fig. 15.3** Manipulating a linked list (part 5 of 6).

```
// Function to test a float List
void testFloatList()
{
   cout << "Testing a List of floating point values" << endl;
   List<float> floatList;
   instructions();
   int choice;
   float value;

   do {
      cout << "? ";
      cin >> choice;

      switch (choice) {
         case 1:
            cout << "Enter a floating point value: ";
            cin >> value;
            floatList.insertAtFront(value);
            floatList.print();
            break;
         case 2:
            cout << "Enter a floating point value: ";
            cin >> value;
            floatList.insertAtBack(value);
            floatList.print();
            break;
         case 3:
            if (floatList.removeFromFront(value))
               cout << value << " removed from list" << endl;
            floatList.print();
            break;
         case 4:
            if (floatList.removeFromBack(value))
               cout << value << " removed from list" << endl;
            floatList.print();
            break;
      }
   } while (choice != 5);

   cout << "End test of float List" << endl;
}

void instructions()
{
   cout << "Enter one of the following:" << endl
        << "  1 to insert at beginning of list" << endl
        << "  2 to insert at end of list" << endl
        << "  3 to delete from beginning of list" << endl
        << "  4 to delete from end of list" << endl
        << "  5 to end list processing" << endl;
}
```

**Fig. 15.3** Manipulating a linked list (part 6 of 6).

```
Testing a List of integer values
Enter one of the following:
  1 to insert at beginning of list
  2 to insert at end of list
  3 to delete from beginning of list
  4 to delete from end of list
  5 to end list processing
? 1
Enter an integer: 1
The list is: 1

? 1
Enter an integer: 2
The list is: 2 1

? 2
Enter an integer: 3
The list is: 2 1 3

? 2
Enter an integer: 4
The list is: 2 1 3 4

? 3
2 removed from list
The list is: 1 3 4

? 3
1 removed from list
The list is: 3 4

? 4
4 removed from list
The list is: 3

? 4
3 removed from list
The list is empty

? 5
End test of integer List

List destroyed

Testing a List of floating point values
Enter one of the following:
  1 to insert at beginning of list
  2 to insert at end of list
  3 to delete from beginning of list
```

**Fig. 15.4** Sample output for the program of 15.3 (part 1 of 2).

```
   4 to delete from end of list
   5 to end list processing
? 1
Enter a floating point value: 1.1
The list is: 1.1

? 1
Enter a floating point value: 2.2
The list is: 2.2 1.1

? 2
Enter a floating point value: 3.3
The list is: 2.2 1.1 3.3

? 2
Enter a floating point value: 4.4
The list is: 2.2 1.1 3.3 4.4

? 3
2.2 removed from list
The list is: 1.1 3.3 4.4

? 3
1.1 removed from list
The list is: 3.3 4.4

? 4
4.4 removed from list
The list is: 3.3

? 4
3.3 removed from list
The list is empty

? 5
End test of float List

List destroyed
```

**Fig. 15.4** Sample output for the program of Fig. 15.3 (part 2 of 2).

***Good Programming Practice 15.3***

*Assign null (zero) to the link member of a new node. Pointers should be initialized before they are used.*

Over the next several pages, we will discuss each of the member functions of the **List** class in detail. Function **insertAtFront** (Fig. 15.5) places a new node at the front of the list. The function consists of several steps:

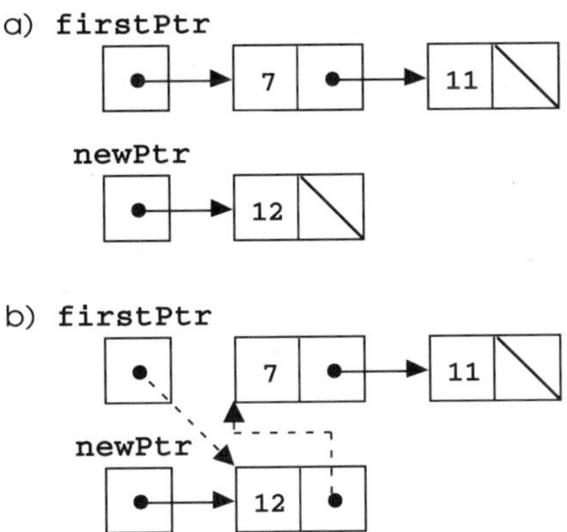


**Fig. 15.5** The **insertAtFront** operation.

1) Call function **getNewNode** passing it **value**, which is a constant reference to the node value to be inserted.
2) Function **getNewNode** uses operator **new** to create a new list node and return a pointer to this list node to **Ptr**. If this pointer is nonzero, **getNewNode** returns a pointer to this newly allocated node to **newPtr** in **insertAtFront**.
3) If the list is empty, then both **firstPtr** and **lastPtr** are set to **newPtr**.
4) If the list is not empty, then the node pointed to by **newPtr** is threaded into the list by copying **firstPtr** to **newPtr->nextPtr** so that the new node points to what used to be the first node of the list, and copying **newPtr** to **firstPtr** so that **firstPtr** now points to the new first node of the list.

Figure 15.5 illustrates function **insertAtFront**. Part a) of the figure shows the list and the new node before the **insertAtFront** operation. The dotted arrows in part b) illustrate the steps 2 and 3 of the **insertAtFront** operation that enable the node containing **12** to become the new list front.

Function **insertAtBack** (Fig. 15.6) places a new node at the back of the list. The function consists of several steps:

1) Call function **getNewNode** passing it **value** which is a constant reference to the node value to be inserted.
2) Function **getNewNode** uses operator **new** to create a new list node and return a pointer to this list node to **Ptr**. If this pointer is nonzero, **getNewNode** returns a pointer to this newly allocated node to **newPtr** in **insertAtBack**.
3) If the list is empty, then both **firstPtr** and **lastPtr** are set to **newPtr**.
4) If the list is not empty, then the node pointed to by **newPtr** is threaded into the list by copying **newPtr** into **lastPtr->nextPtr** so that the new node is pointed to by what used to be the last node of the list, and copying **newPtr** to **lastPtr** so that **lastPtr** now points to the new last node of the list.

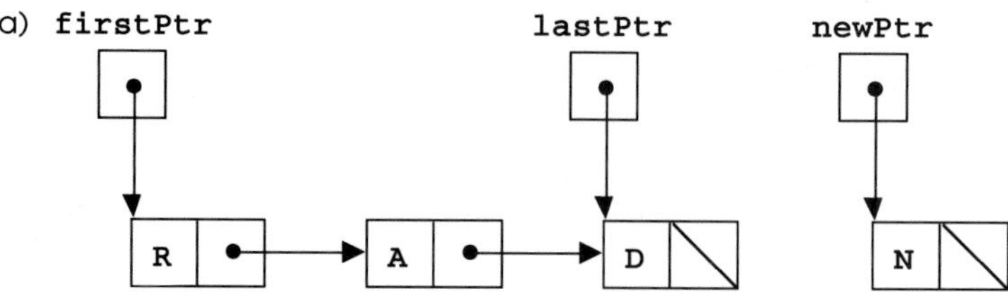


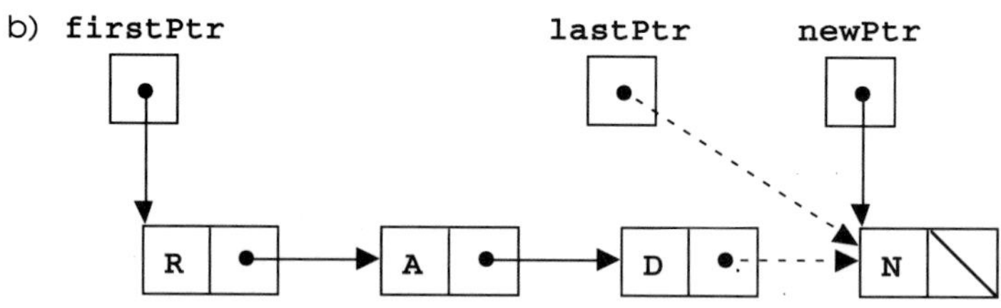


**Fig. 15.6** A graphical representation of the **insertAtBack** operation.

Figure 15.6 illustrates an **insertAtBack** operation. Part a) of the figure shows the list and the new node before the operation. The dotted arrows in part b) illustrate the steps of function **insertAtBack** that enable a new node to be added to the end of a list that is not empty.

Function **removeFromFront** (Fig. 15.7) removes the front node of the list and copies the node value to the reference parameter. The function returns 0 if an attempt is made to remove a node from an empty list, and returns 1 if the removal is successful. The function consists of several steps:

1) Instantiate **tempPtr** as a copy of **firstPtr**. Eventually, **tempPtr** will be used to delete the memory space for the node being removed.
2) If **firstPtr** is equal to **lastPtr**, i.e., if the list has only one element prior to the removal attempt, then set **firstPtr** and **lastPtr** to zero to dethread that node from the list (leaving the list empty).
3) If the list has more than one node prior to removal, then leave **lastPtr** as is and simply set **firstPtr** to **firstPtr->nextPtr**, i.e., modify **firstPtr** to point to what was the second node prior to removal (and now, the new first node).
4) After all these pointer manipulations are complete, copy to reference parameter **value** the **data** member of the node being removed.
5) Now **delete** the memory space for the node pointed to by **tempPtr**.
6) Return 1 indicating successful removal.

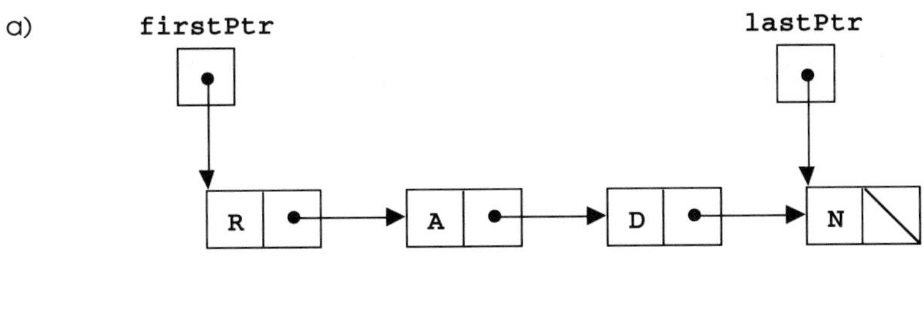


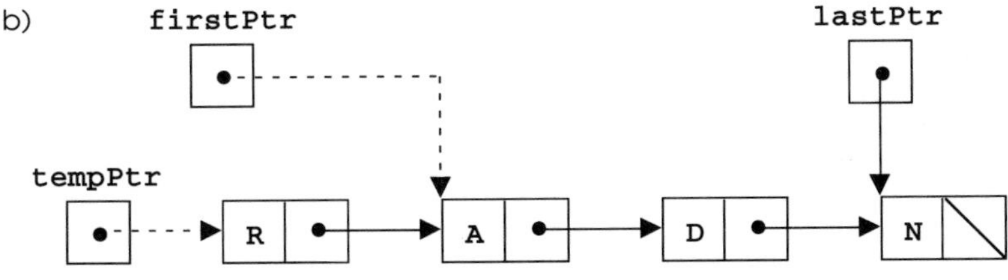


**Fig. 15.7** A graphical representation of the **removeFromFront** operation.

Figure 15.7 illustrates function **removeFromFront**. Part a) of the figure illustrates the list before the removal operation. Part b) of the figure shows actual pointer manipulations.

Function **removeFromBack** (Fig. 15.8) removes the back node of the list and copies the node value to the reference parameter. The function returns 0 if an attempt is made to remove a node from an empty list, and returns 1 if the removal is successful. The function consists of several steps:

1) Instantiate **tempPtr** as a copy of **lastPtr**. Eventually, **tempPtr** will be used to delete the memory space for the node being remove.
2) If **firstPtr** is equal to **lastPtr**, i.e., if the list has only one element prior to the removal attempt, then set **firstPtr** and **lastPtr** to zero to dethread that node from the list (leaving the list empty).
3) If the list has more than one node prior to removal, then instantiate **currentPtr** as a copy of **firstPtr**.
4) Now "walk the list" with **currentPtr** until it points to the node before the last node. This is done with a **while** loop that keeps replacing **currentPtr** by **currentPtr->nextPtr** while **currentPtr->nextPtr** is not **lastPtr**.
5) Copy **currentPtr** to **lastPtr** to dethread the back node from the list.
6) Set the **currentPtr->nextPtr** to zero in the new last node of the list.
7) After all the pointer manipulations are complete, copy to reference parameter **value** the **data** member of the node being removed.
8) Now **delete** the memory space for the node pointed to by **tempPtr**.

a)

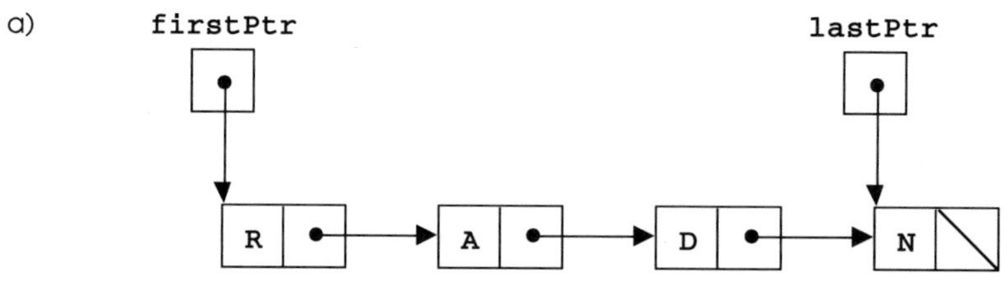


b)

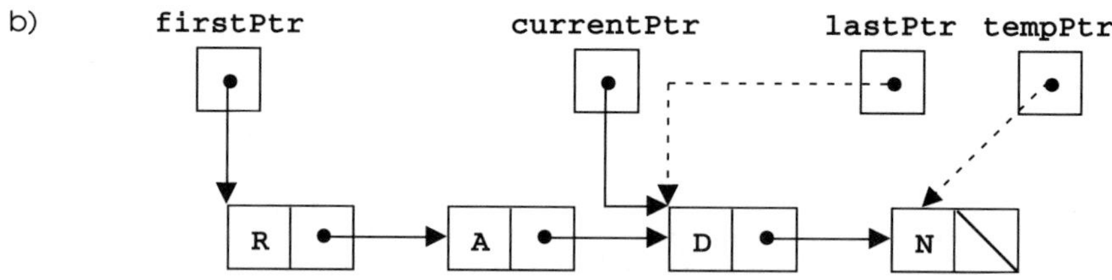


**Fig. 15.8** A graphical representation of the **removeFromBack** operation.

9) Return 1 indicating successful removal.

Figure 15.8 illustrates function **removeFromFront**. Part a) of the figure illustrates the list before the removal operation. Part b) of the figure shows the actual pointer manipulations.

Function **print** first determines if the list is empty. If so, **print** prints **"The list is empty"** and terminates. Otherwise, it prints the data in the list. The function instantiates **currentPtr** as a copy of **firstPtr** and then prints the string **"The list is: "**. While **currentPtr** is not null, **currentPtr->data** is printed and **currentPtr->nextPtr** is assigned to **currentPtr**. Note that if the link in the last node of the list is not null, the printing algorithm will erroneously print past the end of the list. The printing algorithm is identical for linked lists, stacks, and queues.

## 15.5 Stacks

A *stack* is a constrained version of a linked list—new nodes can be added to a stack and removed from a stack only at the top. For this reason, a stack is referred to as a *last-in, first-out (LIFO)* data structure. The link member in the last node of the stack is set to null (zero) to indicate the bottom of the stack.

***Common Programming Error 15.6***

*Not setting the link in the bottom node of a stack to null (zero).*

The primary member functions used to manipulate a stack are **push** and **pop**. Function **push** adds a new node to the top of the stack. Function **pop** removes a node from the top of the stack, stores the popped value in a reference variable that is passed to the calling function, and returns 1 if the **pop** operation was successful (0 otherwise).

Stacks have many interesting applications. For example, when a function call is made, the called function must know how to return to its caller, so the return address is pushed onto a stack. If a series of function calls occurs, the successive return values are pushed onto the stack in last-in, first-out order so that each function can return to its caller. Stacks support recursive function calls in the same manner as conventional nonrecursive calls.

Stacks contain the space created for automatic variables on each invocation of a function. When the function returns to its caller, the space for that function's automatic variables is popped off the stack, and those variables are no longer known to the program.

Stacks are used by compilers in the process of evaluating expressions and generating machine language code. The Exercises explore several applications of stacks, including using them to develop a complete working compiler.

We will take advantage of the close relationship between lists and stacks to implement a stack class primarily by reusing a list class. We use two different forms of reusability. First, we implement the stack class through private inheritance of the list class. Then we implement an identically performing stack class through composition by including a list class as a private member of a stack class. Of course, all of the data structures in this chapter, including these two stack classes, are implemented as templates (see Chapter 12, "Templates") to encourage further reusability.

The program of Fig. 15.9 (whose output is shown in Fig. 15.10) creates a stack class template primarily through private inheritance of a list class template. We want the stack to have member functions **push**, **pop**, **isStackEmpty**, and **printStack**. Note that these are essentially the **insertAtFront**, **removeFromFront**, **isEmpty**, and **print** functions of list class template. Of course, the list class template contains other member functions (i.e., **insertAtBack** and **removeFromBack**) that we would not

```
// STACK.H
// Template Stack class definition
// Derived from class List
#ifndef STACK_H
#define STACK_H

#include "list.h"

template<class STACKTYPE>
class Stack : private List<STACKTYPE> {
public:
   void push(const STACKTYPE &d) { insertAtFront(d); }
   int pop(STACKTYPE &d) { return removeFromFront(d); }
   int isStackEmpty() const { return isEmpty(); }
   void printStack() const { print(); }
};

#endif
```

Fig. 15.9 A simple stack program (part 1 of 2).

```
// STACKDRV.CPP
// Driver to test the template Stack class
#include <iostream.h>
#include "stack.h"

main()
{
   Stack<int> intStack;
   int popInteger;
   cout << "processing an integer Stack" << endl;

   for (int i = 0; i < 4; i++) {
      intStack.push(i);
      intStack.printStack();
   }

   while (!intStack.isStackEmpty()) {
      intStack.pop(popInteger);
      cout << popInteger << " popped from stack" << endl;
      intStack.printStack();
   }

   Stack<float> floatStack;
   float val = 1.1, popFloat;

   cout << "processing a float Stack" << endl;

   for (i = 0; i < 4; i++) {
      floatStack.push(val);
      floatStack.printStack();
      val += 1.1;
   }

   while (!floatStack.isStackEmpty()) {
      floatStack.pop(popFloat);
      cout << popFloat << " popped from stack" << endl;
      floatStack.printStack();
   }

   return 0;
}
```

**Fig. 15.9** A simple stack program (part 2 of 2).

want to make accessible through the public interface to the stack class. So when we indicate that the stack class template is to inherit the list class template, we specify private inheritance. This makes all the list class template's member functions private in the stack class template. When we implement the stack's member functions, we then simply have each of these call the appropriate member function of the list class—**push** calls **insertAtFront**, **pop** calls **removeFromFront**, **isStackEmpty** calls **isEmpty**, and **printStack** calls **print**.

```
processing an integer Stack
The list is: 0

The list is: 1 0

The list is: 2 1 0

The list is: 3 2 1 0

3 popped from stack
The list is: 2 1 0

2 popped from stack
The list is: 1 0

1 popped from stack
The list is: 0

0 popped from stack
The list is empty

processing a float Stack
The list is: 1.1

The list is: 2.2 1.1

The list is: 3.3 2.2 1.1

The list is: 4.4 3.3 2.2 1.1

4.4 popped from stack
The list is: 3.3 2.2 1.1

3.3 popped from stack
The list is: 2.2 1.1

2.2 popped from stack
The list is: 1.1

1.1 popped from stack
The list is empty

All nodes destroyed

All nodes destroyed
```

**Fig. 15.10** Sample output from the program of Fig. 15.9.

The stack class template is used in **main** to instantiate integer stack **intStack** of type **Stack<int>**. Integers 0 through 3 are pushed onto **intStack** and then popped off **intStack**. The stack class template is then used to instantiate float stack **floatStack** of type **Stack<float>**. Float values 1.1, 2.2, 3.3, and 4.4 are pushed onto **floatStack** and then popped off **floatStack**.

Another way to implement a stack class template is by reusing a list class template through composition. The program of Fig. 15.11 uses the files **list.h** and **listnd.h** from the list program. It also uses the same driver program as the previous stack program, except the new header file—**stack_c.h**—is included and replaces **stack.h**. The output is also the same. The stack class template definition now includes member object **s** of type **List<STACKTYPE>**.

```
// STACK_C.H
// Definition of Stack class composed of List object
#ifndef STACK_C
#define STACK_C

#include "list.h"

template<class STACKTYPE>
class Stack {
public:
   // no constructor; List constructor does initialization
   void push(const STACKTYPE &);
   int pop(STACKTYPE &);
   int isStackEmpty() const;
   void printStack() const;
private:
   List<STACKTYPE> s;
};

// Push a value onto the Stack
template<class STACKTYPE>
void Stack<STACKTYPE>::push(const STACKTYPE &value)
   { s.insertAtFront(value); }

// Pop a value off the Stack
template<class STACKTYPE>
int Stack<STACKTYPE>::pop(STACKTYPE &value)
   { return s.removeFromFront(value); }

// Is the Stack empty?
template<class STACKTYPE>
int Stack<STACKTYPE>::isStackEmpty() const { return s.isEmpty(); }

// Display the Stack contents
template<class STACKTYPE>
void Stack<STACKTYPE>::printStack() const { s.print(); }

#endif
```

**Fig. 15.11** A simple stack program using composition.

## 15.6 Queues

Another common data structure is the *queue*. A queue is similar to a checkout line in a supermarket—the first person in line is serviced first, and other customers enter the line only at the end and wait to be serviced. Queue nodes are removed only from the *head* of the queue, and are inserted only at the *tail* of the queue. For this reason, a queue is referred to as a *first-in, first-out (FIFO)* data structure. The insert and remove operations are known as **enqueue** and **dequeue**.

Queues have many applications in computer systems. Most computers have only a single processor, so only one user at a time can be serviced. Entries for the other users are placed in a queue. Each entry gradually advances to the front of the queue as users receive service. The entry at the front of the queue is the next to receive service.

Queues are also used to support print spooling. A multiuser environment may have only a single printer. Many users may be generating outputs to be printed. If the printer is busy, other outputs may still be generated. These are "spooled" to disk (much as thread is wound onto a spool) where they wait in a queue until the printer becomes available.

Information packets also wait in queues in computer networks. Each time a packet arrives at a network node, it must be routed to the next node on the network along the path to the packet's final destination. The routing node routes one packet at a time, so additional packets are enqueued until the router can route them.

A file server in a computer network handles file access requests from many clients throughout the network. Servers have a limited capacity to service requests from clients. When that capacity is exceeded, client requests wait in queues.

***Common Programming Error 15.7***

*Not setting the link in the last node of a queue to null (zero).*

The program of Fig. 15.12 (whose output is shown in Fig. 15.13) creates a queue class template primarily through private inheritance of a list class template. We want the

```
// QUEUE.H
// Template Queue class definition (derived from class list)
#ifndef QUEUE_H
#define QUEUE_H
#include "list.h"

template<class QUEUETYPE>
class Queue: private List<QUEUETYPE> {
public:
   void enqueue(const QUEUETYPE &d) { insertAtBack(d); }
   int dequeue(QUEUETYPE &d) { return removeFromFront(d); }
   int isQueueEmpty() const { return isEmpty(); }
   void printQueue() const { print(); }
};

#endif
```

**Fig. 15.12** Processing a queue (part 1 of 2).

```
// QUEUEDRV.CPP
// Driver to test the template Queue class
#include <iostream.h>
#include "queue.h"

main()
{
   Queue<int> intQueue;
   int dequeueInteger;
   cout << "processing an integer Queue" << endl;

   for (int i = 0; i < 4; i++) {
      intQueue.enqueue(i);
      intQueue.printQueue();
   }

   while (!intQueue.isQueueEmpty()) {
      intQueue.dequeue(dequeueInteger);
      cout << dequeueInteger << " dequeued" << endl;
      intQueue.printQueue();
   }

   Queue<float> floatQueue;
   float val = 1.1, dequeueFloat;

   cout << "processing a float Queue" << endl;

   for (i = 0; i < 4; i++) {
      floatQueue.enqueue(val);
      floatQueue.printQueue();
      val += 1.1;
   }

   while (!floatQueue.isQueueEmpty()) {
      floatQueue.dequeue(dequeueFloat);
      cout << dequeueFloat << " dequeued" << endl;
      floatQueue.printQueue();
   }

   return 0;
}
```

**Fig. 15.12** Processing a queue (part 2 of 2).

queue to have member functions **enqueue**, **dequeue**, **isQueueEmpty**, and **printQueue**. We note that these are essentially the **insertAtBack**, **removeFromFront**, **isEmpty**, and **print** functions of the list class template. Of course, the list class template contains other member functions (i.e., **insertAtFront** and **removeFromBack**) that we would not want to make accessible through the public interface to the queue class. So when we indicate that the queue class template is to inherit the list class template, we specify private inheritance. This makes all the list class template's member

```
processing an integer Queue
The list is: 0

The list is: 0 1

The list is: 0 1 2

The list is: 0 1 2 3

0 dequeued
The list is: 1 2 3

1 dequeued
The list is: 2 3

2 dequeued
The list is: 3

3 dequeued
The list is empty

processing a float Queue
The list is: 1.1

The list is: 1.1 2.2

The list is: 1.1 2.2 3.3

The list is: 1.1 2.2 3.3 4.4

1.1 dequeued
The list is: 2.2 3.3 4.4

2.2 dequeued
The list is: 3.3 4.4

3.3 dequeued
The list is: 4.4

4.4 dequeued
The list is empty

All nodes destroyed

All nodes destroyed
```

**Fig. 15.13** Sample output from the program in Fig. 15.12.

functions private in the queue class template. When we implement the queue's member functions, we simply have each of these call the appropriate member function of the list class—**enqueue** calls **insertAtBack**, **dequeue** calls **removeFromFront**, **isQueueEmpty** calls **isEmpty**, and **printQueue** calls **print**.

The queue class template is used in **main** to instantiate integer queue **intQueue** of type **Queue<int>**. Integers 0 through 3 are enqueued to **intQueue** and then dequeued from **intQueue** in first-in-first-out order. The queue class template is then used to instantiate float queue **floatQueue** of type **Queue<float>**. Float values 1.1, 2.2, 3.3, and 4.4 are enqueued to **floatQueue** and then dequeued from **floatQueue** in first-in-first-out order.

## 15.7 Trees

Linked lists, stacks, and queues are *linear data structures.* A tree is a nonlinear, two-dimensional data structure with special properties. Tree nodes contain two or more links. This section discusses *binary trees* (Fig. 15.14)—trees whose nodes all contain two links (none, one, or both of which may be null). The *root node* is the first node in a tree. Each link in the root node refers to a *child.* The *left child* is the first node in the *left subtree,* and the *right child* is the first node in the *right subtree.* The children of a node are called *siblings.* A node with no children is called a *leaf node.* Computer scientists normally draw trees from the root node down—exactly the opposite of trees in nature.

In this section, a special binary tree called a *binary search tree* is created. A binary search tree (with no duplicate node values) has the characteristic that the values in any left subtree are less than the value in its parent node, and the values in any right subtree are greater than the value in its parent node. Figure 15.15 illustrates a binary search tree with 12 values. Note that the shape of the binary search tree that corresponds to a set of data can vary, depending on the order in which the values are inserted into the tree.

***Common Programming Error 15.8***

*Not setting to null (zero) the links in leaf nodes of a tree.*

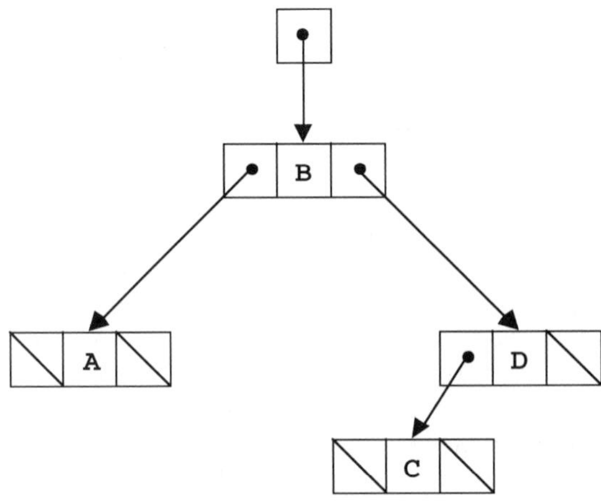


**Fig. 15.14** A graphical representation of a binary tree.

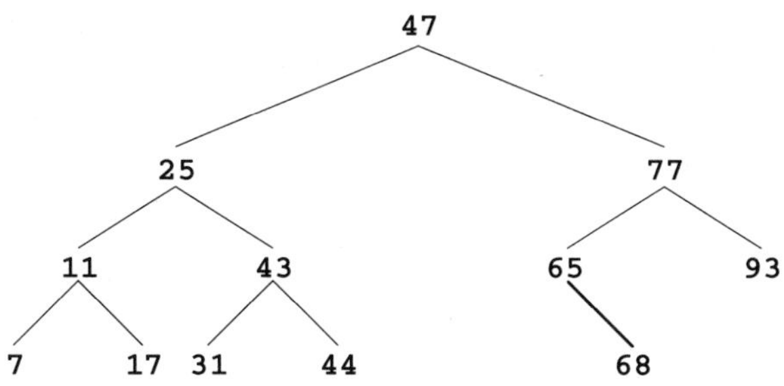


**Fig. 15.15** A binary search tree.

The program of Fig. 15.16 (whose output is shown in Fig. 15.17) creates a binary search tree and traverses it (i.e., walks through all its nodes) three ways—using recursive *inorder, preorder,* and *postorder traversals.* The program generates 10 random numbers and inserts each in the tree, except that duplicate values are discarded.

Let us walk through the binary tree program of Fig. 15.16. Function **main** begins by instantiating integer tree **intTree** of type **Tree<int>**. The program prompts for 10 integers, each of which is inserted in the binary tree through a call to **insertNode**. The program then performs preorder, inorder, and postorder traversals (these will be explained shortly) of **intTree**. The program then instantiates floating point tree **floatTree** of type **Tree<float>**. The program prompts for 10 float values, each of which is inserted in the binary tree through a call to **insertNode**. The program then performs preorder, inorder, and postorder traversals of **floatTree**.

Now, let us walk through the class template definitions and member functions. We begin with the **TreeNode** class template which declares as its friend the **Tree** class template. The **TreeNode** class has as private data the node's **data** value, and pointers **leftPtr** (to the node's left subtree) and **rightPtr** (to the node's right subtree). The constructor sets the **data** value to the value supplied as a constructor argument, and sets pointers **leftPtr** and **rightPtr** to zero (thus initializing this node to be a leaf node). Member function **getData** returns the **data** value.

The **Tree** class has as private data **rootPtr**, a pointer to the root node of the tree. The class has public member functions **insertNode** (that inserts a new node in the tree,) and **preorderTraversal**, **inorderTraversal**, and **postorderTraversal**, each of which walks the tree in the designated manner. Each of these member functions calls its own separate recursive utility function to perform the appropriate operations on the internal representation of the tree. The **Tree** constructor initializes **rootPtr** to zero to indicate that the tree is initially empty.

The **Tree** class's utility function **insertNodeHelper** recursively inserts a node into the tree. *A node can only be inserted as a leaf node in a binary search tree.* If the tree is empty, a new **TreeNode** is created, initialized, and inserted in the tree.

If the tree is not empty, the program compares the value to be inserted with the **data** value in the root node. If the insert value is smaller, the program recursively calls **insertNodeHelper** to insert the value in the left subtree. If the insert value is larger, the program recursively calls **insertNode** to insert the value in the right subtree. If the value to be inserted is identical to the data value in the root node, the program prints the message **" dup"** and returns without inserting the duplicate value into the tree.

```
// TREENODE.H: Definition of class TreeNode
#ifndef TREENODE_H
#define TREENODE_H

template<class NODETYPE>
class TreeNode {
   friend class Tree<NODETYPE>;
public:
   TreeNode(const NODETYPE &);   // constructor
   NODETYPE getData() const;     // return data
private:
   TreeNode *leftPtr;    // pointer to left subtree
   NODETYPE data;
   TreeNode *rightPtr;   // pointer to right subtree
};

// Constructor
template<class NODETYPE>
TreeNode<NODETYPE>::TreeNode(const NODETYPE &d)
{
   data = d;
   leftPtr = rightPtr = 0;
}

//Return a copy of the data value
template<class NODETYPE>
NODETYPE TreeNode<NODETYPE>::getData() const { return data; }
#endif

// TREE.H: Definition of template class Tree
#ifndef TREE_H
#define TREE_H
#include <iostream.h>
#include <assert.h>
#include "treenode.h"

template<class NODETYPE>
class Tree {
public:
   Tree();
   void insertNode(const NODETYPE &);
   void preOrderTraversal() const;
   void inOrderTraversal() const;
   void postOrderTraversal() const;
```

**Fig. 15.16** Creating and traversing a binary tree (part 1 of 4).

```
private:
   TreeNode<NODETYPE> *rootPtr;

   // utility functions
   void insertNodeHelper(TreeNode<NODETYPE> **, const NODETYPE &);
   void preOrderHelper(TreeNode<NODETYPE> *) const;
   void inOrderHelper(TreeNode<NODETYPE> *) const;
   void postOrderHelper(TreeNode<NODETYPE> *) const;
};

template<class NODETYPE>
Tree<NODETYPE>::Tree() { rootPtr = 0; }

template<class NODETYPE>
void Tree<NODETYPE>::insertNode(const NODETYPE &value)
   { insertNodeHelper(&rootPtr, value); }

// This function receives a pointer to a pointer so the
// pointer can be modified.
template<class NODETYPE>
void Tree<NODETYPE>::insertNodeHelper(TreeNode<NODETYPE> **ptr,
                                      const NODETYPE &value)
{
   if (*ptr == 0) {                   // tree is empty
      *ptr = new TreeNode<NODETYPE>(value);
      assert(*ptr != 0);
   }
   else                              // tree is not empty
      if (value < (*ptr)->data)
         insertNodeHelper( &((*ptr)->leftPtr), value);
      else

         if (value > (*ptr)->data)
            insertNodeHelper(&((*ptr)->rightPtr), value);
         else
            cout << value << " dup" << endl;
}

template<class NODETYPE>
void Tree<NODETYPE>::preOrderTraversal() const
   { preOrderHelper(rootPtr); }

template<class NODETYPE>
void Tree<NODETYPE>::preOrderHelper(TreeNode<NODETYPE> *ptr) const
{
   if (ptr != 0) {
      cout << ptr->data << ' ';
      preOrderHelper(ptr->leftPtr);
      preOrderHelper(ptr->rightPtr);
   }
}
```

**Fig. 15.16** Creating and traversing a binary tree (part 2 of 4).

```
template<class NODETYPE>
void Tree<NODETYPE>::inOrderTraversal() const
   { inOrderHelper(rootPtr); }

template<class NODETYPE>
void Tree<NODETYPE>::inOrderHelper(TreeNode<NODETYPE> *ptr) const
{
   if (ptr != 0) {
      inOrderHelper(ptr->leftPtr);
      cout << ptr->data << ' ';
      inOrderHelper(ptr->rightPtr);
   }
}

template<class NODETYPE>
void Tree<NODETYPE>::postOrderTraversal() const
   { postOrderHelper(rootPtr); }

template<class NODETYPE>
void Tree<NODETYPE>::postOrderHelper(TreeNode<NODETYPE> *ptr)
const
{
   if (ptr != 0) {
      postOrderHelper(ptr->leftPtr);
      postOrderHelper(ptr->rightPtr);
      cout << ptr->data << ' ';
   }
}

#endif

// Driver to test class Tree
#include <iostream.h>
#include <iomanip.h>
#include "tree.h"

main()
{
   Tree<int> intTree;
   int intVal;

   cout << "Enter 10 integer values:" << endl;
   for (int i = 0; i < 10; i++) {
      cin >> intVal;
      intTree.insertNode(intVal);
   }

   cout << endl << "Preorder traversal" << endl;
   intTree.preOrderTraversal();

   cout << endl << "Inorder traversal" << endl;
   intTree.inOrderTraversal();
```

**Fig. 15.16** Creating and traversing a binary tree (part 3 of 4).

```
    cout << endl << "Postorder traversal" << endl;
    intTree.postOrderTraversal();

    Tree<float> floatTree;
    float floatVal;

    cout << endl << endl << endl << "Enter 10 float values:"
         << endl << setiosflags(ios::fixed | ios::showpoint)
         << setprecision(1);
    for (i = 0; i < 10; i++) {
       cin >> floatVal;
       floatTree.insertNode(floatVal);
    }

    cout << endl << "Preorder traversal" << endl;
    floatTree.preOrderTraversal();

    cout << endl << "Inorder traversal" << endl;
    floatTree.inOrderTraversal();

    cout << endl << "Postorder traversal" << endl;
    floatTree.postOrderTraversal();

    return 0;
}
```

**Fig. 15.16** Creating and traversing a binary tree (part 4 of 4).

```
Enter 10 integer values:
50 25 75 12 33 67 88 6 13 68

Preorder traversal
50 25 12 6 13 33 75 67 68 88
Inorder traversal
6 12 13 25 33 50 67 68 75 88
Postorder traversal
6 13 12 33 25 68 67 88 75 50


Enter 10 float values:
39.2 16.5 82.7 3.3 65.2 90.8 1.1 4.4 89.5 92.5

Preorder traversal
39.2 16.5 3.3 1.1 4.4 82.7 65.2 90.8 89.5 92.5
Inorder traversal
1.1 3.3 4.4 16.5 39.2 65.2 82.7 89.5 90.8 92.5
Postorder traversal
1.1 4.4 3.3 16.5 65.2 89.5 92.5 90.8 82.7 39.2
```

**Fig. 15.17** Sample output from the program of Fig. 15.16.

Each of the member functions **inOrderTraversal**, **preOrderTraversal**, and **postOrderTraversal** traverse the tree (Fig. 15.18) and print the node values.

The steps for an **inOrderTraversal** are:

1) Traverse the left subtree with an **inOrderTraversal**.
2) Process the value in the node (i.e., print the node value).
3) Traverse the right subtree with an **inOrderTraversal**.

The value in a node is not processed until the values in its left subtree are processed. The **inOrderTraversal** of the tree in Fig. 15.18 is:

```
6 13 17 27 33 42 48
```

Note that the **inOrderTraversal** of a binary search tree prints the node values in ascending order. The process of creating a binary search tree actually sorts the data—and thus this process is called the *binary tree sort.*

The steps for a **preOrderTraversal** are:

1) Process the value in the node.
2) Traverse the left subtree with a **preOrderTraversal**.
3) Traverse the right subtree with a **preOrderTraversal**.

The value in each node is processed as the node is visited. After the value in a given node is processed, the values in the left subtree are processed, then the values in the right subtree are processed. The **preOrderTraversal** of the tree in Fig. 15.18 is:

```
27 13 6 17 42 33 48
```

The steps for a **postOrderTraversal** are:

1) Traverse the left subtree with a **postOrderTraversal**.
2) Traverse the right subtree with a **postOrderTraversal**.
3) Process the value in the node.

The value in each node is not printed until the values of its children are printed. The **postOrderTraversal** of the tree in Fig. 15.18 is:

```
6 17 13 33 48 42 27
```

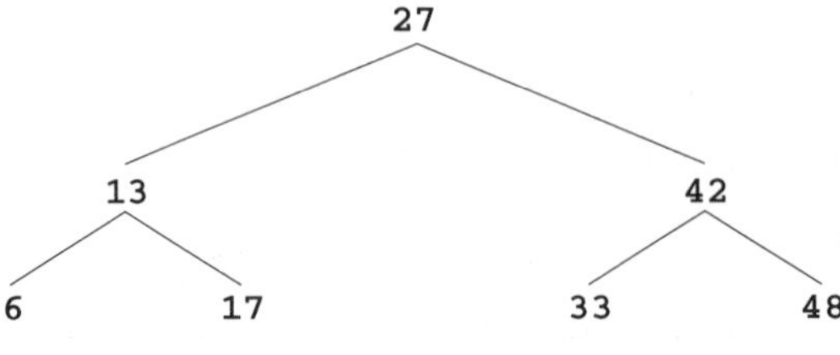


**Fig. 15.18** A binary search tree.

The binary search tree facilitates *duplicate elimination.* As the tree is being created, an attempt to insert a duplicate value will be recognized because a duplicate will follow the same "go left" or "go right" decisions on each comparison as the original value did. Thus, the duplicate will eventually be compared with a node containing the same value. The duplicate value may simply be discarded at this point.

Searching a binary tree for a value that matches a key value is also fast. If the tree is tightly packed, then each level contains about twice as many elements as the previous level. So a binary search tree with $n$ elements would have a maximum of $\log_2 n$ levels, and thus a maximum of $\log_2 n$ comparisons would have to be made either to find a match or to determine that no match exists. This means, for example, that when searching a (tightly packed) 1000-element binary search tree, no more than 10 comparisons need to be made because $2^{10} > 1000$. When searching a (tightly packed) 1,000,000 element binary search tree, no more than 20 comparisons need to be made because $2^{20} > 1{,}000{,}000$.

In the Exercises, algorithms are presented for several other binary tree operations such as deleting an item from a binary tree, printing a binary tree in a two-dimensional tree format, and performing a level-order traversal of a binary tree. The level-order traversal of a binary tree visits the nodes of the tree row-by-row starting at the root node level. On each level of the tree, the nodes are visited from left to right. Other binary tree exercises include allowing a binary search tree to contain duplicate values, inserting string values in a binary tree, and determining how many levels are contained in a binary tree.

## Summary

- Self-referential classes contain members called links that point to objects of the same class type.
- Self-referential classes enable many class objects to be linked together in stacks, queues, lists, and trees.
- Dynamic memory allocation reserves a block of bytes in memory to store an object during program execution.
- A linked list is a linear collection of self-referential class objects.
- A linked list is a dynamic data structure—the length of the list can increase or decrease as necessary.
- Linked lists can continue to grow until memory is exhausted.
- Linked lists provide a mechanism for simple insertion and deletion of data by pointer manipulation.
- Stacks and queues are constrained versions of linked lists.
- New stack nodes are added to a stack and are removed from a stack only at the top of the stack.. For this reason, a stack is referred to as a last-in, first-out (LIFO) data structure.
- The link member in the last node of the stack is set to null (zero) to indicate the bottom of the stack.

- The two primary operations used to manipulate a stack are **push** and **pop**. The **push** operation creates a new node and places it on the top of the stack. The **pop** operation removes a node from the top of the stack, deletes the memory that was allocated to the popped node, and returns the popped value.
- In a queue data structure, nodes are removed from the head and added to the tail. For this reason, a queue is referred to as a first-in, first-out (FIFO) data structure. The add and remove operations are known as **enqueue** and **dequeue**.
- Trees are two-dimensional data structures requiring two or more links per node.
- Binary trees contain two links per node.
- The root node is the first node in the tree.
- Each of the pointers in the root node refers to a child. The left child is the first node in the left subtree, and the right child is the first node in the right subtree. The children of a node are called siblings. Any tree node that does not have any children is called a leaf node.
- A binary search tree has the characteristic that the value in the left child of a node is less than the value in its parent node, and the value in the right child of a node is greater than or equal to the value in its parent node. If there are no duplicate data values, the value in the right child is simply greater than the value in its parent node.
- An inorder traversal of a binary tree traverses the left subtree inorder, processes the value in the root node, then traverses the right subtree inorder. The value in a node is not processed until the values in its left subtree are processed.
- A preorder traversal processes the value in the root node, traverses the left subtree preorder, then traverses the right subtree preorder. The value in each node is processed as the node is encountered.
- A postorder traversal traverses the left subtree postorder, traverses the right subtree postorder, then processes the value in the root node. The value in each node is not processed until the values in both its subtrees are processed.

## Terminology

binary search tree
binary tree
binary tree sort
child node
children
deleting a node
**dequeue**
double indirection
duplicate elimination
dynamic data structures
dynamic memory allocation
**enqueue**
FIFO (first-in, first-out)
head of a queue
inorder traversal of a binary tree
inserting a node
leaf node
left child
left subtree
level-order traversal of a binary tree
LIFO (last-in, first-out)
linear data structure
linked list
node

nonlinear data structure
null pointer
parent node
pointer to a pointer
**`pop`**
postorder traversal of a binary tree
predicate function
preorder traversal of a binary tree
**`push`**
queue
right child
right subtree
root node
self-referential structure
siblings
**`sizeof`**
stack
subtree
tail of a queue
top
traversal
tree
visit a node

## Common Programming Errors

**15.1** Not setting the link in the last node of a list to null (zero).

**15.2** Assuming that the size of a class object is simply the sum of the sizes of its data members.

**15.3** Not returning dynamically allocated memory when it is no longer needed can cause the system to run out of memory prematurely. This is sometimes called a "memory leak."

**15.4** Deleting memory with **`delete`** that was not allocated dynamically with **`new`**.

**15.5** Referring to memory that has been deleted.

**15.6** Not setting the link in the bottom node of a stack to null (zero).

**15.7** Not setting the link in the last node of a queue to null (zero).

**15.8** Not setting to null (zero) the links in leaf nodes of a tree.

## Good Programming Practices

**15.1** When using **`new`**, test for a null pointer return value. Perform appropriate error processing if the requested memory is not allocated.

**15.2** When memory that was dynamically allocated with **`new`** is no longer needed, use **`delete`** to return the memory to the system immediately.

**15.3** Assign null (zero) to the link member of a new node. Pointers should be initialized before they are used.

## Performance Tips

**15.1** An array can be declared to contain more elements than the number of items expected, but this can waste memory. Linked lists can provide better memory utilization in these situations. Linked lists allow the program to adapt at run time.

**15.2** Insertion and deletion in a sorted array can be time consuming—all the elements following the inserted or deleted element must be shifted appropriately.

**15.3** The elements of an array are stored contiguously in memory. This allows immediate access to any array element because the address of any element can be calculated directly based on its position relative to the beginning of the array. Linked lists do not afford such immediate access to their elements.

**15.4** Using dynamic memory allocation (instead of arrays) for data structures that grow and shrink at execution time can save memory. Keep in mind, however, that pointers occupy space, and that dynamic memory allocation incurs the overhead of function calls.

## Portability Tip

**15.1** A class object's size is not necessarily the sum of the sizes of its data members. This is because of various machine-dependent boundary alignment requirements (see Chapter 16) and other reasons.

## Self-Review Exercises

**15.1** Fill in the blanks in each of the following:

a) A self-__________ class is used to form dynamic data structures. that can grow and shrink at execution time
b) Operator __________ is used to dynamically allocate memory; this operator returns a pointer to the allocated memory.
c) A __________ is a constrained version of a linked list in which nodes can be inserted and deleted only from the start of the list; this data structure returns node values in last-in-first-out order.
d) A functionsthat does not alter a linked list, but simply looks at the list to determine if it is empty is referred to as a __________function.
e) A queue is referred to as a __________ data structure because the first nodes inserted are the first nodes removed.
f) The pointer to the next node in a linked list is referred to as a __________.
g) Operator __________ is used to reclaim dynamically allocated memory.
h) A __________ is a constrained version of a linked list in which nodes can be inserted only at the end of the list and deleted only from the start of the list.
i) A __________ is a nonlinear, two-dimensional data structure that contains nodes with two or more links.
j) A stack is referred to as a __________ data structure because the last node inserted is the first node removed.
k) The nodes of a __________ tree contain two link members.
l) The first node of a tree is the __________ node.
m) Each link in a tree node points to a __________ or __________ of that node.
n) A tree node that has no children is called a __________ node.
o) The four traversal algorithms we mentioned in the text for binary search trees are ________, ________, _________ and ________.

**15.2** What are the differences between a linked list and a stack?

**15.3** What are the differences between a stack and a queue?

**15.4** Perhaps a more appropriate title for this chapter would have been "Reusable Data Structures." Comment on how each of the following entities or concepts contributes to the reusability of data structures:

a) classes
b) template classes
c) inheritance
d) private inheritance
e) composition.

**15.5** Manually provide the inorder, preorder, and postorder traversals of the binary search tree of Fig. 15.19.

## Answers to Self-Review Exercises

**15.1** a) referential. b) `new`. c) stack. d) predicate functions. e) first-in-first-out (FIFO). f) link. g) `delete`. h) queue. i) tree. j) last-in-first-out (LIFO). k) binary. l) root. m) child or subtree. n) leaf. o) inorder, preorder, and postorder.

**15.2** It is possible to insert a node anywhere in a linked list and remove a node from anywhere in a linked list. Nodes in a stack may only be inserted at the top of the stack and removed from the top of a stack.

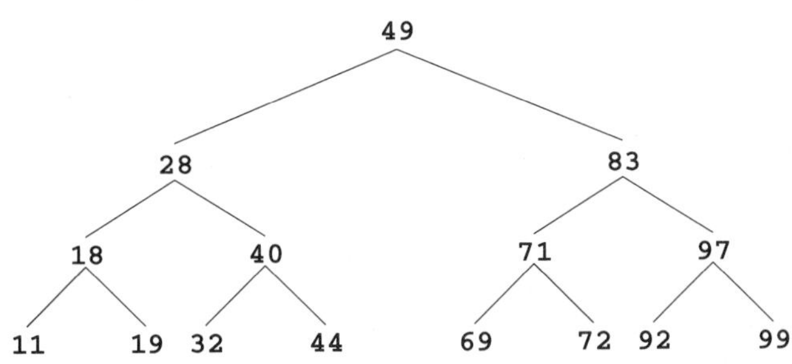


**Fig. 15.19** A 15-node binary search tree.

**15.3** A queue has pointers to both its head and its tail so that nodes may be inserted at the tail and deleted from the head. A stack has a single pointer to the top of the stack where both insertion and deletion of nodes are performed.

**15.4** a) Classes allow us to instantiate as many data structure objects of a certain type (i.e., class) as we wish.

b) Class templates enable us to instantiate related classes—each based on different type parameters—we can then generate as many objects of each template class as we like.

c) Inheritance enables us to reuse code from a base class in a derived class so that the derived class data structure is also a base class data structure (with public inheritance, that is).

d) Private inheritance enables us to reuse portions of the code from a base class to form a derived class data structure; because the inheritance is private, all public base-class member functions become private in the derived class. This enables us to prevent clients of the derived class data structure from accessing base-class member functions that do not apply to the derived class.

e) Composition enables us to reuse code by making a class object data structure a member of a composed class; if we make the class object a private member of the composed class, then the class object's public member functions are not available through the composed object's interface.

**15.5** The inorder traversal is:

```
11 18 19 28 32 40 44 49 69 71 72 83 92 97 99
```

The preorder traversal is:

```
49 28 18 11 19 40 32 44 83 71 69 72 97 92 99
```

The postorder traversal is:

```
11 19 18 32 44 40 28 69 72 71 92 99 97 83 49
```

## Exercises

**15.6** Write a program that concatenates two linked list objects of characters. The program should include function **concatenate** that takes references to both list objects as arguments and concatenates the second list to the first list.

**15.7** Write a program that merges two ordered list objects of integers into a single ordered list object of integers. Function **merge** should receive references to each of the list objects to be merged, and should return a reference to the merged list object.

**15.8** Write a program that inserts 25 random integers from 0 to 100 in order in a linked list object. The program should calculate the sum of the elements, and the floating-point average of the elements.

**15.9** Write a program that creates a linked list object of 10 characters, then creates a second list object containing a copy of the first list, but in reverse order.

**15.10** Write a program that inputs a line of text and uses a stack object to print the line reversed.

**15.11** Write a program that uses a stack object to determine if a string is a palindrome (i.e., the string is spelled identically backwards and forwards). The program should ignore spaces and punctuation.

**15.12** Stacks are used by compilers to help in the process of evaluating expressions and generating machine language code. In this and the next exercise, we investigate how compilers evaluate arithmetic expressions consisting only of constants, operators, and parentheses.

Humans generally write expressions like `3 + 4` and `7 / 9` in which the operator (`+` or `/` here) is written between its operands—this is called *infix notation.* Computers "prefer" *postfix notation* in which the operator is written to the right of its two operands. The preceding infix expressions would appear in postfix notation as `3 4 +` and `7 9 /`, respectively.

To evaluate a complex infix expression, a compiler would first convert the expression to postfix notation, and then evaluate the postfix version of the expression. Each of these algorithms requires only a single left-to-right pass of the expression. Each algorithm uses a stack object in support of its operation, and in each algorithm the stack is used for a different purpose.

In this exercise, you will write a C++ version of the infix-to-postfix conversion algorithm. In the next exercise, you will write a C++ version of the postfix expression evaluation algorithm. Later in the chapter, you will discover that code you write in this exercise can help you implement a complete working compiler.

Write a program that converts an ordinary infix arithmetic expression (assume a valid expression is entered) with single digit integers such as

```
(6 + 2) * 5 - 8 / 4
```

to a postfix expression. The postfix version of the preceding infix expression is

```
6 2 + 5 * 8 4 / -
```

The program should read the expression into character array **infix**, and use modified versions of the stack functions implemented in this chapter to help create the postfix expression in character array **postfix**. The algorithm for creating a postfix expression is as follows:

1) Push a left parenthesis `'('` on the stack.
2) Append a right parenthesis `')'` to the end of **infix**.
3) While the stack is not empty, read **infix** from left to right and do the following:
   If the current character in **infix** is a digit, copy it to the next element of **postfix**.
   If the current character in **infix** is a left parenthesis, push it on the stack.

If the current character in **infix** is an operator,
  Pop operators (if there are any) at the top of the stack while they have equal or higher precedence than the current operator, and insert the popped operators in **postfix**.
  Push the current character in **infix** on the stack.
If the current character in **infix** is a right parenthesis
  Pop operators from the top of the stack and insert them in **postfix** until a left parenthesis is at the top of the stack.
  Pop (and discard) the left parenthesis from the stack.

The following arithmetic operations are allowed in an expression:

| | |
|---|---|
| + | addition |
| - | subtraction |
| * | multiplication |
| / | division |
| ^ | exponentiation |
| % | modulus |

The stack should be maintained with stack nodes that each contain a data member and a pointer to the next stack node.
Some of the functional capabilities you may want to provide are:

a) Function **convertToPostfix** that converts the infix expression to postfix notation.
b) Function **isOperator** that determines if **c** is an operator.
c) Function **precedence** that determines if the precedence of **operator1** is less than, equal to, or greater than the precedence of **operator2**. The function returns -1, 0, and 1, respectively.
d) Function **push** that pushes a value on the stack.
e) Function **pop** that pops a value off the stack.
f) Function **stackTop** that returns the top value of the stack without popping the stack.
g) Function **isEmpty** that determines if the stack is empty.
h) Function **printStack** that prints the stack.

**15.13** Write a program that evaluates a postfix expression (assume it is valid) such as

```
6 2 + 5 * 8 4 / -
```

The program should read a postfix expression consisting of digits and operators into a character array. Using modified versions of the stack functions implemented earlier in this chapter, the program should scan the expression and evaluate it. The algorithm is as follows:

1) Append the null character (**'\0'**) to the end of the postfix expression. When the null character is encountered, no further processing is necessary.
2) While **'\0'** has not been encountered, read the expression from left to right.
   If the current character is a digit,
     Push its integer value on the stack (the integer value of a digit character is its value in the computer's character set minus the value of **'0'** in the computer's character set).
   Otherwise, if the current character is an *operator*,
     Pop the two top elements of the stack into variables **x** and **y**.
     Calculate **y** *operator* **x**.
     Push the result of the calculation onto the stack.
3) When the null character is encountered in the expression, pop the top value of the stack. This is the result of the postfix expression.

Note: In 2) above, if the operator is `'/'`, the top of the stack is `2`, and the next element in the stack is `8`, then pop `2` into **`x`**, pop `8` into **`y`**, evaluate `8 / 2`, and push the result, `4`, back on the stack. This note also applies to operator `'-'`. The arithmetic operations allowed in an expression are:

| | |
|---|---|
| `+` | addition |
| `-` | subtraction |
| `*` | multiplication |
| `/` | division |
| `^` | exponentiation |
| `%` | modulus |

The stack should be maintained with stack nodes that contain an **`int`** data member and a pointer to the next stack node. You may want to provide the following functional capabilities:

a) Function **`evaluatePostfixExpression`** that evaluates the postfix expression.
b) Function **`calculate`** that evaluates the expression **`op1 operator op2`**.
c) Function **`push`** that pushes a value on the stack.
d) Function **`pop`** that pops a value off the stack.
e) Function **`isEmpty`** that determines if the stack is empty.
f) Function **`printStack`** that prints the stack.

**15.14** Modify the postfix evaluator program of Exercise 15.13 so that it can process integer operands larger than 9.

**15.15** *(Supermarket simulation)* Write a program that simulates a check-out line at a supermarket. The line is a queue object. Customers (i.e., customer objects) arrive in random integer intervals of 1 to 4 minutes. Also, each customer is serviced in random integer intervals of 1 to 4 minutes. Obviously, the rates need to be balanced. If the average arrival rate is larger than the average service rate, the queue will grow infinitely. Even with "balanced" rates, randomness can still cause long lines. Run the supermarket simulation for a 12-hour day (720 minutes) using the following algorithm:

1) Choose a random integer between 1 and 4 to determine the minute at which the first customer arrives.
2) At the first customer's arrival time:
   Determine customer's service time (random integer from 1 to 4);
   Begin servicing the customer;
   Schedule the arrival time of the next customer (random integer 1 to 4 added to the current time).
3) For each minute of the day:
   If the next customer arrives,
      Say so,
      Enqueue the customer;
      Schedule the arrival time of the next customer;
   If service was completed for the last customer;
      Say so
      Dequeue next customer to be serviced
      Determine customer's service completion time (random integer from 1 to 4 added to the current time).

Now run your simulation for 720 minutes and answer each of the following:

a) What is the maximum number of customers in the queue at any time?
b) What is the longest wait any one customer experiences?
c) What happens if the arrival interval is changed from 1-to-4 minutes to 1-to-3 minutes?

**15.16** Modify the program of Fig. 15.16 to allow the binary tree object to contain duplicates.

**15.17** Write a program based on the program of Fig. 15.16 that inputs a line of text, tokenizes the sentence into separate words (you may want to use the **`strtok`** library function), inserts the words in a binary search tree, and prints the inorder, preorder, and postorder traversals of the tree. Use an OOP approach.

**15.18** In this chapter, we saw that duplicate elimination is straightforward when creating a binary search tree. Describe how you would perform duplicate elimination using only a single-subscripted array. Compare the performance of array-based duplicate elimination with the performance of binary-search-tree-based duplicate elimination.

**15.19** Write a function **`depth`** that receives a binary tree and determines how many levels it has.

**15.20** *(Recursively print a list backwards)* Write a member function **`printListBackwards`** that recursively outputs the items in a linked list object in reverse order. Write a test program that creates a sorted list of integers and prints the list in reverse order.

**15.21** *(Recursively search a list)* Write a member function **`searchList`** that recursively searches a linked list object for a specified value. The function should return a pointer to the value if it is found; otherwise, null should be returned. Use your function in a test program that creates a list of integers. The program should prompt the user for a value to locate in the list.

**15.22** *(Binary tree delete)* In this exercise, we discuss deleting items from binary search trees. The deletion algorithm is not as straightforward as the insertion algorithm. There are three cases that are encountered when deleting an item—the item is contained in a leaf node (i.e., it has no children), the item is contained in a node that has one child, or the item is contained in a node that has two children.

If the item to be deleted is contained in a leaf node, the node is deleted and the pointer in the parent node is set to null.

If the item to be deleted is contained in a node with one child, the pointer in the parent node is set to point to the child node and the node containing the data item is deleted. This causes the child node to take the place of the deleted node in the tree.

The last case is the most difficult. When a node with two children is deleted, another node in the tree must take its place. However, the pointer in the parent node cannot simply be assigned to point to one of the children of the node to be deleted. In most cases, the resulting binary search tree would not adhere to the following characteristic of binary search trees (with no duplicate values): *The values in any left subtree are less than the value in the parent node, and the values in any right subtree are greater than the value in the parent node.*

Which node is used as a *replacement node* to maintain this characteristic? Either the node containing the largest value in the tree less than the value in the node being deleted, or the node containing the smallest value in the tree greater than the value in the node being deleted. Let us consider the node with the smaller value. In a binary search tree, the largest value less than a parent's value is located in the left subtree of the parent node and is guaranteed to be contained in the rightmost node of the subtree. This node is located by walking down the left subtree to the right until the pointer to the right child of the current node is null. We are now pointing to the replacement node which is either a leaf node or a node with one child to its left. If the replacement node is a leaf node, the steps to perform the deletion are as follows:

1) Store the pointer to the node to be deleted in a temporary pointer variable (this pointer is used to delete the dynamically allocated memory)
2) Set the pointer in the parent of the node being deleted to point to the replacement node
3) Set the pointer in the parent of the replacement node to null

4) Set the pointer to the right subtree in the replacement node to point to the right subtree of the node to be deleted
5) Delete the node to which the temporary pointer variable points.

The deletion steps for a replacement node with a left child are similar to those for a replacement node with no children, but the algorithm also must move the child in to the replacement node's position in the tree. If the replacement node is a node with a left child, the steps to perform the deletion are as follows:

1) Store the pointer to the node to be deleted in a temporary pointer variable
2) Set the pointer in the parent of the node being deleted to point to the replacement node
3) Set the pointer in the parent of the replacement node to point to the left child of the replacement node
4) Set the pointer to the right subtree in the replacement node to point to the right subtree of the node to be deleted
5) Delete the node to which the temporary pointer variable points.

Write member function **`deleteNode`** which takes as its arguments a pointer to the root node of the tree object and the value to be deleted. The function should locate in the tree the node containing the value to be deleted and use the algorithms discussed here to delete the node. If the value is not found in the tree, the function should print a message that indicates whether or not the value is deleted. Modify the program of Fig. 15.16 to use this function. After deleting an item, call the **`inOrder`**, **`preOrder`**, and **`postOrder`** traversal functions to confirm that the delete operation was performed correctly.

**15.23** (*Binary tree search*) Write member function **`binaryTreeSearch`** that attempts to locate a specified value in a binary search tree object. The function should take as arguments a pointer to the root node of the binary tree and a search key to be located. If the node containing the search key is found, the function should return a pointer to that node; otherwise, the function should return a null pointer.

**15.24** (*Level-order binary tree traversal*) The program of Fig. 15.16 illustrated three recursive methods of traversing a binary tree—inorder, preorder, and postorder traversals. This exercise presents the *level-order traversal* of a binary tree in which the node values are printed level-by-level starting at the root node level. The nodes on each level are printed from left to right. The level-order traversal is not a recursive algorithm. It uses a queue object to control the output of the nodes. The algorithm is as follows:

1) Insert the root node in the queue
2) While there are nodes left in the queue,
   - Get the next node in the queue
   - Print the node's value
   - If the pointer to the left child of the node is not null
     - Insert the left child node in the queue
   - If the pointer to the right child of the node is not null
     - Insert the right child node in the queue.

Write member function **`levelOrder`** to perform a level-order traversal of a binary tree object. Modify the program of Fig 15.16 to use this function. (Note: You will also need to modify and incorporate the queue processing functions of Fig. 15.12 in this program.)

**15.25** (*Printing trees*) Write a recursive member function **`outputTree`** to display a binary tree object on the screen. The function should output the tree row-by-row with the top of the tree at the left of the screen and the bottom of the tree toward the right of the screen. Each row is output vertically. For example, the binary tree illustrated in Fig. 15.19 is output as follows:

```
                    99
               97
                    92
          83
                    72
               71
                    69
     49
                    44
               40
                    32
          28
                    19
               18
                    11
```

Note the rightmost leaf node appears at the top of the output in the rightmost column and the root node appears at the left of the output. Each column of output starts five spaces to the right of the previous column. Function **outputTree** should receive an argument **totalSpaces** representing the number of spaces preceding the value to be output (this variable should start at zero so the root node is output at the left of the screen). The function uses a modified inorder traversal to output the tree—it starts at the rightmost node in the tree and works back to the left. The algorithm is as follows:

While the pointer to the current node is not null
  Recursively call **outputTree** with the right subtree of the current node and **totalSpaces** + 5
  Use a **for** structure to count from 1 to **totalSpaces** and output spaces
  Output the value in the current node
  Set the pointer to the current node to point to the left subtree of the current node
  Increment **totalSpaces** by 5.

## Special Section: Building Your Own Compiler

In Exercises 5.18 and 5.19, we introduced Simpletron Machine Language (SML) and you implemented a Simpletron computer simulator to execute programs written in SML. In this section, we build a compiler that converts programs written in a high-level programming language to SML. This section "ties" together the entire programming process. You will write programs in this new high-level language, compile these programs on the compiler you build, and run the programs on the simulator you built in Exercise 7.19. You should make every effort to implement your compiler in an object-oriented manner.

**15.26** (*The Simple Language*) Before we begin building the compiler, we discuss a simple, yet powerful, high-level language similar to early versions of the popular language BASIC. We call the language *Simple*. Every Simple *statement* consists of a *line number* and a Simple *instruction*. Line numbers must appear in ascending order. Each instruction begins with one of the following Simple *commands*: **rem**, **input**, **let**, **print**, **goto**, **if/goto**, or **end** (see Fig. 15.20). All commands except **end** can be used repeatedly. Simple evaluates only integer expressions using the **+**, **-**, *****, and **/** operators. These operators have the same precedence as in C. Parentheses can be used to change the order of evaluation of an expression.

| Command | Example statement | Description |
|---|---|---|
| `rem` | `50 rem this is a remark` | Any text following the command `rem` is for documentation purposes only and is ignored by the compiler. |
| `input` | `30 input x` | Display a question mark to prompt the user to enter an integer. Read that integer from the keyboard and store the integer in `x`. |
| `let` | `80 let u = 4 * (j - 56)` | Assign `u` the value of `4 * (j - 56)`. Note that an arbitrarily complex expression can appear to the right of the equal sign. |
| `print` | `10 print w` | Display the value of `w`. |
| `goto` | `70 goto 45` | Transfer program control to line `45`. |
| `if/goto` | `35 if i == z goto 80` | Compare `i` and `z` for equality and transfer program control to line `80` if the condition is true; otherwise, continue execution with the next statement. |
| `end` | `99 end` | Terminate program execution. |

**Fig. 15.20** Simple commands.

Our Simple compiler recognizes only lowercase letters. All characters in a Simple file should be lowercase (uppercase letters result in a syntax error unless they appear in a `rem` statement in which case they are ignored). A *variable name* is a single letter. Simple does not allow descriptive variable names, so variables should be explained in remarks to indicate their use in a program. Simple uses only integer variables. Simple does not have variable declarations—merely mentioning a variable name in a program causes the variable to be declared and initialized to zero automatically. The syntax of Simple does not allow string manipulation (reading a string, writing a string, comparing strings, etc.). If a string is encountered in a Simple program (after a command other than `rem`), the compiler generates a syntax error. The first version of our compiler will assume that Simple programs are entered correctly. Exercise 15.29 asks the student to modify the compiler to perform syntax error checking.

Simple uses the conditional `if/goto` statement and the unconditional `goto` statement to alter the flow of control during program execution. If the condition in the `if/goto` statement is true, control is transferred to a specific line of the program. The following relational and equality operators are valid in an `if/goto` statement: `<`, `>`, `<=`, `>=`, `==`, or `!=`. The precedence of these operators is the same as in C++.

Let us now consider several programs that demonstrate Simple's features. The first program (Fig. 15.21) reads two integers from the keyboard, stores the values in variables `a` and `b`, and computes and prints their sum (stored in variable `c`).

The program of Fig. 15.22 determines and prints the larger of two integers. The integers are input from the keyboard and stored in `s` and `t`. The `if/goto` statement tests the condition `s >= t`. If the condition is true, control is transferred to line `90` and `s` is output; otherwise, `t` is output and control is transferred to the `end` statement in line `99` where the program terminates.

```
10 rem   determine and print the sum of two integers
15 rem
20 rem   input the two integers
30 input a
40 input b
45 rem
50 rem   add integers and store result in c
60 let c = a + b
65 rem
70 rem   print the result
80 print c
90 rem   terminate program execution
99 end
```

**Fig. 15.21** Simple program that determines the sum of two integers.

```
10 rem   determine the larger of two integers
20 input s
30 input t
32 rem
35 rem   test if s >= t
40 if s >= t goto 90
45 rem
50 rem   t is greater than s, so print t
60 print t
70 goto 99
75 rem
80 rem   s is greater than or equal to t, so print s
90 print s
99 end
```

**Fig. 15.22** Simple program that finds the larger of two integers.

Simple does not provide a repetition structure (such as C++'s **`for`**, **`while`**, or **`do/while`**). However, Simple can simulate each of C++'s repetition structures using the **`if/goto`** and **`goto`** statements. Figure 15.23 uses a sentinel-controlled loop to calculate the squares of several integers. Each integer is input from the keyboard and stored in variable **`j`**. If the value entered is the sentinel **`-9999`**, control is transferred to line **`99`** where the program terminates. Otherwise, **`k`** is assigned the square of **`j`**, **`k`** is output to the screen, and control is passed to line **`20`** where the next integer is input.

Using the sample programs of Fig. 15.21, Fig. 15.22, and Fig. 15.23 as your guide, write a Simple program to accomplish each of the following:

a) Input three integers, determine their average, and print the result.
b) Use a sentinel-controlled loop to input 10 integers and compute and print their sum.
c) Use a counter-controlled loop to input 7 integers, some positive and some negative, and compute and print their average.
d) Input a series of integers and determine and print the largest. The first integer input indicates how many numbers should be processed.

e) Input 10 integers and print the smallest.
f) Calculate and print the sum of the even integers from 2 to 30.
g) Calculate and print the product of the odd integers from 1 to 9.

**15.27** *(Building A Compiler; Prerequisite: Complete Exercises 5.18, 5.19, 15.12, 15.13, and 15.26)* Now that the Simple language has been presented (Exercise 15.26), we discuss how to build a Simple compiler. First, we consider the process by which a Simple program is converted to SML and executed by the Simpletron simulator (see Fig. 15.24). A file containing a Simple program is read by the compiler and converted to SML code. The SML code is output to a file on disk, in which SML instructions appear one per line. The SML file is then loaded into the Simpletron simulator, and the results are sent to a file on disk and to the screen. Note that the Simpletron program developed in Exercise 5.19 took its input from the keyboard. It must be modified to read from a file so it can run the programs produced by our compiler.

The Simple compiler performs two *passes* of the Simple program to convert it to SML. The first pass constructs a *symbol table* (object) in which every *line number* (object), *variable name* (object) and *constant* (object) of the Simple program is stored with its type and corresponding location in the final SML code (the symbol table is discussed in detail below). The first pass also produces the corresponding SML instruction object(s) for each of the Simple statements (object, etc.). As we will see, if the Simple program contains statements that transfer control to a line later

```
10 rem   calculate the squares of several integers
20 input j
23 rem
25 rem   test for sentinel value
30 if j == -9999 goto 99
33 rem
35 rem   calculate square of j and assign result to k
40 let k = j * j
50 print k
53 rem
55 rem   loop to get next j
60 goto 20
99 end
```

**Fig. 15.23** Calculate the squares of several integers.

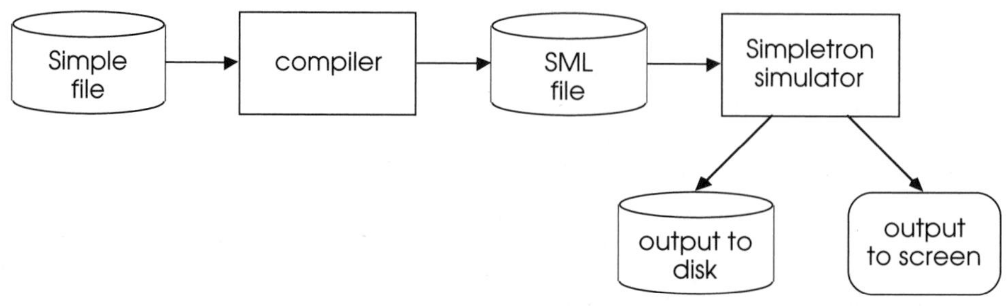


**Fig. 15.24** Writing, compiling, and executing a Simple language program.

in the program, the first pass results in an SML program containing some "unfinished" instructions. The second pass of the compiler locates and completes the unfinished instructions, and outputs the SML program to a file.

**First Pass**

The compiler begins by reading one statement of the Simple program into memory. The line must be separated into its individual *tokens* (i.e., "pieces" of a statement) for processing and compilation (standard library function `strtok` can be used to facilitate this task). Recall that every statement begins with a line number followed by a command. As the compiler breaks a statement into tokens, if the token is a line number, a variable, or a constant, it is placed in the symbol table. A line number is placed in the symbol table only if it is the first token in a statement. The `symbolTable` object is an array of `tableEntry` objects representing each symbol in the program. There is no restriction on the number of symbols that can appear in the program. Therefore, the `symbolTable` for a particular program could be large. Make the `symbolTable` a 100-element array for now. You can increase or decrease its size once the program is working.

Each `tableEntry` object contains three members. Member `symbol` is an integer containing the ASCII representation of a variable (remember that variable names are single characters), a line number, or a constant. Member `type` is one of the following characters indicating the symbol's type: `'C'` for constant, `'L'` for line number, or `'V'` for variable. Member `location` contains the Simpletron memory location (`00` to `99`) to which the symbol refers. Simpletron memory is an array of 100 integers in which SML instructions and data are stored. For a line number, the location is the element in the Simpletron memory array at which the SML instructions for the Simple statement begin. For a variable or constant, the location is the element in the Simpletron memory array in which the variable or constant is stored. Variables and constants are allocated from the end of Simpletron's memory backwards. The first variable or constant is stored in location at `99`, the next in location at `98`, etc.

The symbol table plays an integral part in converting Simple programs to SML. We learned in Chapter 5 that an SML instruction is a four-digit integer comprised of two parts—the *operation code* and the *operand*. The operation code is determined by commands in Simple. For example, the simple command `input` corresponds to SML operation code `10` (read), and the Simple command `print` corresponds to SML operation code `11` (write). The operand is a memory location containing the data on which the operation code performs its task (e.g., operation code `10` reads a value from the keyboard and stores it in the memory location specified by the operand). The compiler searches `symbolTable` to determine the Simpletron memory location for each symbol so the corresponding location can be used to complete the SML instructions.

The compilation of each Simple statement is based on its command. For example, after the line number in a `rem` statement is inserted in the symbol table, the remainder of the statement is ignored by the compiler because a remark is for documentation purposes only. The `input`, `print`, `goto` and `end` statements correspond to the SML *read*, *write*, *branch* (to a specific location) and *halt* instructions. Statements containing these Simple commands are converted directly to SML (note that a `goto` statement may contain an unresolved reference if the specified line number refers to a statement further into the Simple program file; this is sometimes called a forward reference).

When a `goto` statement is compiled with an unresolved reference, the SML instruction must be *flagged* to indicate that the second pass of the compiler must complete the instruction. The flags are stored in 100-element array `flags` of type `int` in which each element is initialized to `-1`. If the memory location to which a line number in the Simple program refers is not yet known (i.e., it is not in the symbol table), the line number is stored in array `flags` in the element with the same subscript as the incomplete instruction. The operand of the incomplete instruction is set to `00` temporarily. For example, an unconditional branch instruction (making a forward reference) is left as `+4000` until the second pass of the compiler. The second pass of the compiler will be described shortly.

Compilation of `if/goto` and `let` statements is more complicated than other statements—they are the only statements that produce more than one SML instruction. For an `if/goto` statement, the compiler produces code to test the condition and to branch to another line if necessary. The result of the branch could be an unresolved reference. Each of the relational and equality operators can be simulated using SML's *branch zero* and *branch negative* instructions (or possibly a combination of both).

For a `let` statement, the compiler produces code to evaluate an arbitrarily complex arithmetic expression consisting of integer variables and/or constants. Expressions should separate each operand and operator with spaces. Exercises 15.12 and 15.13 presented the infix-to-postfix conversion algorithm and the postfix evaluation algorithm used by compilers to evaluate expressions. Before proceeding with your compiler, you should complete each of these exercises. When a compiler encounters an expression, it converts the expression from infix notation to postfix notation, then evaluates the postfix expression.

How is it that the compiler produces the machine language to evaluate an expression containing variables? The postfix evaluation algorithm contains a "hook" where the compiler can generate SML instructions rather than actually evaluating the expression. To enable this "hook" in the compiler, the postfix evaluation algorithm must be modified to search the symbol table for each symbol it encounters (and possibly insert it), determine the symbol's corresponding memory location, and *push the memory location on the stack (instead of the symbol).* When an operator is encountered in the postfix expression, the two memory locations at the top of the stack are popped and machine language for effecting the operation is produced using the memory locations as operands. The result of each subexpression is stored in a temporary location in memory and pushed back onto the stack so the evaluation of the postfix expression can continue. When postfix evaluation is complete, the memory location containing the result is the only location left on the stack. This is popped and SML instructions are generated to assign the result to the variable at the left of the `let` statement.

### Second Pass

The second pass of the compiler performs two tasks: resolve any unresolved references and output the SML code to a file. Resolution of references occurs as follows:

1) Search the `flags` array for an unresolved reference (i.e., an element with a value other than `-1`).
2) Locate the object in array `symbolTable` containing the symbol stored in the `flags` array (be sure that the type of the symbol is `'L'` for line number).
3) Insert the memory location from member `location` into the instruction with the unresolved reference (remember that an instruction containing an unresolved reference has operand `00`).
4) Repeat steps 1, 2, and 3 until the end of the `flags` array is reached.

After the resolution process is complete, the entire array containing the SML code is output to a disk file with one SML instruction per line. This file can be read by the Simpletron for execution (after the simulator is modified to read its input from a file). Compiling your first Simple program into an SML file and then executing that file should give you a real sense of personal accomplishment.

### A Complete Example

The following example illustrates a complete conversion of a Simple program to SML as it will be performed by the Simple compiler. Consider a Simple program that inputs an integer and sums the values from 1 to that integer. The program and the SML instructions produced by the first pass of the Simple compilerare illustrated in Fig. 15.25. The symbol table constructed by the first pass is shown in Fig. 15.26.

Most Simple statements convert directly to single SML instructions. The exceptions in this program are remarks, the **`if/goto`** statement in line **`20`**, and the **`let`** statements. Remarks do not translate into machine language. However, the line number for a remark is placed in the symbol table in case the line number is referenced in a **`goto`** statement or an **`if/goto`** statement. Line **`20`** of the program specifies that if the condition **`y == x`** is true, program control is transferred to line **`60`**. Because line **`60`** appears later in the program, the first pass of the compiler has not as yet placed **`60`** in the symbol table (statement line numbers are placed in the symbol table only when they appear as the first token in a statement). Therefore, it is not possible at this time to determine the operand of the SML *branch zero* instruction at location **`03`** in the array of SML instructions. The compiler places **`60`** in location **`03`** of the **`flags`** array to indicate that the second pass completes this instruction.

We must keep track of the next instruction location in the SML array because there is not a one-to-one correspondence between Simple statements and SML instructions. For example, the **`if/goto`** statement of line **`20`** compiles into three SML instructions. Each time an instruction is produced, we must increment the *instruction counter* to the next location in the SML array. Note that the size of Simpletron's memory could present a problem for Simple programs with many statements, variables and constants. It is conceivable that the compiler will run out of memory. To test for this case, your program should contain a *data counter* to keep track of the location at which the next variable or constant will be stored in the SML array. If the value of the instruction counter is larger than the value of the data counter, the SML array is full. In this case, the compilation process should terminate and the compiler should print an error message indicating that it ran out of memory during compilation. This serves to emphasize that although the programmer is freed from the burdens of managing memory by the compiler, the compiler itself must carefully determine the placement of instructions and data in memory, and must check for such errors as memory being exhausted during the compilation process.

### A Step-by-Step View of the Compilation Process

Let us now walk through the compilation process for the Simple program in Fig. 15.25. The compiler reads the first line of the program

```
5 rem sum 1 to x
```

into memory. The first token in the statement (the line number) is determined using **`strtok`** (see Chapters 5 and 16 for a discussion of C++'s string manipulation functions). The token returned by **`strtok`** is converted to an integer using **`atoi`** so the symbol **`5`** can be located in the symbol table. If the symbol is not found, it is inserted in the symbol table. Since we are at the beginning of the program and this is the first line, no symbols are in the table yet. So, **`5`** is inserted into the symbol table as type **`L`** (line number) and assigned the first location in SML array (**`00`**). Although this line is a remark, a space in the symbol table is still allocated for the line number (in case it is referenced by a **`goto`** or an **`if/goto`**). No SML instruction is generated for a **`rem`** statement, so the instruction counter is not incremented.

| Simple program | SML location and instruction | Description |
|---|---|---|
| `5 rem  sum 1 to x` | *none* | **rem** ignored |
| `10 input x` | 00 +1099 | read **x** into location 99 |
| `15 rem  check y == x` | *none* | **rem** ignored |
| `20 if y == x goto 60` | 01 +2098 | load **y** (98) into accumulator |
| | 02 +3199 | sub **x** (99) from accumulator |
| | 03 +4200 | *branch zero to unresolved location* |
| `25 rem  increment y` | *none* | **rem** ignored |
| `30 let y = y + 1` | 04 +2098 | load **y** into accumulator |
| | 05 +3097 | add 1 (97) to accumulator |
| | 06 +2196 | store in temporary location 96 |
| | 07 +2096 | load from temporary location 96 |
| | 08 +2198 | store accumulator in **y** |
| `35 rem  add y to total` | *none* | **rem** ignored |
| `40 let t = t + y` | 09 +2095 | load **t** (95) into accumulator |
| | 10 +3098 | add **y** to accumulator |
| | 11 +2194 | store in temporary location 94 |
| | 12 +2094 | load from temporary location 94 |
| | 13 +2195 | store accumulator in **t** |
| `45 rem  loop y` | *none* | **rem** ignored |
| `50 goto 20` | 14 +4001 | branch to location 01 |
| `55 rem  output result` | *none* | **rem** ignored |
| `60 print t` | 15 +1195 | output **t** to screen |
| `99 end` | 16 +4300 | terminate execution |

**Fig. 15.25** SML instructions produced after the compiler's first pass.

The statement

```
10 input x
```

is tokenized next. The line number **10** is placed in the symbol table as type **L** and assigned the first location in the SML array (**00** because a remark began the program so the instruction counter is currently **00**). The command **input** indicates that the next token is a variable (only a variable can appear in an **input** statement). Because **input** corresponds directly to an SML operation code, the compiler simply has to determine the location of **x** in the SML array. Symbol **x** is not found in

| Symbol | Type | Location |
|---|---|---|
| 5 | L | 00 |
| 10 | L | 00 |
| 'x' | V | 99 |
| 15 | L | 01 |
| 20 | L | 01 |
| 'y' | V | 98 |
| 25 | L | 04 |
| 30 | L | 04 |
| 1 | C | 97 |
| 35 | L | 09 |
| 40 | L | 09 |
| 't' | V | 95 |
| 45 | L | 14 |
| 50 | L | 14 |
| 55 | L | 15 |
| 60 | L | 15 |
| 99 | L | 16 |

**Fig. 15.26** Symbol table for program of Fig. 15.25.

the symbol table. So, it is inserted into the symbol table as the ASCII representation of **x**, given type **V**, and assigned location **99** in the SML array (data storage begins at **99** and is allocated backwards). SML code can now be generated for this statement. Operation code **10** (the SML read operation code) is multiplied by 100, and the location of **x** (as determined in the symbol table) is added to complete the instruction. The instruction is then stored in the SML array at location **00**. The instruction counter is incremented by 1 because a single SML instruction was produced.

The statement

```
15 rem   check y == x
```

is tokenized next. The symbol table is searched for line number **15** (which is not found). The line number is inserted as type **L** and assigned the next location in the array, **01** (remember that **rem** statements do not produce code, so the instruction counter is not incremented).

The statement

```
20 if y == x goto 60
```

is tokenized next. Line number **20** is inserted in the symbol table and given type **L** with the next location in the SML array **01**. The command **if** indicates that a condition is to be evaluated. The variable **y** is not found in the symbol table, so it is inserted and given the type **V** and the SML location **98**. Next, SML instructions are generated to evaluate the condition. Since there is no direct equivalent in SML for the **if/goto**, it must be simulated by performing a calculation using **x** and **y** and branching based on the result. If **y** is equal to **x**, the result of subtracting **x** from **y** is zero, so the *branch zero* instruction can be used with the result of the calculation to simulate the **if/goto** statement. The first step requires that **y** be loaded (from SML location **98**) into the accumulator. This produces the instruction **01 +2098**. Next, **x** is subtracted from the accumulator. This produces the instruction **02 +3199**. The value in the accumulator may be zero, positive, or negative.

Since the operator is `==`, we want to *branch zero*. First, the symbol table is searched for the branch location (`60` in this case), which is not found. So, `60` is placed in the `flags` array at location `03`, and the instruction `03 +4200` is generated (we cannot add the branch location because we have not assigned a location to line `60` in the SML array yet). The instruction counter is incremented to `04`.

The compiler proceeds to the statement

```
25 rem   increment y
```

The line number `25` is inserted in the symbol table as type `L` and assigned SML location `04`. The instruction counter is not incremented.

When the statement

```
30 let y = y + 1
```

is tokenized, the line number `30` is inserted in the symbol table as type `L` and assigned SML location `04`. Command `let` indicates that the line is an assignment statement. First, all the symbols on the line are inserted in the symbol table (if they are not already there). The integer `1` is added to the symbol table as type `C` and assigned SML location `97`. Next, the right side of the assignment is converted from infix to postfix notation. Then the postfix expression (`y 1 +`) is evaluated. Symbol `y` is located in the symbol table and its corresponding memory location is pushed onto the stack. Symbol `1` is also located in the symbol table and its corresponding memory location is pushed onto the stack. When the operator `+` is encountered, the postfix evaluator pops the stack into the right operand of the operator and pops the stack again into the left operand of the operator, then produces the SML instructions

`04 +2098` *(load* `y`*)*
`05 +3097` *(add* `1`*)*

The result of the expression is stored in a temporary location in memory (`96`) with instruction

`06 +2196` *(store temporary)*

and the temporary location is pushed on the stack. Now that the expression has been evaluated, the result must be stored in `y` (i.e., the variable on the left side of `=`). So, the temporary location is loaded into the accumulator and the accumulator is stored in `y` with the instructions

`07 +2096` *(load temporary)*
`08 +2198` *(store* `y`*)*

The reader will immediately notice that SML instructions appear to be redundant. We will discuss this issue shortly.

When the statement

```
35 rem   add y to total
```

is tokenized, line number `35` is inserted in the symbol table as type `L` and assigned location `09`.

The statement

```
40 let t = t + y
```

is similar to line `30`. The variable `t` is inserted in the symbol table as type `V` and assigned SML location `95`. The instructions follow the same logic and format as line `30`, and the instructions `09 +2095`, `10 +3098`, `11 +2194`, `12 +2094`, and `13 +2195` are generated. Note that the result of `t + y` is assigned to temporary location `94` before being assigned to `t` (`95`). Once again, the reader will note that the instructions in memory locations `11` and `12` appear to be redundant. Again, we will discuss this shortly.

The statement

```
45 rem   loop y
```

is a remark, so line **45** is added to the symbol table as type **L** and assigned SML location **14**.

The statement

```
50 goto 20
```

transfers control to line **20**. Line number **50** is inserted in the symbol table as type **L** and assigned SML location **14**. The equivalent of **goto** in SML is the *unconditional branch* (**40**) instruction that transfers control to a specific SML location. The compiler searches the symbol table for line **20** and finds that it corresponds to SML location **01**. The operation code (**40**) is multiplied by 100 and location **01** is added to it to produce the instruction **14 +4001**.

The statement

```
55 rem   output result
```

is a remark, so line **55** is inserted in the symbol table as type **L** and assigned SML location **15**.

The statement

```
60 print t
```

is an output statement. Line number **60** is inserted in the symbol table as type **L** and assigned SML location **15**. The equivalent of **print** in SML is operation code **11** (*write*). The location of **t** is determined from the symbol table and added to the result of the operation code multiplied by 100.

The statement

```
99 end
```

is the final line of the program. Line number **99** is stored in the symbol table as type **L** and assigned SML location **16**. The **end** command produces the SML instruction **+4300** (**43** is *halt* in SML) which is written as the final instruction in the SML memory array.

This completes the first pass of the compiler. We now consider the second pass. The **flags** array is searched for values other than **-1**. Location **03** contains **60**, so the compiler knows that instruction **03** is incomplete. The compiler completes the instruction by searching the symbol table for **60**, determining its location, and adding the location to the incomplete instruction. In this case, the search determines that line **60** corresponds to SML location **15**, so the completed instruction **03 +4215** is produced replacing **03 +4200**. The Simple program has now been compiled successfully.

To build the compiler, you will have to perform each of the following tasks:

a) Modify the Simpletron simulator program you wrote in Exercise 5.19 to take its input from a file specified by the user (see Chapter 14). The simulator should output its results to a disk file in the same format as the screen output. Convert the simulator to be an object-oriented program. In particular, make each part of the hardware an object. Arrange the instruction types into a class hierarchy using inheritance. Then execute the program polymorphically simply by telling each instruction to execute itself with an **executeInstruction** message.

b) Modify the infix-to-postfix evaluation algorithm of Exercise 15.12 to process multi-digit integer operands and single-letter variable name operands. Hint: Standard library function **strtok** can be used to locate each constant and variable in an expression, and constants can be converted from strings to integers using standard library function **atoi**. (Note: The data representation of the postfix expression must be altered to support variable names and integer constants.)

c) Modify the postfix evaluation algorithm to process multi-digit integer operands and variable name operands. Also, the algorithm should now implement the "hook" discussed above so that SML instructions are produced rather than directly evaluating the expression. Hint: Standard library function **strtok** can be used to locate each constant and variable in an expression, and constants can be converted from strings to integers using standard library function **atoi**. (Note: The data representation of the postfix expression must be altered to support variable names and integer constants.)

d) Build the compiler. Incorporate parts (b) and (c) for evaluating expressions in **let** statements. Your program should contain a function that performs the first pass of the compiler and a function that performs the second pass of the compiler. Both functions can call other functions to accomplish their tasks. Make your compiler as object oriented as possible.

**15.28** (*Optimizing the Simple Compiler*) When a program is compiled and converted into SML, a set of instructions is generated. Certain combinations of instructions often repeat themselves, usually in triplets called *productions*. A production normally consists of three instructions such as *load*, *add*, and *store*. For example, Fig. 15.27 illustrates five of the SML instructions that were produced in the compilation of the program in Fig. 15.25 The first three instructions are the production that adds **1** to **y**. Note that instructions **06** and **07** store the accumulator value in temporary location **96**, then load the value back into the accumulator so instruction **08** can store the value in location **98**. Often a production is followed by a load instruction for the same location that was just stored. This code can be *optimized* by eliminating the store instruction and the subsequent load instruction that operate on the same memory location, thus enabling the Simpletron to execute the program faster. Figure 15.28 illustrates the optimized SML for the program of Fig. 15.25. Note that there are four fewer instructions in the optimized code—a memory-space savings of 25%.

Modify the compiler to provide an option for optimizing the Simpletron Machine Language code it produces. Manually compare the non-optimized code with the optimized code, and calculate the percentage reduction.

**15.29** (*Modifications to the Simple compiler*) Perform the following modifications to the Simple compiler. Some of these modifications may also require modifications to the Simpletron Simulator program written in Exercise 5.19.

a) Allow the modulus operator (**%**) to be used in **let** statements. Simpletron Machine Language must be modified to include a modulus instruction.
b) Allow exponentiation in a **let** statement using **^** as the exponentiation operator. Simpletron Machine Language must be modified to include an exponentiation instruction.
c) Allow the compiler to recognize uppercase and lowercase letters in Simple statements (e.g., **'A'** is equivalent to **'a'**). No modifications to the Simpletron Simulator are required.
d) Allow **input** statements to read values for multiple variables such as **input x, y**. No modifications to the Simpletron Simulator are required.
e) Allow the compiler to output multiple values in a single **print** statement such as **print a, b, c**. No modifications to the Simpletron Simulator are required.

```
04 +2098    (load)
05 +3097    (add)
06 +2196    (store)

07 +2096    (load)
08 +2198    (store)
```

**Fig. 15.27** Unoptimized code from the program of Fig. 15.25.

f) Add syntax-checking capabilities to the compiler so error messages are output when syntax errors are encountered in a Simple program. No modifications to the Simpletron Simulator are required.
g) Allow arrays of integers. No modifications to the Simpletron Simulator are required.
h) Allow subroutines specified by the Simple commands **gosub** and **return**. Command **gosub** passes program control to a subroutine and command **return** passes control back to the statement after the **gosub**. This is similar to a function call in C++. The same subroutine can be called from many **gosub** commands distributed throughout a program. No modifications to the Simpletron Simulator are required.
i) Allow repetition structures of the form

```
for x = 2 to 10 step 2
    Simple statements
next
```

This **for** statement loops from **2** to **10** with an increment of **2**. The **next** line marks the end of the body of the **for** line. No modifications to the Simpletron Simulator are required.

| Simple program | SML location and instruction | | Description |
|---|---|---|---|
| `5 rem sum 1 to x` | | *none* | **rem** ignored |
| `10 input x` | 00 | +1099 | read **x** into location **99** |
| `15 rem    check y == x` | | *none* | **rem** ignored |
| `20 if y == x goto 60` | 01 | +2098 | load **y** (**98**) into accumulator |
| | 02 | +3199 | sub **x** (**99**) from accumulator |
| | 03 | +4211 | branch to location **11** if zero |
| `25 rem    increment y` | | *none* | **rem** ignored |
| `30 let y = y + 1` | 04 | +2098 | load **y** into accumulator |
| | 05 | +3097 | add **1** (**97**) to accumulator |
| | 06 | +2198 | store accumulator in **y** (**98**) |
| `35 rem    add y to total` | | *none* | **rem** ignored |
| `40 let t = t + y` | 07 | +2096 | load **t** from location (**96** ) |
| | 08 | +3098 | add **y** (**98**) accumulator |
| | 09 | +2196 | store accumulator in **t** (**96**) |
| `45 rem    loop y` | | *none* | **rem** ignored |
| `50 goto 20` | 10 | +4001 | branch to location **01** |
| `55 rem    output result` | | *none* | **rem** ignored |
| `60 print t` | 11 | +1196 | output **t** (**96**) to screen |
| `99 end` | 12 | +4300 | terminate execution |

**Fig. 15.28** Optimized code for the program of Fig. 15.25.

j) Allow repetition structures of the form

```
for x = 2 to 10
    Simple statements
next
```

This `for` statement loops from `2` to `10` with a default increment of `1`. No modifications to the Simpletron Simulator are required.

k) Allow the compiler to process string input and output. This requires the Simpletron Simulator to be modified to process and store string values. Hint: Each Simpletron word can be divided into two groups, each holding a two-digit integer. Each two-digit integer represents the ASCII decimal equivalent of a character. Add a machine language instruction that will print a string beginning at a certain Simpletron memory location. The first half of the word at that location is a count of the number of characters in the string (i.e., the length of the string). Each succeeding half word contains one ASCII character expressed as two decimal digits. The machine language instruction checks the length and prints the string by translating each two-digit number into its equivalent character.

l) Allow the compiler to process floating-point values in addition to integers. The Simpletron Simulator must also be modified to process floating-point values.

**15.30** *(A Simple interpreter)* An interpreter is a program that reads a high-level language program statement, determines the operation to be performed by the statement, and executes the operation immediately. The high-level language program is not converted into machine language first. Interpreters execute slowly because each statement encountered in the program must first be deciphered. If statements are contained in a loop, the statements are deciphered each time they are encountered in the loop. Early versions of the BASIC programming language were implemented as interpreters.

Write an interpreter for the Simple language discussed in Exercise 15.26. The program should use the infix-to-postfix converter developed in Exercise 15.12 and the postfix evaluator developed in Exercise 15.13 to evaluate expressions in a `let` statement. The same restrictions placed on the Simple language in Exercise 15.26 should be adhered to in this program. Test the interpreter with the Simple programs written in Exercise 15.26. Compare the results of running these programs in the interpreter with the results of compiling the Simple programs and running them in the Simpletron Simulator built in Exercise 5.19.

**15.31** *(Insert/Delete Anywhere in a Linked List)* Our linked list class template allowed insertions and deletions at only the front and the back of the linked list. These capabilities were convenient for us when we used private inheritance and composition to produce a stack class template and a queue class template with a minimal amount of code simply by reusing the list class template. Actually linked lists are more general that those we provided. Modify the linked list class template we developed in this chapter to handle insertions and deletions anywhere in the list.

**15.32** *(List and Queues without Tail Pointers)* Our implementation of a linked list (Fig. 15.3) used both a `firstPtr` and a `lastPtr`. The `lastPtr` was useful for the `insertAtBack` and `removeFromBack` member functions of the `List` class. The `insertAtBack` function corresponds to the `enqueue` member function of the `Queue` class. Rewrite the `List` class so that it does not use a `lastPtr`. Thus, any operations on the tail of a list must begin searching the list from the front. Does this affect our implementation of the `Queue` class (Fig. 15.12)?

**15.33** Use the composition version of the stack program (Fig. 15.11) to form a complete working stack program. Modify this program to inline the member functions. Compare the two approaches. Summarize the advantages and disadvantages of inlining member functions.

**15.34** *(Performance of Binary Tree Sorting and Searching)* One problem with the binary tree sort is that the order in which the data is inserted affects the shape of the tree—for the same collection of data, different orderings can yield binary trees of dramatically different shapes. The performance of the binary tree sorting and searching algorithms is sensitive to the shape of the binary tree. What shape would a binary tree have if its data were inserted in increasing order? in decreasing orde? What shape should the tree have to achieve maximal searching performance?

**15.35** *(Indexed Lists)* As presented in the text, linked lists must be searched sequentially. For large lists, this can result in poor performance. A common technique for improving list searching performance is to creatre and maintain an index to the list. An index is a set of pointers to various key places in the list. For example, an application that searches a large list of names could improve performance by creating an index with 26 entries—one for each letter of the alphabet. A search operation for a last name beginning with 'Y' would then first search the index to determine where the 'Y' entries begin, and then "jump into" the list at that point and search linearly until the desired name is found. This would be much faster than searching the linked list from the beginning. Use the **`List`** class of Fig. 15.3 as the basis of an **`IndexedList`** class. Write a program that demonstrates the operation of indexed lists. Be sure to include member functions **`insertInIndexedList`**, **`seatrchIndexedList`**, and **`deleteFromIndexedList`**.

# 16

# Bit, Characters, Strings and Structures

### Objectives

- To be able to create and use structures.
- To be able to pass structures to functions call-by-value and call-by-reference.
- To be able to manipulate data with the bitwise operators and to create bit fields for storing data compactly.
- To be able to use the functions of the character handling library (`ctype`), general utilities library (`stdlib`), string handling library (`string`).
- To appreciate the power of function libraries as a means of achieving software reuseability.

*The same old charitable lie*
*Repeated as the years scoot by*
*Perpetually make a hit—*
"You really haven't changed a bit!"
Margaret Fishback

*The chief defect of Henry King*
*Was chewing little bits of string.*
Hilaire Belloc

*Vigorous writing is concise. A sentence should contain no unnecessary words, a paragraph no unnecessary sentences.*
William Strunk, Jr.

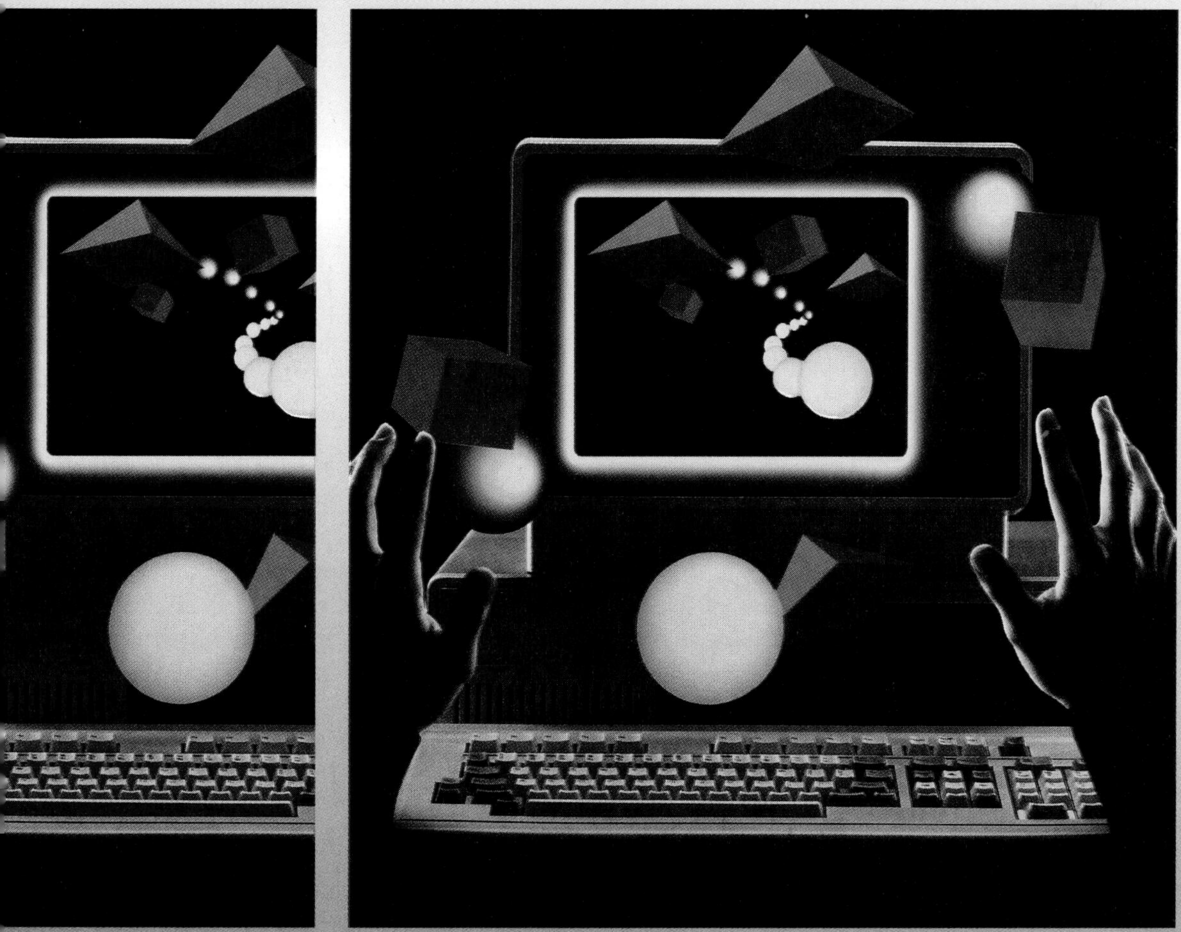

## Outline



## 16.1 Introduction

In this chapter, we say more about structures, then we discuss the manipulation of bits, characters, and strings.

Structures may contain variables of many different data types—in contrast to arrays that contain only elements of the same data type. This fact, and most of what we say about structures in the next several pages, applies to classes as well. Again, the only real difference between structures and classes in C++ is that structure members default to public access and class members default to private access. Structures are commonly used to define data records to be stored in files (see Chapter 14, "File Processing and String Stream I/O"). Pointers and structures facilitate the formation of more complex data structures such as linked lists, queues, stacks, and trees (see Chapter 15, "Data Structures"). We discuss how to declare structures, initialize them, and pass them to functions. Then, we present a high-performance card shuffling and dealing simulation.

## 16.2 Structure Definitions

Consider the following structure definition:

```
struct Card {
   char *face;
   char *suit;
};
```

The keyword **struct** introduces the definition for structure **Card**. The identifier **Card** is the *structure name* and is used in C++ to declare variables of the *structure type* (in C, the type name of the preceding structure is **struct Card**). In this example, the structure type is **Card**. Data (and possibly functions—just as with classes) declared within the braces of the structure definition are the structure's *members*. Members of the same structure must have unique names, but two different structures may contain members of the same name without conflict. Each structure definition must end with a semicolon.

*Common Programming Error 16.1*

*Forgetting the semicolon that terminates a structure definition.*

The definition of **Card** contains two members of type **char ***—**face** and **suit**. Structure members can be variables of the basic data types (e.g., **int**, **float**, etc.), or aggregates, such as arrays and other structures. As we saw in Chapter 4, each element of an array must be of the same type. Data members of a structure, however, can be of a variety of data types. For example, an **Employee** structure might contain character string members for the first and last names, an **int** member for the employee's age, a **char** member containing **'M'** or **'F'** for the employee's gender, a **float** member for the employee's hourly salary, and so on.

A structure cannot contain an instance of itself. For example, a structure variable **Card** cannot be declared in the definition for structure **Card**. A pointer to a **Card** structure, however, can be included. A structure containing a member that is a pointer to the same structure type is referred to as a *self-referential structure*. Self-referential structures are used in Chapter 15 to build various kinds of linked data structures.

The preceding structure definition does not reserve any space in memory; rather, the definition creates a new data type that is used to declare structure variables. Structure variables are declared like variables of other types. The declaration

```
Card a, deck[52], *c;
```

declares **a** to be a structure variable of type **Card**, **deck** to be an array with 52 elements of type **Card**, and **c** to be a pointer to a **Card** structure. Variables of a given structure type may also be declared by placing a comma-separated list of the variable names between the closing brace of the structure definition and the semicolon that ends the structure definition. For example, the preceding declaration could have been incorporated into the **Card** structure definition as follows:

```
struct Card {
   char *face;
   char *suit;
} a, deck[52], *c;
```

The structure name is optional. If a structure definition does not contain a structure name, variables of the structure type may be declared only in the structure definition—not in a separate declaration.

*Good Programming Practice 16.1*

*Provide a structure name when creating a structure type. The structure name is convenient for declaring new variables of the structure type later in the program.*

The only valid built-in operations that may be performed on structures are: assigning a structure to a structure of the same type, taking the address (**&**) of a structure, accessing the members of a structure (see Chapter 6, "Classes and Data Abstraction"), and using the **sizeof** operator to determine the size of a structure. As with classes, most operators can be overloaded to work with objects of a structure type.

*Common Programming Error 16.2*

*Assigning a structure of one type to a structure of a different type.*

Structure members are not necessarily stored in consecutive bytes of memory. Sometimes there are "holes" in a structure because computers may store specific data types only on certain memory boundaries such as halfword, word, or doubleword boundaries. A word is a standard memory unit used to store data in a computer—usually 2 bytes or 4 bytes. Consider the following structure definition in which structure variables (objects really) **sample1** and **sample2** of type **Example** are declared:

```
struct Example {
   char c;
   int i;
} sample1, sample2;
```

A computer with 2-byte words may require that each of the members of **Example** be aligned on a word boundary, i.e., at the beginning of a word (this is machine dependent). Figure 16.1 shows a sample storage alignment for an object of type **Example** that has been assigned the character **'a'** and the integer **97** (the bit representations of the values are shown). If the members are stored beginning at word boundaries, there is a 1-byte hole (byte **1** in the figure) in the storage for objects of type **Example**. The value in the 1-byte hole is undefined. If the member values of **sample1** and **sample2** are in fact equal, the structures do not necessarily compare equal because the undefined 1-byte holes are not likely to contain identical values.

*Common Programming Error 16.3*

*Comparing structures is a syntax error because of the different alignment requirements on various systems.*

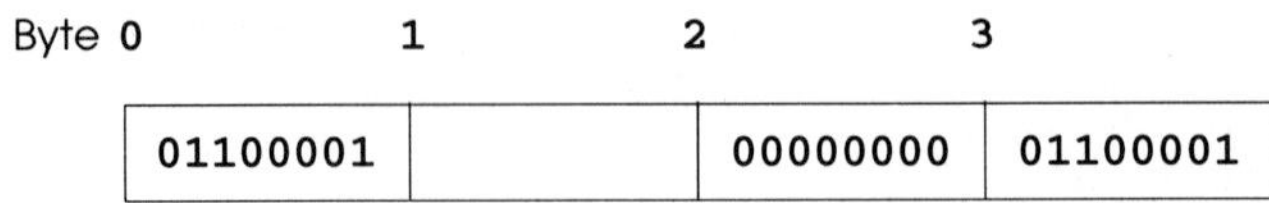


**Fig. 16.1** A possible storage alignment for a variable of type **Example** showing an undefined area in memory.

***Portability Tip 16.1***

*Because the size of data items of a particular type is machine dependent, and because storage alignment considerations are machine dependent, so too is the representation of a structure.*

## 16.3 Initializing Structures

Structures can be initialized using initializer lists as with arrays. To initialize a structure, follow the variable name in the structure declaration with an equal sign and a brace-enclosed, comma-separated list of initializers. For example, the declaration

```
Card a = {"Three", "Hearts"};
```

creates variable **a** to be a **Card** structure (as defined previously) and initializes member **face** to **"Three"** and member **suit** to **"Hearts"**. If there are fewer initializers in the list than members in the structure, the remaining members are automatically initialized to **0** (or **NULL** if the member is a pointer). Structure variables declared outside a function definition (i.e., externally) are initialized to **0** or **NULL** if they are not explicitly initialized in the external declaration. Structure variables may also be initialized in assignment statements by assigning a structure variable of the same type, or by assigning values to the individual data members of the structure.

## 16.4 Using Structures with Functions

There are two ways to pass the information in structures to functions. You can either pass the entire structure or you can pass the individual members of a structure. By default, the data (except individual array members) passes call-by-value. Structures and their members can also be passed call-by-reference by passing either references or pointers.

To pass a structure call-by-reference, pass the address of the structure variable. Arrays of structures—like all other arrays—are automatically passed call-by-reference.

In Chapter 4, we stated that an array could be passed call-by-value by using a structure. To pass an array call-by-value, create a structure (or a class) with the array as a member. Since structures are passed call-by-value, the array is passed call-by-value.

***Common Programming Error 16.4***

*Assuming that structures, like arrays, are automatically passed call-by-reference and trying to modify the caller's structure values in the called function.*

***Performance Tip 16.1***

*Passing structures (and especially large structures) call-by-reference is more efficient than passing structures call-by-value (which requires the entire structure to be copied).*

## 16.5 Typedef

The keyword **typedef** provides a mechanism for creating synonyms (or aliases) for previously defined data types. Names for structure types are often defined with **typedef** to create shorter or more readable type names. For example, the statement

```
typedef Card* CardPtr;
```

defines the new type name **CardPtr** as a synonym for type **Card ***.

***Good Programming Practice 16.2***

*Capitalize* **typedef** *names to emphasize that these names are synonyms for other type names.*

Creating a new name with **typedef** does not create a new data type; **typedef** simply creates a new type name which may then be used in the program as an alias for an existing type name.

Synonyms for built-in data types can be created with **typedef**. For example, a program requiring 4-byte integers may use type **int** on one system and type **long int** on another system that has 2-byte integers. Programs designed for portability can use **typedef** to create an alias such as **Integer** for 4-byte integers. **Integer** can then be aliased to **int** on systems with 4-byte integers and can be aliased to **long int** on systems with 2-byte integers where **long int** values occupy 4 bytes. Then, to write portable programs, the programmer simply declares all 4-byte integer variables to be of type **Integer**.

***Portability Tip 16.2***

*Using* **typedef** *can help make a program more portable.*

## 16.6 Example: High-Performance Card Shuffling and Dealing Simulation

The program in Fig. 16.2 is based on the card shuffling and dealing simulation discussed in Chapter 5, "Pointers and Strings." The program represents the deck of cards as an array of structures and uses high-performance shuffling and dealing algorithms. The output is shown in Fig. 16.3.

In the program, function **fillDeck** initializes the **Card** array in order with character strings representing Ace through King of each suit. The **Card** array is passed to function **shuffle** where the high-performance shuffling algorithm is implemented. Function **shuffle** takes an array of 52 **Card** structures as an argument. The function loops through all 52 cards (array subscripts 0 to 51). For each card, a number between 0 and 51 is picked randomly. Next, the current **Card** structure and the randomly selected **Card** structure are swapped in the array. A total of 52 swaps are made in a single pass of the entire array, and the array of **Card** structures is shuffled! This algorithm does not suffer from indefinite postponement like the shuffling algorithm presented in Chapter 5. Because the **Card** structures were swapped in place in the array, the high-performance dealing algorithm implemented in function **deal** requires only one pass of the array to deal the shuffled cards.

***Common Programming Error 16.5***

*Forgetting to include the array subscript when referring to individual structures in an array of structures.*

```
// Card shuffling and dealing program using structures
#include <iostream.h>
#include <iomanip.h>
#include <stdlib.h>
#include <time.h>

struct Card {
   char *face;
   char *suit;
};

void fillDeck(Card *, char *[], char *[]);
void shuffle(Card *);
void deal(Card *);

main()
{
   Card deck[52];
   char *face[] = {"Ace", "Deuce", "Three", "Four", "Five",
                   "Six", "Seven", "Eight", "Nine", "Ten",
                   "Jack", "Queen", "King"};
   char *suit[] = {"Hearts", "Diamonds", "Clubs", "Spades"};

   srand(time(NULL));            // randomize
   fillDeck(deck, face, suit);
   shuffle(deck);
   deal(deck);
   return 0;
}

void fillDeck(Card *wDeck, char *wFace[], char *wSuit[])
{
   for (int i = 0; i < 52; i++) {
      wDeck[i].face = wFace[i % 13];
      wDeck[i].suit = wSuit[i / 13];
   }
}

void shuffle(Card *wDeck)
{
   for (int i = 0; i <= 51; i++) {
      int j = rand() % 52;
      Card temp = wDeck[i];
      wDeck[i] = wDeck[j];
      wDeck[j] = temp;
   }
}

void deal(Card *wdeck)
{
   for (int i = 0; i < 52; i++)
      cout << setiosflags(ios::right) << setw(5) << wdeck[i].face
           << " of " << setiosflags(ios::left) << setw(8)
           << wdeck[i].suit << ((i + 1) % 2 ? '\t' : '\n');
}
```

**Fig. 16.2** High-performance card shuffling and dealing simulation.

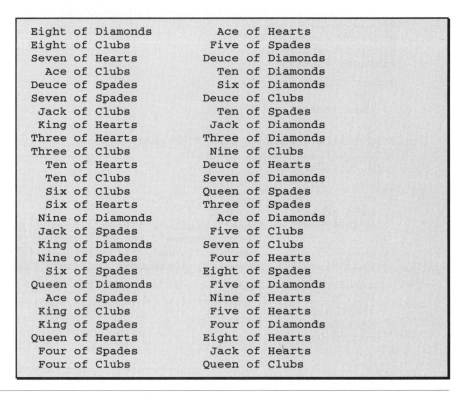

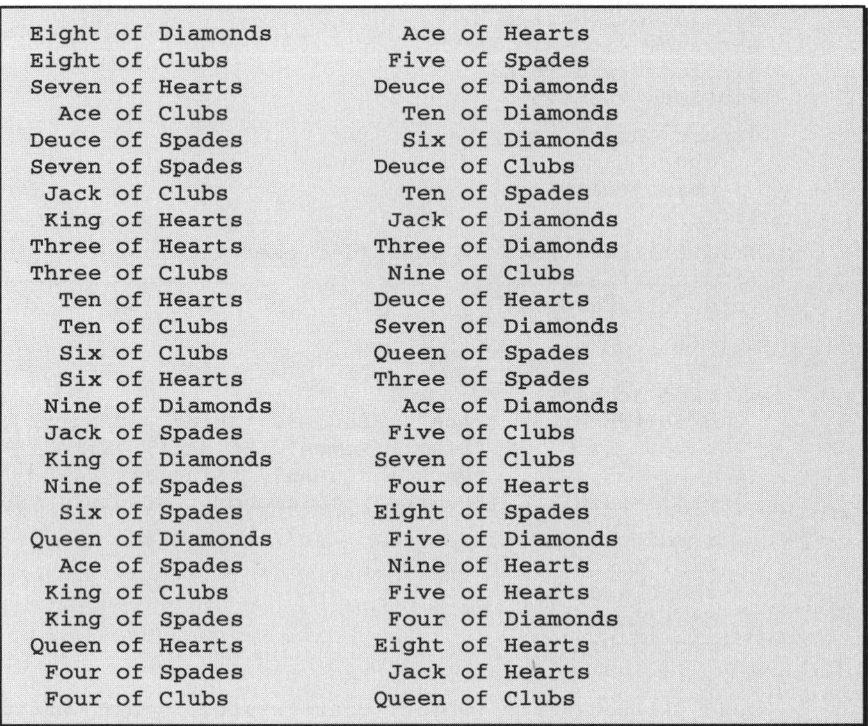

```
Eight of Diamonds          Ace of Hearts
Eight of Clubs            Five of Spades
Seven of Hearts          Deuce of Diamonds
  Ace of Clubs             Ten of Diamonds
Deuce of Spades            Six of Diamonds
Seven of Spades          Deuce of Clubs
 Jack of Clubs             Ten of Spades
 King of Hearts           Jack of Diamonds
Three of Hearts          Three of Diamonds
Three of Clubs            Nine of Clubs
  Ten of Hearts          Deuce of Hearts
  Ten of Clubs           Seven of Diamonds
  Six of Clubs           Queen of Spades
  Six of Hearts          Three of Spades
 Nine of Diamonds          Ace of Diamonds
 Jack of Spades           Five of Clubs
 King of Diamonds        Seven of Clubs
 Nine of Spades           Four of Hearts
  Six of Spades          Eight of Spades
Queen of Diamonds         Five of Diamonds
  Ace of Spades           Nine of Hearts
 King of Clubs            Five of Hearts
 King of Spades           Four of Diamonds
Queen of Hearts          Eight of Hearts
 Four of Spades           Jack of Hearts
 Four of Clubs           Queen of Clubs
```

**Fig. 16.3** Output for the high-performance card shuffling and dealing simulation.

## 16.7 Bitwise Operators

C++ provides extensive bit manipulation capabilities for programmers who need to get down to the so-called "bits-and-bytes" level. Operating systems, test equipment software, networking software, and many other kids of software require that the programmer communicate "directly with the hardware." In this and the next several sections, we discuss C++'s bit manipulation capabilities. We introduce each of C++'s many bitwise operators and we discuss how to save memory by using bit fields.

All data is represented internally by computers as sequences of bits. Each bit can assume the value **0** or the value **1**. On most systems, a sequence of 8 bits forms a byte—the standard storage unit for a variable of type **char**. Other data types are stored in larger numbers of bytes. The bitwise operators are used to manipulate the bits of integral operands (**char**, **short**, **int**, and **long**; both **signed** and **unsigned**). Unsigned integers are normally used with the bitwise operators.

*Portability Tip 16.3*

*Bitwise data manipulations are machine dependent.*

Note that the bitwise operator discussions in this section show the binary representations of the integer operands. For a detailed explanation of the binary (also called base 2) number system see Appendix E, "Number Systems". Also, the programs in Sections 16.7 and 16.8 were tested on a PC compatible using Borland C++. This system uses 16-bit (2-byte) integers. Because of the machine-dependent nature of bitwise manipulations, these programs may not work on your system.

The bitwise operators are: *bitwise AND (&), bitwise inclusive OR ( |), bitwise exclusive OR ( ^), left shift ( <<), right shift (>>),* and *complement (~).* (Note that we have been using **&**, **<<**, and **>>** for other purposes. This is a classic example of operator overloading.) The bitwise AND, bitwise inclusive OR, and bitwise exclusive OR operators compare their two operands bit-by-bit. The bitwise AND operator sets each bit in the result to 1 if the corresponding bit in both operands is 1. The bitwise inclusive OR operator sets each bit in the result to 1 if the corresponding bit in either (or both) operand(s) is 1. The bitwise exclusive OR operator sets each bit in the result to 1 if the corresponding bit in exactly one operand is 1. The left shift operator shifts the bits of its left operand to the left by the number of bits specified in its right operand. The right shift operator shifts the bits in its left operand to the right by the number of bits specified in its right operand. The bitwise complement operator sets all `0` bits in its operand to `1` in the result and sets all `1` bits to `0` in the result. Detailed discussions of each bitwise operator appear in the following examples. The bitwise operators are summarized in Fig. 16.4.

When using the bitwise operators, it is useful to print values in their binary representation to illustrate the precise effects of these operators. The program of Fig. 16.5 prints an **unsigned** integer in its binary representation in groups of eight bits each. Function **displayBits** uses the bitwise AND operator to combine variable **value** with variable **displayMask**. Often, the bitwise AND operator is used with an operand called a *mask*—an integer value with specific bits set to **1**. Masks are used to hide some bits in a value while selecting other bits. In **displayBits**, mask variable **displayMask** is as-

| Operator | | Description |
|---|---|---|
| & | bitwise AND | The bits in the result are set to `1` if the corresponding bits in the two operands are both `1`. |
| \| | bitwise inclusive OR | The bits in the result are set to `1` if at least one of the corresponding bits in the two operands is `1`. |
| ^ | bitwise exclusive OR | The bits in the result are set to `1` if exactly one of the corresponding bits in the two operands is `1`. |
| << | left shift | Shifts the bits of the first operand left by the number of bits specified by the second operand; fill from the right with `0` bits. |
| >> | right shift | Shifts the bits of the first operand right by the number of bits specified by the second operand; the method of filling from the left is machine dependent. |
| ~ | one's complement | All `0` bits are set to `1` and all `1` bits are set to `0`. |

**Fig 16.4** The bitwise operators.

signed the value **1 << 15** (**10000000 00000000**). The left shift operator shifts the value **1** from the low order (rightmost) bit to the high order (leftmost) bit in **displayMask**, and fills in **0** bits from the right. The statement

```
cout << (value & displayMask ? '1' : '0');
```

determines whether a **1** or a **0** should be printed for the current leftmost bit of variable **value**. Assume variable **value** contains **65000** (**11111101 11101000**). When **value** and **displayMask** are combined using **&**, all the bits except the high order bit in variable **value** are "masked off" (hidden) because any bit "ANDed" with **0** yields **0**. If the leftmost bit is **1**, **value & displayMask** evaluates to **1**, and **1** is printed—otherwise, **0** is printed. Variable **value** is then left shifted one bit by the expression **value <<= 1** (this is equivalent to **value = value << 1**). These steps are repeated for each bit

```
// Printing an unsigned integer in bits
#include <iostream.h>
#include <iomanip.h>

main()
{
   unsigned x;
   void displayBits(unsigned);

   cout << "Enter an unsigned integer: ";
   cin >> x;
   displayBits(x);
   return 0;
}

void displayBits(unsigned value)
{
   unsigned c, displayMask = 1 << 15;

   cout << setw(7) << value << " = ";

   for (c = 1; c <= 16; c++) {
      cout << (value & displayMask ? '1' : '0');
      value <<= 1;

      if (c % 8 == 0)
         cout << ' ';
   }

   cout << endl;
}
```

```
Enter an unsigned integer: 65000
  65000 = 11111101 11101000
```

**Fig. 16.5** Printing an unsigned integer in bits.

in **unsigned** variable **value**. Figure 16.6 summarizes the results of combining two bits with the bitwise AND operator.

*Common Programming Error 16.6*

*Using the logical AND operator (&&) for the bitwise AND operator (&) and vice versa.*

The program of Fig. 16.7 demonstrates the use of the bitwise AND operator, the bitwise inclusive OR operator, the bitwise exclusive OR operator, and the bitwise complement operator. The program uses function **displayBits** to print the **unsigned** integer values. The output is shown in Fig. 16.8.

| Bit 1 | Bit 2 | Bit 1 & Bit 2 |
|---|---|---|
| 0 | 0 | 0 |
| 1 | 0 | 0 |
| 0 | 1 | 0 |
| 1 | 1 | 1 |

**Fig 16.6** Results of combining two bits with the bitwise AND operator &.

```
// Using the bitwise AND, bitwise inclusive OR, bitwise
// exclusive OR, and bitwise complement operators.
#include <iostream.h>
#include <iomanip.h>

void displayBits(unsigned);

main()
{
   unsigned number1, number2, mask, setBits;

   number1 = 65535;
   mask = 1;
   cout << "The result of combining the following" << endl;
   displayBits(number1);
   displayBits(mask);
   cout << "using the bitwise AND operator & is" << endl;
   displayBits(number1 & mask);

   number1 = 15;
   setBits = 241;
   cout << endl << "The result of combining the following" << endl;
   displayBits(number1);
   displayBits(setBits);
   cout << "using the bitwise inclusive OR operator | is" << endl;
   displayBits(number1 | setBits);
```

**Fig. 16.7** Using the bitwise AND, bitwise inclusive OR, bitwise exclusive OR, and bitwise complement operators (part 1 of 2).

```
   number1 = 139;
   number2 = 199;
   cout << endl << "The result of combining the following" <<
endl;
   displayBits(number1);
   displayBits(number2);
   cout << "using the bitwise exclusive OR operator ^ is" << endl;
   displayBits(number1 ^ number2);

   number1 = 21845;
   cout << endl << "The one's complement of" << endl;
   displayBits(number1);
   cout << "is" << endl;
   displayBits(~number1);

   return 0;
}

void displayBits(unsigned value)
{
   unsigned c, displayMask = 1 << 15;

   cout << setw(7) << value << " = ";

   for (c = 1; c <= 16; c++) {
      cout << (value & displayMask ? '1' : '0');
      value <<= 1;

      if (c % 8 == 0)
         cout << ' ';
   }

   cout << endl;
}
```

**Fig. 16.7** Using the bitwise AND, bitwise inclusive OR, bitwise exclusive OR, and bitwise complement operators (part 2 of 2).

In Fig. 16.7, variable **mask** is assigned the value **1** (**00000000 00000001**), and variable **number1** is assigned value **65535** (**11111111 11111111**). When **mask** and **number1** are combined using the bitwise AND operator (**&**) in the expression **number1 & mask**, the result is **00000000 00000001**. All the bits except the low order bit in variable **number1** are "masked off" (hidden) by "ANDing" with variable **mask**.

The bitwise inclusive OR operator is used to set specific bits to 1 in an operand. In Fig. 16.7, variable **number1** is assigned **15** (**00000000 00001111**), and variable **setBits** is assigned **241** (**00000000 11110001**). When **number1** and **setBits** are combined using the bitwise OR operator in the expression **number1 | setBits**, the result is **255** (**00000000 11111111**). Figure 16.9 summarizes the results of combining two bits with the bitwise inclusive OR operator.

***Common Programming Error 16.7***

*Using the logical OR operator (**||**) for the bitwise OR operator (**|**) and vice versa.*

```
The result of combining the following
  65535 = 11111111 11111111
      1 = 00000000 00000001
using the bitwise AND operator & is
      1 = 00000000 00000001

The result of combining the following
     15 = 00000000 00001111
    241 = 00000000 11110001
using the bitwise inclusive OR operator | is
    255 = 00000000 11111111

The result of combining the following
    139 = 00000000 10001011
    199 = 00000000 11000111
using the bitwise exclusive OR operator ^ is
     76 = 00000000 01001100

The one's complement of
  21845 = 01010101 01010101
is
  43690 = 10101010 10101010
```

**Fig. 16.8** Output for the program of Fig. 16.7.

| Bit 1 | Bit 2 | Bit 1 \| Bit 2 |
|---|---|---|
| 0 | 0 | 0 |
| 1 | 0 | 1 |
| 0 | 1 | 1 |
| 1 | 1 | 1 |

**Fig 16.9** Results of combining two bits with the bitwise inclusive OR operator **|**.

The bitwise exclusive OR operator (**^**) sets each bit in the result to 1 if *exactly* one of the corresponding bits in its two operands is 1. In Fig. 16.7, variables **number1** and **number2** are assigned the values **139** (**00000000 10001011**) and **199** (**00000000 11000111**). When these variables are combined with the exclusive OR operator in the expression **number1 ^ number2**, the result is **00000000 01001100**. Figure 16.10 summarizes the results of combining two bits with the bitwise exclusive OR operator.

The *bitwise* complement operator (**~**) sets all **1** bits in its operand to **0** in the result and sets all **0** bits to **1** in the result—otherwise referred to as "taking the *one's complement* of the value." In Fig. 16.7, variable **number1** is assigned the value **21845** (**01010101 01010101**). When the expression **~number1** is evaluated, the result is (**10101010 10101010**).

| Bit 1 | Bit 2 | Bit 1 ^ Bit 2 |
|---|---|---|
| 0 | 0 | 0 |
| 1 | 0 | 1 |
| 0 | 1 | 1 |
| 1 | 1 | 0 |

**Fig 16.10** Results of combining two bits with the bitwise exclusive OR operator `^`.

The program of Fig. 16.11 demonstrates the left shift operator (`<<`) and the right shift operator (`>>`). Function **displayBits** is used to print the **unsigned** integer values.

```
// Using the bitwise shift operators
#include <iostream.h>
#include <iomanip.h>
void displayBits(unsigned);

main()
{
   unsigned number1 = 960;

   cout << "The result of left shifting" << endl;
   displayBits(number1);
   cout << "8 bit positions using the left shift operator << is"
        << endl;
   displayBits(number1 << 8);
   cout << endl << "The result of right shifting" << endl;
   displayBits(number1);
   cout << "8 bit positions using the right shift operator >> is"
        << endl;
   displayBits(number1 >> 8);
   return 0;
}

void displayBits(unsigned value)
{
   unsigned c, displayMask = 1 << 15;

   cout << setw(7) << value << " = ";

   for (c = 1; c <= 16; c++) {
      cout << (value & displayMask ? '1' : '0');
      value <<= 1;

      if (c % 8 == 0)
         cout << ' ';
   }

   cout << endl;
}
```

**Fig. 16.11** Using the bitwise shift operators (part 1 of 2).

```
The result of left shifting
    960 = 00000011 11000000
8 bit positions using the left shift operator << is
  49152 = 11000000 00000000

The result of right shifting
    960 = 00000011 11000000
8 bit positions using the right shift operator >> is
      3 = 00000000 00000011
```

**Fig. 16.11** Using the bitwise shift operators (part 2 of 2).

The left shift operator (**<<**) shifts the bits of its left operand to the left by the number of bits specified in its right operand. Bits vacated to the right are replaced with **0**s; **1**s shifted off the left are lost. In the program of Fig. 16.11, variable **number1** is assigned the value **960** (**00000011 11000000**). The result of left shifting variable **number1** 8 bits in the expression **number1 << 8** is **49152** (**11000000 00000000**).

The right shift operator (**>>**) shifts the bits of its left operand to the right by the number of bits specified in its right operand. Performing a right shift on an **unsigned** integer causes the vacated bits at the left to be replaced by 0s; **1**s shifted off the right are lost. In the program of Fig. 16.11, the result of right shifting **number1** in the expression **number1 >> 8** is **3** (**00000000 00000011**).

***Common Programming Error 16.8***

*The result of shifting a value is undefined if the right operand is negative or if the right operand is larger than the number of bits in which the left operand is stored.*

***Portability Tip 16.4***

*The result of right shifting a signed value is machine dependent. Some machines fill with zero and others use the sign bit.*

Each bitwise operator (except the bitwise complement operator) has a corresponding assignment operator. These *bitwise assignment operators* are shown in Fig. 16.12 and are used in a similar manner to the arithmetic assignment operators introduced in Chapter 2.

| Bitwise assignment operators | |
|---|---|
| **&=** | Bitwise AND assignment operator. |
| **\|=** | Bitwise inclusive OR assignment operator. |
| **^=** | Bitwise exclusive OR assignment operator. |
| **<<=** | Left shift assignment operator. |
| **>>=** | Right shift assignment operator. |

**Fig 16.12** The bitwise assignment operators.

Figure 16.13 shows the precedence and associativity of the various operators introduced to this point in the text. They are shown top to bottom in decreasing order of precedence.

## 16.8 Bit Fields

C++ provides the ability to specify the number of bits in which an **unsigned** or **int** member of a class or a structure (or a union—see Chapter 18, "Other Topics") is stored. Such a member is referred to as a *bit field.* Bit fields enable better memory utilization by storing data in the minimum number of bits required. Bit field members *must* be declared as **int** or **unsigned**.

***Performance Tip 16.2***

*Bit fields help conserve storage.*

Consider the following structure definition:

```
struct BitCard {
   unsigned face : 4;
   unsigned suit : 2;
   unsigned color : 1;
};
```

<table>
<tr><th>Operator</th><th>Associativity</th><th>Type</th></tr>
<tr><td>:: (unary; right to left) :: (binary; left to right)</td><td></td><td>scope resolution</td></tr>
<tr><td>() [] . -></td><td>left to right</td><td>miscellaneous</td></tr>
<tr><td>+ - ++ -- ! (type) & * ~ sizeof</td><td>right to left</td><td>unary</td></tr>
<tr><td>* / %</td><td>left to right</td><td>multiplicative</td></tr>
<tr><td>+ -</td><td>left to right</td><td>additive</td></tr>
<tr><td><< >></td><td>left to right</td><td>shifting</td></tr>
<tr><td>< <= > >=</td><td>left to right</td><td>relational</td></tr>
<tr><td>== !=</td><td>left to right</td><td>equality</td></tr>
<tr><td>&</td><td>left to right</td><td>bitwise AND</td></tr>
<tr><td>^</td><td>left to right</td><td>negation</td></tr>
<tr><td>|</td><td>left to right</td><td>bitwise OR</td></tr>
<tr><td>&&</td><td>left to right</td><td>logical AND</td></tr>
<tr><td>||</td><td>left to right</td><td>logical OR</td></tr>
<tr><td>?:</td><td>right to left</td><td>conditional</td></tr>
<tr><td>= += -= *= /= %= &= |= ^= <<= >>=</td><td>right to left</td><td>assignment</td></tr>
<tr><td>,</td><td>left to right</td><td>comma</td></tr>
</table>

**Fig. 16.13** Operator precedence and associativity.

The definition contains three **unsigned** bit fields—**face**, **suit**, and **color**—used to represent a card from a deck of 52 cards. A bit field is declared by following an **unsigned** or **int** member with a colon (**:**) and an integer constant representing the *width* of the field (i.e., the number of bits in which the member is stored). The width must be an integer constant between 0 and the total number of bits used to store an **int** on your system. Our examples were tested on a computer with 2-byte (16 bit) integers.

The preceding structure definition indicates that member **face** is stored in 4 bits, member **suit** is stored in 2 bits, and member **color** is stored in 1 bit. The number of bits is based on the desired range of values for each structure member. Member **face** stores values between 0 (Ace) and 12 (King)—4 bits can store a value between 0 and 15. Member suit stores values between 0 and 3 (0 = Diamonds, 1 = Hearts, 2 = Clubs, 3 = Spades)—2 bits can store a value between 0 and 3. Finally, member **color** stores either 0 (Red) or 1 (Black)—1 bit can store either 0 or 1.

The program in Fig. 16.14 (output shown in Fig. 16.15) creates array **deck** containing 52 **struct bitCard** structures. Function **fillDeck** inserts the 52 cards in the **deck** array, and function **deal** prints the 52 cards. Notice that bit field members of structures are accessed exactly as any other structure member. The member **color** is included as a means of indicating the card color on a system that allows color displays.

It is possible to specify an *unnamed bit field* in which case the field is used as *padding* in the structure. For example, the structure definition

```
struct Example {
   unsigned a : 13;
   unsigned   : 3;
   unsigned b : 4;
};
```

```
// Example using bit fields to store a deck of cards
#include <iostream.h>
#include <iomanip.h>

struct BitCard {
   unsigned face : 4;
   unsigned suit : 2;
   unsigned color : 1;
};

void fillDeck(BitCard *);
void deal(BitCard *);

main()
{
   BitCard deck[52];

   fillDeck(deck);
   deal(deck);
   return 0;
}
```

**Fig. 16.14** Using bit fields to store a deck of cards (part 1 of 2).

```
void fillDeck(BitCard *wDeck)
{
   for (int i = 0; i <= 51; i++) {
      wDeck[i].face = i % 13;
      wDeck[i].suit = i / 13;
      wDeck[i].color = i / 26;
   }
}

// Output cards in two column format. Cards 0-25 subscripted with
// k1 in column 1. Cards 26-51 subscripted with k2 in column 2.
void deal(BitCard *wDeck)
{
   for (int k1 = 0, k2 = k1 + 26; k1 <= 25; k1++, k2++) {
      cout << "Card:" << setw(3) << wDeck[k1].face << "  Suit:"
           << setw(2) << wDeck[k1].suit << "  Color:" << setw(2)
           << wDeck[k1].color << "   ";
      cout << "Card:" << setw(3) << wDeck[k2].face << "  Suit:"
           << setw(2) << wDeck[k2].suit << "  Color:" << setw(2)
           << wDeck[k2].color << endl;
   }
}
```

Fig. 16.14 Using bit fields to store a deck of cards (part 2 of 2).

uses an unnamed 3-bit field as padding—nothing can be stored in those three bits. Member **b** (on our 2-byte word computer) is stored in another storage unit.

An *unnamed bit field with a zero width* is used to align the next bit field on a new storage unit boundary. For example, the structure definition

```
struct Example {
   unsigned a : 13;
   unsigned   : 0;
   unsigned b : 4;
};
```

uses an unnamed **0**-bit field to skip the remaining bits (as many as there are) of the storage unit in which **a** is stored, and align **b** on the next storage unit boundary.

***Portability Tip 16.5***

*Bit field manipulations are machine dependent. For example, some computers allow bit fields to cross word boundaries, whereas others do not.*

***Common Programming Error 16.9***

*Attempting to access individual bits of a bit field as if they were elements of an array. Bit fields are not "arrays of bits."*

***Common Programming Error 16.10***

*Attempting to take the address of a bit field (the **&** operator may not be used with bit fields because they do not have addresses).*

```
Card:  0  Suit: 0  Color: 0   Card:  0  Suit: 2  Color: 1
Card:  1  Suit: 0  Color: 0   Card:  1  Suit: 2  Color: 1
Card:  2  Suit: 0  Color: 0   Card:  2  Suit: 2  Color: 1
Card:  3  Suit: 0  Color: 0   Card:  3  Suit: 2  Color: 1
Card:  4  Suit: 0  Color: 0   Card:  4  Suit: 2  Color: 1
Card:  5  Suit: 0  Color: 0   Card:  5  Suit: 2  Color: 1
Card:  6  Suit: 0  Color: 0   Card:  6  Suit: 2  Color: 1
Card:  7  Suit: 0  Color: 0   Card:  7  Suit: 2  Color: 1
Card:  8  Suit: 0  Color: 0   Card:  8  Suit: 2  Color: 1
Card:  9  Suit: 0  Color: 0   Card:  9  Suit: 2  Color: 1
Card: 10  Suit: 0  Color: 0   Card: 10  Suit: 2  Color: 1
Card: 11  Suit: 0  Color: 0   Card: 11  Suit: 2  Color: 1
Card: 12  Suit: 0  Color: 0   Card: 12  Suit: 2  Color: 1
Card:  0  Suit: 1  Color: 0   Card:  0  Suit: 3  Color: 1
Card:  1  Suit: 1  Color: 0   Card:  1  Suit: 3  Color: 1
Card:  2  Suit: 1  Color: 0   Card:  2  Suit: 3  Color: 1
Card:  3  Suit: 1  Color: 0   Card:  3  Suit: 3  Color: 1
Card:  4  Suit: 1  Color: 0   Card:  4  Suit: 3  Color: 1
Card:  5  Suit: 1  Color: 0   Card:  5  Suit: 3  Color: 1
Card:  6  Suit: 1  Color: 0   Card:  6  Suit: 3  Color: 1
Card:  7  Suit: 1  Color: 0   Card:  7  Suit: 3  Color: 1
Card:  8  Suit: 1  Color: 0   Card:  8  Suit: 3  Color: 1
Card:  9  Suit: 1  Color: 0   Card:  9  Suit: 3  Color: 1
Card: 10  Suit: 1  Color: 0   Card: 10  Suit: 3  Color: 1
Card: 11  Suit: 1  Color: 0   Card: 11  Suit: 3  Color: 1
Card: 12  Suit: 1  Color: 0   Card: 12  Suit: 3  Color: 1
```

**Fig. 16.15** Output of the program in Fig. 16.14.

***Performance Tip 16.3***

*Although bit fields save space, using them can cause the compiler to generate slower-executing machine language code. This occurs because it takes extra machine language operations to access only portions of an addressable storage unit. This is one of many examples of the kinds of space-time tradeoffs that occur in computer science.*

## 16.9 Character Handling Library

Most data is entered into computers as characters—including letters, digits, and various special symbols. In this section, we discuss C++'s capabilities for examining and manipulating individual characters. In the remainder of the chapter, we continue the discussion of character string manipulation that we began in Chapter 5.

The character handling library includes several functions that perform useful tests and manipulations of character data. Each function receives a character—represented as an **`int`**—or **`EOF`** as an argument. Characters are often manipulated as integers. Remember that **`EOF`** normally has the value –1 and some hardware architectures do not allow negative values to be stored in **`char`** variables. Therefore, the character handling functions manipulate characters as integers. Figure 16.16 summarizes the functions of the character handling library. When using functions from the character handling library, be sure to include the **<ctype.h>** header file.

The program of Fig. 16.17 demonstrates functions ***isdigit***, ***isalpha***, ***isalnum***, and ***isxdigit***. Function **isdigit** determines whether its argument is a digit (**0-9**). Function **isalpha** determines whether its argument is an uppercase letter (**A-Z**) or a lowercase letter (**a-z**). Function **isalnum** determines whether its argument is an uppercase letter, a lowercase letter, or a digit. Function **isxdigit** determines whether its argument is a hexadecimal digit (**A-F**, **a-f**, **0-9**).

| Prototype | Function description |
|---|---|
| `int isdigit(int c)` | Returns a true value if **c** is a digit, and 0 (false) otherwise. |
| `int isalpha(int c)` | Returns a true value if **c** is a letter, and 0 otherwise. |
| `int isalnum(int c)` | Returns a true value if **c** is a digit or if **c** is a letter, and 0 otherwise. |
| `int isxdigit(int c)` | Returns a true value if **c** is a hexadecimal digit character, and 0 otherwise. (See Appendix E, "Number Systems," for a detailed explanation of binary numbers, octal numbers, decimal numbers, and hexadecimal numbers.) |
| `int islower(int c)` | Returns a true value if **c** is a lowercase letter, and 0 otherwise. |
| `int isupper(int c)` | Returns a true value if **c** is an uppercase letter, and 0 otherwise. |
| `int tolower(int c)` | If **c** is an uppercase letter, **tolower** returns **c** as a lowercase letter. Otherwise, **tolower** returns the argument unchanged. |
| `int toupper(int c)` | If **c** is a lowercase letter, **toupper** returns **c** as an uppercase letter. Otherwise, **toupper** returns the argument unchanged. |
| `int isspace(int c)` | Returns a true value if **c** is a white-space character—newline (**'\n'**), space (**' '**), form feed (**'\f'**), carriage return (**'\r'**), horizontal tab (**'\t'**), or vertical tab (**'\v'**)—and 0 otherwise |
| `int iscntrl(int c)` | Returns a true value if **c** is a control character, and 0 otherwise. |
| `int ispunct(int c)` | Returns a true value if **c** is a printing character other than a space, a digit, or a letter, and 0 otherwise. |
| `int isprint(int c)` | Returns a true value if **c** is a printing character including space (**' '**), and 0 otherwise. |
| `int isgraph(int c)` | Returns a true value if **c** is a printing character other than space (**' '**), and 0 otherwise. |

**Fig. 16.16** Summary of the character handling library functions.

```
// Using functions isdigit, isalpha, isalnum, and isxdigit
#include <iostream.h>
#include <ctype.h>

main()
{
   cout << "According to isdigit:" << endl
        << (isdigit('8') ? "8 is a" : "8 is not a") << " digit" << endl
        << (isdigit('#') ? "# is a" : "# is not a") << " digit" << endl;

   cout << endl << "According to isalpha:" << endl
        << (isalpha('A') ? "A is a" : "A is not a") << " letter" << endl
        << (isalpha('b') ? "b is a" : "b is not a") << " letter" << endl
        << (isalpha('&') ? "& is a" : "& is not a") << " letter" << endl
        << (isalpha('4') ? "4 is a" : "4 is not a") << " letter" << endl;

   cout << endl << "According to isalnum:" << endl
        << (isalnum('A') ? "A is a" : "A is not a")
        << " digit or a letter" << endl
        << (isalnum('8') ? "8 is a" : "8 is not a")
        << " digit or a letter" << endl
        << (isalnum('#') ? "# is a" : "# is not a")
        << " digit or a letter" << endl;

   cout << endl << "According to isxdigit:" << endl
        << (isxdigit('F') ? "F is a" : "F is not a")
        << " hexadecimal digit" << endl
        << (isxdigit('J') ? "J is a" : "J is not a")
        << " hexadecimal digit" << endl
        << (isxdigit('7') ? "7 is a" : "7 is not a")
        << " hexadecimal digit" << endl
        << (isxdigit('$') ? "$ is a" : "$ is not a")
        << " hexadecimal digit" << endl
        << (isxdigit('f') ? "f is a" : "f is not a")
        << " hexadecimal digit" << endl;

   return 0;
}
```

**Fig. 16.17** Using `isdigit`, `isalpha`, `isalnum`, and `isxdigit` (part 1 of 2).

The program of Fig. 16.17 uses the conditional operator (**`?:`**) with each function to determine whether the string **`" is a "`** or the string **`" is not a "`** should be printed in the output for each character tested. For example, the expression

```
isdigit('8') ? "8 is a " : "8 is not a "
```

indicates that if **`'8'`** is a digit, i.e., **`isdigit`** returns a true (nonzero) value, the string **`"8 is a "`** is printed, and if **`'8'`** is not a digit, i.e., **`isdigit`** returns **`0`**, the string **`"8 is not a "`** is printed.

The program of Fig. 16.18 demonstrates functions ***`islower`***, ***`isupper`***, ***`tolower`***, and ***`toupper`***. Function **`islower`** determines whether its argument is a lowercase letter

```
According to isdigit:
8 is a digit
# is not a digit

According to isalpha:
A is a letter
b is a letter
& is not a letter
4 is not a letter

According to isalnum:
A is a digit or a letter
8 is a digit or a letter
# is not a digit or a letter

According to isxdigit:
F is a hexadecimal digit
J is not a hexadecimal digit
7 is a hexadecimal digit
$ is not a hexadecimal digit
f is a hexadecimal digit
```

Fig. 16.17 Using **isdigit**, **isalpha**, **isalnum**, and **isxdigit** (part 2 of 2).

(**a-z**). Function **isupper** determines whether its argument is an uppercase letter (**A-Z**). Function **tolower** converts an uppercase letter to a lowercase letter, and returns the lowercase letter. If the argument is not an uppercase letter, **tolower** returns the argument unchanged. Function **toupper** converts a lowercase letter to an uppercase letter, and returns the uppercase letter. If the argument is not a lowercase letter, **toupper** returns the argument unchanged.

```
// Using functions islower, isupper, tolower, toupper
#include <iostream.h>
#include <ctype.h>

main()
{
   cout << "According to islower:" << endl
        << (islower('p') ? "p is a" : "p is not a")
        << " lowercase letter" << endl
        << (islower('P') ? "P is a" : "P is not a")
        << " lowercase letter" << endl
        << (islower('5') ? "5 is a" : "5 is not a")
        << " lowercase letter" << endl
        << (islower('!') ? "! is a" : "! is not a")
        << " lowercase letter" << endl;
```

Fig. 16.18 Using **islower**, **isupper**, **tolower**, and **toupper** (part 1 of 2).

```
   cout << endl << "According to isupper:" << endl
        << (isupper('D') ? "D is an" : "D is not an")
        << " uppercase letter" << endl
        << (isupper('d') ? "d is an" : "d is not an")
        << " uppercase letter" << endl
        << (isupper('8') ? "8 is an" : "8 is not an")
        << " uppercase letter" << endl
        << (isupper('$') ? "$ is an" : "$ is not an")
        << " uppercase letter" << endl;

   cout << endl << "u converted to uppercase is "
        << (char) toupper('u') << endl
        << "7 converted to uppercase is "
        << (char) toupper('7') << endl
        << "$ converted to uppercase is "
        << (char) toupper('$') << endl
        << "L converted to lowercase is "
        << (char) tolower('L') << endl;
   return 0;
}
```

```
According to islower:
p is a lowercase letter
P is not a lowercase letter
5 is not a lowercase letter
! is not a lowercase letter

According to isupper:
D is an uppercase letter
d is not an uppercase letter
8 is not an uppercase letter
$ is not an uppercase letter

u converted to uppercase is U
7 converted to uppercase is 7
$ converted to uppercase is $
L converted to lowercase is l
```

**Fig. 16.18** Using **islower**, **isupper**, **tolower**, and **toupper** (part 2 of 2).

Figure 16.19 demonstrates functions ***isspace***, ***iscntrl***, ***ispunct***, ***isprint***, and ***isgraph***. Function **isspace** determines if its argument is a white-space character such as space (' '), form feed ('\f'), newline ('\n'), carriage return ('\r' ), horizontal tab ('\t' ), or vertical tab ('\v' ). Function **iscntrl** determines if its argument is a control character such as horizontal tab, vertical tab, form feed, alert ('\a'), backspace ('\b'), carriage return, or newline. Function **ispunct** determines if its argument is a printing character other than a space, digit, or letter such as $, #, (, ), [, ], {, }, ;, :, %, etc. Function **isprint** determines if its argument is a character that can be displayed on the screen (including the space character). Function **isgraph** tests for the same characters as **isprint**, however the space character is not included.

```
// Using functions isspace, iscntrl, ispunct, isprint, isgraph
#include <iostream.h>
#include <ctype.h>

main()
{
   cout << "According to isspace:" << endl
        << "Newline " << (isspace('\n') ? "is a" : "is not a")
        << " whitespace character" << endl
        << "Horizontal tab "
        << (isspace('\t') ? "is a" : "is not a")
        << " whitespace character" << endl
        << (isspace('%') ? "% is a" : "% is not a")
        << " whitespace character" << endl;

   cout << endl << "According to iscntrl:" << endl
        << "Newline " << (iscntrl('\n') ? "is a" : "is not a")
        << " control character" << endl
        << (iscntrl('$') ? "$ is a" : "$ is not a")
        << " control character" << endl;

   cout << endl << "According to ispunct:" << endl
        << (ispunct(';') ? "; is a" : "; is not a")
        << " punctuation character" << endl
        << (ispunct('Y') ? "Y is a" : "Y is not a")
        << " punctuation character" << endl
        << (ispunct('#') ? "# is a" : "# is not a")
        << " punctuation character" << endl;

   cout << endl << "According to isprint:" << endl
        << (isprint('$') ? "$ is a" : "$ is not a")
        << " printing character" << endl
        << "Alert " << (isprint('\a') ? "is a" : "is not a")
        << " printing character" << endl;

   cout << endl << "According to isgraph:" << endl
        << (isgraph('Q') ? "Q is a" : "Q is not a")
        << " printing character other than a space" << endl
        << "Space " << (isgraph(' ') ? "is a" : "is not a")
        << " printing character other than a space" << endl;
   return 0;
}
```

Fig. 16.19 Using `isspace`, `iscntrl`, `ispunct`, `isprint`, and `isgraph` (part 1 of 2).

## 16.10 String Conversion Functions

In Chapter 5, we discussed several of C++'s most popular character string manipulation functions. In the next several sections, we cover the remaining functions including functions for converting strings to numeric values, functions for searching strings, and functions for manipulating, comparing, and searching blocks of memory.

```
According to isspace:
Newline is a whitespace character
Horizontal tab is a whitespace character
% is not a whitespace character

According to iscntrl:
Newline is a control character
$ is not a control character

According to ispunct:
; is a punctuation character
Y is not a punctuation character
# is a punctuation character

According to isprint:
$ is a printing character
Alert is not a printing character

According to isgraph:
Q is a printing character other than a space
Space is not a printing character other than a space
```

**Fig. 16.19** Using **isspace**, **iscntrl**, **ispunct**, **isprint**, and **isgraph** (part 2 of 2).

This section presents the *string conversion functions* from the *general utilities library* (**stdlib**). These functions convert strings of digits to integer and floating-point values. Figure 16.20 summarizes the string conversion functions. Note the use of **const** to declare variable **nPtr** in the function headers (read from right to left as "**nPtr** is a pointer to a character constant"); **const** declares that the argument value will not be modified. When using functions from the general utilities library, be sure to include the **<stdlib.h>** header file.

| Function prototype | Function description |
|---|---|
| `double atof(const char *nPtr)` | Converts the string **nPtr** to **double**. |
| `int atoi(const char *nPtr)` | Converts the string **nPtr** to **int**. |
| `long atol(const char *nPtr)` | Converts the string **nPtr** to long **int**. |
| `double strtod(const char *nPtr, char **endPtr)` | Converts the string **nPtr** to **double**. |
| `long strtol(const char *nPtr, char **endPtr, int base)` | Converts the string **nPtr** to **long**. |
| `unsigned long strtoul(const char *nPtr, char **endPtr, int base)` | Converts the string **nPtr** to **unsigned long**. |

**Fig. 16.20** Summary of the string conversion functions of the general utilities library.

Function ***atof*** (Fig. 16.21) converts its argument—a string that represents a floating point number—to a **double** value. The function returns the **double** value. If the converted value cannot be represented—for example, if the first character of the string is not a digit—the behavior of function **atof** is undefined.

Function ***atoi*** (Fig. 16.22) converts its argument—a string of digits that represents an integer—to an **int** value. The function returns the **int** value. If the converted value cannot be represented, the behavior of function **atoi** is undefined.

```
// Using atof
#include <iostream.h>
#include <stdlib.h>

main()
{
   double d = atof("99.0");

   cout << "The string \"99.0\" converted to double is "
        << d << "\nThe converted value divided by 2 is "
        << (d / 2.0) << endl;
   return 0;
}
```

```
The string "99.0" converted to double is 99
The converted value divided by 2 is 49.5
```

Fig. 16.21 Using atof.

```
// Using atoi
#include <iostream.h>
#include <stdlib.h>

main()
{
   int i = atoi("2593");

   cout << "The string \"2593\" converted to int is " << i
        << "\nThe converted value minus 593 is " << (i - 593)
        << endl;
   return 0;
}
```

```
The string "2593" converted to int is 2593
The converted value minus 593 is 2000
```

Fig. 16.22 Using atoi.

Function **atol** (Fig. 16.23) converts its argument—a string of digits representing a long integer—to a **long** value. The function returns the **long** value. If the converted value cannot be represented, the behavior of function **atol** is undefined. If **int** and **long** are both stored in 4 bytes, function **atoi** and function **atol** work identically.

Function **strtod** (Fig. 16.24) converts a sequence of characters representing a floating-point value to **double**. The function receives two arguments—a string (**char ***) and a pointer to a string. The string contains the character sequence to be converted to **double**. The second argument is assigned the location of the first character after the converted portion of the string. The statement

```
d = strtod(string, &stringPtr);
```

from the program of Fig. 16.24 indicates that **d** is assigned the **double** value converted from **string**, and **&stringPtr** is assigned the location of the first character after the converted value (**51.2**) in **string**.

```
// Using atol
#include <iostream.h>
#include <stdlib.h>

main()
{
   long l = atol("1000000");

   cout << "The string \"1000000\" converted to long is " << l
        << "\nThe converted value divided by 2 is " << (l / 2)
        << endl;
   return 0;
}
```

```
The string "1000000" converted to long int is 1000000
The converted value divided by 2 is 500000
```

Fig. 16.23 Using atol.

Function **strtol** (Fig. 16.25) converts to **long** a sequence of characters representing an integer. The function receives three arguments—a string (**char ***), a pointer to a string, and an integer. The string contains the character sequence to be converted. The second argument is assigned the location of the first character after the converted portion of the string. The integer specifies the *base* of the value being converted. The statement

```
x = strtol(string, &remainderPtr, 0);
```

in the program of Fig. 16.25 indicates that **x** is assigned the **long** value converted from **string**. The second argument, **&remainderPtr**, is assigned the remainder of **string** after the conversion. Using **NULL** for the second argument causes the remainder

```
// Using strtod
#include <iostream.h>
#include <stdlib.h>

main()
{
   double d;
   char *string = "51.2% are admitted", *stringPtr;

   d = strtod(string, &stringPtr);
   cout << "The string \"" << string << "\" is converted to the\n"
        << "double value " << d << " and the string \""
        << stringPtr << "\"" << endl;
   return 0;
}
```

```
The string "51.2% are admitted" is converted to the
double value 51.20 and the string "% are admitted"
```

**Fig. 16.24** Using `strtod`.

of the string to be ignored. The third argument, `0`, indicates that the value to be converted can be in octal (base 8), decimal (base 10), or hexadecimal (base 16) format. The base can be specified as 0 or any value between 2 and 36. See Appendix E, "Number Systems," for a detailed explanation of the octal, decimal, hexadecimal, and binary number systems. Numeric representations of integers from base 11 to base 36 use the characters A–Z to represent the values 10 to 35. For example, hexadecimal values can consist of the digits 0–9 and the characters A–F. A base 11 integer can consist of the digits 0–9 and the character A. A base 24 integer can consist of the digits 0–9 and the characters A–N. A base 36 integer can consist of the digits 0–9 and the characters A–Z.

```
// Using strtol
#include <iostream.h>
#include <stdlib.h>

main()
{
   long x;
   char *string = "-1234567abc", *remainderPtr;

   x = strtol(string, &remainderPtr, 0);
   cout << "The original string is \"" << string
        << "\"\nThe converted value is " << x
        << "\nThe remainder of the original string is \""
        << remainderPtr << "\"\nThe converted value plus 567 is "
        << (x + 567) << endl;
   return 0;
}
```

**Fig. 16.25** Using `strtol` (part 1 of 2).

```
The original string is "-1234567abc"
The converted value is -1234567
The remainder of the original string is "abc"
The converted value plus 567 is -1234000
```

Fig. 16.25 Using `strtol` (part 2 of 2).

Function ***strtoul*** (Fig. 16.26) converts to **`unsigned long`** a sequence of characters representing an **`unsigned long`** integer. The function works identically to function **`strtol`**. The statement

```
x = strtoul(string, &remainderPtr, 0);
```

in the program of Fig. 16.26 indicates that **`x`** is assigned the **`unsigned long`** value converted from **`string`**. The second argument, **`&remainderPtr`**, is assigned the remainder of **`string`** after the conversion. The third argument, 0, indicates that the value to be converted can be in octal, decimal, or hexadecimal format.

## 16.11 Search Functions of the String Handling Library

This section presents the functions of the string handling library used to search strings for characters and other strings. The functions are summarized in Fig. 16.27. Note that func-

```
// Using strtoul
#include <iostream.h>
#include <stdlib.h>

main()
{
   unsigned long x;
   char *string = "1234567abc", *remainderPtr;

   x = strtoul(string, &remainderPtr, 0);
   cout << "The original string is \"" << string
        << "\"\nThe converted value is " << x
        << "\nThe remainder of the original string is \""
        << remainderPtr
        << "\"\nThe converted value minus 567 is " << (x - 567)
        << endl;
   return 0;
}
```

```
The original string is "1234567abc"
The converted value is 1234567
The remainder of the original string is "abc"
The converted value minus 567 is 1234000
```

Fig. 16.26 Using `strtoul`.

tions **strcspn** and **strspn** specify return type **size_t**. Type **size_t** is a type defined by the standard as the integral type of the value returned by operator **sizeof**.

*Portability Tip 16.6*

*Type* `size_t` *is a system dependent synonym for either type* `unsigned long` *or type* `unsigned int`.

Function ***strchr*** searches for the first occurrence of a character in a string. If the character is found, **strchr** returns a pointer to the character in the string, otherwise **strchr** returns **NULL**. The program of Fig. 16.28 uses **strchr** to search for the first occurrences of **'a'** and **'z'** in the string **"This is a test"**.

Function ***strcspn*** (Fig. 16.29) determines the length of the initial part of the string in its first argument that does not contain any characters from the string in its second argument. The function returns the length of the segment.

| Function prototype | Function description |
|---|---|
| `char *strchr(const char *s, int c)` | Locates the first occurrence of character c in string **s**. If **c** is found, a pointer to **c** in **s** is returned. Otherwise, a **NULL** pointer is returned. |
| `size_t strcspn(const char *s1, const char *s2)` | Determines and returns the length of the initial segment of string **s1** consisting of characters not contained in string **s2**. |
| `size_t strspn(const char *s1, const char *s2)` | Determines and returns the length of the initial segment of string **s1** consisting only of characters contained in string **s2**. |
| `char *strpbrk(const char *s1, const char *s2)` | Locates the first occurrence in string **s1** of any character in string **s2**. If a character from string **s2** is found, a pointer to the character in string **s1** is returned. Otherwise a **NULL** pointer is returned. |
| `char *strrchr(const char *s, int c)` | Locates the last occurrence of **c** in string **s**. If **c** is found, a pointer to **c** in string **s** is returned. Otherwise, a **NULL** pointer is returned. |
| `char *strstr(const char *s1, const char *s2)` | Locates the first occurrence in string **s1** of string **s2**. If the string is found, a pointer to the string in **s1** is returned. Otherwise, a **NULL** pointer is returned. |

**Fig. 16.27** Search functions of the string handling library.

```
// Using strchr
#include <iostream.h>
#include <string.h>

main()
{
   char *string = "This is a test";
   char character1 = 'a', character2 = 'z';

   if (strchr(string, character1) != NULL)
      cout << '\'' << character1 << "' was found in \""
           << string << "\"." << endl;
   else
      cout << '\'' << character1 << "' was not found in \""
           << string << "\"." << endl;

   if (strchr(string, character2) != NULL)
      cout << '\'' << character2 << "' was found in \""
           << string << "\"." << endl;
   else
      cout << '\'' << character2 << "' was not found in \""
           << string << "\"." << endl;
   return 0;
}
```

```
'a' was found in "This is a test".
'z' was not found in "This is a test".
```

Fig. 16.28 Using `strchr`.

```
// Using strcspn
#include <iostream.h>
#include <string.h>

main()
{
   char *string1 = "The value is 3.14159";
   char *string2 = "1234567890";

   cout << "string1 = " << string1 << "\nstring2 = " << string2
        << "\n\nThe length of the initial segment of string1"
        << "\ncontaining no characters from string2 = "
        << strcspn(string1, string2) << endl;
   return 0;
}
```

```
string1 = The value is 3.14159
string2 = 1234567890

The length of the initial segment of string1
containing no characters from string2 = 13
```

Fig. 16.29 Using `strcspn`.

Function ***strpbrk*** searches for the first occurrence in its first string argument of any character in its second string argument. If a character from the second argument is found, **strpbrk** returns a pointer to the character in the first argument, otherwise **strpbrk** returns **NULL**. The program of Fig. 16.30 locates the first occurrence in **string1** of any character from **string2**.

Function ***strrchr*** searches for the last occurrence of the specified character in a string. If the character is found, **strrchr** returns a pointer to the character in the string, otherwise **strrchr** returns **NULL**. The program of Fig. 16.31 searches for the last occurrence of the character **'z'** in the string **"A zoo has many animals including zebras"**.

```
#include <iostream.h>
#include <string.h>

main()
{
   char *string1 = "This is a test";
   char *string2 = "beware";

   cout << "Of the characters in \"" << string2 << "\"\n'"
        << *strpbrk(string1, string2) << '\''
        << " is the first character to appear in\n\""
        << string1 << '\"' << endl;
   return 0;
}
```

```
Of the characters in "beware"
'a' is the first character to appear in
"This is a test"
```

Fig. 16.30 Using strpbrk.

```
// Using strrchr
#include <iostream.h>
#include <string.h>

main()
{
   char *string1 = "A zoo has many animals including zebras";
   int c = 'z';

   cout << "The remainder of string1 beginning with the\n"
        << "last occurrence of character '" << (char) c
        << "' is: \"" << strrchr(string1, c) << '\"' << endl;
   return 0;
}
```

Fig. 16.31 Using strrchr (part 1 of 2).

```
The remainder of string1 beginning with the
last occurrence of character 'z' is: "zebras"
```

Fig. 16.31 Using `strrchr` (part 2 of 2).

Function ***strspn*** (Fig. 16.32) determines the length of the initial part of the string in its first argument that contains only characters from the string in its second argument. The function returns the length of the segment.

Function ***strstr*** searches for the first occurrence of its second string argument in its first string argument. If the second string is found in the first string, a pointer to the location of the string in the first argument is returned. The program of Fig. 16.33 uses **strstr** to find the string **"def"** in the string **"abcdefabcdef"**.

## 16.12 Memory Functions of the String Handling Library

The string handling library functions presented in this section facilitate manipulating, comparing, and searching blocks of memory. The functions treat blocks of memory as character arrays. These functions can manipulate any block of data. Figure 16.34 summarizes the memory functions of the string handling library. In the function discussions, "object" refers to a block of data.

```
// Using strspn
#include <iostream.h>
#include <string.h>

main()
{
   char *string1 = "The value is 3.14159";
   char *string2 = "aehilsTuv ";

   cout << "string1 = " << string1 << "\nstring2 = " << string2
        << "\n\nThe length of the initial segment of string1\n"
        << "containing only characters from string2 = "
        << strspn(string1, string2) << endl;
   return 0;
}
```

```
string1 = The value is 3.14159
string2 = aehilsTuv

The length of the initial segment of string1
containing only characters from string2 = 13
```

Fig. 16.32 Using `strspn`.

```
// Using strstr
#include <iostream.h>
#include <string.h>

main()
{
   char *string1 = "abcdefabcdef";
   char *string2 = "def";

   cout << "string1 = " << string1 << "\nstring2 = " << string2
        << "\n\nThe remainder of string1 beginning with the\n"
        << "first occurrence of string2 is: "
        << strstr(string1, string2) << endl;
   return 0;
}
```

```
string1 = abcdefabcdef
string2 = def

The remainder of string1 beginning with the
first occurrence of string2 is: defabcdef
```

Fig. 16.33 Using `strstr`.

| Function prototype | Function description |
|---|---|
| `void *memcpy(void *s1, const void *s2, size_t n)` | Copies **n** characters from the object pointed to by **s2** into the object pointed to by **s1**. A pointer to the resulting object is returned. |
| `void *memmove(void *s1, const void *s2, size_t n)` | Copies **n** characters from the object pointed to by **s2** into the object pointed to by **s1**. The copy is performed as if the characters are first copied from the object pointed to by **s2** into a temporary array, then from the temporary array into the object pointed to by **s1**. A pointer to the resulting object is returned. |
| `int memcmp(const void *s1, const void *s2, size_t n)` | Compares the first **n** characters of the objects pointed to by **s1** and **s2**. The function returns **0**, less than **0**, or greater than **0** if **s1** is equal to, less than, or greater than **s2**. |
| `void *memchr(const void *s, int c, size_t n)` | Locates the first occurrence of **c** (converted to **unsigned char**) in the first **n** characters of the object pointed to by **s**. If **c** is found, a pointer to **c** in the object is returned. Otherwise, **NULL** is returned. |

Fig. 16.34 The memory functions of the string handling library (part 1 of 2).

| Function prototype | Function description |
|---|---|
| `void *memset(void *s, int c, size_t n)` | Copies **c** (converted to **unsigned char**) into the first **n** characters of the object pointed to by **s**. A pointer to the result is returned. |

Fig. 16.34 The memory functions of the string handling library (part 2 of 2).

The pointer parameters to these functions are declared **void ***. In Chapter 5, we saw that a pointer to any data type can be assigned directly to a pointer of type **void ***. For this reason, these functions can receive pointers to any data type. Remember that a pointer of type **void *** cannot be assigned directly to a pointer to any data type. Because a **void *** pointer cannot be dereferenced, each function receives a size argument that specifies the number of characters (bytes) the function will process. For simplicity, the examples in this section manipulate character arrays (blocks of characters).

Function ***memcpy*** copies a specified number of characters from the object pointed to by its second argument into the object pointed to by its first argument. The function can receive a pointer to any type of object. The result of this function is undefined if the two objects overlap in memory, i.e., they are parts of the same object. The program of Fig. 16.35 uses **memcpy** to copy the string in array **s2** to array **s1**.

Function ***memmove***, like **memcpy**, copies a specified number of bytes from the object pointed to by its second argument into the object pointed to by its first argument. Copying is performed as if the bytes are copied from the second argument to a temporary array of characters, then copied from the temporary array to the first argument. This allows characters from one part of a string to be copied into another part of the same string.

```
// Using memcpy
#include <iostream.h>
#include <string.h>

main()
{
   char s1[17], s2[]  = "Copy this string";

   memcpy(s1, s2, 17);
   cout << "After s2 is copied into s1 with memcpy,\n"
        << "s1 contains \"" << s1 << '\"' << endl;
   return 0;
}
```

```
After s2 is copied into s1 with memcpy,
s1 contains "Copy this string"
```

Fig. 16.35 Using **memcpy**.

*Common Programming Error 16.11*

*String manipulation functions other than* **memmove** *that copy characters have undefined results when copying takes place between parts of the same string.*

The program in Fig. 16.36 uses **memmove** to copy the last **10** bytes of array **x** into the first **10** bytes of array **x**.

Function ***memcmp*** (Fig. 16.37) compares the specified number of characters of its first argument to the corresponding characters of its second argument. The function returns a value greater than 0 if the first argument is greater than the second argument, returns 0 if the arguments are equal, and returns a value less than zero if the first argument is less than the second argument.

```
// Using memmove
#include <iostream.h>
#include <string.h>

main()
{
   char x[] = "Home Sweet Home";

   cout << "The string in array x before memmove is: " << x << endl
   cout << "The string in array x after memmove is:  "
        << (char *) memmove(x, &x[5], 10) << endl;
   return 0;
}
```

```
The string in array x before memmove is: Home Sweet Home
The string in array x after memmove is:  Sweet Home Home
```

**Fig. 16.36** Using **memmove**.

```
// Using memcmp
#include <iostream.h>
#include <iomanip.h>
#include <string.h>

main()
{
   char s1[] = "ABCDEFG", s2[] = "ABCDXYZ";

   cout << "s1 = " << s1 << "\ns2 = " << s2 << endl
        << "\nmemcmp(s1, s2, 4) = " << setw(3) << memcmp(s1, s2, 4)
        << "\nmemcmp(s1, s2, 7) = " << setw(3) << memcmp(s1, s2, 7)
        << "\nmemcmp(s2, s1, 7) = " << setw(3) << memcmp(s2, s1, 7)
        << endl;
   return 0;
}
```

**Fig. 16.37** Using **memcmp** (part 1 of 2).

```
s1 = ABCDEFG
s2 = ABCDXYZ

memcmp(s1, s2, 4) =   0
memcmp(s1, s2, 7) = -19
memcmp(s2, s1, 7) =  19
```

Fig. 16.37 Using **memcmp** (part 2 of 2).

Function ***memchr*** searches for the first occurrence of a byte, represented as **unsigned char**, in the specified number of bytes of an object. If the byte is found, a pointer to the byte in the object is returned, otherwise **NULL** is returned. The program of Fig. 16.38 searches for the character (byte) **'r'** in the string **"This is a string"**.

Function ***memset*** copies the value of the byte in its second argument into a specified number of bytes of the object pointed to by its first argument. The program in Fig. 16.39 uses **memset** to copy **'b'** into the first **7** bytes of **string1**.

```
// Using memchr
#include <iostream.h>
#include <string.h>

main()
{
   char *s = "This is a string";

   cout << "The remainder of s after character 'r' is found is \""
        << (char *) memchr(s, 'r', 16) << '\"' << endl;
   return 0;
}
```

```
The remainder of s after character 'r' is found is "ring"
```

Fig. 16.38 Using **memchr**.

```
// Using memset
#include <iostream.h>
#include <string.h>

main()
{
   char string1[15] = "BBBBBBBBBBBBBB";

   cout << "string1 = " << string1 << endl;
   cout << "string1 after memset = "
        << (char *) memset(string1, 'b', 7) << endl;
   return 0;
}
```

Fig. 16.39 Using **memset** (part 1 of 2).

```
string1 = BBBBBBBBBBBBBB
string1 after memset = bbbbbbbBBBBBBB
```

Fig. 16.39 Using **memset** (part 2 of 2).

## 16.13 Other Functions of the String Handling Library

The remaining function of the string handling library is **strerror**. Figure 16.40 summarizes the **strerror** function.

Function ***strerror*** takes an error number and creates an error message string. A pointer to the string is returned. The program of Fig. 16.41 demonstrates **strerror**.

***Portability Tip 16.7***

*The message generated by* **strerror** *is system dependent.*

### *Summary*

- Structures are collections of related variables, sometimes referred to as aggregates, under one name.
- Structures can contain variables of different data types.

| Function prototype | Function description |
|---|---|
| **char *strerror(int errornum)** | Maps **errornum** into a full text string in a system dependent manner. A pointer to the string is returned. |

Fig. 16.40 Another string manipulation function of the string handling library.

```
// Using strerror
#include <iostream.h>
#include <string.h>

main()
{
   cout << strerror(2) << endl;
   return 0;
}
```

```
No such file or directory
```

Fig. 16.41 Using **strerror**.

- The keyword **`struct`** begins every structure definition. Within the braces of the structure definition are the structure member declarations.
- Members of the same structure must have unique names.
- A structure definition creates a new data type that can be used to declare variables.
- A structure can be initialized with an initializer list by following the variable in the declaration with an equal sign and a comma-separated list of initializers enclosed in braces. If there are fewer initializers in the list than members in the structure, the remaining members are automatically initialized to zero (or **`NULL`** for pointer members).
- Entire structure variables may be assigned to structure variables of the same type.
- A structure variable may be initialized with a structure variable of the same type.
- Structures variables and individual structure members are passed to functions call-by-value. Array members are, of course, passed call-by-reference.
- To pass a structure call-by-reference, pass the address of the structure variable.
- An array of structures is automatically passed call-by-reference.
- To pass an array call-by-value, create a structure with the array as a member.
- Creating a new name with **`typedef`** does not create a new type; it creates a name that is synonymous to a type defined previously.
- The bitwise AND operator (**`&`**) takes two integral operands. A bit in the result is set to 1 if the corresponding bits in each of the operands are 1.
- Masks are used to hide some bits while preserving others.
- The bitwise inclusive OR operator (**`|`**) takes two operands. A bit in the result is set to 1 if the corresponding bit in either operand is set to 1.
- Each of the bitwise operators (except the unary bitwise complement operator) has a corresponding assignment operator.
- The bitwise exclusive OR operator (**`^`**) takes two operands. A bit in the result is set to 1 if exactly one of the corresponding bits in the two operands is set to 1.
- The left shift operator (**`<<`**) shifts the bits of its left operand left by the number of bits specified by its right operand. Bits vacated to the right are replaced with **`0`**s.
- The right shift operator (**`>>`**) shifts the bits of its left operand right by the number of bits specified in its right operand. Performing a right shift on an unsigned integer causes bits vacated at the left to be replaced by 0s. Vacated bits in signed integers can be replaced with 0s or 1s—this is machine dependent.
- The bitwise complement operator (**`~`**) takes one operand and reverses its bits—this produces the one's complement of the operand.
- Bit fields reduce storage use by storing data in the minimum number of bits required.
- Bit field members must be declared as **`int`** or **`unsigned`**.

- A bit field is declared by following an **unsigned** or **int** member name with a colon and the width of the bit field.
- The bit field width must be an integer constant between 0 and the total number of bits used to store an **int** variable on your system
- If a bit field is specified without a name, the field is used as padding in the structure.
- An unnamed bit field with width **0** is used to align the next bit field on a new machine word boundary.
- Function **islower** determines whether its argument is a lowercase letter (**a-z**).
- Function **isupper** determines if its argument is an uppercase letter (**A-Z**).
- Function **isdigit** determines whether its argument is a digit (**0-9**).
- Function **isalpha** determines whether its argument is an uppercase letter (**A-Z**) or a lowercase letter (**a-z**).
- Function **isalnum** determines whether its argument is an uppercase letter (**A-Z**), a lowercase letter (**a-z**), or a digit (**0-9**).
- Function **isxdigit** determines whether its argument is a hexadecimal digit (**A-F**, **a-f**, **0-9**).
- Function **toupper** converts a lowercase letter to an uppercase letter.
- Function **tolower** converts an uppercase letter to a lowercase letter.
- Function **isspace** determines whether its argument is one of the following white-space characters: **' '** (space), **'\f'**, **'\n'**, **'\r'** , **'\t'**, or **'\v'**.
- Function **iscntrl** determines whether its argument is one of the following control characters: **'\t'**, **'\v'**, **'\f'**, **'\a'**, **'\b'**, **'\r'**, or **'\n'**.
- Function **ispunct** determines whether its argument is a printing character other than a space, a digit, or a letter.
- Function **isprint** determines whether its argument is any printing character including the space character.
- Function **isgraph** determines whether its argument is a printing character other than the space character.
- Function **atof** converts its argument—a string beginning with a series of digits that represents a floating-point number—to a **double** value.
- Function **atoi** converts its argument—a string beginning with a series of digits that represents an integer—to an **int** value.
- Function **atol** converts its argument—a string beginning with a series of digits that represents a long integer—to a **long** value.
- Function **strtod** converts a sequence of characters representing a floating-point value to **double**. The function receives two arguments—a string (**char ***) and a

pointer to **char ***. The string contains the character sequence to be converted, and the pointer to **char *** is assigned the remainder of the string after the conversion.

- Function **strtol** converts a sequence of characters representing an integer to **long**. The function receives three arguments—a string (**char ***), a pointer to **char ***, and an integer. The string contains the character sequence to be converted, the pointer to **char *** is assigned the remainder of the string after the conversion, and the integer specifies the base of the value being converted.
- Function **strtoul** converts a sequence of characters representing an integer to **unsigned long**. The function receives three arguments—a string (**char ***), a pointer to **char ***, and an integer. The string contains the character sequence to be converted, the pointer to **char *** is assigned the remainder of the string after the conversion, and the integer specifies the base of the value being converted.
- Function **strchr** searches for the first occurrence of a character in a string. If the character is found, **strchr** returns a pointer to the character in the string, otherwise **strchr** returns **NULL**.
- Function **strcspn** determines the length of the initial part of the string in its first argument that does not contain any characters from the string in its second argument. The function returns the length of the segment.
- Function **strpbrk** searches for the first occurrence in its first argument of any character that appears in its second argument. If a character from the second argument is found, **strpbrk** returns a pointer to the character, otherwise **strpbrk** returns **NULL**.
- Function **strrchr** searches for the last occurrence of a character in a string. If the character is found, **strrchr** returns a pointer to the character in the string, otherwise **strrchr** returns **NULL**.
- Function **strspn** determines the length of the initial part of the string in its first argument that contains only characters from the string in its second argument. The function returns the length of the segment.
- Function **strstr** searches for the first occurrence of its second string argument in its first string argument. If the second string is found in the first string, a pointer to the location of the string in the first argument is returned.
- Function **memcpy** copies a specified number of characters from the object to which its second argument points into the object to which its first argument points. The function can receive a pointer to any type of object. The pointers are received by **memcpy** as **void** pointers, and converted to **char** pointers for use in the function. Function **memcpy** manipulates the bytes of the argument as characters.
- Function **memmove**, copies a specified number of bytes from the object pointed to by its second argument to the object pointed to by its first argument. Copying is accomplished as if the bytes are copied from the second argument to a temporary character array, then copied from the temporary array to the first argument.

- Function **memcmp** compares the specified number of characters of its first and second arguments.
- Function **memchr** searches for the first occurrence of a byte, represented as **unsigned char**, in the specified number of bytes of an object. If the byte is found, a pointer to the byte is returned, otherwise a **NULL** pointer is returned.
- Function **memset** copies its second argument, treated as an **unsigned char**, to a specified number of bytes of the object pointed to by the first argument.
- Function **strerror** maps an integer error number into a full text string in a system dependent manner. A pointer to the string is returned.

## Terminology

^ bitwise exclusive OR operator
~ one's complement operator
& bitwise AND operator
&= bitwise AND assignment operator
<< left shift operator
<<= left shift assignment operator
^= bitwise exclusive OR assignment operator
>> right shift operator
>>= right shift assignment operator
| bitwise inclusive OR operator
|= bitwise inclusive OR assignment operator
array of structures
ASCII
**atof**
**atoi**
**atol**
bit field
bitwise operators
character code
character constant
character set
complementing
control character
**ctype.h**
delimiter
general utilities library
hexadecimal digits
initialization of structures
**isalnum**
**isalpha**
**iscntrl**
**isdigit**
**isgraph**
**islower**
**isprint**
**ispunct**
**isspace**
**isupper**
**isxdigit**
left shift
literal
mask
masking off bits
**memchr**
**memcmp**
**memcpy**
**memmove**
**memset**
one's complement
padding
pointer to a structure
printing character
record
right shift
search string
self-referential structure
shifting
space-time tradeoffs
**stdlib.h**
**strchr**
**strcspn**
**strerror**
string
string constant
string conversion functions
string literal
string processing
**string.h**

**strpbrk**
**strrchr**
**strspn**
**strstr**
**strtod**
**strtol**
**strtoul**
**struct**
structure assignment
structure initialization
structure type
**tolower**
**toupper**
**typedef**
unnamed bit field
whitespace characters
width of a bit field
word processing
zero-width bit field

## Common Programming Errors

**16.1** Forgetting the semicolon that terminates a structure definition.

**16.2** Assigning a structure of one type to a structure of a different type.

**16.3** Comparing structures is a syntax error because of the different alignment requirements on various systems.

**16.4** Assuming that structures, like arrays, are automatically passed call-by-reference and trying to modify the caller's structure values in the called function.

**16.5** Forgetting to include the array subscript when referring to individual structures in an array of structures.

**16.6** Using the logical AND operator (**&&**) for the bitwise AND operator (**&**) and vice versa.

**16.7** Using the logical OR operator (**||**) for the bitwise OR operator (**|**) and vice versa.

**16.8** The result of shifting a value is undefined if the right operand is negative or if the right operand is larger than the number of bits in which the left operand is stored.

**16.9** Attempting to access individual bits of a bit field as if they were elements of an array. Bit fields are not "arrays of bits."

**16.10** Attempting to take the address of a bit field (the **&** operator may not be used with bit fields because they do not have addresses).

**16.11** String manipulation functions other than **memmove** that copy characters have undefined results when copying takes place between parts of the same string.

## Good Programming Practices

**16.1** Provide a structure name when creating a structure type. The structure name is convenient for declaring new variables of the structure type later in the program.

**16.2** Capitalize **typedef** names to emphasize that these names are synonyms for other type names.

## Performance Tips

**16.1** Passing structures (and especially large structures) call-by-reference is more efficient than passing structures call-by-value (which requires the entire structure to be copied).

**16.2** Bit fields help conserve storage.

**16.3** Although bit fields save space, using them can cause the compiler to generate slower-executing machine language code. This occurs because it takes extra machine language operations to access only portions of an addressable storage unit. This is one of many examples of the kinds of space-time tradeoffs that occur in computer science.

## Portability Tips

16.1 Because the size of data items of a particular type is machine dependent, and because storage alignment considerations are machine dependent, so too is the representation of a structure.

16.2 Using **typedef** can help make a program more portable.

16.3 Bitwise data manipulations are machine dependent.

16.4 The result of right shifting a signed value is machine dependent. Some machines fill with zero and others use the sign bit.

16.5 Bit field manipulations are machine dependent. For example, some computers allow bit fields to cross word boundaries, whereas others do not.

16.6 Type **size_t** is a system dependent synonym for either type **unsigned long** or type **unsigned int**.

16.7 The message generated by **strerror** is system dependent.

## Self-Review Exercises

16.1 Fill in the blanks in each of the following:

a) A __________ is a collection of related variables under one name.
b) The bits in the result of an expression using the __________ operator are set to 1 if the corresponding bits in each operand are set to 1. Otherwise, the bits are set to zero.
c) The variables declared in a structure definition are called its __________ .
d) The bits in the result of an expression using the __________ operator are set to 1 if at least one of the corresponding bits in either operand is set to 1. Otherwise, the bits are set to zero.
e) The keyword __________ introduces a structure declaration.
f) The keyword __________ is used to create a synonym for a previously defined data type.
g) The bits in the result of an expression using the __________ operator are set to 1 if exactly one of the corresponding bits in either operand is set to 1. Otherwise, the bits are set to zero.
h) The bitwise AND operator **&** is often used to __________ bits, that is to select certain bits from a bit string while zeroing others.
i) The name of the structure is referred to as the structure __________.
j) A structure member is accessed with either the __________ operator or the __________ operator.
k) The __________ and __________ operators are used to shift the bits of a value to the left or to the right, respectively.

16.2 State whether each of the following is true or false. If false, explain why.

a) Structures may contain only one data type.
b) The members of different structures must have unique names.
c) The keyword **typedef** is used to define new data types.
d) Structures are always passed to functions call-by-reference.

16.3 Write a single statement or a set of statements to accomplish each of the following:

a) Define a structure called **Part** containing **int** variable **partNumber**, and **char** array **partName** whose values may be as long as 25 characters.
b) Define **PartPtr** to be a synonym for the type **Part ***.
c) Declare variable **a** to be of type **Part**, array **b[10]** to be of type **Part**, and variable **ptr** to be of type pointer to **Part**.

d) Read a part number and a part name from the keyboard into the individual members of variable **a**.
e) Assign the member values of variable **a** to element 3 of array **b**.
f) Assign the address of array **b** to the pointer variable **ptr**.
g) Print the member values of element 3 of array **b** using the variable **ptr** and the structure pointer operator to refer to the members.

**16.4** Find the error in each of the following:

a) Assume that **struct Card** has been defined containing two pointers to type **char**, namely **face** and **suit**. Also, the variable **c** has been declared to be of type **Card** and the variable **cPtr** has been declared to be of type pointer to **Card**. Variable **cPtr** has been assigned the address of **c**.

```
cout << *cPtr.face << endl;
```

b) Assume that **struct Card** has been defined containing two pointers to type **char**, namely **face** and **suit**. Also, the array **hearts[13]** has been declared to be of type **Card**. The following statement should print the member **face** of element 10 of the array.

```
cout << hearts.face << endl;
```

c)
```
struct Person {
   char lastName[15];
   char firstName[15];
   int age;
}
```

d) Assume variable **p** has been declared as type **Person**, and variable **c** has been declared as type **Card**.

```
p = c;
```

**16.5** Write a single statement to accomplish each of the following. Assume that variables **c** (which stores a character), **x**, **y**, and **z** are of type **int**, variables **d**, **e**, and **f** are of type **float**, variable **ptr** is of type **char ***, and arrays **s1[100]** and **s2[100]** are of type **char**.

a) Convert the character stored in variable **c** to an uppercase letter. Assign the result to variable **c**.
b) Determine if the value of variable **c** is a digit. Use the conditional operator as shown in Fig. 16.17, 16.18, and 16.19 to print **" is a "** or **" is not a "** when the result is displayed.
c) Convert the string **"1234567"** to **long** and print the value.
d) Determine if the value of variable **c** is a control character. Use the conditional operator to print **" is a "** or **" is not a "** when the result is displayed.
e) Assign **ptr** the location of the last occurrence of **c** in **s1**.
f) Convert the string **"8.63582"** to **double** and print the value.
g) Determine if the value of **c** is a letter. Use the conditional operator to print **" is a "** or **" is not a "** when the result is displayed.
h) Assign **ptr** the location of the first occurrence of **s2** in **s1**.
i) Determine if the value of variable **c** is a printing character. Use the conditional operator to print **" is a "** or **" is not a "** when the result is displayed.
j) Assign **ptr** the location of the first occurrence in **s1** of any character from **s2**.
k) Assign **ptr** the location of the first occurrence of **c** in **s1**.
l) Convert the string **"-21"** to **int** and print the value.

## Answers to Self-Review Exercises

**16.1** a) structure. b) bitwise AND (`&`). c) members. d) bitwise inclusive OR (`|`). e) `struct`. f) `typedef`. g) bitwise exclusive OR (`^`). h) mask. i) tag. j) structure member (`.`), structure pointer (`->`). k) left shift operator (`<<`), right shift operator (`>>`).

**16.2**
a) False. A structure can contain many data types.
b) False. The members of separate structures can have the same names, but the members of the same structure must have unique names.
c) False. `typedef` is used to define aliases for previously defined data types.
d) False. Structures are always passed to functions call-by-value.

**16.3**
a)
```
struct Part {
    int partNumber;
    char partName[26];
};
```
b) `typedef Part * PartPtr;`
c) `Part a, b[10], *ptr;`
d) `cin >> a.partNumber >> a.partName;`
e) `b[3] = a;`
f) `ptr = b;`
g)
```
cout << (ptr + 3)->partNumber << ' '
     << (ptr + 3)->partName) << endl;
```

**16.4**
a) Error: The parentheses that should enclose `*cPtr` have been omitted causing the order of evaluation of the expression to be incorrect.
b) Error: The array subscript has been omitted. The expression should be `hearts[10].face`.
c) Error: A semicolon is required to end a structure definition.
d) Error: Variables of different structure types cannot be assigned to one another.

**16.5**
a) `c = toupper(c);`
b)
```
cout << '\'' << c << "\' " << (isdigit(c) ? "is a" : "is not a")
     << " digit" << endl;
```
c) `cout << atol("1234567") << endl;`
d)
```
cout << '\'' << c << "\' " << (iscntrl(c) ? "is a" : "is not a")
     << " control character" << endl;
```
e) `ptr = strrchr(s1, c);`
f) `cout << atof("8.63582") << endl;`
g)
```
cout << '\'' << c << "\' " << (isalpha(c) ? "is a" : "is not a")
     << " letter" << endl;
```
h) `ptr = strstr(s1, s2);`
i)
```
cout << '\'' << c << "\' " << (isprint(c) ? "is a" : "is not a")
     << " printing character" << endl;
```
j) `ptr = strpbrk(s1, s2);`
k) `ptr = strchr(s1, c);`
l) `cout << atoi("-21") << endl;`

## Exercises

**16.6** Provide the definition for each of the following structures and unions:
a) Structure `Inventory` containing character array `partName[30]`, integer `partNumber`, floating point `price`, integer `stock`, and integer `reorder`.

b) A structure called **Address** that contains character arrays **streetAddress[25]**, **city[20]**, **state[3]**, and **zipCode[6]**.

c) Structure **Student** that contains arrays **firstName[15]** and **lastName[15]**, and variable **homeAddress** of type **struct Address** from part (b).

d) Structure **Test** containing 16 bit fields with widths of 1 bit. The names of the bit fields are the letters **a** to **p**.

**16.7** Given the following structure definitions and variable declarations,

```
struct Customer {
   char lastName[15];
   char firstName[15];
   int customerNumber;

   struct {
      char phoneNumber[11];
      char address[50];
      char city[15];
      char state[3];
      char zipCode[6];
   } personal;

} customerRecord, *customerPtr;

customerPtr = &customerRecord;
```

write a separate expression that can be used to access the structure members in each of the following parts.

a) Member **lastName** of structure **customerRecord**.
b) Member **lastName** of the structure pointed to by **customerPtr**.
c) Member **firstName** of structure **customerRecord**.
d) Member **firstName** of the structure pointed to by **customerPtr**.
e) Member **customerNumber** of structure **customerRecord**.
f) Member **customerNumber** of the structure pointed to by **customerPtr**.
g) Member **phoneNumber** of member **personal** of structure **customerRecord**.
h) Member **phoneNumber** of member **personal** of the structure pointed to by **customerPtr**.
i) Member **address** of member **personal** of structure **customerRecord**.
j) Member **address** of member **personal** of the structure pointed to by **customerPtr**.
k) Member **city** of member **personal** of structure **customerRecord**.
l) Member **city** of member **personal** of the structure pointed to by **customerPtr**.
m) Member **state** of member **personal** of structure **customerRecord**.
n) Member **state** of member **personal** of the structure pointed to by **customerPtr**.
o) Member **zipCode** of member **personal** of structure **customerRecord**.
p) Member **zipCode** of member **personal** of the structure pointed to by **customerPtr**.

**16.8** Modify the program of Fig. 16.14 to shuffle the cards using a high-performance shuffle (as shown in Fig. 16.2). Print the resulting deck in two column format as in Fig. 16.3. Precede each card with its color.

**16.9** Write a program that right shifts an integer variable 4 bits. The program should print the integer in bits before and after the shift operation. Does your system place 0s or 1s in the vacated bits?

**16.10** If your computer uses 4-byte integers, modify the program of Fig. 16.5 so that it works with 4-byte integers.

**16.11** Left shifting an **unsigned** integer by 1 bit is equivalent to multiplying the value by 2. Write function **power2** that takes two integer arguments **number** and **pow**, and calculates

```
number * 2pow
```

Use the shift operator to calculate the result. The program should print the values as integers and as bits.

**16.12** The left shift operator can be used to pack two character values into a 2-byte unsigned integer variable. Write a program that inputs two characters from the keyboard and passes them to function **packCharacters**. To pack two characters into an **unsigned** integer variable, assign the first character to the **unsigned** variable, shift the **unsigned** variable left by 8 bit positions, and combine the **unsigned** variable with the second character using the bitwise inclusive OR operator. The program should output the characters in their bit format before and after they are packed into the **unsigned** integer to prove that the characters are in fact packed correctly in the **unsigned** variable.

**16.13** Using the right shift operator, the bitwise AND operator, and a mask, write function **unpackCharacters** that takes the **unsigned** integer from Exercise 16.12 and unpacks it into two characters. To unpack two characters from an **unsigned** 2-byte integer, combine the unsigned integer with the mask **65280** (**11111111 00000000**) and right shift the result 8 bits. Assign the resulting value to a **char** variable. Then combine the **unsigned** integer with the mask **255** (**00000000 11111111**). Assign the result to another **char** variable. The program should print the **unsigned** integer in bits before it is unpacked, then print the characters in bits to confirm that they were unpacked correctly.

**16.14** If your system uses 4-byte integers, rewrite the program of Exercise 16.12 to pack 4 characters.

**16.15** If your system uses 4-byte integers, rewrite the function **unpackCharacters** of Exercise 16.13 to unpack 4 characters. Create the masks you need to unpack the 4 characters by left shifting the value 255 in the mask variable by 8 bits 0, 1, 2, or 3 times (depending on the byte you are unpacking).

**16.16** Write a program that reverses the order of the bits in an unsigned integer value. The program should input the value from the user and call function **reverseBits** to print the bits in reverse order. Print the value in bits both before and after the bits are reversed to confirm that the bits are reversed properly.

**16.17** Modify the **displayBits** function of Fig. 16.5 so it is portable between systems using 2-byte integers and systems using 4-byte integers. Hint: Use the **sizeof** operator to determine the size of an integer on a particular machine.

**16.18** Write a program that inputs a character from the keyboard, and tests the character with each of the functions in the character handling library. The program should print the value returned by each function.

**16.19** The following program uses function **multiple** to determine if the integer entered from the keyboard is a multiple of some integer **X**. Examine the function **multiple**, then determine the value of **X**.

```
// This program determines if a value is a multiple of X
#include <iostream.h>

int multiple(int);

main()
{
   int y;

   cout << "Enter an integer between 1 and 32000: ";
   cin >> y;

   if (multiple(y))
      cout << y << " is a multiple of X" << endl;
   else
      cout << y << " is not a multiple of X" << endl;

   return 0;
}

int multiple(int num)
{
   int mask = 1, mult = 1;

   for (int i = 0; i < 10; i++, mask <<= 1)
      if ((num & mask) != 0) {
         mult = 0;
         break;
      }

   return mult;
}
```

**16.20** What does the following program do?

```
#include <iostream.h>

int mystery(unsigned);

main()
{
   unsigned x;

   cout << "Enter an integer: ";
   cin >> x;
   cout << "The result is " << mystery(x) << endl;
   return 0;
}

int mystery(unsigned bits)
{
   unsigned mask = 1 << 15, total = 0;

   for (int i = 0; i < 16; i++, bits <<= 1)
      if ((bits & mask) == mask)
         ++total;

   return total % 2 == 0 ? 1 : 0;
}
```

**16.21** Write a program that inputs a line of text with `istream` member function `getline` (see Chapter 11) into character array `s[100]`. Output the line in uppercase letters,then in lowercase letters.

**16.22** Write a program that inputs 4 strings that represent integers, converts the strings to integers, sums the values, and prints the total of the 4 values.

**16.23** Write a program that inputs 4 strings that represent floating-point values, converts the strings to double values, sums the values, and prints the total of the 4 values.

**16.24** Write a program that inputs a line of text and a search string from the keyboard. Using function `strstr`, locate the first occurrence of the search string in the line of text, and assign the location to variable `searchPtr` of type `char *`. If the search string is found, print the remainder of the line of text beginning with the search string. Then, use `strstr` again to locate the next occurrence of the search string in the line of text. If a second occurrence is found, print the remainder of the line of text beginning with the second occurrence. Hint: The second call to `strstr` should contain `searchPtr + 1` as its first argument.

**16.25** Write a program based on the program of Exercise 16.24 that inputs several lines of text and a search string, and uses function `strstr` to determine the total number of occurrences of the string in the lines of text. Print the result.

**16.26** Write a program that inputs several lines of text and a search character, and uses function `strchr` to determine the total number of occurrences of the character in the lines of text.

**16.27** Write a program based on the program of Exercise 16.26 that inputs several lines of text and uses function `strchr` to determine the total number of occurrences of each letter of the alphabet in the text. Uppercase and lowercase letters should be counted together. Store the totals for each letter in an array, and print the values in tabular format after the totals have been determined.

**16.28** The chart in Appendix D shows the numeric code representations for the characters in the ASCII character set. Study this chart and then state whether each of the following is true or false.

a) The letter "`A`" comes before the letter "`B`."
b) The digit "`9`" comes before the digit "`0`."
c) The commonly used symbols for addition, subtraction, multiplication, and division all come before any of the digits.
d) The digits come before the letters.
e) If a sort program sorts strings into ascending sequence, then the program will place the symbol for a right parenthesis before the symbol for a left parenthesis.

**16.29** Write a program that reads a series of strings and prints only those strings beginning with the letter "`b`."

**16.30** Write a program that reads a series of strings and prints only those strings that end with the letters "`ED`."

**16.31** Write a program that inputs an ASCII code and prints the corresponding character. Modify this program so that it generates all possible three-digit codes in the range 000 to 255 and attempts to print the corresponding characters. What happens when this program is run?

**16.32** Using the ASCII character chart in Appendix D as a guide, write your own versions of the character handling functions in Fig. 16.16.

**16.33** Write your own versions of the functions in Fig. 16.20 for converting strings to numbers.

**16.34** Write your own versions of the functions in Fig. 16.27 for searching strings.

**16.35** Write your own versions of the functions in Fig. 16.34 for manipulating blocks of memory.

**16.35** *(Project: A Spelling Checker)* Many popular word processing software packages have built-in spell checkers. We used the spell-checking capabilities of Microsoft Word 5.0 in preparing this book and discovered that no matter how careful we thought we were in writing a chapter, Word was always able to find a few more spelling errors than we were able to catch manually.

In this project, you are asked to develop your own spell-checker utility. We make suggestions to help get you started. You should then consider adding more capabilities. You may find it helpful to use a computerized dictionary as a source of words.

Why do we type so many words with incorrect spellings? In some cases, it is because we simply do not know the correct spelling, so we make a "best guess." In some cases, it is because we transpose two letters (e.g., "defualt" instead of "default"). Sometimes we double-type a letter accidentally (e.g., "hanndy" instead of "handy"). Sometimes we type a nearby key instead of the one we intended (e.g., "biryhday" instead of "birthday"). And so on.

Design and implement a spell-checker program in C++. Your program maintains an array **`wordList`** of character strings. You can either enter these strings or obtain them from a computerized dictionary.

Your program asks a user to enter a word. The program then looks up that word in the **`wordList`** array. If the word is present in the array, your program should print "**`Word is spelled correctly`**."

If the word is not present in the array, your program should print "**`word is not spelled correctly`**." Then your program should try to locate other words in **`wordList`** that might be the word the user intended to type. For example, you can try all possible single transpositions of adjacent letters to discover that the word "default" is a direct match to a word in **`wordList`**. Of course, this implies that your program will check all other single transpositions such as "edfault," "dfeault," "deafult," "defalut," and "defautl." When you find a new word that matches one in **`wordList`**, print that word in a message such as, "**`Did you mean "default?"`**."

Implement other tests such as replacing each double letter with a single letter and any other tests you can develop to improve the value of your spell checker.

# 17

# The Preprocessor

## Objectives

- To be able to use `#include` for developing large programs.
- To be able to use `#define` to create macros and macros with with arguments.
- To understand conditional compilation.
- To be able to display error messages during conditional compilation.
- To be able to use assertions to test if the values of expressions are correct.

*Hold thou the good; define it well.*
Alfred, Lord Tennyson

*I have found you an argument; but I am not obliged to find you an understanding.*
Samuel Johnson

*A good symbol is the best argument, and is a missionary to persuade thousands.*
Ralph Waldo Emerson

*Conditions are fundamentally sound.*
Herbert Hoover (December 1929)

*The partisan, when he is engaged in a dispute, cares nothing about the rights of the question, but is anxious only to convince his hearers of his own assertions*
Plato

## Outline



## 17.1 Introduction

This chapter introduces the *preprocessor.* Preprocessing occurs before a program is compiled. Some possible actions are: inclusion of other files in the file being compiled, definition of *symbolic constants* and *macros, conditional compilation* of program code, and *conditional execution of preprocessor directives.* All preprocessor directives begin with **#**, and only whitespace characters may appear before a preprocessor directive on a line.

## 17.2 The #include Preprocessor Directive

The ***#include*** *preprocessor directive* has been used throughout this text. The **#include** directive causes a copy of a specified file to be included in place of the directive. The two forms of the **#include** directive are:

```
#include <filename>
#include "filename"
```

The difference between these is the location the preprocessor searches for the file to be included. If the file name is enclosed in angle brackets (**<** and **>**)—used for *standard library header files*—the preprocessor searches for the specified file in an implementation-dependent manner, normally through predesignated directories. If the file name is enclosed in quotes, the preprocessor searches first in the same directory as the file being compiled, then in the same implementation-dependent manner as a file name enclosed in angle brackets. This method is normally used to include programmer-defined header files.

The **#include** directive is normally used to include standard header files such as **iostream.h** and **iomanip.h**. The **#include** directive is also used with programs consisting of several source files that are to be compiled together. A *header file* containing declarations and definitions common to the separate program files is often created and included in the file. Examples of such declarations and definitions are classes, structures, unions, enumerations, and function prototypes.

## 17.3 The #define Preprocessor Directive: Symbolic Constants

The **#define** *preprocessor directive* creates *symbolic constants*—constants represented as symbols—and *macros*—operations defined as symbols. The **#define** preprocessor directive format is

**#define** *identifier replacement-text*

When this line appears in a file, all subsequent occurrences of *identifier* will be replaced by *replacement-text* automatically before the program is compiled. For example,

```
#define PI 3.14159
```

replaces all subsequent occurrences of the symbolic constant **PI** with the numeric constant **3.14159**. Symbolic constants enable the programmer to create a name for a constant and use the name throughout the program. If the constant needs to be modified throughout the program, it can be modified once in the **#define** preprocessor directive—and when the program is recompiled, all occurrences of the constant in the program will be modified automatically. Note: *Everything to the right of the symbolic constant name replaces the symbolic constant.* For example, **#define PI = 3.14159** causes the preprocessor to replace every occurrence of **PI** with **= 3.14159**. This is the cause of many subtle logic and syntax errors. Redefining a symbolic constant with a new value is also an error. Note that **const** variables in C++ are preferred over symbolic constants. Constant variables have a specific data type and are visible by name to a debugger. Once a symbolic constant is replaced with its replacement text, only the replacement text is visible to a debugger. A disadvantage of **const** variables is they may require a memory location of their data type size—symbolic constants do not require any additional memory.

*Good Programming Practice 17.1*

*Using meaningful names for symbolic constants helps make programs more self-documenting.*

## 17.4 The #define Preprocessor Directive: Macros

A *macro* is an operation defined in a **#define** preprocessor directive. As with symbolic constants, the *macro-identifier* is replaced with the *replacement-text* before the program is compiled. Macros may be defined with or without *arguments*. A macro without arguments is processed like a symbolic constant. In a macro with arguments, the arguments are substituted in the replacement text, then the macro is *expanded*—i.e., the replacement-text replaces the macro-identifier and argument list in the program.

Consider the following macro definition with one argument for the area of a circle:

```
#define CIRCLE_AREA(x) ( PI * (x) * (x) )
```

Wherever **`CIRCLE_AREA(x)`** appears in the file, the value of **`x`** is substituted for **`x`** in the replacement text, the symbolic constant **`PI`** is replaced by its value (defined previously), and the macro is expanded in the program. For example, the statement

```
area = CIRCLE_AREA(4);
```

is expanded to

```
area = ( 3.14159 * (4) * (4) );
```

Since the expression consists only of constants, at compile time the value of the expression is evaluated and the result is assigned to **`area`** at run time. The parentheses around each **`x`** in the replacement text and around the entire expression force the proper order of evaluation when the macro argument is an expression. For example, the statement

```
area = CIRCLE_AREA(c + 2);
```

is expanded to

```
area = ( 3.14159 * (c + 2) * (c + 2) );
```

which evaluates correctly because the parentheses force the proper order of evaluation. If the parentheses are omitted, the macro expansion is

```
area = 3.14159 * c + 2 * c + 2;
```

which evaluates incorrectly as

```
area = (3.14159 * c) + (2 * c) + 2;
```

because of the rules of operator precedence.

***Common Programming Error 17.1***

*Forgetting to enclose macro arguments in parentheses in the replacement text.*

Macro **`CIRCLE_AREA`** could be defined as a function. Function **`circleArea`**

```
double circleArea(double x) { return 3.14159 * x * x; }
```

performs the same calculation as **`CIRCLE_AREA`**, but the overhead of a function call is associated with function **`circleArea`**. The advantages of **`CIRCLE_AREA`** are that macros insert code directly in the program—avoiding function overhead—and the program remains readable because **`CIRCLE_AREA`** is defined separately and named meaningfully. A disadvantage is that its argument is evaluated twice. Also, every time a macro appears in a program, the macro is expanded. If the macro is large, this produces an increase in program size. Thus, there is a tradeoff between execution speed and program size (disk space may be low). Note that **`inline`** functions (see Chapter 3) are preferred to obtain the performance of macros and the software engineering benefits of functions.

*Performance Tip 17.1*

*Macros can sometimes be used to replace a function call with inline code prior to execution time. This eliminates the overhead of a function call. Inline functions are preferable.*

The following is a macro definition with 2 arguments for the area of a rectangle:

```
#define RECTANGLE_AREA(x, y)   ( (x) * (y) )
```

Wherever **RECTANGLE_AREA(x, y)** appears in the program, the values of **x** and **y** are substituted in the macro replacement text, and the macro is expanded in place of the macro name. For example, the statement

```
rectArea = RECTANGLE_AREA(a + 4, b + 7);
```

is expanded to

```
rectArea = ( (a + 4) * (b + 7) );
```

The value of the expression is evaluated and assigned to variable **rectArea**.

The replacement text for a macro or symbolic constant is normally any text on the line after the identifier in the **#define** directive. If the replacement text for a macro or symbolic constant is longer than the remainder of the line, a backslash (\) must be placed at the end of the line indicating that the replacement text continues on the next line.

Symbolic constants and macros can be discarded using the ***#undef** preprocessor directive*. Directive **#undef** "undefines" a symbolic constant or macro name. The *scope* of a symbolic constant or macro is from its definition until it is undefined with **#undef**, or until the end of the file. Once undefined, a name can be redefined with **#define**.

Functions in the standard library sometimes are defined as macros based on other library functions. A macro commonly defined in the **<stdio.h>** header file is

```
#define getchar() getc(stdin)
```

The macro definition of **getchar** uses function **getc** to get one character from the standard input stream. Function **putchar** of the **<stdio.h>** header, and the character handling functions of the **<ctype.h>** header often are implemented as macros as well. Note that expressions with side effects (i.e., variable values are modified) should not be passed to a macro because macro arguments may be evaluated more than once.

## 17.5 Conditional Compilation

*Conditional compilation* enables the programmer to control the execution of preprocessor directives and the compilation of program code. Each of the conditional preprocessor directives evaluates a constant integer expression. Cast expressions, **sizeof** expressions, and enumeration constants cannot be evaluated in preprocessor directives.

The conditional preprocessor construct is much like the **if** selection structure. Consider the following preprocessor code:

```
#if !defined(NULL)
   #define NULL 0
#endif
```

These directives determine if **NULL** is defined. The expression **defined(NULL)** evaluates to **1** if **NULL** is defined; **0** otherwise. If the result is **0**, **!defined(NULL)** evaluates to **1**, and **NULL** is defined. Otherwise, the **#define** directive is skipped. Every **#if** construct ends with **#endif**. Directives ***#ifdef*** and ***#ifndef*** are shorthand for **#if defined(*name*)** and **#if !defined(*name*)**. A multiple-part conditional preprocessor construct may be tested using the **#elif** (the equivalent of **else if** in an **if** structure) and the **#else** (the equivalent of **else** in an **if** structure) directives.

During program development, programmers often find it helpful to "comment out" large portions of code to prevent it from being compiled. If the code contains C-style comments, **/*** and ***/** cannot be used to accomplish this task. Instead, the programmer can use the following preprocessor construct

```
#if 0
   code prevented from compiling
#endif
```

To enable the code to be compiled, the **0** in the preceding construct is replaced by **1**.

Conditional compilation is commonly used as a debugging aid. Many C++ implementations provide *debuggers*. However, debuggers often are difficult to use and understand, so they are rarely used by students in a first programming course. Instead, output statements are used to print variable values and to confirm the flow of control. These output statements can be enclosed in conditional preprocessor directives so the statements are only compiled while the debugging process is not completed. For example,

```
#ifdef DEBUG
   cerr << "Variable x = " << x << endl;
#endif
```

causes the **cerr** statement to be compiled in the program if the symbolic constant **DEBUG** has been defined (**#define DEBUG**) before directive **#ifdef DEBUG**. When debugging is completed, the **#define** directive is removed from the source file and the output statements inserted for debugging purposes are ignored during compilation. In larger programs, it may be desirable to define several different symbolic constants that control the conditional compilation in separate sections of the source file.

*Common Programming Error 17.2*

*Inserting conditionally compiled output statements for debugging purposes in locations where C++ currently expects a single statement. In this case, the conditionally compiled statement should be enclosed in a compound statement. Thus, when the program is compiled with debugging statements, the flow of control of the program is not altered.*

## 17.6 The #error and #pragma Preprocessor Directives

The ***#error*** *directive*

```
#error tokens
```

prints an implementation-dependent message including the *tokens* specified in the directive. The tokens are sequences of characters separated by spaces. For example,

```
#error 1 - Out of range error
```

contains 6 tokens. In Borland C++, for example, when a **#error** directive is processed, the tokens in the directive are displayed as an error message, preprocessing stops, and the program does not compile.

The ***#pragma*** *directive*

```
#pragma tokens
```

causes an implementation-defined action. A pragma not recognized by the implementation is ignored. Borland C++, for example, recognizes several pragmas that enable the programmer to take full advantage of the Borland C++ implementation. For more information on **#error** and **#pragma**, see the documentation for your C++ implementation.

## 17.7 The # and ## Operators

The **#** and **##** preprocessor operators are available in C++ and ANSI C. The **#** operator causes a replacement text token to be converted to a string surrounded by quotes. Consider the following macro definition:

```
#define HELLO(x) cout << "Hello, " #x << endl
```

When **HELLO(John)** appears in a program file, it is expanded to

```
cout << "Hello, " "John" << endl
```

The string **"John"** replaces **#x** in the replacement text. Strings separated by whitespace are concatenated during preprocessing, so the above statement is equivalent to

```
cout << "Hello, John" << endl
```

Note that the **#** operator must be used in a macro with arguments because the operand of **#** refers to an argument of the macro.

The **##** operator concatenates two tokens. Consider the following macro definition:

```
#define TOKENCONCAT(x, y)  x ## y
```

When **TOKENCONCAT** appears in the program, its arguments are concatenated and used to replace the macro. For example, **TOKENCONCAT(O, K)** is replaced by **OK** in the program. The **##** operator must have two operands.

## 17.8 Line Numbers

The ***#line*** *preprocessor directive* causes the subsequent source code lines to be renumbered starting with the specified constant integer value. The directive

```
#line 100
```

starts line numbering from **100** beginning with the next source code line. A file name can be included in the **#line** directive. The directive

```
#line 100 "file1.c"
```

indicates that lines are numbered from **100** beginning with the next source code line, and that the name of the file for the purpose of any compiler messages is **"file1.c"**. The directive normally is used to help make the messages produced by syntax errors and compiler warnings more meaningful. The line numbers do not appear in the source file.

## 17.9 Predefined Symbolic Constants

There are five *predefined symbolic constants* (Fig. 17.1). The indentifiers for each of the predefined symbolic constants begin and end with *two* underscores. These identifiers and the **defined** identifier (used in Section 17.5) cannot be used in **#define** or **#undef** directives.

## 17.10 Assertions

The ***assert** macro*—defined in the **<assert.h>** header file—tests the value of an expression. If the value of the expression is **0** (false), then **assert** prints an error message and calls function ***abort*** (of the general utilities library—**<stdlib.h>**) to terminate program execution. This is a useful debugging tool for testing if a variable has a correct value. For example, suppose variable **x** should never be larger than **10** in a program. An assertion may be used to test the value of **x** and print an error message if the value of **x** is incorrect. The statement would be:

```
assert(x <= 10);
```

If **x** is greater than **10** when the preceding statement is encountered in a program, an error message containing the line number and file name is printed, and the program terminates. The programmer may then concentrate on this area of the code to find the error. If the symbolic constant **NDEBUG** is defined, subsequent assertions will be ignored. Thus, when assertions are no longer needed (i.e., when debugging is complete), the line

| Symbolic constant | Explanation |
|---|---|
| `__LINE__` | The line number of the current source code line (an integer constant). |
| `__FILE__` | The presumed name of the source file (a string). |
| `__DATE__` | The date the source file is compiled (a string of the form **"Mmm dd yyyy"** such as **"Jan 19 1994"**). |
| `__TIME__` | The time the source file is compiled (a string literal of the form **"hh:mm:ss"**). |
| `__STDC__` | The integer constant 1. This is intended to indicate that the implementation is ANSI compliant. |

**Fig. 17.1** The predefined symbolic constants.

```
#define NDEBUG
```

is inserted in the program file rather than deleting each assertion manually.

## Summary

- All preprocessor directives begin with **#**.
- Only whitespace characters may appear before a preprocessor directive on a line.
- The **#include** directive includes a copy of the specified file. If the file name is enclosed in quotes, the preprocessor begins searching in the same directory as the file being compiled for the file to be included. If the file name is enclosed in angle brackets (**<** and **>**), the search is performed in an implementation-defined manner.
- The **#define** preprocessor directive is used to create symbolic constants and macros.
- A symbolic constant is a name for a constant.
- A macro is an operation defined in a **#define** preprocessor directive. Macros may be defined with or without arguments.
- The replacement text for a macro or symbolic constant is any text remaining on the line after the identifier in the **#define** directive. If the replacement text for a macro or symbolic constant is too long to fit clearly on one line, a backslash (****) is placed at the end of the line indicating that the replacement text continues on the next line.
- Symbolic constants and macros can be discarded using the **#undef** preprocessor directive. Directive **#undef** "undefines" the symbolic constant or macro name.
- The scope of a symbolic constant or macro is from its definition until it is undefined with **#undef**, or until the end of the file.
- Conditional compilation enables the programmer to control the execution of preprocessor directives and the compilation of program code.
- The conditional preprocessor directives evaluate constant integer expressions. Cast expressions, **sizeof** expressions, and enumeration constants cannot be evaluated in preprocessor directives.
- Every **#if** construct ends with **#endif**.
- Directives **#ifdef** and **#ifndef** are provided as shorthand for **#if defined(***name***)** and **#if !defined(***name***)**.
- A multiple-part conditional preprocessor construct may be tested using the **#elif** (the equivalent of **else if** in an **if** structure) and the **#else** (the equivalent of **else** in an **if** structure) directives.
- The **#error** directive prints an implementation-dependent message that includes the tokens specified in the directive and terminates preprocessing and compiling.
- The **#pragma** directive causes an implementation-defined action. If the pragma is not recognized by the implementation, the pragma is ignored.

- The **#** operator causes a replacement text token to be converted to a string surrounded by quotes. The **#** operator must be used in a macro with arguments because the operand of **#** must be an argument of the macro.
- The **##** operator concatenates two tokens. The **##** operator must have two operands.
- The **#line** preprocessor directive causes the subsequent source code lines to be renumbered starting with the specified constant integer value.
- There are five predefined symbolic constants. Constant **__LINE__** is the line number of the current source code line (an integer). Constant **__FILE__** is the presumed name of the file (a string). Constant **__DATE__** is the date the source file is compiled (a string). Constant **__TIME__** is the time the source file is compiled (a string). Constant **__STDC__** is **1**; it is intended to indicate that the implementation is ANSI compliant. Note that each of the predefined symbolic constants begins and ends with two underbars.
- The **assert** macro—defined in the **assert.h** header file—tests the value of an expression. If the value of the expression is **0** (false), then **assert** prints an error message and calls function **abort** to terminate program execution.

## Terminology

**#define**
**#elif**
**#else**
**#endif**
**#error**
**#if**
**#ifdef**
**#ifndef**
**#include <filename>**
**#include "filename"**
**#line**
**#pragma**
**#undef**
\ (backslash) continuation character
**__DATE__**
**__FILE__**
**__LINE__**
**__STDC__**
**__TIME__**
**abort**
argument
**assert**
**assert.h**
concatenation preprocessor operator **##**
conditional compilation
conditional execution of preprocessor directives
convert-to-string preprocessor operator **#**
debugger
expand a macro
header file
macro
macro with arguments
predefined symbolic constants
preprocessing directive
preprocessor
replacement text
scope of a symbolic constant or macro
standard library header files
**stdio.h**
**stdlib.h**
symbolic constant

## Common Programming Errors

**17.1** Forgetting to enclose macro arguments in parentheses in the replacement text.

**17.2** Inserting conditionally compiled output statements for debugging purposes in locations where C++ currently expects a single statement. In this case, the conditionally compiled statement should be enclosed in a compound statement. Thus, when the program is compiled with debugging statements, the flow of control of the program is not altered.

## Good Programming Practice

**17.1** Using meaningful names for symbolic constants helps make programs more self-documenting.

## Performance Tip

**17.1** Macros can sometimes be used to replace a function call with inline code prior to execution time. This eliminates the overhead of a function call. Inline functions are preferable.

## Self-Review Exercises

**17.1** Fill in the blanks in each of the following:

a) Every preprocessor directive must begin with ________.
b) The conditional compilation construct may be extended to test for multiple cases by using the ________ and the ________ directives.
c) The ________ directive creates macros and symbolic constants.
d) Only ________ characters may appear before a preprocessor directive on a line.
e) The ________ directive discards symbolic constant and macro names.
f) The ________ and ________ directives are provided as shorthand notation for **#if defined(***name***)** and **#if !defined(***name***)**.
g) ________ enables the programmer to control the execution of preprocessor directives and the compilation of program code.
h) The ________ macro prints a message and terminates program execution if the value of the expression the macro evaluates is 0.
i) The ________ directive inserts a file in another file.
j) The ________ operator concatenates its two arguments.
k) The ________ operator converts its operand to a string.
l) The character ________ indicates that the replacement text for a symbolic constant or macro continues on the next line.
m) The ________ directive causes the source code lines to be numbered from the indicated value beginning with the next source code line.

**17.2** Write a program to print the values of the predefined symbolic constants listed in Fig. 17.1.

**17.3** Write a preprocessor directive to accomplish each of the following:

a) Define symbolic constant **YES** to have the value **1**.
b) Define symbolic constant **NO** to have the value **0**.
c) Include the header file **common.h**. The header is found in the same directory as the file being compiled.
d) Renumber the remaining lines in the file beginning with line number **3000**.
e) If symbolic constant **TRUE** is defined, undefine it, and redefine it as **1**. Do not use **#ifdef**.
f) If symbolic constant **TRUE** is defined, undefine it, and redefine it as **1**. Use the **#ifdef** preprocessor directive.

g) If symbolic constant **ACTIVE** is not equal to **0**, define symbolic constant **INACTIVE** as **0**. Otherwise define **INACTIVE** as **1**.

h) Define macro **CUBE_VOLUME** that computes the volume of a cube. The macro takes one argument.

## Answers to Self-Review Exercises

**17.1** a) **#**. b) **#elif**, **#else**. c) **#define**. d) whitespace. e) **#undef**. f) **#ifdef**, **#ifndef**. g) Conditional compilation. h) **assert**. i) **#include**. j) **##**. k) **#**. l) ****. m) **#line**.

**17.2**
```
#include <iostream.h>
main()
{
   cout << "__LINE__ = " << __LINE__ << endl;
   cout << "__FILE__ = " << __FILE__ << endl;
   cout << "__DATE__ = " << __DATE__ << endl;
   cout << "__TIME__ = " << __TIME__ << endl;
   cout << "__STDC__ = " << __STDC__ << endl;
   return 0;
}
```

```
__LINE__ = 5
__FILE__ = macros.c
__DATE__ = Mar 08 1994
__TIME__ = 10:23:47
__STDC__ = 1
```

**17.3**

a) `#define YES 1`

b) `#define NO 0`

c) `#include "common.h"`

d) `#line 3000`

e)
```
#if defined(TRUE)
   #undef TRUE
   #define TRUE 1
#endif
```

f)
```
#ifdef TRUE
   #undef TRUE
   #define TRUE 1
#endif
```

g)
```
#if ACTIVE
   #define INACTIVE 0
#else
   #define INACTIVE 1
#endif
```

h) `#define CUBE_VOLUME(x)   ( (x) * (x) * (x) )`

## Exercises

**17.4** Write a program that defines a macro with one argument to compute the volume of a sphere. The program should compute the volume for spheres of radius 1 to 10, and print the results in tabular format. The formula for the volume of a sphere is:

```
(4/3) * π * r³
```

where π is **3.14159**.

**17.5** Write a program that produces the following output:

```
The sum of x and y is 13
```

The program should define macro **SUM** with two arguments, **x** and **y**, and use **SUM** to produce the output.

**17.6** Write a program that uses macro **MINIMUM2** to determine the smallest of two numeric values. Input the values from the keyboard.

**17.7** Write a program that uses macro **MINIMUM3** to determine the smallest of three numeric values. Macro **MINIMUM3** should use macro **MINIMUM2** defined in Exercise 17.6 to determine the smallest number. Input the values from the keyboard.

**17.8** Write a program that uses macro **PRINT** to print a string value.

**17.9** Write a program that uses macro **PRINTARRAY** to print an array of integers. The macro should receive the array and the number of elements in the array as arguments.

**17.10** Write a program that uses macro **SUMARRAY** to sum the values in a numeric array. The macro should receive the array and the number of elements in the array as arguments.

**17.11** Rewrite the solutions to 17.4 to 17.10 as inline functions.

# 18

# Other Topics

## Objectives

- To be able to redirect keyboard input from a file.
- To be able to redirect screen output to a file.
- To be able to write functions that use variable-length argument lists.
- To be able to process command-line arguments.
- To be able to provide types to numeric constants.
- To be able to process unexpected events.
- To be able to allocate memory dynamically for arrays using C-style dynamic memory allocation.
- To be able to change the size of memory dynamically allocated using C-style dynamic memory allocation.

*We'll use a signal I have tried and found far-reaching and easy to yell. Waa-hoo!*
Zane Grey

*It is quite a three-pipe problem.*
Sir Arthur Conan Doyle

*But yet an union in partition;*
William Shakespeare

*I could never make out what those damned dots meant.*
Winston Churchill

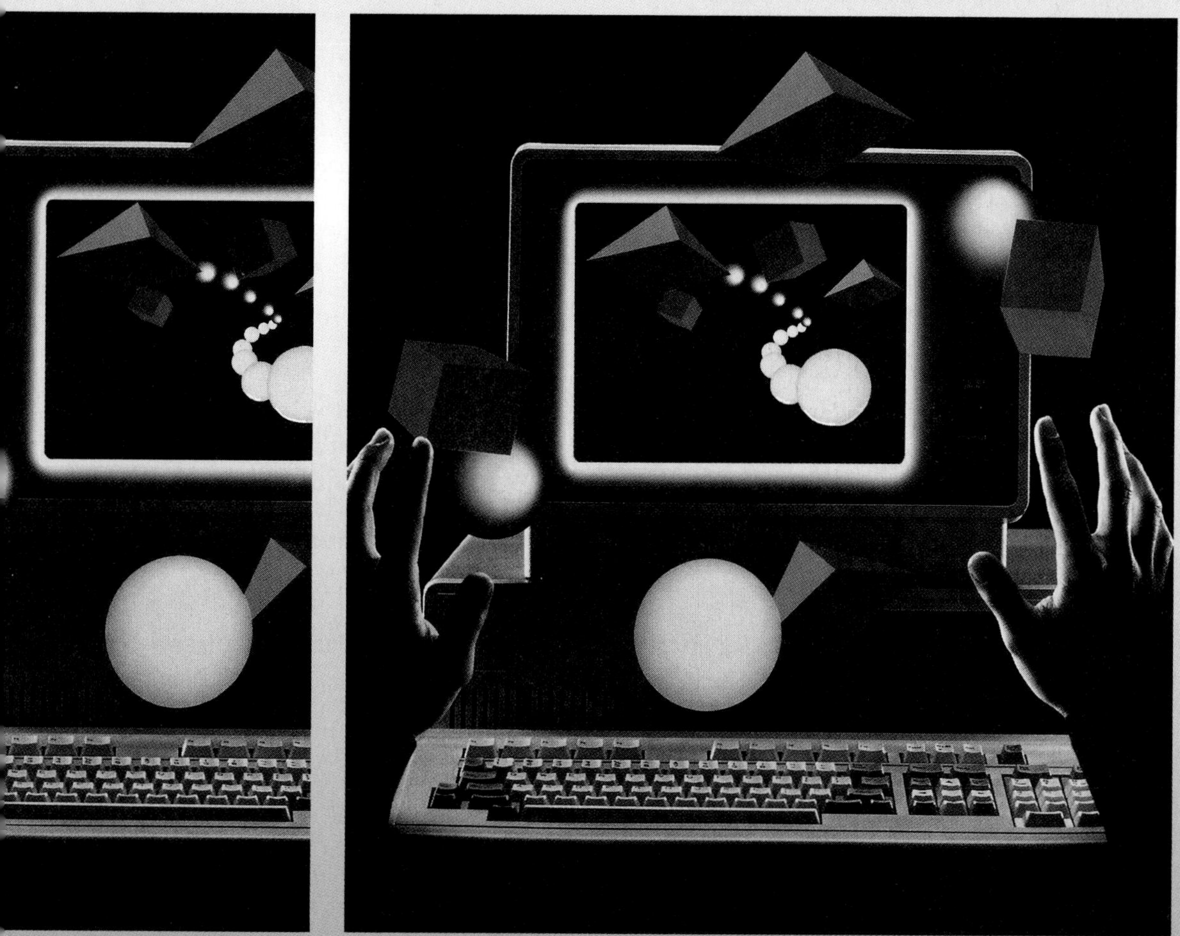

## Outline



## 18.1 Introduction

This chapter presents several advanced topics not ordinarily covered in introductory courses. Many of the capabilities discussed here are specific to particular operating systems, especially UNIX and/or DOS.

## 18.2 Redirecting Input/Output on UNIX and DOS Systems

Normally the input to a program is from the keyboard (standard input), and the output from a program is displayed on the screen (standard output). On most computer systems—UNIX and DOS systems in particular—it is possible to *redirect* inputs to come from a file, and redirect outputs to be placed in a file. Both forms of redirection can be accomplished without using the file processing capabilities of the standard library.

There are several ways to redirect input and output from the UNIX command line. Consider the executable file **sum** that inputs integers one at a time and keeps a running total of the values until the end-of-file indicator is set, then prints the result. Normally the user inputs integers from the keyboard and enters the end-of-file key combination to indicate that no further values will be input. With input redirection, the input can be stored in a file. For example, if the data is stored in file **input**, the command line

```
$ sum < input
```

causes program **sum** to be executed; the *redirect input symbol (<)* indicates that the data in file **input** (instead of the keyboard) is to be used as input by the program. Redirecting input on a DOS system is performed identically.

Note that **$** is the UNIX command line prompt (some UNIX systems use a **%** prompt). Students often find it difficult to understand that redirection is an operating system function, not another C++ feature.

The second method of redirecting input is *piping*. A *pipe (|)* causes the output of one program to be redirected as the input to another program. Suppose program **random** outputs a series of random integers; the output of **random** can be "piped" directly to program **sum** using the UNIX command line

```
$ random | sum
```

This causes the sum of the integers produced by **random** to be calculated. Piping can be performed in UNIX and DOS.

Program output can be redirected to a file by using the *redirect output symbol (>)* (the same symbol is used for UNIX and DOS). For example, to redirect the output of program **random** to file **out**, use

```
$ random > out
```

Finally, program output can be appended to the end of an existing file by using the *append output symbol (>>)* (the same symbol is used for UNIX and DOS). For example, to append the output from program **random** to file **out** created in the preceding command line, use the command line

```
$ random >> out
```

## 18.3 Variable-Length Argument Lists

It is possible to create functions that receive an unspecified number of arguments. An ellipsis (**...**) in a function's prototype indicates that the function receives a variable number of arguments of any type. Note that the ellipsis must always be placed at the end of the parameter list, and there must be at least one named parameter.

The macros and definitions of the *variable arguments header* ***stdarg.h*** (Fig. 18.1) provide the capabilities necessary to build functions with variable-length argument lists. The program of Fig. 18.2 demonstrates function **average** that receives a variable number of arguments. The first argument of **average** is always the number of values to be averaged.

Function **average** uses all the definitions and macros of header **stdarg.h**. Object **ap**, of type **va_list**, is used by macros **va_start**, **va_arg**, and **va_end** to process

| Identifier | Explanation |
|---|---|
| **va_list** | A type suitable for holding information needed by macros **va_start**, **va_arg**, and **va_end**. To access the arguments in a variable-length argument list, an object of type **va_list** must be declared. |
| **va_start** | A macro that is invoked before the arguments of a variable-length argument list can be accessed. The macro initializes the object declared with **va_list** for use by the **va_arg** and **va_end** macros. |
| **va_arg** | A macro that expands to an expression of the value and type of the next argument in the variable-length argument list. Each invocation of **va_arg** modifies the object declared with **va_list** so that the object points to the next argument in the list. |
| **va_end** | A macro that facilitates a normal return from a function whose variable-length argument list was referred to by the **va_start** macro. |

**Fig. 18.1** The type and the macros defined in header **stdarg.h**.

the variable-length argument list of function **average**. The function begins by invoking **va_start** to initialize object **ap** for use in **va_arg** and **va_end**. The macro receives two arguments—object **ap** and the identifier of the rightmost argument in the argument list before the ellipsis—**i** in this case (**va_start** uses **i** here to determine where the variable-length argument list begins). Next, function **average** repeatedly adds the arguments in the variable-length argument list to variable **total**. The value to be added to **total** is retrieved from the argument list by invoking macro **va_arg**. Macro **va_arg** receives two arguments—object **ap**, and the type of the value expected in the argument list—**double** in this case. The macro returns the value of the argument. Function **average** invokes macro **va_end** with object **ap** as an argument to facilitate a normal return to **main** from **average**. Finally, the average is calculated and returned to **main**.

***Common Programming Error 18.1***

*Placing an ellipsis in the middle of a function parameter list. An ellipsis may only be placed at the end of the parameter list.*

## 18.4 Using Command-Line Arguments

On many systems—DOS and UNIX in particular—it is possible to pass arguments to **main** from a command line by including parameters **int argc** and **char *argv[]** in the parameter list of **main**. Parameter **argc** receives the number of command-line arguments. Parameter **argv** is an array of strings in which the actual command-line arguments are stored. Common uses of command-line arguments include printing the arguments, passing options to a program, and passing filenames to a program.

```
// Using variable-length argument lists
#include <iostream.h>
#include <iomanip.h>
#include <stdarg.h>

double average(int, ...);

main()
{
   double w = 37.5, x = 22.5, y = 1.7, z = 10.2;

   cout << setiosflags(ios::fixed | ios::showpoint)
        << setprecision(1) << "w = " << w << endl << "x = " << x
        << endl << "y = " << y << endl << "z = " << z << endl;
   cout << setiosflags(ios::fixed | ios::showpoint)
        << setprecision(3) << endl << "The average of w and x is "
        << average(2, w, x) << endl
        << "The average of w, x, and y is " << average(3, w, x, y)
        << endl << "The average of w, x, y, and z is "
        << average(4, w, x, y, z) << endl;

   return 0;
}

double average(int i, ...)
{
   double total = 0;
   int j;
   va_list ap;

   va_start(ap, i);

   for (j = 1; j <= i; j++)
      total += va_arg(ap, double);

   va_end(ap);

   return total / i;
}
```

```
w = 37.5
x = 22.5
y = 1.7
z = 10.2

The average of w and x is 30.000
The average of w, x, and y is 20.567
The average of w, x, y, and z is 17.975
```

**Fig. 18.2** Using variable-length argument lists.

The program of Fig. 18.3 copies a file into another file one character at a time. The executable file for the program is called **copy**. A typical command line for the **copy** program on a UNIX system is

```
$ copy input output
```

This command line indicates that file **input** is to be copied to file **output**. When the program is executed, if **argc** is not **3** (**copy** counts as one of the arguments), the program prints an error message and terminates. Otherwise, array **argv** contains the strings **"copy"**, **"input"**, and **"output"**. The second and third arguments on the command line are used as file names by the program. The files are opened by creating **ifstream** object **inFile** and **ofstream** object **outFile**. If both files are opened successfully, characters are read from file **input** with member function **get** and written to file **output** with member function **put** until the end-of-file indicator for file **input** is set. Then the program terminates. The result is an exact copy of file **input**. Note that not all computer systems support command-line arguments as easily as UNIX and DOS. Macintosh and VMS systems, for example, require special settings for processing command-line arguments. See the manuals for your system for more information on command-line arguments.

## 18.5 Notes on Compiling Multiple-Source-File Programs

As stated earlier in the text, it is possible to build programs that consist of multiple source files (see Chapter 6, "Classes and Data Abstraction"). There are several considerations

```
// Using command-line arguments
#include <iostream.h>
#include <fstream.h>

main(int argc, char *argv[])
{
   if (argc != 3)
      cout << "Usage: copy infile outfile" << endl;
   else {
      ifstream inFile(argv[1], ios::in);
      if (!inFile)
         cout << argv[1] << " could not be opened" << endl;

      ofstream outFile(argv[2], ios::out);
      if (!outFile)
         cout << argv[2] << " could not be opened" << endl;

      while ( !inFile.eof() )
         outFile.put( (char) inFile.get() );
   }

   return 0;
}
```

**Fig. 18.3** Using command-line arguments.

when creating programs in multiple files. For example, the definition of a function must be entirely contained in one file—it cannot span two or more files.

In Chapter 3, we introduced the concepts of storage class and scope. We learned that variables declared outside any function definition are of storage class static by default and are referred to as global variables. Global variables are accessible to any function defined in the same file after the variable is declared. Global variables also are accessible to functions in other files, however, the global variables must be declared in each file in which they are used. For example, if we define global integer variable **flag** in one file, and refer to it in a second file, the second file must contain the declaration

```
extern int flag;
```

prior to the variable's use in that file. In the preceding declaration, the storage class specifier **extern** indicates to the compiler that variable **flag** is defined either later in the same file or in a different file. The compiler informs the linker that unresolved references to variable **flag** appear in the file (the compiler does not know where the **flag** is defined, so it lets the linker attempt to find **flag**). If the linker cannot locate a definition of **flag**, a linker error is reported, and no executable file is produced. If a proper global definition is located, the linker resolves the references by indicating where **flag** is located.

***Performance Tip 18.1***

*Global variables increase performance because they can be accessed directly by any function—the overhead of passing data to functions is eliminated.*

***Software Engineering Observation 18.1***

*Global variables should be avoided unless application performance is critical because they violate the principle of least privilege, and they make software difficult to maintain.*

Just as **extern** declarations can be used to declare global variables to other program files, function prototypes can extend the scope of a function beyond the file in which it is defined (the **extern** specifier is not required in a function prototype). This is accomplished by including the function prototype in each file in which the function is invoked, and compiling the files together (see Section 17.2). Function prototypes indicate to the compiler that the specified function is defined either later in the same file or in a different file. Again, the compiler does not attempt to resolve references to such a function—that task is left to the linker. If the linker cannot locate a proper function definition, an error is generated.

As an example of using function prototypes to extend the scope of a function, consider any program containing the preprocessor directive **#include <string.h>**. This directive includes in a file the function prototypes for functions such as **strcmp** and **strcat**. Other functions in the file can use **strcmp** and **strcat** to accomplish their tasks. The **strcmp** and **strcat** functions are defined for us separately. We do not need to know where they are defined. We are simply reusing the code in our programs. The linker resolves our references to these functions automatically. This process enables us to use the functions in the standard library.

***Software Engineering Observation 18.2***

*Creating programs in multiple source files facilitates software reusability and good software engineering. Functions may be common to many applications. In such instances, those functions should be stored in their own source files, and each source file should have a corresponding header file containing function prototypes. This enables programmers of different applications to reuse the same code by including the proper header file, and compiling their application with the corresponding source file.*

***Portability Tip 18.1***

*Some systems do not support global variable names or function names of more than 6 characters. This should be considered when writing programs that will be ported to multiple platforms.*

It is possible to restrict the scope of a global variable or function to the file in which it is defined. The storage class specifier **static**, when applied to a global variable or a function, prevents it from being used by any function that is not defined in the same file. This is referred to as *internal linkage*. Global variables and functions that are not preceded by **static** in their definitions have *external linkage*—they can be accessed in other files if those files contain proper declarations and/or function prototypes.

The global variable declaration

```
static float pi = 3.14159;
```

creates variable **pi** of type **float**, initializes it to **3.14159**, and indicates that **pi** is known only to functions in the file in which it is defined.

The **static** specifier is commonly used with utility functions that are called only by functions in a particular file. If a function is not required outside a particular file, the principle of least privilege should be enforced by using **static**. If a function is defined before it is used in a file, **static** should be applied to the function definition. Otherwise, **static** should be applied to the function prototype.

When building large programs in multiple source files, compiling the program becomes tedious if small changes are made to one file, and the entire program must be recompiled. Many systems provide special utilities that recompile only the modified program file. On UNIX systems the utility is called ***make***. Utility **make** reads a file called ***makefile*** that contains instructions for compiling and linking the program. Systems such as Borland C++ and Microsoft Visual C++ for PCs provide **make** utilities and "projects". For more information on **make** utilities, see the manual for your particular system.

## 18.6 Program Termination with Exit and Atexit

The general utilities library (**stdlib.h**) provides methods of terminating program execution other than a conventional return from function **main**. Function ***exit*** forces a program to terminate as if it executed normally. The function often is used to terminate a program when an error is detected in the input, or if a file to be processed by the program cannot be opened. Function ***atexit*** *registers* a function in the program to be called upon successful termination of the program—i.e., either when the program terminates by reaching the end of **main**, or when **exit** is invoked.

Function **atexit** takes a pointer to a function (i.e., the function name) as an argument. Functions called at program termination cannot have arguments, and cannot return a value. Up to 32 functions may be registered for execution at program termination.

Function **exit** takes one argument. The argument is normally the symbolic constant ***EXIT_SUCCESS*** or the symbolic constant ***EXIT_FAILURE***. If **exit** is called with **EXIT_SUCCESS**, the implementation-defined value for successful termination is returned to the calling environment. If **exit** is called with **EXIT_FAILURE**, the implementation-defined value for unsuccessful termination is returned. When function **exit** is invoked, any functions previously registered with **atexit** are invoked in the reverse order of their registration, all streams associated with the program are flushed and closed, and control returns to the host environment. The program of Fig. 18.4 tests functions **exit** and **atexit**. The program prompts the user to determine whether the program should be terminated with **exit** or by reaching the end of **main**. Note that function **print** is executed at program termination in each case.

```
// Using the exit and atexit functions
#include <iostream.h>
#include <stdlib.h>

void print(void);

main()
{
   atexit(print);          // register function print
   cout << "Enter 1 to terminate program with function exit"
        << endl << "Enter 2 to terminate program normally"
        << endl;

   int answer;
   cin >> answer;

   if (answer == 1) {
      cout << endl << "Terminating program with function exit"
           << endl;
      exit(EXIT_SUCCESS);
   }

   cout << endl << "Terminating program by reaching end of main"
        << endl;

   return 0;
}

void print(void)
{
   cout << "Executing function print at program termination"
        << endl << "Program terminated" << endl;
}
```

**Fig. 18.4** Using functions **exit** and **atexit** (part 1 of 2).

```
Enter 1 to terminate program with function exit
Enter 2 to terminate program normally
: 1

Terminating program with function exit
Executing function print at program termination
Program terminated
```

```
Enter 1 to terminate program with function exit
Enter 2 to terminate program normally
: 2

Terminating program by reaching end of main
Executing function print at program termination
Program terminated
```

**Fig. 18.4** Using functions **`exit`** and **`atexit`** (part 2 of 2).

## 18.7 The Volatile Type Qualifier

In Chapters 4 and 5, we introduced the **`const`** type qualifier. C++ also provides the **`volatile`** type qualifier. The evolving C++ standard (Cb94) indicates that when **`volatile`** is used to qualify a type, the nature of the access to an object of that type is implementation dependent. Kernighan and Ritchie (Ke88) indicate that the **`volatile`** qualifier is used to suppress various kinds of optimizations.

## 18.8 Suffixes for Integer and Floating-Point Constants

C++ provides integer and floating-point suffixes for specifying the types of integer and floating-point constants. The integer suffixes are: **`u`** or **`U`** for an **`unsigned`** integer, **`l`** or **`L`** for a **`long`** integer, and **`ul`** or **`UL`** for an **`unsigned long`** integer. The following constants are of type **`unsigned`**, **`long`**, and **`unsigned long`**, respectively:

```
174u
8358L
28373ul
```

If an integer constant is not suffixed, its type is determined by the first type capable of storing a value of that size (first **`int`**, then **`long int`**, then **`unsigned long int`**).

The floating-point suffixes are: **`f`** or **`F`** for a **`float`**, and **`l`** or **`L`** for a **`long double`**. The following constants are of type **`long double`** and **`float`**, respectively:

```
3.14159L
1.28f
```

A floating-point constant that is not suffixed is automatically of type **`double`**.

## 18.9 Signal Handling

An unexpected event, or *signal*, can cause a program to terminate prematurely. Some unexpected events include *interrupts* (typing **<ctrl> c** on a UNIX or DOS system), *illegal instructions, segmentation violations, termination orders from the operating system,* and *floating-point exceptions* (division by zero or multiplying large floating-point values). The *signal handling library* provides the capability to *trap* unexpected events with function ***signal***. Function **signal** receives two arguments—an integer signal number and a pointer to the signal handling function. Signals can be generated by function ***raise*** which takes an integer signal number as an argument. Figure 18.5 summarizes the standard signals defined in header file ***signal.h***. The program of Fig. 18.6 demonstrates functions **signal** and **raise**.

The program of Fig. 18.6 uses function **signal** to trap an interactive signal (**SIGINT**). The program begins by calling **signal** with **SIGINT** and a pointer to function **signal_handler** (remember that the name of a function is a pointer to the beginning of the function). When a signal of type **SIGINT** is generated, control is passed to function **signal_handler**, a message is printed, and the user is given the option to continue normal execution of the program. If the user wishes to continue execution, the signal handler is reinitialized by calling **signal** again (some systems require the signal handler to be reinitialized), and control returns to the point in the program at which the signal was detected. In this program, function **raise** is used to simulate an interactive signal. A random number between **1** and **50** is chosen. If the number is **25**, then **raise** is called to generate the signal. Normally, interactive signals are initiated outside the program. For example, typing **<ctrl> c** during program execution on a UNIX or DOS system generates an interactive signal that terminates program execution. Signal handling can be used to trap the interactive signal and prevent the program from being terminated.

## 18.10 Dynamic Memory Allocation: Functions Calloc and Realloc

In Chapter 7, when we discussed C++-style dynamic memory allocation with **new** and **delete**, we compared new and delete with the C functions **malloc** and **free**. C++

| Signal | Explanation |
|---|---|
| **SIGABRT** | Abnormal termination of the program (such as a call to **abort**). |
| **SIGFPE** | An erroneous arithmetic operation, such as a divide-by-zero or an operation resulting in overflow. |
| **SIGILL** | Detection of an illegal instruction. |
| **SIGINT** | Receipt of an interactive attention signal. |
| **SIGSEGV** | An invalid access to storage. |
| **SIGTERM** | A termination request sent to the program. |

**Fig. 18.5** The signals defined in header **signal.h**.

```
// Using signal handling
#include <iostream.h>
#include <iomanip.h>
#include <signal.h>
#include <stdlib.h>
#include <time.h>

void signal_handler(int);

main()
{
   signal(SIGINT, signal_handler);
   srand(time(NULL));

   for (int i = 1; i < 101; i++) {
      int x = 1 + rand() % 50;

      if (x == 25)
         raise(SIGINT);

      cout << setw(4) << i;

      if (i % 10 == 0)
         cout << endl;
   }

   return 0;
}

void signal_handler(int signalValue)
{
   cout << endl << "Interrupt signal (" << signalValue
        << ") received." << endl
        << "Do you wish to continue (1 = yes or 2 = no)? ";

   int response;
   cin >> response;

   while (response != 1 && response != 2) {
      cout << "(1 = yes or 2 = no)? ";
      cin >> response;
   }

   if (response == 1)
      signal(SIGINT, signal_handler);
   else
      exit(EXIT_SUCCESS);
}
```

**Fig. 18.6** Using signal handling (part 1 of 2).

programmers should use **new** and **delete** not **malloc** and **free**. However, most C++ programmers will find themselves reading a great deal of C legacy code, and therefore we include this additional discussion on C-style dynamic memory allocation.

```
  1   2   3   4   5   6   7   8   9  10
 11  12  13  14  15  16  17  18  19  20
 21  22  23  24  25  26  27  28  29  30
 31  32  33  34  35  36  37  38  39  40
 41  42  43  44  45  46  47  48  49  50
 51  52  53  54  55  56  57  58  59  60
 61  62  63  64  65  66  67  68  69  70
 71  72  73  74  75  76  77  78  79  80
 81  82  83  84  85  86  87  88
Interrupt signal (4) received.
Do you wish to continue (1 = yes or 2 = no)? 1
 89  90
 91  92  93  94  95  96  97  98  99 100
```

**Fig. 18.6** Using signal handling (part 2 of 2).

The general utilities library (**stdlib.h**) provides two other functions for dynamic memory allocation—**calloc** and **realloc**. These functions can be used to create and modify *dynamic arrays.* As shown in Chapter 5, "Pointers and Strings," a pointer to an array can be subscripted like an array. Thus, a pointer to a contiguous portion of memory created by **calloc** can be manipulated as an array. Function **calloc** dynamically allocates memory for an array. The prototype for **calloc** is

```
void *calloc(size_t nmemb, size_t size);
```

It receives two arguments—the number of elements (**nmemb**) and the size of each element (**size**)—and initializes the elements of the array to zero. The function returns a pointer to the allocated memory, or a null pointer (**0**) if the memory is not allocated.

Function **realloc** changes the size of an object allocated by a previous call to **malloc**, **calloc**, or **realloc**. The original object's contents are not modified provided that the amount of memory allocated is larger than the amount allocated previously. Otherwise, the contents are unchanged up to the size of the new object. The prototype for **realloc** is

```
void *realloc(void *ptr, size_t size);
```

Function **realloc** takes two arguments—a pointer to the original object (**ptr**) and the new size of the object (**size**). If **ptr** is **0**, **realloc** works identically to **malloc**. If **size** is **0** and **ptr** is not **0**, the memory for the object is freed. Otherwise, if **ptr** is not **0** and size is greater than zero, **realloc** tries to allocate a new block of memory for the object. If the new space cannot be allocated, the object pointed to by **ptr** is unchanged. Function **realloc** returns either a pointer to the reallocated memory, or a null pointer.

## 18.11 The Unconditional Branch: Goto

Throughout the text we have stressed the importance of using structured programming techniques to build reliable software that is easy to debug, maintain, and modify. In some cases, performance is more important than strict adherence to structured programming techniques. In these cases, some unstructured programming techniques may be used. For example, we can use **break** to terminate execution of a repetition structure before the loop continuation condition becomes false. This saves unnecessary repetitions of the loop if the task is completed before loop termination.

Another instance of unstructured programming is the ***goto** statement*—an unconditional branch. The result of the **goto** statement is a change in the flow of control of the program to the first statement after the *label* specified in the **goto** statement. A label is an identifier followed by a colon. A label must appear in the same function as the **goto** statement that refers to it. The program of Fig. 18.7 uses **goto** statements to loop ten times and print the counter value each time. After initializing **count** to **1**, the program tests **count** to determine whether it is greater than **10** (the label **start** is skipped because labels do not perform any action). If so, control is transferred from the **goto** to the first statement after the label **end**. Otherwise, **count** is printed and incremented, and control is transferred from the **goto** to the first statement after the label **start**.

In Chapter 2, we stated that only three control structures are required to write any program—sequence, selection, and repetition. When the rules of structured programming are followed, it is possible to create deeply nested control structures from which it is difficult to efficiently escape. Some programmers use **goto** statements in such situations as a quick exit from a deeply nested structure. This eliminates the need to test multiple conditions to escape from a control structure.

```
// Using goto

#include <iostream.h>

main()
{
   int count = 1;

   start:                        // label
      if (count > 10)
         goto end;

      cout << count << "  ";
      ++count;
      goto start;

   end:                          // label
      cout << endl;

   return 0;
}
```

```
1  2  3  4  5  6  7  8  9  10
```

Fig. 18.7 Using **goto**.

***Performance Tip 18.2***

*The `goto` statement can be used to exit deeply nested control structures efficiently.*

***Software Engineering Observation 18.3***

*The `goto` statement should be used only in performance-oriented applications. The `goto` statement is unstructured and can lead to programs that are more difficult to debug, maintain, and modify.*

## 18.12 Unions

A ***union*** is a memory location that, over time, can contain objects of a variety of types. However, at any moment, a union can contain a maximum of one object because the members of a union share the same storage space. It is the programmer's responsibility to ensure that the data in a union is referenced with a member name of the proper data type.

***Common Programming Error 18.2***

*The result of referenceing a union member other than the last one stored is undefined. It treats the stored data as the different type.*

***Portability Tip 18.2***

*If data is stored in a union as one type and referenced as another type, the results are implementation dependent.*

At different times during a program's execution, some objects may not be relevant, but one other object is—so a union shares the space instead of wasting storage on objects that are not being used. The number of bytes used to store a union must be at least enough to hold the largest member.

***Performance Tip 18.3***

*Unions conserve storage.*

***Portability Tip 18.3***

*The amount of storage required to store a union is implementation dependent.*

***Portability Tip 18.4***

*Some unions may not port easily to other computer systems. Whether a union is portable or not often depends on the storage alignment requirements for the union member data types on a given system.*

A union is declared with the **union** keyword in the same format as a structure or a class. The **union** declaration

```
union Number {
   int x;
   float y;
};
```

indicates that **`Number`** is a **`union`** type with members **`int x`** and **`float y`**. The union definition normally precedes **`main`** in a program so the definition can be used to declare variables in all the program's functions.

***Software Engineering Observation 18.4***

*As with a **`struct`** or a **`class`** declaration, a **`union`** declaration simply creates a new type. Placing a **`union`** or **`struct`** declaration outside any function does not create a global variable.*

The only valid built-in operations that can be performed on a union are: assigning a union to another union of the same type, taking the address (**`&`**) of a union, and accessing union members using the structure member operator (**`.`**) and the structure pointer operator (**`->`**). Unions may not be compared for the same reasons that structures cannot be compared.

***Common Programming Error 18.3***

*Comparing unions is a syntax error because the compiler does not know which member of each is active, and hence which member of one to compare to which member of the other.*

A union is similar to a class in that it can have a constructor to initialize any of its members. A union that has no constructor can be initialized with another union of the same type, with an expression of the type of the first member of the union, or with an initializer (enclosed in braces) of the type of the first member of the union. Unions can have other member functions, such as destructors, but a union's member functions cannot be declared **`virtual`**. The members of a union are public by default.

***Common Programming Error 18.4***

*Initializing a union in a declaration with a value or an expression whose type is different from the type of the union's first member.*

A union cannot be used as a base class in inheritance, i.e., classes may not be derived from unions. Unions can have objects as members only if these objects do not have a constructor, a destructor, or an overloaded assignment operator. None of a union's data members can be declared **`static`**.

The program in Fig. 18.8 uses the variable **`value`** of type **`union number`** to display the value stored in the union as both an **`int`** and a **`float`**. The program output is implementation dependent. The program output shows that the internal representation of a **`float`** value can be quite different from the representation of an **`int`**.

An *anonymous union* is a union without a type name, that does not attempt to define objects or pointers before its terminating semicolon. Such a union does not create a type but does create an unnamed object. An anonymous union's members may be accessed directly in the scope in which the anonymous union is declared just as any other local variable—there is no need to use the dot (**`.`**) or arrow (**`->`**) operators.

Anonymous unions have some restrictions. Anonymous unions can contain only data members. All members of an anonymous union must be public. And, an anonymous union declared globally (i.e., at file scope) must be explicitly declared **`static`**.

Figure 18.9 illustrates the use of an anonymous union.

```
// An example of a union
#include <iostream.h>

union Number {
   int x;
   float y;
};

main()
{
   Number value;

   value.x = 100;
   cout << "Put a value in the integer member" << endl
        << "and print both members." << endl << "int:   "
        << value.x << endl << "float: " << value.y << endl << endl;

   value.y = 100.0;
   cout << "Put a value in the floating member" << endl
        << "and print both members." << endl << "int:   "
        << value.x << endl << "float: " << value.y << endl;
   return 0;
}
```

```
Put a value in the integer member
and print both members.
int:   100
float: 3.504168e-16

Put a value in the floating member
and print both members.
int:   0
float: 100
```

**Fig. 18.8** Printing the value of a union in both member data types.

## 18.13 Linkage Specifications

It is possible from a C++ program to call functions written and compiled with a C compiler. As stated in Section 3.20, C++ specially encodes function names for type-safe linkage. C, however, does not encode its function names. Thus, a function compiled in C will not be recognized when an attempt is made to link C code with C++ code because the C++ code expects a specially encoded function name. C++ enables the programmer to provide *linkage specifications* to inform the compiler that a function was compiled on a C compiler, and to prevent the name of the function from being encoded by the C++ compiler. Linkage specifications are useful when large libraries of specialized functions have been developed, and the user either does not have access to the source code for recompilation into C++ or time to convert the library functions from C to C++.

```
// Using an anonymous union
#include <iostream.h>

main()
{
   // Declare an anonymous union.
   // Note that members b, d, and f share the same space.
   union {
      int b;
      float d;
      char *f;
   };

   // Declare conventional local variables
   int a = 1;
   float c = 3.3;
   char *e = "Anonymous";

   // Assign a value to each union member
   // successively and print each.
   cout << a << ' ';
   b = 2;
   cout << b << endl;

   cout << c << ' ';
   d = 4.4;
   cout << d << endl;

   cout << e << ' ';
   f = "union";
   cout << f << endl;

   return 0;
}
```

```
1 2
3.3 4.4
Anonymous union
```

**Fig. 18.9** Using an anonymous union.

To inform the compiler that one or several functions have been compiled in C, write the function prototypes as follows:

```
extern "C" function prototype     // single function

extern "C"              // multiple functions
{
   function prototypes
}
```

These declarations inform the compiler that the specified functions are not compiled in C++, so name encoding should not be performed on the functions listed in the linkage specification. These functions can then be linked properly with the program. C++ environments normally include the standard C libraries and do not require the programmer to use linkage specifications for those functions.

## 18.14 Closing Remarks

We sincerely hope you have enjoyed learning C++ and object-oriented programming in this course. The future seems clear. We wish you success in pursuing it!

We would greatly appreciate your comments, criticisms, corrections, and suggestions for improving the text. We will acknowledge all contributions in the next edition of the book. Please address all correspondence to our email address:

`deitel@world.std.com`

Good luck!

### *Summary*

- On many computer systems—UNIX and DOS systems in particular—it is possible to redirect input to a program and output from a program.
- Input is redirected from the UNIX and DOS command lines using the redirect input symbol (<) or using a pipe ( | ).
- Output is redirected from the UNIX and DOS command lines using the redirect output symbol (>) or the append output symbol (>>). The redirect output symbol simply stores the program output in a file, and the append output symbol appends the output to the end of a file.
- The macros and definitions of the variable arguments header `stdarg.h` provide the capabilities necessary to build functions with variable-length argument lists.
- An ellipsis (`...`) in a function prototype indicates that the function receives a variable number of arguments.
- Type `va_list` is suitable for holding information needed by macros `va_start`, `va_arg`, and `va_end`. To access the arguments in a variable-length argument list, an object of type `va_list` must be declared.
- Macro `va_start` is invoked before the arguments of a variable-length argument list can be accessed. The macro initializes the object declared with `va_list` for use by the `va_arg` and `va_end` macros.
- Macro `va_arg` expands to an expression of the value and type of the next argument in the variable-length argument list. Each invocation of `va_arg` modifies the object declared with `va_list` so that the object points to the next argument in the list.
- Macro `va_end` facilitates a normal return from a function whose variable argument list was referred to by the `va_start` macro.

- On many systems—DOS and UNIX in particular—it is possible to pass arguments to **main** from the command line by including the parameters **int argc** and **char *argv[]** in the parameter list of **main**. Parameter **argc** receives the number of command-line arguments. Parameter **argv** is an array of strings in which the actual command-line arguments are stored.
- The definition of a function must be entirely contained in one file—it cannot span two or more files.
- Global variables must be declared in each file in which they are used.
- Function prototypes can extend the scope of a function beyond the file in which it is defined (the **extern** specifier is not required in a function prototype). This is accomplished by including the function prototype in each file in which the function is invoked and compiling the files together.
- The storage class specifier **static**, when applied to a global variable or a function, prevents it from being used by any function that is not defined in the same file. This is referred to as internal linkage. Global variables and functions that are not preceded by **static** in their definitions have external linkage—they can be accessed in other files if those files contain proper declarations and/or function prototypes.
- The **static** specifier is commonly used with utility functions that are called only by functions in a particular file. If a function is not required outside a particular file, the principle of least privilege should be enforced by using **static**.
- When building large programs in multiple source files, compiling the program becomes tedious if small changes are made to one file, and the entire program must be recompiled. Many systems provide special utilities that recompile only the modified program file. On UNIX systems the utility is called **make**. Utility **make** reads a file called **makefile** that contains instructions for compiling and linking the program.
- Function **exit** forces a program to terminate as if it executed normally.
- Function **atexit** registers a function in a program to be called upon normal termination of the program—i.e., either when the program terminates by reaching the end of **main** or when **exit** is invoked.
- Function **atexit** takes a pointer to a function (i.e., a function name) as an argument. Functions called at program termination cannot have arguments, and cannot return a value. Up to 32 functions may be registered for execution at program termination.
- Function **exit** takes one argument. The argument is normally the symbolic constant **EXIT_SUCCESS** or the symbolic constant **EXIT_FAILURE**. If **exit** is called with **EXIT_SUCCESS**, the implementation-defined value for successful termination is returned to the calling environment. If **exit** is called with **EXIT_FAILURE**, the implementation-defined value for unsuccessful termination is returned.
- When function **exit** is invoked, any functions registered with **atexit** are invoked in the reverse order of their registration, all streams associated with the program are flushed and closed, and control returns to the host environment.

- The evolving C++ standard indicates that when **volatile** is used to qualify a type, the nature of the access to an object of that type is implementation dependent. Kernighan and Ritchie indicate that the **volatile** qualifier is used to suppress various kinds of optimizations.
- C++ provides integer and floating-point suffixes for specifying the types of integer and floating-point constants. The integer suffixes are: **u** or **U** for an **unsigned** integer, **l** or **L** for a **long** integer, and **ul** or **UL** for an **unsigned long** integer. If an integer constant is not suffixed, its type is determined by the first type capable of storing a value of that size (first **int**, then **long int**, then **unsigned long int**). The floating-point suffixes are: **f** or **F** for a **float**, and **l** or **L** for a **long double**. A floating-point constant that is not suffixed is of type **double**.
- The signal handling library provides the capability to trap unexpected events with function **signal**. Function **signal** receives two arguments—an integer signal number and a pointer to the signal handling function.
- Signals can also be generated with function **raise** and an integer argument.
- The general utilities library (**stdlib.h**) provides functions **calloc** and **realloc** for dynamic memory allocation. These functions can be used to create dynamic arrays.
- Function **calloc** receives two arguments—the number of elements (**nmemb**) and the size of each element (**size**)—and initializes the elements of the array to zero. The function returns either a pointer to the allocated memory, or a **NULL** pointer if the memory is not allocated.
- Function **realloc** changes the size of an object allocated by a previous call to **malloc**, **calloc**, or **realloc**. The original object's contents are not modified provided that the amount of memory allocated is larger than the amount allocated previously.
- Function **realloc** takes two arguments—a pointer to the original object (**ptr**) and the new size of the object (**size**). If ptr is **NULL**, **realloc** works identically to **malloc**. If **size** is **0** and the pointer received is not **NULL**, the memory for the object is freed. Otherwise, if **ptr** is not **NULL** and size is greater than zero, **realloc** tries to allocate a new block of memory for the object. If the new space cannot be allocated, the object pointed to by **ptr** is unchanged. Function **realloc** returns either a pointer to the reallocated memory, or a **NULL** pointer.
- The result of the **goto** statement is a change in the program's flow of control. Program execution continues at the first statement after the label in the **goto** statement.
- A label is an identifier followed by a colon. A label must appear in the same function as the **goto** statement that refers to it.
- A union is a derived data type whose members share the same storage space. The members can be any type.
- The storage reserved for a union is large enough to store its largest member. In most cases, unions contain two or more data types. Only one member, and thus one data type, can be referenced at a time.

- A union is declared with the **union** keyword in the same format as a structure.
- A union can be initialized only with a value of the type of its first member.
- C++ enables the programmer to provide linkage specifications to inform the compiler that a function was compiled on a C compiler, and to prevent the name of the function from being encoded by the C++ compiler.
- To inform the compiler that one or several functions have been compiled in C, write the function prototypes as follows:

```
extern "C" function prototype     // single function

extern "C"                        // multiple functions
{
    function prototypes
}
```

  These declarations inform the compiler that the specified functions are not compiled in C++, so name encoding should not be performed on the functions listed in the linkage specification. These functions can then be linked properly with the program.
- C++ environments normally include the standard C libraries and do not require the programmer to use linkage specifications for those functions.

## Terminology

append output symbol >>
**argc**
**argv**
**atexit**
**calloc**
command-line arguments
**const**
dynamic arrays
event
**exit**
external linkage
**extern** storage class specifier
**EXIT_FAILURE**
**EXIT_SUCCESS**
**float** suffix (**f** or **F**)
floating-point exception
**goto** statement
I/O redirection
illegal instruction
internal linkage
interrupt
**long double** suffix (**l** or **L**)
**long integer** suffix (**l** or **L**)
**make**
**makefile**
**union**
pipe |
piping
**raise**
**realloc**
redirect input symbol <
redirect output symbol >
segmentation violation
**signal**
signal handling library
**signal.h**
**static** storage class specifier
**stdarg.h**
trap
**unsigned** integer suffix (**u** or **U**)
**unsigned long** integer suffix (**ul** or **UL**)
**va_arg**
**va_end**
**va_list**
**va_start**
variable-length argument list
**volatile**

## Common Programming Errors

**18.1** Placing an ellipsis in the middle of a function parameter list. An ellipsis may only be placed at the end of the parameter list.

**18.2** The result of referenceing a union member other than the last one stored is undefined. It treats the stored data as the different type.

**18.3** Comparing unions is a syntax error because the compiler does not know which member of each is active, and hence which member of one to compare to which member of the other.

**18.4** Initializing a union in a declaration with a value or an expression whose type is different from the type of the union's first member.

## Performance Tips

**18.1** Global variables increase performance because they can be accessed directly by any function—the overhead of passing data to functions is eliminated.

**18.2** The `goto` statement can be used to exit deeply nested control structures efficiently.

**18.3** Unions conserve storage.

## Portability Tips

**18.1** Some systems do not support global variable names or function names of more than 6 characters. This should be considered when writing programs that will be ported to multiple platforms.

**18.2** If data is stored in a union as one type and referenced as another type, the results are implementation dependent.

**18.3** The amount of storage required to store a union is implementation dependent.

**18.4** Some unions may not port easily to other computer systems. Whether a union is portable or not often depends on the storage alignment requirements for the union member data types on a given system.

## Software Engineering Observations

**18.1** Global variables should be avoided unless application performance is critical because they violate the principle of least privilege, and they make software difficult to maintain.

**18.2** Creating programs in multiple source files facilitates software reusability and good software engineering. Functions may be common to many applications. In such instances, those functions should be stored in their own source files, and each source file should have a corresponding header file containing function prototypes. This enables programmers of different applications to reuse the same code by including the proper header file, and compiling their application with the corresponding source file.

**18.3** The `goto` statement should be used only in performance-oriented applications. The `goto` statement is unstructured and can lead to programs that are more difficult to debug, maintain, and modify.

**18.4** As with a `struct` or a `class` declaration, a `union` declaration simply creates a new type. Placing a `union` or `struct` declaration outside any function does not create a global variable.

## Self-Review Exercises

**18.1** Fill in the blanks in each of the following:

a) Symbol ________ redirects input data from the keyboard to come from a file.

b) The __________ symbol is used to redirect the screen output to be placed in a file.
c) The __________ symbol is used to append the output of a program to the end of a file.
d) A __________ is used to direct the output of a program as the input of another program.
e) An __________ in the parameter list of a function indicates that the function can receive a variable number of arguments.
f) Macro __________ must be invoked before the arguments in a variable-length argument list can be accessed.
g) Macro __________ is used to access the individual arguments of a variable-length argument list.
h) Macro __________ facilitates a normal return from a function whose variable argument list was referred to by macro **va_start**.
i) Argument __________ of **main** receives the number of arguments in a command line.
j) Argument __________ of **main** stores command-line arguments as character strings.
k) The UNIX utility __________ reads a file called __________ that contains instructions for compiling and linking a program consisting of multiple source files. The utility only recompiles a file if the file has been modified since it was last compiled.
l) Function __________ forces a program to terminate execution.
m) Function __________ registers a function to be called upon normal termination of the program.
n) Type qualifier __________ indicates that an object should not be modified after it is initialized.
o) An integer or floating-point __________ can be appended to an integer or floating-point constant to specify the exact type of the constant.
p) Function __________ can be used to trap unexpected events.
q) Function __________ generates a signal from within a program.
r) Function __________ dynamically allocates memory for an array and initializes the elements to zero.
s) Function __________ changes the size of a block of dynamically allocated memory.
t) A __________ is a class containing a collection of variables that occupy the same memory, but at different times.
u) The __________ keyword is used to introduce a union definition.

## Answers to Self-Review Exercises

**18.1** a) redirect input (<). b) redirect output (>). c) append output (>>). d) pipe (|). e) ellipsis (**...**). f) **va_start**. g) **va_arg**. h) **va_end**. i) **argc**. j) **argv**. k) **make**, **makefile**. l) **exit**. m) **atexit**. n) **const**. o) suffix. p) **signal**. q) **raise**. r) **calloc**. s) **realloc**. t) union. u) **union**.

## Exercises

**18.2** Write a program that calculates the product of a series of integers that are passed to function **product** using a variable-length argument list. Test your function with several calls each with a different number of arguments.

**18.3** Write a program that prints the command-line arguments of the program.

**18.4** Write a program that sorts an integer array into ascending order or descending order. The program should use command-line arguments to pass either argument **-a** for ascending order or **-d** for descending order. (Note: This is the standard format for passing options to a program in UNIX.)

**18.5** Read the manuals for your system to determine what signals are supported by the signal handling library (`signal.h`). Write a program with signal handlers for the signals `SIGABRT` and `SIGINT`. The program should test the trapping of these signals by calling function `abort` to generate a signal of type `SIGABRT`, and by typing `<ctrl> c` to generate a signal of type `SIGINT`.

**18.6** Write a program that dynamically allocates an array of integers. The size of the array should be input from the keyboard. The elements of the array should be assigned values input from the keyboard. Print the values of the array. Next, reallocate the memory for the array to half of the current number of elements. Print the values remaining in the array to confirm that they match the first half of the values in the original array.

**18.7** Write a program that takes two file name command-line arguments, reads the characters from the first file one at a time, and writes the characters in reverse order to the second file.

**18.8** Write a program that uses `goto` statements to simulate a nested looping structure that prints a square of asterisks, as follows:

```
*****
*   *
*   *
*   *
*****
```

The program should use only the following three output statements:

```
cout << '*';
cout << ' ';
cout << endl;
```

**18.9** Provide the definition for union `Data` containing `char c`, `short s`, `long l`, `float f`, and `double d`.

**18.10** Create union `Integer` with members `char c`, `short s`, `int i`, and `long l`. Write a program that inputs values of type `char`, `short`, `int` and `long`, and stores the values in union variables of type `union Integer`. Each union variable should be printed as a `char`, a `short`, an `int`, and a `long`. Do the values always print correctly?

**18.11** Create union `FloatingPoint` with members `float f`, `double d`, and `long double l`. Write a program that inputs value of type `float`, `double`, and `long double`, and stores the values in union variables of type `union FloatingPoint`. Each union variable should be printed as a `float`, a `double`, and a `long double`. Do the values always print correctly?

**18.12** Given the union

```
union A {
   float y;
   char *z;
};
```

which of the following are correct statements for initializing the union?

a) `A p = B;   // B is of same type as A`
b) `A q = x; // x is a float`
c) `A r = 3.14159;`
d) `A s = { 79.63 };`
e) `A t = { "Hi There!" };`
f) `A u = { 3.14159, "Pi" };`

# Appendix A*

## *C++ Syntax*

**Deliberately Omitted**

As of the time of the reprint of this text, *C++* had not become an *ANSI* or *ISO* Standard. The draft standard is still rapidly evolving, and the reader may request a summary of the latest version of the *C++* grammar by contacting the Secretariat of Accredited Standards Committee, X3, 1250 Eye Street NW, Suite 200, Washington DC 20005-3922. Phone: (202) 626-5738.

# Appendix B*

## *Standard Library*

### B.1 Errors `<errno.h>`

**EDOM**
**ERANGE**

These expand to integral constant expressions with distinct nonzero values, suitable for use in **#if** preprocessing directives.

**errno**

A value of type **int** which is set to a positive error number by several library functions. The value of **errno** is zero at program startup, but is never set to zero by any library function. A program that uses **errno** for error checking should set it to zero before a library function call, and inspect it before a subsequent library function call. A library function can save the value of **errno** on entry and then set it to zero, as long as the original value is restored if **errno**'s value is still zero just before the return. The value of **errno** may be set to nonzero by a library function call whether or not there is an error, provided the use of **errno** is not documented in the function description in the standard.

### B.2 Common Definitions `<stddef.h>`

**NULL**

An implementation-defined null pointer constant.

**offsetof(*type*, *member-designator*)**

Expands to an integral constant expression of type **size_t**, the value of which is the offset in bytes to the structure member (designated by *member-designator*) from the beginning of its structure type (designated by *type*). The *member-designator* shall be such that given

**static** *type* **t;**

* Permissions Acknowledgement: This material has been condensed and adapted from American National Standard for Information Systems—Programming Language—C, ANSI/ISO 9899: 1990. Copies of this standard may be purchased from the American National Standards Institute at 11 West 42nd Street, New York, NY 10036.

then the expression `& (t.`*member-designator*`)` evaluates to an address constant. (If the specified member is a bit-field, the behavior is undefined.)

`ptrdiff_t`

The signed integral type of the result of subtracting two pointers.

`size_t`

The unsigned integral type of the result of the **sizeof** operator.

`wchar_t`

An integral type whose range of values can represent distinct codes for all members of the largest extended character set specified among the supported locales; the null character shall have the code value zero and each member of the basic character set shall have a code value equal to its value when used as the lone character in an integer character constant.

## B.3 Diagnostics <assert.h>

**`void assert(int expression);`**

Macro **assert** puts diagnostics into programs. When it is executed, if **expression** is false, the **assert** macro writes information about the particular call that failed (including the text of the argument, the name of the source file, and the source line number—the latter are respectively the values of the preprocessing macros **__FILE__** and **__LINE__**) on the standard error file in an implementation-defined format. Te message written might be of the form

**Assertion failed:** *expression*, **file** *xyz*, **line** *nnn*

Macro **assert** then calls function **abort**. If the preprocessor directive

```
#define NDEBUG
```

appears in the source file where **assert.h** is included, any assertions in the file are ignored.

## B.4 Character Handling <ctype.h>

The functions in this section return nonzero (true) if and only if the value of the argument c conforms to that in the description of the function.

**`int isalnum(int c);`**

Tests for any character for which **isalpha** or **isdigit** is true.

**`int isalpha(int c);`**

Tests for any character for which **isupper** or **islower** is true.

**`int iscntrl(int c);`**

Tests for any control character.

**`int isdigit(int c);`**

Tests for any decimal-digit character.

**`int isgraph(int c);`**

Tests for any printing character except space (`' '`).

**`int islower(int c);`**

Tests for any character that is a lowercase letter.

**`int isprint(int c);`**

Tests for any printing character including space (`' '`).

**`int ispunct(int c);`**

Tests for any printing character that is neither space (`' '`) nor a character for which **isalnum** is true.

**int isspace(int c);**
Tests for any character that is a standard white-space character. The standard white-space characters are: space (' '), form feed ('\f'), new-line ('\n'), carriage return ('\r'), horizontal tab ('\t'), and vertical tab ('\v').

**int isupper(int c);**
Tests for any character that is an uppercase letter.

**int isxdigit(int c);**
Tests for any hexadecimal-digit character.

**int tolower(int c);**
Converts an uppercase letter to the corresponding lowercase letter. If the argument is a character for which **isupper** is true and there is a corresponding character for which **islower** is true, the **tolower** function returns the corresponding character; otherwise, the argument is returned unchanged.

**int toupper(int c);**
Converts a lowercase letter to the corresponding uppercase letter. If the argument is a character for which **islower** is true and there is a corresponding character for which **isupper** is true, the **toupper** function returns the corresponding character; otherwise, the argument is returned unchanged.

## B.5 Localization <locale.h>

**LC_ALL**
**LC_COLLATE**
**LC_CTYPE**
**LC_MONETARY**
**LC_NUMERIC**
**LC_TIME**
These expand to integral constant expressions with distinct values, suitable for use as the first argument to the **setlocale** function.

**NULL**
An implementation-defined null pointer constant.

**struct lconv**
Contains members related to the formatting of numeric values. The structure shall contain at least the following members, in any order. In the "C" locale, the members shall have the values specified in the comments.

```
char *decimal_point;          /* "." */
char *thousands-sep;          /* "" */
char *grouping;               /* "" */
char *int_curr_symbol;        /* "" */
char *currency_symbol;        /* "" */
char *mon_decimal_point;      /* "" */
char *mon_thousands_sep;      /* "" */
char *mon_grouping;           /* "" */
char *positive_sign;          /* "" */
char *negative_sign;          /* "" */
char int_frac_digits;         /* CHAR_MAX */
char frac_digits;             /* CHAR_MAX */
```

```
    char p_cs_precedes;        /* CHAR_MAX */
    char p_sep_by_space;       /* CHAR_MAX */
    char n_cs_precedes;        /* CHAR_MAX */
    char n_sep_by_space;       /* CHAR_MAX */
    char p_sign_posn;          /* CHAR_MAX */
    char n_sign_posn;          /* CHAR_MAX */
```

`char *setlocale(int category, const char *locale);`

Function `setlocale` selects the appropriate portion of the program's locale as specified by the `category` and `locale` arguments. Function `setlocale` may be used to change or query the program's entire current locale or portions thereof. The value `LC_ALL` for `category` names the program's entire locale; the other values for `category` name only a portion of the program's locale. `LC_COLLATE` affects the behavior of the `strcoll` and `strxfrm` functions. `LC_CTYPE` affects the behavior of the character handling functions and the multibyte functions. `LC_MONETARY` affects the monetary formatting information returned by the `localeconv` function. `LC_NUMERIC` affects the decimal-point character for the formatted input/output functions, the string conversion functions, and the nonmonetary formatting information returned by `localeconv`. `LC_TIME` affects the behavior of `strftime`.

A value of `"C"` for `locale` specifies the minimal environment for C translation; a value of `""` for `locale` specifies the implementation-defined native environment. Other implementation-defined strings may be passed to `setlocale`. At program startup, the equivalent of

```
setlocale(LC_ALL, "C");
```

is executed. If a pointer to a string is given for `locale` and the selection can be honored, the `setlocale` function returns a pointer to the string associated with the specified `category` for the new locale. If the selection cannot be honored, the `setlocale` function returns a null pointer and the program's locale is not changed.

A null pointer for `locale` causes the `setlocale` function to return a pointer to the string associated with the `category` for the program's current locale; the program's locale is not changed.

The pointer to string returned by the `setlocale` function is such that a subsequent call with that string value and its associated category will restore that part of the program's locale. The string pointed to shall be modified by the program, but may be overwritten by a subsequent call to the `setlocale` function.

`struct lconv *localeconv(void);`

The `localeconv` function sets the components of an object with type `struct lconv` with values appropriate for the formatting of numeric quantities (monetary and otherwise) according to the rules of the current locale.

The members of the structure with type `char *` are pointers to strings, any of which (except `decimal_point`) can point to `""`, to indicate that the value is not available in the current locale or is of zero length. The members with type `char` are nonnegative numbers, any of which can be `CHAR_MAX` to indicate that the value is not available in the current locale. The members include the following:

`char *decimal_point`

The decimal-point character used to format nonmonetary quantities.

`char *thousands_sep`

The character used to separate groups of digits before the decimal-point character in formatted nonmonetary quantities.

**`char *grouping`**
A string whose elements indicate the size of each group of digits in formatted nonmonetary quantities.

**`char *int_curr_symbol`**
The international currency symbol applicable to the current locale. The first three characters contain the alphabetic international currency symbol in accordance with those specified in ISO 4217:1987. The fourth character (immediately preceding the null character) is the character used to separate the international currency symbol from the monetary quantity.

**`char *currency_symbol`**
The locale currency symbol applicable to the current locale.

**`char *mon_decimal_point`**
The decimal-point used to format monetary quantities.

**`char *mon_thousands_sep`**
The separator for groups of digits before the decimal-point in formatted monetary quantities.

**`char *mon_grouping`**
A string whose elements indicate the size of each group of digits in formatted monetary quantities.

**`char *positive_sign`**
The string used to indicate a nonnegative-valued formatted monetary quantity.

**`char *negative_sign`**
The string used to indicate a negative-valued formatted monetary quantity.

**`char int_frac_digits`**
The number of fractional digits (those after the decimal-point) to be displayed in a internationally formatted monetary quantity.

**`char frac_digits`**
The number of fractional digits (those after the decimal-point) to be displayed in a formatted monetary quantity.

**`char p_cs_precedes`**
Set to 1 or 0 the **`currency_symbol`** respectively precedes or succeeds the value for a nonnegative formatted monetary quantity.

**`char p_sep_by_space`**
Set to 1 or 0 the **`currency_symbol`** respectively is or is not separated by a space from the value for a nonnegative formatted monetary quantity.

**`char n_cs_precedes`**
Set to 1 or 0 the **`currency_symbol`** respectively precedes or succeeds the value for a negative formatted monetary quantity.

**`char n_sep_by_space`**
Set to 1 or 0 the **`currency_symbol`** respectively is or is not separated by a space from the value for a negative formatted monetary quantity.

**`char p_sign_posn`**
Set to a value indicating the positioning of the **`positive_sign`** for a nonnegative formatted monetary quantity.

**char n_sign_posn**
Set to a value indicating the positioning of the **negative_sign** for a negative formatted monetary quantity.

The elements of **grouping** and **mon_grouping** are interpreted according to the following:

| | |
|---|---|
| **CHAR_MAX** | No further grouping is to be performed. |
| **0** | The previous element is to be repeatedly used for the remainder of the digits. |
| *other* | The integer value is the number of digits that comprise the current group. The next element is examined to determine the size of the next group of digits before the current group. |

The values of **p_sign_posn** and **n_sign_posn** are interpreted according to the following:

0 Parentheses surround the quantity and **currency_symbol**.

1 The sign string precedes the quantity and **currency_symbol**.

2 The sign string succeeds the quantity and **currency_symbol**.

3 The sign string immediately precedes the **currency_symbol**.

4 The sign string immediately succeeds the **currency_symbol**.

The **localeconv** function returns a pointer to the filled-in object. The structure pointed to by the return value shall not be modified by the program, but may be overwritten by a subsequent call to the **localeconv** function. In addition, calls to the **setlocale** function with categories **LC_ALL**, **LC_MONETARY**, or **LC_NUMERIC** may overwrite the contents of the structure.

## B.6 Mathematics <math.h>

**HUGE_VAL**
A symbolic constant representing a positive **double** expression.

**double acos(double x);**
Computes the principal value of the arc cosine of **x**. A domain error occurs for arguments not in the range [-1, +1]. The **acos** function returns the arc cosine in the range [0, π] radians.

**double asin(double x);**
Computes the principal value of the arc sine of **x**. A domain error occurs for arguments not in the range [-1, +1]. The **asin** function returns the arc sine in the range [-π/2, +π/2] radians.

**double atan(double x);**
Computes the principal value of the arc tangent of **x**. The **atan** function returns the arc tangent in the range [-π/2, +π/2] radians.

**double atan2(double y, double x);**
The **atan2** function computes the principal value of the arc tangent **y/x**, using the signs of both arguments to determine the quandrant of the return value. A domain error may occur if both arguments are zero. The **atan2** function returns the arc tangent of **y/x**, in the range [-π, +π] radians.

**double cos(double x);**
Computes the cosine of **x** (measured in radians).

**double sin(double x);**
Computes the sine of **x** (measured in radians).

**double tan(double x);**
Returns the tangent of **x** (measured in radians).

**double cosh(double x);**
Computes the hyperbolic cosine of **x**. A range error occurs if the magnitude of **x** is too large.

**double sinh(double x);**
Computes the hyperbolic sine of **x**. A range error occurs if the magnitude of **x** is too large.

**double tanh(double x);**
The **tanh** function computes the hyperbolic tangent of **x**.

**double exp(double x);**
Computes the exponential function of **x**. A range error occurs if the magnitude of **x** is too large.

**double frexp(double value, int *exp);**
Breaks the floating-point number onto a normalized fraction and an integral power of 2. It stores the integer in the **int** object pointed to by **exp**. The **frexp** function returns the value **x**, such that **x** is a **double** with magnitude in the interval [1/2, 1] or zero, and **value** equals **x** times 2 raised to the power ***exp**. If **value** is zero, both parts of the result are zero.

**double ldexp(double x, int exp);**
Multiplies a floating-point number by an integral power of 2. A range error may occur. The **ldexp** function returns the value of **x** times 2 raised to the power **exp**.

**double log(double x);**
Computes the natural logarithm of **x**. A domain error occurs if the argument is negative. A range error may occur if the argument is zero.

**double log10(double x);**
Computes the base-ten logarithm of **x**. A domain error occurs if the argument is negative. A range error may occur if the argument is zero.

**double modf(double value, double *iptr);**
Breaks the argument **value** into integral and fractional parts, each of which has the same sign as the argument. It stores the integral part as a **double** in the object pointed to by **iptr**. The **modf** function returns the signed frantional part of **value**.

**double pow(double x, double y);**
Computes **x** raised to the power **y**. A domain error occurs if **x** is negative and **y** is not an integral value. A domain error occurs if the result cannot be represented when **x** is zero and **y** is less than or equal to zero. A range error may occur.

**double sqrt(double x);**
Computes the nonnegative square root of **x**. A domain error occurs if the argument is negative.

**double ceil(double x);**
Computes the smallest integral value not less than **x**.

**double fabs(double x);**
Computes the absolute value of a floating-point number **x**.

**double floor(double x);**
Computes the largest integral value not greater than **x**.

**`double fmod(double x, double y);`**
Computes the floating-point remainder of **`x/y`**.

## B.7 Nonlocal Jumps <`setjmp.h`>

**`jmp_buf`**
An array type suitable for holding the information needed to restore a calling environment.

**`int setjmp(jmp_buf env);`**
Saves its calling environment in argument **`jmp_buf`** for later use by the **`longjmp`** function.

If the return is from a direct invocation, the **`setjmp`** macro returns the value zero. If the return is from a call to the **`longjmp`** function, the **`setjmp`** macro returns a nonzero value.

An invocation of the **`setjmp`** macro shall appear only in one of the following contexts:

- the entire controlling expression of a selection or iteration statement;
- one operand of a relational or equality operator with the other operand an integral constant expression, with the resulting expression being the entire controlling expression of a selection or iteration statement;
- the operand of a unary **`!`** operator with the resulting expression being the entire controlling expression of a selection or iteration statement; or
- the entire expression of an expression statement.

**`void longjmp(jmp_buf env, int val);`**
Restores the environment saved by the most recent invocation of the **`setjmp`** macro in the same invocation of the program, with the corresponding **`jmp_buf`** argument. If there has been no such invocation, or if the function containing the invocation of the **`setjmp`** macro has terminated execution in the interim, the behavior is undefined.

All accessible objects have values as of the time **`longjmp`** was called, except that the values of objects of automatic storage duration that are local to the function containing the invocation of the corresponding **`setjmp`** macro that are not volatile type and have been changed between the **`setjmp`** invocation and **`longjmp`** invocation call are indeterminate.

As it bypasses the usual function call and return mechanisms, **`longjmp`** shall execute correctly in context of interrupts, signals, and any of their associated functions. However, if the **`longjmp`** function is invoked from a nested signal handler (that is, from a function invoked as a result of a signal raised during the handling of another signal), the behavior is undefined.

After **`longjmp`** is completed, program execution continues as if the corresponding invocation of the **`setjmp`** macro had just returned the value specified by **`val`**. The **`longjmp`** function cannot cause the **`setjmp`** macro to return the value 0; if **`val`** is 0, the **`setjmp`** macro returns the value 1.

## B.8 Signal Handling <`signal.h`>

**`sig_atomic_t`**
The integral type of an object that can be accessed as an atomic entity, even in the presence of asynchronous interrupts.

**`SIG_DFL`**
**`SIG_ERR`**
**`SIG_IGN`**
These expand to constant expressions with distinct values that have type compatible with the second argument to and the return value of the **`signal`** function, and whose value compares

unequal to the address of any declarable function; and the following, each of which expands to a positive integral constant expression that is the signal number for the specified condition:

**SIGABRT** abnormal termination, such as is initiated by the **abort** function

**SIGFPE** an erroneous arithmetic operation, such as zero divide or an operation resulting in overflow

**SIGILL** detection of an invalid function image, such as an illegal instruction

**SIGINT** receipt of an interactive attention signal

**SIGSEGV** an invalid access to storage

**SIGTERM** a termination request sent to the program

An implementation need not generate any of these signals, except as a result of explicit calls to the **raise** function.

**void (*signal(int sig, void (*func)(int)))(int);**

Chooses one of three ways in which receipt of the signal number **sig** is to be subsequently handled. If the value of **func** is **SIG_DEF**, default handling for that signal will occur. If the value of **func** is **SIG_IGN**, the signal will be ignored. Otherwise, **func** shall point to a function to be called when that signal occurs. Such a function is called a *signal handler.*

When a signal occurs, if **func** points to a function, first the equivalent of **signal(sig, SIG_DFL);** is executed or an implementation-defined blocking of the signal is performed. (If the value of **sig** is **SIGILL**, whether the reset to **SIG_DFL** occurs is implementation-defined.) Next the equivalent of **(*func) (sig);** is executed. The function **func** may terminate by executing a **return** statement or by calling the **abort**, **exit**, or **longjmp** function. If **func** executes a **return** statement and the value if **sig** was **SIGFPE** or any other implementation-defined value corresponding to a computational exception, the behavior is undefined. Otherwise, the program will resume execution at the point it was interrupted.

If the signal occurs other than as the result of calling the **abort** or **raise** function, the behavior is undefined if the signal handler calls any function in the standard library other than the **signal** function itself (with a first argument of the signal number corresponding to the signal that caused the invocation of the handler) or refers to any object with static storage duration other than by assigning a value to a static storage duration variable of type **volatile sig_atomic_t**. Furthermore, if such a call to the **signal** function results in a **SIG_ERR** return, the value of **errno** in indeterminate.

At program startup, the equivalent of

```
signal(sig, SIG_IGN);
```

may be executed for some signals selected in an implementation-defined manner; the equivalent of

```
signal(sig, SIG_DFL);
```

is executed for all other signals defined by the implementation.

If the request can be honored, the **signal** function returns the value of **func** for the most recent call to **signal** for the specified signal **sig**. Otherwise, a value of **SIG_ERR** is returned and a positive value is stored in **errno**.

**int raise(int sig);**

The **raise** function sends the signal **sig** to the executing program The **raise** function returns zero if successful, nonzero if unsuccessful.

## B.9 Variable Arguments <stdarg.h>

**va_list**

A type suitable for holding information needed by the macros **va_start**, **va_arg**, and **va_end**. If access to the varying arguments is desired, the called function shall declare an object (referred to as **ap** in this section) having type **va_list**. The object **ap** may be passed as an argument to another function; if that function invokes the **va_arg** macro with parameter **ap**, the value of **ap** in the calling function is determinate and shall be passed to the **va_end** macro prior to any further reference to **ap**.

**void va_start(va_list ap, *parmN*);**

Shall be invoked before any access to the unnamed arguments. The **va_start** marco initializes **ap** for subsequent use by **va_arg** and **va_end**. The parameter *parmN* is the identifier of the rightmost parameter in the variable parameter list in the function definition (the one just before the **,** ...). If the parameter *parmN* is declared with the **register** storage class, with a function or array type, or with a type that is not compatible with the type that results after application of the default argument promotions, the behavior is undefined.

*type* **va_arg(va_list ap, *type*);**

Expands to an expression that has the type and value of the next argument in the call. The parameter **ap** shall be the same as the **va_list ap** initialized by **va_start**. Each invocation of **va_arg** modifies **ap** so that the values of successive arguments are returned in turn. The parameter *type* is a type name specified such that the type of a pointer to an object that has the specified type can be obtained simply by postfixing a ***** to *type*. If there is no next argument, or if *type* is not compatible with the type of the next argument (as promoted according to the default argument promotions), the behavior is undefined. The first invocation of the **va_arg** macro after that of the **va_start** macro returns the value of the argument after that specified by *parmN*. Successive invocations return the values of the remaining arguments in succession.

**void va_end(va_list ap);**

Facilitates a normal return from the function whose variable argument list was referred to by the expansion of **va_start** that initialized **va_list ap**. The **va_end** macro may modify **ap** so that it is no longer usable (without an intervening invocation of **va_start**). If there is no corresponding invocation of the **va_start** macro, or if the **va_end** macro is not invoked before the return, the behavior is undefined.

## B.10 Input/Output <stdio.h>

**_IOFBF**
**_IOLBF**
**_IONBF**

Integral constant expressions with distinct values, suitable for use as the third argument to the **setvbuf** function.

**BUFSIZ**

An integral constant expression, which is the size of the buffer used by the **setbuf** function.

**EOF**

A negative integral constant expression that is returned by several functions to indicate end-of-file, that is, no more input from a stream.

**FILE**

An object type capable of recording all the information needed to control a stream, including its file position indicator, a pointer to its associated buffer (if any), an error indicator that records whether a read/write error has occurred, and an end-of-file indicator that records whether the end of the file has been reached.

**FILENAME_MAX**
An integral constant expression that is the size needed for an array of **char** large enough to hold the longest file name string that the implementation guarantees can be opened.

**FOPEN_MAX**
An integral constant expression that is the minimum number of files that the implementation guarantees can be open simultaneously.

**fpos_t**
An object type capable of recording all the information needed to specify uniquely every position within a file.

**L_tmpnam**
An integral constant expression that is the size needed for an array of **char** large enough to hold a temporary file name string generated by the **tmpnam** function.

**NULL**
An implementation-defined null pointer constant.

**SEEK_CUR**
**SEEK_END**
**SEEK_SET**
Integral constant expressions with distinct values, suitable for use as the third argument to the **fseek** function.

**size_t**
The unsigned integral type of the result of the **sizeof** operator.

**stderr**
Expression of type "pointer to **FILE**" that points to the **FILE** object associated with the standard error stream.

**stdin**
Expression of type "pointer to **FILE**" that points to the **FILE** object associated with the standard input stream.

**stdout**
Expression of type "pointer to **FILE**" that points to the **FILE** object associated with the standard output stream.

**TMP_MAX**
An integral constant expression that is the minimum number of unique file names that shall be generated by the **tmpnam** function. The value of the macro **TMP_MAX** shall be at least 25.

**int remove(const char *filename);**
Causes the file whose name is the string pointed to by **filename** to be no longer accessible by that name. A subsequent attempt to open that file using that name will fail, unless it is created anew. If the file is open, the behavior of the **remove** function is implementation-defined. Thr **remove** function returns zero if the operation succeeds, nonzero if it fails.

**int rename(const char *old, const char *new);**
Causes the file whose name is the string pointed to by **old** to be henceforth known by the name given by the string pointed to by **new**. The file named **old** is no longer accessible by that name. If a file named by the string pointed to by **new** exists prior to the call to the **re-**

**name** function, the behavior is implementation-defined. The **rename** function returns zero if the operation succeeds, nonzero if it fails, in which case if the file existed previously it is still known by its original name.

**FILE *tmpfile(void);**

Creates a temporary binary file that will automatically be removed when it is closed or at program termination. If the program terminates abnormally, whether an open temporary file is removed is implementation-defined. The file is opened for update with "**wb+**" mode. The **tmpfile** function returns a pointer to the stream of the file that is created. If the file cannot be created, the **tmpfile** function returns a null pointer.

**char *tmpnam(char *s);**

The **tmpnam** function generates a string that is a valid file name and that is not the same as the name of an existing file. The **tmpnam** function generates a different string each time it is called, up to **TMP_MAX** times. If it is called more than **TMP_MAX** times, the behavior is implementation-defined.

If the argument is a null pointer, the **tmpnam** function leaves its result in an internal static object and returns a pointer to that object. Subsequent calls to the **tmpnam** function may modify the same object. If the argument is not a null pointer, it is assumed to point to an array of at least **L_tmpnam char**s; the **tmpnam** function writes its result in that array and returns the argument as its value.

**int fclose(FILE *stream);**

The **fclose** function causes the stream pointed to by **stream** to be flushed and the associated file to be closed. Any unwritten buffered data for the stream are delivered to the host environment to be written to the file; any unread buffered data are discarded. The stream is disassociated from the file. If the associated buffer was automatically allocated, it is deallocated. The **fclose** function returns zero if the stream was successfully closed, or **EOF** if any errors were detected.

**int fflush(FILE *stream);**

If **stream** points to an output stream or an update stream in which the most recent operation was not input, the **fflush** function causes any unwritten data for that stream to be delivered to the host environment or to be written to the file; otherwise, the behavior is undefined.

If **stream** is a null pointer, the **fflush** function performs this flushing action on all streams for which the behavior is defined above. The **fflush** function returns **EOF** if a write error occurs, otherwise zero.

**FILE *fopen(const char *filename, const char *mode);**

The **fopen** function opens the file whose name is the string pointed to by **filename**, and associates a stream with it. The argument **mode** points to a string beginning with one of the following sequences:

| | |
|---|---|
| **r** | open text file for reading |
| **w** | truncate to zero length or create text file for writing |
| **a** | append; open or create text file for writing at end-of-file |
| **rb** | open binary file for reading |
| **wb** | truncate to zero length or create binary file for writing |
| **ab** | append; open or create binary file for writing at end-of-file |
| **r+** | open text file for update (reading and writing) |

| | |
|---|---|
| `w+` | truncate to zero length or create text file for update |
| `a+` | append; open or create text file for update, writing at end-of-file |
| `r+b` or `rb+` | open binary file for update (reading and writing) |
| `w+b` or `wb+` | truncate to zero length or create binary file for update |
| `a+b` or `ab+` | append; open or create binary file for update, writing at end-of-file |

Opening a file with read mode (`'r'` as the first character in the **mode** argument) fails if the file does not exist or cannot be read. Opening the file with append mode (`'a'` as the first character in the **mode** argument) causes all subsequent writes to the file to be forced to the then current end-of-file, regardless of intervening calls to the **fseek** function. In some implementations, opening a binary file with append mode (`'b'` as the second or third character in the above list of **mode** argument values) may initially position the file position indicator for the stream beyond the last data written, because of null character padding.

When a file is opened with update mode (`'+'` as the second or third character in the above list of **mode** argument values), both input and output may be performed on the associated stream. However, output may not be directly followed by input without an intervening call to the **fflush** function or to a file positioning function (**fseek**, **fsetpos**, or **rewind**), and input may not be directly followed by output without an intervening call to a file positioning function, unless the input operation encounters end-of-file. Opening (or creating) a text file with update mode may instead open (or create) a binary stream in some implementations.

When opened, a stream is fully buffered if and only if it can be determined not to refer to an interactive device. The error and end-of-file indicators for the stream are cleared. The **fopen** function returns a pointer to the object controlling the stream. If the open operation fails, **fopen** returns a null pointer.

**`FILE *freopen(const char *filename, const char *mode, FILE *stream);`**

The **freopen** function opens the file whose name is the string pointed to by **filename** and associates the stream pointed to by **stream** with it. The **mode** argument is used just as in the **fopen** function.

The **freopen** function first attempts to close any file that is associated with the specified stream. Failure to close the file successfully is ignored. The error and end-of-file indicators for the stream are cleared. The **freopen** function returns a null pointer if the open operation fails. Otherwise, **freopen** returns the value of **stream**.

**`void setbuf(FILE *stream, char *buf);`**

The **setbuf** function is equivalent to the **setvbuf** function invoked with the values **_IOFBF** for **mode** and **BUFSIZ** for **size**, or (if **buf** is a null pointer), with the value **_IONBF** for **mode**. The **setbuf** function returns no value.

**`int setvbuf(FILE *stream, char *buf, int mode, size_t size);`**

The **setvbuf** function may be used only after the stream pointed to by **stream** has been associated with an open file and before any other operation is performed on the stream. The argument **mode** determines how **stream** will be buffered, as follows: **_IOFBF** causes input/output to be fully buffered; **_IOLBF** causes input/output to be line buffered; **_IONBF** causes input/output to be unbuffered. If **buf** is not a null pointer, the array it points to may be used instead of a buffer allocated by the **setvbuf** function. The argument **size** specifies the size of the array. The contents of the array at any time are indeterminate. The **setvbuf** function returns zero on success, or nonzero if an invalid value is given for **mode** or if the request cannot be honored.

**int fprintf(FILE *stream, const char *format, ...);**

The **fprintf** function writes output to the stream pointed to by **stream**, under control of the string pointed to by **format** that specifies how subsequent arguments are converted for output. If there are insufficient arguments for the format, the behavior is undefined. If the format is exhausted while arguments remain, the excess arguments are evaluated (as always) but are otherwise ignored. The **fprintf** function returns when the end of the format string is encountered. See Chapter 9, "Formatted Input/Output," for a detailed description of the output conversion specifications. The **fprintf** function returns the number of characters transmitted, or a negative value if an output error occurred.

**int fscanf(FILE *stream, const char *format, ...);**

The **fscanf** function reads input from the stream pointed to by **stream**, under control of the string pointed to by **format** that specifies the admissible input sequences and how they are to be converted for assignment, using subsequent arguments as pointers to the objects to receive the converted input. If there are insufficient arguments for the format, the behavior is undefined. If the format is exhausted while arguments remain, the excess arguments are evaluated (as always) but are otherwise ignored. See Chapter 9, "Formatted Input/Output," for a detailed description of the input conversion specifications.

The **fscanf** function returns the value **EOF** if an input failure occurs before any conversion. Otherwise, the **fscanf** function returns the number of input items assigned, which can be fewer than provided for, or even zero, in the event of an early matching failure.

**int printf(const char *format, ...);**

The **printf** function is equivalent to **fprintf** with the argument **stdout** interposed before the arguments to **printf**. The **printf** function returns the number of characters transmitted, or a negative value if an output error occurred.

**int scanf(const char *format, ...);**

Function **scanf** is equivalent to **fscanf** with the argument **stdin** interposed before the arguments to **scanf**. Function **scanf** returns the value of the macro **EOF** if an input failure occurs before any conversion. Otherwise, **scanf** returns the number of input items assigned, which can be fewer than provided for, or even zero, in the event of an early matching failure.

**int sprintf(char *s, const char *format, ...);**

Function **sprintf** is equivalent to **fprintf**, except that the argument **s** specifies an array into which the generated output is to be written, rather than to a stream. A null character is written at the end of the characters written; it is not counted as part of the returned sum. The behavior of copying between objects that overlap is undefined. Function **sprintf** returns the number of characters written by the array, not counting the terminating null character.

**int sscanf(const char *s, const char *format, ...);**

The **sscanf** function is equivalent to **fscanf**, except that the argument **s** specifies a string from which the input is to be obtained, rather than from a stream. Reaching the end of the string is equivalent to encountering end-of-file for the **fscanf** function. If copying takes place between objects that overlap, the behavior is undefined.

The **sscanf** function returns the value **EOF** if an input failure occurs before any conversion. Otherwise, the **sscanf** function returns the number of input items assigned, which can be fewer than provided for, or even zero, in the event of an early matching failure.

**int vfprintf(FILE *stream, const char *format, va_list arg);**

Function **vfprintf** is equivalent to **fprintf**, with the variable argument list replaced by **arg**, which is initialized by the **va_start** macro (and possibly subsequent **va_arg** calls).

Function **vfprintf** does not invoke the **va_end** macro. The **vfprintf** function returns the number of characters transmitted, or a negative value if an output error occurred.

**int vprintf(const char *format, va_list arg);**

The **vprintf** function is equivalent to **printf**, with the variable argument list replaced by **arg**, which shall have been initialized by the **va_start** macro (and possibly subsequent **va_arg** calls). Function **vprintf** does not invoke the **va_end** macro. Function **vprintf** returns the number of characters transmitted, or a negative value if an output error occurred.

**int vsprintf(char *s, const char *format, va_list arg);**

Function **vsprintf** is equivalent to **sprintf**, with the variable argument list replaced by **arg**, which shall have been initialized by the **va_start** macro (and possibly subsequent **va_arg** calls). Function **vsprintf** does not invoke the **va_end** macro. If copying takes place between objects that overlap, the behavior is undefined. Function **vsprintf** returns the number of characters written in the array, not counting the terminating null character.

**int fgetc(FILE *stream);**

The **fgetc** function obtains the next character (if present) as an **unsigned char** converted to an **int**, from the input stream pointed to by **stream**, and advances the associated file position indicator for the stream (if defined). The **fgetc** function returns the next character from the input stream pointed to by **stream**. If the stream is at end-of-file, the end-of-file indicator for the stream is set and **fgetc** returns **EOF**. If a read error occurs, the error indicator for the stream is set and **fgetc** returns **EOF**.

**char *fgets(char *s, int n, FILE *stream);**

The **fgets** function reads at most one less than the number of characters specified by **n** from the stream pointed to by **stream** into the array pointed to by **s**. No additional characters are read after a new-line character (which is retained) or after end-of-file. A null character is written immediately after the last character read into the array.

The **fgets** function returns **s** if successful. If end-of-file is encountered and no characters have been read into the array, the contents of the array remain unchanged and a null pointer is returned. If a read error occurs during the operation, the array contents are indeterminate and a null pointer is returned.

**int fputc(int c, FILE *stream);**

The **fputc** function writes the character specified by **c** (converted to an **unsigned char**) to the output stream pointed to by **stream**, at the position indicated by the associated file position indicator for the stream (if defined), and advances the indicator appropriately. If the file cannot support positioning requests, or if the stream was opened with append mode, the character is appended to the output stream. The **fputc** function returns the character written. If a write error occurs, the error indicator for the stream is set and **fputc** returns **EOF**.

**int fputs(const char *s, FILE *stream);**

The **fputs** function writes the string pointed to by **s** to the stream pointed to by **stream**. The terminating null character is not written. The **fputs** function returns **EOF** of a write error occurs; otherwise it returns a nonnegative value.

**int getc(FILE *stream);**

Function **getc** is equivalent to **fgetc**, except that if it is implemented as a macro, it may evaluate **stream** more than once—the argument should be an expression without side effects.

Function **getc** returns the next character from the input stream pointed to by **stream**. If the stream is at end-of-file, the end-of-file indicator for the stream is set and **getc** returns **EOF**. If a read error occurs, the error indicator for the stream is set and **getc** returns **EOF**.

**int getchar(void);**

The **getchar** function is equivalent to **getc** with the argument **stdin**. The **getchar** function returns the next character from the input stream pointed to by **stdin**. If the stream is at end-of-file, the end-of-file indicator for the stream is set and **getchar** returns **EOF**. If a read error occurs, the error indicator for the stream is set and **getchar** returns **EOF**.

**char *gets(char *s);**

The **gets** function reads characters from the input stream pointed to by **stdin**, into the array pointed to by **s**, until end-of-file is encountered or a new-line character is read. Any new-line character is discarded, and a null character is written immediately after the last character read into the array. The **gets** function returns **s** if successful. If end-of-file is encountered and no characters have been read into the array, the contents of the array remain unchanged and a null pointer is returned. If a read error occurs during the operation, the array contents are indeterminate and a null pointer is returned.

**int putc(int c, FILE *stream);**

The **putc** function is equivalent to **fputc**, except that if it is implemented as a macro, it may evaluate **stream** more than once, so the argument should never be an expression with side effects. The **putc** function returns the character written. If a write error occurs, the error indicator for the stream is set and **putc** returns **EOF**.

**int putchar(int c);**

The **putchar** is equivalent to **putc** with the second argument **stdout**. The **putchar** function returns the character written. If a write error occurs, the error indicator for the stream is set and **putchar** returns **EOF**.

**int puts(const char *s);**

The **puts** function writes the string pointed to by **s** to the stream pointed to by **stdout**, and appends a new-line character to the output. The terminating null character is not written. The **puts** function returns **EOF** if a write error occurs; otherwise it returns a nonnegative value.

**int ungetc(int c, FILE *stream);**

The **ungetc** function pushes the character specified by **c** (converted to an **unsigned char**) back onto the input stream pointed to by **stream**. The pushed-back characters will be returned by subsequent reads on that stream in the reverse order of their pushing. A successful intervening call (with the stream pointed to by **stream**) to a file positioning function (**fseek**, **fsetpos**, or **rewind**) discards any pushed-back characters for the stream. The external storage corresponding to the stream is unchanged.

One character of pushback is guaranteed. If the **ungetc** function is called too many times on the same stream without an intervening read or file positioning operation on that stream, the operation may fail. If the value of c equals that of the macro **EOF**, the operation fails and the input stream is unchanged.

A successful call to the **ungetc** function clears the end-of-file indicator for the stream. The value of the file position indicator for the stream after reading or discarding all pushed-back characters shall be the same as it was before the characters were pushed back. For a text stream, the value of its file position indicator after a successful call to the **ungetc** function is unspecified until all pushed-back characters are read or discarded. For a binary stream, its file position indicator is determined by each successful call to the **ungetc** function; if its value was zero before a call, it is indeterminate after the call. The **ungetc** function returns the character pushed back after conversion, or **EOF** if the operation fails.

**size_t fread(void *ptr, size_t size, size_t nmemb, FILE *stream);**

The **fread** function reads, into the array pointed to by **ptr**, up to **nmemb** elements whose size is specified by **size**, from the stream pointed to by **stream**. The file position indicator for the stream (if defined) is advanced by the number of characters successfully read. If an error occurs, the resulting value of the file position indicator for the stream is indeterminate. If a partial element is read, its value is indeterminate.

The **fread** function returns the number of elements successfully read, which may be less than **nmemb** if a read error or end-of-file is encountered. If **size** or **nmemb** is zero, **fread** returns zero and the contents of the array and the state of the stream remain unchanged.

**size_t fwrite(const void *ptr, size_t size, size_t nmemb, FILE *stream);**

The **fwrite** function writes, from the array pointed to by **ptr**, up to **nmemb** elements whose size is specified by **size**, to the stream pointed to by **stream**. The file position indicator for the stream (if defined) is advanced by the number of characters successfully written. If an error occurs, the resulting value of the file position for the stream is indeterminate. The **fwrite** function returns the number of elements successfully written, which will be less than **nmemb** only if a write error is encountered.

**int fgetpos(FILE *stream, fpos_t *pos);**

The **fgetpos** function stores the current value of the file position indicator for the stream pointed to by **stream** in the object pointed to by **pos**. The value stored contains unspecified information usable by the **fsetpos** function for repositioning the stream to its position at the time of the call to the **fgetpos** function. If successful, the **fgetpos** function returns zero; on failure, the **fgetpos** function returns nonzero and stores an implementation-defined positive value in **errno**.

**int fseek(FILE *stream, long int offset, int whence);**

The **fseek** function sets the file position indicator for the stream pointed to by **stream**. For a binary stream, the new position, measured in characters from the beginning of the file, is obtained by adding **offset** to the position specified by **whence**. The specified position is the beginning of the file if **whence** is **SEEK_SET**, the current value of the file position indicator if **SEEK_CUR**, or end-of-file if **SEEK_END**. A binary stream need not meaningfully support **fseek** calls with a **whence** value of **SEEK_END**. For a text stream, either **offset** shall be zero, or **offset** shall be a value returned by an earlier call to the **ftell** function on the same stream and **whence** shall be **SEEK_SET**.

A successful call to the **fseek** function clears the end-of-file indicator for the stream and undoes any effects of the **ungetc** function on the same stream. After an **fseek** call, the next operation on an update stream may be either input or output. The **fseek** function returns nonzero only for a request that cannot be satisfied.

**int fsetpos(FILE *stream, const fpos_t *pos);**

The **fsetpos** function sets the file position indicator for the stream pointed to by **stream** according to the value of the object pointed to by **pos**, which shall be a value obtained from an earlier call to the **fgetpos** function on the same stream. A successful call to the **fsetpos** function clears the end-of-file indicator for the stream and undoes any effects of the **ungetc** function on the same stream. After an **fsetpos** call, the next operation on an update stream may be either input or output. If successful, the **fsetpos** function returns zero; on failure, the **fsetpos** function returns nonzero and stores an implementation-defined positive value in **errno**.

**`long int ftell(FILE *stream);`**

Function `ftell` obtains the current value of the file position indicator for the stream pointed to by `stream`. For a binary stream, the value is the number of characters from the beginning of the file. For a text stream, its file position indicator contains unspecified information, usable by the `fseek` function for returning the file position indicator for the stream to its position at the time of the `ftell` call; the difference between two such return values is not necessarily a meaningful measure of the number of characters written or read. If successful, the `ftell` function returns the current value of the file position indicator for the stream. On failure, the `ftell` function returns `-1L` and stores an implementation-defined positive value in `errno`.

**`void rewind(FILE *stream);`**

The `rewind` function sets the file position indicator for the stream pointed to by `stream` to the beginning of the file. It is equivalent to

```
(void)fseek(stream, 0L, SEEK_SET)
```

except that the error indicator for the stream is also cleared.

**`void clearerr(FILE *stream);`**

The `clearerr` function clears the end-of-file and error indicators for the stream pointed to by `stream`.

**`int feof(FILE *stream);`**

The `feof` function tests the end-of-file indicator for the stream pointed to by `stream`. The `feof` function returns nonzero if and only if the end-of-file indicator is set for `stream`.

**`int ferror(FILE *stream);`**

The `ferror` function tests the error indicator for the stream pointed to by `stream`. The `ferror` function returns nonzero if and only if the error indicator is set for `stream`.

**`void perror(const char *s);`**

The `perror` function maps the error number in the integer expression `errno` to an error message. It writes a sequence of characters to the standard error stream thus: first (if `s` is not a null pointer and the character pointed to by `s` is not the null character), the string pointed to by `s` followed by a colon (:) and a space; then an appropriate error message string followed by a new-line character. The contents of the error message strings are the same as those returned by the `strerror` function with argument `errno`, which are implementation-defined.

## B.11 General Utilities `<stdlib.h>`

**`EXIT_FAILURE`**
**`EXIT_SUCCESS`**

Integral expressions that may be used as the argument to the `exit` function to return unsuccessful or successful termination status, respectively, to the host environment.

**`MB_CUR_MAX`**

A positive integer expression whose value is the maximum number of bytes in a multibyte character for the extended character set specified by the current locale (category `LC_CTYPE`), and whose value is never greater than `MB_LEN_MAX`.

**`NULL`**

An implementation-defined null pointer constant.

**`RAND_MAX`**

An interval constant expression, the value of which is the maximum value returned by the `rand` function. The value of the `RAND_MAX` macro shall be at least 32767.

`div_t`

A structure type that is the type of the value returned by the `div` function.

`ldiv_t`

A structure type that is the type of the value returned by the `ldiv` function.

`size_t`

The unsigned integral type of the result of the `sizeof` operator.

`wchar_t`

An integral type whose range of values can represent distinct codes for all members of the largest extended character set specified among the supported locales; the null character shall have the code value zero and each member of the basic character set shall have a code value equal to its value when used as the lone character in an integer character constant.

`double atof(const char *nptr);`

Converts the initial portion of the string pointed to by `nptr` to `double` representation. The `atof` function returns the converted value.

`int atoi(const char *nptr);`

Converts the initial portion of the string pointed to by `nptr` to `int` representation. The `atoi` function returns the converted value.

`long int atol(const char *nptr);`

Converts the initial portion of the string pointed to by `nptr` to `long` representation. The `atol` function returns the converted value.

`double strtod(const char *nptr, char **endptr);`

Converts the initial portion of the string pointed to by `nptr` to `double` representation. First, it decomposes the input string into three parts: an initial, possibly empty, sequence of white-space characters (as specified by the `isspace` function), a subject sequence resembling a floating-point constant; and a final string of one or more unrecognized characters, including the terminating null character of the input string. Then, it attempts to convert the subject sequence to a floating-point number, and returns the result.

The expanded form of the subject sequence is an optional plus or minus sign, then a nonempty sequence of digits optionally containing a decimal-point character, then an optional exponent part, but no floating suffix. The subject sequence is defined as the longest initial subsequence of the input string, starting with the first non-white-space character, that is of the expected form. The subject sequence contains no characters if the input string is empty or consists entirely of white space, or if the first non-white-space character is other than a sign, a digit, or a decimal-point character.

If the subject sequence has the expected form, the sequence of characters starting with the first digit or the decimal-point character (whichever occurs first) is interpreted as a floating constant, except that the decimal-point character is used in place of a period, and that if neither an exponent part nor a decimal-point character appears, a decimal point is assumed to follow the last digit in the string. If the subject sequence begins with a minus sign, the value resulting from the conversion is negated. A pointer to the final string is stored in the object pointed to by `endptr`, provided that `endptr` is not a null pointer.

If the subject sequence is empty or does not have the expected form, no conversion is performed; the value of `nptr` is stored in the object pointed to by `endptr`, provided that `endptr` is not a null pointer.

The `strtod` function returns the converted value, if any. If no conversion could be performed, zero is returned. If the correct value is outside the range of representable values, plus or minus **HUGE_VAL** is returned (according to the sign of the value), and the value of the macro **ERANGE** is stored in **errno**. If the correct value would cause underflow, zero is returned and the value of the macro **ERANGE** is stored in **errno**.

**`long int strtol(const char *nptr, char **endptr, int base);`**

Converts the initial portion of the string pointed to by **nptr** to **long int** representation. It decomposes the input string into three parts: an initial, possibly empty, sequence of white-space characters (as specified by the **isspace** function), a subject sequence resembling an integer represented in some radix determined by the value of **base**, and a final string of one or more unrecognized characters, including the terminating null character of the input string. Then, it attempts to convert the subject sequence to an integer, and returns the result.

If the value of **base** is zero, the expected form of the subject sequence is that of an integer constant, optionally preceded by a plus or minus sign, but not including an integer suffix. If the value of **base** is between 2 and 36, the expected form of the subject sequence is a sequence of letters and digits representing an integer with the radix specified by **base**, optionally preceded by a plus or minus sign, but not including an integer suffix. The letters from **a** (or **A**) through **z** (or **Z**) are ascribed the values 10 to 35; only letters whose ascribed values are less than that of **base** are permitted. If the value of **base** is 16, the characters **0x** or **0X** may optionally precede the sequence of letters and digits, following the sign if present.

The subject sequence is defined as the longest initial subsequence of the input string, starting with the first non-white-space character, that is of the expected form. The subject sequence contains no characters if the input string is empty or consists entirely of white space, or if the first non-white-space character is other than a sign or a permissible letter or digit.

If the subject sequence has the expected form and the value of **base** is zero, the sequence of characters starting with the first digit is interpreted as an integer constant. If the subject sequence has the expected form and the value of **base** is between 2 and 36, it is used as the base for conversion, ascribing to each letter its value as given above. If the subject sequence begins with a minus sign, the value resulting from the conversion is negated. A pointer to the final string is stored in the object pointed to by **endptr**, provided that **endptr** is not null.

If the subject sequence is empty or does not have the expected form, no conversion is performed; the value **nptr** is stored in the object pointed to by **endptr**, provided that **endptr** is not a null pointer.

The **strtol** function returns the converted value, if any. If no conversion could be performed, zero is returned. If the correct value is outside the range of representable values, **LONG_MAX** or **LONG_MIN** is returned (according to the sign of the value), and the value of the macro **ERANGE** is stored in **errno**.

**`unsigned long int strtoul(const char *nptr, char **endptr, int base);`**

Converts the initial portion of the string pointed to by **nptr** to **unsigned long int** representation. The **strtoul** function works identically to the **strtol** function. The **strtoul** function returns the converted value, if any. If no conversion could be performed, zero is returned. If the correct value is outside the range of representable values, **ULONG_MAX** is returned, and the value of the macro **ERANGE** is stored in **errno**.

**`int rand(void);`**

The **rand** function computes a sequence of pseudo-random integers in the range 0 to **RAND_MAX**. The **rand** function returns a pseudo-random integer.

**`void srand(unsigned int seed);`**

Uses the argument as a seed for a new sequence of pseudo-random numbers to be returned by subsequent calls to **rand**. If **srand** is then called with the same seed value, the sequence of pseudo-random numbers shall be repeated. If **rand** is called before any calls to **srand** have been made, the same sequence shall be generated as when **srand** is first called with a seed value of 1. The following functions define a portable implementation of **rand** and **srand**.

```
static unsigned long int next = 1;

int rand(void)   /* RAND_MAX assumed to be 32767 */
{
   next = next * 1103515245 + 12345;
   return (unsigned int) (next/65536) % 32768;
}

void srand(unsigned int seed)
{
   next = seed;
}
```

**void *calloc(size_t nmemb, size_t size);**
Allocates space for an array of **nmemb** objects, each of whose size is **size**. The space is initialized to all bits zero. The **calloc** function returns either a null pointer or a pointer to the allocated space.

**void free(void *ptr);**
Causes the space pointed to by **ptr** to be deallocated, that is, made available for further allocation. If **ptr** is a null pointer, no action occurs. Otherwise, if the argument does not match a pointer earlier returned by the **calloc**, **malloc**, or **realloc** function, or if the space has been deallocated by a call to **free** or **realloc**, the behavior is undefined.

**void *malloc(size_t size);**
Allocates space for an object whose size is specified by **size** and whose value is indeterminate. The **malloc** function returns a null pointer or a pointer to the allocated space.

**void *realloc(void *ptr, size_t size);**
Changes the size of the object pointed to by **ptr** to the size specified by **size**. The contents of the object shall be unchanged up to the lesser of the new and old sizes. If the new size is larger, the value of the newly allocated portion of the object is indeterminate. If **ptr** is a null pointer, the **realloc** function behaves like the **malloc** function for the specified size. Otherwise, if **ptr** does not match a pointer earlier returned by the **calloc**, **malloc**, or **realloc** function, or if the space has been deallocated by a call to the **free** or **realloc** function, the behavior is undefined. If the space cannot be allocated, the object pointed to by **ptr** is unchanged. If **size** is zero and **ptr** is not null, the object it points to is freed. Function **realloc** returns either a null pointer or a pointer to the possibly moved allocated space.

**void abort(void);**
Causes abnormal program termination to occur, unless the signal **SIGABRT** is being caught and the signal handler does not return. Whether open output streams are flushed or open streams closed or temporary files removed is implementation-defined. An implementation-defined form of the status *unsuccessful termination* is returned to the host environment by means of the function call **raise(SIGABRT)**. The **abort** function cannot return to its caller.

**int atexit(void (*func)(void));**
Registers the function pointed to by **func**, to be called without arguments at normal program termination. The implementation shall support the registration of at least 32 functions. The **atexit** function returns zero if the registration succeeds, nonzero if it fails.

**`void exit(int status);`**

Causes normal program termination to occur. If more than one call to the **exit** function is executed by a program, the behavior is undefined. First, all functions registered by the **atexit** function are called, in the reverse order of their registration. Each function is called as many times as it was registered. Next, all open streams with unwritten buffered data are flushed, all open streams are closed, and all files created by the **tmpfile** function are removed.

Finally, control is returned to the host environment. If the value of **status** is zero or **EXIT_SUCCESS**, an implementation-defined form of the status *successful termination* is returned. If the value of **status** is **EXIT_FAILURE**, an implementation-defined form of the status *unsuccessful termination* is returned. Otherwise the status returned is implementation-defined. The **exit** function cannot return to its caller.

**`char *getenv(const char *name);`**

Searches an *environment list,* provided by the host environment, for a string that matches the string pointed to by **name**. The set of environment names and the method for altering the environment list are implementation-defined. Returns a pointer to a string associated with the matched list member. The string pointed to shall not be modified by the program, but may be overwritten by a subsequent call to the **getenv** function. If the specified **name** cannot be found, a null pointer is returned.

**`int system(const char *string);`**

Passes the string pointed to by **string** to the host environment to be executed by a *command processor* in an implementation-defined manner. A null pointer may be used for **string** to inquire whether a command processor exists. If the argument is a null pointer, the **system** function returns nonzero only if a command processor is available. If the argument is not a null pointer, the **system** function returns an implementation-defined value.

```
void *bsearch(const void *key, const void *base, size_t nmemb,
              size_t size, int (*compar)(const void *, const void *));
```

Searches an array of **nmemb** objects, the initial element of which is pointed to by **base**, for an element that matches the object pointed to by **key**. The size of each element of the array is specified by **size**. The comparison function pointed to by **compar** is called with two arguments that point to the **key** object and to an array element, in that order. The function shall return an integer less than, equal to, or greater than zero if the **key** object is considered, respectively, to be less than, to match, or to be greater than the array element. The array shall consist of: all the elements that compare less than, all the elements that compare equal to, and all the elements that compare greater than the **key** object, in that order.

Function **bsearch** returns a pointer to a matching element of the array, or a null pointer if no match is found. If two elements compare as equal, the element matched is unspecified.

```
void qsort(void *base, size_t nmemb, size_t size, int
           (*compar)(const void *, const void *));
```

Sorts an array of **nmemb** objects. The initial element is pointed to by **base**. The size of each object is specified by **size**. The array contents are sorted into ascending order according to a comparison function pointed to by **compar**, which is called with two arguments that point to the objects being compared. The function returns an integer less than equal to, or greater than zero if the first argument is considered to be respectively less than, equal to, or greater than the second. If two elements compare as equal, their order in the sorted array is undefined.

**`int abs(int j);`**

Computes the absolute value of an integer **j**. If the result cannot be represented, the behavior is undefined. The **abs** function returns the absolute value.

**`div_t div(int numer, int denom);`**

Computes the quotient and remainder of the division of the numerator **`numer`** by the denominator **`denom`**. If the division is inexact, the resulting quotient is the integer of lesser magnitude that is the nearest to the algebric quotient. If the result cannot be represented, the behavior is undefined; otherwise, **`quot * denom + rem`** shall equal **`numer`**. The **`div`** function returns a structure of type **`div_t`**, comprising both the quotient and the remainder. The structure shall contain the following members, in either order:

```
int quot;    /* quotient */
int rem;     /* remainder */
```

**`long int labs(long int j);`**

Similar to the **`abs`** function, except that the argument and the returned value each have type **`long int`**.

**`ldiv_t ldiv(long int numer, long int denom);`**

Similar to the **`div`** function, except that the arguments and the members of the returned structure (which has type **`ldiv_t`**) all have type **`long int`**.

**`int mblen(const char *s, size_t n);`**

If s is not a null pointer, the **`mblen`** function determines the number of bytes contained in the multibyte character pointed to by **`s`**. If **`s`** is a null pointer, the **`mblen`** function returns a nonzero or zero value, if multibyte character encodings, respectively, do or do not have state-dependent encodings. If **`s`** is not a null pointer, the **`mblen`** function either returns 0 (if **`s`** points to the null character), or returns the number of bytes that are contained in the multibyte character (if the next **`n`** or fewer bytes form a valid multibyte character), or returns -1 (if they do not form a valid multibyte character).

**`int mbtowc(wchar_t *pwc, const char *s, size_t n);`**

If **`s`** is not a null pointer, the **`mbtowc`** function determines the number of bytes that are contained in the multibyte character pointed to by **`s`**. It then determines the code for the value of type **`wchar_t`** that corresponds to that multibyte character. (The value of the code corresponding to the null character is zero.) If the multibyte character is valid and **`pwc`** is not a null pointer, the **`mbtowc`** function stores the code in the object pointed to by **`pwc`**. At most n bytes of the array pointed to by **`s`** will be examined.

If **`s`** is a null pointer, the **`mbtowc`** function returns a nonzero or zero value, if multibyte character encodings, respectively, do or do not have state-dependent encodings. If **`s`** is not a null pointer, the **`mbtowc`** function either returns 0 (if **`s`** points to the null character), or returns the number of bytes that are contained in the converted multibyte character (if the next **`n`** or fewer bytes form a valid multibyte character), or returns -1 (if they do not form a valid multibyte character). In no case will the value returned be greater than n or the value of the **`MB_CUR_MAX`** macro.

**`int wctomb(char *s, wchar_t wchar);`**

The **`wctomb`** function determines the number of bytes needed to represent the multibyte character corresponding to the code whose value is **`wchar`** (including any change in shift state). It stores the multibyte character representation in the array object pointed to by s (if **`s`** is not a null pointer). At most **`MB_CUR_MAX`** characters are stored. If the value of **`wchar`** is zero, the **`wctomb`** function is left in the initial shift state.

If **`s`** is a null pointer, the **`wctomb`** function returns a nonzero or zero value, if multibyte character encodings, respectively, do or do not have state-dependent encodings. If **`s`** is not a null pointer, the **`wctomb`** function returns -1 if the value of **`wchar`** does not correspond to a valid multibyte character, or returns the number of bytes that are contained in the multibyte character corresponding to the value of **wchar**. In no case will the value returned be greater than the value of the **MB_CUR_MAX** macro.

**size_t mbstowcs(wchar_t *pwcs, const char *s, size_t n);**

The **mbstowcs** function converts a sequence of multibyte characters that begins in the initial shift state from the array pointed to by **s** into a sequence of corresponding codes and stores not more than **n** codes into the array pointed to by **pwcs**. No multibyte characters that follow a null character (which is converted into a code with value zero) will be examined or converted. Each multibyte character is converted as if by a call to the **mbtowc** function, except that the shift state of the **mbtowc** function is not affected.

No more than **n** elements will be modified in the array pointed to by **pwcs**. The behavior of copying between objects that overlap is undefined. If an invalid multibyte character is encountered, function **mbstowcs** returns **(size_t)-1**. Otherwise, the **mbstowcs** function returns the number of array elements modified, not including a terminating zero code, if any.

**size_t wcstombs(char *s, const wchar_t *pwcs, size_t n);**

The **wcstombs** function converts a sequence of codes that correspond to multibyte characters from the array pointed to by **pwcs** into a sequence of multibyte characters that begins in the initial shift state and stores these multibyte characters into the array pointed to by **s**, stopping if a multibyte character would exceed the limit of **n** total bytes or if a null character is stored. Each code is converted as if by a call to the **wctomb** function, except that the shift state of the **wctomb** function is not affected.

No more than **n** bytes will be modified in the array pointed to by **s**. If copying takes place between objects that overlap, the behavior is undefined. If a code is encountered that does not correspond to a valid multibyte character, the **wcstombs** function returns **(size_t)-1**. Otherwise, the **wcstombs** function returns the number of bytes modified, not including a terminating null character, if any.

## B.12 String Handling <string.h>

**NULL**

An implementation-defined null pointer constant.

**size_t**

The unsigned integral type of the result of the **sizeof** operator.

**void *memcpy(void *s1, const void *s2, size_t n);**

The **memcpy** function copies n characters from the object pointed to by **s2** into the object pointed to by **s1**. If copying takes place between objects that overlap, the behavior is undefined. The **memcpy** function returns the value of **s1**.

**void *memmove(void *s1, const void *s2, size_t n);**

The **memmove** function copies **n** characters from the object pointed to by **s2** into the object pointed to by **s1**. Copying takes place as if the **n** characters from the object pointed to by **s2** are first copied into a temporary array of **n** characters that does not overlap the objects pointed to by **s1** and **s2**, and then the **n** characters from the temporary array are copied into the object pointed to by **s1**. The **memmove** function returns the value of **s1**.

**char *strcpy(char *s1, const char *s2);**

The **strcpy** function copies the string pointed to by **s2** (including the terminating null character) into the array pointed to by **s1**. If copying takes place between objects that overlap, the behavior is undefined. The **strcpy** function returns the value of **s1**.

**`char *strncpy(char *s1, const char *s2, size_t n);`**

The **`strncpy`** function copies not more than **`n`** characters (characters that follow a null character are not copied) from the array pointed to by **`s2`** to the array pointed to by **`s1`**. If copying takes place between objects that overlap, the behavior is undefined. If the array pointed to by **`s2`** is a string that is shorter than **`n`** characters, null characters are appended to the copy in the array pointed to by **`s1`**, until **`n`** characters in all have been written. The **`strncpy`** function returns the value of **`s1`**.

**`char *strcat(char *s1, const char *s2);`**

The **`strcat`** function appends a copy of the string pointed to by **`s2`** (including the terminating null character) to the end of the string pointed to by **`s1`**. The initial character of **`s2`** overwrites the null character at the end of **`s1`**. If copying takes place between objects that overlap, the behavior is undefined. The **`strcat`** function returns the value of **`s1`**.

**`char *strncat(char *s1, const char *s2, size_t n);`**

The **`strncat`** function appends not more than **`n`** characters (a null character and characters that follow it are not appended) from the array pointed to by **`s2`** to the end of the string pointed to by **`s1`**. The initial character of **`s2`** overwrites the null character at the end of **`s1`**. A terminating null character is always appended to the result. If copying takes place between objects that overlap, the behavior is undefined. The **`strncat`** function returns the value of **`s1`**.

**`int memcmp(const void *s1, const void *s2, size_t n);`**

The **`memcmp`** function compares the first **`n`** characters of the object pointed to by **`s1`** to the first **`n`** characters of the object pointed to by **`s2`** The **`memcmp`** function returns an integer greater than, equal to, or less than zero, accordingly as the object pointed to by **`s1`** is greater than, equal to, or less than the object pointed to by **`s2`**.

**`int strcmp(const char *s1, const char *s2);`**

The **`strcmp`** function compares the string pointed to by **`s1`** to the string pointed to by **`s2`**. The **`strcmp`** function returns an integer greater than, equal to, or less than zero, accordingly as the string pointed to by **`s1`** is greater than, equal to, or less than the string pointed to by **`s2`**.

**`int strcoll(const char *s1, const char *s2);`**

The **`strcoll`** function compares the string pointed to by **`s1`** to the string pointed to by **`s2`**, both interpreted as appropriate to the **`LC_COLLATE`** category of the current locale. The **`strcoll`** function returns an integer greater than, equal to, or less than zero, accordingly as the string pointed to by **`s1`** is greater than, equal to, or less than the string pointed to by **`s2`** when both are interpreted as appropriate to the current locale.

**`int strncmp(const char *s1, const char *s2, size_t n);`**

The **`strncmp`** function compares not more than **`n`** characters (characters that follow a null character are not compared) from the array pointed to by **`s1`** to the array pointed to by **`s2`**. The **`strncmp`** function returns an integer greater than, equal to, or less than zero, accordingly as the possibly null-terminated array pointed to by **`s1`** is greater than, equal to, or less than the possibly null-terminated array pointed to by **`s2`**.

**`size_t strxfrm(char *s1, const char *s2, size_t n);`**

The **`strxfrm`** function transforms the string pointed to by **`s2`** and places the resulting string into the array pointed to by **`s1`**. The transformation is such that if the **`strcmp`** function is applied to two transformed strings, it returns a value greater than, equal to, or less than zero, corresponding to the result of the **`strcoll`** function applied to the same two original strings. No more than **`n`** characters are placed into the resulting array pointed to by **`s1`**, including the terminating null character. If **`n`** is zero, **`s1`** is permitted to be a null pointer. If copying takes place between objects that overlap, the behavior is undefined. The **strxfrm** function returns the length of the transformed string (not including the terminating null character). If the value is **n** or more, the contents of the array pointed to by **s1** are indeterminate.

**void *memchr(const void *s, int c, size_t n);**

The **memchr** function locates the first occurrence of **c** (converted to an **unsigned char**) in the initial **n** characters (each interpreted as **unsigned char**) of the object pointed to by **s**. The **memchr** function returns a pointer to the located character, or a null pointer if the character does not occur in the object.

**char *strchr(const char *s, int c);**

The **strchr** function locates the first occurrence of **c** (converted to a **char**) in the string pointed to by **s**. The terminating null character is considered to be part of the string. The **strchr** function returns a pointer to the located character, or a null pointer if the character does not occur in the string.

**size_t strcspn(const char *s1, const char *s2);**

The **strcspn** function computes the length of the maximum initial segment of the string pointed to by **s1** which consists entirely of characters not from the string pointed to by **s2**. The **strcspn** function returns the length of the segment.

**char *strpbrk(const char *s1, const char *s2);**

The **strpbrk** function locates the first occurrence in the string pointed to by **s1** of any character from the string pointed to by **s2**. The **strpbrk** function returns a pointer to the character, or a null pointer if no character from **s2** occurs in **s1**.

**char *strrchr(const char *s, int c);**

Function **strrchr** locates the last occurrence of **c** (converted to a **char**) in the string pointed to by **s**. The terminating null character is considered part of the string. The **strrchr** function returns a pointer to the character, or a null pointer if **c** does not occur in the string.

**size_t strspn(const char *s1, const char *s2);**

The **strspn** function computes the length of the maximum initial segment of the string pointed to by **s1** which consists entirely of characters from the string pointed to by **s2**. The **strspn** function returns the length of the segment.

**char *strstr(const char *s1, const char *s2);**

The **strstr** function locates the first occurrence in the string pointed to by **s1** of the sequence of characters (excluding the terminating null character) in the string pointed to by **s2**. The **strstr** function returns a pointer to the located string, or a null pointer if the string is not found. If **s2** points to a string with zero length, the function returns **s1**.

**char *strtok(char *s1, const char *s2);**

A sequence of calls to the **strtok** function breaks the string pointed to by **s1** into a sequence of tokens, each of which is delimited by a character from the string pointed to by **s2**. The first call in the sequence has **s1** as its argument, and is followed by calls with a null pointer as their first argument. The separator string pointed to by **s2** may be different from call to call.

The first call in the sequence searches the string pointed to by **s1** for the first character that is not contained in the current separator string pointed to by **s2**. If no such character is found, then there are no tokens in the string pointed to by **s1** and the **strtok** function returns a null pointer. If such a character is found, it is the start of the first token.

The **strtok** function then searches from there for a character that is contained in the current separator string. If no such character is found, the current token extends to the end of the string pointed to by **s1**, and subsequent searches for a token will return a null pointer. If such a character is found, it is overwritten by a null character, which terminates the current token. The **strtok** function saves a pointer to the following character, from which the next search for a token will start.

Each subsequent call, with a null pointer as the value of the first argument, starts searching from the saved pointer and behaves as described above. The implementation shall behave as if no library function calls the **strtok** function. The **strtok** function returns a pointer to the first character of a token, or a null pointer if there is no token.

**void *memset(void *s, int c, size_t n);**

Function **memset** copies the value of **c** (converted to an **unsigned char**) into each of the first **n** characters in the object pointed to by **s**. The **memset** function returns the value of **s**.

**char *strerror(int errnum);**

The **strerror** function maps the error number in **errnum** to an error message string. The implementation shall behave as if no library function calls the **strerror** function. The **strerror** function returns a pointer to the string, the contents of which are implementation-defined. The array pointed to shall not be modified by the program, but may be overwritten by a subsequent call to the **strerror** function.

**size_t strlen(const char *s);**

The **strlen** function computes the length of the string pointed to by **s**. The **strlen** function returns the number of characters that precede the terminating null character.

## B.13 Date and Time <time.h>

**CLOCKS_PER_SEC**

The number per second of the value returned by the **clock** function.

**NULL**

An implementation-defined null pointer constant.

**clock_t**

An arithmetic type capable of representing time.

**time_t**

An arithmetic type capable of representing time.

**size_t**

The unsigned integral type of the result of the **sizeof** operator.

**struct tm**

Holds the components of a calendar time, called the *broken-down time.* The structure shall contain at least the following members, in any order. The semantics of the members and their normal ranges are expressed in the comments.

```
int tm_sec;      /* seconds after the minute—[0, 61] */
int tm_min;      /* minutes after the hour—[0, 59] */
int tm_hour;     /* hours since midnight—[0, 23] */
int tm_mday;     /* day of the month—[1, 31] */
int tm_mon;      /* months since January—[0, 11] */
int tm_year;     /* years since 1900 */
int tm_wday;     /* days since Sunday—[0, 6] */
int tm_yday;     /* days since January 1—[0, 365] */
int tm_isdst;    /* Daylight Saving Time flag */
```

The value `tm_isdst` is positive if Daylight Saving Time is in effect, zero if Daylight Saving Time is not in effect, and negative if the information is not available.

**`clock_t clock(void);`**

The `clock` function determines the processor time used. The `clock` function returns the implementation's best approximation to the processor time used by the program since the beginning of an implementation-defined era related only to the program invocation. To determine the time in seconds, the value returned by the `clock` function should be divided by the value of the macro `CLOCKS_PER_SEC`. If the processor time used is not available or its value cannot be represented, the function returns the value `(clock_t)-1`.

**`double difftime(time_t time1, time_t time0);`**

The `difftime` function computes the difference between two calendar times: `time1 - time0`. The `difftime` function returns the difference expressed in seconds as a `double`.

**`time_t mktime(struct tm *timeptr);`**

The `mktime` function converts the broken-down time, expressed as local time, in the structure pointed to by `timeptr` into a calendar time value with the same encoding as that of the values returned by the `time` function. The original values of the `tm_wday` and `tm_yday` components of the structure are ignored, and the original values of the other components are not restricted to the ranges indicated above. On successful completion, the values of the `tm_wday` and `tm_yday` components of the structure are set appropriately, and the other components are set to represent the specified calendar time, but with their values forced to the ranges indicated above; the final value of `tm_mday` is not set until `tm_mon` and `tm_year` are determined. The `mktime` function returns the specified calendar time encoded as a value of type `time_t`. If the calendar time cannot be represented, the function returns the value `(time_t)-1`.

**`time_t time(time_t *timer);`**

The `time` function determines the current calendar time. The `time` function returns the implementation's best approximation to the current calendar time. The value `(time_t)-1` is returned if the calendar time is not available. If `timer` is not a null pointer, the return value is also assigned to the object it points to.

**`char *asctime(const struct tm *timeptr);`**

The `asctime` function converts the broken-down time in the structure pointed to by `timeptr` into a string in the form

```
Sun Sep 16 01:03:52 1973\n\0
```

The `asctime` function returns a pointer to the string.

**`char *ctime(const time_t *timer);`**

The `ctime` function converts the calendar time pointed to by `timer` to local time in the form of a string. It is equivalent to

```
asctime(localtime(timer))
```

The `ctime` function returns the pointer returned by the `asctime` function with that broken-down time as argument.

**`struct tm *gmtime(const time_t *timer);`**

The `gmtime` function converts the calendar time pointed to by `timer` into a broken-down time, expressed as Coordinated Universal Time (UTC). The `gmtime` function returns a pointer to that object, or a null pointer if UTC is not available.

**`struct tm *localtime(const time_t *timer);`**

The **`localtime`** function converts the calendar time pointed to by **`timer`** into a broken-down time, expressed as local time. The **`localtime`** function returns a pointer to that object.

**`size_t strftime(char *s, size_t maxsize, const char *format, const struct tm *timeptr);`**

The **`strftime`** function places characters into the array pointed to by **`s`** as controlled by the string pointed to by **`format`**. The **`format`** string consists of zero or more conversion specifiers and ordinary multibyte characters. All ordinary characters (including the terminating null character) are copied unchanged into the array. If copying takes place between objects that overlap, the behavior is undefined. No more than **`maxsize`** characters are placed into the array. Each conversion specifier is replaced by appropriate characters as described in the following list. The appropriate characters are determined by the **`LC_TIME`** category of the current locale and by the values contained in the structure pointed to by **`timeptr`**.

**`%a`** is replaced by the locale's abbreviated weekday name.

**`%A`** is replaced by the locale's full weekday name.

**`%b`** is replaced by the locale's abbreviated month name.

**`%B`** is replaced by the locale's full month name.

**`%c`** is replaced by the locale's appropriate date and time representation.

**`%d`** is replaced by the day of the month as a decimal number (`01-31`).

**`%H`** is replaced by the hour (24-hour clock) as a decimal number (`00-23`).

**`%I`** is replaced by the hour (12-hour clock) as a decimal number (`01-12`).

**`%j`** is replaced by the day of the year as a decimal number (`001-366`).

**`%m`** is replaced by the month as a decimal number (`01-12`).

**`%M`** is replaced by the minute as a decimal number (`00-59`).

**`%p`** is replaced by the locale's equivalent of the AM/PM designations associated with a 12-hour clock.

**`%S`** is replaced by the second as a decimal number (`00-61`).

**`%U`** is replaced by the week number of the year (the first Sunday as the first day of week 1) as a decimal number (`00-53`).

**`%w`** is replaced by the weekday as a decimal number (`0-6`), where Sunday is `0`.

**`%W`** is replaced by the week number of the year (the first Monday as the first day of week 1) as a decimal number (`00-53`).

**`%x`** is replaced by the locale's appropriate date representation.

**`%X`** is replaced by the locale's appropriate time representation.

**`%y`** is replaced by the year without century as a decimal number (`00-99`).

**`%Y`** is replaced by the year with century as a decimal number.

**`%Z`** is replaced by the time zone name or abbreviation, or by no characters if no time zone is determinable.

**`%%`** is replaced by `%`.

If a conversion specifier is not one of the above, the behavior is undefined. If the total number of resulting characters including the terminating null character is not more than **`max-`**

**size**, the **strftime** function returns the number of characters placed into the array pointed to by **s** not including the terminating null character. Otherwise, zero is returned and the contents of the array are indeterminate.

## B.14 Implementation Limits

### <limits.h>

The following shall be defined equal to or greater than in magnitude (absolute value) to the values below.

**#define CHAR_BIT** **8**
The number of bits for the smallest object that is not a bit-field (byte).

**#define SCHAR_MIN** **-127**
The minimum value for an object of type **signed char**.

**#define SCHAR_MAX** **+127**
The maximum value for an object of type **signed char**.

**#define UCHAR_MAX** **255**
The maximum value for an object of type **unsigned char**.

**#define CHAR_MIN** **0** ***or*** **SCHAR_MIN**
The minimum value for an object of type **char**.

**#define CHAR_MAX** **UCHAR_MAX** ***or*** **SCHAR_MAX**
The maximum value for an object of type **char**.

**#define MB_LEN_MAX** **1**
The maximum number of bytes in a multibyte character, for any supported locale.

**#define SHRT_MIN** **-32767**
The minimum value for an object of type **short int**.

**#define SHRT_MAX** **+32767**
The maximum value for an object of type **short int**.

**#define USHRT_MAX** **65535**
The maximum value for an object of type **unsigned short int**.

**#define INT_MIN** **-32767**
The minimum value for an object of type **int**.

**#define INT_MAX** **+32767**
The maximum value for an object of type **int**.

**#define UINT_MAX** **65535**
The maximum value for an object of type **unsigned int**.

**#define LONG_MIN** **-2147483647**
The minimum value for an object of type **long int**.

**#define LONG_MAX** **+2147483647**
The maximum value for an object of type **long int**.

**#define ULONG_MAX** **4294967295**
The maximum value for an object of type **unsigned long int**.

## <float.h>

**#define FLT_ROUNDS**

The rounding mode for floating-point addition.

- `-1` indeterminable
- `0` toward zero
- `1` to nearest
- `2` toward positive infinity
- `3` toward negative infinity

The following shall be defined equal to or greater than in magnitude (absolute value) to the values below.

**#define FLT_RADIX** 2

The radix of exponent representation, *b*.

**#define FLT_MANT_DIG**
**#define LDBL_MANT_DIG**
**#define DBL_MANT_DIG**

The number of base-**FLT_RADIX** digits in the floating-point significand, *p*.

**#define FLT_DIG** 6
**#define DBL_DIG** 10
**#define LDBL_DIG** 10

The number of decimal digits, *q*, such that any floating-point number with *q* decimal digits can be rounded into a floating-point number with *p* radix *b* digits and back again without change to the *q* decimal digits.

**#define FLT_MIN_EXP**
**#define DBL_MIN_EXP**
**#define LDBL_MIN_EXP**

The minimum negative integer such that **FLT_RADIX** raised to that power minus 1 is a normalized floating-point number.

**#define FLT_MIN_10_EXP** -37
**#define DBL_MIN_10_EXP** -37
**#define LDBL_MIN_10_EXP** -37

The minimum negative integer such that 10 raised to that power is in the range of normalized floating point numbers.

**#define FLT_MAX_EXP**
**#define DBL_MAX_EXP**
**#define LDBL_MAX_EXP**

The maximum integer such that **FLT_RADIX** raised to that power minus 1 is a representable finite floating-point number.

**#define FLT_MAX_10_EXP** +37
**#define DBL_MAX_10_EXP** +37
**#define LDBL_MAX_10_EXP** +37

The maximum integer such that 10 raised to that power is in the range of representable finite floating point numbers.

The following shall be defined equal to or greater than the values shown below.

```
#define FLT_MAX                                        1E+37
#define DBL_MAX                                        1E+37
#define LDBL_MAX                                       1E+37
```

The maximum representable finite floating-point number.

The following shall be defined equal to or less than the values shown below.

```
#define FLT_EPSILON                                     1E-5
#define DBL_EPSILON                                     1E-9
#define LDBL_EPSILON                                    1E-9
```

The difference between 1.0 and the least value greater than 1.0 that is representable in the given floating point type.

```
#define FLT_MIN                                        1E-37
#define DBL_MIN                                        1E-37
#define LDBL_MIN                                       1E-37
```

The minimum normalized positive floating-point number.

# Appendix C

## *Operator Precedence Chart*

<table>
<tr><th>Operator</th><th>Associativity</th></tr>
<tr><td>:: (unary; right to left)    :: (binary; left to right)</td><td></td></tr>
<tr><td>( )   [ ]   ->   .</td><td>left to right</td></tr>
<tr><td>++   --   +   -   !   ~   (type)   *   &   sizeof</td><td>right to left</td></tr>
<tr><td>.*   ->*</td><td>left to right</td></tr>
<tr><td>*   /   %</td><td>left to right</td></tr>
<tr><td>+   -</td><td>left to right</td></tr>
<tr><td><<   >></td><td>left to right</td></tr>
<tr><td><   <=   >   >=</td><td>left to right</td></tr>
<tr><td>==   !=</td><td>left to right</td></tr>
<tr><td>&</td><td>left to right</td></tr>
<tr><td>^</td><td>left to right</td></tr>
<tr><td>|</td><td>left to right</td></tr>
<tr><td>&&</td><td>left to right</td></tr>
<tr><td>||</td><td>left to right</td></tr>
<tr><td>? :</td><td>right to left</td></tr>
<tr><td>=   +=   -=   *=   /=   %=   &=   ^=   |=   <<=   >>=</td><td>right to left</td></tr>
<tr><td>,</td><td>left to right</td></tr>
</table>

The operators are shown in decreasing order of precedence from top to bottom.

# Appendix D

## *ASCII Character Set*

| | **0** | **1** | **2** | **3** | **4** | **5** | **6** | **7** | **8** | **9** |
|---|---|---|---|---|---|---|---|---|---|---|
| **0** | nul | soh | stx | etx | eot | enq | ack | bel | bs | ht |
| **1** | nl | vt | ff | cr | so | si | dle | dc1 | dc2 | dc3 |
| **2** | dc4 | nak | syn | etb | can | em | sub | esc | fs | gs |
| **3** | rs | us | sp | ! | " | # | $ | % | & | ‘ |
| **4** | ( | ) | * | + | , | - | . | / | 0 | 1 |
| **5** | 2 | 3 | 4 | 5 | 6 | 7 | 8 | 9 | : | ; |
| **6** | < | = | > | ? | @ | A | B | C | D | E |
| **7** | F | G | H | I | J | K | L | M | N | O |
| **8** | P | Q | R | S | T | U | V | W | X | Y |
| **9** | Z | [ | \ | ] | ^ | _ | ’ | a | b | c |
| **10** | d | e | f | g | h | i | j | k | l | m |
| **11** | n | o | p | q | r | s | t | u | v | w |
| **12** | x | y | z | { | \| | } | ~ | del | | |

The digits at the left of the table are the left digits of the decimal equivalent (0-127) of the character code, and the digits at the top of the table are the right digits of the character code. For example, the character code for 'F' is 70, and the character code for '&' is 38.

# APPENDIX E

# Number Systems

## Objectives

- To understand basic number systems concepts such as base, positional value, and symbol value.
- To understand how to work with numbers represented in the binary, octal, and hexadecimal number systems.
- To be able to abbreviate binary numbers as octal numbers or hexadecimal numbers.
- To be able to convert octal numbers and hexadecimal numbers to binary numbers.
- To be able to convert back and forth between decimal numbers and their binary, octal, and hexadecimal equivalents.
- To understand binary arithmetic, and how negative binary numbers are represented using two's complement notation.

*Here are only numbers ratified.*
William Shakespeare

*Nature has some sort of arithmetic-geometrical coordinate system, because nature has all kinds of models. What we experience of nature is in models, and all of nature's models are so beautiful. It struck me that nature's system must be a real beauty, because in chemistry we find that the associations are always in beautiful whole numbers–there are no fractions.*
Richard Buckminster Fuller

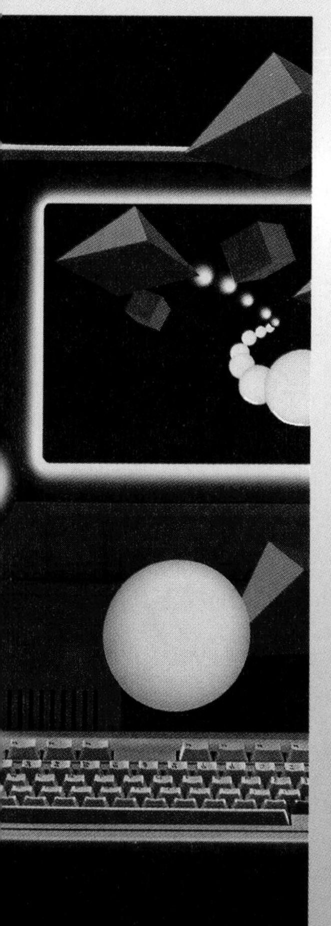

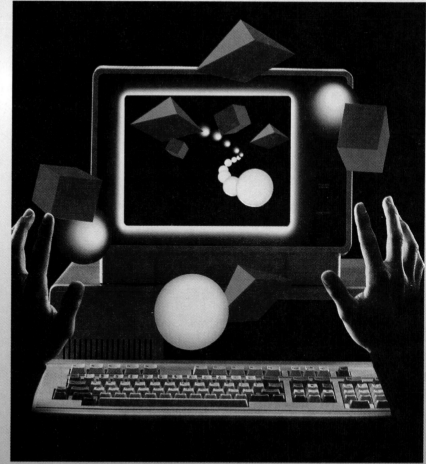

## Outline



## E.1 Introduction

In this appendix, we introduce the key number systems that C++ programmers use, especially when they are working on software projects that require close interaction with "machine-level" hardware. Projects like this include include operating systems, computer networking software, compilers, database systems, and applications requiring high performance.

When we write an integer such as 227 or -63 in a C++ program, the number is assumed to be in the *decimal (base 10) number system.* The *digits* in the decimal number system are 0, 1, 2, 3, 4, 5, 6, 7, 8, and 9. The lowest digit is 0 and the highest digit is 9—one less than the *base* of 10. Internally, computers use the *binary (base 2) number system.* The binary number system has only two digits, namely 0 and 1. Its lowest digit is 0 and its highest digit is 1—one less than the base of 2.

As we will see, binary numbers tend to be much longer than their decimal equivalents. Programmers who work in assembly languages and in high-level languages like C++ that enable programmers to reach down to the "machine level," find it cumbersome to work with binary numbers. So two other number systems the *octal number system (base 8)* and the *hexadecimal number system (base 16)*—are popular primarily because they make it convenient to abbreviate binary numbers.

In the octal number system, the digits range from 0 to 7. Because both the binary number system and the octal number system have fewer digits than the decimal number system, their digits are the same as the corresponding digits in decimal.

The hexadecimal number system poses a problem because it requires sixteen digits—a lowest digit of 0 and a highest digit with a value equivalent to decimal 15 (one less than the base of 16). By convention, we use the letters A through F to represent the hexadecimal digits corresponding to decimal values 10 through 15. Thus in hexadecimal we can have numbers like 876 consisting solely of decimal-like digits, numbers like 8A55F consisting of digits and letters, and numbers like FFE consisting solely of letters. Occasionally, a hexadecimal number spells a common word such as FACE or FEED—this can appear strange to programmers accustomed to working with numbers.

Each of these number systems uses *positional notation*—each position in which a digit is written has a different *positional value.* For example, in the decimal number 937 (the 9, the 3, and the 7 are referred to as *symbol values*), we say that the 7 is written in the *ones position,* the 3 is written in the *tens position,* and the 9 is written in the *hundreds position.* Notice that each of these positions is a power of the base (base 10), and that these powers begin at 0 and increase by 1 as we move left in the number (Fig. E.3).

| Binary digit | Octal digit | Decimal digit | Hexadecimal digit |
|---|---|---|---|
| 0 | 0 | 0 | 0 |
| 1 | 1 | 1 | 1 |
| | 2 | 2 | 2 |
| | 3 | 3 | 3 |
| | 4 | 4 | 4 |
| | 5 | 5 | 5 |
| | 6 | 6 | 6 |
| | 7 | 7 | 7 |
| | | 8 | 8 |
| | | 9 | 9 |
| | | | A (decimal value of 10) |
| | | | B (decimal value of 11) |
| | | | C (decimal value of 12) |
| | | | D (decimal value of 13) |
| | | | E (decimal value of 14) |
| | | | F (decimal value of 15) |

**Fig. E.1** Digits of the binary, octal, decimal, and hexadecimal number systems.

| Attribute | Binary | Octal | Decimal | Hexadecimal |
|---|---|---|---|---|
| Base | 2 | 8 | 10 | 16 |
| Lowest digit | 0 | 0 | 0 | 0 |
| Highest digit | 1 | 7 | 9 | F |

**Fig. E.2** Comparison of the binary, octal, decimal, and hexadecimal number systems.

| Positional values in the decimal number system | | | |
|---|---|---|---|
| Decimal digit | 9 | 3 | 7 |
| Position name | Hundreds | Tens | Ones |
| Positional value | 100 | 10 | 1 |
| Positional value as a power of the base (10) | $10^2$ | $10^1$ | $10^0$ |

**Fig. E.3** Positional values in the decimal number system.

For longer decimal numbers, the next positions to the left would be the *thousands position* (10 to the 3rd power), the *ten-thousands position* (10 to the 4th power), the *hundred-thousands position* (10 to the 5th power), the *millions position* (10 to the 6th power), the *ten-millions position* (10 to the 7th power), and so on.

In the binary number 101, we say that the rightmost 1 is written in the *ones position,* the 0 is written in the *twos position,* and the leftmost 1 is written in the *fours position.* Notice that each of these positions is a power of the base (base 2), and that these powers begin at 0 and increase by 1 as we move left in the number (Fig E.4).

For longer binary numbers, the next positions to the left would be the *eights position* (2 to the 3rd power), the *sixteens position* (2 to the 4th power), the *thirty-twos position* (2 to the 5th power), the *sixty-fours position* (2 to the 6th power), and so on.

In the octal number 425, we say that the 5 is written in the *ones position,* the 2 is written in the *eights position,* and the 4 is written in the *sixty-fours position.* Notice that each of these positions is a power of the base (base 8), and that these powers begin at 0 and increase by 1 as we move left in the number (Fig. E.5).

For longer octal numbers, the next positions to the left would be the *five-hundred-and-twelves position* (8 to the 3rd power), the *four-thousand-and-ninety-sixes position* (8 to the 4th power), the *thirty-two-thousand-seven-hundred-and-sixty eights position* (8 to the 5th power), and so on.

In the hexadecimal number 3DA, we say that the A is written in the *ones position,* the D is written in the *sixteens position,* and the 3 is written in the *two-hundred-and-fifty-sixes position.* Notice that each of these positions is a power of the base (base 16), and that these powers begin at 0 and increase by 1 as we move left in the number (Fig. E.6).

**Positional values in the binary number system**

| | | | |
|---|---|---|---|
| Binary digit | 1 | 0 | 1 |
| Position name | Fours | Twos | Ones |
| Positional value | 4 | 2 | 1 |
| Positional value as a power of the base (2) | $2^2$ | $2^1$ | $2^0$ |

**Fig. E.4** Positional values in the binary number system.

**Positional values in the octal number system**

| | | | |
|---|---|---|---|
| Decimal digit | 4 | 2 | 5 |
| Position name | Sixty-fours | Eights | Ones |
| Positional value | 64 | 8 | 1 |
| Positional value as a power of the base (8) | $8^2$ | $8^1$ | $8^0$ |

**Fig. E.5** Positional values in the octal number system.

| Positional values in the hexadecimal number system | | | |
|---|---|---|---|
| Decimal digit | 3 | D | A |
| Position name | Two-hundred-and-fifty-sixes | Sixteens | Ones |
| Positional value | 256 | 16 | 1 |
| Positional value as a power of the base (16) | $16^2$ | $16^1$ | $16^0$ |

**Fig. E.6** Positional values in the hexadecimal number system.

For longer hexadecimal numbers, the next positions to the left would be the *four-thousand-and-ninety-sixes position* (16 to the 3rd power), the *thirty-two-thousand-seven-hundred-and-sixty-eights position* (16 to the 4th power), and so on.

## E.2 Abbreviating Binary Numbers as Octal Numbers and Hexadecimal Numbers

The main use for octal and hexadecimal numbers in computing is for abbreviating lengthy binary representations. Figure E.7 highlights the fact that lengthy binary numbers can be expressed concisely in number systems with higher bases than the binary number system.

| Decimal Number | Binary representation | Octal representation | Hexadecimal representation |
|---|---|---|---|
| 0 | 0 | 0 | 0 |
| 1 | 1 | 1 | 1 |
| 2 | 10 | 2 | 2 |
| 3 | 11 | 3 | 3 |
| 4 | 100 | 4 | 4 |
| 5 | 101 | 5 | 5 |
| 6 | 110 | 6 | 6 |
| 7 | 111 | 7 | 7 |
| 8 | 1000 | 10 | 8 |
| 9 | 1001 | 11 | 9 |
| 10 | 1010 | 12 | A |
| 11 | 1011 | 13 | B |
| 12 | 1100 | 14 | C |
| 13 | 1101 | 15 | D |
| 14 | 1110 | 16 | E |
| 15 | 1111 | 17 | F |
| 16 | 10000 | 20 | 10 |

**Fig. E.7** Decimal, binary, octal, and hexadecimal equivalents.

A particularly important relationship that both the octal number system and the hexadecimal number system have to the binary system is that the bases of octal and hexadecimal (8 and 16 respectively) are powers of the base of the binary number system (base 2). Consider the following 12-digit binary number and its octal and hexadecimal equivalents. See if you can determine how this relationship makes it convenient to abbreviate binary numbers in octal or hexadecimal. The answer follows the numbers.

```
Binary Number      Octal equivalent    Hexadecimal equivalent
100011010001       4321                8D1
```

To see how the binary number converts easily to octal, simply break the 12-digit binary number into groups of three consecutive bits each, and write those groups over the corresponding digits of the octal number as follows

```
100    011    010    001
4      3      2      1
```

Notice that the octal digit you have written under each group of thee bits corresponds precisely to the octal equivalent of that 3-digit binary number as shown in Fig. E.7.

The same kind of relationship may be observed in converting numbers from binary to hexadecimal. In particular, break the 12-digit binary number into groups of four consecutive bits each and write those groups over the corresponding digits of the hexadecimal number as follows

```
1000   1101   0001
8      D      1
```

Notice that the hexadecimal digit you have written under each group of four bits corresponds precisely to the hexadecimal equivalent of that 4-digit binary number as shown in Fig. E.7.

## E.3 Converting Octal Numbers and Hexadecimal Numbers to Binary Numbers

In the previous section, we saw how to convert binary numbers to their octal and hexadecimal equivalents by forming groups of binary digits and simply rewriting these groups as their equivalent octal digit values or hexadecimal digit values. This process may be used in reverse to produce the binary equivalent of a given octal or hexadecimal number.

For example, the octal number 653 is converted to binary simply by writing the 6 as its 3-digit binary equivalent 110, the 5 as its 3-digit binary equivalent 101, and the 3 as its 3-digit binary equivalent 011 to form the 9-digit binary number 110101011.

The hexadecimal number FAD5 is converted to binary simply by writing the F as its 4-digit binary equivalent 1111, the A as its 4-digit binary equivalent 1010, the D as its 4-digit binary equivalent 1101, and the 5 as its 4-digit binary equivalent 0101 to form the 16-digit 1111101011010101.

## E.4 Converting from Binary, Octal, or Hexadecimal to Decimal

Because we are accustomed to working in decimal, it is often convenient to convert a binary, octal, or hexadecimal number to decimal to get a sense of what the number is "really" worth. Our diagrams in Section E.1 express the positional values in decimal. To convert a number to decimal from another base, multiply the decimal equivalent of each digit by its positional value, and sum these products. For example, the binary number 110101 is converted to decimal 53 as shown in Fig. E.8.

| Converting a binary number to decimal | | | | | | |
|---|---|---|---|---|---|---|
| Positional values: | 32 | 16 | 8 | 4 | 2 | 1 |
| Symbol values: | 1 | 1 | 0 | 1 | 0 | 1 |
| Products: | 1*32=32 | 1*16=16 | 0*8=0 | 1*4=4 | 0*2=0 | 1*1=1 |
| Sum: | = 32 + 16 + 0 + 4 + 0 + 1 = 53 | | | | | |

**Fig. E.8** Converting a binary number to decimal.

To convert octal 7614 to decimal 3980, we use the same technique, this time using appropriate octal positional values as shown in Fig. E.9.

To convert hexadecimal AD3B to decimal 44347, we use the same technique, this time using appropriate hexadecimal positional values as shown in Fig. E.10.

## E.5 Converting from Decimal to Binary, Octal, or Hexadecimal

The conversions of the previous section follow naturally from the conventions of positional notation. Converting from decimal to binary, octal, or hexadecimal also follows these conventions.

Suppose we wish to convert decimal 57 to binary. We begin by writing the positional values of the columns right to left until we reach a column whose positional value is greater than the decimal number. We do not need that column, so we discard it. Thus, we first write:

| Converting an octal number to decimal | | | | |
|---|---|---|---|---|
| Positional values: | 512 | 64 | 8 | 1 |
| Symbol values: | 7 | 6 | 1 | 4 |
| Products | 7*512=3584 | 6*64=384 | 1*8=8 | 4*1=4 |
| Sum: | = 3584 + 384 + 8 + 4 = 3980 | | | |

**Fig. E.9** Converting an octal number to decimal.

| Converting a hexadecimal number to decimal | | | | |
|---|---|---|---|---|
| Positional values: | 4096 | 256 | 16 | 1 |
| Symbol values: | A | D | 3 | B |
| Products | A*4096=40960 | D*256=3328 | 3*16=48 | B*1=11 |
| Sum: | = 40960 + 3328 + 48 + 11 = 44347 | | | |

**Fig. E.10** Converting a hexadecimal number to decimal.

| | | | | | | | |
|---|---|---|---|---|---|---|---|
| Positional values: | 64 | 32 | 16 | 8 | 4 | 2 | 1 |

Then we discard the column with positional value 64 leaving:

| | | | | | | |
|---|---|---|---|---|---|---|
| Positional values: | 32 | 16 | 8 | 4 | 2 | 1 |

Next we work from the leftmost column to the right. We divide 32 into 57 and observe that there is one 32 in 57 with a remainder of 25, so we write 1 in the 32 column. We divide 16 into 25 and observe that there is one 16 in 25 with a remainder of 9 and write 1 in the 16 column. We divide 8 into 9 and observe that there is one 8 in 9 with a remainder of 1. The next two columns each produce quotients of zero when their positional values are divided into 1 so we write 0s in the 4 and 2 columns. Finally, 1 into 1 is 1 so we write 1 in the 1 column. This yields:

| | | | | | | |
|---|---|---|---|---|---|---|
| Positional values: | 32 | 16 | 8 | 4 | 2 | 1 |
| Symbol values: | 1 | 1 | 1 | 0 | 0 | 1 |

and thus decimal 57 is equivalent to binary 111001.

To convert decimal 103 to octal, we begin by writing the positional values of the columns until we reach a column whose positional value is greater than the decimal number. We do not need that column, so we discard it. Thus, we first write:

| | | | | |
|---|---|---|---|---|
| Positional values: | 512 | 64 | 8 | 1 |

Then we discard the column with positional value 512, yielding:

| | | | |
|---|---|---|---|
| Positional values: | 64 | 8 | 1 |

Next we work from the leftmost column to the right. We divide 64 into 103 and observe that there is one 64 in 103 with a remainder of 39, so we write 1 in the 64 column. We divide 8 into 39 and observe that there are four 8s in 39 with a remainder of 7 and write 4 in the 8 column. Finally, we divide 1 into 7 and observe that there are seven 1s in 7 with no remainder so we write 7 in the 1 column. This yields:

| | | | |
|---|---|---|---|
| Positional values: | 64 | 8 | 1 |
| Symbol values: | 1 | 4 | 7 |

and thus decimal 103 is equivalent to octal 147.

To convert decimal 375 to hexadecimal, we begin by writing the positional values of the columns until we reach a column whose positional value is greater than the decimal number. We do not need that column, so we discard it. Thus, we first write

| | | | | |
|---|---|---|---|---|
| Positional values: | 4096 | 256 | 16 | 1 |

Then we discard the column with positional value 4096, yielding:

| | | | |
|---|---|---|---|
| Positional values: | 256 | 16 | 1 |

Next we work from the leftmost column to the right. We divide 256 into 375 and observe that there is one 256 in 375 with a remainder of 119, so we write 1 in the 256 column. We divide 16 into 119 and observe that there are seven 16s in 119 with a remainder of 7 and write 7 in the 16 column. Finally, we divide 1 into 7 and observe that there are seven 1s in 7 with no remainder so we write 7 in the 1 column. This yields:

| | | | |
|---|---|---|---|
| Positional values: | 256 | 16 | 1 |
| Symbol values: | 1 | 7 | 7 |

and thus decimal 375 is equivalent to hexadecimal 177.

## E.6 Negative Binary Numbers: Two's Complement Notation

The discussion in this appendix has been focussed on positive numbers. In this section, we explain how computers represent negative numbers using *two's complement notation.* First we explain how the two's complement of a binary number is formed, and then we show why it represents the negative value of the given binary number.

Consider a machine with 32-bit integers. Suppose

```
int value = 13;
```

The 32-bit representation of **value** is

```
00000000 00000000 00000000 00001101
```

To form the negative of **value** we first form its *one's complement* by applying C++'s bitwise complement operator (~):

```
ones_complement_of_value = ~value;
```

Internally, **~value** is now **value** with each of its bits reversed—ones become zeros and zeros become ones as follows:

```
value:
00000000 00000000 00000000 00001101

~value (i.e., value's ones complement):
11111111 11111111 11111111 11110010
```

To form the two's complement of **value** we simply add one to **value**'s one's complement. Thus

```
Two's complement of value:
11111111 11111111 11111111 11110011
```

Now if this is in fact equal to -13, we should be able to add it to binary 13 and obtain a result of 0. Let us try this:

```
 00000000 00000000 00000000 00001101
+11111111 11111111 11111111 11110011
------------------------------------
 00000000 00000000 00000000 00000000
```

The carry bit coming out of the leftmost column is discarded and we indeed get zero as a result. If we add the one's complement of a number to the number, the result would be all 1s. The key to getting a result of all zeros is that the twos complement is 1 more than the one's complement. The addition of 1 causes each column to add to 0 with a carry of 1. The carry keeps moving leftward until it is discarded from the leftmost bit, and hence the resulting number is all zeros.

Computers actually perform a subtraction such as

```
x = a - value;
```

by adding the two's complement of **value** to **a** as follows:

```
x = a + (~value + 1);
```

Suppose **a** is 27 and **value** is 13 as before. If the two's complement of **value** is actually the negative of **value**, then adding the two's complement of **value** to **a** should produce the result 14. Let us try this:

```
a (i.e., 27)          00000000 00000000 00000000 00011011
+(~value + 1)        +11111111 11111111 11111111 11110011
                     ------------------------------------
                      00000000 00000000 00000000 00001110
```

which is indeed equal to 14.

## Summary

- When we write an integer such as 19 or 227 or -63 in a C++ program, the number is automatically assumed to be in the decimal (base 10) number system. The digits in the decimal number system are 0, 1, 2, 3, 4, 5, 6, 7, 8, and 9. The lowest digit is 0 and the highest digit is 9—one less than the base of 10.
- Internally, computers use the binary (base 2) number system. The binary number system has only two digits, namely 0 and 1. Its lowest digit is 0 and its highest digit is 1—one less than the base of 2.
- The octal number system (base 8) and the hexadecimal number system (base 16) have become popular primarily because they make it convenient to abbreviate binary numbers.
- The digits of the octal number system range from 0 to 7.
- The hexadecimal number system poses a problem because it requires sixteen digits—a lowest digit of 0 and a highest digit with a value equivalent to decimal 15 (one less than the base of 16). By convention, we use the letters A through F to represent the hexadecimal digits corresponding to decimal values 10 through 15.
- Each number system uses positional notation—each position in which a digit is written has a different positional value.
- A particularly important relationship that both the octal number system and the hexadecimal number system have to the binary system is that the bases of octal and hexadecimal (8 and 16 respectively) are powers of the base of the binary number system (base 2).
- To convert an octal number to a binary number, simply replace each octal digit with its three-digit binary equivalent.
- To convert a hexadecimal number to a binary number, simply replace each hexadecimal digit with its four-digit binary equivalent.
- Because we are accustomed to working in decimal, it is often convenient to convert a binary, octal, or hexadecimal number to decimal to get a better sense of what the number is "really" worth.
- To convert a number to decimal from another base, multiply the decimal equivalent of each digit by its positional value, and sum these products.

- Computers represent negative numbers using two's complement notation.
- To form the negative of a value in binary, first form its one's complement by applying C++'s bitwise complement operator (~). This reverses the bits of the value. To form the two's complement of a value, simply add one to the value's one's complement.

## Terminology

base
base 2 number system
base 8 number system
base 10 number system
base 16 number system
binary number system
bitwise complement operator (~)
conversions
decimal number system
digit
hexadecimal number system
negative value
octal number system
one's complement notation
positional notation
positional value
symbol value
two's complement notation

## Self-Review Exercises

**E.1** The bases of the decimal, binary, octal, and hexadecimal number systems are ________, ________, ________, and ________ respectively.

**E.2** In general, the decimal, octal, and hexadecimal representations of a given binary number contain (more/fewer) digits than the binary number contains.

**E.3** (True/False) A popular reason for using the decimal number system is that it forms a convenient notation for abbreviating binary numbers simply by substituting one decimal digit per group of four binary bits.

**E.4** The (octal / hexadecimal / decimal) representation of a very large binary value is the most concise (of the given alternatives).

**E.5** (True/False) The highest digit in any base is one more than the base.

**E.6** (True/False) The lowest digit in any base is one less than the base.

**E.7** The positional value of the rightmost digit of any number in either binary, octal, decimal, or hexadecimal is always ________.

**E.8** The positional value of the digit to the left of the rightmost digit of any number in binary, octal, decimal, or hexadecimal is always equal to ________.

**E.9** Fill in the missing values in this chart of positional values for the rightmost four positions in each of the indicated number systems:

| | | | | |
|---|---|---|---|---|
| decimal | `1000` | `100` | `10` | `1` |
| hexadecimal | `...` | `256` | `...` | `...` |
| binary | `...` | `...` | `...` | `...` |
| octal | `512` | `...` | `8` | `...` |

**E.10** Convert binary `110101011000` to octal and to hexadecimal.

**E.11** Convert hexadecimal `FACE` to binary.

**E.12** Convert octal `7316` to binary.

**E.13** Convert hexadecimal **4FEC** to octal. (Hint: First convert **4FEC** to binary then convert that binary number to octal.)

**E.14** Convert binary 1101110 to decimal.

**E.15** Convert octal 317 to decimal.

**E.16** Convert hexadecimal **EFD4** to decimal.

**E.17** Convert decimal 177 to binary, to octal, and to hexadecimal.

**E.18** Show the binary representation of decimal **417**. Then show the one's complement of **417**, and the two's complement of **417**.

**E.19** What is the result when the one's complement of a number is added to itself?

## *Self-Review Answers*

**E.1** 10, 2, 8, 16.

**E.2** Fewer.

**E.3** False.

**E.4** Hexadecimal.

**E.5** False—The highest digit in any base is one less than the base.

**E.6** False— The lowest digit in any base is zero.

**E.7** 1 (the base raised to the zero power).

**E.8** The base of the number system.

**E.9** Fill in the missing values in this chart of positional values for the rightmost four positions in each of the indicated number systems:

| | | | | |
|---|---|---|---|---|
| decimal | 1000 | 100 | 10 | 1 |
| hexadecimal | 4096 | 256 | 16 | 1 |
| binary | 8 | 4 | 2 | 1 |
| octal | 512 | 64 | 8 | 1 |

**E.10** Octal 6530; Hexadecimal D58.

**E.11** Binary 1111 1010 1100 1110.

**E.12** Binary 111 011 001 110

**E.13** Binary 0 100 111 111 101 100; Octal 47754 .

**E.14** Decimal 2+4+8+32+64=110.

**E.15** Decimal 7+1*8+3*64=7+8+192=207.

**E.16** Decimal 4+13*16+15*256+14*4096=61396.

**E.17** Decimal 177

to binary:

```
256 128 64 32 16 8 4 2 1
128 64 32 16 8 4 2 1
(1*128)+(0*64)+(1*32)+(1*16)+(0*8)+(0*4)+(0*2)+(1*1)
10110001
```

to octal:

```
512 64 8 1
64 8 1
(2*64)+(6*8)+(1*1)
261
```

to hexadecimal:

```
256 16 1
16 1
(11*16)+(1*1)
(B*16)+(1*1)
B1
```

**E.18** Binary:

```
512 256 128 64 32 16 8 4 2 1
256 128 64 32 16 8 4 2 1
(1*256)+(1*128)+(0*64)+(1*32)+(0*16)+(0*8)+(0*4)+(0*2)+
(1*1)
110100001
```

One's complement: `001011110`
Two's complement: `001011111`
Check: Original binary number + its two's complement

```
110100001
001011111
---------
000000000
```

**E.19** Zero.

## Exercises

**E.20** Some people argue that many of our calculations would be easier in the base `12` number system because `12` is divisible by so many more numbers than `10` (for base `10`). What is the lowest digit in base `12`? What might the highest symbol for the digit in base `12` be? What are the positional values of the rightmost four positions of any number in the base `12` number system?

**E.21** How is the highest symbol value in the number systems we discussed related to the positional value of the first digit to the left of the rightmost digit of any number in these number systems?

**E.22** Complete the following chart of positional values for the rightmost four positions in each of the indicated number systems:

| | | | | |
|---|---|---|---|---|
| decimal | 1000 | 100 | 10 | 1 |
| base 6 | ... | ... | 6 | ... |
| base 13 | ... | 169 | ... | ... |
| base 3 | 27 | ... | ... | ... |

**E.23** Convert binary **100101111010** to octal and to hexadecimal.

**E.24** Convert hexadecimal **3A7D** to binary.

**E.25** Convert hexadecimal **765F** to octal. (Hint: First convert **765F** to binary, then convert that binary number to octal.)

**E.26** Convert binary **1011110** to decimal.

**E.27** Convert octal **426** to decimal.

**E.28** Convert hexadecimal **FFFF** to decimal.

**E.29** Convert decimal **299** to binary, to octal, and to hexadecimal.

**E.30** Show the binary representation of decimal **779**. Then show the one's complement of **779**, and the two's complement of **779**.

**E.31** What is the result when the two's complement of a number is added to itself?

**E.32** Show the two's complement of integer value **-1** on a machine with 32-bit integers.

# Appendix F
## *C++ and OOP Resources*

**Apple Programmers and Developers Association**
290 Southwest 43rd Street
Renton, WA 98055
Tel: 206-251-6548

**AT&T C++ Language System**
AT&T Computer Systems
225 Littleton Road
Morris Plains, NJ 07950
Tel: 800-922-4787

**Borland C++**
**Borland ObjectVision**
Borland International, Inc.
1800 Green Hills Road
Scotts Valley, CA 95067
Tel: (800) 331-0877
Tel: (408) 438-8400
Fax: (408) 439-8088

***C Users Journal***
R & D Publications, Inc.
1601 W. 23rd Street, Suite 200
Lawrence, Kansas 66046
Tel: (913) 841-1631

***C++ Journal***
2 Haven Avenue
Port Washington, NY 11050-9768
Tel: (516) 767-7107

***C++ Report***
588 Broadway, Suite 604
New York, NY 10012
Tel: 212-274-0640
Fax: 212-274-0646

**Centerline**
(Formerly Saber Software)
10 Fawcett Street
Cambridge, MA 02138-1110
Tel: 617-498-3000
Fax: 617-868-6655
Publications:

*Key Requirements for Evaluating C++ Programming Environments*

*Moving From C to C++: A Real World Approach*

*The Easiest Way to Build GUIs in C++*

**Digitalk**
9841 Airport Blvd
Los Angeles, CA 90045
Tel: 310-645-1082
Tel: 800-922-8255
Fax: 310-645-1306

**Eiffel**
Interactive Software Engineering Inc.
270 Storke Road, Suite 7
Goleta, CA 94043
Tel: 805-685-1006

**Glockenspeil C++**
Glockenspeil Ltd.
39 Lower Dominick Street
Dublin 1, Ireland
Tel: +353-1-733166
Fax: 353 (1) 733034

**Hewlett Packard**
5301 Stevens Creek Blvd.
P.O. Box 58059, MS 51LSG
Santa Clara, CA 95052-8059
Tel: 800-637-7740
C++ SoftBench
800-752-0900, Ext. 2703

**Hotline on Object-Oriented Technology**
Subscriber Services
P. O. Box 3000
Denville, New Jersey 07834
212-274-0640

**IBM Corp.**
Old Orchard Road
Armonk, NY 10504
Tel: 914-765-1900

**ImageSoft**
1-800-245-8840
2 Haven Avenue
Port Washington, New York 11050
Fax: 516-767-9067
Tel: 516-767-2233

**Intel Corp.**
3065 Bowers Ave.
Santa Clara, CA 95052
Tel: 800-538-3373

**Interactive Development Environments**
595 Market Street
San Franciso, CA 94105
Tel: 415-543-0900
Fax: 415-543-0145

**Journal of Object-Oriented Programming**
588 Broadway, Suite 604
New York, New York 10012
212-274-0640

**Liant Software Corporation**
959 Concord Street
Framingham, MA 01701
Tel: 508-872-8700
Fax: 508-626-2221

**Micro Focus**
Object COBOL
(ANSI is developing draft standard)
Palo Alto, CA
800-872-6265

**Microsoft C/C++ 7.0**
Microsoft Corp.
1 Microsoft Way
Redmond, WA 98052
Tel: 206-882-8080-
In USA: 800-426-9400
Outside US and Canada: 206-936-8661
Canada: 800-563-9048
Fax: 206-883-8101

**Oasys**
One Cranberry Hill
Lexington, MA 02173
Tel: 617-862-2002
Fax: 617 863-2633

**Objectcenter**
(Integrated C++ development environment)
CenterLine Software, Inc.
(formerly Saber Software)
10 Fawcett Street, Cambridge, MA 02138
Tel: 617-498-3000

**Object Cobol**
Micro Focus
Palo Alto, CA
800-872-6265

**Object Design**
One New England Executive Park
Burlington, MA 01803
Tel: 617-270-9797
Fax: 617-270-3509

**Object Expo**
Conference presented by:
Object Expo
588 Broadway, Suite 604
New York, NY 10012

**Object Magazine**
155 E 31st Street, Suite 225
New York, NY 10016
Fax: 212-274-0646
Subscriber Services
Dept. OBJ
P. O. Box 3000
Denville, New Jersey 07834

**Object Management Group**
492 Old Connecticut Path
Framingham, MA 01701
508-820-4300
Fax: 508-820-4303
3823 Birchwood Drive
Boulder, CO 80304
Tel: 303-444-8129
Fax: 303-444-8172

**Object View**
MAT SYS Corp., N.A.
900 Larkspur Landing Circle, Suite 175
Larkspur, CA 94939
Tel: 415-925-2900

**Object World Conference**
Presented by: Object World
P.O. Box 9107
111 Speen Street
Framingham, MA 01701

**ObjectCraft**
2124 Kittredge Street, Suite 118
Berkeley, CA 94704
415-540-4889

**Objective C**
Stepstone Corp.
75 Glen Road
Sandy Hook, CT 06482
Tel: 203-426-1875

**Objectivity, Inc.**
800 El Camino Real
Menlo Park, CA 94025
Tel: 415-688-8000
Email: info@objy.com

**Objectworks**
(SmallTalk and C development environment)
ParcPlace Systems Inc.
1550 Plymouth Street
Mountain View, CA 94043
Tel: 415-691-6700

**Oregon Software**
7352 S.W. Durham Road
Portland, OR 97224
800-874-8501
503-624-6883

**ParcPlace Systems**
1550 Plymouth Street
Mountain View, CA 94043
Tel: 415-691-6700

**Rational**
(C++ Booch Components)
3320 Scott Blvd.
Santa Clara, CA 95054-3197
408-496-3700

**Saber Software, Inc.**
(now CenterLine Software)
185 Alewife Brook Parkway
Cambridge, MA 02138
617-876-7636

**Simula**
Simula
Simula a.s.
Postboks 4403 Torshov
N-0402 Oslo, Norway
473 720530

**Smalltalk Report**
SIGS Publications Group
588 Broadway, Suite 604
New York, NY 10012
212-274-0640

**Smalltalk/V**
Digitalk
9841 Airport Blvd
Los Angeles, CA 90045
Tel: 310-645-1082
Tel: 800-922-8255

**SPARCworks Professional C++**
Sun Microsystems Inc.
2550 Garcia Avenue
Mountain View, CA 94043
Tel: 415-960-1300

**Stepstone Corp.**
75 Glenn Road
Sandy Hook, CT 06482
Tel: 203-426-1875

**Symantec Corp.**
10201 Torre Ave.
Cupertino, CA 95014-2132
(Zortech C++)
Tel: 408-253-9600
In Canada: 800-465-2266
In Europe: 31-71-353111
In Australia: 612-879-6577

**Versant Object Technology**
4500 Bohannon Drive
Menlo Park, CA 94025
1-800-9-OBJECT
415-325-2300

**Zortech Inc.**
Zortech C++
4-C Gill Street
Woburn, MA 01801
800-848-8408
617-937-0696

# Bibliography

(Ak93) Akerbaek, T., "C++, Coroutines, and Simulation," *The C Users Journal,* March 1993, 99. 74–86.

(Al93) Allison, C., "Code Capsules: A C++ Date Class, Part 1," *The C Users Journal,* Vol. 11, No. 2, February 1993, pp. 123–131.

(An90) ANSI, *American National Standard for Information Systems—Programming Language C (ANSI Document ANSI/ISO 9899: 1990),* New York, NY: American National Standards Institute, 1990.

(An94) American National Standard, Programming Language C++. [Approval and technical development work is being conducted by Accredited Standards Committee X3, Information Technology and its Technical Committee X3J16, Programming Language C++, respectively. For further details, contact X3 Secretariat, 1250 Eye Street, NW, Washington, DC 20005.]

(An92) Anderson, A.E., and W.J. Heinze, *C++ Programming and Fundamental Concepts,* Englewood Cliffs, NJ: Prentice-Hall, 1992.

(An88) Anderson, K. J.; R. P. Beck; and T. E. Buonanno, "Reuse of Software Modules," *AT&T Technical Journal,* Vol. 67, No. 4, July/August 1988, pp. 71–76.

(Ar92) Aranow, E., "Object Technology Means Object-Oriented Thinking," Vol. 12, No. 3, *Software Magazine,* March 1992, pp. 41–48.

(Ba93) Bar-David, T., *Object-Oriented Design for C++,* Englewood Cliffs, NJ: Prentice-Hall, 1993.

(Be91) Beck, B., "Shared-Memory Parallel Programming in C++," *IEEE Software,* Vol. 7, No. 4, July 1991, pp. 38–48.

(Be93) Becker, P., "Shrinking the Big Switch Statement," *Windows Tech Journal,* Vol. 2, No. 5, May 1993, pp. 26–33.

(Be93a) Berard, E. V., Essays on Object-Oriented Software Engineering: Volume I, Englewood Cliffs, NJ: Prentice-Hall, 1993.

(Bi92) Bilow, S. C., "X Application Development with C++ and InterViews—Part I," *The X Journal,* November/December 1992, pp. 36–41.

(Bl91) Bloom, E. P., *The Turbo C++ Trilogy,* Blue Ridge Summit, PA: Windcrest, 1991.

(Bl92) Blum, A., *Neural Networks in C++: An Object-Oriented Framework for Building Connectionist Systems,* New York, NY: John Wiley & Sons, 1992.

(Bo91) Booch, G., *Object-Oriented Design with Applications,* Redwood City, CA: The Benjamin/Cummings Publishing Company, Inc., 1991.

(Bo91a) Booch, G., "Using the Booch OOD Notation," *Object Magazine,* Vol. 1, No. 2, July/August 1991, pp. 76–84.

(Br91) Borland, *Borland C++ Programmer's Guide,* Part No. 14MN-TCP04, Scotts Valley, CA: Borland International, Inc., 1991.

(Br91a) Borland, *Borland C++ Getting Started,* Part No. 14MN-TCP02, Scotts Valley, CA: Borland International, Inc., 1991.

(Br91b) Borland, *Borland C++ 3.0 Programmers Guide,* Scotts Valley, CA: Borland International, Inc., 1991.

(Bl91) Borland International, *Borland C++ Version 3: Library Reference,* Scotts Valley, CA: Borland International, Inc., 1991.

(Bl91a) Borland International, *The World of C++: The Fastest Way to Become a C++ Programmer,* Scotts Valley, CA: Borland International, Inc., 1991.

(Bo91) Bowles, A., (moderator), "Evolution vs. Revolution: Should Structured Methods be Objectified?" *Object Magazine,* Vol. 1, No. 4, November/December 1991, pp. 30–41.

(Br93) Brumbaugh, D., Object-Oriented Development: Building CASE Tools with C++, John Wiley & Sons, 1993.

(Bu87) Budd, T., *A Little Smalltalk,* Reading, MA: Addison-Wesley, 1987.

(Bu91) Budd, T., *An Introduction to Object-Oriented Programming*, Reading, MA: Addison-Wesley, 1991.

(Ch91) Chin, R. S., and S. T. Chanson, "Distributed Object-Based Programming Systems," *ACM Computing Surveys,* Vol. 23, No. 1, March 1991, pp. 91–124.

(Co91) Coad, P., and E. Yourdon, *Object-Oriented Analysis,* Second Edition, Englewood Cliffs, NJ: Yourdon Press, 1991.

(Co91a) Coad, P., and E. Yourdon, *Object-Oriented Design,* Englewood Cliffs, NJ: Yourdon Press, 1991.

(Co93) Colborn, K., "OOP Should Be Your Object," *Datamation,* May 1, 1993, p. 102.

(Co93a) Computerworld, "The CW Guide to Object-Oriented Programming," *Computerworld,* June 14, 1993, pp. 107–130.

(Co91b) Connell, J. L.; L. Shafer; and D. M. Gursky, "Object-Oriented Rapid Prototyping," *Embedded Systems,* Vol. 4, No. 9, September 1991, pp. 24–33.

(Co91c) Cox, B. J., and A. J. Novobilski, *Object-Oriented Programming: An Evolutionary Approach,* Reading, MA: Addison-Wesley, 1991.

(Co91d) Cox, B. J., and A. Novobilski, *Object-Oriented Programming,* Second Edition, Reading, MA: Addison-Wesley, 1991.

(Cu93) Custer, H., *Inside Windows NT,* Redmond, WA: Microsoft Press, 1993.

(Da93) Davis, J., and T. Morgan, "Object-Oriented Development at Brooklyn Union Gas," *IEEE Software Magazine,* Vol. 10, No. 1, January 1993, pp. 67–74.

(De90) Deitel, H. M., *Operating Systems,* Second Edition, Reading, MA: Addison-Wesley, 1990.

(De94) Deitel, H. M., and P. J. Deitel, *C How to Program (Second Edition),* Englewood Cliffs, NJ: Prentice-Hall, 1994.

(De91) Deutsch, L. P., and A. Goldberg, "Smalltalk Yesterday, Today, and Tomorrow," Vol. 16, No. 8, *BYTE,* August 1991, pp. 108–115.

(De89) Dewhurst, S. C., and K. T. Stark, *Programming in C++,* Englewood Cliffs, NJ: Prentice-Hall, 1989.

(Du90) Duncan, R., "Managing the Complexity of the GUI Environment: The Promise of OOPLs," Vol. 9, No. 20, *PC Magazine,* November 27, 1990, pp. 475–478.

(Du90a) Duncan, R., "Redefining the Programming Paradigm: The Move Toward OOPLs," Vol. 9, No. 19, *PC Magazine,* November 13, 1990, pp. 526–529.

(Du91) Duncan, R., "Inside C++: Friend and Virtual Functions, and Multiple Inheritance," Vol. 10, No. 17, *PC Magazine,* October 15, 1991, pp. 417–420.

(Du91a) Duncan, R., "Containers and Objects: Object Linking and Embedding in Windows," Vol. 10, No. 10, *PC Magazine,* May 28, 1991, pp. 379–384.

(Dy89) Dyke, R. P. T., and J. C. Kunz, "Object-Oriented Programming," *IBM Systems Journal,* Vol. 28, No. 3, 1989, pp. 465–478.

(Eg92) Ege, R. K., *Programming in an Object-Oriented Environment,* San Diego, CA: Academic Press, Inc., 1992.

(El90) Ellis, M.A. and B. Stroustrup, *The Annotated C++ Reference Manual,* Reading, MA: Addison-Wesley, 1990.

(Em92) Embley, D. W.; B. D. Kurtz; and S. N. Woodfield, *Object-Oriented Systems Analysis,* Englewood Cliffs, NJ: Yourdon Press, 1992.

(En90) Entsminger, G., *The Tao of Objects: A Beginner's Guide to Object-Oriented Programming,* Redwood City, CA: M&T Books, 1990.

(Ew93) Ewald, A., and M. Roy, "Why OT is Good for System Integration," *Object Magazine,* Vol. 2, No. 5, January/February 1993, pp. 60–63.

(Fa92) Faison, T., *Borland C++ 3 Object-Oriented Programming,* Carmel, IN: SAMS, 1992.

(Fa92a) Farrow, R., "Object-Oriented Network Management," *UNIXWorld,* November 1992, pp. 93–96.

(Fl93) Flamig, B., *Practical Data Structures in C++,* John Wiley & Sons, 1993.

(Fo90) Ford, W. R., "Object-Oriented Programming: Will it Work for Real-Time Systems?" Vol. 29, No. 5, *Computer Design,* March 1, 1990, pp. 44–46.

(Ge89) Gehani, N., and W. D. Roome, *The Concurrent C Programming Language,* Summit, NJ: Silicon Press, 1989.

(Gi92) Giancola, A., and L. Baker, "Bit Arrays with C++," Vol. 10, No. 7, The C Users Journal, July 1992, pp. 21–26.

(Go83) Goldberg, A., and D. Robson, *Smalltalk-80: The Language and its Implementation,* Reading, MA: Addison-Wesley, 1983.

(Go92) Gopinath, P.; T. Bihari; and R. Gupta, "Compiler Support for Object-Oriented Real-Time Software," Vol. 9, No. 5, *IEEE Software,* September 1992, pp. 45–50.

(Go93) Gordon, E., and D. Kara, "CASE for C and C++," *CASE Trends,* Vol. 5, No. 1, February 1993, pp. 8–12, 68.

(Gr93) Grimshaw, A. S., "Easy-to-Use Object-Oriented Parallel Processing with Mentat," *IEEE Computer Magazine,* May 1993, pp. 39–51.

(Gu93) Guttman, M., and J. A. King, "A Methodology for Developing Distributed Applications," *Object Magazine,* Vol. 2, No. 5, January/February 1993, pp. 54–59.

(Ha93) Hagan, T., "C++ Class Libraries for GUIs," *Open Systems Today,* February 15, 1993, pp. 54, 58.

(Ha93a) Halbleib, H., "Modeling Real-Time Software Systems Using Object-Oriented Analysis and Design," *CASE Trends,* September 1993, pp. 30–42.

(Ha90) Hansen, T. L., *The C++ Answer Book,* Reading, MA: Addison-Wesley, 1990.

(He92) Herman, J., "Object-Oriented Programming Moves Industry Toward Integrated Network Management," Vol. 22, No. 10, *Business Communications Review,* October 1992, pp. 66–72.

(Ho92) Holub, A., "Heavyweight Champ: The Last Word on Microsoft's C++ Compiler," Vol. 1, No. 10, *Windows TECH Journal,* November 1992, pp. 49–58.

(Ho93) Honiden, S.; N. Kotaka; and Y. Kishimoto, "Formalizing Specification Modeling in OOA," *IEEE Software Magazine,* Vol. 10, No. 1, January 1993, pp. 54–66.

(Ho91) Horstmann, C. S., *Mastering C++: An Introduction to C++ and Object-Oriented Programming for C and Pascal Programmers,* New York, NY: John Wiley & Sons, 1991.

(Ja93) Jacobson, I., "Is Object Technology Software's Industrial Platform?" *IEEE Software Magazine,* Vol. 10, No. 1, January 1993, pp. 24–30.

(Ja89) Jaeschke, R., *Portability and the C Language,* Indianapolis, IN: Hayden Books, 1989.

(Ka89) Karakostas, V., "Requirements for CASE Tools in Early Software Reuse," Vol. 14, No. 2, *ACM Software Engineering Notes,* April, 1989, pp. 39–41.

(Ke92) Kehler, T., "Users Discover Objects," Vol. 12, No. 13, *Software Magazine,* September 1992, pp. 16–23.

(Ke88) Kernighan, B. W., and D. M. Ritchie, *The C Programming Language* (Second Edition), Englewood Cliffs, NJ: Prentice-Hall, 1988.

(Kh90) Khoshafian, A. and R. Abnous., *Object Orientation: Concepts, Languages, Databases, User Interfaces,* New York, NY: John Wiley, 1990.

(Ki92) Kim, W., "Unifying the Relational and Object Models," *Datamation,* November 1, 1992, pp. 56–57.

(Ko90) Koenig, A., and B. Stroustrup, "Exception Handling for C++ (revised)," *Proceedings of the USENIX C++ Conference,* San Francisco, CA, April 1990.

(Ko91) Koenig, A., "What is C++ Anyway?," *Journal of Object-Oriented Programming,* April/May 1991, pp. 48-52.

(Ko92) Kornfeld, K., and K. Gilhooly, "OOPS Via DDE," *BYTE,* June 1992, pp. 145–154.

(Ko92a) Korzeniowski, P., "Object-Oriented DBMSs Strive to Differentiate," Vol. 12, No. 6, *Software Magazine,* May 1992, pp. 68–75.

(Ko93) Kozaczynski, W., and A. Kuntzmann-Combelles, "What It Takes to Make OO Work," *IEEE Software Magazine,* Vol. 10, No. 1, January 1993, pp. 20–23.

(Kr91) Kruse, R. L.; B. P. Leung; and C. L. Tondo, *Data Structures and Program Design in C,* Englewood Cliffs, NJ: Prentice-Hall, 1991.

(Ku90) Kung, C., "Object Subclass Hierarchy in SQL: A Simple Approach," Vol. 33, No. 7, *Communications of the ACM,* July 1990, pp. 117–124.

(La93) Ladd, S. R., *C++ Components and Algorithms,* M&T Books, 1993.

(La91) Lane, A., "Demystifying Objects—A Framework for Understanding," *Object Magazine,* Vol. 1, No. 1, May/June 1991, pp. 58–63.

(Le92) Lejter, M.; S. Meyers; and S. P. Reiss, "Support for Maintaining Object-Oriented Programs," *IEEE Transactions on Software Engineering,* Vol. 18, No. 12, December 1992, pp. 1045–1052.

(Li92) Linthicum, D., "Object-Oriented Software Development Tools," Vol.4, No. 6, *CASE Trends,* September 1992, pp. 14–25.

(Li93) Linthicum, D., "Object-Oriented CASE: State of the Technology," *CASE Trends,* September 1993, pp. 8–18, 26.

(Li91) Lippman, S. B., *C++ Primer* (Second Edition), Reading, MA: Addison-Wesley Publishing Company, 1991.

(Lo93) Longo, T., "OO: New Technology for the Open System's Movement," *Risc 6000 World,* September 1993, p. 14.

(Lo93a) Loomis, M. E. S., "Cooperation Between Object and Relational Technology," *Object Magazine,* Vol. 2, No. 5, January/February 1993, pp. 34–40.

(Lo93b) Lorenz, M., *Object-Oriented Software Development: A Practical Guide,* Englewood Cliffs, NJ: Prentice-Hall, 1993.

(Lu92a) Lu, C., "Objects for End Users," Vol. 17, No. 14, *BYTE,* December 1992, pp. 143–152.

(Lu92) Lucas, P. J., *The C++ Programmer's Handbook,* Englewood Cliffs, NJ: Prentice-Hall, 1992.

(Ma93) Magedson, B., "Building OT From the Bottom Up," *Object Magazine,* Vol. 2, No. 5, January/February 1993, pp. 45–47.

(Ma92) Mantel, K., "Easy Object Orientation," *Datamation,* July 1, 1992, p. 92.

(Ma93) Marco, L., "Object-Oriented Programming: Simplifying Systems Development and Maintenance," *Enterprise Systems Journal,* Vol. 8, No. 6, June 1993, pp. 57–68.

(Ma93a) Martin, J., *Principles of Object-Oriented Analysis and Dyesign,* Englewood Cliffs, NJ: Prentice-Hall, 1993.

(Me93) Matsche, J. J., "Object-oriented programming in Standard C," *Object Magazine,* Vol. 2, No. 5, January/February 1993, pp. 71-74.

(Me90) Meng, B., "Object-Oriented Programming," *Macworld,* January 1990, pp. 174–180.

(Me88) Meyer, B., *Object-Oriented Software Construction,* C. A. R. Hoare Series Editor, Englewood Cliffs, NJ: Prentice-Hall, 1988.

(Me92) Meyer, B., *Advances in Object-Oriented Software Engineering,* Edited by D. Mandrioli and B. Meyer, Englewood Cliffs, NJ: Prentice-Hall, 1992.

(Me92a) Meyer, B., *Eiffel: The Language,* Englewood Cliffs, NJ: Prentice-Hall, 1992.

(Mi91) Microsoft, *Microsoft C/C++ Class Libraries Reference* (Version 7.0), Redmond, WA: Microsoft Corporation, 1991.

(Mi91a) Microsoft, *Microsoft C/C++ C++ Language Reference* (Version 7.0), Redmond, WA: Microsoft Corporation, 1991.

(Mi91b) Microsoft, *Microsoft C/C++ C++ Tutorial* (Version 7.0), Redmond, WA: Microsoft Corporation, 1991.

(Mi91) Microsoft Corporation, *C/C++ Language Reference,* Part Number 24772, Redmond, WA: Microsoft Corporation, 1991.

(Mi91a) Microsoft Corporation, *Microsoft C/C++ Version 7.0: Environment and Tools,* Part Number 24778, Redmond, WA: Microsoft Corporation, 1991.

(Mi92) Microsoft Corporation, *Microsoft C/C++ Version 7.0: Getting Started,* Part Number 24777, Redmond, WA: Microsoft Corporation, 1992.

(Mi91b) Mikes, S., "New Ways to Program in Object-Oriented X," Vol. 8, No. 8, *UNIXWorld,* August 1991, pp. 103–108.

(Mo92) Monarchi, D. E., and G. I. Puhr, "A Research Typology for Object-Oriented Analysis and Design," *Communications of the ACM,* Vol. 35, No. 9, September 1992, pp. 35–47.

(Ne92) Nerson, J. M., "Applying Object-Oriented Analysis and Design," *Communications of the ACM,* Vol. 35, No. 9, September 1992., pp. 63–74.

(Ni92) Nierstrasz, O.; S. Gibbs; and D. Tsichritzis, "Component-Oriented Software Development," *Communications of the ACM,* Vol. 35, No. 9, September 1992., pp. 160–165.

(No91) Novobilski, A., "From Concept to Code—An Electronic Calendar Application in Objective-C," *Object Magazine,* Vol. 1, No. 1, May/June 1991, pp. 84–91.

(No91a) Novobilski, A., "From Concept to Code—An Electronic Calendar Application in Objective-C (part 2)," *Object Magazine,* Vol. 1, No. 2, July/August 1991, pp. 86–96.

(No91b) Novobilski, A., "From Concept to Code—An Electronic Calendar Application in Objective-C (part 3)," *Object Magazine,* Vol. 1, No. 3, September/October 1991, pp. 80–84.

(Ob92) Object Design, *Objectstore: Technical Overview,* Object Design, One New England Executive Park, Burlington, MA, 01803, 1992.

(Os91) Osher, H., "Distributed Object Management," *Object Magazine,* Vol. 1, No. 3, September/October 1991, pp. 62–66.

(Pa90) Pappas, T. L., "Object-Oriented Programming," Vol. 23, No. 11, *Computer,* November 1990, pp. 94–100.

(Pa92) Pappas, C. H., and W. H. Murray, III, *Borland C++ Handbook,* Third Edition, Berkeley, CA: Osbourne McGraw-Hill, 1992.

(Pa93) Parker, J., "Windows Developers Get Object Lessons," *Datamation,* March 15, 1993, pp. 94–97.

(Pa92) Parshall, J. H., "Mac OOP Explained," Vol. 17, No. 10, *BYTE,* October 1992, pp. 267–274.

(Pa93) Pascal, F., "Objection!" *Computerworld,* The CW Guide to Object-Oriented Programming, June 14, 1993, pp. 127–128, 130.

(Pi90) Pinson, L. J., and R. S. Wiener, *Applications of Object-Oriented Programming,* Reading, MA: Addison-Wesley, 1990.

(Pi93) Pittman, M., "Lessons Learned in Managing Object-Oriented Development," *IEEE Software Magazine,* Vol. 10, No. 1, January 1993, pp. 43–53.

(Pl92) Plauger, P. J., *The Standard C Library,* Englewood Cliffs, NJ: Prentice-Hall, 1992.

(Pl93) Plauger, D., "Making C++ Safe for Threads," *The C Users Journal,* Vol 11, No. 2, February 1993, pp. 58–62.

(Pl92) Plauger, P. J., "Embedded Programming in C++," *Embedded Systems Programming,* November 1992, pp. 97–100.

(Pl91) Plum, T., and D. Saks, *C++ Programming Guidelines,* Lawrence, KS: Plum Hall, 1991.

(Po92) Polese, K., and T. C. Goldstein, "Choosing an Object-Oriented Language," Vol. 1, No. 1, *SunProgrammer,* Winter 1992, pp. 11–13.

(Pr93) Prieto-Diaz, R., "Status Report: Software Reusability," *IEEE Software,* Vol. 10, No. 3, May 1993, pp. 61–66.

(Ra90) Rabinowitz, H., and C. Schaap, *Portable C,* Englewood Cliffs, NJ: Prentice-Hall, 1990.

(Ra92) Rasmus, D. W., "Relating to Objects," Vol. 17, No. 14, *BYTE,* December 1992, pp.161–165.

(Ra93) Ray, G., "Distributed Objects Take Step Forward," *Computerworld,* February 8, 1993, p. 51.

(Re91) Reed, D. R., "Moving from C to C++," *Object Magazine,* Vol. 1, No. 3, September/October, 1991, pp. 46–60.

(Re92) Reichbach, J. D., and R. A. Kemmerer, "SoundWorks: An Object-Oriented Distributed System for Digital Sound," Vol. 25, No. 3, *IEEE Computer,* March 1992, pp. 25–37.

(Rl93) Rettig, M.; G. Simmons; and J. Thomson, "Extended Objects," *Communications of the ACM,* Vol. 36, No. 8, August 1993, pp. 19–24.

(Ri92) Ricciuti, M., "The Road to Objects: RDBMS Vendors Face an Object Future," *Datamation,* November 1, 1992, pp. 41–48.

(Ri78) Ritchie, D. M.; S. C. Johnson; M. E. Lesk; and B. W. Kernighan, "UNIX Time-Sharing System: The C Programming Language," *The Bell System Technical Journal,* Vol. 57, No. 6, Part 2, July–August 1978, pp. 1991–2019.

(Ri84) Ritchie, D. M., "The UNIX System: The Evolution of the UNIX Time-Sharing System," *AT&T Bell Laboratories Technical Journal,* Vol. 63, No. 8, Part 2, October 1984, pp. 1577–1593.

(Ro84) Rosler, L., "The UNIX System: The Evolution of C—Past and Future," *AT&T Bell Laboratories Technical Journal,* Vol. 63, No. 8, Part 2, October 1984, pp. 1685–1699.

(Ru92) Rubin, K. S., and A. Goldberg, "Object Behavior Analysis," *Communications of the ACM,* Vol. 35, No. 9, September 1992., pp. 48–62

(Ru93) Rubin, K. S., and A. Goldberg, "Getting to Why," *Object Oriented Analysis & Design,* Finding Your Path, Supplement to SIGS Publications. 1993, pp. 5–10.

(Ru91) Rumbaugh, J.; M. Blaha; W. Premerlani; F. Eddy; and W. Lorensen, *Object-Oriented Modeling and Design,* Englewood Cliffs, NJ: Prentice-Hall, 1991.

(Sa93) Saks, D., "Inheritance," *The C Users Journal,* May 1993, pp. 81–89.

(Se92) Sedgewick, R., *Algorithms in C++,* Reading, MA: Addison-Wesley, 1992.

(Se92a) Sessions, R., *Class Construction in C and C++,* Englewood Cliffs, NJ: Prentice-Hall, 1992.

(Sh92) Shammas, N. C., *Advanced C++,* SAMS Publishing, 1992.

(Sh91) Shapiro, J. S., *A C++ Toolkit,* Englewood Cliffs, NJ: Prentice-Hall, 1991.

(Sh90) Shaw, R. H., "Based Pointers: Combining Far Pointer Addressability and the Small Size of Near Pointers," Vol. 5, No. 5, *Microsoft Systems Journal,* September 1990, pp. 51–63.

(Sh91) Shiffman, H., "C++ Object-Oriented Extensions to C," *SunWorld,* Vol. 4, No. 5, May 1991, pp. 63–70.

(Sk93) Skelly, C., "Pointer Power in C and C++," *The C Users Journal,* Vol. 11, No. 2, February 1993, pp. 93–98.

(Sm92) Smaer, S., and S. J. Mellor, *Object Lifecycles: Modeling the World in States,* Englewood Cliffs, NJ: Yourdon Press, 1992.

(Sm90) Smith, J. D., *Reusability & Software Construction C & C++,* New York, NY: John Wiley & Sons, 1990.

(Sm91) Smith, J. T., *C++ for Scientists & Engineers,* New York, NY: McGraw-Hill, 1991.

(Sn93) Snyder, A., "The Essence of Objects: Concepts and Terms," *IEEE Software Magazine,* Vol. 10, No. 1, January 1993, pp. 31–42.

(St84) Stroustrup, B., "The UNIX System: Data Abstraction in C," *AT&T Bell Laboratories Technical Journal,* Vol. 63, No. 8, Part 2, October 1984, pp. 1701–1732.

(St88) Stroustrup, B., "What is Object-Oriented Programming?" *IEEE Software,* Vol. 5, No. 3, May 1988, pp. 10–20.

(St88a) Stroustrup, B., "Parameterized Types for C++," *Proceedings of the USENIX C++ Conference,* Denver, CO, October 1988.

(St91) Stroustrup, B. *The C++ Programming Language* (Second Edition), Reading, MA: Addison-Wesley Series in Computer Science, 1991.

(St93) Stroustrup. B., "Why Consider Language Extensions?: Maintaining a Delicate Balance" *C++ Report,* September 1993, pp. 44–51.

(Su91) SunSoft, "Project DOE: Distributed Objects Everywhere," Sun Microsystems, Inc., 1991.

(Ta92) Taylor, D., *Object-Oriented Information Systems,* New York, NY: John Wiley & Sons, 1992.

(To89) Tondo, C. L., and S. E. Gimpel, *The C Answer Book,* Englewood Cliffs, NJ: Prentice-Hall, 1989.

(Un93) UniNews, "AT&T Licenses Follow-On to C++," Vol. 7, No. 2, *UniNews,* January 25, 1993, pp. 1–2.

(Ur92) Urlocker, Z., "Polymorphism Unbounded," Vol. 1, No. 1, *Windows Tech Journal,* January 1992, pp. 11–16.

(Ur90) Urlocker, Z., "Object-Oriented Programming for Windows," Vol. 15, No. 5, *BYTE,* May 1990, pp. 287–294.

(Va91) VanCamp, D., "Inherit the Win," Vol. 16, No. 9, *BYTE,* September 1991, pp. 325–340.

(Va93) Vasan, R., "Relational Databases and Objects—A Hybrid Solution," *Object Magazine,* Vol. 2, No. 5, January/February 1993, pp. 41–44.

(Ve93) Verhoest, C., and J. L. Barbe, "Object Oriented Business Application Development: The Business Class Approach," *CASE Trends,* April 1993, pp. 40–49.

(Ve91) Verity, J. W., and E. I. Schwartz; "Software Made Simple: Will Object-Oriented Programming Transform the Computer Industry?" *Business Week*, September 30, 1991, pp. 92–100.

(Vo91) Voss, G., *Object-Oriented Programming: An Introduction,* Berkeley, CA: Osbourne McGraw-Hill, 1991.

(Vo93) Voss, G., "Objects and Messages," *Windows Tech Journal,* February 1993, pp. 15–16.

(We92) Weiskamp, K., and B. Flamig, *The Complete C++ Primer,* Second Edition, Academic Press, 1992.

(Wh91) Whitefield, B., and K. Auer, "You Can't Do That in Smalltalk! Or Can You?" *Object Magazine,* Vol. 1, No. 1, May/June 1991, pp. 64–73.

(Wi93) Wiebel, M., and S. Halladay, "Using OOP Techniques Instead of *switch* in C++," Vol. 10, No. 10, *The C Users Journal,* October 1992, pp. 105–112.

(Wi88) Wiener, R. S., and L. J. Pinson, *An Introduction to Object-Oriented Programming and C++,* Reading, MA: Addison-Wesley, 1988.

(Wi92) Wilde, N., and R. Huitt, "Maintenance Support for Object-Oriented Programs," *IEEE Transactions on Software Engineering,* Vol. 18, No. 12, December 1992, pp. 1038–1044.

(Wl93) Wilde, N.; P. Matthews and R. Huitt, "Maintaining Object-Oriented Software," *IEEE Software Magazine,* Vol. 10, No. 1, January 1993, pp. 75–80.

(Wi91) Williams, J., "The Object Paradigm Requires Object-Oriented Methods and Tools," *Object Magazine,* Vol. 1, No. 4, November/December 1991, pp. 50–58.

(Wi92) Williams, T., "Object-Oriented Methods Transform Real-Time Programming," Vol. 31, No. 9. *Computer Design,* September 1992, pp. 101–118.

(Wt93) Wilt, N., "Templates in C++," *The C Users Journal,* May 1993, pp. 33–51.

(Wi90) Wirfs-Brock, R.; B. Wilkerson; and L. Wiener, *Designing Object-Oriented Software,* Englewood Cliffs, NJ: Prentice-Hall, 1990.

(Wy92) Wyatt, B. B.; K. Kavi; and S. Hufnagel, "Parallelism in Object-Oriented Languages: A Survey," Vol. 9, No. 7, *IEEE Software,* November 1992, pp. 56–66.

(Ya93) Yamazaki, S.; K. Kajihara; M. Ito; and R. Yasuhara, "Object-Oriented Design of Telecommunication Software," *IEEE Software Magazine,* Vol. 10, No. 1, January 1993, pp. 81–87.

# Index

# A

# B

# C

# D

# E

# F

# I

# J



# K



# L

# M

# N

# O

# P

## R

# S

# T